# third edition
# Family Violence
## across the lifespan

2011

# third edition
# Family Violence
## across the lifespan
### AN INTRODUCTION

Ola W. Barnett
Cindy L. Miller-Perrin
Robin D. Perrin
*Pepperdine University*

**SAGE**

Los Angeles | London | New Delhi
Singapore | Washington DC

*For information:*

SAGE Publications, Inc.
2455 Teller Road
Thousand Oaks, California 91320
E-mail: order@sagepub.com

SAGE Publications India Pvt. Ltd.
B 1/I 1 Mohan Cooperative Industrial Area
Mathura Road, New Delhi 110 044
India

SAGE Publications Ltd.
1 Oliver's Yard
55 City Road
London EC1Y 1SP
United Kingdom

SAGE Publications Asia-Pacific Pte. Ltd.
33 Pekin Street #02-01
Far East Square
Singapore 048763

Printed in the United States of America

*Library of Congress Cataloging-in-Publication Data*

Barnett, Ola W.
Family violence across the lifespan : an introduction / Ola Barnett, Cindy L. Miller-Perrin, Robin D. Perrin.—3rd ed.
    p. cm.
Includes bibliographical references and index.
ISBN 978-1-4129-8178-1 (pbk.)
    1. Family violence. I. Miller-Perrin, Cindy L. (Cindy Lou), 1962- II. Perrin, Robin D. III. Title.

HV6626.B315 2011
362.82′92—dc22                    2010032332

This book is printed on acid-free paper.

10   11   12   13   14   10   9   8   7   6   5   4   3   2   1

| | |
|---|---|
| *Acquisitions Editor:* | Kassie Graves |
| *Associate Editor:* | Leah Mori |
| *Editorial Assistant:* | Courtney Munz |
| *Production Editor:* | Astrid Virding |
| *Copy Editor:* | Terri Paulsen |
| *Permissions Editor:* | Adele Hutchinson |
| *Typesetter:* | C&M Digitals (P) Ltd. |
| *Proofreaders:* | Scott Oney, Dennis Webb |
| *Indexer:* | Molly Hall |
| *Cover Designer:* | Bryan Fishman |

# Brief Contents

# Detailed Contents

# Case Histories

# Preface

Family violence is *not* a new phenomenon—it has probably existed in families since the beginning of time. Only in modern times, however, has society begun to recognize violence against family members as a social problem.

The well-publicized findings of multiple fractures appearing in the X-rays of abused children by Dr. C. Henry Kempe of Colorado propelled the problem of child abuse into public view. The advent of the women's movement in the 1970s helped spawn the battered women's shelter movement. The vast number of reports of family violence made to the police and other officials also heightened concern about abuse of children, dating partners, spouses, and elders.

Family violence research has expanded across the globe, illuminating the vastness of the problem of violence. Now, the World Health Organization expends considerable effort on reducing violence against women and children. Some of these atrocities have come to light through the media coverage of the wars in Iraq and Afghanistan. With worldwide attention focused on family violence, Human Rights Conventions (documents containing stipulations for government action) have incorporated authoritative language to protect women and children.

Progress within the field of family violence has been rapid. Many grassroots organizations, mental health workers, researchers, lawmakers, legal and medical professionals, criminal justice authorities, book writers, and the media have mobilized their efforts to understand the phenomenon of family violence. In the past three decades, the general public has become familiar with family violence through news coverage of highly publicized cases, television programs, and movies. At the same time, researchers have made great strides in recognizing the scope of family violence and the context in which it occurs. Despite these advances, academicians have only examined the "tip of the iceberg" of this crisis.

*Family Violence Across the Lifespan, 3rd Edition* has been written to continue the "discovery" of violence between intimates. There is a great need to go on with the work of bringing the topic into the mainstream of public knowledge. To achieve these goals, the book draws together a voluminous research literature that describes the magnitude, consequences, and causes of family violence. The amount of published research available since the first edition (1997) and the second edition (2005) of the text has tripled, if not quadrupled. The third edition includes a new chapter on abused and abusive adolescents and another on abused and abusive adult partners in understudied populations. The chapter on understudied populations incorporates scholarship on abused persons among marginalized groups. These populations include rural women, disabled individuals, same-sex couples, military adults, immigrant/ethnic groups within the United States, and cultures worldwide. Other topics cover the social and professional responses to family violence, including clinical treatments, educational efforts within schools, social service agency practices, governmental policies, criminal justice system procedures, and policy and prevention efforts.

Because of the breadth of the topic and the enormous amount of available literature, the chapters present a broad overview and summary of research findings. Throughout the volume, the focus has been on providing responsible scholarship by presenting data relevant to both sides of a debatable issue. Along the way, graphic case histories have enlivened statistical accounts, and controversial topics frequently appear within boxed inserts. For readers who are interested in obtaining further details on specific topics, there are additional resources in appendixes and on the book's website (www.sagepub.com/barnett3e).

In particular, the glossary appendix aids readers in understanding unfamiliar phrases and statistical nomenclature. Its inclusion facilitates readers' access to a broader coverage of the field. Another appendix contains abbreviations (acronyms) of the names of organizations and phrases used by researchers. These appendixes will simplify the reader's task of understanding the research findings.

We hope that we have presented the content in such a way that readers can find their own personal roles in the struggle to end family violence. We invite you, our readers, to contact us to express your impressions of the book, to send us your personal case histories, or to provide us with additional references and resources. Furthermore, we hope the book offers information to victims and perpetrators that will change their lives for the better. Finally, we hope this text in some measure decreases the isolation and suffering of victims and ultimately contributes to solutions to end family violence.

Ola W. Barnett

Cindy L. Miller-Perrin

Robin D. Perrin

# Acknowledgments

First, we wish to acknowledge Kassie Graves, senior acquisitions editor of Human Services at Sage Publications, and C. Terry Hendrix, consulting editor, for reviving the prospects of a third edition of the text. Their expertise in recognizing and shaping changes in the third edition expanded the scope of the content to include a more global approach. Without their proficiency and guidance, the book would not have become available to academia and the public in general. We are also grateful to the instructor-reviewers of the second edition for their analyses of the book's content. Their extensive knowledge of the field and constructive comments provided new insights and directions for the third edition.

Another person we wish to thank is Carol V. Harnish, who read and reread chapters from a "common man's" (woman's in this case) perspective, adding clarity to the scientific writing style. She also collected current case histories and up-to-date newspaper stories that helped bring the topic of family violence to life. Among her many contributions was the important idea of a glossary of unfamiliar terms as an appendix to the book.

The original authors of the research discussed in this volume are among those who deserve recognition for helping to create the field of family violence. It is their knowledge and dedication that has laid the foundation for the text. They have not rested on their laurels but have soldiered onward always trying to prevent one more victimization, one more shattered life. Although sometimes disagreeing with each other's methodologies or research interpretations, these professionals are totally united in their commitment to ending family violence. They serve as models to the generation of scholars to follow.

In general, we wish to thank the survivors of family violence who provided data for family violence researchers, even when doing so was painful. These men, women, and children seldom receive the acknowledgment they deserve. We are grateful to the staff of Sage Publications for executing the many detailed tasks that accompany publication of a book this size. They are a noteworthy team of experts. Finally, we thank our families who supported us during the many long months of writing.

The publisher and the authors thank the following who reviewed earlier drafts of this book:

Dr. Kathryn A. Branch, University of Tampa

J. Michael Cruz, Southern Methodist University

Ronald Dolon, Ball State University

George W. Holden, Southern Methodist University

Jan Ricks, LISW, ACSW, University of Cincinnati

Melanie Shepard, University of Minnesota–Duluth

# About the Authors

**Ola W. Barnett** is a Distinguished Professor Emerita of Psychology at Pepperdine University, Malibu, California. She earned her undergraduate and doctoral degrees in psychology at the University of California Los Angeles, specializing in learning. Her initial research centered on batterers and her later work on battered women and dating violence. She has coauthored two editions of a best-selling Sage book (with A. D. LaViolette) on why battered women stay with abusive partners: *It Could Happen to Anyone: Why Battered Women Stay*. These books provide a scientific explanation grounded in learning theory for understanding the obstacles battered women face in trying to break free of their violent relationships.

**Cindy Miller-Perrin** is Professor of Psychology and Blanche E. Seaver Professor of Social Science at Pepperdine University in Malibu, California. She is also a clinical psychologist and has worked with developmentally delayed, maltreated, and other troubled children and their families. She has coauthored two other books, including *Child Sexual Abuse: Sharing the Responsibility* (with S. Wurtele, University of Nebraska Press, 1992) and *Child Maltreatment: An Introduction* (with R. Perrin, 1999, 2007). She is also the author or coauthor of numerous articles and book chapters on topics including child sexual abuse prevention, perceptions associated with child maltreatment, family violence, and psychology and religion. She enjoys teaching and researching with undergraduates and is the recipient of the 2008 Howard A. White Award for Teaching Excellence. She has also received honors for her research, including the 2008 Pro Humanitate for a paper published in *Child Maltreatment*. She recently served as the President of the Section on Child Maltreatment of APA and is currently serving as Member-At-Large for Division 37 Society for Child and Family Policy and Practice. She received her doctorate from Washington State University in 1991 and completed postdoctoral studies in child clinical psychology at the University of Washington.

**Robin D. Perrin** is currently Professor of Sociology at Pepperdine University in Malibu, California. His research interests and publications are in the areas of family violence, deviance theory, the social construction of social problems, and the sociology of religion. He is the coauthor of two other books: *Social Deviance: Being, Behaving, and Branding* (with D. Ward & T. Carter, 1991) and *Child Maltreatment: An Introduction* (with C. Miller-Perrin, Sage, 1999). He is also the author or coauthor of numerous articles on a variety of topics, including the satanism scare, the growth of conservative churches, the relationship between religious commitment and honesty, and religion as deviant behavior. He teaches Introduction to Sociology, Introductory Statistics, Deviant Behavior and Social Control, and Sociology of Religion and is the recipient of the 2004 Howard A. White Award for Teaching Excellence. He received his doctorate in sociology from Washington State University in 1989. Following his doctoral studies he was assistant professor of sociology at Seattle Pacific University in Seattle, Washington.

# 1

# History and Definitions of Family Violence

**May 14, 2009, *Daily Press* (Victorville, CA):** On Mother's Day, sheriff's deputies discovered a 94-year-old woman living in a wooden shed with no running water or cooling. The deputies arrested her 59-year-old son Ronald Rego and his wife for elder abuse. They were living on the property in a travel trailer. Adult protective services placed the woman in the house of a neighbor who was willing to take her in ("Calif. Husband, Wife," 2009).

**May 21, 2009, *Sun News* (Myrtle Beach, SC):** A woman told police that her husband tied her up with duct tape, assaulted her, and tried to kill her with a roach-killing gel. After other abuses, he asked her if she was "ready to meet her maker." Police arrested her 24-year-old husband for intent to kill, criminal domestic violence, and kidnapping ("SC Husband Jailed," 2009).

**June 6, 2009, *Santa Fe New Mexican* (Santa Fe, NM):** A 22-year-old father-to-be, Marino Leyba, intentionally killed his unborn son by shooting his 17-year-old wife in the stomach and upper torso. He also shot the mother's father after bursting into his father in-law's apartment. Although the district attorney could prosecute Lebya for two murders, she could not lawfully prosecute him for killing the fetus. There was no law against killing a baby in the womb, she said ("Police: N.M. Suspect," 2009).

**May 7, 2007, *Houston Chronicle* (TX):** Two young women thought they could manage the persistent unwanted attention of their ex-boyfriends. They were wrong. Rachel Pendray, a 20-year-old Sam Houston University cheerleader, died when the man she rejected

*(Continued)*

---

Unless otherwise noted, all of the case histories presented in this volume come from our own personal knowledge of the cases described, which we have gathered through our experience as researchers and practitioners in the field of family violence. Also, unless otherwise noted, all of the names used in these case histories are pseudonyms.

shot her and then killed himself. Tynesha Stewart, a 19-year-old Texas A&M freshman, disappeared during a spring break. Her ex-boyfriend later admitted to choking her to death, dismembering her body, and burning the remains in his apartment barbecue pit. Although both men were controlling, constantly e-mailing, and showing anger, no one recognized the warning signs ("Ignoring Warning," 2007).

The newspaper articles cited above represent a sample of the diverse stories about family violence that recently appeared across the United States. Although news media accounts of family violence often represent the most sensational cases, there is no reason to believe that the particular stories above are in any way unique. Because of sensationalism in the media, readers hear little about the commonplace, routine violence that occurs within families. To comprehend the complexity of family violence, this text offers an examination of family violence that is both comprehensive and scientific. Even though this chapter serves as a preview, readers will be able to grasp a deeper understanding of many different issues associated with family violence. A list of some of these issues is as follows: (a) the estimates of the different types of assault, (b) the scientific research involved, (c) the various theories that try to explain family violence, (d) the definitions, (e) the various forms of abuse, (f) the physical and psychological consequences of family violence, (g) current treatments for both victims and perpetrators, and (h) various policy recommendations aimed at ending family violence. The first chapter begins by considering two important questions: "When (and how) did family violence come to be recognized as a social problem?" and "How is family violence defined?" The successive chapters in the text will round out the information presented here.

## VIOLENCE IN FAMILIES

Society tends to think of the family as a relatively safe place, a safe harbor, a place of sustenance and care. It is a place where spouses love each other and their children. Regrettably, this view of families is idealized. Far too often, families are a source of maltreatment and violence. How common is child abuse, sibling abuse, abuse of parents, dating abuse, spouse abuse, and elder abuse? For a variety of reasons, this question is very difficult to answer. First of all, there is little agreement on exactly what constitutes family violence. Even when definitional consensus is achieved, however, the fact remains that most family violence occurs behind closed doors. It is often hidden, unnoticed, and ignored. As a result, it does not come to the attention of authorities and become part of official estimates. In addition, victims may not recall abuse, may not perceive the behavior as abusive, may not wish to disclose the abuse, or may not even be able to report the behavior. Given these numerous impediments, any statistics on family violence should be interpreted with a degree of caution; most are underestimates. In actuality, there is simply no way to know with certainty how much family violence exists in society.

There are a number of data sources that provide a sense of the scope of the problem. Some, for example, monitor the number of criminal assaults, while others record the number of homicides. With the advent of computers, governmental organizations have inaugurated one or more electronic databases to better track family violence. A few of the standard and newer *government* systems are the following:

Centers for Disease Control and Prevention (CDC)

National Child Abuse and Neglect Data System (NCANDS)

National Institute of Justice (NIJ)

National Center for Injury Prevention and Control (NCIPC)

Youth Risk Behavior System (YRBS)

National Electronic Injury Surveillance System (NEISS)

Federal Bureau of Investigation (FBI)

U.S. Department of Health and Human Services (DHHS)

National Crime Victimization Survey (NCVS)

Morbidity and Mortality Weekly Review (MMWR)

U.S. Department of Justice (DOJ)

Behavioral Risk Factor Surveillance System (BRFSS)

National Comorbidity Survey (NCS)

Adoption & Foster Care Analysis & Reporting System (AFCARS)

National Violent Death Reporting System (NVDRS)

National Survey of Children Exposed to Violence (NatSCEV)

National Incident-Based Reporting System (NIBRS)

In addition, there are a number of surveys conducted by university *academics* and by nongovernmental agencies. A few of these are the following:

National Family Violence Surveys (NFVS)

Severity of Violence Against Women Scales (SVAWS)

National Violence Against Women Survey (NVAWS)

National Survey of Families and Households (NSFH)

## Intrafamilial Nonfatal Abuse

The statistical summaries on family violence that follow document that women and children are more likely to be victimized in their own homes than they are on the streets of America's most violent cities (Bachman & Saltzman, 1995; Hotaling, Straus, & Lincoln, 1990). Family violence has significant ramifications for a number of personal, societal, and health problems that affect people in the United States (e.g., A. S. Jones, 2000). Overall, family interactions comprise the single greatest determinant of an individual's level of violence outside the home. Children who are abused, or who witness violence, are far more likely to engage in violence themselves, both as children and when they are adults.

- *Child maltreatment.* U.S. Department of Health & Human Services (DHHS; 2009) specified that for the year 2007, social service agencies across the United States received approximately 3.5 million reports of child maltreatment, a rate of 10.6 per 1,000 children. The 2007 rate of abuse is below the all-time high of 15.3 per 1,000, which was recorded in 1993. Parents were the perpetrators of the abuse in 80% of these cases.

- *The National Violence Against Women Survey (NVAWS;* Tjaden & Thoennes, 2000b) found that 52% of adult women and 66% of adult men in the survey sample reported being assaulted as children by adult caretakers.

- *The National Crime Victimization Survey* (*NCVS;* Rand, 2009), based on telephone interview data, reported that 255,630 rapes occurred in 2006. Strangers perpetrated 39.1%, and intimates perpetrated 60.9%. Of those raped, 22.9% were 18 to 20 years old and 22.8% were 21 to 29 years old.

- *The NVAWS* (Tjaden & Thoennes, 2000b) found that rape by an intimate partner occurred against nearly 10% of women.

- *The NVAWS* (Tjaden & Thoennes, 2000a) presented data on ***intimate partner violence (IPV)*** showing that 22% of women and 7% of men reported experiencing IPV at some point in their lifetimes.

## Intrafamilial Fatal Abuse

- *The U.S. Department of Health & Human Services* (2009b) estimated that in 2007 approximately 1,760 children in the United States died as a result of abuse and neglect. Of these children, 42.2% were under the age of 1 year and 75.7% were under the age of 4. One or both parents caused 70% of the fatalities.

- *The Office of Juvenile Justice and Delinquency Prevention (OJJDP; U.S. Department of Justice,* 2006) reported that of juvenile murder victims with known offenders, 39% were killed by family members, 46% by acquaintances, and 15% by strangers.

- *Surveillance for Violent Deaths—The National Violent Death Reporting System (NVDRS—within the Centers for Disease Control and Prevention [CDC]; Karch et al., 2009)* tabulated 616 deaths of intimate partners with 16 states reporting. Of these, 370 (60.1%) were females and 246 (39.9%) were males. The largest number of victims and offenders were in the 35 to 44 age range.

- *Surveillance for Violent Deaths—The NVDRS* (Karch et al., 2009) found that of *homicide-suicide deaths,* IPV problems preceded the crimes in 73.0% of the cases (see also Felthous et al., 2001; see Regoeczi, 2001, for Canadian IPV homicides).

- *The U.S. Bureau of Justice Statistics* (2007) summarized gender differences among *homicide victims* from 1976 to 2005. For females, intimates killed 30.0%, family members killed 11.7%, known acquaintances killed 21.8%, strangers killed 8.8%, and unknown assailants killed 27.7%.

For males, intimates killed 5.3%, family members killed 6.7%, known acquaintances killed 35.6%, strangers killed 15.5%, and unknown assailants killed 37.8%.

- *The National Center for Injury Prevention and Control* (CDC, 2007) reported that in 2005, homicide was the fourth-leading cause of death for children ages 1 through 11.

*Combined homicide-suicide.* In *combined homicide-suicides,* a perpetrator commits suicide after killing others, most often an intimate partner. The perpetrators may also kill their children, in-laws, romantic partners of the victim, and others. A related category of deaths are the *collateral deaths of family and friends.* In a claims-making move, scholars in the state of Washington asserted that family homicide rates ought to include these collateral deaths occurring with an *IPV homicide/suicide* (Washington State Coalition Against Domestic Violence, 2000). Because of family violence researchers' interest in these IPV-related deaths, statisticians are now beginning to tabulate the frequencies of these occurrences.

## WHY ARE FAMILIES VIOLENT?

All families have tensions, and all families may occasionally resolve these tensions in inappropriate ways. Even the best parents and the most loving couples display inappropriate behaviors. They sometimes lose their tempers, say intentionally hurtful things to one another, raise their voices when arguing, and even lash out physically. In many respects, aggression is a normal (i.e., common and culturally approved) part of family life. Since these behaviors are so common and widespread, one has to ask "Why," and "Why are women and children so often the ones who are victimized?"

*Structural factors.* Many structural factors make families particularly prone to violence. One of these is the amount of time family members spend together, which increases the opportunity for violence. In addition, power differentials often exist among family members, and those who are less powerful run a greater risk for victimization. Children are subordinate to parents, wives often must be subordinate to husbands, and sometimes elderly parents are subordinate to their adult children. Further complicating matters is that children and women usually cannot fight back; nor can they always choose with whom they will or will not interact. Children are dependent on their parents, and wives are very frequently dependent on their husbands. Whereas many interpersonal conflicts can be resolved simply through the dissolution of relationships, most family relationships are protected by law and are not so easily severed. Even when child maltreatment comes to the attention of authorities, states are reluctant to break up families. Instead, authorities give dysfunctional families multiple opportunities to change. Finally, the privacy and autonomy traditionally granted to families make violence relatively easy to hide (Brinkerhoff & Lupri, 1988).

*Idealization of the family.* Levesque (2001) asserts that the problem begins with an *idealized notion of the family.* This image of the family includes several beliefs: (a) parental rights supersede children's rights; (b) parents can and should have control over the development of their children; (c) family members will act in the best interests of children and elderly parents who are incapable of caring for themselves; (d) families rooted in traditional cultures are *strong families,* even if some of their customs justify family violence; and (e) families have the right to privacy and autonomy, even if this right results in harm to vulnerable members. This perception of the family serves to "justify what otherwise could be construed as violent, abusive, and worthy of intervention" (p. 5).

*Family norms.* There is little doubt that *family norms,* such as spanking, contribute to a certain amount of family aggression. Summarized by Bender et al. (2007), Phoenix Children's Hospital reported the following *rates of physical punishment* by parents: (a) Nearly 66% of 1- and 2-year-olds, (b) 80% by the time children reach 5th grade, and (c) 85% by the time adolescents are in high school. Along the same lines, the National Opinion Research Center (1998) disclosed that 73% of surveyed Americans agreed or strongly agreed that it is "sometimes necessary to discipline a child with a good hard spanking."

*Social tolerance of violence.* In addition, social scientists almost universally maintain that *society's acceptance,* encouragement, and glorification of violence contributes to abuse in the family. Such tolerance may have a ***spillover effect,*** raising the likelihood of violence in the home (Tolan & Guerra, 1998). Depiction of women in advertising and in video games, for example, often characterizes women as sex objects and as victims (Stankiewicz & Rosselli, 2008). Objectification of males in the media appears to be problematic, as well (Johnson, McCreary, & Mills, 2007). As a case in point, a Japanese-produced video game, *Rapelay,* features players stalking and raping a mother and her two daughters. At least in this one situation, Amazon, eBay, and other sellers banned the sale of this "game" ("NYC Official: Ban," 2009). Although a minority of social scientists may still contend that attributing any youth violence to the media is empirically unjustified, most now disagree (C. A. Anderson et al., 2003). Watching media violence constitutes a form of *social learning,* a broadly accepted theory that explains learning through observation.

## CASE HISTORY  Ben and Lori—Making Up Is Not Hard to Do

At an after-theater party that Ben and Lori attended on their vacation, Ben struck up a conversation with Vanessa, a 20-year-old ingénue from the Dominican Republic. When Lori noted Ben's interest in Vanessa, she began flirting with one of the theater company's young male dancers, Danny. Lori made a show of *kicking back* with Danny, requesting slow music, rubbing up against him while dancing, and asking him to bring her several glasses of wine. The next thing she knew, Ben was out of sight and so was Vanessa. Lori stormed out of the party with Danny in hot pursuit.

As Lori walked down Broadway at midnight, Ben came out of nowhere and pleaded with her to come back to the party. Lori slapped his face, screamed that he was a cheat, and marched on toward their hotel. Ben tried to stop her by pinning her to a wall. He accused her of being turned on by Danny, so Lori taunted Ben, saying things like "Young guys in tight pants look good to me!" When Ben couldn't shut Lori up, he slapped her once and twisted her arm behind her back. When he let go, Lori ran crying to their hotel.

Inside their room, Lori slammed things around and insisted that Ben no longer loved her. She threw Ben's jacket to the floor and stomped all over it. Ben said that Lori ought to know that he loved her. Didn't she know that he thought she was the "sexiest woman at the party, so blond, so cool, so beautiful"? Lori burst into tears and told Ben that she wanted only him. He grabbed her and began kissing her passionately. The real party lasted until 3 a.m. Lori and Ben had learned long ago that a few slaps here and there were just part of their relationship. After all, they weren't really violent, because they loved each other and no one ever got hurt.

This case history provides an example of how many couples view a certain amount of aggression as acceptable in their relationships.

*Social acceptance of violence.* Scientific polls gauging the attitudes of large segments of the U.S. population toward IPV have identified an antiwoman bias, enhanced somewhat by the gender of the respondent. In a cynical vein, McMahon and Pence (2003) asserted that society would prefer that battered women be "perfect victims," those who neither instigate abuse nor fight back. Although significant changes in attitudes toward drunk driving and littering were evident over the years 1982 to 1992, changes concerning IPV were more limited. Younger males, but not older males or any-age females, drawn from a random community sample said they would be worried about *legal repercussions* if they hurt someone else. Men also said they would be *embarrassed* if their friends and acquaintances found out that they hurt someone, but they did not report any substantial increases in feeling guilt or shame if others did find out (Grasmic, Blackwell, Bursik, & Mitchell, 1993).

Another poll taken during 1992 uncovered some typical attitudes toward IPV. Americans ranked domestic violence as *fifth* on a list of public concerns, with only 34% of the total respondents agreeing that it is an extremely important topic. The general public *failed to endorse arrest* as the proper response to spouse abuse; that is, most IPV is not seen as a crime. At a minimum, many respondents said a man would have to hit a woman hard (53%) to deserve arrest, but if he punched her, 94% agreed that arrest was appropriate. One disturbing and persistent belief among 38% of respondents was that "Some women provoked men into abusing them" (E. Klein, Campbell, Soler, & Ghez, 1997).

By 1995, domestic violence ranked first among social concerns, with 83% of respondents evaluating it as an extremely important social issue. At that time, the respondents also thought that public intervention was necessary (82%), especially if an injury occurred (96%). The principal reason they cited for the necessity of public intervention, however, was to protect children, not women (E. Klein et al., 1997; see also Nabi & Horner, 2001).

*Cultural factors.* Cultural factors can also be useful in explaining male-to-female intimate partner violence (MFIPV). Some cultures accept violence; others condemn it. In some cultures, such as Brazil and the Arab world, a husband's violence against an unfaithful wife presumably restores the husband's honor (Kulwicki, 2002; Vandello & Cohen, 2003). Many authorities place partial blame for the widespread acceptance of violence in U.S. culture on the content of television programming as well as movies, sports, toys, and video games (Bushman & Anderson, 2001). Others cite approval of violence within the home as a contributing factor. For some, the most crucial element is cultural acceptance of male dominance.

*Individual factors.* In addition to powerful social forces that may foster family violence, there are a number of more individual factors that do so as well. One factor, of course, is some type of *mental illness or mental disorder,* such as schizophrenia. Another factor is individual differences, such as vulnerability to *jealousy,* or *anger.* One powerful precursor of family violence that may flow across the lifespan is level of *attachment.* Attachment refers to the affectional bond between a parent and a child or, later as an adult, the bond between romantic partners. Disruptions in attachment are related to numerous correlates of family violence, such as intense emotional dependence (D.G. Dutton & Painter, 1993a; Holtzworth-Munroe & Hutchinson, 1993).

## DISCOVERING FAMILY VIOLENCE: HOW SOCIAL CONDITIONS BECOME SOCIAL PROBLEMS

Although historians have characterized America as a violent nation, their focus has been on collective social violence. Consistently overlooked was the significant amount of interpersonal violence and even violence in wars. This oversight helps explain why Americans expressed surprise over the enormous amount of violence among family members (Leonard, 2003). Presumably, few knowledgeable people would now question the assertion that family violence is a serious social problem.

In addition to increased coverage in the media, the academic community has covered the topic in textbooks on social problems and deviant behavior, and increasingly universities are offering specific courses on family violence. The amount of research on the topic has grown exponentially, leading to countless new publications related to family violence. Articles reporting on family violence research have also become increasingly common in mainstream journals in other fields: sociology, psychology, social work, law, criminal justice, epidemiology, cross-cultural issues, human rights, homosexuality, and health. In addition, numerous social movement organizations and federal agencies are increasingly dedicated to assisting victims and preventing family violence (see Adair & Vohra, 2003). Others point to the overall advances in the field (Kendall-Tackett, 2009). Despite all these encouraging signs, Pyles and Postmus (2004) complain that theorizing has not kept pace with the upsurge in research.

Concern and outrage about family violence has also increased around the world, and several *international treaties* explicitly include human rights protection from violent family members. The 1989 *United Nations Convention on the Rights of the Child* proclaimed that all children should be protected from "physical or mental violence, injury or abuse, neglect or negligent treatment, maltreatment or exploitation including sexual abuse, while in the care of parent(s), legal guardian(s) or any other person who has the care of the child" (quoted in Levesque, 2001, p. 7). The United Nations Declaration on the *Elimination of Violence Against Women* (1994) condemned any "act of gender-based violence that results in, or is likely to result in, physical, sexual, or psychological harm or suffering to women, including threats of such acts, coercion or arbitrary deprivation of liberty, whether occurring in public or private life" (quoted in Levesque, 2001, p. 7). In these documents, the United Nations rejected *cultural relativism,* declaring that all U.N. member countries must eliminate any cultural practices or customs that permit the abuse of women or children. In the ensuing years, however, it is clear that progress in reducing violence against children and women has proceeded at a snail's pace.

*Children's human rights.* The customary view of children's rights is through the lens of family law, and to date, observers have justly concluded that "international law and the human rights jurisdiction can be surprisingly disappointing in allowing children's rights" (Sawyer, 2006). Children need much more protection in terms of property rights and in custodial decisions. International law seems inoperative in compelling various countries to honor agreements, such as the Hague Convention. A custodial dispute concerning an 8-year-old American boy and his biological father clarifies the problem. A Brazilian court awarded custody of the boy to his Brazilian stepfather following the death of his mother, even though she had abducted him illegally when he was only 3 years old (Simao, 2009).

*Women's human rights.* Improvement in the status of women across the globe has been painstakingly slow. An *International News* report on October 12, 2006, proclaimed that the U.N. found violence against women to be severe, pervasive, and worldwide. A 2006 *BBC News* report on October 11 stated that Ethiopian women were the most abused women in the world, with 60% reporting sexual violence and marital rape. In addition, 100 countries had no domestic violence laws whatsoever. Emblematic of the sheer needless cruelty toward women, Ghanaian communities punish widows in many of the following ways: "by seclusion, pouring pepper into the eyes and private parts of a widow and preventing her from eating as signs of mourning" (Amoakohene, 2004, p. 2375). Clearly, family violence is a universal problem, receiving recognition on the social agendas of the United States and many other nations. It is important to recognize, however, that concern about family violence is a fairly recent phenomenon.

*Social constructionism.* When and how did family violence come to be seen as a social problem? According to many sociologists, social conditions become social problems through a process of social constructionism (Loseke, 2003; Spector & Kitsuse, 1977). From this perspective, *societal reactions* are central to the process through which a social condition is redefined as a social problem. Societal reactions to various situations, such as child abuse, can come from many sources: individual citizens, religious groups, social movement organizations, political interest groups, and the media, to name but a few. Through their reactions to particular social conditions, individuals and institutions play a crucial role in transforming public perceptions.

*Claims-making.* Various interest groups change social conditions into social problems by actively engaging in the process of raising awareness about that condition. The term *claims-making* has been applied to the activities of such groups; it refers to the "activities of individuals or groups making assertions of grievances or claims with respect to some putative condition" (Spector & Kitsuse, 1977, p. 75). Generally speaking, the process begins when claims-makers express anger or distress about a particular condition that they see as highly objectionable. Claims-makers may have vested interests in the outcomes of their protests, or they may simply be *moral entrepreneurs* engaged in what they see as a purely moral crusade (Becker, 1963). As the cause of a particular claims-making group becomes acknowledged by society more generally, the social condition comes to be defined as a social problem. Social problems, then, are essentially *discovered* through this process of societal reactions and social definitions. From this perspective, social problems come and go as societal reactions to given conditions change.

Among other things, the *social constructionist perspective* helps to explain cross-cultural variations in definitions of family violence. That is, what is condemned as abuse in one culture is not always condemned in another. The social constructionist perspective also helps to illustrate how research is used in ongoing debates about social problems. The findings from family violence research have not uniformly settled disagreements about family violence–related topics. Instead, the research has become one of the most contentious areas in the social sciences. Experts pose many significant and far-reaching questions: Is family violence increasing or decreasing? Are men as likely as women to be the victims of intimate partner violence? Should parents be allowed to hit their children? And what constitutes rape? Although one might hope that research could settle such debates, the reality is that competing claims-makers interpret research data differently. Furthermore, those on both sides in any given debate typically arm themselves with their own sets of empirical findings, which they espouse as *the truth.* From a social constructionist perspective, the "winners" of these debates define the nature and the facts of social problems (Best, 2001).

## Discovering Child Maltreatment: The Historical Context

> This history of childhood is a nightmare from which we have only recently begun to awaken. The further back in history one goes, the lower the level of child care, and the more likely children are to be killed, abandoned, beaten, terrorized, and sexually abused. (deMause, 1974, p. 1)

Contemporary conceptions of children and childhood in the United States—that childhood is a special phase of life and that children should be loved, nurtured, and protected from the cruel world—emerged only within the past few hundred years. As Empey, Stafford, and Hay (1999) noted, in previous times children were "regarded more as small or inadequate versions of their parents than as sacred beings in need of special protection" (pp. 6–7). One illustration of the previous indifference to children as a group with special status is the historical practice of infanticide. Some scholars maintain infanticide was the most frequent crime in all of Europe and remained a relatively common practice until about 1800 (Piers, 1978).

Over the centuries, the value of children grew in developed societies, and by the 1900s in the United States, the government's interest in the welfare of children resulted in *child protection laws* including child labor laws, the creation of a juvenile court system, and mandatory education requirements. Although these changes likely reflect an increase in the value U.S. society placed on children, they no doubt also came about because of the state's interest in protecting itself from troubled children and the troubled adults these children often become (Pfohl, 1977).

*Discovering child physical abuse.* In many ways, the indifference to childhood evidenced in previous centuries is not difficult to explain. The harshness of life, the high rates of disease, and the visibility of death all contributed to a general devaluation of life and of children's lives in particular. In addition, most societies regarded children as the property of their parents, who were allowed to treat their property as they saw fit. In some cases, parents probably viewed their children as economic liabilities—as little more than more mouths to feed (Walker, Bonner, & Kaufman, 1988; Wolfe, 1991).

Many scholars trace the actual discovery of child abuse in the United States to the *house of refuge movement* of the early 1800s. The medieval principle of *parens patriae*—that is, the right and responsibility of the state to protect those who cannot protect themselves—guided this movement (Pfohl, 1977). As a result of reforms brought about by the movement in the early to mid-1800s, authorities began to house children who were neglected, abused, or otherwise *on the road to ruin* in one of many state-supported institutions. The house of refuge movement represents the government's first attempt to intervene in neglect and abuse cases (Empey, et al., 1999).

*First child abuse court case.* Probably the most famous early court case involving child abuse was tried in 1874. Church social worker Etta Wheeler discovered that 8-year-old Mary Ellen Wilson was being beaten and starved by her stepmother. After unsuccessfully seeking help to remedy the situation, Wheeler took the case to Henry Bergh, founder of the *Society for the Prevention of Cruelty to Animals.* Mary Ellen was, after all, a member of the animal kingdom. A courtroom full of concerned New Yorkers, many of them upper-class women, heard the shocking details of Mary Ellen's life. The stepmother had beaten her almost daily and did not allow her to play with other children or even to leave the house. Mary Ellen had an unhealed gash on the left side of her face, where her stepmother had struck her with a pair of scissors. The jury took only 20 minutes to find the stepmother guilty of assault and battery (Pleck, 1987).

*Child-saving movement.* Because of the resulting public outcry, concerned citizens eventually founded the *Society for the Prevention of Cruelty to Children* in 1874 (Pagelow, 1984). This organization, and the larger *child-saving movement* of which it was a part, advocated for dramatic changes in society's treatment of children. Increasingly, child protection advocates argued that children need to be loved and nurtured, and if parents fail to protect their children, the state should intervene. They argued, in effect, that parents should not have complete authority over their children (Finkelhor, 1996).

Largely as a result of the claims-making of child advocacy groups, many state legislatures passed child protective statutes in the early 1900s, criminalizing parents' abusive and neglectful behavior and specifying procedures for meeting the needs of abused and neglected children (Pleck, 1987). Although there was considerable movement toward child protection during this time, sociolegal reactions to the problem of child abuse remained somewhat sporadic. For example, no laws existed to make the reporting of suspected child abuse mandatory for certain professionals.

*The battered child syndrome.* The full recognition of child abuse as a social problem in the United States was not complete until the 1960s, when Dr. C. Henry Kempe and his colleagues first described the **battered child syndrome.** They further suggested that physicians should report any observed cases of abuse (Kempe, Silverman, Steele, Droegemueller, & Silver, 1962). Kempe et al. defined child abuse as a *clinical condition with diagnosable medical and physical symptoms resulting from deliberate physical assault.* This declaration was important because it marked the addition of the considerable clout of the medical community to claims-making about the child abuse problem. When medical doctors combined forces with other professionals and child protection advocacy groups, the movement rapidly gained momentum. Before the end of the 1960s, every U.S. state had created laws mandating that professionals report suspected cases of abuse, and in 1974, Congress enacted the *Child Abuse Prevention and Treatment Act,* which provided federal funding to help states fight child abuse.

*Discovering child sexual abuse.* Throughout history, and particularly in certain cultures, sexual interactions involving children have been commonplace. Some cultures have regarded these interactions as appropriate, even healthy for children. As one illustration, the ancient Greeks sexually exploited children, especially boys (deMause, 1974). Despite dramatic changes over the centuries, condemnation of sexual contact between adults and children is still not universal. One extreme minority perspective is that of the North American Man/Boy Love Association (NAMBLA). This organization, founded in 1978, supports "the rights of all people to engage in consensual relations, and opposes laws which destroy loving relationships merely on the basis of the age of the participants" (NAMBLA, 2002). Robert Rhodes, a NAMBLA spokesman, made the following comments when asked whether the group views itself as an advocacy group for children:

> Yes. Considering the legitimacy of sexual relationships with children, there are two main theories that you can work from. One was the classical Greek theory—that is to say that the older partner in a sexual relationship served as initiator and tutor of the younger partner. You can also take a children's liberationist viewpoint—that is to say that children insofar as is possible—and it's far more possible than the current structure allows—should be given liberty to run their own lives as they choose, including the ability to determine how and with whom they should have sex. (quoted in Hechler, 1988, pp. 193–194)

Fortunately, mainstream America totally rejects the philosophy of NAMBLA. Even though freedom of speech allows NAMBLA members the right to express their beliefs, laws forbid any sexual contact between adults and children. Legislatures and attorneys continue their struggle to update legislation to protect children more effectively.

*Discovering child neglect and psychological maltreatment.* Child neglect is probably the *most forgotten* form of maltreatment (Daro, 1988). Such limited interest in neglect is surprising, however, given that it is much more common than physical or sexual child abuse. Psychological maltreatment is also pervasive and overlooked, even though it is a central component in all child maltreatment. The most obvious reason for these oversights is that physical and sexual abuse are far more likely to result in observable harm, and the definition of child physical abuse tends to be defined only in terms of *harm*. By contrast, the many negative effects of neglect and psychological maltreatment may not result in observable harm.

Although child neglect is a very old phenomenon, society did not come to acknowledge and define it as a social problem until the 20th century (Wolock & Horowitz, 1984). Psychological maltreatment of children has received even less recognition. Professionals have tended to look at psychological abuse as a *side effect* of other forms of abuse, rather than as a unique form of maltreatment. Only since the early 1990s have experts established psychological maltreatment as a discrete form of child maltreatment (see Hart & Brassard, 1993; Loring, 1994; Wiehe, 1990). Now, surveys suggest that Americans have finally come to consider psychological maltreatment a serious problem. Of those surveyed, 75% indicated that exposure to "repeated yelling and swearing" is harmful to a child's well-being (Daro & Gelles, 1992).

# Discovering Intimate Partner Violence:
# The Historical Context

WOMAN'S RIGHTS CONVENTION. A Convention to discuss the social, civil, and religious condition and rights of women, will be held in the Wesleyan Chapel, at Seneca Falls, N.Y., on Wednesday and Thursday, the 19th and 20th of July, current; commencing at 10 o'clock am. (*Seneca Falls Convention*, 1848)

Social conditions in the United States were not conducive to the recognition of wife abuse until the women's movement of the mid-1800s called attention to the subordination of women. This movement, which was followed by the suffragist movement of the early 1900s and the feminist movement of the mid- to late 1900s, was an important precursor to the discovery of marital violence. The Seneca Falls Convention in 1848 planted the seed for a women's rights movement in a Wesleyan Methodist church in Seneca Falls, New York. Lucretia Mott, wife of an antislavery reformer and Quaker preacher, and women's rights advocate Elizabeth Stanton organized the Seneca Falls Convention. In the days prior to the convention, Stanton wrote the convention's Declaration of Sentiments, a document modeled after the Declaration of Independence. The declaration begins with the following pronouncement:

We hold these truths to be self-evident; that all men and women are created equal; that they are endowed by their Creator with certain inalienable rights; that among these are life, liberty, and the pursuit of happiness; that to secure these rights governments are instituted, deriving their just powers from the consent of the governed. (*Seneca Falls Convention*, 1848)

In strong language, the document asserts that throughout history men have injured and controlled women in hopes of establishing absolute tyranny over them. It concludes: "In view of this entire disfranchisement of one-half the people of this country . . . we insist that they have immediate admission to all the rights and privileges which belong to them as citizens of the United States."

Through the early 1900s, the struggle for women's rights in the United States focused mainly on securing the *right to vote*. Presumably, the right to vote would give women the necessary power to challenge many injustices, including violence in the family (Ashcraft, 2000). The efforts of the suffragist movement culminated with the passage of the 19th Amendment to the U.S. Constitution in 1920. Another advance for women occurred during World War II when women's joining the labor force changed some opinions about the adage, "women's place is in the home." During the 1960s, interest in women's rights revived as a new feminist movement gained momentum. The 1965 Supreme Court decision giving women access to birth control in every state freed women to limit the size of their families, to undertake alternative roles, and to pursue their autonomy. Now, the movement's major concerns turned to the subordination and victimization of women within the family.

*Discovering battered women.* Many historians have noted that early marriage laws actually gave men the legal right to hit their wives (R. E. Dobash & Dobash, 1979). Thus, the marriage license became "a hitting license" (Straus, 1983). English common law held that women were inferior to men, and a married woman had *no legal existence* apart from her husband. The husband, in effect, owned and controlled her, and he also was accountable for her actions. Because social norms expected husbands to govern their wives, the law allowed them a great deal of latitude in using force to do so (Sigler, 1989). Early *British rape laws* also reflected the status of women as property, stating that when a woman was raped, restitution should be paid to her husband (or, if she was unmarried, to her father) (Sigler, 1989).

Recognizing the vulnerability of women within the family, Elizabeth Stanton argued that the rights of women should be acknowledged in all spheres of life. In doing so, she listed a number of facts, several of which related specifically to the family:

> He has made her, if married, in the eye of the law, civilly dead. He has taken from her all right in property, even to the wages she earns. In the covenant of marriage, she is compelled to promise obedience to her husband, he becoming, to all intents and purposes, her master—the law giving him power to deprive her of her liberty and to administer chastisement. He has so framed the laws of divorce, as to what shall be the proper causes, and in case of separation, to whom the guardianship of the children shall be given, as to be wholly regardless of the happiness of women—the law, in all cases, going upon a false supposition of the supremacy of man, and giving all power into his hands. (*Seneca Falls Convention*, 1848)

Despite the efforts of Stanton and other influential reformers, the problem of wife abuse attracted little attention in the first half of the 20th century. As Pleck (1987) has noted, the campaign was, "compared to the child abuse movement of roughly the same time period, an abysmal failure" (p. 109). The modern feminist movement that arose in the 1960s renewed public interest in the problem of the subordination of women, in general, and in marital relationships in particular. Initially, however, leaders of the movement, including the National Organization for Women (NOW), tended to ignore wife abuse. Instead, NOW focused on passage of the Equal Rights Amendment, elimination of discrimination against women in the workplace, public funding for child care, and abortion rights. To the degree that feminists did advocate for battered women, the public, suspicious of their claims, often dismissed the movement as too radical and antifamily (Pleck, 1987).

The battered women's movement gained momentum when *Chiswick Women's Aid,* the first shelter for battered women to gain widespread public attention, opened in England in 1971. Chiswick's founder, Erin Pizzey, published the influential book *Scream Quietly or the Neighbours Will Hear* in 1974. The publicity that surrounded the book, and the subsequent radio and television exposure it generated, helped spread the battered women's movement in Europe. American activists, influenced by visiting Chiswick in the early 1970s, were eager to open similar shelters in the United States. A flood of media attention in the mid-1970s further increased public awareness of the domestic violence problem (R. E. Dobash & Dobash, 1978, 1979; Pleck, 1987).

In 1976, NOW decided to make wife battering a priority issue. As advocates founded organizations such as the *National Coalition Against Domestic Violence,* they effectively brought attention to battered women's issues at the national level. Their work led to improvements in social services for battered wives and changes in legal statutes that failed to protect women

(Studer, 1984). Several other organizations, such as the *National Organization for Victim Assistance* and the *National Council on Child Abuse and Family Violence,* actively fought for the rights of women. Although these organizations had somewhat dissimilar social and political agendas, their combined efforts raised awareness of the significance of violence against women as a *social problem.* Public health scholars recently pronounced violence against women to be a serious national *health problem,* because of the countless negative physical and mental health consequences of IPV (Chrisler & Ferguson, 2006). To some extent, the battered women's movement is a victim of its own success. Broad-based organizations, such as health care and government entities, have become so embedded in the movement that it is now mainstream, no longer in need of specialized advocates (Allen, Lehner, Marrison, Miles, & Russel, 2007).

*Discovering marital rape.* The women's movement has been influential in the relatively recent discovery of another form of domestic violence: *marital rape.* Historically, rape laws have pertained only to sexual assault outside of marriage. In the 1700s, Sir Matthew Hale, a chief justice of the Court of Kings Bench in England, originated the *marital exemption law.* The exemption held that by mutual matrimonial consent and contract, a wife had given her consent to sexual intercourse with her husband and could not retract it. Countering this longstanding assumption, early reformers viewed a woman's right to control her own body as key to eliminating her subordination, and they waged a vigorous campaign against a man's right to force sex in marriage. Their attempts to change marital exemption laws, however, were unsuccessful, and in the 19th century, the *status quo* continued. There were no criminal charges against any husband for raping his wife (Pleck, 1987).

Not until the modern feminist movement of the 1960s and 1970s did the topic of marital rape materialize once again. Contemporary defenders of the marital exemption law have challenged feminist claims-making during the past 40 years, arguing that the state has no business intervening in the private affairs of married couples. Defenders claimed that once the state intervenes, the love, trust, and closeness in a marriage will disintegrate, unlikely ever to be recovered (Hasday, 2000). Another defense of the marital exemption is that a husband may need protection from a vindictive wife who might falsely accuse him of marital rape as leverage in a divorce case. Diana Russell, however, illustrated the problem of uninformed legislators and others in the 1990 revision of her book *Rape in Marriage,* in which she quotes a telltale statement made by California state senator Bob Wilson: "But if you can't rape your wife, who can you rape?" (p. 18).

Fortunately, feminists have made substantial legal inroads in their attempts to prevent married men from forcing their wives to have sex. Laws against marital rape, while still imperfect, made rape a crime in all 50 states in July 1993. Although marital rape laws now exist, changes in feelings of entitlement among male partners have not always kept pace. In a 1996 inquiry, Raquel Bergen relayed a statement reiterated frequently by a husband to his wife: "That's my body—my ass, my tits, my body. You gave that to me when you married me and that belongs to me" (p. 20).

*Discovering dating violence.* In 1981, James Makepeace published the results of a seminal study on dating violence. The apparent similarity between the victimization of women in dating relationships and in marital relationships led advocates and academicians to view dating violence as a form of violence against women (R. E. Dobash & Dobash, 1979). Given this renewed interest and availability of university students for research participation, surveys of dating violence became as prevalent as surveys of wife abuse. As the unresolved issues surrounding female-to-male dating violence resurfaced, advocates were successful in their claims-making, and today many high school and college campuses offer programs educating students about dating violence (Levy, 1991).

*Discovering sexual assault among dating couples.* In recent years, society has also come to recognize *date rape* as a serious social problem. Surprisingly, researchers determined that *sexual assault by an acquaintance* was far more likely than a violent sexual assault by a stranger. Date rape came more fully into view in the late 1980s when *Ms.* magazine published the results of a study called Campus Project on Sexual Assault (Koss, 1992, 1993). The study, which was funded by the National Institute of Mental Health, found that 27% of the college women surveyed had been victims of a completed rape (15%) or attempted rape (12%). Journalists in the popular press publicized the findings widely, and the study was the subject of a 1991 U.S. Senate hearing on sexual assault. Of late, experts have begun to abandon the term *date rape* in favor of *sexual assault* because the term *sexual assault* goes far beyond forceful intercourse and includes many forms of unwanted sexual touching (Clay-Warner & Burt, 2005).

*Discovering stalking.* Another form of abuse that is loosely related to dating violence (and wife battering) is *stalking,* which Tjaden and Thoennes (2000b) define as "visual or physical proximity; nonconsensual communication; verbal, written, or implied threats; or a combination thereof that would cause fear in a reasonable person" (p. 5). To provide an empirical definition of stalking, researchers queried battered women via a 13-item inventory. The women responded once for themselves and once for their stalker. See Table 1.1 for percentages of perpetrations and victimizations (items collapsed into subscale scores) reported by battered women (Langhinrichsen-Rohling, 2006).

These data round out the meaning (operationalization) of stalking and demonstrate the gendered nature of the behavior. Although stalking has always existed, criminal codes largely ignored it until the 1990s. Women's advocates and other groups were successful in attracting considerable media and scholarly attention to this behavior in the last few years, and today it is a criminal offense in all 50 states (Rosenfeld, 2000). Ongoing research has recognized stalking

**TABLE 1.1**  Stalking Perpetration and Victimization

| Perpetration | Victimization |
|---|---|
| Begging—29.3% | Begging—87.9% |
| Unwanted pursuit—41.3% | Unwanted pursuit—87.0.3% |
| Stalking—25.0% | Stalking—74.4% |
| Threatening—25.3% | Threatening—78.8% |

as a more serious crime, capable of causing traumatic reactions in its victims (Logan & Cole, 2007). With access to computers, *cyberstalking* has also become a frequent tool of stalking perpetrators (Moriarty & Freiberger, 2008).

*Discovering elder abuse.* Elder abuse has been one of the last forms of family violence to receive societal attention, following the discovery of child abuse in the 1960s and marital violence in the early 1970s (Wolf & Pillemer, 1989). The first research on elder abuse did not appear in the *Social Science Index* until 1981–1982 (Baumann, 1989). It was not until 1989 that a scholarly journal dedicated solely to the topic began publishing. The earliest federal government involvement in addressing elder abuse came in 1962, when Congress authorized payments to states to provide protective services for "persons with physical and/or mental limitations, who are unable to manage their own affairs . . . or who are neglected or exploited" (U.S. DHHS, as quoted in Wolf, 2000, p. 6). In 1974, Congress mandated adult protective services (APS) programs for all states.

For some observers, the image of the stressed and burdened adult daughter abusing an elderly parent *linked elder abuse to child abuse* and resulted in considerable media attention. Following the child abuse model, claims-makers successfully advocated for laws that make the reporting of suspected elder abuse mandatory for certain professionals (Wilber & McNeilly, 2001). Legal progress in the area continues with ongoing attempts to pass the *Elder Justice Act* and related bills. It has become increasingly clear that it is necessary to help protect seniors from financial fraud, phony marketers, and social security misuse. Efforts have resulted in improved emergency law enforcement and rape prevention (Stiegel & Klem, 2007). Most of the legal amendments have centered on advancing guardianship rules and court oversight (Cook-Daniels, 2008a). The *Elder Justice Coalition* originated in early 2003 and included *five* founding organizations, such as the National Committee for the Prevention of Elder Abuse (NCPEA). Finally, advocates inaugurated an Elder Abuse Awareness Day on June 15, 2006.

*Discovering battered (?) men.* One vigorous debate in the field of family violence centers on the issue of female-to-male intimate partner violence (IPV). The debate can in many respects be traced to survey data from the 1970s and 1980s that suggest that wives are violent toward their spouses as frequently as husbands are violent toward their spouses (Gelles & Straus, 1988; Straus, Gelles, & Steinmetz, 1980). Most of these data emanated from research using the Conflict Tactics Scale (CTS), a self-report instrument that measures the frequency of various kinds of violent interpersonal interactions between couples (see the discussion of the CTS in Chapter 2). Findings from the *National Family Violence Resurvey* indicated that 12% of the women and 11% of the men surveyed engaged in at least one act of interpersonal violence (usually minor violence) in the previous year.

The assertion that women are as violent as men troubles and angers many battered women's advocates who perceive the "real" marital violence problem to be wife battering. Critics charge that the CTS fails to measure the degree to which women who report committing violent acts may be acting in *self-defense* or out of *fear* (Kurz, 1989). As the debate progressed, Saunders (2002) reviewed the available IPV literature and found no consensus among experts that female-to-male partner violence is even a social problem, let alone a behavioral equivalent to male-to-female violence. While strenuously defending gender equivalence of IPV, Straus and his colleagues (1980) stated that it would be unfortunate if the data on wife-to-husband violence "distracted us from giving first attention to wives as victims as the focus of social policy" (p. 43). Arguably, however, the data derived from their research showing extensive female-to-male violence via the CTS have fed a backlash against the battered women's movement (George, 2003).

Whatever the case may be, it is reassuring to note that the issue of male victimization has attracted more academic attention in the last decade. As researchers found evidence of some female-to-male IPV, the debate evolved into a comparison of gender similarities and differences in IPV (Miller & Meloy, 2006). As an illustration, *coercive control* of one's partner is not only a feature of male-to-female IPV, but also of female-to-male IPV, although to a much lesser extent (Swan & Snow, 2006). Competing claims-makers continue to negotiate the scope and nature of domestic violence. For the time being, the issue of women's violence against men remains in the background to some extent, as the real problem of IPV has emerged as *woman battering*.

## The Co-occurrence of Child Maltreatment and Marital Violence

It may come as no surprise that child maltreatment and marital violence very frequently occur within the same family. Co-occurrence refers to situations in which one or both adult partners are abusive not only toward the other but also toward a child within the same family (Knickerbocker, Heyman, Slep, Jouriles, & McDonald, 2007). The exact amount of abusive behaviors that overlap is unknown but seems to extend between 30% and 60% (Appel & Holden, 1998). According to M. A. Dutton (as cited in Dingfelder, 2006b), child maltreatment and partner abuse are linked to such an extent that scholars *must* address them jointly.

Funding sources and advocate organizations are beginning to note this linkage and are altering their approaches accordingly. Scholars have commented on the vastly different mandates of the agencies involved. *Child Protective Services (CPS)* primarily focus on protecting children with much less concern toward mothers. Battered women's advocates focus primarily on the safety of both mothers and children and on the rights of the mother. These different goals came to a head in an adversarial manner when CPS charged a battered mother with child neglect because she *allowed* her children to see her husband beat her. Incredibly, a New York court in 1999 sided with CPS and found the mother guilty. Although higher courts later soundly reversed the decision, the case made it clear that co-occurring violence urgently requires professional attention (Clarke, 2006). For now, representatives from both factions are attempting to resolve their different approaches through collaborative exchanges.

## International and Understudied Groups in the Discovery of Family Violence

Most Americans probably did not know much about Osama bin Laden, the Taliban, or the views of radical Islamic fundamentalists prior to the terrorist attacks on September 11, 2001.

These attacks not only awakened Americans to the threat of terrorism, but also served to raise awareness about another shocking reality: the oppression of women and children around the world. Many of these practices constitute *human rights violations.* Only after the attacks did the mistreatment of women in Afghanistan make headlines in major U.S. newspapers and magazines. Such mistreatment, however, is not unique to radical Islamic fundamentalism. Other conservative extremist groups across the globe cling to similar cruel customs.

Women and children (especially girls) around the world have been and continue to be victimized by a vast array of cultural practices, including genital mutilation, foot binding, dowry death, child abandonment and infanticide, selective abortion of female fetuses, sexual exploitation, forced prostitution, and violent pornography (Holloway, 1994; Levesque, 2001). Many of these practices continue today essentially as customary laws—that is, customs that predate international legal reforms and are still widely observed (Levesque, 2001). These customs are deeply rooted in some cultures and continue to influence contemporary practices.

In China, for example, the state's one-child policy (which penalizes married couples for having more than the prescribed number of children) appears to have increased infanticide. Demographers estimate that approximately 12% of Chinese girl infants go missing each year (Riley, 1996). Another example of a cultural practice that indirectly contributes to abuse is India's dowry system. Wives whose families cannot pay dowries (payments to a groom) are often abused and sometimes killed by their husbands or their husbands' families (Levesque, 2001).

Levesque (2001) cites estimates made by the United Nations that between 17% and 38% of the world's women are victims of intimate violence, with rates as high as 60% in developing countries. McWhirter (1999) reported that in Chile, *private* violence probably affects 25% of wives and 60% of families. The country's cultural history of machismo, alcohol use, and acceptance of violence, in general, has hindered reform efforts. Illustrative of the seriousness of male violence against women are the criminal penalties for wife abuse. In Chile, legal sanctions apply only if the abuse resulted in at least 14 days of hospitalization for the victim or her loss of work (Levesque, 2001).

*Cross-cultural family abuse.* For the most part, American academicians have failed to blend into their definitions of IPV nuanced interpretations of family violence derived from other cultures. One indication of cultural variation comes from battered Japanese women who emphasize unprotected sex as a particularly onerous type of *male-to-female intimate partner violence* (**MFIPV**; Yoshihama, 2002). Chinese people living in Hong Kong are especially sensitive to the selection of terms, such as violence versus abuse, when responding to questionnaires about IPV (Tang, Cheung, Chen, & Sun, 2002). For a comprehensive discussion of definitions across cultures, see Malley-Morrison and Hines (2004).

*Immigrant family violence.* As American culture has become more diverse, the need to study, understand, and respond to cultural variations in family violence has received priority consideration from organizations, such as the American Psychological Association (APA 2003). Scholars in every field have forcefully called for enhanced cultural competence among practitioners and researchers. There is a great need to translate assessment tools, recognize some of the subtleties of cultures that influence behaviors, and expand programs aimed at minorities (e.g., Calvete, Corral, & Estévez, 2007; Keller, Gonzales, & Fleuriet, 2005).

Immigrant women are especially vulnerable to IPV because they may be socially isolated and economically dependent on their spouses. Husbands can easily threaten their spouses with deportation (LaViolette & Barnett, 2000). Latino immigrants in the United States are more likely than Anglo families to live in poverty and to experience the stresses associated with recent immigration—factors that are likely to contribute to violence in the family. Latino parents tend to be relatively authoritarian and are more likely than Anglo-American parents to *punish their children physically*. As Fontes (2002) notes, the vast majority of these families are not dysfunctional or abusive, and they do not need the strong arm of the state. What these parents need are culturally competent counselors who can apply their knowledge in several ways: (a) to explain the dangers of punishing children physically, (b) to teach nonviolent parenting skills, and (c) to help families to cope with the isolation and other stressors they may be experiencing.

*Violence among ethnic and racial minorities.* Findings about *ethnic and racial differences* in IPV are mixed. Although several studies have uncovered higher rates of IPV among several minority groups, others have found few, if any, differences (McFarlane, Groff, O'Brien, & Watson, 2005; Smith & Chiricos, 2003). Caution in interpreting these findings is warranted because of other factors: (a) Police bias accounts for some racial disparity in felony arrest rates for black women (Bourg & Stock, 1994); (b) Demographic and socioeconomic factors help explain some racial disparities (Lauritsen & White, 2001); (c) Combining data from several diverse ethnic groups (e.g., Native American Indians and Asian Americans) distorts the findings (Sokoloff & Dupont, 2005); (d) Providing research respondents with inventories labeled as *crime surveys* versus *personal safety* surveys alters the results (McFarlane et al., 2005); and (e) Lack of knowledge of the impact of current and historical parameters of racism have influenced responses. Finally, there is no empirical evidence suggesting that racial differences in family violence are rooted in biology.

*Violence between gay and lesbian partners.* One form of interpartner violence that has only lately attracted academic research is IPV between *gay and lesbian partners*. One of the first influential books covering same-sex IPV (Renzetti, 1992) appeared in the early 1990s. The amount of contemporary research on the topic, however, has eclipsed expectations and is having a strong impact on the field of family violence. For one reason, findings about same-sex IPV have challenged the attribution of partner violence to the patriarchy (D. G. Dutton, 1994). Research continues to suggest that while the rates of some forms of violence within homosexual relationships are similar to those found within heterosexual relationships, the *forms* of abuse vary considerably. Same-sex assaults produce substantially more injuries, and same-sex homicides tend to be much more brutal than heterosexual homicides (Bartholomew, Regan, White, & Oram, 2008; Mize & Shackelford, 2008).

*Abuse of disabled intimates.* A 2000 definition of *disability* from the National Center for Injury Prevention and Control defines disability as "limitations in physical or mental function, caused by one or more health conditions, in carrying out socially defined tasks and roles that individuals generally are expected to be able to do" (p. 1). Research on disabled women and children is especially sad and especially limited. Perpetrators do things such as move furniture around the house so that a blind spouse will trip over it. The prevalence of IPV in various disabled populations is unknown, but specialists theorize that disabled women may be 10 times more likely than nondisabled women to be abused (Sobsey, 1994; see also Sundram, 2000).

*Religious diversity.* Some current religious groups in the United States rob women of equality with men, going so far as to embed male dominance into their by-laws (Niebuhr, 1998). "The major religions legitimize the power of men over women as a God-given right, and there are strong historical traditions indicating approval of men beating their wives—within certain limits—as a way of controlling their behavior" (Archer, 2006, p. 149). Mormons, for instance, usually believe in rigid gender roles that give preference to men. A smattering of Mormons operating *under the radar* appear to cling to bygone and illegal practices, such as forced early marriage of teenage girls, and polygamy (Tresniowski, Atlas, Lang, & Cardwell, 2009). Because of the dual combination of religious freedom and an emphasis on parental rights in the United States, authorities hesitate to interfere with child-rearing practices that are simply unusual.

Some doctrines, though, incorporate beliefs that are so extreme, that agents of the mainstream culture must intervene. One exemplar is the rejection of modern medicine by Christian Scientists. In the news on May 16, 2009, was a story about a judge who ruled that the parents of a 13-year-old cancer victim must allow the boy to undergo chemotherapy. The doctors feared that the delay in obtaining a court order might already have cost the boy his life (Forliti, 2009). In addition, most denominations condemn homosexuality, thus threatening homosexuals' self-esteem and complicating their help-seeking efforts for same-sex IPV (Lacayo, Barovick, Cloud, & Duffy, 1998). On a more positive note, several studies of female IPV victims judged spiritual beliefs to be beneficial and important to their ability to cope (Farrell, 1996; Goodman, Dutton, Weinfurt, & Cook, 2003; Humphreys, Lee, Neylan, & Marmar, 1999).

*Abuse of rural residents.* Rural abused women are another subpopulation in dire need of aid, because they are isolated in a cultural enclave of patriarchy (Websdale, 1995). There are several elements that make it especially difficult for rural battered women: (a) a more patriarchal social order, (b) greater gun use, (c) inadequate or no criminal justice response to incidents of male-to-female IPV, and (d) a lack of confidentiality, phones, shelters, transportation, social support, and legal representation (Thompson, 1995; Websdale, 1995).

*Abuse among intimates serving in the military.* There are reasons to ask whether military training and service negatively influence family harmony and the safety of all family members. The emphases on killing and weapons training, the increased stress caused by family separations, male dominance, and other factors intimate that IPV rates would be very high. Research in the area is ongoing, but the attitudes of some military commanders hamper efforts to identify problems. Some studies have found that IPV rates among military personnel are higher and that deployment may increase the rates. In one respect, however, military discipline can be somewhat effective in compelling treatment and in enforcing regulations requiring nonviolence in the home (e.g., McCarroll, Thayer, et al., 2000).

## Defining Family Violence: Understanding the Social Construction of Deviance Definitions

Just as the claims-making process has played a role in the history and discovery of family violence, it plays an important role in how family violence is defined. Claims-making influences people's understanding of what the problem is and, in turn, impacts academia and policy. Claims-making among researchers has sometimes led to use of vastly different research methodologies that have often produced competing definitions. Because of claims-making and other factors, any given definition is rarely accepted as universally correct. Two examples help to illustrate this point.

### Corporal Punishment

Many social scientists and child advocates believe that corporal punishment is morally wrong, harmful to children, and counterproductive. Some go so far as to argue that corporal punishment is a form of child abuse (Gershoff, 2008). Such claims-makers offer their arguments in an attempt to influence societal definitions of child maltreatment. Despite the worries of child abuse experts, surveys have shown that a majority of U.S. parents spank, and every U.S. state protects the right of a parent to spank as long is the child is not injured. But if the voices of these claims-makers become more persuasive in the future, spanking could conceivably be criminalized in the United States, as it is now in some Scandinavian countries (Straus, 1994).

### Defining Rape

Equally controversial is how to define rape. Currently, the FBI defines rape as "carnal knowledge of a female forcibly and against her will" (U.S. Department of Justice, 2004). Ordinarily, experts define *carnal knowledge* so narrowly that it excludes a number of onerous sexual acts. In the past 20 years, feminists have convincingly argued that all forced sexual acts should be legally condemned. In response, most states have rewritten and expanded their legal definitions of rape. Feminists have also advocated, with some success, for a broadening of the interpretation of *against her will,* arguing that where there is no female desire or explicit consent there is, by definition, male coercion. From this more inclusive perspective, a woman whose ability to consent is compromised by alcohol/drugs or through some form of coercion is judged to be a victim of rape.

### Defining Family

In general, the term *family violence* refers to violence that takes place between immediate family members: husbands, wives, children, and parents. Yet, consideration of the topic invariably leads to the discussion of interpersonal violence outside the bounds of the traditional family. Cultural and legal definitions of what constitutes a family are changing, and as a result it has become impossible to discuss marital violence, for example, without also considering violence between unmarried intimates. Today, the term *intimate* is more commonly used to refer to anyone in a very close personal relationship, frequently a sexual relationship, even same-sex relationships. The *U.S. Bureau of Justice and the Centers for Disease Control and Prevention* currently use the term *intimate partner violence* to refer to violence between spouses, ex-spouses, or separated spouses; between cohabiters or ex-cohabiters; between boyfriends or ex-boyfriends and girlfriends or ex-girlfriends; and between same-sex partners or ex-partners.

Many of the forms of violence discussed in this volume occur outside of families as well as within them. Child sexual abuse most often occurs within the family, but not always. Elders may suffer abuse at the hands of family members, but society neglects them more generally. Although the primary focus in this text is on the family, there are a few discussions of abusive settings that exist outside the family unit, such as those of persons in a position of trust in the caretaking of children.

## Defining Violence

Violence may be defined as "an act carried out with the intention of, or an act perceived as having the intention of, physically hurting another person" (Steinmetz, 1987, p. 729). Although this definition offers a clear and concise starting point, it can be overly narrow when it fails to include some forms of maltreatment, such as child neglect or controlling a spouse's right to leave the house. On the other hand, it may be *overly broad* when it includes corporal punishment or slightly pushing a spouse once in 20 years.

## Defining Family Violence

The focus of this text is primarily violence that has been successfully labeled *abusive* by claims-makers. Roger Levesque (2001) offers one suitable definition: "Family violence includes family members' acts of omission or commission resulting in physical abuse, sexual abuse, emotional abuse, neglect, or other forms of maltreatment that hamper individuals' healthy development" (p. 13). A government-convened panel of experts suggests defining violence against intimate partners as consisting of three kinds of behaviors: (a) physical violence, (b) sexual violence, and (c) threats of physical and/or sexual violence. The panel concluded that *abuse* should be defined broadly to include the above three types of violent behaviors *and* two more forms: (d) stalking and (e) psychological/emotional abuse (Saltzman, Fanslow, McMahon, & Shelley, 1999). The *APA Dictionary of Psychology* defines domestic violence as "any action by a person that causes physical harm to one or more members of his or her family unit" (VandenBos, 2007, p. 295).

The imprecision of definitions has contributed to differences of opinion and in some cases to contentious debates about methods for assessing family violence. The terminology selected by various scholars may *not* convey the *extent of harm* a specific act may cause. Some forms of physical violence, such as cutting with a knife, cause observable physical harm, while others, such as emotional abuse, cause less visible harm. Hence, *observable harm* is not a perfect yardstick. Sexual abuse, for example, may have near-incapacitating effects that last a lifetime but do not inevitably cause physical injury. A spouse can be emotionally tormented and controlled by the other spouse without a blow being struck. Elders can be harmed through neglect and financial exploitation, rather than physical assault.

Perhaps, some acts of family violence should be referred to as *abuse* rather than violence, because they do not meet a *physical harm* standard. Because the definition is so unsettled, most definitions of family violence use the terms *violence* and *abuse* interchangeably. To offset confusion and dissension, progressive social scientists are now calling for **operationalized** definitions for *every* type of family violence (Knickerbocker et al., 2007). An operationalized definition is one developed through empirical measurement. Intelligence, for instance, gains its meaning through standardized IQ tests.

New knowledge from other fields may help resolve these dilemmas. Neurobiological studies have documented actual *brain changes* resulting from childhood abuse. The major alteration was an increased sensitivity to stress (McGowan et al., 2009). Similarly, brain scans have exposed size reductions of the frontal lobe (i.e., thinking) and hippocampus (i.e., memory) of children reared in poverty. The scientists attributed the decreased brain volume to the constant stresses of being poor, especially being at the bottom of the social ladder. The brain deficits caused a decrease in ability to learn that probably will last a lifetime ("I Am Just a Poor Boy," 2009).

## Legally Defining Family Violence

Ultimately, societal norms associated with the legitimacy of family-violent acts are formalized into laws. The difficulty of specifying a norm, of course, varies across dissimilar forms of abuse, because beliefs about the legitimacy of behavioral practices diverge across individuals and whole cultures. One set of laws that is not especially ambiguous are the child sexual abuse laws, because they focus on *perpetrator actions.* The laws concerning physical abuse, neglect, and psychological abuse, in contrast, tend to focus on the *injury outcomes* for the victim and, as a result, are far less clearly defined. The legal distinction between legitimate and illegitimate forms of verbal abuse is less clear yet, and making a legal distinction between neglectful parents and poor parents is especially problematic. Legal definitions of physical marital violence may seem relatively unambiguous, because in the eyes of the law there is no legitimate marital violence. Nevertheless, current scholars evaluate legal definitions of IPV as so narrow as to be unacceptable (DeKeseredy & Schwartz, 1998).

Defining family violence is compounded by historical approaches to enforcement of laws, laws that apply to single violent incidents. In reality, IPV rarely occurs as a *single incident,* but more accurately occurs as an ongoing series of violent events (Hirschel & Buzawa, 2002). Furthermore, the law does not take into account many obvious disparities in violence associated with gender. The law considers a hit by a woman to be just as serious as a hit by a man

(Osthoff, 2002). Battered women's motivation for female-to-male violence may be distinctly different from those of a batterer. While advocates view battered women's violence as likely to be self-defensive, criminal justice personnel are just as likely to view it as a form of *mutual combat.* Battered women's motivation for IPV may also be unimportant to some judges or other personnel who are attempting to avoid gender bias in implementing laws (Kernsmith, 2005a; Osthoff, 2002). All these factors emphasize the critical need to understand the dynamics of violent relationships.

## Monetary and Other Costs of Family Violence

In addition to concern for children's and women's safety and well-being, society should be concerned about the staggering costs of IPV. Researchers trying to capture the monetary cost of IPV have taken several broad approaches. One tactic is to estimate the financial burden of *treating injuries* and providing *mental health care* for victims. Another line of attack has been to investigate the costs of IPV-related *homelessness and welfare.* Finally, agencies within the U.S. *criminal justice system* have begun to scrutinize the costs of *processing* battery cases. Analyzing the National Violence Against Women Survey (NVAWS; Tjaden & Thoennes, 1998a) and several other data sources, a panel of experts determined the 1995 economic toll of IPV in the United States to be $5.8 billion, or if updated to 2003 dollars, $8.3 billion. Another team of analysts determined the cost for the 45.1% of the 8,000 female victims of IPV surveyed for the NVAWS (Ulrich et al., 2003). Categorizing the costs produced the figures in Table 1.2 (Max, Rice, Finkelstein, Bardwell, & Leadbetter, 2004).

**TABLE 1.2**    Costs for IPV

| Total Costs | Medical Costs for Injuries |
|---|---|
| Rapes—$320 million | Hospital care, 78.6% |
| Physical assaults—$4.2 billion | Physician care, 51.5% |
| Stalking—$342 million | Ambulance/paramedic, 14.9% |
| Murders—$893 million | Dental care, 9.5% |
|  | Physical therapy, 8.9% |

Battered women also took more time off from *paid work* and more time off from *child care and household* responsibilities. A comparison of the average number of injuries multiplied by the average cost of services for each injury yielded significant gendered differences. For men, the total cost of female-to-male IPV was $386.76 per person; for women, the total cost of male-to-female IPV per person was $948. These results emphasize the crucial toll of IPV beyond medical costs of assaults (Arias & Corso, 2005; see also T. R. Miller, Cohen, & Wiersema, 1996). Of course the costs of child abuse are similarly astounding. *Prevent Child Abuse America* published the estimates displayed in Table 1.3 (Wang & Holton, 2007).

**TABLE 1.3** Total Annual Cost of Child Abuse and Neglect in the United States

| Direct Costs | Estimates of Annual Costs (in 2007 Dollars) |
|---|---|
| Hospitalization | $6,625,959,263 |
| Mental health care system | $1,080,706,049 |
| Child welfare services system | $25,361,329,051 |
| Law enforcement | $33,307,770 |
| **Total Direct Costs** | **$33,101,302,133** |
| Indirect Costs | Estimates of Annual Costs (in 2007 Dollars) |
| Special education | $2,410,306,242 |
| Juvenile delinquency | $7,174,814,134 |
| Mental health and health care | $67,863,457 |
| Adult criminal justice system | $27,979,811,982 |
| Lost productivity to society | $33,019,919,544 |
| **Total Costs** | **$103,754,017,492** |

## PRACTICE, POLICY, AND PREVENTION ISSUES

It is useful to conclude this history of the discovery of family violence with a discussion of the numerous policies and practices introduced in recent years to help prevent family violence. As with the prevention of crime more generally, family violence prevention is confronted with two pervasive tensions. The first concerns the relative importance of prevention versus intervention.

- *Prevention* refers to social support and education programs designed to stop family violence before it occurs in the first place.
- *Intervention* refers to societal responses to family violence after it occurs. Such responses include programs to identify and protect victims, criminal justice sanctions for perpetrators, and various treatment options for offenders and victims.

In terms of intervention, the question arises about who the target of the intervention should be. Should society focus on protecting victims and punishing offenders, or on providing treatment and services for offenders and victims? A variety of *legal interventions* exist, such as mandatory reporting laws, mandatory arrest laws, criminal sanctions, and restraining orders. *Rehabilitative interventions* primarily include various types of counseling and medical treatment.

History helps to put the current social policy debates in context. Once family violence became fully recognized in the 1960s and 1970s, the most immediate concerns of authorities were the identification and protection of abuse victims and the punishment of offenders. This response, however, has often come at the expense of a societal commitment to *primary prevention* and efforts to help abusive families. With most of the resources available to combat family violence committed to the criminal justice response, little is left for the support and services needed by vulnerable families. Table 1.3 lists a number of family violence prevention and intervention strategies targeted toward children and adults. The following discussions introduce these strategies briefly.

It is possible to approach the subject of family violence prevention on many different levels. Because there are so many precursors to family violence, there are multiple opportunities to prevent it. One might begin with a discussion of the social problems directly or indirectly related to family violence (e.g., poverty, unemployment, inadequate housing, inadequate health care, and inadequate welfare assistance). Although these enduring and complicated problems are causally relevant, an expanded discussion of them is well beyond the scope of this book. More manageable are the various prevention strategies that focus specifically on community education and social services for families.

*Family support and training programs.* A teenager cannot legally drive an automobile without first receiving appropriate training and passing a driver's license test, but that same teenager can become a parent without any oversight from the state. Many who assume the role of parent are not adequately prepared to do so (Pogarsky, Thornberry, & Lizotte, 2006). In recent years, family support and training programs have become increasingly common as part of community efforts to enhance the knowledge and competence of new parents. Many involve home visits with at-risk (i.e., poor, single, young) parents of newborns or expectant mothers. These contacts give the service providers opportunities to work with the parents in a safe, nonconfrontational environment, and they may also prevent some of the social isolation that is often associated with abuse. Although in-home intervention programs typically focus on child abuse prevention, it is important to note that they could potentially influence marital violence rates as well (Wolfe & Jaffe, 1999).

*School-based programs.* School-based programs have obvious appeal because they are an inexpensive way to reach many children, teens, and college students. The most common sexual abuse prevention programs target school-age children (ages 6–12) and emphasize primary prevention and detection (Reppucci, Land, & Haugaard, 1998). The overwhelming majority of school districts in the United States offer sexual abuse programs, and research suggests that these programs are successful in increasing children's knowledge and in teaching prevention skills. Whether school-based programs actually reduce the incidence of sexual abuse is a matter of some debate (Wurtele, 2002).

Schools can also be suitable places for identifying children exposed to marital violence (Wolfe & Jaffe, 1999). Many scholars see the adolescent years (ages 13–18), when children often form their first intimate relationships, as an ideal time to teach children about the importance of violence-free intimate relationships (Godenzi & De Puy, 2001). High schools commonly offer a variety of school assemblies, lectures, videos, drama groups, and discussion groups in hopes of promoting healthy relationships and reducing dating and marital violence. Evaluation research suggests that such programs result in positive changes in knowledge and attitudes, and some reduction of violence perpetration (Wekerle & Wolfe, 1999). Although less common, there are growing numbers of school-based programs designed to educate parents (Hébert, Lavoie, & Parent, 2002). See Table 1.4 for a summary of prevention and intervention types of approaches.

At the *college level*, administrators often broaden discussions about the importance of healthy relationships to include more information about dating violence and sexual assault. Programs can have both primary prevention and intervention goals, including teaching definitions and providing information on its prevalence, its relationship to alcohol and drug misuse, and how to identify a potentially abusive partner. Aspects of the programs may include consciousness-raising regarding the sexual rights of women, rape myths, traditional sex roles,

**TABLE 1.4**  A Model for Prevention and Intervention

| Age-Group Targeted | Prevention (Designed to Stop Violence Before It Occurs) | Intervention (Response to Victims and Offenders) |
|---|---|---|
| Infants and preschoolers (ages 0–5) | *Family support and training programs:* | *Family support and training programs:* |
| | Education and social support for at-risk families | Intervention services for marginally abusive families |
| | | *Foster care and adoption programs:* |
| | | Provide alternative homes when conditions warrant removal |
| | | *Treatment programs:* |
| | | Programs for victims |
| School age to high school (ages 6–17) | *School-based education:* | *Foster care and adoption programs:* |
| | Programs to educate young children about inappropriate touching; programs to educate junior high and high school students about violence-free intimate relationships | Provide alternative homes when conditions warrant removal |
| | | *Treatment programs:* |
| | | Programs for victims and offenders |
| College age and adults (over age 17) | *College-based education:* | *Mandatory reporting policies:* |
| | Programs on violence-free intimate relationships and rape | Professional mandates to report child abuse, elder abuse, and, in some states, domestic violence |
| | *Community awareness campaigns:* | *Mandatory arrest and no-drop policies:* |
| | Campaigns to promote awareness about family violence | Policies that essentially force police and the courts to arrest and prosecute offenders |
| | | *Treatment programs:* |
| | | Programs for offenders and victims |

SOURCE: Adapted from Wolfe and Jaffe (1999, p. 137).

and assertiveness training for women (Holcomb, Savage, Seehafer, & Waalkes, 2002). Some special programs focus on the role of college men in preventing assaults on college women, with a few fraternities taking the lead. Universities also publish material for students relevant to prevention, intervention, and help-seeking sources. More and more colleges and universities are requiring attendance at such programs.

*Community awareness campaigns.* One of the easiest and most cost-efficient family violence prevention techniques is public education through advertisements and public service announcements. Many of the social movement organizations and federal agencies devoted to the family violence problem see themselves, at least in part, as public educators. One prominent example is the *Family Violence Prevention Fund* which, in collaboration with the *Advertising Council,* has initiated several public service campaigns. Among these is *Teach Early,* a domestic violence campaign directed toward men that sends the message, "What they learn as boys, they do as men. That's why we need to teach our sons and other boys in our lives that violence against women is wrong. Now, when they need to hear it most." The campaign includes a 30-second television announcement, radio and print spots, and a toll-free information number (Family Violence Prevention Fund, 2002). Evaluation research on education campaigns like this one have found that following the periods of the campaigns, people have more knowledge about family violence and are more willing to report family violence (Wolfe & Jaffe, 1999).

Another example comes from Canada, where the "Violence—You Can Make a Difference" campaign attempted to raise awareness about both child and adult family violence. Television and radio advertisements, along with fact sheets distributed nationally, provided tips on anger management, how to help abuse victims, safety plans, coping with family violence, and getting help. The campaign focused specifically on identifying early warning signs of violence, especially from the perspective of the aggressor (Godenzi & De Puy, 2001).

It is becoming more common for corporations to become involved in family violence prevention. A few employer-based initiatives aimed at preventing family violence include conscious attempts to facilitate stress-free working environments. More common, however, are workplace education and information campaigns designed to help employees who are dealing with family violence. Many of these programs focus specifically on IPV, in part because of the potential costs of reduced employee performance that result from such violence (Urban & Bennett, 1999).

## Intervention Strategies

*Mandatory reporting laws.* Within 5 years following the publication of Kempe's influential research on the *battered child syndrome,* every U.S. state had enacted laws mandating that professionals report all cases of suspected child abuse. Arguably, no other kind of legislation has been as widely and as rapidly adopted in the history of the United States (Zellman & Fair, 2002). Initially, the laws pertained primarily to medical personnel who suspect physical abuse, but since their initial passage the list of professionals required to report has grown, as has the list of abusive behaviors they must report. Today, doctors, nurses, social workers, mental health professionals, teachers, and other school staff are required to report any suspected physical, sexual, or emotional child abuse. Family violence advocacy groups have generally heralded mandatory reporting laws as a triumph. No doubt the benefits of these laws include increased identification of abuse, which has led to improvements in protecting the powerless and holding perpetrators accountable.

Mandatory reporting protections for adult victims have also become more common. Almost all states, for example, now require medical and social services professionals to report suspected cases of elder abuse (Moskowitz, 1997), and a few states mandate the reporting of suspicions of marital violence (Hyman, Schillinger, & Lo, 1995). Increasingly, however, such laws have been the source of some controversy because of a number of unintended consequences. It is possible that mandatory reporting laws might inhibit women from seeking care or might make them more vulnerable to retaliation (Hyman et al., 1995). These laws also often put people in the helping professions in a difficult position, essentially forcing them to violate the confidences of their clients. Furthermore, many professionals choose to ignore the reporting laws because they see themselves as better equipped to help needy families than the overburdened CPS and APS systems (Melton, 2002; Zellman & Fair, 2002). Research evidence suggests that the more professionals know about the child protection system (i.e., the more formal training they have), the *less* likely they are to report suspected cases of child maltreatment (Melton, 2002).

*Family preservation, foster care, and adoption.* Child protective services agencies are mandated to make child protection their top priority, but when a child is being abused, what course of action will serve the best interests of the child? How to protect abused children is an especially controversial issue. Some scholars are proponents of the *family preservation model,* a model that maintains that the best place to raise a child is in a nuclear family. Their approach is to provide intensive in-home help in the areas of financial management, nonviolent discipline, anger management, and education (Melton, 2002). Another option is out-of-home-placement, or foster care. This system, however, is not a panacea because of the high rates of maltreatment and inadequate oversight by child welfare bureaus. Some factions within this group believe that the best alternative may be orphanages (e.g., McKenzie, 1998).

*Criminal justice responses.* Although there is little debate over the necessity of arresting and prosecuting child abusers, a large number of issues concerning children in the courtroom have arisen. How serious is the stress placed on child witnesses? Can a child's testimony be accepted as accurate? Removing parental abusers from the home constitutes another set of challenges. What happens to the family if the breadwinner is no longer present? These concerns are especially pronounced in cases of sex abuse where the traumatic reactions of the victim may supersede all other concerns (Borowski & Ajzenstadt, 2007; Lesher, 2009).

Not in My Backyard

In one neighborhood known to the authors, a series of events led to an intense reaction by a local school administrator and parents in the community. The episode began in a routine manner when school officials placed *all* parents' names for the fourth grade on a list of potential chaperones for school trips. As the school year progressed and an overnight excursion was imminent, parents began to volunteer to accompany the children. Unbeknownst to one father in the neighborhood, a school employee inadvertently placed his name on the list. Next, one parent undertook the task of checking the local sex offender registry. Readers can almost predict the end of this narrative. The father's arrest record came to light. Of course, the school superintendent removed the man's name as a potential chaperone from the list, a volunteer position that the father never agreed to fulfill in the first place. In the uproar that followed, the sex offender's wife divorced him, and the embarrassed wife and children moved because they felt driven from their home.

Despite the fact that domestic violence has long been recognized as a crime, police discretion in making arrests—combined with family privacy norms, cultural tolerance, and the reluctance of women to press charges—has meant that criminal sanctions have often been the exception rather than the rule. Research routinely indicates that courts rarely sanction even the most assaultive men in IPV cases. A synthesis of investigations revealed that police arrest about one fourth of batterers, prosecutors prosecute about a third of those arrested, and about 1% of those prosecuted receive jail time beyond the time served at arrest (often just a few hours) (see Coulter, Kuehnle, Byers, & Alfonso, 1999; Davis, 1998; Holmes, 1993).

Criminologists and women's advocates saw these data as a sign of societal indifference to and continuing tolerance of the abuse of women (E.S. Buzawa & Buzawa, 2003). Citing the deterrence doctrine, they argued that a society that punishes violent family members should have less family violence (see Chapter 2). Advocates argued that punishing family offenders would begin with the limiting of discretion in the criminal justice system. Mandatory arrest and *no-drop prosecution* policies became the centerpiece of improved criminal justice processing. The no-drop rule requires prosecutors to move forward with criminal proceedings, even if the victim has recanted or asked that the prosecution cease (see Robbins, 1999).

*Treating offenders.* There are a few criminal justice responses to family violence that include some form of treatment. Treatment for IPV rests mainly on court-ordered group counseling over a period of 6 months to a year (Healey, Smith, & O'Sullivan, 1998). Debate about the effectiveness of court-ordered counseling is ongoing and unsettled. Practitioners in the counseling fields increasingly point out the wide variety of mental health problems associated with violent behavior. Empirical assessments indicate that many family-violent individuals suffer from trauma reactions, abnormal socialization factors, impulsivity, addictions, psychopathology, and personality disorders. In fact, receiving a dual diagnosis is quite common among offenders. Consequently, calls for treatment via psychiatric medications are mounting (Royce & Coccaro, 2001; Silver, 2006).

Mandating perpetrators of family violence to counseling is a part of a more general trend toward *medicalization.* Instead of punishing perpetrators for their harmful behavior, it is more reasonable and effective to treat them for their illness (Conrad & Schneider, 1992). This trend has been the source of some controversy because, taken to its extreme, medicalization suggests that the perpetrators of violence have little or no control over their behavior and, therefore, should not be held accountable. Finally, some theory-based thinkers contend that family violence perpetrators should be both punished *and* treated. The punishment communicates that violence will not be tolerated, and the treatment helps the perpetrators to recognize why they are prone to violence.

Treatments for the perpetrators of child physical abuse, emotional abuse, and neglect most often focus on the unlearning (i.e., extinction) of inappropriate parenting techniques as well as on anger control and stress management (Miller-Perrin & Perrin, 1999). In treatments for perpetrators of sexual abuse, a *mental illness model* is more uniformly endorsed, with some employing drug therapies designed to control sexual impulses (Maletzky & Field, 2003).

*Treating victims.* Victims of IPV may experience the same types of mental health problems ascribed to perpetrators. A duo of practitioners has pointed out that victims display considerable individual variability. Consequently, victims need individualized responses that include a wide variety of medical, mental health, and social support (Briere & Jordan, 2004). In addition, treating victims can sometimes reduce subsequent rates of violence by empowering victims to take an active role in preventing their abuse. A battered woman may learn in counseling, for example, that she is not responsible for the violence, that her children are adversely affected by the violence, and that she can and should take steps to protect herself and her children (Busch & Valentine, 2000).

*Shelters and hotlines.* Perhaps the most visible form of intervention for IPV victims is the battered women's shelter. Since the first such shelter opened in England in the early 1970s, battered women's shelters have become more commonplace. Today, most large metropolitan areas have shelters that provide numerous services, including counseling, social support groups, child care, economic support, job training, and some minor legal assistance. The U.S. government took an active role in promoting the shelter movement in 1994 when it passed the first Violence Against Women Act (VAWA). The VAWA, which was reauthorized in 2000 and 2005, has provided funding for shelters and established the National Domestic Violence Hotline (1-800-799-SAFE). Some observers have argued that although implementing VAWA provisions has been expensive, it may have saved U.S. taxpayers billions of dollars in medical costs and social services (Clark, Biddle, & Martin, 2002).

*Coordinated community responses.* Many communities have attempted to coordinate the implementation of a number of kinds of prevention and intervention strategies. (See the table on the website : www.sagepub.com/barnett3e) Such a coordinated community response to child abuse prevention, for example, might include education campaigns to raise awareness, in-home visitations of at-risk and marginally abusive families, school-based education on sex abuse, and treatment programs for victims and offenders. A newer approach is to mandate parent education (Pollet & Lombreglia, 2008). A truly communitywide effort of this magnitude would involve doctors, nurses, social workers, police, lawyers, judges, and others in the community willing to take an active role.

The most commonly cited coordinated community response to the problem of domestic violence is the Domestic Abuse Intervention Project (DAIP), which was implemented in the 1980s in Duluth, Minnesota. The DAIP was the first community project to coordinate the responses of police, lawyers, and judges in an effort to limit justice system discretion and ensure at least a minimum legal reaction against perpetrators and the protection of victims. The "Duluth model," as the design of the DAIP has come to be known, has also been influential in the creation of community education and treatment programs for male batterers. Various aspects of this model have been adopted in communities across the United States, and the model has been the subject of much discussion and research (Shepard & Pence, 1999).

## Common Myths About Family Violence

Family violence is a topic that generates both strong opinions and strong emotional reactions. These attitudes, however, are not always well informed. Without sufficient knowledge, people are likely to develop *common sense* understandings that are not necessarily accurate. Some overly simplistic explanations for the occurrence of family violence have been repeated so often that they have taken on the semblance of well-established fact (Gelles & Cornell, 1990). A new assessment tool shows promise in measuring myth acceptance and elaborates how acceptance functions to promote victim blaming, exonerating the perpetrator, and minimizing the violence (Peters, 2008). Sometimes it seems as if society is aware of many more myths than facts; some myths have been particularly hard to dispel, because they contain a kernel of truth. Providing accurate information regarding such myths is one important role of the social scientist. Gelles and Cornell (1990) were the first writers to call attention to the myths in family violence.

*Myth 1: Family violence is uncommon.* Because family violence is hidden, subjectively defined, and difficult to measure, it is impossible to estimate precisely how frequently it occurs. These observations, however, should not be taken to mean that it rarely occurs. In fact, if there is one point about which all family violence experts seemingly agree, it is this: Family violence is far more common than is generally realized (Straus & Gelles, 1986). Although approximately 3,000 people died on September 11, 2001, it is important to remember that in the same year, 2,387 people were killed by family members or by their boyfriends or girlfriends (U.S. Department of Justice, Federal Bureau of Investigation, 2002). The loss of life on September 11 was an anomaly, an aberration, but the number of intimate homicides in 2001 was normal.

*Myth 2: Only poor people are violent.* A substantial body of evidence does show higher rates of family violence in lower socioeconomic groups. First, the link between family violence and low socioeconomic status is largely unquestioned, but this empirical connection should be interpreted with a degree of caution for two reasons: (a) People who are poor and lack other resources may be more likely than those who are better off to turn to police and social service agencies, and therefore have their violence represented in official estimates of family violence (Hampton & Newberger, 1988); and (b) Even if social class is a statistically viable risk marker, it does not suggest that *only* poor families are violent or that poor families are always violent.

*Myth 3: Abused children always become abusive partners or parents.* A history of family violence is commonly recognized as a correlate of family violence. Studies have consistently found that abusive adults have been exposed to significantly more childhood violence than nonabusive adults (Egeland, 1993). As with socioeconomic status, however, one must be careful not to overinterpret the data. A childhood history of abuse is neither a necessary nor a sufficient cause of adult violence. At best, the data suggest that individuals who were abused as children, or who witnessed abuse in childhood, are more likely to be abusive adults. Children growing up in abusive households are not predetermined to be abusive adults. In fact, the majority of abused children do not grow up to be abusive adults (Widom, 1989b).

*Myth 4: Battered women "ask for it."* Some commentators and scholars have chosen to explain family violence by focusing on the victims. A woman is beaten because she *nags, drinks too much,* or comes from a *dysfunctional family* (Tilden, 1989). She might even be a masochistic martyr who actually enjoys being beaten (Shainess, 1979). Those who blame battered women for not just leaving violent men often say, "If she didn't like it, wouldn't she leave? If she just left, the whole problem would go away." Implicit in many of these assertions are assumptions that something must be wrong with battered women, that they somehow deserve the violence directed at them, and that they should do something to alleviate the violence. This shifting of the blame from the perpetrator to the victim is inherently unfair (see Hotaling & Sugarman, 1990). No one deserves to be hit, and no one "asks for it." The perpetrator, not the victim, bears responsibility for the abuse.

*Myth 5: Family violence sometimes "just happens."* Some members of society believe that family members can be expected to "lose control" from time to time, that parents and spouses sometimes need to "blow off steam." They may rationalize that a man who hits his wife is not really violent; he just had a bad day at work and lost his temper. Or they may rationalize that a woman is generally a good mother, but her kids were really acting up and she only hit them because she lost control for a minute. Some people believe that such actions are inevitable—*even natural*—and are hardly worthy of serious societal reaction.

The ludicrous nature of the "it-just-happens" justification becomes clear when one recognizes that stranger violence is not so summarily dismissed (Gelles & Straus, 1988). When one stranger assaults another, society does not allow the assailant to set aside his actions as a momentary loss of control, a need to blow off steam, or a reaction to a bad day at work. According to Gelles and Straus (1988), family members hit family members because "they can." That is, because society has generally accepted the "it-just-happens" justification, the social and legal costs attached to family violence are very low.

*Myth 6: Minor acts of family violence are always trivial and inconsequential.* Although minor acts of violence are not equivalent to severe violence (Emery & Laumann-Billings, 1998), it is not true that minor violence is always trivial and inconsequential. Parents who push, shove, and occasionally hit one another are implicitly endorsing such violence as the way to settle disagreements. The same can be said for parents who condone pushing and hitting between siblings and for parents who hit their children. Furthermore, emotional abuse is not always less serious than physical abuse. Battered women nearly always say, for example, that the psychological abuse they endured is far worse than the physical abuse (see Currie, 1998; Lynch & Graham-Bermann, 2000).

*Myth 7: Alcohol and drugs are the real cause of family violence.* Men and women who drink are more likely than those who do not to hit each other and to hit their children (Greenfeld et al., 1998). The rate of husband-to-wife violence is approximately 3 times higher for *binge* drinkers (19.2%) than for abstainers, and alcohol is involved in roughly 1 out of 4 instances of wife beating (Kantor & Straus, 1990). Heavy drinking by abusive partners and parents, nevertheless, may *not* actually be the cause (K. D. O'Leary, Slep, & O'Leary, 2007; Zubretsky & Digirolamo, 1994). Abusive individuals are abusive whether sober or drunk (Barnett & Fagan, 1993). Drunkenness, however, often serves as a justification or explanation for abuse, thus allowing some couples to maintain the belief that their marriage is salvageable (LaBell, 1979). Finally, the vast majority of men who drink do not hit their wives (Kantor & Straus, 1990).

*Myth 8: Women who claim date rape are "lying," "deserve what they got," or were "asking for it."* Probably the most common myth about women who report date rape is that they are lying (Burt, 1991). The purpose of rape myths may be to cloud interpretation about consent and shift the blame to the victims. Implicit in this myth is the assumption that the raped woman actually consented to sexual intercourse. This trend has contributed to some observers' belief that women who report date rape were not really raped. Perhaps the woman led the man on and was essentially asking for it. Perhaps she feels guilty about a sexual experience she now sees as negative, so she alleges rape out of vindictiveness or to conceal an unwanted pregnancy. Associated with the myth about lying is the myth that most rapes are committed by strangers in a *blitz* rape (a violent attack by a stranger). True, many women are raped by strangers, but college rape statistics show that a woman is most vulnerable at a party where the alcohol is flowing (Mohler-Kuo, Dowdall, Koss, & Wechsler, 2004). In truth, rape is such an underreported crime that exaggerations and false reports, while not unheard of, are especially unlikely (National Center for Victims of Crime, 1992).

*Myth 9: Some people cannot be raped, and anyway, coercive sexual contact is not damaging.* Even the FBI has contributed to this long-standing belief that men cannot be raped, despite well-known assaults in prisons ("Prison Rape Panel," 2008). Presumably homosexuals cannot rape their partners, nor can legally married husbands rape their wives, but they do (Merrill, 1996; Tjaden & Thoennes, 2000b).

*Myth 10: If he ever laid a hand on me I would leave.* People tend to believe that love and violence are so opposite that they cannot coexist, but in reality, love does not preclude violence. Children learn that parents who love them may also hit them (Straus, 2001). Violent couples express love for one another also hit each other (Muldary, 1983). The statement who "If he ever lays a hand on me, I'll leave" does not mirror reality. Physical aggression does not herald the demise of a marriage (Lloyd, 1988; Margolin & Fernandez, 1987).

## GOALS OF THIS BOOK

There are many reasons for writing this book. First, it is important to summarize the available research on the topic of family violence so that readers will gain a substantive knowledge of the scientific information available. In the process, it is also important to challenge many common myths about family violence. Second, greater factual knowledge of the topic should foster an understanding of the magnitude of the problem and the devastation it causes. Finally, the book should help alleviate the problem of family violence by providing practical information on prevention and policy, and by motivating people to get involved. Providing numerous sources of information will give students, practitioners, researchers, academicians, advocates, and policymakers a better foundation for their work. The compelling nature of the topic motivated the authors to write this book, and they hope it will generate interest and concern among readers. Readers will find that exploration of the field of family violence is fascinating, relevant, and worthwhile.

## CHAPTER SUMMARY

The intent of this chapter, in part, is to inform readers about the *significance and prevalence* of family violence in U.S. society. The United States is one of the most violent industrialized countries in the world, and a remarkably high proportion of this violence occurs within families. To expound upon this theme, two tables detail several statistical summaries about the frequencies of nonfatal and fatal family violence.

The next section focuses on *why* there is violence in families. Theories suggests that male dominance, an idealized notion of the family, various family norms about behavior, and the influence of the media combine to create a cultural acceptance of violence within families. Family violence is an overwhelming problem that has finally captured international reactions that have led to the developments of a *human rights convention* for children and women.

In the United States, *claims-makers* began to define the various forms of family violence as social problems. Despite history's long record of abusing children and women, the *mistreatment of children* began to receive serious attention during the child-saving movement of the mid- to late 1800s. The medical and academic communities essentially ignored child abuse until the 1960s. Society similarly ignored the victimization of women until the late 1800s, and the social problem of *woman battering* was not fully discovered until the early 1970s. *Other forms of family violence* kept emerging: child sexual abuse, child neglect, marital rape, dating violence, sexual assault, stalking, elder abuse, and battered men. As claims-makers continued, their work resulted in the recognition of intimate violence among special populations: cross-cultural groups, immigrants, ethnic/racial minorities, disabled women, religious communities, rural women, and personnel in the military.

Defining such terms as *child neglect* or *wife battering* are integral parts of the claims-making process. *Definition*s of family violence are, to some degree, subjective and always evolving. Words such as *abuse, battering, assault, maltreatment,* and *violence* are commonly used in discussions of family violence, but there is sometimes little agreement on exactly what these words mean. Their meanings are negotiated by claims-makers, and the winners in these negotiations earn the right to define particular behaviors and to estimate their prevalence. Most recently, claims-makers in the health field have declared family violence a *national health problem,* not just a social problem. Definitions are a crucial part of any research or social policy endeavor, as can be seen in the necessity to legally define maltreatment terms. Social scientific progress in the field of family violence depends, to some extent, on a shared understanding of what constitutes family violence.

A series of evaluations have determined the surprising estimates of the *monetary costs* of family violence. Governmental and nongovernmental organizations have compiled some estimates of the costs, which encompass hospitalization, mental health services, welfare services, criminal justice processing, and costs arising from other entities. These costs are staggering, and even those presented here are underestimates.

To address family violence, society has relied upon a number of *prevention and intervention strategies.* Prevention efforts are attempts to keep family violence from occurring in the first place, whereas intervention strategies are responses to family violence after it occurs. Prevention efforts usually include support of families in their own homes, school-based informational programs, and community awareness campaigns. Interventions encompass mandatory reporting, criminal justice responses, and often an emphasis on family preservation and family reunification. To date, U.S. social policies have tended to emphasize intervention rather than prevention, and many of the intervention strategies have focused on protecting victims and deterring perpetrators from committing further violence.

The chapter ends with a presentation of examples of common myths about family violence. Only a smattering of myths appear, but they provide a glimpse into how little members of society actually know about the tragedy of family violence.

## DISCUSSION QUESTIONS

1. Are family members violent compared with nonfamily members of society?
2. Women and children in the United States are in more danger at home than on the streets of the most violent cities. Is this an empirically defensible claim?
3. Why would some people say "the marriage license is a hitting license"?
4. What are some of the rationales for family violence? What is your opinion?

5. Who defines family violence? Why is it important to examine the influence of claims-making on definitions of social problems?

6. How would you judge the degree of consensus on the meaning of family violence?

7. What categories of monetary costs are now apparent? What is your reaction to these costs?

8. Are children more valued today than at any time in history?

9. What claims-making have you heard about family violence?

10. Why have greater societal resources been directed toward intervention in cases of family violence than toward prevention?

11. Do you have any perceptions about family violence that have been challenged by anything you have read in this opening chapter?

For chapter-specific resources including audio and video links, SAGE research articles, additional case studies, and more, please visit www.sagepub.com/barnett3e.

# 2

# Research Methodology, Assessment, and Theories of Family Violence

**CASE HISTORY**  Juanita's Broken Heart and Broken Body

When I was a child, my father switched my legs when I failed to clean my room right, and he belted me if I "ran my mouth." My mother said nothing about my father's "discipline."

When I was 17, I met Miguel at school. He told me I was beautiful and that he couldn't live without me. He said he loved me. He was always gentle and kind and we did everything together. He transformed my whole world.

Everything was perfect, like living in a dream. When Miguel said he wanted to marry me, I knew that I was going to have a home of my own where I would be loved and protected. It was the happiest time of my life.

When I was 18, Miguel and I got married. The week after the wedding, Miguel slapped me across the face and pushed me to the floor. I couldn't believe it. Why? Why? Why? I couldn't figure it out. What had gone wrong? I was stunned and heartbroken. I still loved him, of course. I didn't know what to do. I decided Miguel must have been upset and that he probably wouldn't hit me again.

After we had been married about 3 months, Miguel no longer made love to me. Instead, he forced me to have sex whenever he wanted, and he made me do some things I still can't talk about. He told me I was an ugly slut, the house looked like a pigpen, and the food wasn't fit for a dog to eat. He told me what to wear and where I could go. Once he socked me and blackened my eye. After that, I was afraid of him. My older brother and father guessed what was going on and threatened to beat up Miguel. I begged them not to, and they didn't. Actually, no one did anything. When I got pregnant, Miguel was really angry and he took to punching me in the stomach. He kept saying that the baby wasn't his, and if it wasn't, he was going to kill me.

Sometimes he woke me up in the middle of the night, screaming, "Who is the baby's father?" He said I wasn't fit to be a mother. He told me he hoped the baby would die, and he forbade me to see a doctor. One time he hit me so hard I began hemorrhaging. A neighbor took me to the doctor.

Miguel started going out without me and staying out all night with other women. He said I was a fat slob and he couldn't stand to be seen with me. I felt alone . . . unloved, afraid . . . very, very sad. I sometimes thought he hated me. I cried a lot, but I kept it to myself. Finally, I went to our priest and told him about Miguel. He told me to pray and try harder. It was my duty to obey my husband. So I tried harder to make Miguel happy. I kept the house clean and cooked good meals. I told him how much I loved him. Nothing changed. I did not know what to do, where to turn. One thing I did know was that staying with him wouldn't help.

This case history contains many elements that exemplify the issues encompassed by the field of family violence and why research and theory development are central to intervention and prevention. Why did these events transpire? Who was to blame? What would you do if you were in Juanita's situation? What would you do if you had ever acted like Miguel? How would you, as a researcher or practitioner, define and measure the variety of experiences that Juanita endured? How would you assess Miguel's behavior or explain why Juanita did what Miguel told her to do, or why she kept trying to make him happy? Who could Juanita have told about her predicament? Will Miguel hurt her again if she goes back to him?

This chapter presents an overview of family violence research. The information presented illuminates the diverse and sometimes complex approaches that family violence experts use in attempting to understand and intervene in family violence. The text describes the various kinds of specialists working in the field and the different theories used to explain why family violence occurs. This chapter also elaborates on the research methodologies that family violence researchers employ and covers some of the practice and policy issues associated with family violence. Because conclusions about how to prevent and intervene effectively in family violence are derived from these scientific investigations, a basic understanding of these concepts is essential.

## STUDYING FAMILY VIOLENCE: A MULTIDISCIPLINARY EFFORT

No single social institution or group has been able to come to grips with the enormity of family violence in the United States, although many have tried, including the criminal justice system, the medical and mental health communities, social welfare agencies, schools, and researchers. The diversity of approaches has resulted in a knowledge base that looks very much like a colossal jigsaw puzzle: Some parts of the picture are relatively clear, some are obscured, some do not fit together, some seem as if they will never fit together, and some are totally missing.

As interest in family violence has heightened, the field has expanded beyond its initial academic borders. Among the disciplines that are highly involved in the study of family violence are criminology, social work, sociology, psychology, and public health. Also connected to the field are such tangentially related disciplines as family studies/sciences, political science, victimology, neuroscience, and women's studies. In addition, professionals in the areas of law and medicine, especially nursing, pediatrics, obstetrics, and psychiatry, are actively engaged in family violence research.

*Advocates* for the victims of family violence have emerged as a forceful group with a specific value-centered and political agenda. Whereas academic researchers who study family violence have spent years in graduate school learning the procedures they use in their work, activists have spent years "on the firing line" trying to awaken the public, legislators, and law enforcement personnel to the plight of victims. Without the tireless work of advocates for children, the abuse of children probably would have continued many more years. In parallel fashion, advocates for sexually assaulted and battered women have worked diligently to increase public awareness about the unrecognized plight of battered women. As a group, these advocates deserve acknowledgment and appreciation. Most advocates are feminists. Despite the importance of feminism in enlightening society about the salience of family violence, the label *feminist* tends to evoke mixed, if not negative, associations in the minds of some individuals (Breen & Karpinski, 2008).

The interest of so many *divergent groups* in the same subject has posed a serious challenge to the field of family violence research in terms of accommodating opposing points of view (e.g., Jacobson, 1994). Contentious debates have arisen between experts schooled within different academic disciplines and among researchers, clinicians, and victims' advocates. Various factions have formulated their own definitions and theoretical frameworks, applied differing research methodologies, and developed specialized interventions. These dissonant perspectives are examples of claims-making, the process through which groups and individuals with differing views compete for society's attention.

Thoughtful diversity of opinion is one cornerstone of science, but fractious debate generated by opposing academic and political groups is detrimental to progress in stopping the violence. In the field of family violence, conflict has exceeded customary levels and has occasionally created an atmosphere of distrust and acrimony (see Gelles & Loseke, 1993). In an extreme instance, Dr. Murray Straus of the Family Violence Laboratory at the University of New Hampshire received a bomb threat from someone who was trying to stop a presentation of his research findings (see Straus, 1991c). Apparently, Dr. Straus's stance on gender equivalence, which flows from his research, infuriates some groups. As another example, Dr. Amy Holtzworth-Munroe (2005) was challenged twice in different grant applications, first because she planned to study violent women, and second because she planned not to study violent women. (For a more thorough description of these problems, see Box 2.1 about issues related to research.)

### BOX 2.1 Issues Related to Family Violence Research

Research results rest on a number of factors that may vary widely from study to study. This extensive variability makes it difficult to interpret findings and affects their generalizability. The following questions illustrate some of the issues faced by family violence researchers:

1. Who asks the questions? (Researcher, practitioner, government interviewer, medical personnel, school personnel, police officer?)

2. What questions are asked? (Items about abuse, sexual assault, or neglect; identity of perpetrator(s); questions about frequency, duration, severity, or outcomes of abuse?)

*(Continued)*

(Continued)

3. What referent period of abuse is selected? (Last month, last 6 months, last 12 months, last 2 years, over a lifetime, during relationship, other time frame or historical period?)

4. How are the questions asked? (By an interviewer, over the phone or in person, by mail, on a paper questionnaire, in an online questionnaire?)

5. What is the context of the questions asked? (Length of the questionnaire and terminology, items within the context of conflict resolution, criminal acts, violence against women, sexual abuse, health problems, human rights abuses?)

6. What is the setting in which questions are asked? (Shelter, emergency room, home, classroom, university laboratory, prison or other institution, military setting? With others present or respondent alone?)

7. What is the cultural context? (Language spoken, reading ability, freedom to speak honestly, views of women and children, roles of men and women?)

8. What is the purpose of asking the questions? (For information on victims' perspectives, utility of perpetrators' arrest, prevalence and incidence rates, effects of violence on physical and mental health?)

9. When are the questions asked? (On arrival at a shelter, following an assault, several years after the incident, or when the victim is pregnant, drunk, injured, or afraid?)

10. Who answers the questions? (Child, man, woman, mother, father, stepparent, brother, sister, husband, wife, cohabitor, same-sex partner, dating partner, racial or ethnic minority group member, elder, immigrant, institutionalized person, homeless person, non–English speaker, doctor, nurse, social worker, agency personnel?)

11. What relationship factors exist between abusers and victims? (Parent-child, stepparent-stepchild, acquaintances, siblings, dating partners, intimate partners—cohabiting, divorced, separated; duration and quality of relationship, degree of relationship intimacy, previous battering relationships?)

12. What historical data are gathered? (Respondent's abuse as a child, criminal victimization, exposure to interparental aggression, criminal arrest record, education, employment, welfare recipient status, children and their health status, religious preference, injuries, illnesses, other events?)

13. What types of sociodemographic data are gathered? (Age, race, socioeconomic status, education, area of residence?)

One difference of opinion has erupted primarily over the issue of the causes of family violence. Another is whether sex offenders or wife beaters can be rehabilitated. The question of gender mutuality in adult *intimate partner violence* (IPV) and its measurement has sparked other bitter clashes. Experts and laypersons alike have become entrenched in their own opinions, and scientific findings alone have not resolved the impasses. It may seem strange that academicians and advocates in the field of family violence are at such odds. Such disputes among factions intensify when the interested parties must compete for limited resources (R. E. Dobash & Dobash, 1988; Schechter, 1988). The problem of child molestation provides an illustration: Should tax and charitable money go to treatment programs for child molesters, who, without treatment, will go on to molest hundreds of children, or should it go to treatment programs for molested children whose lives have been shattered by their victimization and whose futures are in jeopardy?

## Sociological Research

Sociologists were the first social scientists to grapple with the problem of family violence. Sociologists conducting research in this field often survey large numbers of people about their experiences with interpersonal violence and use the data they gather to examine the relationships between these experiences and variables such as age, gender, and socioeconomic class (e.g., Steffensmeir & Hayne, 2000). They also conduct surveys with smaller samples to study a vast array of related topics, such as gender-role conflicts among immigrants and the impact of interpersonal violence on women's employment (Min, 2001; Raphael, 1996). Feminist researchers may come from any field, but most are anchored in sociology (Orme, 2003).

## Social Work Research

Specialists with degrees in social work often investigate family violence using handy clinical samples. Some of the topics they have considered include the effects of poverty and welfare on rates of abuse, the effectiveness of parenting classes, and the functioning of child protective services (e.g., Busch & Wolfer, 2002). Additionally, clinical social workers are frequently on the front lines of treatment, working in agencies that serve individuals affected by interpersonal violence. Here they may collaborate on issues of how best to identify battered elders.

## Criminological Research

Criminologists who study family violence are most often sociologists who focus on family crime. Frequently, these researchers analyze the very large banks of crime statistics gathered and published by government agencies such as the Federal Bureau of Investigation. It is important to note, however, that criminologists did not categorize violent acts between family members as crimes until the 1970s (Ohlin & Tonry, 1989). Criminologists also investigate forensic samples, such as incarcerated teenagers. Typical kinds of criminological inquiry into family violence are investigations of the role of prosecutors in domestic violence cases (Finn & Stalans, 2002; Gaarder & Belknap, 2002). Even subsections of the criminal justice system, such as police departments, have become more involved in evaluating and comparing various police interventions (e.g., "Sacramento Police Department," n.d.).

## Psychological and Psychiatric Research

Psychologists and psychiatrists who study family violence often collect data from small *clinical samples,* although some conduct large surveys. Clinical samples are groups of people, such as those undergoing counseling, living in a shelter, or in other similar groups. They customarily evaluate the effects of individual factors, such as psychopathology or the dynamics of interpersonal functioning on the treatment effectiveness and prevention of family violence. These specialists have also conducted research concerning such questions as the role of alcoholism in violent behavior (e.g., Feiring, Deblinger, Hoch-Espada, & Haworth, 2002).

## Public Health and Medical Research

As the near-universal occurrence of family violence became more evident, public health officials declared that family violence was *a public health issue* rather than a social problem. Public health specialists tend to conduct epidemiological studies by gathering data on large representative samples and by bringing advanced statistical methodology to bear on family violence questions (e.g., A. S. Jones, 2000). As one might anticipate, the subjects of interest to these researchers include prevalence and incidence statistics, the role that health care providers can play in preventing or intervening in family violence, the nature of victims' injuries, the mental and physical effects that stem from family violence, and the training that health providers receive (McNutt, Carlson, Rose, & Robinson, 2002; Phelan et al., 2005). Public health statisticians have gathered some of the most influential data in the field (e.g., Bachman & Saltzman, 1995). Currently, medical researchers have begun to evaluate intervention programs within a medical setting.

## Neuroscience and Genetics Research

Neuroscience (behavioral neuroscience) is the study of the nervous system and the application of its findings to psychology and psychiatry. These specialists often use laboratory equipment, for example to perform brain scans and to produce electrocardiograms. As an example of the contributions of experts in this field, neuroscientists compared battered and nonbattered women's *reactions to fear* stimuli in the laboratory. Results showed that battered women's brains underwent significant increased activation in one part of the brain (anterior/middle insula). The researchers concluded that since this pattern of neuronal activity could have been caused by factors other than IPV, longitudinal studies are needed to determine if abuse actually caused the difference (Simmons, Paulus, Thorp, Norman, & Stein, 2008). Geneticists frequently study twins to determine the heritability of various traits. Specialists have found evidence of *genetic bases* for such correlates of family violence as **antisocial personality disorder**, aggression, and alcoholism (Lesch & Merschdorf, 2000; van den Bree, Svikis, & Pickens, 1998).

## Legal Research

Because of the acceleration of family violence reports in recent years, along with mounting public pressures for authorities to prevent such violence, growing numbers of legal scholars have doubled their involvement in the field. Many such researchers have conducted reviews of both family violence laws and the academic literature, and what changes in the laws are needed (Barata & Senn, 2003). Some legal scholars have become advocates, delving into controversial issues, such as whether battered women should be charged with failure to protect their children when the father has abused them. Some other areas of legal research have concerned the financial abuse of elders and the identification of legal steps needed to end stalking (Dennison & Thomson, 2005; Elder Justice Coalition, 2009).

## Cross-Cultural/Global Inquiry

Several academic and professional fields have accelerated their coverage of cross-cultural and international family violence concerns because of ethics regarding the inclusion of all societal subgroups. Racial minorities, sexual orientation minorities, immigrants, individuals living in rural areas, those assigned to military duty, and individuals from countries around the world are all worthy of scientific focus. No longer can educational institutions and governmental entities prioritize the study of white, Christian, heterosexual European Americans (Belar, 2008).

## Biobehavioral Research: An Emerging Field

Scholars in both medicine and psychology are currently discussing the merit, or lack thereof, of combining the two fields into a single field. Although the tenor of this dialogue has been of an inquiring nature, various forums have distinct opinions. Some psychologists have questions about the possible loss of psychology as a separate science, while others focus on the pressing need to incorporate biological principles into clinical health psychology. Despite psychologists' success in altering behavior in clinical settings (e.g., stress reduction) and evidence of cost savings (e.g., fewer heart attacks), psychological research has only limited dissemination into medical practice. It has taken a considerable length of time to convince medical personnel, for example, to screen patients for family violence (see the *Journal of Clinical Psychology in Medical Settings,* 2008, Vol. 15, No. 1).

## Interdisciplinary Science

Increasingly, experts have called for greater collaborative efforts among several groups: (a) researchers and practitioners, (b) agencies and practitioners, and (c) researchers from different scientific areas. The American Psychological Association's (APA's) Board of Scientific Affairs conducted a preliminary trial to determine how to encourage research psychologists to become more interdisciplinary (Young, 2009). Several ideas emerged, such as recommending that graduate programs mandate student training in different techniques, models, and theoretical perspectives.

## Expansion of Federal Government Research

Government researchers, statisticians, and epidemiologists working in the field of family violence often design surveillance systems (i.e., monitoring/tracking) and collect data on violence-related incidents from very large population samples. In recent years, government agencies have increasingly funded family violence research and expanded their collaborations with other experts and agencies ("Legislation Advances," 2007; "Victims Office," 2008). The National Criminal Justice Reference Service, the Office of Violence Against Women, and the National Institute on Drug Abuse produce and update many important articles on family violence and make most of them available free of charge over the Internet. The National Child Abuse and Neglect Data System compiles lists of the incidence of child abuse.

---

**SECTION SUMMARY**

### Studying Family Violence—A Multidisciplinary Effort

Scholars and practitioners in the field of family violence come from a wide range of academic disciplines and professions. Since these researchers and theorists use diverse research methodologies, they do not always agree on data interpretations. Along with the impressions of advocates, disagreements have erupted. Nonetheless, groups and institutions with disparate agendas have begun to unite behind their shared desire to find solutions to family violence. A list of academic disciplines involved in family research include the following: sociologists, social workers, criminologists, the police, psychologists and psychiatrists, neuroscientists and geneticists, biobehavioralists, legal and medical professionals, public health researchers, and cross-cultural specialists. In the past decade, the U.S. government has become proactive in improving *surveillance systems* (gathering data for monitoring/tracking events/behavior), such as the number and type of injuries treated in emergency rooms. Finally, advocates have continued their valuable work of improving awareness of family violence issues.

---

## THEORETICAL EXPLANATIONS FOR FAMILY VIOLENCE

In many respects, family violence is seemingly incomprehensible. How could a husband who supposedly loves his wife be physically violent toward her? How could a mother purposely hurt her infant? In considering family violence, it may be fruitful to look at the many social and cultural conditions that make such violence not only comprehensible but also, in some respects, a normal (or at least culturally approved) part of family life. Researchers' and practitioners' ideological convictions are pivotal because they typically dictate the selection of research designs and preferences for intervention (Hamby, 1998; Kim & Ahn, 2002).

No one theory can fully explain what causes family violence. A **theory** may be defined as "an integrated set of ideas that explain a set of observations" (O'Neill, 1998, p. 459). Without empirical support, theories are only speculations about what may or may not be sound. Without evidence, no one can say with total assurance which theory derived from which academic discipline is the most explanatory, the most heuristic. Ostensibly distinctive theories put forward by academics from divergent disciplines may actually be identical, their likeness obscured by variations in terminology. The *micro and macro* framework used in the next section should be useful for clarifying and organizing the most prominent theoretical formulations for understanding the causes of family violence.

*Readers:* The case history at the opening of this chapter can serve as a launching point for discussing the theories outlined below. These theories provide ideas about what may have caused Miguel's violence against Juanita.

## Macrotheory: Explaining Patterns of Family Violence

The task of a macrotheory of family violence is to identify the *broad factors* that make families prone to violence. Macro-level explanations incorporate cultural factors (e.g., acceptance of violence, patriarchy), social-structural variables (e.g., poverty), structural characteristics of the family (e.g., age, family stresses), the inadequacies of deterrence (e.g., punishment and costs of family violence), situational impetus (e.g., a gun in the house), and even evolutionary theory.

*Cultural and broad socialization factors.* On many levels, family violence is an accepted, encouraged, and even glorified form of cultural expression in the United States and elsewhere (O'Neill, 1998). Cultural explanation rests on socialization (learning). Socialization takes note of children's strong tendency to be influenced by parents, peers, the media, and other factors within their own culture.

*Social acceptance of family violence.* Social approval of corporal punishment, for example, is consonant with the moral obligation that parents have to train, protect, and control their children. From this point of view, spanking (hitting) children is normative (Ellison, Bartkowski, & Segal, 1996; Flynn, 1996). Striking a spouse may be viewed as less tolerable than striking a child, and presumably hitting a woman is less acceptable than hitting a man (Felson, 2000). A sizable minority of Americans, however, still thinks that slapping an intimate partner is permissible under certain circumstances, such as when a partner has been unfaithful (Simon et al., 2001). In one study of East Asian and Southeast Asian immigrants to the United States, a little more than one-fourth of the study sample agreed that marital violence is justified under certain circumstances (Yoshioka, DiNoia, & Ullah, 2001).

*Patriarchy.* In many ways, complaints about the *patriarchal* nature of U.S. culture have been the foundation on which the American anti–domestic violence movement has been built. In a patriarchal culture, *men hold greater power and privilege in the social hierarchy than do women.* In its extreme form, patriarchy literally gives men the right to dominate and control women and children (R. E. Dobash & Dobash, 1979). Many common theological doctrines have incorporated patriarchal beliefs into the basic marital contract. Unfortunately, socialization of the acceptance of male dominance contributes to a certain moral disengagement about female abuse (Heggen, 1996). In an article published in 1976, Murray Straus identified four *cherished cultural standards* in the United States that not only permit but encourage husband-to-wife violence: (a) men rightfully have greater authority than women; (b) male aggressiveness is a sign of maleness and an acceptable tool for a man to demonstrate male identity; (c) the wife/mother role is the preferred status for women; and (d) the criminal justice system is male dominated and operates under a male orientation and thus may provide little legal relief for female victims.

Going beyond the borders of the United States, there is little doubt that in many countries *men have the power to imprison, punish, enslave, or even kill women and children with impunity* (Levesque, 2001). Patriarchy in the United States, however, is inadequate to account for the IPV perpetrated by American husbands. Although many Americans hold patriarchal values, the influence of patriarchy is not all-embracing. Only 10% to 11% of American men can be classified as "wife beaters" (D. G. Dutton, 1994), and no more than 30% of American men ever abuse their female partners (Straus & Gelles, 1990). Furthermore, one cannot easily account for female-to-male violence or same-sex violence under the umbrella of patriarchy. Strangely, some women who kill their children believe they "own" the children whom they ultimately kill because they adhere to a matriarchal corollary to patriarchal ideology (Messing & Heeren, 2004). One theorist has resurrected patriarchy to explain male partner abuse because it keeps the focus on dominance, gender, power, and social conditions (Hunnicutt, 2009).

*Feminist theories* regarding family violence typically include *four principal perspectives:* (a) gender and power relationships and their utility in accounting for IPV, (b) the historical salience of the family as a social institution, (c) the importance of understanding and validating women's experiences, and (d) the use of family violence research findings to help women (Bograd, 1988). Feminists decry the widespread use of so-called gender-neutral research methodologies that contain a patriarchal bias and therefore are damaging to women (Yllö, 1993). In fact, Yllö (2005) says that "domestic violence cannot be adequately understood unless gender and power are taken into account" (p. 19). Without its influence, some questions would never be asked. Until Russell (1982) and Finkelhor and Yllö (1982) conducted their landmark research surveys, for instance, the law did not recognize marital rape as a crime. Despite the salutary effects that feminism has had on U.S. society as a whole, and on academia in particular, the scope of feminist family violence research, until lately, has been confined almost entirely to male-to-female IPV. Feminist scholars have not yet offered satisfactory accounts of other forms of family violence, such as child abuse or same-sex aggression (see Waldner-Haugrud, Gratch, & Magruder, 1997).

*Social-structural variables as a theory.* Theories founded upon social-structural formulations link family violence to certain socially defined classifications, such as minority status, gender, and low income. Although abuse occurs at every social-structural level, a large volume of research has identified all of the aforementioned factors as correlates of family violence (Magdol et al., 1997; Rennison & Welchans, 2000). Also, the presence of stressors such as *unequal opportunity* and *poverty* produces high levels of personal frustration, which increase the risk of aggression (e.g., Copenhaver, Lash, & Eisler, 2000).

Early on, scholars identified another cluster of factors woven throughout family living that make families especially prone to violence (Brinkerhoff & Lupri, 1988). Some of these typically stress-producing elements of family life are close proximity, emotional investment, privacy concerns, and power imbalances. There is some evidence that these stresses can be passed down from one generation to the next (Kiever, 2005). Two obvious power imbalances in the family are the subordination of children to parents and, frequently, the subjugation of women to men. These family stressors foster conflict and aggression (Lambert & Firestone, 2000). Nevertheless, social-structural explanations fall short of accounting for the violence because the vast majority of lower-class family members do not assault each other.

*Deterrence theory: The low cost of family violence.* Deterrence theory is the backbone of the criminal justice system, but does deterrence work? From a *social control* standpoint, deviant behavior is common when it does not engender social or legal costs. Logically then, family violence occurs so frequently because the offender suffers no adverse consequences. Legal sanctions, in fact, are lacking. Arrest and prosecution for family violence are unlikely, and incarceration or other punishments are even less probable (Healey, Smith, & O'Sullivan, 1998; Office for Victims of Crime, 1999).

According to deterrence theory, intensifying the legal consequences for antisocial behavior should lessen its frequency within the general population (general deterrence) and among individual offenders (specific deterrence). When legal sanctions are applied, however, the theory may still be inadequate for explaining family violence (Sitren & Applegate, 2007). As one illustration, court-ordered interventions with batterers are *not* very effective in reducing IPV (e.g., Gondolf, 2000b). Furthermore, researchers have found no relationship between incarceration and recidivism among sex offenders (Nunes, Firestone, Wexler, Jensen, & Bradford, 2007).

*Punishment.* Research on punishment helps to explain why deterrence theory has garnered little empirical support. Punishment entails either the administration of a *negative event* (e.g., a spanking) or the removal of a *positive event* (e.g., watching television) with the goal of reducing an unwanted behavior (e.g., swearing). The problem is that punishment procedures do *not* have the desired outcome of reducing unwanted behaviors. Following the rules that make punishment effective is often unmanageable. As an example, to be effective, a punishment needs to be dispensed immediately after the unwanted behavior and consistently. Rarely are parents able to carry out immediate, consistent punishment (see a learning psychology text for more clarification).

## Microtheory: Explaining the Behaviors of Individual Violent Family Members

Although macrotheories help to explain why families within certain societies are violent, they are insufficient to explain violence on an individual level. As a case in point, selling teenage girls into prostitution is a widespread practice in some African and South Asian countries, yet most parents in these societies do not sell their daughters. Social scientists want to know why individuals vary. Several types of theories address individual proclivities toward aggression, including learning theories, individual (intrapersonal) differences theories, and interpersonal interaction theories. These theories make family violence understandable, but not justifiable.

## Learning Theories (Individual Experiences)

Although specific types of socialization such as gender socialization depend on learning, this section examines learning by individual family members. A large body of research extending across academic disciplines has documented the importance of childhood experiences in the backgrounds of family-violent offenders. Abusive parents provide children with a veritable classroom for learning specific forms of abusive behaviors, particular attitudes, and distinct cognitions that justify violence (Dunlap, Golub, Johnson, & Wesley, 2002). Over the years, researchers have expanded applications of basic learning principles to a broad repertoire of behaviors. The following paragraphs explain and provide examples of the principles of learning: (a) *modeling* (social imitation, social learning), (b) *classical conditioning* (emotional learning), (c) *operant conditioning* (modification of behavior), and (d) *avoidance conditioning* (both classical and operant conditioning). At the foundation of learning are the overarching principles of reinforcement and punishment. (See Moffitt & Caspi, 1999, for a discussion of learning effects based on results from a longitudinal study.)

*Social learning.* A widely accepted account of how learning plays a role in family violence hinges on *social learning (vicarious learning, imitation, or observational learning).* In layman's vernacular, this is a "monkey see; monkey do" truism. At the core of this theory is a process called *modeling* (or *imitation*), by which people learn social behaviors and cognitions simply by observing others (Bandura, 1977). The popularity of social learning theory rests on two primary lines of evidence. First, a wealth of laboratory experiments with animals and humans lends strong validation to the claim that aggression can be learned through observation (e.g., Bandura, Ross, & Ross, 1961). Second, research has shown that violence tends to be perpetuated from one generation to the next (transgenerational/intergenerational learning) (e.g., Ehrensaft et al., 2003). Abuse during childhood is associated with later dating violence, marital violence, and the eventual abuse of one's own children (e.g., Carr & VanDeusen, 2002; Cunningham, 2003). The childhoods of gay men who are violent show the same patterns (Craft & Serovich, 2005). Some sorts of childhood abuse are also linked more with victimization than perpetration of interpersonal violence (National Criminal Justice Reference Service, 2007).

Social learning theory applied to family violence proposes that children model specific family-violent behaviors and attitudes, conflict resolution styles, and alcohol misuse. Although the social learning theory explanation of family violence has many proponents, some skeptics find this explanation to be either overstated or too narrow, and others believe that the research thus far has had methodological shortcomings (Newcomb & Locke, 2001). Also counting against this theory as causal is the fact that many, if not most, individuals exposed to violent family models do not go on to emulate abusive behaviors later in life (e.g., Mihalic & Elliott, 1997).

Even when behavior is observed, there are other factors such as reinforcement that contribute to its actual imitation.

Neuroscientists have introduced a new line of evidence from **mirror cell** (neuron) research in *primates* that is compatible with observational learning (E. Jaffe, 2007). Mirror cells in the brain of an observer respond to the actions (behaviors) of the observed person in the same way they would if the observer had executed the action himself. That is, the mirror cells of an observer fire in the same pattern as the actual cells do in the person who has performed the action. Extrapolating from this primate research to humans, the mirror cells in a child observing his father assault his mother would react as if the child were carrying out the assault herself. Neuroscientists have now uncovered evidence of mirror cells in humans (Saey, 2009).

The stability of findings about the associations between childhood experiences and adult behaviors reaffirms *intergenerational accounts* of family violence, even though the magnitudes of the relationships are not uniformly robust (Stith et al., 2000). In a recent 20-year longitudinal, prospective (follows subjects forward in time) study, Ehrensaft et al. (2003) uncovered very strong intergenerational effects for partner violence. The models of both victim and perpetrator behavior provide social learning opportunities. The observation of violence (e.g., father hits mother for "mouthing off"—punishment for the mother) and the outcome of the violence (i.e., mother "shuts up"—reinforcement for the offender) teaches children exactly how to be abusive and how to be victims. In the past decade, researchers have demonstrated that forms of behaviors other than assault reflect intergenerational (transgenerational) leaning. Illustrative of these efforts is the finding that the level of a father's insecure romantic attachment is closely associated with the self-reported insecure attachment of his children (Roelofs, Meesters, & Muris, 2008).

*Classical, operant, and avoidance learning theories.* Some family violence formulations incorporate classical and operant conditioning (learning) principles. Basically, academicians have extrapolated learning principles gleaned from laboratory studies with animals to humans. The reactions of *Pavlov's* dogs and *Skinner's* rats form the basis for these types of learning. Of course, caution is warranted in assuming that any extrapolations are accurate descriptions of human behavior. Research based on animals does not automatically apply to humans.

*Classical conditioning* concerns the emotional changes that take place in an individual as a result of experience. Fear, for example, can be classically conditioned in humans through the pairing of a signal or cue (e.g., angry voice) with a subsequent frightening and painful event (e.g., assault). Thus theories of family violence that encompass classical conditioning can explain the intense levels of fear experienced by battered women (see O'Keefe & Treister, 1998). If a husband repeatedly comes home drunk and then threatens his wife with a beating, the wife will learn to fear her husband's drunken arrival. Children can be classically conditioned to fear being bullied at school or to react with conditioned *trauma reactions* (e.g., startle responses). Psychotherapists and even researchers may acquire *vicarious trauma* as a consequence of listening to and treating abuse victims (Campbell, 2005).

*Trauma theory* is a contemporary learning theory that helps to illuminate more complex kinds of learning, such as prolonged reactions to traumatic events. Research concerning *trauma, posttraumatic stress disorder (PTSD), and revictimization* has demonstrated the deleterious effects of exposure to trauma or abuse victimization. Children traumatized by abuse suffer from **PTSD** (Famularo, Fenton, Kinscherff, Ayoub, & Barnum, 1994). Battered women also very frequently develop PTSD brought about by the effects of battering trauma (Babcock, Roseman, Green, & Ross, 2008). Soldiers exposed to the trauma of war may suffer serious and long-lasting effects (Taft, Street, Marshall, Dowdall, & Riggs, 2007).

Trauma and PTSD have continuing effects on experiencing subsequent traumas (Breaslau, Peterson, & Schultz, 2008). *Revictimization* is an unfortunate type of learning that is evident when a response to an initial victimization is predictive of a second victimization (Fisher, Cullen, & Turner, 2000). Vulnerability to repeat victimization appears to be a long-term consequence of abuse, and there appear to be a number of factors that increase or decrease repeat victimization. Congruent with this thesis, evidence has substantiated that childhood sexual abuse (CSA) places both adolescent and adult women at *greater risk* for a variety of revictimization experiences by partners and other males (e.g., Messman-Moore & Brown, 2006). Sexually victimized gays, lesbians, and bisexuals report comparable revictimization experiences (Marx, Heidt, & Gold, 2005). The most scientifically grounded model of sexual revictimization is a *learning* model tied to the uncontrollability and unpredictability of child or adult sexual assault incidents (Marx et al., 2005).

*Operant conditioning* entails the individual's understanding of the relationship between his or her actions and their consequences. For example, in learning to drive a car, people learn that stepping on the brakes stops the car (which shapes their behavior in a step-by-step fashion). An instance of operant conditioning occurs when a perpetrator learns that the use of violence (actions) coerces a victim's compliance (consequences). Victim compliance reinforces (rewards) the perpetrator's aggression. When abusive persons learn that they get what they want by mistreating others, they are likely to become even more violent (see Felson, 1992). Similarly, when abusive persons are not punished for their violent behavior, they learn to hone their aggressive skills (Patterson, 1982).

*Avoidance conditioning* encompasses classically conditioned fear and operantly conditioned escape or avoidance. As a case in point, a bullied child will avoid going to school because he is afraid of being bullied. A constantly criticized husband will avoid going home because of the abusive criticism. A raped college student will avoid the locations where she was assaulted. Traumatized individuals indulge in a great deal of avoidance behavior.

### Individual (Intrapersonal) Differences Theories

Some scholars have searched for the causation of family violence in individual differences among offenders and sometimes among victims. Some individual differences include **psychopathology,** psychological **trait** differences, and psychobiological mechanisms. There is considerable evidence supporting this theory. Countering this theory as the cause of family violence, however, is evidence showing that although many abusive individuals manifest unusual personal characteristics, most do not.

*Psychopathology.* One recurrent explanation for family violence is *psychopathology (mental disorder)* in perpetrators, victims, or both. This supposition proposes that individuals who mistreat children, dating partners, spouses, elders, or other family members are seriously disturbed. Their psychopathology may distort their view of the world or serve as a disinhibitor to prohibited behavior. Over the years, scientifically sound studies have supported the mental illness model of family violence by demonstrating higher rates of mental disorders among family violence offenders relative to individuals in comparison groups. **Narcissism,** clinical depression, and **antisocial personality disorder** are examples of the kinds of pathology typical of family violence offenders (e.g., see Kessler, Molnar, Feurer, & Appelbaum, 2001; Krueger, Moffitt, Caspi, Bleske, & Silva, 1998). Increasingly, *geneticists* have shown substantial contribution to psychopathology via inheritance.

*Psychological traits.* Other research has focused on *psychological traits* of persons involved in family violence that are not necessarily defined as pathological. Some authorities have theorized that certain personality traits typical of offenders or victims (e.g., high hostility, jealousy) contribute to their perpetration or experience of family violence. Such characteristics help to explain (but do not justify) abusive behaviors (Blanchard, 2001). Although traits are simply constructs (labels) that do not exist in reality, they describe characteristic ways in which people behave in different situations. The trait formulation alleges that traits reside within the individual and are *not* situation specific. For example, a person who has the trait of cheerfulness would be cheerful at home, at work, and in other settings. If true, quantification of traits can help practitioners predict behavior and provide a clear point for therapeutic intervention.

Taking trait proscriptions a step further, social scientists during the 1990s concentrated heavily on devising patterns of traits, or **typologies** (Holtzworth-Munroe & Stuart, 1994). As one illustration, trait research has found that perpetrators of child sexual abuse tend to exhibit feelings of vulnerability, dependency, inadequacy, and loneliness and to experience cognitive distortions (e.g., Hanson, Gizzarelli, & Scott, 1994). Studies have also identified several psychological traits that are associated with aggression among abusive parents and assaultive partners, including low self-esteem, anger, hostility, emotional dependency, and poor problem-solving skills (e.g., Sedlar & Hansen, 2001; see Dixon & Browne, 2003, for a review of typology research).

Until the early 1990s, possible *psychobiological bases* for family violence escaped scrutiny for the most part (DiLalla & Gottesman, 1991). More and more so-called psychological traits that have a very strong genetic or physiological basis are coming into view. Illustrative of a psychobiological approach is research showing that physical child abusers exhibit hyper-responsive physiological activity to both positive and negative child stimuli (Milner & Chilamkurti, 1991). Such unusual physiological responses might contribute to diminished tolerance for proximity to children in such individuals, which in turn might elicit physical aggression. Investigators have further explored possible links between the hormone testosterone and aggression (see Book, Starzyk, & Quinsey, 2001, for a meta-analysis). Understanding how psychobiological determinants are connected to aggression is important, because such a link suggests that alternative interventions, such as drug treatments, may be successful in reducing family violence (Paris, 2001).

## Systems Theory and Interactional Theories

*Systems theory* is the assumption that family violence is a product of interactions between individuals in a specific relationship. Certain aspects of specific relationships, in and of themselves, may foster family violence. Proponents of this view think that violence in a relationship is not the result of the behavior of only one person, such as the perpetrator, but also a result of the victim's behavior (Giles-Sims, 1983). As Lane and Russell (1989) contend, one cannot separate victim from victimizer, dominance from submission, or aggression from passivity. More specifically, there cannot be a victimizer unless someone allows herself or himself to be a victim. Feminist theoreticians deplore systems theory because it places an equal portion of the blame on victims, and thus fails to make perpetrators totally responsible for their violence.

A number of researchers have pinpointed *marital dysfunction (dyadic/relationship stress)* as a factor that promotes IPV. The supposition is that a violent partner's behavior may be a response to the other partner's conduct. Accordingly, it is the interactions of both partners that preserve the homeostatic balance (e.g., violence) of the relationship (another concept from systems theory; see S. Johnson & Lebow, 2000; Tyrell, 2002). Support for this premise comes from research that has shown that both partners in abusive relationships experience high rates of discord or have deficits in communication skills. Evidence apparently contradicting dyadic stress (marital dysfunction) formulations demonstrates that men scoring above the median on marital satisfaction tests may still beat their wives, and some of those scoring below may not (e.g., Barnett & Hamberger, 1992; Rosenbaum & O'Leary, 1981).

*Interpersonal interaction theory.* **Interpersonal interaction theory** is similar to systems theory, but without a victim-blaming component or the concept of equally shared responsibility for the violence. This theory also avoids the supposition that the violence is specific to a relationship. It is premised on the idea that members of a couple or parent-child dyad are responsive to the actions of the other in terms of such issues as *attachment needs* and *anger.* Although the previous discussion of *marital dysfunction* appeared within the framework of systems theory, others would place the topic under interpersonal interaction theory. How does one partner's behavior influence the other partner's level of marital satisfaction? Is aggression an antecedent or a consequence of dyadic stress? Application of newer statistical techniques is finally allowing researchers to answers such questions (see Marcus & Swett, 2002). One analysis, for example, showed that low marital adjustment *was* a "causal" factor in partner aggression (K. D. O'Leary, Slep, & O'Leary, 2007).

**Attachment** research provides strong evidence that interpersonal interactions influence family violence (Rothbaum, Weisz, Pott, Miyake, & Morelli, 2000). **Infant attachment** refers to the enduring emotional bond that develops between a dependent infant and his or her primary caretaker during the first year of life (Bowlby, 1980). Research findings from several areas allude to the occurrence of disturbed patterns of attachment in abusive and neglecting families (e.g., Ward, Lee, & Lipper, 2000). **Adult attachment** is an affectionate bond with a romantic partner that is a relatively long-lasting connection typified by wanting to be close to the partner (Feeney & Noller, 1996). According to some theorists, an inadequately attached adult suffers anxiety and anger when faced with a partner who threatens to leave, and these intense feelings may fuel an assault against that partner (Bookwala, 2002).

## Correlates and Single-Factor Variables Related to Family Violence

A section on correlates and single causal factors is appropriate to place within the theories section because correlates are often viewed as explanations (semitheories) for family violence. Most students, however, have heard over and over again the warning that "correlations are not causal." Using correlations only, a researcher never knows the direction of causality between the linked variables or whether a third unknown variable is responsible for the association.

### *Poverty*

Poverty is probably the correlate most associated with IPV and child maltreatment (e.g., Rennison & Welchans, 2000). Poverty is linked with *social disorganization,* more specifically *neighborhood disadvantage.* Disadvantaged neighborhoods are characterized by numerous factors: (a) a high percentage of people living below the poverty line, (b) a high rate of unemployment and employment instability, (c) a high percentage of female-headed households, women often living on welfare, (d) social isolation, and (e) general financial strain, all of which are individually related to IPV (Kohl & Macy, 2008). As if these factors were not enough, injection drug use among African Americans is also related to social isolation within certain metropolitan areas (Cooper, Friedman, Tempalski, & Friedman, 2007). The relationship between poverty and IPV also occurs in countries other than the United States. An Australian study, for instance, showed that an index of socioeconomic disadvantage is a significant predictor of reported IPV (Di Bartolo, 2001).

### *Alcohol and Drug Use (AOD)*

Probably the earliest proposed correlate of family violence was alcohol abuse. Many, many cases of known family violence occurred while a family member, usually the perpetrator, was drunk. Accordingly, drunkenness seemed causal in the minds of many experts and laypersons alike. Government statisticians report that alcohol and other drug abuse (AOD) is highly linked with family violence at all levels.

- AOD by parents is one of the many risk factors for child abuse (Greenfeld et al., 1998).
- AOD is significantly correlated with sexual assault and/or risky sexual behaviors (e.g., Girard & Senn, 2008).
- AOD is also highly correlated with adult IPV. IPV victimization occurred in three fourths of the spousal cases when examined separately and two thirds of the combined group of intimate partners: current/former spouses and boyfriends/girlfriends cases (Greenfeld, 1998).

- AOD is a significant correlate not only of physical violence but also of sexual and emotional abuse (Coker, Smith, McKeown, & Melissa, 2000).
- AOD is a significant factor in *intimate partner homicides* (IPHs). Indicative of such findings, Jeffrey Fagan (1993) reported that AOD was involved in more than half of intimate homicides.
- AOD was evident in 39% of three geographically different samples of elder abusers (Wolf & Pillemer, 1988).
- AOD was present in over half the reports of male abusers of disabled women (Milberger et al., 2003).
- AOD was linked with a lifetime of physical abuse, sexual abuse, battering, and marriage to an alcoholic, according to one group of older women (Osgood & Manetta, 2002).
- AOD of parents is linked with adolescents' externalizing behavior and alcoholism (Hussong et al., 2007).

See Table 2.1 for additional theories of family violence.

**TABLE 2.1**  Additional Theories of Family Violence

| Explanation | Description |
|---|---|
| Social exchange theory | Explores interactions between victim and perpetrator from a cost-benefit point of view, assuming that humans enter and maintain relationships only when they judge that the benefits (such as love and security) outweigh the costs (such as increased workload) (Gelles, 1983). Social exchange principles may apply to several family and intimate relationships, including adult child–elder parent, parent-child, husband-wife, and boyfriend-girlfriend. When benefits outweigh costs, one member of the pair may perceive the relationship as inequitable and terminate it (see Blum, 1997; Call, Finch, Huck, & Kane, 1999; Sprecher, 2001). When termination is impossible, the aggrieved party experiences frustration and may become aggressive (frustration-aggression hypothesis; see Rodriguez & Henderson, 1995; Worden, 2002). |
| Symbolic interactionism | Emphasizes the symbolic communication between humans. Within the ongoing process of social interactions, the actors construct and reconstruct their own social reality, which, in turn, propels behavior. From this point of view, it is simplistic to assume that human behavior can be understood merely on the basis of objectively specifiable variables, such as the actors' background characteristics or external stimuli (see Felson & Tedeschi, 1993; Snow, 2001). Through this lens, the key to understanding family violence can be found in the meanings that family members attach to various interactions. A real-life illustration of this "meaning in the making" process is a case in which an infant-abusing mother interprets her baby's crying as repetitive complaints about the mother's ineptitude. Refusing to be labeled "bad," the mother decides to shut the baby up by hitting her (for an application, see Hill & Amuwo, 1998). |
| Routine activities theory | Especially useful for explaining stalking patterns (Tjaden & Thoennes, 1998b). Cohen and Felson (1979) define routine activities as "any recurrent and prevalent activities which provide for basic population and individual need (e.g., working, schooling, leisure outings, shopping" (p. 590). Schwartz and Pitts (1995) have applied parts of this theory to explain sexual assault of college women. Presumably, women's regular attendance at classes, restaurants, and other settings makes it easier for men to target them. |

# Multidimensional Theories

Multidimensional models endeavor to *integrate several unidimensional theories.* Attempts to develop such models flow logically from the failure of single-concept frameworks to account for family violence. The need for a multidimensional theory is especially salient when one is attempting to interpret the causes of family violence in other cultures or when one is striving to delineate a worldview (Perilla, Bakeman, & Norris, 1994). As a wide-ranging illustration, suppose that a very hostile man (psychological trait) who was abused as a child (learning), who is currently unhappily married (interpersonal interaction), who has inherited a genetic predisposition for antisocial personality disorder (psychopathology), and who has just lost his job (stress) uses male privilege (patriarchy) as a justification for assaulting his wife. Clearly, no singular etiological framework fully explains his violence. (See www.sagepub.com/barnett3e for a discussion of common models used by researchers studying family violence.)

---

**SECTION SUMMARY**

## Theoretical Explanations of Family Violence

Logicians have promulgated numerous theories to explain and unify disparate research findings. No one conceptual framework adequately explains family violence, but evidence has emerged that supports several theories. One practical organization classifies theories into two major groups: macrotheories and microtheories.

Macrotheories account for family violence by explaining how broad, cultural forces allow or even promote it. *Cultural acceptance of violence* applied to family violence is the product of widespread social acceptance of violence, such as spanking. The ideology of some cultures, such as *patriarchy*, allows men to dominate and control families. Patriarchal formulations attribute family violence to male privilege and power in a society. Through this lens, men beat women because they can get away with it. *Feminist analysis* focuses on gender inequality and the damage done to women because of male-dominance beliefs. Peer-group influence theories suppose that male peers support male-to-female aggression and domination and thereby constitute a *subculture of violence.*

*Deterrence theory* presumes that the criminal justice response to assaults against family members is too minimal to be effective. The idea of *situational impetus* is that environmental elements, such as guns in homes, engender violence. *Social-structural explanations* have noted the many correlations between youthfulness, low income, and other variables. These parameters may create stress and anger, which lead to aggression. *Evolutionary theory* may explain some aggressive behaviors. *Punishment procedures* are supposed to reduce unwanted behaviors, but their implementation is so challenging that they cannot succeed under ordinary circumstances.

*(Continued)*

(Continued)

*Microtheories,* in contrast, are anchored in individual behaviors. Learning explanations of family violence, the most empirically grounded of this group of theories, rest primarily on the concepts of social learning (modeling) and classical and operant conditioning. People learn to be fearful through *classical conditioning,* and they learn how to perform an action through *operant conditioning. Avoidance conditioning* is a type of learning that includes both classical and operant conditioning. Contemporary learning theories make use of all of these theories to explain reactions to *trauma and PTSD.* They can explain learned fear and individuals' attempts to avoid situations (cues) that induce fear. Learning principles form the basis for arguments concerning the intergenerational transmission of violence, trauma reactions, and revictimization.

Individual intrapersonal theories (psychopathology, psychological traits, and psychobiological traits) are especially important concepts when providing treatment. *Psychopathological* explanations for family violence assume the presence of mental illness in perpetrators. Therefore, family members who abuse other members lack the ability to be normally reasonable. *Psychological traits* theories attribute family violence to individual variation in personality traits such as empathy. *Psychobiological traits,* such as physiological reactivity, may contribute to abusive behaviors.

When dealing with couples or families, *systems theory* and interpersonal interaction theories (dyadic stress, parent-child stress, and insecure attachment) may offer useful ideas. These theories hold that the actions of both perpetrator and victim interact to promote violence or to maintain it. *Attachment theory* asserts that children who have bonded insufficiently with their primary caregivers are at risk for abuse. Such early difficulties with attachment may set the stage for later anxieties about adult romantic attachments.

Although family violence research would benefit from the development of multidimensional theories, the complexity of the family violence problem has made such theories elusive. It is hoped that newer statistical techniques can provide more insight in the future into multiple causations. There are a number of *correlates* of family violence. Two of the best known correlates are *poverty* and *alcohol/drug dependence.* Given that no single-concept theory has been able to explain the complex phenomenon of family violence fully, the development of *multidimensional theories* should be a priority.

## METHODOLOGY: HOW RESEARCHERS TRY TO ANSWER QUESTIONS ABOUT FAMILY VIOLENCE

This section of the chapter elaborates on the deficiencies of the research carried out in the field of family violence. Conducting research in this area is a daunting challenge for investigators. Gathering data is especially problematic because of the delicate and private nature of the subject matter. In addition, by reporting subjects' experiences, researchers may accidentally stigmatize or shame individual research subjects, or generate fears of reprisal or even legal sanctions (Sullivan & Cain, 2004). From a newer perspective, however, experts are calling attention to the ethical question of *not* asking about abuse. To avoid asking "plays directly into the social forces that perpetuate IPV (intimate partner violence) and other forms of violence" (Black & Black, 2007, p. 329). Furthermore, the connection between childhood abuse and adult health problems almost compels health providers to ask about abuse (Edwards, Dube, Felitti, & Anda, 2007). Moreover, abuse directly affects the data obtained in many related studies, such as those linked with personality and health (Becker-Blease, 2006). Taken together, researchers must thoroughly consider the well-being of their subjects and the ramifications of their study in recruiting study participants.

The earliest investigations of family violence tended to be *exceedingly weak methodologically.* The first researchers in this area "swept with a wide broom," desperately searching for commonalities in hopes of gaining insight into the phenomenon. This approach led to a proliferation of essentially pilot studies that failed to produce the crucial information researchers so eagerly sought (Rosenbaum, 1988). Among the many shortcomings of the early research mentioned throughout the literature are the following: (a) the researchers' lack of understanding of ethical principles, (b) inadequate methods for obtaining data, (c) underdeveloped theory, (d) imprecise definitions and methods of measurement, (e) faulty sampling, (f) failure to use optimal comparison groups, (g) overreliance on descriptive and cross-sectional investigations, (h) the use of univariate rather than **multivariate methods** of analysis, (i) failure to replicate studies or integrate findings, and (j) insufficient adjustments for cultural and ethnic differences.

With the advent of advanced statistical techniques (e.g., **structural equation modeling),** researchers can pinpoint *causality* with greater certainty (B. M. Byrne, 2001; Pearl, 2000). In one productive undertaking, researchers identified a number of single dimensions, such as jealousy, anger, and marital dissatisfaction, and combined them to generate preliminary models of both men's and women's interpersonal aggression (K. D. O'Leary et al., 2007). According to Hearn (2006), however, it is possible that a search for a final cause of IPV may well be futile. Overall, the research on family violence to date has been "extensive but not definitive" (see Gartner, 1993).

To pinpoint specific deficits, researchers assessed the methodological strengths and weaknesses of nine extant studies on *IPV prevention.* Drawing upon previous work evaluating family preservation programs, researchers used a standardized list of 15 criteria for judging the characteristics of the nine quantitative prevention studies (C. E. Murray & Graybeal, 2007). Results revealed that none of the nine studies satisfied all 15 criteria and only two met 12 of the 15 criteria. The *primary strengths* of the studies were as follows: (a) specification of eligibility criteria, (b) adequate description of the intervention for the treatment group, (c) the use of suitable statistical procedures, and (d) adequate documentation of the treatment and control groups' similarity. The most notable limitations of the prevention studies included the following: (a) insufficient use of representative sampling procedures, (b) deficient specification of exclusion criteria, (c) nonuse of random assignment to groups, and (d) failure to use psychometrically sound assessment tools. The authors concluded that more government funding, along with methodological changes, was needed to advance prevention research in the field of IPV.

A major problem in studying family violence is the *lack of random assignment.* Individuals familiar with the principles of research are well aware of the importance of random assignment to enhance the potential of producing generalizable results. Researchers, however, cannot use random assignment in many studies because they have no control over some of the important variables (e.g., individuals' AOD). Examples include conditions such as judges' behavior when mandating offenders to a treatment condition, such as alcohol treatment, counseling, community service, or fines. In a crime setting it is preferable to rule out the effects of arrest and other powerful factors that may affect behavioral change.

Despite universal preference for random assignment, it is possible that this methodology is *problematic.* As a case in point, implementation of random assignment designs for assessment of batterer treatment may *lack utility, be impossible to achieve,* or both. One solution is to follow the methodology adopted by statisticians in the public health field when investigating populations such as alcoholics. Note that investigators cannot randomly assign people to either the experimental alcoholic group or the control group. Epidemiologists often turn to **quasi-experimental designs** (cannot use random assignment) because they seem to yield *more meaningful results.* By analogy, quasi-experimental designs may be the most appropriate for batterer treatment evaluation (see Feder & Ford, 2000; Maxwell, Garner, & Fagan, 2001; Taylor, Davis, & Maxwell, 2001).

Although researchers have made *methodological advances in the past 10 years,* deficiencies are still the rule rather than the exception. Of great promise, however, are the growing numbers of working partnerships between *researchers* in the *private sector* and those working within *federal government agencies*, such as the National Institutes of Health, the National Institute of Mental Health, the National Institute of Child Health and Development, and the Centers for Disease Control and Prevention. With federal funding, these researchers have undertaken a number of large-scale, representative surveys and other highly significant studies (Felson, Messner, Hoskin, & Deane, 2002; Tjaden & Thoennes, 1998a, 2000b). Government agencies also accumulate all types of health and violence information that is often generalizable across large regions. The National Data Archive on Child Abuse and Neglect (NDACAN), for example, makes available sizable datasets covering a host of topics (e.g., adoption and foster care).

## Sources of Data

Data on family violence come from several kinds of sources. Weis (1989) separates these into five principle types: (a) *Official records* come from FBI summaries of police department reports and reports from social service agencies and reflect amounts of "officially" reported family violence; (b) *self-reports* are mail, phone, or face-to-face surveys about violence in the family conducted with members of the general public; (c) *victimization and perpetration surveys* are mail, phone, or face-to-face surveys conducted with victims of family violence; (d) *informant reports* are mail, phone, or face-to-face surveys conducted with observers (e.g., parents) of violent behaviors (e.g., fights between siblings) that do not inquire directly of the individual agents involved (e.g., siblings); and (e) *direct observations* are empirical observations (e.g., measurement of physiological responses during a quarrel) made by social scientists in a laboratory. No one type of data source is inherently superior to the others; rather, each has its own strengths and weaknesses (Verhoek-Oftedahl, Pearlman, & Babcock, 2000). (For descriptions of government and large private surveys from a criminological perspective, see Buzawa and Buzawa, 2003.)

*Official statistics* reflect the rates of reported intimate violence—that is, cases reported to police or to other public agencies. The Federal Bureau of Investigation's *Uniform Crime Reports* (*UCR*) are the most commonly cited sources of official data. These reports, which are published annually, include data on all reported crimes and arrests made for those crimes across the United States. Government statisticians also track injuries recorded by hospital emergency department personnel through the National Electronic Injury Surveillance System. Another newer data collection tool is the National Incident-Based Reporting System (Centers for Disease Control and Prevention [CDC], 2000; Orchowsky & Weiss, 2000). State agencies such as those devoted to adult protective services and child protective services accumulate reports of family violence against vulnerable groups.

It should be noted, however, that official statistics on family violence are plagued by a *number of flaws*. The most glaring of these is that individuals report only a small proportion of the violence that takes place within families. The violence that is reported, furthermore, tends to be the most serious, and therefore it is not representative of family violence as a whole (Chalk & King, 1998). Other problems with official data include the failure of government agencies to track criminal acts against children under the age of 12 (Finkelhor & Ormrod, 2001).

Occasionally, government agencies have categorized certain kinds of acts of family violence as other types of crimes (Steinman, 1991). Agencies collecting data have often merged specific information on the relationships between offenders and victims (e.g., boyfriend-girlfriend, spouses, ex-spouses) into two less precise offender categories: stranger and nonstranger. Gradually, however, the FBI has modified the crime classifications in the *UCR* and has improved the coverage, reliability, and detail of these reports (Jensen & Karpos, 1993; Langford, Isaac, & Kabat, 1998). Since the UCR provides data only on crimes actually reported and excludes data on crimes not reported, it cannot ascertain information on rates of reporting.

*Self-report surveys.* Self-report surveys are especially useful for gathering information about crimes such as spouse abuse and date rape, in which the victims may be reluctant to talk to police but may be willing to share information about the crimes in anonymous surveys. They also are particularly useful for gathering information on subabusive behavior, such as corporal punishment of a child or light pushing between marital partners. In family violence *perpetration* self-report surveys, respondents answer questions about their own violent behavior directed toward other intimates (children, spouses, partners, and parents). In *victimization* self-report surveys, victims answer questions about the violent behaviors they have experienced. The obvious advantage of such surveys is that they provide access to information about violence that is not reported to official agencies. The most commonly cited data source of this kind in the United States is the *National Crime Victimization Survey (NCVS)*. This survey collects data from a stratified sample of 60,000 households and is conducted semiannually by the U.S. Bureau of the Census.

On the other hand, self-reports have numerous inherent problems, one of which arises because of their *retrospective* nature (recalled events). Thus, respondents may not answer questions accurately because of *memory lapses* or reluctance to recall. The possibility for differential interpretations of questions and motivated or unconscious response errors suggests that respondents might lie, underreport, or minimize the severity of the violent acts (Kessler et al., 2001). Even though research participants are promised anonymity and confidentiality, they might not tell the truth because they think what they have gone through is a *private matter,* because they have *already reported it* to another official, or because they *fear retaliation* (U.S. Bureau of Justice Statistics, 1992).

Also, the fact that surveys ask respondents about *specific time periods* (e.g., the previous 6 months) fails to tap the chronic and repetitive nature of family violence (Weis, 1989). What is more, a number of *reporting biases* can influence respondents' answers in such surveys. One bias is the tendency to perceive one's own violence as justified and therefore not reportable (see Kruttschnitt & Dornfeld, 1992). Another weakness is that women's violence, relative to men's, is more likely to be recalled and reported because it is unexpected behavior (Morse, 1995). Interestingly, new research in neuropsychology has revealed that the hippocampus (which includes emotional memory) is larger in women. It is probable that its greater capacity allows women to remember emotional events, such as IPV, in greater detail (see Tyre & Scelfo, 2006).

The relationship between victim and perpetrator strongly influences reporting: Victims often do not want to report violence perpetrated on them by family members (Waltermaurer, Ortega, & McNutt, 2003). In addition, research has shown that the interviewer's gender has strong effects on reporting, with women revealing sexual assault more readily to female interviewers (Sorenson, Stein, Siegel, Golding, & Burnam, 1987).

*Informant data.* Informant data is information that requires individuals to report their observations of violence used by others. For example, children might report what they saw when their parents hurt each other (e.g., Cronin, 1995). Although seemingly valid at first glance, informant reports may lack validity because informants (e.g., teachers) may not always know the extent of the behavior about which they are reporting (e.g., children's sexualized behaviors with peers). Researchers in some family violence studies more frequently ask parents to report on their children's behaviors than they ask children to provide self-report data (Wilkens, 2002). These reports may also be biased for other reasons, such as informants' defensiveness or level of psychological distress (Levendosky, Huth-Bocks, Semel, & Shapiro, 2002).

***Direct observation*** of violent acts is a rarely used mode of data collection, but it may provide unusual insight into the dynamics of interpersonal violence (Weis, 1989). Direct observation also circumvents overreliance on self-reports. Urquiza and Timmer (2002) recommend that family violence researchers videotape study participants' social interactions or observe the interactions directly. As an illustration, researchers might watch couples as they quarrel in their own homes (Margolin, Burman, & John, 1989) or monitor the physiological responses of couples as they quarrel in laboratory settings (Jacobson & Gottman, 1993).

## Assessment and Research Design Issues

Given the record of the 1980s and early 1990s, it is clear that progress in understanding family violence depends on improvements in the quality of research. The discussion below calls attention to the extraordinary difficulties of conducting family violence research in the field and proposes some solutions. Although researchers may well be aware of the value of including certain elements in their study designs, they typically must compromise some of their goals. Access to appropriate research subjects, for instance, may be extremely limited (Kinard, 2001). On the other hand, researchers often appear oblivious to research design defects that they could avoid with a reasonable amount of forethought. Students of family violence will obtain a deeper understanding of the issues if they become aware of the many pitfalls in executing research on the topic.

*Lack of theoretical foundation.* Even though causation of family violence may be the most hotly contested issue in the field, a surprisingly large number of family violence studies lack any stated theoretical premise. Without some foundation, research findings run the risk of appearing to arise from isolated events. By proposing a conceptual base and then testing it within a controlled study, a researcher can put forward the basic determinants of family violence. Because selection of treatment flows from etiological conceptions, debates concerning the causes of family violence spill over into quarrels about interventions.

*Definitions and disagreements.* Without a doubt, the most problematic issue in family violence research is the lack of well-established and agreed-upon definitions. An assortment of definitions has emerged among cultural communities, legal scholars, health specialists, and persons involved in interpersonal violence (Bonomi, Allen, & Holt, 2005). S. Torres (1991), for example, found that Latinas tended not to label a behavior as abuse until it had occurred frequently. Overcoming this obstacle is challenging (see Fincham, 2000). Definitions of abuse need to be sufficiently comprehensive to capture the experiences of victims, yet not so broad as to encompass behaviors that cannot be validly assessed (Centers for Disease Control and Prevention, 2000). Some scholars or agencies have tailored their definitions very restrictively, and others have employed definitions that are quite broad. Obviously, definitions guide and restrain the type of measurement selected and therefore the nature of results reported (Bonomi et al., 2005).

What sense can be made of the term *rape,* for example, if the FBI excludes rape of males while all other government agencies include it? This exclusion is unwarranted in that rapes of males in settings like prisons can present serious health and violence problems ("Weak Laws Encourage," 2005). It is encouraging to see that there now is a National Prison Rape Elimination Commission that has issued new "zero tolerance" standards ("Prison Rape Panel," 2008). In addition, some females *do* sexually assault male intimates, and gay males may sexually assault gay male partners.

Whose definition should prevail? Suppose researchers and those individuals actually involved in family violence do not agree? Should victims define their own condition? In one inquiry where respondents used their own definitions, abusive men judged some behaviors as violent that were not included in the researchers' constructs (Chamberland, Fortin, Turgeon, & Laporte, 2007). Language influences victims' and listeners' interpretations of abuse, and therefore controls, for example, who gets identified as a victim or perpetrator of abuse in medical settings (Bonomi et al., 2005). A serious current problem is the overuse of the term *violence,* yet the milder term *abuse* seems too innocuous to capture the meaning of some behaviors.

It has become increasingly clear that researchers need to differentiate **battering** (repetitive, severe physical and psychological abuse accompanied by fear and control) from "normative" abuse or common couple violence (a few slaps or shoves, not accompanied by fear or control) (Schumacher, 2002). One group of commentators has pointed out shortcomings in defining customarily accepted dichotomies, such as victim/perpetrator or male/female within the study of IPV (McHugh, Livingston, & Ford, 2005). As an illustration, a term like *violence* does not have a monolithic meaning. Each gender differentially evaluates the meaning and acceptability of an action. IPV is not a single truth but a "complex, multifaceted, and dynamic aspect of human interaction that occurs in multiple forms and patterns" (p. 323).

Others underscore the need to view IPV from a holistic stance, taking into account the *multiple intersecting factors* involved in conceptualizing IPV. It is essential to incorporate many dimensions, such as social-economic-status, heterosexism, and race, which interact with each other to influence the types and levels of abusive behavior (Lindhorst & Tajima, 2008). Still others have focused on the term *battering* for two reasons. First, battered women do *not* think of their own abuse using this terminology. Second, the term *battering* is not especially useful to professionals (e.g., lawyers) who do not have a deep understanding of violent relationships.

Such ambiguity can be perplexing. Family violence researchers' *definitions of ancillary terms* such as *child, neglect, elder,* and *date rape* have also been vague or inconsistent. In some studies, the appellation *child* may refer to an individual under age 12, whereas in others it may include all persons up to age 18 (Goldman & Padayachi, 2000). Recently, researchers ascertained that divorced nonresidential parents felt confused over how to define the meaning of "family" once their own family had changed (Bailey, 2007). In one survey, researchers reported that in 31 articles covering the co-occurrence of physical child abuse and IPV, 15 different definitions of abuse appeared (Appel & Holden, 1998). Failure to reach accord on the meanings of such terms has significantly handicapped scientific inquiry, limited interpretations of research findings, restricted generalizations across studies, and impeded understanding of the very nature of family violence. In many circumstances, lack of standardized definitions has even precluded the development of effective preventions and interventions (Portwood, 1999).

*Populations sampled.* Should researchers rely on college student research participants for their samples? Family violence researchers have recruited widely divergent samples of research participants including the following: (a) individuals randomly chosen from the general population; (b) volunteers recruited from clinics or through door-to-door or telephone solicitation, or by advertisement; (c) individuals who are members of special groups, such as military recruits, college students, or postpartum mothers; and (d) people referred by agencies, such as elders or probationers. Researchers have also examined the records of hospital emergency room visits and police calls to gather data. Obviously, systematic differences exist between any two such sample populations, and this noncomparability hampers comparisons across studies (see Ohlin & Tonry, 1989). Lack of comparability contributes to consequential disputes, such as the question of prevalence of male-to-male versus female-to-male partner violence (Holtzworth-Munroe, 2005).

The representativeness of study samples is another challenge in family violence inquiries. A *representative sample* is one in which the sample's characteristics are proportionally similar to those of the population from which the sample was drawn. Without random assignment, causal inferences are difficult to make. Representative samples, such as those used in the National Family Violence Surveys (NFVS), the National Crime Victimization Survey, and the National Violence Against Women Survey, can be used to make inferences about entire populations. Some supposedly representative samples, however, may still exclude certain kinds of people, such as those who have no telephones or those who fall into circumscribed categories (e.g., gay men, non–English speakers, homeless people, and those living in institutions) (Centers for Disease Control and Prevention, 2000). Some surveys limit their samples to cohabiting couples, thus excluding the extensive amount of abuse that occurs between ex-intimates (Bachman & Saltzman, 1995). Furthermore, scholars interested in assessing lesbian IPV have almost uniformly studied participants who are White, well educated, and middle class (Turrell, 2000). Nonresponse is also a complication, because it raises questions about the representativeness of a sample (Koss et al., 1994).

Another type of sample, a *clinical sample,* can be drawn from any number of sources. In the case of family violence research, typical sources might be group homes for abused children, shelters for battered women, and social service agencies. Clinical samples are usually small "handy" samples, and data derived from them commonly lack generalizability, even within small subgroups of the population. Findings generated by data gathered from children living in battered women's shelters, for example, cannot be generalized to children living in violent homes or in foster care. Notwithstanding these serious limitations, research conducted with clinical samples provides useful information about the dynamics and causes of abuse and often generates initial impressions about prevention and treatment (see Weis, 1989). A related type of sample is a *forensic sample,* comprised of individuals who may be involved in family violence. Forensic samples are frequently drawn from prisons, probation caseloads, court cases, or criminal justice records.

*Comparison groups.* Most family violence research designs have failed to include satisfactory comparison groups of subjects. Comparison groups provide critical details about how target groups differ from or are similar to other groups. Without them, it is difficult to present a useful interpretation of research findings (see Chalk & King, 1998). When researchers have enlisted comparison groups, moreover, they have all too frequently failed to conceptualize sufficiently the kinds of individuals appropriate for comparison. This failure has led to serious errors in the classification of subjects and, in turn, meaningless results (P. H. Smith, Thornton, DeVellis, Earp, & Coker, 2002). For example, as Rosenbaum (1988) has noted, in a study of maritally violent men, a suitable comparison group is not simply men who are maritally nonviolent, but rather men who are both unhappily married and maritally nonviolent. Some researchers have contrasted maritally violent men with generally violent men (Mowat-Leger, 2002).

When researchers cannot readily obtain comparison group data, they sometimes use normative data (i.e., data from published test standards). As an illustration, a researcher might initially obtain a clinical sample of foster mothers' ratings of children on the *Child Behavior Checklist* (CBCL), a standardized instrument designed to measure a variety of behavior problems (Achenbach & Edelbrock, 1983). The investigator might then compare the foster mothers' ratings with CBCL ratings obtained previously from a representative sample of mothers from the general population (the normative group ratings).

A disadvantage of relying on normative group scores is that the comparison does not control for any confounding variables (e.g., drug abuse) inherent in the target group. This critique can apply to comparisons between any naturally occurring groups. That is, when the researcher does not randomly assign participants to the *conditions that are being compared,* such as children in foster care versus children not in foster care, the findings may lack clarity. Variables that obscure interpretation (confounds) may affect the results on dependent variables (e.g., CBCL ratings) (see Randolf & Conkle, 1993). Of course, researchers cannot randomly assign children to foster care or non–foster care conditions just for the sake of research. Consequently, they settle for methods such as those described above, which are basically correlational in nature.

*Longitudinal (outcome) studies.* Experts generally advocate the use of research designs that extend over time, rather than cross-sectional designs, even though the data are still correlational (National Research Council, 1993). Longitudinal investigations are expensive and difficult to conduct, in part because it can be hard to recruit sufficient numbers of research participants, and attrition (or dropout) rates among participants are high. As might be expected, longitudinal studies also may have serious flaws. Typical of such shortcomings are instances in which test score variations can be attributed to children's age differences over time (e.g., Yoshihama & Gillespie, 2002). (For an impressive example of a longitudinal analysis conducted by family violence researchers, see Runyan et al., 1998; and for a review of recruitment and retention problems in IPV research, see M. A. Dutton et al., 2003.)

One practical approach to collecting retrospective data is to use a *Life History Calendar method* (Freedman, Thornton, Camburn, Alwin, & Young-DeMarco, 1988). To increase recall, this methodology advises participants to first recall personal memorable events, such as marriages or deaths of family members. Next, participants try to remember less easily remembered events, such as occurrences of interpersonal violence. Research indicates that this method does enhance memory. Sophisticated analyses of these records further allow researchers to obtain more accurate information about the sequence of events (e.g., Belli, Shay, & Stafford, 2001).

*Diversity awareness.* Although the American Psychological Association has in recent years made cultural sensitivity a hallmark of its organizational goals, implementing these policy changes is a "work in progress" (Crawford, 2002). American family violence scholars have systematically indulged in what Hall (1997) calls "cultural malpractice." Individuals from certain communities (e.g., immigrants) have been understudied and underserved (Daniels, 2001; for a review, see Harway et al., 2002). To improve their studies of family violence, investigators must employ research designs that include minority groups (Fernández, 2006). To help improve researchers' cultural sensitivity, the American Psychological Association (2003) has issued a set of guidelines on multicultural education, training, research, and organizational changes.

A less considered type of diversity awareness centers on sociopolitical diversity in psychology. Redding (2001) suggests that the lack of conservative viewpoints on social policy issues "damages psychology's credibility with policymakers and the public, impedes serving conservative clients, results in de facto discrimination against conservative students and scholars, and has a chilling effect on liberal education." He makes a compelling case by furnishing examples in such areas as adolescent competence. That is, psychologists ordinarily hold that adolescents are competent enough to make some medical decisions (e.g., about abortion) but not competent enough to be held culpable for crimes in the same way that adults are. Another example is whether gay and lesbian parenting is harmful to children. Psychologists usually report few if any ill effects on children but have no longitudinal data to support this assumption.

## Family Violence Scales and Measurement Issues

Just as research design features are important, it is equally important that researchers address measurement dilemmas. Incorrect or inadequate measurements lead to faulty assumptions about family violence that narrow understanding. Family violence scholars have had many disagreements about measuring family violence because optimal assessment methods remain uncertain. To date, there is no *gold standard* of measuring interpersonal violence between family members (Hamby, 2005). One of the most critical needs in the field is the development of better measurement of intimate partner violence (Frieze, 2008b).

*Conflict Tactics Scale (CTS1).* As noted in Chapter 1, the most widely used measure in family violence research is the Conflict Tactics Scale (Straus, 1979). The construction of the first version of this scale, or CTS1, represented an impressive leap forward in identification and quantification of specific violent interpersonal behaviors. Most important, the CTS1 is highly *empirical* and thus represents a marked advance over anecdotal reports. Respondents to the CTS1 test indicate how many times in a given period (the previous year, the individual's lifetime) they used reasoning and negotiation, verbal and symbolic aggression, or physical aggression during *interpersonal disagreements*. Overall, the scale has served as the basis for estimating family violence in a variety of groups, including adolescents, college students, same-sex partners, and elders.

In an unexpected turn of events, nearly all research using CTS1 to examine rates of IPV among community and college samples reported that women are as interpersonally violent as men (Magdol et al., 1997). These surprising results seemed totally unbelievable to several groups, especially feminist researchers and battered women's advocates (e.g., Loseke

& Kurz, 2005). Findings anchored on CTS1 data led to ongoing heated exchanges over the scale's use to assess violence against women by male intimates, especially battering. Bolstered by advocates' impressions that vigorously repudiated the idea of gender equivalence, researchers deduced that women rarely struck men, and when they did it was necessitated by self-preservation (Cascardi, Langhinrichsen-Rohling, & Vivian, 1992; Hamberger & Potente, 1994; Saunders, 1995). Several government incidence surveys, such as the NCVS, also reported compelling evidence contradicting CTS-based surveys. Both sides, however, agreed that women suffered more frequent and serious injuries than men. The inconsistencies generated concerns that seem to represent a microcosm of the many problems inherent in family violence research. While the CTS1 clearly found *gender equivalence* in interpersonal violence, battered women calling hotlines, calling the police, and living in shelters clearly suffered more violence than men.

*Revised Conflict Tactics Scale (CTS2).* To address the concerns of feminist researchers and others, Straus and his colleagues remedied some of CTS1's perceived weaknesses by developing CTS2. CTS2 assesses IPV more broadly than does CTS1. Its improvements include clarified wording, improved differentiation between minor and severe degrees of violence, and a simplified format. CTS2 includes five subscales: (a) the original three, negotiation, psychological aggression, and physical assault, and (b) two new ones, sexual coercion and injury. The scales have become more inclusive by taking into account some acts that may be more prevalent among men's assaults than women's, such as "slamming someone against a wall" (see Cascardi, Avery-Leaf, O'Leary, & Slep, 1999). All but the negotiation subscale incorporate both *minor* and *severe* forms of violence (Straus, Hamby, Boney-McCoy, & Sugarman, 1996).

For IPV assessment, investigators interview one or both members of a randomly selected couple. Like CTS1, a CTS2 respondent is still asked to rate the frequencies of his or her own behaviors or those of someone else, such as a spouse, cohabitant, boyfriend, or girlfriend. The following test items are similar in nature to the items found in CTS2:

- You discussed the disagreement calmly.
- You refused to talk about your feelings.
- You threw a hard object at your partner.
- You punched your partner in the face.
- You threatened your partner with a weapon.
- You coerced your partner to have unwanted sex.
- You had to see a doctor because you were injured.

*Dispute about using CTS1 or CTS2.* Development of CTS2 did not end the debate about how best to measure interpersonal violence and whether CTS2 was the best index available. Experts representing the two main factions adopted diverse approaches to resolve this issue. Those convinced that the CTS data were an accurate reflection of IPV primarily emphasized the statistical properties of the scales. Those convinced the scales were not measuring the experiences of battered women offered numerous verbal analyses of the scales' lack of applicability. Thus the disagreement continues and, to a large extent, has evolved into a gender debate. Because measurement of IPV is so critical—politically, legally, and economically—it is crucial to understand the debate when evaluating the literature that appears throughout the book. See Boxes 2.2A and 2.2B for a more comprehensive analysis of the CTS2.

---

### BOX 2.2A  The Psychometric Properties of CTS2

- Scholars have demonstrated the utility of the scales with a wide variety of populations.
- Over several decades and numerous studies, the scales have demonstrated their **reliability.** That is, research participants answer the test items very similarly if asked to complete the test a second time. There is a consistency in their answers.
- At least one factor-analytic inquiry has shown that the scales have construct **validity.** In this study, the CTS scales obtained roughly the same results as another scale assumed to assess interpersonal violence.
- Several studies using factor analysis identified clusters of test items that tended to match or nearly match the categories of items (e.g., injury) used in the CTS subscales, thus providing evidence of factorial validity.
- Several studies have shown that it is possible to translate the English-language version of the CTS2 into a usable scale in a foreign language.
- Many studies have demonstrated that the scale has predictive validity because it can be used to forecast other behaviors.
- In the face of the empirical evidence, those insisting on refuting the outcomes seem to be guilty of a feminist bias.

SOURCES: Archer, 2000; Cascardi, Avery-Leaf, O'Leary, & Slep, 1999; Calvete, Corral, & Estévez, 2007; N. T. Jones, Ji, Beck, & Beck, 2002; Lucente, Fals-Stewart, Richards, & Goscha, 2001; Moore et al., 2008; Newton, Connelly, & Landsverk, 2001.

---

With the undisputed psychometric excellence of CTS1 and CTS2, one might assume that there would be universal agreement about their appropriateness for use as an IPV index, but this is not the case. The essence of this dispute may be summed up as a question of validity (measuring what the scale purports to measure). The question is whether the CTS scales truly assess *women's experiences* of interpersonal violence, especially the experience of battering, or rather some other sort of aggression? How is it that test results provided by community couples or college students generalize to battered women? As a more familiar example of validity, would the scores on the *Scholastic Aptitude Test* (SAT; Educational Testing Service, 2009) be valid predictors of college success (i.e., grades in college) if the test items actually measured teaching ability or interest in astronomy? Those who believe that the CTS findings are not an accurate reflection of women's experiences of intimate partner violence have raised a number of issues. A sample of these objections follows.

## BOX 2.2B Does CTS2 Measure "Battering"?

*Measurement/interpretation issues*

- What does it mean when couples' answers about their interpersonal violence are divergent?
- Does asking test-takers to answer questions about IPV that occurred only within the context of an argument provide a total picture of their IPV?
- Does counting the frequency of abusive acts actually capture the chronic nature of IPV?
- Do the test items capture what many experts consider to be the essence of IPV, control of one's partner?
- Are experts within the field of family violence and others, such as judges, misinterpreting CTS findings to the detriment of battered women?

*Sample issues*

- Community samples and young dating couples do not represent "battered" women who go to the police, shelters, or other agencies.
- The CTS may be quite suitable for college students but less adequate for battered spouses.
- Separated women (i.e., those at the greatest risk for abuse and homicide) are usually not included in samples of community couples.
- Can researchers assume that the CTS test questions are as applicable to same-sex intimates as heterosexual intimates?

*Gender differences*

- When measuring IPV, is it necessary to take size and strength into account?
- What is the context of IPV? Are fears and/or control present? How much gender equality do women have?
- The motivations for IPV may be quite different for men compared with women. Is there a fear factor that creates gender differences?

SOURCES: Archer, 2006; Armstrong, Wernke, Medina, & Schafer, 2002; Caetano, Field, Ramisetty-Mikler, & Lipsky, 2009; Cunradi, Bersamin, & Ames, 2009; DeKeseredy & Schwartz, 1998; Frieze, 2008b; Graham-Kevan & Archer, 2003; Hamberger, 2005; National Coalition of Antiviolence Programs, 2001; K. D. O'Leary & Williams, 2006; Renzetti, 1992; P. H. Smith, Smith, & Earp, 1999; Swan, Gambone, Caldwell, Sullivan, & Snow, 2005; White, Smith, Koss, & Figueredo, 2000; Yllö, 1993. (See Finn & Bettis, 2006, for a review.)

*Parent-child CTS.* This measurement debate concerning the CTS has not appeared to be an issue when assessing child abuse. A slightly modified version of the scale is available for use by children and teenagers. The items on the *Parent-Child Conflict Tactics Scale*, which is known as CTSPC (Straus, Hamby, Finkelhor, Moore, & Runyan, 1998), are similar to the following:

- Mother told me why some things were bad to do.
- Father spanked me with a belt or chain.

- Father threatened to burn me but didn't do it.
- Mother pushed me down the stairs.
- Father told me I was really stupid.
- Mother left me alone in the house without a babysitter.

*Growing recognition of psychological abuse.* In recent years, ever-expanding numbers of individuals concerned about family violence have called for additional recognition of psychological (emotional) abuse that goes beyond what the CTS measures (e.g., Elliston, 2001). Definitions of psychological abuse include verbal or nonverbal behaviors that demean, belittle, or undermine one's self-worth (e.g., Tolman, 1989). Advocates argue that understanding the parameters of emotional abuse is essential because this kind of maltreatment appears to be even more damaging than physical abuse (e.g., Lewis, Griffing, et al., 2006). In fact, psychological abuse is the strongest predictor of PTSD (Pico-Alfonso, 2005). Despite its documented harm, verbal abuse of adults is only illegal in its extreme forms, such as verbal threats.

Although constructs of child and adult psychological aggression overlap, distinctions remain. Some forms of psychological abuse, such as rejection, may have comparable effects across ages and genders (e.g., shame or sadness). Other forms of abuse, such as inducing an individual to engage in antisocial behavior (e.g., bullying), may produce dissimilar outcomes across the same variables. As one might suspect, it is even more difficult for family violence researchers to reach accord about defining and measuring psychological abuse than it is for them to agree about measurements of physical abuse (Schumacher, Slep, & Heyman, 2001). Should scholars assess the construct of emotional abuse in terms of frequency, intent, duration, perceptions of victims, or harm done to victims? Who has the authority to decide the true meaning of the construct? Will empirical research resolve disagreements? (See www.sagepub.com/barnett3e for an interview with Dan O'Leary.)

*Need for multiple measurements.* Because no single scale is sufficient to gauge every dimension of family violence, researchers should use multiple measures. They also should obtain both *quantitative and qualitative data* (Strauchler et al., 2004). Interview data, for instance, yield more comprehensive information than do data gathered through the examination of records kept by health agencies (Verhoek-Oftedahl et al., 2000). Furthermore, questionnaires designed to measure given constructs (e.g., abuse) sometimes yield disparate results (Hamby, Poindexter, & Gray-Little, 1996). Researchers have devised scales to compensate for these perceived shortcomings. An Australian team, for instance, developed a composite abuse scale to classify women according to the *type and severity of abuse* suffered (Hegarty, Bush, & Sheehan, 2005).

*Cultural competence in assessment.* Family violence researchers have for many years often excluded persons who belong to minority groups from research samples. To make matters worse, when researchers have recruited minority study participants, they have usually assessed them using inappropriate questionnaires or inappropriate test administration. It is important, for example, that researchers use correct appellations for minority groups and that they test minority group members in ways that meet with these individuals' cultural mores (see Ratner, 2008). Of course, it is expensive and time-consuming to translate existing tests into other languages and to validate the translated versions, but this may not be the only reason researchers have tended to ignore minority populations. Perhaps, scholars' disinterest in minorities may actually lie at the heart of the oversight. (For a set of guidelines concerning multicultural education and other variables, see American Psychological Association, 2003.)

In recent years, government funding and other inducements have allowed social and public health scientists to make some inroads into the evaluation of family violence among more diverse populations. Representative of these fledgling efforts are studies of American Indian families (Gone, 2008), families in developing countries (e.g., Gupta et al., 2008), Blacks and Hispanics (Cunradi, Caetano, & Schafer, 2002), and Asian American immigrants (Leung & Cheung, 2008). One example of progress in measurement is that researchers have substantiated the validity of CTS2 with both battered and community Spanish women. The women sampled experienced substantial amounts of sexual abuse (Calvete, Corral, & Estévez, 2007).

*Estimating rates of family violence.* When the question arises, how many family members are being abused, it is obvious that the answer depends on whom you ask. Family violence is such a complex multidimensional problem that no single set of numbers can adequately capture the phenomenon (U.S. Department of Justice, 2000). Researchers, students, and members of the lay public all need to recognize that statistical estimates of the prevalence and incidence of various forms of family violence are *not empirical facts.* Rather, they are conjectures based on quantitative data that are easily influenced by many factors, such as the nature of the sources and kinds of samples from which they come. Note, for example, that estimates of the proportion of U.S. families in which violent acts occur range from 20% to 55%, and estimates of severe acts of violence extend from 1% to 9% (for a minor review, see M. Gordon, 2000). The wide span of these appraisals is a clear indication that nobody knows exactly how much family violence actually takes place.

In discussing family violence, scientists typically report **prevalence** rates, **incidence** rates, or both. Family violence research, however, has been plagued by considerable confusion over the precise meanings of these terms (Brownridge & Halli, 1999). In general, *prevalence* of family violence refers to the number of people in the population of interest who are affected by the occurrence of family-violent acts. *Incidence* refers to the frequency of family-violent acts occurring within this subgroup of affected individuals.

## Statistical and Evaluation Matters

In addition to the pitfalls described above, statistical analysis is another area of methodological weakness in the family violence research. Statistical evaluation is extremely important in the social sciences to add empirical clarity through summarization of what is known.

*Researcher training.* Some statisticians have denounced the ways social science researchers in general analyze and present their data, implying that the basic problem is inadequate training of researchers. The American Psychological Association's Task Force on Statistical Inference has asserted that scholars need to learn the importance of describing their data fully, characterizing their analyses thoroughly, scrutinizing the results of their analyses carefully for anomalies, and reporting the magnitude of relationships. The task force also recommends that researchers employ research designs and analyses that are as *simple as possible* (cited in B. Azar, 1997). Other commentators have noted that the academic training researchers receive in conducting longitudinal studies appears to be suboptimal (Stouthamer-Loeber, van Kammen, & Loeber, 1992).

Finally, there has been a growing movement to encourage scientists to function as *advocates* to clarify their findings to nonscientists. Such a supposition contradicts the long-held tradition of portraying science in as neutral a language as possible. Furthermore, scientists should improve their communications to experts in policy and law. They should present their findings in *comprehensible language and state how it applies to the decisions at hand.* That is, in order to meet the needs of policymakers, researchers should translate their findings into simple terms and illustrate them with graphs. They should also offer clear policy recommendations based on their findings. Frequently, legislators lack sufficient staff to search through journals and websites for research applicable to their needs (Feldman, Nadash, & Gursen, 2001).

*Univariate versus multivariate designs.* Although simplicity in research designs is commendable, overreliance on *univariate* (single-variable, e.g., gender) analyses tends to fragment and narrow family violence researchers' findings in the field. Comparisons based on *multivariate* designs (multiple variables, e.g., gender, age, abuse type), in contrast, can deepen researchers' understanding of the dynamics of violent families (K. R. Williams, 1992).

Assessments of **risk markers** are multivariate approaches that allow statisticians to pinpoint the degree of *association between antecedent and consequent variables.* Emblematic of this approach is a risk-factor study that uncovered several precursors of sexual offending, such as childhood emotional abuse and family dysfunction (J. K. P. Lee, Jackson, Pattison, & Ward, 2002). Also see an analysis using a German-language version of the *Violence Risk Appraisal* Guide to predict violent delinquency (Urbaniok, Noll, Grunewald, Steinbach, & Endrass, 2006). Another multivariate technique useful for making sense of vast quantities of data derived from individual studies is **meta-analysis,** which has been described as a set of "quantitative procedures for summarizing or integrating findings obtained from a literature review of a subject" (Vogt, 1993, p. 138). By combining findings from a large number of studies, meta-analysis adds clarity to areas where individual studies have had conflicting results.

*Case histories and qualitative studies.* Case histories such as those presented throughout this book enliven dissemination of information about family violence. Qualitative studies accomplish similar goals by adding richness and meaning to quantitative data. As Vogt (1993) observes, "Qualitative components are crucial to most good quantitative research, which begins with theories, concepts, and constructs" (pp. 183–184). A Swedish inquiry of battered women, for example, provided readers with a disturbing, first-hand account of victims' fears and stresses (Lindgren & Renck, 2008). Frieze (2008a), on the other hand, sounds a note of caution by setting forth *scientific* criteria for publication of qualitative research in the journal *Sex Roles.* Finally, Straus (2004b) emphasizes that research must include large-scale surveys and "cannot be limited to in-depth qualitative studies" (p. 71). (See Chalk & King, 1998, for an extensive evaluation of research practices in family violence.)

## Ethical Issues

The most central ethical requirement of any form of research with *human subjects* is the protection of those subjects (M. D. Schwartz, 2000). Fears regarding the possibility that human research participants may somehow be harmed as a result of their participation have so far prompted four U.S. states (California, Maryland, New York, and Virginia) to create regulations governing the procedures that researchers must follow when working with human subjects (Kessler, 2002). If someone is injured while participating in a medical or psychological inquiry (e.g., receives the wrong medicine dosage, is made to feel stupid), a legal response may ensue.

Although ethical constraints are necessary, there is no denying that they hamper the progress of research (e.g., researchers cannot compel anyone to participate in their studies). In working with human subjects, family violence researchers must meet several important ethical requirements. Specifically, they must (a) ensure the safety of research participants, investigators, and mental health workers; (b) obtain informed consent from all research subjects and make sure that those giving consent are competent to do so; (c) guarantee anonymity (where possible) and confidentiality to research participants and use methods that honor this pledge; (d) disclose research findings carefully, describing methodology, conclusions, and limitations of the work meticulously and with political sensitivity; (e) implement the legal duty to warn and protect certain groups endangered by violent subjects; and (f) display cultural competence in working with participants whose cultures are different from the researchers' own (e.g., members of ethnic minority groups, immigrants, disabled persons, or gay, lesbian, bisexual, and transgendered persons).

The number of publications devoted to the ethical concerns involved in research and practice with human research participants has mushroomed over the past few years. (For a list of some of these resources, see the link for this volume on the Sage Publications website at the www.sagepub.com/barnett3e). In addition, *Monitor on Psychology* has featured an ongoing series of ethical rounds beginning in 2005 that help clinicians and researchers learn to deal with particularly difficult and unexpected issues. Finally, the American Psychological Association maintains an ethics office that may be of service to researchers and practitioners.

Universities have been at the forefront of the movement toward *improved ethical standards* in research and practice with human subjects. Indeed, psychology instructors are finding ways to incorporate the subject of research and practice ethics across the entire curriculum (e.g., Handelsman, Gottlieb, & Knapp, 2005; Kitchener, 2000; Margolin et al., 2005). The American Psychological Association commissioned a task force to formulate recommendations for ethical guidelines for those who work in the field of family violence (Harway et al., 2002). To further ensure protection of subjects, universities have established Internal Review Boards composed of faculty who verify the appropriateness of research proposals (Panicker, 2008). Several disciplines associated with family violence research, such as nursing, counseling, psychiatry, psychology, education, medicine, social work, sociology, public health, and criminal justice, have also expanded their emphasis on ethics in their curricula (Melville, 2005).

An example of *questionable ethical behavior* in family violence research would be a study that required a child victim in a child sexual assault study to spend time alone in the same room with the perpetrator of the abuse. Looking back at the case history that opens this chapter, how do you think it would have worked out if a researcher had interviewed Juanita in her living room while Miguel was reading in the adjacent dining room? How would Juanita have felt if a male interviewer had asked her whether she had been raped by her husband? Would it be ethical for interviewers to quiz Juanita and Miguel's neighbors about the couple's marriage? Would it be safe for an investigator to check on Juanita's situation 36 months later?

# PRACTICE, POLICY, AND PREVENTION ISSUES

The literature covered in this chapter has several implications for advocates, practitioners, and researchers.

## Research Issues

Family violence scholars could improve their contributions to the field by doing the following: (a) keeping abreast of emerging ethical and legal issues and applying them in their work, (b) finding ways to collaborate with family violence practitioners harmoniously, (c) participating in interdisciplinary research (Cacioppo, 2007), (d) making a concerted effort to disseminate research findings to practitioners, policymakers, and the general public (see Byrd, 2007), and (e) framing findings (honestly) to avoid polarization of opposing groups (Pruett, 2007).

*Collaboration.* A number of experts have observed the schism between agencies, such as shelters and researchers, and have called for collaborative research and dissemination of research. There is a great need for increased partnerships to produce the highest caliber of research possible (Radford & Gill, 2006). Including agency personnel and research participants throughout the entire research project helps accomplish this goal. Representatives from these various groups should begin their teamwork during the initial planning phase of the research. They should continue sharing ideas during the summarizing of the data and their interpretations. Last, the individuals should jointly determine the best way to present the research in a clear and understandable way and how to disseminate the findings. To reach the widest audience possible, researchers need to publish in academic journals, magazines, organizational newsletters, bulletins, and websites. Just as important, if not more so, is to make sure legislators receive copies. Other possibilities are to investigate preparing video materials and other media presentations. With careful planning, research conducted in this manner should improve the possibility of influencing policy (Chronister, Wettersten, & Brown, 2004). See Box 2.3 for a discussion of collaboration issues.

---

### BOX 2.3 Conflicting Goals of Researchers and Practitioners: The Need for Collaboration

Through their training, researchers learn to value as ideal a number of procedures related to implementing the scientific method. In particular, they want to test large samples, recruit suitable comparison groups, and be able to control variables, such as age, socioeconomic status, minority status of subjects, and the timing of tests. They may also have other incentives, such as winning research grants, obtaining academic promotions, or gaining status in their field. Most, if not all, family violence researchers are strongly committed to the mission of preventing or ending family violence through the application of research findings.

Practitioners who work with the victims of family violence, in contrast, are principally concerned with improving their clients' functioning, such as helping them cope with anger.

*(Continued)*

(Continued)

Therapists want to protect their clients from undue intrusions and from emotionally upsetting experiences. Practitioners often must consider whether using valuable clinical time for research purposes is warranted. They may have reservations about collaborating with researchers if the studies proposed appear to be irrelevant to their clients' current needs. Furthermore, there are problems in dissemination of research knowledge to practitioners, so that research participation fails to have a maximum beneficial impact ("National Symposium," 1998). Participating in research also generates added paperwork and responsibility for clinicians.

Because of these differences in priorities, clashes sometimes arise between researchers and clinicians in agencies such as those that administer shelters or outreach programs (Levin, 1999). Researchers may unthinkingly expect clinical staff to conduct their investigations for them or to supervise students as they conduct research-related interviews. Some investigators with higher-level academic degrees may behave as though they are superior to master's-degree-level clinical personnel.

In addition, the two factions may hold different opinions about various issues associated with family violence, especially about treatments. Researchers may appear insensitive to the needs of agency staff, as they frequently fail to grasp the fact that agency personnel face endless tasks and responsibilities, such as answering hotlines and supervising trainees. Agency personnel, on the other hand, may experience difficulties in attempting to fulfill a research role. They may not allow investigators to interact with research participants directly, yet neglect to administer tests on behalf of the investigators when scheduled. They may fail to keep data in a locked location. On occasion, overworked practitioners may even lose research data. Some agency personnel may go so far as to cancel a research agreement when other obligations become more compelling.

Some opposition toward researchers arises from the suspicion that researchers (or others) may push back the clock by casting battered women in a bad light, perhaps by conceptualizing battering as mutual. Missteps may have egregious consequences on shelter funding. Some agency directors have become hostile toward researchers in general. Such directors might require would-be investigators to supply vast quantities of written materials as part of requesting permission for research access, knowing that they intend all along to reject their requests.

In recent years, the strain between practitioners and researchers has motivated some who work in the field of family violence to promote a significant shift in conceptualization—the need to establish a collaborative culture (see Mohr, 1998). Within such an environment, investigators, practitioners, and victims' advocates can reach agreement on fundamental standards, encourage individual contributions, learn how to listen to each other, value different perspectives, develop trust in each other, and work toward equalizing power and making joint decisions (Block, Engel, Naureckas, & Riordan, 1999; C. M. Murphy & Dienemann, 1999).

The need for collaboration extends beyond that between researchers and practitioners to collaboration among different social service agencies. Alcohol treatment personnel and domestic violence personnel, for instance, need to join forces to reduce both alcohol misuse and domestic violence. There are numerous calls for increased partnering between law enforcement, child and adult protective services, alcohol and drug treatment staff, shelters, and batterer intervention practitioners staff.

*Methodology.* One of the clearest messages from the literature is that family violence researchers should recruit more *representative samples*. This admonition is important because sampling has such widespread effects on the data obtained. Yet, how to obtain representative samples is an understudied aspect of research methodology. According to one group of researchers, the use of random telephone sampling is a feasible approach. Many epidemiological studies rely on *random digit dialing* (RDD) to identify potential participants for in-laboratory research (Slep, Heyman, Williams, Van Dyke, & O'Leary, 2006). Despite this fact, RDD appears not to be the hoped-for panacea in family violence research.

Farris and Holtzworth-Munroe (2007) assessed three potential methods for obtaining a representative sample of maritally violent and nonviolent couples from the community. They used RDD, another method known as directory-assisted recruitment, and a hybrid of the two. Their results were exceptionally discouraging. Their calculations revealed that using unpaid students to make the necessary number of telephone calls needed to obtain a single screening interview with a violent couple would cost $210. Unbelievably, the cost would rise to $2,908 per violent couple if the researcher had to fund the screening. Hence, employment of methodologically sound sampling methods for some family violence research seems problematic.

*Cultural awareness.* Finally, researchers must become more *culturally conversant*. Expert information is now available on adjusting informed consents, interviewing techniques, and testing for cross-cultural research (Adams, Miller, Craig, Sonam, Droyoung, & Varner, 2007). More and more questionnaires are now available and suitable for non–English speaking research participants (e.g., Calvete et al., 2007). Similarly, researchers need to become familiar with and follow the guidelines set forth by the American Psychological Association in regard to conducting multicultural research (American Psychological Association, 2002; see also Keller, Gonzales, & Fleuriet, 2005; Zebian, Alamuddin, Maalouf, & Chatila, 2007).

The terms *race* and *ethnicity* have distinct meanings, although people use the terms interchangeably. Initially, biologists classified humans into different racial groups based on genetic variation, just as they classify plants and animals. Ethnicity, by contrast, implies a psychological and social identity based on one's background—his cultural allegiance. As an illustration, an Asian is likely to have recognizable external features of his *race,* but he may consider himself to be Muslim or a Buddhist. What racial markers might a geneticist studying golfer Tiger Woods find given that both of his parents had mixed racial backgrounds? Over time, social scientists have been less inclined to classify people on the basis of race and more inclined to group them by their cultural identification. Ethnicity is a better predictor of behavior than race, but there are some who claim that race and ethnicity cannot predict anything.

## Practice Issues

Because practitioners play such a major role in the treatment of family violence, their work has received heightened scrutiny over the last decade. First, of course, practitioners need advanced training in family violence to help victims and perpetrators as effectively as possible.

*Clinical assessment is no easy task.* One area of deep concern is whether practitioners are using *multiple measures* when assessing clients' problems and behavior, and clinical assessment is no easy task. Practitioners need to know if clients are abusive, have alcohol problems, suffer from a brain disorder (bipolar disorder), are dangerous or manipulative, and so forth (see Whisman, Snyder, & Beach, 2009). Expertise is especially required when counselors' findings and opinions will be used to make decisions that may alter the clients' lives, such as recommending that a child be placed in foster or institutional care. Clinicians may be called upon to testify in court or work behind the scenes in a custody dispute or explain the so-called battered woman syndrome to jurors (Osthoff & Maguigan, 2005).

*Vicarious (secondary) traumatization–burnout.* All of these activities, along with counseling clients whose problems are so dreadful, may easily lead to counselor burnout. As this situation has surfaced more clearly, professionals are calling for a number of strategies, such as coworker support, to offset the problem (Ducharme, Knudsen, & Roman, 2008; also see Ben-Porat & Itzhaky, 2009, for a non-confirmatory study). In addition to coworker support, working in an environment where power is shared helps protect advocates from secondary traumatic stress (Slattery & Goodman, 2009).

*Insufficient training.* In some settings, counselors or advocates may *lack sufficient training in research methods and statistical analysis* (Long, 2008). To enhance partnering and sharing with others in collaborative research, practitioners must have a basic understanding of research designs and statistics. To help meet this challenge, a series of clearly written articles about research for practitioners has appeared in the *Domestic Violence Report* beginning in 2007. Messing (2007a, 2007b) has written a series of very short articles to help practitioners (untrained in research methodology) to understand research methods.

*Evidence-based therapy.* Practitioners need to increase *awareness of their own personal preferences* for interventions and whether their choices have sufficient empirical foundation to merit their use. If preferred interventions *lack a scientific foundation,* they may actually do more harm than good, and health providers may not be willing to pay for patients' counseling services. Although insufficient guidelines for treatment may have existed in the past, more effective methods are now available (Rubin, 2007). Therapists must "connect clinical practice to scientific progress" (Mischel, 2009, p. i). Policymakers and funding agencies are broadening demands that counseling methods be *evidence-based* and that treatment outcomes be evaluated empirically (American Psychological Association, 2006; Stoltenberg & Pace, 2007; see also *Research on Social Work Practice,* 2008, Vol. 18, No. 4 [the whole issue]).

*Cultural competence/sensitivity.* Practitioners need to enhance their *cultural competence* (American Psychological Association, 2003). Sue (1998), the leading expert in cultural competence, says that "one [a therapist] *is culturally competent when one possesses the cultural knowledge and skills of a particular culture to deliver effective interventions to members of that culture"* (p. 441). Clients often face barriers to culturally sensitive care including the following: (a) practitioners' lack of knowledge of diverse cultures, (b) practitioners' tendencies to view cultural differences as pathological, and (c) practitioners' lack of culturally sensitive therapeutic skills (Suyemoto, Liem, Kuhn, Mongillo, & Tauriac, 2007). Some believe that the core principles of culturally sensitive treatment may not be a homogeneous set of principles but may consist of a variety of perspectives suitable for each cultural group (Cardemil, 2008).

Guidelines suggesting culturally sensitive techniques have only recently become available. Practitioners can develop their competence by following the guidelines suggested by the American Psychological Association (2003). In-service training programs may also be especially informative (e.g., Payne, Carmody, Plichta, & Vandecar-Burdin, 2007). Training, therefore, should include *knowledge about and sensitivity to cultural, ethnic, and racial differences* (Ristock, 2003). Cultural-specific interventions "utilize language and settings familiar to the target population as well as staff who share the target populations' culture. . . . They take into account their *culture-specific values, norms, attitudes, expectations and customs*" (Gillum, 2009, p. 58).

Much of the time, domestic violence programs try to achieve the goal of cultural competence by training and hiring counselors who are proficient in a *second language* or by establishing *racial-specific intervention groups.* Hiring counselors who are members of the specific minority group receiving treatment may demonstrate a certain degree of cultural sensitivity. As another illustration, a culturally sensitive female counselor would avoid wearing a short skirt and heavy makeup if she were working with a Muslim group, and assigning a male therapist to a male Muslim group would be best. More advanced efforts include altering the appearance or ambiance of a meeting place or clinic so it appears to be welcoming to minority groups. Having a radio playing a Mariachi tune in the waiting room of a clinic treating Hispanics, for example, would send a welcoming signal. (For improving cultural competence, see Struther, Lauderdale, Tom-Orme, & Strickland, 2005.)

*Cultural competence and evidence-based counseling.* There is a disagreement about whether evidence-based practice and cultural competence are *complementary or inconsistent.* One faction perceives the two directives to be complementary. From this point of view, there exists sufficient evidence to demonstrate that cultural adaptation of evidence-based therapies, such as cognitive-behavioral therapy, *is effective.* Treatments that work with European Americans can be adapted to work with minority Americans. The use of manuals, homework assignments, and other techniques work with mainstream and minority clients. The idea of both individual empowerment and group empowerment are concepts acceptable to evidence-based psychotherapy (Whaley & Davis, 2007).

A different faction asserts that the two requirements for practice may clash. One disparity is the focus of change. *Evidence-based methods* assume that the goal of psychotherapy is *individual change* (e.g., anger reduction), and little mention is made of contextual factors. Outcome measures include those appropriate for assessment of individual change. *Culturally sensitive therapy* assumes therapy takes place within a cultural context including elements such as amount of community violence, accessibility of health services, and sociopolitical forces (e.g., prejudice). As a result, change not only must occur within an individual but should be broadened to mean *transformation of the cultural context* (e.g., reduction of sexism in the community). By not taking cultural components into account, evidence-based therapies end up confirming the values of White Americans and define cultural differences as deficits (La Roche & Christopher, 2008).

## Advocacy Issues

"Advocacy and science play by different rules, employ different rules of evidence, and cater to different [groups]" (Pruett, 2007, p. 54). Advocacy refers to the techniques individuals use to accomplish change. Science is very tentative in nature, inherently skeptical, and perpetually incomplete. Just as researchers and practitioners need to respect and work closely with family violence advocates, advocates must shoulder adequate responsibility to understand scientific findings. In addition, political misuse of research has the potential for undercutting efforts to prevent family violence (Gelles, 2007). As a recent case in point, see the discussion about the assertions of the Heritage Foundation in Chapter 11.

## Policy Implications

Policymakers have a great deal of power because they control the purse strings. They also frequently have access to the press. As mentioned previously, researchers need to improve their efforts to make their research findings easily understandable to policymakers. Policymakers can contribute to progress in the field of family violence by doing the following: (a) getting as much education on the topic as feasible; (b) focusing on scientifically derived information; (c) improving funding for longitudinal studies; (d) requiring ethics education in applicable graduate schools; (e) encouraging collaborative efforts among researchers, practitioners, and advocates at all levels; (f) convening symposia to reach agreement on definitions and other related questions; and (g) finding ways to keep practitioners abreast of the newest scientific findings.

### BOX 2.4 Answering Questions About Family Violence

#### Methodology—How Researchers Answer Questions About Family Violence

Academicians, professionals, and activists from diverse disciplines have embraced the crisis of family violence and have worked diligently to deepen society's understanding of this problem. Neuroscientists and geneticists have more recently joined the mix. The U.S. government has become more actively involved over the past decade by funding more research, developing new surveillance systems, and convening panels of experts to confer about troublesome issues. Regrettably, the individual nature of research conducted in separate academic fields has resulted in a disorganized representation of family violence.

Conducting research in the field of family violence is a daunting task, in part because of the sensitivity of the topic and the need to shield at-risk target populations. Much of the research in the field has been methodologically weak but is improving. Many variables (e.g., sample selection, type of questionnaire employed, relationship between victim and perpetrator) influence study results. Researchers in various family violence subfields collect data from a wide variety of sources that are compatible with their expertise. Despite long-standing differences in their goals, family violence researchers and practitioners have recently begun to work more collaboratively.

An initial deficiency in family violence research has been the lack of a theoretical footing. In addition, at the core of criticisms of research across the entire field has been the elasticity of definitions. Without such definitions, meaningful comparisons among studies are not possible. Furthermore, many studies have employed different types of samples: representative samples or small clinical or forensic samples, and so their findings have proved insufficient to improve scholars' understanding of the prevalence and incidence of family violence. Other shortcomings of family violence research include the lack of appropriately conceived and assessed comparison groups in research designs, the limited number of longitudinal studies conducted, and the failure to include members of marginalized groups in study samples.

Estimates of the frequency and severity of IPV vary according to the definitions used, the samples investigated, and the types of data collected. Estimates arise from data gathered by the FBI, the NCVS, and several other national surveys. FBI crime statistics on IPV are incomplete because reporting from police departments is voluntary. Data derived from self-reports, of course, are fraught with problems, such as underreporting and even intentional falsification. Newer surveys, such as the National Electronic Injury Surveillance System, are assessing injury data.

The estimates of intimate partner violence rates from these various sources are not concordant. Surveys set within a *crime context* (e.g., FBI, NCVS) indicate that partner violence is gendered, with males committing a disproportionate amount. National surveys incorporating a *conflict context* (e.g., NFVS, CTS) usually show gender equivalence. Different methods of measuring IPV and findings premised on these assessments have generated considerable debate in the field. In sum, the precise prevalence and incidence of intimate partner abuses and assaults remains unknown.

Measurement complexities have become a focal point, if not a rallying cry, for various subgroups of researchers. The original Conflict Tactics Scale has been the most widely used instrument for measuring family-violent behaviors. Straus and his colleagues have revised this scale to include questions about injury outcomes and sexual assault. Both CTS1 and CTS2 assess violent behaviors through self-reports of perpetrators, victims, and informants. Despite their extensive use and excellent psychometric properties, these scales have drawn extensive criticism by skeptics who assert that they decontextualize family-violent behaviors and fail to get at the heart of male-to-female violence.

In recent years, family violence researchers have increasingly recognized the need to incorporate the phenomenon of emotional abuse into definitions of family violence. Both researchers and practitioners need to use multiple measures in their assessments in order to gather information on all forms of abuse. There also is a need for both groups to become more culturally competent. Several new and improved government surveillance (tracking) systems have expanded to cover reports of violence within special populations. These large studies hold great promise for the field.

*(Continued)*

(Continued)

Statisticians have asserted that researcher training in statistical analysis is faulty. As true experimental studies are impermissible in family violence research, more quasi-experimental studies are needed. More qualitative data is needed to furnish a more personal sense of family violence. Currently, there is an overreliance on uni-variate designs when multivariate designs are needed. The use of sophisticated statistical techniques, such as risk assessment and meta-analysis, have begun to help explain disparate research findings. Structural equation modeling holds the promise of crystallizing more information on the causes of family violence.

The current heightened emphasis on the protection of human research subjects, although necessary, has impeded the application of rigorous research methodologies. The past few years have seen the publication of an avalanche of new or updated ethical guidelines for research with human subjects. In the final analysis, it is important to note that despite the many methodological limitations of research on family violence, a large and growing body of research worthy of academic consideration has emerged, and scholars have established a modest core of principles that have met with general acceptance.

## DISCUSSION QUESTIONS

1. In which major academic and professional fields can one find researchers and practitioners who are concerned with understanding and eliminating family violence?

2. Why do family violence researchers and practitioners sometimes have difficulty working together effectively?

3. What is the difference between macrotheories and microtheories of family violence? Select one theory in each category and evaluate it.

4. Why does the field of family violence pose extraordinary problems for conducting research?

5. What kinds of issues arise when researchers attempt to define and assess family violence?

6. How important is it that definitions of family violence incorporate the concept of emotional abuse?

7. Outline measurement debates from both sides of the argument.

8. Think of a population you would like to study or know more about in relation to family violence. Propose a research design that would answer your specific questions about that population.

9. What ethical issues are associated with family violence research? Why are ethical guidelines for researchers necessary?

10. How can investigators study cases such as that of Juanita and Miguel (presented at the opening of this chapter)? Why did violence occur in Juanita and Miguel's relationship? What should Juanita do?

11. Why is it necessary for practitioners to use empirically based interventions?

For chapter-specific resources including audio and video links, SAGE research articles, additional case studies, and more, please visit www.sagepub.com/barnett3e.

# CHAPTER

## 3

# Child Neglect and Psychological Maltreatment

**CASE HISTORY**   Will and Mark—Where Are the Parents?

Will and Mark arrived at the psychiatric unit of the county hospital after they had been apprehended by the police the night before. Their clothes were covered with dirt, and the odor emanating from their bodies indicated that they had not bathed in quite some time. Both were thin and immediately asked the nursing staff for some food. An interview revealed that they were brothers and part of a family of seven, although many other "friends of the family" often stayed in their house. Neither of their parents worked, and Will and Mark stated that they often had the responsibility of bringing home money for their parents. Their father had taught them how to beg for money on various street corners.

After the interview, the events of the previous evening were clear. Mark and Will had been out wandering around the neighborhood. After roaming the city for hours, they spotted a pickup truck and took it for a ride. After a short drive, they stopped at a local furniture store, broke in, and began to vandalize the merchandise, using Will's knife. A woman from the community spotted the boys and called the police. She told the police that two young boys, probably somewhere between 7 and 9 years of age, had broken into a local business.

The events of this case history clearly reflect parenting practices that are less than ideal. This vignette illustrates a form of child maltreatment—child neglect. Child neglect is typically viewed as an *act of omission* rather than an act of commission. Child neglect may sometimes be unintentional, but that does not make it any less detrimental to a child's development. *Child neglect is the most frequently reported form of child maltreatment* (Sedlak et al., 2010; U.S. Department of Health & Human Services, 2008).

*Historical perspective.* Like all forms of child maltreatment, child neglect is *not new.* It was not until the early 20th century, however, that the neglect of children's basic needs was acknowledged or defined as a social problem (Wolock & Horowitz, 1984). Despite widespread recognition of this form of child maltreatment in recent times and subsequent empirical attention, it has taken a backseat to concerns about physical and sexual child abuse (Berliner, 1994; Dubowitz, 1994). Indeed, scholars often refer to child neglect as the "most forgotten" form of maltreatment (e.g., Daro, 1988). Wolock and Horowitz (1984) coined the phrase "the neglect of neglect" to describe the disinterest in this topic shown by researchers, professionals, and society in general. Dubowitz (1994) blames several beliefs for this *historical inattention:*

1. Neglect does not result in serious consequences.
2. It is a problem because it seems insurmountable.
3. Other forms of child maltreatment are more compelling.
4. Definitions of child neglect are too vague.
5. It provokes negative feelings that make some people feel uncomfortable.

This chapter addresses child neglect and psychological maltreatment by examining issues related to definitions and the magnitude of the problem. Included is a discussion about children exposed to domestic violence. Also included are discussions about the short-term and long-term consequences of these forms of maltreatment, and the characteristics of neglectful and/or psychologically abusive parents and their children. How society addresses these forms of child abuse is outlined, and the chapter concludes with a discussion of potential interventions, policy, and prevention strategies for addressing these concerns.

## SCOPE OF THE PROBLEM

Of all the types of child abuse, child neglect is the most difficult to define and yet occurs the most frequently. Indeed, definitions are still evolving. As is true of other forms of child maltreatment, reaching consensus regarding conceptual and operational definitions and determining the rates of the neglect problem are two of the greatest challenges in the field of family violence.

### What Is Child Neglect?

- Mark, who is 8 years old, is left to care for his 3-year-old sister, Maria, while their parents go out.
- Margaret fails to provide medication for her 10-year-old daughter, who has a seizure disorder.
- Jonathan refuses to allow his 16-year-old son into the family's home and tells him not to return.
- Tyrone and Rachel live with their three children in a home that is thick with dirt and dust, smells of urine, and has nothing but rotting food in the refrigerator.
- Alicia leaves her 10-month-old infant unattended in a bathtub full of water.
- Brad refuses to pay any child support for his three children.

Which, if any, of the above scenarios portrays behaviors that may be defined as child neglect?

## Definitions of Child Neglect

Generally, experts agree that deficits in meeting a *child's basic needs* constitute neglect. In a longitudinal study of 377 children between 4 and 8 years of age, researchers identified three fundamental needs: (a) *perceived support from mothers,* (b) *nonexposure to family conflict,* and (c) *early affection from mothers* (Dubowitz et al., 2005). There is less agreement, however, about the various aspects and specificity of children's needs.

Gaudin (1993) states: "Child neglect is the term used most often to encompass parents' or caretakers' failure to provide basic physical health care, supervision, nutrition, personal hygiene, emotional nurturing, education, or safe housing" (p. 67). (See the National Incidence Study [NIS-4], Sedlak et al., 2010, for a detailed definition.)

Straus and Kaufman Kantor (2005, p. 20) offer a limited definition: "Neglectful behavior by a caregiver that constitutes a failure to act in ways that are presumed by the culture of a society to be necessary to meet the developmental needs of a child and which are the responsibility of a caregiver to provide."

*Comprehensive definitions.* Several researchers have called for a comprehensive definition of child neglect that incorporates a variety of factors that might be neglectful or might lead to neglect (e.g., Dubowitz, Black, Starr, & Zuravin, 1993; Sedlak et al., 2010). Definitions need to be sufficiently long to verbally distinguish between parental *failure to provide* when options *are* available and when options are *not* available. The definition should exclude situations in which the parents were involved in acts of omission because of financial limitations (e.g., inability to afford health care). Inclusion of social factors, such as socioeconomic status in the definition, underscores the complexity of defining neglectful behaviors.

*Lack of agreement.* Another challenge to defining neglect is lack of agreement about *children's basic needs.* Are the parents of Mark and Maria, described in the first scenario, negligent because they leave an 8-year-old boy to care for his 3-year-old sister? Obviously, the answer to that question depends on the specific circumstances: What if Mark was responsible for Maria's care for 5 minutes while she played on the floor?

- For 5 minutes while she played in the bathtub?
- For one evening between 9 p.m. and 1 a.m?
- For every evening between 9 p.m. and 1 a.m?
- While their parents took a 2-week vacation?

*Intentionality.* One unresolved issue concerns the importance of *intentionality* in defining parental failure to provide. Definitions of child neglect that emphasize *parental blame* and/or *responsibility* may focus so narrowly that they fail to understand the caretaker's circumstances. The question of *intentionality* arises in the scenario above, in which Margaret does not provide her child with medication. Suppose Margaret cannot afford to pay for the medication? Without understanding, professionals might confine their strategies to improving Margaret's *parenting skills,* rather than recognizing the problem as *poverty.*

*Harm standard versus endangerment standard.* Scholars typically assess *severity of neglect* according to the degree of demonstrable *harm* (Dubowitz, Black, Harrington, & Verschoore, 1993; U.S. Department of Health & Human Services, 1981). A case in which a *child dies* from bleach poisoning, for example, would be a more severe outcome than a case in which a child receives a *minor burn* from an iron. Although the same parental behavior (i.e., lack of supervision) contributed to both injuries, the consequences of the behavior differ dramatically. One problem with including a criterion of *demonstrable harm* is that some outcomes are *difficult to measure* and difficult to prove in court (e.g., emotional consequences). A second problem is that some *delayed consequences* will not be readily identified. The children of Tyrone and Rachel, described above, may suffer no demonstrable immediate harm as a result of living in unsanitary conditions for a month. Nevertheless, professionals might still characterize the parents' behavior as neglectful (Champagne & Curley, 2009; Kaffman, 2009).

In recognition of this dilemma, the *National Incidence Studies* (NIS-2) included an *endangerment standard.* This new standard allowed for the reporting of cases in which children demonstrated no actual harm (the *harm standard*), but in which *potential harm* (i.e., future risk of injury) was probable. The laws in most U.S. states include *risk* of harm or endangerment in their definitions of child neglect (Child Welfare Information Gateway, 2009). Professionals who are mandated reporters (e.g., nurses) of child neglect are prone to inconsistencies and underreporting (Daka, 2009; Eckenrode, Izzo, & Smith, 2007; Sege & Flaherty, 2008). Complaints about social workers' reporting practices have, among other influences, led to a call for more empirically based procedures (e.g., City News Service, 2010, March 24; Kindler, 2008; Mullen, Bledsoe, & Bellamy, 2008).

*Frequency and duration.* The frequency and duration of neglecting behaviors are also important definitional considerations. A single incident of neglectful behavior is usually considered a normal characteristic of parenting, rather than an indication of serious child neglect. Few would allege child neglect if a child occasionally misses a bath or a meal. In contrast, a pattern of frequent and repeated failures to bathe or feed a child is likely to be considered child neglect (Dubowitz et al., 2005). Some isolated incidents or brief omissions in care *can* result in serious consequences. As a case in point, if a parent fails to buckle a young child into a car seat properly just one time, that child may die in a car accident.

*Chronicity of neglect.* **Chronically neglectful** families in one study, for instance, experienced multiple problems and deficits, including lack of knowledge, skills, and tangible resources. *Nonchronically neglectful* families, by comparison, had experienced recent significant crises (e.g., parental divorce or illness) that appeared to overwhelm their normally sufficient coping abilities. Analysts suggest that chronically neglectful families need multiple treatment interventions of long duration, whereas nonchronically neglectful families need short-term crisis, stress management, and support group interventions (English, Graham, Litrownik, Everson, & Bangdiwala, 2005).

*Cultural issues.* Societal values largely determine the point at which child care practices transition from adequate to inadequate. The age at which a minor is considered capable of being responsible for preparing his or her own meals, for instance, differs among cultural groups. The social context of a family's culture and beliefs is an important factor in both defining and intervening in child neglect. Research has consistently indicated that there is strong agreement about the basic elements of child care, with similar standards of care found for rural, urban, working-class, and middle-class individuals (Sedlak & Broadhurst, 1996; see also Shor, 2000). On the other hand, there is some discrepancy internationally about the acceptability of physical discipline and parental substance use (International Society for Prevention of Child Abuse and Neglect [ISPCAN], 2008; Tajima & Harachi, 2010).

## BOX 3.1 Neglecting the Unborn Child

The term *prenatal neglect* refers generally to any actions of a pregnant woman that could potentially harm her unborn child. Most conceptualizations of prenatal neglect focus on women who abuse illicit drugs and alcohol during pregnancy, exposing infants to the effects of these substances *in utero*. As stated by the National Center on Substance Abuse and Child Welfare (2009), 400,000 infants (10% to 11% of all births) are exposed to substances annually (see also the National Survey on Drug Use and Health, 2009).

*Drug exposure.* Most of the concern about prenatal drug exposure has arisen because of the strong relationship between prenatal drug exposure and negative child developmental outcomes (see Ondersma, Simpson, Brestan, & Ward, 2000, for a review). Research has consistently demonstrated that children born of mothers who consumed large quantities of *alcohol* during pregnancy incur definitive and irreversible effects. A constellation of symptoms, known as *fetal alcohol syndrome,* includes growth deficiency, anomalies of brain structure and function, and mental retardation (Streissguth, 1997). There has also been concern, based on *rat* studies, that prenatal exposure to alcohol primes organisms to drink more alcohol as adults than nonexposed fetuses (Chamberlin, 2008). There may be a relationship between pregnant women's smoking and aggression among their children (Brook, Zhang, Rosenberg, & Brook, 2006).

*Effects of prenatal exposures.* Other research examining the link between fetal harm and prenatal *use of illicit drugs* has focused on the effects of *cocaine* on developmental outcomes. *Short-term effects,* such as jitteriness and irritability in newborns, appear to be well established, and more recently, research has produced some evidence of *long-term effects.* A trio of researchers was able to link prenatal *cocaine* use with a mild reduction in boys'—but not girls'—cognitive abilities over a 9-year period (Bennett, Bendersky, & Lewis, 2008).

A different team of researchers presented an overview of prenatal drug effects. Deficits associated with cocaine exposure "appear to be associated with what has been described as statistically significant but subtle decrements in neurobehavioral, cognitive, and language function . . ." (Bandstra, Morrow, Mansoor, & Accornero, 2010,

*(Continued)*

(Continued)

p. 245). Another reviewer concluded that despite a few findings of negative effects (Lester et al., 2010), prenatal drug consumption of cocaine and heroin *failed to show* "devastating child consequences" when environmental factors are controlled (H. E. Jones, 2006). A study under way in Denmark will test 5-year longitudinal effects to provide a more definitive answer to long-term effects of prenatal drug use (Kesmodal et al., 2010).

***Identifying the precursors.*** One explanation for these equivocal findings may be the many methodological constraints on this research, which limit the establishment of definitive cause-effect relationships. The *quantity of cocaine* that pregnant women consume, for example, may determine whether any negative effects manifest in their infants (Schuler & Nair, 1999). Maternal drug use also often occurs in association with *poor maternal nutrition* and other factors, so it is difficult to determine which variable is responsible for negative developmental outcomes. As one illustration, *iron deficiency* is the most common micronutrient deficiency in infants and toddlers (Goldberg et al., 2010; Hartfield, 2010).

***Stress.*** In addition to a mother's drug use during pregnancy, more and more research has accumulated about the devastating effects of *maternal stress in utero.* Stress caused by numerous circumstances (e.g., *abuse by an intimate partner,* illness of another child in the family) takes a neurobiological toll that leaves the child vulnerable to psychiatric ills and other negative outcomes (Neigh, Gillespie, & Nemeroff, 2009). Researchers suggest that *postnatal high maternal stress* influences the developmental outcomes of drug-exposed infants (Kelley, 2002; Talley, Heitkemper, Chiez-Demet, & Sandman, 2006). Indicative of the interplay of such variables are the effects of *smoking.* A child may be exposed to cigarette or marijuana smoke both *in utero* and after birth when the mother continues to smoke (see Goldberg et al., 2010). Going beyond the scope of this text are findings about *possible* effects on the fetus of certain drugs prescribed by doctors to combat depression during pregnancy (see Gaidos, 2010).

***Physical abuse of pregnant women effects.*** Male-to-female partner violence occurs during some *pregnancies,* and the literature on this crime is extensive. Abuse of pregnant women is not just a crime against the woman but also a form of abuse of a fetus. Just as the mother's consumption of alcohol and illegal drugs can cause severe fetal problems, so too can the father's abuse of his pregnant wife. Although doctors have increased screening for drug problems and other potential harms to the fetus, they have not totally undertaken the task of screening for spouse abuse. More education in medical schools is needed. Obstetricians for immigrant women need to be especially alert to wife beating because it is quite common in some immigrants' countries of origin (Quelopana, Champion, & Salazar, 2008; see Kiely, El-Mohandes, El-Khorazaty, & Gantz, 2010, for a brief intervention program).

***Drug testing/screening.*** Despite inconsistent research findings, many observers have called for drug testing of newborns, asserting that such testing could identify infants at risk for developmental problems. Infant drug screening, however, is problematic. For one thing, not all tests can detect drugs reliably. Screening also raises financial costs; it may cause pregnant drug users to avoid medical care, and there is a potential for discriminatory screening practices (Ondersma et al., 2000).

***Criminalization versus treatment.*** Although some scholars have recommended criminalizing illicit drug use by women during pregnancy, the Supreme Court did not agree. In 2001, the Court banned mandatory screening aimed at providing police with evidence for prosecutions (see Harris & Paltrow, 2003). Instead, federal law (Child Abuse Prevention and Treatment Act [CAPTA] 2006) mandates that all medical and other professionals report drug-exposed infants or substance-abusing pregnant women to Child Protective Services (CPS). The Washington State Department of Health (2009) has produced a manual with guidelines for screening during pregnancy. Their abbreviated message is as follows: ASK, ADVISE, ASSESS, ASSIST, ARRANGE.

Special local support programs for such mothers have sprung up in several communities. CPS established one *postnatal* treatment for mothers of drug-exposed infants that relied on intensive services. A termination status variable, a score that included the number of treatments, the length of treatment, and progress in treatment revealed a reduction in follow-up reports to CPS (Mullins, Bard, & Ondersma, 2005).

***Prevention.*** Providing special programs to meet the challenge of prenatal neglect may be more appealing than criminalization. Project Prevention, for instance, offers up to $200 of privately donated funds to women for limiting their reproductive capabilities. Not surprisingly, the women most affected are poor, non-White, and drug-using. Also not surprisingly, various groups find such a program to be discriminatory (Gregory, 2010). The National Abandoned Infants Assistance Resource Center (NAIARC; 2010) offered a series of programs on substance-exposed newborns, such as "A Helping Hand: Mother to Mother Program" under the auspices of the Massachusetts Department of Public Health (see NAIARC, 2010). Although the problem of prenatal neglect continues to be the focus of much theoretical discussion and empirical research, solutions will likely remain elusive for some time.

## Typologies of Neglect

Additional efforts to define the *precise nature* of child neglect have led researchers to propose numerous typologies to clarify the various situations that constitute child neglect. Most experts agree that child neglect exists in many forms, such as physical neglect, educational neglect, developmental neglect, and emotional neglect. Some experts in the field have proposed an additional category, *prenatal neglect,* for neglect that occurs even before a child is born. Others urge society to categorize fathers who abandon children and provide no child support as guilty of neglect (J. Currie & Widom, 2010; see also Zorza, 2003).

*Specific behaviors.* Despite general agreement concerning the *broad categories* of neglect, disagreement exists regarding the *specific behaviors* that should be included under each category. The strongest consensus exists for *physical neglect,* which is generally defined as failure to provide a child with basic necessities of life, such as food, clothing, and shelter. The Third National Incident Study (NIS-3) broadened the concept of physical neglect to include refusal to seek or a delay in seeking health care, desertion or abandonment, refusing custody responsibilities, and inadequate supervision. *Educational* or *developmental neglect* is generally defined as failure to provide a child with the experiences necessary for growth and development, such as intellectual and educational opportunities (Sedlak et al., 2010).

*Emotional neglect versus psychological maltreatment.* Defining the category of *emotional neglect* has stimulated the greatest disagreement among scholars. Although most agree on broad conceptual parameters of emotional neglect that include failure to provide a child with emotional support, security, *and* encouragement, they disagree on the specific operationalizations of such behaviors. Part of the problem is the considerable overlap between definitions of *emotional neglect* and *psychological maltreatment.* Some experts, for example, consider a parent's failure to express affection and caring for a child to be *psychological maltreatment,* whereas others define this behavior as emotional neglect (Erickson & Egeland, 2010). Despite such lack of consensus and overlap, several subtypes of neglect are repeatedly reported in the literature. See Table 3.1 for a list of major types of neglect with examples.

**TABLE 3.1**   Subtypes of Child Neglect

| Subtype | Description | Examples |
|---|---|---|
| Health care neglect | Refusal to provide, or a delay in providing, physical/mental health care | Failing to obtain immunizations<br>Failing to attend to dental needs<br>Failing to obtain necessary counseling<br>Failing to attend to exercise needs |
| Personal hygiene neglect | Failure to meet basic standards of personal care and cleanliness | Infrequent bathing<br>Failure to provide clothing adequate for weather conditions or of the correct size<br>Failure to provide sleeping arrangements that allow adequate sleep |
| Nutritional neglect | Failure to provide a sufficient and nutritionally balanced diet | Providing insufficient calories to support growth<br>Providing meals that do not include all of the basic food groups |
| Neglect of household safety | Failure to eliminate safety hazards in and around the child's living area | Allowing structural hazards to exist in and around the home, such as broken stair railings or broken windows<br>Allowing fire hazards, such as frayed wiring, to exist<br>Storing/leaving chemicals or drugs where they are accessible to a child |

| Subtype | Description | Examples |
|---------|-------------|----------|
| Neglect of household sanitation | Failure to meet basic standards of housekeeping care and cleanliness | Allowing garbage and trash to accumulate in the home<br>Failing to control vermin and insects<br>Failing to provide clean bedding |
| Inadequate shelter | Failure to provide adequate physical shelter and/or a stable home | Refusing responsibilities of custody of a child—forcing the child to leave home<br>Providing an overcrowded home (e.g., 10 people living in a 2-bedroom home) |
| Abandonment | Physical desertion | Placing a child in a dumpster; leaving the child in a park<br>Failing to return after placing a child in the care of others (e.g., babysitters)<br>Failing to pay child support; economic neglect |
| Supervisory neglect | Failure to provide a level of parental supervision necessary to avoid child injury | Leaving a child in the home without adult supervision for prolonged periods<br>Allowing a child to roam the streets at night |
| Educational neglect | Failure to provide care and supervision necessary to promote education | Failing to enroll a child of mandatory school age in school<br>Permitting a child's frequent/chronic truancy |
| Emotional neglect | Failure to provide encouragement, security, and emotional support | Being emotionally unavailable to a child<br>Being indifferent toward or rejecting a child |
| Fostering delinquency | Encouragement of the development of illegal behaviors in the child | Rewarding a child for stealing |

SOURCES: A representative but not exhaustive list of sources for the information displayed in this table includes American Professional Society on the Abuse of Children, 2008; U.S. Department of Health & Human Services, 2008; Erickson & Egeland, 2010; Mezzich et al., 2007; Sedlak et al., 2010.

*Medical neglect.* Medical neglect has attracted increasing concern. Resting on a *broad definition,* medical neglect occurs when children's basic health care needs are not met. Legal definitions rest upon the *narrow definition* of caretaker omissions, thus adopting a *parental blame model.* Child Protective Services, bound by law, must follow the narrow definition. Nonetheless, the broader definition based on *children's rights* is more helpful to professionals trying to intervene. **Addressing the child's needs rather than the parents' failures is a more constructive approach** (Dubowitz, 2010). A recent improvement is the establishment of a Children's Rights Council to help children in times of crisis, such as parental divorce (D. L. Levy, 2009).

Parents' *refusal to allow medical treatment* for their children constitutes a unique form of medical neglect. When parents' refusal is founded on *religious beliefs,* the case can become more complex. As an illustration, Christian Scientists reject Western medicine and rely on the "healing ministry" of nonmedical practitioners. Respect for such religious beliefs becomes intertwined with society's concern for children's rights. Although legal challenges have resulted in plaintiffs winning some religious exemptions based on constitutional rights to practice religion, such decisions may be overturned. Courts have ruled against parents in some cases, stating that parents cannot martyr their children based on parental beliefs or deny them essential medical care (*Jehovah's Witnesses of Washington v. King County Hospital,* 1968, cited in Dubowitz, 2010).

Some parents even refuse to have their children vaccinated, even though they have no legal right to expose the *community or the child* to communicable diseases (see Omer, Salmon, Orenstein, deHart, & Halsey, 2009). The California Department of Health has declared an outbreak of pertussis (whooping cough) to be a pandemic. In 2010, 5 infants died of this vaccine-preventable disease. Vaccinations against whooping cough or actually having the disease do not protect people over a lifetime because immunity dissipates over time. Children in middle school, adolescents, and adults all need booster shots. Unfortunately, California is one of the few states that does not require children to have a booster vaccination before entering middle school (Abram, 2010).

## Cross-Cultural Abuse

International efforts continue to track information about child abuse and neglect, and as of 2006, 72 countries contributed their findings. In regard to *definitions,* all but three countries included sexual touching/pornography and physical abuse as abusive behaviors. More than 80% of respondents included *physical neglect, abandonment,* child prostitution, *children living on the street, physical beatings, forcing a child to beg,* and *infanticide.* Three events elicited nonagreement: *medical neglect, parental substance abuse,* and *physical discipline* (International Society for Prevention of Child Abuse and Neglect [ISPCAN], 2008).

*Dutch prevalence study.* One study in the Netherlands replicated the *methodology of the National Incidence Study (NIS)* employed in the United States. In 2005, the population of children between the ages of 0 and 18 in Holland was 3,597,591. The Dutch NIS findings were as follows: (a) 107,200 children were maltreated in 2005; (b) the estimated rate of maltreatment was 30 per 1,000 children; (c) the *largest number (56%) was neglected;* (d) 4% were sexually abused; and (e) 47% of those maltreated suffered **polyvictimization** (multiple forms of abuse). A study of *Dutch CPS agency data* yielded 13,538 *registered* cases. Percentages of subtypes included the following: (a) Physical neglect—10.3%, (b) Educational/emotional neglect—15.1%, (c) Emotional abuse—13.7%, (d) Observing intimate partner violence (IPV)—13.7%, (e) Physical abuse—10.5%, (f) Sexual abuse—4.0%, and (g) Other unknown types of abuses—35.4% (Euser, Ijendoorn, Prinzie, & Bakerman-Kranenburg, 2010).

*Romanian infants.* The institutionalization and neglect of Romanian infants has become legendary. A 2009 study examined the effects of institutionalization on 136 children, half of whom were placed in foster care between the ages of 6 and 30 months. Researchers later compared these children with 59 typically reared infants when the children were 4½ years of age. The results revealed that the children who were institutionalized at *any time* (i.e., even at 6 months) suffered significantly more psychiatric symptoms, 53.2% versus 22.0%. Also, 44.2% of those placed in foster care had psychiatric symptoms compared with 22.0% of the typically raised children. One additional important finding was that "boys were more symptomatic than girls regardless of their caregiving environment, [and they] had no reduction in total psychiatric symptoms following foster placement" (Zeanah et al., 2009, p. 777).

## SECTION SUMMARY

### Defining Child Neglect

Child neglect is one of the most elusive yet most frequent forms of child maltreatment and, as a result, has received less attention than other forms. The vague nature of child neglect is evident in the fact that a significant proportion of the research devoted to this topic has focused on definitional issues. At present, no single definition of child neglect is universally accepted. Although experts generally agree on conceptual definitions of child neglect (i.e., failure to provide for a child's basic needs), little consensus exists regarding operational definitions. Problems in defining neglect include questions about the need for comprehensiveness, intentionality, whether to use harm or endangerment standards, and frequency/chronicity variables. Other cultures' viewpoints about neglect, while basically similar to those in the United States, do manifest some variability.

# PREVALENCE/INCIDENCE OF CHILD NEGLECT

During the past 20 years, child neglect has emerged as the *most frequently reported and substantiated form of child maltreatment* (U.S. Department of Health & Human Services, 2008; NIS-4, Sedlak et al., 2010). Estimates of child neglect come primarily from official reports made to *professionals and CPS agencies*. Recent research has also employed *parent self-report techniques* to determine estimates of neglecting behavior.

## Official Estimates

Official reporting statistics over the past several years indicate that reports of child neglect have increased and then decreased.

*U.S. Department of Health & Human Services (DHHS) [CPS records]. Child maltreatment. (2009)*

The number of substantiated (i.e., found to be true) victims of child abuse and neglect was 794,000. The victimization rate was 10.6/1,000. Of this number, 468,460 (59%) *were neglected.*

*National Incidence Studies (NIS-4)*
*(Data from multiple sources—goes beyond DHHS to capture data from individuals such as school counselors and psychologists in private practice)*

**TABLE 3.2** Numbers of Children Reported for Neglect on the Harm Standard in the National Incidence Studies

| All Neglect Categories | | | | | |
|---|---|---|---|---|---|
| NIS-2 for 1986 | | NIS-3 for 1993 | | NIS-4 for 2005–2006 | |
| *Number of Children* | *Rate per 1,000 Children* | *Number of Children* | *Rate per 1,000 Children* | *Number of Children* | *Rate per 1,000 Children* |
| 474,800 | 7.5 | 897,000 | 13.1 | 771,700 | 10.5 |
| *Physical Neglect* | | *Educational Neglect* | | *Emotional Neglect* | |
| | *Number of Children* | *Rate per 1,000 Children* | *Number of Children* | *Rate per 1,000 Children* | *Number of Children* | *Rate per 1,000 Children* |

| | Physical Neglect Number of Children | Physical Neglect Rate per 1,000 Children | Educational Neglect Number of Children | Educational Neglect Rate per 1,000 Children | Emotional Neglect Number of Children | Emotional Neglect Rate per 1,000 Children |
|---|---|---|---|---|---|---|
| NIS-2 | 167,800 | 2.7 | 284,800 | 4.5 | 49,200 | 0.8 |
| NIS-3 | 338,900 | 5.0 | 397,300 | 5.9 | 212,800 | 3.2 |
| NIS-4 | 295,300 | 4.0 | 360,500 | 4.9 | 193,400 | 2.6 |

SOURCES: Sedlak, 1990; Sedlak & Broadhurst, 1996; Sedlak et al., 2010.

NOTE: The increase in the numbers of children reported for child neglect between NIS-2 and NIS-3 likely reflects heightened awareness and knowledge of child neglect on the part of community professionals, but it may also reflect a real increase in child neglect during this period (Sedlak & Broadhurst, 1996). The decrease in the number of children reported for neglect between NIS-3 and NIS-4 was not significantly different overall or for individual categories (Sedlak et al., 2010).

*Adverse Childhood Experiences (ACE) Study. Data from Kaiser Permanente–San Diego in collaboration with the Centers for Disease Control and Prevention (2006);*
*N = 17,337 adult patients reporting on childhood neglect.*

**TABLE 3.3** Adverse Childhood Experiences (ACE) of Neglect

| *ACE Category of Neglect* | *Women: N = 9,367* | *Men: N = 7,970* |
|---|---|---|
| Emotional neglect | 16.7% | 12.4% |
| Physical neglect | 9.2% | 10.7% |

## Self-Report Surveys

*The Centers for Disease Control and Prevention (CDC-MMWR, 2008).* The Morbidity and Mortality Weekly Report (2008) reported that 905,000 infants were maltreated between October 2005 and September 2006. Of these, 68.5% were neglected.

A study that employed a nationally representative sample of parents using the *Parent-Child Conflict Tactics Scales* provided self-report estimates of child neglect (Straus, Hamby, Finkelhor, Moore, & Runyan, 1998). Questions that focused on lack of parental supervision, nutritional neglect, alcohol abuse, medical neglect, and emotional neglect defined child neglect. Of parents responding to this survey, 27% reported engaging in some form of *child neglect* at least once during the past year. The most common form of neglect reported was *leaving a child alone* even when the parent thought an adult should be present. In this sample, 11% of the parents also reported that they were unable to ensure that their children obtained the food they needed, and approximately 2% reported an inability to care for their children adequately because of problem drinking. (See www.sagepub.com/barnett3e for additional statistics.)

---

**SECTION SUMMARY**

## Prevalence of Child Neglect

Official estimates of child neglect, despite their limitations, provide most of the available information on the subject. Official estimates are lower than self-report estimates, although self-report data is not current. The difference in prevalence rates attributable to definitional disparity is acute, especially when comparing findings when using the harm standard (evidence-based, more conservative) versus the endangerment standard (more speculative, encompasses more measurements). When using the NIS harm standards and CPS standards, neglect among identified maltreatment cases is approximately 60%, or 10.5 per 1,000. Morbidity and Mortality Weekly Report (CDC) tallies are higher, 68% for infants, and fatality estimates attributable to neglect are 31.9%. Differences between subtypes of neglect (physical, educational, emotional, and medical) are also divergent, extending from 2.6 per 1,000 to 4.9 per 1,000. What little is known about the prevalence of prenatal neglect suggests that 10% to 11% of infants may be subjected.

---

# EFFECTS OF CHILD NEGLECT

Researchers have approached the topic of neglect from several directions, such as early versus later effects, unique versus general effects, and the negativity of the effects. They have also pinpointed and emphasized several interactional effects (e.g., attachment difficulties) that may harm children. Some researchers have documented differences in specific behavioral and emotional problems between nonneglected and neglected children (e.g., Shields, Ryan, & Cicchetti, 2001). Others, however, have failed to find differences (e.g., Wodarski, Kurtz, Gaudin, & Howing, 1990). These conflicting findings demonstrate the difficult nature of studying the complex effects associated with child neglect.

## Early Neglect

A team of researchers conducted an 8-year longitudinal study of the effects of child neglect among 1,318 at-risk children. A contemporary comparison of earlier and later neglect and earlier and later abuse yielded a very important result. "Child neglect in the first two years of life may be a more important precursor of childhood aggression than later neglect or physical abuse at any age" (Kotch et al., 2008). Sadly, ongoing *neurobiological research* has also established that early neglect has the potential to modify the body's stress response. *Cortisol levels* (stress hormones) are altered, and their pattern of abnormality continues into adulthood even when the child is placed in a foster home (van der Vegt, van der Ende, Kirschbaum, Verhulst, & Tiemeier, 2009; see also Kaffman, 2009).

## Unique Effects

Relatively little research has examined the *unique effects* of child neglect on children's functioning. The limited research in this area is surprising given that child neglect is the most frequently reported form of child maltreatment and can have serious consequences for children. Many children experience more than one major form of maltreatment, such as physical abuse *and* child neglect. Consequently, it is difficult to determine which specific effects are associated with the various forms of child neglect. Table 3.4 provides a summary of the possible negative effects that have been associated with child neglect.

# EXPANDED RESEARCH ON THE EFFECTS OF NEGLECT

Research has expanded to cover some types of child-parent interactions that are involved with neglect (and other forms of abuse).

## Attachment Difficulties

A number of studies suggest a relationship between neglect and disturbed patterns of infant-caretaker attachment. About 70% of the infants in the United States experience

**TABLE 3.4**    Possible Negative Effects Associated With Child Neglect

| Effects | Examples |
|---|---|
| Social and attachment difficulties | Disturbed parent-child attachment (e.g., anxious and disorganized) |
| | Disturbed parent-child interactions (e.g., child is passive and withdrawn; parent exhibits low sensitivity to and involvement with child) |
| | Disturbed peer interactions (e.g., deficits in prosocial behavior, social withdrawal, isolation, few reciprocal friendships) |
| Cognitive and academic deficits | Receptive and expressive language deficits |
| | Low academic achievement and repetition of grades |
| | Deficits in overall intelligence |
| | Low level of creativity and flexibility in problem solving |
| | Deficits in language comprehension and verbal abilities |

| Effects | Examples | |
|---|---|---|
| Emotional and behavioral problems | Apathy and withdrawal | Conduct problems and noncompliance |
| | Low self-esteem | Personality disorder symptoms |
| | Ineffective coping | Psychiatric symptoms (e.g., anxiety and depression) |
| | Physical aggression | |
| | Verbal aggression | Difficulty recognizing/discriminating emotion |
| | Attention problems | Negative affect (e.g., anger, frustration) |
| Physical consequences | Death, failure to thrive | |
| Long-term consequences | Cognitive deficits (e.g., low IQ scores and reading ability) | |
| | Illegal behavior (e.g., delinquency, prostitution, violent assault) | |
| | Psychiatric disorders (e.g., dysthymia, PTSD, major depressive disorder, disruptive disorders, antisocial personality disorder) | |
| | Alcohol problems, poverty, need for special education, school drop-out | |
| | Poor parenting—intergenerational cycle of abuse | |

SOURCES: A representative but not exhaustive list of sources for the information displayed in this table includes P. Cohen, Brown, & Smailes, 2001; Conron, Beardslee, Koenen, Buka, & Gortmaker, 2009; Erickson & Egeland, 2010; Gil et al., 2009; Hildyard & Wolfe, 2002; Sroufe, Egeland, Carlson, & Collins, 2005; Widom, Czaja, & Dutton, 2008.

secure attachment. Their caretakers are sensitive and responsive to the infant. Theoretically, these parental behaviors allow babies to feel that they can trust their caretaker, to feel effective in soliciting help when needed, and thus to feel competent. These infants develop into children who have confidence and enthusiasm. Generally, they can regulate their emotions, and they can cope with life.

About 30% of babies develop *insecure (anxious) attachment.* Parents of these babies, by contrast, lack sensitivity to the baby's needs. They are inconsistent and chronically unresponsive to the baby's needs. These infants feel powerless, and they manifest an *avoidant or ambiguous type of attachment* (see Erickson & Egeland, 2010). Infants who develop avoidant attachment often manifest behavior problems, such as aggression, bullying, or social withdrawal. They do not regulate their emotions well, and they do not cope well with life. *Ambiguously attached* infants grow into school-aged children who are extremely dependent on others for help; have low self-esteem; and are unpopular (see Crittenden, Kozlowska, & Landini, 2010).

In a minority of cases, parent-infant interactions are so chaotic that infants develop a *disorganized attachment* style. In these circumstances, the infant shows a number of symptoms, such as contradictory *approach-avoidance behavior,* and this behavior is evident by 12 months of age (Hennighausen & Lyons-Ruth, 2010). In particular, these children are likely to develop some form of psychopathology (see Hildyard & Wolfe, 2002; Erickson & Egeland, 2010; Sroufe et al., 2005). Attachment styles are even more crucial because they are passed on from one generation to the next (intergenerational transmission) (Belsky, 2005).

## Minnesota Longitudinal Study

To study *attachment*, the *Minnesota Longitudinal Study of High Risk Parents and Children* (starting in 1975) tested mother-infant dyads. The mother-child pairs participated in a series of situations designed to assess the quality of attachment during the first 2 years of life (see Egeland, Sroufe, & Erickson, 1983). Investigators observed mother-infant interactions as follows: (a) *feeding and play situations*, (b) a *stressful situation* in which a *stranger* appeared in the environment, and (c) a *problem-solving task*. Results indicated that, compared with children in the control group, a significantly higher proportion of *neglected children were anxiously attached* at both 12 and 18 months, and the social difficulties they experienced continued throughout elementary school (see Crittenden, 1992). At 17½ years of age, they completed an interview for *mental illness*. Results were as follows: (a) 90% received at least one diagnosis, (b) children who had been in the emotional neglect group were most likely to receive a diagnosis, and (c) 73% of the children received one or more diagnoses (e.g., depression and anxiety). Of children physically neglected, 54% had a dual diagnosis (comorbid) compared with 30% of the control group of nonneglected children (Sroufe et al., 2005).

## Cognitive and Academic Deficits

An additional area of functioning often affected by neglect in childhood is intellectual ability. Findings from a large group of studies comparing neglected infants, children, and adolescents with matched comparisons have indicated that neglect victims show deficits in language abilities, academic skills, intelligence, and problem-solving skills (e.g., Erickson & Egeland, 2010; Kendall-Tackett & Eckenrode, 1996). One team of investigators, for example, evaluated 139 school-aged children classified into three groups: (a) physically abused, (b) neglected, and (c) nonmaltreated. Analyses indicated that both neglected and abused children evidenced significantly poorer overall school performance and math skills than their nonmaltreated peers. The neglected children, but not the abused children, also had lower scores on measures of language and reading skills (Wodarski et al., 1990). Furthermore, a 3-year follow-up study demonstrated that these performance patterns were generally stable over time (Kurtz, Gaudin, Wodarski, & Howing, 1993). Along with other research findings, it now seems clear that cognitive and academic deficits are generally more severe for neglected children than for physically abused children (Erickson & Egeland, 2010; Hildyard & Wolfe, 2002).

## Emotional and Behavioral Problems

Child neglect victims frequently, but not uniformly, exhibit emotional and behavioral difficulties (e.g., Erickson & Egeland, 2010; Williamson, Borduin, & Howe, 1991). A group of researchers compared the associations between types of childhood abuse and adult personality disorders for 105 adults from a community sample. The researchers grouped the participants into three groups on the basis of retrospective reports of childhood abuse: (a) *a physically and/or sexually abused group, n* = 38; (b) *an emotional abuse/neglect* group, *n* = 32; and (c) a control group with no reported abuses, *n* = 35. Briefly summarized, the results for significant difference in diagnoses and diagnostic clusters were as follows (Tyrka, Wyche, Kelly, Price, & Carpenter, 2009):

- More maltreated subjects in either group *met criteria for at least one clinical diagnosis* (e.g., anxiety, cognitive, or impulse-control disorders) contrasted with the nonmaltreated subjects.
- More subjects in the maltreatment groups reported being *treated for a psychiatric condition* than subjects in the nonmaltreated group.
- The maltreatment groups differed from the nonmaltreatment group in the *frequency of personality disorder symptoms* included in Clusters A, B, and C personality disorders:
  - ○ *Cluster A (odd):* Paranoid  Schizoid  Schizotypal
  - ○ *Cluster B (dramatic):* Antisocial  Borderline  Histrionic  Narcissistic
  - ○ *Cluster C (anxious):* Avoidant  Dependent  Obsessive-compulsive
- The two maltreatment groups did *not* differ significantly from each other on any of the clusters.
- The specific personality disorders within each cluster were significant for *paranoid, borderline, avoidant, dependent, and obsessive-compulsive,* but not for passive-aggressive (a personality disorder not included in the clusters). (See *Diagnostic and Statistical Manual of Mental Disorders,* Fourth Edition (DSM-IV), published by the American Psychiatric Association, for more details about psychiatric classification.)

## Physical Consequences

Child neglect also has physical consequences for victims. The most serious physical consequence, of course, is death, and neglect is the form of maltreatment most often associated with death (U.S. Department of Health & Human Services, 2008). Research on whether neglect is a risk factor for either obesity or underweight has produced mixed results (Bennett, Sullivan, Thompson, & Lewis, 2010). An additional physical consequence often associated with neglect is failure to thrive (FTT), a syndrome characterized by marked retardation or cessation of growth during the first 3 years of life (Kempe, Cutler, & Dean, 1980). Because FTT also includes nonphysical components, its designation as a consequence of physical neglect versus psychological maltreatment is controversial (for more on this, see Box 3.2).

---

### BOX 3.2  Failure to Thrive

One extreme consequence of possible child maltreatment is a clinical disorder known as *failure to thrive* (FTT). This term was initially coined to describe infants and young children hospitalized or living in institutions in the early 1900s who exhibited marked deficits in growth as well as abnormal behaviors such as withdrawal, apathy, excessive sleep, unhappy facial expressions, and self-stimulatory behaviors, including body rocking or head banging (e.g., Bakwin, 1949). Although many cases of FTT stem from *organic* causes (e.g., kidney or heart disease), other cases appear to arise from *nonorganic* causes (e.g., physical and emotional neglect) (Block & Krebs, 2005). Contemporary analysis attributes many past cases of organic FTT to undiagnosed subtle organic problems and presents a *combination organic and nonorganic* category (Rabinowitz, Katturupalli, & Rogers, 2010).

*(Continued)*

(Continued)

Medical professionals have operationalized the anthropometric aspects of FTT as *height and weight gain below the third to the fifth percentile* on standardized growth charts of expected development (e.g., Marino, Weinman, & Soudelier, 2001). They further dichotomized the *organic* causes of FTT into *prenatal* (e.g., complications of prematurity, interuterine infections, toxins [smoking]) and *postnatal* (e.g., conditions of defective swallowing, metabolic disease) (Rabinowitz et al., 2010; see also Kerzner, 2009).

Although the strongest correlate of nonorganic FTT is *poverty,* mental health professionals have identified a number of other *nonorganic* causes of FTT. *Nonorganic* causes usually include *combinations of parenting problems* as follows (Marino et al., 2001; Rabinowitz et al., 2010; Wekerle & Wolfe, 1996):

| Mother's insensitivity toward the child | Child neglect | Difficult parent-child interactions |
|---|---|---|
| Less adaptive social interactional behavior | Family dynamics | Arbitrary terminations of feedings |
| Disturbed patterns of attachment | Difficult child | Less positive feelings |
| Lack of preparation for parenting | POVERTY | Poor feeding skills |

Fortunately, the newer referral/screening program for children under 3 years of age established under the Child Abuse Prevention and Treatment Act (CAPTA see the discussion below) will be able to recognize FTT problems and institute treatment sooner (Herman-Smith, 2009).

## SECTION SUMMARY

### Effects of Child Neglect

Relative to other forms of maltreatment, less research has examined the unique effects of child neglect on children's functioning, although an increasing number of methodologically sound investigations are appearing. This oversight is troubling, given the high frequency with which neglect occurs and the serious consequences associated with this form of child maltreatment. Available research to date suggests that child neglect is associated with a variety of problems, including social difficulties, cognitive and academic deficits, behavioral and emotional problems, and physical dysfunction. Studies that have evaluated child neglect victims of various ages (e.g., infants, school-age children, and adolescents) consistently demonstrate that experiences of child neglect result in significant developmental problems and negative outcomes that are similar across developmental stages. Research also indicates that the effects associated with child neglect are cumulative and extend into adulthood. Long-term effects that have been documented include cognitive deficits, illegal behaviors, and psychiatric disturbances. Future studies should continue to be sensitive to developmental issues and also attend to additional variables potentially associated with child neglect outcomes, such as the victim's gender, the severity of neglect, and various subtypes of neglect.

Studies that have examined the negative effects associated with child neglect have so far been limited in both number and quality, making the interpretation of findings difficult. Nonetheless, this research has consistently shown a variety of problems to be associated with child neglect, including social difficulties, intellectual deficits, and emotional and behavioral problems. Although many scholars believe that the negative effects of child neglect extend into adulthood, more research is needed to establish the relationship between a childhood history of neglect and adjustment problems in adulthood.

## CHARACTERISTICS OF NEGLECTED CHILDREN AND THEIR FAMILIES

Agencies that receive official reports of abuse and survey data collected from representative samples of the U.S. population have provided much of the information currently available on the sociodemographic characteristics of parents and children involved in child neglect. Clinical as well as community studies have also provided information relevant to the psychosocial characteristics of neglecting parents. Much of the research that has evaluated risk factors for child neglect has been limited by methodological weaknesses: inconsistent definitions of neglect, the retrospective nature of some data, biased sampling, and overreliance on studies of mothers (rather than fathers or both parents) as perpetrators of neglect. Although the studies described below are limited by these biases, their findings nonetheless shed some light on the general characteristics of neglected children and their parents.

### Characteristics of Neglected Children

Two large government surveys (NIS and DHHS) draw data yearly from different populations.

*NIS-4. Between 2005 and 2006; N = 771,700 (61%) were neglected according to the harm standard.*

- Educational neglect (47%) was highest for children 9 to 11 years of age (7.5 per 1,000) and then declined somewhat.
- Emotional neglect (25%) was highest for adolescents 15 to 17 years of age (4.1 per 1,000). Emotional neglect rose steadily from birth through the late teens.
- Physical neglect occurred at a rate of 38%.

*U.S. Department of Health & Human Services (2008)* identified 758,289 maltreated children. Uses only records from Child Protective Services.

*NIS-4 (2005–2006)* identified 1,256,600 maltreated children.

The National Incidence Study—uses data from CPS, professionals, school counselors, and others (Sedlak et al., 2010).

*U.S. Department of Health & Human Services, 2008; 758,289 maltreated children (lowest rate of neglect in 5 years).*

- 71.1% were neglected.
- 2.2% were medically neglected.

*Sex of Neglected Children*

- Male = 48.3%; Female = 51.3%; Unknown = 0.4%

*Race of Neglected Children*
NIS- 4 (Sedlak et al., 2010)

- 58% of children physically neglected by a biological parent were White.
- 53% of children physically neglected by a nonbiological parent (or parent's partner) were Black.

*U.S. Department of Health & Human Services (2008):* No significant racial disparities in percentages of *neglect,* but significant differences for *medical neglect.* See Table 3.5 for a distribution of neglect by race.

**TABLE 3.5**　Child Neglect Victims by Race

| Race | Medical Neglect | Neglect | Race | Medical Neglect | Neglect |
|---|---|---|---|---|---|
| African American | 3.2% | 70.9% | Multiple race | 2.1% | 78.2% |
| American Indian | 1.7% | 79.4% | Pacific Islander | 1.4% | 43.3% |
| Asian | 1.4% | 69.3% | Unknown | 1.6% | 63.2% |
| Hispanic | 2.3% | 72.9% | White | 1.8% | 72.1% |

*Disability.* The rate of *emotional neglect* for *disabled* children was 4.7 per 1,000 and for children without disabilities 2.3 per 1,000 (NIS-4, Sedlak et al., 2010).

## Disabled Children in Eastern Europe

In Eastern Europe and Russia, the number of disabled children has grown from roughly 500,000 in 1990 to 1.5 million in 2000. Governments *neglect* these children in almost every measurable way. International conventions state that all children, including disabled children, have the *human right* to grow up in families. The laws in Eastern Europe and Russia, however, make such a right impossible. Although laws require that the State must establish *preschools* for handicapped children, they do not. Local schools say they cannot afford the extra equipment required (e.g., a wheelchair ramp). Parents of disabled children face many obstacles in obtaining schooling and other services for their children that would allow them to stay with their families. Since community services are rarely available and parents cannot afford to pay for services on their own, they often send their children to institutions. Parents assume that institutions will provide the special services children need to return home, but this is not the case. Disabled children are simply "*written off.*" Without services, they make little progress and cannot return to the community. When they turn 18, they simply enter an adult institution (Sundram, 2006b).

## Characteristics of Neglectful Parents

### Demographic Characteristics

*NIS-4,* prevalance and incidence rates, using the harm standard, reported the following (Sedlak et al., 2010):

- 92% of neglect perpetrators were the biological parents.
- 86% of neglect perpetrators were female.

- 12.1 per 1,000 parental neglect perpetrators were unemployed.
- 4.1 per 1,000 parental neglect perpetrators were employed.

- 16.1 per 1,000 neglected children were in low socioeconomic status (SES) families.
- 2.2 per 1,000 neglected children were not in low SES families.

*Gender differences.* **It is not uncommon in two-parent families for only mothers,** not fathers, **to be labeled as neglectful** (Azar, Povilaitis, Lauretti, & Pouquette, 1998). The higher proportion of **females reported for neglect may reflect the general** *social attitude* that mothers, rather than fathers, **are responsible for meeting the needs of their children** (Turney, 2000). When fathers feel effective as parents, there is significantly less child neglect in the household (Dubowitz, Black, Kerr, Starr, & Harrington, 2000). Gender differences may also reflect gender bias among CPS workers. In one study, workers *incorrectly classified* mothers as co-batterers when the mothers were the victims of marital violence (see Hulbert, 2008, below).

The Adverse Childhood Experiences study ("Prevalence of Individual," 2006), a retrospective report of childhood experiences of parents found to be neglectful, found that

- 26.9% had a substance abuse problem in the household;
- 19.4% had a mental illness problem in the household;
- 23.3% involved a parental divorce or separation; and
- 4.7% had an incarcerated household member.

*Risk factors.* An analysis of 499,330 child maltreatment records from Florida's Child Protective Services (CPS) revealed the following risk factors (Yampolskaya & Banks, 2006):

a. *Risk factors for neglect and threatened harm:* **Caregiver's alcohol/substance abuse**
b. *Risk factors for recurrent maltreatment*
   - **Prior referral**
   - More than one type of maltreatment during initial incident
   - Caregiver absence
c. *Risk factors for incident severity*
   - Nonminority girls with prior referral
   - Substance use (not alcohol use)

## Parent-Child Interactions

One consistent finding is that, compared with nonneglecting parents, neglecting parents generally *interact less* with their children, and when they do interact, the interactions are less positive. Neglectful parents, for example, engage in less verbal instruction and play behavior with their children, show their children less nonverbal affection, and exhibit less warmth in discussions with their children. There is also evidence that neglecting parents are involved in more *negative interactions* with their children, including issuing commands and engaging in verbal aggression (Barth, 2009; Hurlburt, Barth, Leslie, Landsverk, & McCree, 2007).

---

**SECTION SUMMARY**

### Characteristics of Neglected Children and Neglecting Parents

Research has demonstrated that the majority of children reported for neglect are under the age of 5 and that risk for the severity of child neglect generally decreases with age. Several studies have revealed that despite controlling for the effects of several related factors, African American children had a 44% higher chance (compared with other racial groups) of foster care placement.

Official statistics concerning demographic, psychological, and behavioral characteristics of neglecting parents are preliminary and so should be viewed cautiously. One of the strongest predictors of child neglect is economic disadvantage, and low-income families with unemployed parents and children residing in single-female-headed households are at greatest risk. Consistent findings indicate that neglecting mothers have low levels of positive interactions with their children and high levels of emotional and psychological distress. Neglecting families also exhibit high levels of daily stress and family stress and low levels of community integration and social support. Neglecting parents are also characterized by low educational achievement and often have become parents at a young age.

---

## CHILD PSYCHOLOGICAL MALTREATMENT

**CASE HISTORY**   Brian and His "Stupid" Son, Mikie

Seven-year-old Mikie and 2-year-old Melanie were the children of Brian and Colleen. Brian was a batterer who was completing a court-mandated counseling program for assaulting Colleen. He was 26 years old, married for 5 years, and a semi-employed roofer by trade. Although he loved Colleen, she caused him a lot of trouble by quarreling with the neighbors over the neighbors' dog. The dog kept coming into Brian's yard and Mikie was always throwing rocks at it. Because Colleen wasn't punishing Mikie enough, Brian had little choice but to "shape her up." He locked her out of the house and tried to "slap some sense into her" every now and again.

Brian was puzzled and alarmed that Mikie had nightmares and often "peed in his pants." Worst of all, Mikie was failing in school. Brian loved little Mikie, but Mikie was dumb, just like him. According to Brian, a lot of the problem was Colleen's poor parenting. She didn't know how to discipline the children, cook well, or even keep the house clean. She couldn't even get Mikie to stop hitting the baby. As a lesson to Mikie and baby Melanie, who "might just as well learn early," Brian had the children watch the way he reprimanded Colleen. Colleen wouldn't shut up, so Brian had to "show her who was boss" by pushing her around.

Brian tried to help Mikie do better in school, just like his own father had tried to help him, by telling Mikie he was dumb. He also thrashed Mikie when he came home with any failing grades "to make him work harder." He occasionally threatened Mikie by saying that if he didn't study harder he would lock him out of the house "just like he had to lock his mother out." On the positive side, Brian bought Mikie a little school desk, but on the negative side, he made Mikie sit at it for 2 hours every night. Brian was puzzled over Mikie's poor performance despite all the "discipline" he gave him.

The group counselor asked Brian whether his own father had actually called him "dumb." "Oh yes, nearly every day," Brian replied. "Sometimes he put a dunce cap on me and had me sit at the table without any dinner." The therapist asked Brian how he felt when his own father said he was dumb.

Suddenly, tears welled up in Brian's eyes, and he got all choked up. He couldn't say a word. He just sat there racked with emotion. His shoulders seemed to shake on the outside in rhythm with his weeping on the inside. He didn't speak the remaining 30 minutes of the group session. At the next weekly meeting, Brian proudly reported that he hadn't told Mikie that he was dumb all week! The group beamed smiles of approval toward him. Perhaps it was not too late to help Brian change his behavior. He had already quit hitting Colleen. Maybe Mikie could be saved too.

## Lack of Focus on Child Maltreatment

Researchers have tended to marginalize psychological maltreatment over the years, and they did not acknowledge it as a distinct form of child maltreatment until quite recently. There are several viewpoints about psychological maltreatment that may seem discordant:

- It is a *side-effect* of other forms of abuse and neglect.
- It is a *co-occurrence* of all other forms of abuse.
- It is a *unique* form of child maltreatment.
- It is the *basic element* of all forms of child abuse together.
- It may be the *most pervasive and destructive* form of child maltreatment.

Researchers' greater focus on child physical and sexual abuse than on psychological mal-treatment may stem from several sources. The most obvious explanation is that physical abuse and, to a lesser degree, sexual abuse result in immediate and observable harm. The negative consequences of psychological maltreatment, by contrast, are much more elusive. A single act of psychological maltreatment is unlikely to result in significant and immediate harm, but the cumulative effects of this form of abuse are insidious. Research has shown that child psycho-logical maltreatment is associated with negative consequences for victims that are just as serious, if not more so, than those related to physical and sexual abuse (e.g., Ney, Fung, & Wickett, 1994).

## Scope of the Problem

Community surveys indicate that Americans in general are concerned about the psycho-logical maltreatment of children. The National Center for Prosecution of Child Abuse, for example, conducted a nationally representative public opinion poll between 1987 and 1992 and found that approximately 75% of adults who were surveyed during this period viewed "repeated yelling and swearing" at children as harmful to the children's well-being (Daro & Gelles, 1992).

### Definition of Psychological Maltreatment

The consensus among those who have debated conceptual issues is that psychological maltreat-ment should be defined primarily on the basis of specific parental behaviors rather than on the basis of the effects those behaviors may produce (Hamarman & Bernet, 2000). Some scholars who support this approach, however, also emphasize the need to consider secondarily the effect of maltreatment (S. N. Hart & Brassard, 1991).

> Psychological maltreatment means a repeated pattern of caregiver behavior or extreme incident(s) that convey to children that they are worthless, flawed, unloved, unwanted, endan-gered, or only of value in meeting another's needs. (American Professional Society on the Abuse of Children, 1995, p. 2)

### What Is Psychological Maltreatment?

- A mother locks her 3-year-old son in a dark closet as a method of punishment.
- A father shackles his 7-year-old son to his bed at night to prevent him from getting out of bed repeatedly.
- A mother says to her daughter, "You are the stupidest, laziest kid on earth. I can't believe you're my child. They must have switched babies on me at the hospital."
- A father tells his daughter that he will kill her new puppy if she or the puppy misbehaves.
- A mother and father provide alcohol to their 16-year-old son and his friends at a party.
- A mother refuses to look at or touch her child.
- A father repeatedly states to one of his children, "I don't love you."

Would you characterize the behaviors depicted in all of these vignettes as "abusive"? Why or why not? How, then, does one determine when child psychological maltreatment has occurred? Which verbal interactions are abusive, which behaviors are psychologically neglecting, and which interactions are necessary parts of parenting?

*Focus of definitions.* One conceptual dilemma that scholars face in defining psychological maltreatment is whether to focus on *child outcomes, parental behavior,* or *parent-child interactions.*

*Child outcomes.* Those focusing on child outcomes, for example, may define psychological maltreatment as *mental injury* or impaired psychological functioning and development (Hamarman, Pope, & Czaja, 2002; S. N. Hart, Brassard, Binggeli, & Davidson, 2002). One problem associated with this approach is that the definition requires *demonstration of harm.* Such a definition fails to recognize that the harm associated with psychological maltreatment may not be evident immediately; it could take months or even years to develop (Glaser, 2002).

*Parental behaviors.* Some logicians propose that the behaviors of the parent define psychological maltreatment. A typical classification of such behaviors includes the following: (a) spurning, (b) terrorizing, (c) isolating, (d) exploiting/corrupting, and (e) denying emotional responsiveness. See Table 3.6 for a description of psychologically maltreating behaviors. Researchers have developed organizational frameworks that identify various subtypes of psychological maltreatment (e.g., S. N. Hart, Brassard, & Davidson, 2010; O'Hagan, 1995).

**TABLE 3.6**  Subtypes of Child Psychological Maltreatment

| Subtype | Description | Examples |
|---|---|---|
| Rejecting | Verbal or symbolic acts that express feelings of rejection toward the child | Singling out a specific child for criticism and/or punishment<br>Refusing to help a child<br>Routinely rejecting a child's ideas |
| Degrading/spurning (i.e., verbally abusing) | Actions that deprecate a child | Insulting a child or calling a child names<br>Telling a child she is ugly<br>Publicly humiliating a child<br>Continually yelling or swearing at a child |
| Terrorizing | Actions or threats that cause extreme fear and/or anxiety in a child | Threatening to harm a child or a loved one<br>Exposing a child to spouse abuse<br>Threatening suicide or to leave a child |
| Isolating | Preventing a child from engaging in normal social activities | Locking a child in a closet or room<br>Refusing to allow a child to interact with others, outside or inside the family |

*(Continued)*

**TABLE 3.6** (Continued)

| Subtype | Description | Examples |
|---------|-------------|----------|
| Missocializing (i.e., corrupting) | Modeling, permitting, or encouraging antisocial behavior in a child | Encouraging delinquent behavior in a child<br><br>Encouraging alcohol or substance abuse<br><br>Indoctrinating a child in racist values |
| Exploiting/corrupting | Using a child for the needs, advantages, or profits of the caretaker | Treating a child as a surrogate parent (i.e., *parentification*)<br><br>Using a child for child pornography or prostitution<br><br>Using a child to fulfill the caretaker's dreams |
| Denying emotional responsiveness (i.e., ignoring) | Acts of omission whereby the caretaker does not provide a child with necessary stimulation and responsiveness | Behaving toward a child in a detached and uninvolved manner<br><br>Interacting with a child only if absolutely necessary<br><br>Failing to express affection, caring, and love toward a child |
| Mental health/medical/educational neglect | Forms of psychological maltreatment not specified under other categories | Withholding food, shelter, sleep, or other necessities from a child as a form of punishment<br><br>Chronically applying developmentally inappropriate expectations to a child (i.e., *overpressuring*) |

SOURCES: A representative but not exhaustive list of sources for the information displayed in this table includes American Professional Society on the Abuse of Children, 1995; Greenfield & Marks, 2010; S. N. Hart & Brassard, 1991; Hooper, Marotta, & Lanthier, 2008; Sedlak et al., 2010; and U.S. Department of Health & Human Services, 2008.

*Parent-child interactions.* Still others define psychological maltreatment as the *violation or failure to respect the elements of a child's psychosocial being.* Every child, for example, is a social being and needs to experience *interaction and communication with other human beings* in a variety of settings. Parents who fail to respect this element of a child's psychological being (e.g., by isolating the child or by denying the child emotional responsiveness) are committing psychological maltreatment (Glaser, 2002).

## Prevalence of Psychological Maltreatment

The true prevalence of psychological maltreatment remains obscured. One challenge to identifying psychological maltreatment is definitional ambiguity. Another is the paucity of reporting to government agencies. These factors influence the observation that psychological maltreatment is the *least common form* of *reported and substantiated child maltreatment.* This state of affairs is troublesome for three reasons: (a) Psychological (emotional) maltreatment is assumed to be the *most common* type of maltreatment; (b) Psychological maltreatment appears to be as *damaging* as physical abuse if not more so; and (c) Experts assume that *every subtype* of child abuse (physical, sexual, neglect) *encompasses* an element of psychological abuse (e.g., Hollins & Hankin, 2005). The latest recommendation, in fact, is to be alert to the *polyvictimization* (i.e., multiple forms of abuse) of children (Finkelhor, Ormrod, & Turner, 2007a).

One type of evidence, however, did *not* corroborate the idea that emotional abuse is the most common type of abuse (see the Adverse Childhood Experiences ["Prevalence of Individual," 2006] study). See Table 3.7 for a summary of these findings.

*Adverse Childhood Experiences (ACE) Study. Data from Kaiser Permanente–San Diego in collaboration with the Centers for Disease Control and Prevention (2006); N = 17,337 adult patients reporting on childhood experiences.*

**TABLE 3.7**  Adverse Childhood Experiences (ACE) of Emotional Abuse

| ACE Categories of Abuse | Women: N = 9,367 | Men: N = 7,970 |
|---|---|---|
| Emotional (psychological) abuse | 13.1% | 7.6% |
| Physical abuse | 27.0% | 29.9% |
| Sexual abuse | 24.7% | 16.0% |

More research is required to determine why the results in the ACE study are incongruent with expectations. Possibly, adults may *not* have recognized their childhood treatment as psychologically abusive. Alternatively, they may simply have *not* reported it. It is always possible, of course, that the assumptions about the frequency of psychological abuse are simply incorrect.

*Mandating record keeping.* The federal government, by the *Keeping Children and Families Safe Act, of 2003 (Public Law 108-36),* has mandated the DHHS to measure the incidence of child maltreatment along many dimensions such as age, gender, and race. Some prevalence estimates of emotional/psychological abuse are as follows:

- 58,196 (7.3%) of 758,289 maltreated children experience psychological maltreatment each year (U.S. Department of Health & Human Services, 2008).
- One third or more of all children experience psychological maltreatment (Binggeli, Hart, & Brassard, 2001).
- 26.8% of 553,330 abused children were *emotionally* abused (NIS-4).

*Self-report surveys of psychological maltreatment.* Researchers collected parent self-reports of psychological maltreatment using the *Parent-Child Conflict Tactics Scales.* Investigators found that approximately 86% of the parents in their sample reported using some form of psychological aggression toward their children (e.g., yelling, screaming or shouting, using threats, and swearing) at least once during the preceding year. The parents who reported engaging in such behaviors did so an average of 22 times during the preceding 12 months. The most common form of psychological aggression used by parents in this study was verbal—shouting, yelling, or screaming at the child. In addition, psychological aggression was almost as common in this sample of parents as nonviolent means of discipline, such as distraction or time-outs (Straus et al., 1998).

## Effects of Psychological Maltreatment

Imagine the potential consequences to children who grow up hearing constantly that they are worthless or stupid or ugly. When children regularly hear that they are worthless, stupid, unlovable, or ugly, they come to believe these things are true. As sociologists and psychologists have discovered, individuals perceive themselves as others see them. Perhaps even more tragic, children who are exposed to such maltreatment may begin to *act* as though they are worthless, stupid, unlovable, or ugly. Studies have consistently attested to the adverse effects of psychological maltreatment. It is possible to categorize the effects into four basic groupings. See Table 3.8 for a summary of negative impacts.

**TABLE 3.8**    Possible Effects Associated With Psychological Maltreatment

| Effects Observed in Infants and Children | | |
|---|---|---|
| Interpersonal maladjustment Social incompetence | Insecure attachment to caregiver Antisocial functioning Aggression Sexual maladjustment Dependency Low empathy Social phobia | Difficulties making and retaining friends Difficulties with peers |
| Intellectual deficits/learning problems | Academic problems Low educational achievement Deficits in cognitive ability Impaired moral reasoning | Deficits in problem solving and intelligence Lack of creativity |

| Effects Observed in Infants and Children | | |
|---|---|---|
| Affective-behavioral problems<br>Interpersonal thought problems | Aggression, hostility, anger<br>Disruptive classroom behavior<br>Noncompliant behavior<br>Lack of impulse control<br>Self-abusive behavior<br>Anxiety<br>Low self-esteem | Shame and guilt<br>Conduct disorder<br>Hyperactivity and distractibility<br>Pessimism and negativity<br>Dependence on adults for help, support, and nurturance |
| Physical health problems | Hypertension<br>Metabolic syndrome | Inflammatory disease |

SOURCES: A representative but not exhaustive list of sources for the information displayed in this table includes the following: Brassard & Donovan, 2006; Finzi-Dottan & Karu, 2006; Gibb, Chelminski, & Zimmerman, 2007; R. M. Johnson et al., 2002; Miller & Chen, 2010; Wolfe, Crooks, Chiodo, & Jaffe, 2003.

## Long-Term Effects of Psychological Maltreatment

Many studies confirm that, relative to other forms of child maltreatment, psychological maltreatment is the *strongest predictor* of *long-term impacts on psychological functioning.* The effects of psychological maltreatment listed in Table 3.8 tend to continue on into adulthood. One evaluation with a sample of 256 university students, for example, found that psychological maltreatment, even without physical abuse, was associated with *negative feelings* and long-term *mental health risks* in adulthood (Greenfield & Marks, 2010). A different analysis determined that subtypes of psychological maltreatment had *specific effects:* (a) parental *terrorizing* predicted anxiety and somatic concerns; (b) parental *ignoring* predicted depression and **Borderline Personality Disorder (BPD)** features; and (c) parental *degradation* also predicted BPD (Allen, 2008).

*Mediators of effects.* A duo of other investigators demonstrated that a group of variables mediated the effects of childhood psychological abuse on adult interpersonal conflict. These **mediators** were early maladaptive schemas adopted in childhood to cope with the following kinds of psychological maltreatment: (a) *mistrust/abuse,* (b) *abandonment,* and (c) *defectiveness/shame.* The association between mistrust/abuse and interpersonal conflict was partially mediated by three patterns of adult maladaptive interpersonal behaviors: (a) *overly accommodating* behavior, (b) *social isolation,* and (c) *domineering/controlling* behavior. Domineering/controlling behavior explained the greatest amount of **variance** in adult maladaptive interpersonal conflict (Messman-Moore & Coates, 2007).

*Neurodevelopmental effects.* Another long-term effect is alteration of neurodevelopmental processes. Just as with neglect, emotional abuse "is likely to result in significant and enduring alterations in the neurobiology of stress response systems" (Yates, 2007, p. 9). More specifically, psychologically maltreated children are significantly more vulnerable than nonmaltreated children to stress, anxiety, depression, and other problems of adaptation.

> **SECTION SUMMARY**
>
> ## Definitions and Prevalence of Child Psychological Maltreatment
>
> Many scholars have described psychological maltreatment as the most difficult form of child maltreatment to define. Some experts emphasize nonphysical behaviors directed at children, such as failing to respond to a child's needs for nurturance and attention, terrorizing a child, or insulting or swearing at a child. Others focus on the nonphysical consequences to the child victim, including a variety of emotional and cognitive symptoms (e.g., anxiety and confusion). Still others define psychological maltreatment broadly to include a combination of physical and nonphysical parental actions that result in negative psychological consequences for the child.
>
> Inadequate definitions and vast underreporting have made estimates of psychological abuse especially difficult to pinpoint. Only recently have large governmental surveys (DHHS, NIS) attempted to assess the prevalence of psychological maltreatment more thoroughly. Of the population of known maltreated children, surveyors have estimated that 7.3% are psychologically maltreated. NIS-4 provides an estimate of 26.8%. ACE retrospective studies found a range of roughly 7.5% to 30%.

## CHILDREN EXPOSED TO INTERPARENTAL VIOLENCE

*Historical introduction.* Historically, the fields of child maltreatment and domestic violence have developed as separate entities. As Graham-Bermann (2002, p. 119) notes, "Researchers in the areas of child abuse and domestic violence have occupied different spheres of inquiry, used disparate sources of data, received funding from different agencies, reported results at different conferences, and published their work in different journals." Research has shown, however, that children suffer *psychological maltreatment* not only directly, but also indirectly, from exposure to violence between others. As a result of the recognition that child and spouse abuse are interconnected, several scholars have begun to consider what place children's exposure to interparental violence should occupy within the field of child maltreatment. From a conceptual perspective, many authorities now view exposure to IPV as a form of child maltreatment (Wekerle & Wolfe, 2003).

*Forms of exposure.* Exposure may take several forms: Some children, for example, *may directly observe violent acts,* some may *overhear violent behaviors,* and some may *see the results of assaults* (e.g., bruises). Such exposure is often conceptualized as a *specific form of psychological maltreatment* (e.g., Sedlak et al., 2010).

### Co-occurrence of Child Abuse and Domestic Violence

There is considerable evidence that interparental violence and child abuse co-occur in families at a significantly high rate (UNICEF, 2006). A review of studies in the United States revealed that *child abuse* is prevalent in 18% to 67% of families experiencing IPV (Jouriles, McDonald, Slep, Heyman, & Garrido, 2008). One explanation for the wide variation in findings is that the source of samples varies—for example, community residents, shelter residents, and children in treatment. Moreover, not every state gathers data on exposure to IPV. More and more frequently, researchers are addressing the overlapping problems of child abuse and IPV (Graham-Bermann & Howell, 2010). One research team was able to demonstrate that among 1,232 partnered women, the following forms and odds ratios of child abuse occurred in homes experiencing domestic violence: (a) 2.7 times the odds of physical abuse; (b) 2.04 times the odds of neglect; (c) 9.8 times the odds of psychological abuse; and (d) 4.90 times the odds of sexual abuse (Zolotor, Theodore, Coyne-Beasley, & Runyan, 2007).

## Defining Exposure to Interparental Violence

Consider the following scenarios that depict the experiences of children who are exposed to interparental violence:

- Alice, a 4-year-old, hears shouting and arguing between her parents on a daily basis.
- On many occasions, 8-year-old Manuel observes his father using his fists to beat Manuel's mother.
- Reza, who is 12, listens in as his mother repeatedly swears at and degrades his father.
- One night, 6-year-old Elizabeth witnesses her father brutally raping her mother.

*Act of omission or commission?* Some experts construe this type of harm as the result of an act of *omission* (i.e., frightening, unsafe environment) and thus classify exposure to interparental violence as child neglect (Kantor & Little, 2003). Others argue that the harm experienced results from an *act of commission,* and thus classify exposure to interparental violence as a form of psychological maltreatment (Somer & Braunstein, 1999).

*Importance of definition.* The way that researchers and scholars define exposure to interparental violence is important, because definitions have significant social and legal implications. Several U.S. states, for example, have adopted laws that make exposing a child to interparental violence a form of *criminal child abuse* (Kantor & Little, 2003). One issue that is unclear about such laws, however, is who would be identified as the perpetrators of child abuse in such cases: (a) Should the father who physically abuses his wife in the presence of their child be held accountable? (b) Should the mother who chooses to reside with her abuser despite his abusiveness be held accountable? or (c) Should both parents be held accountable? These are difficult questions that will need careful consideration. It is particularly important that researchers examine these questions in light of the special circumstances of battered individuals and the potential obstacles associated with leaving a violent relationship (Berliner, 1998; Kantor & Little, 2003).

*Specific aspects of defining exposure to interparental violence.* It may be best to classify exposure to interparental violence broadly, as a form of psychological maltreatment that could involve *acts of omission, acts of commission,* or *both.* In addition, legal statutes that define exposure to interparental violence as child abuse per se need further examination. Rather than defining all cases of exposure to interparental violence as child abuse, legislators and others may find it more useful to consider the specific circumstances under which exposure should be defined as criminal child abuse. Kantor and Little (2003), for example, recommend that Child Protective Services caseworkers ask themselves the following questions when attempting to determine what interventions are in the best interests of the child in such circumstances:

- What types of injuries have both the parent victim and the child sustained?
- How frequent and severe is the interparental violence?
- What is the victim parent's ability to nurture the child?
- How has the victim parent attempted to protect the child?

## Prevalence of Exposure to Marital Violence

Until recently, there were no government-sponsored prevalence studies of children exposed to marital violence. Some of the findings are as follows:

- 3.3 million to nearly 10 million children were exposed to marital violence according to Straus's (1991a) national population survey data.
- 25% of one sample may have *directly observed* interparental violence (national survey of *battered women;* Tomkins et al., 1994).
- 66% of samples *directly observed* interparental violence (studies of battered women; Hilton, 1992; Holden & Ritchie, 1991).
- 25% of children reported witnessing both husband-to-wife and wife-to-husband aggression (child interviews of children 8 to 11 years old; O'Brien, John, Margolin, & Erel, 1994).
- 20% of the children in a sample *saw* their fathers slap their mothers (community sample of children; McCloskey, Figueredo, & Koss, 1995).

*First National Survey on Children's Exposure to Violence* (Finkelhor, Turner, Ormrod, Hamby, & Kracke, 2009). (*Not* reported here are estimates of children's exposure to other types of violence, such as shootings.)

*9.8%* of surveyed children were exposed to violence.

*Adverse Childhood Experiences (ACE) Study. Data from Kaiser Permanente–San Diego in collaboration with the Centers for Disease Control and Prevention (2006);* N = 17,337 adult patients reporting on childhood exposure to male-to-mother intimate partner violence (IPV).

*13.7%* of women and 11.5% of men reported male-to-female IPV.

*Revised estimates.* These early studies, while important and useful, actually served to point out how prone such data were to error. Researchers queried only children of specific ages, and information was derived primarily from nonrandom samples of children (Clements, Oxtoby, & Ogle, 2008). Furthermore, data from multiple informants (e.g., both parents and children) found that mothers' and fathers' reports of children's exposure agreed fairly well, but there was much less agreement between parents' and children's reports (O'Brien et al., 1994). More recent surveys, building upon the foundation of these earlier surveys, have improved research methodology.

## Effects of Children's Exposure to Interparental Violence

Regardless of the particular classification system used, it is clear that children exposed to interparental violence experience multiple threats. Children in these violent homes fear for themselves as well as for the parent who is the direct recipient of violence. In addition, these children are likely to experience direct forms of abuse and neglect (e.g., Holden, 2003). Even psychological interparental violence has significant negative effects on children (J. J. Chang, Theodore, Martin, & Runyan, 2008). A number of controlled studies have found that children exposed to marital violence experience a variety of negative psychosocial problems.

Since the late 1970s, researchers have made progress in documenting a number of problems in children exposed to interparental violence. Research findings on the effects associated with exposure to interparental violence reveal that such children are prone to suffer problems in five general areas: emotional functioning, behavior problems, social competence, cognitive ability, and physical health. Table 3.9 displays the effects most frequently associated with children's exposure to interparental violence.

**TABLE 3.9**  Possible Effects Associated With Children's Exposure to Interparental Violence

| Areas Affected | Examples | |
|---|---|---|
| Emotional functioning | Anxiety/difficult temperament <br> Low self-esteem <br> Depression and suicide | Trauma/stress reactions <br> Negative emotions (e.g., feelings of loss, anger, sadness, self-blame) |
| Behavior problems | Aggression <br> Delinquency <br> Regressive behavior | Alcohol/drug use <br> High levels of physical activity <br> Acting like a child several years younger |
| Social competence | Shyness/withdrawal <br> Social incompetence <br> Low empathy | Aggression, wariness, and hostility in interpersonal relationships |
| Cognitive ability | Academic and achievement problems <br> Poor problem-solving and conflict resolution skills <br> Cognitive deficits | Negative perceptions <br> Deficits in adaptive behavior <br> Altered information-processing ability <br> Increased vigilance for threat situations |
| Physical health | Physical symptoms/ailments <br> Obesity <br> Some chronic diseases (e.g., arthritis) | Somatic complaints <br> Many emergency room visits <br> High medical expenditures |

SOURCES: A representative but not exhaustive list of sources for the information displayed in this table includes C. M. Adams, 2006; Bair-Merritt et al., 2008; Bedi & Goddard, 2007; Finkelhor, Turner, Ormrod, Hamby, & Kracke, 2009; Graham-Bermann, Lynch, Banyard, & Halabu, 2007; Kracke & Hahn, 2008; Russell, Springer, & Greenfield, 2010.

*Research findings about children exposed to violence.* Some specific research findings about children who are exposed to family violence are as follows:

- They tend to exhibit more emotional and behavior problems than do nonexposed children (Repetti, Taylor, & Seeman, 2002).
- They often display multiple problems (Finkelhor, Turner, Ormrod, Hamby, & Kracke, 2009).
- They often exhibit problems that warrant clinical intervention (e.g., O'Keefe, 1994).
- A subgroup of children appears to be well adjusted, resilient (e.g., Hughes & Luke, 1998).

- A trend of exposure increased with age (Finkelhor et al., 2009).
- More than 10% of the children were exposed 5 or more times (Finkelhor et al., 2009).

*Long-term effects of exposure to marital violence.* Children exposed to interparental violence continue to demonstrate psychological difficulties later in life. Several studies have examined problems in adolescents, college students, and national samples of adults that are correlated with childhood exposure to interparental violence. The long-term effects observed include depression, trauma-related symptoms (e.g., anxiety and sleep disturbance), low self-esteem, alcohol and drug use, poor social adjustment, general psychological distress, and ineffective conflict resolution skills (Choice, Lamke, & Pittman, 1995; Henning, Leitenberg, Coffey, Turner, & Bennett, 1996; Silvern et al., 1995).

Other possible long-term effects include verbal and physical violence against one's own spouse, dating partner, or peers; verbal and physical abuse of one's own children; and participation in violence outside the family (e.g., arrests for criminal assault) (Maker, Kemmelmeier, & Peterson, 1998; McCloskey & Lichter, 2003; Straus, 1992). There is also some evidence that outcomes for young adults who were exposed to interparental violence in childhood depend upon whether the violence was initiated by their mothers or fathers. Father-initiated violence was associated with greater risk for psychological problems (Fergusson & Horwood, 1998).

*Need for services.* Social recognition that children exposed to interparental violence are in need of services has grown in the United States because of the work of advocates, clinicians, and researchers since the late 1970s. A 1994 report from the American Bar Association acknowledged, for example, that despite society's obligation to protect children living in violent households, the law has generally failed even to recognize their exposure as a problem (Davidson, 1994). Indeed, some authors have described children in such homes as "the 'forgotten,' 'unacknowledged,' 'hidden,' 'unintended,' and 'silent' victims" of family violence (Holden, 1998, p. 1).

---

### SECTION SUMMARY

### Children Exposed to Marital Violence and Effects of Psychological Maltreatment

Child abuse experts now consider children's exposure to interparental violence to be a specific form of child psychological maltreatment. How such exposure should be defined constitutes another challenge for scholars and lawmakers. Although it is clear that significant numbers of children are exposed to violence between their parents, prevalence estimates lack certitude. While earlier studies suggested the prevalence could range from 20% to 66%, newer population-based studies suggest the prevalence is from 9.8% to 13.7%.

---

> Negative effects associated with psychological maltreatment including exposure to marital violence include difficulties in interpersonal, intellectual, and affective and behavioral realms of functioning. For example, these children demonstrate more problems than comparison children in such areas as aggression, delinquency, self-abuse, anxiety, hostility, and anger. Researchers have found similar problems in adults with childhood histories of psychological maltreatment. Future research should attempt to examine the effects of psychological maltreatment on development, the effects of psychological maltreatment alone or in combination with other forms of maltreatment, and the distinctive effects associated with various subtypes of psychological maltreatment.

## CHARACTERISTICS OF MALTREATED CHILDREN AND THEIR FAMILIES

### Characteristics of Maltreated Children

Most of the available information about sociodemographic characteristics of psychological maltreatment victims comes from official reports made to CPS and other agencies. Because of research factors such as small sample sizes and usage of dissimilar definitions, current knowledge about sociodemographic characteristics of psychological maltreatment victims is tentative at best.

*Age and gender.* The two primary national surveys presented different findings about psychological maltreatment.

    a. *NIS-4, 2010.* Findings from NIS-4 (Sedlak et al., 2010), with its broad definition of psychological maltreatment, indicated that psychological maltreatment increases with children's age and that boys are more likely than girls to experience psychological maltreatment. Still, other researchers have failed to find any gender differences associated with psychological maltreatment.

    b. *U.S. Department of Health & Human Services, 2008.* The *peak* of psychological abuse was between *4* and *11 years of age.* Of the 1,344 *child fatalities,* 1.3% of the fatalities were associated with psychological maltreatment. (U.S. DHHS did not provide information on psychological maltreatment specific to gender and some other variables.)

### Resilient Children

Despite suffering neglect and other abuse, some children appear to survive less encumbered than others suffering from long-term serious effects. Why some children are negatively affected by such experiences and others appear to emerge relatively unscathed is not totally clear. Several factors might mediate the psychological and developmental outcomes for children, such as age, gender, ethnicity, the quality of mothering, social support, the child's exposure to other forms of violence (i.e., polyvictimization), and child characteristics such as temperament and self-esteem (e.g., Spaccarelli, Sandler, & Roosa, 1994). Definitional ambiguity contributes to the lack of comparability across inquiries even further, and this problem extends to the measurement indicators within domains (see Walsh, Dawson, & Mattingly, 2010, for a review; see also Fantuzzo & Fusco, 2007).

Newer research has begun to unravel heretofore-unidentified parameters related to resilience. As one illustration, several comparisons have disclosed that resilience does *not* extend uniformly across every sphere. That is, children exposed to maltreatment may be resilient in only one domain, such as competency (Graham-Bermann, Gruber, Howell, & Girz, 2009; see Walsh et al., 2010, for a review). After controlling for relevant influential factors, recent research has identified three crucial elements contributing to children's resilience: *better parenting performance, fewer maternal mental health problems,* and *less severe exposure to violence* (Howells, Graham-Bermann, Czyz, & Lilly, 2010). More research should be forthcoming with the advent of a trauma resilience scale (Madsen & Abell, 2010).

## Characteristics of Maltreating Parents

Because separating parents who are psychologically maltreating only is a newer undertaking, information about their characteristics is almost not available. One study joined the subtypes (physical, sexual, emotional, psychological, and neglect) of maltreating parents into a single grouping. Based on a literature review, a **meta-analysis** (integration of many studies' findings) identified the following significant parental risk factors that were independent of a child's problems (Stith et al., 2009):

- Parental stress
- Lack social support
- Personal childhood abuse
- Depressed

- Low parent age
- Psychopathology
- Single parenthood
- Unemployed

- Anger
- Low self-esteem
- Poor relationship with own parents

---

**SECTION SUMMARY**

### Characteristics of Psychologically Maltreated Children and Psychologically Maltreating Parents

Research conducted to date indicates that reports of psychological maltreatment increase as children become older, with those ages 4 to 11 being the most likely to be reported for psychological maltreatment. Research findings about possible gender differences or racial differences are inconsistent. Primarily methodological difficulties have precluded generalization. Early studies do show a link, however, between child psychological maltreatment and low income.

One increasingly examined child trait is resilience. Given the potentially devastating effects of psychological maltreatment, it is surprising that a small minority of children escape with only mild or moderate symptoms. One finding is that resilience does not extend across all behavioral domains. Relatively better parenting, fewer maternal health problems, and less exposure to severe violence appear to be factors in the development of resilience.

Female parents are identified most often as the perpetrators of psychological maltreatment. Consistent findings indicate that parents often exhibit interpersonal and social difficulties, poor problem-solving skills, substance abuse, and psychiatric difficulties. Data also provide preliminary support for the hypothesis of potential intergenerational transmission of psychological maltreatment. Additional research is needed to replicate current findings and expand our understanding of the risk factors associated with psychological maltreatment.

## Explaining Child Neglect and Child Psychological Maltreatment

There are many factors contributing to child neglect and psychological maltreatment. The sources of the problems vary from socioeconomic variables, to family structure, to intergenerational transmission of violence. In addition, there are numerous parenting problems, some of which are more typical of neglectful or maltreating families than of nonneglectful and nonmaltreating families.

*Socioeconomic status (SES).* Although child neglect occurs at all levels of U.S. society, studies uniformly affirm that rates of neglect are higher in families with very low income, unemployment, and dependence on social assistance. Indeed, SES is a *stronger predictor of child neglect* than of any other form of child maltreatment (Sedlak et al., 2010). Income level has also been associated with *severity of neglect,* with higher-income families generally associated with less severe forms of neglect (see Claussen & Crittenden, 1991). An analysis of data from the National Comorbidity Survey (1990–1992) ascertained that of the 5,004 respondents, those who had experienced maltreatment, abuse, and/or neglect had lower scores on all economic measures (Zielinski, 2009).

*Family structure/functioning.* Research has also shown that family size and structure are associated with neglect. One comparison indicated that mothers who have a greater number of children during their teen years or who are younger at the birth of their first child are at increased risk for neglecting their children. Furthermore, teenage mothers whose first children were premature or had a low birth weight were more likely to neglect their children than were older mothers whose infants were healthier (Pryce & Samuels, 2010; Landy, Sword, & Valaitis, 2009). An analysis of data from 2,753 mothers from the Fragile Families and Wellbeing Study (Princeton University) established that mothers who left a coresidential relationship with a biological father or entered a coresidential relationship with a nonbiological father experienced significantly more parenting stress than mothers living in a stable coresidential relationship. This finding is especially true for women with less education (Cooper, McLanahan, Meadows, & Brooks-Gunn, 2007). Another team of researchers examining the role of alcohol on family functions concluded that family functioning lies on a *continuum* (Coyle et al., 2009).

*Intergenerational transmission of maltreatment.* Researchers apply *learning theory* to nearly every type of family violence situation, and their research is congruent with this theory. In the case of neglect, some researchers have hypothesized and found that neglectful parents reported childhood histories of *both neglect and abuse* (e.g., Van Ijzendoorn, 1992; Widom, 1989b). A more contemporary study indicated that witnessing IPV was independently related to engaging in IPV in one's own adult relationships (D. S. Black, Sussman, & Unger, 2010). In addition to several previous studies, a group of independent researchers collaborated in editing a special issue of the journal *Developmental Psychology* (Vol. 45, 2009) presenting several contemporary evaluations. Across the five studies presented, the researchers found consistent evidence of *intergenerational transmission of parenting styles*. As an illustration, a trio of investigators conducted a prospective longitudinal study of 61 two-generation sets of respondents. From *observational data of parenting quality,* they determined that the scores from the two generations, each with a child at 24 months of age, were significantly correlated ($r = .43$) (Kovan, Chung, & Sroufe, 2009).

A previous assessment of 200 children revealed that mothers' *anxious attachment* style (via mothers' reports) uniquely predicted children's insecure attachment to both mother and father (Doyle, Markiewicz, Brendgen, Lieberman, & Voss, 2000). From a distinctive perspective, one researcher has suggested that *low socioeconomic status* is the actual *mechanism of transmission.* A rationale for this interpretation is that childhood maltreatment is closely linked with economic measures, such as unemployment, poverty, and Medicaid usage (Zielinski, 2009).

## PARENTING PROBLEMS IN NEGLECTFUL AND PSYCHOLOGICALLY MALTREATING FAMILIES

In addition to their own individual problems and the problems of children who are neglected, neglecting parents have parenting problems associated with specific circumstances that generate additional stress. Some of these are as follows: (a) *single parenting,* (b) *being disabled,* (c) *living in a home where marital violence is occurring,* and (d) *coping with other stresses,* such as being a stepparent, being a homosexual parent, or managing without a spouse/parent who is deployed in the military (La Bash, Vogt, King, & King, 2009). These types of stresses increase the risk for child neglect and maltreatment. A brief discussion of a *few* parenting problems follows:

*Single parenting/presence of fathers.* Children of single parents are at greater risk for all types of neglect compared with children living with both parents, partially because single parenting is often extremely stressful. Fathers who make a positive difference in their children's lives are those not just present in the house but who are involved with their children (e.g., R. Green, 2006; Rentz et al., 2006; Weaver & Coleman, 2010). *Substance-abusing fathers* place their children at much higher risk when they live with their children (Osborne & Berger, 2009). When evaluating *mother*-child interactions, race and ethnicity influence the impact of a father's presence in the house. Having a married father in the home was beneficial in this study. Although marriage was not uniformly associated with *better outcomes, cohabitation* may be associated with *negative outcomes,* especially for Hispanic families (Gibson-Davis & Glassman-Pines, 2010).

*Disabled mothers.* Past conceptions of disability have viewed a disabled person as having deficits or something akin to pathology. Some members of society may criticize a disabled woman for having children; others try to offer the support she needs to care for an infant. Disabled mothers face unique challenges in caring for their children's needs, a challenge that generates stress. The disabled mother also has to struggle to maintain control over her parenting, a situation worsened by lack of funding (Parish, Magaña, & Cassiman, 2008; Pledger, 2003).

*Mothers' parenting in father-violent families.* A growing body of research has highlighted the difficulties of parenting in the face of interparental violence because of the added stress. Diminution of social support risks children's emotional and behavioral adjustment (Casanueva, Martin, Runyan, Barth, & Bradley, 2008; Huth-Bocks & Hughes, 2008; Owen, Mitchell, Paranjape, & Hargrove, 2008; Renner, 2009). Custody and visitation issues usually force the mother to safeguard her child while arranging visitation with her abusive spouse (Dugan, Nagin, & Rosenfeld, 2003; Jaffe & Crooks, 2005).

*Fathers' parenting in violent families.* Researchers have just recently begun to study *fathers* in homes where neglect and maltreatment are occurring. The stereotype that domestically violent men are uninvolved in fathering is not true (Bellamy, 2009). In one study, 65.6% of men arrested for intimate partner violence (IPV) had some type of fathering role, and most of these men returned home and resumed their role. Although the men in the study knew that their children had been exposed to IPV, most did not realize their children had been negatively impacted (Salisbury, Henning, & Holdford, 2009). Many men wish to be involved fathers, but they encounter real impediments, such as unemployment. In well-functioning households, fathers can contribute to the well-being of their female partners and their children. Consequently, more programs (e.g., job training, parenting skills) are needed to help these men achieve their goals (see Lamb, 2010).

*Mothers' legal difficulties coping with a violent father.* Mothers living with violent fathers have serious problems coping with their own fear while trying to protect their children. These problems are especially obvious in court (see Stahly, 2007).

---

### BOX 3.3 Custody Issues and (In)Justice in the Courts

*Custody problems for mothers.* In addition to the pain and fear generated by intimate partner violence (IPV) victimization, women uniformly encounter difficulties in maneuvering through, in, or around the court system. From a legal perspective, juvenile court judges have found that exposing children to IPV can constitute a form of neglect (Myers, 2005).

For the most part, these mothers are in a no-win situation (e.g., Erickson, 2006):

- *Abusive husbands may gain custody*—Only a handful of states have ruled out possible custody for an abusive husband. Judges tend to overlook solid evidence about the harmful effects of exposure to interparental violence.
- *Reporting father's child neglect/abuse*—Failure to report may lead to a loss of custody for "failure to protect." Reporting may lead to loss of custody because

*(Continued)*

of so-called *"parental alienation"* (a non–empirically based syndrome in which one parent forms an alliance with a child to denigrate the other parent, such as getting the child to falsely accuse a father of leaving the child alone in the house all weekend).

- *Financial inequities*—for example, forcing mothers with no assets to pay half the legal fees when fathers have substantial assets, such as $2,000,000.
- *Hostile court settings*—for example, having to wait for the judge with one's children in rooms where an abusive ex-husband may enter and threaten everyone.

*Law guardians and custody disputes.* Of the 50 states, 46 have adopted some form of regulation to guide custody decisions when IPV has occurred. Frequently, the court appoints a law guardian (also referred to by the more formal term guardian *ad litem*) to oversee the process and report back to the court. Regrettably, the practice is in shambles because the guardians appear to act with impunity. No one oversees their work nor holds them accountable. First and foremost, the exact role of a law guardian may *not* be specified legally and may not require training. It is uncertain whether guardians are charged with *acting in the best interest of the child,* or whether they are required to *speak to the child's wishes.* Laws are inconsistent from county to county and even from city to city, and appointment of a guardian may be mandatory or discretionary (e.g., Cuthbert et al., 2002; Erickson, 2000).

A pair of researchers queried divorced women and their children about their interactions with their children's law guardians. Because only 10 women volunteered, all of whom expressed negative viewpoints, the researchers tried vigorously to recruit other women who had positive perceptions, but to no avail. *No* lawyers, judges, law guardians, research participants, or others were able to provide referrals to *a single* woman who was satisfied with her children's law guardians. The women reported a host of negative perceptions as follows (Berger & Rosenberg, 2008):

- Some guardians *lacked expertise* (e.g., lack of knowledge about child development and male domestic violence).
- Some guardians were *unprofessional* (e.g., did not return a child's telephone call or provided false information to the court).
- Some guardians supported abusers' custody petitions despite *known child abuse by the father.*
- All guardians displayed *biases and inequality* (e.g., presented a report on mother's mental health but not the father's).
- Some guardians committed mother bashing (e.g., blamed a mother because a 17-year-old child refused to buy a Father's Day gift for a father who was absent for year).

## Methodological Issues Pertaining to *Effects* Research

One of the problems in understanding and coping with child neglect and child psychological maltreatment is the issue of research methodology. It is difficult to address the actual questions these problems pose when issues such as definitional uncertainty and lack of measurement standards affect the findings so extensively. The results of studies that have examined the negative effects associated with child neglect, psychological maltreatment, and exposure to interparental violence should be interpreted with some caution. There are many methodological problems that complicate both the certainty of the findings and their interpretations. These methodological problems include a lack of *standard definitions*, the use of *biased samples*, and the use of *limited research designs*.

*Lack of a standard definition.* Some researchers have used the term *psychological maltreatment* to refer to a *broad* collection of behaviors, including rejection/degradation, terrorizing, denying emotional responsiveness, and abandonment. Others have used the term to refer to a more *circumscribed* set of behaviors, such as verbal abuse only. A number of inquiries have not considered the *parameters* of maltreatment, such as its frequency, severity, and duration, all of which might influence a child's functional outcome. Vague definitions of maltreatment and neglect impede attempts to enforce the law as well. One idea for improving definitions is to emphasize the "Rights of the Child" under United Nations Conventions (UNICEF, n.d.).

*Inadequate sampling.* Another methodological problem is that most studies to date have used *small, nonrepresentative samples.* The majority of studies have included *mothers and children* temporarily residing in battered women's shelters. Such samples vary greatly from general population samples in many ways.

*Polyvictimization effects.* Many researchers have also failed to control for the fact that child and adult samples often include individuals who have *experienced multiple forms of abuse.* As an illustration, both parent and child may have observed interparental violence *in addition* to experiencing direct physical or sexual abuse— that is, **polyvictimization** (e.g., Finkelhor, Ormrod, Turner, & Hamby, 2005). Such research designs preclude the possibility of separating the effects of *observing* interparental violence from the effects of *experiencing other forms* of maltreatment.

One appraisal with a sample of 1,924 Taiwanese college students examined the long-term effects of exposure to marital violence and direct experience of child physical abuse. Results indicated that students experiencing *two* forms of family violence scored *lower* on self-esteem than students who had experienced only one form of child maltreatment. Furthermore, male students scored lower than female students (Shen, 2009). When researchers have controlled for polyvictimization effects, the findings have suggested that particular forms of child maltreatment are associated with specific problems and that specific forms of abuse have differential power to predict certain types of child and adult functioning (e.g., Allen, 2008).

*Sources of reports.* The source of the report (e.g., mothers, fathers, teachers, parents, adolescents, peers) greatly influences the data obtained. In one study that examined the effects associated with exposure to parental violence, for example, researchers found that mothers' reports of the degree of their children's behavioral difficulties varied depending on whether or not the mothers were victims of spouse abuse (Sternberg et al., 1993).

*Research designs.* Some researchers have used *retrospective study* designs, questioning adults about their childhood memories of their own neglect, psychological maltreatment, and exposure to interparental violence. College students provide a sizable amount of this type of information. Parents who themselves are in treatment or whose children are in treatment provide another source of retrospective information. Other designs query parents about their *current* behaviors of neglect and psychological maltreatment. Obviously, retrospective data differs significantly from current reports. Occasionally, researchers undertake direct observation of parent-child interactions at home or in clinic-based studies.

*Correlational data.* The correlational nature of the research has also weakened the validity of interpretations about the findings. That is, one cannot necessarily assume that psychological maltreatment is the *cause* of the various problems observed in children. Children living in homes characterized by psychological maltreatment often experience *additional risk factors,* such as parental alcoholism, low income, stress, and maternal impairment (e.g., Rossman, 2001). Without appropriate statistical controls or comparison groups, it is impossible to determine which of these many factors contribute to the negative outcomes observed in children. As mentioned in the previous chapter, scholars are more and more frequently analyzing data with sophisticated statistical analyses, making it more possible to narrow and pinpoint cause-effect relationships.

*Lack of theoretical underpinnings.* Two final criticisms are that research is rarely driven by theory and that researchers have paid little attention to the processes that lead to behavioral problems in children and adults with histories of this form of abuse. A new wave of research, however, is addressing both theoretical and conceptual issues within the field and attempting to link findings with implications for intervention and social policy (e.g., Kent & Waller, 2000).

*Noncomparability of comparison groups.* Only about 50% of researchers using samples of child/parent/family clients undergoing typical *community services* collect sociodemographic and other relevant data. Researchers studying clients in agencies using *evidence-based therapy,* by contrast, are able to collect significantly more data, even though the data may not be derived from the same test inventories. These findings are problematic since research has clearly shown that sociodemographic factors and other variables such as parental stress affect treatment effectiveness. Despite these impediments, authors of recent meta-analyses have provided information showing that the characteristics of clients in *clinic samples* undergoing evidence-based therapy are *not* the same as the clients in *community clinic samples* undergoing typical counseling.

Children in the evidence-based programs were younger, less apt to be from a minority race, and male. Children in the typical community programs included many more minority youth. Parents in the evidence-based clinic samples were often more educated and had less depression than parents in the typical community programs. Overall, the families in the evidence-based programs were less disadvantaged and more likely to have two parents. Accordingly, determining the generalizability of evidence-based treatments for general community should *not* be assumed (Baker-Ericzén, Hurlburt, Brookman-Frazee, Jenkins, & Hough, 2010).

## PRACTICE, POLICY, AND PREVENTION ISSUES

**CASE HISTORY** Emmanuelle—Young and Alone

Emmanuelle, an 18-year-old high school senior, was desperate. The father of her child had abandoned her, she was unable to support herself and her child with her waitress job, and her family was unwilling to help. With nowhere to turn, she left her 2-½-year-old child at a Brooklyn hospital with a note:

*To Whom It May Concern:*

*I am an 18-year-old student and I also work. I can't handle the pressure. I sometimes take it out on her. I love her and would not like to hurt her. Please find her a good home where she'll get the love she desires.*

The next day Emmanuelle realized she had made a terrible mistake, so she called the hospital to ask for her baby back. When she arrived, she was arrested and charged with child abandonment (Fontana & Moohnan, 1994, pp. 227–228).

The case of Emmanuelle illustrates the need for *societal intervention* rather than punishment for most psychologically maltreating parents. Emmanuelle felt overwhelmed and desperate with no one to help her, so she decided it would be best to abandon her baby at the hospital where the baby would be safe. When she realized her mistake, she tried to reclaim her baby but was arrested. With help, Emmanuelle might have been able to care for her child, whereas prosecuting her merely put "one more young woman in jail and another child in the city's already overstretched foster care system" (Fontana & Moohnan, 1994, p. 229).

## Practice (Treatment) for Child Neglect and Psychological Maltreatment

Theoretically, practitioners are to provide services that are in the *best interest of the child.* Making decisions about neglect of a child, however, is challenging. A number of entities are involved: child, families, agencies, courts, communities, and the child welfare system. Practitioners use most programs for several types of abuse. Some interventions include the following: (a) interventions with adults to *enhance parenting skills,* (b) interventions with children to *reduce effects associated with maltreatment,* (c) *economic assistance,* and (d) *multiservice interventions* (see Corcoran, 2000). Efficacy of such programs is still controversial (O'Reilly, Wilkes, Luck, & Jackson, 2010).

*Multiservice interventions.* Research examining programs to prevent child neglect suggests that the best way to approach it is to use a combination of interventions simultaneously (O'Reilly et al., 2010). Many neglectful parents, for example, may not know how to parent effectively or may be experiencing pressures that make parenting difficult. They may be young and immature, have economic pressures, and be socially isolated. They or their children may have physical problems, or their children may have especially difficult temperaments. They may be insecurely attached.

Multiservice intervention approaches are ideal for neglecting families because of the multiproblem nature of such families (Erickson & Egeland, 2010). Multiservice interventions typically include the delivery of a broad range of services, including individual, family, and group counseling; social support services; behavioral skills training to eliminate problematic behavior; and parenting education. An example of this type of program is *Healthy Families New York* (Dumont et al., 2008).

A contemporary review of maltreatment interventions essentially found small levels of improvement, with some programs more effective than others (e.g., Dumont et al., 2008; see also Gessner, 2008). This review, however, was able to identify factors that enhanced effectiveness. These included the following: (a) *implementation by highly trained staff,* professionals rather than paraprofessionals; (b) relatively *high dosage* (i.e., high levels) and *intensity of treatment;* and (c) *comprehensiveness* of scope (i.e., multiservice). Several recommendations emanated from the analysis. These primarily included methodological improvements. One special appeal, however, was to increase the focus on economic well-being and, if possible, to obtain a comprehensive two-generation model (Reynolds, Mathieson, & Topitzes, 2009; see also Currie & Widom, 2010).

*Home visitation programs.* Home visitation programs aimed at preventing child neglect typically connect at-risk parents with mentors who come to their homes and provide social support, parenting suggestions, and help with life decisions (see Daro & Donnelly, 2002). Although the specifics of the parental education and support efforts of such programs vary, the World Health Organization and the International Society for Prevention of Child Abuse and Neglect (2008) have identified several successful strategies:

- Increasing parents' knowledge about general child development
- Improving parents' overall child-rearing skills
- Increasing parents' empathy for and awareness of others' needs
- Improving parents' ability to provide sensitive, responsive responding
- Improving family and parent-child communication
- Changing parents' beliefs about the value of abusive parenting
- Increasing parents' ability to handle stress
- Increasing parents' use of nonviolent approaches to child discipline

Many home visitation programs attempt to *identify high-risk parents in a community* (i.e., those who are young, low-income, and single) and intervene during pregnancy, before the first child is born. Early intervention programs have received not only considerable state and federal support, but also the support of several important private foundations (such as the Carnegie Foundation). Unfortunately, the effectiveness of most programs is still unknown (MacMillan et al., 2009). Nonetheless, many scholars in the field remain cautiously optimistic about the potential of home visitation programs for preventing child maltreatment.

*Social support programs.* Another form of intervention for neglecting families that has proven effective is the promotion of social support (for a review, see DePanfilis, 1996). Emotional support groups are the most common type of service (Groves & Gewirtz, 2006). Given that social isolation and lack of social support have been identified as significant risk factors for child maltreatment, some programs try to increase the social support available to neglecting families. Although research examining the effectiveness of such programs is limited, some published studies focused on social support have shown improvements in child mental health and social dysfunction among parents (Lundhal & Harris, 2006; see also O'Reilly et al., 2010).

One group of researchers/practitioners developed a program for mothers and their children who had sought refuge at a battered women's shelter. This weekly *in-home intervention* program extended over an 8-month period. The program focused on providing mothers with social support, parent training (including child management and nurturing skills), and training in problem-solving and decision-making skills. The sessions also included social support for the children: A child mentor served as a "big brother" or "big sister" to each mother-child dyad, engaging the child in interesting activities and providing positive attention and affection. A preliminary outcome evaluation of the program using a randomized control group design found that participating families demonstrated *significant benefits,* including a reduction in child antisocial behavior, enhanced child management and nurturance skills, and decreased parental psychological distress (Jouriles et al., 1998).

## Early Intervention Programs

*Healthy Families New York.* This program is an example of a home visitation program that *has* reported some successes. After treatment, study participants were significantly *less* likely to have the following outcomes: (a) to deliver a low birth-weight baby, (b) to engage in neglectful behaviors, and (c) to engage in severe abuse of any form (Dumont et al., 2008).

*Nurse-Family Partnership (NFP).* The NFP program focuses on low-income, first-time parents and their children. The main focus of this evidence-based program is nurse home visitation that endeavors to improve the health, well-being, and self-sufficiency of parents. Evaluation methods have met scientific scrutiny as demonstrated in an assessment by Olds (2006). The nurse-practitioner model has demonstrated *long-term effectiveness* across a broad spectrum of locations. Components of the program that determined its effectiveness were implementation by professional staff, relatively lengthy intense treatments, and comprehensiveness of scope (Reynolds, Mathieson, & Topitzes, 2009). What is more, the program is cost-effective (Alexander et al., 2003).

*U. S. Triple-P—Positive Parenting Program.* In this program, researchers randomly selected 18 counties across the nation as study sites and worked with 600 service providers. The researchers assigned each county to deliver the Triple P services to half of the counties and services as usual to the other half. To reduce the effects of factors that are associated with parenting (e.g., income, services available), they used a stratified random sampling procedure to select the counties. Triple P programs provide a number of levels and types of treatment.

*Level 1* uses media and informational techniques in the community to reduce stigmatization of parents having difficulties. *Level 2* tries to normalize parenting practices through brief individual consultations and parenting seminars. *Level 3* aims to help parents with discrete child management skills. *Level 4* works with parents whose children have discernable problems. This level provides services such as group discussion, learning through observation and practice, and follow-up telephone calls. *Level 5* addresses additional more intense risk factors, such as mood disturbances.

Results of this well-controlled study are impressive. They showed large effect sizes (i.e., robust results) with three different populations: (a) families in which there is *substantiated child maltreatment,* (b) children living in *out-of-home placements,* and (c) children who *suffer maltreatment injuries.* Using some of the Triple P strategies with a small sample, other researchers have confirmed the effectiveness of Triple P (Boyle et al., 2010).

## Interventions for Children Exposed to Interparental Violence

Although children who have been exposed to interparental violence would likely benefit from involvement with various child welfare and mental health professionals, many such professionals have been slow to respond. The difficulties of these children are often overlooked because the children are often not themselves direct victims of physical or sexual abuse. Children who experience various forms of abuse directly are much more likely to come to the attention of

CPS and other professionals. A variety of new services for the children of battered women are increasingly becoming available, however, including *individual treatment, group therapy,* and *home visitation* (see Graham-Bermann & Hughes, 2003; Groves, 2002).

When responding to the service needs of any at-risk children, practitioners need to *screen for intimate partner violence* given the high rates of co-occurrence and the deleterious outcomes of exposure (English et al., 2008). An evaluation of 520 children demonstrated increased risks of PTSD, self-blaming behaviors, and functional impairments (Olaya, Ezpeleta, de la Osa, Granero, & Doménech, 2010). Similarly, another group of researchers documented the occurrence of *depression* in young adults. In this comparison, researchers assessed 1,175 young adults aged 20 to 24 years by means of an initial test of recollected memories of exposure to IPV and another test 2 years later that measured depression. This result demonstrates that exposure can function independently as a risk factor for later depression. That is, traumas other than exposure need not *co-exist* for the depression to occur (Russell et al., 2010).

*Pediatricians can support IPV screening* as well because of the established negative impact that exposure to IPV has (McColgan et al., 2010; see also Bair-Merritt et al., 2008). Researchers have begun the work of developing interventions for children exposed to IPV. One community-based program with a sample of 181 children between 8 and 12 years of age rendered promising results. Using scales to measure child adjustment problems and attitudes/beliefs, investigators specified that after treatment significantly fewer children were in the clinical range of externalizing and internalizing problems (Graham-Bermann et al., 2007; see also Katz & Windecker-Nelson, 2006).

*Group counseling.* One of the most common treatments for children exposed to interparental violence is group counseling The goals of such treatment for the child typically include the following: (a) *labeling feelings,* (b) *dealing with anger,* (c) *developing safety skills,* (d) *obtaining social support,* (e) *developing social competence* and a *good self-concept,* (f) *recognizing one's lack of responsibility for a parent or for the violence,* (g) *understanding family violence,* and (h) *specifying personal wishes about family relationships* (e.g., Jaffe, Wolfe, & Wilson, 1990). Data about the effectiveness of group counseling for such children are limited, but the technique appears promising. In addition, programs include goals such as helping a child develop a safety plan (Groves & Gewirtz, 2006). Several studies have demonstrated positive treatment effects of group counseling, including improved social skills, increased self-esteem, and decreased problematic behaviors and symptoms (e.g., Wagar & Rodway, 1995).

*Shelter programs.* A number of barriers exist in regard to offering in-shelter programs to children exposed to intimate partner violence. Often, a major shortcoming is *lack of an adequate staff,* especially a professionally trained staff. Interventions with mothers frequently undertake educational projects (Groves & Gewirtz, 2006). Frequently, women and children in shelters require specialized counseling, and programs need to be age-appropriate. Some shelter volunteers simply play with the children while their mothers participate in other therapeutic activities. Although in typical family counseling it is advisable to include fathers, this is not the case in shelter programs (see Poole, Beran, & Thurston, 2008, for a review of shelter programs).

*The Safe Start Initiative.* On the horizon is the Safe Start Initiative program. It centers attention on children exposed to violence in the home and the community. This initiative is developing under the leadership of the U.S. Department of Justice and works in collaboration with national, state, and local public and private agencies. The *goals* of this program are as follows: (a) to *increase awareness* about exposure to violence and identify affected children, (b) to intervene with parents in order to help them ensure the *safety and well-being of their children* at all times, and (c) to assure that practices of *programs are developmentally appropriate.* Implementation and evaluation of this program is under way (Kracke & Cohen, 2008).

---

**SECTION SUMMARY**

### Interventions for Neglected and Psychologically Maltreated Children

Academicians and practitioners have devised a growing number of intervention/prevention strategies to address the *unique aspects* of child neglect or psychological abuse. Preliminary efforts directed at neglecting parents have been effective in increasing positive parent-child interactions and enhancing parents' personal hygiene and nutrition skills. Few programs offer services directly to neglected children, but a few have successfully improved children's social interaction and developmental skills. Multiservice approaches to intervention have demonstrated some effectiveness. There is also evidence that home visitation programs targeting high-risk parents, as well as programs targeting parents with high-risk children, are generally effective in meeting many of their goals.

An exception is research concerning the intervention programs that have been developed for one specific form of child psychological maltreatment: exposure to interparental violence. Such interventions typically include group therapies for children, and some programs use a multiservice approach. Preliminary outcome evaluations suggest that these programs demonstrate significant benefits, including reductions in problem behaviors and symptoms for children and increased skills for parents.

---

## Common Problems in Implementation for All Programs

In addition to possible deficits in program content, at least two events undermine program efficacy: (a) dropping out of therapy and (b) the failure of personnel implementing the program to follow instructions.

*Therapy drop-outs.* One limitation associated with home visitation programs and therapy, in general, is that a significant number of families drop out of treatment before service goals are fully met. A contemporary comparison of completers and drop-outs among families with children ages 2 to 10 produced useful results. Of the 52 families who began treatment, 11 dropped out during assessment, before any counseling had begun. Of the remaining 41 families, 51% dropped out during various stages before completion. Analyses identified four significant predictors of drop-out (Topham & Wampler, 2008):

| | |
|---|---|
| • Lack of satisfactory social support | • Older maternal age |
| • Low acceptance of the child | • Older child age |

*Lack of correct implementation by workers.* One problem may be widespread variability in workers' training causing failures to execute program instructions correctly. Inadequate training is sometimes the result of insufficient funding. In addition, there is little evidence that changes associated with participation in such programs continue over the long term. It is also unclear whether home visitation programs fulfill their broader goal of integrating families into their communities so they can access community resources. Future research should attempt to determine the specific conditions associated with program success, such as the types of families that benefit and the specific components of intervention that are effective (Palusci & Haney, 2010).

*Interactions with difficult children.* The interaction of difficult child behaviors and particular parent characteristics can lead to negative parent-child interactions. Helping parents learn how they can best respond to behaviorally challenging children should help to reduce abuse and neglect. In working with a sample of Dutch parents with irritable children, van den Boom (1994, 1995) observed that the parents often approached the children during times when the children were fussy and ignored the children when the fussiness stopped. Through time, the parent-child interactions became increasingly negative.

To test his observations, van den Boom randomly assigned parents of irritable children to experimental and control groups. Parents in the experimental group attended information sessions and received home visitation, the purposes of which were to promote parent-child attachment and to teach parents how to respond to their children appropriately. Evaluations after 12 months and 18 months indicated that, compared with the control group, *mothers* in the experimental group were *more responsive and attentive,* and their children were more *securely attached* (van den Boom, 1994, 1995, cited in Wekerle & Wolfe, 1998).

## Elements of Successful Programs

Although the findings of studies have provided some reason for optimism, it has not been clear why some programs are effective and some are not. A number of experts have asked, "What are the specific components of prevention/intervention programs that make them effective?" The Centers for Disease Control and Prevention (2009) made considerable headway in answering this question by conducting a **meta-analysis** of parenting programs. The meta-analysis drew from two basic program components, *content* and *delivery,* and centered on two possible outcomes, acquisition of *parenting skills* and decreases in children's *externalizing behavior.* Three program components were *less effective* than others: (a) teaching parents how to problem solve about child behaviors, (b) teaching parents how to promote children's academic and cognitive skills, and (c) including ancillary services as part of the parenting program. See Table 3.10 for a summary of specific components of programs that are effective.

**TABLE 3.10** Components in Effective Parenting Programs

| *Acquisition of Parenting Skills* | *Decreases in Children's Externalizing Behaviors* |
|---|---|
| Teaching parents emotional communication skills | Teaching parents the correct use of time-out |
| Teaching parents positive parent-child interaction skills | Teaching parents to respond consistently to their child |
| Requiring parents to practice with their children during program sessions | Teaching parents to interact positively with their child |

SOURCE: Centers for Disease Control and Prevention, 2009.

## Policy Issues

Dutch sociologists have highlighted the ambiguous status of children. Their position lies somewhere between the private and public domains. Consequently, the division of responsibility for children lies between parents and society's social institutions (van Daalen, 2010).

*Legal issues concerning parental behaviors.* It is likely that nearly all parents, at some level, psychologically mistreat their children at some time by saying or doing hurtful things they later regret. Such mistakes are a characteristic of most intimate relationships. Legislators must determine when parental "mistakes" cross the line and require a legal response. To enforce a law, of course, statutes banning psychological abuse of children depend on specific *definitions* of psychological maltreatment. Hence, operational definitions supersede all other considerations. Terms such as *mental injury* are overly vague, yet requiring that a child's injuries be *substantial* and *observable* is problematic. The effects of psychological maltreatment may not be readily identifiable, or they may be identifiable only in adolescence or later in life. Indeed, some of the most damaging neglect occurs during the first 2 years of life before a child can verbally communicate distress (see Erickson & Egeland's summary of the [2010] Minnesota Longitudinal Study of High Risk Parents and Children).

*Neglect and maltreatment investigations.* Both Child Protective Services (CPS) and law enforcement have made headway in establishing *best practices* for investigating suspected neglect cases. Each agency asks different questions, such as "Does this child need protection?" or "Does someone need to be arrested and prosecuted?" Although there are circumstances in which either CPS or law enforcement works alone, best practices recommend conducting most investigations with a *multidisciplinary team.* Team investigations have many advantages, such as sparing the child from *repeated questioning, sharing expertise,* and *joint decision making.* Also, teams are better equipped to address issues relevant to the nonoffending parent. Is the nonoffending parent being abused? Is he or she overwhelmed by the knowledge that his or her partner has been neglecting the child? (Pence, 2010; see also Cross, Finkelhor, & Ormrod, 2005).

Even severe cases of psychological abuse are difficult to prove in court. Consequently, law enforcement personnel almost never file charges against parents for psychological abuse *only.* To ensure a conviction, prosecutors usually find a *tag-along* charge consisting of some other type of abuse, such as physical abuse. This approach is pragmatic because psychological abuse is nearly always embedded in every other subtype of child abuse (Hollins & Hankin, 2005). At a minimum, legal personnel need to take the following steps to conduct an investigation of potentially illegal psychological maltreatment (S. N. Hart et al., 2010):

- Gather relevant information about the incident, what is observed, and what is suspected
- Question multiple sources, such as family members, neighbors, and school personnel
- Use valid and reliable assessment instruments and procedures
- Confer with other experts as necessary

Because prosecuting child abuse perpetrators is especially challenging, the National Center for Prosecution of Child Abuse (2001) provides specialized classes for prosecutors, field investigators, and other legal personnel.

*Safe Families Act.* Congress passed the Adoption and Safe Families Act of 1997 (P.L. 105-89), which mandates that various agencies make decisions in the best interests of the child. The need for a change in the law arose when interpretations of existing law compelled CPS workers to reunite the child with an abusing parent. Current law, however, instructs caseworkers to remove children from the home only when absolutely necessary for their safety and to provide a rationale for their decision making. Most CPS workers judge exposure to family violence as dangerous to children's mental health.

*Safe-haven laws.* Fortunately, passage of *safe-haven* laws has taken place in the majority of U.S. states. These laws allow biological mothers to give up their *newborn infants* anonymously in specific safe locations (e.g., hospitals, fire stations) with full immunity from prosecution. Since 1999, when Texas's *Baby Moses* abandoned baby law was passed, more than 40 other states have passed similar legislation (see Phillipsen, 2003). In Los Angeles County, the number of safely surrendered infants was 76 (January 1, 2001, to March 2, 2010). During the same period, the number of abandoned babies who survived was 13, and the number of abandoned babies who died was 49 (Inter-Agency Council on Child Abuse and Neglect [ICAN], 2010). Some experts criticize the laws as primarily "crime control theater." More information is needed before declaring the laws a success (Hammond, Miller, & Griffin, 2010).

*The Child Abuse Prevention and Treatment Act (CAPTA; 2003).* CAPTA specifies that maltreated children "must have access to early intervention under Part C of the *Individuals with Disabilities Education Act*" (Stahmer, Sutton, Fox, & Leslie, 2008, p. 99). Accordingly, agencies charged with children's welfare have begun the quest to *refer, screen/evaluate, deliver services,* and *track* maltreated/neglected infants and toddlers 0 to 3 years of age. Much work lies ahead in finding ways to make referrals, but innovative policies are on the horizon.

*Poverty.* A low socioeconomic level is associated with every type of abuse. In some cases, such as *failure to thrive,* the effects of poverty are more demonstrable. The same is true of *medical neglect.* Although progressive governments around the world are more aware of the negative effects of poverty on children, to a large extent, responses to poverty are driven by dissimilar assumptions about its causes and solutions (see Guetzkow, 2010).

## Who Is Accountable for Children's Exposure to Marital Violence?

Many in American society are quick to blame a woman who knowingly allows her child to be exposed to her partner's violence. Under some circumstances, social workers within Child Protective Services (CPS) have been particularly unsympathetic and even harmful to battered women (Douglas & Walsh, 2010; S. P. Johnson & Sullivan, 2008). These workers appear to blame the mother for not protecting her child from an abusive father or husband, but evidence about their official actions is sparse. Some observers argue that workers should *hold the violent person accountable rather than placing the blame on victims,* whether the victims are children or adults (Edleson, 1998). This faction holds that children are better protected when the battered mother is supported and protected (Honer, 2008). How best to grapple with the clash of belief systems of personnel within the different agencies is under investigation (Postmus & Merritt, 2010).

Recent years have seen a number of gains in terms of increasing collaboration between CPS workers and battered women's advocates. The *Greenbook initiative* represents one of the broadest attempts to learn how to improve system responses to families experiencing both child maltreatment and domestic violence (see the *Journal of Interpersonal Violence,* 2008, Vol. 28, No. 7, Special issue). Greenbook programs generally found that to collaborate effectively, agencies needed considerable time to understand organizational differences. Human resources, such as *leadership, material resources, trust,* and *commitment,* were key elements in establishing successful collaborations (D. Banks, Dutch, & Wang, 2008). It is especially helpful if programs help CPS workers to identify a *batterer's controlling behavior,* rather than just his physical violence. It is helpful for workers to understand the battered mother's decision-making process (see Mandel, 2010). More research is still needed (Postmus & Merritt, 2010).

An independent examination of four jurisdictions by an attorney produced actual evidence of events in cases of co-occurrence of domestic violence and child abuse. She examined agency policies, dependency court rulings, and CPS workers' actions. Her 5-year investigation uncovered numerous *shortcomings* including the following (Hulbert, 2008):

- Jurisdictions enact significantly different policies.
- Even counties within the same jurisdiction adopt dissimilar policies.
- A major problem throughout jurisdictions is lack of documentation.
- Some courts do not articulate a ruling, but simply state a return date.
- CPS workers may not state why they removed a child from his home.

- CPS workers may not state the rationale for their out-of-home placements.
- CPS workers had offered referral services to 53% of parents before removing a child.
- CPS workers did believe that exposure to domestic violence was harmful to children.
- They did not uniformly document findings about the identity of the abuser.
- They found the mother to be the victim in 65% of the cases.
- 19% of the victims were incorrectly classified as co-batterers.
- In some cases they unknowingly placed the child in a different abusive home because of an insufficient investigation.
- Child visitation guidelines for the offending parent were not specified.
- 82% of parents investigated voluntarily agreed to their child's removal without court adjudication.

## Lack of Available Programs

To our knowledge, no prevention programs have yet been established with the explicit purpose of preventing only *child psychological maltreatment,* broadly defined. This is a curious state of affairs, particularly given the evidence that psychological maltreatment is a very pervasive form of child maltreatment. In addition, research findings consistent with the notion that psychological maltreatment is the core component of the negative outcomes associated with all forms of child maltreatment suggest the need for prevention efforts specifically targeting this form of abuse. First, psychological maltreatment has only recently been recognized as a distinct form of child maltreatment. Indeed, many experts in the field argue that *awareness* of the problem continues to be limited among some professional groups. In addition, state and federal *funding* has not been available to support intervention and prevention research or program implementation (Binggeli et al., 2001; Thompson & Wilcox, 1995).

Research showing that more than 40% of very young children with substantiated cases of psychological maltreatment have *severe developmental problems* has crystallized the need for further government intervention. Although parents have the principal responsibility for taking care of their children, community professionals and governmental policymakers are accountable as well—"It Takes a Village" (see Dubowitz, 2010). If nothing else, the *cost* in dollars, not to mention lives, has spurred action. Two estimates are as follows: (a) $80 billion annually (Alexander et al., 2003), and (b) $103.8 billion for 2007 (Wang & Holton, 2007).

Binggeli and colleagues (2001) argue that "efforts to prevent psychological maltreatment should be embedded in comprehensive programs designed to prevent a variety of problems" (p. 72). These researchers suggest a two-tier approach to helping families, in which the *first tier* would focus on education and support strategies. Education and support for families could be delivered, for example, through parent education classes that focus on topics such as effective parenting skills, knowledge of child development, stress management techniques, and conflict resolution. Binggeli et al. also suggest the strategy of education through sensitization campaigns. *Media campaigns* such as "Words Can Hurt" could serve to educate the general public regarding the harmful nature of parent-child verbal aggression. The *second tier* in Binggeli et al.'s approach would consist of prevention efforts more typical of those already used by many Child Protective Service agencies, such as home visitation programs.

*Many entities in society are involved in improving the lives of children.* These include government as well as private agencies and institutions. Government tracking of prevalence issues and funding of research forms the foundation of these efforts. In addition, a large number of academicians have devoted their careers to understanding and developing prevention strategies and treatments to reduce the scourge of family violence. Educational institutions have increased their involvement, and more and more members of society have volunteered their time and effort.

**SECTION SUMMARY**

### Chapter Summary for Neglect, Psychological Maltreatment, and Children Exposed to Marital Violence

The definitional complexities of child neglect and psychological maltreatment have left prevalence issues largely undetermined. Researchers have obtained much of their information about rates and correlates of child neglect from official reports. Although such reports are limited, it is clear that hundreds of thousands of cases of child neglect and psychological maltreatment are reported each year in the United States. Child neglect is the most frequently reported form of child maltreatment, accounting for 45% to 55% of reported maltreatment cases. By comparison, psychological maltreatment may be the least frequently reported form of child maltreatment. Estimates of psychological maltreatment range from 7% to 30%. The prevalence of children exposed to marital violence ranges from almost 10% to 66%. The majority of child neglect victims are under age 5, and the risk for neglect appears to decline as children become older. Reports of psychological maltreatment increase as children become older.

The *effects of neglect* are serious and can last a lifetime. Relative to other forms of maltreatment, less research has examined the unique effects of child neglect on children's functioning, although an increasing number of methodologically sound investigations are appearing. This oversight is troubling, given the high frequency with which neglect occurs and the serious consequences associated with child psychological maltreatment. Child neglect is associated with a variety of problems, including social difficulties, cognitive and academic deficits, behavioral and emotional problems, and physical dysfunction.

Studies of the negative effects associated with *psychological maltreatment* are limited in both number and quality, making interpretations of the findings more difficult. One consideration is that while psychological maltreatment is rarely reported to child abuse agencies or the police, it may constitute a part of almost every other form of abuse. A considerable body of knowledge has accumulated concerning one specific form of child psychological maltreatment: *exposure to interparental violence.*

The *methodological problems* inherent in effect studies, particularly the discrepancy among definitions, complicate interpretation of the findings. In addition to the presence of the target variable, a large number of other influential variables may simultaneously influence children's behavior (e.g., parental alcoholism, low income, and maternal impairment). Ferreting out specific effects among behaviors that are multidetermined is difficult, but newer statistical methods are making progress.

The *characteristics of maltreated children and their parents* are gradually coming to light. Available research has shown no consistent gender differences among neglected and psychologically maltreated victims. With regard to neglect, however, research has clearly revealed a pattern of racial differences. African American children are most at risk as are children in low socioeconomic families. No racial differences in psychological maltreatment differences have emerged, but this group of children does more frequently come from low-income families. Victims of psychological maltreatment, including those exposed to marital violence, suffer from social, emotional, and behavioral difficulties and intellectual deficits. The victims also exhibit increased aggression, delinquency, self-abuse, anxiety, and hostility. Worst of all, these effects have repercussions extending into adulthood, thus creating a lifetime legacy of the effects of childhood neglect and maltreatment.

The *characteristics of maltreating parents* are also associated with important psychosocial markers. Most reported cases of neglect and psychological maltreatment show that female parents are more likely than male parents to be the perpetrators. Some variables, such as fathers' neglect to provide for their children financially, are not counted in current surveys of neglect. Findings with regard to variables in psychologically maltreating parents have established that these parents exhibit interpersonal and social difficulties, poor problem-solving skills, substance abuse, and psychiatric maladjustment.

Lack of sufficient knowledge about the traits of child victims and their parents presents several challenges to those who respond to issues of child neglect and psychological abuse. Development of treatment programs is a rapidly growing field. Evaluations of some of the programs show efficacy in assisting families. Multisystem approaches have produced the most clear-cut improvements. Nevertheless, treatment programs are not reliably successful. Policymakers, child social agencies, and practitioners all need evidence-based information to address child neglect and child maltreatment. The legislature, for example, cannot set meaningful legal standards for addressing child neglect and child psychological maltreatment without knowing what it is and why it must be outlawed.

***Future Focus.*** There are at least two important conceptual/scientific areas that could change the current conceptions of child neglect and psychological maltreatment. First is the *growing pre-eminence of children's rights* (International Society for Prevention of Child Abuse and Neglect, 2008). Second is the *emergence of neurobiological and psychobiological science* (see Watts-English, Fortson, Gibler, Hooper, & De Bellis, 2006). Professionals in the field of child maltreatment should focus more effort on increasing public awareness and understanding of child neglect and psychological maltreatment. More societal support is needed to garner support and resources for research efforts aimed at reducing the incidence and harmful effects associated with this form of child abuse.

1.  Why do experts often refer to child neglect as the "most forgotten" form of child maltreatment? What factors have contributed to scholars' historical lack of interest in the topic?

2.  Why has defining child neglect (or psychological maltreatment) been such a challenge? Discuss the many factors that influence definitions.

3.  What are the various forms or subtypes of child neglect, including prenatal neglect (or psychological maltreatment)?

4.  Should prenatal neglect be criminalized? Should exposure to interparental violence be criminalized? Why or why not?

5.  What "causes" child neglect?

6.  What are the short- and long-term effects associated with child neglect?

7.  Why have researchers and practitioners frequently overlooked child psychological maltreatment?

8.  What are the various initial and long-term effects associated with child psychological maltreatment?

9.  What kinds of intervention strategies are used to help neglected and psychologically maltreated children and their families?

10. What factors appear to make treatment for child neglect and psychological maltreatment effective?

For chapter-specific resources including audio and video links, SAGE research articles, additional case studies, and more, please visit www.sagepub.com/barnett3e.

# CHAPTER

# 4

# Child Physical Abuse

**CASE HISTORY**   Kenny Fell Off of His Razor

Kenny was placed in foster care because his community's Department of Child Protective Services (CPS) determined that his family was "in conflict." The placement was made after 10-year-old Kenny was seen at the local hospital's emergency room for bruises, welts, and cuts on his back. According to his mother's report to emergency room personnel, the boy "fell off of his Razor" (scooter) while riding down a hill near the family home. Kenny was very quiet during the visit, never speaking but occasionally nodding his head in affirmation of his mother's report. The attending physician, however, believed that Kenny's injuries were unlikely to have occurred as the result of such a fall. Rather, they appeared consistent with the kinds of injuries a child might have from being slapped repeatedly or possibly whipped with a belt.

Initially, Kenny's mother persisted in her story that Kenny had fallen from his Razor, but after the doctor told her that the injuries could not have resulted from such an accident, she confessed that her boyfriend of several years, Sam, had some strong opinions about how children should behave and how they should be disciplined. She reported that Sam had a "short temper" when it came to difficult behavior in children and that he sometimes "lost his cool" in disciplining Kenny. She also suggested that Kenny's behavior could often be very difficult to control. She said that Kenny had numerous problems, including difficulties in school (e.g., trouble with reading) and with peers (e.g., physically fighting with other children); she described both acting-out behaviors (e.g., setting fire to objects, torturing and killing small animals, stealing) and oppositional behaviors (e.g., skipping school, refusing to do homework, breaking curfew, being noncompliant with requests).

In interviews with a CPS worker, Kenny revealed that he was, in fact, experiencing physical abuse inflicted by his mother's boyfriend. Kenny reluctantly acknowledged that Sam frequently disciplined him by repeatedly slapping a belt across his back. He also talked about an incident when he had been trying to teach the ducks to "swim underwater." When Sam saw Kenny submerging the ducklings' heads under the water, he became very angry and "taught Kenny a lesson" by holding Kenny's head underwater repeatedly. Kenny was tearful as he told this story and stated that at the time, he thought he was going to drown.

After Kenny had been in foster care for several weeks, his foster mother indicated that he was doing very well and described him as a "remarkably adaptive child." She said she found him to be a "warm, loving kid," and he had not exhibited "any behavior problems other than what you might expect from a 10-year-old boy." She reported also that Kenny "hoped to go home soon" because he "missed his mother and Sam." He believed that he was placed in foster care because he was disobedient toward his mother and her boyfriend, and because he hadn't been doing well in school.

T he case history presented above describes a typical case of child abuse. Until the 1960s, society was relatively unaware of the hellish characteristic of abused children's lives. People considered physical child abuse a mythical or rare phenomenon that occurred only in some people's imaginations or in sick, lower-class families. As it is now more widely known, however, child maltreatment is an ugly reality for millions of children. In 1990, the U.S. Advisory Board on Child Abuse and Neglect described the level of child maltreatment in the United States as a national emergency.

This chapter on child physical abuse (CPA) first offers a discourse on the definition and prevalence of child physical abuse. Following these topics, there is a discussion of short-term and long-term consequences associated with CPA. Next, there is a presentation about the typical characteristics of physically abused children and the adults who abuse them. A dialogue of methodological research problems and explanations of child physical abuse appears next. The chapter concludes with recommendations for addressing the problem.

## SCOPE OF THE PROBLEM

### What Is Child Physical Abuse?

One of the most significant issues in understanding the problem of CPA is that of defining the term *child physical abuse*. Consider the following situations:

- Ryan and his brother, Matthew, were playing with their Power Rangers in Ryan's bedroom when they got into a disagreement. Both boys began hitting each other and calling each other names. Their mother heard the commotion and came running into the room and separated the two boys. She then took each boy, pulled down his trousers, put him over her knee, and spanked him several times.

- Angela's baby, Maria, had colic from the day she was born. This meant that from 4:00 in the afternoon until 8:00 in the evening, every day, Maria cried inconsolably. No matter what Angela did, she could not get Maria to stop crying. One evening, after 5-month-old Maria had been crying for 3 hours straight, Angela became so frustrated that she began shaking Maria. The shaking caused Maria to cry more loudly, which in turn provoked Angela into shaking the infant more vigorously. Angela shook Maria until the baby lost consciousness.

- Jimmy, a 3-year-old, was playing with his puppy in his backyard when he tried to make the puppy stay near him by pulling roughly on the dog's tail. Jimmy's father saw the child vigorously pulling on the puppy's tail and yelled at him to stop. When Jimmy did not respond quickly, his father grabbed Jimmy's arm and pulled him away from the dog. The father then began pulling on Jimmy's ear, actually tearing the skin, to "teach him a lesson" about the appropriate way to treat a dog.

These vignettes portray a range of behaviors, from actions that may or may not be considered abusive to those that are clearly abusive. Prior to the 1960s, however, few, if any, of these actions would have been labeled abusive. Society's growing awareness of physical child abuse and researchers' growing understanding helped to evolve more accurate definitions. Furthermore, researchers and practitioners concerned with child physical abuse have also discovered that violence against children may sometimes take an unusual form or be more difficult to recognize.

## Definitions of Child Physical Abuse

While recognition of CPA was increasing, the definition continued to be restrictive. The definitions of CPA that first emerged commonly focused on *acts of violence* that cause some form of *observable harm*. In 1988, the National Center on Child Abuse and Neglect broadened the definition of physical abuse to include two standards (U.S. Department of Health & Human Services, 1988).

- **Harm standard:** Recognizes children as CPA victims *if* they have observable injuries that last at least 48 hours.
- **Endangerment standard:** Recognizes children as abuse victims if they are deemed to be substantially *at risk* for injury (*endangerment*).

Although some discrepancies exist, many experts include the following signs and symptoms as reflective of physical child abuse (see "Signs of Physical Abuse," n.d.; see also Wiehe, 1997):

| | |
|---|---|
| Bruises, black eyes, welts, lacerations, or rope marks | A child's report of physical abuse |
| Physical signs of being punished or signs of being restrained | Bone fractures, broken bones, or skull fractures |
| Open wounds, cuts, punctures, or untreated injuries in stages of healing | Sprains, dislocations, or internal injuries/bleeding |
| A sudden change in behavior | |

- Child Abuse Prevention and Treatment Act (CAPTA) definition of abuse:

"Any recent act or failure to act on the part of a parent or caretaker, which results in death, serious physical or emotional harm, sexual abuse, or exploitation, or an act or failure to act which presents an imminent risk of serious harm." (Child Welfare Information Gateway, 2009, p. 1)

- Centers for Disease Control and Prevention (CDC; 2008, p. 2):

"The *intentional* use of physical force by a parent or caregiver against a child that results in, or has the potential to result in, physical injury."

## Physical Punishment and Child Rearing

Many people consider some of the acts listed (e.g., slapping, paddling, spanking) as *normal* violence. They consider such acts to be acceptable as part of the punishment of children in the course of child rearing. Mainstream Americans use physical punishment as a form of discipline, even with very young children (Watts-English, Fortson, Gibler, Hooper, & De Bellis, 2006). After all, what else can a parent do to manage a noncompliant child? A definition of physical punishment is as follows (Gershoff, 2008, p. 9):

Physical punishment is the use of physical force with the intention of causing the child to experience bodily pain or discomfort so as to correct or punish the child's behavior.

*Protective use of force.* Most authorities make a distinction between *physical punishment* and *protective physical restraint.* This distinction occurs because parents frequently *must* use physical force to prevent a child from touching a hot stove or running into the street. Parents might also hold a child's hand down to stop him from hitting a baby.

As Graziano and Namaste (1990, pp. 459–460) state:

Slapping, spanking, paddling, and, generally hitting children for purposes of discipline are accepted, pervasive, adult behaviors in U.S. families. In these instances, although anger, physical attack, and pain are involved between two people of vastly different size, weight, and strength, such behavior is commonly accepted as a proper exercise of adult authority over children.

## Physical Discipline—The Debate

A heated debate about the use of corporal punishment is ongoing. Social scientists and pediatricians, in particular, decry the use of corporal punishment against children. Children are the only group in society that may be hit legally. Even convicted criminals are safeguarded against corporal punishment.

*Sociological objections.* Perhaps the most significant critic of the cultural acceptance of corporal punishment is Murray Straus, who has attracted considerable attention in recent years for his research and views on spanking. From a *sociological theoretical point of view,* Straus (1991c) argues that spanking is harmful for two reasons: (a) When authority figures spank, they are, in essence, *condoning the use of violence* as a way of dealing with frustration and settling disputes; and (b) the implicit message of acceptance of this form of *violence contributes to violence* in other aspects of society. Others point out that adults who administer punishment that reduces a behavior (even if temporarily) have *modeled how, when, and why* one uses violence against another (Bandura, Ross, & Ross, 1961).

*Learning researchers.* Based on laboratory findings, researchers in learning condemn the use of physical punishment on the grounds that it is *ineffective* in achieving the results anticipated by parents, school administrators, prison officials, and others. According to this group of scientists, *a punisher is an event that decreases responses.* By definition, therefore, punishment *cannot* teach *new,* desirable behaviors. Unfortunately, the research in this area is complex and not readily understandable to nonspecialists. Nevertheless, animal research has led to a number of firm conclusions about the use of punishment, a few of which follow (see LaViolette & Barnett, 2000, for a review):

- A punishment can be either *biologically unlearned* (e.g., physical pain) or *learned* (e.g., unpleasantness of *being sworn at*).
- A punishment is *not the opposite of a reward* (reinforcement).
- Mildly punished behavior *will recover* (i.e., occur again).
- To be more effective, punishment must be delivered *immediately* after an unwanted response.
- To be more effective, punishment must be delivered *consistently* after every unwanted response.
- Punishment that *builds up gradually* in intensity is ineffective.

Even this short list of empirical findings demonstrates how faulty assumptions about punishment as an effective tool for managing children's behavior really are. The findings do, however, point out why members of society are disappointed when their use of corporal punishment lacks long-term effectiveness. In particular, the assumption that gradually building up the intensity of spankings is the correct way to deliver punishment is inaccurate.

*Neurobiological effects of punishment.* Correlational data revealed a significant relationship between harsh childhood physical punishment and the volume of gray matter assessed in adults ages 18 to 25. In this analysis, 1,455 young adults participated in a screening experience for the purpose of subject selection. Among the total, 23 participants had been harshly punished over a minimum of years and 22 had not been harshly punished. Morphometry (neuroimaging of brain anatomy) revealed that harshly punished participants had significantly reduced volumes of gray matter in three brain regions. Correlations between the brain volume measures and IQ scores (WAIS-III) were significant as well. The results suggest that harsh physical punishment has adverse effects on brain development, but correlational data cannot verify causality (Tomoda et al., 2009).

*Counter-productiveness of punishment.* One element of the debate about corporal punishment is whether it is harmful, neutral, or helpful. One faction holds that corporal punishment does *no harm* (Rosemond, 2005). From the other faction, Straus (2005) maintains that such claims are a myth. Using social science research as a foundation, experts have summarized a list of reasons why punishment may be counterproductive (Gershoff, 2008):

1. It does not help children learn why their behavior is wrong or what they could do alternatively, instead of the punished behavior.
2. The physiological response aroused by the pain of the spanking may prevent the child from learning the lesson that the punishment was supposed to teach.
3. It fails to communicate why refraining from certain behaviors is important. That is, children will learn nothing about morality from a spanking.
4. It demonstrates how using force enables one to control others (modeling).
5. It increases the probability that children will attribute hostile motivations to others.
6. It may cause children to experience fear of their parents, or fear of school if punishment is used at school.
7. Since parents *love* their children, adding punishment to parent-child interactions may increase a child's belief that violence and love are linked.

*Spillover effects of spanking.* Research also supports Straus's (1991c) viewpoint that spanking is positively correlated with *other forms of family violence,* including sibling abuse and spouse assault. As one illustration, children who had been physically punished during the previous year were three times more likely to have assaulted a sibling during that year. As another illustration, spanking is correlated with crime outside the home, including self-reported delinquency, arrest, and homicide (Straus, 1991c). Other researchers have shown a connection between *spanking* and *antisocial behaviors* such as cheating, telling lies, and disobedience in school (e.g., Dadds & Salmon, 2003; Grogan-Kaylor, 2005). Findings suggest that parents who use spanking to punish antisocial behavior are actually contributing to subsequent antisocial behavior in their children (Straus, Sugarman, & Giles-Sims, 1997).

Despite calls from a large number of social entities and evidence that physical punishment is ineffective and counterproductive, a majority of Americans remain convinced that spanking is not abusive. Indeed, many U.S. states explicitly exclude acts of corporal punishment from their legislative definitions in child abuse statutes.

*Children's assessments of punishment.* While adults in many spheres of life have voiced their opinions about punishment, social scientists have rarely taken the time to query children about their opinions. To fill this gap, researchers asked 108 children 6 to 10 years old to judge 4 vignettes in which a mother disciplines a child for playing with balls in the living room and breaking a lamp. The types of punishment vary as follows: (a) *time-out,* (b) *withdrawal of a privilege* (e.g., TV viewing), (c) *reasoning/explaining,* and (d) *spanking.*

Effects from exposure to spanking were varied. Some of the results are as follows (Vittrup & Holden, 2010):

- Overall, children judged spanking to be the least fair method of discipline.
- Younger children judged spanking as fairer than older children did.
- Older children judged withdrawal of privileges as fairer than younger children did.
- Older children, relative to younger children, thought recurrence of the punished behavior was less likely in the short term after reasoning.
- Younger children, relative to older children, thought recurrence of the punished behavior was less likely in the short term following time-out.
- The combined group of children thought spanking (or reasoning) would be most effective in the short run.
- The combined group thought that spanking would not reduce recurrence of the punished behavior in the long run, but reasoning would have a longer deterrent effect.
- Although children judged reasoning to be more effective than the other methods in the long run, they did not think reasoning would totally prevent recurrence of the punished behavior.
- The children thought that the spanked children would not misbehave right away because they would be afraid of getting another spanking.
- Neither race nor socioeconomic status (SES) contributed to differences between children.

## SECTION SUMMARY

### Differentiating Abuse From Punishment

The complexity of CPA is evident in attempts to define what specific circumstances constitute abuse. Although most experts agree that CPA includes a range of behaviors that cause observable harm to children, there is less agreement about the boundary between CPA and normal parenting practices, or behaviors that do not result in observable harm (e.g., spanking). Currently, the National Incidence Studies (NIS) report abuse using two standards: (a) The harm standard—Children are CPA victims if they have observable injuries that last at least 48 hours; (b) The endangerment standard—Children are abuse victims if they were deemed to be substantially at risk for injury (endangerment).

Controversy especially centers on behaviors that fall somewhere between normal and excessive corporal punishment. Sociologists criticize spanking because it both models and condones violence. Learning experts within the field of psychology criticize punishment in general for many reasons. Primarily, laboratory research has shown how ineffective punishment is unless it is administered "perfectly," and even then punishment seldom eliminates unwanted behaviors permanently. On the other hand, the trauma of harsh punishment is likely to cause permanent neurobiological changes. Both sociologists and psychologists criticize punishment because it is counterproductive. It might temporarily eradicate a behavior, but it teaches nothing—that is, it teaches no acceptable new behaviors. Some experts believe spanking has spillover effects, increasing the probability of violence throughout the family and society. Children do not always perceive punishment as fair.

## PREVALENCE/INCIDENCE OF CHILD PHYSICAL ABUSE

Researchers generally use one of two methods of estimation: Official estimates come from government agencies, based on the numbers of cases reported to law enforcement and social service agencies. Other estimates come from self-reports of victims and perpetrators as gathered by survey research. As in other areas of family violence, there are several impediments to reporting. First, medical doctors through inexperience may not recognize child abuse. Second, they may decide to delay or not to report the abuse at all for a host of reasons (court time, belief system, disappointing responses from police or CPS). Other mandated reporters may also decide not to report. The general public may not report for reasons such as lack of certainty (CDC, 2008; Daka, 2009; Sege & Flaherty, 2008). Assessment of recalled CPA among adult samples has suffered from a lack of standardized measurement. Uniformity may improve, however, with the development of a new CPA screening tool crafted using opinions of experts in 28 countries and field tested in 7 countries (Dunne et al., 2009).

> **Department of Health & Human Services (DHHS; U.S. Department of Health & Human Services, 2008) [CPS records].**
>
> The number of substantiated (i.e., found to be true) victims of child maltreatment is 758,289.
>
> Of this number, 16.1% were physically abused.

### Official Estimates

Official reporting statistics over the last two decades indicate that reports of child physical abuse from the DHHS have decreased from 1992 to 2004. Presented in the box below are the two major data collections for child abuse.

> **The U.S. Department of Health & Human Services (2008) identified 758,289 maltreated children.** Department of Health & Human Services uses only records from Child Protective Services.
>
> **NIS-4 (2005–2006)** identified 1,256,600 maltreated children.
>
> **National Incidence Study** uses data from CPS, professionals, school counselors, and others (Sedlak et al., 2010).

> *National Incidence Studies (NIS-4, Sedlak et al., 2010) (Data from multiple sources— goes beyond the U.S. DHHS to capture data from individuals such as school counselors and psychologists in private practice)*

See Table 4.1 for a summary of statistics for physical abuse.

| TABLE 4.1 | Numbers of Children Reported for Physical Abuse on the Harm Standard in the National Incidence Studies |
|---|---|

| Physically Abused Children | | | | | |
|---|---|---|---|---|---|
| NIS-2 (1986) | | NIS-3 (1993) | | NIS-4 (2005–2006) | |
| 269,700 | 4.3 per 1,000 children | 381,700 | 5.7 per 1,000 children | 323,000 | 4.4 per 1,000 children |

## Injuries

Some findings about injuries and fatalities are as follows:

*Bureau of Justice Statistics—Special Report (Rand, 1997). Many victims of abuse are unwilling or unable to report information about the perpetrators.*

- Of children <12 years of age presenting at emergency rooms for treatment.
  - Half of those treated were under 5 years of age.
  - The rate of injury was 1.6 per 1,000 children < 12.
- Relatives inflicted 56% of the injuries, acquaintances inflicted 34.1%, and strangers inflicted 9.7%.

*Fatalities by Physical Abuse Only (U.S. Department of Health & Human Services, 2008)*

- 22.9% of fatalities were attributed to physical abuse.
- 69.9% of all child fatalities were caused by parents.

*National Child Abuse and Neglect Data System (NCANDS; 2008), Victims by Age and Race for 2007. NCANDS describes parents/caregivers only.*

- Male infants (18.5%) were more likely than female infants (15.39%) to become a fatality.
- 41.1% of all fatality victims were *White*, 26.1% of victims were *African American*, 16.9% were *Hispanic*, and the remainder was unknown.
- There were 1,400 child fatalities in 2002 (U.S. Department of Health & Human Services, 2002b).

*National Violent Death Reporting System (NVDRS): 1,374 deaths in children under 5 with 16 states reporting (Klevens & Leeb, 2010)*

- 52% occurred in children under 1 year of age.
- 600 were attributable to child maltreatment.

> **The Centers for Disease Control and Prevention (CDC; 2008).** The Morbidity and Mortality Weekly Report (2008):
>
> - CPS investigated roughly 3.6 million cases of abuse of children less than 18 years of age between October 2005 and September 2006.
> - Of these, CPS substantiated the abuse for 905,000 (25.1%) of the cases.
> - An investigation of very young children revealed that 3,957 (13.2%) infants <1 week of age were victims of physical abuse.

- 58.9% were male.
- 41.6% of victims were non-Hispanic White, 36.8% were non-Hispanic Black, 18.9% were Hispanic, and 2.7% were other than Hispanic.
- 63% were attributable to abusive head trauma (AHT), 27.5% to other types of physical abuse, and 10% to neglect.
- Fathers/father substitutes were significantly more likely to be perpetrators of AHT and other physical types of abuse; mothers were significantly more likely to be deemed responsible for neglect.

## Child Death Review Teams

Sometimes, the recorded causes of children's deaths are inaccurate. Lack of such knowledge impedes interventionists' attempts to reduce child deaths. Communities have inaugurated child *death review teams* to understand better the *real causes* of children's deaths. Teams are made up of community leaders in medicine, child services, religion, law enforcement, and other areas. The expectation is that careful scrutiny of the causes will lead to development of methods to intervene and prevent such deaths. As one illustration, identification of factors involved in *sudden infant death syndrome (SIDS)* and *sudden unexpected infant death (SUID)* contributed to several recommendations. *Preventable* factors involved in these deaths were prenatal smoking, second-hand smoke exposure, alcohol/illicit drug use, and unsafe sleeping practices.

One suggestion triggered by these findings was to explore whether it would be feasible for law enforcement to conduct an *immediate drug and alcohol screen* of parents/caretakers who were on scene prior to an infant's death. Another innovation was to establish *cross-reporting online services between agencies* to enhance alertness among first responders. Knowledge of previous CPS investigations, drug arrests, or previous hospitalizations for a child's injuries would be useful for law enforcement, social services, hospitals, the coroner's office, and other agencies.

Another example of the death review team's activities was the inauguration of *safe sleeping campaigns*. The team noted that unsafe sleeping situations caused the deaths of a number of infants. One type of unsafe sleeping arrangements is *co-sleeping* (allowing the baby to sleep with the parents in the parents' bed). Other types of unsafe sleeping include placing the infant on a couch or in a crib with blankets, pillows, and stuffed toys. One study estimated that 40% of SUIDs resulted from co-sleeping accidents. In these accidents, a parent may overlay the baby causing him or her to suffocate. Such an accident is especially likely if the parent is drunk. In other situations, a baby may suffocate when *sleeping on his stomach* on a soft pillow. He may not be able to turn himself over to breathe. Legislation should mandate hospitals to instruct all new parents about safe-sleeping routines. A brochure is available to help with this task. Another proposal by the infant death review team was to have *universal neonatal home visitations* by public health nurses. Trained nurses are capable of noting potential hazards and of assisting parents in providing a safe living area (Inter-Agency Council on Child Abuse and Neglect [ICAN], 2009).

## Neonaticidal Mothers

About 75% of mothers who kill newborns fit a *common profile.* As a group, these women are *not* mentally ill, and they do *not* have a history of arrest. They often *deny their pregnancy* intermittently. Most manage to *deliver the baby on their own* in secret, and most recover sufficiently to *go right on with their daily routines,* such as going to school or work. Much more research is needed to understand this strange and sad set of circumstances (Beyer, Mack, & Shelton, 2008). The case history below is a typical case.

---

**CASE HISTORY**  Juliet—A Neonaticidal Mother

Police responded to a call in a middle-class neighborhood when passersby heard screaming coming from the women's restroom in a neighborhood park. When police arrived at 9:30 in the morning, they found 17-year-old Juliet, a high school senior, walking away from a nearby dumpster. Inside the dumpster lay a newborn baby boy wrapped in a plastic trash bag.

Noting blood on Juliet's jacket, the police took her to the hospital where doctors said she had just delivered a baby. The police called Juliet's parents, who had no idea Juliet was pregnant. How could this happen?

When Juliet's best friend asked if she were pregnant, Juliet said, "No." Juliet had confided in the school nurse about the pregnancy, but then refused any medical or social service referrals the nurse gave her. Instead, day after day, Juliet pretended that she was not pregnant. She had told her boyfriend, and his response was the same. The two of them kept pretending she was not pregnant, as if the pregnancy would just disappear.

Juliet was fearful that if her parents knew about her pregnancy, they would be furious with her for having had sex, let alone for getting pregnant. How ashamed of her they would be. Juliet was a B+ student, and she had never been arrested or been in any kind of trouble before. Although she had not been officially tested for any mental health problems, no one had seen any behavior to make them believe that she was mentally ill.

Juliet had given birth over the toilet and then made sure the baby drowned before placing him in the trash bin. At 17, Juliet was a baby killer.

---

## Self-Report Surveys

Surveys of individuals and families across the United States also provide researchers with data they can use to estimate rates of CPA. Usually, researchers ask parents in the general population to report on their use of various kinds of physical violence against their children. Some research is actually able to query children.

*Family Violence Survey, 1985.* The first National Family Violence Survey–1985 was very influential in revealing the startling amount of self-reported violence toward children (Gelles & Straus, 1987, 1988). In this telephone survey, which used the Conflict Tactics Scale (CTS) to measure abuse, parents reported on the conflict techniques they used with their children in the past year, selecting their responses from a scale that ranged from mild forms of violence (e.g., slapped or spanked child) to severe forms of violence (e.g., beat up child, burned or scalded child, used a knife or gun). Results disclosed that 75% of the parents acknowledged having used at least one violent act in rearing their children. Approximately 2% of the parents had engaged in one act of abusive violence (i.e., an act with a high probability of injuring the child) during the year prior to the survey. The most frequent type of violence in either case was slapping or spanking the child.

*Survey with an improved CTS—1998.* To improve upon measurement of child abuse, researchers developed the *Parent-Child Conflict Tactics Scale (CTSPC)*. This inventory specifically assesses violence between parents and children. In addition to its revised physical assault and psychological aggression scales, the CTSPC expands the CTS by including new scales designed to measure *non-violent discipline, child neglect,* and *sexual abuse* (Straus, Hamby, Finkelhor, Moore, & Runyan, 1998). The CTSPC distinguishes three levels of physical assault: *minor* assault (i.e., corporal punishment), *severe* assault (i.e., physical maltreatment), and *very severe* assault (i.e., severe physical maltreatment). As part of a survey sponsored by the Gallup Organization, Straus and his colleagues administered the CTSPC to a nationally representative sample of 1,000 parents with the following outcomes:

- 75% reported using some method of physical assault during the rearing of their children. Most of the assaults were minor assaults, such as spanking, slapping, and pinching.
- Nearly 50% of parents surveyed said that they had engaged in behaviors from the *severe physical assault subscale* at some point during their parenting. An example of an item from the severe physical assault scale is "hitting the child with an object such as a stick or belt."
- Less than 1% of the parents employed behaviors from the *very severe physical assault* scale. An example of a behavior from this scale is "throwing or knocking down a child."

> **Office of Juvenile Justice and Delinquency Prevention (OJJDP), First National Survey on Children's Exposure to Violence** (Finkelhor, Turner, Ormrod, Hamby, & Kracke, 2009); *N* = 4,549; Comprehensive national population survey of children:
>
> - 46.3% of all children surveyed had been physically assaulted.
> - The peak of assaults occurred between 6 and 9 years of age.
> - Of the assaulted children, boys (50.2%) were more likely than girls (42.1%) to be physically assaulted.

*National Violence Against Women Survey.* In another form of self-report survey, adults in the general population describe their own childhood experiences with various forms of physical violence from adult caretakers. The most significant survey of this type to date is the National Violence Against Women Survey, conducted in 1995–1996 (Tjaden & Thoennes, 2000b). In this telephone survey, a random sample of 16,000 adults (8,000 women and 8,000 men) responded to a modified version of the Conflict Tactics Scale. The respondents reported on the kinds of physical assaults they had experienced as children at the hands of their adult caretakers. Nearly half reported having experienced at least one physical assault by an adult caretaker, with the acts of violence ranging from relatively minor forms of assault (e.g., being slapped or hit) to more serious forms (e.g., being threatened with a knife or gun). For both men and women, most of the assaults consisted of pushing, grabbing, shoving, slapping, hitting, or being hit with an object. Men were more likely than women to have experienced these forms of violence.

## Trends in Rates of Physical Abuse

*What does it mean that the rate of child maltreatment decreased from 1992 to 2004? Is this a true reduction or an artifact?* A pair of child maltreatment experts undertook the task of investigating these questions. For the basis of their comparisons, they used data from the following surveys: (a) National Child Abuse and Neglect Data System (NCANDS), (b) National Crime Victimization Survey (NCVS), (c) Minnesota Student Survey, and (d) Supplementary Homicide Reports. It may be important to acknowledge that they did not use NIS data. NIS abuse data showed a decline of 19% from NIS-3 to NIS-4.

First, they examined the possibility that only one form of maltreatment (e.g., CPA) had decreased, while other forms had not. Inspection of maltreatment trends across maltreatment types, however, did *not* support this possibility. All forms of child maltreatment decreased from 40% to 70%. Inspection of other indicators also showed changes—improvements for *teens.* There were fewer teen pregnancies, teen suicides, and children living in poverty. Hence, they concluded that the downward trend was a valid phenomenon.

Second, they examined a number of possible explanations for the decreases, such as legalization of abortion and improved economic conditions. Their analyses suggested that three explanations appeared more likely than others: (a) *improved economic factors,* (b) *increased agents of social change* (e.g., more social workers), and (c) *psychopharmacological advances,* such as those used to treat sex offenders. Obviously, decreasing trends of such a magnitude must have been related to more than one indicator (Finkelhor & Jones, 2006).

*Other related trends.* Outcomes of two self-report surveys suggested that the level of child maltreatment was staying about the same, at least not increasing. First, the National Violence Against Women survey, for example, found evidence that childhood physical assaults by caretakers, as reported during adulthood, remained relatively unchanged over time (Tjaden & Thoennes, 2000b). In this survey, younger adults (age 25 or younger at the time of the survey) were just as likely as older adults (age 50 or older) to report having experienced physical assault by caretakers during childhood. Second, Gelles and Straus (1987) found that the estimated rate of violence toward children *declined* from 1975 to 1985. The most *substantial decline* was in the use of *severe and very severe violence* (e.g., kicking, using a knife).

---

**SECTION SUMMARY**

### Scope of Physical Child Abuse—Prevalence

Several factors impact reports of incidence and prevalence of child physical abuse. Law enforcement and Child Protective Services must abide by legal standards when reporting abuse. Official estimates of abuse ordinarily rely on legally defined acts of CPA. Official estimates suggest that CPA is a problem for 16% to 25% of children. There are some problems of disclosure of abuse among mandated reporters (e.g., pediatricians).

*(Continued)*

(Continued)

For various reasons, mandated reporters do not always report, thus decreasing prevalence reports from medical settings. Anonymous self-report surveys of parent-to-child physical abuse reveal very high rates of abuse. In one survey of parents, some 75% reported using at least one violent act toward their children at some point during child rearing.

Records suggest that when children are injured and visit an emergency room, over half of their injuries have been inflicted by relatives including parents. Among fatalities associated with CPA those most common are among the youngest children (those under 1 year of age), and male infants are more likely to be murdered than female infants. Child Death Review teams actively study fatalities in order to understand the causes and make recommendations. Some mothers, especially very young mothers, commit neonaticide. Much more research is needed to understand these events and what might reduce their frequency.

CPS agencies receive hundreds of thousands of reports of CPA each year, and the numbers of reports have increased and decreased during certain time periods. The most current analyses show that the rate of CPA is decreasing.

## EFFECTS OF CHILD PHYSICAL ABUSE ON CHILDREN

Children who experience physical maltreatment are more likely than their nonabused counterparts to exhibit *physical, behavioral,* and *emotional impairments.* In some cases, the negative consequences associated with abuse continue to affect individuals well into adulthood (Gershoff, 2008; Sroufe, Coffino, & Carlson, 2010). Until relatively recently, research examining the effects of CPA on children was limited to measures of *physical harm.* Investigators ignored the sometimes subtle, yet significant, social and psychological effects, focusing only on visible signs of trauma, such as physical injuries. Examination of 88 studies uncovered associations between corporal punishment and numerous negative outcomes in childhood on into adulthood, including deficits in moral internalization, poor mental health, and increased aggression, antisocial behavior, and abusive behavior toward others (Gershoff, 2002). Table 4.2 displays the most frequently reported problems associated with CPA for children, adolescents, and adults.

**TABLE 4.2** Effects Associated With Physical Child Abuse for Children, Adolescents, and Adults

| *Effects* | *Examples* | |
|---|---|---|
| Medical and neurobiological complications | Bruises | Head, chest, and abdominal injuries |
| | Fractures | Compromised brain development |
| | Burns | Alteration of biological stress system |
| Cognitive difficulties | Increased need for special education services | Deficits in verbal abilities, memory, problem solving, and perceptual-motor skills |
| | Decreased reading/math skills | Decreased intellectual and cognitive functioning |
| | Poor school achievement | |

| Effects | Examples | |
|---|---|---|
| Behavioral problems | Aggression | Property offenses |
| | Fighting | Defiance |
| | Noncompliance | Arrests |
| Socioemotional deficits | Delayed play skills | Infant attachment problems |
| | Peer rejection | Low self-esteem |
| | Avoidance of adults | Deficits in prosocial behaviors |
| | Poor social interaction skills | Deficits in social competence with peers |
| | Difficulty making friends | Hopelessness |
| | Suicidality | Depressive symptoms |
| Psychiatric disorders | Major depressive disorder | Oppositional defiant disorder |
| | Borderline personality disorder | Attention-deficit/hyperactivity disorder |
| | Conduct disorder | Posttraumatic stress disorder |
| Aggressive and antisocial behavior | Violent interpersonal behavior | Delinquency; violent and criminal offenses |
| Deficits in social competence | Increased levels of conflict and negative affect in interpersonal interactions | Decreased levels of social competence |
| | Low levels of intimacy | |
| Psychiatric disorders | Major depressive disorder | Disruptive behavior disorders |
| | Substance abuse | |
| Other | Attention problems | Sexual risk taking |
| | Deficient school performance | Increased daily stress |
| | Suicidal behavior | Low self-esteem |
| Criminal/violent behavior | Arrests for delinquency | Marital violence (for adult males) |
| | Physical abuse of own children | Received and inflicted dating violence |
| | Prostitution | Violent and/or criminal behavior |
| Substance abuse | Abuse of alcohol and other substances | |
| Socioemotional problems | Self-destructive behavior | Suicidal ideation and behavior |
| | Anxiety | Depression and mania |
| | Dissociation | Unusual thoughts |
| | Poor self-concept | Interpersonal difficulties |
| | Hostility | |
| Psychiatric disorders | Disruptive behavior disorders | Antisocial and other personality disorders |
| | Posttraumatic stress disorder | Major depressive disorder |

SOURCES: A representative but not exhaustive list of sources for information displayed in this table includes Afifi, Brownridge, Cox, & Sareen, 2006; Appleyard, Egeland, van Dulmen, & Sroufe, 2005; English, Widom, & Brandford, 2004; Gershoff, 2008; S. R. Jaffee et al., 2005; D. J. Kolko & Kolko, 2009; Moe, King, & Bailly, 2004; Salzinger, Rosario, & Feldman, 2007; Sedlak et al., 2010; U.S. Department of Health & Human Services, 2008.

# LONG-TERM EFFECTS ASSOCIATED WITH CHILD PHYSICAL ABUSE (CPA)

## Physical and Mental Health

Abused children, relative to nonabused children, suffer numerous health problems extending on into old age. Some of these problems are observable in kindergarten samples and then stretch across the lifespan (Greenfield, 2010).

*Injuries.* The effects of CPA-related injuries may follow an individual throughout life. In particular, head injuries, abdominal injuries, and burns are likely to have long-lasting effects (Wharton, Rosenberg, Sheridan, & Ryan, 2000).

*Pain.* Sadly, victims may experience chronic pain on into old age. Within a sample of 3,381 adults, 14.7% had been physically abused, 5.8% had been sexually abused, and 7.2% suffered both physical and sexual abuse during childhood. Of the abused group, the prevalence of pain was 28.1% (Walsh, Jamieson, MacMillan, & Boyle, 2007).

*Specific illnesses.* A 32-year prospective study of 1,037 Australians centered on the health records of the participants. The records clearly demonstrated that children exposed to adverse childhood experiences (socioeconomic disadvantage, maltreatment, and social isolation) suffered significantly worse health. In particular, the abused group evidenced (a) *depression,* (b) *high inflammation levels,* and (c) a *clustering of metabolic risk factors.* The metabolic risk factors included being overweight, having high blood pressure, high "bad" cholesterol, high blood sugar, and low oxygen consumption (Danese et al., 2009). Relative to a nonabused group in a different inquiry, adults abused as children had elevated risks for allergies, arthritis, asthma, bronchitis, high blood pressure, and other problems (Reece, 2010).

## Criminal and Violent Behavior

One of the most frequently discussed long-term consequences of CPA is criminal and violent behavior (e.g., Lansford et al., 2006).

*Criminal behavior of CPA victims.* Widom (1989a) compared a sample of validated cases of child abuse and neglect (identified 20 years earlier by social service agencies) to a sample of matched comparisons, evaluating juvenile court and probation department records to establish occurrences of delinquency, criminal behavior, and violent criminal behavior. She found that the subjects in the abused-neglected group had a higher likelihood of arrests for delinquency, adult criminality, and violent criminal behavior than did those in the comparison group (see also Mallett, Dare, & Seck, 2009; Salzinger, Rosario, & Feldman, 2007).

*Interpersonal violence.* Other research suggests that the interpersonal relationships of adults with childhood histories of physical abuse are more likely than those of nonabused persons to be characterized by violence (Crooks, Scott, Wolfe, Chiodo, & Killip, 2007). Adults with histories of CPA are more likely both to receive and to inflict dating violence (Rapoza & Baker, 2008;

Wolfe, Crooks, Chiodo, & Jaffe, 2003). In addition, adults (primarily males) who were physically abused as children are more likely to inflict physical abuse on their marital partners (McKinney, Caetano, Ramisetty-Mikler, & Nelson, 2009; Weston, Marshall, & Coker, 2007).

*Genetic contributions.* A team of researchers working in England, New Zealand, and the United States examined the potential role of genetic makeup as a contributor to aggressive, antisocial, or violent behavior in adults who were abused or maltreated as children (Caspi et al., 2002). These researchers speculated that the relationship between childhood maltreatment and violent behavior in adulthood depends on variations in a gene that helps to regulate neurotransmitters in the brain that are implicated in antisocial behavior. They assessed a group of 442 boys in New Zealand for antisocial behavior periodically between the ages of 3 and 28 years and found that maltreated children with a *protective* version of the gene were less likely to develop antisocial problems in adulthood. In contrast, 85% of maltreated children who had the less protective version of the gene later became violent criminal offenders (Jaffee et al., 2005).

## Substance Abuse

Researchers have examined the possible association between CPA and later substance abuse among CPA victims. A prospective longitudinal assessment of substance use among the offspring of 585 abusive families detected gender differences in outcomes. CPA was significantly associated with substance abuse for girls at age 12, and then indirectly related to CPA at age 16 and 24. For boys, however, CPA was *not* related to substance abuse at age 12. Instead, substance abuse at age 12 was related to substance abuse at ages 16 and 24. These seemingly unexpected findings for males *are* consistent with previous research by Wilson and Widom (2009). The investigators suggested that CPA among girls led to a use of substances at age 12 which *then* continued onward (Lansford, Dodge, Petit, & Bates, 2010).

## Socioemotional Difficulties

Well-conducted studies on the long-term socioemotional consequences of physical maltreatment in childhood are now available. Evidence to date indicates that adults with histories of CPA exhibit more significant emotional problems (e.g., De Bellis & Thomas, 2003; Springer, Sheridan, Kuo, & Carnes, 2007). Some of these disorders are as follows:

| Poor self-concept | Attention-deficit disorder | Self-destructive behavior |
|---|---|---|
| Anger/hostility | Reactive attachment disorder | Substance abuse disorder |
| Disruptive disorders | Oppositional defiant disorder | Major depressive disorder |
| Conduct disorder | Dissociative disorders | Negative feelings about interpersonal interactions |
| Panic disorder | Personality disorders | PTSD |
| Anxiety | Mania | Dysthymia |

## Mediators/Moderators of Abuse Effects

To add to the uncertainty regarding the effects of CPA, it is also true that CPA victims do not respond to being abused in consistent or predictable ways. For some, the effects of their victimization may be *pervasive and long-standing*, whereas for others their abuse experiences may *not be invariably disruptive.*

---

CPA → Mediator → Behavior

or

Moderator

---

Knowledge of **mediators and moderators** helps to explain the *variability* of effects, why some effects may be pervasive and others not. The following section outlines *some* detected mediators and moderators:

*Frequency, severity, and duration of the abuse.* More severe and/or chronic maltreatment may have more negative outcomes. Although empirical data on this topic are sparse, some evidence supports this contention (e.g., E. J. Brown, 2003; Wind & Silvern, 1992).

*Polyvictimization.* The greater the number of subtypes of maltreatment (e.g., physical abuse, sexual abuse, neglect) experienced by a child, the more negative the outcomes will be (e.g., Chartier, Walker, & Naimark, 2010; Fischer, Stojek, & Hartzell, 2010).

*Prior involvement with Child Protective Services.* Data from a nationally representative, longitudinal survey revealed that prior involvement with CPS influenced the probability of a second determination of abuse (Kahn & Schwalbe, 2010).

*Child's attributions.* Specific attributions as well as general attributional style were predictive of the level of psychopathology exhibited by CPA victims. Children who tended to blame themselves for the abuse, for example, exhibited greater internalizing symptoms. These findings suggest that the child's *perceptions* of those events may also serve an important mediating role (Kolko & Feiring, 2002; Mash & Wolfe, 2008).

*Family stress.* The negative effects of abuse are greatest for children in families in which there are high levels of stress and parental psychopathology (e.g., schizophrenia) or depression (Huth-Bocks & Hughes, 2008; Kurtz, Gaudin, Wodarski, & Howing, 1993).

*Sociocultural factors.* Reports also demonstrate the negative impact of sociocultural and family variables (e.g., SES) on the effects of CPA. The presence of community violence can be a factor influencing the effects of CPA (E. C. Herrenkohl, Herrenkohl, Rupert, Egolf, & Lutz, 1995; Sedlak et al., 2010).

*Child's intellectual functioning.* Factors such as high *intellectual functioning* and/or the presence of a *supportive parent* figure have a *protective* influence, thus mitigating the effects of CPA (e.g., Lansford et al., 2006).

*Relationships between the victim and abuser.* The quality of the parent-child interaction may attenuate the negative outcomes of CPA (Collishaw et al., 2007; English, Upadhyaya, et al., 2005). *Parental sensitivity,* for example, has a protective influence (see Haskett, Allaire, Kreig, & Hart, 2008). *Lack of empathy* predicted the appearance of adverse symptoms following CPA victimization (Moor & Silvern, 2006).

*Trauma symptoms.* Whether a child victim of CPA became an adult CPA abuser (of his/her children) depended on whether the child developed trauma symptoms. Children whose abuse eventuated in the trauma symptom of *avoidance coping* were more likely than those who did not develop the symptoms to abuse their own child (Milner et al., 2010).

*Child's temperament.* Parenting attempts at socialization were less effective if the child had certain *temperamental features,* such as low fear and low sensitivity to punishment (Edens, Skopp, & Cahill, 2008).

*Social support.* Egeland (1997) found that mothers who were physically abused but did not abuse their own children were significantly more likely than abusing mothers to have received emotional support from a nonabusive adult during childhood, to have participated in therapy during some period in their lives, and to have been involved in nonabusive, stable, emotionally supportive, and satisfying relationships with mates.

## EXPANDED DISCUSSION OF INDIVIDUAL EFFECTS OF CHILD PHYSICAL ABUSE

### Medical and Neurobiological Problems

The medical consequences of CPA are numerous and range from minor physical injuries (e.g., bruising) to serious physical disfigurements and disabilities. In extreme cases, CPA can result in death. Bruises are one of the most common types of physical injuries associated with CPA. CPA victims may also have other marks on their bodies as the result of being grabbed or squeezed or of being struck with belts, switches, or cords. When a child has a series of unusual injuries, this is often an indication of CPA (Myers, 1992).

Other common physical injuries associated with CPA include chest and abdominal injuries, burns, and fractures (Myers, 1992; Schmitt, 1987). Victims may incur abdominal injuries by being struck with objects, by being grabbed tightly, or by being punched or kicked in the chest or abdomen, which can result in organ ruptures or compressions. Burns, which are often inflicted as punishment, can result from immersion in scalding water or from contact with objects such as irons, cigarettes, stove burners, and heaters. Finally, fractures of bones in various areas of the body often result from CPA. Any of a number of actions can cause fractures, including punching, kicking, twisting, shaking, and squeezing.

*Neurobiological injuries.* Negative changes in the brain caused by maltreatment do occur. Several neurobiological consequences are related to CPA head injury including compromised brain development. Victims may exhibit deficits in language skills, memory, spatial skills, attention, sensorimotor functioning, cognitive processing, and overall intelligence. One of the most dangerous types of CPA injury is *head injury.* Various actions on the part of an abuser can result in head injury and inflict neurotrauma. Some of these actions include a blow to the child's head by an object, punching the head with a fist, compressing the head between two surfaces, throwing the child against a hard surface, and shaken baby syndrome (see Leslie et al., 2005; Reece & Nicholson, 2003).

## BOX 4.1  Shaken Baby Syndrome (SBS)

Violently shaking an infant can result in mild to serious *traumatic brain injuries (TBIs)* that are not always readily observable (National Institute of Neurological Disorders and Stroke, 2010). One type of TBI is known as **shaken baby syndrome (SBS).** Shaking a child violently can cause the child's brain to move within the skull, stretching and tearing blood vessels. Damage may include bleeding in the eye or brain, damage to the spinal cord and neck, and rib or bone fractures. For the period 2002–2006, the best estimate of deaths attributable to shaken baby syndrome was 144 (38.4%) of 375 head trauma deaths.

Commonly, parents who bring their children into emergency rooms with nonaccidental head injuries report that the children were hurt when they fell from some item of furniture (e.g., crib, couch, bed). Although 52.2% of TBI hospital deaths were attributed to falls for children age 0 to 14, doctors may be able to determine if such falls were accidental (Jayakumar, Barry, & Ramachandran, 2010).

Brain-injury deaths occurring in emergency rooms (2002–2005) for children 0 to 14 years of age totaled 2,174. Data shed some light on the causes of TBIs, such as motor vehicle deaths and assaults. The estimated average annual death rates associated with TBIs were as follows (Faul, Xu, Wald, & Coronado, 2010):

- 0–4 years of age: 998 deaths, 5.0 per 100,000 children
- 5–9 years of age: 450 deaths, 2.3 per 100,000 children
- 10–14 years of age: 726 deaths, 3.5 per 100,000 children

The estimated annual percentage of TBIs diagnosed in emergency rooms by age and by sex appears in Table 4.3. Note that the preponderance of TBIs occur in male children (Faul et al., 2010).

**TABLE 4.3**  Percentage of TBIs by Age and Sex

| Age | Number | Males | Females |
|-----|--------|-------|---------|
| 0–4 | 139,001 | 55.3% | 44.7% |
| 5–9 | 68,671 | 65.4% | 36.6% |
| 10–14 | 90,221 | 76.9% | 23.1% |

Although medical personnel undertake actions to stop bleeding in the brain, long-term neurological or mental disability may appear (Watts-English et al., 2006)

A Canadian comparison of 11 children who had suffered shaken baby syndrome with 11 matched comparison children found that one long-term consequence was a significant reduction in intelligence scores at 7 to 8 years of age (Stipanicic, Nolin, Fortin, & Gobeil, 2008). To *prevent* SBS, hospitals need to provide information about shaken baby syndrome to new parents in maternity wards (Deyo, Skybo, & Carroll, 2008; Dias et al., 2005).

## Cognitive Problems

Studies have shown that physically abused children exhibit lower intellectual and cognitive functioning relative to comparison groups of children on general intellectual measures as well as on specific measures of verbal facility, memory, dissociation, verbal language, communication ability, problem-solving skills, and perceptual motor skills (e.g., Macfie, Cicchetti, & Toth, 2001; see also U.S. Department of Health & Human Services, 2008). The cognitive deficits that have been observed in physically abused children, however, may be the results of *direct physical injury* (e.g., head injury), *environmental factors* (e.g., low levels of stimulation and communication), or a *combination of both*. Additional research is needed to determine the precise nature of the relationship between CPA and the cognitive problems observed in abused children.

*Academic performance* is another area of substantiated difficulty in physically abused children. Compared with nonabused children, victims of CPA display poor school achievement and adjustment, receive more special education services, score lower on reading and math tests, exhibit more learning disabilities, and are more likely to repeat a grade (e.g., Halambie & Klapper, 2005).

*Biological stress reaction.* The experience of child maltreatment can also result in alterations of the biological stress systems within the body via disruption of various chemicals in the body, such as *neurotransmitters and hormones* (Cicchetti & Rogosch, in press; Veenema, 2009). In one study, for example, researchers found that a sample of abused children exhibited greater concentrations of urinary dopamine, norepinephrine, and free cortisol than did children in a control group. They also found that a number of specific brain regions were smaller in the abused children relative to the nonabused children. Changes in neurobiological systems can have negative impacts on children's ability to regulate both emotional and behavioral responses (De Bellis & Kuchibhatla, 2006).

## Behavioral Problems

Physical aggression and antisocial behavior are among the most common correlates of CPA. In most studies, abused children have exhibited more aggression than nonabused children, even after the researchers have statistically controlled for the poverty, family instability, and wife battering that often accompany abuse (e.g., Springer et al., 2007). In other words, abuse seems to have effects on behavior independent of the potential contribution of other factors. This negative behavioral pattern has been observed across a wide variety of settings, including *summer camps* (Kaufman & Cicchetti, 1989) and *preschool and day-care programs* (Alessandri, 1991), in which researchers have used a variety of data collection procedures (e.g., R. S. Feldman et al., 1995). Other behavioral difficulties displayed by CPA victims include drinking and drug use, noncompliance, defiance, fighting in and outside of the home, property offenses, and arrests (e.g., Conroy, Degenhardt, Mattick, & Nelson, 2009; Ireland, Smith, & Thornberry, 2002). A type of behavioral problem associated with child abuse that has garnered more and more societal and research attention is bullying.

## BOX 4.2 Bullying in Middle School

Bullying is a use of power and aggression to distress a vulnerable person. It can include verbal or physical actions and behaviors such as exclusion and ostracism. Bullying can be conceptualized as the result of the interplay between the child and his or her family, peer group, school, community, and culture.

*Bullies and cliques.* One interesting observation is that bullying is not confined to a bully-victim dyad. Instead, groups of children victimize individual children (Espelage, 2004).

Children may form cliques in which members influence each other to partake in bullying. Peer groups usually form on the basis of similarity, such as sex, propinquity, and race (see Espelage & Swearer, 2003). The most central member of the clique is often the most aggressive bully (Espelage, 2004). Bullies are often popular and socially dominant (Witvliet et al., 2009).

There are three kinds of bully involvement: (a) *bully only,* (b) *victim only,* and (c) *both victim and bully.* Another group of children are involved as bystanders. Bullies like an audience. There are also different forms of bullying, such as physical, emotional, indirect, verbal, sexual, and relational. Relational bullying is aggression aimed at damaging someone else's relationship (e.g., a rival's dating relationship). (See Espelage & Swearer, 2003, for a review.)

*Prevalence of bullying.* Bullying occurs almost universally among children and adolescents. Bullying is more prevalent before age 12, and it continues during adolescence. A survey of 15,686 students in Grades 6 to 11 reported a bully involvement rate of 30% (Nansel et al., 2001). A typical trajectory of bullying is beginning in middle school and reaching a peak during the transition from middle school to high school followed by a decline (Pelligrini & Long, 2002). The frequency of bullying varies by the ethnic background of the students and the ethnic composition of the class. Black students report being victimized more than White students (Nansel et al., 2001).

*Consequences of bullying.* Being the victim of a bully (or clique of bullies) is damaging to one's mental health. A 2-year longitudinal study of 2,232 twins 5 to 7 years old assessed changes via before- and after-test inventories. Of the total, 272 children were bullied by being excluded from school activities, and 137 were involved as both bullies and victims. Contrasting the bullied groups with the 1,387 children who were not bullied uncovered several significant differences. The bullied group suffered from an escalation of symptoms: depression, anxiety, social withdrawal, and physical complaints (Arseneault et al., 2010; see also Gruber & Fineran, 2007; Poteat & Espelage, 2008).

*Characteristics of bullies.* Bullies rank high in antisocial behavior and aggression (Solberg & Olweus, 2003). One group of investigators found that increases in bullying over time were associated with *anger, impulsivity,* and *depression* (Espelage, Bosworth, & Simon, 2001). Regardless of sex, masculine traits predicted bullying (Gini & Pozzoli, 2006). Being bullied by a boy was more detrimental to both boy and girl victims than being bullied by a girl (Felix & McMahon, 2006). A newer study has demonstrated that among 105 students (Grades 4, 6, and 8), students with *lower-quality parental attachment* are significantly more likely to bully and to be bullied (Walden & Beran, 2010; see also Eliot & Cornell, 2009).

*Characteristics of victims.* Students ages 9 to 11 were more likely to be bullied by social exclusion if they were submissive or nonassertive (C. L. Fox & Boulton, 2006). Although any child may become a victim of bullying, the most vulnerable targets are individuals who deviate from the norm, someone who is different because of sexual orientation, race, or disability. Students enrolled in special education classes have a different pattern of bullying than those enrolled in general education. Students in special education reported more bully perpetration, victimization, and physical types of bullying than did general education students. Further, special education students maintained roughly the same level of bullying over the middle school and high school years. General education students who were older, conversely, exhibited less bullying (Rose, Espelage, & Monda-Amaya, 2009).

Victimization is associated with *low self-esteem and depression* (Solberg & Olweus, 2003). Traits of children who do not transition out of victimization indicated that boys were lower in *prosocial behavior* and girls were higher in *impulsivity* compared with those who did transition out of victimization. In addition, a reduction in girls' relational bullying was linked with a cessation of their own victimization (Dempsey, Fireman, & Wang, 2006). Also, some victims react to being bullied with *intensified anxiety and depression.*

*Explanations for bullying. Exposure to parental intimate partner violence (IPV), personal maltreatment, and sibling bullying* are powerful risk factors for future bullying behaviors (Wolfe et al., 2003). A cross-cultural comparison showed a significant relationship between parents' harming a child physically and the child victim's bullying behaviors (Dussich & Maekoya, 2007). Youth from such homes often model the violence and carry out similar abusive patterns of behavior in their own relationships.

Bullies have also witnessed interpersonal aggression at school by peers and some teachers (Twemlow & Fornagy, 2005) and had their own behavior shaped by operant/instrumental learning procedures. Parents or peers may have rewarded (e.g., praised or admired) a child for bullying others or fighting back when insulted. In parallel fashion,

*(Continued)*

(Continued)

parents/peers may have punished (e.g., ridiculed) a child for not "standing up to a bully" (see Button & Gealt, 2010). From a different point of view, an analysis of the data from the Arseneault et al. (2010) study of twins clearly showed that *genetics* as well as the environment played a role in bullying/bully victimization (Ball et al., 2008).

***Treatment/prevention of bullying/victimization.*** Because bullying occurs most frequently at school, society's expectations are that the school has the responsibility for preventing bullying. The school has to manage a problem that has its roots in physical child abuse in the home (Dussich & Maekoya, 2007; see also Totura et al., 2009). Bullying is not harmless. Teachers, parents, and others should intervene when bullying is observed. A violent childhood does not mean that bullying behavior is inevitable, and interventions can change the way schoolchildren relate to others (Poteat & Espelage, 2008).

Experts studying the problem, taking note of the interrelations between bullying and other parameters, have strongly recommended a research-based, social-ecological program. Interventionists must take into account the impacts of "families, schools, peer groups, teacher-student relationships, neighborhoods, and cultural expectations" (Swearer, Espelage, Vaillancourt, & Hymel, 2010, p. 42).

## Difficulties Related to Psychopathology

Additional problems frequently observed in physically abused children are *internalizing behavioral symptom*s that include social and emotional difficulties.

*Attachment problems.* The quality of the parent-child bond consistently reflects *insecure attachment* in *infants* exposed to CPA. For these children, the parent-child relationship presents an *irresolvable paradox* because the caregiver is both the child's source of safety and protection and the source of danger or harm (Hesse & Main, 2000; Zeanah et al., 2004).

*Psychiatric disorders.* A number of studies have examined rates of psychiatric disorders in samples of physically abused children and have found that CPA victims are at increased risk for psychiatric problems. The rate of risk for *social dysfunction,* in general, was nine times greater, and *somatization* risk was four times greater in one longitudinal study (Nomura & Chemtob, 2007). Abused (and neglected) children were at elevated risk for experiencing additional traumas (revictimizations) over their lifetime (Widom, Czaja, & Dutton, 2008). CPA has also been associated with *attention-deficit/hyperactivity disorder* and *borderline personality disorder* (e.g., Liu, 2010). Furthermore, there is an increased risk for *bipolar disorder* among physically abused children.

*Posttraumatic Stress Disorder (PTSD).* Since the late 1980s, researchers have documented PTSD in abused children, but the prevalence rates were inconsistent. For children referred to child welfare ($N = 1,848$), 11% had clinically significant symptoms of PTSD. For children placed in out-of-home care, 19.2% had PTSD (Hurlburt, Zhang, Barth, Leslie, & Burns, 2010; see also Pollak, Vardi,

Bechner, & Curtain, 2005; B. E. Saunders, Berliner, & Hanson, 2004). One inquiry established that 81% of abused children have partial PTSD symptoms (e.g., Runyon, Deblinger, & Schroeder, 2009).

*Depression.* One pair of researchers conducted a longitudinal investigation (birth to age 26) on the combined effects of child physical abuse *and* low birth weight among 1,748 children. Analyses showed a 10-fold greater risk of depression among the abused low birth weight children compared with children in a control group (Nomura & Chemtob, 2007; see also Sternberg, Lamb, Guterman, & Abbott, 2006). In another inquiry, harshly parented kindergartners tested with some insolvable puzzle problems revealed learned helplessness (similar to hopelessness) (Cole et al., 2007).

## Research Issues

It is difficult to be certain that the psychological problems associated with CPA result solely from violent interactions between parent and child. First, child physical abuse often occurs in association with other problems within the family, such as marital violence, alcohol/drug use by parents, and low SES. Determining which factors or combination of factors in the child's environment are responsible for his or her problems is a difficult task. Certainly, it would not be surprising to find that a child who regularly witnesses interparental violence, who is abused by an older sibling, and who is poor might be having problems in school whether or not he or she is being abused by a parent. It would be surprising if such a child were *not* having difficulties. The perennial problems of lack of comparison groups and correlational data are ongoing.

---

### SECTION SUMMARY

### Effects of Child Abuse

Society, the government, experts in the social sciences, education, and medicine, those who work in CPS and law enforcement; and many others are extremely concerned about the effects of CPA on children. In fact, there is international concern about the fate of abused children. Researchers examine and categorize the effects of abuse along numerous dimensions: (a) type and severity of outcomes, and (b) duration of the effects, from infancy to old age. These consequences affect a variety of areas of functioning, including physical, emotional, cognitive, behavioral, and social domains. The experience of CPA, however, does not affect all victims in the same way. Specific factors can mediate the effects of CPA. For example, severity, duration, frequency, and chronicity of abuse impact the effects of the abuse. Additional research efforts are needed to identify potential mediating variables.

It can be quite challenging to link specific parental abusive behaviors to specific outcomes because behavior has so many causes. Sometimes the effects are subtle or do not show up immediately. The effects of shaken baby syndrome are some of the most damaging and long lasting because of irreversible brain damage. Abused children are likely to have cognitive deficits and behavioral and emotional problems that affect others in the family and community. As one example, bullying one's schoolmates can be directly tied to abusive behaviors in the home.

---

# CHARACTERISTICS OF CHILDREN
# WHO ARE PHYSICALLY ABUSED

## Age

Over the years, evidence has suggested that maltreatment as a whole declines with a child's increasing age. This pattern appears *not* to be true of child physical abuse.

*Official estimates.*

**U.S. Department of Health & Human Services (2008): Age and Percentage of Physically Abused Children**

| Age | Percentage | Age | Percentage | Age | Percentage |
|-----|-----------|-----|-----------|-----|-----------|
| <1 | 17.1% | 3 | 12.0% | 12–15 | 19.7% |
| 1 | 11.0% | 4–7 | 15.7% | 16–17 | 21.0% |
| 2 | 11.4% | 8–11 | 16.6% | Unknown | 20.6% |

**NIS-4 (Sedlak et al., 2010). NIS-4 reports of ages of physically abused children as follows:**

- 2.5 per 1,000 for children 0 to 2
- 3.6 per 1,000 for children 3 to 5
- 5.5 per 1,000 for children 6 to 8
- 4.6 per 1,000 for children 9 to 11
- 5.0 per 1,000 for children 12 to 14
- 4.3 per 1,000 for children 15 to 17

**National Child Abuse and Neglect Data System (NCANDS; 2008):**

- 13.2% of physically abused children were <1 week old.

**National Survey of Children Exposed to Violence (NatSCEV survey of 503 children (Finkelhor et al., 2009)**

- 2.1% of children were under 2 years of age.

*Self-report surveys.* Results of self-report surveys are quite different than those from official estimates. Researchers compared three methods of identifying maltreatment incidents: (a) *retrospectively* (self-report via interview*)*, (b) *prospectively* (case record data), and (c) with a *combination* of both methods. Using a sample of 170 participants tracked from birth to age 19, researchers identified maltreatment occurrences as follows: (a) *retrospective* identification—7.1%, (b) *prospective* identification—20.6%, and (c) *combination* method—22.9% (Shaffer, Huston, & Egeland, 2008).

## Gender

NIS-4 (Sedlak et al., 2010) demonstrates that

- *Girls* (8.5 per 1,000 children) are generally more at risk for abuse by the harm standard than are boys (6.5 per 1,000). Inclusion of girls' greater *sexual* victimization appears to account for this overall maltreatment gender differences.
- *Boys* (54%) are generally at slightly greater risk than girls (50%) for child physical abuse.

## Related Variables

*Socioeconomic status.* Although child maltreatment occurs in all socioeconomic groups, official statistics have consistently shown that CPA occurs disproportionately more often among economically and socially disadvantaged families (U.S. Department of Health & Human Services, 2008; NIS-4, Sedlak et al., 2010). Economic stress impacts CPA rates in military families as well (Hennessy, 2009).

NIS-4 (Sedlak et al., 2010) presented the following incidence rate of physical abuse among children categorized by SES (see Table 4.4 also):

- 1.5 per 1,000 children were *not* in low SES families.
- 4.4 per 1,000 children were *in* low SES families.

> *U.S. Department of Health & Human Services [CPS records] (2008).* The number of substantiated (i.e., found to be true) cases of child maltreatment was 758,289 victims (51.3% girls).
>
> *Adverse Childhood Experiences (ACE) Study. Data from Kaiser Permanente–San Diego in collaboration with the Centers for Disease Control and Prevention (2006);* N = 17,337 adult patients reporting on childhood physical abuse.
>
> - *27% of women* (n = 9,367) reported having been physically abused.
> - *29.9% of men* (n = 7,970) reported having been physically abused.

**TABLE 4.4** Incidence Rates of Severity of Harm for Maltreated Children Associated With SES Status

| Severity of Harm | Children Not in Low SES Family | Children in Low SES Family |
| --- | --- | --- |
| Serious | 1.7 per 1,000 | 9.9 per 1,000 |
| Moderate | 2.4 per 1,000 | 11.7 per 1,000 |
| Inferred | 0.2 per 1,000 | 0.9 per 1,000 |

## Race

*NIS-4 incidence rates of physically abused children by race (Sedlak et al., 2010).* For the first time, NIS data found a significant racial disparity showing Black children to be the most physically abused:

- 6.6 per 1,000 physically abused children were Black.
- 4.4 per 1,000 physically abused children were Hispanic.
- 3.2 per 1,000 physically abused children were White.

*U.S. Department of Health & Human Services (2008)* had racial information on 745,962 maltreatment victims of whom 121,137 were physically abused.

| | |
|---|---|
| African American: 19.1% | Multiple race: 14.1% |
| American Indian: 10.6% | White: 15.0% |
| Asian: 19.9% | Unknown/missing: 20.2% |
| Hispanic: 15.1% | Native Hawaiian/Pacific Islander: 20.8% |

The data gathered through national self-report studies of CPA add to the growing body of evidence suggesting that African American families are at the greatest risk for child physical abuse (Wolfner & Gelles, 1993).

*Disabled children.* The special characteristics of disabled children increase their risk for abuse. Several studies, but not all, have found an association between CPA and *birth complications* such as low birth weight and *premature birth* (Benedict, White, Wulff, & Hall, 1990; J. Brown, Cohen, Johnson, & Salzinger, 1998).

*NIS-4 prevalence—2010.* Using the NIS-4 harm standard, the incidence rate of *physical abuse* was *lower* for disabled children (3.1 per 1,000) than for nondisabled children (4.2 per 1,000 children). When the incidence rate included neglect *and* abuse, *severity of harm* findings were reversed. The rate for children with disabilities (8.8 per 1,000) was *higher* than the rate for children without disabilities (5.8 per 1,000).

*NCCAN—1993.* The National Center on Child Abuse and Neglect addressed the incidence of child abuse among children with disabilities (e.g., mental retardation, physical impairments such as deafness and blindness, and serious emotional disturbance) by collecting data from a nationally representative sample of 35 CPS agencies. The results of that analysis indicated that the incidence of child maltreatment was almost twice as high (1.7 times higher) among children with disabilities as it was among children without disabilities. For children who were physically abused, the rate for children with disabilities was 2.1 times the rate for maltreated children without disabilities (versus 1.8 for sexually abused and 1.6 for neglected children). The most common disabilities noted were emotional disturbance, learning disability, physical health problems, and speech or language delay or impairment (U.S. Department of Health & Human Services, 1993).

One difficulty in interpreting these data hinges on the specification of the *sequence* of these events. Were children disabled before the abuse, or did their disabilities result from abuse? CPS caseworkers reported that for 47% of the maltreated children with disabilities, the disabilities directly led to or contributed to child maltreatment; for 37% of the disabled children, abuse presumably caused the maltreatment-related injuries (U.S. Department of Health & Human Services, 1993).

*Child Protective Services.* One analysis suggested CPS workers may treat abuse of disabled children differently than they treat abuse of nondisabled children. In an evaluation of CPS workers' reaction to vignettes, caseworkers were *less likely to initiate an investigation of disabled children* compared with nondisabled children. Children with *behavioral/emotional disabilities* were the most likely group among disabled groups to have abuse allegations substantiated. Workers tended to attribute abuse of disabled children to the *added stress of caring for a disabled child*. The workers had empathy for the parents, but they did not condone abuse. The workers were also especially likely to *recommend services for disabled abused children* instead of services for the abusive parents, reflecting their belief in the difficult child model. The researchers suggested that CPS workers need *specialized training* to work with abused disabled children. They also recommended a *team approach* to evaluating cases. The team should include at least one disability expert (Manders & Stoneman, 2008).

*American Academy of Pediatrics.* In 2001, the American Academy of Pediatrics issued a policy statement on assessing maltreatment of children with disabilities. The organization believes that pediatricians play a significant role in identification, treatment, and prevention of child abuse, especially in cases of maltreatment of disabled children. The group has formulated eight recommendations. As an illustration, "Pediatrician should be actively involved with treatment plans developed for children with disabilities" (Committee on Child Abuse and Neglect and Committee on Children With Disabilities, 2001, p. 511).

## CHARACTERISTICS OF ADULTS WHO PHYSICALLY ABUSE CHILDREN

### Age

There is some evidence that younger parents are more likely than older parents to maltreat their children physically. NIS-4 reported that only 11% of children were abused by a "perpetrator" under the age of 26. These perpetrators (36%) who were younger, however, were more likely to be *nonparents* than parents by contrast. DHHS records indicate that 69.3% of male child abuse perpetrators and 80.4% of female child abuse perpetrators were younger than age 40 (U.S. Department of Health & Human Services, 2008).

### Gender and Parental Type

The gender of the perpetrator varies by the category of abuse according to NIS-4 (Sedlak et al., 2010): More males (62%) *physically* abused children than females (41%). (Sometimes, both a male and a female abuse a child.)

NIS-4 (Sedlak et al., 2010) had information on *types* of 323,000 parental perpetrators of *physical abuse*. See Table 4.5 for a grouping of physically abused children by gender of child and parental type.

**TABLE 4.5**  Percentages of Physically Abused Children by Gender and Parental Type

| Parent Type | Percentage of Male Children Abused (54%) | Percentage of Female Children Abused (50%) |
|---|---|---|
| Biological parent | 48% | 56% |
| Nonbiological parent/partner | 74% | 29% |
| Other person | 56% | 43% |

*Adverse Childhood Experiences (ACE) Study. Data from Kaiser Permanente–San Diego in collaboration with the Centers for Disease Control and Prevention (2006); N = 17,337 adult patients reporting on childhood experiences.* Table 4.6 summarizes differences in household dysfunction reported by gender.

**TABLE 4.6**  Adverse Childhood Experiences (ACE) of Abuse Reported by Adults

| ACE Categories of Household Dysfunction | Women: N = 9,367 | Men: N = 7,970 |
| --- | --- | --- |
| Mother treated violently by male partner | 13.7% | 11.5% |
| Household substance abuse | 29.5% | 23.8% |
| Household mental illness | 23.3% | 14.8% |
| Parental separation/divorce | 24.5% | 21.8% |
| Incarcerated household member | 5.2% | 4.1% |

The ACE survey also reported that 15.2% of women and 9.2% of men had experienced four or more adverse events.

## Race

U.S. Department of Health & Human Services (2008) had racial information on 121,137 *physically abused child victims* and 891,809 *maltreatment perpetrators.* Racial/ethnicity differences for all *child maltreatment perpetrators* (not just perpetrators of physical abuse) were as follows:

| | |
| --- | --- |
| African American: 19.6% | Multiple race: 0.9% |
| American Indian: 1.3% | White: 47.8% |
| Asian: 1.0% | Unknown/missing: 9.5% |
| Hispanic: 19.5% | Native Hawaiian/Pacific Islander: 0.2% |

## Relationship of Perpetrator to the Abused Child

Official statistics indicate that physically abused children's birth parents are the perpetrators of the abuse in the majority of reported cases. Official statistics are difficult to interpret, however, because many states define as child abuse only those cases in which perpetrators are in caretaking roles.

U.S. Department of Health & Human Services (2008) had information on the type of parental perpetrator for *all maltreatment perpetrators* from 6 states. (More than one parent type may maltreat a child.) Their findings for 658,632 parents were as follows:

| Adoptive parent: 0.7% | Stepparent: 4.4% |
|---|---|
| Biological parent: 90.9% | Unknown parental type: 19.5% |

NIS-4 (Sedlak et al., 2010) had information on 323,000 types of parental perpetrators of physical abuse. Among these perpetrators, researchers categorized the perpetrators into three categories as follows:

Biological parent: 72%  Other person: 9%

Nonbiological parent or partner: 19%

NIS-4 (2010) See Table 4.7 for a summary of parental type by severity of harm.

**TABLE 4.7** Percentages of Physically Abused Children by Parental Type Using the *Severity of Harm* Standard

| Parent Type | Fatal/Serious Harm | Moderate Harm |
|---|---|---|
| Biological parent | 22% | 78% |
| Nonbiological parent/partner | 17% | 83% |
| Other person | 31% | 69% |

U.S. Department of Health & Human Services (2008) had information on *types* of 658,632 parental perpetrators of child maltreatment (not physical abuse only; 6 states reporting). See Table 4.8 for a categorization of maltreated children by parental type.

**TABLE 4.8** Relationship of General Maltreatment Victim to Perpetrator Parental Type

| Adoptive Parent | Biological Parent | Stepparent | Unknown Parental Type |
|---|---|---|---|
| 4,816 | 598,815 | 29,064 | 26,937 |

## Nontraditional Parenting

Both official data and survey data show that single parents are overrepresented among abusers (J. Brown et al., 1998; Sedlak et al., 2010). NIS-4 found that the highest rates of child abuse occurred among *single parents who had a cohabiting partner.* Children living in these households had a rate of abuse 10 times higher than children living with married biological parents (Sedlak et al., 2010). The U.S. Department of Health & Human Services (2008) reported a rate of physical abuse at 13.9% for unmarried partners of parents and 9.4% for parents. Grandparents, on the other hand, usually present a safer environment for children. Children cared for by grandparents (3.0 per 1,000) were less apt to be physically abused than children (4.5 per 1,000) cared for by parents (NIS-4, Sedlak et al., 2010).

## PSYCHOLOGICAL, INTERPERSONAL, AND BIOLOGICAL CHARACTERISTICS OF ADULTS WHO PHYSICALLY ABUSE CHILDREN

Many studies have attempted to determine whether adults who physically abuse children share any particular characteristics (see Gershoff, 2008). This type of knowledge has the potential for improving treatment. The rationale underlying research on child abusers was the idea that something about the parent caused the abuse, not the child, not the situation, and not the specific parent-child combination. Although suggestive, the correlational nature of the research cannot definitively establish whether certain characteristics *cause* a parent to abuse a child physically. Even if certain traits were contributory to CPA, behavior generally has several causes. See Table 4.9 for a summary of the most common characteristics of adult perpetrators of CPA.

**TABLE 4.9** Psychological, Interpersonal, and Biological Characteristics of Adults Who Physically Abuse Children

| Characteristics | Examples | |
|---|---|---|
| Emotional and behavioral difficulties | Depression | Deficits in problem-solving skills |
| | Deficits in empathy | Low frustration tolerance |
| | Low self-esteem | Anger control problems |
| | Anxiety | Self-expressed anger |
| | Rigidity | Substance abuse/dependence |
| | | Perceived life stress and personal distress |
| Family and interpersonal difficulties | Spousal tension, abuse, disagreement | Verbal and physical conflict among family members |
| | Parental history of abuse in childhood | Deficits in family cohesion and expressiveness |
| | Deficits in positive interactions | Isolation from friends and the community |
| | | Abuse of children and other family members |
| Parenting difficulties | Disregard for children's needs/abilities | Unrealistic expectations of children |
| | Deficits in child management skills | Poor problem-solving ability with regard to child rearing |
| | Negative bias/perceptions regarding children | High rates of verbal and physical aggression toward children |

| Characteristics | Examples | |
|---|---|---|
| | View of parenting role as stressful | Low levels of communication, stimulation, and interaction with children |
| | Intrusive/inconsistent parenting | |
| Biological factors | Reports of physical health problems and disabilities | Neuropsychological deficits (e.g., problem solving, conceptual ability) |
| | Physiological overreactivity | |

SOURCES: A representative but not exhaustive list of sources for the information displayed in this table includes Borrego, Timmer, Urquiza, & Follette, 2004; Casanueva, Martin, Runyan, Barth, & Bradley, 2008; Estacion & Cherlin, 2010; Francis & Wolfe, 2008; Mammen, Kolko, & Pilkonis, 2003; Milner, 2003; C. M. Rodriguez, 2010; Tajima & Harachi, 2010.

# EXPANDED DISCUSSION OF PSYCHOLOGICAL, INTERPERSONAL, AND BIOLOGICAL CHARACTERISTICS OF ADULTS WHO PHYSICALLY ABUSE CHILDREN

## Biological Factors

Several researchers have suggested that biological factors may distinguish physically abusive parents from nonabusive parents. Studies have examined physiological reactivity in perpetrators of CPA, and the findings have consistently demonstrated that these individuals are hyper-responsive to child-related stimuli such as crying (e.g., Chen, Hou, & Chuang, 2009; Kagan, 2007; McPherson, Lewis, Lynn, Haskett, & Behrend, 2009).

## Emotional and Behavioral Characteristics of Perpetrators

Studies comparing nonabusive parents with physically abusive parents have confirmed several characteristics such as *anger control problems, hostility, low frustration tolerance, depression, low self-esteem, deficits in empathy,* and *rigidity* (e.g., Cicchetti & Rogosch, in press; Sroufe et al., 2010). Such negative emotional and behavioral states may increase the risk of CPA by interfering with the way these parents perceive events, by decreasing their parenting abilities, or by lowering their tolerance for specific child behaviors (Cerezo, Pons-Salvador, & Trenado, 2008). *Substance abuse* problems are significantly related to *recurrence of a CPA report* (Johnson-Reid, Chung, Way, & Jolley, 2010; see also Berger, Slack, Waldfogel, & Bruch, 2010). Along the same lines, some evidence also suggests that abusive parents, relative to nonabusive parents, automatically encode *ambiguous* child behavior in negative ways (Crouch et al., 2010; see also Seng & Prinz, 2008).

## Family and Interpersonal Difficulties of Perpetrators

Physically abusive adults are more likely than nonabusive individuals to exhibit family and interpersonal difficulties. Abusive individuals report more verbal and physical conflict among family members, higher levels of spousal disagreement and tension, and greater deficits in family cohesion and expressiveness. There are several robust linkages between CPA and adult violence:

- Abusive parents report more conflict in their families of origin than nonabusive parents (Henning, Leitenberg, Coffey, Turner, & Bennett, 1996; Messman-Moore & Coates, 2007).

- Abusive parents engage in fewer interactions with their children, such as playing together, providing positive responses to their children, and demonstrating affection (see Boyle et al., 2010).

- Adults with histories of CPA are more likely both to receive and to inflict *dating violence* (Herrenkohl et al., 2004; D. S. Black, Sussman, & Unger, 2010).

- Adults (primarily males) who were physically abused as children are more likely to inflict *physical abuse* on their *marital partners* (Jouriles, McDonald, Slep, Heyman, & Garrido, 2008).

- Adults who were victims of physical abuse as children are more likely to *be perpetrators of CPA as adults* (e.g., Coohey & Braun, 1997; see also Coohey, 2007).

---

## SECTION SUMMARY

### Characteristics of Abusive Parents and Abused Children

A relatively large volume of literature describes the characteristics of perpetrators of CPA. Although no single profile exists, research findings indicate that several attributes may represent elevated risk for CPA. The sociodemographic characteristics of the victims of CPA do not suggest that any particular subpopulation of children is the primary target of violence. Both girls and boys are maltreated, and victims are found in all age-groups. CPA victims also come from diverse ethnic backgrounds. Although studies show that CPA usually differs by race of the victim, there is evidence that some characteristics place certain children at more risk than others. Young children, for example (birth to age 5), are at particularly high risk for CPA, as are children who are economically disadvantaged. Children with special needs, such as those with physical or mental disabilities, may be at higher risk for abuse than other children.

High CPA rates are associated with individuals who are young when they have a child. In the overwhelming majority of reported cases, perpetrators are the parents of the victims. Single parenthood is also associated with abuse. The relationship of stepparenting to abuse has been examined, but the findings do not generally indicate that stepparents are as abusive as biological parents. Live-in boyfriends, however, may be particularly abusive. Data regarding perpetrator gender are mixed, although it is clear that CPA is committed by both males and females.

Studies have found numerous psychological characteristics and biological factors that differentiate abusive parents from nonabusive parents, including depression, anger control problems, parenting difficulties, family difficulties, and neurobiological abnormalities.

# EXPLAINING CHILD PHYSICAL ABUSE

## The Individual Psychopathology Model—Mentally Ill Parent

As CPA has come to be defined more broadly to include greater numbers of adults as perpetrators, it has become increasingly difficult to view child abusers as people who suffer from mental illnesses, personality disorders, alcohol or drug abuse, or any other individual defect. Although research has identified a subgroup of severely disturbed individuals who abuse children, only a small proportion of abusive parents (less than 10%) meet criteria for severe psychiatric disorders (Kempe & Helfer, 1972; Straus, 1980; E. Walker, Downey, & Bergman, 1989). Adults who physically abuse children often do exhibit specific nonpsychiatric psychological, behavioral, and biological characteristics that distinguish them from nonabusive parents, such as anger control problems, depression, parenting difficulties, physiological hyperreactivity, and substance abuse.

### *Postpartum Depression/Psychosis*

The postpartum mental health of a mother is a crucial factor in her child's well-being (Whitaker, Orzoil, & Kahn, 2006). Some mothers with *postpartum depression* experience problems in providing optimal care for their newborns. They have problems in feeding, sleep routines, well-baby clinic visits, vaccinations, and safety practices (Field, 2010). Of interest are findings that the behavior of women with postpartum depression is similar across the globe. Such findings implicate a biological basis for the depression. A small number of mothers with postpartum psychosis may appear to be neglectful, abusive, and even murderous. Although few mothers actually harm their babies because of postpartum depression, many women have recurrent and *disturbing* thoughts of harming their babies (Humenik & Fingerhut, 2007).

*Prevalence of postpartum depression.* Until recently, the number of women affected by postpartum depression has been largely unknown. Within the United States, about 11% to 16% of women experience depression the first year after childbirth (Logsdon, Wisner, Billings, & Shanahan, 2006; Vesga-López et al., 2008; see also Gaidos, 2010). Within Canada, 11.2% of Canadian-born women experienced postpartum depression in one survey. The percentage among majority group immigrant women was 8.3%, and 24.7% among minority group immigrant women (Mechakra-Tahiri, Zunzunegui, & Sequin, 2007).

A large nationally representative sample of 14,549 women aged 18 to 49 participated in face-to-face interviews as part of the 2001–2002 National Epidemiological Survey on Alcohol and Related Conditions. Epidemiologists were able to contrast women who had been pregnant, women who had been pregnant and suffered postpartum depression, nonpregnant women, and currently pregnant women. Women responded to questions about their alcohol/drug use, their mental health, and their sociodemographic information.

Several findings emerged from the analyses: (a) *Currently pregnant* women had *fewer mood disorders* than nonpregnant women; (b) Pregnancy was not associated with mental disorders; (c) Women who had been *pregnant* during the last 12 months and women currently *pregnant,* relative to nonpregnant women, *consumed less alcohol and drugs* (except for illicit drugs);

(d) Women who had been pregnant during the previous 12 months suffered significantly more depression; (e) Pregnant women with psychiatric conditions received very little treatment; and (f) Risk factors for a major depression included the following: young age, not being married, trauma exposure, exposure to stress, pregnancy complications, and overall poor health. The authors concluded that while pregnancy is *not* related to an increased prevalence of mental disorders, depression is associated with the postpartum period (Vesga-López et al., 2008; see also Gaidos, 2010).

*Causes of postpartum depression.* The cause of postpartum depression is unknown, but experts refer to it as a *brain-based disorder.* Newer scholarship is finally shedding a glimmer of light on precursors of postpartum depression. One risk is *elevated corticotrophin-releasing hormones* during pregnancy—hormones that help maintain a pregnancy. A second is *childhood sexual abuse* (Lev-Wiesel, Daphna-Tekoah, & Hallak, 2009; Yim et al., 2009). Some women with postpartum depression must also defend themselves against violent husbands (Ulrich et al., 2006). Congress officially widened the number of possible determinants.

| Rapid decline in hormones | Previous mental illness | Stressful life events |
|---|---|---|
| Lack of social support | Difficulty during labor/ pregnancy | Physical or mental abuse |
| Marital strife | Premature birth or miscarriage | Family history of mood disorders |
| Financial problems | Previous bout of postpartum depression | Feeling overwhelmed by one's role as mother |

*Public reactions.* Persons showing signs and symptoms of any mental health condition (e.g., phobia, bipolar disorder, obsessive-compulsive disorder) may receive harsh treatment from society. Without a definitive neurobiological understanding of postpartum depression, society has viewed the abusive behaviors of these mothers as purely criminal. A mother who kills her own baby, regardless of her mental condition, becomes a pariah (Pinto-Foltz & Logsdon, 2008). The general public is also becoming more aware of postpartum depression because of notorious cases in the media and because a few courageous celebrities who have experienced the condition have spoken publicly about their distressing symptoms.

*Medical responses.* Information is finally making its way into medical journals and hence into doctors' practices. Experts recommend *universal screening* by health care workers for depression during pregnancy and during the postpartum period. In fact, Congress has mandated screening (Tovino, 2010). A first step is to raise awareness among primary care providers (Logsdon et al., 2006). Nevertheless, the stigma attached to any mental illness impedes service delivery (Pinto-Foltz & Logsdon, 2008). Rural women, in particular, face challenges in finding help (Jesse, Dolbier, & Blanchard, 2008).

*Legal responses.* Quite a few factors that may improve services for postpartum mothers are coalescing. The narrowing gap between medical and mental conditions that must be covered by insurance companies represents one such factor. The implications of disability law provide another intertwining legal factor affecting women with postpartum depression. Mandated screening is another illustration (Tovino, 2010).

*Treatment.* Postpartum depression is *underidentified and undertreated*. The most common treatments are psychotherapy and antidepressant medications. Psychosocial interventions may be best for adolescent mothers (Yozwiak, 2010). One effective intervention consisted of an educational element incorporated into postpartum discharge care. The inclusion of information about postpartum depression significantly alleviated depression compared with a comparison group that did not receive the intervention (Ho et al., 2009). Another inquiry found that treatment for postpartum depression resulted in significant stress reduction. A major contributor to stress among postpartum depressed mothers is the perception that their parenting skills are inadequate (Misri, Reebye, Milis, & Shah, 2006).

Another innovative approach for severely depressed women included a 12-week massage therapy component during and after pregnancy administered by a significant male partner. Compared with the nonmassaged depressed women, massaged women were significantly improved: (a) Massaged pregnant and postpartum women had lower cortisol ("stress hormone") levels and less depression; and (b) Massaged pregnant women had fewer preterm births or low birth weight babies. Moreover, the babies had lower cortisol levels and did better on a newborn behavioral assessment test (Field, Diego, Hernandez-Reif, Deeds, & Figuerido, 2009).

*Prevention.* Fortunately, Congress has done more to reduce problems associated with postpartum depression than it has to diminish several other less serious problems. The House passed the Mom's Opportunity to Access Health, Education, Research, and Support for Postpartum Depression Act (2009). Public awareness campaigns are under way in some locales. The California Assembly Concurrent Resolution proclaimed May 2003 as Postpartum Mood and Anxiety Disorder Awareness Month.

## CASE HISTORY   Andrea Yates—The Devil Spoke to Her

In 2001, 35-year-old Andrea Yates drowned her five children, ranging in age from 6 months to 7 years, in the bathtub one by one.

During her trial, facts about her mental state came to light. She had suffered postpartum depression after the births of her last two children. Psychiatrists had diagnosed her as suffering from postpartum depression/postpartum psychosis. She would not always take her powerful antipsychotic medication, Haldol; 2 weeks before the drownings, her doctor discontinued its use. Even to the untrained eye, Andrea appeared *mad*. She refused to feed herself and the children from time to time. She hallucinated and frantically read the Bible.

Adding to her torment were the sermons of their church's pastor. He centered on the wickedness of Eve and claimed that any mother who did not rear her children according to the precepts of Jesus Christ would go to hell—so too would her children. Andrea became convinced that she was a *bad* mother. Satan was inside her, and she had to kill her children to save them from hellfire and damnation. Her husband, an ardent member of the congregation, said he did everything he could to support Andrea. Given Andrea's fragile mental state, her mother-in-law often helped her with the children for hours on end. Despite such support, Andrea remained psychotic, and no one gave her the mental health services she needed.

Strangely, a well-known expert witness for the prosecution said he believed that Andrea was *not* mentally ill and that she was copying a crime she had seen on *Law & Order.* In this episode, a mother who had drowned her children was acquitted on an insanity defense. The jury found Andrea guilty of three of the murders and the judge sentenced her to life in prison. Experts complained about Texas's definition of insanity, and family members blamed the medical community.

*Law & Order,* however, had never taped such a show! This error became the basis for a second trial, in 2006. This time the jury found Andrea *not guilty by reason of insanity.* Prosecutors took no action against the expert witness for his "honest mistake." The judge sentenced Andrea to a maximum-security mental hospital to remain there until psychiatrists deem her no longer a threat (Associated Press, 2006b; Yardley, 2002).

### Munchausen by Proxy

One especially rare and unrecognized type of child abuse is Munchausen syndrome by proxy (MBP). In these strange cases, adult caretakers *falsify* to medical personnel *physical and/or psychological symptoms* in a child to meet their own psychological needs. Typically, children who are victims of MBP are "paraded before the medical profession with a fantastic range of illnesses" (D. A. Rosenberg, 1987, p. 548). The principal routes that caregivers take to produce or feign illness in children include the fabrication of symptoms such as altering laboratory specimens, and the direct production of physical symptoms. For example, caregivers have been known to contaminate children's urine specimens with their own blood and claim that the children have been urinating blood. One mother repeatedly administered laxatives to her child, causing severe diarrhea, blood infection, and dehydration (see D. P. H. Jones, 1994; J. M. Peters, 1989; D. A. Rosenberg, 1987).

An adult's production or feigning of illness in a dependent child is considered *abusive,* primarily because of the serious physical consequences to the child. The procedures that caregivers use to produce illnesses often cause a child physical discomfort or pain (Stirling, 2007). For example, one caregiver administered ipecac to a child to produce recurrent and chronic vomiting and diarrhea (McClung, Murray, & Braden, 1988; see also "Caustic Ingestion," 2010). Such behaviors may result in a child's death. As a case in point, one study of five families with eight children found that all of the victims were poisoned or suffocated by their mothers, and two of the children died (Vennemann et al., 2004). One possible prevention strategy is to place the child in foster care because of the dangerousness of the mother's behavior (Sanders & Bursch, 2002).

### The Difficult Child Model

Other theorists have focused on the *behavior* of the child as the major cause of CPA. From this standpoint, children with certain characteristics (such as mental disabilities, aggressiveness, young age) are at increased risk for abuse (Chen, Hou, & Chuang, 2009). Researchers have also suggested that difficult behavior and specific temperaments in children may contribute to abusive incidents (e.g., Youngblade & Belsky, 1990). Some parents, for example, may lack the skills to manage children who are annoying, defiant, argumentative, or vindictive, and their frustration may lead to child abuse (see J. D. Ford et al., 1999). Children given a psychiatric diagnosis are also at greater risk for abuse than children without psychiatric diagnoses. Furthermore, diagnosed children are at significantly greater risk for **polyvictimization** (Cuevas, Finkelhor, Ormrod, & Turner, 2009).

Regardless of the cause of a child's behavior, CPA is associated with especially demanding and difficult child care. Nonetheless, the behavior of a child should never be accepted as a justification for an adult's violent behavior. Legal statutes governing adult behavior do not grant adults the right to inflict physical injury on children who are difficult. Children cannot be held responsible for their own victimization. In addition, it is important to remember that although characteristics of the child are important, they are only one factor among many that contribute to CPA (Sidebotham & Heron, 2003).

## Parent-Child Interaction Model

Parent-child interaction theories suggest that difficult child behaviors interact with specific parental behaviors to result in CPA (Crittenden, 1998; van Bakel & Ricksen-Walraven, 2002). That is, it is the *behavior of both parent and child,* rather than the behavior of either alone, that promotes violence. Studies have repeatedly demonstrated, for instance, that punitive parenting is associated with negative child behavior and outcomes. Researchers in one study contrasted three groups of adults aged 15 to 54 whose retrospective data were available in the National Comorbidity Survey (NCS; Kessler et al., 1994): (a) those who experienced *no physical punishment* (35.5%), (b) those who experienced *physical punishment only* (48.%), and (c) those who experienced *child abuse* (16.5%). Research participants responded to a number of tests of childhood abuse, parental bonding, psychiatric disorders, *and* socioeconomic variables. The physically punished group experienced *less maternal warmth, less paternal warmth,* and *less protective parental bonding.* The punished group also had a greater chance (odds ratio) of manifesting *psychiatric disorders: major depression, alcohol abuse/dependence,* and *externalizing problems.* These results offer very strong support for an association between childhood spanking and adult psychiatric disorders (Afifi et al., 2006).

Some experts have suggested that difficulties in parent-child relations develop during the abused child's infancy, when early *attachments* between parent and child are formed (Erickson & Egeland, 2010; Hennighausen & Lyons-Ruth, 2010). A child may be born with a particular characteristic, such as a difficult temperament or a physical disability, which creates an excessive challenge for a parent and interferes with the development of a secure attachment between the parent and child. This vulnerability may in turn lead to further difficult child behaviors and increased challenges for the parent. Such a pattern may escalate and result in physical abuse when the challenges exceed the parent's tolerance or capability threshold. Research, however, seems to suggest that the temperament of the infant is *not* causal in forming attachments (Sroufe et al., 2010; see also Cerezo et al., 2008). Nevertheless, these findings do not detract from the many findings of temperamental differences among infants (e.g., Else-Quest, Hyde, Goldsmith, & Van Hulle, 2006).

## Social Learning Theory

As noted throughout this text, many retrospective studies have demonstrated that a significant percentage of adults who abuse children were abused themselves as children. In one study, mothers' childhood physical abuse was associated with outcomes for infants: (a) poorer mother-child interaction, (b) increased vigilance, and (c) difficulty recovering from distress among infants (A. J. Lang, Gartstein, Rodgers, & Lebeck, 2010). Abusive adults presumably learned through experiences with their own parents that violence is an acceptable method of child rearing. They also missed the opportunity as children to learn appropriate and nurturing forms of adult-child interaction (e.g., Medley & Sachs-Ericsson, 2009; Milner et al., 2010).

*Parenting styles.* The findings from prospective studies consistently support the notion that *parenting styles* are passed from one generation to the next (e.g., McKinney et al., 2009; Van Ijzendoorn, 1992). One illustration is the *intergenerational transmission of attachment style* (Belsky, 2005; see also, Doyle, Markiewicz, Brendgen, Lieberman, & Voss, 2000). One investigation identified strong associations between specific types of childhood abuse and adult abuse of one's own children: (a) Parents who had been neglected during their own childhood, relative to those who had not, were 2.6 times more likely to neglect their own children and 2 times more likely to physically abuse their own children, and (b) parents who had been physically abused during childhood, relative to those who had not, were 5 times more likely to physically abuse their own children and 1.4 times more likely to neglect their children (Kim, 2008).

*Observational learning.* Other opportunities for social learning stem from seeing violence. As one example, children who observe (witness) interparental violence are likely to engage as perpetrator or victim in their own adult intimate relationship (Fehringer & Hindin, 2009; see also A. Flynn & Graham, 2010).

## Situational and Societal Conditions

*Economic disadvantage.* D. G. Gil (1970) was one of the first to point out that a high proportion of abused children come from poor and socially disadvantaged families. Subsequent research has supported these early findings, indicating that CPA is more common among low-income families and families supported by public assistance than among better-off families. Children whose fathers are unemployed or work part-time are also at greater risk for abuse than children whose fathers have full-time employment (Sedlak et al., 2010; Zielinski, 2009).

*Social isolation/social support.* One group of studies indicates that perpetrators of CPA report more interpersonal problems outside the family—such as social isolation, limited support from friends and family members, and loneliness—than do nonperpetrators (e.g., Coohey, 2007; Staggs, Long, Mason, Krishnan, & Riger, 2007). Abusive parents often lack an extended family or peer support network. Compared with nonabusive parents, abusive parents have relatively fewer contacts with peer networks as well as with immediate family and other relatives (e.g., Coohey, 2007; Whipple & Webster-Stratton, 1991). As noted previously, children who had grandparents were significantly less likely to be abused than those who did not, suggesting that having an extended family may have functioned to reduce isolation and hence CPA (Sedlak et al., 2010).

## Stress

Research indicates that some situational variables, particularly as they affect the levels of stress within families, are associated with child physical abuse. Research evidence has clearly established that parenting stress strongly influences both parenting behaviors and children's behavioral and emotional problems (Huth-Bocks & Hughes, 2008). The importance of a mother's psychological functioning came to light in a comparison of *intolerance for children's misbehavior.* Abusive mothers ($n = 80$) in contrast to nonabusive mothers ($n = 86$) experienced more stress stemming from children's misbehavior (McPherson et al., 2009; see also McKelvey et al., 2008; C. A. Walker & Davies, 2009).

In their review of the literature, D. A. Black, Heyman, and Slep (2001) found that CPA is generally associated with high numbers of *stressful life events* as well as *stress associated with parenting.* Stressful situations that appear to be risk factors for CPA include the presence in the family of a *new baby, illness, death of a family member, poor housing conditions,* and *larger-than-average family size* (e.g., Wolfner & Gelles, 1993). Other situational variables associated with CPA include high levels of stress in the family from *work-related problems* and pressures, marital discord, conflicts over a child's school performance, illness, and a crying or fussy child (Barton & Baglio, 1993).

*Military families.* Newer research has uncovered strong associations between *stress associated with military service* and physical child abuse and neglect. One inquiry compared military and nonmilitary families on two dimensions derived from *aggregate population data* in Texas: (a) child maltreatment records (from NCANDS), and (b) military deployment records. The research team compared data *before* October 2002 with data from the period *afterward* (October 2002 through June 2003). The rate of substantiated CPA cases per month *doubled during the after period (the deployment period),* and child abuse rates increased both upon deployment *and* upon return from deployment. The rates among nonmilitary families stayed static (Rentz et al., 2007; see also Gibbs, Martin, Kupper, & Johnson, 2007). Other evidence stems from analyses of veterans. An analysis of child physical abuse among *female* military veterans found a prevalence rate of 45% (Sadler, Booth, Mengeling, & Doebbeling, 2004; see also Munsey, 2007a).

*Children's behavior during deployment.* Another inquiry compared children aged 3 to 5 years of age who had a deployed parent (33% of 233 military families) with children who did not. Children with a deployed parent had significantly *higher externalizing scores* than the comparison group. In addition, parents with a deployed spouse had significantly *elevated depression* when contrasted with their counterparts (Chartrand, Frank, White, & Shope, 2008).

*Stress related to intimate partner violence.* It is not surprising that mothers who are experiencing male-to-female intimate partner violence would exhibit more stress and hence decreased parenting efficacy. "Living with violence terrorizes children and presents a formidable barrier to women's resources and confidence to meet their children's needs" (P. G. Jaffe & Crooks, 2005, p. 2). A different comparison of abused and nonabused rural mothers indicated that abused mothers sought health care advice significantly more frequently than nonabused mothers (Ellis et al., 2008). If pediatricians and other health workers would routinely screen mothers for spouse abuse, it might lead to helpful referrals and eventually to a reduction in maternal stress and better parenting (see Glowa, Frasier, & Newton, 2002).

## Cultural Acceptance of Corporal Punishment

Historically, the view of children and wives as "property" permitted the use of violence against them. Physical chastisement of wives is no longer legal and no longer generally socially acceptable in the United States. Unfortunately, the belief in the legitimacy of physical discipline of children still remains (Garbarino, 2005). So far there are *no federal laws against spanking children,* and only half the states ban spanking in child care settings and/or schools. Parents may still hit children at will in their own homes (Bitensky, 2006). (See www.sagepub.com/barnett3e for a list of possible cultural contributions to CPA.)

*Predicting injury from physical punishment.* Some injuries and even fatalities are the result of punishment that got out of control (J. E. B. Myers, 2005). A *prediction* of injury (endangerment) forms the basis of CPS workers' decisions to remove the child from the home. In light of the consequences of their decisions, their assumptions about the likelihood of injury deserve evaluation. Beliefs about assaults include the following: (a) Injurious and noninjurious actions are *qualitatively different,* (b) the *determinants* of injurious assault *differ* from the determinants of noninjurious assault, and (c) *caregiving quality* differs during injurious versus noninjurious assaults.

A study examining whether the characteristics of the child, the family, or the social context might provide valid information about risk factors for injury from physical punishment produced *no* significant results. The researchers interpreted the data to mean that *trying to predict injury* from physical punishment may be questionable (Gonzalez, Durrant, Chabot, Trocmé, & Brown, 2008).

*Evangelical parenting.* Certain *Protestant religious beliefs* (belief in hell, authoritarian parenting) and *sociopolitical conservatism* play a forceful role in the acceptance of physical discipline of children (Ellison & Bradshaw, 2009). Importantly, such beliefs do *not* incorporate acceptance of child physical abuse. In fact, one investigation was able to show that Protestant parents who used corporal punishment were *not* more likely to be guilty of CPA than parents with different beliefs (Dyslin & Thomsen, 2005). A few other findings suggest improved parenting among Protestant religious parents. Evangelical fathers, for instance, were more likely to spend quality time with their children, and Protestant parents were *less* likely to yell at their children (Bartkowski & Wilcox, 2000; Bartkowski & Xu, 2000). The United Methodist Church has now called for a ban on corporal punishment (see Knox, 2010). Another survey noted an association between risk potential for CPA and *extrinsic religiosity* but not for intrinsic religiosity (Rodriguez & Henderson, 2010).

# Risk Factors for Child Physical Abuse

There are multiple risk factors implicated in the empirical literature as playing important roles in the physical abuse of children. Evidence continues to accumulate that cultural acceptance of corporal punishment as a method of discipline is a factor that is conducive to CPA (Gershoff, 2008). With a sample of 1,435 parents interviewed by phone, a group of researchers produced empirical evidence for two hypotheses. First, *frequent spanking* is a predictor of child physical abuse. Second, *spanking the buttocks with an object* (may legally be "spanking") is a very strong predictor of CPA (Zolotor, Theodore, Chang, Berkoff, & Runyan, 2008). See Table 4.10 for a more complete summary of risk factors for CPA.

**TABLE 4.10** Risk Factors Associated With Physical Child Abuse

| Risk Factors Associated With the Parent-Child Relationship | | |
|---|---|---|
| Characteristics of the child | Young age | Physical and mental disabilities |
| | Difficult child behaviors | Insufficiently self-protective |
| Characteristics of the parent | Deficits in parenting skills | View parent role as stressful |
| | Unrealistic expectations of children | Negatively biased perception of children |
| | Power-assertive discipline | |
| **Risk Factors Associated With Family Environment** | | |
| Characteristics of the family | Abuse of spouses and children | Marital discord |
| | Few positive interactions | Spank child frequently |
| | Spank child on bottom with object | |
| **Risk Factors Associated With Situational and Societal Conditions** | | |
| Situational conditions | Low socioeconomic status | Large family size |
| | Single-parent household | Social isolation/lack of social capital |
| | Receiving public assistance | Situational stress |
| | Blue-collar employment | Unemployment or part-time work |
| | Poverty | Family disorganization |
| | Community violence | |
| Societal conditions | Cultural approval of violence in society | |
| | Cultural approval of corporal punishment | |
| | Power differentials in society and the family | |

SOURCES: A representative but not exhaustive list of sources for information displayed in this table includes Annerbäck, Svedin, & Gustafsson, 2010; Cuevas, Finkelhor, Ormrod, & Turner, 2009; de Paúl, Asla, Pérez-Albéniz, & Torres-Gómez de Cádiz, 2006; de Paúl, Pérez-Albéniz, Guibert, Asla, & Ormaechea, 2008; Gershoff, 2008; Leslie et al., 2005; Maker, Shah, & Agha, 2005; C. M. Rodriguez, 2010; Stith et al., 2009; R. Thompson, 2007; H. A. Turner, Finkelhor, & Ormrod, 2010; U.S. Department of Health & Human Services, 2008; Zolotor, Theodore, Chang, Berkoff, & Runyan, 2008.

## Polyvictimization/Overlapping Risk Factors

In a retrospective Canadian health study of 9,953 children 15 years old or older, researchers uncovered important facts about neglect and maltreatment. They tallied negative childhood experiences, such as physical abuse, sexual abuse, exposure to marital conflict, poor parent-child relationship, low parental education, and parental psychopathology (Chartier et al., 2010; see also Appleyard et al., 2005; Greenfield, 2010):

- 72% of respondents reported at least one negative childhood experience.
- 37% reported two or more adverse childhood experiences.
- Effects on health from physical or sexual abuse were stronger than for other types of abuse.
- An aggregate measure of abuse revealed increased negative health effects with each additional abuse experience—cumulative effects.
- Adverse experience overlap can increase the likelihood of becoming risk factors for adult health problems.

## Protective Factors That Reduce Likelihood of Abuse

The Centers for Disease Control and Prevention (n.d.) has summed up research that has identified factors associated with reduced risks of child maltreatment. See Table 4.11 for a list of these factors.

**TABLE 4.11**   Factors Associated With Reduced Occurrence of Child Abuse

| Family Protective Factors | | |
|---|---|---|
| Supportive family environment | Child monitoring | Access to health care |
| Nurturing parenting skills | Parental employment | Access to social services |
| Household rules | Adequate housing | Extended family support |
| Family-protective communities | | |

## Contemporary Theories of Child Physical Abuse

In the past decade, experts have formulated several theories of child physical abuse that build on the models just described and take into account the risk factors known to be associated with CPA. Most of these theories focus on the interplay among individual factors, parent-child interaction factors, family environment factors, and situational and societal factors. **Transactional theories,** as one example, emphasize the interactions among **risk factors** and **protective factors** associated with child physical abuse. Unfortunately, both kinds of theories currently have only limited empirical support. Efforts directed toward conceptualizing such theories, however, are a positive first step in understanding the origins of CPA.

*Transactional theories.* Cicchetti and Lynch (1993) have developed a transactional theory that focuses on the importance of *independent factors* such as characteristics of the individual, the family, the community, and culture. They suggest that child maltreatment results when potentiating factors that increase the likelihood of maltreatment outweigh various compensatory factors that decrease the risk for maltreatment. Transactional theories are unique in that they not only describe various factors that might contribute to CPA but also emphasize the role of the interaction of these factors in the etiology of child maltreatment. One study found, however, that numerous risk factors identified through bivariate correlational analyses did not uniquely contribute to physical child abuse (Slep & O'Leary, 2007).

---

**SECTION SUMMARY**

### Explanations for Child Physical Abuse

The causes of CPA are not well understood, and scholars' views on the primary causes of CPA vary widely. Academic logicians have proposed a number of models to explain the behavior. One theory postulated that abusive behavior arises from psychiatric disturbance (e.g., mental illness, personality disorder, substance abuse). Cases of postpartum psychosis and Munchausen syndrome by proxy exemplify the link between parental mental illness and child abuse.

Others suggest that some children are so difficult (e.g., babies who have colic) that they provoke abusive parental behavior. Still others believe that the problem is rooted in stressed parent-child interactions. As a case in point, the deployment of a military spouse/father might make both parties upset, irritable, and depressed. In turn, each party might antagonize the other leading to increased CPA. A third explanation rests on learning theory. Because children learn to model the violent behavior of parents (CPA), they grow up and repeat the intergenerational cycles of violence by abusing their own children.

A significant shift in the conceptualization of CPA occurred with the birth of sociological models. These models emphasize the possible contributions to CPA of the factors of socioeconomic disadvantage, social isolation, situational stressors, and cultural approval of violence. Most likely, more than one theory may help explain CPA. As research progresses, it will be possible to narrow the determinants of CPA and thus clarify the heuristic value of various models.

---

## PRACTICE, POLICY, AND PREVENTION ISSUES

### Practice (Treatment) for CPA

Historically, the view that the mental illness of parents caused CPA led to treatment efforts directed primarily at individual parents. Treatment approaches gradually broadened to include not only *adult interventions* but also *child-focused* and *family interventions* (Chaffin et al., 2004; Oliver & Washington, 2009). *Community interventions* address other multiple factors believed to contribute to CPA, such as *social isolation, financial stress,* and *excessive child-care demands.* Many parents are aware of their need for more parenting help. In one survey, 94% of parents queried said they had unmet needs for either parental guidance or screening by pediatric providers (Bethell, Reuland, Halfon, & Schor, 2004).

*Treatment for physically abusive adults.* Current maltreatment experts assert that for treatment to be effective it must incorporate four components (Runyon & Urquiza, 2010):

> - Parenting skills. For example, remembering to praise a child's desirable behavior—"I like the way you came to dinner right away when I called you."
> - Correcting distorted cognitions/attributions: For example, "This toddler is old enough to know better than to run in the street. He is trying to make me mad."
> - Coping strategies that are adaptive and nonviolent: For example, "Let me tell you what I need to feel better right now."
> - Better emotional regulation: For example, impulse control—"I'll pull this baby's hair right this minute because she pulled my hair. That will teach her!"

A different scheme derived from a meta-analysis of the literature lists three factors essential to effective treatment (Oliver & Washington, 2009): Anger Management, Child Management, and Stress Management.

## Parent-Focused Treatment

Although practitioners need more *cultural competence,* the *parent-focused treatment programs* consistently demonstrate improvements in parenting skills as a result of treatment (e.g., D. J. Kolko & Kolko, 2009):

| | |
|---|---|
| Positive interactions with their children | Decreases in negative interactions |
| Positive perceptions of their children | Reductions in parenting stress |
| Effective control of unwanted behavior | Decreases in physically punitive parenting techniques |
| Enhanced anger control | Decreases in coercive parenting techniques |
| Improved coping/problem-solving skills | |

## In-Home Treatments

Several in-home treatments are *effective* for reducing CPA. Project SafeCare exemplifies in-home visitation treatments even though it requires more sessions than other programs. The program extends over 24 weeks and features 5 to 6 in-home visits for each component. Although the sessions are instructive, they do not rely on passive listening by parents. Instead, parents *actively* acquire needed skills through techniques such as completing homework assignments and demonstrating (modeling) desirable parental behaviors. Some topics addressed by the training staff include *health risks* (safety hazards, proper health care skills) and *psychosocial risks* resulting from poor parent-child interactions. To check on parents' learning (e.g., parent-child interaction skills), the staff conducts assessments of parental skills according to certain protocols (Gershater-Molko, Lutzker, & Wesch, 2003; Edwards & Lutzker, 2008).

## Behavior-Based Treatment Programs

There are several empirically tested *effective* programs that use cognitive-behavioral techniques. The focus of the program can be on the *parent's behavior,* the *child's behavior, parent-child interactive behaviors,* or all three. Parent training based on *behavioral (learning)* or *cognitive-behavioral principles* involves educating parents about the following elements:

- The effects of reinforcement and punishment on children's behavior
- The appropriate methods of delivering reinforcement and punishment
- The importance of consistency in discipline
- Identification of events that increase negative emotions
- Changing anger-producing thoughts
- Relaxation techniques
- Methods for coping with stressful interactions with their children

*Parent-Child Interaction Therapy (PCIT).* PCIT is a program to eliminate parents' physical abuse of their children. As the child and parent interact in one room, a counselor watching behind a window in another room gives the parent instructions via an electronic hearing device ("bug" in the ear). Parents learn specific skills, such as empathic listening and how to communicate the consequences for specific behaviors (see S. N. Hart, Brassard, & Davidson, 2010).

Several outcome evaluations have demonstrated that PCIT programs accomplish most of their goals (e.g., Chaffin et al., 2004; Timmer, Zebell, Culver, & Urquiza, 2010). One study compared 48 Chinese parent-child dyads that received treatment with 62 dyads that did not. Analysis of pre- and post-intervention *questionnaire* data showed that parents who received the treatment reported fewer child behavior problems and experienced less parental stress. Results from pre- and post-intervention *observational data* also demonstrated a decrease in inappropriate child-management skills and an increase in positive parenting practices (C. Leung, Tsang, Heung, & Yiu, 2009). In a second study of 73 parent-child dyads participating in a clinic-based PCIT program, investigators presented an adjunct treatment. They randomly assigned half the dyads to an in-home PCIT series of treatments and the other half to a social support treatment. Dyads who received the PCIT treatment showed a decrease in parental stress, an increase in parental tolerance for child behaviors, but no significant improvement in child behaviors (Timmer et al., 2010).

*Alternatives for Families: Cognitive-Behavioral Therapy (AF-CBT).* AF-CBT features three phases that focus on psychoeducation, skills training, and application. Embedded within these sections are child-directed, parent-directed, and family-directed components. See Table 4.12 for a summary of the program components.

**TABLE 4.12** Program Components of the Alternative for Families: Cognitive-Behavioral Therapy

| Child Tasks | Parent Tasks | Family Tasks |
|---|---|---|
| Healthy coping | Becoming engaged in the program | Learn about physical abuse—psychoeducation |
| Emotion expression | Understanding the reason for the CPS referral | Clarification of abusive behaviors |
| Emotion recognition, expression, and management | Examining coercive behaviors within the family | Development of safety plans (what to do/where to go when abuse seems imminent) |
| Cognitive processing of their experiences of abuse | Examining parental beliefs about coercion and violence | Communication skills training |
| Social/interpersonal skill learning | Examination of unrealistic expectations of children | Nonviolent problem solving |
|  | Emotion regulation training |  |
|  | Parenting skills training |  |

In one evaluation of the AF-CBT program's efficacy, a researcher compared its results with those of families receiving a *community intervention.* Families receiving AF-CBT manifested less parental distress, risk for child abuse, and family conflict. Results also included better family cohesion and a reduction in children's externalizing behavior (D. J. Kolko & Kolko, 2009).

*The Combined Parent-Child Cognitive Behavioral Treatment (CPC-CBT).* CPC-CBT consists of 16 therapy sessions, each 90 minutes long. Within each session, the therapist meets the parent and child separately and together. First, CPC-CBT initiates the program with engagement strategies to motivate the parent to enter and remain in treatment. Second, implementation of a psychoeducational component provides information about different types of abuse and coercive behavior and their impacts on children and parents. Third, parents receive information about child development and setting realistic expectations for children's behavior. Fourth, children learn how to express their feelings.

During the sessions, parents practice *communication skills, positive parenting,* and *behavior management.* First they practice with the therapist and then with their children. The therapist serves as a *coach,* offering positive reinforcement and corrective feedback. Near the end of the session, the whole family develops a *safety plan* and practices how to implement it. A safety plan guides parents and children about specific actions to take, such as going into a different room, if abuse seems imminent. The family also works on communicating about abuse issues. The sessions end with the parent writing a *letter of apology* for being abusive, and the *child writes about the traumatic elements of his abuse.* An outcome evaluation judged the program to be effective (Runyon et al., 2009).

*Therapeutic day care.* Because abusive parents often find the parenting role challenging and have fewer child care options than other parents, programs that offer *child care* can provide relief for overly burdened parents who need a break (Hay & Jones, 1994; R. A. Thompson, Laible, & Robbennolt, 1997). Most child interventions, however, involve therapeutic day treatment programs, individual therapy, group therapy, and play sessions. Therapeutic day treatment programs typically provide abused children with *group activities, opportunities for peer interactions*, and learning experiences to address *developmental delays*. Group therapy may include sharing experiences, anger management, and social skills training. Play sessions include opportunities for informal interaction between abused children and adults and/or peers (e.g., Culp, Little, Letts, & Lawrence, 1991; Swenson & Kolko, 2000).

*The Incredible Years*. The *Incredible Years Teacher Training Series* is a program that helps children deal with externalizing behaviors (e.g., noncompliance, poor impulse control). Teachers have access to training modules that can be offered once a week. Children in group settings learn how to empathize and behave in prosocial ways. An evaluation of this program indicated that children become less disruptive at home and in class and also improved their academic performance (Webster-Stratton, 2009). A recent evaluation of the program reported a number of beneficial outcomes. Parent training led to many improvements in the area of disciplining children: less harsh discipline, less physical punishment, more praise/incentive behaviors, more appropriate discipline, and positive verbal discipline (Letarte, Normandeau, & Allard, 2010).

*Parental support interventions*. Because research has found that many abusive parents are socially isolated, some experts advocate providing them with assistance in developing social support networks made up of personal friends as well as community contacts. The kinds of community contacts that could benefit these families vary depending on their particular needs. One program that has been judged effective relied on a *group therapy format* that centers on identification of stressors common to parenting and how to cope with them. The participants include both abusive and nonabusive parents whose children attend Head Start programs (Fantuzzo, Bulotsky-Shearer, Fusco, & McWayne, 2005; see also Donohue & Van Hasselt, 1999).

*Treatment by CPS agencies*. Evaluations of *parenting programs* employed by Child Protective Services have shown only weak evidence of effectiveness, apparently because the programs are not necessarily research based (Casanueva et al., 2008). Nevertheless, one element of parental support *infrequently* provided by typical treatment programs is assistance in obtaining services for basic necessities (e.g., Osofsky et al., 2007). Child Protective Services agencies, by contrast, *frequently* provide *assistance in obtaining economic support* (e.g., referral to food banks). CPS also helps parents who need help in completing government forms that will allow them to obtain food stamps and other welfare assistance.

*Family preservation and out-of-home care (foster care)*. Intensive family preservation programs constitute one family-oriented approach that has received a great deal of attention in the literature. In such programs, professionals provide a variety of *short-term intensive and supportive interventions*. Most such programs focus on training parents in child development and parenting skills, as well as in stress reduction techniques and anger management (Wasik & Roberts, 1994). Advocates for family preservation have developed these programs as part of their efforts to *prevent out-of-home placement* of abused and neglected children. Out-of-home placement may occur when CPS responds to reports of child abuse by removing the child from his or her home. Out-of-home care for child maltreatment victims includes *foster care placement, court placements with relatives* (e.g., kinship care), and placement in *residential treatment centers and institutions.*

The Adoption and Foster Care Analysis and Reporting System estimated that as of September 30, 2008, 463,000 children were living in foster care in the United States (U.S. Department of Health & Human Services, 2009a). The federal Adoption and Safe Families Act of 1997 reaffirms the principle of *family reunification* but also holds paramount the concern for children's safety. This act, which President Bill Clinton signed into law on November 19, 1997, is one of the strongest statements regarding child protection ever produced in this country. It establishes child protection as a national goal and specifies procedures for ensuring that protection.

Despite attempts at reunification, some children must return to foster care. Risk factors for re-entry include the following: (a) *prior foster care placement,* (b) *being younger than 4 years of age,* (c) *prior placement with nonrelatives,* and (d) *being neglected or maltreated physically rather than sexually.* Compared with children in foster care for reasons other than maltreatment, risk for re-entry following physical abuse almost doubled and following neglect was tripled (Connell et al., 2009). It remains unclear to what extent family preservation programs are effective in preventing child abuse (see Dagenais, Briére, Gratton, & Dupont, 2009).

*Fathers supporting success.* Psychologists have crafted new abuse intervention/prevention programs for fathers. Instead of holding group therapy sessions to teach fathers how to be less abusive, the experts focus on guiding fathers in methods that "help their children." One less-confrontational part of the program is a video presentation depicting parent-child interactions followed by a group discussion. Fathers evaluate the interactions in the videos and eventually bring up their own issues, thus allowing experts to explain effective and nonviolent ways to parent (see Clay, 2010).

## Policy Toward Physical Child Abuse

*Legal perspectives.* There are several problems involved in the development and **operationalization** of state statutes aimed at addressing CPA. Some of these problems include how to define abuse in as objective a manner as possible, how to balance children's rights with parental rights, and how to apply the legal system to such a complex set of human behaviors (Daro, 1988). Until President George W. Bush signed a revision of CAPTA into law in 2003, no national laws defined CPA in a uniform manner. Now, CAPTA provides a bare-bones definition of child abuse and neglect (Child Welfare Information Gateway, 2006).

In addition, each of the 50 states and the District of Columbia has its own legal definition of CPA and corresponding reporting responsibilities. In general, all states acknowledge that CPA is physical injury caused by other than accidental means that results in a substantial risk of physical harm to the child. Other key features of states' definitions vary according to the specificity of the acts included as physically abusive (e.g., T. J. Stein, 1993). Most emphasize the overt consequences of abuse, such as bruises or broken bones.

*Mandatory reporting.* During the child abuse prevention movement of the 1960s, all U.S. states adopted *mandatory reporting laws.* These laws require certain professionals to report suspected cases of child maltreatment. Professionals who are mandated to report typically include the following:

- Medical personnel (e.g., physicians, dentists, nurses)
- Educators (e.g., teachers, principals)
- Mental health professionals (e.g., psychologists, counselors)
- Public employees (e.g., law enforcement, probation officers)
- Day care personnel

Many individuals mandated to report suspected abuse encounter challenges in carrying out these requirements. One aspect of the problem is the complexity of reporting. To assist mandated reporters, individual states have prepared booklets specifying detailed guidelines (State of California 2003). With training, some personnel (e.g., nurses) can become the key personnel in recognizing and reporting child abuse (Fraser, Mathews, Walsh, Chen, & Dunne, 2010).

Mandated professionals sometimes have qualms about reporting abuse. Imagine, for example, the nature of the relationship that could develop between a clinical social worker and a troubled mother. After working together for several months, the mother, who has come to trust the social worker, confesses that she sometimes spanks her 3-month-old baby very hard. By law, the social worker is required to report the case to CPS. Experience tells her, however, that given the ambiguity of abuse definitions and the limited physical evidence in this particular case, it is unlikely that the abuse allegation would be substantiated. The family needs help and wants help, and the social worker knows that she is in the best position to provide that help. If the social worker reports the case, she violates the trust she has painstakingly built. In addition, the most likely outcome would be no provision of services and no legal action (Emery & Laumann-Billings, 1998).

*Prosecuting individuals who abuse children.* Throughout history there have been few legal or social costs for child maltreatment. For much of human history, adults have physically and sexually abused children with state endorsement. Child maltreatment offenders are still not uniformly prosecuted for their crimes. Prosecution and conviction rates for child abuse are still very low (Dissanaike, 2010). Myers (2010) explains why this statement is true. He likens the criminal justice system to a funnel that begins with all cases that are officially reported at the broad end and ends with convictions at the narrow end. At every step in the system, fewer cases move forward toward prosecution, that is, toward the smaller end of the funnel:

1. The police receive a report of CPA.

2. The police do not investigate every case.

3. The police arrest only some of the accused and then turn the case over to the prosecutor.

4. The prosecutor decides to prosecute a case only if he has sufficient evidence to convict.

5. The prosecutor takes the case to the grand jury or follows a similar process.

6. The jury usually agrees with the prosecutor and indicts the accused.

7. The accused is arraigned and a defense attorney appointed.

8. The judge holds a preliminary hearing so he can decide whether to compel the accused to be tried.

9. Most cases undergo a plea bargaining process in which the accused pleads guilty to a lesser charge and receives a judgment (e.g., 2 years in jail).

10. Only about 10% of the cases actually go to trial.

11. If convicted, the criminal can appeal his conviction or ask for probation.

The process as outlined above calls attention to the vast number of protections afforded a criminal defendant in the American justice system. Despite the difficulty in prosecuting cases of child maltreatment, there is some evidence that child abuse is treated much like other crimes within the American criminal justice system. The proportion of child maltreatment cases that proceed to trial, for example, is approximately 10%, which is similar to the proportion for criminal cases in general (G. S. Goodman et al., 1992; Tjaden & Thoennes, 1992).

*Human rights violations.* "Hitting children is a clear violation of children's human rights" (Knox, 2010, p. 103). Fortunately, international agencies are making clear progress in ending physical discipline of children. Human rights protections for children clearly state that hitting children is not acceptable. The United Nations proclaims that no violence against children is justifiable. As of 2010, 24 nations have banished corporal punishment of children. All nation members of the U.N. have ratified Human Rights Conventions for the protection of the child except Somalia and the United States. In some countries, hitting a child falls under assault laws (see Knox, 2010).

*Cross-cultural responses to CPA.* Other countries across the globe are responding to child physical abuse. A sample of these responses follows:

- *Yemeni* authorities have noted the connection between *harsh physical discipline (beatings)* and two outcomes: (a) *school failure,* and (b) *psychological maladjustment.* Yemen urgently needs programs to teach parents behavior modification techniques (Alyahri & Goodman, 2008).

- *Saudi Arabia* has instituted a series of Child Abuse and Neglect protection centers operating within medical centers. The number of reported cases increased during the period between 2000 and 2008 as the work of the protection centers expanded (Al Eissa & Almuneef, 2010).

- *Korean* maltreated children ($N = 357$) ages 9 to 12 participated in a study of maltreatment. Both CPA and emotional abuse were common. Face-to-face interviews with 14 children provided insight into the lives of these children. Typically, alcoholic parents abandoned the children when they were very young. The children went through several cycles of being put into protective care, then reunified with their parents (whom they usually had not seen for a year), only to be mistreated again and put into protective care again. Communities need to develop a holistic approach to the care of these children (Ju & Lee, 2010).

*Medical policies.* Medical professionals can function as effective sources of support in regard to determinations of physical (and sexual) abuse (Pariset, Feldman, & Paris, 2010). In addition to conducting a medical exam, a doctor needs to understand the context of a child's injuries, the likely biases of any witnesses, and the probability that the injuries he finds could be accidental. He further must receive information about law enforcement's findings, such as where the injury occurred. He must interpret various laboratory tests, take the child's age and developmental status into account, and examine the child's medical history (see Reece, 2010; see also Newman, Holenweg-Gross, Vuillerot, Jeannet, & Roulet-Perez, 2010).

## Research Issues

A review of publications on treatment of CPA perpetrators yielded important analyses (Oliver & Washington, 2009):

- Addressing parents' social needs and providing case management are both important elements of treatment.
- High therapy drop-out rates undermine the interpretations of the findings.
- Male caregivers' participation occurs at a very low level.
- Despite exhortations to improve research designs, studies may still fail to include control groups.
- Pretreatment evaluation measurement may lack validity because parents may minimize their parenting problems.
- Most programs are psychoeducational and therefore do not directly address parents' psychological needs.
- Safety screening should occur before all family members receive treatment.
- Treatment failures do not readily appear in the literature.

## Prevention of Child Physical Abuse

Most experts in the field of child maltreatment agree that, to be successful, strategies for preventing CPA must be aimed at all levels of society (e.g., family, community, social service institutions). One aspect of prevention involves correct and early recognition (CDC, 2008). Another involves specialized programs for groups, such as teenage parents.

*Medical settings.* Approximately 84% of pregnant women in the United States receive some prenatal care, and about 99% of infants are born in medical settings (J. A. Martin, Hamilton, et al., 2007). These circumstances provide medical professionals with an opportunity to detect and manage infant abuse (CDC, 2008). Researchers are crafting a screening tool to identify parental risk of harsh punishment of infants and older children for use by medical workers. When available, it will be a useful adjunct to counseling parents (Feigelman et al., 2009).

*Anticipatory guidance.* An idea forwarded by nursing researchers is to have a concise discussion with parents before any children's major health care problems occur. Information about refraining from hitting, shaking, or spanking their child can be part of the discourse. Other information can include topics such as securing firearms and preventing exposure to violent media (Barkin et al., 2008; Price & Gwin, 2007).

*Public awareness.* Another approach to the prevention of CPA, and child maltreatment more generally, is that of educating the public about the problem through mass-media campaigns. Such campaigns employ public service announcements on radio and television; in newspapers, magazines, and brochures; and on posters and billboards. The rationale behind this approach is that increasing knowledge and awareness about the problem of CPA will result in lower levels of abuse. Media can render a service by striving to publicize the danger of *specific disciplinary practices,* such as spanking a child frequently or hitting a child on the buttocks with an object (Zolotor et al., 2008). One evaluation judged a public awareness campaign effective on the basis of the dramatic increase in the number of calls received by a national child abuse hotline in the period after the campaign (Hoefnagels & Baartman, 1997).

## Grandparenting

Assistance by grandparents may play a role in preventing abuse. Research on grandparents who raise their grandchildren has only recently begun. One group of studies covers the effects on grandparents of providing care for grandchildren. These assessments find that grandparents may suffer from stress and depression associated with providing care. Sometimes, caring for grandchildren poses an economic burden on grandparents or calls into question their legal rights. Another group of studies examines whether grandchildren are safe in their grandmothers' care and whether they are thriving. Because the research has generally relied on small sample sizes, it is too early to draw any definitive conclusions about grandparenting (e.g., Dolan, Casanueva, Smith, & Bradley, 2008; Dunifon & Kowaleski-Jones, 2007; Letiecq, Bailey, & Porterfield, 2008).

One larger inquiry of 1,051 racially diversified grandmothers is available. It found significant differences attributable to race. Latina grandmothers had the highest scores on life satisfaction. African American grandmothers who had custodial care of their grandchildren were more satisfied than grandmothers who had co-parenting responsibilities with the parent. White grandmothers had the highest negative mood about their roles. They frequently stepped in to care for grandchildren when the parents were incapacitated by drugs (C. C. Goodman & Silverstein, 2006).

Generally, the presence of grandparents is associated with fewer incidents of child abuse and fewer incidents of severe child abuse. Using the harm standard, NIS-4 data for all categories of abuse rates were as follows (Sedlak et al., 2010):

- 6.1 per 1,000 *incidents* of child abuse occurred for children *with* an identified grandparent.
- 7.6 per 1,000 *incidents* of child abuse occurred for children *without* an identified grandparent.
- 3.0 per 1,000 children *with* a grandparent caregiver experienced child physical abuse. Inferred harm was *severe* among 2.3 per 1,000 children.
- 4.5 per 1,000 children *without* an identified grandparent caregiver experienced CPA. Inferred harm was *severe* among 3.2 per 1,000 children.

## SECTION SUMMARY

### Practice, Policy, and Prevention of Child Physical Abuse

Proposed solutions to the CPA problem include intervention, policy improvements, and prevention efforts. Because of the complexity of CPA, any single intervention or treatment may be insufficient for fostering change. Psychological approaches for children and their families primarily target parenting skills. For example, abusive parents probably do not know how to discipline a child correctly through a system of rewards and punishment (i.e., time-out). They most likely need education about children's social and developmental skills. Parents may not understand why they are angry or stressed and may therefore need counseling in anger control and stress management.

Treatments may be child-centered, parent-centered, or family oriented, and many treatments incorporate all three areas of concern. Some families may need additional treatment interventions that focus on psychiatric disorders, substance abuse problems, or in-home services (e.g., crisis intervention and assertiveness training). Helping parents become economically stable usually helps to reduce CPA as well.

Furthermore, community interventions have expanded to address situational and social factors that might contribute to CPA, such as social isolation and economic stressors. Efforts to prevent CPA have focused primarily on parental competency programs that include home visitation, parent education, and parent support. Such programs operate on the assumption that by enhancing parental support and parents' knowledge about parenting and child development, they can improve family functioning, which will result in lower levels of physical abuse of children.

Although evaluation studies suggest that many intervention and prevention strategies are promising, additional research is needed to enhance the current state of knowledge about solutions to the CPA problem.

Among policy initiatives, public education campaigns have effectively increased community awareness, recognition, and understanding of the CPA problem. Head Start and school prevention programs have also contributed to the reduction of abusive parenting. The presence of grandparents in the lives of parents and children usually offers some reduction in CPA.

*(Continued)*

(Continued)

Society has not always recognized physical violence directed at children as abusive, but today CPA is illegal in every U.S. state. Most state statutes and experts in the field recognize that CPA includes a range of acts carried out with the intention of harm that puts a child at considerable risk for physical injury. Laws, of course, depend on objective definitions of CPA. Laws also must balance children's rights with parental rights. Examinations of policies regarding legal statutes frequently indicate needed changes.

Fortunately, federal legislators have increased requirements for screening infants and for providing safeguards for their normal development. Medical personnel must become more active in identifying abused children and for screening abused and abusive mothers.

## DISCUSSION QUESTIONS

1. Describe the distinction between harm and endangerment standards.
2. Should corporal punishment be outlawed? Is it effective? Why/why not?
3. Describe a *typical* mother who kills her baby. What might her motives be?
4. List five general categories of the effects of CPA on children.
5. Name three mediators of CPA.
6. Discuss the causes and consequences of bullying.
7. Describe a prototypical adult who abuses children.
8. What is postpartum depression and its effects?
9. Describe two different "causal" models of CPA. Which model is most heuristic?
10. Outline two treatment strategies for adults who commit CPA.

For chapter-specific resources including audio and video links, SAGE research articles, additional case studies, and more, please visit www.sagepub.com/barnett3e.

# CHAPTER

**5**

# Child Sexual Abuse

**CASE HISTORY**   Sashim's Secret

Sashim, an only child, was 6 years old when her parents divorced. Her father had been physically violent toward both Sashim and her mother, and they broke off all ties with him after the divorce. The next 3 years were difficult for Sashim because she rarely saw her mother, who had to work two jobs to make ends meet. When Sashim was 9 years old, her mother became romantically involved with Bhagwan, a 39-year-old construction foreman. Shortly after Sashim's mother met Bhagwan, he moved in with the family and took a serious interest in Sashim. He took her to movies, bought her new clothes, and listened to her when she complained about difficulties at school. He seemed to provide her with the parental attention that she had missed for so many years.

Over the course of several months, Bhagwan's behavior toward Sashim gradually changed. He became much more physical with her, putting his arm around her when they were at the movies, stroking her hair, and kissing her on the lips when he said good night. He began to go into her bedroom and the bathroom without knocking when she was changing her clothes or bathing. He also began "checking on her" in the middle of the night. During these visits, he would stroke and caress her body. In the beginning, he touched only her nonprivate areas (e.g., shoulders, arms, and legs), but after several visits, he began to touch her breasts and genitals. Eventually, he began to kiss her sexually during his touching, all the while telling her how much he loved her and enjoyed being her father. He warned her that she should not tell anyone about their time together because others would not understand their "special" relationship.

One night, Bhagwan attempted to have sexual intercourse with Sashim, and she refused. A few days later, one of Sashim's favorite teachers noticed that Sashim seemed very quiet and asked if something was bothering her. Sashim began crying and told her teacher everything that had happened. Sashim's teacher reassured her that she believed her and would help her. The teacher called Child Protective Services and reported her conversation with Sashim. Two social workers came to Sashim's school and listened to Sashim as she told her story. Bhagwan was arrested. Sashim's mother could not believe that Bhagwan could do such things or that the things Sashim described could occur without her knowledge. She refused to believe Sashim, calling her a liar and a "home wrecker."

As a result, Sashim was placed in a foster home. Shortly thereafter, she was diagnosed with leukemia; the doctors estimated that she had only 6 months to live. Her only request was that she be able to die at "home" with her foster parents, to whom she had become quite attached. The hospital, however, was unable to grant Sashim's request without the consent of her biological mother, who still had legal custody of Sashim. Her mother refused to consent unless Sashim agreed to recant her story about Bhagwan.

As this case history demonstrates, child sexual abuse (CSA) is a multifaceted problem, extraordinarily complex in its characteristics, dynamics, causes, and consequences. As one group of authors have stated, CSA has an intricate history of "discovery and suppression" (Olafson, Corwin, & Summit, 1993). This chapter examines the major issues that contribute to this complexity. The chapter begins by addressing issues related to defining the scope of CSA, including definitions and estimates of the rates of CSA. The focus then changes to the typical effects of abuse and the characteristics of CSA victims and perpetrators. A discourse follows on the dynamics of CSA and its consequences. The chapter concludes with an analysis of potential causes of CSA and responses to the problem. Although the major focus of the content is on intrafamilial (i.e., between family members) sexual abuse, there is some additional discussion on extrafamilial CSA because of its prevalence.

## SCOPE OF THE PROBLEM

### What Is Child Sexual Abuse?

As described throughout this text, one of the greatest barriers to understanding different forms of family violence is the difficulty inherent in defining different categories. Child sexual abuse is a multifaceted type of abuse that is challenging to define as well. As Haugaard (2000) noted, "child sexual abuse has never been unequivocally defined," and this lack of consensus among professionals in the field "continues to inhibit research, treatment, and advocacy efforts" (p. 1036). To illustrate the complexities in defining CSA, consider the following scenarios:

- Naveen and Nadia frequently walked around nude at home in front of their 5-year-old son, Ali.
- John had a homosexual affair with his cousin, and his 10-year-old daughter found out about it.
- Cynthia, a divorced woman of 21, became sexually involved with her 16-year-old nephew, Matt. At the time, Matt was very happy about the affair, but later he regretted it.
- When Cynthia and Matt ended their affair, Matt "hooked up" with his 15-year-old cousin, and they had sex at least once a week.
- Jamie, a 15-year-old, frequently served as the babysitter for his neighbor, 4-year-old Naomi. Each time Jamie was left alone with Naomi, he had her stroke his exposed penis while they watched her favorite video.
- Ernesto, an adult, repeatedly forced his nephew Jorge to have anal intercourse with him when Jorge was between the ages of 5 and 9 years. After the abuse stopped when he was 10, Jorge frequently sneaked into his 6-year-old sister's room and had anal intercourse with her.

- Shu-ping, at 16 years of age, was a self-proclaimed "nymphomaniac." She had physical relationships with numerous boyfriends from school. One evening when Shu-ping was home alone with her 45-year-old stepfather, he asked her if she would like to "mess around." She willingly agreed to have sexual intercourse with him.
- Dexter, a 30-year-old man, invited 7-year-old Jimmy to his house frequently for after-school snacks. After their snacks, Dexter asked Jimmy to undress and instructed him to assume various sexual poses while Dexter videotaped him. Dexter sold the videos for profit.

Which of these interactions should be described as CSA? Why or why not? The above vignettes illustrate two important questions concerning the definition of CSA. First, what behaviors are culturally defined as inappropriately sexual? Second, under what circumstances do sexual interactions become abusive?

## Defining Sexual Abuse

Definitions of child sexual abuse not only include several components, but they also differ in regard to their focus and utility. Definitions are of supreme importance because of their impact on all those involved in a case of CSA. The specifications of legal definitions, of course, can make the difference between going to prison for life or not even being charged with a crime.

*Noncontact CSA.* One component of judging CSA is whether the abusive behavior involves bodily contact. When people think of the behavior that constitutes CSA, they usually think of physical contact such as fondling or intercourse with a child. Although such behaviors with a child *are* clearly regarded as CSA, other noncontact behaviors are also deemed abusive. In the examples of possible CSA above, note that some cultures would consider parental nudity abusive, especially in front of older children. In American culture, the example about the neighbor who takes pornographic pictures of a 7-year-old boy and sells them constitutes both a noncontact form of CSA *and* a form of nonfamily CSA.

*Intention of the perpetrator.* A second component of CSA is the intentionality of the behavior. Many definitions of CSA include the requirement that the activity in question be intentionally sexually stimulating. The requirement of intentionality thus excludes normal family and caregiving interactions (e.g., nudity, bathing, displays of affection). In practice, however, determining whether a behavioral intention is sexual can be difficult. Furthermore, some caregiving behaviors can go beyond normal and become abusive, such as when an adult repeatedly exposes children to genital examinations or cleanings (Berson & Herman-Giddens, 1994).

*Exertion of power/control over the child victim.* A third component of CSA definitions emphasizes an adult's use of his or her authority/power to achieve sexual ends. Implicit in this component is the principle that children are incapable of providing informed consent to sexual interactions with adults for two reasons: (a) Children are not capable of fully understanding what they are consenting to and what the consequences of their consent might be; and (b) children might not be in a position to decline involvement because of the adult's authority status. An illustration of the first principle is a situation in which a 3-year-old "agrees" to pose nude for photographs.

An illustration of the second principle is a 13-year-old girl who showers in front of her mother's live-in boyfriend because he ordered her to do so. As Haugaard and Reppucci (1988) point out, "The total legal and moral responsibility for *any* sexual behavior between an adult and a child is the adult's; it is the responsibility of the adult *not* to respond to the child" (p. 193).

*Age differences between perpetrator and victim.* **The fourth component of CSA definitions addresses the age or maturational advantage of the perpetrator over the victim.** Although many definitions limit abuse to situations involving an age discrepancy of 2 years or more between perpetrator and victim (e.g., California Penal Code, 2010), others include children and adolescents as potential perpetrators if a situation involves the exploitation of a child by virtue of the perpetrator's size, age, sex, or status (see Carlstedt et al., 2009). Broader definitions of CSA include circumstances in which, for example, a 10-year-old boy pulls the underwear off of his 6-year-old sister.

*Types of abuse.* **Some scholars have concluded that categorizing victims by type of abuse has utility. One classification scheme based upon self-report data from children 12 years of age encompassed four categories: (1) No Child Physical Abuse (CPA), no Child Sexual Abuse (CSA); (2) high CPA, low CSA; (3) no CPA, moderate CSA; and (4) high CPA, high CSA.** The probabilities of having a report from Child Protective Services differed among these four categories. **Categories 2, 3, and 4 all had higher odds ratios than Category 1.** Hence, one value of this approach was its ability to account for both type and severity of abuse (Nooner et al., 2010).

*Clusters of definitions.* **There are at least four *clusters* of formal definitions of sexual abuse.** One cluster focuses on definitions suitable for legal purposes. Within the legal group, some statutes may be specialized for child protection purposes and others for criminal prosecution goals. Another cluster of definitions accommodates the needs of clinicians (Faller, 1993a).

---

### BOX 5.1 Definitions of Child Sexual Abuse

*Definitions—Child Protection Example* (Child Abuse Prevention and Treatment Act [CAPTA] of 2003)

"(A) the employment, use, persuasion, inducement, enticement, or coercion of any child to engage in, or assist any other person to engage in, any sexually explicit conduct or simulation of such conduct for the purpose of producing a visual depiction of such conduct; or (B) the rape, molestation, prostitution, or other form of sexual exploitation of children, or incest with children" (cited in Faller, 1993a, p. 2).

*Definition—Criminal Justice System Example* (CAPTA of 2003, 2008)

Criminal definitions involve "crimes committed on Federal property, interstate transport of minors for sexual purposes, and the shipment or possession of child pornography;

State criminal statutes regulate child sexual abuse. Generally, the definitions of sexual abuse found in criminal statutes are very detailed" (cited in Faller, 1993a, p. 2).

### Definition—Legal Stipulations, Examples

(A) All U.S. states have laws prohibiting the sexual abuse of children, but the specifics of criminal statutes vary from state to state (Myers, 2010). CSA laws typically identify an age of consent—that is, the age at which an individual is considered to be capable of consenting to sexual contact. In most states, the age of consent falls somewhere between 14 and 18 years. Sexual contact between an adult and a minor who has not reached the age of consent is illegal (statutory rape). Most states, however, define incest as illegal regardless of the victim's age or consent (Berliner & Saunders, 2010).

(B) Criminal statutes also vary in how they define sexual contact between an adult and a minor. Most define CSA in relatively broad terms that cover sexual contact against a minor's will by means of coercion. CSA consists of acts such as sexual abuse/sexual assault, sexual exploitation, and Internet exploitation. Sexual assault encompasses anal or vaginal penetration by the penis or another object, oral-genital and oral-anal contact, touching of the genitals or other intimate body parts whether clothed or unclothed, and genital masturbation of the perpetrator in the presence of a child (see Faller, 1993a).

(C) Legal considerations: Generally, the younger the child, the greater the force/coercion, the closer the victim/perpetrator relationship, and the perpetration of an actual act of sexual penetration, the worse the crime is considered to be (Faller, 1993a).

### Definitions—Clinical Examples

"Contacts or interactions between a child and an adult when the child is being used for sexual stimulation of the perpetrator or another person when the perpetrator or another person is in a position of power or control over the victim" (cited in Faller, 1993a).

### Definition—Medical Examples

"The engaging of a child in sexual activities that the child cannot comprehend, for which the child is developmentally unprepared and cannot consent, and that violates the social taboos of society" (Botash, 2008, p. 1).

### Definition—Brief

"Sexual abuse involves any sexual activity with a child below the age of consent" (Berliner, 2000, p. 18).

### Incest—Sexually Prohibited Activities Between Blood-Related Individuals

Illegal at any age.

*Impact of definitions.* Broad definitions lead to the labeling of greater numbers of interactions as abusive and, in turn, have led to higher rates of reported abuse. Higher rates of reported abuse have led to greater public concern (Haugaard, 2000). High rates of reporting, however, may have influenced other people to dismiss the statistics as exaggerated (Perrin & Miller-Perrin, 2004). Third, others have voiced the view that all-encompassing definitions of abuse can be practically meaningless (Emery & Laumann-Billings, 1998).

*Cultural context.* As noted previously, sexual interactions between children and adults have occurred throughout history. Only relatively recently, however, has CSA been recognized as a social problem. It is thus apparent that any definition of CSA is dependent on the *historical period* in question, the *cultural context* of the behavior, and the *values and orientations* of specific social groups (Wurtele & Miller-Perrin, 1992).

> Entire Japanese families enjoy the *ofuro* ritual of soaking in a hot tub together naked. Rituals control related activities, such as cleaning with soap, shampoo, and water before entering the tub. Only soaking is allowed in the tub ("Ofuro, Bathing Ritual in Japan," 1995).

## Normal Touching

To define CSA in the United States today, it is essential to know something about what types of behaviors are generally regarded as acceptable within American families. In an early survey of parents, parents rarely bathed with their children at any age, particularly with children of the opposite sex (e.g., mothers with sons), after the children were 3 to 4 years old. Children's touching of mothers' and fathers' private areas (e.g., genitals or breasts) was relatively common among preschoolers but declined as the children became older (e.g., Rosenfeld, Bailey, Siegel, & Bailey, 1986; Rosenfeld, Siegel, & Bailey, 1987).

More recent research confirms these findings and indicates that some types of sexual behavior are common in nonabused children (e.g., children touching their own sex parts), whereas more explicit sexual behaviors (e.g., inserting objects into the anus or vagina and oral-genital contact) are extremely rare (S. L. Davies, Glaser, & Kossoff, 2000; Sandnabba, Santtila, Wannas, & Krook, 2003; Thanasiu, 2004). Additional research is necessary to determine the average frequency of other family behaviors, such as sleeping patterns, nudity, privacy, and other types of touching (e.g., kissing and hugging), as well as cultural differences in such behaviors.

## PREVALENCE OF CHILD SEX ABUSE

### Disclosure Variability

A number of variables influence both the disclosure rate of CSA and its accuracy. In turn, the disclosure rate influences prevalence rates. As one illustration, the more CPS services a state provides, the greater the number of CSA reports generated. From a different vantage point, however, more frequent services by CPS reduce the recurrence rate (U.S. Department of Health & Human Services, 1999). The National Child Abuse and Neglect Data System (NCANDS; 2008) describes only cases of parents and caregivers, not acquaintances and others.

*Accuracy of records compiled by Child Protective Services (CPS).* Research findings have called into question the accuracy of reports made by Child Protective Services (CPS) (e.g., Hussey et al., 2005) and the accuracy of children's memories (or children's willingness to disclose). Abuse findings from a study of adolescents' reports about their childhood abuse did not closely parallel reports made by CPS workers. In this comparison, researchers contrasted two types of data related to 350 young adolescents: (a) CPS records of maltreatment before age 2 and (b) current recollections of adolescents about their childhood abuse collected via Audio-Computer Assisted Self Interview (A-CASI).

One outcome was that the *A-CASI data uncovered prevalence rates of abuse that were 4 to 6 times higher than those found by CPS records.* Another outcome was that the rate (44%) of substantiated abuse before age 2 was not identified by 45 adolescents. Clearly, the occurrence of new abuses after age 2, memory lapses, and nondisclosure rates (especially of sexual abuse) contributed to the lack of concordance. The findings cast doubt on the questions of both the accuracy of adolescents' accounts and the impact of nondisclosure patterns (Everson et al., 2008).

*Victim reluctance to report.* Surveys of child victims, as well as adults victimized as children, indicate that the majority of victims **do *not* disclose their abuse immediately,** and a significant **number do not disclose it for years** (e.g., London, Bruck, Wright, & Ceci, 2008). A mail survey of 61 adult female survivors, however, ascertained that 69% had disclosed CSA to professionals and the remainder would have liked to disclose but were not asked (McGregor, Jolich, Glover, & Gautam, 2010). Nondisclosure is very unfortunate because it prevents parents and professionals from helping. Other variables that influence disclosure rates include the following:

- Victim's relationship to the perpetrator (e.g., Bader, Scalora, Cassady, & Black, 2008)
- Severity of sexual abuse (e.g., Arata, 1998)
- Developmental/cognitive variables (e.g., Mann, Webster, Wakeling, & William, 2007)
- Fear of negative consequences (Leventhal, Murphy, & Asnes, 2010)
- Greater likelihood of females to disclose CSA (Tang, Freyd, & Wang, 2007)
- Improvement of disclosure when parents provide accurate sex education to the child (Smith & Cook, 2008)

**Males** in particular may be *reluctant to disclose abuse.* Several societal norms may contribute to male underreporting, including (a) the expectation that boys should be dominant and self-reliant; (b) the notion that early sexual experiences are a normal part of boys' lives; (c) fears associated with homosexuality, because most boys who are abused are abused by men; and (d) pressure on males not to express helplessness or vulnerability (e.g., Alaggia & Millington, 2008; Romano & De Luca, 2001).

*School-based CSA programs and disclosure.* In one school-based prevention study, school counselors from 5 schools received 20 confirmed reports of inappropriate touching during the 6-month follow-up period compared with no reports from one control school (Kolko, Moser, & Hughes, 1989). Although these findings are promising, data are insufficient to confirm the hypothesis that CSA prevention programs increase victim disclosures (e.g., Topping & Barron, 2009).

*Medical personnel and disclosure.* Since most CSA sufferers do *not* disclose their victimization right away, there is less urgency for doctors to conduct an examination immediately. Of course, a prompt exam is advisable and necessary when a child is in pain, needs medication, or must be tested for a disease, as well as for other reasons (see Berkoff et al., 2008). It is also advisable to perform an examination if forensic materials might still be collectable. Another advantage of providing an examination is to allow the doctor to reassure and comfort the child. Disclosures made to health care workers may be distinctive because of the setting and because of the child's confidence in medical personnel. Fortunately, a nurse or doctor can reiterate a child's disclosures in court and usually the judge will accept them as hearsay evidence, an exception to the hearsay rule of evidence (e.g., J. A. Adams et al., 2007; Finkel, 2009).

## Memory Issues, CSA, and Disclosure

*Memory capacity.* Another relevant issue is whether children have the *capacity* to form memories and recall events accurately. Studies of memory in children indicate that memory capacity is related to both *language skills* and the ability to order and *interpret events*, skills that are not usually well developed in young children (Saywitz, Goodman, & Lyon, 2002). Most studies have found that young children are more suggestible than older children, but by age 10 or 11 children are no more suggestible than adults (Ceci & Bruck, 1993; Saywitz & Snyder, 1993).

*Memory accuracy in the laboratory.* It is clear that several factors can confound the memories of young children (e.g., Saywitz et al., 2002). Some research has examined the suggestibility of children by exposing them to different kinds of events and then asking them to recall those events. Social scientists, for example, describe investigations in which they showed 1-minute films to preschool and kindergarten children and subsequently interviewed them about what they saw. The researchers asked *leading questions* of children in the target group, such as "Did you see a boat?" and "Didn't you see a bear?" The children responded affirmatively that they had seen the specified objects in the films. Because there was no boat or bear in the films, the researchers concluded that they were able to *alter the children's responses*, or possibly even *create false memories* in the children, simply by asking *leading questions* (Loftus & Ketcham, 1991; see also Bernstein & Loftus, 2009).

*Memory accuracy in the real world.* How well do laboratory findings correspond to situations in the real world? One factor that distinguishes experimental situations from actual situations is that real CSA memories are generally *traumatic* for the child. Some memory researchers propose that the CSA-induced trauma has a *debilitating effect* on memory, whereas other researchers conjecture it has an *enhancing effect*. An assessment of 44 adult women in treatment for sexual abuse or assault responded to three autobiographical events: (a) sexual assault, (b) nonsexual trauma, and (c) a positive emotional event. Analyses indicated that memories of sexually traumatic events contained even more detail and sensory components than the other types of events (Peace, Porter, & ten Brinke, 2008). In fact, there is evidence that the greater the severity of posttraumatic stress disorder (PTSD) symptomatology, the greater the accuracy of the memories (Alexander et al., 2005). In addition, there appear to be unique differences among individuals in the ways they remember stressful events (Saywitz et al., 2002).

*Victim fabrication of CSA.* Another contention is that children *lie about sexual abuse.* Available research suggests that *children rarely lie about sexual abuse* (Lanning, 2002). For one thing, child development specialists have found that children under age 7 are unlikely to be successful at telling lies (Morency & Krauss, 1982). Some research suggests that children may not intentionally fabricate stories of CSA, but they may make false reports as a result of developmental limitations or because they are led to do so by parents and professionals, such as doctors and therapists. A 2002 national survey of women (*N* = 711) analyzed data consisting of self-report of forgetting and remembering childhood sexual abuse. Only 1.8% of women who "felt abused" in childhood recovered the memory with the help of a therapist (Wilsnack, Wonderlich, Kristjanson, Vogeltanz-Holm, & Wilsnack, 2002; see also O'Donohue, Benuto, & Fanetti, 2010).

## BOX 5.2 The Repressed Memory Controversy

Questions about children's memories have generated extensive controversy among professionals, and the dispute eventually entered the mainstream media. The statement that "hundreds of thousands of individuals each year are accused falsely of child abuse" angered many child advocates. Soon, an oppositional phrase developed: "Children never lie about sex abuse" (see Hechler, 1988; Bradley & Wood, 1996).

**1989:** A California Court of Appeal extended the statute of limitations for CSA under the doctrine of delayed discovery, allowing individuals who, as adults, claim histories of CSA to sue their parents. An individual bringing such a claim must be able to demonstrate that his or her memories of the abuse were **repressed** (by providing certification from a licensed mental health professional).

> **Repression:** A process of *unconscious* "forgetting" as a protection against anxiety. Stated differently, a repressed memory is one that a person cannot bring to mind under ordinary circumstances because it is so painful and/or frightening. He or she does not/cannot purposefully "forget" the event.

**1990:** Holly Ramona, age 19, accused her father, Gary Ramona, of repeatedly raping her when she was between the ages of 5 and 8. Holly's memories of the abuse surfaced while she was a college student receiving therapy for depression and bulimia. During several months of therapy, Holly experienced flashback memories of her father sexually

*(Continued)*

(Continued)

molesting her. Just before openly accusing her father, Holly received the hypnotic drug Sodium Amytal and under its influence recounted multiple episodes of abuse by her father. After the allegations surfaced, Gary Ramona lost his $400,000-a-year job, his daughters refused to interact with him, and his wife divorced him.

**1991:** Some experts and those concerned about false accusations established the False Memory Syndrome Foundation to provide information and support to individuals who have been victimized by the "rash" of false accusations of CSA (see this organization's website at http://fmsfonline.org). Several similar organizations also sprang up including the British False Memory Society, FACT (Falsely Accused Carers and Teachers), Action Against False Allegations of Abuse, and VOCAL (Victims of Child Abuse Laws).

**1994:** In Napa Valley (California) Superior Court, a jury ruled that Holly Ramona's memories were probably false and that although her therapists did not implant the memories, they negligently reinforced them (Butler, 1994). Gary Ramona, who has sought $8 million in damages, was awarded $500,000.

**1999:** The first criminal trial involving false memories of CSA was against five defendants (two psychologists, two psychiatrists, and one hospital administrator). The prosecutors charged them with several crimes: (a) insurance fraud, (b) falsely diagnosing multiple personality disorder, and (c) implanting memories of satanic ritual abuse. After 5 months of testimony, the judge had to declare a mistrial. In time, the judge and prosecutors concluded that it would be too costly to retry the defendants, so charges were dropped (M. Smith, 1999).

**2002:** Numerous cases of sexual misconduct and cover-up brought the issue of the sexual abuse of parishioners by Catholic priests to the front pages of the nation's newspapers. Although most of the cases did not involve the recovery of repressed memories, the publicity surrounding the cases once again drew attention to the repressed memory controversy.

Animosities reached their peak when Paul McHugh, longtime chair of the Department of Psychiatry at Johns Hopkins University, was appointed to a review board to monitor the Catholic Church's response to the sexual abuse scandal. Members of SNAP (Survivors Network for those Abused by Priests) were critical of the appointment because McHugh had openly supported the False Memory Syndrome Foundation and had testified for defendants in recovered memory cases.

**2010:** Over the decade, SNAP has been active in supporting victims who accuse Catholic Priests of CSA. Accusations across the globe have multiplied, leading to lawsuits, monetary awards, the defrocking of a few priests, and the demotion of several bishops. Pope Benedict XVI has issued apologies and revised instructions to cardinals and bishops about how to handle accusations. No longer will higher-ups fail to notify the police of accusations (see Terry & Tallon, 2008).

> *The believers*: In one camp are experts who believe that repressed memories are common and result from either *repression* of negative feelings associated with the abuse or amnesia associated with *dissociative defenses* (i.e., multiple personality disorder) of a traumatic event (Briere & Conte, 1993).
>
> *The doubters*: In the other camp are critics of the concept of repressed memories, who claim that what some individuals perceive to be memories may be *fantasies* or illusions. They are the results of contextual cues or implantation by therapists or other perceived authority figures (Ganaway, 1989; Loftus, 1993).

The consequences of the recovered memory debate are significant, beyond their importance for prevalence estimates. If therapists are indeed implanting false memories, then people will be falsely accused and innocent families will be ripped apart. If the critics are wrong, on the other hand, then victims of abuse will not be believed (Ost, 2003). In a world that has historically been reluctant to acknowledge many of the unthinkable acts inflicted on children, disbelieving the truth can no longer be tolerated.

*The research findings.* No matter how reluctant one may be to accept the concept of repressed memories, research findings clearly show that repressed memories do exist and some of them are centered on CSA. One study, for example, found a substantial rate of repressed memories (59%) in a clinical sample of sexual abuse victims (Briere & Conte, 1993). Without additional information, however, it is difficult to corroborate the veracity of such memories. Studies are limited because of the *retrospective* and *self-report* nature of the data and because the individuals were *in therapy*. In an attempt to overcome these problems, researchers employed different approaches to determine if memories of CSA were sometimes repressed. One appraisal followed a community sample of 100 documented sexual abuse cases in which the victims were between the ages of 10 months and 12 years when the CSA occurred. When these CSA victims were questioned about their childhood histories *17 years later*, 38% did *not* recall the previously substantiated incidents (L. M. Williams, 1994; see also Widom & Morris, 1997).

Critics of the concept of repressed memories, on the other hand, emphasize the limitations of such studies. Some critics have suggested other potential sources for what are asserted to be repressed memories. For example, some argue that popular writings exaggerate sexual abuse as "nearly universal" (Bower, 1993). Hearing an unvalidated claim, such as "If you are unable to remember any specific instances but still have a feeling that something abusive happened to you, it probably did" (Bass & Davis, 1988, p. 21) may influence memory. Critics further assert that such statements are dangerous given the malleability of memory. Research has shown that memory is subject to several distortions: (a) stress effects, (b) incentives to keep secrets, and (c) suggestion, such as leading questions (Loftus, 2005).

*American Psychological Association.* An American Psychological Association (APA) task force (made up of both skeptics and believers) appointed to examine what is known about repressed memories reached essentially the following conclusion:

> Both ends of the continuum on people's memories of abuse are possible.... It is possible that under some cue conditions, early memories may be retrievable. At the other extreme, it is possible under some conditions for memories to be implanted or embedded. (DeAngelis, 1993, p. 44)

*Explanations for conflicting findings.* One comparison of 120 women has shed light on the cognitive mechanism underlying recovered memories (Geraerts et al., 2009):

- A person who recovered CSA memories through *suggestive therapy* was more likely to exhibit heightened susceptibility to false memory construction. However, there was *no* inclination to underestimate prior remembered CSA incidents.
- A person who recovered CSA *spontaneously* displayed no increased probability of false memory construction. Nonetheless, there was a *heightened proclivity to forget* prior CSA.

A similar study of people whose CSA was *not* experienced as traumatic were *not* inclined to report repressed memory syndrome. Instead, they appeared *not to think of the CSA* for years, or to simply *forget* it. Later, environmental cues triggered their recall which was then verified. The recall of these environmentally cued memories occurred at the same rate as in people who *never forgot* in the first place. The authors concluded that there was no evidence that these memories had been repressed (McNally & Geraerts, 2009).

## ESTIMATES OF CHILD SEXUAL ABUSE

However, it is widely believed that official records are *underestimates* of the actual incidence of sexual crimes (e.g., Berliner & Saunders, 2010), so the true victimization rates are significantly higher. In assessing the prevalence and incidence of CSA, researchers have typically relied on three sources of data: (a) official government reports, (b) self-report survey data obtained from older children and adolescents, and (c) retrospective self-report data from adults who have been sexually victimized during childhood.

### Official Estimates

As stated in the previous chapter, there are two major data collections for child abuse.

*U.S. Department of Health & Human Services (U.S. Department of Health & Human Services, 2008)—CPS records).* With 51 states reporting, 69,184 children were the victims of sexual abuse, which represented 9.1% of all maltreated children ($N = 772,000$). Recall that CPS statistics, also the basis for the National Child Abuse and Neglect Data System (NCANDS), include only cases perpetrated by parents or caregivers (U.S. Department of Health & Human Services, 2009).

*National Incidence Studies (NIS-4; Sedlak et al., 2010).* NIS-4 uses data from multiple sources and goes beyond DHHS to capture data from individuals such as school counselors and psychologists in private practice. Note that the rate of children sexually abused increases over the first three NIS studies, but then falls for NIS-4 (see Table 5.1).

**TABLE 5.1**  Numbers of Children Reported for Sexual Abuse on the Harm Standard in the National Incidence Studies

| Sexually Abused Children | | | | | | | |
|---|---|---|---|---|---|---|---|
| NIS-1 (1980) | | NIS-2 (1986) | | NIS-3 (1993) | | NIS-4 (2005–006) | |
| 42,900 children | 0.7 per 1,000 children | 133,600 children | 2.1 per 1,000 children | 300,200 children | 4.5 per 1,000 children | 323,000 children | 1.838 per 1,000 children |

*National Child Abuse and Neglect Data System (NCANDS; 2008) and National Incident-Based Reporting System (NIBRS).* The data in Table 5.2 show that criminal justice data (NIBRS) generally report more sexual abuse than do Child Protective Agency data (NCANDS) ("Estimates of Child," 2004).

**TABLE 5.2**  Comparison of Criminal Justice Data (NIBRS) and National Child Abuse and Neglect Data System (NCANDS) Data From CPS

| State | Date | NIBRS (Rate per 100,000 Children) | NCANDS (Rate per 100,000 Children) |
|---|---|---|---|
| Alabama | 2001 | 56 child rapes | 174 (all maltreatment) |
| California | 2001 | 141 | 112 |
| Delaware | 1995 | 285 | 112 |
| Idaho | 2001 | 363 | 79 |
| Iowa | 2001 | 198 | 141 |
| Michigan | 2001 | 3,081 incidents | 1,656 incidents |
| South Carolina | 2000/2002 | 2,438 incidents | 610 incidents |
| South Dakota | n.d. | 131 incidents | 169 incidents |
| Tennessee | 2001 | 248 | 166 |

## Self-Report Surveys

Self-report surveys have the potential to present a clearer picture of the true rate of victimization, but they have several drawbacks. The methodology employed by self-report surveys has a dramatic impact on the findings. In one appraisal, researchers compared three self-report methods of identifying maltreatment incidents: (a) retrospectively (self-report via interview), (b) prospectively (case record data), and (c) with a combination of both methods. Using a sample of 170 participants tracked from birth to age 19, researchers identified maltreatment occurrences as follows: (a) retrospective identification—7.1%, (b) prospective identification—20.6%, and (c) combination method—22.9%. As is evident, the retrospective (recall) method produces the smallest percentage of identifications (Shaffer, Huston, & Egeland, 2008). Self-report data likely underestimate actual rates because some adults may not remember their experiences or may be reluctant to report them (see L. M. Williams, 1994). Last, definitional ambiguity across studies contributes to variations in reporting rates. In one review of studies that sampled both college students and community members, for example, the prevalence rates for CSA ranged from 7% to 62% for females and from 3% to 16% for males (Wurtele & Miller-Perrin, 1992).

*Gallup Organization (Finkelhor, Moore, Hamby, &*
*Straus, 1997).* This survey used a random sample ($N = 1,000$ adults). The findings were as follows:

- 23% had been "touched in a sexual way" or "forced to have sex" before the age of 18.
- The women in this survey sample were nearly 3 times as likely as the men to self-report child sexual abuse.

*Nationally Representative Survey of Children Exposed to Violence (NatSCEV)*
*(Finkelhor, Turner, Ormrod, Hamby, & Kracke, 2009;* N = 4,549*).* Results for sexual abuse, from self-reports for children ages 10 through 18 and parent or caregiver reports for children 9 or under, were as follows:

- 6.1%—all children during last year
- 9.8%—all children during lifetime
- 16.3%—adolescents 14 to 17 years old during last year
- 27.3%—adolescents 14 to 17 years old during lifetime

*Adverse Childhood Experiences (ACE) Study.* Data used are from Kaiser Permanente–San Diego in collaboration with the Centers for Disease Control and Prevention (2006); $N = 17,337$ adult patients reporting on childhood sexual abuse.

- 24.7% of women ($n = 9,367$) reported having been sexually abused.
- 16.0% of men ($n = 7,970$) reported having been sexually abused.

*National Health and Social Life Survey (Leung, Curtis, & Mapp, 2010).* This study used a stratified random probability sample of 3,432 adults, 18 to 59 years of age. *Sexual touching* includes kissing, touching, fondling of genitals, oral sex, vaginal intercourse, and anal intercourse.

- 566 respondents (16.5%) reported *sexual touching* before age 12.

*National Violence Against Women Survey (Tjaden & Thoennes, 1998a).* This study used a nationally representative population sample of 16,000 adults, 8,000 women and 8,000 men.

- Completed Rape <18 years of age: Females—9%; Males—2%

*Military samples.* A *retrospective clinical survey* comes from a sample of *female veterans.* Studies set the prevalence rate of CSA between 27% and 49%, thus suggesting an overall rate of at least 33% (e.g., Zinzow, Grubaugh, Frueh, & Magruder, 2008; see also Rentz et al., 2006).

## Trends in Reported Child Sexual Abuse

Data from both CPS records and NIS data indicated an increase in reporting rates for child sexual abuse during the 1980s and early 1990s. Many factors contribute to fluctuating reporting rates, such as the specific definition of CSA employed.

*Increasing rates.* In NIS-2, for instance, rates were higher when the U.S. Department of Health & Human Services (1988) added teenagers to the category of perpetrators of abuse. Although the reasons for the increase remain unclear, it may be that the *increased reporting* reflected legislative changes and increases in public and professional awareness associated with CSA.

*Decreasing rates.* A very different picture emerges during the mid- to late 1990s, however, as data indicate a marked *decline* in reporting rates of CSA (Finkelhor & Jones, 2004; Sedlak et al., 2010). It may be, and hopefully is, that the *actual incidence* of child sexual abuse is *decreasing.* However, there are numerous other determinants that might be artificially deflating the rates (Finkelhor & Jones, 2006):

- Economic prosperity
- Falling crime rates in general
- Psychiatric pharmacology
- Public awareness campaigns
- Increased services (e.g., welfare)
- Changes in public attitudes and policies
- Knowledge and implementation of newer treatment
- Increased criminal justice efforts (e.g., arrest, incarceration)

Ongoing research has lent some support that the decrease is "real," that society's massive effort has reaped some benefits.

---

**SECTION SUMMARY**

### Definitions and Prevalence Estimates of Child Sexual Abuse

Although any definition of CSA is time and culture bound, current definitions focus on types and intent of the behaviors involved, as well as the age and/or power discrepancies between offenders and victims. CSA includes both contact and noncontact experiences, events that occur both within and outside the family, and behaviors that involve the exploitation of authority, status, and physical size to achieve the perpetrator's sexual interests. Also, definitions vary according to the needs of individuals working in diverse organizations and fields, such as the medical field. Legal definitions assume that children are incapable of providing informed consent to sexual interactions with adults. Although all states have laws prohibiting the sexual abuse of children, laws vary from state to state. Definitions are extremely important because of their impact on people's lives.

A large number of factors influence the precision of CSA prevalence assessments, such as memory accuracy. The actual rate of child sexual abuse remains elusive because of the reluctance of victims and families, as well as professionals, to report abuse. Indeed, there is good reason to speculate that official and self-report data vastly underestimate the extent of the problem. As a result, the actual number of children victimized by CSA is unknown. Other variability in research methodology affects both official and self-report estimates. Some of these factors include the type of population sampled and the definition of abuse employed. Of particular note is the disparity between the annual DHHS report of sexually abused children identified by CPS agencies ($N = 69,184$) and the National Incidence Study (NIS-4; $N = 323,200$) that has access to a more comprehensive source of informants. Research during the past several years has documented significant decreases in rates of reported CSA, but it is unclear whether these changes are attributable to social factors or to an actual decrease in the incidence of abuse.

---

## SEARCHING FOR PATTERNS: CHARACTERISTICS OF VICTIMS AND PERPETRATORS

## Characteristics of Sexually Abused Child Victims

### Age of CSA Victims

Some abuse of very young children most certainly goes undetected because these children are less likely, or less able, than older children to report abuse (Hewitt, 1998), and adults responding to self-report surveys may not remember abuse that occurred early in their childhoods (L. M. Williams, 1994). Although some evidence has suggested that *maltreatment as a whole* declines with a child's increasing age, this pattern appears *not* to be true of child sexual abuse.

*Official estimates.* The two most notable official surveys are concordant across some age-groups, but discordant across others: (a) Both surveys show a peak around age 12, and (b) the surveys lack concordance for ages 15 to 17. It is unclear why the two official assessments differ for the older age-groups, but the usual methodological differences may explain some of the disparity. See the following tables for findings about the ages of CSA victims.

*U. S. Department of Health & Human Services (2008): Age and Percentage of Sexually Abused Children (N = 68,002)*

| Age | Percentage | Age | Percentage | Age | Percentage |
|-----|-----------|-----|-----------|-----|-----------|
| <1 | 0.7% | 3 | 3.5% | 12–15 | 35.2% |
| 1 | 0.8% | 4–7 | 22.4% | 16–17 | 11.7% |
| 2 | 1.4% | 8–11 | 23.7% | Unknown | 0.5% |

*NIS-4 (Sedlak et al., 2010). Reports of incidence of sexual abuse per 1,000 children by age as follows:*

| Age | Per 1,000 | Age | Per 1,000 | Age | Per 1,000 |
|-----|-----------|-----|-----------|-----|-----------|
| 0–2 | 0.997 | 6–8 | 1.576 | 12–14 | 2.403 |
| 3–5 | 1.755 | 9–11 | 1.417 | 15–17 | 1.567 |

**Self-report survey: National Health and Social Life Survey (Leung et al., 2010).** (This survey used a stratified random probability sample ($N = 3,432$ adults, 18–59 years of age). Sexual touching includes kissing, touching, fondling of genitals, oral sex, vaginal intercourse, and anal intercourse. Most *sexual touching* is *prepubertal,* occurring at about age 12.

## Gender of CSA Victims

Data from both official sources and self-report surveys consistently indicate that the majority of CSA victims are female. Notwithstanding such congruence of results, many experts believe that boys may be abused more often than the data indicate, because males may be less likely to report sexual abuse. Also, society may fail to identify it (Faller, 1993a).

NIS-4 (Sedlak et al., 2010) demonstrates the following:

- *Girls* (8.5 per 1,000 children) are generally more at risk for *all types* of abuse per the harm standard than are boys (6.5 per 1,000). Inclusion of girls' greater *sexual* victimization appears to account for this overall maltreatment gender difference.
- *Girls* (3.043 per 1,000 children) are at far greater risk for child sexual abuse than *boys* (0.647 per 1,000 children).

*National Survey of Children Exposed to Violence (NatSCEV).* In this self-report survey of 4,549 children from 0 to 17 years of age, the distribution for sexual victimization was as follows (Finkelhor, Turner, Ormrod, Hamby, & Kracke, 2009):

- 7.4%—girls during last year
- 12.2%—girls during lifetime
- 7.9%—girls 14 to 17 years old last year
- 18.2%—girls 14 to 17 years old during lifetime

*International meta-analysis of studies from 22 countries* (Pereda, Guilera, Forns, & Gómez-Benito, 2009). Rates of child sexual abuse were as follows:

- 7.9% of men
- 19.7% of women

## Race of CSA Victims

NIS-4 (Sedlak et al., 2010) presented the following incidence rates for sexually abused children by race:

- 2.606 per 1,000 Black children were sexually abused.
- 1.820 per 1,000 Hispanic children were sexually abused.
- 1.357 per 1,000 White children were sexually abused.

U.S. Department of Health & Human Services (2008) had racial information on 745,962 maltreatment victims, of whom 68,002 were sexually abused.

| Race | Percentage | Race | Percentage |
| --- | --- | --- | --- |
| African American | 6.8% | Multiple race | 5.2% |
| American Indian | 5.2% | White | 10.3% |
| Asian | 6.6% | Unknown/missing | 14.1% |
| Hispanic | 8.3% | Native Hawaiian/Pacific Islander | 9.0% |

*National Health and Social Life Survey (Leung et al., 2010).* This survey used a stratified random probability sample ($N = 3,432$ adults, 18–59 years of age). Of the total, 71.4% were White; 16.0% were Black; 9.4% were Hispanic, and 3.1% were Other. Sexual touching is broadly defined and includes kissing, touching, fondling of genital, oral sex, vaginal intercourse, and anal intercourse. Researchers found the following distribution of *prepubertal* sexual touching among the varying percentage of racial groups:

- Black—17.3%
- Hispanic—18%
- White—16.1%
- Other—15%

## Additional Risk Factors for CSA Victimization

*Socioeconomic status (SES).* Almost without exception, research shows that children living in families with low SES suffer significantly more CSA than children living in homes with higher SES.

NIS-4 (Sedlak et al., 2010) presented the following incidence rates of sexual abuse among children categorized by *SES*:

- 0.587 per 1,000 children *not* in low SES families
- 1.687 per 1,000 children *in* low SES families

*Low socioeconomic status,* in addition to its direct link with child maltreatment (including CSA), is correlated with numerous variables that are independently related to CSA. Some of these are *single parenthood, lower education, parental stress* and *depression,* and *marital conflict/ marital violence* (e.g., Fergusson, Boden, & Horwood, 2008; Greer, 2004; C. G. Moore, 2005; see Evans, Gonnella, Marcynszyn, Gentile, & Salpekar, 2005).

Children whose **fathers are** *unemployed* (2.963 per 1,000) **are** also at **greater risk for sexual abuse than children** whose fathers are *employed* (0.795 per 1,000) (Sedlak et al., 2010). On the other hand, some research suggests that if both parents are out of the house working, children left unmonitored are at increased vulnerability for CSA victimizations (see Leung et al., 2010).

*Others risk factors for CSA.* The number of children in the household had only a minor association with the risk for CSA. Living in a *rural area* (2.828 per 1,000) compared with an urban area (1.447 per 1,000) or major urban area (1.762 per 1,000), however, was a risk factor (NIS-4; Sedlak et al., 2010).

*CSA victims' self-blame.* The potential reaction of self-blame among child sexual abuse victims has attracted considerable research attention. To understand children's changes in attributions of blame for CSA, researchers both *interviewed* victims (8–15 years old) and asked them to *complete a rating scale.* Victims responded at three different stages. The timing sequence was as follows: (a) Within 8 weeks of Child Protective Services notification ($n = 160$), (b) 1 year later ($n = 147$), and (c) 6 years later ($n = 121$). Chi-square analyses yielded several results:

- Blame placed on perpetrators remained high over time ($p < .05$).
- Self-blame decreased over time ($p < .01$).
- Sexual penetration was correlated with more self-blame ($p < .05$).
- The initial level of victims' self-blame predicted the later level of depression ($p < .05$).
- The initial level of self-blame predicted the later level of intrusive thoughts ($p < .05$).
- Perpetrator blame was *not* related to victims' symptomatology.
- The use of force was linked with more perpetrator blame.
- More frequent abuse was associated with greater perpetrator blame over time.
- The youth frequently reported confusion as to *why* the CSA occurred.
- There were no gender differences in level of self-blame.

The investigators concluded that although self-blame attributions are unhealthy, perpetrator blame is *not* particularly healthy either (Feiring & Cleland, 2007).

*Attributions.* Research by Zinzow and her colleagues (Zinzow, Grubaugh, Monnier, Suffoletta-Maierle, & Frueh, 2007; Zinzow & Jackson, 2009; Zinzow, Seth, Jackson, Niehaus, & Fitzgerald, 2010) has illuminated some issues of **attributions** (beliefs about causality) and PTSD symptoms. Undergraduate females ($N = 424$) comprised several subgroups of people victimized by traumatic events, such as natural disasters and serious accidents. Other subgroups included victims of interpersonally violent events, such as violent crimes, sexual assaults, intimate partner violence, and child abuse. Significantly different attributions intervened between specific traumatic events and PTSD levels. The victims of interpersonal violence adopted significantly higher levels of *global* attributions (i.e., other negative events are likely to happen to me) than other victims.

Second, the attributions of *stability* (i.e., negative events will always happen to me) increased in sexual assault survivors while decreasing in natural disaster victims (Zinzow & Jackson, 2009). Thus, *features of the abuse events* are significantly correlated with victims' attributions of blame. In addition, victim blaming by the perpetrator and the family accounted for a significant amount of variability in victims' symptoms of PTSD (Zinzow et al., 2010). (See www.sagepub.com/barnett3e for more details.)

## Characteristics of Child Sexual Abuse Perpetrators

Many people have the impression that CSA perpetrators are *frightening strangers* or "dirty old men." Research findings, however, usually *contradict such stereotypes*. The real attributes of child sex abusers have been the target of a sizable amount of research. Understanding the multiple aspects of an offender's childhood experiences, personality, adult family, and other factors should contribute to the development of effective intervention and prevention strategies.

### Nontraditional Parenting

Families that contain a child molester tend to vary in several critical ways. Both official data and survey data, for instance, show that single parents are overrepresented among sexual abusers (Freeman & Temple, 2010). NIS-4 found that the highest rates of child abuse occurred among *single parents who had a cohabiting partner.* Children living in these households had a rate of abuse 10 times higher than children living with married biological parents (Sedlak et al., 2010). Table 5.3 displays the incidence rate of sexually abused children by family structure.

**TABLE 5.3**  Incidence Rate of Sexually Abused Children by Family Structure

| Family Structure | Per 1,000 Children |
|---|---|
| Married parents, both biological | 0.504 |
| Unmarried parents | 2.371 |
| Single parent, no partner | 2.390 |
| Other married parents (i.e., stepparents and others) | 4.265 |
| Neither parent | 5.280 |
| Single parent with partner | 9.919 |
| Grandparents | 1.592 |
| All parent groups combined | 1.830 |

## Age of CSA Perpetrators

Table 5.4 summarizes the ages and sex of maltreatment perpetrators, *any type of child maltreatment,* not sexual abuse only (U.S. Department of Health & Human Services, 2005).

**TABLE 5.4**  Percentage of Child Maltreatment Perpetrators by Age and Gender

| Age of Offender | Percentage of Male Offenders (n = 89,028) | Percentage of Female Offenders (n = 103,293) |
|---|---|---|
| 20 or younger | 10 | 7 |
| 21 to 30 | 25 | 39 |
| 31 to 40 | 32 | 35 |
| 41 to 50 | 18 | 13 |
| 51 to 60 | 5 | 3 |
| 61 and older | 2 | 1 |

*Juvenile sex offenders.* While the vast majority of sex offenders are adults, a significant proportion of sex crimes are committed by individuals under the age of 18. According to the *U.S. Department of Justice* (2009), juveniles accounted for 17% of arrests for sexual crimes in 2007.

## Gender of CSA Perpetrators

Data have uniformly established that **males** are disproportionately the perpetrators of sexual **crimes against children.** Last, approximately 1% to 2% of males in the general population will be convicted of a sexual offense in their lifetime (P. Marshall, 1997).

*NIS-4.* NIS-4 grouped perpetrators into three major categories for an analysis of relationship by gender as summarized in Table 5.5.

**TABLE 5.5**  Percentage of Child Maltreatment Perpetrators by Relationship and Gender

| Sexual Abuser | Percentage of Children With Perpetrator Whose Sex Was . . . | |
|---|---|---|
| | Male | Female |
| Biological parent | 80% | 22% |
| Nonbiological parent/partner | 97% | 3% |
| Other person | 86% | 6% |
| Total known sexual abuse | 87% | 11% |

NOTE: Sometimes both a male and a female act together to molest a child.

*Inconsistent research findings.* The available scholarship on female child sexual abuse offenders is riddled with inconsistent findings. One major problem among the studies is the *questionable validity of the measurements used* (Bader, Welsh, & Scalora, 2010; Dolan & Völlm, 2009). Some questions that have produced *opposing outcomes* are as follows:

- Whether female offenders molest more girl than boy victims (Bader et al., 2010; Elliott, Eldridge, Ashfield, & Beech, 2010; Lawson, 2008; Vandiver & Kercher, 2004)
- Whether females abuse children primarily when coerced by males or primarily act alone (Bader et al., 2010; Elliott et al., 2010; Lawson, 2008; Peter, 2009; Saradjian, 1996)
- Whether the level of abuse perpetrated by females is as severe as that perpetrated by males (Rudin, Zalewski, & Bodmer-Turner, 1995)
- Whether female sex offenders suffer significant levels of psychopathology (Peter, 2009; Saradjian, 1996)
- Whether females molest relatively younger children than do males (Elliott et al., 2010; Lawson, 2008; Peter, 2009)

*Congruent research findings.* Researchers have detected a number of *similar characteristics of female CSA* (Bader et al., 2010; Elliott et al., 2010; Peter, 2009; Roe-Sepowitz & Krysik, 2008; Strickland, 2008; Vandiver & Kercher, 2004; Whitaker et al., 2008):

- Fondling/touching of genitals is the most frequent type of CSA committed by *both* females and males.
- Female and male CSA offenders have grown up in *highly dysfunctional families.*
- Female and male perpetrators suffered *sexual abuse, sometimes severe abuse during childhood.*
- Female and male CSA offenders manifest *inadequate social skills.*
- Female and male CSA offenders display *cognitive distortions.*

*Explanations of female CSA perpetration.* Researchers have found that female offenders, although not a homogeneous group, *share some common characteristics.* For example. large percentages of offenders are abuse victims themselves (e.g., Roe-Sepowitz & Krysik, 2008; see Vandiver & Kercher, 2004, for a review). One empirically derived description of female sex offenders is as follows (Strickland, 2008, p. 486):

> Female sexual offenders, due to overall severe childhood trauma and deprivation, including severe sexual abuse, have few skills to negotiate their social and sexual contacts. Distorted sexual values, beliefs, and knowledge, coupled with emotional neediness and dependency issues, increase their risk for engaging in dysfunctional relationships. They lack the necessary skills to get their emotional and sexual needs met with appropriate partners—namely healthy, consensual adults. This inability increases their risk of getting their sexual needs met by children.

A qualitative analysis illuminated several pertinent aspects of female sex offenders' thinking gleaned from 20 offenders. (The following excerpts are made up of *individual* sentences and do *not* comprise an entire continuous paragraph.)

> "They idealized children, demonized men, and distrusted other women." "The offenders were ambivalent about themselves" [i.e. their good and bad qualities]. "When discussing their offense, they generally described the effect on themselves, most often in terms of what happened when they got caught." "When they verbalized their regret or said how bad they felt about what they had done, it was in relation to how their behavior had affected them." "They expressed little regret for the impact on the victim." "Their abilities to express intimacy, understanding, empathy, and competency were limited." "They . . . felt out of control of their lives and did not know why." (L. Lawson, 2008, pp. 340–341)

A previous classification of female CSA offenders divided them into three groups: intergenerationally predisposed, teacher/lover, and male-coerced (Saradjian, 1996). A newer categorization of 43 offenders living in England divided the women into four groups: (a) 11—lone offender, victim over 12 years of age; (b) 9—lone offender, victim under 12 years of age; (c) 18—male associated with the assault; and (d) 5—male coerced female in assault. All 5 of the women in the male coerced group and 15 of the 18 women in the male associated group had controlling, violent male partners. *Depression was the primary trigger for abuse* (Elliott et al., 2010).

*Relationship to the abused child.* Male perpetrators of CSA are generally divided into *two categories:* those who commit *intrafamilial (within the family) abuse* and those who commit extrafamilial (outside the family). The most typical type of perpetrator is an *acquaintance* of the family or the child (e.g., Finkelhor, Ormrod, Turner, & Hamby, 2009).

The U.S. Department of Health & Human Services (2008) presented information on the type of *sexual abuse perpetrator* from 47 states. See Table 5.6 for the distribution of perpetrator types.

**TABLE 5.6** Perpetrators by Maltreatment Type and Relationship to Victim

| Parent (n = 706,765) | | Daycare Provider (n = 4,720) | | Foster Parent (n = 3,228) | |
|---|---|---|---|---|---|
| 16,322 | 2.3% | 1,001 | 21.2% | 206 | 6.4% |
| Legal Guardian (n = 1,960) | | Friends/Neighbors (n = 4,007) | | Other (n = 31,858) | |
| 69 | 3.5% | 2,335 | 58.3% | 13,056 | 41% |
| Other Professional (n = 967) | | Other Relative (n = 57,349) | | Residential Staff (n = 2,074) | |
| 349 | 36.1% | 17,688 | 30.8% | 170 | 8.2% |
| Unmarried Partner of Parent (n = 38,269) | | Unknown or Missing (n = 29,247) | | Total Maltreatment Perpetrators (n = 880,444) | |
| 5,276 | 13.8% | 3,781 | 12.9% | 60, 253 | 6.8% |

## SECTION SUMMARY

## Characteristics of CSA Victims and Perpetrators

The age of CSA victims varies from infancy to 18 years of age, with a peak between 12 and 14 years of age. One of the most consistent findings of research evaluating risk factors associated with CSA is that females are more likely than males to be victims of CSA, and males (about 93%) are more likely than females (about 7%) to be perpetrators. Relatively recent research suggests, however, that significant proportions of female perpetrators and male victims may go undetected by researchers, practitioners, and reporting agencies. Female perpetrators are frequently in relationships with violent/controlling male partners, and a large proportion of them have a history of CSA themselves.

Research has shown that widely held stereotypes of CSA perpetrators and victims are inaccurate. For example, rather than being "dirty old men," CSA perpetrators are most likely to be between 30 and 40 years of age. CSA perpetrators are also less likely to be strangers to their victims than is often imagined. Instead, the most likely perpetrator is a male acquaintance who has developed a trusting relationship with the victim/family, or a male relative. Child and family variables that may increase the risk of CSA victimization include victim's age, family composition (e.g., presence of a male live-in partner of the mother), and maternal unavailability (e.g., parents with emotional or drug-related problems). One factor related to the maintenance of CSA is the victim's willingness to accept blame for the incident.

Populations of victims and offenders are heterogeneous, suggesting that sexual abuse occurs in virtually all demographic, social, and family circumstances. Some evidence suggests, however, that children living in families with a low socioeconomic status are more likely to be victimized than their better-off counterparts. Furthermore, because the majority of research has focused on female victims and male perpetrators, most research findings do not pertain to male victims or female perpetrators. As a final caveat, it is important to acknowledge the difficulty in determining whether the variables found to be associated with CSA are actual risk factors for abuse, consequences of abuse, or correlates of abuse history.

# DYNAMICS AND CONSEQUENCES ASSOCIATED WITH CHILD SEXUAL ABUSE

## Dynamics of Child Sexual Abuse

To develop a comprehensive understanding of CSA, it is necessary to examine the characteristics of the victimization experience itself. Most research suggests that sexual offenses against children are most often nonviolent and that long-lasting physical injuries are rare. Physical violence accompanies only about 20% of CSA incidents (Timnick, 1985). Other findings, however, suggest that offenders are more frequently aggressive and often use physical threats (Briere & Elliott, 1994).

*Severity of abuse.* Several inquiries assessed the severity of CSA, and some searched for links between severity and various outcomes, such as adult somatization problems (see Russell, 1983, on www. sagepub.com/barnett3e). Gomes-Schwartz, Horowitz, and Cardarelli (1990), in a study of 156 sexually abused *children,* found the following levels of CSA severity: (a) 6%—sexual touching, voyeurism, or attempted sexual contact (e.g., requests to touch his genitals); (b) 23%—fondling or mutual stimulation; (c) 38%—oral-genital contact or object penetration; and (d) 28%—vaginal or anal intercourse. A team of researchers used data from the 156 adult men and women who had been sexually abused as children to construct a severity of sexual abuse scale by linking the variables to adult outcomes and to compare men's and women's responses. Table 5.7 displays significant associations between CSA and (a) adult trauma and (b) adult somatization. This study is valuable to practitioners trying to craft individualized effective treatment plans for victims (Zink, Klesges, Stevens, & Decker, 2009).

 **TABLE 5.7** Significance of Gender Differences in Associations Between Significant CSA Variables and Significant Adult Somatization and Trauma

| CSA Variable | Somatization Significance Level (Gender) | Trauma Significance Level |
|---|---|---|
| Age at first sex abuse | <.001 | <.001 |
| Coercion used | <.001 | <.001 |
| Nature of abuse | n.s. | <.006 |
| Number of times abused | n.s. | <.024 |
| More than one offender | n.s. | n.s. |

(See www.sagepub.com/barnett3e for more details about the significant differences between males and females on these variables.)

*Initiation of abuse.* Preliminary reports from men incarcerated for CSA or participating in treatment programs for CSA offenders have provided some information about the techniques perpetrators use to identify and recruit child victims. Perpetrators do not molest every child to whom they have access. Instead, they generally select children who are vulnerable, at risk in some way. They also do not use uniform strategies to perpetrate abuse initially. Some use force, threats, or fear. Another approach is to use subterfuge by telling the child the activities are for educational purposes (e.g., B. E. Saunders, Berliner, & Hanson, 2004).

*Grooming.* *"Grooming is a premeditated behavior intended to manipulate the potential victim into complying with the sexual abuse"* (Terry & Tallon, 2004, p. 22). A slightly different perspective makes use of the terminology *modus operandi* to characterize grooming and defines it as "the actions taken by an offender to perpetrate the offense successfully" (J. E. Douglas, Burgess, Burgess, & Ressler, 1997, p. 353).

Offenders resort to a range of coercive tactics to reach their goals. Frequently, a molester conditions the child through *rewards* (e.g., money, toys, candy, and clothes) and *punishments* (e.g., threatening to hit the child or to stop taking the child to Disneyland). Further, he is very likely to *misrepresent moral standards* or to misuse his authority or adult sophistication to seduce a child (e.g., "It's okay, you're my daughter" or "I'm teaching you about sex"). Gradually, the relationship may develop into a *quid pro quo* interaction in which the molester *pays* for sex. Over time, the sexual activity becomes routine. Surveys of child victims confirmed molesters' reports about their techniques (Berliner & Conte, 1990; Pryor, 1996).

According to one researcher who surveyed molesters, there are two *basic categories* of common grooming tactics: (a) *seduction/enticements* and (b) *verbal/physical intimidation*. To gain access to the child, molesters initially try to *separate the child from protective adults*. In seduction, the abuser builds on a preexisting relationship through a progression of nonsexual to sexual touching. One typical scenario begins with seemingly accidental or affectionate touches and then proceeds to sexual touches. Another may start with a game of tickling and move forward. A trio of investigators have reviewed molesters' modus operandi within two domains: (a) stages of grooming and (b) the association between stages of grooming and other characteristics (e.g., deviant sexual fantasies). The studies revealed that the *modus operandi* used by a CSA offender was highly associated with the victim's age and gender (Leclerc, Proulx, & Beauregard, 2009).

*Online molesters.* Online molesters use several common tactics as well: (a) taking over a young person's online account to groom the young person's contacts; (b) hacking into a young person's account to verbally abuse these contacts; and (c) sending or threatening to send a virus to the young person's computer. After gaining access to a contact, the CSA abuser may cajole the child into sending some suggestive pictures of the child him- or herself. Then the abuser can use the picture to blackmail the child into doing other things. Sometimes a pornographer will photoshop an ordinary picture to sexualize it and then blackmail the child with it. Children cannot easily counteract such approaches (Baines, 2008).

# Child Pornography

*Defining child pornography.* The National Center for Missing and Exploited Children (n.d.) notes that federal law defines child pornography as follows:

> Child pornography is "a visual depiction of any kind, including a drawing, cartoon, sculpture, painting, photograph, film, video, or computer/computer-generated image or picture, whether made or produced by electronic, mechanical, or other means, of sexually explicit conduct" involving a minor.

*Legal responses to child pornography.* Until the late 1970s, there were no laws against child pornography in most U.S. states. In 1978, the U.S. Congress passed the *Protection of Children Against Sexual Exploitation Act* in an attempt to halt the production and dissemination of pornographic materials involving children. In addition, the Child Sexual Abuse and Pornography Act of 1986 provided for federal prosecution of individuals engaged in child pornography, including parents who permit their children to engage in such activities (Otto & Melton, 1990). A recent difference of opinion has erupted over research suggesting that child pornographers are frequently the same men who molest children (see Estes & Weiner, 2010; Schell, Martin, Hung, & Rueda, 2007).

There are several federal statutes that govern production of child pornography, possession of child pornography, sexual trafficking, and importation of child pornography (see USC §§ 2251, 2251A, 2252, 2252A, and 2260). As lawmakers have tried to define and curtail child pornography, courts have overturned one law after another on the constitutional basis of freedom of speech. As a case in point, acceptable definitions of child pornography had to exclude computer-generated images and adults who look like minors. Basic free speech rights underlie such decisions (Schell et al., 2007).

Several U.S. states have also passed legislation that requires commercial film and photo processors to inform authorities when they discover suspected child pornography during the processing of film (e.g., Wurtele & Miller-Perrin, 1992). With the advent of the Internet, child pornography has become increasingly complex. Without a doubt, complete elimination of child pornography will require worldwide prohibitions. Only about half of the countries who are members of Interpol, however, have adopted prohibitions against child pornography on the Internet (Baines, 2008).

*Impact of pornography on children.* There are several ways in which child pornography negatively impacts children: (a) by creating a market for the victimization of children, (b) by serving as a tool that perpetrators use to educate and stimulate victims, and (c) as a tool to blackmail victims into maintaining secrecy about the abuse (Estes & Weiner, 2010; Hunt & Baird, 1990).

# Prostitution

Survey findings conducted with adult female prostitutes suggest that significant numbers of these women began to work as prostitutes when they were children. Silbert and Pines (1983) surveyed 200 San Francisco street prostitutes and found that 70% reported that they were less than 21 years of age when they began prostitution. Of these, 60% reported they were under age 16 when they started work as prostitutes. A more recent survey has postulated that about

293,000 American youth were at risk for becoming victims of commercial sexual exploitation. Documented characteristics of adolescent prostitutes often include a history of childhood maltreatment (such as physical and sexual abuse and exposure to interparental violence), personal and parental alcohol or drug abuse, and poor family functioning (Choi, Klein, Shin, & Lee, 2009; Estes & Weiner, 2010). One common factor in the backgrounds of adolescent prostitutes on the street is *runaway or thrown-away youth status* (Estes & Weiner, 2010). Some runaways are too young to obtain legitimate employment (Williamson & Folaron, 2003). (See Edinburgh & Saewyc, 2009, for a fresh therapy approach for this population.)

## EFFECTS OF CHILD SEXUAL ABUSE

The consequences associated with CSA can be classified as either *initial effects* (occurring within 2 years following the abuse) or *long-term effects* (consequences beyond 2 years subsequent to the abuse).

### Initial Effects

Investigators have identified a wide range of emotional, cognitive, physical, and behavioral effects in CSA victims within 2 years of the abuse. The specific manifestation of symptoms appears to depend on the developmental level of the victim (Wurtele & Miller-Perrin, 1992). Table 5.8 displays the most common initial effects associated with CSA for preschool and school-age children. (See www.sagepub.com/barnett3e for adolescent children.)

**TABLE 5.8**  Possible Initial Effects Associated With Sexual Abuse

| Behavioral Effects | Emotional Effects | Cognitive Effects | Physical Effects |
|---|---|---|---|
| *Preschool Children* | | | |
| Regression/immaturity | Anxiety[a] | Learning difficulties | Bruises |
| Social withdrawal | Clinging | | Genital bleeding |
| Sexualized behavior[a] | Nightmares[a] | | Genital pain |
| Sexual preoccupation[a] | Fears | | Genital itching |
| Precocious sexual knowledge[a] | Depression | | Genital odors |
| Seductive behavior[a] | Guilt | | Problems walking |
| Excessive masturbation[a] | Hostility/anger | | Problems sitting |
| Sex play with others[a] | Tantrums | | Sleep disturbance |
| Sexual language | Aggression | | Eating disturbance |
| Genital exposure | | | Enuresis |
| Sexual victimization of others[a] | | | Encopresis |
| Family/peer conflicts | | | Stomachache |
| Difficulty separating | | | Headache |
| Hyperactivity | | | |

| Behavioral Effects | Emotional Effects | Cognitive Effects | Physical Effects |
|---|---|---|---|
| **School-Age Children** | | | |
| Regression/immaturity[a] | Anxiety | Learning difficulties[a] | Stomachache |
| Social withdrawal | Phobias | Poor concentration | Headache |
| Sexualized behavior | Nightmares[a] | Poor attention | Genital pain |
| Sexual preoccupation | Fears[a] | Declining grades | Genital itching |
| Precocious sexual knowledge | Obsessions | Negative perceptions | Genital odors |
| Seductive behavior | Tics | Dissociation | Problems walking |
| Excessive masturbation | Hostility/anger | | Problems sitting |
| Sex play with others | Aggression[a] | | Sleep disturbance |
| Sexual language | Family/peer conflicts | | Eating disturbance |
| Genital exposure | Depression | | Enuresis |
| Sexual victimization of others | Guilt | | Encopresis |
| Delinquency | Suicidality | | |
| Stealing | Low self-esteem | | |
| Poor peer relations | | | |
| Hyperactivity[a] | | | |
| **Physical Effects Any Age** | | | |
| Bruises around breast or genitals | | Unexplained vaginal or anal bleeding | |
| A torn or scarred hymen | | Unexplained venereal disease | |
| Bruising of hard/soft palate, etc. from forced oral penetration | | Frequent urinary tract infections | |

SOURCES: A representative but not exhaustive list of sources for the information displayed in this table includes Botash, 2008; Chaffin, Silovsky, & Vaughn, 2005; Feiring & Cleland, 2007; Fergusson, Boden, & Horwood, 2008; Finkelhor, Ormrod, & Turner, 2007b; Gilbert et al., 2008; Seto & Lalumière, 2010; Tyler & Johnson, 2006.
NOTE: [a]Most common symptoms for this age-group.

*Mimicking sexual behavior.* In a review of 45 empirical studies on initial effects of CSA, Kendall-Tackett, Williams, and Finkelhor (1993) found that one of the two most common symptoms identified in sexually abused children is *sexualized behavior.* Sexualized behavior refers to behaviors such as overt sexual acting out toward adults or other children, compulsive masturbation, excessive sexual curiosity, sexual promiscuity, and precocious sexual play and knowledge. The sexual behaviors of sexually abused children are often associated with intercourse, such as mimicking intercourse and inserting objects into the vagina or anus (Friedrich et al., 2001). Sexualized behavior is also believed to be the behavioral symptom that is most predictive of the occurrence of sexual abuse (Friedrich, 1993).

**CASE HISTORY** "I Love Her but Is She a Nymphomaniac?"

Patty attended a church youth group where she met Tim. She was 16 and he was 18. She was so eager to have sex with him that he felt flattered. They had sex all the time and Patty got pregnant rather quickly. They eloped to avoid any gossip among their church friends about premarital sex.

The youth minister, in an apparent attempt to prevent premarital sex, announced to the young people attending a Sunday evening meeting that the couple was forced to marry because of her pregnancy. Patty and Tim were mortified by their public disgrace. In time, they dropped out of the youth group and stopped going to church altogether. Patty cried, and they never attended the church again.

Patty had been an incest victim since the age of 8, but she had not confided in anyone about her plight until she built up trust in the youth minister. She was happy about her marriage and especially pleased to move away from her father. Although she had nearly finished high school, she had never worked. Tim, on the other hand, got a job delivering laundry, so he was able to support them financially. While Tim worked all day, Patty took a bus downtown and shopped all day, even though she never bought anything.

Patty came home early every day in order to have dinner on the table the minute Tim walked in the door. As soon as she cleared the dishes away, she rushed Tim into the bedroom for sex. If Tim got home early enough and ate dinner early enough, Patty could approach him for sex again around 10 p.m. or in the middle of the night. She also made a point of getting him up early so they could have sex before he left for work. Sometimes she would plead with him to come home in the middle of day to have sex. She said she would not go out shopping if he would just come home for 30 minutes.

After three months, Tim began to feel strange about his sexual relationship with Patty. He was beginning to enjoy sex much less and really wished he had not gotten married so early. Patty finally told Tim about her father, and Tim did what he could to make Patty feel better. He talked to Patty about the frequency of their sex, but she was adamant about her sexual needs. By the fourth month Tim began to feel frantic and desperately needed to "find a way out." He did not know who could help him or offer advice. He had an idea why Patty was like this, but he was not sure and he did not want to upset her by voicing his suspicions. One thing was for sure; he would not seek counsel from the youth minister. Will Patty ever get the help she needs? Will Tim and Patty ever be able to develop a happy marriage?

*Posttraumatic stress disorder (PTSD).* The other most frequent problem noted in sexually abused children is posttraumatic stress disorder.

> PTSD may occur when a person lives through/witnesses an event that appears to be life-threatening and experiences intense fear or helplessness. The PTSD sufferer may suffer from many symptoms, some of which are as follows: (a) diminished responsiveness, (b) chronic physiological arousal leading to symptoms such as sleeplessness, and (c) flashbacks (see the glossary—Goldenson, 1984; see also VandenBos, 2007).
>
> A newly devised factor structure based on 2,378 female survivors of sexual and/or physical abuse or assault suggests that PTSD includes four unique components: (a) avoidance, (b) re-experiencing, (c) dysphoria, and (d) hyperarousal (Hetzel-Riggin, 2009).

Sexually abused children are extremely likely to suffer from high levels of these PTSD symptoms. Using the *DSM-IV* as a guide, more than one-third of sexually abused children meet criteria for PTSD (e.g., Ruggiero, McLeer, & Dixon, 2000; see also Humphreys, Sauder, Martin, & Marx, 2010). Compared with children abused by other kinds of maltreatment or compared with nonabused children, abused children have significantly higher rates of PTSD symptoms (e.g., Dubner & Motta, 1999). Meta-analytic results indicated that females are significantly more likely than males to experience *child abuse, sexual assault,* and *PTSD*. This gender difference in acquisition of PTSD exists even though males are exposed to more traumatic events. Males experience significantly more *accidents, nonsexual assaults, exposure to death or injury, disaster or fire,* and *combat or war.* Because of males' greater exposure to various types of traumatic events, gender differences in PTSD symptoms cannot be completely accounted for by the higher level of sex abuse of females (Tolin & Foa, 2008; see also Maikovich-Fong & Jaffee, 2010).

*Psychopathology effects.* CSA has also been associated with a wide range of psychopathologies, such as borderline personality disorder (McLean & Gallop, 2003). Of the sexually victimized children studied by Gomes-Schwartz et al. (1990), 17% of the preschool group (4 to 6 years of age), 40% of the school-age group (7 to 13 years of age), and 8% of the adolescent group (14 to 18 years of age) evidenced clinically significant pathology, indicating severe behavioral and emotional difficulties. Using a checklist of parent-reported behaviors to assess the effects of sexual abuse on 93 prepubertal children, Dubowitz, Black, Harrington, and Verschoore (1993) found that 36% had significantly elevated scores on the *Internalizing Scale* (e.g., depression and withdrawn behavior) and 38% had elevated scores on the *Externalizing Scale* (e.g., acting-out behaviors). Similar levels of dysfunction would be expected in only 10% of the general population of children. The results from the National Comorbidity Survey of 5,877 adults indicated the following percentages of mood, anxiety, and substance use disorders: (a) 13.5% of women, and (b) 2.5% of men. "CSA, whether alone or in a larger adversity cluster, is associated with substantial increased risk of subsequent psychopathology" (Molnar, Buka, & Kessler, 2001, p. 753; see also R. Schneider, Baumrind, & Kimerling, 2007).

## Long-Term Effects of Child Sexual Abuse

The psychological consequences of childhood sexual victimization can extend not only into adolescence and adulthood but also into old age. Table 5.9 summarizes the long-term effects associated with CSA.

*Anger.* Children may experience varying degrees of anger stemming from the entire CSA experience: (a) not being able to disclose CSA to a parent who is emotionally fragile, (b) people's reactions to their disclosure, (c) no one protected them, (d) they felt singled out for victimization, (e) they were assigned to out-of-home placement because their family broke up, and (f) they (might) have to testify in open court (see S. V. Hunter, 2010; Zinzow et al., 2010).

**TABLE 5.9** · Possible Long-Term Effects Associated With Child Sexual Abuse

| Type of Effect | Specific Problem | Specific Symptoms | | |
|---|---|---|---|---|
| Emotional | Depression | Depressed affect | Suicidality | Guilt |
| | | Low self-esteem | Poor self-image | Self-blame |
| | Anxiety | Anxiety attacks | Migraines | Fears |
| | | Somatic symptoms | Skin disorders | Phobias |
| | | Stomach problems | Aches and pains | |
| Interpersonal | | Difficulty trusting others | Alienation and insecurity | |
| | | Poor social adjustment | Parenting difficulties | |
| | | Feelings of isolation/ loneliness | Revictimization | |
| | | Difficulty forming/maintaining relationships | | |
| Posttraumatic stress disorder | Re-experiencing | Intrusive thoughts | Flashbacks | Nightmares |
| | Numbing Avoidance | Amnesia for abusive events | Dissociation | |
| | | Disengagement ("spacing out") | Emotional numbing | |
| | | Out-of-body experiences | Poor concentration | |
| Sexual adjustment | | Promiscuity | Anorgasmia | |
| | | Sexual guilt | Sexual anxiety | |
| | | Sexual phobia/aversion | Prostitution | |
| | | Arousal/desire dysfunction | | |
| | | Dissatisfaction with sexual relationships | | |
| Behavior dysfunction | Eating disorder | Binging | Purging | Overeating |
| | Substance abuse | Use of illicit drugs | Alcohol misuse | |
| | Medical exams | Did not obtain common medical exams because of fear | | |

SOURCES: A representative but not exhaustive list of sources for the information displayed in this table includes Berliner & Saunders, 2010; C. Browne & Winkelman, 2007; P. Cohen, Brown, & Smailes, 2001; DeLago, Deblinger, Schroeder, & Finkel, 2008; Godbout, Sabourin, & Lussier, 2009; K. Hall, 2008; Klonsky & Moyer, 2008; Maikovich-Fong & Jaffee, 2010; McGregor et al., 2010; Polusny & Follette, 2008; Silverman, Reinherz, & Giaconia, 1996; C. A. Smith, 2009; Smolak & Murnen, 2002; Widom, 1995.

*Polyvictimization, revictimization, and cumulative trauma effects.* Experiencing one type of victimization is associated with experiencing another type. "A child who was physically assaulted in the past year would be five times as likely to have also been sexually victimized . . ." (Finkelhor, Turner, Ormrod, Hamby, & Kracke, 2009, p. 7). Sadly, susceptibility/vulnerability to post-CSA sexual assaults is a common occurrence among victims. *Revictimization* rates are high (e.g., Polusny & Follette, 2008). A consistent finding in the literature is that *any victimization in childhood increases the likelihood of victimization throughout adulthood* (e.g., Finkelhor, Ormrod, & Turner, 2007a). Multiple types of child abuse increase the risk for mental health problems (R. Schneider et al., 2007).

A trio of investigators examined the *cumulative effects* of additional trauma following seven types of childhood abuse as they related to *five forms* of adult abuse. In this investigation, 557 heterosexual women from a *domestic violence* screening intervention in a primary care setting provided data. Results supported the investigators' hypotheses of long-lasting effects in nearly every aspect. Hence, treatment for CSA should be multidimensional (Alaggia, 2010; Litrownick et al., 2005).

- Both physical and sexual child abuse were significantly correlated with both anxiety and depression.
- Recent intimate partner violence and very severe child abuse were risk factors for depression.
- Recent and past male-to-female interpersonal violence and child abuse were risk factors for anxiety.

Last, an analysis revealed *significant cumulative effects on both depression and anxiety*. Even low levels of cumulative abuse were significantly linked with increases in depression and anxiety (Carlson, McNutt, & Choi, 2003; see also Finkelhor, Ormond, & Turner, 2007c).


## Explaining the Variability in Effects of CSA

Not every CSA victim feels equally distressed by CSA. Some older children abused by individuals, such as coaches, teachers, and Boy Scout leaders, may view their sexual interactions as consensual. They may believe the *abuse* to be a sign of true love and the relationship to be unique and valuable. Moreover, no single symptom or pattern of symptoms is present in all victims of CSA. Many CSA victims exhibit no symptoms at all, at least in the short term. Based on their review of CSA effects, Kendall-Tackett et al., (1993) concluded that approximately 20% to 50% of CSA victims are *asymptomatic at initial assessment*, and only 10% to 25% become symptomatically worse during the 2 years following victimization. What causes such variability in responses?

Researchers attempting to answer this question have explored associations between characteristics of the sexually abusive situation or its aftermath and differential psychological effects. Some characteristics of the victim or the incident are factors such as the frequency and the duration of the abuse and the type of CSA activity. As one illustration, mother-daughter CSA has unusually profound effects because of factors such as the betrayal of trust and the inability to cope effectively with such an "unspeakable" offense (Peter, 2008). Other negative effects of CSA include postabuse disclosure outcomes and the extent to which the victim perceives the abuse as harmful (e.g., Chartier, Walker, & Naimark, 2010; Fischer, Stojek, & Hartzell, 2010; Tyler & Johnson, 2006). (See the table on the website, www.sagepub.com/barnett3e, for a list of potential mediators and their effects.)

## Reactions to Disclosure

Research has found that specific postabuse events (e.g., the ways in which family members and institutions respond to disclosure) are related to the overall effects of CSA. It is well established that responses toward the victim by parents, relatives, teachers, and other adults have dramatic effects on the trauma associated with CSA. Studies have consistently found that negative responses tend to aggravate victims' experience of trauma (e.g., Gomes-Schwartz et al., 1990; Runyan, Hunter, & Everson, 1992).

---

**SECTION SUMMARY**

### The Dynamics of Child Sexual Abuse

The sexual activities of CSA perpetrators range from exhibitionism to various forms of penetration. Perpetrators usually target children who are vulnerable or needy in some way and involve the children in a grooming process that involves a gradual progression from nonsexual to sexual touch. To initiate and maintain abuse, perpetrators may use seduction/enticement strategies and/or coercive/controlling tactics. Offenders usually adapt their techniques to the age and gender of the victim.

A relatively new area within CSA research concerns the sexual exploitation of children via the Internet. Perpetrators can be quite successful in obtaining sexual activity with a child by taking over the child's computer account and then exerting control over some of the child's sexual activities, such as talking the child into taking a picture of him- or herself in a sexual pose.

More organized forms of child maltreatment involve groups of children who are abused for the sexual stimulation of perpetrators and often for commercial gain. Children who become involved in pornography and prostitution are often runaways or thrown-away children attempting to escape dysfunctional or abusive home environments. Interventions aimed at alleviating the problem of organized exploitation have focused primarily on policy initiatives and legislation designed to protect children from these activities. Although these approaches have met with some success, more efforts are needed.

Numerous empirical studies have shown that myriad psychological consequences are associated with childhood sexual victimization. These include both short-term and long-term difficulties of an emotional, physical, cognitive, and behavioral nature. Victims exhibit a wide range of effects, varying from just a few problems to experiencing significant psychopathology. The most common effect appears to be PTSD. This heterogeneity in the effects of CSA plus methodological weaknesses in many of the studies conducted have led to equivocal findings. Nevertheless, it appears that the factors most likely to increase the trauma experienced by CSA victims are numerous: (a) long duration of abuse, (b) polyvictimization, (c) the severity of the abuse, (d) abuse by someone who is a parental figure or trusted acquaintance, (e) abuse that involves invasive forms of sexual activity, and (f) negative reactions by significant others to the disclosure of the abuse. Recent research has also established that several variables may mediate the effects of CSA, such as the victim's subjective perceptions of the events and the availability of social support following disclosure.

# EXPLAINING CHILD SEXUAL ABUSE

The victims and perpetrators of CSA are characterized by a great deal of diversity, and such heterogeneity contributes to the difficulty in answering one of the central questions about CSA: Why do some individuals sexually abuse children? Scholars have developed theoretical formulations that focus on different individuals or systems involved in CSA, including the victim, the perpetrator, the abusive family, and society. Table 5.10 displays the risk factors associated with each of these systems.

**TABLE 5.10**    Risk Factors Associated With Child Sexual Abuse

| Analytical Level | Risk Factors | | | |
|---|---|---|---|---|
| Characteristics of the child | Cognitive disability | Passive | Few close friends | Quiet |
| | Unhappy appearance | Needy | Female gender | Trusting |
| | Depressed affect | | | |
| Characteristics of the perpetrator | Male gender | Passive | Poor impulse control | |
| | Childhood sexual/physical victimization | | Sexual attraction to children | |
| | Antisocial disregard for others | | Misuse of alcohol/drugs | |
| | Sensitive about sexual performance | | Sexual fantasies about children | |
| | Use cognitive distortions to justify behavior | | Deficient heterosexual skills | |
| | Neurobiological disorders (e.g., white matter volume in the brain) | | | |
| | Feelings of dependency, inadequacy, vulnerability, loneliness | | | |
| Characteristics of the family | Single parent with live-in partner | | Parents in conflict | |
| | Unhappy home life | | Mother disabled/ill | |
| | Institutionalized parent | | Mother employed | |
| | Mother not high school graduate | | Divorced parents | |
| | Mother sexually abused in childhood | | Residential mobility | |
| | Family isolation | | | |
| Sociocultural characteristics | Over-sexualization of normal emotional needs | | Objectification of sexual partners | |
| | Male-dominated household/patriarchal | | Access to child pornography | |
| | Neglect of children's sexual development | | Socialization of male stoicism | |
| | Blocking of socialization of empathy in males | | | |
| | Permissible sexual relations between adults and children | | | |

SOURCES: A representative but not exhaustive list of sources for the information displayed in this table includes Cantor et al., 2008; Gery, Miljkovitch, Berthoz, & Soussignan, 2009; Gold, Hyman, & Andrés-Hyman, 2004; K. Hall, 2008; Hussey, Chang, & Kotch, 2008; Leung et al., 2010; Stripe & Stermac, 2003; U.S. Department of Health & Human Services, 2008; Wright, Fredrich, Cinq-Mars, & McDuff, 2004.

## Focus on the Victim

Early explanations for the occurrence of CSA focused on the *victim's culpability* for *encouraging* or *allowing* the sexual abuse to occur. Researchers asserted that victims seductively encouraged perpetrators or that they enjoyed the abuse. Little evidence, however, exists to support these positions. Admittedly, many CSA victims exhibit sexualized behavior, but most experts believe that such behavior is the result, rather than the cause, of the abuse. In addition, research evidence contradicts this assumption that children *encourage* or *want* the abuse. Only a *minority of victims* report that their abuse had any pleasurable or positive characteristics (e.g., that they felt *loved* during the abuse; Faller, 1988). As previously discussed, current perspectives on CSA *preclude victim culpability* because, by definition, children are viewed as developmentally incapable of consenting to take part in sexual activities with adults.

## Focus on the Offender

The amount of research on child sexual abusers with a focus on explaining their behavior has proliferated. The earliest researchers relied on the *psychiatric model,* assuming that the causes of abuse stem from the individual psychopathology of male abusers. Later attempts focused additionally on deviant patterns of sexual arousal and a childhood history of sex abuse. Contemporary theories attempt to integrate several factors that might contribute to sexual offending against children. The newer the research, the more likely it is to include the neurobiological basis of psychopathy. This research clearly shows significant differences in the brains of psychopaths compared with nonpsychopaths, such as differences in the amygdala, orbitofrontal cortex, and cortisol levels. More research is needed to track the developmental origins of these neurobiological processes (Gao, Glenn, Schug, Yang, & Raine, 2009).

Most perpetrators of CSA have a variety of personality disorders or less severe forms of psychopathology (Quinsey, Lalumière, Rice, & Harris, 1995). Typical problems include *antisocial tendencies* such as disregard for the interests of others and lack of empathy and impulse control. Such offenders have a willingness to exploit others and to violate social norms (Whitaker et al., 2008). Some researchers have described child molesters as passive; as having feelings of vulnerability, inadequacy, and loneliness; as displaying deficits in intimacy; as being overly sensitive about their sexual performance with women; and as exhibiting deficits in social skills (e.g., Cortoni & Marshall, 2001; see Whitaker et al., 2008). Perpetrators also generally demonstrate ineffective means of coping with stress (Cortoni & Marshall, 2001). Presumably, such difficulties may lead them to avoid the demands of adult relationships by turning to children to fulfill their social and relationship needs.

*Deviant sexual arousal—pedophilia.* Some theorists propose that CSA *perpetrators* seek out sexual encounters with children primarily because they are sexually attracted to children (G. G. Abel, Becker, & Cunningham-Rathner, 1984). It seems apparent, however, that a minority of college males experience sexual arousal to children also. In one sample, 22.2% of *male* undergraduates (*n* = 99) and 2.8% of *female* college students (*n* = 180) reported having experienced sexual attraction to children (Smiljanich & Briere, 1996). Another analysis of 531 undergraduate *males* found the following: (a) 18% had fantasized about CSA, (b) 4% said there was some likelihood they would have sex with a child, and (c) 2.5% admitted to at least one sexually abusive act against a child (Becker-Blease, Friend, & Freyd, 2006). Given these results concerning college males, the assumption that sexual attraction to children is *deviant* may need further research consideration.

The origins of such deviant sexual arousal, however, are undetermined. Some researchers have suggested that *neurobiological factors* may be a cause of **pedophilia,** such as insufficient levels of white matter in the brain (e.g., Cantor et al., 2008). *Learning theorists*, on the other hand, have proposed that deviant sexual arousal develops when it is reinforced through fantasies of sexual activity with children and masturbating to those fantasies (e.g., Cortoni & Marshall, 2001).

*Plethysmography.* The procedure most often used to determine whether a CSA perpetrator is sexually aroused by children is called *penile plethysmography.* In this procedure, a circular gauge is placed around the base of the penis in the privacy of a clinic. The subject then views pictures of different types of people who might be potential sexual partners (e.g., same-age individuals, same-sex and opposite-sex individuals, young children, and adolescents of both sexes). The plethysmograph records even small increases in the circumference of the penis in response to picture viewing. The penile plethysmography procedure itself has also been questioned because of problematic findings (Conte, 1993). Studies examining sexual arousal in specific categories of perpetrators (*child molesters, incest offenders, rapists, nonsexual offenders,* and *nonoffending men*) have yielded contradictory results. (See Clegg & Fremouw, 2009, for a review.)

## Cognitive distortion occurs in some CSA offenders.
.............................................................................

### CASE HISTORY    Alberto—"I Knew What She Wanted"

*Alberto.* Alberto was a 64-year-old grandpa convicted of molesting his 3-year-old granddaughter, Rosie. On a family picnic one day, Rosie had asked to sit on Grandpa's lap. When Grandpa had an erection, Rosie was curious and asked Alberto what was in his pocket. She wanted to see what it was. Grandpa took her aside and showed her his penis. He said she could touch it and kiss it if she wanted to, so she did. Now, he is sitting in prison "unfairly." After all, when she sat on his lap, Alberto knew what she wanted.

### CASE HISTORY    Dave—"Society Doesn't Understand Children's Sexuality"

*Dave.* Dave was serving a 10-year sentence for incest. He was 37, tall, thin, and nice looking, and he had a high IQ. He had been employed all his adult life, and his marital relationship was still intact. He proclaimed loud and long to everyone that he did not belong in prison. He cried real tears and implored people to "do something" to get him out. Yes, it was true that he had had sex with his 13-year-old daughter, Brigette, but that was only half the story. "People did not understand. It was Brigette who instigated the sexual activities. It was Brigette who wanted sex." He had done nothing wrong.

The other half of the story appeared in his jacket (i.e., his case file). Brigette had begged her father to "stop hurting her." She had turned to her mother for help after the first assault, but her mother seemed paralyzed by the news and did nothing. Brigette eventually walked the 2 miles to the local police station alone at 10 p.m. to ask for help. When confronted with this information, Dave still insisted that Brigette wanted to have sex with him. "What is wrong with people?" Why didn't they believe him?

*Cognitive distortion.* The case histories above reflect some of the commonly authenticated cognitive distortions found among child sex offenders (see Hayashino, Wurtele, & Klebe, 1995). Cognitive distortions may function as disinhibitors of CSA. That is, perpetrators may rationalize and defend their behavior through distorted ideas or thoughts, such as "having sex with children is a good way to teach them about sex" or "children need to be liberated from the sexually repressive bonds of society." (Recall the ideas of the North American Man/Boy Love Association, NAMBLA, discussed in Chapter 1.)

In order to tap these distorted beliefs, researchers crafted a measurement called the *Sex With Children* (SWCH) scale. A **factor analysis** identified two distinct types of beliefs held by sex offenders: (a) *sex with children is harmless* and (b) *children provoke adults into sexual activities.* Further inquiry revealed that child molesters, relative to rapists and nonoffenders, scored significantly higher on the SWCH scale. In addition, high-scoring child molesters had more entrenched abuse-supportive beliefs than lower-scoring molesters. Analyses also detected a link between abuse-supportive beliefs and beliefs ascribing responsibility to the child. A link also existed between SWCH scores and conceptions that the victim enjoyed the sexual activities (Mann et al., 2007).

*Childhood history of sexual abuse.* Evidence is mounting that the childhood sexual experiences of *adult sex offenders* differ from those of *nonsexual offenders* and *rapists* as follows:

- CSA adult offenders are more likely than nonsexual offenders to have suffered CSA in childhood (Jesperson, Lalumière, & Seto, 2009).
- CSA adult offenders *against children* are significantly more likely than CSA offenders *against adults* to have been sexually abused during childhood but less likely to have been physically abused (Jesperson et al., 2009).
- CSA victimization levels among three Swiss groups of criminals ($N = 354$) differed: (a) sex offenders—13%, (b) violent offenders—5.8%, and (c) child molesters—18.9% (Rossegger, Endress, Urbaniok, & Maercker, 2010).
- A comparison of rapists with adult CSA abusers uncovered several significant differences (Simons, Wurtele, & Durham, 2008). Table 5.11 summarizes identified traits of child molesters and rapists.

*Adolescent sex offenders.* A meta-analysis based on 59 studies of male *adolescent sex offenders* ($n = 3,855$) and male adolescent *offenders* ($n = 13,393$) whose crimes were not sexual crimes

**TABLE 5.11**  Traits and Events Distinguishing CSA Offenders From Rapists

| Trait/Event | Child Molesters (n = 132) Offense Against a Child |
|---|---|
| Experienced more frequent CSA events | 73% |
| Early exposure to pornography <10 yrs. of age | 65% |
| Early onset of masturbation <11 yrs. of age | 60% |
| Had sexual activities with animals | 38% |
| Displayed anxious parental attachment | 62% |
| | Rapists (n = 137) Offense Against an Adult |
| More frequent CPA | 68% |
| Exposure to parental violence | 78% |
| Experienced emotional abuse | 76% |
| Displayed cruelty to animals | 68% |
| Developed avoidant parental attachment | 76% |

NOTE: See Table 5.12 for a summary of how sex offenders differ and do not differ from nonsex offenders.

also found significant differences between the two groups. The investigators also presented **effect sizes** (i.e., the strength of the relationship) (Seto & Lalumière, 2010). See Table 5.12 for a summary of how sex offenders differ and do not differ from nonsex offenders.

**TABLE 5.12**  Differences and Nondifferences Between Adolescent Sex Offenders and Adolescent Nonsex Offenders

| Sex Offenders Were Significantly Different From Nonsex Offenders on These Measures | | Sex Offenders and Nonsex Offenders Were Not Significantly Different on These Measures |
|---|---|---|
| Fewer antisocial peers[2] | Social isolation | Low intellectual ability |
| Sexual abuse history[1] | Atypical sexual interests[1] | Exposure to nonsexual violence |
| Exposure to sexual violence | Other abuse or neglect | Social incompetence |
| Fewer substance abuse problems[2] | Low self-esteem | Conventional sexual experience |
| Less extensive criminal history[2] | Anxiety | Family communication problems |
| Early exposure to sex/ pornography | | Attitudes/beliefs about women or sexual offending |

NOTES: [1]Largest group difference. [2]Second largest group difference.

*Sexually abused–sexual abuser hypothesis.* Taken together, the findings from the above studies point to several significant differences between CSA offenders and non-CSA offenders (Burton, 2003; Whitaker et al., 2008). Many experts attribute these differences to learning during childhood and adolescence. Having experienced or observed victimization, the offender has *learned* that children can be used for sexual gratification or as a form of *anxiety reduction*. Lack of a nurturing parental relationship, experiencing betrayal as a child, and suffering subordination of his or her own needs to those of an abuser probably would have several effects. It might induce feelings of powerlessness and preclude the learning of *empathy* or *sensitivity* toward others (see Veneziano, Veneziano, & LeGrand, 2000; Wurtele & Miller-Perrin, 1992).

## Focus on the Family

From the perspective of family dysfunction models, CSA is an outcome of family dynamics. Either the family as a whole, or one of its members (e.g., typically the perpetrator or a nonoffending adult), contributes to an environment that permits and possibly encourages the sexual victimization of children.

*Mother's behavior—early view.* Early theories blamed mothers for having poor marital relationships—in particular, infrequent marital sex. Presumably, infrequent marital sex increased a husband's sexual frustration and "drove" him to seek satisfaction elsewhere in the family. Alternatively, mothers were culpable because of their failure to protect the victims from the offenders. Such theories have not been supported by research. In addition, family system approaches do not explain extrafamilial CSA (see Faller, 1993a).

*Mother's behavior—contemporary view.* Contemporary family system explanations view the *mother's role* as contributing to a child's vulnerability, rather than holding her responsible for the abuse. Research, however, suggests that mothers of sexually abused children may actually be covictims rather than coconspirators. Mothers in incestuous families are often abused by the perpetrators as well, and frequently have childhood histories of CSA. In this case, mothers may contribute to their children's vulnerability by withdrawing from their children or being unavailable to them (e.g., Gomes-Schwartz et al., 1990; Lawson, 2008; Strand, 2000).

*General characteristics of the family.* Other family system theorists have identified significant levels of dysfunction in families of CSA victims, although the nature of the dysfunction is unclear (Crittenden, 1996). Many researchers have found that abusive families exhibit conflicted relationships, including marital conflict in the home, poor relationships between children and parents, divorce, and spouse abuse (e.g., Boney-McCoy & Finkelhor, 1995). CSA families are frequently disorganized and lack cohesion, and they are generally more dysfunctional than non-CSA families (e.g., Leung et al., 2010; MacMillan et al., 2009; Runyon, Deblinger, & Schroeder, 2009).

## Focus on Society and Culture

Another theory views CSA as a problem stemming from the inequality between men and women (i.e., the patriarchal social system). Traditionally, women and children have shared the same minority status and have been subject to sexual abuse by men (see Birns & Meyer, 1993).

*Media impact.* A different sociocultural theory implicates mass-media portrayals of sexuality and children as factors in the etiology of CSA (e.g., Wurtele & Miller-Perrin, 1992). Many depictions of sexuality in the popular media contribute to misperceptions that women and girls deserve or desire violent sexual contact (e.g., Millburn, Mathes, & Conrad, 2000). *Child pornography* is another type of media that may stimulate sexual interest in children. The findings of research examining the relationship between child pornography and CSA have been mixed, with some studies failing to support the hypothesized relationship and others indicating that child molesters do use pornography (Howe, 1995).

## Integrative Theories

One comprehensive etiological model of sexual offending incorporates multiple components, including biological, social, and attachment processes. According to this theory, the early developmental environment of a sexual offender includes several stressful events, such as poor **attachment** between parent and child, low self-esteem, limited coping abilities, low-quality relationships with others, and a history of sexual abuse. The presence of such stressors leads the child to rely on *sexualized coping methods,* including masturbation and sexual acts with others, as a way to avoid current stressors. When other factors are present (e.g., access to a victim, disinhibition owing to alcohol use), the offender is predisposed to engage in sexually abusive behavior (W. L. Marshall & Marshall, 2000; see also Covell & Scalora, 2002).

---

### SECTION SUMMARY

#### Explaining the Determinants of Child Sexual Abuse

Despite the work of numerous researchers in academia and government, it is still not totally clear what causes individuals to abuse children sexually. Some theories focus on the child, especially the characteristics of the child that may make him or her vulnerable to CSA (e.g., being passive, quiet, trusting, young, unhappy, and needy). Other theories focus on perpetrator characteristics, such as psychological dysfunction, deviant sexual arousal, and childhood history of victimization. Some perpetrators clearly lack empathy. Some female perpetrators may additionally be influenced by their violent male partners. Numerous family characteristics are also associated with CSA, including family conflict and dysfunction. Mothers in CSA families are also more likely than those in other families to have histories of CSA. Other theories propose that sociocultural forces such as social attitudes (e.g., inequality between men and women) and child pornography may contribute to CSA. Currently, no existing theory or combination of theories successfully explains CSA.

---

# PRACTICE, POLICY, AND PREVENTION ISSUES

Society continues to show a high level of outrage about sexual crimes committed against children. Public pressure has driven the implementation of sex offender registries, Megan's Law, and efforts to incarcerate offenders for life. Scholars in the field of CSA who have judged the quality of therapeutic expertise to be inadequate have begun to advocate for better training (e.g., Knight, 2004). Along the same lines, Oz (2010) has crystallized the need for therapists who treat CSA clients to have *specialized training* in the area of sexual abuse. Child Protective Service workers in particular need more training to provide services (see Dixon, 2005; Dugmore & Channell, 2010).

## Practice (Treatment) Issues

Treatment programs for the child victim, the adult survivor, or the perpetrator of CSA must take several issues into account. First, victims and offenders are diverse in their *preabuse histories,* the *nature of their abuse experiences,* and the *social supports and coping resources* available to them. As a result, treatment programs need to tailor the services they offer to meet the particular needs of each individual client (Zink et al., 2009). No single treatment plan will be effective for all victims, all perpetrators, or all families. Second, therapists need to be aware of several core issues:

1. *Countertransference*—a therapist's own personal reactions toward victims, perpetrators, and victims' families. A counselor may have feelings of anger or hatred toward the offender, making it difficult to respond in a therapeutic manner. As Haugaard and Reppucci (1988) put it, "The image of a 5-year-old girl performing fellatio on her father in submission to his parental authority does not engender compassion" for the father (p. 191).

2. *A victim's sexualized behavior.* Clinicians may feel uncomfortable working with victims who may behave sexually in their office.

3. *Recollecting one's own victimization.* A significant number of professionals who work with CSA victims have histories of CSA themselves (e.g., Nuttall & Jackson, 1994). Their childhood abuse might affect their views of CSA and its victims.

4. Therapists' susceptibility to *vicarious traumatization* as a result of being exposed to victims and their traumatic histories. **Vicarious traumatization** (secondary trauma) results in the therapist's modification of his or her worldview. The therapist changes his or her beliefs about how fair and safe the world is (VandenBos, 2007).

### *Therapy for Child CSA Survivors*

Many kinds of mental health professionals conduct therapy with child victims. Treatment can take a variety of forms, such as individual counseling and/or group therapy. Three major categories of variables interact to determine which type(s) of therapy would be most effective: (a) one domain includes variables related to the *CSA incident* (e.g., type of abuse); (b) a second domain centers on the *victim's reactions* to the CSA (e.g., trauma). Some research indicates that not all survivors need treatment (Saywitz, Mannarino, Berliner, & Cohen, 2000). Nonetheless, the many long-term deficits associated with CSA require early interventions for those who do (Finkelhor et al., 2009; Silverman, Reinherz, & Giaconia, 1996); and (c) the third domain includes the *variety of existing effective therapeutic modalities* (e.g., individual, group, family).

The variability of elements in the first and second domains dictates the selection of variables (treatment) in the third domain.

*Goals of therapy.* The major goal of therapy is to alleviate any significant symptoms presented by the individual child or adult. There is value in providing *CSA-specific psychotherapy.* "One size does not fit all" (Boxer & Terranova, 2008). Some symptoms of CSA victimization are so common that therapists should expect to address them in the majority of victims. On the other hand, the therapist must develop a specialized treatment strategy to meet each individual's needs. A child victim who presents with self-injurious behaviors, for example, might benefit most from a behavior modification program designed expressly to alleviate such behaviors (e.g., Osmond, Durham, Leggett, & Keating, 1998). Alternatively, for a child who displays self-denigrating beliefs, group therapy is a particularly effective modality for countering issues of secrecy and stigmatization. Participation in a discussion with one's peers about personal abuse experiences appears to be helpful (Cahill, Llewelyn, & Pearson, 1991). For a list of a therapist's core tasks see Meichenbaum (2004).

*Acceptance of self-blame.* Therapists will likely need to help victims overcome negative **attributions** and cognitive distortions such as guilt, shame, and stigmatization. Here, therapists often undertake some form of **cognitive restructuring.** They help victims change their perceptions of "being different" or "to blame" for the abuse, and they help victims to relocate the responsibility for the abuse onto the offender (Cahill et al., 1991; Osmond et al., 1998).

*Anxiety and fear.* Another task of therapy is to give victims the opportunity to defuse these feelings by talking about their abuse experiences in the safety of a supportive therapeutic relationship. With children, therapists may need to explore avenues such as reenacting the abuse through play. Therapists need to teach child victims the strategies they will need for managing the fear and anxiety that may accompany the processing of the abuse, such as relaxation techniques, problem-solving skills, and how to use positive coping statements and positive imagery (e.g., Berliner, 1991).

*Anger/depression/low self-esteem.* Therapists also need to teach the client to express anger in appropriate ways (C. F. Johnson, 2004; Steel, Sanna, Hammond, Whipple, & Cross, 2004). To combat depression and low self-esteem, therapists may use cognitive and interpersonal exercises and role-play to emphasize the clients' survival skills and personal strengths (e.g., Corder, Haizlip, & DeBoer, 1990). In addition, CSA victims may gain a sense of empowerment through sex education and training in self-protection skills that may also prevent any further victimization (Berliner, 1991).

*Treatment efficacy.* Early on, researchers began to evaluate variables that enhance or inhibit treatment efficacy and have singled out the following factors: (a) *therapist and victim gender,* (b) *victim's current social supports,* (c) *victim's educational level,* and (d) *victim's relationship to the perpetrator.*

*Meta-analytic study of treatment efficacy.* A New Zealand team completed a massive undertaking to expand understanding of the complexity of therapy outcomes. This fresh approach used a meta-analysis of 39 studies to determine which therapies significantly affect specific symptoms. The research plan called for two major types of analyses: (a) the relationship between specific symptoms and specific techniques effective for symptom reduction, and (b) numerous analyses to identify significant **moderators** (e.g., number of CSA incidents) of treatment effectiveness (Harvey & Taylor, 2010). The complexity of the research design, statistical procedures, and findings call for an abbreviation of the study in this text.

Over the 39 studies, analyses ascertained that the reported types of therapy provided were as follows: (a) 27.1%—individual, (b) 50%—group, (c) 8.3%—family, and (d) 14.6%—mixed. Most participants were girls over the age of 6. Results indicated that most of the treatments evaluated had beneficial effects. Treatments were able to improve significantly the following seven CSA-evoked symptoms among children and nonoffending caregivers:

| Large Effect Sizes | Moderate Effect Sizes | Small to Moderate Effect Sizes |
| --- | --- | --- |
| Global symptoms | Internalizing symptoms | Coping/functioning |
| PTSD/trauma | Self-esteem | (Nonoffending) Caregiver outcome |
| | Externalizing symptoms | Social skills/competence |
| | Sexualized behavior | |

The investigators computed *individual* analyses to determine if any statistically significant moderators existed for *each treatment outcome*. Furthermore, improvements remained over a follow-up period of 6 months. These findings clearly show that psychotherapy "has differing effects according to the outcome measured" (Harvey & Taylor, 2010, p. 517).

## Treatments for Offenders

Given the large number of children victimized by sex offenders and the severe and long-lasting psychological effects of CSA, responses to offenders are often vindictive.

*Categorization of CSA offenders.* More and more, practitioners throughout the field of family violence search for adequate categorizations of victims and offenders with several goals in mind. Primarily, interventionists aim to **improve treatment** by presenting a program that is tailored to the offender's needs in order to provide the most effective treatment possible. Secondarily, they hope to use the statistical analyses to **predict recidivism** more accurately, thus better protecting the public. Finally, they expect to understand the offender's childhood history to understand the determinants of CSA, and thus be able to devise better prevention programs (Mandeville-Norden & Beech, 2009).

A duo of specialists emphasized **two fundamental types of empirical categorization used to organize sex offenders:** (a) a classification founded upon an *offense*—a *deviancy* model, and (b) a classification founded on the *social needs* of the offender. The *offense grouping* includes the following scales: (a) Victim Empathy Distortion, (b) Cognitive Distortion, and (c) Emotional Identification. This arrangement yields two classifications: high and low deviancy groups. The *social needs* grouping includes the following scales: (a) *Self-Esteem,* (b) *UCLA Loneliness,* (c) *Underassertiveness,* and (d) *Personal Distress.* This arrangement yields three classifications: high, medium, and low needs.

A comparison of 437 sex offenders revealed that *both classification schemes have utility*. The deviancy model was successful in accurately placing offenders into High-Deviancy or Low-Deviancy groups. Lengthening the number of treatment sessions for the high-deviancy group lowered recidivism. Using the social needs classification identified a medium-needs subgroup *within* the low-deviancy group. The researchers anticipate clarifying whether treating this intermediate group with an intermediate number of sessions would improve treatment outcomes. That is, would using three different lengths of treatment improve outcomes compared with using two levels of treatment (Mandeville-Norden & Beech, 2009)? Further research is needed.

*Goals of treatment for CSA offenders.* The primary treatment goal in working with CSA offenders is to *reduce the likelihood of recidivism* (repeated offenses). The measurement of recidivism is challenging, however, because of the need to conduct follow-up studies for an indefinite length of time.

*Types of treatments.* There are several broad categories of treatment that are currently in use.

*Medical approaches.* Medical approaches for treating sexual offenders include *castration* (surgical removal of the testicles), *brain surgery,* and *drug therapy* (e.g., Bradford, 1990; Maletzky & Field, 2003). Most medical treatments are based on the notion that some sort of biological mechanism affects the offender's sex drive and causes the abusive behavior. Early approaches focused on castration and removal of certain brain areas (e.g., hypothalamus) in attempts to control sexual behavior. Although some outcome studies show that these techniques resulted in a reduction in sex offenses, the presence of methodological problems in the evaluations, ethical concerns, and negative side effects cast doubt on the usefulness of these techniques (Maletzky & Field, 2003).

Newer approaches focus on the use of medications to reduce sexual drive. This type of treatment, sometimes referred to as *chemical castration,* usually involves the administration of hormonal agents that reduce sexual drive. Judges often allow an offender to be out of prison on probation if he will submit to hormonal therapy. One drug that has received considerable attention in Canada and Europe is cyproterone acetate, a synthetic steroid that reduces testosterone levels. Unfortunately, no well-controlled research has yet been carried out to determine the efficacy of this treatment. Because there is no clear evidence of the drug's efficacy, and because it may have long-term negative effects on liver functioning, cyproterone acetate cannot be prescribed in the United States (C. L. Scott & Holmberg, 2003; Weinberger, Sreenivasan, Garrick, & Osran, 2005).

Another hormonal agent employed to reduce testosterone levels is medroxyprogesterone acetate, which is generally known by its brand name, Depo-Provera. This drug is available in injectable form in a long-acting formula (i.e., the substance is slowly released into the bloodstream). Several outcome studies have evaluated the efficacy of Depo-Provera treatment. Although clinical evidence suggests that it is somewhat effective in reducing sexual crimes, controlled and methodologically rigorous studies are lacking. Drug therapy may be beneficial for some offenders, but it should be used conservatively in conjunction with other treatments or as a temporary method until psychological treatments can begin (Giltay & Gooren, 2009; Maletzky & Field, 2003).

*Insight therapies.* Although some therapists conduct group sessions for sex offenders, insight-oriented approaches primarily involve individual counseling for offenders to help them understand the role sexual abuse plays in their life (Zgoba, 2004). Studies that have evaluated the outcomes of various insight-oriented approaches have been mixed probably because of methodological differences across studies. Results of a meta-analysis, however, suggest that insight therapies are as beneficial as other therapies (Harvey & Taylor, 2010).

*Family system approaches.* Some treatment programs for offenders emphasize a family system approach. The goal of these therapies is to *reunify* families in which incest has occurred. One approach includes a series of meetings both with individual family members and with different (sub)groups of family members (e.g., nonoffending parent, the child victim, and the alleged abuser) (Hewitt, 1998). Typical counseling themes include (a) a parent's failure to protect the victim from abuse, (b) feelings of guilt and depression, (c) the inappropriateness of secrecy, (d) the victim's anger toward the parents, (e) the perpetrator's responsibility for the abuse, (f) acceptable forms of touching, (g) confusion about blurred role boundaries, (h) poor communication patterns, and (i) the effect of the abuse on the child (e.g., Osmond et al., 1998).

Family therapy may also address, as a distinct issue, the needs of family members indirectly affected by the abuse, such as the nonoffending parent and siblings. In addition to the psychological problems suffered by these family members, they also face disruptions caused by the disclosure of abuse, incarceration, financial hardship, and parental separation (Hernandez, 2009).

It should be noted that whenever therapists see victims and abusers together in therapy, they must pay special attention to protecting the victims from intimidation. In fact, a number of therapists reject therapies that force child victims to interact with offenders. Although few studies to date have evaluated the outcomes of the family therapy approach to treating CSA perpetrators, and none have included long-term follow-up, the research that is available appears to demonstrate the effectiveness of the approach (see Harvey & Taylor, 2010; Hernandez, 2009).

*Cognitive-behavioral techniques.* Cognitive-behavioral approaches are the most widely implemented and actively researched forms of therapy for CSA offenders (for a review, see Marshall, Jones, Ward, Johnston, & Barbaree, 1991). *Behavioral* interventions are primarily concerned with altering the deviant sexual arousal patterns of CSA perpetrators. These approaches predominantly use some form of *aversive therapy* to replace an offender's sexual excitement over CSA with repugnance. (See www.sagepub.com/barnett3e for a description of masturbatory satiation.) *Cognitive therapies,* in contrast, are designed to teach offenders how to recognize and change their distorted beliefs, such as insisting that molesting a 7-year-old boy was simply "teaching" him about sex (Mandeville-Norden & Beech, 2009). Some programs include a component of *relapse prevention* by assisting perpetrators to identify patterns in their behavior that are precursors to abuse, that is, which environmental cues are connected with offending (Marques, Nelson, West, & Day, 1994).

## CASE HISTORY   Dantrell and the Dirty Laundry

Dantrell had been released from prison 7 months previously after serving 8 years for raping a 10-year-old girl. Dantrell was currently participating in a community behavioral program geared to help him avoid situations that might trigger his CSA. Dantrell did not know how he happened to end up assaulting his victim when he had no intention of committing the offense in the first place.

One evening when Dantrell returned home after working outside in 103-degree heat, he sat down with a beer and turned on the TV. The first thing he saw was a huge pile of dirty laundry near the front door. He suddenly felt enraged by his wife's sloppy housekeeping. After all, she didn't have to work. She had all day to do the laundry. He didn't want to get into another argument with her, however, so he said nothing and left the house for a walk. Soon, he passed by a park, and there was a young girl, about 11, lying down in the shade by herself. He decided it probably wouldn't hurt anything if he just dropped over to chat with her for a few minutes. Maybe she would like to join him for an ice cream cone.

Would Dantrell and his therapist recognize the initial cue that set off the chain of events triggering Dantrell's walk past the park? If so, what therapeutic approach might the therapist take?

Most experts agree that the therapeutic value of *cognitive-behavioral* approaches has been clearly demonstrated (Harvey & Taylor, 2010; W. L. Marshall & Pithers, 1994). Many CSA offender treatment programs use *multidimensional approaches* that combine both cognitive and behavioral techniques with other components (e.g., improving social and life skills). These approaches recommend that treatment should also focus on perpetrators' nonsexual difficulties, such as anxiety (Chaffin et al., 2005). Experts are likely to recommend multidimensional programs because "implementation of a single therapeutic intervention, even by the most highly skilled practitioners, cannot be considered sufficient treatment for most sex offenders" (Marshall & Pithers, 1994, p. 25; see also Oz, 2010).

*Recidivism studies.* Recidivism studies have several methodological limitations, including overreliance on self-report data and lack of appropriate comparison groups. One overarching variable in these studies is the need for accurate diagnosis of the seriousness of the offender's crime. There are good data to support the effectiveness of treatment for *less severe offenders*. Criticism of some studies, however, is that treatment showing perpetrator changes in prisons and clinic settings do not necessarily apply to behavior with children in the "real world" (Chaffin, 1994). Whatever the case may be, there is obviously room for improvement (Kirsch, Fanniff, & Becker, 2010). Some recidivism findings are as follows:

- 5.3% of sex offenders recidivated after 3 years (Durose, Landon, & Schmitt, 2003).
- 13% of juvenile offenders recidivated after 5 years (Reitzel & Carbonell, 2006).
- 24% of Canadian sex offenders recidivated after 15 years (Harris & Hanson, 2004).
- 27% of Canadian sex offenders recidivated after 20 years (Hanson, Morton, & Harris, 2003).

# Policy for Child Sexual Abuse

## *Legal Issues*

Society has steadily demanded more control of offenders by the criminal justice system. One impetus for these legal policies has been the social concern about rising crime rates in the 1980s. One major outcome of social outrage has been a greater focus on the development and use of **sex offender registries.** Another has been the *continual updating and expanding of laws* governing sex offenders in the community, such as their place of residence and areas within the city where they cannot go. A third has been increasing demands for offenders to wear electronic positioning devices. A series of laws have led to the passage of the federal *Adam Walsh Child Protection and Safety Act of 2006.* The foundation of these legislative efforts has been the concerns of the public, rather than the findings of scientific research. Representative of such outcomes are the effects of AMBER alerts. (See Letourneau & Levenson, 2010, for a review.) Although the alerts have successfully resulted in the recovery of many abducted children, most recoveries have involved familial situations, not the stranger abductions for which they were intended (T. Griffin, Miller, Hoppe, Rebideaux, & Hammack, 2007).

*Adam Walsh Child Protection and Safety Act of 2006.* The Adam Walsh Act includes very comprehensive legislation aimed at protecting children. Four of the most important provisions include (a) integration of state sex offender registries into a national registry available to every state, (b) imposition of mandatory sentences for crimes against children and civil provisions to detain dangerous sex offenders after incarceration, (c) increased prosecution of individuals who perpetrate Internet crimes against children, and (d) establishment of a new registry that would allow designated individuals to conduct background checks of prospective adoptive and foster parents ("President Signs Legislation," 2006).

*Case management considerations.* Initial responders to CSA accusations must respond to several very important issues: (a) whether the child must be separated from his or her home; (b) whether the offenders must leave home; (c) whether the case merits involvement of the juvenile court or the criminal court; and (d) what type of treatment plan should be inaugurated that might necessarily include visitation and eventually family reunification (Faller, 1993a).

*Interviewing child abuse victims.* Over the decades, sexually abused children and their caregivers have complained about various aspects of the criminal justice system (e.g., Westcott & Kynan, 2006). The failure to keep language simple when interviewing children comprises one type of complaint. As a case in point, the language used in 43 interviews for children ages 3 to 8 included the following problems: (a) long and complex sentences, (b) multiple questions presented consecutively without allowing the child to answer, and (c) vague references to persons and situations. A further analysis of the data ascertained that this type of interviewing evoked less detailed responses from the children (Korkman, Santtila, Drzewiecki, & Sandnabba, 2007). A different inquiry identified some language, *"what and how"* questions that were associated with *more disclosure* (Cheung, 2008; see also Bala, Lee, Lindsay, & Talwar, 2010). Two particularly worrisome problems were *insensitive forensic interviewing* and the *lack of a child-friendly setting* (e.g., office suite, converted house). To ameliorate the situation, advocates have established Child Advocacy Centers (CACs).

*Child Advocacy Centers (CACs).* The first CAC began serving victims and nonoffending caregivers in 1986, and the number of CACs grew to more than 600 by 2006. The Office of Juvenile Justice and Delinquency Prevention funded four more CACs with the idea that they would work on communicating across the nation about improvement in services to victimized children (OJJDP News @ a Glance, 2006). "Improving criminal justice outcomes for child sexual abuse cases helps protect children and is a critical goal of CACs" (p. 6). CACs are to provide the following: (a) *an appropriate setting*, (b) *multidisciplinary investigation team* and *coordinated forensic interviews*, (c) *team case reviews* (how is the victim responding?), and (d) *medical evaluation, therapeutic intervention*, and *victim advocacy*. Later on, a therapist working to improve the quality of therapy asserted that multidisciplinary teams should be involved in ongoing CSA treatment, not just first-response interventions (Oz, 2010).

A team of investigators conducted a comparison of outcomes of CAC services and ordinary community services with the following results. See Table 5.13 for an abbreviated summary of outcomes.

**TABLE 5.13** Abbreviated Comparison of CAC Outcomes Versus Community Outcomes

| Outcome | CAC Percentage | Community Percentage |
| --- | --- | --- |
| Joint police and CPS investigation | 81 | 52 |
| Team forensic interview | 28 | 5 |
| Medical exams | 48 | 21 |
| Mental health services | 72 | 21 |
| Child Protective Services | 17 | 4 |
| Caregiver satisfaction | 70 | 54 |
| Child satisfaction | 75 | 80 |

Although the CAC was superior to community services in many ways, it did not achieve its goal of satisfying the children to the extent desired (Cross et al., 2008). Subsequently, a team of researchers took a closer look at the reasons for the findings above. The subjects of the study were a subsample of nonoffending caregivers ($n = 203$) and CSA victims ($n = 65$). The youth were between 8 and 18 years of age, with an average age of 8.6 years. Participants responded to a series of quantitative and open-ended questions. Facsimiles of two items are as follows: (a) "Were you able to discuss the details and everything with the investigator?" and (b) "How well did the investigator understand kids?" Families who participated received a payment of $50 to compensate for their time.

For the most part, both caregivers and children evaluated their experiences as satisfactory. Caregivers especially appreciated the interviewers' emotional support and interviewing skill, while the youth especially liked their communication about the case. About a quarter of the children/adolescents said they *felt worse* after the interview and a third felt repeatedly questioned. Some caregivers felt their cases were not being pursued vigorously enough and that they received too little information about where the case stood or how it was progressing. Greater clarity in understanding these frustrations suggests avenues for future research (L. M. Jones et al., 2010). Other researchers have pinpointed a gap in assessing domestic violence during CAC interviewing (Thackeray, Scribano, & Rhoda, 2010).

*Police interviewing of CSA victims.* An analysis of 27 CSA victims' disclosures to police during forensic interviews yielded beneficial information. In this study, experts, such as CPS and medical personnel, had verified that CSA had occurred before the *police* questioned the children. Some of the findings were as follows:

- Children disclosed more nonsexual information than sexual information.
- Children avoided the topic as much as possible.
- Children sometimes denied the CSA despite its documentation.
- The second and third interviews yielded twice as many sexual details as the first interview.
- Children denied and avoided more during the first interview than during subsequent interviews.

Results imply that children are sometimes especially resistant to disclosures of CSA, and legal personnel need to know this information (Leander, 2010; see also Wright, Powell, & Ridge, 2006). Some evidence suggests that accuracy increased with increased numbers of interviews; this was true even with misleading questions embedded in the protocol (G. S. Goodman & Quas, 2008). The need for repetitive questioning should diminish as the number and availability of Child Advocacy Centers increase.

*Prosecution of CSA perpetrators.* Prosecutors file charges in only about 66% of child abuse cases, and only 49% of these reach a verdict. In other words, the common practice is to plea-bargain down to a lesser offense (Cross, Walsh, Simone, & Jones, 2003).

*Mandatory reporting laws.* A debate between scholars has emerged over mandatory reporting of child sexual abuse. One research duo has asserted that using child safety as the primary criterion for continuing mandatory reporting laws *demands* an approach beyond *voluntary* reporting by specified professionals (e.g., doctors, teachers). Opponents call mandatory reporting a "*policy without reason*" (G. B. Melton, 2005, p. 9). Such a lack of agreement requires much investigation and resolution (Mathews & Bross, 2008).

## Prevention of Child Sexual Abuse

Efforts aimed at eliminating child sexual abuse through prevention have focused primarily on equipping children with the skills they need to respond to, or protect themselves from, sexual abuse. Such approaches include programs that educate children about the problem of CSA as well as to teach them specific methods for coping with potentially abusive situations. Some CSA prevention programs are geared toward parents, who are often in a position to empower children to protect themselves. However, "as with child sexual abuse in any population, effective prevention policies are challenging to implement due to the interaction of many variables related to the abuse process" (Terry, 2004, p. 31).

## Education Programs for Children

During the 1980s, *school-based empowerment programs* to help children avoid and report victimization became popular across the United States. Such programs generally teach children knowledge and skills that experts believe will help them to protect themselves from a variety of dangers. Most focus on sexual abuse and emphasize two goals: *primary prevention* (keeping the abuse from occurring) and *detection* (encouraging children to report past and current abuse) (Reppucci, Land, & Haugaard, 1998). Empowerment programs have obvious appeal because they are an inexpensive way to reach many school-age children, who, for the most part, are eager to learn (Daro & McCurdy, 1994).

A 1990 survey of elementary school districts found that 85% of districts offered CSA education programs, with 65% of those programs mandated by law (Breen, Daro, & Romano, as cited in Finkelhor, Asdigian, & Dziuba-Leatherman, 1995). In their National Youth Victimization Prevention Study, a telephone survey of 2,000 children and their caretakers, Finkelhor et al. (1995) found that 67% of children reported being exposed to victimization prevention programs, with 37% reporting participation within the previous year.

*Outcomes of school-based programs.* A meta-analysis examined 27 school-based prevention programs and found that children who participated in prevention programs *scored higher on measures of prevention-related knowledge and skills* than did children in comparison groups. In addition, this study's results suggest that long-term programs (e.g., four or more sessions) and programs that involved participants physically are most effective. Unfortunately, no research has demonstrated a relationship between prevention programs and a decline in actual numbers of victimizations (M. K. Davis & Gidycz, 2000). Another review of school-based education programs has shown that they result in significant increases in *knowledge* about "good touch" and "bad touch," for example, and about *protective behaviors.* A few actually resulted in increased *harm,* such as *anxiety* among children and/or parents (Zwi et al., 2008; see also Topping & Barron, 2009).

A South Carolina program attempting to prevent rape among students transitioning to high school was able to decrease belief in rape myths, but it did not change attitudes (Fay & Medway, 2006). While primary and secondary prevention efforts would yield the greatest reductions in victimization, *treatment of known sex offenders* also holds much promise for decreasing CSA (Kirsch et al., 2010). Another proposal centered on children left alone. "Policies should focus on *supporting single mothers* and parents who both work outside of the home to reduce the likelihood that children are left vulnerable and at risk of being sexually touched" (Leung et al., 2010, p. 650).

*Critics of programs.* CSA prevention programs are not without their critics. For one thing, they may imply that children rather than adults must shoulder the responsibility of protection against CSA. Reppucci et al. (1998) have questioned whether the "relatively exclusive focus on children as their own protectors is appropriate" (p. 332). Many children may not be developmentally ready to protect themselves, and an overreliance on these types of programs may give parents and society a *false sense of security*. At the same time, it seems reasonable to conclude the following:

> Children and adolescents have a right to be enlightened about sexuality and sexual abuse and to know about their right to live free from such abuse. The more pertinent question is not whether to educate children about sexual abuse but rather how to do so in an effective, sensitive manner. (Wurtele & Miller-Perrin, 1992, p. 89; see also Bennett, Hart, & Svevo-Cianci, 2010)

*Parental role in child education.* Prevention efforts should include programs that attempt to target adults who can help children avoid sexually abusive experiences. Endeavors that focus on parents primarily attempt to educate them about CSA. Various program formats designed for parents include audiovisual materials, books, and educational workshops (Wurtele & Miller-Perrin, 1992). Studies indicate that parents not only want to be involved in preventing CSA but also are somewhat effective in teaching their children about sexual abuse and appropriate protective skills (Wurtele, Kast, & Melzer, 1994). Parents are particularly effective if they are given specific instruction in how to talk to their children about sexual abuse (E. S. Burgess & Wurtele, 1998).

A more recent investigation queried 289 child caretakers about their efforts to educate their children ($M = 8.5$ years old). Responses to questionnaires from this convenience sample ($N = 218$; 94.8% female) disclosed the following *percentages of parental discussions about CSA topics and abusers* (Deblinger, Thakkar-Kolar, Berry, & Schroeder, 2010):

| Topic | Potential Abusers |
|---|---|
| Person might try to touch your genitals—81% | Strangers—97% |
| Person might try to touch your genitals and tell you to keep it secret—61% | Other children or adolescents—62% |
| | Adults the child knows—67% |
| | Relatives—45% |

Parents can play other roles in CSA prevention. For example, parents might interrupt abuse by learning to identify behaviors in children that are associated with CSA. Parents also play an important role when a child victim discloses abuse. By responding appropriately they can reduce the child's feelings of self-blame, isolation, and anger (Wurtele & Miller-Perrin, 1992). These prevention approaches can also effectively be extended to other adults in a child's environment, such as teachers. Teachers are in a unique position to detect possible abuse by learning to identify behaviors indicative of abuse (Renk, Liljequist, Steinberg, Bosco, & Phares, 2002). Future research should assess the effectiveness of these programs as well as programs that attempt to help other adults identify CSA and respond appropriately.

## Practice, Policy, and Prevention

In recognition of the significance of the problems associated with CSA, many professionals are involved in responding to the needs of victims and the treatment of perpetrators. Researchers and mental health practitioners have developed an array of treatment interventions in an effort to address the multiple causes and far-reaching consequences of CSA.

Regardless of any specific counseling approach, the therapeutic goals for child victims and adult survivors of CSA generally include addressing significant symptoms as well as common emotions associated with abuse, such as guilt, shame, anger, depression, and anxiety. Psychotherapists themselves must manage their own reactions of anger and sadness when listening to victims talk about their sexual abuse experiences. Therapists can suffer vicarious traumatization. They also need to be on guard against any recollections of their own childhood sexual abuse and a victim's inappropriate sexualized behavior.

Specialists often recommend group therapy for CSA victims as a beneficial intervention to reduce self-denigrating beliefs, secrecy, and stigmatization. Therapists also address CSA-induced anxiety and methods for coping with anger. Meta-analytic reviews have shown that treatment for victims has beneficial effects. Progress in ameliorating PTSD is particularly apparent. Therapists also treat other members in a CSA family who are suffering from the disclosure of CSA, especially nonoffending parents.

In order to provide more effective treatment for sex offenders, some scholars have attempted to classify sex offenders into subtypes. One classification rests on the CSA offense, while the other takes social needs into account. Statistical analyses demonstrated that both models have predictive utility. Treatment programs for offenders include a variety of approaches but most typically incorporate cognitive and behavioral components to reduce deviant sexual arousal and cognitive distortions associated with abuse. Drug treatments, in conjunction with cognitive-behavioral therapy, are common in some clinical settings. Whereas cognitive-behavioral programs focus on altering behavior without regard to its origin, insight therapies attempt to alter behavior by helping the offender understand the causes of his deviancy. All these approaches demonstrate some promise, but further studies are needed to address the limitations of extant research methodologies and potential alternative treatments (e.g., improving social and life skills) to accompany therapeutic interventions. The specific treatment needs of female offenders have yet to be identified.

Policy considerations most commonly center reforms on legislation expected to manage sex offenders' criminal tendencies. Public outrage against sex offenders, rather than scientific findings, has spawned the formation of most sex offender laws. According to some authorities, however, the overall consequences of current legislation are more likely to be deleterious instead of efficacious. The potential benefits of sex offender registries, for instance, have been especially disappointing.

*(Continued)*

(Continued)

How to question children successfully about their CSA experiences has been another active area of policy deliberation. The most active area under scrutiny is the formation of Child Advocacy Centers (CACs), to function as first responders to CSA reports. To date, the CACs have shown an ability to help victims superior to that of typical community centers. Along the same lines, researchers have examined the efficacy of police interviews to obtain details about the CSA incident.

The prevention of child sexual abuse begins with social awareness, plus the recognition that expertise, energy, and money are needed to alleviate the conditions that produce CSA. Many experts maintain, however, that society has not yet sufficiently demonstrated a commitment to prevention. In most communities, monetary resources are tied up in responding to, rather than preventing, CSA. Increasing commitment to the prevention of CSA, however, is evidenced in the many prevention programs appearing across the United States.

Several of the strategies employed in these programs seem especially promising. School-based CSA education for children is appealing because it has the potential to reach large numbers of young people, and it is at least moderately effective. Parental competency programs target at-risk parents (poor, young, single) and at-risk children with the goal of providing training and social support before any abuse can occur. Although additional evaluations are needed, available research indicates that these programs have positive potential.

## DISCUSSION QUESTIONS

1. How common is CSA? Are rates of CSA currently increasing or decreasing?

2. Discuss the characteristics of sexually abused children and describe a typical victim.

3. Discuss the characteristics of adults who sexually abuse children and describe a typical perpetrator.

4. Describe female sex abusers and how they compare with male abusers.

5. What tactics do CSA perpetrators use to involve and maintain children's participation in sexual activities?

6. What are the potential long-term effects of CSA on children? List the major categories of effects and give at least one example of a symptom in each category.

7. Which etiological model or models best explain why CSA occurs?

8. What are the common goals of therapy for child survivors of CSA? How effective are these therapies?

9. Which treatment interventions appear to be most promising for CSA offenders? What do recidivism rates suggest?

10. Evaluate legal policies aimed at controlling CSA in the United States. Discuss the major obstacle(s) to establishing effective laws. What is your opinion about how to manage child molesters?

11. Which CSA prevention approaches are useful? What can parents do to prevent CSA?

For chapter-specific resources including audio and video links, SAGE research articles, additional case studies, and more, please visit www.sagepub.com/barnett3e.

# CHAPTER

## 6

# Abused and Abusive Adolescents

Society has focused considerable attention on adolescents' problems, such as juvenile delinquency, alcohol/drug use, school truancy, gang participation, and running away from home. Historically, society viewed most of them as *criminal*. Accordingly, recalcitrant teenagers needed physical discipline and incarceration. In time, various social scientist researchers reported on how *parental behavior,* such as alcoholism, negatively impacted juvenile behavior. Eventually, family violence researchers/practitioners began to see specific connections between parental use of corporal punishment and juvenile violence.

The inclusion in this volume of a separate chapter on adolescent violence highlights several impressions. First, because law classifies adolescents as children, should legal precepts constrain researchers' constructs? Probably not, because adolescents' development of strength, cognition, and sexual interest differentiate them from infants, toddlers, and younger children. Second, should adolescents be classified with adults? Probably not, because adolescence is a time of transition; the adolescent brain has not reached maturity, and the circumstances of adolescents vary from those of adults. *Adolescents are neither identical to adults nor the same as children.* See Table 6.1 for a summary of differences between adolescents and adults and children.

**TABLE 6.1**   Differences Between Adolescents and Adults *and* Adolescents and Children

| *Adolescents Are Not Adults* | *Adolescents Are Not Children* |
|---|---|
| Less dating experience | Adolescents can fight back and run away from abuse |
| Seldom live with intimate partner | Running away puts them in harm's way |
| Economically independent from partner | Society believes adolescents deserve punishment |
| Gender imbalances are less prominent | Society thinks punishment may not hurt adolescents |
| Coping skills are less well developed | Adolescents are potential victimizers, not just victims |
| See Mulford & Giordano (2008) | See Kimball & Golding (2004) and Gil (1996) |

This chapter highlights brief overviews of research that illuminates connections between *adolescent family violence* and *adolescent psychological* and *behavioral problems*. The first section covers types of abuse that occur in families and among intimates: (a) *adolescent abuse by parents*, (b) *parent abuse by adolescents*, (c) *sibling abuse*, and (d) *same-sex violence*. A second section describes some of the internalizing effects of abusiveness on adolescents' behavior: (e) *trauma*, (f) *psychopathology and substance abuse*, (g) *lifetime decreased well-being*, (h) *homelessness*, and (i) *teenage pregnancy and parenting*. A third section examines some externalizing effects of abusiveness: (j) *bullying/cyberbullying*, the contribution of *media* to teen violence, (k) *dating violence*, and (l) *juvenile delinquency*. Next there is (m) some coverage of the *criminal justice system response* to abused/abusive teens, and finally a discussion of (n) *revictimization*.

## PARENTAL ABUSE OF ADOLESCENTS

**CASE HISTORY**   Tough Love or Psychological Maltreatment?

The Machnicks[1] appeared to be a typical all-American family. Grady Machnick was a sergeant with the Los Angeles County Sheriff's Department, and Deborah Machnick was an elementary school principal. The couple was raising three children, including a 14-year-old boy, Grady Machnick's biological son and Deborah's stepson. They lived in an attractive Southern California neighborhood.

In 2001, Orange County prosecutors charged the Machnicks with child abuse, even though Grady stated that "any actions that were taken were appropriate to the circumstances of disciplining a teenager." The circumstances were so unusual, nonetheless, that a deputy district attorney stated, "It's very, very bizarre. I have not seen this type of conduct in my entire career." The allegations included the following:

- Punishment for not finishing homework was to spend nights outside, sleeping on a dog mat.
- The teen was not allowed to use the home's bathroom but had to use a restroom at a nearby park.
- The parents poured water on the boy to wake him from sleep.
- The parents sent the teen to school with dog feces in his backpack as punishment for not cleaning up after the family dog.
- The parents forced the teen to strip and be photographed naked as a form of punishment.
- If the parents left at night, the boy had to stay outside because he was untrustworthy.
- The teen had to "earn" items like clean clothing through good behavior.
- The parents withheld the teen's lunch money.

At trial, Grady and Deborah Machnick testified that they employed these parenting practices because they were attempting to discipline their defiant son. The teen reportedly earned poor grades in school, refused to help with chores at home, and was often caught lying and stealing (e.g., shoplifting, taking money from his parents). The Machnicks insisted that their discipline was designed to keep the boy from engaging in questionable behavior.

In his closing argument, one of the Machnicks' attorneys described the couple's parenting behavior as follows: "It's not a great parenting technique. If you're grading, A, B, C, D, or F, maybe it's an F. But it's not a crime."

In December 2002, the Machnicks were *acquitted on felony charges* of conspiring to abuse their teenage son. The jurors agreed that the parents' discipline was inappropriate and inconsistent with their own parenting practices, but they were reluctant to condemn the Machnicks' behavior as criminal. A judge has ruled in favor of the Machnicks being retried on the lesser charge of misdemeanor child abuse, but the case has not gone forward (Leonard, 2001).

NOTE: 1. Sources for the details and quotes in this case history are as follows: "Judge OKs Retrial," 2003; Leonard, 2001; Pfeifer, 2002; Pfeifer & Anton, 2002. Grady and Deborah Machnick are the subjects' real names.

What is your opinion of the parenting of the Machnicks? Should the laws be changed to cover this type of parenting? If not, what should society do about such harsh disciplining?

## Defining Adolescent Maltreatment

Child maltreatment is a "broad spectrum of behaviors that are harmful to children, including physical, psychological, and sexual abuse, as well as neglect" (C. A. Smith, Thornberry, & Ireland, 2004, p. 7). Much of what society labels as physical abuse today, people viewed as merely stern discipline or punishment 25 years ago. A common example of past standards would be whipping a child with a lightweight stick for his failure to do his chores.

Historically, official agencies have paid scant attention to parental abuse of adolescents. Various experts have suggested that this lack of attention may have reflected societal perceptions that adolescents' difficult behavior makes them complicit in the abuse. Alternatively, abusive parental behavior may appear to be legitimate attempts to maintain parental control. In addition, compared with younger children, adolescents may appear to be less physically vulnerable or in danger of bodily harm (see Gelles & Cornell, 1990; J. L. Powers & Eckenrode, 1988).

## Types of Maltreatment

*Maltreatment* is an action or failure to act by a caregiver that results in physical abuse, neglect, medical neglect, sexual abuse, emotional abuse, or an act or failure to act which presents an imminent risk of serious harm to a child or adolescent. The U.S. Department of Health & Human Services (DHHS) has provided all but the last definition of child maltreatment (0 through 18 years) by a caregiver, abbreviated below:

> *Medical neglect:* Failure to provide for appropriate health care of a child though the caregiver is financially able to do so, or has access to other financial resources

*Neglect/deprivation of necessities:* Failure to provide needed age-appropriate care though the caregiver is able to do so, or has access to other financial resources

*Physical abuse:* Physical acts that caused or can cause physical injury to a child

*Psychological/emotional abuse:* Nonphysical/nonsexual acts that caused or could cause behavioral, cognitive, affective, or other mental injury that frequently occurs as verbal abuse or excessive demands on the child's performance

*Sexual abuse:* The involvement of the child in sexual activity to provide sexual gratification or financial benefit to the perpetrator. Includes sexual contacts, molestation, statutory rape, prostitution, pornography, exposure, incest, or other sexually exploitive activities.

*Polyvictimization:* Two or more *victimization types* (e.g., psychological and sexual) within a stated time frame (Finkelhor, Ormrod, & Turner, 2007a)

## Timing of Maltreatment

It can be difficult to determine the precise effects of maltreatment on adolescents. One measurement problem entails the identity of the informant: parents, teachers, or the child/adolescent himself (Sternberg, Lamb, Guterman, & Abbott, 2006). Another quandary revolves around differences in the timing of the abuse. In some cases the abuse begins in childhood and continues through adolescence. In other cases the abuse begins during adolescence. The problem of delineating potentially different outcomes of the timing and duration of abuse became a focus of a trio of researchers (Thornberry, Ireland, & Smith, 2001). They divided data from 736 abused youth into four age-groups: (a) 0 to 5 *only*—early childhood, (b) 6 to 11 *only*—late childhood, (c) 12 to 17 adolescence *only,* and (d) 0 to 17 (persistent abuse). The researchers obtained self-reported and official delinquency measures at two times: (a) early adolescence, 14 to 16, and (b) late adolescence, 16 to 18. A brief summary of their findings is as follows:

- Maltreatment in *only late* childhood doubled the odds of delinquency in *early* adolescence.
- Maltreatment *only during adolescence* increased the odds of delinquency in *early* adolescence by more than 4 times.
- Maltreatment only *during adolescence* increased the odds of delinquency in *late* adolescence by nearly 3 times.
- Maltreatment during *childhood* and *adolescence* (persistent abuse) increased the odds of delinquency during *late* adolescence. Maltreatment during *childhood* and *adolescence* (persistent abuse) did *not* increase the odds of delinquency during *early* adolescence.

## Prevalence of Parent-to-Adolescent Physical/Psychological Abuse

The largest database of estimates of child abuse comes from the U.S. Department of Health & Human Services (DHHS), which collects yearly reports from Child Protective Services (CPS). See Tables 6.2 and 6.3 for a summary of findings about age and types of adolescent maltreatment.

> *U.S. Department of Health & Human Services (DHHS) [CPS records]. Child maltreatment. (2009b)* 794,000 children were *victims* of abuse. See Table 6.2 for percentages of age, amount, and type of abuse.

TABLE 6.2
Percentage of Adolescent Maltreatment by Age and Type of Maltreatment

| Adolescent Maltreatment | | Type of Abuse | Ages 12–15 | Ages 16–17 |
|---|---|---|---|---|
| Ages 12–15 | Ages 16–17 | Medical neglect | 16.4% | 5.0% |
| 18.5% | 6.1% | Neglect | 15.2% | 5.0% |
| 8.7 per 1,000 | 5.4 per 1,000 | Physical abuse | 22.6% | 8.2% |
| | | Psychological abuse | 18.6% | 5.2% |

TABLE 6.3   Age and Sex of Adolescent Maltreatment Victims, 2008

| Age | Boys | | | Girls | | | Total Victims | | | |
|---|---|---|---|---|---|---|---|---|---|---|
| | Population | Number | Rate/ 1,000 | Population | Number | Rate/ 1,000 | Population | Number | Rate/ 1,000 | Percentage |
| 12–15 | 8,259,206 | 55,051 | 6.7 | 7,866,086 | 79,950 | 10.2 | 16,125,292 | 135,306* | 8.4 | 18.1% |
| 16–17 | 4,327,364 | 17,576 | 4.1 | 4,124,531 | 29,107 | 7.1 | 8,451,895 | 46,795** | 5.5 | 6.3% |

SOURCE: National Incidence Studies (NIS-4; Sedlak et al., 2010). Data from multiple sources—goes beyond DHHS to capture data from individuals such as school counselors and psychologists in private practice.

NOTE: Adapted from Sedlak et al. (2008), Table 3–8; *305 Unknown victims; **112 Unknown victims.

## Consequences of Adolescent Maltreatment

The list of problematic behaviors exhibited by adolescents who were abused when they were younger is extensive. Numerous independent and federal government researchers have studied the consequences of child maltreatment. A few researchers have separated the consequences by age-groups, thus making it possible to examine the results for youth 12 to 17 distinct from younger children. See Table 6.4 for a summary of the results.

TABLE 6.4   Consequences of Maltreatment of Adolescents by Caregivers

| Externalizing Behaviors | | Internalizing Behavior Problems |
|---|---|---|
| Violent dating behavior | Delinquency | Suicidal thoughts |
| Violence toward parents | Violent crime | Low self-esteem |
| Violence toward siblings | Risky sex behavior | Poor anger management |
| Antisocial behavior | Sexually transmitted diseases | High levels of daily stress |

*(Continued)*

TABLE 6.4 (Continued)

| Externalizing Behaviors | | Internalizing Behavior Problems |
|---|---|---|
| Arrest or incarceration | Social-skills deficit | Vulnerable to sexual coercion |
| Self-reported crime | Low academic achievement | Attention problems |
| Suicide | Body cutting | Obesity |
| Substance abuse | | |

SOURCES: Daversa & Knight, 2007; De Luca, 2010; R. C. Herrenkohl, Egolf, & Herrenkohl, 1997; Kaplan, Pelcovitz, Salzinger, Mandel, & Weiner, 1997; Lansford, Dodge, Petit, & Bates, 2010; Parker & Herrera, 1996; Pelcovitz, Kaplan, Goldenberg, & Mandel, 1994; Thornberry, Henry, Ireland, & Smith, 2010; Zingraff, Leiter, Myers, & Johnsen, 1993.

## Psychiatric Disorders Among Adolescent Victims of Child Maltreatment

In the past decade, several studies have examined rates of *psychiatric disorders* in samples of physically abused adolescents. They have found that adolescent child physical abuse (CPA) victims are at increased risk for a number of the same psychiatric disorders found in younger victims: depression, disruptive behavior disorders (e.g., conduct disorder, attention-deficit/hyperactivity disorder, oppositional defiant disorder), and drug abuse (e.g., Kaplan et al., 1997).

*Trauma.* As authorities across many disciplines and professions have increasingly come to realize the devastating effects of trauma, the concept of **polyvictimization** has surfaced as a more important dimension of family violence. In a nationally representative sample of 1,000 adolescents aged 10 to 17 who had experienced polyvictimization (different kinds of victimization), predictors of trauma symptomatology included polyvictimization and either *sexual assault* by a known perpetrator or emotional *bullying* (Finkelhor, Ormrod, Turner, & Hamby, 2005).

*Psychopathology.* A different longitudinal study of psychopathology assessed 250 males at age 13 and again at age 24. The researchers found that adolescents rated high in psychopathology at 13 were significantly likely to be rated high at age 24. For 13-year-olds scoring low on psychopathology, several variables acted as **mediators** to increase it. The presence of low socioeconomic status, delinquent friends, and heightened physical punishment were associated with higher psychopathology scores at age 24. This study accentuates the importance of environmental factors in the development of psychopathology (Lynam, Loeber, & Stouthamer-Loeber, 2008).

*Genetics.* Criminal behavior and psychopathology may have their roots in genetic differences. Confirming this assertion, one study of more than 1,000 school-age boys detected a taxon (a distinct genetic unit) for serious antisocial behavior in children (Skilling, Quinsey, & Craig, 2001). Other analyses established that disinhibition and negative affectivity served as **mediators** for the effects of parental psychopathology (e.g., borderline personality disorder [BPD] features). Childhood abuse measures were linked with the two personality traits and directly to BPD features among 18-year-olds. Further, childhood trauma constitutes one etiological correlate of borderline personality disorder, and disinhibition and negative affectivity appear to be core personality traits underpinning BPD (Trull, 2001). Although replication studies are needed, such findings provide an important account of the relationship between variability in childhood experiences of abuse and adult individual differences in battering (Dutton, 1998). (See www.sagepub.com/barnett3e for a longitudinal study of antisocial personality disorder.)

*National Survey of Child and Adolescent Well-Being (NSCAW).* NSCAW (n.d.) has provided an accounting of circumstances and outcomes for *adolescents transitioning to young adulthood.* The longitudinal data came from Wave 5 (5th set of measures, 2006–2007). The 620 youth drawn from the sample had been in contact with the Child Welfare System 6 to 7 years previously when child protective services investigated their family for child abuse. The participants were 12 to 15 years of age at the time, and almost 60% were female. A wealth of important findings emerged reflecting strong associations between the participants' *childhood experiences* and their functioning during *young adulthood,* ages 18 to 21:

- 83% reported being in good health, but 56.6% were overweight or obese.
- One short mental health questionnaire suggested the group was slightly below average.
  - They were significantly more depressed; some had trauma symptoms and dissociative experiences.
  - They had scores in the clinical range for internalizing and externalizing behavior problems.
- Academic achievement was extremely low with significantly low scores on separate comprehension, calculations, and applied problem scores.
- 75% were sexually active, but less than 50% used a condom during their last sexual encounter.
- 26.7% were married/living with a boy/girlfriend, 37.4% had had children, and 29% were raising a child.
- 61.8% of the young mothers were living in poverty.
- 55% used corporal punishment; about 50% were psychologically abusive.
- 16.7% had been arrested, and more than 25% of the women experienced domestic violence.
- 58.1% were employed full- or part-time.
- 59% had incomes below the poverty level; females were significantly poorer than males.
- 88.6% had contact with their biological mother.

*Gender difference in effects.* One interesting gender difference that is emerging is that girls' behavior is more adversely affected by abuse than boys'. Even though boys' *base rate* of violence is customarily higher than girls, maltreatment of girls disturbs their behavior comparatively more than boys along some dimensions (Magdol, Moffitt, Caspi, & Silva, 1998). In one study, for example, child maltreatment of girls was a risk factor for later intimate partner violence perpetration (T. I. Herrenkohl et al., 2004). Obviously, more research is needed to illuminate the pathways that improve adolescents' resilience to abuse (see C. A. Smith et al., 2004).

## BOX 6.1 Adolescent Homelessness

Almost without exception, researchers have documented a link between childhood abuse and adolescent running away and homelessness. Government funding of three studies conducted between 1992 and 1999 and published in the 2000s produced some of the most comprehensive and pertinent information on the topic (see Cauce, Tyler, & Whitbeck, 2004; U.S. Department of Health & Human Services, n.d.).

*(Continued)*

(Continued)

The three funded studies include the Street Youth at Risk for AIDS (SYRA, *N* = 775), the Midwest Homeless and Runaway Adolescent Project (MHRAP, *N* = 595), and the Seattle Homeless Adolescent and Research and Evaluation Project (SHARE, *N* = 295). Some of the differences in methodology are as follows: (a) *Definitions* [1 night away to 3 months]; (b) *Ages* [12–17 years old, but SHARE included 18–21 years old]; and (c) *Gender balance* [about 65% male for SYRA, about 40% male for MHRAP, and 53% male for SHARE]. The *definitions of sexual abuse* varied substantially as well (from any unwanted sexual behavior to explicit sexual behaviors, and the abuser being 5 years older). Homeless girls and boys frequently turn to *prostitution* as a way of earning a livelihood. Although the police tend to think of these juveniles as victims, they arrest them anyway as a paternalistic response to help protect them (Halter, 2010).

A few findings are as follows:

- Age at first leaving home ranged from 12.4 to 13.9 years.
- 40% of SHARE and 34% of MHRAP participants had been beaten up at home.
- Sexual abuse before leaving home ranged from 23% to 34.2%.
- Age at first sexual abuse was 7.1 years (SHARE).
- The largest percentage of sexual abusers was adult acquaintances (32%); stepfathers were fourth at 14.4%, and biological fathers were fifth at 9.9%.
- 59.9% of participants in the SYRA study had attempted suicide.
- 38.7% of abused and 29.7% of nonabused males in the SYRA study had gotten someone pregnant.
- 52.7% of abused and 32.7% of nonabused girls had gotten pregnant.

Less than a handful of studies have gathered data on treatment effectiveness for adolescent *homelessness per se,* rather than for substance abuse (see Nebbitt, House, Thompson, & Pollio, 2007). A 2007 treatment program added a *12-session individual therapy* component along with the customary drop-in services for food, shelter, and a talk with a case manager. The *specialized program* showed significant reductions in alcohol/drug abuse and depression, and increased social stability (Slesnick, Prestopnik, Meyers, & Glassman, 2004). Obviously, much more needs to be done to protect youth from abusive parents and to assist runaway/homeless youth more effectively.

## Risk Factors for Parent-to-Adolescent Maltreatment

Several studies have identified adolescent risk factors for delinquency (e.g., Mulford & Redding, 2008). Analysis of 1,411 data sets from the Chicago Longitudinal Study supplied information on risk factors for adolescent maltreatment (Mersky, Berger, Reynolds, & Gromoske, 2009; see also Daversa & Knight, 2007). See Table 6.5 for risk factor findings for three studies.

**TABLE 6.5** Studies of Risk Factors for Parent-to-Adolescent Maltreatment

| DeMatteo & Marczyk (2005) | Mersky et al. (2009) and Daversa & Knight (2007) | U.S. Public Health Service (2001): Risk Factors for Adolescent Onset |
|---|---|---|
| Low parental warmth | Receiving public assistance | Low parental involvement |
| Parent-child conflict | Young maternal age at child's birth | Poor parent/child relationship |
| Poor supervision | Exposure to antisocial male role models | Poor monitoring, supervision, and harsh or lax discipline |
| Harsh discipline and ineffective punishment | Observation of interparental violence | Low socioeconomic status/poverty and a broken home |
| Parental antisocial behavior | | Antisocial and abusive parents |

## Explaining Parent-to-Adolescent Maltreatment

Some of conflicts giving rise to adolescent maltreatment are issues surrounding adolescent development (e.g., sexual interest) (C. A. Smith et al., 2004). As detailed in previous chapters, experts have drawn from several *standard theories* to explain the effects of caregiver maltreatment of children and adolescents:

| Family's social/economic status | Caregivers' psychopathology | Social learning theory |
|---|---|---|
| Caregiver's personality characteristics | Community and school violence | Cultural factors |
| Child's personality characteristics | Family's characteristics | |

See www.sagepub.com/barnett3e for a list of formal theories explaining parent maltreatment effects.

## SEXUAL ABUSE OF ADOLESCENTS

Adolescent sexual abuse (ASA) is a multifaceted problem that is extraordinarily complex in its characteristics, dynamics, causes, and consequences. The section that follows primarily examines ASA within the first two contexts: (a) caregiver/adolescent incest and (b) as an element of adolescent maltreatment. Measurement of these behaviors, as throughout the field of family violence, is unsettled. Different definitions, samples, assessments, and statistical analyses have undermined clarity. In this section, most measurement divisions are along *gender lines*. Further delineations may partition the sample for statistical analysis along variables of age, race, culture, or sexual orientation. These various foci of research have led to overlapping information.

## Definition of Caregiver-to-Adolescent Sexual Abuse

A concern of sexual abuse experts working in the field is that child/adolescent sexual abuse has lacked unequivocal definition to such an extent that it "inhibits research, treatment, and advocacy efforts" (Haugaard, 2000, p. 1036). The Office of Violence Against Women (OVW) (2009, p. 1) offers a number of helpful definitions:

- *Sexual abuse* is a term commonly used when discussing sexual assault, and refers to a series of repeated acts.
- *Sexual violence* includes the following behaviors:
  - Unwanted oral, anal, and vaginal penetration by penis, hand, finger, or other foreign object that is attempted or completed; commonly known as rape
  - Unwanted contact between the mouth and penis, vulva, or anus
  - Unwanted sexual touching, both above and underneath clothing
  - Forcing an individual to masturbate or masturbate another party
  - Physical sexual acts forced through threats of violence or coercion
- *Sexual victimization* also includes noncontact acts which may include exhibitionism, voyeurism, and sexual photography.
- *Sexual harassment* includes unwelcome sexual advances, requests for sexual favors, inappropriate sexual comments, and any hostile environment (workplace, school, etc.) where sexual joking, viewing of pornography, and/or degrading images are present.

## Context and Relationship to Offender of Sexually Victimized Adolescents

A team of researchers compared adolescent and adult sexual victimization experiences. Adolescent sexual victimization seems to occur for adolescent girls within four contexts. See the following two-part table for a summary of adolescent girl's contexts of assaults and their relationship to their offenders from Livingston, Hequembourg, Testa, and VanZile-Tamsen (2007).

| Context/Setting of Sexual Assaults of Adolescent Girls (n = 106) | Adolescent Girls' (n = 112) Relationship to the Offender |
|---|---|
| 42—within an intimate relationship | 15—stranger/just met |
| 38—at parties/social gathering | 45—friend/acquaintance |
| 18—abused by an authority figure | 41—partner/ex-partner |
| 8—while alone with a friend | 11—other (relative, authority figure) |

The researchers presented details about the vulnerability factors within the contexts associated with the sexual assault gleaned from 106 interviews with adolescents.

- Lack of guardianship ($n = 77$) … E.g., Attending a party when parents were away.
- Inexperienced ($n = 59$) … E.g., He fondled me; I was confused; I didn't know his intentions.
- Offender-substance ($n = 51$) … E.g., He got out of control; I think it was the alcohol.
- Victim-substance ($n = 36$) … E.g., I was so drunk I didn't know what I was doing.

- Social concerns ($n = 22$) ... E.g., He was a "catch," so I said "yes," then "no." He got angry.
- Powerlessness ($n = 13$) ... E.g., He drove me to his house to babysit, but no baby was there.

The adolescent women differed significantly from the adult *women* along two dimensions.

1. Adolescents were significantly *more* likely than adults to have been assaulted (a) after a party/ social gathering, and (b) at a party/social gathering.

2. Adolescents were significantly *less* likely than adults (a) to have had consensual sex previously, before being assaulted; (b) to have been assaulted after going to a bar; and (c) tended to have been assaulted by a current partner (Livingston et al., 2007).

## Prevalence of Sexual Abuse of Adolescents

Some of the statistical summaries below present a sampling of current findings on the sexual abuse of adolescents. (See www.sagepub.com/barnett3e for a table of information about sexual experiences with persons other than the primary sibling [B. E. Carlson, Maciol, & Schneider, 2006]).

### BOX 6.2 Pregnant Adolescents

Findings from surveys have definitively established that teen mothers usually come from homes typified by interparental violence, physical and/or sexual violence toward the children, poverty, low educational attainment of the parents, and low school achievement by the children. The lives of the young mothers-to-be leaving such backgrounds are quite difficult as well. One qualitative study of only eight pregnant teens ascertained that varying numbers of the young women suffered from an array of problems, such as lack of stable housing, lack of economic support, alcohol/drug problems, difficult family relationships, mental health problems, and relationship abuse (Saewye, 2003; see also Brace, Hall, & Hunt, 2008).

The United States has more teenage pregnancies than any other country in the industrialized world. Kids Count (2008) reports a national rate of 41.9/1,000. The Centers for Disease Control and Prevention (CDC; 2009b) reported 435,436 births to mothers aged 15 to 19 in 2006. More than half of these pregnancies were unintended. Teen pregnancies are problematic for a number of reasons. Compared with pregnancies for mothers 20 to 21 years of age, the following events are more likely for teen mothers: (a) Infants are born prematurely, (b) Infant birth weights are lower, and (c) Infant mortality rates are higher. For the younger mothers, the following events are more likely to occur than for the older mothers: (a) dropping out of school, and (b) remaining a single parent. Sadly, these teens frequently give birth a second time before age 19. The race/ethnic status of pregnant teens differs significantly. The groups in descending order of teen pregnancies are as follows: Hispanics, Blacks, Whites, American Indians/Native Alaskans, and Asian/Pacific Islanders.

*(Continued)*

(Continued)

*Children of the younger mothers* compared with children of the older mothers also have problems contributing to a *transgenerational cycle of early pregnancies:* (a) lower cognitive attainment, (b) behavior problems, (c) chronic medical conditions, (d) more reliance on public health care, and (e) more likely to be incarcerated. Younger mothers do not have the maturity and knowledge to care for an infant and they are also more abusive to their own children. Finally, the costs of unintended teen pregnancies before age 18 are enormous—$9.1 billion annually (CDC, 2009b; Brace et al., 2008).

In an effort to reduce costs and improve the quality of life for these young women and their families, a county in Georgia developed an intervention/prevention program titled Circle of Care. The program is a collaborative effort of more than five social agencies and schools to provide multilevel services. At a minimum, services include case management, family assessment, parenting classes, and home visits. Case management activities consist of providing transportation to obtain services, child care, contraception information, abstinence training, and help obtaining medical care. The program successfully met its goals to reduce costs and reduce the list of problems outlined above, such as school drop-out and abusive parenting (Brace et al., 2008).

---

- *U.S. Department of Health & Human Services (DHHS) [CPS records]. Child maltreatment (2009)*

  794,000 children were victims of abuse.
  Sexual Abuse:  Ages 12–15—35.2%
  Ages 16–17—10.6%

- *National Violence Against Women Survey (NVAWS; Tjaden & Thoennes, 2000b). (Self-reported on modified CTS; data from 16, 000 adults.)*
  Rape:     Female Victims—32.4%
  Male Victims— 23.0%

For a discussion of both *father-to-daughter incest* and *sibling incest,* see the section below under Sibling Abuse. Also see the previous chapter for a more thorough coverage of parent-to-child sexual abuse.

## Practice, Policy, and Prevention of Adolescent Maltreatment

Previous chapters have already discussed many of the programs for parents who abuse their children; however, in the words of Smith et al. (2004, p. 10), "Our results indicate the need for much greater attention to adolescent victims of maltreatment." While some practitioners are striving to treat *specific problems*, such as sexual abuse or bullying, others say "that it is problematic to study these in isolation or to focus on 'pure victimization groups' which may not truly exist" (Koverola, Murtaugh, Connors, Reeves, & Papas, 2007, p. 38). Researchers also call attention to the observation that most types of parent-to-adolescent abuse occur simultaneously. Adapting programs for different age-groups is certainly warranted as are *some* adaptations for types of abuse.

## Program Effectiveness

As the call for effective psychotherapy intensifies, researchers have focused more expressly on comparing program effectiveness. A contemporary evaluation of *seven* types of *pro bono* therapy revealed that individual and group cognitive behavioral therapy was able to decrease trauma symptoms among abused children/adolescents (Wethington et al., 2008). This result is impressive considering the span of treatments tested (e.g., psychodynamic, pharmacologic).

*Treatment retention.* On a related theme, researchers examined differences in attrition/retention of 118 children/adolescents aged 4 to 17 years who scored in the low-average range of intelligence. Overall, 64% of the sample completed therapy, 20% did *not* engage in treatment (i.e., attended no treatment session after completing entry questionnaires), and 16% terminated prematurely. Some of the significant findings follow (Koverola et al., 2007):

- Caregivers initially reporting high levels of *parental* distress were more likely to drop out early.
- Nonengaging caregivers were significantly older than the other completers and drop-outs.
- Families who received multimodal treatment were significantly more likely to complete therapy.
- Children in the completer group had higher externalizing scores than the other two groups.

*Classroom program.* One team of experts has conclusively demonstrated the effectiveness of a *prevention and treatment classroom program* for adolescents. Modules within *health education* classes discussed *healthy nonviolent relationships* and found a reduction in aggression contrasted with classes that did not receive the module (Wolfe et al., 2009). A different team judged that four types of treatment were superior to others and that Multisystemic Therapy (MST) was best of all. MST includes a coordinated, community, parent, and adolescent intervention strategy (Mulford & Redding, 2008). Now that some successful treatments are available, adolescents should actually receive treatment. There is a possibility, however, that victimized adolescents whose behavior puts them at risk for arrest will be "*criminalized instead of treated*" (Smith et al., 2004, p. 10).

All too frequently, the effects of past child/adolescent abuse are lingering on in the lives of the victims, as seen in the case history that follows.

**CASE HISTORY**  Country Singing Star Billy Currington Confronts the Past

Despite producing a No. 1 hit single, Billy suffered from attacks of rage that spoiled his relationships with his professional associates, his girlfriend, and his fans. While Billy was enduring a case of laryngitis that forced him to cancel a forthcoming tour, his manager and his then-girlfriend helped him face up to his life—it was unmanageable.

Billy entered a 30-week trauma recovery program, the best decision of his whole life, he says now. From the time he was 8 months old until he was age 7, he lived with an abusive, alcoholic stepfather who hit him, threw him, and hurt him whenever the mood struck him. During a visit to his stepfather after his mother's divorce, his stepfather took the opportunity to hit Billy so hard it knocked him out. Even though Billy was now an adolescent, the police arrived but made no arrest. Later, Billy wrote a song about his stepfather, entitled "Living With the Devil."

Although Billy drank, he was not an alcoholic—his challenge in life was his anger. During his stay at Sierra Tucson Treatment Center, he wrote notes about his life and learned to be *still*, a word that was not in his vocabulary. He learned to meditate and he learned the beatings were not his fault. He still has a few outbreaks of rage when "Little Billy" comes out for 2 seconds yelling and blowing up, so he is continuing his therapy.

He has forgiven his stepfather, now deceased, and he does not blame his mother. He let his band go because they needed to work, and his girlfriend left because she could not really understand what he had gone through. He has no attachments. He does not even know where his mother is, but he loves her (Keel, 2007).

### Welfare Services

Despite all the difficulties discussed previously in the National Survey of Child and Adolescent Well-Being (n.d.) study, the number of welfare services available to young adults abused as children is insufficient. One must ask, "How will these young people break the transgenerational cycle of abuse?" In this study, over a third had *no health insurance,* and 67.1% of those in need of *mental health services* did not receive them. At least 91% *did* receive help in one or more of the following areas: education, jobs, housing, daily living, and managing finances. Although only 4.8% of the males received *food stamps,* 70.7% of females with children received more extensive *nutrition benefits,* and 26.6% of the females were enrolled in the Temporary Assistance for Needy Families *welfare program.* The young adults lost many of the basic supports they had as adolescents and were now charged with "navigating a confusing social service system, with diminished access to services to address their risks for negative developmental outcomes" (NSCAW, n.d., p. 10). (See www.sagepub.com/barnett3e for more studies.)

## ABUSE OF PARENTS BY ADOLESCENTS AND PARRICIDE

One understudied area of family violence is abuse of parents by their children. Society has been fascinated with famous cases of parricide, but parent nonfatal abuse did not begin to capture attention until 30 years ago. It is a pervasive problem with many ramifications. Only a handful of studies have investigated parent abuse, and there is little public awareness of the problem. Child-to-parent violence (CPV) has qualities that differ in some ways from other types of abuse encompassed by family violence (Kennair & Mellor, 2007; J. A. Walsh & Krienert, 2009).

### Nonfatal Abuse of Parents

An attempt to differentiate normal adolescent defiance and oppositional behavior from abuse of parents has generated one acceptable definition of parent abuse (Paterson, Luntz, Perlesz, & Cotton, 2002).

Parent abuse is any act perpetrated by a child/adolescent that inflicts injury on a parent and/or threatening and controlling acts aimed at a parent. [Examples include hitting a parent and stealing money from a parent.]

*Prevalence of adolescent-to-parent abuse.* One consideration in responding to the problem of parent abuse is *parents' unwillingness to disclose* the problem to law enforcement or to professional counselors. According to a Canadian *qualitative study,* a mother who was bruised by her son's kicking "did not want anyone to know." Another issue is the *reactions of police.* A policeman responding to a different mother asked her, "Well, don't you have a husband to take care of this" (Cottrell & Monk, 2004, p.1089). Surveys of CPV have produced the following rates:

- 9% to 14% of *all juveniles* abused a parent according to a review article (Cottrell & Monk, 2004).
- 16% of *female juvenile offenders* assaulted a parent (H. N. Snyder & McCurley, 2008).
- 10% of *all juvenile offenders* assaulted a parent (H. N. Snyder & McCurley, 2008).
- 18% of two-parent families and 29% of one-parent families suffered CPV (J. A. Walsh & Krienert, 2009).

*Risk factors for adolescent-to-parent abuse.* A clearly recognized factor influencing CPV is whether there are two parents or only one living in the home. *Single parents* are more at risk than parents with partners in the home. Although studies usually find that gender differences in prevalence rates are modest, males more frequently use *physical aggression* against a parent than females (Nock & Kazdin, 2002). Some risk factors are below (Kennair & Mellor, 2007).

Risk Factors for Adolescent Perpetration of Abuse Against Parents

| Greater age | Larger size/strength | Low attachment to parents |
| --- | --- | --- |
| White race | Previous deviant behavior | Exposure to interparental violence |
| Substance abuse | Negative peer influence | |

Risk Factors for Parent Victimization by Adolescents

| Female gender | Permissive parenting style | High family stress level |
| --- | --- | --- |
| Single parent | Middle-to-higher socioeconomic status | |

## Adolescent-to-Parent Violence Versus Parricide

An illuminating comparison of CPV with parricides concluded that the two crimes are distinct and unique. A duo of researchers extracted data from the National Incident-Based Reporting System (NIBRS) covering the years 1995 to 2005 for 108,231 CPV offenders and 79 parricide offenders. The NIBRS database provides information about the victim, the offender, and the event—far more completely than other databases. The criminologists found that when the data were combined, males committed 63% of the crimes, while females committed 37%. Most victims were 35 to 44 years of age and most offenders were 14 to 16 years of age (J. A. Walsh & Krienert, 2009). See Table 6.6 for a comparison of CPA and Parricide offenders and victims.

TABLE 6.6   Adolescent Child-to-Parent Violence and Parricide Offenders/Victims

| CPV Offenders | Parricide Offenders | CPV Victims | Parricide Victims |
|---|---|---|---|
| Younger (14–16 years) | Older (17–21 years) | Younger (55%, 35–44 years) | Older (60%, 45+ years) |
| Female more likely | Male more likely | Mother more likely | Father more likely |
| Males were the majority of offenders overall | | Stepparent *less* likely | Stepparent *more* likely |
| Black more likely | White most likely | Race shows no significant differences overall | |
| Weapon use *less* likely | Weapon use *more* likely | Biological parents are the majority of victims overall | |

*Parricide (Matricide and Patricide), Filicide, and Siblicide.* Murder of family members by other family members is a rare event, yet society is interested in these events. Typically, parricide comprises less than 2% of homicides in which the victim-perpetrator relationship is known (Heide & Frei, 2010). Other than topics covered previously, such as infanticide, this section will cover murder of other family members. Murders of specific individuals in the family have designated names:

| |
|---|
| Parricide: The killing of one's parent(s) |
| Patricide: The killing of one's father |
| Matricide: The killing of one's mother |
| Filicide: The killing of one's son or daughter |
| Fratricide/Siblicide: The killing of one's brother or sister |

## Prevalence of Family Murders

The total number of homicides for the 2008 report was 14,180. The relationship between the perpetrator and the victim is unknown in about one third of the cases. These data do not provide information on whether the sons, daughters, brothers, and sisters are adolescents. See the figures below for details on murdered family members (U.S. Department of Justice, Federal Bureau of Investigation, 2010).

| | |
|---|---|
| Filicide: Son: 270; Daughter: 211 | Fratricide: Brother: 98; Sister: 15 |
| Patricide: 120<br>Matricide: 117 | Other Family Member: 314 |

## Matricide Analysis

An analysis of matricide (1976–1999) revealed interesting findings. First, most mothers are killed by their adult sons. Daughters under 18 are the least likely to kill their mothers. Second, from 1976 to 1999, the group of juvenile matricide offenders under 18 were 80% male ($n = 332$) and 20% female ($n = 83$). Third, adult offenders older than 18 were 84% male ($n = 1,702$) and 16% female ($n = 319$) (Heide & Frei, 2010). According to one researcher-practitioner, it is possible to classify juvenile matricide offenders into three types: (a) *severely abused adolescents*— who thought it was the only way to end the abuse, (b) *severely mentally ill adolescents,* and (c) *dangerously antisocial adolescents* (Heide, 1992).

## Explaining Adolescent-to-Caregiver (Parent) Abuse

In addition to some of the explanations presented in previous chapters, rationales specifically tied to adolescent abuse of parents include the following: (a) The parent has previously physically/sexually abused the adolescent, (b) The adolescent has low attachment to parents; and (c) The adolescent has witnessed interparental abuse (J. A. Walsh & Krienert, 2009). In regard to matricide, the evidence points to long-standing abuse and dysfunction in the family. Adolescents cannot find the help they need to escape the abuse and in desperation kill the parent in order to end the abuse (Heide & Frei, 2010).

## SIBLING ABUSE

During the early 1980s, discussion of sibling abuse as a form of child maltreatment emerged, but questions arose as to whether quarreling/fighting between siblings should be labeled *abusive*. Perhaps it is just normal sibling rivalry. Because aggressive interactions between siblings are almost universal, society has rarely defined such behavior as family violence (Gelles & Cornell, 1990; Wiehe, 1990). In the view of some child abuse scholars, it is inappropriate to consider sibling quarrels and fights as a form of family violence. These very common behaviors entail relatively minor physical acts and result in little or no measurable harm (Emery & Laumann-Billings, 1998). Other child abuse scholars, however, contend that harmful encounters between siblings should be recognized as serious forms of family violence. Scientific rigor requires that assumptions such as these provide empirical verification (Finkelhor & Dziuba-Leatherman, 1994).

## Definitions of Sibling Abuse

Briefly, sibling abuse refers to the physical, emotional/psychological, and/or sexual abuse of a brother or sister. Other definitions of *sibling aggression* are as follows:

- "A repeated pattern of aggression directed toward a sibling with the intent to inflict harm, and motivated by an internal emotional need for *power*" (Caffaro & Conn-Caffaro, 2005, p. 609)
- Psychological sibling aggression: "Ridicule, which involved both words and action that express contempt, degradation, or degradation which deprives the victim of a sense of self-worth" (Whipple & Finton, 1995, p. 35)

*Normative sibling interaction.* A complicating factor in defining sibling abuse is determining when so-called *normal* intersibling play becomes abusive. Where should society draw the line between normal sibling aggression and those behaviors that are damaging and abusive? Most, if not all, siblings at some time or another hit, slap, and/or punch each other, and they often call each other names. Presumably, a moderate number of sibling squabbles may be one basis for the development of social behavior (see Caffaro & Conn-Caffaro, 2005). Notwithstanding these facts, adolescent maltreatment experts do *not* assume that frequency of conflict is equivalent to acceptability of conflict. Many of these behaviors are too violent, controlling, and harmful to be overlooked (Eriksen & Jensen, 2009).

*Broad or narrow definitions.* Many academicians prefer to define sibling abuse *broadly.* From this perspective, even such *common behaviors* as hitting or pushing are labeled abusive. Other scholars have reasoned that overly inclusive definitions may make it difficult for professionals to respond appropriately to adolescent maltreatment (Emery & Laumann-Billings, 1998).

As one comparison has clearly shown, definitions (operationalizations) of sibling abuse affect prevalence rates (Mackey, Fromuth, & Kelly, 2009). To improve understanding of sibling abuse, it is essential to know the context of the aggression. Is this behavior an instance of bullying or playful wrestling? The most objective method for defining sibling abuse may be to develop *criteria* that specify whether a behavior rises to the level of abuse. Several scholars have proposed specific factors that might distinguish between sibling abuse and normal sibling rivalry and sex play (e.g., De Jong, 1989; Wiehe, 1997). See Table 6.7 for a list of criteria that differentiate sibling abuse from nonabusive sibling interactions.

In some cases, it may be necessary for sibling interactions to meet only *one* of these criteria to establish abusiveness. Getting into a knife fight, for instance, is never appropriate. In other cases, siblings' behaviors may need to meet *several* of these criteria.

**TABLE 6.7**    Criteria That Differentiate Sibling Abuse From Nonabusive Sibling Interactions

| Criterion | Descriptions of Negative Sibling Interactions |
|---|---|
| Power disparity between siblings | Involve significant differences in the distribution of power in age, physical size/strength, or social status |
| Frequency/duration of interactions | Occur over many months or years and include multiple incidents |
| Elements of pressure or secrecy | Involve coercion for involvement or occur in secret |
| Outcomes of interactions | Result in harm (e.g., physical/emotional) to the sibling victim |
| Developmental appropriateness | Fall outside the realm of typical sibling rivalry or normal sex play exploration |
| Type of parental intervention | Include lack of appropriateness, such as no response, indifference to the victim's suffering, and blaming of the victim |

SOURCES: Adler & Schutz, 1995; Caffaro & Conn-Caffaro, 2005; Eriksen & Jensen, 2009; Laviola, 1992; Wiehe, 1997.

## Attitudes Toward Sibling Abuse

A group of researchers examined whether violence against siblings is currently acceptable in American society. Presumably, acceptance can act as a precipitant of abusive behaviors. They first exposed 506 college students to four scenarios that depicted siblings of different genders perpetrating various types of *sibling aggression,* such as fighting over a TV remote. Next, the students rated the *acceptability* of the violence. Then the researchers administered a modified Conflict Tactics Scale (CTS) to assess the students' *personal experiences* with perpetration and victimization of sibling abuse. The researchers submitted the data to a factor analysis that grouped the responses into three factors: (a) *verbal/emotional aggression,* (b) *physical aggression,* and (c) *severe violence.* Last, they correlated the *acceptability ratings* with the three *perpetration/victimization factors.*

Results indicated that *men* were significantly more *accepting of sibling violence* than women. Second, *perpetrating* sibling violence was positively correlated with *acceptability ratings,* especially for women perpetrators. *Victimization* experiences of sibling violence were significantly associated with *acceptability* of sibling violence, but only for *men.* Hence, a critical gender difference was that men's childhood *victimization* experiences and women's childhood *perpetration* experiences were differentially correlated with their judgments of acceptability of sibling abuse (Hardy, Beers, Burgess, & Taylor, 2010). Evaluate the following case history.

### CASE HISTORY   Revenge Is Sweet

Nicolette, who was 15 years old, was infuriated with her big brother, Lenny. He lied to the three boys who came to her birthday party by saying that she was eager to "hook up" with all of them. One day just as Lenny was trying to exit quickly in and out of the balcony to hang out a wet towel, Nicolette happened to enter the room. When she saw that Lenny was wearing only underwear, she raced to the patio door and locked him outside on the balcony. Now it was Lenny's turn to be embarrassed and infuriated with Nicolette.

On a different day, a male friend visited Lenny when he and Nicolette were home alone. Nicolette had been showering and did not know her brother's friend was in the house. When she exited the bathroom wrapped in a large towel, Lenny ran over and pulled off her towel. As she ran screaming into her room, Lenny pinched her bottom, and he and his friend had a good laugh.

In the case history above, how helpful would it be to label the interactions abusive? Which behaviors are abusive: Lenny's comment at the birthday party? Nicollete's action of locking Lenny out on the balcony? Lenny's decision to pull off Nicollete's towel?

## Prevalence of Sibling Abuse

Experts point out that sibling abuse is far more prevalent than parent-to-child abuse (Kiselica & Morrill-Richards, 2007). Means of studying sibling abuse have varied. Initially, researchers reported only physical sibling abuse. Currently, some researchers report individual types of abuse separately, while others combine all types. Some differentiate severe from mild (e.g., Khan & Cooke, 2008).

- **Office of Juvenile Justice and Delinquency Prevention (H. N. Snyder & McCurley, 2008)**

  24% of juvenile domestic assault offenders (spouses, family members, intimate partners) victimized a sibling. Both genders may assault a same-sex sibling and some offenders are legally adults. When limiting domestic assaults to siblings, males more frequently assaulted than females:

  27% of domestic assaults by juvenile male offenders were of siblings.

  19% of domestic assaults by juvenile female offenders were of siblings.
- **N = 8,122 [8th Grade: n = 4,548; 11th Grade: n = 3,574] (Button & Gealt, 2010)**

  42% reported sibling violence.
- **Siblicides and Genetic Relatedness in Chicago, 1870–1930 (Michalski, Russell, Shackelford, & Weekes-Shackelford, 2007)**

| 11,018 total murders | 2 stepsiblings |
|---|---|
| 134 siblicides | 66 siblings-in-law |
| 70 full siblings and 2 half siblings | 14 of 68 offenders (ages known) were less than 18 years old |

(See www.sagepub.com/barnett3e for additional statistics on sibling abuse.)

# SIBLING SEXUAL ABUSE

## Definitions of Sibling Sexual Abuse

A commonly held view is that sexual activity between siblings is generally benign and within the context of *normal play or exploration,* and that it is not abusive, particularly when the children are close in age (Finkelhor, 1980; Pittman, 1987; Steele & Alexander, 1981). Others contend that such interactions between siblings are always harmful (Brickman, 1984; Canavan, Meyer, & Higgs, 1992). One study found that when others discover sibling incest, they sometimes have a morally engendered state of nausea, gagging, and diminished appetite, while those involved in incest feel humiliated and ashamed (Royzman, Leeman, & Sabini, 2008; see also Caffaro & Conn-Caffaro, 2005).

*Types of sibling sexual abuse.* Inappropriate sexual behaviors between siblings range from fondling and genital touching to oral contact to penetration. The most common sexual behavior between siblings appears to be *genital fondling* (Wiehe, 1997). Survivors have reported rates of sibling incest ranging from 42% to 89%. One small clinical study provided details about types of sibling sexual abuse. See Table 6.8 for a listing of percentages of different types of sibling sexual abuse reported by clinical patients.

**TABLE 6.8**   Forms of Sibling Incest Victimization

| Type of Sibling Incest Experienced | % Females (n = 34) | % Males (n = 7) |
|---|---|---|
| Fondled | 94.1 | 71.4 |
| Genitals rubbed against my body | 73.5 | 51.7 |
| Touched sibling's genitals | 58.8 | 71.4 |
| Sexualized kissing | 52.9 | 28.6 |
| Oral sex | 44.1 | 71.4 |
| Vaginal intercourse | 41.2 | 14.3 |
| Subjected to sexual comments | 41.2 | 42.9 |
| Fingers inserted into vagina or anus | 38.2 | 14.3 |
| Objects inserted into vagina or anus | 21.1 | – |
| Exposure to pornography | 20.6 | 14.3 |
| Ritually abused, physically/sexually tortured | 14.7 | – |
| Anal sex | 11.8 | – |
| Made to watch sexual acts | 11.8 | – |
| Made to pose for seductive/sexual photographs | 11.8 | – |
| Sadomasochistic activities | 8.8 | – |

SOURCE: Adapted from Carlson, Maciol, & Schneider, 2006.

*Brother-sister versus father-daughter incest.* The degree to which brother-sister incest is harmful has sparked interest among a range of researchers. One inquiry determined that the widely held belief that father-daughter incest is much worse than brother-sister incest is mistaken. A team of Canadian researchers separated 72 incest victims between the ages of 5 and 16 into three groups: (a) *brother-sister incest,* (b) *father-daughter incest,* and (c) *stepfather-stepdaughter incest.* Analyses of questionnaire data about the *types of sexual abuse* experienced uncovered few significant differences between the groups. Among other predictions, the researchers hypothesized that brothers would use more *force* than fathers or stepfathers. Although the brothers did use more force, the differences between groups did not achieve statistical significance. Unexpectedly, the brothers engaged in *intercourse* significantly more *often* than the fathers or stepfathers (Cyr, Wright, McDuff, & Perron, 2002).

## Prevalence of Sibling Sexual Abuse

Although father-daughter incest has fostered some research, less than a handful of studies have investigated sibling incest. Most published articles focus on clinical findings rather than upon incidence and prevalence (Phillips-Green, 2002). Nonetheless, some experts suggest that sibling incest is the most common form of incest, that is, more common than father-daughter incest (Carlson et al., 2006; see also Shaw, Lewis, Loeb, Rosado, & Rodriguez, 2000).

- 15% of female and 10% of male undergraduates ($N = 796$) reported some type of sexual experience involving a sibling (Finkelhor, 1980).
- 29% of 367 college students raised with opposite-sex siblings engaged in some type of sexual activity with a sibling. Males and females were nearly equally likely to report having had such experiences (Bevc & Silverman, 1993).

Differences among these findings and others are easily attributable to sample variations, such as the age of the victim, whether the data are retrospective, and whether Child Protective Services have substantiated the cases.

## Consequences of Negative Psychological, Physical, and Sexual Sibling Interactions

In most abusive sibling interactions, there is an aspect of *victimization* whereby the recipient of the behavior is "hurt or injured by the action or actions of another" (Wiehe, 1997, p. 167). Hurt or injury might be *psychological* in nature, including feelings of depression or anxiety, or it might take a *physical* form, such as bruises or cuts. Depression and anxiety are especially prevalent reactions (Mackey, Fromuth, et al., 2009). Other consequences such as poor academic achievement also occur. As one illustration of another consequence, sibling aggression is linked with lower competence in peer relationships (J. Y. Kim, McHale, Crouter, & Osgood, 2007).

Virtually no controlled studies of the effects of sibling sexual abuse are available. Most of the research to date has relied on a small number of clinical case studies of individuals seeking therapy, and most studies have failed to include control groups or to use standardized assessment instruments. As a result, the research evaluating the effects of sexual violence between siblings has produced inconclusive findings. Although lacking in methodological rigor, the studies conducted so far have demonstrated some consistency in the types of difficulties that sibling abuse victims experience. See Table 6.9 for a summary of findings about the negative consequences of sibling sexual assault.

*Collateral effects of child/adolescent sexual maltreatment.* The preceding chapters have included several discussions on the myriad negative consequences associated with being a victim of child maltreatment, so it is not necessary to reiterate them here. The negative outcomes associated with child maltreatment, however, affect not only the children who experience abuse but also those who live and/or work with these children. It is important to be aware of these "spillover" effects for the victimized child's family members and professionals who interact with the

| TABLE 6.9 | Negative Consequences of Sibling Psychological, Physical, and Sexual Assaults |

| Externalizing Problems | | Internalizing Problems | |
| --- | --- | --- | --- |
| Poor academic performance | Substance abuse | Revictimization | Low self-esteem |
| Sexual risk taking | Health problems | Negative emotions | Helplessness |
| Eating-disordered behavior | Aggression | Interpersonal problems | Fear |
| Sexually abusing others | Pregnancy | Anger control problems | Shame |
| Sexual promiscuity | Delinquency | Depression | Humiliation |
| Sexualized behavior | Suicidality | PTSD symptoms | Anxiety |
| Sexual response difficulty | | Self-blame | Mistrust of others |

SOURCES: Ackard & Neumark-Sztainer, 2002; Burgess, Hartman, & Clements, 1995; Button & Gealt, 2010; Graham-Bermann, Cutler, Litzenberger, & Schwartz, 1994; Kim et al., 2007; Mackey, Fromuth, et al., 2009; Marx, Calhoun, Wilson, & Meyerson, 2001; Thompson, 2009; Wiehe, 1997; Wordes & Nunez, 2002.

victims. Interactions with the victims, the adult perpetrators, nonperpetrating parents, and child witnesses are difficult and emotionally provocative. The following subsections review the research findings with regard to *negative collateral effects* as well as some approaches to treating and preventing such effects.

*Vicarious/secondary traumatization.* Relatively few studies have examined the effects of child maltreatment on nonabusive family members of victims, such as *nonoffending parents* and siblings. Family members of abuse victims are often referred to as *secondary victims* because they can experience a number of psychological difficulties associated with the abuse (McCourt, Peel, & O'Carroll, 1998; V. C. Strand, 2000). Several research findings published in the mid-1980s and early 1990s contributed to this new perspective.

*Attitudes toward mothers.* The first studies in this area were concerned with the characteristics of nonoffending mothers of children who had been *sexually abused.* Researchers who examined this topic tended to view mothers of sexual abuse victims as *coconspirators* in their children's abuse. They hypothesized that *dysfunction* in such mothers was a *cause* of the sexual abuse. Professionals often viewed mothers of sexual abuse victims as "unprotective," "collusive," "inadequate," or "conspiratorial" due to their own psychopathology (V. C. Strand, 2000). Within the past 15 years, however, a greater understanding of the problem of sexual abuse has led researchers to view nonoffending mothers as covictims rather than as conspirators.

One line of research, using a variety of samples, demonstrated that *most mothers of child victims support and believe their children* when told about sexual victimization (Sirles & Franke, 1989). Another collection of studies, which evaluated various factors that might potentially affect a mother's willingness and ability to support and believe her child, indicated the following about nonoffending mothers (Faller, 1988; Leifer, Shapiro, & Kassem, 1993).

> Mothers were *more supportive* when they were no longer living with or married to the perpetrator.
>
> Mothers were *less supportive* if they were abusing substances themselves or had little social support following their children's disclosures of abuse.

One team of investigators studying brother-sister, father-daughter, and stepfather-stepdaughter incest discriminated some disparity in their reactions. From 70% to 90% believed their daughter. The level of support varied significantly as a reflection of the accused male. Mothers gave the most support to girls in the father-daughter incest group (65%), some support to girls in the brother-sister incest group (50%), and the least support to girls in the stepfather-stepdaughter group (30.4%). Approximately 70% of the mothers offered protection to their daughter in all three groups. About 50% of the mothers had been incest victims themselves, but the researchers found no significant link between their victimization and their reactions to their daughters' victimization (Cyr et al., 2002).

In addition, one review of empirical studies that assessed *mothers' pathology* during this time judged the evidence as *inconclusive* (Tamraz, 1996). Some feminist advocates for mothers critiqued the entire line of research as just one more expression of blaming mothers for the fathers' behavior (see Berliner, 1998; Bolen, 2003).

## Characteristics of Sibling Abusers

Researchers have evaluated a number of characteristics of individuals who perpetrate sibling abuse. The most common variables under scrutiny are gender and age.

*Age.* At least one representative sample of adolescents in 30 states (National Incident-Based Reporting System [NIBRS]) reported on juvenile domestic offenders (spouses, siblings, other family members, and dating partners). Physical assaults by adolescents increased with age, while sexual assaults declined (H. N. Snyder & McCurley, 2008). The Button and Gealt (2010) study found opposing results using *victimization data*. "With each year of age, a respondent's odds of experiencing sibling aggression decreased. . . ." (p. 136).

*Gender.* It is unclear whether gender is a discriminating variable in characterizing adolescents who inflict harm on their sibling(s). The evidence is mixed. The 30-state study assessing violence via the NIBRS clearly identified males as more aggressive (Snyder & McCurley, 2008). The Delaware study of 8,122 high school students also found significant gender differences, with males significantly more aggressive with siblings (Button & Gealt, 2010). A survey of 506 college students using recollected memories assessed with a modified CTS scale found no overall significant sibling gender differences (Hardy et al., 2010).

## Explaining Sibling Psychological, Physical, and Sexual Abuse

The numerous forms of detrimental sibling interactions are similar to the forms of child maltreatment perpetrated by adults, giving rise to at least three theories.

*Learning theory.* Learning theory incorporates three broad types of learning: *social learning* (imitation, modeling), *classical conditioning* (emotional learning—e.g., fear), and *operant conditioning* (behavioral learning—e.g., to hit/kick someone). One research group has expanded the idea of parent-to-child learning to sibling-to-sibling learning. In this case, getting along with siblings carries over to getting along with peers, and the reverse direction of learning is undoubtedly true as well (J. Y. Kim et al., 2007).

The families in which these siblings live offer ample exposure to violent and immoral sexual behaviors that can be imitated (i.e., learned). Violent adolescents have *seen parent-to-child abuse and witnessed interparental violence* (see Button & Gealt, 2010). An extensive series of studies have, in fact, observed these kinds of family dysfunction and many others (e.g., Akers, 2000; Button & Gealt, 2010; Caffaro & Conn-Caffaro, 1998, 2005). Some evidence suggests that *specific* childhood experiences are significantly associated with later types of offending (D. A. Simons, Wurtele, & Durham, 2008; see also Worling, 1995). See Table 6.10 for a summary of characteristics of the juvenile's home and family.

**TABLE 6.10** Characteristics of Families of Sibling-Abusive Adolescents

| Heightened degree of marital discord | Childhood sexual abuse | Family stress |
|---|---|---|
| Negative communication patterns | Physical child abuse | Neglect |
| Chaotic family environment | Excessive caretaking of siblings | Parental absence |
| Lack of parental involvement | Parental deprivation | Parental rejection |
| Poor parental sexual boundaries | Physical discipline | Family secrets |
| Mother's childhood victimization | Lack of parental supervision | |

*Feminist theory.* As a rule, males feel they have the prerogative to dominate females regardless of age differences (Laviola, 1992). Moreover, when a male experiences powerlessness, he may use violence to achieve control over others. The structure of families and cultural acceptance of violence make it permissible for older siblings and male siblings to aggress against younger siblings and female siblings. Several investigations have revealed that offending siblings are usually older, stronger, or both than the victims (see Button & Gealt, 2010). The obvious age disparity between offenders and victims supports the *power differential* theme so central to feminism. As explained throughout the text, the use of power as a control tactic to maintain dominance is a reflection of patriarchal ideology.

*Conflict theory.* Family members resort to violence to resolve conflict. Parental behavior, such as comparing siblings, triggers a chain of behaviors: sibling rivalry → conflict, → sibling aggression. Siblings also compete for resources, such as toys, and may disagree over the distribution of household chores. An empirical theory-testing comparison using retrospective data from 651 young adults gave some support to conflict theory, more support to feminist explanations, and most to social learning theory (Hoffman, Kiecolt, & Edwards, 2005; Ng Tseung & Schott, 2004; Wiehe, 1997).

## PRACTICE, POLICY, AND PREVENTION FOR ABUSIVE/ABUSED SIBLINGS

### Practice With Sibling Abusers

Classic treatment for sibling abusers is that used throughout the field of family violence: cognitive behavior therapy. But is this approach sufficient? When few specialized treatments are available, practitioners try to adapt empirically supported interventions into new frameworks. In a review article, experts crystallized the thinking in the field of adolescent abuse: Juvenile offenders are unique and therefore require distinctive treatment (Fanniff & Becker, 2006). Dissatisfied with the lack of well-defined sibling abuse treatment, one practitioner began development on a new format. Some elements of the intervention were to assign homework tasks for the whole family and to provide knowledge about sibling aggression. Although untested, clients' preliminary responses to the treatment were promising (Caspi, 2008).

*Treatments for juvenile sex offenders.* Despite the widespread belief that juvenile sex offenders are distinctive, treatment for sexually abusive adolescents initially followed those developed for adult treatment. There are three types of frequently used treatments:

1. *Cognitive behavioral therapy (CBT)* treatment was and is the preferred mode for intervening with adults and adolescents. In addition to group therapy, counselors provide individual and family treatment. Because sex-offending is most likely a *learned behavior* accompanied by learned attitudes, the goal of CBT is to help the client "unlearn" these behaviors and attitudes and replace them with more acceptable behaviors and attitudes. Concomitantly, juveniles learn to improve their social skills and take a class in sex education. Finally, therapists offer treatment for trauma-related symptoms (McGrath, Cumming, & Burchard, 2003).

2. *Multisystemic Treatment (MST)* features a social ecological approach that offers intensive therapeutic services delivered in the juvenile's home and community. Counselors work with the individual offender, his family, his peers, and his school. Under this system, the therapist and the family are accountable for the juvenile offender's improvement. MST therapists may also incorporate cognitive behavior therapy in the intervention (see Henggeler, Schoenwald, Borduin, Rowland, & Cunningham, 1998).

3. *The Good Lives Model* centers on the construction of a positive self-image for the offender (Thakker, Ward, & Tidmarsh, 2006).

Juvenile sex-offender programs have reduced recidivism but still need improvement (e.g., Reitzel & Carbonell, 2006). (See Fanniff & Becker, 2006, for a comprehensive and empirical evaluation of adolescent sex-offender treatments.)

*Treatment of sibling incest victims.* One practitioner has provided suggestions for providing group therapy for *adult* female survivors of sibling incest (K. M. Thompson, 2009). Her general method can be subsumed under the umbrella of *Cognitive Processing Therapy* for Sexual Abuse adapted from Chard (2005) and Chard, Weaver, and Resick (1997). In this program, facilitators follow a 12-week format in which women group members discuss issues such as family relationships, reactions to abuse disclosure, and current relationship with their brother (K. M. Thompson, 2009). Some women survivors had problems in defining incest as coerced because of their humiliation. It took insight gained in counseling sessions to realize they had *not freely consented* but *acquiesced out of fear* (see Caffaro & Conn-Caffaro, 2005).

*Survivors of sibling physical and sexual abuse.* In a broader study of 73 *adult* siblings from a convenience sample (49 females; 24 males), researchers acquired data by conducting structured interviews. Of the total sample, 29 were incest survivors, 26 were physical assault survivors, and 18 survived both physical assault and incest. Brother-sister incest ($n = 18$) comprised the largest category of incest survivors followed by brother-brother ($n = 6$), sister-brother ($n = 4$), and sister-sister ($n = 2$). Other interesting characteristics of the sample came to light: (a) More than half of the brother-sister incest victims had never married, even 25 years after the incest experience; and (b) when adults, 35% of the victims distanced themselves emotionally from the abuser, having no contact whatsoever.

The researcher-practitioners made a number of observations that can help therapists working with sibling abuse survivors. Many of the participants had never disclosed their abuse to anyone before, and the disclosure to the researchers was beneficial. Another element to surface was the faulty misconception that the incest was consensual, a belief that provoked confusion and shame. Last, the families in which incest occurs seem especially likely to be characterized by parental abandonment—physical, psychological, or both (Caffaro & Conn-Caffaro, 2005).

*Effects of disclosure of sibling incest.* Three focus groups of adult female sibling abuse survivors in Australia described the reactions of others to their disclosures of sibling sexual abuse. The women's comments clearly indicate how unhelpful the responses were and point to the need for much more education of psychotherapists (Rowntree, 2007):

1.  Boys are just being boys: Bullying is natural for boys; sexual interactions were mutual.
2.  The abuse is the victim's fault: She asked for it; she should not be a troublemaker by telling the family; she has to prove it.
3.  The abuse is not serious: He is only your brother; get over it.
4.  It is a family matter: It can't be abuse because he is your brother; she should not betray her family by telling the secret.
5.  The topic is taboo: My counselor said we did not have to talk about it (but I wanted to).
6.  It is abuse: It's not your fault; it is abuse.

## Policy for Sibling Abuse

*Caseworkers' conceptualizations of sibling abuse.* One instructive study examined several variables about caseworker training: (a) specific college discipline of Child Protective

Services workers, and (b) caseworkers' definitions of sibling abuse. As these assessments took place, other crucial variables came to light, such as the existence/nonexistence of laws defining sibling abuse, political policy regarding CPS's functions, caseworkers' interpretations of the laws, and agency practices. Finally, the researcher raised the issue of how these multiple factors and their interactions affected the safety and developmental outcomes for abused siblings. Results of her analyses might be startling to some readers (Kominkiewicz, 2004).

*Social welfare training.* First, the assumption that social welfare is the discipline charged with child welfare is questionable. The idea that the prerequisite for functioning as a caseworker in CPS agencies is social welfare training is unfounded. Moreover, there is a problem in the actual training of social welfare workers. A social welfare department might not include any curriculum on caseworker training, and there is no known uniformity about the curriculum across social welfare departments (see Woody, D'Souza, & Dartman, 2006). Additionally, students appropriately trained in case management do not usually seek jobs in CPS agencies. Finally, the background training of those who undertake child case management seems inexplicable. Beyond the majority of students who are trained in the social sciences, workers come from a variety of disciplines, such as history, political science, and chemistry. Some workers have no academic training but are trained in the field.

*Nonagreement with legal definitions.* Second, child caseworkers' acknowledgement and/or agreement with the elements in the legal or commonly accepted definitions of sibling abuse are low. This finding applies to workers whose background training is in social welfare. Those with backgrounds in psychology reached the highest levels of agreement. These dismal findings suggest that caseworkers may not recognize sibling abuse when it exists.

*Lack of interventions.* Third, it is all too likely that the lack of adequate training and the hiring practices of CPS agencies make it a near certainty that some abused sibling will receive no intervention whatsoever. Consequently, these adolescents will suffer long-lasting emotional damage, or even be physically injured (Kominkiewicz, 2004).

*Police arrests.* "Child Protective Services and the legal system are reluctant to accept and respond to sibling abuse reports that are filed" (Caffaro & Conn-Caffaro, 2005, p. 604). Other researchers' findings lent credence to this assertion. A pair of investigators examined 109 adolescents, 12 to 17 years of age, who had been *sexually victimized more than once*. The researchers categorized the offenders according to their relationship to the victim. Some of the categories were friends, parents/stepparents, other child relatives (including siblings), and neighbors.

A tally of 338 *incidents* revealed that 44.4% of the offenders were friends and 11.8% were other child relatives. The majority of *boys* did *not* turn to adults for help, but of those who did, 37.8% told their mother and 42.8% told a close friend. The boys were most likely to tell a friend if the offender was a friend and tell their mother if the offender was a family member. Of the disclosed cases, police received a report of the assault for 35%. Of the 34 police notifications by mothers, the police arrested 25 juvenile offenders, and of the 9 police notifications by close friends, the police arrested 3. Apparently, confiding in a mother is often a good choice, but confiding in a friend may be less effective. Adolescents lack the experience and resources to help a victimized friend. Of all the arrests made including those reported to the police by other confidants, the police were significantly more likely to arrest an adult than a juvenile. Police discretion probably reflects society's perception that adult offenders are the most dangerous (R. F. Stein & Nofziger, 2008).

---

**SECTION SUMMARY**

## Abuse of Adolescent Offspring and Abuse of Parents

Parental maltreatment of adolescents takes many forms (neglect, physical abuse, emotional abuse, and sexual abuse). Several forms of abuse are likely to occur simultaneously, creating an appalling home environment for adolescents. General abuse prevalence rates of adolescents range from about 4% to 22% and sexual abuse rates from about 11% to 35%. Different rates arise from the diverse samples such as confirmed cases from Child Protective Services or questionnaire data from broader samples. For general abuse, girls (17.3%) are significantly more likely than boys (10.8%) to be abused, and for sexual abuse the gender differences are very large (girls = 32.4%; boys = 23.0%). Younger juveniles, 12 to 15 years old (18.1%), are more likely to be abused than older juveniles, 16 to 17 years old (6.3%).

Adolescent abuse of parents ranges from 9% to 29% depending on factors such as whether the juvenile is living in a two-parent family. *Males* were more likely overall than females to abuse or kill a parent. Younger females (ages 14–16) were more likely than younger males (ages 14–16) to abuse a parent.

Historically, society has tended to view sibling abuse as normative and nonsevere, but this belief has not stood the test of time. Sibling physical and sexual abuse occurs at rates of about 42%. As such it is the most frequent form of family violence. Sibling incest rates range from 42% to 89% among *clinic* clients.

Adolescents abused by parents and/or siblings suffer from a number of far-ranging psychological (e.g., anger, shame) and behavioral effects (e.g., substance misuse). Adolescents may run away from home, and some very young runaway girls become teenage mothers, thus starting the cycle all over again. Although some experts initially thought mothers ignored their children's complaints of sexual abuse, research has not supported this point of view. Treatments for victims and offenders are available and helpful. Child Protective Services, however, has received criticisms from a number of quarters for their selection of workers, lack of worker training, and inappropriate decision making.

## EFFECTS OF FAMILY ABUSE ON ADOLESCENT INTERPERSONAL RELATIONSHIPS

There are numerous adverse effects related to abuse of adolescents in addition to homelessness and teenage pregnancy. Abused adolescents are very likely to strike out at family members, friends, dates, and others. Some of these areas of violence include juvenile delinquency, bullying, dating violence, and same-sex violence. When adolescents do strike out, they often become involved with the dysfunctional juvenile justice system. Rehabilitating juveniles at this stage is more difficult, and society is often more interested in punishment than rehabilitation.

## Juvenile Delinquency

---

### BOX 6.3 Juvenile Delinquency

One of the most frequently discussed long-term consequences of child maltreatment is juvenile delinquency. Almost without exception, studies have documented the relationship between child maltreatment and juvenile delinquency (Button & Gealt, 2010; Mallett, Dare, & Seck, 2009; Zingraff, Leiter, Myers, & Johnsen, 1993). Juvenile arrests for 2008 were 3.8/100,000 juveniles. Juveniles accounted for 16% of all violent crime, 10% of all murders, and 47% of all arson (Puzzanchera, 2009).

The Office of the Surgeon General (2001) has divided risk factors into early onset (ages 6–11) and late onset (ages 12–14). Within these two categories there are five domains: individual, family, school, peer group, and community (see Table 6.5 for a summary of family risk factors). Peer risk factors are weak social ties, antisocial delinquent peers, and gang membership.

A 2-year longitudinal investigation of 18,676 children revealed that victims of substantiated child maltreatment have a delinquency rate that is 47% higher than that of children without such a background. In this study, conducted in Cook County, Illinois, 62% of the sample experienced abuse: (a) 46% *physical abuse,* (b) 15% *sexual abuse,* (c) 2% *exposure to substances,* and (d) less than 1% *emotional abuse* (Ryan & Testa, 2005).

*Race.* The race of adolescents arrested for juvenile delinquency differs significantly: (a) African American—69%, (b) White—19%, and (c) Hispanic—12%.

*Age.* Older children are more apt to be delinquent than younger children. For every year of increasing age, the odds ratio for delinquency increases by 1.09 for males and by 1.06 for females.

*Recurrence of maltreatment.* Males with two or more recurrences of substantiated maltreatment are 1.78 times more likely to be delinquent than those with only one report.

*Out-of-home-placement.* Approximately 25% of the children experienced at least one out-of-home placement. Those sent to at least one placement had a delinquency rate of 16% compared with only 7% for children without a placement. Race is a factor in placements. African American children suffer the highest number of out-of-home placements, followed by Hispanics and then Whites (Ryan & Testa, 2005).

*Multiple victimizations.* An evaluation of children victimized differentially found that children who experienced multiple forms of maltreatment (**polyvictimization**) exhibited the highest rates of aggression, delinquency, and interpersonal problems compared with those victimized by a single *form of maltreatment* (Vissing, Straus, Gelles, & Harrop, 1991).

*Incarcerated parent.* Among 1,112 juvenile offenders, 31% had a parental history of incarceration (Dannerbeck, 2005).

*Violent teenage girls.* A number of academicians have addressed the possibility of a steep rise in violence by teenage girls. Reports in the media have suggested that adolescent girls' violence is rapidly approaching that of teenage boys. To investigate these speculations, a team of 10 criminologists analyzed 3 large databases: (a) Uniform Crime Reports (UCR)—arrest data; (b) National Crime Victimization Survey (NCVS)—victimization data; and (c) MTF (Monitoring the Future)—self-reported delinquency. Along with a number of independent studies, they reached some convincing conclusions (Zahn et al., 2008):

- The UCR reported significant increases in *arrests* of juvenile girls from 1996 to 2005. Girls' arrests for simple assault increased, while boys' decreased. Boys maintained much higher arrest rates for *aggravated assault,* on the *violent crime index,* and for *all crimes together.*
- *Delinquency assault indexes* (MTF) for both boys and girls remained stable over the period of 1980 to 2003.
- Girls' *victimization rates* (NCVS) contrasted with boys' remained fairly constant over the same period, 1980 to 2003, but both rates evidenced sharp declines in assaults.
- The research team suggests these findings imply that *police arrest policies changed,* and that girls were not becoming more violent. One reason might be enhanced police attention to domestic violence crimes.
- Prior victimizations in the home, community, or school are the most likely precursors to girls' violent behavior. Girls are more likely to assault household members, while boys are most likely to assault individuals outside the home.
- Girls who mature early are at greater risk for delinquent behavior than their later-maturing counterparts.

## Bullying

### BOX 6.4 Adolescent Bullying/Cyberbullying—Perpetration/ Victimization

*Schoolyard bullying.* Although bullying is more prevalent before age 12, it continues during adolescence and may have dramatic consequences (Nansel et al., 2001). There are strong connections between bullying, gender-based harassment, and adolescent dating violence (Connolly & Friedlander, 2009; Wolfe, Crooks, Chiodo, & Jaffe, 2003). Although some studies show that adolescent peers are attracted to bullies, one study of 36 adolescent girls indicated that masculinity was a *negative* predictor of girls' attraction (J. Field, Crothers, & Kolbert, 2007).

*(Continued)*

(Continued)

Presumably, a major purpose of male-to-male bullying is for *embedding masculine norms* of toughness, strength, and dominance/control (D. A. Phillips, 2007; Wolfe et al., 2009). *Punking,* a term used interchangeably with *bullying,* is a form of *humiliating and shaming* adopted by boys to achieve these goals (D. A. Phillips, 2007). Of course, this explanation does not suffice for female-to-female bullying, a type of very hurtful aggression that incorporates *spreading rumors* about a girl and *excluding her* from important activities (see the special issue of *The Prevention Researcher* on juvenile bullying, 2004).

Nonetheless, bullying may have less of an impact on high school students than on middle school students. Possibly, high school students have better coping skills or have fewer developmental challenges to conquer. The consequences of high school bullying victimization can be extremely serious: leaving school, or feeling impelled to kill oneself or someone at school. In one study, 71% of 41 school shooters had been bully victims (Vossekuil, Fein, Reddy, Borum, & Modzeleski, 2002). Bullying may carry over into adult relationships (e.g., Button & Gealt, 2010; Stambor, 2006). Some corporations and organizations, in fact, have held mandatory seminars to prevent bullying at work (see Dingfelder, 2006a, for a brief review).

School antibullying programs are much more prevalent in Europe than in the United States. A duo of social scientists reviewed 16 programs with the following results: (a) 8 produced desirable results; (b) 2 produced mixed results; (c) 4 produced negligible results, and (d) 2 produced undesirable results. The investigators were unable to perform a meta-analysis because of insufficient information. They concluded that although the weight of the evidence did not allow them to state unequivocally that antibullying programs are effective, they could say the results are promising (Baldry & Farrington, 2007). (Return to Chapter 4 for a general discussion of bullying.)

***Internet harassment/Cyberbullying.*** Cyberbullying has captured national attention with the hanging deaths of two high school girls who had been bullied. Although one bully was the mother of an adolescent (Missouri), the other case involved a seven-member group of adolescents (Massachusetts) (FoxNews, 2008; Smolowe, Herbert, Egan, Rakowsky, & Mascia, 2010). Within the last two decades, bullying behaviors have spread to the Internet, more so among *high school* than middle school students (Ybarra & Mitchell, 2004). Electronic communications, such as e-mails, text messages, chat rooms, and cell phones, provide bullies with anonymity. *Cyberbullying* is the "willful and repeated harm inflicted through the medium of electronic text" (Patchin & Hinduja, 2006, p. 152). The National Survey of Children Exposed to Violence revealed that 7.9% of adolescents 14 to 17 years of age reported Internet harassment (Finkelhor, Turner, Ormrod, & Hamby, 2009).

*Internet harassment,* however, may be a better term than cyberbullying because the overlap between schoolyard bullying and Internet harassment is much lower than expected. Reports from a sample of 1,588 children and adolescents aged 10 to 15 found that 64% of students harassed online were *not* concurrently bullied at school (Ybarra, Diener-West, & Leaf, 2007; Wolak, Mitchell, & Finkelhor, 2007). Among a group of 1,378 adolescents, over 32% of boys and over 36% of girls reported online *victimization.*

From the same sample, 18% of the boys and 16% of the girls reported cyberbully *offending.* No significant racial or gender differences appeared (Hinduja & Patchin, 2008).

According to a meta-synthesis, the major difference is that *boys* are overrepresented as both *offenders* and *victims* in traditional bullying, but there appear to be *no gender differences in cyberbullying* (Tokunaga, 2010). As a side note, some colleges now have websites for the sole purpose of spreading gossip (Westfall, Triggs, & Grossman, 2008).

Researchers, practitioners, educators, and policymakers are establishing programs to deal with the problem. Antibullying school programs have shown promise in reducing unacceptable behavior. Likewise, supervising/monitoring adolescents' online activities can reduce the possibility of detrimental choices on the Internet (I. R. Berson, Berson, & Ferron, 2002). A further requirement is to educate teachers, law enforcement personnel, and mental health staff in how to identify *red flags of bully victimization,* especially those that may lead to suicide or homicide.

*Is Internet harassment illegal?* An Internet source listed only a *few* states with anticyberbullying laws. These range from school dismissal to a Class D felony (CyberBully Alert, 2008). There is no federal legislation banning the practice, and some analysts think that outlawing Internet harassment is impractical because it is too *anonymous* (J. Strickland, 2010). As social scientists and legal experts search for a way to curtail cyberbullying, one concerned attorney has a website offering specific advice to educators about responding to cyberbullying and cyberthreats (Willard, 2005–2007).

## ADOLESCENT DATING VIOLENCE

National Teen Dating Abuse Helpline: 886-331-9474

Rape, Abuse & Incest National Network (RAINN) Hotline: 800-656-HOPE

### CASE HISTORY   Claudia and Roberto's Last Dance at the High School Prom

Claudia met Roberto when she was a junior in high school. It was love at first sight. All Claudia ever wanted was a boyfriend who loved her and made her feel special. One problem Claudia and Roberto had was that they fought like cats and dogs. It didn't matter what the situation was—what movie to see, where to get a hamburger, or whether to go out on Friday or Saturday.

As the couple sat in Roberto's car one night, Claudia accused Roberto of flirting with an old girlfriend. The argument got heated, and Roberto leaned over and slapped Claudia across the face. She slapped him back. They always fought like this, just like a couple of kids, the way they thought "most" couples do. After all, don't all couples who love each other fight and hit each other?

Over the next 10 months, Claudia and Roberto continued fighting, and Claudia occasionally had bruises. One time she got a black eye. The next morning, she told her parents that the bruises on her face came from a minor car accident. She wore a long-sleeved turtleneck shirt to hide her other bruises. A month later, she was badly bruised again. In fact, Roberto bit her arm several times and pulled her hair. She tried to bite him back.

Claudia loved Roberto, and she knew he loved her. In fact, she believed that he would not hit her if he didn't love her. One thing she did to please him was give up her participation on the debate team, because Roberto hated it when she stayed after school once a week for practice. In fact, she stopped seeing nearly all of her old friends. Roberto told her that it was her "nagging" that set him off, and he had to get her to stop. She tried harder and harder to please him and thought that their quarrels would cease, especially if she stopped provoking him.

Claudia's greatest fear was not that she would get seriously injured, but that Roberto would never call her again. He was her whole world. She worried that if her parents found out about Roberto's violence, they would forbid her to see him again, and that her two brothers might decide to beat him up. Every time she got hurt, Claudia renewed her efforts to hide her injuries.

On the night of their senior prom, Claudia was ecstatic. High school was almost over. She thought that she and Roberto would get married and she would finally have everything she always wanted, but it didn't work out that way. At the prom, Claudia and Roberto got into a quarrel as usual, but this time Roberto's buddies overheard the argument and he felt humiliated because he "couldn't keep Claudia in line." Roberto decided that they should leave the prom. On the way to the car, however, Roberto got out of control. He punched and kicked Claudia over and over again, letting out all of his rage about everything in his whole life. He was so infuriated that he left Claudia in the parking lot, bleeding and unconscious.

Another couple found Claudia and called the paramedics, who took her to the hospital. When Claudia regained consciousness the next morning, her parents were in a state of shock. They could not believe that Roberto had ever hit her. Her brothers vowed to beat him up, and the police were out looking to arrest him. Claudia was worried when the doctors told her she might lose the vision in one of her eyes. She was even *more* worried that she would never see Roberto again, that he would never call her again, and that he might stop loving her. Without Roberto, she thought, her life would be over.

Society has largely ignored dating violence. Although the media has addressed adult intimate partner violence (IPV), it pays scant attention to similar problems occurring among teens. The same can be said for health professionals, law enforcement, and legislatures (Betz, 2007). What is more, several investigations have determined that adolescent dating violence is a risk factor for adult IPV (Jaycox et al., 2006; Noonan & Charles, 2009). Although research on the topic of teen dating violence has improved, knowledge about its prevalence and risk factors remains tentative. Theoretical explanations are incomplete, and intervention/prevention programs need refinement (see Hickman, Jaycox, & Aronoff, 2004).

## Definition of Dating Violence (DV)

The majority of measurements on teen dating violence consist of frequency tallies of specific acts. A typical question is: "How many times did your boy/girlfriend push you in the past 12 months?"

## Prevalence of Dating Violence

Although the amount of research conducted on dating violence has increased over the last three decades, the prevalence of adolescent dating violence remains uncertain. *Variations* in research *methodology* have hampered attempts to understand the reality of the problem. In some cases, questionnaires have been especially inadequate. Even though government-sponsored large representative surveys have asked about adolescent DV, they generally have *not* probed for answers with multiple questions. They most commonly track issues such as alcohol/drug use, carrying weapons, gang membership, condom use, health, and injuries.

An obstacle to obtaining a representative sample of adolescent research participants is that researchers must obtain parental consent for adolescents to take the tests (S. M. Jackson, 1998; C. E. Murray & Graybeal, 2007). Finally, understanding the statistical results may be confusing. Researchers, for instance, collect data from victims and offenders who are *not* necessarily coupled with each other. Thus, boys who respond to the questionnaires are not necessarily the boyfriends of the girls who respond. Some estimates of adolescent dating violence include the following.

*Injury data.* In 1994, the injuries of boy/girlfriends treated in emergency rooms totaled 139,600 (9.8%) of the 1,417,500 emergency room patients. Of the 139,600 injured adolescent daters, the number of boys injured was 23,600, and the number of girls treated was 116,000 (Rand, 1997). According to MMWR (2008), about 10% of students nationwide suffered an injury caused by a boyfriend or girlfriend.

> **Centers for Disease Control & Prevention (CDC):** Physical, sexual, or psychological violence within a dating relationship.
>
> - Physical abuse—occurs when a teen is pinched, hit, shoved, or kicked
> - Emotional abuse—threatening a teen or harming his/her sense of self-worth
> - Sexual abuse—forcing a teen to engage in a sex act (e.g., fondling and rape)
>
> **National Youth Violence Prevention Resource Center (n.d.)** "Dating violence can take many forms, including psychological and emotional abuse, physical abuse, and sexual abuse."
>
> **Sabina & Straus's (2008) definition of dating violence:** The definition is operationalized by CTS2 questions. Polyvictimization: Two or more victimization types within the prior year.
>
> **Sugarman & Hotaling's (1989) definition of dating violence:** "Dating violence involves the perpetration of physical, emotional, or threat abuse by at least one member of an unmarried dating couple" (p. 5).

*Gender distinctions—dating violence.* Some disagreement exists over possible gender differences of victims and perpetrators of DV. Inconsistent findings are attributable to numerous factors. *Measurement* and *sample dissimilarities* account for many of the *inconsistencies.*

**TABLE 6.11**    Reported Percentages of Dating Violence by Gender, Race, and Grade

| Girls | Boys | Whites | Blacks | Hispanics | Grade | | | |
|---|---|---|---|---|---|---|---|---|
| 8.8% | 11.0% | 8.4% | 14.2% | 11.1% | 9th 8.5% | 10th 8.9% | 11th 10.6% | 12th 12.1% |

| TABLE 6.12 | Percentage of Dating Violence Victimization in North Carolina |
| --- | --- |

| 2005–Physical DV; N = 375–11.6% | | 2007–Physical DV; N = 372–12.5% | |
| --- | --- | --- | --- |
| Males: n = 167 44.7% | Females: n = 207 55.3% | Males: n = 188 51.1% | Females: n = 180 48.9% |

*Morbidity and Mortality Weekly Report (MMWR)* (Lobach, 2008)

Nationwide Victimization Survey: 14,041 completed questionnaires from students in Grades 7–12 (data from Youth Risk Behavior Surveillance System). The overall rate of dating violence was 9.9%. See Table 6.11 for percentages of dating violence by gender, race, and grade.

*Office of Juvenile Justice and Delinquency Prevention (OJJDP) (H. N. Snyder & McCurley, 2008). Data is from the National Incident-Based Reporting System (FBI)*:

3% of juvenile assaults are assaults of intimate partners.

73% of victims of juvenile boy/ girlfriends are females.

*Two North Carolina Dating Violence Surveys (Youth Risk Behavior Survey; Kim-Godwin, Clements, McCuiston, & Fox, 2010).* See Table 6.12 for DV victimization in North Carolina.

*National Longitudinal Study of Adolescent Health. Victimization data for same-sex DV (Halpern, Young, Waller, Martin, & Kupper, 2004) (N = 117)* Ages 12 to 17.

22% Same-sex dating violence

*Self-report surveys,* especially those derived from CTS2 data, reveal that DV is largely reciprocal or gender neutral (Hines & Saudino, 2003). See some of the findings below for information about contrasting gender findings (e.g., Banyard, Cross, & Modecki, 2006; Rand, 2009; M. Schwartz, O'Leary, & Kendziora, 1997; H. N. Snyder & McCurley, 2008):

- *Police reports* clearly reveal that teenage boys perpetrate more dating violence than girls.
- *Boys* are more likely than girls to engage in violent tactics like beating, while girls are more prone to hit, slap, or kick.
- *Injury statistics* document that girls suffer more frequent and severe injuries from DV than boys.
- *Sexual assault* statistics show a strong gendered effect with boys committing by far the largest number.
- *Motivations for DV* indicate that girls report more fear and self-defensive violence, while boys report a greater incentive to control a partner.
  - Girls' violence was self-defensive 37% of the time.
  - Boys' was self-defensive 6% of the time.
- Adolescent boys may judge themselves as less culpable for relationship violence than adolescent girls and thus not report their violence.
- Males may lie, minimize, or underreport DV.

*A qualitative gender analysis.* In an attempt to learn more about possible motivations for violent acts, a team of researchers conducted interviews with 116 boys and girls who had previously completed an *act scale* similar to CTS2. *Act scales* provide information about the frequency of acts (e.g., kicking) but no information about the context (e.g., self-defense). After completing the act scale, adolescents viewed a blank copy of the same scale and provided a narrative account of the *first and worst* times they had engaged in the behavior. The research team grouped the responses on the basis of similarity.

The team was able to classify the girls' responses into *four categories* and the boys into *one category* plus a *miscellaneous grouping*. The data indicated that over one third (38.5%) of the girls' responses were *self-defensive*, followed by *anger* responses (25%), *rule/value violation* responses (e.g., openly flirting with another girl) (19.2%), and *first-time aggression* (17.3%). The one category for boys was *escalation prevention* (e.g., holding her down so she would not hurt him), which was cited by most of the boys (64.3%). These findings suggested that boys and girl's have different reasons for dating violence (Foshee, Bauman, Linder, Rice, & Wilcher, 2007).

*Prevalence of same-sex peer violence versus dating violence.* One interesting inquiry compared the gender violence in dating couples and among same-sex peers (not selected for same-sex attraction). From a large pool of 7th, 9th, and 11/12th grade students, 4,131 students participated. Of this group, researchers identified 2,888 who had dated in the past year. A noteworthy aspect of this study was its use of the same measurement scale for assessing both dating and same-sex peer violence. In brief, the scale was a modified version of a scale used with high school students previously (Foshee, 1996). Data analyses yielded the customary gender distinctions among *dating students:* (a) *Girls* reported perpetrating more physical violence and psychological aggression than boys reported; and (b) *boys* were more likely to physically injure a date than girls were. For *same-sex peer violence,* boys reported more physical victimization and perpetration against their male peers than girls reported. Dating students were significantly *older* than nondating students (Swahn, Simon, Arias, & Bossarte, 2008). Using a similar methodology with 5,404 6th grade students, researchers found very similar results (Simon, Miller, Gorman-Smith, Orpinas, & Sullivan, 2010).

## Risk Factors for Dating Violence

Research has unveiled a number of factors that are associated with dating violence. Awareness of these indicators should be useful to teens trying to avoid dating violence (Centers for Disease Control and Prevention, 2006; see also Simon et al., 2010; see the review by Jouriles, Platt, & McDonald, 2009).

| | |
|---|---|
| Use of violence for conflict resolution | Alcohol/drug use |
| Inability to manage anger/frustration | Poor social skills |
| Association with violent friends | Problems at school |
| Acceptance of dating violence | Witnessing abuse at home |

Contemporary Canadian research has uncovered risk factors for "sustained psychological, sexual, and physical violence in romantic relationships of young women 12 to 24 years old" (Vézina & Hébert, 2007, p. 33).

| Depression | Beliefs that violence is justifiable |
| --- | --- |
| Substance use | Risky sexual practices |
| Prior victimization | Lack of parental supervision |
| Harsh discipline | Interacting with delinquent peers |

## Consequences of Dating Violence

In addition to an increased risk for *injury,* victims of dating violence are at increased risk for *binge drinking, suicide attempts, physical fights,* and *sexual activity* (CDC, 2006). Research has also highlighted other negative outcomes, such as injuries, ongoing abuse, revictimization, school drop-out, low self-esteem, depression, and anxiety (e.g., Collin-Vézina, Hébert, Manseau, Blais, & Fernet, 2006).

*Suicide.* A survey of 8,080 teenagers 14-plus years of age demonstrated that dating violence among girls and a lifetime history of sexual assault for boys were associated with suicide (Olshen, McVeigh, Wunsch-Hitzig, & Rickert, 2007; see also Ang, Chia, & Fung, 2006). Since suicide is the third-leading cause of death among teenagers, recognition of precipitants is vital (Centers for Disease Control and Prevention, 2007).

## Adolescents' Responses to Dating Violence

How to cope with relationship aggression presents another quandary for adolescent girls. Although some girls cope with a practical problem-solving response, others cope with ineffective coping strategies such as wishful thinking (Remillard & Lamb, 2005; Vashchenko, Lambidoni, & Brody, 2007). Frequently, victims take a *number of actions.* One post-assault survey of 183 *high school students* discerned the following reaction(s) to DV: (a) sought help from an informal source (e.g., friend, parent)—43%; (b) broke up or threatened to break up—37%; (c) fought back—35%; (d) took no action—32%; and (e) sought help from a professional—8% (J. M. Watson, Cascardi, Avery-Leaf, & O'Leary, 2001).

## Helpseeking Among Teen Dating Violence Victims

The sources of help adolescents seek out for help with DV have significant repercussions. Some isolated teens do not seek any help, and teens from different racial groups have different patterns of disclosure. At a developmental stage when teens are striving for independence, they most often turn to other teens for help while avoiding seeking help from their parents. Neither choice is entirely satisfactory (B. M. Black, Tolman, Callahan, Saunders, & Weisz, 2008). Both teens and parents lack professional knowledge of how best to help. Teens may be unaware about sources of help, and parents may try to take over or give unhelpful advice, such as suggesting the teen focus on the good aspects of the relationship (B. M. Black & Weisz, 2004). Nevertheless, teens generally receive support when they disclose the DV to their friends (Weisz, Tolman, Callahan, Saunders, & Black, 2007).

Social scientists trying to formulate adequate responses have suggested several program elements expected to be helpful. One is to help teens identify behaviors that are abusive. Another is to provide knowledge about where to seek help. Currently, the Internet has several websites that offer information about what to do and whom to tell. Teens witnessing DV also need facts about appropriate actions. Some scholars (Black et al., 2008) have suggested bystander intervention programs (Weisz & Black, 2009).

## Characteristics of Adolescents Who Are Violent in Intimate Relationships

Individuals who are *hypersensitive to rejection* by the important people in their lives are more likely to aggress against a date. According to specialists in the field, adolescents who felt rejected by their parents may develop a cognitive expectation of rejection. If other adolescents in their peer group are rejecting, their worst fears have come to fruition. To manage the anxiety they feel about ongoing interactions with peers, they may become aggressive in anticipation of rejection (see Purdie & Downey, 2000).

## Explaining Dating Violence

*Family-of-origin violence.* Contemporary research has repeatedly shown that family-of-origin violence is significantly related to dating violence for both males and females. The *interpersonal relationships* of juveniles with childhood histories of physical abuse are more likely than those of nonabused persons to be characterized by violence (Moylan et al., 2010; Pflieger & Vazsonyi, 2005; Windle & Mrug, 2009). There is also an association for adolescent males between involvement in *sibling abuse* and *later dating violence* (Simonelli, Mullis, Elliott, & Pierce, 2002). *Social learning theory* is the most frequently offered theory for associations such as these. (See the Sibling Abuse section above for an expanded discussion of social learning and adolescent violence.) Some analyses have uncovered specific associations between types of childhood abuse and involvement in DV (Sappington, Pharr, Tunstall, & Rickert, 1997). For instance, analysis of longitudinal data from the National Youth Survey ($N = 1,725$) found an association between adolescent physical abuse and DV (A. A. Fagan, 2005).

*Shaming/rejecting children.* One set of childhood feelings that may play a role in DV is shame or humiliation, and development of *shame* is influenced by parenting practices. Recent research has linked *harsh parenting* to *shame-proneness* among adolescents, with *parental rejection* during adolescence serving as a **mediator.** *Shame-proneness among adolescents* was also related to depression 2 years later. In brief, researchers assert that childhood abuse influences what children believe about violence, which, in turn, affects their involvement with antisocial peers (Stuewig & McCloskey, 2005).

*Family dysfunction.* Other scholars have evaluated the negative impacts of *family dysfunctions,* such as divorce, alcoholism, mental illness, inadequate parental monitoring, and possible genetic contributions (see Chapple, 2003; Kellogg, Burge, & Taylor, 2000; Lesch & Merschdorf, 2000).

*Attachment issues.* Attachment to a caretaker (Bowlby, 1980) represents a pivotal type of early learning, in this case learning in early life. As children develop into adolescents, they begin to fulfill some of their attachment needs by way of best friends and romantic partners (Markiewicz, Lawford, Doyle, & Haggart, 2006; Mayseless, 1991). Evidence is now available demonstrating that the quality of childhood attachment (e.g., secure, avoidant, fearful, preoccupied) extends into adulthood and profoundly affects the nature of an individual's later intimate relationships (see Rapoza & Baker, 2008).

*Socialization of girls.* S. A. Lloyd (1991) has proposed that two major facets of the culture increase the likelihood of dating violence: *gender-related themes* (i.e., male control and female dependency) and *romanticism* (the idea that "love conquers all"). First, young women who believe in the male control/female dependency model become more vulnerable to abuse. Second, romanticism may encourage dating partners to believe that their relationship problems are mainly situational (e.g., just an angry outburst) and will dissolve upon marriage. The case history of Claudia and Roberto represents a situation in which a young girl wants a romantic relationship no matter what the cost. The belief that love conquers all may prompt some individuals to accept DV on the grounds that their dating partners may change. (See www.sagepub. com/barnett3e for a brief discussion of dominance/romanticism.)

*Socialization of males.* One belief (among males) is that DV is acceptable (Foshee, Linder, MacDougall, & Bangdiwala, 2001); another is that DV is justifiable (O'Keefe, 1997; M. D. Schwartz et al., 1997). Violent families seem to spawn the formation of negative opinions about women and the development of male adolescent sexual promiscuity. These attitudes, in turn, appear to generate sexual assault (see Forbes & Adams-Curtis, 2001; Reitzel-Jaffe & Wolfe, 2001; Senn, Desmarais, Verberg, & Wood, 2000). Schools specifically and the broader society more generally perpetuate sexism by adopting the attitude that "boys will be boys," so nothing needs to be done to stop their violence. As a result, girls face harassment on a daily basis not only from other school-children, but also from some adult male teachers and administrators. Even the targets of many school shootings seem to be girls who have rejected a dating relationship with the shooter (J. Klein, 2006).

*Peer influences on dating violence.* Peers are more important during adolescence than in any other time of life. Social interactions with a mixed-gender adolescent peer group provide opportunities to find a romantic partner. Interactions with peers also help adolescents learn how to relate to the opposite sex (Connolly & Friedlander, 2009). A slow but steady stream of research has demonstrated that adolescent peer-group support for aggressive behavior encourages DV (Arriaga & Foshee, 2004; Connolly & Friedlander, 2009; Leff, 2005).

*Media influences.* For many years, researchers have been documenting the harmful effects on juveniles from being exposed to violent and sexual media. Although some disagreement remains, the majority of research studies have shown that viewing violence on television stimulates aggression. If nothing else, viewing violence desensitizes viewers (Bushman & Anderson, 2001, 2009).

## BOX 6.5 Media Influences on Adolescent Interpersonal Violence

Developmental psychologists have voiced alarm over the negative effects of exposure to TV violence and certain types of sexual content in the media. Despite scientific evidence linking exposure to violence and aggression, some skeptics have raised continuing doubts. Regrettably, political interests have fueled further questions about the generalizability of the findings (Ceci & Bjork, 2003).

*Television violence.* Consistent with theory, academicians in many fields and experts in medical professions have shown strong associations between media violence and aggression in children and adolescents. The generally accepted theories explaining the connection ". . . fall under the rubric of social-cognitive, information processing models. Such models focus on how people perceive, think, learn, and come to behave in particular ways" (C. A. Anderson et al., 2003, p. 94). Exposure to violence is linked with *learning* how to be violent. Knowing *how* to be violent, however, is not the same thing as *being* violent. Other factors, such as age, gender, and personality traits (e.g., anger, aggression), influence actual *performance* of behaviors (C. A. Anderson et al., 2003).

*Violent video games.* Questions have arisen about potential links between exposure to violent video games and violent behavior. The rationale for an even stronger link is that video game players are more *actively* involved than adolescents *passively* watching TV. Not surprisingly, findings stemming from research on video games are similar to those found for watching TV (e.g., Gentile, Lynch, Linder, & Walsh, 2004). The American Psychological Association, after examining the evidence, has reached the following conclusions (see Carll, 2006):

- Violent media, including video games, can increase thoughts of violence in teenagers.
- Suspicions of others' motives increases due to violent video game play.
- Teens who spend more time playing violent video games are more likely to argue with others than teens who do not spend as much time playing violent video games.
- Teens who play violent video games act aggressively soon after playing (while the effects may wear off, right after a game, a teen is more likely to be hostile).

Despite criticisms from some skeptics, a meta-analysis using over 18,000 participants in two cultures found robust support for game-elicited aggression. Specific effects included significant changes in the following domains: (a) *increased aggressive behavior,* (b) *increased aggressive cognition,* (c) *increased aggressive affect,* (d) *decreased prosocial behavior,* (e) *decreased empathy* (more desensitization), and (f) *increased physiological arousal* (Anderson et al., 2010).

*(Continued)*

(Continued)

*Sexually explicit media.* A third body of research has conducted some investigations of the negative effects of sexually explicit media (e.g., rape) on teen behavior. Some research has found links between this type of exposure and acceptance of rape myths (e.g., most women are raped by strangers; many women lie about being raped) (e.g., Franiuk, Seefelt, Cepress, & Vandello, 2008). Very little, if any, longitudinal research has appeared in the literature. Although information is sparse, a study of 433 adolescents found differences between those exposed to sexually explicit websites (SEWs) and several undesirable variables. Differences between the 55.4% who had visited a SEW and those who had not were as follows (Braun-Courville & Rojas, 2009):

- More than one sexual partner in the last 3 months
- More sexual partners overall
- Used alcohol or other substance during last sexual encounter
- Had anal sex
- Displayed higher sexual permissiveness scores

The battle to regulate exposure to television violence and videogame violence for children and adolescents continues.

## Legal Issues for Victims of Psychological/Physical Dating Violence

Until recently, teenagers had no option but to depend on their parents to obtain necessary legal protections. The *legal status of adolescents* (minors) based on age is especially relevant to the responses of the criminal justice system. By and large, the criminal justice system is *adult-centered* and has failed to acknowledge dating violence among adolescents. Any laws governing DV were often subsumed under adult laws. The Violence Against Women Act of 2000 for the first time extended many provisions protecting adult women to teenage women. Later, the House submitted H.R. 789: Teen Dating Violence Prevention Act of 2009. As of the writing of this book, the bill is pending in the Subcommittee on Crime, Terrorism, and Homeland Security.

All 50 states and the District of Columbia have civil laws to protect *adult victims* of domestic violence, but most states still lag behind on legislation to protect teens from DV because legally adolescents are minors. Many states fail to provide sufficient procedural and remedial provisions for teen victims. In fact, 13 states have *no laws* acknowledging dating violence as a basis for a protection order, and 6 states specifically exclude same-sex couples from obtaining protective orders. Many other states are simply *silent* in regard to same-sex teens. In 30 states, laws require a parent, guardian, or other adult to be involved in obtaining a protective order for a teen (see Lorenz, Davis, Ramakrishnan, & Chun, 2008; "Welcome to the Commission," 2009).

*Provisions for juvenile abusers.* Many states do not indicate whether laws are applicable to minor abusers, thus leaving the interpretation up to the judge. Some states specifically *exclude abusive minors* from their domestic violence statutes. Other states allow victims to obtain protective orders against minors, but the procedures available to enforce protective orders provide far less protection to victims. For example, in Oklahoma, some judges are failing to require abusive minors to undergo batterer treatment/counseling, anger management, or substance abuse counseling. In Michigan, minors who violate a protective order cannot be subject to a sentence that could have been imposed on an adult for the same offense (Lorenz et al., 2008).

## DATING/INTIMATE SEXUAL ASSAULT

### Prevalence

Some statistical summaries concerning dating/intimate assault of adolescents include the following.

*Centers for Disease Control and Prevention. Youth Risk Behavior Surveillance, United States. 2005 Surveillance Summaries, 2006. MMWR, 2006. Sexual Assault.* A 2005 survey of high school students disclosed the following rates of first rape victimization between the ages of 12 and 17.

| Females | Males |
|---------|-------|
| 34.9% | 27.9% |

*Age/gender/race of adolescents involved in sexual assault.* In one account, rates of assaults against juveniles making unwanted sexual advances were 17.1% against boys and 3% against girls (Molidor & Tolman, 1998).

*Morbidity and Mortality Weekly Report (MMWR)—Victimization (Easton, Shackelford, & Schipper, 2008).* A nationwide victimization survey consisting of 14,041 questionnaires from students in grades 7 through 12 found 7.8% forced sexual intercourse overall, 11.3% for girls overall and 4.5% for boys overall. See Table 6.13 for a summary of these findings.

**TABLE 6.13** Reported Percentages of Forced Sexual Intercourse by Race, Grade, and Gender

| White Females 11.0% | Black Females 13.3% | Hispanic Females 11.4% | *Grade* | *Boys* | *Girls* |
|---------------------|---------------------|------------------------|---------|--------|---------|
| | | | 9th | 4.1% | 9.2% |
| White Males 3.2% | Black Males 7.8% | Hispanic Males 6.2% | 10th | 3.4% | 13.1% |
| | | | 11th | 5.0% | 12.0% |
| — | | | 12th | 5.7% | 10.9% |

## Consequences of Dating Sexual Abuse

Sexual abuse has devastating consequences for victims that can take several forms. **Posttraumatic stress disorder (PTSD)** is an anxiety disorder produced by an extremely stressful event(s) and characterized by a number of adverse reactions. A summary of 19 studies revealed 7 clusters of symptoms: (a) *general disturbance*, (b) *emotional reaction* (e.g., terror), (c) *cognitive changes* (e.g., feeling confused), (d) *physical health* (e.g., alcohol consumption), (e) *social health* (e.g., avoiding certain locations), (f) *resource health* (e.g., disruption of school performance), and (g) *resilience* (e.g., decreased symptoms) (Spitzberg, 2002; see also Lewis, Jospitre, et al., 2006). A strong *risk factor* for sexual victimization in young adolescents is mental health problems (Turner, Finkelhor, & Ormrod, 2010).

## Explaining Sexual Abuse From Peers

Factors explaining sexual aggression from peers are beginning to emerge. Investigators conducted a 4-year longitudinal study of 200 adolescents by evaluating them annually beginning in the 10th grade. They assessed events occurring in the previous year along several dimensions: (a) *sexual experience*, (b) *romantic style*, (c) *romantic competence*, and (d) *rejection sensitivity*. The researchers analyzed the four waves of data via **survival analysis** (a time-to-event analysis, such as the length of time that elapses before an adolescent experiences another sexual assault). The analyses ascertained that 46.6% of the participants suffered sexual aggression from a peer, and as expected, girls (49%) suffered significantly more sexual assaults than boys (33%). Astoundingly, 65% of those victimized suffered another assault. The average time to revictimization was 1.33 years. The interpersonal dimension most predictive of sexual assault was *rejection sensitivity*. Adolescents above the median on the rejection sensitivity test were 31% more likely to be sexually aggressed upon than those below the median (B. J. Young & Furman, 2008).

## Legal Issues Concerning Dating Sexual Abuse

*Capacity to consent to sexual activity.* The legal age for consent varies across the United States from 16 to 18 years of age. Most states have *no laws* regarding age of consent for same-sex individuals. Some prosecutors only prosecute so-called *consensual* sexual cases of sexual assault if the offender is 2-plus years older than the victim (often referred to as statutory rape should the girl be young, perhaps 14 years old) (Livingstrong.com, 2009). Statutory rape charges may necessitate an assessment of the victim in cases where the girl is mentally retarded or mentally ill. The American Psychological Association states that therapists in court have the ethical obligation to explain to the court the limitations of any assessment procedure (American Psychological Association, 2002). As a side note, the criminal justice system does not often convict females of *female-to-male* sexual assault.

*Sexting.* Modern technology has currently created an unusual type of adolescent sex offender—one who sends sexual pictures and messages via e-mail (i.e., "sexting") to another adolescent friend. If a 35-year-old man e-mailed a picture of his genitals to a 14-year old girl, he would face criminal charges. If a 14-year-old girl sends a nude picture of herself to her current 15-year-old boyfriend, and he later e-mails it to his friends, she would face criminal charges. Authorities would place both persons' names on a sex registry. Advocates for teenagers assert that to place the girl's name on the registry goes beyond the intentions of the law. Many states are beginning to amend their laws, but the requirements are complex because of age limitations, the relationship between the sender and recipient of the e-mail, and the status of the person who distributes the pictures thereafter (T. Lewis, 2010).

## SAME-SEX ASSAULTS AMONG ADOLESCENTS

Although little information is available about gay, lesbian, bisexual, and transgendered (GLBT) youths, studies suggest that *dating violence and sexual assault* occur more frequently among same-sex youths than among non-same-sex youths. For example, a survey of high school students in Massachusetts revealed that those who reported same-sex sexual activities were twice as likely as those reporting only heterosexual contacts to be threatened or injured (Faulkner & Cranston, 1998).

## Same-Sex Adolescent Development

A number of investigators have speculated that same-sex adolescents have developmental issues such as limited friendships, poor parental relationships, and victimization experiences. Research on the topic has proliferated over the last 30 years. Still, most of the scholarship has placed same-sex questions within the framework of deficiencies, victimization, and resilience. Research with adolescent samples that could include sexual orientation variables fails to include them. As a case in point, the *mainstream* literature on bullying pays scant attention to the prevalence of bullying among adolescents attracted to same-sex peers (Horn, Kosciw, & Russell, 2009). One variable rarely included in current research is whether the student has "come out" to proclaim his or her attraction to same-sex persons.

A Canadian research team devised a comprehensive investigation that called for a passive parental consent procedure (e.g., send parents information about the research, etc.) to help achieve a close approximation to a *representative sample.* Researchers separated the 3,876 participants into four groups on the basis of their stated sexual attraction (not specifically sexual orientation): (a) *exclusively heterosexual attraction (EHA)*—3,594, (b) *mostly heterosexual attraction (MHA)*—124, (c) *bisexual attraction (BSA)*—122, and (d) *same-sex attraction (SSA)*—36. Measures consisted of four intrapersonal variables (e.g., attitudes toward risk-taking), three interpersonal variables (e.g., parental relationships), two environmental variables (*school climate*), and demographic information. From a large number of significant results, two seem most informative: (a) The EHA group compared with the other three had the most positive scores across each developmental domain, and (b) MHA, BSA, and SSA groups were not significantly different from each other across domains. Thus, "the primary difference between the four groups was between youth reporting exclusively heterosexual attractions and individuals reporting any degree of same-sex attraction" (Busseri, Willoughby, Chalmers, & Bogaert, 2006).

Dutch social scientists collected computer-based questionnaire data from 866 young adolescents (including 74 SSA students) whose average age was 13.61 years. Data analyses detected that SSA students rated the quality of their relationships with their fathers as lower than that of their heterosexual peers. Related to these lower-quality relationships, SSA adolescents suffered from more depression and lower self-esteem. SSA students, contrasted with non-SSA students, also identified less with their schools. The findings suggest that young Dutch SSA adolescents may have both mental health and school problems (Bos, Sandfort, de Bruyn, & Hakvoort, 2008).

## CASE HISTORY "I Just Want to Be Me"

Ceara Sturgis, a 17-year-old honor student in Jackson, Mississippi, encountered resistance when she went to get photographed for her senior yearbook picture. Ceara is a lesbian who has always been "out" about her sexuality. School officials critiqued her selection of clothing—a tuxedo—because only males were allowed to wear tuxedos. One problem was that Ceara did not even own a dress; she wore only boys' clothing. Ceara said she should be able to decide how she looks in the photo and that she just wanted to be herself (R. Smith, 2009). Later, the American Civil Liberties Union became involved, stating that the school was violating Ceara's constitutional rights, and the judge decided in favor of Ceara. The school cancelled the senior prom in response to the whole episode, and many of the students held Ceara responsible.

## Prejudice/Victimization of GLBT Youth

A study of 528 lesbian, gay, and bisexual youth disclosed more victimization than youth who are not SSA: (a) verbal—nearly 80%, (b) physical—11%, and (c) sexual—9%. Also, males reported more victimization than females (D'Augelli, Grossman, & Starks, 2006). A survey of two large middle school and high school samples (sample 1: $n = 20,509$; sample 2: $n = 16,917$) questioned students about friendships and school attendance with gay and lesbian (GL) peers. Data analyses revealed two major significant findings about willingness of heterosexual students to remain friends with and attend a school with GL peers: (a) Boys were less willing than girls; and (b) students in a more racially diverse school were more willing than those in a less racially diverse school (Poteat, Espelage, & Koenig, 2009).

*Nonconformity.* Prejudice may or may not be centered on a peer's sexual orientation as much as upon other factors. One inquiry of 264 high school youth examined their judgments of acceptability of their peers in regard to peers' conformity to gender norms related to appearance and mannerisms. Students judged straight, gay, and lesbian peers who did *not conform* as *less acceptable* than those who did. Unexpectedly, boys evaluated straight but nonconforming peers as less acceptable than conforming homosexual peers (Horn, 2007).

*Anti-harassment programs.* Schools make use of several types of programs to prevent victimization of same-sex youth. An analysis of 1,069 youths (14–18 years old) found that intimate/close contact between heterosexual and nonheterosexual youth reduces prejudice. That is, having acquaintances/friends who are homosexual reduces **heterosexism** among students (Heinze & Horn, 2009). Heterosexism refers to attitudes conveying that heterosexuality is superior to homosexuality and that stigmatize any nonheterosexual form of behavior. Researchers obtained survey data from a different sample of 2,037 heterosexual and homosexual (including those "Questioning"— ["Q"] their sexual orientation) high school students. The goal of the study was to determine whether associations existed between the two sets of variables.

> Perceptions about one set of school variables (e.g., policies, programs, social features)
>
> Perceptions of student experience variables (e.g., anti-GLBTQ harassment)

First, *policy* statements simply *referred* to the existence of antidiscrimination policies. Second, certain *programs* (e.g., classroom discussions) communicated attitudes of inclusion of persons of all sexual orientations. Third, the *social features* of the school referred to activities that allowed participation of everyone regardless of sexual orientation. The findings indicated that students were aware of whether the school tolerated antigay harassment. Also, the analyses indicated that there were associations between the two sets of variables. School policies and inclusive social activities were directly associated with perceptions of less GLBTQ harassment and outright victimization. Inclusive programs were associated, but not directly, with less antigay harassment and victimization. The researchers interpreted the results as showing that the ecology of the school affected levels of heterosexism and students' personal experiences of less exclusion based on sexual orientation (Chesir-Teran & Hughes, 2009).

## Medical Screening

Professionals also need to reach out to GLBT youths. Medical providers seldom query teenage patients about same-sex violence, nor do youths usually disclose their sexual orientations to their providers. Future research should investigate how professionals can best communicate with GLBT teens (N. D. Hoffman, Swann, & Freeman, 2003).

## PRACTICE, POLICY, AND PREVENTION FOR DATING VIOLENCE

### Practice

Developing general strategies to work with adolescents should be helpful for dating violence (Carlson, McNutt, & Choi, 2003). Experts recommend starting treatment with younger adolescents in middle school because current research suggests that the risk for dating violence increases with age (e.g., Howard, Wang, & Yan, 2007a, 2007b; Wolitzky-Taylor et al., 2008). (See the section on Revictimization below.) According to one teen DV prevention specialist, researchers must adopt multidimensional perspectives: (a) *developmental*, (b) *sociocultural*, and (c) *gendered* (Zurbriggen,

2009). Adolescent girls need help in recognizing the signs of an abusive partner, such as jealousy (K. A. Murphy & Smith, 2010). Legal scholars and legislators have obligations to devise and pass legislation to protect victims of dating violence and to rehabilitate offenders.

*Perpetrator treatment.* It is important to begin addressing dating violence among perpetrators. It is not too early to offer treatment/prevention programs to young men during their *teenage years.* Fortunately, culturally sensitive treatments are becoming better researched and more applicable (K. F. Jackson & Hodge, 2010). Because the vast majority of male batterers are young men, providing *community batterer intervention programs* aimed at this age-group should be beneficial (Bennett, Stroops, Call, & Flett, 2007; Peacock & Rothman, 2001).

*Peer counselors.* Finally, some experts believe that schools should consider preparing teens to be *peer counselors* for abused friends (Creighton & Kivel, 1993), because teens are most likely to disclose abuse to their peers. Others suggest harnessing peer influence as a *prevention strategy* to reduce dating aggression (Connolly & Friedlander, 2009).

## Policy

### BOX 6.6 Juvenile Justice System

Early on, the Court's goal was to rehabilitate juveniles before they entered a life of crime. At that time, policymakers deemed it appropriate to have judges make decisions about what treatment or punishment to order. Unexpectedly, assumptions about judges' wisdom and compassion were misplaced in a number of cases. As a case in point, a judge sentenced a juvenile for up to 5.5 years in prison for a crime that an adult committing the same crime would receive a maximum of 60 days. Such an egregious miscarriage of justice ended in the 1967 Supreme Court decision *In re Gault.* The Court required that henceforth juvenile courts must ensure legal representation for juveniles charged with a felony. Although a considerable amount of time has passed since the *Gault* (1967) decision, the majority of judges are not following the Court's mandates (see Bishop, 2010).

Despite the unambiguous nature of the ruling, courts and attorneys failed to follow through. Researchers demonstrated that an analysis contrasting data first gathered in 1994 and then again in 1999 showed no real improvement in implementing *In re Gault:* (a) In some courts, youths charged with a felony in 1999 were actually *less likely* to be represented by an attorney than youths charged with a misdemeanor; (b) "Justice by geography" statistics indicated that suburban youths were more likely to have representation than urban youths, and urban youths were more likely to be represented than rural youths; (c) In both 1994 and 1999, *younger* juveniles and *males* were more likely to be represented than older juveniles and females; and (d) Whites were more likely than Blacks to receive representation. Much of the problem rests with the added costs of implementation (Feld & Schaefer, 2010). Obviously, judicial inconsistencies need monitoring and remediation.

When juvenile crime exploded in the early 1990s, the criminal justice system responded with a "get tough" policy. One such strategy was to *transfer* juveniles who had committed serious crimes to the adult courts, where adult penalties prevailed. In making the determination to transfer, judges are to consider the juvenile's age and I.Q. as well as the seriousness of the crime. Juveniles adjudicated in adult courts typically receive *longer sentences* than those adjudicated in juvenile courts and even *harsher penalties* than their adult counterparts (see Kurlychek & Johnson, 2004; J. E. B. Myers, 2005). What is worse, juvenile transfers had *higher rearrest rates* and shorter times to reoffending then their nontransferred counterparts (e.g., Bishop, Frazier, Lanza-Kaduce, & Winner, 1996). Finally, juvenile transfers have no known deterrent effect on *adolescent crime,* although there *may* be a deterrent effect after the adolescents reach the *age of criminal responsibility.*

More and more organizations are joining efforts to prevent teen dating violence. As one example, the American Bar Association's Steering Committee on the Unmet Needs of Children has been actively engaged in trying to prevent teen dating violence.

*American Bar Association.* The American Bar Association wrote a pamphlet entitled "We Need to Talk." The ABA hopes to send a tool kit to every high school in the country (Tebo, 2005). The ABA has also written a book describing opportunities for attorneys to engage in pro bono work with youth ("Welcome to the Commission," 2009).

*Legal policy changes.* A duo of experts has proposed ideas on needed policy changes regarding adolescents (Lowenberg & Fulcher, 2008):

- States should ensure that *protective order laws* reflect typical teen relationships. Even the youngest victims of teen dating violence should be able to seek a protective order.

- Domestic violence laws must cover dating/cohabiting/marital relationships of minors.
  - They must provide minors with access to courts and legal counsel.
  - They must ensure minors' confidentiality.

- Whether a young person wishes to confide in his or her parents about being abused should *not* determine whether a state should provide protection.

- Minor petitioners seeking protective orders without parental involvement need a legal advocate. The court's inability to find a legal advocate should not prevent a minor from continuing the case.

- Statutes must ensure two factors, and services must be accessible to minors in the community and be affordable.
  - Minors are legally able to consent to services necessary to cope with the abuse.
  - Minors are able to contract/pay for legal services when they are not available free of charge.

- When abusers are under 18 years of age, laws must still protect victims and hold perpetrators accountable.

- Courts must also consider the perpetrating youth's age and consider confidentiality needs.

*Public awareness campaigns.* Congress designated the first full week of February as National Teen Dating Awareness Week. A Teen Kids News television broadcast honored the second year of the awareness campaign by interviewing Regina Schofield, assistant attorney general for the Office of Justice Programs. She promoted community action by stating that banding together would lead to vast improvements in the lives of children (News @ a Glance, 2007).

*Medical screening.* Health care professionals have been slow to recognize teen dating violence among their patients, and teenage patients have been equally slow to recognize their abuse (Forcier, Patel, & Kahn, 2003). In one survey, teenagers strongly endorsed medical screening, even if they did not feel like disclosing abuse at the time. Whether teens will disclose abuse to a health provider, of course, depends upon a configuration of factors: *personal factors* (e.g., fear of retaliation), *patient-provider factors* (e.g., trusting relationship), and *provider factors* (e.g., explaining screening procedures) (Freed, Gupta, Hynes, & Miller, 2003).

Variables such as race and lack of insurance coverage prevent many teens with psychological problems from obtaining help. One experienced nurse practitioner advises that it is necessary for health providers to provide screening for dating violence on every health maintenance visit and to provide anticipatory guidance. It is essential that teenagers have mental health care available to them. Obviously, one policy recommendation would be to modify insurance policies so that teens have access to mental health professionals (L. K. Brown, Puster, Vazquez, Hunter, & Lescano, 2007; Callahan, Tolman, & Saunders, 2004; Close, 2005).

## Prevention of Dating Violence and Sibling Abuse

The most appropriate time to begin prevention is at the onset of adolescence (Magdol et al., 1998). Although programs may successfully improve knowledge and attitudes about dating violence, not many have reported a reduction in *DV behavior* (e.g., Hickman et al., 2004; see D. J. Whitaker et al., 2006, for a comprehensive review of programs). Almost without exception, the program developers and counselors emphasized the need for a gendered approach. Separating boys and girls into same-sex groups was essential, and one pair of researchers/ practitioners remarked upon the necessity of providing culturally sensitive programs. As one illustration, the interventions included discussions about how racism hurt and how a target of racism felt victimized. Then they helped the largely African American group of incarcerated juveniles to think about how it felt to be victimized by sexism (Salazar & Cook, 2006).

*Safe Dates.* One progressive and successful DV prevention program is *Safe Dates,* which combines ongoing school activities (e.g., theater production) and community activities (e.g., support groups). To evaluate this program empirically, researchers provided a control group with community activities only. A 1-year follow-up assessment revealed a 25% reduction in emotional abuse and a 60% reduction in sexual abuse among Safe Dates participants (Foshee et al., 1998; Foshee et al., 2000).

*Break the Cycle.* Teen dating violence specialists have also examined the role of the school in providing assistance to abused adolescents. The Internet describes several programs for teens and their helpers. "Break the Cycle is an organization that works directly with young people, ages 12–14, providing innovative preventive education that is practical, teen-friendly, and effective" (Break the Cycle, n.d.). Break the Cycle holds focus groups with adolescents to learn their needs. Break the Cycle gathered a group of gay, lesbian, bisexual, transsexual, and questioning (**GLBTQ**) youth to solicit their feelings and opinions (Gallopin & Leigh, 2009):

- Most of these teens would tell a friend before a parent.
- A *few* had a trusted teacher that they could tell.
- A sizable minority dismissed the idea that a counselor could help.
- Most doubted the police could serve as a resource.
- They valued the idea of talking with a counselor specializing in these issues. They presumed that the conversation would be similar to talking with a stranger on a train—they would never have to see the provider again.
- They only have a responsibility to intervene in DV if a close friend is involved.
- The teens would help by offering a safe place to stay or to stay close to the victim in public.
- They thought that schools' responses are inconsistent and inadequate. Their suggestions follow:
  - Staff needs training
  - Schools should reach out to teens
  - Need a confidentiality policy
  - Have a dating violence policy
  - Create a safe place for GLBTQ teens

A legal intern working in the Break the Cycle program and the director of the program in Washington, DC, conducted follow-up evaluations at three sites. Staff conducted interventions with a variety of teens (not specifically same-sex teens), and then assessed differences between pre- and posttests. First, the teens enjoyed the program, and nearly 80% said they would share the new information they learned with others. The percentage of teens aware of the frequency of dating violence before the program doubled after the program. Knowledge regarding the warning signs of DV changed from 46.5% to 63.2%, and there was some improvement in recognizing how difficult it was to leave an abusive relationship (Dalal & Fulcher, 2006).

*Coaching Boys into Men Campaign (CBIM).* One fresh idea for preventing male-to-female dating violence enlists high school athletic coaches to act as role models. With funding from the Family Violence Prevention Fund (http://www.endabuse.org), Brian O'Connor originated the CBIM program and blended his talents with those of Juan Areán, program manager at the prevention fund, to launch the program. Their thinking was that coaches already serve as mentors and must deal with problems such as steroid use. In consultation with coaches, the duo devised the *CBIM Playbook,* a manual (tips) for coaches to use in trying to change violent behavior toward women, and they then *invited* (not directed) the coaches to participate. Future research will need to evaluate this promising adjunct to the effort to end male-to-female violence.

*Teen's opinions about dating.* As part of the Centers for Disease Control and Prevention's (CDC's) efforts to prevent teen dating violence, representatives planned a qualitative study. They conducted 12 focus groups of six to seven young teens drawn from a carefully selected sample (selected on dimensions of race, age, etc.). Carefully selected experienced group facilitators asked the teens' opinions on a number of themes. Some of their findings revealed highly gendered ideas (Noonan & Charles, 2009):

- *Healthy Relationships:* Boyfriends give girls gifts and protect them. Girls support boys and do things to please them.

- *Peer Group Norms:* Male peers refer to boys who treat their girlfriends well as weak and not manly. Girls who are nice to their boyfriends show that they really love them.

- *Unhealthy Relationships:* Couples argue a lot, spread rumors about each other, stop talking eventually, and break up. Boys try to save face if rejected, and may try to "put the girl down."

- *Physical Abuse:* Both boys and girls said physical abuse was wrong. Very few had witnessed physical abuse. African American youth, compared with others, said abuse was more frequent.

- *Sexual Abuse:* Sexual abuse refers to touching and kissing when the girl doesn't want to. Younger adolescents said it never happened. Girls in the eighth grade said sexual abuse was rare, but that some girls were willing. Most girls just "do it" if the boy wants to. Boys manipulate girls to get sex by threatening to break up and by other threats. Subtle acts of coercion are more acceptable than overt tactics such as grabbing. Girls feel pressured to have sex but run the risk of being called a slut.

- *Bystander Intervention:* Adolescents would probably *not* intervene if they saw abuse taking place. They would only intervene if the couple involved were their friends. It is dangerous to intervene, and older people (probably men) are more likely to intervene. Boys do not want to get involved.

- *Trusted and Credible Sources of Information:* If victimized, participants said that they would tell a friend first and some said they would consult with an older sibling. A few said they would tell their mother. A majority said they would not seek help from the school counselor or a teacher.

On the basis of these comments, the CDC researchers concluded that prevention programs would profit from several activities. The programs should try to make physical violence totally unacceptable. They should try to prevent low-level abuses such as spreading rumors, and they would help youth build skills (e.g., communication), especially in terms of intervening if witnessing physical or sexual abuse. Interventionists should devise gender-specific approaches to prevention as well as tailoring their efforts to different racial groups. Another approach is to inform boys about organizations such as *My Strength (http://www.mystrength.org)*, which uses the slogan "*My strength is not for hurting.*" It may be wise to educate peer counselors so that they would know what to say and how to make referrals.

*Expect respect.* Shaped from the above findings, researchers/practitioners crafted a *qualitative study* of students' statements and reactions to the Expect Respect program. Participants selected on the basis of their *gender, age,* and *ethnicity* met in separate gender groups for 24 support sessions with two same-gender group facilitators. Most of the 28 groups of 10 students each consisted of middle school and high school students, but members of 2 of the 14 groups for boys were inmates in juvenile detention settings. At the end of the 24-week sessions, the participants made a number of favorable comments that have proved fundamental to understanding what adolescents value in a program to change beliefs and behavior:

- *The group leader is like a friend.* The leader understands, empathizes, respects, and remains nonjudgmental about the content of the group discussions.
- *The group is like a special type of family.* Participants said they could say what they need to say and still be respected.
- *Effective group activities* included interactive games, mixed-gender discussions, and educational videos (e.g., "It Ain't Love"). Some of the boys felt empathy for the victim, a feeling they had not experienced before.
- *Challenges* consisted of finding it difficult to talk at first and the short length of the sessions. The next step is to draw upon these results to construct a usable outcome scale. A final step is to assess behavioral outcomes to determine if the programs reduce actual dating violence (Ball, Kerig, & Rosenbluth, 2009).

## SECTION SUMMARY

### Effects of Abuse on Adolescents' Behaviors

*Juvenile delinquency.* One particularly well-known adolescent behavioral problem that is related to adolescent maltreatment is juvenile delinquency. Juveniles commit an inordinate amount of crime. Family-related risk factors are the same as those mentioned previously, such as parental substance abuse, mental illness, and low socioeconomic status. One longitudinal survey reported that the delinquency rate is 47% higher for abused compared with nonabused adolescents. Polyvictimized adolescents registered the highest frequency of delinquency. Although the media has taken note of increasing arrest rates for teenage girls, these rates probably do not reflect increased female delinquency. Instead, police most likely have changed their arrest policies for female juveniles.

*(Continued)*

*Bullying.* Bullying at school is another unfortunate behavior related to abusive maltreatment of children at ages 6 to 11 and 12 to 17. Males display significantly more bullying behavior than girls, and while boys often bully physically, girls more often bully indirectly by spreading gossip, telling lies, and excluding certain girls. One force motivating boys to bully seems to be to enforce masculine norms for behavior. Bully victims may drop out of school or be unable to perform well academically. Antibullying programs appear to be effective, but schools may not implement them.

Internet bullying/Internet harassment is a newer form of hurting one's peers. Its anonymity makes it an easier behavior to perform. Few gender differences exist among cyberbullying offenders. Internet harassment is rarely outlawed, but it has some of the same negative outcomes as schoolyard bullying. Several cases of suicide following teen bully victimization have appeared in the media. Policies need to be in place to intervene and prevent Internet harassment.

*Teen dating violence.* More and more research has accumulated about adolescent dating violence. A number of DV surveys suggest that dating violence is gender equivalent, but others do not. The Office of Juvenile Justice and Delinquency Prevention found that boys perpetrated 73% of DV assaults. Other studies show that girls perpetrate as much or more than boys. Injury data clearly indicate that girls are more victimized than boys. The motivations for assaulting a dating partner vary by gender. While boys say they may prevent girls from striking them by "holding them down," girls may perpetrate abuse in self-defense, because the boy has broken a rule (e.g., flirted with another girl) or as a first use of aggression. Male same-sex adolescents reported more physical offending and victimization than females.

Not surprisingly, more teenage girls report a sexual assault than teenage boys. Unfortunately, girls assaulted once are likely to suffer another assault. Laws govern the age of legal consent, usually 16 or 17. Older boys or men are subject to charges of statutory rape if they have sex with an underage girl even if she consents. Prevention programs should be offered in school during the teenage years. Fortunately, a number of programs are available.

Teens are frequently reluctant to disclose their abuse to others. Most often they tell a friend who usually is too inexperienced to offer good advice. Because of this pattern, some experts suggest that some teens receive peer counseling training. Teens also break up if their partner is abusive. Significantly more violent dating partners come from violent/dysfunctional homes than do nonviolent dating partners. Nevertheless, peers and the media influence adolescents' dating violence.

*Media exposure.* Another cause of adolescent violence is exposure to the media. Although this connection has been evident for many years, political interests have successfully prevented management of violence on TV and in video games. Teens exposed to media violence display more aggressive behavior, have more aggressive thoughts, show more anger, show less empathy, exhibit decreased prosocial behavior, and display increased physiological arousal contrasted with those less exposed. Moreover, viewing sexually explicit media appears to increase sexual activities among teens and increase substance use.

***Juvenile justice system.*** The ruling known as *In re Gault* requires that all juveniles charged with a felony be provided with legal representation. Much to the dismay of legal scholars, however, juvenile court judges across the nation are not obeying legal mandates set forth by state legislatures or even by the Supreme Court. A second important consideration is transferring juveniles to adult courts. Here they often receive harsher sentences than adults convicted of the same crime.

Adolescents involved in dating violence need legal protections. Organizations such as the American Bar Association (ABA) have offered some assistance by recommending specific changes, such as allowing teens to obtain orders of protection. To help teens, the ABA has also written a booklet that ought to be available in every high school in the nation.

## REVICTIMIZATION

Understanding the phenomenon of revictimization is vital to the topic of family violence because traumatic experiences, with their long-lasting negative effects, are so frequently perpetrated by family members and intimates. *Victimization* evokes psychological repercussions, such as *anxiety, depression, substance abuse,* and *PTSD* (Kimmerling, Alverez, Pavao, Kaminiski, & Baumrind, 2007). An especially widespread and disturbing finding is that *any* victimization in childhood is likely to increase the likelihood of continued victimization in adolescence and young adulthood (Finkelhor, Ormrod, & Turner, 2007b). Unfortunately, revictimization studies authenticate Koss's (1990, p. 374) early observation:

> Experiencing violence transforms people into victims and changes their lives forever. Once victimized, one can never again feel quite as invulnerable.

One illuminating study from Canada provided considerable detail about traumas among 774 adolescents. The researchers collected several types of data: (a) *mothers' reports* of life events (traumas) that occurred in the girls' 14th years, (b) *teachers' reports* of externalizing behaviors (restlessness and bullying) during kindergarten, (c) *adolescent girls' retrospective reports* of child sexual abuse (CSA), (d) *dating violence* at age 15, and (e) *mental health problems.* Results revealed that 46% of girls with a history of CSA reported significantly more psychological, physical, and sexual abuse than the 25% of the girls without a history of CSA. Both CSA and DV were separately and significantly linked with mental health symptoms. Nonetheless, 53.3% of the CSA victims were *not* victimized by dating violence at age 15 (Hébert, Lavoie, Vitaro, McDuff, & Tremblay, 2008).

1. What is your opinion about separating adolescent abuse from child abuse?

2. What are the forms of adolescent maltreatment?

3. Of the various consequences of adolescent maltreatment, which is the most damaging in your opinion?

4. Should adolescents who run away from home be placed in juvenile hall? Why or why not?

5. Discuss parricide, its frequency, gender of perpetrator/victim, and causes.

6. Why is defining sibling abuse such a challenge? Should society be concerned about sibling abuse?

7. Should society be concerned with adolescent bullying perpetrators and victims? What are some of the causes of perpetration and victimization?

8. What factors help explain adolescent dating violence?

9. Should schools help same-sex adolescents feel more comfortable at school? What student attitudes do school administrators need to address?

10. Evaluate the juvenile criminal justice system.

For chapter-specific resources including audio and video links, SAGE research articles, additional case studies, and more, please visit www.sagepub.com/barnett3e.

# 7

# Dating Aggression, Sexual Assault, and Stalking

## *Primarily Unmarried, College-Age Individuals*

### CASE HISTORY   Ivana and Bruce—Teaching Her a Lesson

Ivana and Bruce met during their senior year in high school. After a few dates they fell madly in love, and by the end of high school they began talking about marriage. Most of the time, Ivana felt very proud and lucky to have "landed" Bruce. Occasionally, however, Bruce was unexpectedly moody and jealous. He voiced numerous suspicions about whether Ivana was lying to him. Eventually, he secretly began to follow Ivana. He liked to follow her unobtrusively in his car as she walked to her house after school, and later he would ask her detailed questions about her trip home. In time, Ivana noticed Bruce's car parked here and there on the route to her house. Although Bruce's angry outbursts were unpleasant, Ivana felt that his possessiveness was a sign of true love. His constant watchfulness actually made her feel secure.

On one occasion, Bruce accused Ivana of being insensitive to his feelings. After thinking it over, Ivana decided that Bruce was probably right, and she resolved to be very careful about how she treated him. This didn't seem to help Bruce feel more relaxed, however. He began complaining about Ivana's many friends, who "took up all her time." Ivana felt somewhat confused, so she discussed the situation with her best friend, who urged her to work it out with Bruce if she really loved him. Ivana decided to try even harder to please Bruce, because they had been dating for nearly a year and a half and she believed that Bruce really loved her.

Next, Bruce started to call Ivana several times a day, "just to check in." Although Ivana felt pressured by these calls, she thought that Bruce was just insecure and that he surely would finally come to believe that she loved him and no one else. She still had a lot of hope that Bruce would change.

One evening when Bruce came to pick Ivana up for a date, he became angry because she was wearing a tight sweater. He wanted to know why she was "trying to turn on other guys";

wasn't he enough for her? Ivana was shocked, but she assured Bruce that she loved only him and she would be glad to change her clothes. After all, changing into a loose blouse wasn't too much to ask, she thought. Bruce appreciated her effort and was very attentive and loving during the date, but for the first time Ivana felt vaguely disturbed by Bruce's behavior. She also felt disappointed that he couldn't seem to trust her.

When it came time for Ivana to go on vacation with her family to Tahiti, Bruce forbade her to go. Ivana still planned to go, but she stopped talking to Bruce about the trip. One day, however, Bruce came over while Ivana was packing for the vacation. When he saw what she was doing, he searched her suitcases and removed all her bathing suits. Ivana still loved him, but she felt burdened, restricted, and uneasy. Bruce seemed to be watching her every move. She hoped that the trip to Tahiti, and the break from school and from Bruce it provided, might help her to relax and clear her mind. It didn't.

When Ivana returned home with her family, she put together an album of snapshots from the trip. Bruce visited soon after, and he decided to look through the album. When he saw snapshots of Ivana in a bikini, he "went ballistic," screaming, shaking Ivana, and finally tearing out sections of the album. Ivana broke off her relationship with Bruce with a heavy heart. She felt she had failed somehow to convince him that she really loved him.

After a few weeks, Ivana decided to accept a date with Bruce and to try again to work out their relationship. After all, he had apologized and promised never to become violent again. The date went fine until the end of the evening, when they drove out to the beach; although Bruce had seemed nonchalant up to that point, his mood suddenly turned ugly. He began to yell at Ivana, saying that she had never loved him. He called her a "no-good, f—g bitch." Although Ivana was upset and furious, she did everything she could think of to calm Bruce down. She told him that she loved him, but that simply seemed to enrage him further. Suddenly, Bruce grabbed Ivana by the throat and began to slap her and choke her. She tried to fight back by scratching him and pulling his hair, but she was no match for him. She could hardly believe what was happening. Bruce ripped off her clothes and raped her, all the time cursing at her and screaming, "I'll teach you to fool around behind my back." Finally he pushed Ivana out of the car and left her sobbing on the beach.

Ivana did not call the police or tell anyone what had happened to her that night for more than 2 years. Although Bruce eventually apologized to her for his behavior, Ivana refused to see him ever again.

T he case history above contains a number of elements typical of dating violence in a college-age couple. Note how Ivana wanted to please Bruce and how he felt he needed to control her. Also noteworthy is that the abuse eventually led to a sexual assault. For some, the term dating violence (DV) is inclusive of sexual assault (SA) and stalking (ST). Research, however, usually focuses on one of the three types: DV, SA, or ST. Individuals involved in dating violence are typically adolescents in middle school or high school (12–19 years old) or unmarried college students (18–26 years old). Research concerning interpersonal violence among individuals younger than 12 and among young adults who are not students is rare. Although cohabiters constitute a group of unmarried intimates, their similarities to married couples usually place them out of the realm of typical dating couples.

*Difference between dating violence and marital violence.* One major difference between DV and marital violence is the greater focus on sexual assault factors within the DV framework. A second dissimilarity exists in the amounts and kinds of information available. A third is that young people do not construe the meaning of intimate partner violence the same way that older, midlife couples do (Kimmel, 2002). In fact, a perusal of the available literature reveals that the majority of researchers use the term dating violence as a reference to adolescents' interpersonal violence, while IPV is used more frequently for older and often married individuals. Only recently have government agencies begun to classify intimate violence by boyfriends and girlfriends as a separate category of crime. A fourth difference between DV and marital violence lies in society's attitudes toward violence between adolescents/college-age persons compared with those between adults. Society has been more concerned with protecting unmarried than married women.

*Beginning of study.* The formal beginning of research on dating violence appears to be Kanin's (1957) landmark study of male aggression toward female dates. It soon became clear that being young and in love does not protect adolescents and young adults from interpersonal violence. A sampling of the DV research reveals an emphasis on proviolence attitudes, especially in terms of sex-role attitudes, male peer-group support, the relationship between alcohol consumption and DV, and gender dissimilarities in acceptance of rape myths. Academicians have also made some headway in understanding the configurations of individual psychological and dyadic factors that promote aggression. Experts do not agree on what causes dating violence, although many offer a social learning explanation. Media violence may play a role as well. Finally, advocates working in the field of DV have actively pursued programs of *education and prevention.*

## FACTORS IN PREVALENCE ESTIMATES OF DATING VIOLENCE, SEXUAL ASSAULT, AND STALKING

As is true of other forms of intimate violence, when dating violence occurs, it usually takes place in private so it is difficult to detect. The problems in interpersonal violence research in general that are summarized in Chapter 2 are all too obvious in estimates of DV, SA, and ST. Lack of theoretical anchors, ambiguous definitions, inadequate questions, inappropriate questionnaire contexts, and suboptimal data collection methods have impeded disclosure of DV, SA, and ST and account for the wide variability in estimates. Problems with sample selection and data analysis techniques have further obscured interpretations of findings (Hilton, Harris, & Rice, 1998).

*Age.* The frequency of dating violence tends to be inversely correlated with age. That is, as age increases, DV decreases. Female college students reported using more DV as adolescents than as college students and more as college freshmen than as college seniors (Graves, Sechrist, White, & Paradise, 2005). Actually, a decrease in DV with age is not surprising, since experts have reported historically that general violence and crime also decreases with age. Between 1998 and 2002, adults 18 to 24 years of age comprised 11.7% of the population over age 12, but 17.6% of the family violence victims (Durose, et.al, 2005).

*Sources of estimates.* In the past, one obstacle in deciphering prevalence rates for DV, SA, and ST was the lack of specificity inherent in the statistical summaries published by government agencies. Until the 1990s, statisticians placed interpersonal violence data into one of two categories: "known offender" or "unknown offender (stranger)." Data from the 1992–1993 National Crime Victimization Survey (NCVS), based on self-reports, were the first assault data available disaggregated by relationship status. Researchers were finally able to report information about dating partners (current and former combined) as a category separate from other intimate couples (Bachman & Saltzman, 1995).

In addition to government surveys, independent researchers have conducted numerous smaller studies of DV, SA, and ST. They have slowly expanded their scope to include ethnic minorities, immigrants, and other seldom-evaluated groups in their study sample. Experts in countries other than the United States have also begun to assess the various aspects of interpersonal violence.

## DATING VIOLENCE

### Defining Dating Violence

Researchers often assume that the term dating violence is so easily understood that they have no need to define it. In the same vein, they rarely bother to define the meaning of the word dating. Dating may be defined as couple interaction with emotional commitment, with or without sexual intimacy and may or may not be heterosexual. The definition of DV used in this text is a modified and updated version of Sugarman and Hotaling's (1989) definition: "*Dating violence involves the perpetration of physical, emotional, or threat abuse by at least one member of an unmarried dating couple*" (p. 5).

*Operational definitions of DV.* Operational definitions of dating violence are quite similar to those developed for intimate partner violence (IPV; see Chapter 8 for more details). That is, researchers define DV in terms of the *frequency and severity* of interpersonally violent behaviors. The items that investigators use to assess DV are most commonly anchored in the Revised Conflict Tactics Scale (CTS2; Straus, Hamby, Boney-McCoy, & Sugarman, 1996) and vary along the same dimensions (refer back to Chapter 2).

*Legal definitions?* It is necessary to keep in mind that many victims/perpetrators of dating violence do not recognize that the behaviors involved are those legally defined as DV. For individuals over the age of 16 to 18, most laws pertaining to individuals involved in DV have been the same as those applying to unpartnered individuals. That is, laws prohibit physically assaulting others (for a review, see Ferguson, 1998). Since the inception and updating of the Violence Against Women Act (Violence Against Women Office, 2000, 2005; see also Conyers, 2007), laws protecting women from male assault have increased and been refined. Few legal definitions of dating violence exist.

### Mutual/Reciprocal Dating Violence

One account of *reciprocal intimate partner abuse* among a *national sample* of 11,370 young adults based its findings on three questions about IPV (Whitaker, Haileyesus, Swahn, & Saltzman, 2007).

There was one item about one's own violence, another about one's partner's violence, and a third about reciprocal IPV. This research group reported that *reciprocal (bilateral, mutual, bidirectional) violence* was the *most common form* of partner violence. Bilateral IPV occurred more frequently (49%) than any other type of DV. These data are not totally convincing, however, because they are based upon only three test items, and they fail to reveal the severity of the violence. Further, they do not take into account sexual violence, underreporting, contextual influences, or a host of other appraisal issues.

*Measurement and gender difference issues.* Do men and women exhibit dissimilar patterns of interpersonal violence? Both male and female college students participate in DV, SA, and ST. Whether gender discrepancies appear varies according to the type of data gathered. Self-report surveys, primarily derived from CTS2 scores, reveal that DV is largely reciprocal or gender neutral (Archer, 2000). Some analysts have found even greater DV perpetration by women than by men (see L. W. Bennett & Fineran, 1998; Majdan, 1998; Moffitt, 1997).

In contrast, studies based on other data sources give the impression that young men perpetrate far more DV than do young women. Results derived from other measurements, such as the revised NCVS self-reports, the FBI's accumulation of police reports, and the National Violence Against Women Survey (NVAWS) (Tjaden & Thoennes, 1998b) all substantiate *large gender disparities* in dating violence and sexual assault. Analyses indicate that disproportionately, boyfriends/ex-boyfriends assault girlfriends/ex-girlfriends (Rand, 2009).

Scholars concerned with accounting for the gender parity results arising from CTS2-based dating violence have searched for explanations beyond those generally plaguing self-report data. Some suggest that the equivalence stems from gender differences in reporting. Men may judge themselves as less culpable for relationship violence than women, or men may lie, minimize the severity of violence, or underreport. (See Finn & Bettis, 2006, for a review.) Contemporary research has attributed serious deficiencies to partner violence assessment as a whole. Researchers do not think summing the frequency of abuse items is sufficient given that the severity of items varies (Hays & Emelianchik, 2009).

## Prevalence Estimates of Dating Violence

**TABLE 7.1**    Assaults by Gender and Relationship of the *Victim*

| Victim Category | % Males | % Females | All Offenses |
|---|---|---|---|
| Boyfriends/Girlfriends | 14.1 | 85.9 | 100% |
| Friend or Acquaintance | 53.7 | 46.3 | 100% |
| Strangers | 68.3 | 31.7 | 100% |

SOURCE: Rand, 2009.

**TABLE 7.2** Assaults by Gender and Relationship of the *Offender*

| Offender Category | % Males | % Females | All Offenses |
|---|---|---|---|
| Boyfriends/girlfriends | 81.9 | 18.1 | 100% |
| Friend or acquaintance | 74.0 | 26.0 | 100% |
| Strangers | 85.8 | 14.2 | 100% |

SOURCE: Federal Bureau of Investigation, 2000.

(See the tables at www.sagepub.com/barnett3e for estimates along several dimensions of interpersonal violence among large samples of adolescents, college students, and young people; also see Sabina & Straus, 2008.)

## Consequences of Dating Violence

There are many costs related to interpersonal violence victimization. For some victims, the worst outcome is injury. Both men and women sustain *injuries* as a result of dating violence, but without exception surveys show that women receive more physical injuries from male intimates than the reverse. The National Violence Against Women Survey (Tjaden & Thoennes, 2000a) reported that 42% of women and 20% of men who were assaulted by intimates received injuries, mainly minor injuries (see also Breiding, Black, & Ryan, 2008). For others, the worst outcome is negative health consequences, such as chronic pain and sleep disorders. For still others, it is long-lasting psychological distress, such as posttraumatic stress disorder (PTSD) (e.g., A. L. Coker, Davis et al., 2002; Crofford, 2007; Ismail, Berman, & Ward-Griffin, 2007).

## Explaining Dating Violence

As is common in other subareas of family violence research, experts have hypothesized that patriarchal *beliefs and attitudes* encourage dating violence. Hostility toward women is another attitude that contributes to DV. Most young people disavow DV in general, but find it acceptable under some circumstances. Some well known **risk factors** for dating violence entail *alcohol use* and *observing interparental violence* in one's childhood home. One child abuse investigator reported that the *impact of child maltreatment* extended into young adulthood where it became a risk factor for intimate partner violence (T. I. Herrenkohl et al., 2004; Black, Sussman, & Unger, 2010). Harsh physical punishment also has a direct effect on perpetration of dating violence among college males (L. G. Simons, Burt, & Simons, 2008). Although far less common, *mental illness* is another risk factor, and some suggest *peer pressure* (DeKeseredy & Kelly, 1993) is yet another.

*Women's rationales for dating violence.* One investigation drew upon and expanded previous research on women's rationales for perpetrating physical dating violence. Research participants were 127 college women who completed five questionnaires, including one with an open-ended portion. For the dating violence questionnaire, they completed one for themselves and one for their male partner. Data analyses revealed several significant differences in types of abuse. Women pushed/grabbed/shoved, slapped, kicked/bit/hit their male partner significantly more often than the reverse, while men physically restrained and forced oral sex more than women did. Responses given on the open-end section indicated that the six most frequently reported *reasons* for DV, in descending order, were anger, escalating verbal argument, frustration, emotional hurt, retaliation for a verbal act, and poor communication. Closed-end responses for the *main cause* of their DV, in descending order of frequency, were anger, partner lied, poor communication, temper, embarrassment, and jealousy.

*Not self-defense.* One especially illuminating finding was that college women did *not* use self-defensive DV in the same manner as battered women and community women do. Although verbal arguments often preceded women's DV, the content/topic of the arguments is unstated. The researchers point out that their findings and those of others raise doubts about whether interpersonal violence among college students and married couples, in which both partners are research participants, is comparable to that of couples involved in battering relationships (Hettrich & O'Leary, 2007; also see Mahlstedt & Welsh, 2005). Results of an investigation with a primarily Hispanic sample were somewhat contradictory to the previous two studies. A path analysis using data from 232 college students found gender-equivalent frequency of dating violence; women's but not men's DV was *reactive.* That is, men initiated DV and then women responded with female-to-male violence (C. T. Allen, Swan, & Raghavan, 2009).

*Preferences for abusive partners or partners to abuse.* Do *college women's* prior *psychologically abusive experiences* lead to their preference for *college* male dating partners who have traits associated with an *abusive personality?* Do college women with *lower self-esteem* prefer male dating partners who have traits associated with an *abusive personality?* Do psychologically abusive men show a preference for dating women with *high attachment anxiety (overly concerned with abandonment)?* A complex, multistep investigation shed light on two events: (a) *the trajectory of events* determining women's preferences for a psychologically abusive male date, and (b) *men's preferences* for a dating partner with high attachment anxiety (Zayas & Shoda, 2007). (See www.sagepub.com/barnett3e for some of the interesting experimental details about the composition of dating ads on a computer dating service used in this experiment.)

*Study 1.* A group of 65 women rated their own level of *attachment anxiety and self-esteem. These variables* were significantly and negatively correlated for these women. They also completed questionnaires about *previous psychological and physical abuse* experiences. In another phase of the experiment, the women participated in a computer dating procedure to select a preferred date. The ads of the 16 possible dates appeared on the experimenter-prepared dating service list. Results revealed that *abusiveness* was generally negatively associated with dating preference. Then again, a more detailed analysis supported the researchers' hypotheses. Women who received *higher psychological abuse* scores preferred an *abusive date* significantly more than women with lower psychological abuse scores.

*Study 2.* In a separate inquiry, 93 men responded to ads about potential female daters who manifested the following combination of attachment variables: (a) *low anxiety/low avoidance;* (b) *high anxiety/high avoidance;* (c) *low anxiety/high avoidance;* and (d) *high anxiety/low avoidance.* The men also indicated the extent to which they had psychologically abused a female dating partner. Overall the men preferred women who had *low anxiety/low avoidance traits.* As hypothesized, however, men who reported *more* instances of inflicting *psychological abuse* toward a dating partner preferred *women* who suffered from *high attachment disorder* (i.e., high attachment/high avoidance). These studies suggest that the combination of vulnerable college women's choices of a dating partner and abusive men's choices may be a factor in dating violence (Zayas & Shoda, 2007). (See the section in the previous chapter on Revictimization.)

## Attachment Issues

Adult attachment is a relatively long-lasting *affectional bond* that is typified by wanting to be close to a romantic partner (Feeney & Noller, 1996). An advantage of attachment theory is its ability to explain the *co-occurrence of love and violence. Attachment* can account for a partner's "on-again, off-again" romantic behavior as well as the stress caused by its variability (e.g., Billingham, 1987; see also Gormley & Lopez, 2010; Sbarra & Ferrer, 2006; Seiffge-Krenke, 2006).

Attachment consists of both *cognitive and emotional mental representations* that guide attachment-related behavior (Collins, Guichard, & Ford, 2006). As the concept of adult attachment evolved, theorists reconceptualized it as featuring two dimensions: (a) *positive/negative view of the self,* and (b) *anxious/avoidance responding* (Bartholomew & Horowitz, 1991; see also Roisman, 2009). Combining self-views with views of others yields four types of attachment: *secure, preoccupied, dismissing,* and *fearful. Dismissing, fearful,* and *preoccupied* attachment styles are all insecure types of attachment. Table 7.3 presents these attachment orientations:

**TABLE 7.3**  Prototypical Attachment Orientations

| View of Self | Positive View of Others | Negative View of Others |
|---|---|---|
| Positive | **Secure attachment**<br>Low attachment anxiety<br>Low avoidance | **Dismissing attachment**<br>Low attachment anxiety<br>High avoidance of others<br>Avoid dyadic closeness<br>Use distancing strategies |
| Negative | **Preoccupied attachment**<br>High attachment anxiety<br>Low avoidance of others<br>Seek dyadic closeness<br>Use pursuit strategies | **Fearful attachment**<br>High attachment anxiety<br>High avoidance of others<br>Avoid dyadic closeness<br>Use distancing strategies |

SOURCES: Bartholomew & Horowitz, 1991; Fraley & Waller, 1998.

Attachment *research* has proliferated in the past decade, with most results confirming the concept's usefulness in accounting for interpersonally violent behaviors (e.g., Chapple, 2003; Wigman, Graham-Kevan, & Archer, 2008). Evidence indicates that attachment styles vary among dating pairs, with *securely attached* couples reporting higher levels of *relationship satisfaction* than insecurely attached couples (see Bartholomew, 1997; Frazier, Byer, Fischer, Wright, & DeBord, 1996). To explain the role of *dysfunctional attachment* in DV, researchers have proposed a model that includes a four-step sequence of events: *Anxious attachment (dysfunctional)* to a romantic partner evokes *anger,* which in turn precipitates efforts to *control* one's partner, which then leads to *DV* (Follingstad, Bradley, Helff, & Laughlin, 2002).

*High partner commitment.* One of the most disheartening findings in the literature is that inter-partner *aggression* occurs more frequently in relationships typified by *high commitment levels.* Indeed, research has shown that both *length of relationship* and *commitment level* are positively correlated with dating violence (Doumas, Pearson, Elgin, & McKinley, 2008). The link between commitment and DV seems illogical because unmarried persons can simply break off an abusive relationship (Carlson, 1996). After all, dating couples rarely share income or children. One explanation is that commitment in an abusive relationship may represent *strong emotional feelings* that can be linked with *attachment and dependency needs* (Griffing et al., 2002; see also Barry, Lawrence, & Langer, 2008). (For a discussion on the effects of *normative beliefs* on college women's commitment/persistence in a dating relationship, see www.sagepub.com/barnett3e.)

### Jealousy

Whether jealousy is a *sign of love* or a dangerous *precipitant of dating violence* and *sexual assault* is "in the eye of the beholder." Many college students consider jealousy to be a sign of love, a normal reaction to the possibility of losing a valuable mate. Family violence experts, in contra-distinction, think jealousy is *not* a sign of love, but possibly a sign of controlling behavior and may even be a danger sign that signifies partner violence. Can both viewpoints be true? One consideration is that there are *multiple meanings of jealousy* and *several scales* that operationalize the concept. As a construct, jealousy comprises several intense feelings, such as *anger, blame,* and *hurt* (Stenner & Rogers, 1998). (See www.sagepub.com/barnett3e for a table of diverse viewpoints about jealousy.)

*The meaning of jealousy.* One series of investigations with undergraduates tried to shed light on the *meaning of jealousy* (Puente & Cohen, 2003):

- When jealousy is the motivation for violence, it *changes the meaning of violence.*
- Students are likely to construe *jealousy as a sign of romantic love.*
- The results are similar for emotional and sexual abuse contexts.
- Students also judge *jealousy-related abuse,* relative to nonjealousy-related abuse, as more *understandable* and therefore less likely to indicate a relationship will end soon.
- On balance, students perceive jealousy-related violence as *qualitatively different* from nonjealousy-related violence.

(See www.sagepub.com/barnett3e for details of the Puente & Cohen, 2003, study.)

*Gender differences in jealousy.* An early study of jealousy identified several gender distinctions (Paul & Galloway, 1994):

- Men are more *uncertain* of women's fidelity than the reverse.
- The majority of students said they would *take no action* against a jealousy-evoking partner.
  - More women than men said they would take some *action* (e.g., show anger) against a sexually unfaithful partner.
  - More *men* than women said they would do *nothing* against a sexually unfaithful partner.
  - More *women* than men said that they would respond by *breaking up.*

One study of 777 college students ascertained that both genders expressed more *anger and blame* toward *sexual infidelity* but more *hurt* over *emotional infidelity* (M. C. Green & Sabini, 2006). In a different inquiry, both men and women also reported a greater likelihood of jealousy instigated by a partner's *emotional relationship* with a potential rival than by a *sexual relationship* (e.g., T. Hines, 2003). A third study found that dating *men accurately perceived* their female dating partner's *interest in other men* which, in turn, was associated with their controlling behavior. *Controlling behavior* was then significantly linked with male-to-female DV (Cousins & Gangestad, 2007).

## Historical and Learning Factors in Dating Violence

There is every reason to expect that abusive childhood socialization experiences are associated with later involvement in dating violence. It is also probable that the gender of a socializing parent (or imitated parent) influences the strength of socialization effects (e.g., Jankowski, Leitenberg, Henning, & Coffey, 1999). Studies have consistently determined that one of the strongest childhood factors associated with DV is *witnessing interparental violence* (Chapple, 2003; Gover, Kaukinen, & Fox, 2008). Although progression from childhood abuse to adult violence is not inevitable, it is common (J. P. Smith & Williams, 1992; K. D. O'Leary, Woodin, & Fritz, 2006). Research convergent with *learning principles* emerged as reflected in violent men's belief that *aggression will be positively reinforced* (i.e., rewarded) (Riggs & Caulfield, 1997).

*Intergenerational transfer of violence.* In furtherance of the *intergenerational transfer* of *violence theory,* academicians have explored *specific mechanisms of transfer* (R. L. Simons, Lin, & Gordon, 1998). In a longitudinal inquiry, Capaldi and Clark (1998) tested male children in 4th grade and at ages 17 to 20 and obtained data from the children's parents at specified intervals. Their results displayed the transfer effect: *Boys' development of antisocial behavior* was prerequisite to dating violence, and unskilled parenting was the major precursor to boys' antisocial behavior. Over the decades, research on the relationship between childhood experiences and adult interpersonal violence has grown. The most illuminating information to date originated from a longitudinal study of youths and their mothers recruited from community samples. Data from this study specify the following predictors of perpetrating dating violence (Ehrensaft et al., 2003).

- Development of a conduct disorder in childhood
- Exposure to interparental violence
- Power-assertive punishment

Substance abuse disorder **mediated** (intervening variable—its presence or absence) the effects of adolescent conduct disorder on risks of perpetrating injuries. That is, substance abuse was needed as an intervening variable to affect the risk of perpetrating and injury.

Adolescent Conduct Disorder → Substance Abuse → Perpetration of Injuries

In addition, the researchers pointed out that many of their findings were *gender neutral.* Another line of research with a sample of 2,500 college students showed that *childhood exposure to violence* is a consistent *predictor* of involvement in *relationship violence* for both men and women (Gover et al., 2008).

*Gender socialization.* Gender socialization represents another type of learning. Research has revealed that individuals use *gender of the perpetrator* as a guide to expected outcomes of interpersonal violence. College students, for example, almost uniformly consider male-to-female violence a far more serious threat than female-to-male violence (Bethke & De Joy, 1993; Riggs, O'Leary, & Breslin, 1990). Additionally, students tend to trivialize the severity of female-to-male violence (see S. L. Miller & Simpson, 1991; Molidor & Tolman, 1998). Both genders view self-defensive DV as justifiable, but women more so than men (Foo & Margolin, 1995).

*Relationship importance.* In one study, women in male-to-female dating violent (MFDV) relationships felt *desperate for a man.* Related to these feelings were *misinterpretations of the male partner's behavior.* The women reported that the *cues of MFDV* were present early in the relationship, but that their feelings of *romantic love masked the cues.* The women misinterpreted the man's jealous behavior as a sign of love (Power, Koch, Kralik, & Jackson, 2006). (See the discussion on jealousy in this chapter.) In a different study, male and female victims of relationship aggression were significantly more likely than nonvictims to state that their *self-worth* was *contingent on their romantic relationship,* and they rated their romantic relationship as *very important* to them (S. E. Goldstein, Chesir-Teran, & McFaul, 2008). These kinds of findings help explain why young women (and perhaps men) involved in a violent dating relationship accept partner abuse as part of the relationship.

## Traits of Individuals Involved in Dating Violence

In addition to sociocultural variables, certain kinds of *personality characteristics,* such as hostility, seem to precipitate abusive behavior. Whether dating aggression stems primarily from the presence of a violent person (personality trait) or more from a violent relationship (situation) remains unresolved (see Marcus & Swett, 2002). A growing number of researchers have searched for both clinical and normal personality differences between men who perpetrate interpersonal violence and those who do not. One common finding among batterers is that they suffer from depression and anxiety. Similar personality differences typify college-age male abusers.

*Anger—men.* In an examination of 33 college men, Eckhardt, Jamison, and Watts (2002) uncovered substantial distinctions between dating violent and non-DV college men on responses to the *State-Trait Anger Expression Inventory* (Spielberger, 1988). DV males had significantly higher scores on four subscales: State Anger (intense anger at time of test), Trait Anger (ongoing, recurrent angry feelings), Anger-In (withholding of angry expression), and Anger-Out (expression of anger). DV men's scores were significantly lower than non-DV men's on Anger Control (reduction of angry feelings). Replication of this study with a larger sample is warranted (see also Dye & Davis, 2003; Gidycz, Van Wynsberghe, & Edwards, 2008).

*Hypermasculinity and power.* Hypermasculinity is a recently developed *trait* construct that may play a role in men's anger, sexual coercion, aggression, and lack of empathy toward women (callousness) (Vass & Gold, 1995). Mosher and Sirkin (1984) operationally defined hypermasculinity as a personality trait that predisposes men to engage in behaviors that assert *physical power and dominance* in interactions. Using a deception paradigm, Parrott and Zeichner (2003a) compared college men's delivery of (presumed) "painful shocks" to fictitious *female* opponents. Men high in hypermasculinity (HH) were significantly more apt to administer shocks than were men low in hypermasculinity (LH). Most convincing, HH men were more likely than LH men to have *abused a woman* during the past year. In addition, HH men's shock delivery scores correlated significantly with other trait measures: (a) *adversarial sexual beliefs,* (b) *acceptance of interpersonal violence,* and (c) *hostility toward women.* (See the discussion in the policy section below for a meta-analytic review of male athletes' and fraternity members' hypermasculinity.)

*Interpersonal control—DV.* Some analysts believe that *perpetrators of DV* have *high needs for control* and that this need can be conceptualized as a *personality trait.* Another line of research indicates that desire for interpersonal control of one's partner lies at the heart of DV (e.g., Chung, 2007; K. E. Davis, Ace, & Anda, 2000; Tjaden & Thoennes, 1998b). Interpersonal control can take many forms, such as "threatening to leave" in order to get one's way about living situations or sexual activities. Both patriarchy and learning theory provide compelling theoretical foundations for this view. Hamby (1996) found that on an interpersonal control scale assessing authority, disparagement, and restrictiveness, restrictiveness is most closely linked with DV (J. Katz, Carine, & Hilton, 2002; see also Rondfeldt, Kimmerling, & Arias, 1998). Although males, relative to females, may use more control tactics against dating partners, women also try to control their partners. (For a review, see S. M. Jackson, 1998.)

## Attitudes Toward Dating Violence

In a survey published in 2002, college *men* were significantly more likely than college women to hold attitudes *condoning partner violence,* and the women in the sample were significantly more likely than the men to *condemn it* (West & Wandrei, 2002). Researchers have been very productive in producing research on college students' attitudes toward both violent and nonviolent DV. (See www.sagepub.com/barnett3e for research details of Basow, Cahill, Phelan, Longshore, & McGillicuddy-DeLise, 2007.) Some research outcomes from this study and others follow:

- Student participants ($N = 314$) rated *male-to-female physical aggression* as less acceptable and more harmful than male-to-female *relational (nonphysical) aggression* (Basow et al., 2007).
- Men's inclination to *blame dating partners* was associated with men's own *denial and minimization* of their own *dating aggression,* while women's partner aggression was associated only with *blaming* their partner (K. Scott & Straus, 2007).
- Both men and women research participants ($N = 428$) believed that *hitting* by a *sexually betrayed* partner was unjustified, but male-to female hitting because of betrayal was even less justified than female to-male (Forbes, Jobe, White, Bloesch, & Adams-Curtis, 2005).
- Relationship satisfaction was significantly linked with relationship commitment among 572 college students (Kaura & Lohman, 2009).

(Relationship Satisfaction → Acceptability of Woman's DV Perpetration → Relationship Commitment)

- Among 263 male college students, measures of *anger/hostility toward women,* and *calloused sexual beliefs* were positively related to the *frequency of physical DV* (Parrott & Zeichner, 2003b). (See www.sagepub.com/barnett3e for expanded version of these studies.)

Other contemporary research has explored the relationship between benevolent sexism and dating violence. (An example of benevolent sexism, as opposed to hostile sexism, is the belief that rescuers should save women from a sinking ship first. Strangely, benevolent sexism is associated with hostile sexism suggesting that benevolent sexism is not entirely harmless.) In an inquiry of 232 Hispanics, social scientists discerned that a belief in benevolent sexism had a protective effect against male-to-female DV (C. T. Allen et al., 2009).

## Treatment of Dating Violence

Counselors in schools, community agencies, and private practice play the largest role in treatment. Practitioners have uniformly emphasized the necessity of treatment for victims of any type of interpersonal violence because of the *long-lasting adverse effects* (see Henning, Leitenberg, Coffey, Turner, & Bennett, 1996). Others believe that intervention in violent premarital relationships is crucial to prevent patterns of conflict and violence from *carrying over into marriage* (e.g., Carr & VanDeusen, 2002). Given such possible outcomes, schools should offer services to victims, and treatment strategies should take note of gender differences (Advisory Council on Violence Against Women, 1996).

*Changing attitudes.* Research has long established that the *relationship* between *attitudes* and *behavior is low* and *inconsistent.* As a case in point, a person may state he deplores classroom cheating but writes a term paper for a classmate for pay. Consequently, programs attempting to change attitudes about the acceptability of dating violence may or may not be successful in actually diminishing violence. Regardless, most of the research on treatment programs assesses changes in post-treatment attitudes. To this end, test developers used factor analysis to construct an Intimate Partner Violence Attitude Scale. The analyses identified three major factors comprising the scale: *abuse, control,* and *violence.* An example of an item on the abuse factor is the following: "It is no big deal if my partner insults me in front of others" (Fincham, Cui, Braithwaite, & Pasley, 2008, p. 263).

*Victim treatment.* Once victims are in treatment, their therapists need to help them with *safety planning first.* If a woman is in danger, she does not know where to go, whom to call, and so forth. There is a host of topics that are appropriate to cover in treatment for dating violence:

- Labeling one's own or one's partner's behavior as a form of violence (Sousa, 1999; Truman-Schram, Cann, Calhoun, & Vanwallendael, 2000)
- Avoiding control by others (Follingstad et al., 2002)
- Modifying one's beliefs about the legitimacy of physical aggression (Coffey, Leitenberg, Henning, Bennett, & Jankowski, 1996)
- Adopting appropriate coping methods (Coffey et al., 1996)
- Exploring the victim's satisfaction with her investment in the relationship (Truman-Schram et al., 2000)
- Addressing the developmental trauma caused by abuse (T. I. Herrenkohl, Huang, Tajima, & Whitney, 2003)
- Focusing on romantic attachment styles—helping insecure daters to feel more secure (McCarthy & Taylor, 1999)
- Encouraging/empowering a victim (or even a perpetrator) to leave a violent relationship when appropriate (Filson, Ulloa, Runfola, & Hokado, 2010; see Rosen & Stith, 1995)
- Pointing out that expectations for DV is correlated with actual experiences of DV among women college students (A. L. Stein, Tran, & Fisher, 2009)

As a learned behavior, counselors can use behavioral techniques to help reduce PTSD symptoms (see Ehlers, Michael, Chen, Payne, & Shan, 2006).

## Policy–Dating Violence

Policy efforts directed at physical violence against women most often focus on teen women and married women. By contrast, advances in sexual assault policies have often focused on college women. Beth Richie (2004) covers the following broad strategies to address DV: (a) Identify and fill in research gaps, (b) Produce qualitative as well as quantitative studies, and (c) Encourage collaboration between practitioners and researchers, and (d) apply new knowledge as quickly as possible.

## Prevention

Schools, medical facilities, law enforcement agencies, advocates, and community organizations are on the front lines in terms of prevention. One evaluated program centered on differences between couples who had received premarital education and those who had not ($N = 2,533$). Program participation *was* associated with higher levels of satisfaction and commitment in marriage and lower levels of conflict. The numbers of divorces were fewer as well (Stanley, Amato, Johnson, & Markman, 2006).

Prevention programs have myriad goals, many of which reflect beliefs about causation. Some proposals are as follows: (a) Offer clinics for victims of childhood abuse(s) and at-risk daters; (b) alert college women to the dangers of interpersonal control; (c) provide guidance about avoiding date-rape drugs; (d) address sexist attitudes and problems of peer-group support for aggression; (e) teach anger management, conflict resolution skills, and stress-reduction skills; (f) present antidrug messages and alcohol misuse awareness programs; and (g) discuss attachment, commitment, and stress (Eckhardt et al., 2002; Gormley & Lopez, 2010; Rickert, Sanghvi, & Wiemann, 2002; J. P. Schwartz, Magee, Griffin, & Dupuis, 2004; P. Smith & Welchans, 2000; Weisz & Black, 2001).

A 2004 experiment (J. P. Schwartz et al., 2004) assessed whether exposure to a program about risk and protective factors might improve attitudes toward prevention among 102 college students. The experimental group participated in four 1½-hour psychoeducational programs. Compared with the control group, the experimental group showed a reduction in acceptance of traditional, stereotypical gender roles, the use of escalating strategies during a conflict, and emotion restriction. The experimental group showed an increase in self-awareness of anger and healthy entitlement.

*Violence screening by physical and mental health providers.* Clinical and medical screening for interpersonal violence can identify young people involved in violence so that professionals can find ways to assist them. Family violence experts provide physicians and counselors with a research-tested screening instrument accompanied by a list of appropriate behavioral responses. A professional asks the client a series of questions from the screening test and follows up by selecting actions from the response list. One question might be "Has anyone hurt you?" or "Are you afraid of any of your acquaintances?" An appropriate response by the professional to an affirmative answer to such a question might be "No one deserves to be hit" (Hamberger & Ambuel, 1998). Referrals for additional sources of treatment follow as needed.

*School/university prevention programs.* Schools and universities have the responsibility to make their campuses safe for women by evaluating and modifying their services as needed (Advisory Council on Violence Against Women, 1996). Federal legislation supporting these goals includes the 1992 Campus Sexual Assault Victim's Bill of Rights and the Student Right-to-Know and Campus Security Act of 1990, which requires schools to give students *access to campus crime reports* (see Ferguson, 1998). These laws may encourage reporting of violence, and thus facilitate efforts to help victims and make perpetrators accountable (Advisory Council on Violence Against Women, 1996). Some universities now routinely present violence prevention programs to incoming students, partly to avoid liability (Marcus & Swett, 2003; Senn, Desmarais, Verberg, & Wood, 2000). One study, focused on the meaning of jealousy among undergraduates, also included some data on the effects of a prevention workshop (Puente & Cohen, 2003). Findings tentatively indicated that attendance lessened participants' tendency to excuse jealousy-related violence such as rape.

*Internship and mentoring program.* An internship mentoring program trains young men to engage with *peers* to prevent dating violence. These programs join an ever-growing number of programs, such as Men Can Stop Rape, to enlist the unique perspectives of men to help stop violence against women.

*Discouraging alcohol misuse.* Another strategy that is helpful on college campuses is to *discourage alcohol misuse* (Wechsler, Lee, Kuo, & Lee, 2000). On the basis of a new study, parents, administrators, counselors, and students themselves might wish to consider *housing* as a factor in alcohol misuse. Page and O'Hegarty (2006) uncovered significant differences in drinking habits among students living in fraternities or sororities contrasted with those living in apartment complexes and residence halls. Both male and female Greeks (members of fraternities and sororities), relative to non-Greeks, consumed more alcohol, engaged more frequently in heavy episodic drinking, and drank more when "partying." Furthermore, Greek students' estimates concerning an amount of alcohol consumption deemed normative were significantly higher than those of the comparison groups.

---

## SECTION SUMMARY

### Dating Violence

Dating violence (DV) is an extremely important topic, partially because the age group covered includes adolescents as well as college-age couples, and society is concerned with protecting them. Family violence experts have *not* identified robust differences between dating violence and marital violence. DV, however, ordinarily refers to younger persons—adolescents through college age—who are unmarried. Although the term intimate partner violence (IPV) is also appropriate terminology for younger daters who are intimate, IPV most commonly refers to older, sexually intimate couples. One difference between DV and marital violence is that sexual assaults occur more frequently among dating couples. Sometimes DV refers to all forms of interpersonal violence among younger couples, including psychological, physical, and sexual aggression, as well as stalking.

More than other areas of family violence, with the exception of sibling abuse, DV tends to be more gender reciprocal (mutual). Estimates of incidence and prevalence rates rest upon ambiguous definitions, and a few of the assessments used are questionable. Of course, the index used to measure these behaviors greatly affects the level of reported mutuality. The CTS, for instance, almost uniformly finds evidence of gender equivalence. Findings from the National Criminal Violence Survey and the FBI, however, show a clear-cut predominance of male-to-female violence. The consequences of DV can be severe. Although physical injuries are generally minor, there remain health consequences that can be serious. The emotional damage can be even more devastating, especially if it includes posttraumatic stress disorder (PTSD).

There are several risk factors for dating violence: Exposure to parental violence during childhood is a consistent risk factor, and alcohol misuse among perpetrators and victims is common. Often, female victims state that their DV is self-defensive and some evidence supports this claim. Some other rationales include anger, escalating arguments, poor communication, bad temper, embarrassment, and jealousy. A broader cause stems from the choice of dating partners. There is some evidence that women who have been psychologically abused select abusive dating partners, and those men who are abusive select women who are vulnerable because of their attachment needs. In any event, the type of DV usually reported does not match the kind of behavior called *battering* that occurs in intimate partner violence.

Attachment issues among dating-violent couples have attracted increasing research attention and have confirmed that insecure attachment is related to DV. A developing application of attachment theory ties feelings of anger and insecurity learned in childhood with later fears of abandonment that subsequently elicit DV. Surprisingly, high commitment to one's partner and longer relationships are linked with DV. Possibly, those who are highly committed are highly attached to their partner and have high dependency needs. Insecure attachment can also lead to ambivalence leading to an "on-again, off-again" relationship. Jealousy is a factor in dating violence, partially because some daters think it is a sign of love. There is strong evidence that many college students find DV quite acceptable if the perpetrator's motive for his violence is jealousy. Gender differences in jealousy exist, but more research is necessary to interpret the piecemeal findings now available.

Historical variables such as direct or indirect exposure to family violence show a relationship to DV. Closely related is the question of whether DV is either a stepping stone to or a training ground for marital violence. Gender-role socialization and individual personality traits, such as need for control, feelings of powerlessness, hypermasculinity, and anger are associated with DV, but more research is needed to establish such generalizations.

Researchers have looked for maladaptive attitudes as the cause of dating violence. One finding, however, is that young people as a general rule do *not* endorse interpersonal violence. They view male-to-female violence as far more detrimental than female-to-male violence. Men, nonetheless, accept violence toward women as more acceptable than women do, and there are individual differences among men in terms of how acceptable and justifiable DV is. Although available evidence is inconclusive, endorsement of traditional male gender attitudes may propel some men toward DV. Similarly, accepting more modern sex-role attitudes may encourage women not to tolerate DV. It is also true that members of couples often think their partners (and sometimes themselves) are the cause of DV.

Treatment of dating violence presents several challenges, yet it is essential to prevent violent patterns of behavior from extending into adult relationships. One impediment is that young people seldom disclose dating violence to adults, teachers, or others who might help them. Trying to change attitudes, such as acceptance of violence, may be successful. A change, nevertheless, may still not translate into a reduction in violence. In addition to providing safety planning for victims, counselors can provide information about helpful resources and focus on problems such as insecure attachment.

Prevention efforts often entail special programs, putting up posters around campus, and teaching conflict resolution skills. Medical doctors and counselors can use intake forms that screen for violence and then take necessary actions. Having programs about alcohol abuse is useful as well, not only to prevent interpersonal violence but also to protect physical health.

## SEXUAL ASSAULT, SEXUAL COERCION, AND RAPE

Several types of unwanted sex-related behaviors occur among unmarried young people on college campuses and elsewhere. This section discusses the problems of *sexual coercion, sexual assault, and rape.* Sexual crimes constitute a highly charged topic that tends to polarize opinions, commonly along gender lines. Polarization is especially apparent in legal matters.

These disputes and other factors have made the definition and assessment of sexual assault especially problematic. Research on these offenses has increased more than research on either dating violence or stalking, possibly because the impact of these crimes is so devastating.

## Defining Sexual Assault

Some definitions of unwanted sexual behaviors are as follows.

> SEXUAL COERCION is "any situation in which one person uses verbal or physical means to obtain sexual activity *against consent* (including the administration of drugs or alcohol, with or without the other person's consent)" (Adams-Curtis & Forbes, 2004, p. 91).
>
> RAPE, within the confines of dating violence, is the perpetration of sexual aggression against an (unmarried) date or acquaintance. Rape, more than the other terms, refers to some form of bodily penetration (see Centers for Disease Control and Prevention, 2002).
>
> SEXUAL ASSAULT (SA) is a more inclusive term that places sex-related behaviors on a *continuum* from unwanted sexual contact (e.g., fondling) through sexual intercourse, and it usually *connotes violence*. Experts often prefer this term because it is more inclusive (see Clay-Warner & Burt, 2005).

*Subjective definitions of sexual assault.* The importance of subjective definitions of sexual assault (SA) must be acknowledged. Evidence persists that *college women do not uniformly define SAs as assaults* (Hannon, Hall, Nash, Formanti, & Hopson, 2000). The point at which any individual involved in a sexual encounter will label unwanted sexual behavior as SA is strongly influenced by factors such as age, sex, race, socioeconomic status, and the person's relationship with the offender (see Banyard et al., 2007). Victims who are romantically involved with their assailants are much less likely to characterize sexual coercion as rape (Bondurant, 2001). From a male perspective, college *men* in one study were able to *identify* behavior that is sexually aggressive but failed to *recognize* it as inappropriate (Loh, Orchowski, Gidycz, & Elizaga, 2007). (See a summary of the Hammond & Calhoun, [2007], study later in this chapter.)

*Legal definitions of sexual assault.* The legal definitions used in statutes covering SA across the United States have evolved over time. A general definition refers to sexual contact against one's will and without consent and includes rape. An unfortunate opinion offered by a 17th century jurist, Matthew Hale, set the stage for gender-based sex laws that still influence court trials. He proclaimed that rape is "an accusation easily made . . . and harder to be defended by the party accused, tho never so innocent" (Matthew Hale [Jurist], 2010). One outcome from this admonition was that for sexual acts to be considered legal rape, victims had to prove that they had physically resisted sexual intercourse. Accordingly, judges were prone to ruling that women had not resisted even if they required stitches resulting from the assault. In some states, extreme laws required any woman who claimed rape to undergo a psychiatric evaluation. Before the 1980s, many Americans viewed rape as a crime stemming purely from sexual desire.

They believed that once a male was fully aroused, he was not capable of stopping short of sexual intercourse (B. Miller & Marshall, 1987). Society as a whole, and legislatures in particular, mistakenly judged sexual assaults to be crimes of sexual passion instead of crimes of violence. Over the past three decades, fortunately, increased knowledge has contributed to a shift in both the sensibilities of the American public and laws concerning sexual assault. By *1984, all 50 states had revised their legal definitions of rape* (Largen, 1987), and improvements are ongoing (WomensLaw, 2009).

*Consent.* At the root of this dissension is the question of *consent* (see Margolin, Moran, & Miller, 1989). The use of powerful illegal *drugs* such as gamma hydroxybutyrate (GHB) and Rohypnol ("roofies")—so-called date-rape drugs—is related to this problem. By administering such drugs to stupefy potential rape victims, perpetrators seek to bypass women's ability to consent to sex. For rapists, these drugs are advantageous because they render victims unable to resist and they cause memory loss (R. H. Schwartz, Milteer, & LeBeau, 2000). The victim's lack of memory in drug-related rapes hampers police investigations and prosecutors' certainty about whether to proceed (Girard & Senn, 2008). Based on the different consequences of drug-related rapes and non-drug-related rapes, advocates have recently advanced their thinking to designate these crimes as distinct, *drug-incapacitated rapes* (A. L. Brown, Testa, & Messman-Moore, 2009).

There are also many less dramatic and more common examples of questions about consent. Does the way a woman dresses on a date, such as her lack of underwear, convey that she is willing to have sexual intercourse with any available male? If she has consented to sex with a particular person in the past, does she give up the right to decline on subsequent occasions? Are there circumstances that excuse SA, such as a woman's drinking too much alcohol? How would you describe Ivana and Bruce's last sexual encounter in the case history that opens this chapter?

Some aspects of lack of consent, defined in New York State's Penal Law, are described in "Forcible Compulsion" (New York Alliance Against Sexual Assault, Factsheets, n.d.):

- Actual physical force
- The threat of physical force, expressed or implied, that puts the victim in fear of being physically harmed or of another person being physically harmed (e.g., one's child)
- The threat to kidnap the victim or a third person

The lack of consent further applies to situations in which a person cannot give consent, such as when the victim is drunk/drugged, under age, or disabled. In 2007, a team of researchers devised a measurement of sexual consent for research use that should yield more comparable results across studies (Humphreys & Herold, 2007).

*Rape laws redefined.* Undoubtedly, statutes enacted before 1975 amounted to a type of *institutionalized sexism.* Rape laws stood alone in their requirements for standards of proof. The victim had to inform her attacker that she did *not* consent in an unmistakable, clear fashion. She also had to demonstrate an extremely high level of forceful resistance. The prosecution had to prove that actual (not attempted) penetration of the vagina by the perpetrator's penis (not an object or finger) had taken place. Last, the laws did not shield a woman from court exposure of her prior sexual history. Hence, defense attorneys attempted to attack a woman's character to label her a liar.

Through the efforts of feminist advocates, rape laws now forbid many of these biased practices (see Clay-Warner & Burt, 2005), but they still need refinement (Schuller & Klippenstine, 2004). Several facets of laws, such as rape shield laws, continue to undergo refinements (e.g., Flowe, Ebbensen, & Putcha-Bhagavatula, 2007; J. Torres, 2008). An example of other more proactive efforts to improve protections for victims is a California law passed in 2006. This law advises the Department of Motor Vehicles to issue immediately a new car license plate for victims of SA and stalking ("Fewer New Laws," 2006).

*FBI–No male rape.* For purposes of data gathering, the FBI formerly defined rape narrowly, as "sexual intercourse or attempted sexual intercourse with a female against her will by force or threat of force" (Flanagan & Maguire, 1991, p. 779). Some have asserted that this narrow definition of rape, promulgated in 1929, totally overlooks and trivializes *same-sex male rape* (see Stop Prisoner Rape, 2002). A narrow definition also ignores an *entire spectrum of forced sexual behaviors* (e.g., oral sex) that the laws of most U.S. states categorize as forms of SA (Clay-Warner & Burt, 2005).

## Prevalence Estimates of Sexual Assault

Factors such as sample variation, differences in interpretations of sexually aggressive behaviors, lack of acknowledgement, and failure to disclose rape, produce differences in reported sexual assaults.

*Nondisclosure of sexual assault.* There are many reasons affecting women's decisions not to inform others about their sexual assault. These entail privacy concerns, embarrassment, lack of understanding, and feelings of self-blame and failure. Typically, a victim does not want her family to know, or she fears that others will blame her, blame her partner, pressure her to end the relationship, and take over for her (e.g., Rennison, 2007). Fears of stigmatization, inability to offer proof of abuse, or being treated with hostility are concerns for victims who contemplate reporting to officials (e.g., Fisher, Cullen, & Turner, 2002). Male victims have even more difficulty disclosing sexual assault than female victims.

*Underreporting of sexual assault.* By any standards, *SA is one of the most underreported crimes.* In a controlled comparison of raped college women, Bondurant (2001) found that 64% did not acknowledge the rape, much less report it. Disclosure seems to be dependent on how questions have been formulated. Behaviorally specific questions will increase disclosure, while ambiguous items will decrease it (Thorensen & Øverlien, 2009). Also disquieting is that a dispute has arisen about how the Bureau of Justice Statistics (BJS) estimates sexual assaults. For 2006, BJS estimated rape/sexual assault at 182,000. Kilpatrick and McCauley (2009) subsequently estimated the number at over 1 million. One cause of the incongruity stemmed from BJS's reckoning that 47% of the rapes had been reported to the police, while Kilpatrick construed the rate to be 16%. Such methodological inconsistencies may be responsible for the difference ("New U.S. Crime Reports," 2009).

As an influential methodological difference, a team of researchers found that telephoning male research participants rather than asking them to take a web-based survey improved the quality of the information obtained (DiNitto et al., 2008). Obviously, methodological variation other than question formatting influenced prevalence rates.

## CASE HISTORY   "I Was Raped; I WAS RAPED!"

Mandy was a freshman at a private women's university. By chance, she enrolled in a popular freshman seminar entitled Dating Relationships. Mandy's professor did not understand Mandy's strange academic behavior. Mandy skipped classes, came late, left early, and did not turn in assignments on time. She talked with no one and seemed isolated among her talkative classmates. Mandy was in danger of failing a fairly easy course.

Two guest speakers from a local Rape Crisis Center addressed the class one day. A woman rape counselor talked about her work at the clinic. A retired older gentleman spoke about his volunteer role in accompanying rape victims to court as a source of support. Next, the speakers opened up the class for questions.

Just before the class was due to take a short break, Mandy stood up. She was trembling and seemed oblivious to her surroundings. She slowly walked toward the counselor while blurting out several times, "I was raped," her voice rising each time, until she was talking very loudly. The speakers stopped talking and the class members sat silently stunned by Mandy's outburst. The professor waved the students out of the classroom on to their break. The rape counselor took Mandy to the professor's office and spent the rest of the hour counseling her.

Mandy visited the professor during office hours a few weeks later. Mandy almost managed a smile as she sat down. She had been in intensive counseling for several weeks, and she was finally able to disclose the identity of her attacker (a male assistant to the campus minister). Although he had raped her 3 months earlier, she had told no one about the rape until that day in class. The administrators confronted the rapist and subsequently fired him. At last, Mandy could walk around campus without feeling terrified that she would encounter her rapist again, and she would no longer have to contend with his attempts to "*date* her again."

*NCVS Self-Report Estimates.* Some estimates of sexual assault victimization compiled by the National Crime Victimization Survey appear in Table 7.4.

**TABLE 7.4**   Estimates of Sexual Assault Victimization by Degree of Relatedness

|  | Intimate | Relative | Friend/ Acquaintance | Stranger | Total Sexual Assaults |
|---|---|---|---|---|---|
| Male Victims | 9.1% | 0.0% | 33.6% | 57.3% | 100% |
| Female Victims | 21.4% | 3.2% | 44.3% | 31.1% | !00% |

SOURCE: NCVS—2006, Table 43a (Rand, 2009).

- 8.3% of 6,790 women and 2.4% of 7,122 men experienced physical aggression, forced sex, or stalking by an intimate (Slashinski, Coker, & Davis, 2003).
- A newer nationwide survey of rapes and assaults has suggested that decreases have occurred that are attributable to the Violence Against Women Act (Boba & Lilley, 2009).

## Women's Responses to Sexual Victimization

The question of how women respond to sexual aggression and whether their protective behavior is successful is critical to understanding the broader complexity of sexual assault. The findings from 4,446 female college students provided a number of insights:

- The majority of women do take protective action when confronted with rape.
- A large proportion of women take protective action during other types of sexual assaults.
- Protective action generally reduces the probability of rape completion.
- Rape evokes forceful reactions while coercion evokes nonforceful responses.
- Actions vary across types of sexual assaults and may reflect parity with the attacker.

In addition, the findings suggested that responses that *are on a par* (i.e., similar in choice of forceful resistance) with those of the assaulter are most effective in preventing completion of the act. The results, however, must be replicated (Fisher, Daigle, Cullen, & Santana, 2007).

## Criminal Justice System Responses

Readers may be familiar with the proposition made by advocates that going through the criminal justice system following a rape constitutes a *second rape.* Despite massive efforts on the part of women's advocates, victims still have a challenging time receiving effective and nonbiased treatment in the criminal justice system. The following case history depicts such a situation.

**CASE HISTORY**  "Rape"—A Word That Dare Not Be Spoken

In Nebraska in 2006, a judge presiding over a rape trial restricted the language used in the courtroom. He banned anyone (e.g., witnesses, police, attorneys) from using the words "rape," "rape kit," or "victim." The case ended in a mistrial. The victim later stated that the language restrictions caused her to hesitate during testimony, thus giving the false impression that she was unsure about what happened. During a second trial, the same judge dismissed the case on the grounds that news coverage had tainted the jury pool. An appeals court upheld the judge's ruling, and the U.S. Supreme Court has declined to hear the case (Ortiz, 2006).

*Law enforcement responses.* Although police have now been trained *not* to ask questions such as what were you wearing, some experts claim that police continue to put up barriers against prosecutions of rapists. Very frequently, law enforcement officials discourage a victim from reporting the rape by telling her that the cross-examination will be grueling or that her identity will probably slip out at trial (R. Campbell, 2009). Another unfortunate circumstance is that some police officers, like others in society, accept rape myths. As might be expected, the higher a police officers' Rape Myth Acceptance score, the less likely he is to believe a rape victim (Page, 2008).

*Law enforcement—sex crimes unit.* Some police departments are working diligently to meet the needs of sexual assault victims. The San Diego Police Department has been able to adopt a two-pronged approach by fully funding a sex crimes unit—about $1 million a year (Littel, Malefyt, Walfer, Buel, & Tucker, 1998). (See www.sagepub.com/barnett3e for a summary of the San Diego Sexual Assault Response Team.)

*Prosecutorial discretion.* Prosecutorial discretion in cases involving interpersonally violent crimes has received mixed reviews. As is true for other crimes, police and prosecutors use discretion in their decisions to make arrests and to prosecute offenders in cases of dating violence, sexual assault, and stalking. Although discretion may be necessary, its use in interpersonal violence cases often comes across as biased. One of the most recent analyses used changes in four potentially influential blocks of factors to track the progress of cases through the system: (a) law-enforcement agency, (b) victim characteristics, (c) assault characteristics, and (d) medical forensic evidence. Results substantiated that significant influence from every block occurred and that criminal justice personnel allowed non-evidentiary information to influence their decision making.

Similar to police officers, prosecutors also enlisted "extralegal" information (e.g., victim's "character") to guide their decision making. Extralegal information may even overshadow the strength of the evidence (Spears & Spohn, 1997; see also J. M. Brown, Hamilton, & O'Neill, 2007). In one analysis, however, medical forensic evidence, not extralegal information, accounted for much of the variability in the conviction rate (R. Campbell, Patterson, Bybee, & Dworkin, 2009).

*Mishandling of DNA evidence.* An especially distressing lapse in Criminal Justice System practices is the mishandling of crime evidence in rape cases. It was a big step forward for women when emergency rooms began routinely using rape kits to collect DNA evidence. DNA evidence is often critical in jury deliberations. When this practice became widespread, members of the public, victims' advocates, and SA victims all assumed that crime labs would analyze the samples gathered and try to identify perpetrators. Not so. As of 2002, across the United States 180,000 rape kits awaiting analysis have been in storage, presumably because of cost constraints (the processing of each kit costs approximately $40; Hewitt, Podesta, & Longley, 2002; also see Pratt, Gaffney, Lovrich, & Johnson, 2006).

As of 2007, there were promising developments concerning the growth of forensic databases for use by law enforcement, including the *Combined DNA Index System (CODIS)* (Bowen & Schneider, 2007). As these databases become readily available to all law enforcement agencies and are regularly used, it should be possible to prosecute and incarcerate more SA perpetrators and hence prevent more sexual assaults. In October 2008, the Los Angeles City Council approved $7 million to hire more crime analysts. This is the first step in clearing up the backlog of 7,000 cases in the Los Angeles City Crime Lab (Orlov, 2008).

*Measuring sexual assault.* The methods the U.S. Bureau of Justice Statistics used to determine SA prevalence rates for the *National Crime Victimization Survey* (NCVS) presumed that respondents knew when sexual encounters in which they had been involved qualified as crimes (for the NCVS questions, see Bachman & Saltzman, 1995). A different index, the *Sexual Experiences Survey* (SES; Koss, Gidycz, & Wisniewski, 1987), provides a broad assessment of sexual assault perpetration and victimization. In addition, it does *not* assume that individuals make use of legal definitions in classifying their experiences. Revisions of this popular and methodologically sound scale include improvements in the behavioral specificity and the gender neutrality of the questions (Koss et al., 2007). (See www.sagepub.com/barnett3e for a debate on the scope of sexual assault.)

## Attitudes Toward Sexual Assault

Attitudes toward sexual assault encompass a number of variables, such as adversarial sexual beliefs, sexism, hostility toward women, lack of empathy, and rape myth acceptance.

*Adversarial sexual beliefs.* Investigators assessed 149 *college and military men* on several inventories including the *Adversarial Sexual Beliefs* (ASB) scale (Burt, 1980). High scores on the ASB scale reflect assumptions that sexual relationships will be *exploitative and manipulative*. Results showed that of four inventories, only scores on the ASB scale discriminated violent and nonviolent groups (Hastings, 2000). A further study examined potential relationships between sexism and hostility toward women among 264 college students. *Sexism* and *rape-supportive beliefs* were correlated with each other and with *aggressive and sexually coercive behavior* (Forbes, Adams-Curtis, & White, 2004).

*Lack of empathy.* A study of 32 rapists, 28 violent non-sex offenders, and 40 nonoffender males produced several significant results: (a) Rapists were *less empathic* toward a woman raped by an *unknown assailant* than toward two other female victims (car accident victims and their own rape victim); (b) they were *less empathic* toward their *own victim than* toward the car accident victim; (c) they were *more hostile toward women than toward men* in the other two groups; and (d) their *hostility* toward women scores were *negatively related to their empathy toward their own victims* (W. L. Marshall & Moulden, 2001; see also P. A. Lopez, George, & Davis, 2007).

*Rape myths/rape myth acceptance (RMA)—against women.* Recall that a cluster of frequently accepted myths centers on date rape: "She deserves what she got" and "She was asking for it" (see Chapter 1). Probably the most common myth about women who report date rape is that they *"are lying"* (Burt, 1991; Franiuk, Seefelt, Cepress, & Vandello, 2008). Acceptance of rape myths is correlated with a number of variables, such as an actual date rape. A new index of RMA is now available, and it should prove heuristic in coming years (G. H. Burgess, 2007).

Several studies have demonstrated a connection between viewing *sexually violent media* and *significant changes in RMA*. One appraisal of film content predilection indicated, as hypothesized, that men prefer films with sex and violence more than women do, whereas preferences are reversed for love stories. Individuals who prefer sex and violence themes are more accepting of RMAs than those who do not, and they are less accepting of film editing to reduce sex and violence. Last, film content functions as a moderator of RMAs for women but not for men (Emmers-Sommer, Pauley, Hanzal, & Triplett, 2006).

*Rape myths/rape myth acceptance (RMA)—against men.* There are myths about male rape as well. The following is a list of myths compiled by Chapleau, Oswald, and Russell (2008):

- Male rape is tantamount to loss of masculinity (Groth & Burgess, 1980).
- Men should be able to defend themselves against rape (Groth & Burgess, 1980).
- Men who get raped must be gay (Stermac, Del Bove, & Addison, 2001).
- Men cannot be forced against their will to have sex (Stermac et al., 2001).
- Men are less affected by sexual assault than women (Stermac et al., 2001).
- Men are always ready to accept any sexual opportunity (Clements-Schreiber & Rempel, 1995).
- Men must be sexually aroused to be raped (Smith, Pine, & Hawley, 1988).

*Blame for sexual assault.* One comparison of college students' assignment of responsibility for date rape rested on the victim's *voluntary consumption* of alcohol/drugs. Randomly selected students ($N = 280$) viewed one of five scenarios about John and Cathy: (a) Both were drinking the same thing voluntarily; (b) Both were sober; (c) Both took date rape drugs voluntarily and were drinking; (d) Both were drinking, but John slipped a date rape drug into Cathy's drink; and (e) Both were drinking, but John tripled the strength of Cathy's drink. The higher the RMA, the more both genders held Cathy relatively *more responsible* and John relatively less responsible and the more both genders *blamed* Cathy. Not surprisingly, results indicated that male research participants held significantly higher *Rape Myth Acceptance* than females did.

Additional results emerged after statistically controlling (removing the effects) for gender differences in RMA. Students differentiated assignment of responsibility and blame on the basis of *voluntary consumption of alcohol.* If John had facilitated the rape with alcohol/drug administration, both genders held him primarily responsible. In contrast, they held John relatively less responsible and the victim relatively more responsible when she *voluntarily* consumed drugs or drank enough to get drunk. The researchers suggested that students held John more responsible and blameworthy when Cathy's consumption was involuntary because they viewed the rape as a *real* rape. The students may have thought of involuntary drug/alcohol consumption as a *weapon,* as if John had used physical force or threats. They also may have thought Cathy was an *unworthy victim* if she voluntarily consumed drugs/excessive alcohol (Girard & Senn, 2008; see also Crawford, Wright, & Birchmeir, 2008; Maurer & Robinson, 2008).

*Gender differences in attitudes toward rape.* Studies of gender differences in attitudes toward rape have routinely uncovered significant differences (e.g., Gerber & Cherneski, 2006). One inquiry disclosed significant gender divergence in placing responsibility on characters in a scenario based on *socioeconomic status* of the *perpetrator* and *victim's level of resistance.* The variables were as follows: (a) *perpetrator*—a bus driver or a doctor; and (b) *victim*'s resistance—verbal objection only or verbal objection *and* physical resistance. As a general response, men placed more blame on the victim than women did. When *judging the perpetrator,* men assigned more blame to the bus driver than to the doctor. When *evaluating the victim,* women blamed the victim of the bus driver more than the victim of the doctor (K. A. Black & Gold, 2008).

## Traits of Individuals Involved in Unwanted Sexual Behaviors

In searching for causes of rape, researchers wonder whether the characteristics of rapists are distinct compared with those of nonrapists. An analysis of 223 nonoffending college men with 81 sexually coercive men differentiated the two groups along several dimensions (DeGue & DiLillo, 2004). The sexually coercive men were *significantly more* likely than the nonoffending men to be described as follows:

| | |
|---|---|
| Subscribe to Rape Myths | Signs of Psychopathy |
| View DV as acceptable | Have empathic deficits |
| Experienced childhood abuse | Are hostile toward women |
| Perceive male/female relationships as adversarial | Are promiscuous/delinquent |

Serbin and Karp (2003) underscore the need for researchers to examine multiple variables, such as genetic contributions, inadequate parenting, and risk and protective factors in addition to trait variables. An analysis of responses of 343 *college men* yielded a very large number of both personality *trait*s (9 of 10 measured) and *situational* components (5 of 5) that *discriminated* between men who are sexually assaultive and those who are not. The appraisal further produced distinctions between types of adult sexual assault (ASA) *tactics* (forced, coercive, attempted/completed rape) of perpetrators, *attributions* for assault, and *outcomes.* The results indicated that both traits and situations played a role in men's ASA (Abbey, McAuslan, Zawacki, Clinton, & Buck, 2001; see also Hersch & Gray-Little, 1998).

## Consequences of Sexual Assault

**CASE HISTORY**  Mary and Her Date at a Fraternity Bash

Mary, a freshman at Florida State University, had been drinking tequila before attending a fraternity party as the date of 23-year-old Daniel Oltarsh, a junior and member of Pi Kappa Alpha.[1] When she arrived at the fraternity house already intoxicated, Oltarsh gave her wine and left her alone in his room. Police lab tests later placed Mary's blood-alcohol level at over .349%, a level that under some circumstances is enough to cause death.

Later, Oltarsh returned and forced Mary to have sex with him. He then took her to the fraternity house's shower room, where at least two other fraternity brothers raped her in a group and further used a toothpaste pump as a means of penetration. Afterward, they dumped her in the hallway of a second fraternity house, where members of yet a third fraternity wrote their house's initials on Mary's thigh with a ballpoint pen.

As news of these assaults got out and gossip pervaded the campus, Mary started to believe she might have been to blame for her own rape, perhaps an accessory of some sort. She tried to take measures to avoid being recognized, such as changing her hair color, but that did not lessen her notoriety. Eventually, Mary was unable to cope with her life any longer and checked into a psychiatric hospital for treatment of alcoholism, bulimia, and depression. Oltarsh was arrested and pleaded no contest to forcible rape. He received a prison sentence of 1 year, a stiff sentence by most standards. His fraternity brothers were allowed to plea-bargain to lesser charges.

---

The preceding case history emphasizes the seriousness of sexual assault and illustrates the widespread nature and acceptance of this type of violence in some settings. It also demonstrates the likelihood that *rape and physical violence are often linked.* At least three men in one fraternity participated in raping Mary, men from another fraternity partook in initialing her thigh, and men from a third fraternity seemed willing to play host to still other assaults on this woman. In a magazine interview conducted more than a year after the rapes, Mary said that it had been therapeutic for her to see her assailants convicted: "These men robbed me of any pride or hope or self-esteem that I had and replaced it with anger and self-hate and fear. To see their lives affected is some vindication" (quoted in Bane et al., 1990, p. 100).

*Injuries and negative health outcomes.* Researchers have uniformly shown that adverse health outcomes, such as sexually transmitted diseases (STDs) or chronic headaches, arise from sexual assaults (Straight, Harper, & Arias, 2003). Early pregnancies among young women are another unwelcome outcome (Spitzberg, 2002). Although most female victims are not physically injured during a sexual assault, one area in need of further research is the identification of any specific pattern of genital injuries (Sommers, 2007). Contrasted with female victims, *most male victims* are injured during a sexual assault. Nevertheless, data from the National Violence Against Women Survey disclosed that of 219 male SA victims only 29% sought medical or psychological assistance and these were those who had most likely suffered sexual penetration (Light & Monk-Turner, 2009). (See www.sagepub.com/barnett3e for injury estimates.)

*Psychological outcomes.* Probably the most common mental health repercussions of rape encompass a variety of *post-assault fears,* such as sexual aversion and feelings of paranoia (e.g., "It is safer to trust no one."). They may *blame themselves* for the assault, *feel ashamed, depressed,* or *even suicidal* (e.g., H. N. Harris & Valentiner, 2002). "Rape is one of the most severe of all traumas, causing multiple, long-term negative outcomes, such as posttraumatic stress disorder (PTSD), depression, substance abuse, suicidality, repeated sexual victimization, and chronic physical health problems" (R. Campbell, 2008, p. 703). Of 103 rape victims seeking help in an emergency room, 74% experienced PTSD (Valentiner, Foa, Riggs, & Gershuny, 1996). In the *California Women's Health Survey* of 11,056 women, 12% suffered anxiety, depression, and PTSD following sexual assault (Kimmerling, Alvarez, Pavao, Kaminski, & Baumrind, 2007).

There is a host of other *mental health consequences,* such as obsessive-compulsive disorder, sexual dysfunction, substance abuse, relationship abuse, phobias, unhealthy weight control, sexual risk behavior, pregnancy, and suicide (Goodman, Koss, & Russo, 1993; Silverman, Raj, Mucci, & Hathaway, 2001). Survivors even had difficulty in parenting as reflected in reduced quality of the parent-child relationship (Reid-Cunningham, 2009). Victims can become *classically conditioned* so that reminder cues (e.g., smell of the aftershave lotion worn by a rapist) reinstate *strong fear reactions* years later. Finally, one study reported that victims of SA increased their sexual *activity post-assault* (Deliramich & Gray, 2008; see also Ellis, Widmayer, & Palmer, 2009).

## Medical Responses to Sexual Assault

Medical responses to sexual assault victims, especially in emergency rooms, are still in need of improvement. An especially important obligation is to document injuries and make their findings available to prosecutors (Sommers, 2007). Medical personnel may be brusque and lack understanding of the victim's state of mind. They may ask victim-blaming questions such as "what did you do to make him attack you?" (R. Campbell, 2008). In fact, a duo of researchers ascertained that the responses of *police and medical personnel exacerbated the impact of sexual assault* (Kaukinen & DeMaris, 2009). Last, victim advocates have found a number of barriers in collaborating with health care workers (Payne, 2007; see also Ullman & Townsend, 2007). One extremely important shortcoming is the lack of *medical interpreters* who can assist victims with limited English proficiency (Nakajima, 2005).

*Sexual assault nurse examiner (SANE) protocol.* An illustration of current efforts to improve emergency room treatment is the establishment of sexual assault nurse examiner (SANE) programs. SANE nurses are highly trained in gathering evidence (i.e., rape kit) and in attending to victims' other medical, emotional, and legal problems. As of 2007, the National Institute of Justice and the Office of Violence Against Women funded a state-of-the-art training tool available over the Internet and on a CD entitled, "*Sexual Assault: Forensic and Clinical Management*" (K. Rose, 2007). Research by others provided evidence of some favorable reactions to the SANE program: (a) It is helpful; (b) Health care–based treatment settings are more attractive to survivors than forensic settings; and (c) Survivors often prefer a combination of medical and psychological care. Two criticisms are that (a) Many survivors do not carry through with HIV prophylaxis; and (b) Delivery of the program does not uniformly offer post-rape pregnancy protection (S. L. Martin, Young, Billings, & Bross, 2007).

Other welcome changes entail the availability of the "*National Protocol for Sexual Assault Medical Forensic Examination*" (SAFE Protocol). This protocol includes an assessment of the roles of other sexual assault response team (SART) members. In communities where these programs are available, victims are more satisfied and cooperative and more evidence is made available for criminal prosecution (Nugent-Borakove et al., 2006; see also info@safeta.org for additional information).

*Male sexual assault medical needs.* A Thai doctor has highlighted the need for medical treatment of male sexual assault victims similar to that afforded to females. Some males experience sexual assault at the hands of bullies, as prisoners, as a form of hate crime, by same-sex partners, and by females. Most often, officials show little concern (e.g., Krienert & Fleisher, 2005). Doctors or nurses should obtain seminal fluid samples, take smears for gonorrhea and other STDs, prescribe HIV tests, and prescribe medicine as needed. Health professionals should document their findings for future use in criminal trials (Wiwanitkit, 2005).

## Explaining Sexual Assault

Most young people disavow sexual assault in general but find it acceptable under some circumstances (Hannon et al., 2000). As already described, two of the most salient concepts in the etiology of sexual assault among college students are *rape myth* and *rape myth acceptance* (RMA). Willingness to rape a woman may not be limited to a few drunk or psychopathic men. It seems ominous that in an early study, Malamuth (1989) found that 35% of college men reported "some likelihood" of committing rape if they were certain they could get away with it. Similarly troublesome are the results of a laboratory study of men's sexual arousal in response to audiotaped rape scenarios (Lohr, Adams, & Davis, 1997). Last, some rapists are *sadistically motivated;* they want to hurt women. Others are motivated by their view of *women as sex objects.* A third group experience feelings—*anger/resentment* toward others including *hostility toward women;* they may also have a perception that *women are dangerous* (Beech, Ward, & Fisher, 2006). (See www.sagepub.com/barnett3e for a study about women's vulnerability profiles by Macy, Nurius, & Norris, 2007.)

*Is women's resistance sincere?* In one of the most telling accounts, Van Wie and Gross (2001) explored men's ability to discriminate female partners' entreaties to stop sexual activities. Men ($N = 185$) listened to one of six audiotaped vignettes of an after-date scenario. The vignettes varied in *intimacy levels* (kissing or breast contact) and in the *female's explanation for asking the man to stop* (waiting for marriage, too soon in the relationship, or fear of pregnancy). Researchers measured how long it took (*latency*) for a participant to press a switch when he thought the *woman first refused* to continue. The researchers found a significant interaction effect between the woman's explanation given in the vignette "*too early in the relationship*" and intimacy level described "*breast contact.*" Latencies were substantially longer for this vignette than for others. Van Wie and Gross interpreted the results as indicating that *men felt the woman's resistance was not entirely sincere,* or that she was indecisive and wanted to be convinced. One strength of this study was its use of objective measures generated by laboratory equipment, instead of self-reports.

*Role of alcohol and sexual assault.* A number of studies have examined the role of alcohol in sexual assault. A web-based survey of 1,564 students asked the participants several questions about reactions to their own alcohol consumption. Percentages of endorsed behaviors correlated positively with a test of alcohol-use disorders, and results revealed some gender differences (Cashell-Smith, Connor, Kypri, 2007). See Table 7.5 for a summary of these results.

| **TABLE 7.5** | Harmful Effects of Alcohol on Sexual Behavior | | |
|---|---|---|---|

| *Drinking Effects on Woman Subject* | *Females* | *Males* |
|---|---|---|
| Had unprotected sex | 11% | 15% |
| Were *not* happy at the time | 6% | 7% |
| Regretted sex later | 16% | 19% |
| *Drinking Effects on Other People Who Were Present (same place)* | | |
| People present received unwanted sexual advances *by others* who were drinking | 34% | 25% |

Some other findings are as follows:

- Men reported more alcohol-related sexual disinhibition than women (Heese & Tutenges, 2008).
- Intoxicated women were less aware and less uncomfortable with sexual assault cues (K. C. Davis, Stoner, Norris, George, & Masters, 2009).

*Fraternity men/athletes and sexual assault.* Off-the-field violence is seemingly a daily occurrence among some American athletes. Also making the news are reports of drunken brawls and even deaths at fraternity houses. Impressions of this sort have led to empirical examinations of sexual assaults perpetrated by fraternity brothers and members of athletic organizations. These investigations have regularly demonstrated linkages between fraternity membership and SA (T. J. Brown, Sumner, & Nocera, 2002; Humphrey & Kahn, 2000). One explanation is that fraternity norms and practices encompass viewing sexual coercion of female acquaintances (a felony) as a sport, a contest, or a game (P. Y. Martin & Hummer, 1995). Researchers have found that increased likelihood of SA is correlated with a number of features typical of fraternities: (a) promotion of toughness, dominance, and aggressiveness (Boeringer, 1999); (b) endorsement of traditional, conservative, sex-role attitudes (Lackie & de Man, 1997); and (c) engagement in heavy alcohol consumption (Cashin, Presley, & Meilman, 1996).

A more contemporary inquiry compared the gender attitudes of 279 college students divided into four groups: (a) *fraternity membership,* (b) *sorority membership,* (b) *nonfraternity membership,* and (d) *nonsorority membership.* The findings were as follows: *Fraternity members,* compared with sorority members and nonsorority/nonfraternity members, held significantly more *stereotypical gender attitudes:*

| | |
|---|---|
| Accept stereotypical beliefs about women | Endorse casual sex by women |
| Accept stereotypical beliefs about male IPV | Reject female political leadership |
| Believe in gendered work roles | Oppose women's rights |

The researchers suggest that fraternity men's *double standard* of denying women's rights while endorsing women's casual sex might contribute to sexual assaults (D. T. Robinson, Gibson-Beverly, & Schwartz, 2004). A contemporary inquiry with a sample of 779 college women reported that 29% of the sorority women relative to 7% of non-sorority women had suffered sexual assault while in college (Minow & Einolf, 2009; see also Bleecker & Murnen, 2005). (See www.sagepub.com/barnett3e for a contrasting finding.)

*Male misperception.* Early on, researchers began to explore the possibility that male-to-female SA occurs in part because of *male misperceptions.* Starting with Abbey (1982), social scientists consistently noted that men tend *to misperceive women's friendliness* as a sign of sexual interest (e.g., George et al., 2006). Another line of inquiry uncovered gender dissimilarities in flirting motivations that could, in fact, evoke misperceptions. *Men* viewed flirting as more *sexual* than women, while women more often than men attributed flirting to *having fun* and to *intensifying one's relationship* (Henningsen, 2004). Perhaps misperceptions are more widespread?

A more complex research endeavor explored *misperceptions* of both *sexual* and *romantic interest* in opposite-sex friendships. First, a person's friends' self-reported interest in the participants was a significant predictor of the participants' perceptions of the friends' sexual and romantic interest. Hence, the participants' perceptions were grounded in reality. Male perceivers *overperceived* and women perceivers *underperceived* their opposite-sex friends' *sexual* interest in them (i.e., in the perceiver). This duality did *not* occur when perceiving an opposite-sex friend's *romantic* interest (in the perceiver). Furthermore, both men and women *projected* their own sexual and romantic interests into their perceptions of their opposite-sex friend's sexual and romantic interests (in the perceiver) (Koenig, Kirkpatrick, & Ketelaar, 2007; see Lindgren, Parkhill, George, & Hendershot, 2008, for a comprehensive review of misperception).

*Gender socialization.* Gender socialization represents another type of learning. Gender is an important organizing variable in explaining the various forms of interpersonal violence. As has been evident over the years, men's *traditional sex-role beliefs* are an element in their sexually aggressive behavior (Lackie & de Man, 1997; Lavoie, Vezina, Piche, & Boivin, 1995). One of the most informative studies to date examined associations between several rough classifications of men's beliefs and their behavior. These classifications were as follows: (a) *masculine gender role,* (b) *general and sexual entitlement attitudes,* and (c) *rape-related attitudes and behaviors.* Using a sample of 114 college men, Hill and Fischer (2001) identified these linkages by making 9 assessments in a path analysis. Aspects of masculine gender role predicted general entitlement attitudes, which in turn predicted sexual entitlement attitudes, which finally predicted rape-related attitudes and behaviors. In fact, both entitlement attitudes were **mediators** (transmitter variables) between masculine gender role and rape-related variables.

*Biological substrates of gender differences.* Such results dovetail with common perceptions of men's sexual inclinations. Contemporary neurophysiolgical evidence has uncovered a number of dissimilarities between men's and women's brain structures (see Tyre & Scelfo, 2006).

One divergence occurs in a brain region referred to as the insula (home to gut instincts). The insula helps regulate intuition and empathy, and it is larger in women than men. Since *women are better at reading nonverbal cues* like facial expressions, it seems likely that *men* do, in fact, *suffer* from some *misperceptions* of women's willingness to have sex.

## Treatment of Sexual Assault

Most victims benefit from professional assistance after SA. Analyses in one study identified the following four predictors of help-seeking: physical injury, perpetration by a family member, history of rape before age 18, and threat to do harm (Masho & Alvanzo, 2009).

*Sexual assault treatment* has attracted extensive research attention. Whereas some of the aforementioned counseling techniques for dating violence might be suitable for SA victims, others may not. Counseling for sexual assault occurs most frequently at rape crisis centers, but crisis intervention is far from sufficient (R. Campbell, Wasco, Ahrens, Sefl, & Barnes, 2001). One of the most relevant topics to cover in treatment is the effect of previous sexual assaults (as a child and/or adult [e.g., Cashell-Smith et al., 2007; Stoner et al., 2007]). Prior sexual assaults may place an SA victim at risk for several negative outcomes, such as increased alcohol consumption, another assault, pregnancy, a sexually transmitted disease, and decreased or increased sexual activity. Counselors might recommend classes in rape avoidance or suggest enrolling in an alcohol reduction program. Nevertheless, it is essential that counselors and others realize that rape vulnerability, such as child sexual assault, does not remove the responsibility for rape from male rapists (Macy et al., 2007; see also Deliramich & Gray, 2008). (See www.sagepub.com/barnett3e for some specific treatment ideas.)

## Policy—Sexual Aggression

A meta-analytic review of sexual aggression among college athletes and fraternity members provided insight into potential policy changes at high schools and universities that might reduce rape (and dating violence) (Murnen & Kohlman, 2007). A summary of findings includes the following points:

- *All-male groups* endorse hypermasculine attitudes more than non-all-male groups.
- Male *athletes* are significantly higher in hypermasculinity than fraternity men.
- Male athletes, more than fraternity men, enter college with hypermasculine attitudes.
- *Hypermasculinity is the strongest predictor of sexual aggression.*
- *Research variants* (e.g., male test administrator) alter the results.
- The higher the *validity of the studies* in the analysis, the stronger the effects of hypermasculinity.
- *Hypermasculinity increased with age* among fraternity men (e.g., possible learning effect).
- Disguising the purpose of a study increases hypermasculinity effects.
- Men in *smaller colleges* hold stronger acceptance of rape myths and acceptance of sexual aggression than their counterparts in larger colleges.

*Male athletes.* One policy recommendation centers on the *preferential treatment often given to athletes* accused of SA. Advocates call for stricter rules regulating athletic eligibility. Universities tend to ignore crimes against women in their quest to maintain strong athletic teams that draw important revenue. As Reed (1999) notes, violence against women is "serious misconduct," at least as serious as drug use or gambling. Why not deny eligibility to athletes who assault women?

A number of policy implications flow from these findings and others. Since athletes enter universities from high schools where hypermasculinity may prevail among athletic teams, high school coaches have a special responsibility to undertake prevention programs (see "Working With Athletes," 2007). Universities need to have regulations banning protection of athletes (e.g., against rape charges) at the expense of women's safety. The National Collegiate Athletic Association also needs to develop policies against athletes' violence. Last, it might be helpful to position men in more caretaking roles to develop more empathic attitudes toward women. Much like this study, a researcher explored possible gender attitude distinctions between athletes and nonathletes (Gage, 2008; see also Jakupcak, 2003). (See www.sagepub.com/barnett3e for details.)

*Targeting a wider audience.* One policy proposed by a duo of program reviewers was to sharpen attention efforts going beyond those directed at changing individual behaviors. They recommended targeting *peer networks* and *community-level factors* that support sexual assault. The researchers, for instance, suggested focusing more attention on bullying and bystander intervention programs (Casey & Lindhorst, 2009). This idea may have merit in terms of rape myth acceptance. A German inquiry, as one illustration, showed that the RMA level of *other men* (a social norm) influenced the research participants' rape proclivity (Eyssel, Bohner, & Siebler, 2006).

*Public awareness.* Education of the public about the realities of *rape* is essential if victims are ever to receive justice. A substantial problem in obtaining SA convictions is jurors' misperceptions of rape. Despite judges' instructions and other courtroom procedures, jurors' subjective impressions of rape are incredibly different from legalistic definitions, and these impressions affect jurors' decisions (Churchill, 1993). Illustrative of this problem is that jurors may fail to define nonconsensual intercourse as rape if the victim had consented to sex with the rapist on a previous occasion. Just like police and prosecutors, jurors take extralegal information into account when making their judgments. That is, a jury might find a rape defendant not guilty because the victim wore a miniskirt to court or because the victim was acquainted with the rapist (Candell, Frazier, Arikan, & Tofteland, 1993; Goldberg-Ambrose, 1992).

## Prevention of Sexual Assault

Most rape avoidance programs occur on college campuses and center on date rape and stranger rape. Nearly every program pinpoints alcohol consumption as a risk factor for women's victimization and men's perpetration. As a result of poor correspondence between attitudes and behavior, *attempting to change attitudes about rape may be of limited value.*

*Victim-focused rape prevention programs.* In their infancy, the vast majority of college rape prevention programs *address women's responsibilities* to take precautionary measures. Focusing on women's conduct may seem misdirected and aggravating given that it is basically *male behaviors that necessitate change* if rape is to be prevented but this emphasis continues.

*College courses.* Colleges could offer more *courses in family violence and interpersonal relation-ships.* Some programs have shown changes in student attitudes, such as a reduction in rape myth acceptance (Currier & Carlson, 2009; see also Malkin & Stake, 2004). One focus of atten-tion should be to *encourage disclosure* of sexual assault. Another should be to explicate *real-istic concerns* (P. P. Hughes, Marshall, & Sherrill, 2003). Some of the most *relevant information* is as follows:

- Not recognizing that as the *degree of victim-perpetrator relatedness* increases, the likelihood of rape and injury rises (i.e., stranger to little-known acquaintance, to well-known acquaintance, to boyfriend, cohabitant, and spouse) (See Stermac, Del Bove, Brazeau, & Bainbridge, 2006)
- *Trusting a man she knows* well as a positive dating partner is risky (Macy et al., 2007)
- *Being drunk* around little-known acquaintances is far more dangerous than encountering an *angry driver* (P. P. Hughes et al., 2003)
- *Leaving a drink unattended is risky* (Crawford et al., 2008)
- *Feeling physically ill at a party* may be a sign of being drugged (Crawford et al., 2008)
- A *prior victimization* makes women more vulnerable to rape (Macy et al., 2007)
- Not being *aware of threatening situations* (e.g., being with a man who keeps *trying to get a woman alone)* is risky (Macy et al., 2007)
- Self-defense training helps reduce women's fear of rape (Brecklin & Ullman, 2005)
- Women's rape scripts (perceptions/expectations of a rape experience) concerning the forceful-ness of their resistance was a novel factor associated with women's actual rape during an 8-week follow-up period (Turchik, Probst, Irvin, Chau, & Gidycz, 2009)

*Perpetrator-focused prevention.* Cumulatively, early outcome data indicated that prevention efforts aimed at *all-male groups* are more successful in *changing attitudes* than are those aimed at mixed-gender groups (e.g., Foubert & Marriott, 1997). In the past two decades, the number of rape prevention programs for male college students have mushroomed. As Berkowitz (2000) points out, "All institutions of higher education have the responsibility to devote significant resources to programs that engage men in the task of preventing sexual assault" (p. 67). One element of a prevention program should be to help men iden-tify behaviors considered by others to be sexually aggressive. This approach might be helpful since men's assessments of their own sexually aggressive behavior do not coincide with others' evaluations (Loh et al., 2007). (See www.sagepub.com/barnett3e for an all-male peer program.)

*Rape attitude scale.* Researchers have crafted a relatively new scale on attitudes about date rape based on recognition of attitudinal elements associated with rape. A factor analysis identified four principal attitudinal components: (a) *entitlement,* (b) *blame-shifting,* (c) *traditional roles,* and (d) *overwhelming sexual arousal.* The authors suggested administering the scale and then devising a prevention program to *change the detected attitudes* (Lanier & Green, 2006; see also Breitenbecher, 2008).

*A review of rape prevention programs.* Rape prevention programs have effectively *improved par-ticipants' knowledge, attitudes about rape,* and *intentions to change behaviors* (L. A. Anderson & Whiston, 2005). No research, however, has convincingly demonstrated that prevention programs reduced the *actual incidence of rape,* and some programs fail to have any impact on students' attitudes at all (Ullman, 2007; see also Casey & Lindhorst, 2009). Notwithstanding such bleak results, work on formulating effective programs has continued (Packard, 2007).

*Changing athletes' and fraternity men's attitudes.* Recently, one researcher reviewed all the outcome research on rape-prevention programs over the last 10 years. She pinpointed several salient findings (Ullman, 2007):

- Appropriate program evaluation rarely occurs.
- It is more important to address the risk of rape by boyfriends than by strangers.
- Follow-up studies of rape myth acceptance prevention programs find little lasting change. Increased knowledge about rape is inadequate to prevent it.
- There are no attitudinal distinctions among raped women and non-raped women.
- Programs are inadequate in illuminating the characteristics of risky situations.
- The largest cost of rape (emotional, physical, social) occurs when a rape is actually *completed.*
- Fighting back physically or physically/verbally is the *most effective* in preventing rape completion.
- The content of program evaluations is insufficient.
- Teaching women self-defense is probably the wisest choice.
- Women cannot be held responsible for preventing rape.

(See www.sagepub.com/barnett3e for several other rape prevention programs.)

---

### SECTION SUMMARY

## Sexual Assault

Some definitions of unwanted sexual behaviors are the following: (a) sexual coercion (verbal/physical/drug induced means to obtain sexual activity against consent), (b) rape (perpetration of sexual aggression against an unmarried person, often referring to bodily penetration), and (c) sexual assault (sex-related behaviors on a continuum from unwanted sexual contact through sexual intercourse). Experts often prefer the term sexual assault (SA) because it is more inclusive. Subjective definitions often exclude behaviors that legally define sexual assault, because people do not know or recognize legal definitions. Consent is the critical legal concept in prosecuting SA charges. Because of the early beliefs voiced by a male jurist about women's willingness to make a false charge and men's difficulty in defending themselves, laws have made it especially difficult to obtain rape convictions. Feminists have been somewhat successful in getting laws passed (e.g., rape shield laws) that have offered more protection to women.

Problems of nondisclosure of sexual assault, for reasons such as shame, have made SA one of the most underreported crimes, rather than frequently made false claims. Rapists, of course, are not especially willing to disclose their criminal behavior. As a consequence, estimates of SA are especially likely to underestimate the true prevalence of the crime. The National Crime Violence Survey (telephone-based) reveals how gender disproportionate SA is. Males commit over 90% of sexual assaults, but it is still true that

*(Continued)*

(Continued)

they can be sexually assaulted and even raped. While most men are assaulted by strangers, most women are assaulted by friends and acquaintances.

Women most often resist SAs by taking various protective actions. A fascinating new study suggests that women's reactions are often proportionate to the perpetrator's tactics. That is, women tend to use forceful actions to fend off rape and nonforceful (e.g., verbal protestations) actions to resist sexual coercion. Responses by the criminal justice system continue to be far from optimal despite continual work by women's advocates. Many law enforcement personnel accept rape myths and treat rape victims as if they were to blame. Police officers may actually try to dissuade rape victims from filing a complaint. Along a similar vein, the FBI has refused to acknowledge male rape. Prosecutors' actions have been equally problematic. Personnel throughout the system have mishandled DNA evidence, thus allowing hundreds of rapists to go unchecked. Very few rapists are arrested, prosecuted, convicted, and incarcerated.

With funding by the federal government and driven by women's advocates, law enforcement agencies have begun trial programs to determine the most effective procedures for responding to sexual assaults. A common approach in large urban centers is to develop a sex crimes unit which offers special education to police officers, prosecutors, and judges. Although recognized as a problem and remedied to some extent, defining rape has also proved challenging. Subjective definitions are often far removed from legal definitions.

Attitudes toward sexual assault reflect men's adversarial beliefs, their lack of empathy toward rape victims, their acceptance of rape myths (about both women and men), victim blaming, and gender differences. Acceptance of rape myths is strongly associated with hostile attitudes toward women and lack of empathy. Myths about male rape (e.g., male rape victims must be gay) can be devastating to male victims. Whatever the myths may be, society is quite likely to blame the victims—What was she wearing? How much did she drink?

The consequences of rape are serious. Although injuries occur and can require lengthy surgical and other medical treatment, psychological reactions seem to be even more severe. Unexpectedly, physical injuries to male rape victims are generally more severe than those suffered by females. Both sexes suffer from PTSD which can be exceptionally long-lasting, extending over a lifetime. Problems continue with increased rates of suicide, parenting problems, and sexual dysfunction. The Sexual Assault Nurses Examination (SANE) protocol can be highly useful in prosecutions. Medical personnel, however, can be quite insensitive during rape examinations, and they need training in the use of protocols.

The causes of sexual assault are far-ranging. Peer support of male-to-female violence, beliefs of one's friends, and male misperceptions of female behavior are associated with SA. Males are generally more likely than females to perceive a dating partner's behavior both as giving consent and as sexual. Some other explanations include rape myth acceptance, hostility toward women, alcohol expectancies, attitudes toward women promulgated by fraternities, gender socialization, and possible biological factors. Men who perpetrate severe SA show more signs of psychopathology than do perpetrators of less severe SA. What meager information is available implies that individuals with high needs to control others or with feelings of powerlessness are more likely to be involved in SA than others. The same is true of men high in hypermasculinity. Each of these rationales has received some research support. Sexual assault, for instance, occurs more frequently among fraternities and athletic organizations. How best to provide treatment for SA victims has been an active field of research.

Policy suggestions include working with male athletes and fraternity members and their peer networks. Prevention efforts are increasing. Some programs are victim-focused, while others are centered on men. Although prevention programs have increased knowledge about date rape and how to avoid it, researchers have not conducted program evaluations to see if prevention programs actually reduce the incidence of rape.

## STALKING

Stalking of celebrities first brought wide public attention to stalking, and California passed the first antistalking legislation in 1990. By 2000, all 50 states had antistalking laws (Rosenfeld, 2000). Stalking (ST), like assault, is a "stand-alone" offense in that it does not necessarily fall under the umbrella of intimate partner violence. As knowledge of interpersonal partner violence (IPV) began to surge in the late 1980s, it became evident that abusive partners sometimes perpetrated stalking. When the victim-offender relationship is or was *intimate*, stalking can be a form of intimate partner violence. Moreover, stalking is significantly correlated with dating violence and sexual assault (e.g., H. C. Melton, 2007; Slashinski et al., 2003). Other experts have pointed out that IPV and ST are dissimilar. Stalkers relentlessly pursue their target. They are obsessional, whereas partner-violent men are not as obsessive (Cox & Speziale, 2009).

There are several reasons why stalking (ST) should not be overlooked as a probable component of dating violence and IPV. It is a very intrusive behavior that can be very frightening. It can have the effect of forcing the target of ST to "turn his/her life upside down by quitting school, moving, or leaving a job" (e.g., Spitzberg, 2002). Moreover, it is a *significant predictor* of *serious injury, femicide,* and a *woman's decision to leave* an abusive partner (see McFarlane, Campbell, & Watson, 2002). Last, it is a costly crime. According to economists, stalking cost $342 million ($438 million inflation adjusted) for 1995 (Max, Rice, Finkelstein, Bardwell, & Leadbetter, 2004; Sahr, 2006). (See www.sagepub.com/barnett3e for a case history of a husband who stalked his wife via her computer.)

## Defining Stalking

As with so many forms of family violence, definitions of stalking (harassment or unwanted pursuit) have evolved with increased scholarship. Some scholars recommend separating stalking from normal *courtship persistence,* hence narrowing the types of behaviors recognized as ST (Davis, Frieze, & Maiuro, 2002). Subsequent research has detected several distinctions. An Australian inquiry of 868 community members determined that research participants evaluated ST behavior that lasted only two days as courtship persistence, even when the intent of the stalking was to upset the target (Dennison, 2007). Examples of stalking and harassment definitions follow:

- Stalking is "harassing or threatening behavior that an individual engages in repeatedly, such as following a person, appearing at a person's home or place of business, making harassing phone calls, leaving written messages or objects or vandalizing a person's property" (Tjaden & Thoennes, 1998b, p. 3)Stalking is "a pattern of repeated and unwanted attention, harassment, contact, or any course of conduct directed at a specific person that would cause a reasonable person to feel fear" (The Office for Victims of Crime, 2002, p. 1).
- Seven types of *harassing or unwanted behavior* are as follows (U.S. Department of Justice, Supplemental Victimization Survey—2006a):

| | |
|---|---|
| Making unwanted phone calls | Showing up at a place where they had no reason to be |
| Sending unsolicited/unwanted e-mails | Leaving unwanted items, presents, flowers |
| Following/spying on the victim | Posting information/rumors about the victim on the Internet and elsewhere |
| Waiting at places for the victim | |

- *Harassment* (as distinguished from stalking)—an annoying but *not* a frightening behavior intended to upset or disturb someone.
- A novel form of stalking is stalking by a friend/family member of the stalker who pursues/harasses a target at the behest of the stalker, thus becoming a *proxy stalker* (H. C. Melton, 2007).

*Subjective definitions.* Victims frequently hold perceptions of interpersonal violence crimes that are at variance with legal definitions. As a case in point, stalked college students ($N = 292$) in one survey did *not* consider themselves to have been stalked (Spitzberg & Veksler, 2007). In a separate study, the subjective definitions of 841 college students' included not only behaviors identified by a team of researchers (Baum, Catalano, Rand, & Rose, 2009), but added supplementary items, such as *vandalizing property* and *contacting the victim's friends or family to find out the victim's whereabouts.* All the various forms of stalking were significantly correlated with each other (Amar, 2007; see also Kinkade, Burns, & Fuentes, 2005).

*Cyberstalking.* Cyberstalking involves the following: (a) repeated threats and/or harassment, (b) the use of electronic mail or other computer-based communication, and (c) which would make a reasonable person afraid or concerned for his or her safety (D'Olvidio & Doyle, 2003). In addition to electronic stalking previously listed, some specific forms of cyberstalking are as follows (e.g., Barak, 2005; Finn & Banach, 2000; Spitzberg & Hoobler, 2002):

| | |
|---|---|
| Monitoring e-mails directly or through "sniffer" programs | Using the victim's e-mail identity to send false messages to others or to purchase goods |
| Disrupting the target's e-mails through flooding his/her e-mail box | Using the Internet to seek and compile a victim's personal information |
| Sending a virus to the target's e-mail | |

Some experts in the field believe that the term cyberstalking is too limited because so many other technologies are available. A more inclusive and accurate term might be *stalking with technology* (Southworth, Finn, Dawson, Fraser, & Tucker, 2007).

Some of the other kinds of electronic equipment that is used for stalking include the following: (a) fax machines, (b) TTY and TTD phones (for the deaf), (c) hidden cameras, (d) GPS and location services, (e) cordless telephones, (f) computer and Internet technology such as spy ware and keystroke logging hardware, and (g) use of government databases when made public, such as Department of Motor Vehicles Records. As an illustration, a Pennsylvania court began publishing the names and addresses of victims who obtained protective orders (see Southworth et al., 2007, for a detailed explanation of computer stalking methods and terms).

*Legal definition. A legal definition* of a stalker—"A person who intentionally and repeatedly follows or harasses another person and who makes a credible threat, either expressed or implied with the intent to place that person in reasonable fear of death or serious bodily harm is guilty of the crime of stalking" (http://www.USLegal.com, 2010). For information on laws governing cyberstalking, see Stalking Resource Center (n.d.). *Fear standard*—Just as early rape laws demanded that women demonstrate they had resisted a rape by fighting back, current ST legislation demands that the stalker's targets *experience fear.* According to Dietz and Martin (2007, p. 750), the fear requirement leads to "a miscarriage of justice, an undercount of the crime, and an abandonment of women (and others) who need validation from the state and protection from stalkers." After all, people react differently to events. What if the victim is angry rather than fearful? Why should ST behaviors require a victim to be fearful when crimes of rape and assault do not? For one thing, even implicit threats can be fear-provoking (Logan & Walker, 2009b).

## Prevalence Estimates of Stalking

For the most part, researchers have presented data on stalking that are disaggregated by gender, age, and the nature of the perpetrator's acquaintance with the victim.

[1] Of 16,000 individuals 18 years of age and over, Tjaden and Thoennes (1998b) found the following:

- 74% of ST victims fell between the ages of 18 and 39.
- 8.1% of women and 2.2% of men were victims of stalking.

[2] Of 9,684 individuals 18 years of age or older reached in a national household random-digit dialing survey, Basile, Swahn, Chen, and Saltzman (2006) reported the following:

- 7% of women and 2% of men had been stalked at any time in the past.
- Persons who were never married/divorced/separated/widowed suffered significantly more victimization than others.
- African Americans experienced significantly less stalking than non-African Americans.

[3] Of 65,270 persons 18 years of age or older in a government study (U.S. Department of Justice, Supplemental Victimization Survey [SVS], 2006a), males were more victimized than

women, thus *contradicting* the majority of other findings. Further research needs to untangle these disparities (Baum et al., 2009).

*Disclosure/reporting of stalking.* Of course, disclosure rates impact results. Surveys have found various *rates of reporting to police.*

- 42% of stalked college students (Westrup, Fremouw, Thompson, & Lewis, 1999)
- 54.6% of a representative sample of 16,000 people (Tjaden & Thoennes, 1998b)
- 41% of the females and 36.6% of the males in a government survey (Baum et al., 2009).

An analysis of 130 female victims yielded variations in patterns of disclosure. These women often made multiple disclosures: (a) to friends—80%; (b) to their sisters—47%; (c) to their mothers—43%; and (d) to criminal justice authorities—9% (Mahlstedt & Keeny, 1993; see also Fisher, Cullen, & Turner, 2000). One qualitative study found male listeners, even fathers, trivialized stalking saying such things as, "He is young and socially awkward." Mothers and females, on the other hand, took the stalking seriously and offered support (Cox & Speziale, 2009).

*Measurement of stalking.* Stalking, like dating violence and sexual assault, suffers from measurement ambiguity. There is no stalking inventory that has gained widespread consensus. Accordingly, findings across studies lack comparability. What is more, stalking victims do not uniformly recognize behaviors defined as stalking as ST. Baum et al. (2009) have provided comprehensive information on stalking victimization. Some results are as follows:

| | |
|---|---|
| Nearly 75% of victims knew their stalker | Stalkers stalked about 11% of the victims for 5 years or more |
| More males than females stalked females | Stalkers stalked low-income more than high-income victims |
| Males and females stalked males about equally | Stalkers threatened various family, friends, coworkers, or pets |
| Stalkers threatened to harm 40% of victims | Stalkers stalked divorced/separated people more than others |
| Stalkers were about the same age as their victims | 85% of victims received unwanted e-mail messages |
| 30% of stalkers stalked for retaliation/anger | About 10% used electronic monitoring devices (e.g., GPS) |
| | 46% of victims were contacted one or more times/week |

## Miscellaneous Findings

- The *largest subcategory of stalkers* is made up of the *former partners* of the victims (Sheridan, Gillett, Blaauw, Davies, & Patel, 2003).
- Stalkers occasionally enlist the support of friends to join with them on stalking activities (i.e., "proxy stalking" [Logan & Walker, 2009b]). (See www.sagepub.com/barnett3e for other statistical results.)

## Consequences of Stalking

The ramifications of stalking are more damaging than the average citizen knows. In addition to the effects of physical and psychological abuse, stalkers frequently cause their victims to have *employment problems* and *financial problems*. (See www.sagepub.com/barnett3e for more details.)

*Psychological ramifications.* Mental health problems are frequently associated with stalking. These reactions are comparable to those of victims of dating violence and sexual assault. Possibly the most common reaction to stalking is to be *angry, fearful, or both* (Baum et al., 2009; M. C. Johnson & Kercher, 2009). Not only can stalking last for years, but also victims may not feel safe for years after the stalking stops (Cox & Speziale, 2009).

*Environmental protective reactions.* In one survey, the most common self-protective action was to improve one's home security system, followed by getting caller ID, traveling with a companion, buying a weapon, and taking a self-defense class. The victims also undertook avoidance actions, such as not returning e-mail, moving their place of residence, changing universities, quitting their job, changing majors, and trying to avoid encountering the stalker (Fisher et al., 2002). Even after obtaining a protective order, female intimate partner violence victims who continued to be stalked suffered the most severe physical, sexual, and psychological abuse compared with those who were not stalked. This enhanced abuse even occurred among women who reconciled with their abuser after receiving a protective order (Logan & Cole, 2007).

*Criminal justice system responses.* In addition to reports to law-enforcement, stalking victims responded by seeking a protective order, filing a grievance or initiating an action with campus authorities, proceeding with criminal charges, and filing civil charges (Fisher et al., 2002). In regard to *prosecution of stalking,* outcomes are similar to those found for sexual assault. That is, there is a winnowing down of cases from arrest, to prosecution, to conviction, to incarceration, so that the consequences of ST for the abuser are mild (e.g., Tjaden & Thoennes, 1998b).

## Traits of Individuals Involved in Stalking

The media coverage of celebrities piqued interest about the mental state of stalkers. What sort of person would dedicate his/her life to following someone he/she did not even know? What sort of person would claim their target loved them despite clear contraindications? On the surface, it seemed that stalkers suffered from some form of *mental illness/personality disorder.*

Subsequent research has supported these early assessments—there is a subset of stalkers who are mentally ill. Some other viewpoints cast stalkers as common criminals, rejected lovers, and attachment disordered. Surprisingly, research by independent laboratories across the entire field of ST has frequently reached very similar conclusions about the traits of stalkers.

*Different degrees of stalking.* Researchers have differentiated several levels of stalking behavior (none, minor, severe). Using scales to assess attachment, emotional dependence, IPV, jealousy, verbal victimization, verbal perpetration, physical victimization, and physical perpetration, researchers have been able to classify 177 undergraduates as follows: (a) NONHARASSERS—45 (25.6%); (b) MINOR HARASSERS—96 (54.5%); and (c) SEVERE HARASSERS—35 (19.9%) (Wigman, Graham-Kevan, & Archer, 2008).

*Attachment/dependency/jealousy.* Researchers have very frequently found relationships between attachment and ST and between ST, dependency, and jealousy (Wigman et al., 2008; see also Dye & Davis, 2003). Jealousy is a trait that is characteristic of a number of stalkers among both dating and married partners (Langhinrichsen-Rohling, Palarea, Cohen, & Rohling, 2000; K. A. Roberts, 2005). Another researcher showed that insecure attachment (fearful, preoccupied, dismissing) differentiated stalkers from both a community sample and a forensic sample (Tonin, 2004).

*Personality disorders/mental illness.* Other classifications of stalkers encompass such categories as *paraphilic stalkers* (i.e., persons needing bizarre fantasies for sexual excitement), *love obsessionals, cyberstalkers,* and *antisocial stalkers* (see Radosevich, 2000; Sheridan, Blaauw, & Davies, 2003). A qualitative study of only nine female stalking survivors revealed that men who initially appeared charming (i.e., nice dates) underwent a metamorphosis. The women claimed that they saw no clues to warn them about the dangerousness of these men (Cox & Speziale, 2009).

In another investigation, a pair of researchers enlisted 292 university students as research participants in a study of stalking. Of this group, 46.3% reported having *ever* suffered from unwanted pursuit/stalking/harassment. Based on a review of the literature, the researchers selected and administered questions from an assortment of tests measuring personality disorders, social interaction competence, and obsessional-relational factors. Analyses of the trait ratings of the stalkers by the victims determined significant differences between stalkers and nonstalkers on all 15 scales (Spitzberg & Veksler, 2007). See the following list of personality disorders on which stalkers are significantly more disordered than nonstalkers.

When the stalkers were divided into three groups of *acquaintances, friends, or romantic partners* of the victims, significant differences occurred on 7 of the 15 scales. Victims of the *romantic partners* evaluated the stalkers as significantly *less normal* on the following dimensions:

| | | |
|---|---|---|
| Antisocial | Avoidant | Borderline |
| Dependent | Histrionic | Narcissistic |
| Obsessive-compulsive | Paranoid | Schizotypal |

Antisocial, Borderline, Histrionic, Narcissistic, Paranoid, and the two Obsessional-Relational factors. The investigators concluded that their findings are sufficient to claim that *a profile of stalkers exists* (Spitzberg & Veksler, 2007). (See www.sagepub.com/barnett3e for a discussion of risk assessments.)

*Common criminals?* Based on their interactions with the criminal justice system, there is reason to believe male stalkers are criminal, or violent, or both. One review of 346 male stalkers (both intimate and nonintimate) revealed that 27.4% had been convicted of a property crime in the same year as their ST conviction. These men had criminal records of drug arrests, resisting arrest, and other crimes suggestive of *antisocial personality disorder* (Jordan, Logan, Walker, & Nigoff, 2003). According to the U.S. Justice Department survey (Baum et al., 2009), stalkers committed many additional crimes against their victim, such as *identity theft, burglary, assault,* and *attacking pets.* Such criminal patterns of behaviors may lay the groundwork for a stalking profile (e.g., Rosenfeld, 2000).

*Typology of stalkers.* Attempting to categorize stalkers into offender types captured the interest of early researchers. Holmes (1993), for example, classified stalkers into six categories: celebrity, lust, hit, scorned, domestic, and political. Another classification that remains popular with some is a three-category grouping: *erotomaniac, love obsessional,* and *simple obsessional* (see Cox & Speziale, 2009). Over time, experts attempted to classify stalkers along other dimensions: (a) *motivation for stalking,* (b) *psychopathology of the stalker,* (c) *the stalker-victim relationship,* or (d) the *stalker's method of stalking.* Building on this foundation, investigators provided a typology of stalkers based on records of 1,005 stalkers drawn from prosecutorial agencies, entertainment security agencies, police departments, and the authors' files. The RECON typology uses information about *stalkers' relationships* and the *context of their stalking* to construct a four-category typology of stalkers. The typology is easy to use in the criminal justice setting, in research, and elsewhere (Mohandie, Meloy, McGowan, & Williams, 2006). See Table 7.6 for a simplified version of a stalker typology.

(See www.sagepub.com/barnett3e for some *criticisms of typologies* advanced by attorney Joan Zorza, 2001.)

**TABLE 7.6**  Simplified Categorization of Stalkers

| Intimate (n = 502) | Acquaintance (n = 129) | Public Figure (n = 271) | Private Stranger (n = 103) |
|---|---|---|---|
| Sense of rejection | Desire bond with target | Desire love and help | Want to communicate with target |
| Insecure attachment | | | |
| Most likely male to female | 21% are female | 27% female | Many are men |

*(Continued)*

**TABLE 7.6** (Continued)

| Intimate (n = 502) | Acquaintance (n = 129) | Public Figure (n = 271) | Private Stranger (n = 103) |
|---|---|---|---|
| Violent criminal records | | Less violent criminals | Fewer violent criminals |
| Likely to escalate | | Less likely to escalate | |
| Abuse drugs/alcohol | | | Less likely drug/alcohol use |
| 50% assaulted target | 33% assaultive | | One-third are violent with target |
| | Pursue relentlessly | | Do not pursue as much |
| Personality disorder | Females maybe borderline | | |
| Not psychotic | Some psychosis | More likely psychotic | Many are mentally ill |
| Nearly all reoffend | | Majority reoffend | Moderate reoffending |
| Prior sex increases danger | | | No prior relationship with target |
| | | Older | |
| | | | Primary targets are women |

## Victims' Responses to Stalking

Given that individuals vary in their responses to the same situation, it should not be surprising that an evaluation of stalking victims' reactions revealed inconsistencies. Close to half of the victims in one survey, however, did take various actions to protect themselves, such as changing their daily routine, changing their telephone number, and seeking help from friends, attorneys, and others (Baum et al., 2009). Analyzing data from the subsample of 1,336 stalked women who responded to the National Violence Against Women Survey, Dietz and Martin (2007) found several types of significant differences. Black women, for example, were less likely to feel fear as a consequence of stalking than White women were. Being *frequently stalked* evoked more fear than being stalked only once, and being stalked by an intimate aroused more fear than being stalked by a stranger. Last, being stalked via physical or communicative modes elicited more fear than did other types of stalking. (See www.sagepub.com/barnett3e for information on coping with ST.)

## Explaining Stalking

Explanations and theories of ST have not been as uniform as findings in other research areas. It is unclear why certain individuals, especially after a romantic break-up, carry out ST behavior. Investigators have frequently surmised that a motive for stalking of ex-romantic partners is *to prevent a romantic partner from leaving*. *Preoccupied attachment* and *emotional reliance* (dependence) may be the two major variables that make severe harassers *qualitatively different* from *nonharassers* and *minor harassers*. The stalking behavior may have been *motivated* by continued interest in the partner's activities, a desire to seek revenge for a perceived wrongdoing during the relationship, or a desire to exert control over the target (Wigman et al., 2008).

Because the stalker and the victim are usually acquainted, the stalker knows something about the victim's life, if she works, goes to school, and so forth. *Routine activities theory* is especially useful for explaining stalker victimization. Victims' habitual activities (their routines), such as going to classes or working at regular hours, make it relatively easy for stalkers to track them (Fisher et al., 2002). *Attachment theory* also provides a useful framework for explaining stalking. Individuals suffering from insecure attachment, especially preoccupied, fear abandonment, and it is hard for them to let their partner go (Tonin, 2004; Wigman et al., 2008).

*Courtship persistence.* In a study with comprehensive measurements, social scientists uncovered a number of similarities between specific *courtship approach* behaviors and *break-up* behaviors among 300 students. The major finding was that with one exception (intimidation), students behaved *very similarly* when either approaching a courtship or when breaking up. Students who sent notes as an approach behavior, for example, often sent notes as break-up behavior. Based on legal definitions of *stalking behaviors,* the behaviors examined included four types as follows (with examples): (a) *approach*—asking the other out on a date, (b) *surveillance*—showing up at events where the other will be, (c) *intimidation*—spying on the other, and (d*) mild aggression*—making threats (Williams & Frieze, 2008).

*Childhood factors—stalking and control.* One thread of evidence about the effects of childhood factors on stalking comes from Dye and Davis's (2003) research. They found several strong associations: (a) *Harsh parental discipline* was significantly associated with the *need to control a dating partner through stalking; and (b) harsh discipline, anxious attachment,* and *stalking were all associated with each other.*

## Practice, Policy, and Prevention of Stalking

### Treatment of Stalking

According to one group of researchers, the literature does not yet provide guidance on what counseling treatment or other services *stalking victims* need (Logan, Shannon, & Cole, 2007). Although dating violence victims and sexual assault victims share some common needs with ST victims, each form of intimate partner violence has some unique aspects calling for specialized counseling. There are extremely few service centers that have trained stalking experts available for victims (Cox & Speziale, 2009). Advocates and others working in shelters need education about stalking, especially cyberstalking. *Safety planning* ought to include Internet and computer safety information (Southworth et al., 2007). Advocates need to advise ST victims to document every infraction by keeping messages and gifts sent by the stalker and by keeping a diary (Cox & Speziale, 2009). Counselors working with stalking perpetrators could try to determine if their client is a minor or major harasser and then work on the troublesome traits identified, such as *insecure attachment* and *jealousy* (Wigman et al., 2008).

*Stalking victims and offenders.* Because ST victimization takes many forms and symptoms vary, therapists can best serve ST victims by helping them to enhance their general coping skills and finding ways to help them decrease their vulnerability (Blaauw, Winkel, Arensman, Sheridan, & Freeve, 2002). Currently, no specific psychological treatments exist for ST offenders (B. D. Rosenfeld, 2000). For the subgroup of stalkers who have diagnosable mental disorders, psychotropic medicine may be beneficial (Sheridan, Blaauw et al., 2003). It is probable, however, that laws protecting the mentally ill would shield ST perpetrators from forced medication (B. D. Rosenfeld, 2000). Given these obstacles, criminal and civil options may be the only choices available. Nonetheless, Spitzberg (2002) examined 32 studies and found that stalkers violated restraining orders 40% of the time.

## Policy—Stalking

First and foremost, education about stalkers and stalking for the general public has lagged behind public awareness campaigns for other forms of DV.

*College campuses.* In the 2002 survey by Fisher, Cullen, and Turner, they make the following policy recommendation: "Due to its prevalence, college and university administrators need to rectify their current neglect of stalking" (p. 257). Administrators should institute educational programs, hold crime prevention seminars, reduce opportunities for stalking, and increase both formal and informal controls over stalkers.

*Criminal justice system approaches.* Disparate *definitions* of stalking, either *broad or narrow,* help shape the reactions of the criminal justice system. Obviously, the use of broader definitions casts a larger net and captures more stalkers than narrowly written definitions (Logan & Walker, 2009b). An interesting outcome of a Dutch analysis of 77 convicted stalkers indicated that the *passage of laws* may be even more important in curtailing ST than the imposition of punishment (Malsch, 2007). Several assessments in the United States determined that criminal justice *interventions appear to decrease* the amount of stalking. Accordingly, policies should emphasize a criminal justice approach (Logan & Cole, 2007; H. C. Melton, 2007). Judges can improve the safety of victims and others by issuing orders of protection that cover the victim's workplace (Logan, Shannon, Cole, & Swanberg, 2007). An opposite opinion suggests that prioritizing prosecution may either exclude victims from participating in the process or force them to become a part of the prosecution, neither of which meets victims' needs (Römkens, 2006).

*Safe at Home.* Typical of progressive laws and programs is California's Safe at Home program, a coordinated system that works to protect the addresses of victims of partner violence and stalking (see California Secretary of State, 1998). Legislators updated this program to include sexual assault victims ("October Is Domestic," 2007).

*Definition/patterns of abuse.* Legislation should try to alter the *incident approach* to criminal justice processing. Along with other abuses, such as physical abuse, the criminal justice system fails to take into account that the repetitive nature of these crimes represents *patterns of behavior.* In the case of ST, a policeman might not understand a woman's claim of being stalked if he is aware of only a single harassing phone call. The current phone call she is complaining about, however, might be 1 of 50 calls made during the current month along with 40 e-mails, and 10 drive-bys of her home. In addition, these harassments may have been continuing for 60 months.

## Prevention—Stalking

*Antistalking legislation.* The current state of affairs dictates the *need for antistalking legislation.* The most obvious improvement would be the modification of current laws to enable victims to obtain lifetime protective orders. A second would be the modification of bail rules to keep stalkers off the streets, and a third would be the passage of legislation to stop cyberstalking (Merschman, 2001). The phenomenon of cyberstalking also raises the need for improvements in law enforcement training, as most police officers are inexperienced in investigating this type of crime ("Police Agencies," 2001; "Successes Seen," 2003).

*Precautions at work.* One team of investigators recommended a number of precautions that *employers* might undertake in order to diminish workplace stalking. "First and foremost, safety planning at work may be especially important to protect the stalking victim, other employees, and workplace customers from harassment" (Logan, Shannon et al., 2007, p. 287). To this end, it is important to provide employers and their workers with educational information. Currently, employers tend to *discipline the victim* and *pressure her to handle the situation.* In addition, personnel within the criminal justice system and public health fields should collaborate to craft prevention programs and to provide timely protection for victims (Logan, Shannon et al., 2007). Finally, government agencies that have databases, such as courts, tax assessors, and departments of motor vehicles, need to have opt-out plans or some system whereby ST victims can prevent stalkers from gaining personal information about them (Southworth et al., 2007).

---

**SECTION SUMMARY**

### Stalking

Stalking definitions include some commonalities. The behavior must be repetitious and unwanted. Some experts use the term harassment or stalking interchangeably, while still others conceptualize harassment as less serious and unlikely to produce fear. Most legal definitions include the fear standard, a standard that some advocates find unacceptable. Most examples of stalking (ST) include pursuit behaviors, such as following the target around and showing up wherever she is. Although ordinary ST includes sending unwanted

*(Continued)*

---

e-mails, *cyberstalking* is much more inclusive and extraordinarily intrusive. It includes many sophisticated assaults dependent upon technology, such as using spyware to keep track of a target's activities or attaching GPS equipment to a target's car. One particularly aspect of ST is its duration—possibly multiple years. Some government agencies add to the target's problem by publishing certain semi-private documents online.

Victims may be somewhat more willing to report stalking than sexual assault. At least victims are likely to confide ST victimization to a friend or relative. Females are more likely to be targets than males, and males are more likely to stalk both males and females. About 8% of women and 2% of men have been stalked. The largest subcategory of stalkers is former intimate partners.

Stalkers' targets respond by taking a large variety of behavioral and environmental activities to protect themselves. Victims truly are fearful and usually angry as well. They change their telephone numbers, acquire caller ID, get alarm systems in their homes, change their place of residence, change cars, and other actions to improve their safety. Stalking is notably interruptive in that victims may have to change jobs or drop out of school. The worry that the stalker will reappear is pervasive and may consume the victim's attention for years. In addition to making a complaint to the police, victims may file for orders of protection. Stalkers often extend their pursuit to the woman's place of employment, causing her excessive stress. The stalker may annoy coworkers, spread gossip about the victim to coworkers, and cause the victim to miss work. Supervisors are prone to hold the victim accountable by expecting her to resolve the stalker's criminal behavior. The victim may perform poorly on the job because of stalking, and she may lose her job.

Several researchers have tried to establish a typology of stalkers by using their traits as classification indicators. Stalkers do vary in degrees of ST between minor and severe. They frequently suffer from attachment disorders, feeling dependent on the target and fearful of abandonment. A subset of stalkers manifest symptoms of personality disorder, such as antisociality or paranoia. Stalkers who harass former intimates may manifest the greatest number of abnormalities. A substantial minority of stalkers have criminal records, thus increasing the possibility that they may carry through with a threat to hurt the victim, her children, her pets, and so forth. There are enough significant differences between stalkers that researchers have been able to form a typology of four subtypes: intimate, acquaintance, public figure, and private stranger.

Victims' responses to ST indicate that victims are very responsive but differ in terms of race, effects of frequency of ST, and whether the stalker is an ex-intimate. Victims try to cope, but the unpredictability and uncontrollability of the stalking takes a toll. Although more research is needed, it may be that problem-focused coping is not as effective in recovery as might be expected.

Explanations for ST fit well into an attachment framework. The stalker is trying to prevent his romantic partner from leaving. Preoccupied attachment and emotional dependence may separate minor from severe harassers. Routine activities theory plays a role because stalkers are aware of a target's habits (routines) of going to class or work, and they use this knowledge to advance their stalking activities. Courtship persistence is a popular explanation for ST. In fact, an insightful study was able to draw a parallel between an individual's courtship approach behaviors and his or her courtship persistence behaviors.

Treatment of ST is not well formulated yet. Counselors accustomed to treating PTSD, for example, are less likely to be as experienced with stalking victims. ST victims need to document events, avoid interacting with the stalkers, and try to find safety. Counselors should help victims develop effective coping skills. Stalking perpetrators may need special help with attachment disorders or medication for their mental illness problems. There are few public awareness campaigns, and colleges are not yet involved in providing programs. It is possible that legislation is more effective in dealing with some stalkers than actual punishment. Accordingly, victims should definitely pursue orders of protection and other legal options. Legislation very much needs to abandon the single-incident approach to enforcement and develop a pattern of behavior approach. Single stalking incidents may not constitute a problem, but the typical series of incidents occurring over many months certainly does. Not enough is known about how to prevent stalking; hence, there are many gaps in the research that must be addressed.

## SAME-SEX DATING VIOLENCE, SEXUAL ASSAULT, AND STALKING

Despite the potential usefulness of data on interpersonal violence among *gay, lesbian, bisexual, and transgendered* (GLBT) young people, data on this population are usually meshed with data about adult IPV. In an investigation of DV conducted with 521 youths, ages 13 to 22, who attended a rally for gays, lesbians, and bisexuals, researchers asked respondents about their sexual orientation among other questions. Data yielded the following *DV victimization rates* for the 171 male participants: gays, 44.6%; bisexuals, 57.1%; and heterosexuals, 28.6%. *Comparable dating violence rates* for the 350 female participants were as follows: lesbians, 43.4%; bisexuals, 38.3%; and heterosexuals, 32.4%. Relative to gay and lesbian respondents, bisexuals experienced the highest level of "outing" threats (i.e., threats to expose their nonheterosexual orientation). Collectively, these findings demonstrate that bisexual males are at greater risk of DV victimization than either gay males or lesbians (Freedner, Freed, Yang, & Austin, 2002).

*Disclosure of same-sex sexual assault.* Chi-square tests and MANCOVAs revealed many similarities between groups in terms of disclosures, perceived helpfulness of listeners, and attribution of blame, but found significant differences in frequency of SA by sexual orientation membership: (a) *heterosexual women* more frequently experienced a *completed rape* than did the other two groups; and (b) *lesbians* were more frequently assaulted by a *family member* than were the other two groups.

The experiences of **bisexuals** differed significantly from those of lesbian and heterosexual women. Bisexuals more than the other two groups disclosed as follows: (a) to *formal sources of support* (e.g., religious personnel, medical personnel, police, rape crisis personnel; (b) to mental health professionals; or (c) to a romantic partner (*one informal source of support)* (Freedner et al., 2002). (See www.sagepub.com/barnett3e for further details about bisexuals.)

*Types of disclosure and their effects.* If a sexual assault victim discloses her victimization to others, what might listeners' responses be? In the survey above, *bisexuals* also received a larger number of *negative reactions* for disclosing their sexual assaults than did the other two groups. An inquiry of 103 sexual assault survivors reported the following consequences:

- Counselors and friends were significantly more supportive than romantic partners.
- Counselors offered high levels of tangible aid and lower levels of negative responses.
- Romantic partners offered a moderate level of tangible aid.
- Romantic partners delivered the highest level of blame, controlling behaviors, and egocentric behaviors, and treated their female partners differently.

Listeners who either did not appear upset or who became overwrought upon hearing about the assault seemed to trigger negative feelings from the survivors. The survivors who received *tangible* support from the police felt blamed by police who failed to offer emotional support. The ratings of the survivors' represent interpretations (Ahrens, Cabral, & Abeling, 2009).

*Students' attitudes about dating violence among same-sex pairs.* A team of researchers investigated whether undergraduates took *sexual orientation* into account when evaluating DV described in scenarios. Although sexual orientation had some effects on students' judgments, the *gender of the victim* in the scenario and the *gender of the participants* had greater effects. Students said that violence against women, whether male-to female DV or female-to-female DV, was more serious than violence against men (Seelau, Seelau, & Poorman, 2003).

*Prevention of same-sex sexual assault.* Although laws based on sexual orientation do not determine victimization status, they do impact execution of the laws by police and other personnel within the criminal justice system. Last but not least, university education and prevention programs must refrain from excluding male victims of same-sex rape (Scarce, 1997). (See Chapter 11 for more information about same-sex intimate partner violence.)

## CROSS-CULTURAL DATING VIOLENCE, SEXUAL ASSAULT, AND STALKING

Researchers have just begun to obtain estimates of dating violence and sexual assaults among other cultural populations. Willingness to disclose DV or SA varies across cultures. According to C. S. Lewis, Griffing et al. (2006, p. 342), "Cultures may be clannish, even vindictive about negative extra-familial exposure, favoring stability of the family over protection from harm." This belief suggests that victims in some countries may be less likely to inform their family if they experience DV or SA. Using the *CTS2*, Straus (2004 a) examined physical assaults among 31universities across the globe. See Table 7.7 for a few estimates of the prevalence of cross-cultural dating violence.

Some researchers have begun to use this international data as a basis of additional cross-cultural comparisons. Lysova and Douglas (2008) surveyed Russian university students and Doroszewicz and Forbes (2008) surveyed Polish students, and both research teams arrived at the usual gender-symmetric rates. Others also found a link between punishment and dating violence (E. M. Douglas & Straus, 2006).

**TABLE 7.7** Physical Dating Violence in a Sample of Foreign Nations

| Country | Males | | Females | | Total Number | |
|---|---|---|---|---|---|---|
| Belgium | 26.0% | n = 126 | 32.5% | n = 406 | 31.0% | n = 532 |
| Brazil | 22.4% | n = 152 | 23.8% | n = 280 | 23.3% | n = 432 |
| Germany | 38.5% | n = 64 | 27.7% | n = 137 | 31.1% | n = 201 |
| Hong Kong (China) | 19.5% | n = 70 | 34.6% | n = 150 | 29.8% | n = 220 |
| Israel | 22.6% | n = 86 | 20.4% | n = 356 | 20.8% | n = 442 |
| Mexico (Juarez) | 30.8% | n = 47 | 44.3% | n = 207 | 41.8% | n = 254 |
| Singapore | 11.6% | n = 87 | 27.8% | n = 192 | 22.7% | n = 279 |

*Arabs/Jews—rape.* An Israeli study contrasted Arabs and Jews. Arab males attributed more responsibility to an Arab victim raped by a Jew, while Arab females attributed more responsibility to a Jewish female victim raped by an Arab. Among Jews, males attributed more responsibility to an Arab victim raped by an Arab, and females attributed more responsibility to a Jewish victim raped by a Jew. One interpretation of the findings was that the *minority status* of Arabs fosters preservation of a separate identity, so that Arab women mingling with Jews are viewed as lesser victims than Arab women raped by Arab men. The Jewish participants, as the *majority group,* assign more responsibility to women interacting with their own group (Korn, 2009; also see Ben-David & Schneider, 2005).

*Australians—dating violence.* There is some evidence that persons involved in dating violence and sexual assault in Australia exhibit distinct patterns of sociostructural variables, but findings are not definitive (O'Keefe, 1998). One survey uncovered *chronic unemployment and low educational levels* as characteristics of abusive male daters (Magdol et al., 1997). In another *Australian* comparison, *insecure parent-child attachment* was significantly correlated with *college men's antisocial dispositions, aggression,* and *sexual assault* (Smallbone & Dadds, 2001).

*Chinese—dating violence.* An accounting of 145 *Chinese* students found that the act of *harm by another* aroused two major emotional complexes: *anger* and *worry.* Significant correlational analyses demonstrated that both *blame* and *loss of image* were linked with *anger,* and *image loss* and *relationship harm* were linked with *worry* (Y-Y Lee, Kam, & Bond, 2007*).* An unusual study of Chinese students exposed to a popular film (*My Sassy Girl*—a woman uses dating violence to fight back), assessed men's and women's attitudes about the woman's behavior in the film. Generally, men rejected the woman and women had empathy for her. Reactions in focus groups of students, however, revealed that both genders *tend to normalize her violence* and justify it when displayed against a cheating boyfriend. They refused to label the behavior as violence and thought of it as a form of playful fighting, a means of communicating, and a way of increasing affection (Xiying, Wang, & Petula, 2007).

*Ethiopians—dating violence risk factors.* A survey of 1,330 female Ethiopian college students pinpointed risk factors for women. Some of these entailed the following: protestant religious affiliation, rural residence as a child, alcohol/drug consumption, and witnessing domestic violence as a child (Arnold, Geylaye, Goshu, Berhane, & Williams, 2008).

*Koreans—date rape.* A survey of 163 South Korean university students found that men were more tolerant of rape myths than females. A sexual assault education program decreased female students' rape myth acceptance but not males' (J. Lee, Busch, Kim, & Lim, 2007).

*Japanese—rape.* Japanese college students ($n = 150$), contrasted with American students ($n = 150$), minimized the seriousness of rape, blamed the victims, and excused the rapist more. *Gender role traditionality* (intervening variable—its presence or absence) **mediated** the cultural disparity between Japanese and American students (Yamawaki & Tschanz, 2005).

*Turks—rape.* Among 425 college students, Belief in a Just World (i.e., you deserve what you get) and level of ambivalent sexism were correlated with *less positive* attitudes toward rape victims. Rape victim *empathy* was linked with more *positive attitudes* toward victims (Sakalli-Uğurlu, Yalçin, & Glick, 2007).

*Multi-nation dating violence.* In a 17-nation survey, researchers analyzed the relationship between parental childhood treatment and college students' involvement in *dating violence.* The authors used the Multidimensional Neglectful Behavior Scale designed by Straus (2006b) to assess neglect, and the CTS to assess DV. Using retrospective data, the researchers determined that from 15% to 45% (median = 28%) of the research participants had experienced neglectful behavior in childhood. Furthermore, statistical modeling revealed that "the more neglectful behaviors experienced as a child the greater the probability of assaulting and injuring a dating partner" (Straus & Savage, 2006, p. 124; see also Maker & deRoon-Cassini, 2007).

*Male victims' stress reactions.* Usually, women are more victimized by stress reactions than men. Despite this general finding, female-to-male IPV was a predictor of severe stress symptoms, as shown by a 60-site worldwide DV study (Hines, 2007).

*Culture's effects on jealousy.* New research on the effects of culture on jealousy may help explain a persistent paradox in the literature: Cultures appear to condemn violence against women as a general principle but still accept it under some conditions. To clarify this contradiction, investigators adopted a methodology similar to the one used by Puente and Cohen (2003) described previously. The researchers recruited and compared several culturally diverse university groups (Vandello Cohen, Grandon, & Franiuk, 2009):

*Honor societies*—(a) Latinos, (b) southern U.S. Anglos, and (c) Chileans

versus

*Nonhonor societies*—(d) northern U.S. Anglos and (e) Anglo-Canadians

Honor societies hold that the honor of the family rests on the public behavior of the women in the family—wives, daughters and daughters-in-law. To preserve their honor, men can kill women for virtually any offense that they consider dishonorable, such as sexual infidelity, refusing to wear prescribed clothing, failure to keep her hair covered, being raped, or refusing to enter into an arranged marriage. (See Box 10.2.)

The results indicated that honor societies do not uniformly condone all types of violence against women. Instead, they accept the culturally driven belief that *men are less culpable for partner abuse when it occurs because of jealousy.* Data analyses demonstrated that students from honor societies felt significantly more *positive about wives who stay with abusive husbands* than did students from non-honor societies (Vandello et al., 2009).

## ETHNIC DATING VIOLENCE, SEXUAL ASSAULT, AND STALKING

Investigators have almost completely ignored the possibility that rates of DV, SA, and ST may differ among various racial and ethnic minority groups. Only recently have social scientists obtained ethnic samples and indexed important dating relationship information. Consequently, some of the research on minorities is independent from other studies on minorities. It is important to be aware that certain racial groups, such as Hispanics, are significantly less likely to report the most serious crimes (Rennison, 2007).

### NCVS Racial/Minority Prevalence Rates of Nonlethal Assaults

In the National Criminal Victimization Survey (NCVS) survey for 2002, females were about 50% of romantic nonmarried partners, but 85.9% of dating violence victims (cited in Durose et al., 2005). See Table 7.8 for racial differences among boy/girlfriends and friends/acquaintances.

**TABLE 7.8** Racial Differences of Family Violence *Victims* Compared to Nonfamily Violence *Victims* in Nonlethal Assaults 1998–2002

| Race | *Victims* N = 28,618,970 | *Boy/Girlfriend* N = 2,037,800 | *Friend/Acquaintance* N = 11,775,660 | *Strangers* N = 14,805,510 |
|---|---|---|---|---|
| White | 72.1% | 71.0% | 74.5% | 70.3% |
| Black | 14.3% | 17.2% | 14.6% | 13.7% |
| Hispanic | 10.5% | 9.0% | 8.8% | 12.2% |
| Other | 3.1% | 2.8% | 2.1% | 3.8% |
| | 100% | 100% | 100% | 100% |

SOURCE: Durose et al., 2005, Table 2.3.

## Asian/Latinas—Dating Violence

Samples of Latina, East Asian, South Asian, and Middle Eastern American college women ($N = 276$) participated in a survey about witnessing parental violence during childhood and involvement in DV in college. Participants completed scales of the CTS Parental Violence Scale and CTS2 for DV. Although the results of the analyses supported a number of the hypotheses, they did not confirm several expectations. Consequently, interpreting the findings was problematic. Some findings were as follows (Maker & deRoon-Cassini, 2007):

- Overall *rates of DV were significantly higher* than those reported by previous researchers for both ethnic and nonethnic college samples.
- Specific forms of abuse (psychological, physical injury) did not differ significantly between groups.
- The South Asian/Middle Eastern research participants reported *no significant differences in witnessing paternal/maternal interparental abuse.*
- *Latina and East Asia*n women reported *significantly more father-to-mother abuse* than the converse.
- Only *Latina*s reported *significantly higher rates of victimization than perpetration.*
- Hispanics were less likely to experience stalking than non-Hispanics (U.S. Department of Justice, 2006a). (See www.sagepub.com/barnett3e for additional Latin and Asian studies.)

## Ethnic Comparisons—Dating Violence/Intimate Partner Violence (IPV)

A criminological investigation compared 476 research participants divided into four groups of *ethnic males* (Asians, Latinos, Blacks, and Whites). Measurement dimensions included (a) *exposure to community violence*, (b) *male* social support *network violence,* (c) *female* social support *network victimization,* and (d) *levels of IPV.* The data validated nearly every hypothesis (Raghavan, Rajah, Gentile, Collado, & Kavanagh, 2009):

- Witnessing community violence (CV) was directly and positively associated with *perpetrating IPV.*
- Male social *support network violence* was positively associated with *perpetrating IPV.*
- Female social support network *victimization* was positively linked with *perpetrating IPV.*
- Male social support network violence also *partially* **mediated** (intervening variable—its presence or absence) the relationship between witnessing CV and perpetrating IPV.
- Male social support network violence (intervening variable—increased/decreased) **moderated** the relationship between CV and IPV.
- Therefore, males reporting the highest CV exposure and the highest level of affiliation with violent males perpetrated the highest levels of IPV. This result held more for Whites and Asians than for Latinos and Blacks.

The research team furnished several interpretations of the findings. The ethnic and cultural context of male-to-female IPV varies. Male peers may actively encourage male-to-female IPV. The many IPV victims in perpetrators' female social networks may have *normalized the experience of IPV.* Network influence varies across cultural groups (Raghavan et al., 2009).

## Stalking

Several studies have found that African Americans experience significantly less stalking than non-African Americans (e.g., Basile et al., 2006; Littleton, Axsom, & Grills-Taqueschel, 2009). A different survey discerned that American Indians were the least likely to be stalked (Fisher et al., 2002).

## Counseling Services

One researcher/practitioner urges *campus counseling services* to tailor their treatment as needed for ethnic minorities. She sees counseling centers as ideal training grounds for psychology interns to hone their cultural competence skills (Resnick, 2006).

# ALCOHOL/DRUG CONSUMPTION ASSOCIATED WITH DATING VIOLENCE AND SEXUAL ASSAULT

Generally, alcohol consumption is significantly correlated with both perpetration and victimization of dating violence and/or sexual assault. It is a powerful risk factor for interpersonal violence (Centers for Disease Control and Prevention, 2009b; Messman-Moore, Coates, Gaffey, & Johnson, 2008; Roudsari, Leahy, & Walters, 2009).

## Resistance Strategies

One multifaceted investigation scrutinized several sets of variables and their influences on women's *resistance strategies* to rape. Cognitive appraisals were core concepts in the study. A *secondary appraisal* consisted of the woman's reappraisal of the danger she is in—the source of the risk, the type of risk, and possible options for resisting the rape. The major findings were as follows:

- Both *alcohol consumption* and *prior sexual assault* influenced *secondary appraisals,* which in turn influenced intended mode of resistance. That is, alcohol consumption or prior sexual assault **mediated** (intervening variable—its presence or absence) the intended resistance strategy.
  - Alcohol or Prior Assault → **Secondary Appraisal** → Resistance Strategy
- A prior *adult sexual assault (ASA)* directly and *negatively* predicted *assertive resistance*
  - ASA → Decreased Assertive Resistance
- Prior *Childhood Sexual Assault (CSA)* directly and positively predicted *passive resistance*
  - CSA → Increased Passive Resistance

Extrapolating the results to an actual threatened rape situation suggests that women previously assaulted would have more difficulty resisting a rape than nonassaulted women. Alcohol consumption would also impair a woman's resistance strategy. (For more details see Stoner et al., 2007; see also Norris et al., 2006; Gidycz et al., 2008).

## Alcohol-Related Treatment

Information gained from a study of 1,251 Icelandic youth 18 to 19 years of age seems to suggest another useful treatment approach to alcoholism. Several types of statistical analyses revealed a significant association between coping through alcohol use (coping motive for drinking) and both major life stress assessments and negative daily events measures. A significant correlation also occurred between depression and both emotion-focused coping and avoidance coping (Rafnsson, Jonsson, & Windle, 2006; Windle & Windle, 1996). Future research might seek to determine if such relationships exist among adult alcoholic batterers. If so, teaching these individuals specific problem-oriented ways of coping might reduce alcohol consumption and levels of depression.

## DISCUSSION QUESTIONS

1. What crucial elements should be included in definitions of dating violence, sexual assault, and stalking?
2. How do the measurement instruments used to assess DV, SA, and ST affect research results?
3. What cultural variables best explain DV, SA, and ST?
4. Is it true that women are more victimized than men by interpersonal violence? Why or why not?
5. Can a man be raped by a lone woman? Can males be sexually coerced?
6. What should society do to prevent DV, SA, and ST?
7. If you were planning to conduct research, which of the topics covered in this chapter would you like to pursue? What gaps have you noted? Why?
8. How would you assist a friend who informed you that she had been raped?
9. What advice would you give your son or daughter about alcohol use and fraternity membership?
10. Should society hold a man responsible for date rape if the woman asserts she did not consent, but she was dressed in a provocative way? Suppose she said "No" to sex and the perpetrator did not use force. Is this rape?

## NOTE

1. In this case history, the name Mary is a pseudonym, but the name of Mary's attacker, Daniel Oltarsh, is real.

 For chapter-specific resources including audio and video links, SAGE research articles, additional case studies, and more, please visit www.sagepub.com/barnett3e.

# 8

# Abused Heterosexual Partners

## *Primarily Women*

---

**CASE HISTORY**   Lisa—For Better or for Worse

I believe that you stay with your partner for better or for worse. I didn't know what "worse" was when I made that promise, but I promised. I believe my husband loves me, and I'm starting to believe he could kill me. I'm not sure how long I should stay and how "bad" is "too bad." I know I don't believe I should be hit. But I do believe if my relationship is a mess, I should stay to help make it better.[1]

---

It should be clear from previous discussions that although both males and females are sometimes violent, women are more likely than men to be victims of injurious abuse and homicide. The focus of this chapter is on the impact of intimate partner violence (physical, sexual, verbal, and psychological) as experienced by women. Because battered women are not a homogeneous group, the effects of their victimization by intimate partner violence (IPV) vary. The chapter begins by addressing some of the misconceptions that have contributed to the public propensity to blame battered women for being victimized. The chapter continues with descriptions of the consequences of intimate partner violence. Part of the chapter addresses the evolving responses of the criminal justice system and health care community to IPV. There is also a section on the problematic relationship between welfare agencies and female victims. Next, there is a consideration of the reasons women stay in abusive relationships and how they manage to survive. Also included is a section on abused men.

## BLAMING VICTIMS OF INTIMATE PARTNER VIOLENCE

One might think that being physically or sexually assaulted by one's male partner would be enough pain for a lifetime, but battered women experience many other adverse incidents that compound their misery. One wounding outcome with very negative consequences is the tendency of others to blame survivors of *male-to-female intimate partner violence* (MFIPV). It appears as if everyone is ready, if not eager, to place the blame for being in a violent relationship on battered women. Perpetrators, families, members of the public, agency personnel, professionals, and entire cultures blame victims rather than perpetrators. Victims even blame themselves. It is especially disturbing to note that some of society's agents whose job it is to assist battered women hold these same damaging attitudes. Far too many law enforcement and criminal justice personnel, welfare workers, and medical personnel perceive MFIPV survivors as blameworthy.

**CASE HISTORY**   Hedda Nussbaum—When the Protector Needs Protection

One of the most notorious cases of both male-to-female IPV and child abuse on record is that of Hedda Nussbaum and Joel Steinberg. In 1987, police arrived at the couple's apartment to find their 6-year-old adopted daughter, Lisa, beaten to death. Although left alone with the beaten and dying child for several hours, Hedda failed to take any action, such as calling 911, to save Lisa's life for fear of angering Joel. She spent much of the time free-basing cocaine, at Joel's direction.

At first, the New York district attorney booked Hedda for second-degree murder of Lisa. As the case unfolded, however, evidence of Hedda's horrifying life with Joel came to light. After the couple had been together for 2 years, Joel began to beat Hedda periodically, and the beatings continued over the ensuing 10 years. He choked her, burned her with a propane torch, beat her with a metal exercise bar, broke her knee and ribs, forced her to sleep handcuffed to a chinning bar, pulled her hair out, and urinated on her. Sometimes, he alternated his abuse with affectionate behavior. Hedda occasionally went to a hospital for medical treatment, but eventually lied about the source of her injuries for fear of the consequences at home if she told the truth. Her appearance gradually changed from that of a normal, attractive woman to one resembling a boxer, with a swollen disfigured face, and she lost her job because she was so often absent from work.

Psychiatrists explained Hedda's behavior in various ways. One said, "It's like what happens to someone in a concentration camp. They are reduced, by virtue of physical torture, to a mere existence level. They shut off normal human emotions" (quoted in Hackett, McKillop, & Wang, 1988, p. 61). Another said that Hedda "was a slave, totally submissive to this man, with no ability or will to save her own daughter" (p. 57). Others observed the gradual buildup of the abuse and the episodic nature of the abuse and affection she received from Joel.

The district attorney eventually dropped all charges against her, because he thought "she was physically and emotionally incapable either of harming Lisa or coming to her aid" (quoted in Hackett et al., 1988, p. 57). Given her state of mind, prosecutors wondered if Hedda would be able to testify against Joel, but she did manage to do so. Hedda's former acquaintances gasped and even cried at her appearance. Joel was convicted of first-degree manslaughter and sent to prison, and Hedda received inpatient psychiatric services for more than a year.[2]

Hedda Nussbaum's experience illustrates an extreme case of family violence in which the adult female victim was unable to save herself or her child. It is crucial to note that police and prosecutors and news writers blamed Hedda at first. It took greater understanding of the victimization process for these criminal justice personnel and the lay public to eventually understand Hedda's helplessness. The lay public did not understand why Hedda did not just take Lisa and run away. This chapter will suggest some research-based explanations for Hedda's puzzling behavior. Several theories might explain her behavior, such as *traumatic bonding* or *learned helplessness.*

## Blaming by Partner

Male IPV perpetrators hold their female partner responsible for their own abusive behavior. (L. W. Bennett, Tolman, Rogalski, & Srinivasaraghavan, 1994). Batterers tell their female partner that their violence happened because she did not clean the house or discipline the kids as he directed her to so. In one analysis, 70.5% of 485 battered women said their partners blamed them for all the abuse, while blaming themselves for none of it (M. A. Anderson et al., 2003).

## Blaming by Society

When negative events occur, a frequent human reaction is to search out the party or parties at fault. This proclivity is especially apparent with regard to abused women in comparison with abused children or elders, who receive much less blame. Because an adult woman's relationship with a batterer is *consensual,* she *is* unworthy of empathy but worthy of blame. No matter how unfair to battered women, the public seems reluctant to place blame for violent behavior solely on perpetrators. In the research studies that follow, respondents focused their attention on what the female victim may have done wrong, not on what the perpetrator had actually done wrong.

Investigators surveyed a random sample of adult community members regarding their attributions of responsibility to both of the partners in violent relationships. Each participant completed a questionnaire after reading a scenario about a violent couple. More than 40% reported that the woman in the scenario *must* have been at least partly to blame for her husband's assaults, even though the story provided *no rationale whatsoever* for such an assumption. More than 60% agreed that if a battered woman were really afraid, she would simply leave. There was an inclination for respondents to believe that the woman must have been emotionally disturbed or that she could have prevented the beatings if she had entered counseling (Ewing & Aubrey, 1987).

A study of college students indicated that they felt some sympathy for female victims of partner abuse under a limited number of conditions. Both sympathy and justifiability ratings were higher if the victim stayed with her abuser for *externally imposed reasons* (e.g., being threatened with death), rather than for reasons such as *loneliness* or *feeling helpless* to change her situation. Women were generally more empathic with victims than men (Follingstad, Runge, Ace, Buzan, & Helff, 2001).

In the following study, however, gender differences in blaming MFIPV victims did not occur. Data from a different group of college students revealed that reliance on *stereotypes* is another factor in societal blaming, including (a) a **battered woman's** *traditionalism (i.e., patriarchal marriages),* and (b) her *reactions* to being psychologically abused. Students judged scenarios that manipulated these two characteristics about an abused woman. The findings indicated that students were more willing to blame a *nontraditional* (i.e., career) woman than a traditional woman (i.e., housewife). The assumed personal *warmth* of the housewife, contrasted with the assumed *coldness* of the career woman, was the major factor in the students' evaluation of her blameworthiness. Students also blamed victims who reacted *negatively* (e.g., yelling) to the abuse, rather than those who responded *passively* (Capezza & Arriaga, 2008). Taken together, these studies show that holding battered women responsible for male battering occurs along a number of dimensions.

## Blaming by Professionals

The extent to which professionals (mental health, social services, corrections, shelters, criminal justice professionals, and coroners) fault battered women for their own victimization has a profound effect on the *treatment* they receive. Clearly, this situation is especially egregious because these professionals are the very individuals expected to treat these victims. Some professionals in the fields of mental health, social services, medicine, and criminal justice seem ready to assume that female victims are *accomplices* or at least indirectly responsible for the violence directed at them (Whatley & Riggio, 1991). One feminist suggests that even researchers have contributed to this tendency by placing the occurrence of MFIPV within the context of a *family conflict model.* The conflict model contends that partner violence occurs in the context of an argument, not for some reason such as being unemployed. This inclination "degenders the problem and genders the blame" (Berns, 2001).

*Blaming by shelter workers.* Even battered women's shelter workers seem disinclined to hold male perpetrators solely responsible for their own behavior. Note, however, that holding perpetrators solely responsible only solves some problems related to stopping IPV. In one survey, McKell and Sporakowski (1993) found that 8.4% of workers held the husband and wife *equally* responsible for physical violence, and 53.8% held the husband primarily responsible. Only *37.8%* held the husband completely responsible. In a 1991 Kentucky survey of service providers, 13.9% agreed, or strongly agreed, with the statement, "*victims 'ask' for it*" (D. G. Wilson & Wilson, 1991). (See Chapter 10 for more detail about the value of perpetrators' internalizing self-blame for violence.)

*Blaming because of welfare needs.* Because many women and children on welfare are the victims of family violence, welfare policies have become a focus of a subgroup of battered women's experts and child advocates (e.g., Edleson, 1998; Tolman & Raphael, 2000). Politicians and others blame welfare recipients for their lack of economic independence, no matter the source of their needs, such as a *father's desertion* (L. Gordon, 2001; Yoshihama, Hammock, & Horrocks, 2006). In respect to women who receive welfare, there are numerous erroneous opinions:

- Welfare-reliant women do not want to work (e.g., Edin & Lein, 1997). It is true, however, that many women on welfare have even stronger inclinations to place their *role as mother* above that of worker.

- Welfare clients lack a *work ethic.*
- Women on welfare do not deserve assistance, especially women of color because they do not adhere to *traditional family values* (Ciabattari, 2006).
- Welfare encourages *irresponsible* women to have too many children and to have them out of wedlock.

Do the real facts match these stereotypes? According to an *APA report,* "Poverty is the result of low wages, most welfare recipients are children, and the average welfare family is not larger than the average non-welfare family" (cited in DeAngelis, 2001, p. 71).

*Blaming by child protective service workers.* Another group of professionals who blame battered women are child protective services (CPS) workers. The problem has arisen because of the clashing mandates between agencies that have left battered mothers *in the middle.* The primary directive of CPS is to safeguard children, to act in the *best interest of the child,* while the primary directive of battered women's services is to help both women and children achieve *safety,* even if a mother does *not* leave her partner (Edleson, 1998). The solution, as applied by CPS workers, is to hold women accountable for *remaining* with an intimate male partner who concurrently abuses the children.

CPS faces a dilemma about how to protect children (their mandate) in homes where fathers are physically or sexually abusing both mothers and children or abusing the mother in front of the children. Instead of resolving the problem by focusing on the father's abusive behaviors, Child Protective Services has expected mothers to protect their children by *leaving* the abusers. If a mother does not do so, CPS may threaten to remove her children (Berliner, 1998). The legal system may even go so far as to classify a *nonoffending* mother as a criminal sexual abuser, while simultaneously classifying her as an assault victim (Bolen, 2003; Davidson, 1995; Sierra, 1997). Because society imposes on mothers the immense task of protecting children, even when they lack sufficient means to do so, Rich (1976) terms the situation, *powerless responsibility.* Society rarely, if ever, holds fathers responsible for failing to protect their children, however, even when their behavior is the same as the mothers' (e.g., leaves a child alone in the house) (National Council of Juvenile and Family Court Judges, 1994).

In addition to being morally objectionable to many, CPS policies do not really protect children (McKay, 1994). How can Child Protective Services legally assert that putting a child in foster care is less harmful than allowing the child to be exposed to the father's abuse of the mother? How would a separation affect the parent-child relationship? What about the financial cost to the state for foster care? Faulting the mother simply provides the batterer with another weapon of intimidation. He can threaten her by pointing out that if she discloses his abusive behavior, she may lose her children (H. A. White, 2003). Just how CPS workers can best respond to battered mothers needs further research (Postmus & Merritt, 2010).

The assumption that women can protect their children simply by leaving their abusers, as highly touted by CPS, is *not* borne out by facts. Women who try to leave abusive partners may place their own lives and those of their children at risk (Harper & Voigt, 2007; Morton, Runyan, Moracco, & Butts, 1998). Fatefully, no government agency can guarantee their safety (e.g., Epstein, 1999; L. A. Goodman, Bennett, & Dutton, 1999).

*Blaming by health care workers.* Health care professionals have a difficult time in dealing with battered women for a host of reasons tied to their training and expectations. Because battered women's problems do not fit neatly into the *medical model,* some health workers classify them as *noncompliant.* Also, advocates' efforts to reposition battering as a medical or health problem, rather than a social problem, is not a simple change. A closer look at these issues explains why. A typical medical consultation entails a doctor's diagnosis of the cause of a disorder and a prescription for alleviating the problem. If the doctor diagnoses a woman as having high blood pressure, he is likely to recommend a diet with restricted salt intake, more exercise, and a drug prescription. In this scenario, the doctor is the expert and the patient is expected to be compliant.

In contrast, a doctor encountering a woman with injuries caused by battering (diagnosis) cannot simply prescribe that she avoid the battering by leaving. If the doctor does tell her to leave and she does not, she is labeled noncompliant. It is as if she refused to take prescribed medicine. Furthermore, she is more of an expert than the doctor on how she can avoid further beatings or even death (e.g., Heckert & Gondolf, 2004). Obviously, health care providers will feel frustrated about their so-called *medical* role in reducing family violence and the demands placed upon them to screen women for male-to-female intimate partner violence, document their injuries, and refer them to social agencies (Lavis, Horrocks, Kelly, & Barker, 2005). No matter how the doctor feels about the battered woman as a patient, he is mandated by law in six states to report her abuse to the police or social service agencies. (Search the Colorado Coalition Against Domestic Violence on the Internet for a debate about mandatory reporting.) See www.sagepub.com/barnett3e for a case history of victim-blaming by judges.

## Blaming Oneself

Given the near-uniform censure of battered women's actions, it is no wonder that they may blame themselves. A common attribution battered women make about themselves is that they somehow provoked the violence or that they should have been able to prevent it by changing their own behavior (Hydén, 1999; Towns & Adams, 2000). Women feel guilt and shame for not leaving their abuser, thereby exposing their children to MFIPV. As a result, many women are reluctant to disclose their problems to family and friends or to seek help (Lindgren & Renck, 2008). Relying on results of a 61-item test and two comparison groups of nonbattered women, Barnett, Martinez, and Keyson (1996) found significantly higher levels of self-blame in battered women than in nonbattered women. They endorsed questionnaire items, such as the following: (a) "I was to blame because I did not listen to him," and (b) "I was to blame because I was too afraid to leave" (see also Nichols & Feltey, 2003).

Battered women both regret some of their actions (e.g., isolating themselves from social support) and some of their inactions (e.g., failure to seek help) (Fry & Barker, 2001; see also Langhinrichsen-Rohling, 2006). An important finding from a different inquiry disclosed that battered women were prone to blame themselves for *initiating aggression* despite actual narrative transcripts contradicting their claims. Further scrutiny showed that it was the women's *subjective interpretations* of the word *initiation* (e.g., being angry) that influenced their judgments (L. N. Olson & Lloyd, 2005; see also Stets & Straus, 1990).

## Attitudes of Faith Community Leaders

In general, pastoral counselors have a vast amount of community responsibility (Nason-Clark, 1997). They have to incorporate numerous doctrinal and belief issues into their counseling of congregants about mental health problems. Confronting male partner abuse is one of the most challenging problems they confront (A. J. Weaver, 1993). Faith leaders need to understand how deeply spouse abuse wounds the inner person (Lyon, 2010). Responses of clergy are crucial in that many abused women turn first to their faith leaders for counseling, and clergy's zealotry can strongly impact battered women's decision making. In a noteworthy inquiry, researchers interviewed a mixed group of 22 religious leaders espousing various faiths (e.g., Catholicism, Judaism, and Islam). Although none of the religious leaders condoned violence, their responses to questions about responsibility for it and whether violence is an acceptable reason for divorce exhibit the diversity of beliefs systems (Levitt & Ware, 2006). A qualitative analysis revealed the following responses:

1. Who is responsible for male-to-female violence?
   a. 20/22 said that perpetrators must assume responsibility, but victims bear some of the blame.
   b. 9/20 thought staying with the abuser made victims blameworthy.

2. What are the causes of male-to-female intimate partner violence?
   a. 15/22 thought some causes were lack of control and respect.
   b. 15/22 thought social learning was the cause.
      - Respondents' additional comments: Conflict is the culprit, and couples (especially women) must halt the escalation of an argument before abuse starts. Battered women's low self-esteem and their wish to be victims play a role in male partner violence.

3. *What is the best approach for dealing with male-to-female intimate partner violence?* 21/22 supported a proactive approach that fostered healthy marriages before violence occurred.

4. Is divorce acceptable?
   a. 20/22 declared that divorce should be a last resort.
   b. 4/20 said that women's power to divorce is limited by sacred documents.
   c. Scientific evidence about the harm done to child observers of male assaults is a lesser issue than divorce.
   d. 6/22 claimed the only acceptable rationale for divorce is infidelity or desertion, and the severity of abuse cannot be considered.

(See Neergaard, Lee, Anderson, & Wong Gengler, 2007, for a review of battered women's experiences with clergy.)

In addition to the role of clergy, the *actions of other congregants* can be problematic for survivors of partner violence. While religious groups can be a source of emotional support and practical assistance, they may also tend to perpetuate silence about male IPV. Overall, religious groups are ill-equipped to help provide a safe environment for IPV survivors (Pyles, 2007).

### Blaming Victims

Male-to-female offenders are notorious for blaming the women they assault, and many other people do so as well. Society blames battered women partially because they think she must have done something wrong. People do not understand why battered women do not leave, and they blame some victims (e.g., career women) more than others (traditional women). If a battered woman is receiving welfare benefits, society blames her even more, holding to such notions as "she must lack a work ethic." Even individuals *trained* to help others in critical situations, such as shelter workers, seem inclined to place some of the blame on victims. Research shows that untrained welfare workers can be downright hostile toward battered women. Some even fail their own responsibilities to follow the laws regarding helping battered women find safety.

Currently, there are conflicts between Child Protective Services personnel and battered women's advocates concerning the attribution of blame for the abuse of children in households where *both* mothers and children are being abused. CPS workers, in their zeal to protect children, may blame battered mothers for the fathers' abuse of the children. CPS workers may *falsely* believe that leaving an abuser would not only protect the children but also the battered woman.

Health care workers often blame battered women for not following customary health care protocols, and workers often find their efforts to help battered women are fruitless. Finally, the attitudes of some faith community leaders toward battered women are upsetting and counterproductive. These faith leaders also believe battered women bear some responsibility for the abuse. *A number contend that doctrinal beliefs prevent divorcing a batterer for his assaults.* He would have to abandon the family or be unfaithful for a divorce to be acceptable. It is not surprising that with so much blame heaped upon them from all quarters, battered women blame themselves. They may believe they provoked the abuse, should have taken a different approach, or should not have followed some other course of action. Some battered women, however, manage not to accept blame.

## CONSEQUENCES OF VIOLENCE AND VICTIMIZATION

Violence affects people and changes them *forever.* The most immediate feeling that most crime victims experience following an assault is *helplessness.* Anger, anxiety, depression, fear, **posttraumatic stress disorder (PTSD),** and many other negative reactions usually occur concurrently or later. The time frame in which the abuse occurs, such as the last six months or last year, and the victim's history of abuse with prior partners, greatly influence the effects of male-to-female violence on victims (Bogat, Levendosky, Theran, von Eye, & Davidson, 2003; Kernsmith, 2005a). A comparison of health statuses of 74 sheltered women with survey results of 65,000 women responding to the 1995 National Health Survey revealed significant differences. Sheltered women had higher rates of mental problems and functional impairments that impinged on women's performances at work, school, and social functioning. Battered women were less well educated and used more health services than the women from the population survey (Helfrich, Fujiura, & Rutkowski-Kmitta, 2008). As the studies below amply demonstrate, researchers have found a massive amount of evidence for *abuse-related damage* among battered women.

## Fear

Once victimized, victims are likely to fear offenders, and their fear varies with their gender, age, and income (Kury & Ferdinand, 1997). *Classical conditioning* (i.e., emotional learning) can explain fear learning scientifically (Mineka & Zinbarg, 2006). Because of conditioning, cues such as the abuser's yelling, hurling insults, drinking heavily, and particular facial expressions become aversive and the cues often become even more recognizable over time (Werner-Wilson, Zimmerman, & Whalen, 2000; Zeelenberg, Wagenmakers, & Rotteveel, 2006); for a review, see Davey, 1992). When these cues have been followed by an assault, they generalize to current situations, keeping female victims in a *chronic state* of fear or anxiety (e.g., Nurius, Furrey, & Berliner, 1992; Pontius, 2002).

One woman described her fear and uncertainty as "being so tense that it was like standing up although you were lying in bed" (Lindgren & Renck, 2008, p. 222). As an example, a woman who had left her abuser 3 years earlier reported that her hands began to sweat when certain assault cues appeared (Lindgren & Renck, 2008). (See Chapter 2 for a review of classical conditioning.) Even if a *battered woman leaves her abusive partner,* the necessity of having to continue to interact with him (e.g., child visitation) makes her apprehensive (Shalansky, Ericksen, & Henderson, 1999).

The search for *gender dissimilarity* (e.g., fear reactions) within violent relationships mounted sharply as claims of *gender symmetry (gender equality),* based on the use of the Conflict Tactics Scales (CTS) permeated the field. A strong faction of disbelievers began presenting alternative explanation and evidence countering assertions of gender symmetry. Several studies have now found that *women are significantly more fearful of IPV* than men are. Although both men and women express feeling fearful of a *partner's violence,* their levels of fear are *not* equivalent (Hamberger & Guse, 2002; see also Cercone-Keeney, Beach, & Arias, 2005). In reality, it is not surprising that women find partner violence more frightening than men do because women are significantly more intimidated by a partner's physical size and strength (Phelan et al., 2005).

A preponderance of experts now suggests that *victim fear* provoked by male IPV *is* a potent factor distinguishing male and female IPV. These experts claim that these gender differences make male IPV *qualitatively* different, despite similarities in frequency rates. Not only do battered women feel fearful, but extended family members and others close to battered women also fear batterers. In fact, it is not uncommon for family and friends to refuse to interact with a battered woman out of fear (Riger, Raja, & Camacho, 2002). Even the police, as discussed elsewhere, find dealing with "*domestics*" fear-provoking. Some social scientists contend that fear level should be integrated into the *definition* of IPV (Heyman & Slep, 2006; O'Leary, 1999).

*Neurological changes.* The most empirically sound explanation for persisting *fear* responses is *fear conditioning,* a type of learning that is now known to cause neurological alterations in the brain ("Emotional Judgments," 1999; Pontius, 2002). Several independent studies have begun to present a picture of these changes in the brain (A. Banks, 2001; Rausch, van der Kolk, Fisler, & Alpert, 1996). A large number of studies have implicated certain structures in the brain (e.g., amygdala) as the areas responsive to stress reactions (e.g., Rogan, 1997). Changes also seem to entail memory for vivid or traumatic experiences (Brewin, 2001).

Several investigations have found high rates of *head injury* among female victims. One study uncovered a prevalence rate for head injury of 35% (Monahan & O'Leary, 1999). Another found a rate of 74% for *one* partner-related brain injurie and 50% for multiple partner-related head injuries (Valera & Berenbaum, 2003). An innovative analysis comparing *brain damage* among 19 female IPV victims and 9 comparison women revealed appalling results. Victims suffered an average of 2.8 concussions, 219.7 head blows, and 725.4 body blows during the average 5.9 years of their relationships (Deering, Templer, Keller, & Canfield, 2001). Concussions can worsen over time and increase the amount of impairment. A unique battering case of considerable interest is that of a 34-year-old woman who was medically diagnosed with "shaken adult (not baby) syndrome." The woman suffered from blood clots and swelling of the brain, hemorrhaging, bleeding in one eye, vision impairment, arm bruises, apparent cigarette burns on her arms, vomiting, chest pain, and a concussion (Carrigan, Walker, & Barnes, 2000). Doctors are identifying similar types of brain injuries in soldiers exposed to roadside bombs in Iraq and Afghanistan (Okie, 2005).

## Stress, Trauma, Posttraumatic Stress Disorder, and Cumulative Stress

Despite women's strength in surviving abusive relationships, battered women suffer from an array of emotional repercussions. MFIPV is associated with inadequate *cognitive processing, trauma memory,* and *judgment.* A host of negative outcomes, such as p*oor problem solving, depression,* and *low self-esteem* are linked to violence-related variables, such as anxiety, sleep problems, and suicidal ideation. These findings lend weight to the claims that women are much more victimized by intimate partner violence than men are (e.g., Beach et al., 2004; Halligan, Michael, Clark, & Ehlers, 2003; J. E. Hathaway et al., 2000; Zlotnick, Johnson, & Kohn, 2006).

*Stress.* Abusive behavior, like other forms of violence, produces stress and chronic apprehension, and female victims experience significantly more stress than nonvictims (Eby, 2004; T. L. Weaver & Clum, 1995). *Stress is a physiological or psychological response to internal or external stressors (e.g., pain, humiliation).* "Stress involves changes affecting nearly every system of the body, influencing how people feel and behave" (VandenBos, 2007, p. 898) and can cause temporary or even permanent changes in the brain. Reactions to stress include *cognitive impairment* (e.g., confusion and poor test performance), *emotional responses* (e.g., anxiety, anger, aggression, depression), and *physical illness* (e.g., headaches and gastrointestinal problems) (Pianta & Egeland, 1994; see Kiecolt-Glaser, 2009). Despite numerous commonalities among stress reactions, an emerging concept supposes that *specific stressors* elicit *specific patterns of activation* (D. S. Goldstein & Kopin, 2007).

*Trauma.* According to the fourth edition of the American Psychiatric Association's (1994) *Diagnostic and Statistical Manual of Mental Disorders* (*DSM-IV*), a **traumatic event** is one in which the individual experiences, witnesses, or is confronted with an event or events that entail actual or threatened death or serious injury, or a threat to the physical integrity of the individual or others. The responses that such an event entails include *intense fear, helplessness, and horror,* and includes *symptoms* of depression, aggression, substance abuse, physical illness, lowered self-esteem, difficulties in interpersonal relationships, identity problems, and guilt and shame (Carlson & Dalenberg, 2000). Clearly, exposure to trauma can be debilitating.

*PTSD.* Because of the wars in Iraq and Afghanistan, and disasters such as Hurricane Katrina and school shootings, research on PTSD has escalated. When a traumatic event causes an acute, *prolonged* emotional reaction, psychiatrists designate the reaction as *posttraumatic stress disorder,* or PTSD. PTSD is a common response to trauma and terror. T. P. Sullivan, Meese, Swan, Mazur, & Snow (2005) determined that both *child abuse and adult victimization* were predictive of PTSD. Some symptoms of PTSD are *disturbed sleep, re-experiencing the trauma in painful recollections, numbing of responses, an exaggerated startle response, difficulty in concentrating or remembering, anger, and avoidance of activities that rekindle memories of the traumatic event* (Gore-Felton, Gill, Koopman, & Spiegel, 1999).

Almost without exception, research has acknowledged the association between male violence and its short- and long-term effects on PTSD. In general, studies suggest that between 40% and 60% of female victims suffer from PTSD (Mertin & Mohr, 2001). Research has further shown that both *extent and severity of exposure* to male abuse are significantly correlated with *severity* of PTSD symptoms (Follette, Polusny, Bechtle, & Naugle, 1996). Even emotional abuse or mild MFIPV can trigger PTSD. One meta-analytic review found that male partner abuse was an even stronger risk factor for PTSD than child sex abuse (Golding, 1999). One markedly salient finding is that abused women were still experiencing PTSD as long as 9 years after the last abusive episode (Woods, 2000). Occasionally, however, victims' *traumatic symptoms* decrease after they have been away from their abusers for six months to three years (Lerner & Kennedy, 2000).

According to contemporary learning theory, a host of variables, such *as prior learning experiences,* can account for individual differences in the development of PTSD. One type of prior learning stems from exposure to trauma. Cumulative trauma exposure (e.g., IPV) and collective trauma (e.g., child sexual abuse followed by IPV) are known to be highly associated with stress and PTSD (Clemmons, Walsh, DiLillo, & Messman-Moore, 2007; Sledjeski, Speisman, & Dierker, 2008). A National Comorbidity Survey-Replication documented that PTSD was significantly correlated with the degree of trauma exposure (Sledjeski et al., 2008). (See the section on revictimization in Chapter 7.)

*Problem-solving deficits.* The possibility that one of the effects of male battering would be to diminish battered women's problem-solving abilities attracted research attention early in the battered women's movement. **Problem solving** is a higher mental process that people use to overcome difficulties, achieve a goal, or reach a conclusion (VandenBos, 2007). The connotation of problem solving as a way to overcome difficulties may not be totally separate from that of coping. Research has uncovered a vast array of problems in cognitive processing, trauma memory, and appraisals in female victims (Halligan et al., 2003). Although longitudinal research on problem solving among MFIPV survivors is lacking, the anxiety generated by the abuse must certainly be detrimental (see also Evans, Gonnella, Marcynyszyn, & Salpekar, 2005). In one early study, female victims were less effective problem-solvers than nonvictims in a few experimental settings (e.g., with everyday problems) (Launius & Jensen, 1987; see also Claerhout, Elder, & Jensen, 1982). In a different study using diverse situations (e.g., involving relationship problems), female partner violence victims were able to outperform nonvictims in problem solving (J. C. Campbell, 1989a).

One survey disclosed that 80% of female victims had sustained facial injuries, but doctors frequently overlooked the possibility of consequent brain damage. Some of these brain injuries cause permanent disabilities (M. E. Banks, 2007). A small subset of female IPV survivors may be poor problem-solvers as the result of *head injuries* or because of cognitive distortions associated with PTSD (Strom & Kosciulek, 2007; see also Winerman, 2006, for a different perspective).

## Health Problems

Research consistently shows that battered women have significantly poorer health than nonbattered women, including physical illness, disabilities, and injuries (Afifi et al., 2009; Bonomi et al., 2009). Not only does stress evoke PTSD, but it also exacerbates health problems. Stress levels are strongly associated with the severity of their psychological and physical abuse, as assessed by the *Minnesota Multiphasic Personality Inventory-2 (MMPI-2)* (Rollstin & Kern, 1998).

*Physical illness.* Both men and women IPV victims, relative to nonvictims, smoke more, consume more alcoholic beverages, and have a higher risk for HIV and sexually transmitted diseases (STDs). Female victims also have a higher body mass index (Morbidity and Mortality Weekly Report [MMWR], 2008). What is more, female victims suffer from more cervical cancer, unwanted pregnancies, and pelvic pain than nonvictims, and they also exhibit greater fear about negotiating condom use with their partner (e.g., J. C. Campbell, 2002; Coker, Sanderson, Fadden, & Pirisi, 2000; Wingood, DiClemente, & Raj, 2000). (See www.sagepub.com/barnett3e for other illness and injuries resulting from sexual assault.)

On a related note, partner abuse victims report significantly *more disabilities* and take significantly *longer sick leaves* than nonvictims. They further suffer from disturbed sleep. As an interesting side observation, mice exposed to fear conditioning suffer from disturbed sleep as well (J. E. Hathaway et al., 2000; Hensing & Alexanderson, 2000; Sanford, Tang, Ross, & Morrison, 2003).

*Injuries.* It has been clear from the beginning that physical injuries are one of the most serious consequences of IPV. Injuries may be severe, even disabling, and the emotional, economic, and societal costs are enormous. As might be expected, there is a consistent *gender disparity in the severity of injuries.* A major reason for the difference is that topographically similar behaviors (e.g., slapping by a woman or slapping by a man) cause far more injuries, and more severe injuries, to women than to men (Cantos, Neidig, & O'Leary, 1994). The National Crime Victimization Survey (NCVS) found that about 50% of female victims of partner aggression report some sort of injury, and about 20% seek medical assistance (Greenfeld et al., 1998).

Medical injury records show a *gendered pattern of injuries* that is typical of female victims ("Physical Violence," 1996; Rand, 1997). According to two researchers at Johns Hopkins University School of Nursing, the most common injuries result from *blunt force trauma to the face* (i.e., being hit with a fist) and *being strangled* (D. J. Sheridan & Nash, 2007). Research on plastic surgery records of 326 female facial trauma patients revealed significant differences between male battering victims' facial traumas and those of other female crime victims or women with other types of facial traumas. Victims of male batterers, for example, suffered more complex fractures, orbital blow-outs, and intracranial injuries than the other two groups (Arosarena, Fritsch, Hsueh, Aynehchi, & Haug, 2009). (See www.sagepub.com/barnett3e for additional tables of information.)

## Coping With Violence

**Coping** refers to "the use of cognitive and behavioral strategies to *manage* the demands of a situation when these are appraised as taxing or exceeding one's resources or to reduce the negative emotions and conflict caused by *stress*" (VandenBos, 2007, p. 232). Because of its significance to general health, coping, along with stress, has generated a vast amount of research, especially by epidemiologists (e.g., Clements & Sawhney, 2000; Penley, Tomaka, & Wiebe, 2002). Coping by battered women comprises an entire spectrum of ongoing research. A general problem in the coping literature is a lack of validated measures, although scale development is underway.

**Coping style** refers to the *typical method(s) an individual uses to handle stress.* Coping skills are important for several reasons. They are strongly correlated with physical and mental health, and their use overlaps a number of specialized areas, such as problem solving, PTSD, and therapeutic practices. Coping style is highly correlated with outcomes such as depression and marital satisfaction level. Some social scientists contend that battered women have inadequate coping skills that were present even before battering began, while others hold that any inadequacies are the result of male assaults. As a matter of fact, the effects of personality on coping outcomes do vary by situational factors (DeLongis & Holtzman, 2005). See Table 8.1 for details about coping.

These findings validate the usefulness of emphasizing research on coping when studying family violence. Future research should try to identify the coping strategies battered women and other trauma victims *need* to develop in order to maintain their safety.

Brief Findings About Coping Strategies Among Battered Women

| Findings | Researchers |
|---|---|
| MFIPV diminishes a victim's ability to cope effectively | Anson & Sagy, 1995; Kemp, Green, Hovanitz, & Rawlings, 1995. |
| MFIPV victims seem less apt to use active coping strategies but significantly more *prone to use passive or avoidance strategies* | Bernhard, 2000; Finn, 1985; Nurius et al., 1992; Valentiner, Foa, Riggs, & Gershuny, 1996; Waldrop & Resick, 2004 |
| *Use of avoidance coping* actually *generates stress* | Holahan, Moos, Holahan, Brennan, & Schutte, 2005 |
| *Problem-focused coping is associated with decreased hopelessness* | Clements & Sawhney, 2000; Clements, Sabourin, Spilby, 2004 |
| *Placating and resisting* are the strategies used early, most often, and are the least effective | L. A. Goodman, Dutton, Weinfurt, & Cook, 2003 |
| *The characteristics of the situation and one's resources* are associated with the specific stressor variables | DeLongis & Holtzman, 2005; De Ridder, 1997 |
| *Stressor type* is a predictor of coping strategy selected | Lee-Baggley, Preece, & DeLongis, 2005 |
| Women with a *high Sense of Coherence (SOC)* cope *more effectively* than those with a lower SOC. SOC is a *tendency to view the world as comprehensible and manageable.* | Lindgren & Renck, 2008 |
| *Change over time* occurs with coping strategies. If one coping method does not work, a battered women may try a different strategy | Bowker, 1983; Dougall, Hyman, Hayward, McFeely, & Baum, 2001 |
| *Leaving an abuser* may lead to a change in a victim's coping strategies. Emotionally focused coping may decrease, while problem-focused coping may increase | Lerner & Kennedy, 2000 |
| *Couples tend to use similar coping styles* and their styles become more similar over 10 years | Holahan et al., 2007 |
| *Racial minorities and subgroups,* such as rural battered women, may use *different coping strategies* | T. M. Greer, 2007; Shannon, Logan, Cole, & Medley, 2006 |
| *Religious* coping reduces the impact of *stress on depression* | B-J. Lee, 2007 |

## The Hostage Syndrome, Traumatic Bonding, and Attachment

Three related theories describe how violence affects the behaviors of some victims in close relationships: the hostage syndrome (also known as Stockholm syndrome), traumatic bonding, and attachment. These theories account for the intriguing finding that love and violence may coexist (Borochowitz & Eisikovits, 2002; Kesner, Julian, & McKenry, 1997).

*Hostage syndrome.* One possible consequence of intimate partner violence is the development of symptoms characteristic of the hostage syndrome (Mega, Mega, Mega, & Harris, 2000). In some circumstances of extreme threat and isolation, imprisoned men and women may exhibit *strange behaviors* that encompass praising the abusers, denying that abuse has taken place, and blaming themselves. Together they constitute what has become known as the *Stockholm syndrome* or *hostage syndrome.* Bizarre as these behaviors are, they may in actuality represent a struggle for survival ("Abusive Relationships," 1991). Captor-controlled conditions of alternating threats and kindness, along with power differentials between captor and captive, appear to make *hostages emotionally dependent on those who have subjugated them.* Captives come to believe that the only way to survive is to avoid angering their captors. Captives may even profess to love their captors (Kuleshnyk, 1984; see Fitzpatrick, 2009, for a description of the Jaycee Dugard case).

Some abusive individuals create *prison-like settings* for their partners. The sheer *terror* of being held captive dictates victims' responses to all events in their lives. One victim, for instance, felt terrorized by her abuser even *after* she had killed him (Loring, Smith, & Bolden, 1997). The case history of Hedda Nussbaum demonstrates how an abused woman might develop a hostage syndrome. Recall how Hedda did not dare to anger Joel Steinberg and how she said that she loved him. In fact, the researchers who examined her case proposed hostage theory as a likely explanation for her strange reactions. An application of the hostage syndrome to female victims suggests that they may adopt such survival techniques (Rawlings, Allen, Graham, & Peters, 1994). Threats to survival and isolation are the most powerful antecedents for predicting development of the Stockholm syndrome (Nielsen, Endo, & Ellington, 1992). The following case history describes a woman kept as a prisoner.

## CASE HISTORY  Sophia and Boris—Lockdown

Boris seemed to get angrier every day. He was convinced that Sophia was having an affair, even though she was 8 months pregnant. He brought some lumber home from work one day and began boarding up all the windows in the house. He also removed the telephone. When he left for work in the mornings, he locked the front door from the outside with a new lock he had installed. One day, he just never came back.

Boris went to work every day and stayed with a girlfriend at night. Boris felt sad a lot of the time, so he went out to bars after work. Although he drove by his house every night, he never checked on Sophia's situation because "she deserved what she got"; she never cared how he felt about anything. Probably the baby wasn't his, he thought, because she was "such a whore."

Apparently, Sophia could not get out of the house, even though she screamed and tried to break through a window. There was almost no food in the house and no medicines. Sixty days later, Sophia was finally rescued; she had lost 20 pounds. A man from the gas company making a meter repair had heard her and called police and paramedics.

In the hospital, Sophia lay in a state of emotional and medical shock. Boris was her first visitor. He brought her flowers and apologized. When he tried to "make love" to Sophia in the hospital, a nurse caught him and called police. Boris was arrested. Although the judge did not sentence Boris to any jail time because he "was working," he did order Boris to attend a 10-week counseling program for batterers. One reason Boris agreed to counseling was that he wanted Sophia to come back.

*Attachment.* Adult attachment is a relatively *long-lasting affectional bond* that is typified by wanting to be close to a romantic partner. Attachment incorporates the view of the partner as a unique individual who is not exchangeable with any other (Feeney & Noller, 1996; Hazan & Shaver, 1987). Attachment theory is important in explaining the impetus for developing relationships with others, and attachment between romantic partners influences the quality of adult intimate relationships (Markiewicz, Lawford, Doyle, & Haggart, 2006). A primary advantage of attachment theory is its ability to explain not only the *co-occurrence of love and violence* but also the *ups and downs* in commitment that couples experience in a relationship.

Attachment consists of both *cognitive and affective mental representations* that guide attachment-related behavior (Collins, Guichard, & Ford 2006). As the concept of adult attachment evolved, theorists reconceptualized it as featuring two dimensions: (a) *positive/negative view of the self,* and (b) *anxious/avoidance responding* (see Roisman, 2009). Combining self-views with response style yields four types of attachment: *secure, preoccupied, dismissing, and fearful* (Bartholomew & Horowitz, 1991; Fraley and Waller, 1998).

Of particular significance in this area of research is the connection between attachment patterns and *proximity/distance regulating strategies* and the idea that *dyadic attachment orientations might be incompatible.* That is, one partner might have a predominantly preoccupied pattern leading to a desire for more proximity, while the other might have a dismissing pattern leading to a desire for greater distance. This type of *attachment conflict,* with each partner attempting a variety of unsuccessful strategies to regulate proximity, produces frustration and sometimes escalates to intimate partner violence (Allison, Bartholomew, Mayseless, & Dutton, 2008; see also K. C. Gordon & Christman, 2008).

*Traumatic bonding.* Another possible consequence of violence on victims' behaviors is that the victim becomes *traumatically bonded* to the abuser, a concept related to attachment theory. D. G. Dutton and Painter's (1981) analysis of traumatic bonding in MFIPV rests on the well-established fact that *intermittently rewarded behavior* is extremely persistent (i.e., resistant to extinction). A cyclical pattern of loving behaviors (rewards) coupled with sporadic violence (assaults) may actually increase the abused partner's dependence on the abuser. Consequently, traumatic bonding is a negative outcome because it may play a role in a *battered woman's persistence* in the relationship and diminish her resolve to leave (Dutton & Painter, 1993b; Towns & Adams, 2000). Insecurely attached women may form very intense bonds (Langhinrichsen-Rohling, 2006).

## Learned Helplessness Versus Survivor Theory

The meaning of learned helplessness rests upon a laboratory experiment with dogs in an *unavoidable, unpredictable shock* paradigm. In an initial phase of the experiment, "nothing they did during conditioning mattered and that the expectation that shock was uncontrollable undermined their trying to escape" ("Martin E. P. Seligman," 2006, p. 772). In a second phase, the dogs could *take an action* (jump over a low barrier) to avoid the painful shock, but they would *not* do so. They became *passive* and did nothing to escape, even though escape was possible. The case of Hedda Nussbaum described previously, for example, can be seen through the lens of learned helplessness. She was not helpless initially but became helpless over time.

"To be assaulted is to be subjected to an illegal action and confronted with one's own helplessness and powerlessness" (Hydén 2005, p. 169). Repetitions of assaults may in time lead to a pattern of behavior called **learned helplessness** (see Gerow, 1989, p. 193). Learning experts liken the *unpredictable and uncontrollable shocks* given to experimental animals (dogs) to the experiences of abused children and assault victims who have no power over their predicament. Further, the effects of *unpredictable and uncontrollable* stress are consistent with PTSD (Mineka & Zinbarg, 2006). Indicative of feeling helpless, is the comment made below by a battered women:

> For the longest time, I would just stand with my arms down and let it happen. Because what I found out later is if you put your hands up, to defend yourself or whatever, he'd make it worse. (R. E. Davis, 2002, p. 1255)

Various experts *disagree* strongly about whether learned helplessness accurately represents the behavior of female partner abuse victims because victims actively search for solutions by help-seeking (L. A. Goodman et al., 2003). Other skeptics point out that even if a woman uses a passive strategy, it may be the safest choice. Whatever she does, she most likely makes a *risked-based analysis* of what might work best (Hamby & Gray-Little, 2009). One new finding may temper the debate to some extent. Steven Maier and his colleagues (2009) at the University of Colorado have been able to show that animals in the *uncontrollable/unpredictable shock paradigm* were actually *failing to learn control* (not learning to be helpless) because of complex brain reactions to stress. In the case history below, a husband made his wife helpless.

## CASE HISTORY  She Was Her Husband's Pet

On Saturday, April 5, 2003, police arrested Jerry Thomason for aggravated assault and unlawful restraint. A witness at the school where Thomason and his wife, Patricia, dropped off their children had noticed a chain around Patricia's neck. When asked about the 25-foot chain, Jerry jerked it and told the witness that he used it so his wife could not run off.

After the witness called the police, Officer Kenny Hagen arrived at the Thomason house, where he found Patricia with the chain wrapped around her neck twice and padlocked in place. Officer Hagen said that it was difficult for Patricia to talk because she was distraught and "kinda beat down," as if she had accepted the chain as her lot in life. Police did not know how long Patricia had had the chain around her neck or if Jerry ever attached the other end to something stationary to tie her down.

Firefighters used bolt cutters to remove the chain, and doctors checked Patricia at the local hospital. When asked, Jerry said he "loved his wife," and that he had been making an effort to take care of her. Currently, he is in jail, awaiting trial; his bail is set at $53,000. The Thomason children are living with their maternal grandmother.[3]

*Survivor Theory—an alternative to Learned Helplessness Theory.* Because early research found that female IPV victims averaged six help-seeking behaviors (e.g., calling police, contacting a clergyman) before they entered a shelter, Gondolf and Fisher (1988) espoused a substitute for learned helplessness theory termed *survivor theory.* They held that battered women *do* seek help to resist male battering, but their actions may not be apparent because social organizations thwart their efforts (see also R. E. Davis, 2002). Ptacek (1999) developed a similar concept of *social entrapment* in which he proposed that women cannot escape abuse when they try because social institutions, such as the welfare system, present insurmountable obstacles.

Survivors can respond to intimate partner violence in various ways. An examination of National Criminal Victimization Survey data revealed three distinctive domains of responses to battering: (a) *nonconfrontational*—43% (e.g., trying to escape or calling the police); (b) *confrontational*—34% (e.g., struggled and shouted; 4% defied their partners with weapons); and (c) *did nothing*—23% (e.g., took no self-protection) (Greenfeld et al., 1998). Women victims of IPV do *not* appear to use self-defensive violence frequently. An analysis of 9,919 crisis calls to a battered woman's shelter indicated that only 5% of the women had used any self-defensive counterattacks during their most recent battering. All of these self-defensive attempts were unsuccessful and resulted in even more physical injury to the women (Murty & Roebuck, 1992).

## Perceived Control

Some battered women may try to offset feelings of helplessness by striving for control. One characterization of *interpersonal control* is the degree to which the individual *believes* he or she can impose control over the environment through his or her own actions and intentions (R. J. Turner & Noh, 1983). One investigation of perceptions about the use of partner abuse showed that women more than men believe that the motivation for male-to-female intimate partner violence is control (Ehrensaft, Langhinrichsen-Rohling, Heyman, O'Leary, & Lawrence, 1999). L. E. Walker (1984) conjectured that female IPV victims may have false beliefs about control. One terminology for this perception is *illusion of control* (see Fast, Gruenfeld, Sivanathan, & Galinsky, 2009). Battered women may think that their personal focus on their batterer's happiness and their own use of *coping strategies* allow them to exert control over the MFIPV in their relationship:

> I gradually started doing what I could to please … so I started thinking, if I give him the food that he likes, that he wants, if I look after the home so it is perfect, and I try to do everything I can not to arouse his anger and attention, perhaps it might be reasonably quiet. (Lindgren & Renck, 2008, p. 223)

A question has arisen over how one's beliefs about control in one's interpersonal relationships might affect them. In regard to *perceived control,* some theory-based reasoners speculate that high perceived control might be maladaptive in situations which are objectively uncontrollable (C. Peterson, Maier, & Seligman, 1993). A trio of researchers examined the beliefs of 100 MFIPV victims about their *perceived control* over *current and future* battering (Clements, Sabourin, & Spilby, 2004). Two distinct findings flowed from the analyses.

First, women's *high perceived control* over their *current* abuse was linked with greater drug use, increased dysphoria (depression), low self-esteem, and employment of disengagement coping strategies (i.e., self-blame). One explanation was that the outcome stemmed from helplessness, when the women's efforts to control the abuse were unsuccessful. Second, *high expectations* for control over *future male abuse,* conversely, had positive outcomes. They were associated with decreased depression and hopelessness and increased self-esteem (Clements et al., 2004).

There is an entirely different type of objection, however. It is argued that expectations for control may have no basis in reality. In terms of *real control,* one study of abusive couples' arguments showed that none of a wife's behaviors successfully suppressed a husband's violence once it began (Jacobson et al., 1994; see also Lindgren & Renck, 2008). Researchers also showed that physical abuse was related to women's *decrease in their beliefs about their ability to manage their relationships* (Raghavan, Swan, Snow, & Mazure, 2005). Other researchers showed that female-to-male IPV was ineffective as a control strategy because men were able to achieve greater decision-making power than women through IPV (Frieze & McHugh, 1992).

## Psychological/Brain Disorder Effects of Male-to-Female Intimate Partner Violence

In addition to acute brain injuries, as mentioned above, male violence against women may precipitate psychological effect as well as actual brain disorder effects.

*Depression.* Until recently, depression among battered women received more research effort than other possible effects save physical injuries and then PTSD. Almost without exception, researchers have documented *clinical depression* in battered women (e.g., D. K. Anderson, Saunders, Yoshihama, Bybee, & Sullivan, 2003; Arboleda-Florez & Wade, 2001; Dienemann, Boyle, Resnick, Wiederhorn, & Campbell, 2000). Clinical depression goes far beyond just feeling blue for a few days or feeling sad over a lost relationship. When practitioners discuss clinical depression, they are referring to a *serious medical illness* that can affect one's ability to function. Afflicted individuals have sleep disturbances, changes in appetites, and fatigue. Using data from the 1985 National Family Violence Re-Survey, Straus and Smith (1990) found that depression and *suicide attempts* were four times more likely in female victims of severe male battering than among their nonvictimized counterparts (see also Seedat, Stein, & Forde, 2005).

*Correlates of depression.* Although male-to-female physical and psychological abuses are an important *correlate of depression* in battered women, they are not the only correlate (B. E. Carlson, McNutt, & Choi, 2003). Various forms of male-to-female intimate partner violence are related to depression:

- Stalking . . . . . . . . . . . . . . . . . . . . . . . . . . . . . . . . . . . (Langhinrichsen-Rohling, 2006)
- Self-blame . . . . . . . . . . . . . . . . . . . . . . . . . . . . . . . . . . . . . . . . . (Clements et al., 2004)
- Low marital satisfaction . . . . . . . . . . . . . . . . . . . . . . . . . . . . . (e.g., Beach et al., 2004)
- Childhood abuse . . . . . . . . . . . . . . . . . . . . (Swan, Gambone, Fields, Sullivan, & Snow, 2005)

Studies are beginning to show, on the other hand, that male abuse is more than a correlate of depression; it is a *cause* (T. P. Sullivan et al., 2005; Von Eye & Anne Bogat, 2006). Over time, male aggression is associated with an increase in women's depression but not men's. One encouraging finding from a *longitudinal investigation* was that when male-to-female abuse stopped, depression decreased (Kernic, Holt, Stoner, Wolf, & Rivara, 2003). Findings from the T. P. Sullivan et al. (2005) study also suggested that depression among MFIPV victims stems from the abuse and is not an inherent trait of the women. Taken together, studies suggest that battering causes depression.

*Mental disorder effects.* For those who disparagingly ask, "What *is* wrong with her?" or "Why does she act like that?" the answer may be that she is suffering from the effects of being battered. Because cross-sectional studies cannot provide evidence of causation, it is impossible to determine whether women's psychopathology precipitates abuse, whether male partner violence precipitates mental problems, or if some third variable is causing the association. Researchers have, nevertheless, found a significant correlation between abuse severity and victims' **psychopathology** ratings. According to Lindgren and Renck (2008, p. 223), a victim in one narrative study said, "You can't live like this, you go mad, because you are exhausted from fear."

A synthesis of studies has shown that female victimization is a *risk factor,* or *a correlation that predicts,* for mental disorders, especially depression and PTSD (Golding, 1999; Pico-Alfonso, 2005). One study compared personality profiles of three groups of women classified by abusive relationships: (a) *multiple abusive relationships,* (b) *one abusive relationship,* and (c) *no abusive relationship.* Using scores based on the *Diagnostic and Statistical Manual of Mental Disorders,* 4th revision and the Coolidge Axis II Inventory, women with multiple abusive relationships fared worse than the other two groups. They had significantly *higher rates and levels of psychopathology* (i.e., dependent, paranoid, and self-defeating personality disorders). Women with only one abusive relationship, however, were similar to women in the control group; they did not evidence significantly more psychopathology (Coolidge & Anderson, 2002). (See www.sagepub.com/barnett3e for a discussion of self-esteem diminishment.)

---

## SECTION SUMMARY

### Consequences of Violence and Victimization

Violence has so many negative consequences that it is challenging to acknowledge each one and understand its impact. *Fear* is a pivotal response that often becomes chronic and long-lasting. Because of past violence, MFIPV victims realize that further assaults might happen at any time. Victims often become acutely sensitive to cues that foretell an imminent assault.

Violence can have many *severe physical and mental repercussions.* A group of related responses, such as stress and PTSD, are very potent aspects of victimization. Stress can cause chronic symptoms of physical illness and may impair thinking, memory, and problem solving. Anger is another common element of victimization. Violence qualifies as a traumatic event capable of inducing trauma symptoms. For many MFIPV victims, the trauma becomes severe enough to be labeled PTSD, which is a common repercussion of sexual assault and IPV and can be very debilitating. It may cause severe symptoms and last a very long time. Unfortunately, stress and traumas can build up cumulatively, one upon the other, causing even greater vulnerability.

*Physical health problems* are very common consequences of MFIPV. Some victims have life-threatening problems like heart attacks. Other consequences may be less serious but very troublesome such as obesity. Battered women have many reproductive problems, somatoform disorders, and acquire many more disabilities. Not surprisingly, victims have significantly more injuries. *Trying to cope* with so much emotional and physical pain places a heavy burden on victims. Many adopt ineffective strategies such as avoidance coping with additional negative outcomes such as depression. Highly stressed MFIPV victims often fail to find any effective methods for *coping* with their violent partners.

Another set of related consequences revolves around identifying with the abuser and forming attachment bonds with him. Certain types of abuse, such as near-imprisonment, create odd symptoms similar to those seen in hostages (the *Stockholm syndrome*). Childhood insecurities may continue into adulthood and combine with partner attachment issues. Couples involved in violent relationships often form close *romantic attachments* that fall into the insecure category, making it difficult for them to interact. The couple may have ongoing and severe challenges in regulating closeness, causing more relationship disruption. Alternatively, victims may form very close bonds with their abusers as a result of patterns of sporadic violence followed by periods of loving behavior (*traumatic bonding*).

Repeated violence when no escape is possible may lead to *learned helplessness,* a condition in which the victim tends to "give up" and accept the assaults. On the other hand, battered women do not uniformly appear to be helpless but exhibit remarkable *initiative* seeking help from friends, faith leaders, police, and mental health agencies. Their efforts may be thwarted by various organizations, such as Child Protective Services, whose functioning often entraps them. An *active coping style* is highly correlated with a battered woman's *help-seeking* activities. A very serious issue for battered women is being *controlled* by the abuser. Certain theorizing suggests that some female violence victims falsely believe they can control battering, an essentially uncontrollable behavior. High *perceived control* has negative effects, while *high expectations of control* have positive effects.

One of the most common correlates of MFIPV is *depression,* and depression is correlated with many other variables, such as low marital satisfaction and tendencies toward self-blame. Although psychopathology has strong genetic components, MFIPV appears to be an environmental factor that contributes to mental illnesses. Last, low self-esteem often is a consequence of male-partner violence.

## EMPLOYMENT

Lack of financial resources is a serious dilemma for most battered women, and employment may offer some solutions. Many women say, however, that assaults increase their risk for unemployment, reduce their incomes, and frequently precipitate divorce. Although many battered women manage to work, it is apparent that battering can cause serious problems in both finding and holding down a job (Swanberg, Logan, & Macke, 2005). A later population-based study of 6,698 women in California demonstrated that both *PTSD* and *psychological abuse* predicted *unemployment.* Although a link between physical IPV and unemployment also occurred, the correlation was no longer significant after the researchers made statistical adjustments for demographics and education (Kimmerling et al., 2009).

## Male-to-Female IPV and Barriers to Employment

Participants in four studies reviewed by the U.S. Government Accounting Office (GAO; 1998) reported that some batterers (16% to 60%) discouraged their female partners from working, and other batterers (33% to 46%) actually prevented their female partners from working. Batterers' harassment includes actions such as turning off an alarm clock so a woman will be late for work, cutting off her hair to embarrass her, and failing to fulfill childcare obligations so she cannot leave. Women attending school to get a better job encounter barriers as well. Some of these tactics encompass destroying her homework or hiding her books so she will fail (Raphael, 1996).

In one inquiry, female IPV victims reported that their abusive partners made the following demands about the female partners' work: (a) 33% prohibited working, (b) 21% prevented searching for employment, (c) 59% discouraged working, (d) 24% did not allow attending school, and (e) 50% discouraged attending school. MFIPV resulted in absenteeism from work for 55% of battered women, lateness or leaving early for 62%, job loss for 24%, and batterer harassments at work for 56%. Ending the abuse, however, enabled 48% of these women to make some kind of change in their employment or school status (Shepard & Pence, 1988; see also Moe & Bell, 2004). According to the Corporate Alliance to End Partner Violence (CAEPV; 2002), the number of episodes of male violence against women at work is 13,000 every year.

In a contemporary web-based, on-the-job survey, researchers categorized workers as nonvictims, current victims, or lifetime victims. Table 8.2 exhibits the victim classification of workers.

**TABLE 8.2** Partner Violence Victimization Classification of Workers

| Category | Men (n = 823) | Women (n = 1,550) |
|---|---|---|
| Nonvictims | 579 | 923 |
| Current victims | 85 | 160 |
| Lifetime victims | 159 | 467 |

Although women, relative to men, reported significantly more *current* victimization on every type of abuse except physical abuse, the frequency of reported female-to-male physical abuse obviated an overall significant gender difference. *Lifetime* rates of victimization, nonetheless, were significantly greater for women than for men. Absenteeism was significantly higher for lifetime victims than for current victims, and victimized workers missed significantly more work hours because of distraction at work than nonvictimized workers. The annual costs of *absenteeism, tardiness,* and *distraction* at work were all significantly greater for victimized than nonvictimized workers. Salary comparison demonstrated that males earned significantly more than females, and nonvictims earned significantly more than victims (Reeves & O'Leary-Kelly, 2007). (See www.sagepub.com/barnett3e for some additional detail.)

## Welfare Assistance Dilemmas

Battered women wishing to leave their abusive relationships often do not have adequate economic resources to support their children without relying on their abusive partner (Lien, Jacquet, Lewis, Cole, & Williams, 2001; C. M. Sullivan, 1991). In fact, the *lack of economic support is the major reason that MFIPV victims seek welfare.*

*MFIPV among welfare-reliant women.* There is a high prevalence of male battering among women on welfare (e.g., Riger & Krieglstein, 2000). Exact percentages are unknown, partially because the studies lack uniformity of definitions, samples, and methodology (U.S. Government Accounting Office [GAO], 1998). A 1997 review established that 15% to 32% of one pool of welfare recipients reported male IPV. Victimization rates among women on welfare may be twice as high as those for community women not on welfare (Raphael & Tolman, 1997; see also Tjaden & Thoennes, 2000b).

*MFIPV mothers among child welfare populations.* The problem of the co-occurrence of male-to-female battering and child maltreatment sparked an interest in mothers whose children are part of the welfare system. Data drawn from this population, that is mothers investigated for child maltreatment, revealed that levels of MFIPV range from 30% to 40% (Tjaden & Thoennes, 2000b).

To understand the problems of women whose children are on welfare, researchers examined data from 1,229 female caretakers using a nationally representative sample. The women studied had experienced a mean frequency of 6.8 severe assaults during the year prior to the research. The investigators used **latent class analysis (LCA)** (a special statistical technique) to differentiate *four group profiles* based on the needs and resources of the women. They also gathered information on continued male partner violence re-assessed after 18 months and new maltreatment allegations (Kohl & Macy, 2008).

---

*Group 1* (13% of women) had multiple problems (e.g., depression), a high rate of child maltreatment, and little support. After 18 months, they continued to have a moderate amount of male partner abuse, and 46% received new allegations of child maltreatment. They received the highest level of welfare support.

*Group 2* (2% of women) had substance abuse problems but received the most social support. This group had the lowest rate of new child maltreatment allegations.

*Group 3* (20% of women) had some drug abuse, very high stress levels, some childhood abuse, and low social support. Their victimization by their male partner was higher than that of the first two groups.

*Group 4* (65% of women) received low social support and low welfare support but had fewer problems such as drug abuse. This group had the highest level of partner abuse and the greatest number of new allegations of child maltreatment.

---

*Obstacles to success in welfare-to-work program.* For several reasons, welfare policy has evolved over the years with the end product being the welfare-to-work programs. Regrettably, these programs have not solved the problems of women on welfare. A contemporary study disclosed that a number of factors, such as the actions of male batterers, make it close to impossible for battered women to manage economically. One prospective survey focused on the effects of social support among 1,315 *welfare-reliant women* who also had a background of male abuse (Staggs, Long, Mason, Krishnan, & Riger, 2007). A pivotal variable in the analyses was whether *perceived level of support affected* both the women's *employment* and receiving male battering. A series of questions assessed the variables of interest: (a) demographic and human capital (e.g., *possessed job skills*), (b) *job turnover,* (c) amount of male-to-female *abuse,* and (d) *social support,* tangible and informal support items. The analyses looked for changes in the consequences of these variables over a *3-year period.* The following findings apply to the "next time interval," after a measurement:

- Women with higher levels of current MFIPV and lower levels of current social support reported *less employment stability.*
- Working steadily did *not protect women* from male violence.
- Working steadily did not help the women *acquire more social support.*
- Receiving higher levels of social support did *not reduce male abuse.*
- Receiving of social support did *not* **mediat**e the link between MFIPV and employment.

These results highlight some of the complexities in understanding the relationship between male-to-female intimate partner violence and employment. (See Riger & Staggs, 2004, for a comprehensive set of tables about the effects of male abuse among welfare-reliant female survivors.) Besides, male violence may not be the major barrier in obtaining and holding down a job for all welfare recipients. Although abuse may hinder or prevent battered women's employment, the *lack of job-supporting programs* may be more blameworthy. One group of welfare recipients disclosed that the two most serious impediments were the *lack of child care* and *lack of transportation* (E. K. Scott, London, & Myers, 2002). Without job support, some employed women reported the necessity of relying on their abusive or alcoholic male partner for child care (Sable, Libbus, Huneke, & Anger, 1999; E. K. Scott et al., 2002).

*The family violence option (FVO).* The federal government fashioned a special program called *the Family Violence Option (FVO)* for Temporary Assistance for Needy Families (TANF) women experiencing harassment from their violent male partners . This program helps women deal with batterer harassment at their work site and has the authority to allow welfare clients *more flexibility* in meeting the TANF work requirements. Another important function of an FVO is to allow TANF recipients some latitude in meeting the requirement to name the father of their children, so that authorities can collect child support from fathers. Some fathers forced to pay child support become even more violent. If TANF allows abusive men to find out the whereabouts of a woman in hiding, it places her in greater danger. In the Lien et al. (2001) study, one TANF recipient stated her concerns this way:

I figured if they was to pursue child support from him, he really would come after me in a violent way. I know him like a book. He's just looking for a reason. He was just waiting for a reason to come at me in some way. He even threatened to kill me and bury me at the side of my sister. So I take things like that serious. . . . I just told her [the caseworker] I didn't want them pursuing child support. (p. 204)

Furthermore, it may be useless to identify fathers to make them pay child support. Many young fathers in poor communities are at risk for substance abuse, unemployment, and criminal activities. They lack employment skills and life experience skills. They may be ill and lack health insurance. All these stressors make it difficult for them to fulfill marital and parental relationships.

---

**SECTION SUMMARY**

### Employment

Battered women experience a host of problems in the employment area. They often must earn a living, but trying to do so may place them in dangerous situations. Many batterers try to control whether a woman works or even hunts for a job. They may sabotage their partner's every effort to get a job, keep a job, or go to school. Nonetheless, some victims manage to work. Their abuser-caused problems such as tardiness and absenteeism make them appear to be poor workers.

Given the need for income for themselves and their children, a number of battered women turn to welfare. The welfare rolls are disproportionately filled with female victims, and battered women's children are frequently among the child welfare population. Because of society's negative attitudes toward welfare recipients, Congress changed the welfare laws in 2001, making recipients enter a welfare-to-work program. Many women received some sort of job training and many of this group obtained employment. Nonetheless, a substantial number of women did not appear on the employment roles. In addition, employment did not save women from male victimization or the abusive behaviors that undermined women's work.

Because female victims in the welfare-to-work program were so endangered, advocates successfully lobbied for changes in the welfare laws that recognized MFIPV victims' precarious situation. Welfare departments were ordered to provide the Family Violence Option (FVO) to battered women on welfare that granted them some leniency in fulfilling the welfare-to-work programs requirements. Furthermore, battered women were eligible to disregard provisions for naming the father(s) of their children because doing so could be life-threatening.

---

## CRIMINAL JUSTICE SYSTEM RESPONSES TO INTIMATE PARTNER VIOLENCE

The criminal justice system (CJS) has played a central role in the battered women's movement by virtue of its responses to the plight of family violence victims. This section elaborates on legal issues such as protective orders and weapon possession. The section also describes what happens when battered women call the police for help, work with prosecutors, and interact with judges. A paragraph or two of historical context sets the stage for changes in the laws and the consequences of these changes. The question underlying these topics is whether the criminal justice system can improve the safety of the women and children caught up in the violence.

## CASE HISTORY   Karen and Richard Graves

Over a year's time, 2 different police departments responded to 22 calls from Karen and Richard Graves' residence. None of the police officers involved was aware of any of the previous calls. Although Richard seriously injured Karen by hitting her with the baby's car seat, stomping on her ear, and assaulting her, several different judges set aside 6 different warrants for Richard's arrest.

Karen and Richard appeared before 10 different judges (none of whom had any notification of previous cases and rulings) at 16 hearings in the local family and criminal courts. Three different judicial officers at 8 separate hearings heard Karen's petitions for divorce, custody, and child support. Richard participated in 3 separate court-ordered counseling programs for alcohol and drug abuse and anger management. Advocates from 4 different agencies (e.g., Child Protective Services) addressed various problems the couple had, but none of the agencies communicated with any of the others.

When Karen started seeing a new boyfriend, Richard fired a gun near Karen and made repeated death threats that Karen reported. Eventually, Karen wrote a letter to the court begging the court to read the entire file of her case, to force Richard to follow the court's directives, and to protect her and her children. Six months later, Richard killed Karen with a shotgun and then killed himself (Epstein, 1999).

The preceding case history is a vivid example of the barriers that battered women face in seeking services from the *criminal justice system (CJS)* and what some of the problems are (Epstein, 1999). An analysis of calls to the *National Domestic Violence Hotline (NDVH)* revealed that the *second most pressing problem* facing IPV victims is the combination of a large gap in legal resources and inadequate responses on the part of the criminal justice system (Danis, Lewis, Trapp, Reid, & Fisher, 1998). Even when the CJS is functioning, sanctions seem ineffective. In one distressing account, batterers who were prosecuted and convicted were actually *more* likely to re-abuse (Hirschel, Buzawa, Pattavina, & Faggiani, 2007).

## Legal Issues

The laws governing spouse abuse have undergone an evolution as the Battered Woman's Movement took foothold. Advocates deserve credit for lobbying legislatures to both change laws and to force the implementation of laws. As will be clearer in the following sections, devising and implementing laws that protect women and children has been long in coming and has not yet successfully improved women's safety. Counterintuitively, males appear to have benefited more than females from legal or social changes geared to protect women. Although there have been numerous disappointments along the way, experts in the field have made remarkable progress (A. Klein, 2009).

Revelations about these kinds of inadequacies continue to surface from a variety of quarters. As an illustration, a judge in Florida found that a father who told his 6-year-old son to "kill" his mother was found not guilty of child abuse. In truth, there were no laws covering this kind of behavior. The mother's response was to begin working with an attorney to have the child abuse laws expanded to include this type of emotional child abuse (Perry, 2007). One could imagine that given a different situation, the child might actually have heeded his father's directive.

In addition to inadequacies in the law, a very serious deficit in helping battered women achieve safety is that they have few affordable legal services available to them. Poor women often have to wait 2 years to obtain legal services for divorce or custody issues. In cases of male battering, victims must remain connected to their abusers in the interim. At least as of 2000, the *Violence Against Women Act (VAWA)* included provisions that should help victims get legal help. As of 2009, the American Bar Association launched a program to provide services to battered women that includes a *National Domestic Violence Pro Bono Directory* sponsored by Verizon Wireless (American Bar Association, 2009).

*Protective orders.* One change in the laws has been to make *protective orders (POs)* more available to victims of IPV. A protective order is essentially a stay-away order forbidding an abuser from contact with the victim. Presumably, obtaining both *criminal and civil POs* would enhance IPV victims' safety, yet only a small number of victims obtain POs (Tjaden & Thoennes, 2000a). Police, when called to the scene of male violence, have stepped up their activities in recommending that women get POs. One survey found that 43% of IPV victims who obtained POs credited the police for informing them about POs or encouraging them to obtain one. Women who apply for POs have usually first tried several other methods to improve their safety, such as leaving the abuser, forcing the abuser out of the house, calling police, and calling a hotline (Ptacek, 1999). (See www.sagepub.com/barnett3e for a copy of a California Protective Order form.)

Justifiably so, experts specializing in partner abuse regularly assert that battered women's need for access to protective orders is acute (M. J. Carlson, Harris, & Holden, 1999). One expert, in fact, called for *mandatory POs* following an arrest for probable cause as a technique for strengthening victims' rights (Adler, 1999). Although POs have several functions, such as forcing an assaultive partner to vacate the family residence, their primary function is to *protect victims from physical abuse, harassment, and threats.* A protective order can literally be lifesaving. Because male partner aggression has a radiating effect that places the *victims' families and friends* in harm's way, these relatives, friends, and coworkers also have a great need for protective orders (Riger, Raja, & Camacho, 2002). (See above.)

*Using civil protective orders.* A fresh review of *civil and criminal* protective orders revealed that female victims petition the courts for very similar reasons with one exception. Women filing for civil POs were more likely to cite emotional abuse as the reason, whereas those filing for criminal protective orders usually cited documented physical abuse. This similarity prevailed even though the rationale behind the two types of orders varied. The rationale for a criminal protective order is a felony arrest for criminal battering. The reason battered women have selected civil POs is that they do not want to formally process the respondent through the criminal justice system. *Civil protective orders* allow women more flexibility in having their individual needs met through specific constraints on the offender. Having some control over these specifics often provides women with a sense of empowerment. Another important advantage of the civil protective order is that the abuser is not jailed and may still be able to provide economically for the woman and her children. The researchers believe that more female victims need to know about the benefits of civil protective orders (Kethineni & Beichner, 2009).

Within the criminal justice system, it is judges who have the authority to issue protective orders. Given the serious threat to the safety of victims and their families, it is disturbing that the courts are unwilling to issue protective orders routinely *or to enforce them.* Regrettably, as is the case throughout the criminal justice system, *judges' decision making about POs is problematic.* As a consequence, many victims may simply not be able to obtain protective orders or keep them in effect (Keilitz, 1994). Considering these stumbling blocks and others, some advocates have begun to urge the adoption of *permanent* protective orders (National Center for Victims of Crime, 2002). From a contrasting viewpoint, some suggest that *mandatory* protective orders may go too far, causing the equivalent of a *de facto divorce* (Suk, 2006). As one sign of progress, at least, female victims no longer have to pay a fee to obtain a protective order ("Congress Votes," 2000).

*Serving protective orders.* In light of a battered woman's struggle to obtain a protective order, one might think that actors in the legal system charged with serving POs would proceed to serve it as quickly as possible. This is *not* the case. A 2004 California study, for instance, found that 34% of restraining orders issued in Los Angeles County and 18% in Ventura County were *never* served on male defendants (offenders). Moreover, protective order violation is a very common occurrence, with as many as 51% of violators re-abusing their victims (A. Klein, Wilson, Crowe, & DeMichele, 2005). Since MFIPV victims cannot count on the legal system to implement judges' orders, other measures are necessary. Some shelters provide services such as photographic documentation of injuries that help with obtaining POs (Gibson & Gutierrez, 1991). Advocates working in some battered women's shelters have undertaken the task of hiring private agencies to serve protective orders (Kleinbaum, 2005).

*Adherence to sentencing guidelines.* The outcome of a recent analysis of judges' adherence to state/federal sentencing *mandates* for *violation of permanent* protective orders "paints a grim picture" (Diviney, Parekh, & Olson, 2009, p. 1215). Sentencing guidelines *mandate* that 100% of the protective order violators receive certain sentences. Examples of sentencing breakdowns were as follows: (a) *sent to batterer intervention program—only 24.1%,* (b) *arrested and incarcerated—only 48.9%,* (c) *firearm surrender—only 4.5%,* and (d) *electronic monitoring—only 3.8%.* Such a lackadaisical judicial performance sends a demoralizing message to victims, not to mention endangers their lives. This state of affairs portrays the judicial dispositions included in the survey as failing to meet legal standards. The results seem to depict judges failing in their judicial duties, as individuals who do not follow federal or state laws themselves, but who nevertheless are charged with controlling the lawbreaking of others.

*Protective order violation rates.* Once a woman has obtained a protective order and it has been served, will she finally be safe? The answer is "no." PO violation rates vary with typical estimates ranging from 44% to 48% (A. Klein et al., 2005). One reason for failure is that judges do not routinely issue arrest warrants for violators (R. Kane, 1999). Enforcement has been so lax in many jurisdictions that women have been forced to sue police departments to make them liable for nonenforcement ("Municipal Liability," 1998; see also R. L. Davis, 1998). One study of protective orders found that there were two key risk factors associated with violations: (a) *stalking* and (b) *victim's resumption and continuation of their relationship* (Logan & Walker, 2009a). Ultimately, POs are so ineffective that many experts suggest that judges inform victims about their limitations.

If a battered woman is not entirely safe after obtaining a protective order, will she be any better off? The answer is "yes, probably." Several studies have found that victims' safety improved after obtaining a PO (Logan & Walker, 2009a; Vigdor & Mercy, 2006). A 2003 survey of female IPV victims who procured protective orders in Seattle, Washington, ascertained that safety was enhanced along several dimensions, including *fewer injuries* and *fewer threats* (Holt, Kernic, Wolf, & Rivara, 2003). Although 59% of women in one survey called the police because of a violation, 86% said the order had stopped or reduced the abuse (Fischer & Rose, 1995; Ptacek, 1999). In conclusion, even without total safety, some women reported *feeling empowered* by the process of obtaining a protective order. Others felt POs were worthwhile because they documented the abuse, sent a message that abuse was wrong, and punished the abuser (Stewart, 2000).

*Weapons.* Weapons possession by batterers is extremely hazardous because the most frequently used weapon in IPV male-to-female homicides (**femicide**) is a gun, and having access to a gun is a potent predictor of a fatal assault (J. C. Campbell et al., 2003; Paulozzi, Saltzman, Thompson, & Holmgreen, 2001). Even when gun possession does not result in a fatality, abusers use guns to coerce and terrorize their victims (Gwinn, 2006). Despite the observation that many more males kill females than the reverse, females may be more likely to use a weapon during an IPV incident than males. This discrepancy may occur because of size and strength sex differentials (Kernsmith & Craun, 2008).

In 1997, the U.S. Congress modified the Gun Control Act of 1968 through an amendment known as the **Lautenberg Amendment** (after its author, Senator Frank Lautenberg). The Lautenberg Amendment bans individuals who have been convicted of domestic assault from carrying weapons, and it does *not* exempt law enforcement officers ("Domestic Violence Conviction," 1997). This amendment sparked investigations of IPV among law enforcement officers across the nation. One investigation revealed that authorities commonly disregard implementing the 1994 Violence Against Women Act policies that call for police IPV perpetrators to suffer severe job consequences (Lonsway & Conis, 2003). Another dangerous situation is that individuals forbidden by law to purchase guns are often able to do so. The FBI has determined that between 1998 and 2001, almost 11,000 illegal gun purchases transpired, and of these, about 26% were to protective order violators. The 3-day limit on background checks appears to be the predominant stumbling block in completing background checks effectively (U.S. General Accounting Office [GAO], 2002a), yet Congress remains unable to pass laws removing restrictions on database sharing ("Restrictions on Gun," 2007).

Finally, federal laws prohibit persons convicted of an IPV offense or who have a partner violence protective order issued against them from having a gun. Pursuant to the law, all those convicted of partner violence must surrender any guns they may have in their possession, and law enforcement must confiscate them. Nevertheless, *many offenders still have guns,* and many of the guns used by males in femicides are illegal because of previous male partner abuse convictions (D. C. Adams, 2007). In a survey of shelters in California, 36% of the women reported that there was a firearm in the house (S. B. Sorenson & Wiebe, 2004). Only one duo of researchers seems to have evaluated the effectiveness of gun confiscation laws, and they found no effect on femicides (Vigdor & Mercy, 2006).

## Arrest Policies

Historically, laws regarding the handling of male-to-female intimate partner violence have mirrored American society's "hands-off" approach—it's a private matter. Police departments traditionally *trivialized family violence* as noncriminal, noninjurious, inconsequential, and primarily consisting of verbal *spats* (Berk, Fenstermaker, & Newton, 1988). In addition to historical mind-sets, police attitudes toward female IPV victims help explain why getting police protection, to which they are entitled, has been almost insurmountable in some instances. Research findings suggest that if an officer holds certain beliefs, he or she may be reluctant to make an arrest:

- If male assaults are the victim's fault they are justified (D. A. Ford, 1999)
- If he beats her and she stays, there is no real victim (see Waaland & Keeley, 1985)
- If battered women are manipulative and unbelievable (Rigakos, 1995)
- If police involvement is not the best way to stop MFIPV (Feder, 1998)
- If responding to domestic abuse calls is not *real* police work or that real police work is catching *real* criminals (see Mastrofski, Parks, Reiss, & Worden, 1998)
- If intervening in partner violence is the most dangerous work police must undertake (Garner & Clemmer, 1986)

Illustrative of negative police attitudes is the statement of one police officer who said during a training session that he found arresting batterers hard to accept because a perpetrator might have married a "Nazi bitch from Hell, like I did" (quoted in D. A. Ford, 1999, p. 14).

*History of inadequate legislation.* Given the legacy of police inaction regarding MFIPV, victims' advocates became more progressive in documenting police behaviors and in trying to shape the policies of police departments. Accordingly, the *decision to arrest* became the dependent variable researchers believed would most likely reveal police attitudes and policies (see A. L. Robinson & Chandek, 2000).

*Double standard of probable cause.* One troubling observation about police conduct was their slowness in responding to domestic violence calls. Another was that police used a double standard in determining *probable cause* for making an arrest: one for domestic violence and the other for stranger assaults (see Avakame & Fyfe, 2001; Bourg & Stock, 1994; Mordini, 2004). This perception turned out to be accurate. *Police have failed to arrest some of the most violent male perpetrators when they had probable cause.* These perpetrators' violence included using guns, knives, or clubs, and throwing female partners down flights of stairs (Buzawa & Buzawa, 2003; Fyfe, Klinger, & Flavin, 1997). In fact, findings from a review of 25 studies documented that police typically *avoid arresting batterers* compared with other violent perpetrators (Erez & Belknap, 1998). Research outcomes such as these led to an evolution in police policies based on the principle of *pro-arrest: mandatory,* to *dual,* to the *primary aggressor statutes.*

*Mandatory arrest.* In the mid-1990s, growing dissatisfaction with police irregularities in handling IPV cases led to strong criticism of police *discretion* (police have the authority to decide if, when, and whom to arrest). Women's frustrations served as a springboard for the establishment of a *pro-arrest policy* that is a heightened *preference for arrests.* If arrests were mandatory, perhaps police would take male battering seriously and treat it as crime. Under such policies, police received notice that *arrest is the preferred response,* and that they *must* make an arrest (mandatory arrest) if there is probable cause (e.g., violence, weapon use, drugs on premises). Police were to abandon policies such as sending the abuser out to "take a walk and cool off" (Hirschel et al., 2007). In addition to making the arrest, police were to fulfill certain *statutory requirements* as follows (Buzawa & Hotaling, 2006):

| | |
|---|---|
| Inform victims of their legal rights | Inquire about suspect's prior abuse |
| Offer assistance in obtaining a PO | Inquire if suspect has access to weapons |
| Inform victims of community services | |

The next question was whether the new policies would finally protect women and children from family violence. A few studies, such as the *Spouse Assault Replication Program,* did detect a decrease in assaults (e.g., Berk et al., 1988). Victim interview data from this accounting revealed that aggression occurred 30% less often following arrest, and police reports showed a 60% drop in reoffending during the 6-month follow-up period. In another analysis, researchers concluded that mandatory arrest policies brought about a drop in *intimate partner homicides* (IPHs) (Rennison & Welchans, 2000).

Nonetheless, *mandatory arrest policies* did *not* consistently exert a deterrent effect on IPV or even serve the best interests of victims. Instead, many unfortunate problems occurred. Some studies uncovered persisting *police resistance,* if not a downright *backlash effect* (strong adverse reaction) presumably tied to the removal of police discretion. Police in one state actually arrested a greater proportion of women for assault than men, 34% and 23%, respectively (M. E. Martin, 1997). Other appraisals using data from court transcripts revealed that many of the women arrested and charged with female partner abuse were actually female *victims* (Melton & Belknap, 2003). A particularly *comprehensive* study with the *largest sample* of cases ($N = 57,000$) used data recorded by the National Incident-Based Recording System (NIBRS) and the Law Enforcement Management and Administrative Statistics (LEMAS). (NIBRS tracks offender and arrest records, and

LEMAS tracks information about police departmental organization). This review reached *four conclusions about mandatory arrest:*

- It increases the arrest rate of individuals involved in IPV.
- The arrest rate is still only 50% (meaning that officers still use arrest discretion).
- Factors contributing to racial bias in arrests are reduced under mandatory arrests.
- Certain organizational differences among police departments, such as access to written arrest instructions, increase the arrest rate.

The author concluded that mandatory arrest is not a panacea, but it does modestly increase arrests for partner violence (Eitle, 2005). Thus, the hopes of advocates, that *mandatory arrest policies* would guarantee aggressive police intervention on behalf of battered women, did not materialize. One very untoward outcome of pro-arrest policies was the tendency to make a dual arrest (see Leisenning, 2008, for an evaluative review of mandatory arrest).

*Dual arrest.* When an overall pro-arrest policy is in place, any involvement in IPV is sufficient to warrant an arrest. A number of police departments decided to manage domestic assault by arresting both parties, that is, making a *dual arrest regardless* of who was the primary aggressor. A dual arrest may also ensue when police cannot truly determine who the perpetrator is and who the victim is. A summary indicated that the percentage of women arrested for female-to-male IPV under this policy ranged from 17.4% to 30.8% (Hirschel et al., 2007). Negative outcomes other than arrest may occur. Some women feel disempowered or blameworthy for being arrested. As a case in point, one woman said she was arrested because she was unable to communicate adequately when talking with the police (Rajah, Frye, & Haviland, 2006).

Once more the hopes of advocates collapsed as research illuminated the unanticipated and very negative effects of *dual arrest* policies. Instead of protecting and assisting battered women, the policies led to an unexpected increase in female arrests, arrests of *females thought to be victims,* not offenders (S. L. Miller & Meloy, 2006). As a case in point, one researcher determined that only 12% of a sample of female IPV offenders, court-ordered into counseling, qualified as primary aggressors (Kernsmith, 2005b).

*Primary aggressor laws.* Primary aggressor provisions expect officers making a decision whether to arrest to evaluate the *context* of the IPV, such as self-defensive aggression (Avakame & Fyfe, 2001; Hofford & Harrell, 1993). Even the primary aggressor laws, however, were often misapplied and used against battered women. Dual arrests did decline following the passage of these laws if arresting officers had received specific training (see Hirschel & Buzawa, 2002; S. L. Miller, 2001). Finally, one seldom-considered issue is that when police make a dual arrest, the prosecutors must still try to decide who the primary aggressor is.

*Persisting problems in law enforcement.* These findings seemed to escalate several ongoing controversies. One dispute centered on how the police should handle partner violence. Are new laws needed, do police officers need more training, or are departments not implementing policies correctly? Are the police practicing a form of over-enforcement? Another dispute focused on what the increased number of female arrests means in terms of gender. Some thought that, perhaps at long last, gender-neutral arrests are reflecting an unsuspected number of *real female batterers.* These questions sparked myriad research endeavors and eventually became a research priority of the federal government (see A. Klein, 2009). (See www.sagepub.com/barnett3e for more details.)

Smaller studies expanded the knowledge base by considering the impact of other decision-making variables. As found in most studies, police are significantly more apt to make an arrest if someone has been *injured. Department policies,* which vary from department to department, also influenced police arrest decisions, as did a police officer's experience. *Experienced officers* were more likely to make dual arrests than inexperienced officers. Even when the *wife was viewed as the primary aggressor,* some police made dual arrests, presumably believing that males were generally more violent (Finn, Blackwell, Stalans, Studdard, & Dugan, 2004). In a later inquiry, researchers established that two rationales usually governed officers' decision to make a dual arrest: (a) believing the *law required it* and (b) thinking an *arrest might force both parties to seek relationship counseling* (Finn & Bettis, 2006). (See www.sagepub.com/barnett3e for information on victim precipitation and its effects.)

*Philosophy of law enforcement.* On balance, existing research implies that police interventions, no matter how well implemented, may still be ill-suited to meet the challenges of male partner violence. The reason may be that *criminal justice system philosophy does not accurately reflect the realities of battering.* Law enforcement's orientation is to view assaults as *incident-based* and as crimes in which there is a *victim-offender dichotomy.* IPV rarely occurs as a single event but rather as an ongoing facet of violent relationships (Hirschel & Buzawa, 2002). The fact that victims frequently fight back gives the impression that the violence is mutual, without a distinction between victim and offender. Another problem is the tendency to judge as equivalent, assaults that are *topographically similar* (i.e., a fist to the mouth). Hence, a wife's hit is just as illegal as a man's hit despite obvious differences (Osthoff, 2002). This type of thinking seems odd given the outcome of gender differentials in dynamic upper torso muscular strength. Military studies have disclosed that women's strength is 50% to 60% that of men's ("Army Gender-Integrated Basic Training," 2003).

*Outcomes of gender-neutral law enforcement for IPV.* Gender-neutral approaches contribute to incarceration of *battered female victims* and to the provision of inappropriate court-ordered treatment for female perpetrators (Kernsmith, 2005b; Osthoff, 2002). An arrested battered victim loses a large number of rights and privileges. She might lose her job, have restrictions placed upon her employment, and/or risk losing custody of her children. Moreover, the arrested victim is not entitled to services for "true" victims, such as being eligible to obtain a restraining order or access to a victim assistance program. Shelters will not accept her because of her arrest record, and there is an increased risk of deportation if she is an immigrant woman. Inappropriate arrests may actually place victims in greater danger because some female victims may not try to protect themselves physically for fear of being arrested (Downs, Rindels, & Atkinson, 2007).

## Law Enforcement/Victim Interactions

The practices of police can play a pivotal role in helping partner abuse victims escape, or they can put up serious barriers that make it difficult or even dangerous for victims to leave (Grigsby & Hartman, 1997). Even though police services have improved over the last decades, research on police responses to calls for IPV-related services reveals notable inconsistencies.

*Calling the police.* There are several reasons governing victims' decisions to call or not to call the police for help. Circumstances that make it more likely victims will call police are *self-protection needs* (current and future), *perception of IPV assaults as serious, victim injury, perpetrator history of abuse,* and *offender intoxication* (Bent-Goodley, 2001; Felson, Messner, Hoskin, & Deane, 2002; Hutchison, 1999). The following rates are estimates of calls for service: (a) 50%—*police estimates,* (b) 54%—*NCVS estimates,* (c) 58%—*sheltered women,* and (d) 23%—pregnant *Hispanic women.* Other surveys have unearthed the reasons why victims do not uniformly seek help from police (Coulter, Kuehnle, Byers, & Alfonso, 1999; Greenfeld et al., 1998; Rennison & Welchans, 2000; Wiist & McFarlane, 1998). See Table 8.3 for MFIPV victims' reasons not to call the police.

| TABLE 8.3 | MFIPV Victims' Reasons for Not Calling the Police |

| | |
|---|---|
| Do not perceive assaults as crimes | Privacy concerns |
| Think assaults are minor | Victim wants to protect offender |
| Fear reprisal—economic/physical | Threat by offender to report victim for child abuse |

SOURCES: Felson, Messner, Hoskin, & Deane, 2002; Rennison & Welchans, 2000; M. E. Wolf, Ly, Hobart, & Kernic, 2003.

*Expectations of the police.* Data are emerging that IPV victims who call the police do not have uniform needs or expectations about police services. Not all victims want their abusers arrested. Female victims' intentions in asking for police services may vary markedly from society's goals or, more specifically, from those of the criminal justice system. Female victims who called but were *not seeking arrest,* according to one survey, wanted the police to *tell him off* or *warn him.* Some of the women's other purposes for calling the police were as follows: *to get even, to shock him into straightening up, to get advice, to get help for the abuser* (e.g., drug treatment), or to ask police to *take the woman and her children to a safe place* (Hoyle & Sanders, 2000).

*Improvements.* Two more studies have indicated that battered women's perceptions of police responses may be improving. One report about 95 female victims indicated that 75% endorsed the highest rating possible for police intervention, and only 9% endorsed the lowest rating (Apsler, Cummins, & Carl, 2003). Another qualitative undertaking of victims revealed that about 70% described police behavior in positive terms. The other 30% were very critical of officers' behaviors and attitudes, claiming that officers threatened them with a dual arrest or made jokes about the violence (Stephens & Sinden, 2000). The most promising advance has been the inauguration of *specialized police units.* Although confirmatory evidence is sparse, one comparison found that in a 2-year follow-up, 29% of abusers handled by specialized units were re-arrested for IPV contrasted with 37% re-arrested by ordinary patrols (Friday, Lord, Exum, & Hartman, 2006).

## Criminal Justice System Processing

As mentioned throughout the text, most families never report abusers. Police arrest only a small proportion of batterers, and courts convict only a very few. It is important to know how the courts process the perpetrators that do enter the system and how the victims react. Identification of obstacles in the criminal justice system for partner abuse victims and improvement of the criminal justice system response to intimate partner violence have generally become especially active areas of research (for an overview, see National Institute of Justice & American Bar Association, 2009).

## Prosecution of MFIPV Perpetrators

Research on the prosecution of IPV offenders has dramatically increased over the last decade and has provided a large number of constructive ideas about improving prosecution because of the numerous problems identified. A review of over a hundred studies revealed that the decision to prosecute was as low as 4.6%. An analysis of 2,670 IPV court cases revealed that 44% of prosecuted cases resulted in a guilty verdict, 5% resulted in a not guilty verdict, and the court dismissed 51% (Belknap et al., 1999). Furthermore, male perpetrators received significantly shorter sentences than did perpetrators of other crimes (Erez & Tontodonato, 1990). A Michigan study disclosed that judges often deferred male abusers from prosecution more frequently than non-IPV offenders. Last, punishments did not fit the crimes and did not necessarily follow the dictates of family law (Canales-Portalatín, 2000).

Additional legal reforms had a positive impact on arrest rates. More victims called the police and more arrests were made as laws were implemented (S. S. Simpson, Bouffard, Garner, & Hickman, 2006). A later review corroborated improvement in criminal justice processing. Criminologists analyzed data from 135 English-language assessments. Results indicated that despite great variability, about one-third of reported offenses and more than three-fifths of arrests resulted in prosecutorial action—filing of charges. More than half of those charged were subsequently convicted. Hence, prosecution and conviction are *not* rare as so many have claimed (Garner & Maxwell, 2009).

*Complaints.* Both prosecutors and female victims have lodged complaints about each others' actions. One contentious issue among prosecutors is the perception that IPV victims waste their time by seeking help and then refusing to testify. In some jurisdictions, IPV is a *crime against the state,* so prosecutors execute their duties whether or not the victims are willing to testify. In other jurisdictions, the prosecution decision is left to the discretion of their victims. Whether to leave the prosecution decision up to the victim is unsettled (e.g., Belknap, 2000).

*Women's reluctance to testify.* Research has uncovered several reasons battered women may not cooperate: (a) *fear of retaliation by the abuser;* (b) *lack of tangible victim support,* such as transportation and babysitting; (c) worry that the *prosecutor would not prepare them adequately* for testifying; (d) *fear of not being believed,* (e) *fear the abuser would not be found guilty;* (f) being *dependent on the abuser for housing,* and (g) surprisingly, *failure to inform victims of their court dates* (see Belknap et al., 1999; L. A. Goodman, Bennett, & Dutton, 1999; Tomz & McGillis, 1997). Notwithstanding these findings, an in-depth 2,670 court case analysis ascertained that prosecutors normally view *women victims as cooperative* (Belknap et al., 1999; Hartley & Frohmann, 2003). Sadly, women's fear of involvement in prosecution has merit, because so many abusers re-abuse their victims even before the trial begins. Depending upon several factors, such as the length of time before trial, re-abuse rates range between 30% and 50% (Hartley & Frohmann, 2003).

The many problems associated with women's reluctance to testify against their abusers has led to the establishment in many locations of mandatory (no-drop) prosecution policies. That is, a battered woman cannot recant her testimony. (For a brief overview of varying opinions on no-drop policies, see Box 8.1at www.sagepub.com/barnett3e.)

More than half the female victims in one inquiry failed to cooperate with criminal prosecutions (Rebovich, 1996). A major stumbling block in gaining victim cooperation was the negative effect *prosecutors' lack of time had on victims.* Prosecutors had never spoken to 90% of the victims even by phone before the trial and had never met with the victim in person in 52% of the cases. When communications did take place, it was usually for only a few minutes (Belknap et al., 1999). Interactions with a victims' advocate or enhanced police services increased the percentage of women willing to cooperate.

Often prosecutors have very little physical evidence because of malfunctions in the system elsewhere. For example, prosecutors may not be able to read doctors' or nurses' *handwriting* in medical reports (Isaac & Enos, 2001). An end result of evidentiary deficiency is that the need for victim testimony is heightened. Several interesting comparisons established that it was not the presence of evidence that controlled prosecution rates but the *prosecutors' determination* to prosecute (see A. Klein, 2004). As with police services, the establishment of specialized prosecutor offices greatly increased prosecution and conviction rates. These units must be adequately staffed to make a difference (Hartley & Frohmann, 2003).

## Judicial Behavior and Decision Making

Judges' decisions have puzzled, angered, and frightened individuals connected to the family violence community. As such, judicial demeanor has attracted detailed research attention. In one inquiry, more than 75% of attorneys responding to a questionnaire said that judges allowed inappropriate questioning of female victims. Further, male perpetrators' defense attorneys could ask questions such as "What did you do to provoke your husband's assault?" (Hemmens, Strom, & Schlegel, 1998). On the other hand, the rulings and pronouncements of *proactive judges* send an unmistakable message that society will not tolerate violence against women.

*Judges' sentencing practices.* Research routinely indicates that courts rarely sanction even the most assaultive men in IPV cases, and that an imposition of a usual sentence rarely deters high-risk abusers. Variations in judicial responses are extreme. Typical of sentences given to IPV offenders are those stipulated in a Chicago survey: 33%—conditional discharge, 24%—probation, and 23%—sent to jail (Hartley & Frohmann, 2003). In one Massachusetts county, judges dismissed more than 60% of cases, whereas in another county the dismissal rate was

18% ("Records Show," 1994). A serious flaw reflected by these sentences is that judges did not follow sentence guidelines and disregarded the offenders' prior criminal history (Belknap, 2000). In a surprising contrast, however, an examination of over 1,000 intimate partner homicides revealed two unexpected outcomes: (a) male defendants are treated more sternly than female defendants at all stages of criminal justice processing, and (b) male intimate partner homicide defendants are sanctioned more severely than are male non-IPH defendants (Auerhahn, 2007).

Ineffective institutional support came to light in a qualitative study of sheltered women (Moe, 2007). In this series of interviews, one woman related how the judge sentenced her abuser to only 37 days in jail, even though her assault included *47 stab wounds*. In another study, a very *intrusive disposition* was responsible for deterring re-abuse. The disposition included the following sanctions: jail, work release, electronic monitoring, and probation. The intrusive disposition group's re-arrest rate was 23.3% in contrast to a comparison control group's rate of 66% (Ventura & Davis, 2006). Additionally, the greater the court involvement by the criminal justice system after the arrest, the less the recidivism (Murphy, Musser, & Maton, 1998). Last, a program that trained service providers to teach survivors how to obtain information from the Internet was highly successful (Finn & Atkinson, 2009).

*Three types of judges.* One scholar conducting a multisite study of the judiciary was able to classify judges into three categories: (a) *good-natured judges* who were supportive of victims and firm with abusers; (b) *bureaucratic judges* who were formal and firm with both victims and abusers; and (c) *condescending, harsh, and demeaning judges* who treated women unfavorably but were often good-natured with abusers. Fortunately, most judges fell into the first category. Victims under the supervision of these judges felt empowered and were more likely to cooperate with judicial orders (Ptacek, 1999).

*Shocking judicial behavior.* In one court study, Deborah Epstein (1999) presented several accounts of *shocking judicial conduct.* One judge presided over a case in which testimony described the behavior of a man who doused his wife with lighter fluid and set her on fire. The judge broke into song in open court, singing, "You light up my wife," to the tune of "You Light Up My Life." Another expressed resentment about having to deal with a husband who pleaded guilty to killing his wife after finding her in bed with another man. The judge complained that his job was very difficult when he was "called upon to sentence noncriminals as criminals" (p. 25).

*Lack of judicial training.* All empirical studies and criminal justice experts' analyses cite *judges' lack of training* in male-to-female IPV as a serious problem (Burt, Newmark, Olson, Aron, & Harrell, 1997; Epstein, 1999; Family Violence Project, 1995). One concern that has come to light is the judges' lack of scientific rigor observed in the courtroom. It appears that court precedents based on various biases sometimes become established in the judicial system. One example is the reliance on the concept of "*parental alienation,*" a debunked concept proposing that one parent alienates the child by making false allegations of abuse against the other, or by coaching the child to lie about abuse in custody hearings (See the National Council of Juvenile and Family Court Judges at http://www.ncjfc.org/content/view/20/94/.)

## SECTION SUMMARY

### Criminal Justice System

The criminal justice system is the major social institution involved in combating IPV, and the first line of defense against IPV is police intervention. Protective orders (POs) are widely sought by battered women, but the court may refuse to issue one. Victims should probably petition for a civil PO because of its greater utility. Certainly, protective orders are not a panacea because agents in the criminal justice system may neither serve them nor prosecute those who violate them.

Historically, the police have been unwilling to intervene in IPV cases. A number of studies have investigated what happens when women call the police. How do the police respond? The failure to respond to calls for protection generated strong political action in recent years. Attempts to improve procedures led to the passage of a series of laws (mandatory arrest, dual arrest, and primary aggressor). None of these, though, have been completely successful in helping women achieve safety. In fact, police often arrested a disproportionate number of women, and gender disparity in arrest rates varied widely between jurisdictions. Attempts to alter procedures through a gender-neutral approach have proved to be a dismal failure. It is useful to note that battered women may want the police to take some action other than arrests (e.g., get drug treatment for the abuser). The most promising improvement has been the establishment of specialized police units. As of 2006, experts concluded that female survivors were justified in their complaints about the police.

Prosecution of male perpetrators brings into a focus another host of issues. There is some debate about how cooperative with the prosecutor female victims are. Specialized prosecution units seem to work the best. If prosecutors take time to communicate with victims even minimally, the victims are more cooperative.

Some excellent laws fail not because of their content but because of poor implementation. An assortment of law enforcement personnel continue to balk at enforcing the laws. Starting with antiwoman and antivictim biases, other preconceived notions and past experiences, as well as several nonlegal variables (whether the woman had called several times previously) may factor into arrest decisions. Judges, though charged with enforcing IPV laws, do not even come close to following the sentencing guidelines. Most seem unwilling even to implement weapon-removal laws. Finally, the performance of the judiciary has been so suboptimal that a totally different approach is needed to compel judges to obey the laws. Some experts believe that the criminal justice system's incident-based philosophy is unsuitable for implementing justice in domestic violence cases because battering is unconfined to a single incident.

## EFFECTS OF MFIPV ON BATTERED WOMEN'S LIVES AND THEIR LEAVE/STAY DECISIONS

Male-to-female intimate partner violence permeates every area of a woman's life: health, happiness, emotional well-being, family welfare, personal and family safety including immediate family, relationship to the abuser, marital satisfaction level, relationship to one's faith, living conditions, employment, economic status, education, and one's future. Coping with the abuse often becomes transformed into a life-altering decision: whether to leave or stay. How can she be safe? Who can help her? Can she protect her children?

In light of the countless negative outcomes of male partner abuse, it is puzzling why all battered women do not leave. When victims decide to stay with abusive men, it evokes a mixture of reactions in others. "Why does she stay?" is often the first question people ask about battered women. The problem with this question, however, is that it implicitly emphasizes the actions of the victimized woman rather than those of her abusive partner. Some commentators have suggested that instead, the first questions should be, "Why does he do it?" and "How can society stop him?" Or perhaps people should ask, "How did she survive the violence?" A number of authorities prefer the term *survivors* to *victims* for women who escape battering because of the numerous obstacles they have to overcome to free themselves.

To better understand leave/stay decisions, researchers have generally assessed specific dependent variables. Some investigators have reported data, such as *percentage* of survivors *who actually left or intended to leave,* and the *consequences of leaving.* Others have explored the *decision-making process* itself. Probably the largest number of researchers have looked at *why, when,* and *how* survivors leave. The findings can be organized in several different ways. One useful way is to conceptualize rationales for *not* leaving as either *external inhibitors* (e.g., inadequate responses from social agencies or the CJS) or *internal inhibitors* (e.g., fear, love). Scholars in this area often espouse the necessity of *understanding the women's perceptions* of their situations and what their stumbling blocks are (Barnett, 2000, 2001).

## Leave/Stay Decision-Making Process

A descriptive study of female IPV victims yielded results in line with the Grigsby and Hartman (1997) barrier model of explaining leave/stay decisions. The *barrier model* is a practical, easy-to-understand model that envisions the impediments to finding safety as lying within four concentric circles with the victim in the center. The other three rings, beginning with the outermost, include the following: (a) environmental barriers, (e.g., lack of money), (b) family and social role expectations (e.g., she should love her abusive husband), and (c) psychological impact of abuse (e.g., fear). The women's responses to 20 qualitative and quantitative questions developed at the Artemis Center in Dayton, Ohio, highlighted differences between external and internal barriers influencing decision making. The most frequently reported barriers in descending order were partner's promise to change (70.5%), partner's apology (60.0%), lack of money (45.9%), and nowhere to go (28.5%). These authors propose that the safety of many battered women is still elusive because of inadequate responses by society, their childhood socialization, and the psychological impact of abuse (M. A. Anderson et al., 2003).

*Factors associated with actually leaving.* In one longitudinal investigation, Seattle women who had had police contact because of their abuse served as research participants (Koepsell, Kernic, & Holt, 2006). At follow-up 9 months later, participants completed questionnaires dealing with a number of relevant variables. A multivariate analysis differentiated between women who left and those who stayed. Those who *left* were significantly more likely to vary along several dimensions: (a) *younger age,* (b) *possession of a protective order,* (c) *previous relationship partings,* (d) *higher psychological vulnerability,* (e) *abuse-related physician visit,* and (f) *successful procurement of external supports,* such as food stamps, Social Security benefits, assistance with employment, transportation, or housing (Koepsell et al., 2006; see also Panchanadeswaran & McCloskey, 2007; E. Rodriguez, 2001; Zlotnick, Johnson, & Kohn, 2006).

In a different sort of study, investigators were able to identify the *help-seeking activities* that MFIPV victims took that enabled them to leave and eventually obtain a *divorce.* These help-seeking actions were as follows: (a) *education/information seeking* (e.g., got information about available resources), (b) *interpersonal help-seeking* (e.g., disclosed the problem to a health care professional), (c) *self-empowerment* (e.g., opened a bank account), and (d) *protection/separation activities* (e.g., called the police) (J. C. Chang et al., 2006).

An especially illuminating study examined the role of (a) *physical and emotional abuse,* (b) *resource utilization,* and (c) *childhood abuse* on leave/stay decisions (Raghavan, Swan, Snow, & Mazure, 2005). This research, based on a sample of nonsheltered female victims, had two important measurement strengths. One was its use of a scale to examine whether *women's beliefs* about their relationship influenced their *leave/stay decisions.* These questions dealt with beliefs about relationship interactions, such as dealing with disagreements or anger in their relationship. The other strong point was its assessment of participants' *help-seeking attempts,* both informal (e.g., friends) and formal (e.g., shelters) sources of assistance. In addition, participants responded to a small sample of physical and emotional abuse items drawn from other scales. Results revealed a number of interesting contrasts.

The majority of women (56.5%) were currently involved in abusive relationships, while the other 43.5% had recently terminated a relationship. *Increased physical abuse* and *degree of psychological abuse were directly associated with leaving.* Physical abuse is also related to women's *increased utilization of resources* and to *a decrease in their beliefs about their ability to manage their relationships.* Finally, the investigators determined that *childhood abuse* was associated with *remaining* with the abusive male partner (Raghavan et al., 2005).

*Physical assaults in leave/stay decision making.* Another widely held false belief is that physical violence is the most important factor in a woman's decision to terminate a relationship (Gortner, Berns, Jacobson, & Gottman, 1997). Although male violence within a relationship may not be the most important factor, *it is one factor. Escalation of the violence,* for instance, is a factor in leave/stay decisions also. Researchers found that 70% of aggressive newlyweds had experienced marriage failure by the end of their first 4 years. In contrast, only 38% of the nonaggressive couples had failed marriages (Lawrence & Bradbury, 2001). Analogously, severe asymmetrical (i.e., one partner more violent than the other) partner violence led to more dissolutions than minor/symmetrical IPV (i.e., partners comparably violent) (K. L. Anderson, 2007). Conversely, results from a 10-year longitudinal inquiry reported that leave/stay decisions were not associated with various dimensions of abuse in totally expected ways. Community survivors (a) exposed to more severe physical assaults and (b) for a longer duration were *less* likely to leave than their counterparts who received shelter services. These results imply that shelter services made it possible for battered women to leave (Panchanadeswaran & McCloskey, 2007).

Data used in the analyses from the National Survey of Families and Households (NSFH) study disclosed that it was *dissatisfaction* related to the violence, not violence per se, that was associated directly with leaving (DeMaris, 2000). A different analysis still based on the NSFH data indicated that the odds of leaving a violent relationship depends somewhat on structural gender inequality, especially *economic dependency* (K. L. Anderson, 2007).

*Psychological/emotional abuse.* Emotional abuse plays a pivotal role in diminishing a victim's ability to leave an abusive relationship (Follingstad & DeHart, 2000; Glaser, 2002; Mazzeo & Espelage, 2002). Women exposed to *higher levels of emotional abuse* were more *likely to leave* than those exposed to lesser levels. Even without taking physical abuse into account, emotional abuse is related to victims' perceptions of *threat* and their plans to *leave the relationship* (Henning & Klesges, 2003; Raghavan et al., 2005; see also Lawrence, Yoon, Langer, & Ro, 2009). Furthermore, emotional abuse is more highly correlated with *actual leaving* than is physical abuse (Jacobson, Gottman, Gortner, Berns, & Shortt, 1996). Last, degree of *emotional abuse* is significantly correlated with female victims' level of *relationship dissatisfaction.*

*Entrapment.* Simply assuming that victims can leave if they *really wanted to* ignores a number of critical constraints these women face (Attala, Weaver, Duckett, & Draper, 2000; Rose, Campbell, & Kub, 2000; Short et al., 2000). Studies find that even when such major obstacles as poverty are not present, women may still judge themselves unable to leave (e.g., Purewal & Ganesh, 2000). In the words of Panchanadeswaran and McCloskey (2007, p. 62), "Decisions about staying in or exiting abusive relationships encompass a plethora of complex, intertwined factors." Some authorities refer to the changes brought about by various conflicting factors (e.g., fear vs. hope) as *entrapment* (Landenburger, 1998). Although increasingly used, the word *entrapment* is bothersome to some observers because they see it as implying that battered women are unable to exercise choice. Others see the fact that many women do leave violent relationships as *proof* that battered women are *not* really trapped. It may be better to conceptualize *entrapment* in terms of factors that sometimes make it extremely difficult for women to leave (e.g., religious beliefs).

*Approach-avoidance conflicts.* Battered women are often overwhelmed by ambivalent feelings that can be likened to approach-avoidance behavior (for a review, see LaViolette & Barnett, 2000). One well-established conflict described by *learning* theorists is termed *double approach-avoidance conflict.* This type of conflict entails making a decision about an object (or person) that contains *both desirable and undesirable features* (the house you want to buy is affordable, but it is 70 miles from your job). People caught in this kind of conflict vacillate, first going toward one goal and then retreating, next going toward the other goal and then retreating, and so forth. This type of push/pull conflict may continue over an extended length of time.

In the case of a battered woman, her relationship meets many of her needs (see L. E. Simpson, Atkins, Gattis, & Christensen, 2008). She wants to approach her partner's love for her, which is hopeful, and run from his battering, which is frightening (Hydén, 1999). In a controlled comparison that demonstrates such a conflict, female victims rated several factors associated with stay/leave decisions: (a) *deciding to leave*—fear of harm, child care needs, poor social support, financial problems; (b) *deciding to stay*—fear of loneliness (Hendy, Eggen, Gustitus, McLeod, & Ng, 2003).

Application of approach-avoidance paradigms suggests that battered women will leave when the avoidance factors build up in intensity, stay when the approach factor predominates, and vacillate for some period of time before making a final decision.

## Do Battered Women Stay?

In light of such heated discussions about why battered women stay, it is useful to find out if battered women actually do stay. Although most female victims eventually leave, not all do so or even voice intentions to leave violent relationships (e.g., Raghavan et al., 2005).

*Leave rates.* A few longitudinal studies have examined *leave rates* among women living in shelters and samples of battered women living in the community:

- *43%* of sheltered women left within 2 years (Okun, 1986).
- *38%* of women living in the community divorced or separated within 2 years (Jacobson et al., 1996; see also Bowlus & Seitz, 2006).
- *43%* of community victims left within *5 years* (Zlotnick et al., 2006).
- *71%* of community victims, and sheltered women left within 10 years (Panchanadeswaran & McCloskey, 2007).

*Return rates.* Two studies measuring women's *return rates* after *shelter* treatment found these percentages: (a) 33% (I. M. Johnson, Crowley, & Sigler, 1992) and (b) 24% to 33% (Gondolf, 1988). One analysis of male-to-female intimate partner violence victims living in the community (nonsheltered) indicated a 33% return rate (Herbert, Silver, & Ellard, 1991; see also Langhinrichsen-Rohling, 2006). On average, women leave and return to their abusers five to six times before they leave for good (see R. E. Davis, 2002; Rhodes & McKenzie, 1998; Stroshine & Robinson, 2003).

## Dangers of Leaving an Abusive Partner

A major reason that people in the lay public think battered women should leave is because they think leaving will finally make them safe. Even many battered women predict less violence if the relationship ends and higher risk if it continues (Harding & Helweg-Larsen, 2008). As a matter of fact, research has shown that abusive behaviors often stop when a female victim does leave (M. E. Bell, Goodman, & Dutton, 2007). Intimate relationships, however, can end in two ways: (a) leaving, separating, and divorce, and (b) death, by natural causes or by intimate partner homicide. *"Just leaving"* an abuser does not guarantee a woman's safety (Horton & Johnson, 1993; Hydén, 1999). In fact, just the opposite is true in far too many cases. To leave can be dangerous, if not fatal (DeKeseredy, Schwartz, Fagen, & Hall, 2006). As a consequence, some women stay because it is safer (Hamby & Gray-Little, 2009; L. E. Walker, 1984). Every resource person (e.g., police, counselors) should help victims deal with their leave/stay decisions because it might lead to better self-protection whether they leave or stay (R. B. Stuart, 2005).

*Worries about a backlash.* It is possible that increases in domestic violence services and changes in women's social status may provoke a *backlash* (retaliation) among male partners that increases male partner violence. In one study, two variables were correlated with an upsurge in the rate of intimate partner homicides: (a) prosecutors' willingness to pursue cases of protective order violations, and (b) the relative education of the partners. Prosecutors' willingness to track violators of protective orders was associated with an *elevation* in the intimate partner homicide rate among some but not all racial groups. That is, prosecutors' following up on POs actually increased victimization of White married partners but not of Black married partners. (See Dugan, Nagin, & Rosenfeld, 2003, for specific details and additional references.)

*Dangerous assaults associated with leaving.* In 1992, the MFIPV assault victimization rate of women who were separated from their husbands was about 3 times higher than that of divorced women and about 25 times higher than that of married women (Bachman & Saltzman, 1995). When female victims try to leave, the risk of femicide is at its highest (H. Johnson & Bunge, 2001). In one sample of abused women, 75% of women who were killed by their male partners and 85% of those who were severely beaten had left or had tried to leave during the previous year (Sharps, Campbell, Campbell, Gary, & Webster, 2003). For some victims, the decision is not whether to leave, but whether to live (Hydén, 1999). Therefore, recommending that all survivors leave should *not* be the only counsel that mental health and physical health care workers make. Petitioning the court for a restraining order, or moving out of state, for instance, might be a viable option.

*Forgiveness.* A wave of contemporary research has investigated the role that forgiveness plays in women's leave/stay decisions. One well-conducted investigation found that forgiveness was a strong predictor of *intention* to return to an abusive partner among 121 sheltered women. Forgiveness was a more powerful predictor of returning than constraints (e.g., pressure to leave), severity of the male aggression, and malicious (negative) attributions about the male partner's rationales for the violence. The results also indicated that forgiveness **mediated** the role between malicious attributions and intent to return. The greater the severity of the violence, the more likely the women were to form malicious attributions. The authors speculated that forgiveness may have reduced the cognitive dissonance generated by the constraints (e.g., inadequate income) (K. C. Gordon, Burton, & Porter, 2004).

## Economic Dependence and Its Diffuse Impact

One of the clearest messages from the literature is that societal practices play a large role in women's economic dependence. *Economic dependency, low income,* and *poverty* are all highly associated with male-to-female IPV and child abuse.

*Women's economic dependency and leaving.* The perennial question about why battered women do not leave their abusers often harks back to their economic situation. Many researchers have called attention to the connection between women's *economic dependence and their inability to leave.* When women leave or divorce in an attempt to end an abusive relationship, their incomes nearly always decline, while men's usable incomes remain relatively constant (Bartfield, 2000). Some impoverished female survivors may not leave their abusers because even basic survival is such a struggle (C. A. Byrne, Resnick, Kilpatrick, Best, & Saunders, 1999; Toews, McHenry, & Catless, 2003). In three inquiries, abused women did *not* leave because of economic needs—58% of one sample, 30% of another, and 45.9% of a third (M. Anderson et al., 2003; Hofeller, 1982;

Stacey & Shupe, 1983). By the same token, many female *survivors return* if they cannot financially provide for their children, and a review determined that *having sufficient funds* was the strongest predictor of leaving (D. K. Anderson & Saunders, 2003; Morrow, Hankivsky, &Varcoe, 2004).

*The radiating impact of IPV.* Other people inhabiting a battered woman's social world are vulnerable to violence, as well; that is, battered women are not the only targets of men who assault their female partner. In one study, battered women leaving a shelter described the harmful impacts of IPV on children and extended family members. During the year following a shelter stay, many women necessarily had to ask relatives to provide a place to live, financial support, and child care. Some women's relatives, however, denied help. Other women did not ask relatives for help because of the perpetrators' threats to harm the family. Either way, the lack of housing, financial resources, credit cards, child care, and transportation make it difficult for nearly all women to reestablish independent households (Riger et al., 2002).

## Society's Inadequate Support for Battered Women

Will society help battered women leave? By and large, the responses of some individuals or agencies that are potential sources of social support for battered women are, in essence, problematic (Krugman et al., 2004). Some of the actions of the police or the responses of emergency personnel may exert a strong influence on a victim's leave/stay decision, either positive or negative (L. V. Davis & Srinivasan, 1995).

When criminal justice, social service, and health care organizations follow detrimental policies, battered women may not be able to leave. A major problem for many women is *navigating access to helping agencies.* Within this realm, a major difficulty is encountering *poorly trained service providers* who are unpleasant and unhelpful. Such workers display a lack of therapeutic skills and are insensitive to the woman's experiences. In one inquiry, the major complaint of 61% of the clients was *helpers' attitudes.* Some of these behaviors encompassed actions, such as "did not listen to me," "blamed me," "dismissed my ideas," "judged me," "mocked me," "excluded certain topics of discussion," "adopted and insisted on following a specific program format," "told me what to do," and "rushed me in and out of sessions" (Stenius & Veysey, 2005). Another study noted that clients greatly disliked having to change therapists or to be cut off from services. (See Goodman & Epstein, 2008, for an analysis of service provisions.) (See www.sagepub.com/barnett3e for information on intimate partner homicides.)

## Responses by Faith Communities

Although most women who seek religious counseling do so because they prefer clergy's religious values, some nonreligious women also seek clergy assistance, possibly for economic reasons or at the request of a family member (Lount & Hargie, 1997). Thus, clergy serve as a general, community resource (Horton & Johnson, 1993). Most secular professionals and the community agencies described below are *first responders* who have an obligation to determine whether violence has occurred and what services are needed (Glowa, Frasier, & Newton, 2002; Harway et al., 2002; C. E. Marshall, Benton, & Brazier, 2000). Some responders are more effective than others in counseling battered women. As described previously, various faith leaders respond differently. Some, for example, blame battered women to various degrees for male battering and find no acceptable rationale for helping them find a way to leave.

*Effectiveness of clergy counseling.* To understand the effects of confiding in clergy, researchers studied psychological outcome data from community-dwelling women who revealed their abuse to clergy. Admission of male-to-female assault was correlated with higher self-esteem and lower negative effects from lack of social support, and 80% of the women rated clergy as helpful. The researchers suggested that confiding in clergy was protective of battered women's self-esteem. Clergy giving less helpful counseling tended to ask women questions such as, "Why were you drawn to an abusive man?" Their behaviors reflect the basic tension between some psychological models and religious ones that may conflict. There are several useful documents that can assist faith leaders: (a) a list of warning signs that partner violence is present, (b) actions clergy should take to provide compassion to IPV victims, and (c) a list of clergy resources (e.g., books, manuals) (Neergaard, Lee, Anderson, & Wong-Gengler, 2007).

*Recommending change.* Two other surveys suggested that members of the clergy have little enthusiasm for training geared toward improving their assistance to female victims (J. M. Johnson & Bondurant, 1992; Reyes, 1999). In reaction, a number of concerned individuals within faith communities advocated that members of the clergy change their responses to male violence. Family violence experts have made the following *recommendations:*

> Hold Christian men accountable for their partner violence and stop blaming victims (Miles, 2002)
>
> Include the topic of battering in premarital counseling (Neuger, 2002)
>
> Help congregants understand IPV and its signs in sermons (Neergaard et al., 2007)

## Welfare Failures and Leave/Stay Decisions

As welfare workers tried to *implement the Family Violence Option (FVO),* a number of obstacles—too numerous to detail—arose. In some cases, the impasse originated with the women. Some women did not know about the program, and others did not disclose IPV for myriad reasons. They might want to avoid the stress of talking about the situation, for example, or they might worry about whether CPS would become involved and try to take away their children (Saunders, Holter, Pahl, Tolman, & Kenna, 2005; E. K. Scott et al., 2002).

As discussed previously, welfare failures are a major problem for IPV survivors. First, guidelines about allowing abusive male partners to know the location of their children presents serious dangers to mothers. The women could not risk revealing this information for the sake of a welfare check (Moe, 2007). Second, there was mishandling of information about the Family Violence Option. An analysis of 782 transcribed interviews between welfare workers and welfare clients found that workers *screened clients for IPV in only 9.3% of the cases.* Screenings usually entailed informing clients about FVOs but did include asking the woman if she had been abused (Lindhorst, Meyers, & Casey, 2008).

Third, there was a mismatch between the type of services offered to welfare recipients and what they thought they required. Welfare staff did not always provide assistance with practical problems such as finding child care. Without child care, the female IPV victims could not meet the welfare staff's expectations to become economically independent. Fourth, surveys of staff's attitudes toward welfare applicants revealed a lack of civility. Workers' rude behavior extended across a broad spectrum of situations. Some recipients felt blamed, disrespected, humiliated, and threatened. Some workers seemed to bully women by issuing threats, perhaps every month, to cut off the woman's benefits (Laakso & Drevdahl, 2006).

## Shelters and Transitional Supportive Housing and Leaving

Women trying to escape male partner violence must find a safe place to stay and a place where they can find help with the multiplicity of problems facing them. How will they feed their children? Will they be able to find a job? Should they try to get help from the criminal justice system? Will they ever feel safe again? Shelter and transitional housing staff help with these issues and many more.

*Shelter help.* Shelters for battered women have saved many lives. Shelters offer a temporary separation from an abuser that assists female victims by helping them feel safe and by providing them with people who will listen to their concerns. First and foremost, shelter programs emphasize *safety planning* for female abuse victims planning to leave their abusers: finding a safe place to go, having money hidden in a separate account, getting a second set of keys for the car, and packing a bag with important documents in it. In one survey of female IPV victims, participants rated safety measures, such as hiding important papers, as the most helpful tactic they used to cope with male battering (L. A. Goodman et al., 2003). M. A. Douglas (1987) alleges that shelter counseling can help victims accept personal responsibility for their own safety while rejecting personal responsibility for the violence.

Helping victims obtain *temporary welfare benefits* and helping them prepare for employment (e.g., referral to training programs) are usually top priorities for shelter programs (C. Brown, Reedy, Fountain, Johnson, & Dichiser, 2000). Shelter staff often help victims complete the legal forms needed to get restraining orders, teach them (nonviolent) parenting skills, and help them enroll in substance abuse programs. It is encouraging to note that in one 10-year longitudinal study, women who accessed shelter services compared with those who did not were significantly more likely to leave abusive relationships (Panchanadeswaran & McCloskey, 2007). Then again, not all studies have shown such striking results (Koepsell et al., 2006).

Although most people assume that battered women can always escape to a shelter, this is not the case. Shelters employ selective admittance policies that require them to deny admission to some women: those with *medical conditions or disabilities* that the staff cannot handle, those with *teenage boys* over the age limit of 13, those with felony *drug convictions,* and those who *admit female-to-male abuse* (see Melbin, Sullivan, & Cain, 2003). If these battered women have no shelter or food, they usually feel forced to return to their abuser. (See www.sagepub.com/barnett3e for an interview with Maria Michaels.)

*Transitional Supportive Housing (TSH).* Battering increases homelessness. Although unemployment and lack of education are the primary causes of homelessness in general, family violence and other forms of victimization appear to be the major causes of female homelessness (e.g., Virginia Coalition for the Homeless, 1995; Waxman & Trupin, 1997). Various researchers have estimated that male violence affects 21% to 64% of homeless shelter clients (e.g., Bassuk et al., 1996; National Low Income Housing Commission, 1998). Sadly, one funding agency had doubts about providing funds for housing because they feared it would support unwed pregnancy, single parenthood, or economic migrants (Pascall, Lee, Morley, & Parker, 2001).

Affordable permanent housing is an especially pressing need among female victims whose safety depends upon their leaving (Baker, Niolon, & Oliphant, 2009). In their analysis of calls to the National Domestic Violence Hotline, Danis et al. (1998) found that the third largest gap in society's response to partner abuse victims is permanent affordable housing. The lack of availability of nonshelter affordable housing forces many women to return to their abusive relationships (Beechey & Payne, 2002; see also Lien et al., 2001). These problems have led to the establishment of *transitional supportive housing (TSH)*. TSH furnishes access to affordable housing and other support for battered women during the period of time when they are trying to establish their independence (Melbin et al., 2003). During a stay in TSH, staff provide counseling and practical support for up to two years.

## Emotional Factors in Leave/Stay Decisions

Just as reasons for male abusers are multidimensional, so are decisions for leaving or staying with an abuser. In addition to economic factors, victims must come to grips with a host of emotional and psychological factors. In order to leave, victims must traverse several changes in beliefs: (a) acknowledging that the relationship is unhealthy, (b) realizing that the relationship will not get better, (c) experiencing some catalytic event, such as abuse of an infant, (d) giving up the dream of an idealized committed relationship, and (e) accepting that, to some extent, the relationship will never be over (e.g., because of the constraints imposed by shared child custody) (Moss, Pitula, Campbell, & Halstead, 1997; see also Enander & Holmberg, 2008).

*Relationship commitment.* Commitment to a relationship is usually seen as a positive attribute. Over the years, numerous well-known women have demonstrated respect for their marital commitment in spite of very painful and humiliating revelations of their partners' infidelity (e.g., Hillary Clinton, Kathie Lee Gifford, and Elizabeth Edwards). So strong is public sentiment about the virtue of marital sacrifice and fidelity that Hillary Clinton's approval ratings skyrocketed when she remained with Bill after his sexual improprieties came to light (Rogers, Krammer, Podesta, & Sellinger, 1998; Schindehette, 1998). Believing that they should stay with their partners "no matter what" is significantly related to female victims' decisions to stay (Roloff, Soule, & Carey, 2001; Vandello, Cohen, Grandon, & Franiuk, 2009).

A victim may remain with her abuser in part because she has adopted *socially approved attitudes* of love, hope, and commitment to the relationship (Hendy et al., 2003; Short et al., 2000). She loves her partner with whom her life has been entwined, and she hopes the violence will end (see Moss et al., 1997). Although she is aware of the discrepancy between her actual marital relationship and her ideal relationship (Shir, 1999), she has come to believe it is her duty to stay (Towns & Adams, 2000).

*Investment model.* Theorists have tried to explain the unexpected behavior of individuals who continue a relationship that has suffered a serious setback. Rusbult's (1980) *investment model* tries to account for women's failure to give up and leave when the relationship includes MFIPV. The model holds that the degree of commitment to an intimate relationship rests on the fulfillment of certain needs: (a) one's *relationship satisfaction level* (relationship's perceived rewards minus its perceived costs), (b) the *quality of one's alternatives* (perceived relationship rewards minus the costs of a better option—another partner, advanced education), and (c) *the magnitude of one's investment*—time and effort, financial resources, and having children together. The woman's commitment level rests on the sum of these three factors, and commitment is a **mediating** variable between these factors and leave/stay decisions.

The results of a survey of 60 female victims court-ordered into treatment for female partner abusers were congruent with the model. The researchers reported that "lesser relationship satisfaction, greater alternatives, and fewer investments" contributed to "lower levels of commitment and greater intentions to leave those relationships" (p. 313). In this study, male violence levels, but not female violence levels, were inversely related to relationship satisfaction. Male-to-female sexual coercion was significantly and inversely related to women's investments. In other words, male partner violence was not directly related to leaving. Instead, male abuse was associated with lowered relationship satisfaction and lowered investments which, in turn, were associated with lowered commitment and hence to a greater probability of exiting the relationship (Rhatigan, Moore, & Stuart, 2005).

In one study, Bauserman and Arias (1992) showed that female IPV victims' commitment to their relationships was related to their level of *failed investment*. That is, the victims may have stayed and worked harder to make their relationships work to justify the time and effort they had already expended. When a relationship is not going well, *frustration* may motivate the victim to try even harder to work things out (see LaViolette & Barnett, 2000). One interesting new conceptualization of commitment may affect future research on MFIPV. Researchers have demonstrated that commitment is not unidimensional but rather composed of several dimensions, such as *personal commitment* (desire to remain with partner) and *constraint commitment* (e.g., structural factors like marital status) (Givertz & Segrin, 2005). Some other dimensions of commitment have more recently emerged: *past/planned* and *tangible/intangible* (Goodfriend & Agnew, 2008). Finally, personality factors (e.g., narcissism) **moderate** investment. Individuals high in narcissism reported less commitment associated with low satisfaction, high quality of alternatives, and low investment (Foster, 2008).

*Relationship hope.* Relationship hope is an especially powerful influence on female victims. Just feeling optimistic appears to be beneficial. Optimism is generally linked with greater persistence toward goals, better coping, and improved health (Sweeny, Carroll, & Shepperd, 2006). Both men and women usually want their marriages to succeed. The failure of a marriage to meet one's expectations causes bitter disappointment (Procci, 1990). Female victims often stay in their marriages because they hope and need to believe that their abusers will stop the violence, a need that Muldary (1983) has termed *learned hopefulness.* Women in Muldary's study of shelter residents listed several reasons for staying in or returning to a battering relationship. They "wanted to save the relationship" or "thought we could solve our problems."

Pagelow (1981) found that 73% of the female victims in one shelter sample returned to their homes because the batterers repented and the women believed the *men would change.* Both Okun (1986) and C. Thompson (1989) discovered that the hopes of battered women were rekindled by their male partners' attendance at even one counseling session, even before the men had made any real changes in their behavior. Similarly, 95% of female victims whose husbands were in court-ordered counseling believed their husband would complete the program, although only half typically do (Gondolf, 1998). The two most frequently reported justifications for staying among a group of female abuse victims were that her partner promised to change (70.5%) and that he apologized (60.0%) (M. Anderson et al., 2003).

Hope also springs from the fact that an *abusive male's behavior is intermittently rewarding* rather than continuously abusive (see above). Male offenders can be kind, romantic, and intimate as well as intimidating and assaultive (Hastings & Hamberger, 1988). Episodes of kindness, interspersed with violence, not only create hope but also allow the victim to deny the side of the abuser that terrifies her (Graham, Rawlings, & Rimini, 1988). Periodic abuse, as in traumatic bonding, strengthens the romantic attachment bond and makes it more difficult for a victim to leave her abusive partner permanently (D. G. Dutton & Painter, 1993b). Exposure to negative events, however, *can* foster a downward shift in optimism that can also be beneficial. A downward shift allows an individual to prevent overwhelming disappointment by better preparing him- or herself for a negative outcome (Sweeny et al., 2006).

Perhaps hope that the violence will stop is justified in some cases. From a qualitative analysis of community women, investigators found that women tended to stay if the violence ceased. These researchers used a procedure that permitted detection of three types of changing/shifting abusive patterns: (a) *taking control,* (b) *counteracting abuse,* and (c) *living differently.* One key element in men's change was *reducing their various addictions* (e.g., alcohol). Another essential element was the *woman's historical or religiously driven sense of competence.* As women acquired personal capacity and autonomy, many male partners "sat up and took notice" and gradually ended their violence. The *crucial indicator* of whether the couple might be able to live nonviolently was whether *the man backed off and de-escalated his battering* in response to the *changes she made.* Even if the violence ceased, not all relationships became happy. For some couples, a nonviolent coexistence was in and of itself sufficient, but for others it did not prevent women from leaving. For still others, renegotiating the couple's relationship by re-investing in the relationship led to *living differently* (e.g., becoming more assertive) and living more successfully (Wuest & Merritt-Gray, 2008).

*Marital dissatisfaction and leaving.* Research shows that another important link with leave/stay decisions can be seen in *marital satisfaction levels.* In a national sample of 185 female survivors who had endured abuse for an average of 10 years, 27 were able to retain their relationship with their abusive partner. Then again, of these only 16 rated themselves as feeling "satisfied" or "very satisfied" with the relationships. Compared with dissatisfied survivors in this sample, *satisfied survivors* were quite different. They tended to be younger, had been more severely abused, pursued more methods for ending the abuse, were more committed to their partners, and felt more hopeful about their relationship. What is more, they had abusive partners who tended to become involved in the therapeutic change process and sought drug and alcohol treatment more readily than their counterparts. By comparison, *dissatisfied survivors* had fewer job opportunities, had a strong fear of failure, had more children, and had male partners who were more likely to sexually abuse them and physically abuse their children. In fact, dissatisfied survivors were more than 3 times as likely as satisfied survivors to have been forced to have sex (Horton & Johnson, 1993).

*Attachment needs.* One explanation for women's decisions to stay is that both members of a couple are strongly *attached t*o each other (Griffing et al., 2002; Henderson, Bartholomew, & Dutton, 1997). Feelings of attachment can be very powerful motives for seeking proximity to a partner (Allison et al., 2008), and attachment to a violent partner can be linked directly with persistence in an abusive relationship. It is a potent emotional force in blocking a battered woman from leaving (Griffing et al., 2002). Like widows, battered women mourn the loss of their relationships. Of the female IPV victims in S. F. Turner and Shapiro's (1986) study sample, 70% said that they returned to their perpetrators because of *feelings of loneliness and loss* generated by the separation. As Allison et al. (2008) have pointed out, violent individuals may have very strong attachments to their partner.

*Afraid to leave and afraid to stay—approach-avoidance conflict.* Female IPV victims may *not leave* their partners because the abuse they have experienced has generated extremely high levels of *fear* (Gore-Felton et al., 1999; Healey, 1995; Hendy et al., 2003; Short et al., 2000). Leaving a perpetrator may not put an end to fear-provoking events. In the M. A. Anderson et al. (2003) inquiry, 36.7% of the sample of battered women feared their partner. Fear changes over time, and for some women contemplating leaving, *terror comes to dominate their lives.* Male partners threaten to retaliate, stalk, assault, take the children, and engage in numerous other frightening activities to force female partners to stay (Fleury, Sullivan, & Bybee, 2000).

One of the most common reasons women do not leave is their sense of foreboding over the *possibility of losing their children.* An analysis of telephone calls to the National Domestic Violence Hotline revealed that more than half of the callers cited *apprehension about revenge* as their principal reason for staying with an abusive partner (Danis et al., 1998). Just the opposite occurs in other situations. Recognizing the deleterious effects that being exposed to male violence can have on their children serves as a catalyst for some battered women to leave. Concern about one's children is often the ultimate reason victims give for leaving their abusive partners (Hilton, 1992; R. E. Davis, 2002). In defense of their children, some battered women find the courage to mobilize their resources and change their own lives (Levendosky, Lynch, & Graham-Bermann, 2000).

## Effects on Battered Women's Lives and Leave/Stay Decisions

The damage done to MFIPV victims is life-altering, permeating every aspect of their lives. The traumatic features of a violent relationship are so numerous and intertwined that deciding whether and how to leave is very stressful. A wrong decision could eventuate in death. One study uncovered a number of characteristics, such as young age and abuse-related physician visits, which were associated with women who left. A different investigation identified help-seeking behaviors, such as finding available resources and actually using them, were the factors that enabled some women to escape. Although physical and emotional abuse levels and escalation of abuse are not the only factors in leave/stay decisions, they do increase the probability of leaving for many women residing in shelters, not those living in the community.

A majority of battered women appear to become entrapped in their violent relationship because of its many conflicting elements. At a basic level, feelings of love and hope counter feelings of terror and pain. Her need for economic support and the need for a father for the children complicate her decision making, further ending in what psychologists refer to as an approach-avoidance conflict. Although approximately 40% of sheltered women and 70% of community battered women do finally leave, about 33% return. This leave-return cycle may repeat itself five or six times before a woman finally leaves for good.

Although the public believes that leaving a violent relationship will secure a woman's safety, just the opposite is often true. Studies of lethality consistently show that the actual time of departure is the most dangerous period of the leaving process. As one example, 75% of women who were murdered and 85% who were severely beaten had tried to leave their partner. Social support is crucial, just after a woman has left.

Commencing with the earliest research evidence, it was clear that economic dependency is a major factor in women's leave/stay decisions and continues to impact return decisions. Women very frequently turn to family and friends for help, such as providing temporary housing. Batterers have usually threatened the victim's family during the course of the relationship. If the family helps her after she leaves, they may become victims of his violence as well.

Regrettably, society responses to battered women's needs have evolved very slowly. Responses have been and still are problematic in far too many instances. Every type of agency, the police, health care, and social service agencies, needs personnels' behavior to improve. The behaviors of faith leaders also fall into this group. Shelter staffs are often the personnel most dedicated and able to help battered women. They provide crisis counseling and then take on the task of helping women "get back on their feet." They explain safety planning and help women obtain protective orders and apply for welfare benefits. In brief, shelter services have been effective in helping women leave. Shelter workers have also been at the forefront in establishing and staffing transitional supportive housing services, thus helping women avoid homelessness.

*(Continued)*

(Continued)

Emotional factors are frequently at the heart of leave/stay decisions as reflected in decisions to stay even when economic factors are not paramount. Society praises the "good" women who maintain their marital relationships in the face of infidelity. Some women stay because they have not only invested a great deal in their relationships, but they may also have evaluated their alternatives as unappealing. Many women keep hoping the violence will end and that their abuser will return to "the man she married." Any sign of change, such as the husband's attendance at one counseling session, provides hope—often misplaced hope. Women often hope that a change in their own behavior (i.e., taking control) will motivate him to change, and sometimes it does. When marital satisfaction is high in other areas of the relationship, some survivors stay despite the violence.

Experts in the field of IPV are increasingly aware of the role of attachment needs in leave/stay decisions. Many violent couples are strongly attached to each other, and attachment is linked with staying. She loves him, for example, and feels lonely without him, so she seeks proximity to him. She wants to be with him whether or not he can financially contribute. Some women find themselves in the position of begging their abusive male partner to stay. Battered women are both afraid to stay and afraid to leave. They are entrapped.

## MALE VICTIMS OF INTIMATE PARTNER VIOLENCE (FMIPV): HOW MUCH OF A PROBLEM?

Researchers are slowly beginning to investigate the parameters of male IPV victimization. In an early deduction, Suzanne Steinmetz (1977) argued that some men suffer from a battered husband syndrome comparable to the battered woman syndrome (see also, e.g., M. J. George, 2003). As noted previously, Conflict Tactics Scale–measured prevalence and incidence data derived from a broad spectrum of community-based (nonclinical) samples indicate that women and men commit physical and psychological intimate partner with almost equal frequency (Archer, 2000). In contrast, data collected within a *crime context* (National Crime Victimization Survey, *Uniform Crime Reports, Supplementary Homicide Reports*) or in *clinical settings* present markedly different findings. These latter data sources establish that women comprise the vast majority of victims.

This gender war has persisted with the two sides providing more and more evidence to back their position. Straus (1993) and D. G. Dutton (2008) continually reaffirm the position that assaults by women (e.g., "slaps") are a serious social problem. Along the same lines, one analysis of a large data set found that men are just as victimized by nonphysical types of abuse as women are (Outlaw, 2009). While Gelles (2004) observes that women are the most likely to be injured, he believes that society focuses so much attention on battered women, that male victims become invisible. He articulates his views as follows: "The real horror is the continued status of battered men as the 'missing persons' of the domestic violence problem" (p. 61) (see also Dalsbeimer, 1998). If nothing else, Frieze (2003) asserts that researchers need to pay more attention to FMIPV. In a review of IPV studies, however, D. G. Saunders (2002) found no consensus among experts that female-to-male intimate partner violence is even a major social problem, let alone a behavioral equivalent to male-to-female intimate partner violence (see also James, 1996).

Studies other than CTS-based gender comparisons have begun to show some real gender distinctions. A 2004 account of female-to-male IPV and male-to male IPV indicated that 24% of 346 men admitted to an emergency room reported female violence (including physical, emotional, and sexual abuse). Only 1% of these men had been injured by partner violence, and 3% said they had perpetrated partner violence themselves. Of the 271 men from the sample of 346 who reported the gender of their abuser, 11% of the offenders were male and 89% were female. In other words, some of the abusers were male partners. The authors concluded that the injured men were likely to be "batterers injured while committing battery" (C. Johnson & Gorchynski, 2004, p. 43). Compared with males who are not victims of female violence, male victims suffer significantly more illness, disabilities, and risk factors for disease (Morbidity and Mortality Weekly Report, 2008). Overall, these findings attest to the fact that some males really are true victims of female partner abuse (and some are victims of male-to-male IPV).

Criminal justice studies find clear differences between male and female victims of IPV (Macmillan & Kruttschnitt, 2004). Males identified as victims in one episode of IPV are likely to be the suspected perpetrators in a second, new episode; 41% of male victims were subsequently identified as suspected male perpetrators and 26% of female victims were later identified as suspected female perpetrators. Males first identified as suspects were far less likely to be identified as victims (26%) in a later episode, and female suspects were more likely to be seen as victims (44%) later (D. A. Ford & Regoli, 1992). Male homicide victims are far more likely than female homicide victims to have been identified previously as abusers (e.g., Starr, Hobart, & Fawcett, 2004).

An analysis of data from the National Survey of Families and Households found gender differences in leave/stay decisions. As an example, men are less likely than women to leave if they are the economic providers and the female-to male IPV is minor/symmetrical. Men experiencing severe female-to-male are less likely to leave than women if they have young children (K. L. Anderson, 2007). Last, one government reporting system has uncovered vast health disparities for both male and female IPV victims. Some of these include statistically significant increased levels of *asthma and stroke.* Moreover, male partner-abuse victims suffer from significantly more heart attacks, heart disease, and higher cholesterol than nonvictims (Morbidity and Mortality Weekly Report, 2008).

On the other hand, it is possible that "commonalities found in past research on wife abuse can be used in the analysis of husband abuse, regardless of the size and the strength of the individual" (Migliaccio, 2002, p. 47). Some expected commonalities include age, race, and drug addiction. Dalsbeimer (1998) convincingly speaks to some of the resemblances of concerns that both male and female victims voice. Some victimized men may feel or believe the following: (a) It is too embarrassing to report female IPV victimization; (b) They might lose their children in a custody battle; (c) They can protect their children if they remain; (d) If they leave, they will be less financially solvent because of the costs of child support and maintaining two residences; (e) The violence is too minor to break up their families; (f) They love their wives; and (g) Stress or alcohol is the real culprit. One gender disparity between victims may be a man's fear that fighting back might lead to his killing the woman. (For further descriptions of abused men, see Cook, 1997.)

## Cluster Analysis of Male and Female IPV-Involved Individuals

Although information about female partner abusers has increased, almost no information is available about male victims at this time. In one study, Hamberger and Guse (2005) presented data from 87 male IPV offenders and 38 female IPV offenders court-ordered into abuse abatement programs. The purpose of this evaluation was to discover empirically based *subtypes* of behavioral and emotional *responses* to partner-initiated IPV. Using **cluster analysis,** these investigators isolated three clusters of response subtypes as shown in the table at www.sagepub.com/barnett3e. These investigators conclude that, "There is *no one way* people involved in a violent relationship react, behaviorally and emotionally, when their partners initiate violence against them" (p. 313).

### DISCUSSION QUESTIONS

1. Name three consequences for women victimized by male partner violence.

2. Should battered mothers be held legally responsible for protecting their children from abusers in their households? Why or why not?

3. What are the symptoms of trauma and PTSD? What causes it? How easily does it dissipate over time?

4. Discuss battered women's fear and its consequences.

5. Describe the following three theories: traumatic bonding, Stockholm syndrome, and attachment. How do these theories explain a victim's entrapment in the relationship?

6. Discuss the difficulties women experience when trying to leave abusive male partners.

7. What are the economic problems faced by battered women?

8. What services do shelters provide?

9. Why is it difficult for health care providers to respond to battered women's problems?

10. Why can't battered women count on the criminal justice system to protect them from an abusive male partner?

11. Evaluate welfare services for battered women. Should Americans have to pay taxes that go toward welfare costs?

### NOTES

1. This case history, which was prepared by Alyce LaViolette, is quoted directly from LaViolette and Barnett (2000, p. 15).

2. The main source for the details in this case history is Hackett et al. (1988). The names used are the subjects' real names.

3. The source for this case history is "Man Held" (2003). The names used are the subjects' real names.

For chapter-specific resources including audio and video links, SAGE research articles, additional case studies, and more, please visit www.sagepub.com/barnett3e.

# CHAPTER

# 9

# Abusive Heterosexual Partners

## *Primarily Men*

**CASE HISTORY**  Ari and Bernadette—When a Little Slap Is a Knockout Punch

Ari came into group counseling like many other men arrested and ordered into counseling. He seemed calm and collected, dressed nicely from his day's work as a department store manager. He protested his arrest, claiming that it was "all a mistake." All he did was give Bernadette a little push in the car because she wouldn't "shut up."

Ari's story was that he came home exhausted from a long day at work only to find Bernadette all dressed up and saying that she "had to get out of the house; she wanted to go out to dinner." Ari said he was too tired, but Bernadette got angry and started screaming that he only "thought of himself." Ari gave in.

It was already 8:30 by the time they pulled into the restaurant parking lot. The restaurant was crowded and noisy, and Ari was angry and sullen as they waited for their dinner. He and Bernadette each had several drinks, but Ari could not calm down. "No one ever cares about my feelings," he thought. When they returned to the car after dinner, Bernadette launched into a diatribe about Ari's "failure" to accept her 6-year-old son by a previous marriage. She kept "mouthing off as usual," and Ari's driving became erratic. As they arrived home, Ari reached across the front seat of the car and slapped her because he "had to do something to get her attention." When he went around to open the passenger-side door for Bernadette, she "fell out and hit her head on the pavement."

The neighbors called paramedics and the police, and Ari was arrested. Bernadette's medical report said that she had been "knocked out"; she did not "fall and hit her head." It took more than 10 weeks of group counseling before Ari would admit that his little slap was really a knockout punch.

$A$ ri's actions in the above case history are typical spouse-abusive behaviors, and they illustrate some of the specific problems batterers have. Note that he dismissed the violent incident as a mistake, and he minimized the harm he had done. Ari's anger and stress contributed to his assault on his wife. To Ari, Bernadette did not seem understanding or accommodating, and he believed that she had provoked his physical attack by behaving in such a demanding manner. She was to blame—not him.

This chapter examines the behaviors of batterers, *primarily men* who abuse and control their female partners through threats and physical, psychological, verbal, and sexual aggression. Men are the primary injury-producing perpetrators of *intimate partner violence* (IPV) (Tjaden & Thoennes, 2000b). Men kill more female intimates than the reverse, and women are the more likely victimized partners. Although this chapter focuses primarily on men, mounting information about women who are violent toward their male partners makes it appropriate to include female abusers here as well.

There has been such an expansion of research on *male spouse abusers* that the topic needs to be subdivided. Research examines the types and estimates of intimate partner violence, descriptions of batterers including their personality traits, and some of the better-known theoretical causes of IPV. The chapter contains updated information on some trait determinants of IPV, such as jealousy and partner control. Some of the latest information is beginning to show how biology influences violence. There is a section on the similarities and differences between generally violent men and those who primarily assault only members of their own family. These topics have fostered work on typologies of batterers which attempt to group abusers along trait dimensions. Scholarship about *female spouse abusers* includes an expanded section on differences between abusive men's and women's motives for abuse.

## MALE-TO-FEMALE INTIMATE PARTNER VIOLENCE (MFIPV)

One social scientist has boldly commented that, "Thorough knowledge and understanding of battering continues to elude both scholars and practitioners" (D. M. Lawson et al., 2001, p. 86). Nonetheless, advances over the last decade are noteworthy. This first section presents some of the sociodemographic descriptions of male batterers and various definitions and estimates of male-to-female intimate partner violence. Some knowledge exists about how best to investigate male-to-female partner abusers starting with the sources of information about them, which includes criminal justice statistics, female partners' reports, and batterers' self-reports. Where does one find the most accurate information? Do different sources provide similar information? This section raises questions about different sorts of data, such as clinical descriptions, legal definitions, criminal history data, observational research, pen-and-pencil tests, or other assessments.

### Sociodemographic Characteristics of Batterers

It is important to remember that while sociodemographic characteristics (e.g., age, gender, race, income, education) help explain patterns and variation in rates of intimate partner violence, they do not cause the battering and cannot predict precisely which individuals will or will not become perpetrators or victims. This knowledge, however, can assist psychotherapists and agents of the criminal justice system to be alert to the variables that differentiate abusers from nonabusers.

*Age/gender/race.* The information from all these sources shows that *current/former intimate partners* are the *most likely to be involved in a homicide-suicide events,* with females the most likely victims and males the most likely offenders. The majority of studies show that in 2000 in 18 states and the District of Columbia, women 18 to 54 years of age comprised 85% of spousal violence victims. Recall that for some, there is a debate about whether women are as abusive as men. Large representative samples using self-report data from the Conflict Tactics Scales (CTS) indicate that women perpetrate IPV as frequently as men do and are as likely to initiate violence toward intimates (Archer, 2000; Schafer, Caetano, & Clark, 1998; Straus & Gelles, 1986). Others, relying on government data collections that cover injury reports, homicide reports, and police reports, find that women, relative to men, are much less likely to be the perpetrators of partner violence. Data from the National Crime Victimization Survey (NCVS), as an illustration, show that females were 50% of spouses, but 84.3% of family violence victims (Durose et al., 2005).

Race comparisons are more challenging since the federal government data-gathering agencies have changed classifications. The White category includes both Hispanic and non-Hispanics now, thus eliminating the Hispanic category. The Black category includes both Hispanic and non-Hispanics. These categories are vague and lack comparability with previous datasets. See Tables 9.1A and 9.1B at www.sagepub.com/barnett3e for summaries of racial differences in nonlethal assaults.

*Socioeconomic diversity.* Although IPV occurs in every socioeconomic group, the National Family Violence Surveys provide self-report evidence that *partner abuse is more prevalent in blue-collar and lower-class families than in others* (O'Donnell, Smith, & Madison, 2002). NCVS data for 1993 to 1998 also demonstrated significantly higher male partner violence rates for women with annual incomes less than $7,500. These rates were 7 times higher than those for women with the highest incomes, $75,000 or more (Rennison & Welchans, 2000). This disparity continues as data indicate that lower socioeconomic status (SES) is a stronger predictor of IPV than higher SES (Stalans & Ritchie, 2008).

## DEFINITIONS OF INTIMATE PARTNER VIOLENCE AND ABUSE

Definitions of intimate partner violence are evolving as the science of family violence advances. In the past, scholars used the term *marital abuse* or *spouse abuse* in reference to verbal abuse, threats, and physical assaults ranging from minor to severe, including weapon use. *Sexual assault* (e.g., marital rape) constituted a separate dimension of abuse. In the 1990s, experts began including *stalking* as a form of intimate abuse (described in Chapter 8). Beginning in the late 1990s, the concept of *psychological abuse* expanded to encompass behaviors such as damaging property, evoking fear, exploiting finances, and partner-controlling behaviors. The latest trend in defining IPV is to reserve the term *violence* for physically violent behaviors and to use the term *aggression* to note other forms of intimate partner abuse. Also, as the focus of IPV research has developed to include both genders in various combinations, it is helpful to be gender-specific in discussions. Terms and abbreviations for adult IPV in this book use the following notations:

| IPV—Intimate partner violence: A general term—any age, gender, or gender orientation | |
|---|---|
| MFIPV—Male-to-female IPV | MMIPV—Male-to-male IPV (Gay IPV) |
| FMIPV—Female-to-male IPV | FFIPV—Female-to-female IPV (Lesbian IPV) |
| SSIPV—Same-sex IPV (Homosexual IPV) | |

## Comprehensive Government-Crafted Definitions

To assess interpersonal violence, the National Crime Victimization Survey (NCVS) has relied on a series of questions covering various forms of criminal acts, such as assaults, threats of violence, robberies, and rapes. In the NCVS, government specialists categorize the data for each respondent into the following classifications: race, sex, age, ethnicity, education, income, marital status, location, and offender-victim relationship. The NCVS has not only changed some questions (see the section on rape in Chapter 8) in recent years, but it has also increased its victim-offender relationship categories to classify intimates more precisely. Categories vary but may include spouses/ex-spouses, husband, wife, ex-husband, ex-wife, boyfriend/girlfriend, ex-boyfriend/ex-girlfriend, acquaintance, and stranger (Bachman & Saltzman, 1995). The newest definitions are beginning to incorporate the instigation of fear in the victim, and some are focusing on partner control as the pre-eminent aspect of psychological abuse.

## Defining MFIPV Through Factor Analysis

In one study, investigators searched for subcomponents of male-to-female intimate partner violence in the 64-item *Artemis Intake Questionnaire* (AIQ). Next, they recruited female *victims* to respond to the AIQ and used the data as the basis of a **factor analysis.** The factor analysis yielded seven factors (dimensions) of MFIPV and their variances as follows:

| | |
|---|---|
| Control—8.64% | Humiliation/blame—8.7% |
| Monitoring—3.46% | Physical violence and injury—5.93% |
| Pet abuse—3.94% | Severe physical violence and injury—6.37%. |
| Child abuse—3.90% | |

The first two factors, *humiliation/blame* and *control,* accounted for 17.34% of the **variance,** an amount greater than the 12.30% of the variance accounted for by the two physical violence factors. The researchers interpreted these results as demonstrating that MFIPV is far more than physical abuse alone. The results strongly indicated that *partner control* is an element of intimate partner violence. Hence, restricting assessments of IPV to physical behaviors misses the true meaning of IPV for victims (Strauchler et al., 2004). (Note: Of course, factor analyses are limited in their ability to identify factors by the constructs provided by the test instrument and by the types of analyses selected.) Findings such as these, that incorporate blame and control into the meaning of partner violence, have led Frieze (2008b) to speculate whether the term *violence* is appropriate. Perhaps *aggression* is the more apt descriptor.

## Patterns of IPV

Using anecdotal data, Lenore Walker (1979) delineated a sequence in male spouses' battering that she termed the *cycle of violence.* Her work rested on interviews with female victims. According to this theory, MFIPV not only intensifies in degree and frequency over time, but it binds the people involved into a repetitive pattern of behavior. The cycle of violence consists of three phases: (a) *Tension building:* In this phase, minor incidents of violence may occur along with a buildup of anger. This phase may include verbal put-downs, jealousy, threats, and breaking things, and can eventually escalate to Phase 2; (b) *Acute or battering:* In this phase, the major violent outburst occurs, the actual physical violence. Following this phase, the couple often enters Phase 3; (c) *Honeymoon or loving respite:* In this phase, the perpetrator is remorseful and afraid of losing his partner. He may promise her anything, beg forgiveness, buy gifts, and basically seem to be "the man she fell in love with." The words of a battered woman personalize the cycle:

> That was my life. Waiting to get hit, getting hit, recovering; forgetting, starting all over again.
> (R. Doyle, quoted in Heath, 2001, p. 376)

For quite a period of time, people working in the field accepted the cycle of violence pattern as an established fact, although no one had actually verified it. Furthermore, the pattern of escalating violence, as inevitable, seemed to hold. Indeed, some research suggested that the violence increases in severity and frequency over time until the woman is killed, injured, or escapes (e.g., Rand & Saltzman, 2003; Tjaden & Thoennes, 2000b). In one comparison of battered women, for example, 74.2% typified their abuse as escalating (M. Anderson et al., 2003). As researchers moved forward, however, quantitative research findings did *not* substantiate the cycle of violence, or an escalating pattern of abuse as the defining characteristic or only pattern of male abusive behaviors.

Escalating abuse is only one of several possible patterns of intimate partner violence, and *IPV actually ceases in some cases* (Aldarondo, 1996; Woffordt, Mihalic, & Menard, 1994; also see Cavanaugh & Gelles, 2005). One male IPV pattern uncovered by researchers was that while *one form of abuse stops, another persists.* As a case in point, one inquiry reported that although male physical aggression decreased in 54% of the couples together after two years, emotional abuse persisted. All forms of abuse ceased in 7% of the couples (Jacobsonet al., 1996; see Connelly et al., 2006 and Holtzworth-Munroe, Meehan, Stuart, Herron, & Rehman, 2003).

## ESTIMATES OF INTIMATE PARTNER VIOLENCE

Over the years, family violence researchers have attempted to estimate the prevalence and incidence of partner violence. Scholars from various disciplines, holding dissimilar ideologies and using different research methods, have produced a *multiplicity* of IPV estimates. Knowledge of how the sources of information vary is useful for anyone trying to make sense of the many disparate estimates. Information is derived from *crime reports* made to police, *injury reports* collected in emergency rooms, and from *self-report/partner-report* data. A wealth of self-report data comes from social service agencies, such as shelters, rape crisis clinics, and batterer intervention groups.

All sources of data underestimate the amount and seriousness of IPV (e.g., Archer, 1999). Although data from one study indicated that both men and women tend to *underreport* their own partner abuse (Regan, Bartholomew, Kwong, Trinke, & Henderson, 2006), other researchers found *gender disparity* in underreporting. One analysis showed that 57.1% of males arrested for MFIPV did not subsequently admit it (Babinski, Hartsough, & Lambert, 2001; Swan & Snow, 2002). Taken together, these divergent results mean that the true amount of underreporting is not known.

Researchers draw data from many different government and nongovernmental reports, as well as from academic surveys. *Sources of* data emanate from several diverse settings: criminal, medical, clinical, community, academic, and from the military (Cronin, 1995). (See Chapter 1 for a list of some of the organizations and agencies.) Reports of *nonlethal violence* arising from police reports sent to the FBI's Uniform Crime Reports (UCR) are not as comprehensive as the data available on *lethal assaults* from the FBI's Supplementary Homicide Reports (SHR). Currently, the NCVS offers some of the most extensive data on nonlethal IPV. Physical acts of partner aggression are *most often in the less severe range* (Aldarondo, 1996; Holtzworth-Munroe & Stuart, 1994; Straus, 1993). These episodes include hitting, throwing things, slapping, and pushing that result in cuts and bruises that rarely require hospitalization.

### Homicides/Suicides/Familicides

*Homicide is* the *least likely outcome* of a domestic assault (IPV), but it is the most feared and is a primary basis for formulating criminal justice policy. It also "is the most objective source of data because it does not depend on self-report" (L. Garcia, Soria, & Hurwitz, 2007, p. 370). Although U.S. government statistics concerning homicides may be the most accurate statistics collected within crime categories, they suffer from several shortcomings. Primarily, they do not capture all of the homicides or all of victim-offender relationships. In 2002, there were 9,102 spousal murders. In 58.6%, the victim/offender relationship was known. Of the known cases, women committed 19.0% of the spousal homicides, and men committed 81.0%. Spouses included current and ex-spouses and cohabitants (Durose et al., 2005).

The following statistics reflect some contemporary findings about intimate partner homicides in the United States for 2008 (U.S. Department of Justice, 2010). *Male intimates,* rather than strangers, committed the majority of known female homicides:

- The Supplementary Homicide Reports recorded 14,841 homicides for the year.
- Expanded Homicide Data revealed that there were 696 known spousal murders.
- Of the 696 spousal murders (a) wives killed 119 husbands; and (b) husbands killed 577 wives.
- Hence, 82.10% were husband-to-wife killings, and 17.10% were wife-to-husband killings.

*Suicide.* Partner-violent men evidence significantly elevated rates of suicidal behavior compared with community epidemiological survey norms (R. C. Kessler, Borges, & Walters, 1999). One comparison provided evidence that within an alcoholic sample, male perpetrators were significantly more likely to commit suicide than nonperpetrators. The suicide group was also more likely to be separated from a domestic partner at the time of suicide (Conner, Duberstein, & Conwell, 2000; see also Conner, Cerulli, & Caine, 2002).

*Homicide/suicide/familicides.* A four-state assessment of homicide-suicide events uncovered significant differences based on the victim-offender relationship. Data for 2003–2004 from the National Violent Death Reporting System (NVDRS) from 17 states disclosed the following: (a) Of 209 *homicide-suicide events,* 58% involve a current or a former intimate partner, and (b) Of *victims,* 74.6% were female and among perpetrators; 91.9% were male (Bossarte, Simon, & Barker, 2006; see also L. Banks, Crandall, Sklar, & Bauer, 2008; Barber et al., 2008; Harper & Voigt, 2007). All this evidence shows that current/former intimate partners are the most likely to be involved in a homicide-suicide event, with females the most likely victims and males the most likely offenders (see also Palermo, 2010b). (See www.sagepub.com/barnett3e for further details.)

## Sexual Assault

An article prepared by the Centers for Disease Control and Prevention (CDC; 2002) presents this broad definition of sexual assault:

> A sex act completed against a victim's will or when a victim is unable to consent due to age, illness, disability, or the influence of alcohol or other drugs. It may involve actual or threatened physical force, use of guns or other weapons, coercion, intimidation or pressure. Sexual violence also includes intentional touching of the genitals, anus, groin, or breasts against a victim's will or when a victim is unable to consent, as well as voyeurism, exposure to exhibitionism, or undesired exposure to pornography. The perpetrator of sexual violence may be a stranger, friend, family member, or intimate partner. (p. 3)

*Narrow definition.* Narrow definitions of rape lack a true correspondence with a sexual assault experience. An example of a narrow definition is to define sexual behaviors as rape only if the assault included *force.* The force inclusion means that a woman's verbal refusal *alone* is insufficient in some states to make a claim of rape. Saying "No" is not enough. Another type of narrow definition is to count only vaginal penetrations as sexual assault, not an entire spectrum of forced sexual behaviors (e.g., oral sex). Generally, there is much more information available about nonsexual assaults of intimate partners than about sexual assaults.

Survey data from community or clinical samples of women suggest that sexual assault and rape occur frequently in *violent marital relationships*. From 7.7% to 14% of ever-married/ever-cohabiting women have been raped by their partner. Intimate rape is much more common than stranger rape (Finkelhor & Yllö, 1987; D. E. H. Russell, 1990; Tjaden & Thoennes, 1998a). More contemporary research has validated the long-held suspicion that rape by an intimate partner evokes far more psychological damage than rape by nonpartners or ex-partners (Temple, Weston, Rodriguez, & Marshall, 2007). Abusive male partners may also try to interfere with birth control and/or refuse to wear condoms (Thiel de Bocanegra, Rostovtseva, Khera, & Godhwani, 2010).

*Sample estimates.* Among a sample of *battered wives,* 87.4% reported that their husbands thought it was their right to have sex with their wives even against a wife's will. These women suffered from various forms of extreme, sexually related degradation, such as having objects inserted (28.6%) and being sexually abused in front of their children (17.8%); 46% had been coerced into having sex immediately after being discharged from a hospital (often after giving birth). Forced anal intercourse (52.8%) actually occurred more frequently than vaginal rape (Campbell, 1989b; Campbell & Alford, 1989; also see Schollenberger et al., 2003).

## Psychological/Emotional Abuse of Intimate Partners

Research reveals that psychological abuse is the most common form of partner abuse. It can be extremely debilitating and have long-lasting effects, such as chronic physical illnesses. Over the last several decades, family violence experts have claimed that *psychological aggression is more damaging to victims than physical aggression.* It was not until 2009 that researchers presented experimental evidence to support this claim. Researchers showed that psychological abuse had detrimental effects on depression and anxiety levels even after controlling for the effects of physical abuse (Lawrence, Yoon, Langer, & Ro, 2009). Some of the earliest operational definitions of emotional abuse appeared in the work of Richard Tolman (1989). Tolman crafted the *Psychological Maltreatment of Women Inventory* (PMWI), which assesses two dimensions: *dominance-isolation* and *emotional-verbal*. It has been possible to discriminate seven major types of psychological abuse based on the PMWI:

- Isolation
- Economic abuse
- Degradation
- Rigid sex-role expectations
- Withholds emotional responsivity

- Monopolization (abuser must be center of woman's life)
- Psychological destabilization (makes woman feel crazy)

Many male partner abuse survivors across studies have asserted that emotional abuse is worse than physical abuse (see Currie, 1998; Lynch & Graham-Bermann, 2000). Emotional abuse is a significant predictor of *posttraumatic stress disorder* (PTSD) and, combined with *partner control,* is a significant predictor of *negative mood and psychosomatic complaints* (see Arias & Pape, 1999; Pitzner & Drummond, 1997; Street, 1998; Tang, 1997).

*Controlling behaviors.* Almost without exception, experts in family violence have asserted that controlling behavior is especially typical of *male batterers.* Controlling behavior seems to be similar or equivalent to behaviors usually classified as physical or psychological abuse (Stark, 2007). Some specialists list controlling behaviors as a *subtype of psychological abuse* (M. A. Dutton & Goodman, 2005; Frieze & McHugh, 1992; Lewis, Griffing et al., 2006; Swan & Snow, 2002). According to one scholar, *coercive control* is so *archetypical* among batterers that it should be the *central feature of any definition* of male-partner IPV (Stark, 2007). One definition states that battering is "a process whereby one member of an intimate relationship experiences vulnerability, loss of power and control, and entrapment as a consequence of the other member's exercise of power through the patterned use of physical, sexual, psychological, and/or moral force" (as quoted in P. H. Smith, Thornton, DeVellis, Earp, & Coker, 2002, p. 1210). Last, men's coercive control of women can be viewed as a *human rights violation* because by entrapping women through intimidation, isolation, and control, men rob them from developing their personhood (Stark, 2007).

Because the construct of control is manifold, its *multiple meanings* have added to the complexity of investigating its role in male aggressive behaviors. There are at least three different ways of conceptualizing control: (a) *coercive control,* (b) *feeling powerless,* and (c) a *personal need for control.* Current research has not clearly illuminated which connotation of control is the most relevant to intimate partner violence.

For some academicians, *coercive control* encompasses *instrumental control*—a method for getting one's own way. An abusive partner, for example, might threaten to leave and go to a bar and pick up another woman to get his way about the couple's sexual activities (see Barnett, Lee, & Thelen, 1997; K. E. Davis, Ace, & Anda, 2000). Most female victims report being controlled by their male partners in this way. In one study, 78.4% of MFIPV victims said they also reported feeling controlled in this way (M. A. Anderson et al., 2003). Some of the male-to-female controlling behaviors noted in this study are as follows:

| | |
|---|---|
| Controlling her reading choices | Not letting her use the phone or go to school |
| Preventing her from getting a job | Controlling the household money |
| Calling/coming home to check up on her | |

*Making decisions* for oneself and one's partner can be viewed as a form of controlling behavior. An analysis of *power strategies* used by husbands and wives (as reported by wives) indicated several significant differences. First, violent husbands and wives with violent husbands used a larger number of influence strategies and used them more frequently than did their counterparts. Second, decision-making power in nonviolent marriages was more equally shared than in violent marriages. Third, the level of male aggression was highly associated with wives' making fewer decisions. This association suggests that male abuse is instrumental in reducing wives' decision-making power (Frieze & McHugh, 1992; see also Hamberger, 2005).

*Powerlessness.* A second area of research deals with the question of MFIPV perpetrators' avoidance of *feeling powerless.* Feeling powerless, rather than seeking partner control, may be the more salient aspect of control behavior among some male perpetrators (Kimmel, 2002). A number of events, such as unemployment, could easily engender feelings of powerlessness (Tollefson, 2002). Nonetheless, an early investigation of powerlessness found that batterers' use of control did *not* enhance their sense of control (Umberson, Anderson, Glick, & Shapiro, 1998). Furthermore, perpetrators did *not* experience greater feelings of being in control than did nonperpetrators. These findings weigh against the idea that intimate partner violence is motivated by powerlessness.

A different evaluation, however, did find results congruent with the powerlessness concept. These investigators used data from a large sample (*N* = 1,392) of ethnically diverse cohabiting and married couples (Caetano, Vaeth, & Ramisetty-Mikler, 2008). Using 11 CTS measures, investigators identified 87% of the sample as uninvolved in intimate partner violence (Straus, 1990). They classified the remaining participants into three groups: (a) *mutually violent—8%,* (b) *male perpetrator only—4%,* and (c) *female perpetrator only—2%.* As a measure of powerlessness, they used three modified questions from *Antonovsky's Sense of Coherence scale* (1993) starting with "How often have you …" as follows: (a) felt that you were treated unfairly?, (b) been in situations where you didn't know what to do?, and (c) felt that "bad things always happen to me?" Analyses revealed that men in the *male perpetrator-only group* reported higher levels of *powerlessness* than either the mutually violent or partner-nonviolent control men (Caetano et al., 2008).

*Need for power/control/dominance.* Several personality theorists note that some individuals, not just males, have a greater *need for power* than others (Mauricio & Gormley, 2001). As other researchers say, "The cause [of MFIPV] is presumed to be a need to be dominant and to exercise power over another, fueled by a strong sense of patriarchal rights" (Arriaga & Capezza, 2005, p. 91). From this view, male perpetrators typically perceive female partners who do not follow their commands to perform certain chores (e.g., cook dinner on time, iron their shirts expertly) as "not obeying their rules." Consequently, wives who fail to follow orders deserve abuse for challenging their male partner's authority as head of the household (Kernsmith, 2005a). (See www.sagepub.com/barnett3e for other control studies.)

*Economic exploitation.* One definition of economic abuse is abuse that "involves restricting access to resources, such as bank accounts, spending money, funds for household expenses, telephone communication, transportation, or medical care" (Harway et al., 2002, p. 10). Without funds, battered victims and their children usually cannot leave their abusers. Even women receiving welfare benefits find it difficult to leave. Also, the snail's pace with which bureaucratic entities move may cause such a long delay in funding that women cannot leave (Moe, 2007).

## Nonlethal Assault Estimates

- *Department of Justice.* Of all crimes (e.g., assaults, rapes, and robberies) committed against intimates in 1998, females experienced 5 times as many incidents of *nonfatal violence* as did males (Rennison & Welchans, 2000).
- *The National Crime Victimization Survey* (*NCVS; U.S. Bureau of the Census*) (**Bachman & Saltzman, 1995; Greenfeld et al., 1998; also see Rand, 2009**):
  - ○ Women were the victims in about 85% of the cases.
  - ○ Separated women tend to be victimized at a rate 3 times higher than the rate for divorced women and 25 times higher than the rate for married women.
- *National Violence Against Women* (NVAW; *Center for Policy Research,* Tjaden & Thoenness, **1998a, 1998b, 2000b**). Modified CTS1 survey of 8,000 men and 8,000 women. Of women, 22.1% experienced abuse by an intimate as did 7.4% of men.
- *National Incident-Based Reporting System* (NIBRS) reported in 2005 on the pattern of IPV incidents for 7 years in Idaho:
  - ○ Number of victims: 36,693
  - ○ Female victims: 79.5%
  - ○ Male victims: 20.5%
  - ○ Number of offenses: 40,977
  - ○ Number of arrests: 29, 882
  - ○ Number of offenders: 47,498
  - ○ Patterns: Mainly in the evening and mainly on the weekends
  - ○ Largest number: New Year's Eve, 4th of July, and Super Bowl Sunday

(See www.sagepub.com/barnett3e for more estimates of IPV.)

## Male-to-Female Intimate Partner Violence

Although there has been a massive influx of new research on IPV, the findings have not essentially changed earlier information about age and gender. Several more databases have come online, and each one describes different data sources, such as police reports or self-report telephone survey information. It is still true that adults (aged 18–54) perpetrate the most frequent violence against intimate partners. The data on gender differences in IPV remain somewhat controversial because of differences in measurement scales. Data from the NCVS, as an illustration, show that females were 50% of spouses, but 84.3% of violence victims. Also, government organizations have changed their methodology for defining race categories, thus making racial comparisons more challenging. It remains true that significantly more abusive behavior occurs among lower-income individuals.

*Defining* intimate partner violence remains unresolved. A factor analysis provided one empirical definition of IPV that includes seven types of abuse: humiliation/blame, control, severe physical violence and injury, child abuse, monitoring, and pet abuse. There also is a movement underfoot to change the terminology from violence to aggression for nonphysical kinds of abuse.

There are numerous ways to *emotionally abuse* an intimate partner. Psychological abuse is the most common form of partner aggression. A large proportion of psychological abuse victims rate it as worse than physical abuse. Psychological abuse is linked with depression, anxiety, and PTSD. There are several types of *economic exploitation,* such as restricting access to bank accounts. Women and their children often cannot leave if economic abuse is occurring. One still unanswered question concerns *patterning* (e.g., escalation) of MFIPV.

Research on *control tactics* has received a very large amount of research attention. A number of female victims, advocates, and academically trained practitioners have conceptualized *control tactics* as central to battering. A handicap in researching the topic of control is the *lack of adequate measurement* of the concept. There are several subtypes of partner control. *Coercive control* refers to the use of power to force one partner to comply with the demands of the other partner, and it may be instrumental. Another connotation envisages control as a *need-for-power trait.* Some individuals use power to negate unwanted feelings of *powerlessness.* Research findings do suggest that batterers use violence to *control victims* and to get their own way.

Although early theorizing suggested a cycle of violence with three phases, later evidence discovered several *patterns of violence.* Newer evidence also indicates that MFIPV does not uniformly escalate over time. *Sexual assaults* are less common than IPV, but a larger percentage of ever-married/ever-cohabiting women have been raped than their counterparts. Even though the victim/offender relationship in *homicides* is not always known, males kill significantly more spouses than females (81% and 19%, respectively). Current/former intimate partners are the most likely to be involved in a *homicide-suicide* event, with females the most likely victims and males the most likely offenders.

# ATTITUDES AND CLASSIFICATIONS OF BATTERERS

This section addresses attitudes toward batterers and batterers' attributions for male partner violence. At the same time that the social problem of IPV has been provoking more and more public outrage among Americans, on a personal level its acceptance remains at surprisingly high levels. In addition, there are gender differences in men's and women's perception and evaluation of IPV (Sorenson & Taylor, 2005). Another part of this section begins a discussion on classifying couples' different types of partner violence into categories. Most of the section describes individual differences (traits) that may distinguish batterers from other men (or women). Some of these traits include denial and minimization, anger and hostility, depression, lack of awareness, attachment difficulties, jealousy, and marital dissatisfaction.

## Society's Attitudes Toward Batterers

When pictures of battered women appear in the media, one would expect members of society to be outraged, but, surprisingly, there is a lot of approval of male-to-female violence.

---

**CASE HISTORY**   Kree Kirkman—Getting Even With the Woman You No Longer Love

Upon learning that his wife had begun divorce proceedings, Kree Kirkman of Enumclaw, Washington, got a demolition permit and bulldozed his wife's home into shambles. The city's police dispatcher reported getting calls from men across the nation offering to set up a defense fund for Kirkman.

"He's got a real cheering section out there," the dispatcher noted (quoted in Brower & Sackett, 1985, p. 108). An informal tally of opinions offered by men frequenting a bar in a nearby working-class neighborhood showed that the men thought it was "just wonderful; he really got even with her!"

They seemed to ignore the information that Kirkman had told his wife that he no longer loved her and that the couple had agreed jointly to a separation. The predominant feeling seemed to be that this type of violence is not only permissible, but also "macho" and praiseworthy.[1]

NOTE: 1. Kree Kirkman is the real name of the man in this case history.

---

## Batterers' Attributions for Male-to-Female Intimate Partner Violence

One hallmark of batterers is their tendency to *blame* their own aggression on nearly *anyone or anything* but themselves. Illustrative of this proclivity, abusers in one survey blamed their MFIPV on external stressors or temporary states, such as substance abuse or jealousy (Cantos, Neidig, & O'Leary, 1994). Male offenders entering group counseling habitually offer explanations for their violence that go something like this: "I told her not to do it (e.g., stay late after work). She knew what would happen if she did, but she did it anyway. She got what she asked for; she brought it on herself" (see Barrera, Palmer, Brown, & Kalaher, 1994). In addition to exemplifying batterers' habit of externalizing blame, this scenario epitomizes male perpetrators' propensity to formulate *household rules* that their female partner must obey. In contrast, a small study of male and female *abusers' attitudes* discerned that even some of the abusers rejected IPV as unacceptable and that the opinions of others about partner abuses are important to them. Women in the study stated that others are less accepting of FMIPV than MFIPV (Kernsmith, 2005a).

In an effort to provide more empirical data on perpetrators' attributions (i.e., ascriptions—who is to blame) for their IPV, researchers conducted a comparison of three groups of men classified by two variables: (a) marital violence and (b) marital satisfaction level. The three groups were (a) *maritally violent, maritally dissatisfied;* (b) maritally *nonviolent, maritally dissatisfied;* and (c) *maritally nonviolent, maritally satisfied.* Participants judged women's behavior in vignettes depicting problematic marital conditions. Maritally violent, unhappily married men attributed more responsibility for negative behaviors to wives in the vignettes than did non maritally violent, satisfactorily married men. Maritally violent, unhappily married men also attributed more negative intentions, selfish motivation, and blame for behaviors to wives than did maritally nonviolent, satisfactorily married men. Vignettes depicting jealousy and wife's rejection elicited particularly negative attributions by the two unhappily married groups of men (Holtzworth-Munroe & Hutchinson,1993; see also Tonizzo, Howells, Day, Reidpath, & Froyland, 2000).

## Johnson's Violent Couple Categories

A number of social scientists in the field of family violence have concluded that battering is not unidimensional or totally male-to-female. One increasingly popular description of intimate partner abuse classifies partner abuse along a *severity dimension* and a *control dimension* while taking into account whether the abuse is *unidirectional* or *bidirectional* (reciprocal, mutual, bilateral, symmetrical). After developing several models of partner violence, Johnson and his collaborators more strongly emphasized partner control (M. P. Johnson, 1995, 2006; M. P. Johnson & Ferraro, 2000; J. B. Kelly & Johnson, 2008):

---

*Situational Couple Violence* (SCV). SCV is the most frequently occurring type of IPV. It is low-level (not severe) and is perpetrated by both members of a couple. One individual is violent, but neither the individual nor the partner is both violent and controlling. This type of IPV is gender symmetric and occurs most often in general populations. (SCV was formerly called Common Couple Violence—CCV.)

*Mutual Violent Control* (MVC). Both the individual and the partner are violent and controlling. This type of IPV is gender symmetric.

*Violent Resistance* (VR). This type of IPV is actually a self-defensive form of IPV. The person is violent but not controlling. This type of IPV is most common in agency samples (e.g., shelter agency) and is perpetrated almost exclusively by women.

*Intimate Terrorism* (IT). Only one partner is violent and controlling, and IT is most common in shelters, other agencies, and forensic samples. This type of IPV is perpetrated almost exclusively by men. It is frequent and often injurious. (IT was formerly called patriarchal terrorism.)

---

To test these theoretical categories, researchers used a **discriminate functions analysis** on data collected from students, sheltered women, and prisoners. The analyses substantiated the basic dichotomy by identifying the anchor points (SCV and IT) as two significant functions and by classifying 75% of the cases correctly (Graham-Kevan & Archer, 2003). (Recall that the inference that IPV is bidirectional is part of the contentious debate about measurement; see Chapter 2.) (See www.sagepub.com/barnett3e for Whitaker, Haileyesus, Swahn, & Saltzman's [2007] account of mutual IPV.)

*Gender dissimilarities.* A team of investigators conducted a rigorous examination of gender dissimilarities within a subgroup of couples who were nominally *mutually violent* (Weston, Temple, & Marshall, 2005). This comparison of 445 racially and ethnically diverse poor women employed L. L. Marshall's inventories: *The Severity of Violence Against Women Scale* (SVAWS; 1992a) and *The Severity of Violence Against Men Scale* (SVAMS; 1992b) as tests of intimate partner violence. Through a series of test phases, she developed several subscales applicable to either female-to-male or male-to-female partner violence. She cleverly constructed both *behavioral gender similarity* scales and *behavioral sameness* (topographic sameness) scales. She also integrated both *sexual aggression* and *injury aftereffects* items into the scales. The respondents completed two versions of the scales, one version about their own female aggression and a second about their partner's battering behavior.

Through advanced statistical techniques, the researchers crafted a *gender-weighted scale, weighted frequency scores* (of abusive actions), *gender-based difference scores* for each scale item, and total scores for each gender. Last, they used these scores as the basis for classifying the women into three subcategories within the presumed single violent group designated as mutually violent (Weston et al., 2005). Table 9.1 shows the gender differences within the mutually violent group.

**TABLE 9.1**  Gender Disparity in IPV Within a Bidirectional (Mutual IPV) Group

| Type of Perpetration Group | Percentage of Group | Results of Analyses of IPV Within the Bidirectional (Mutual) Group |
|---|---|---|
| Gender symmetrically violent | 35% | Low frequency of IPV by both genders |
| Males are the primary perpetrators | 54% | Females suffered significantly more MFIPV than males suffered FMIPV |
| Females are the primary perpetrators | 11% | Males suffered significantly more FMIPV than females suffered MFIPV |

These critical findings make it clear that IPV is *not gender symmetrical* even within a subgroup of so-called mutually violent couples. Women's FMIPV is not equal to men's MFIPV (Weston et al., 2005). See Próspero, 2008, for a topical study of coercion among college students based on J. B. Kelly and Johnson's (2008) model of couple violence; see Langhinrichsen-Rohling, 2010, for a comprehensive discussion of the gender debate.

## INDIVIDUAL DIFFERENCES (TRAITS)
## BETWEEN BATTERERS AND OTHERS

The earliest attempts to examine male intimate partner violence perpetrators generally consisted of anecdotal descriptions provided by IPV victims in counseling (Elbow, 1977). Slowly, researchers began to use psychological tests to assess batterers empirically. Given that patriarchal explanations for male IPV are incomplete, it is essential that researchers look for *individual differences* in personality traits, disorders, or other variables that can account for male aggressive behaviors (O'Leary, 1993).

The concept of a **trait** implies that a strong impetus for behavior *lies within an individual*. Statements such as, "He is always angry, no matter what," or "He is the most jealous person I know" exemplify the trait approach.

A second premise for explaining behavior lies within a *situation*—it is the situation that controls behavior. Statements such as, "She was happy until the bank would not cash her check," or "She did not want to hurt his feelings, but he insulted her first," indicate that the situation has a strong effect on her behavior.

A third view combines trait and situation concepts into an *interactional* approach. "She always tended to be depressed, but when her pet died she just fell apart and had to take anti-depressants," illustrates an interaction.

There is research evidence supporting each of these paradigms. Personality traits are among the most compelling *risk factors* for IPV and *violence severity* (Ehrensaft, Cohen, & Johnson, 2006). Currently, researchers tend to use general personality inventories to assess a broad range of both normal and abnormal traits.

A fresh analysis has yielded a fascinating new *interactionist* position designated the Traits as Situational Sensitivities (TASS). This model adopts the viewpoint that there is an *inseparable interdependence between traits and situations*. Part of the rationale for developing this model is research showing that the idea of a *trait as stable* across diverse situations does not fit the facts. An individual's predisposition (trait level) to respond in a certain manner actually represents a level of *sensitivity to provocation* inherent in various situations. As an illustration, a person measuring high in trait hostility is more likely than a person low in trait hostility to display hostility in certain situations, but not others. Hence, the provocation level of the situation interacts with an individual's sensitivity to provocation level to produce behavior. Research affirming the TASS model has emerged (M. A. Marshall & Brown, 2006).

Some kinds of personality tests try to identify characteristics that differentiate individuals within *normal* populations. These investigators have looked for *individual differences* between partner-violent and nonpartner-violent men on various personality tests. A duo of researchers analyzed responses provided by three groups of men: (a) partner-violent men, (b) nonpartner-violent, unhappily married men, and (c) nonpartner-violent, happily married men on the *California Psychological Inventory* (Gough, 1975). In this survey, partner-violent men clearly displayed different personality traits than nonviolent men in three general areas: *intimacy, impulsivity,* and *problem-solving skills.* Overall, the MFIPV perpetrators were less well adjusted than nonviolent men (Barnett & Hamberger, 1992). To understand batterers more clearly, numerous investigators have examined which traits might be applicable to partner violence. Below are some of the traits commonly identified in the literature. See Table 9.2 for a preview of these descriptors.

**TABLE 9.2**  Commonly Identified Characteristic of Male Batterers

| Abusive | Patriarchal | Lacking awareness |
|---------|-------------|-------------------|
| Rigid | Controlling | Fearful but aggressive |
| Aloof | Ashamed | Emotionally dependent |
| Anxious | Impulsive | Stereotypically masculine |
| Angry | Un-empathic | Poor problem solvers |
| Jealous | Self-centered | Nonmutual intimate relationships |
| Moody | Poor self-image | |
| Depressed | Inhibited emotions | |

## Denial and Minimization

Abusers tend to downplay or minimize the significance and seriousness of their violence, claiming they did not really hurt their female partner. They often totally *deny* having hurt their partner in any way whatsoever (e.g., Hamberger, 1997). In a different study of 2,824 men convicted of MFIPV, investigators found very convincing evidence of denial and minimization as follows (Henning & Holdford, 2006):

- 50% claimed self-defense.
- 72% denied MFIPV harmed victim/children.
- 38% to 53% faked answers to look good.
- 63% denied accuracy of current police report.
- 66% blamed partner more than themselves.
- 54% to 59% denied aspects of current offense.

*Correlations* revealed that an overall *minimization* score and a *denial that male aggression* was harmful to the victim/children score were significantly associated with new police reports (28% recidivated during follow-up). *Sociodemographic variables* (e.g., age, education, and employment status), however, were *better predictors* of *new recidivism* than the denial/minimization variables. Nonetheless, information about the denial/minimization variables is needed to inform clinicians and criminal justice system personnel who might otherwise be deceived by MFIPV perpetrators' erroneous reports (Henning & Holdford, 2006).

## Anger, Hostility, and Intermittent Explosive Disorder (IED)

Because specialists in wide-ranging disciplines have implicated *anger* as a precursor to violence, anger has become one of the most frequently studied traits in personality psychology.

Anecdotal observations about the extreme anger in maritally violent men prompted incorporation of anger research into the field of family violence. One challenge researchers face is that anger can be a trait, a situation, or an interaction. The construct lacks a uniform meaning. One line of research views anger as (a) a *trait* (i.e., a relatively stable characteristic), (b) a *state* (i.e., temporary feelings elicited by a specific situation), or (c) *both*. (See www.sagepub.com/barnett3e for more information on anger and hostility concepts.)

*Multidimensional concept* DSM-IV-TR (Diagnostic and Statistical Manual, Fourth Edition, Text Revision) *(American Psychiatric Association, 2000)*. Many theorists conceptualize anger as an *emotion* that involves a physiological response. Others consider *anger* to be a multidimensional construct that includes *cognitive* and *behavioral components,* as well as *physiological aspects.* Anger may extend from feeling mildly annoyed to feeling enraged. Anger may even be pathological in some cases, even though the DSM-IV-TR (2000) does not currently recognize a spectrum of anger-disordered behaviors. Some logicians distinguish between *trait anger* and *hostile cognitions,* and others use anger and hostility interchangeably. Still others differentiate subtypes of *hostility,* such as *irritability and resentment.* Given the diversity of meanings, researchers **operationalize** the constructs of anger and hostility they think pivotal to their research (see Norlander & Eckhardt, 2005, for a review).

*Anger as a motive for IPV.* Anger seems to be more than just a feeling or a type of situation. It may function as a motive for male assaults. Within the field of IPV, anger research has primarily centered upon trait anger among male offenders and responsive anger among victims. Available studies have found that high levels of *trait anger* are characteristic of *both MFIPV and FMIPV* perpetrators as well as MFIPV victims (see Norlander & Eckhardt, 2005, for a review). The discovery that violent partner abusers experience more trait anger than nonviolent partner abusers is important because of the interpretations flowing from the results. Although the data are correlational in nature, commentators have almost uniformly reached two conclusions on the basis of trait studies. First, men's anger (or hostility) motivates them to perpetrate male-partner IPV. Over the decades, specialists in wide-ranging disciplines have implicated anger as a precursor to violence. Researchers using dyadic interaction methods have begun to show the causal role of anger in mutual IPV, although they cannot specify whether IPV perpetrators are *experiencing* anger during their actual assaults (Norlander & Eckhardt, 2005; see also Jacobson et al., 1994). It is essential, however, to keep in mind that anger does not inevitably lead to aggression.

A *meta-analytic review* provided fresh insights about *anger* among male-to-female intimate partner violence offenders. A summary of 28 independent samples indicated that while the majority of perpetrators do not have anger disturbance, perpetrators had moderately higher levels of anger and hostility than nonperpetrators. Additional analyses showed that these group differences held up across self-report, observational, and spouse-specific data. Last, offenders classified as moderate to high in partner violence severity had significantly higher anger and hostility scores than offenders classified as low to moderate in partner abuse severity. These results imply that *MFIPV perpetrators are angrier* and more hostile *than non-MFIPV* perpetrators. The correlational nature of the results, nonetheless, do not permit assumptions that anger and/or hostility cause intimate partner violence (Norlander & Eckhardt, 2005; see also

Schumacher, Feldbau-Kohn, Slep, & Heyman, 2001). Nonetheless, situations vary in their provocation levels. (See the website case history of an angry husband.)

*Classifying angry MFIPV men.* One of the most recent inquiries examined anger disturbances among male offenders and their relationship to abusive behaviors. First, the researchers administered several tests to the research participants enrolled in a batterer intervention program to assess their anger: (a) *anger factors*, (b) *partner aggression*, (c) *childhood abuse*, (d) **psychopathology**, (e) *alcohol/drug use*, and (f) *criminal justice variables*. Second, a *cluster analysis* of the data produced three clusters of men: (a) *low anger (LA)*, (b) *moderate anger—inexpressive (MA-I)*, and (c) *high anger—expressive* (HA-E). See Table 9.3 for a summary of group differences.

**TABLE 9.3** Some *Significant* Differences Between Three Groups of Men in Treatment for MFIPV

| Variable | Low Anger (LA) n = 118; 63.1% | Moderate Anger—Inexpressive (MA-I) n = 13; 7.0% | High Anger—Expressive (HA-E) n = 56; 29.9% |
|---|---|---|---|
| Batterer intervention program completion | Most likely to complete | | |
| Anger | Lowest anger expression | Highest anger–in(ward) | Highest trait anger |
| | | | Highest anger-out |
| | | | Lowest anger control |
| IPV | | | Highest amount MFIPV |
| Childhood abuse | | | Highest childhood abuse |
| Psychopathology | | | Higher than LA/MA-I |
| Alcohol | | | Higher than LA (only) |
| Drug use | | | Highest drug use |
| CJS data | Least likely re-arrested | | |

SOURCE: Eckhardt, Samper, & Murphy, 2008.

Although the researchers do not advise that clinicians use an anger typology to separate MFIPV offenders, they do advise that clinicians be aware that about one-third of the men suffer dysfunctional levels of anger and lack effective strategies for dealing with it.

*Hostility and partner violence.* Even though hostility and anger appear to be similar constructs, academicians generally define *hostility* as an *attitude* reflecting one's dislike and negative evaluation of others. In contrast, anger has more than one connotation and is more of an emotion than an attitude. Despite some generalities, there is no overwhelming agreement concerning the true meaning of hostility or how anger and hostility may differ. Consequently, there are numerous assessment instruments (see Eckhardt, Norlander, & Deffenbacher, 2004, for a review).

In a highly controlled study, researchers investigated differences on the *Buss-Durkee Hostility Inventory* (Buss & Durkee, 1957) among men screened for battering behaviors, marital satisfaction level, and counseling status. They then divided the 227 men into five groups: (a) partner-violent men in counseling; (b) partner-violent men not in counseling; (c) nonpartner-violent, maritally distressed men; (d) nonpartner-violent satisfactorily married men; and (e) generally violent men. Partner-violent men were more hostile overall than men in any of the other groups, and nonpartner-violent men had lower mean scores on every subscale. Partner-violent men differed from at least one of the nonpartner-violent groups on five of eight dimensions: *assault, indirect hostility, irritability, resentment,* and *verbal hostility* (Barnett, Fagan, & Booker, 1991).

In a complex multimethod, comparison of five groups of men screened for partner abusive behaviors and marital satisfaction level, Holtzworth-Munroe, Rehman, and Herron (2000) administered anger and hostility questionnaires. They also obtained observational measures of couples' discussions and coded participants' responses to hypothetical marital/nonmarital conflict situations. Their results yielded several significant differences. First, measures of anger and hostility tended to be correlated. Second, anger and hostility were related to levels of MFIPV across groups. Third, men reported more general anger than spouse-specific anger (anger toward wife) except on one inventory. Fourth, the angriest, most hostile men were those in two groups: *the borderline/dysphoric* group and the *generally violent group,* and these two groups were not significantly different from each other. (For reviews of anger/hostility studies with MFIPV offenders see Eckhardt, Barbour, & Stuart, 1997; Holtzworth-Munroe, Bates, Smutzler, & Sandin, 1997.)

*Intermittent explosive disorder.* A newer construct that seems somewhat analogous to anger is the little-recognized *psychiatric condition* referred to as **intermittent explosive disorder** (IED) in DSM-IV. The characteristic behaviors of individuals afflicted with IED are periodic, dangerous assaultive actions that represent extreme responses to stressors and are not attributable to other mental disorders or the effects of psychotropic drugs. Because impulsive violence can be an important aspect of mental disorders, researchers undertook an analysis of data gleaned from the National Comorbidity Survey Replication (NCS-R) carried out between 2001 and 2003 (Kessler et al, 2006). These researchers analyzed data from a subset of NCS-R data from 5,692 persons, which excluded any individuals whose anger attacks were associated with physiological impairments such as epilepsy. One survey found that over *two-thirds of individuals with a history of partner violence suffered an IED episode during an* anger *attack.* It seems reasonable to assume that some partner violence involving rage reactions may be attributable to IED. (See www.sagepub.com/barnett3e for more details on this study.)

## Depression, Self-Esteem, Shame, Guilt, and Humiliation

Several personality traits may be related to depression, including low self-esteem, shame, guilt, and humiliation. It is probable that these traits arose during childhood as an outgrowth of parental psychologically abusive behavior.

*Depression.* Just as battered women suffer from depression, sometimes at a clinical level, so do the men who perpetrate the assaults. Most of the research conducted to date on the relationship between depression and IPV has relied on the *Beck Depression Inventory* (Beck, 1978). Several investigations that enlisted comparison groups to assess moods have demonstrated that male perpetrators are substantially more depressed than nonperpetrators (Hamberger & Hastings, 1991; Julian & McKenry, 1993; C. M. Murphy, Meyer, & O'Leary, 1993). Using the *DSM-III-R* with a probability subsample of 1,738 men and 1,799 women, researchers showed that partner-violent men perpetrating minor violence registered significantly higher levels of major depression than did their female counterparts (Kessler, Molnar, Feurer, & Appelbaum, 2001).

*Self-esteem.* Low self-esteem appears to be a key symptom in depression in naturalistic studies (see Bothwell & Scott, 1997). Some scholars have suggested that male IPV perpetrators engage in intimate partner aggression because they suffer from low self-esteem. Indeed, several comparisons found significantly lower self-esteem scores in partner-violent men compared with nonpartner-violent men (Boney-McCoy & Sugarman, 1999; D. Goldstein & Rosenbaum, 1985; Neidig, Friedman, & Collins, 1986). (For studies about self-esteem in relationships, see S. L. Murray, Bellavia, Rose, & Griffin, 2003; Murray, Rose, Bellavia, Holmes, & Kusche, 2002.) (See www.sagepub.com/barnett3e for a controversy about self-esteem.) (See Baumeister, Dale, & Sommer, 1996, for an opposing viewpoint.)

*Shame, guilt, and humiliation.* A set of childhood feelings, shame, humiliation, and guilt, may play a role in MFIPV. One inquiry correlated parent-to-child shaming and guilt inducement with chronic adult anger, trauma symptoms, IPV, and borderline personality organization (BPO) (Dutton, van Ginkel, & Landolt, 1995). On the basis of additional analyses, Dutton and his colleagues determined that shame developed through *parental punishments* and that childhood *abuse* was the *central precursor to men's adult abusiveness.* Other appraisals revealed that men's recollections of being shamed by parents were linked with adult anger, abusiveness, trauma symptoms, and borderline personality organization. Some have suggested that shame in adult batterers is linked with *anxious attachment* during childhood (Wallace & Nosko, 1993). (See www.sagepub .com/barnett3e for additional details of the Dutton et al., 1995, research methodology and a theoretical paper by Jennings and Murphy, 2000).

## Lack of Awareness/Automaticity

One rarely explored behavioral pattern is automaticity, a concept that is akin to *habit.* It is probable that some batterers have stopped thinking about their battering in such terms as "how hard to hit this time," and simply strike out automatically with or without any provocation by the victim. Some violent men are *unaware of the feelings* underlying their behaviors, such as feelings of anger, worthlessness, depression, and fear (e.g., Barnett et al., 1997; Chamberland, Fortin, Turgeon, & Laporte, 2007; Yelsma, 1996). They may also have automatic cognitive biases that lead them to misinterpret events. What is more, there might be certain cues (similar to fear cues) that set off anger automatically (Norlander & Eckhardt, 2005), and they may have repressed many painful childhood memories that become apparent in the form of *dissociative coping styles.* A dissociative coping style allows perpetrators to carry out extremely violent assaults (Stosny, 1995). **Dissociation** is an extreme experience falling at the high end of a continuum of nonawareness (Braun, 1988). This continuum runs from suppressed awareness to denial, to repression, and finally to dissociation.

## Empathy

Another line of reasoning postulates that empathic responses might inhibit aggression. Given that partner-violent men are aggressive, perhaps they lack empathy. Very little information, however, is known about empathy and how it might relate to MFIPV. Future research holds the promise of integrating newer knowledge of hypothesized *mirror cell phenomena* with the empathy literature to expand understanding of the association between empathy and aggression. Briefly, mirror cells within a monkey's brain fire when he *executes* some specific action and also when he *observes* another monkey executing the same specific action (see E. Jaffe, 2007; Saey, 2009).

## Attachment Difficulties and Emotional Dependence

Research on attachment and emotional dependency has been particularly worthwhile for understanding the dynamics in violent relationships. Research has increasingly implicated attachment difficulties as a precursor to partner violence among both men and women. Attachment is involved in several relevant reactions. IPV-involved males and females exhibit attachment difficulties by emotional dependency, childhood attachment insecurity, and adult attachment difficulties. Attachment is further involved in conflicted proximity and distancing strategies, jealousy, and marital satisfaction and as a predictor of IPV.

*Emotional dependency.* Findings across studies have consistently shown that partner-violent men are *more emotionally dependent* than other men. Male IPV perpetrators have profound dependency needs and are very sensitive to themes of abandonment (D. G. Dutton & Painter, 1993a; Holtzworth-Munroe & Hutchinson, 1993). Researchers testing the dependency needs in three groups of men found significant differences between groups. Aggressive males had significantly higher dependency needs than two other partner-nonviolent groups, (a) unhappily married men and (b) happily married men (Murphy, Meyer, & O'Leary, 1994; see also Holtzworth-Munroe, Stuart, & Hutchinson, 1997). Finally, other investigators found corroborative results using different nonclinical samples of research participants. Abusive males were significantly more emotionally dependent than a group of football players and community service volunteers (Kane, Staiger, & Ricciardelli, 2000).

*Attachment and IPV.* Adults who felt safe and secure with their caretaker during infancy are likely to feel secure in their adult partner's presence and enjoy being close to him or her (e.g., Feeney & Noller, 1996; Morton & Browne, 1998). On the other hand, insecure attachment in childhood may lead to feelings in adulthood of anxiety, anger, and fear of abandonment. Such intense feelings may fuel an assault against an adult intimate partner (Bookwala, 2002; McCarthy & Taylor, 1999). Although evidence of the *importance of adult attachment* as a factor in MFIPV has been mounting steadily, not all the findings coincide (e.g., Babcock, Jacobson, Gottman, & Yerington, 2000; Henderson, Bartholomew, Trinke, & Kwong, 2005; Kesner & McKenry, 1998).

*Regulating closeness.* As outlined in the previous chapter, one's type of attachment pattern is closely associated with one's *proximity/distance regulating strategies.* When one member of a couple desires more intimacy and the other member does not, a *frustration response* may escalate into intimate partner violence. In a focal inquiry, investigators recruited couples selected on the basis of the male member's violence level. All of the males were participating in a batterers' counseling program, and nearly all of the females had engaged in some female-to-male intimate partner violence judged not to be self-defensive. Qualitative analyses suggested that the attachment patterns of secure, preoccupied, dismissing, and fearful were *not consistently unitary.* Rather, participants often manifested both a *primary and secondary pattern of attachment (e.g., primarily dismissing; secondarily preoccupied).* Although preoccupied attachment patterns were the most common for men, within the couples there was a surprising variability of attachment patterns.

The most intriguing findings emerged from an examination of themes revealed in the interviews: All the couples commonly used both emotional and physical *strategies for regulating levels of proximity.* The investigators termed these strategies *pursuit and distancing.* Individuals whose attachment patterns are *primarily preoccupied* usually sought high levels of *dyadic closeness* and used pursuit strategies to achieve greater proximity. Individuals whose attachment patterns are primarily *dismissing or fearful* typically wanted to avoid too much closeness, and they tended to use *distancing strategies* (Allison, Bartholomew, Mayseless, & Dutton, 2008; see also K. C. Gordon & Christman, 2008).

Recognition of these proximity/distancing strategies led to some insightful constructs. Some behaviors, such as having a sexual affair outside the relationship, could be either pursuit behaviors to gain the partner's attention or distancing behaviors to create an emotional distance from the partner. Partners often undertook first one strategy and then another, trying a number of strategies to achieve their desired level of proximity (or distance). Although partners used IPV for regulating both proximity and distance, IPV was usually a strategy of last resort. Of particular significance was the connection between attachment patterns and proximity/distance regulating strategies.

Of major consequence was the revelation that *dyadic attachment orientations might be incompatible.* That is, one partner might have a predominantly preoccupied pattern leading to a desire for more proximity, while the other partner might have a dismissing pattern leading to a desire for greater distance. In an up-to-date comparison, this type of attachment conflict, with each partner attempting a variety of unsuccessful strategies to regulate proximity, produced frustration and sometimes escalated to intimate violence (Allison et al., 2008).

*Predicting IPV.* One comparison revealed that two variables predicted both male and female IPV. These variables were as follows: (a) females' anxious attachment and (b) the interaction between male avoidance and female anxious attachment patterns. Further testing ascertained that male behaviors **mediated** the association between female anxious attachment and female violence. Stated differently, when *female anxious attachment* was followed by *male battering,* female *responsive violence occ*urred.

> Female Anxious Attachment → Male Battering → Female-to-Male IPV
>
> [Mediator]

"One interpretation of these findings is that *avoidant males* may respond to anxious females with violence, and females may then respond with violence as a *self-protective* behavior" (Doumas, Pearson, Elgin, & McKinley, 2008, p. 629). Alternatively, highly anxious females may believe that their male partner's violence toward them signifies *rejection,* and they retaliate with female-partner abuse.

*Attachment, jealousy, and borderline traits. Disordered attachment* was associated with *jealousy* in two independent comparisons (see D. G. Dutton et al., 1996; Holtzworth-Munroe et al., 1997; see also Goldenson, Geffner, Foster, & Clipson, 2007; D. M. Lawson, 2008). Furthermore, there is a growing body of evidence indicating a pattern of connections between attachment insecurity and *borderline traits* among both men *and* women (e.g., Henderson, Bartholomew, & Dutton, 1997; Henning, Jones, & Holdford, 2003; Mauricio, Tein, & Lopez, 2007). Last, some personality traits, such as low empathy, high impulsivity, and anxious attachment, may be more closely related to personality disorders than previously thought (see D. G. Dutton, 2008).

## Jealousy

> Let's say I committed this crime [the murder of ex-wife Nicole Brown Simpson]. Even if I did do this, it would have to have been because I loved her very much, right?—O. J. Simpson (quoted in Puente & Cohen, 2003, p. 449)

The topic of jealousy has captured the attention of numerous popular writers and academicians, both within and without the field of family violence. For conventional men and women, not involved in IPV, jealousy is a common source of relational dissatisfaction, relational conflict, and relationship dissolution (Andersen, Eloy, Guerrero, & Spitzberg, 1995). Within the field of family violence, clinicians, researchers, social service agencies, police, and victims have all recognized that jealousy often becomes entwined with IPV perpetrators' violent behavior (e.g., Holtzworth-Munroe, Meehan, Stuart, Herron, & Rehman, 2000). Abusive men themselves have confirmed that jealousy may be a factor in their partner violence (Babcock, Green, Webb, & Graham, 2004; Cantos et al., 1994). In a Chinese inquiry of IPV, surprisingly it was the jealous person who got hit (Wang, Parish, Laumann, & Luo, 2009). When researchers presented evidence asserting that jealousy is the motivation for a substantial percentage of intimate partner homicides (IPHs), jealousy took on greater urgency (Cazenave & Zahn, 1992).

**CASE HISTORY** Kevin and Kim—"She Didn't Clean the Lint Trap"

Kevin was a handsome, 32-year-old video cameraman for a local TV station. He frequently was called out of town to cover stories and even went overseas on work assignments occasionally.

His beautiful wife, Kim, who earned money modeling, went with him if she wasn't working. They had no children.

On the job, Kevin felt fearful from time to time when he had to shoot at a location in a ghetto neighborhood. He was afraid that local hoods would try to beat him up, and he thought he wouldn't be able to defend himself because he *thought of himself as too "small."* He was anxious about Kim's behavior as well. Other guys were always flirting with her, and she saw nothing wrong with "just being friends" with them. Kevin saw a lot wrong with it, and he warned her to watch her step. In Kevin's mind, Kim was very sloppy around the house. No matter what he said, she was always forgetting to empty the lint trap in the clothes dryer. It was clear to him that Kim didn't care how he felt, and he was desperate to do something to make her "treat him better."

The night Kevin got arrested for beating Kim up (for the first time, according to Kevin), he had come home around 6:30 in the evening after several weeks in Australia. He had caught an early flight back to surprise Kim with an expensive pearl ring and some champagne that he bought on the way home from the airport. He really loved her, and he was looking forward to a romantic reunion.

The first thing that went wrong was that Kim was not home. Kevin was both disappointed and suspicious. He did not think she was at work, but probably she was out having a drink with some guy who picked her up at a bar. He had never actually caught her doing this, but he thought she did it a lot when he was out of town. The second thing that happened was that there were some dirty dishes on the sink counter, and when he decided to do his laundry, he discovered Kim had failed to empty the lint trap again!

At 7:30, Kevin looked out a window and saw Kim coming out of the neighbor's house. He grabbed a shotgun and ran up and down the side yard, shooting into the air over the neighbor's house. He then took a sharp tool out of the garage and sliced his neighbor's tires. By the time the police arrived, Kim was on the living room floor with a broken nose and two broken ribs. Her 6-foot, 4-inch batterer was sitting on the couch sobbing. Kim was threatening to leave him. He hadn't meant to hurt her, but what other options did he have?

---

The case history above reflects the high level of distress suffered by many batterers. Kevin is constantly mistrustful and worried about his wife's fidelity. He feels jealous every time another man looks at her. He is miserable but does not know how to handle his hurt and anger. In the batterers' group therapy, where he has been court-ordered into treatment, he can barely hold back the tears. As much as he feels attached to Kim and needs her, he cannot get what he wants from her. He ends up blaming her for all their "relationship" problems. His reaction is to lash out impulsively and violently and then to regret his actions. He fears he will lose her, so he tries harder to control her. Nothing is working; he is desperate.

To understand Kevin, a therapist will probably want to determine if Kevin is more jealous than other men (high trait jealousy), or alternatively if his jealousy is more situational (his wife's friendship with a male neighbor). Last, his jealousy may be a combination of both his strong tendency to feel jealous and because of the situation (as described in the case history).

As important as *jealousy* is, as a construct it is not fully formed, and *definitions of jealousy* are imprecise and inconsistent. One common definition considers jealousy to be "*a complex of thought, emotion and actions that follows loss or threat to self-esteem and/or the existence or quality of the romantic relationship*" (G. L. White, 1980, p. 2). Some thinkers construe jealousy to be a unidimensional emotion, while others view it as multidimensional. As a prototypical multidimensional emotional construct, jealousy comprises several intense feelings, such as anger, blame, and hurt (Sharpsteen, 1991; Stenner & Rogers, 1998; G. L. White & Mullen, 1980). (See www.sagepub.com/barnett3e for a table of diverse viewpoints about jealousy.)

Cultural mores affect the existence and expression of both violence and jealousy (Vandello, Cohen, Grandon, & Franiuk, 2009). There are several rationales that have a bearing on cultural attitudes about jealousy. First, feminists allege that jealousy-related MFIPV occurs because of the patriarchal nature of societies. When women have less power and control than men because of patriarchy, the likelihood of their abuse for any reason is greater (Levesque, 2001). Learning theorists point out that transmission of cultural mores, such as the devaluation of women, is heavily reliant on learning. As an illustration, if a culture approves of (rewards) *honor killings,* the probability of their occurrence will increase. In analogous fashion, if a culture approves of (reinforces) female acceptance of MFIPV, the probability of its occurrence will increase.

*Jealousy as a trait.* The literature provides ample evidence indicating that jealousy can be studied as a trait and is characteristic of male perpetrators. Research using comparison groups and fairly large research samples has shown that *jealousy trait* scores are significantly higher for partner-violent men than for partner-nonviolent men (D. G. Dutton et al., 1996; Holtzworth-Munroe, Meehan et al., 2000; see also Barnett, Martinez, & Bluestein, 1995). The most conclusive research indicated that among 453 representative couples, a combined *dominance/jealousy score* was one of the *strongest predictors* of both male and female *aggression,* and it accounted for 50% of the **variance** (K. D. O'Leary, Slep, & O'Leary, 2007).

*Operationalization and research methodology.* Although jealousy is far from an understudied topic, researchers have not been able to resolve the ambiguities regarding its meaning and hence its measurement. As a result, operationalizing the concept has proven to be elusive. Nevertheless, test developers have constructed various scales representing divergent conceptions, such as *The Interpersonal Jealousy Scale* (Mathes & Severa, 1981) and *The Multidimensional Jealousy Scale* (Pfeiffer & Wong, 1989). A number of pivotal methodological differences have characterized research on jealousy, such as whether research samples are drawn from community or college student populations (see Penke & Asendorpf, 2007, for a review). As one illustration, research based on young, relatively well-educated college students is not automatically generalizable to noncollege adults. In sum, several factors render research on jealousy only partly applicable to intimate partner violence behaviors (Green & Sabini, 2006; C. R. Harris, 2003).

*Jealousy and gender.* Debate continues as to whether there are evolved sex differences in jealousy (C. R. Harris, 2003; Sagarin, 2005). A number of logicians have theorized that experiences related to romantic jealousy differ broadly by gender. One line of reasoning is rooted in *evolutionary theory.* Presumably, evolutionary forces have prepared males to *mate-guard* to ensure paternity. Thus, male jealousy is focused on sexual infidelity. Observations of male primates fighting over sexual access to females are congruent with this viewpoint. Females may also mate-guard to prevent the diluting of male-provided resources (e.g., food) needed to raise offspring. Thus, females are centered on emotional infidelity (e.g., Buss, Larsen, Westen, & Semmelroth, 1992). There is some support for an evolutionary approach. (See www.sagepub .com/barnett3e for an elaboration of evolution's impact on women's jealousy.)

*Reactive (normal), anxious, and possessive jealousy.* From another perspective, researchers examined gender dissimilarities in jealousy. When they examined the three types they found that women rated both their levels of reactive and anxious jealousy higher than men did in two of three studies (Barelds & Dijkstra, 2006). In one of the three studies, women also rated themselves higher than men on possessive jealousy. According to a different account, men differed significantly from women in their predictions of the effects of male partner violence on the length of marriage. If the abuse followed a nonjealousy-related conflict, their predictions were less dire than if the abuse followed a jealousy-related conflict (Puente & Cohen, 2003).

*Relationship implications of jealousy.* A clear-cut divergence of opinion among both academicians and the lay public exists about what it means to attribute jealousy to someone's feelings or behaviors. *Is jealousy a sign of love* (e.g., valuing a partner) and thus a positive feeling or behavior (Staske, 1999) or a sign of insecurity (e.g., fearing loss of a partner) and thus a negative condition (Carson & Cupach, 2000). Perhaps jealousy incorporates both positive and negative signals. It might be a sign of (positive) possessiveness—used as a mate-retention tactic (Buss & Shackelford, 1997), or of (negative) possessiveness—used to control the partner's behavior (Tjaden & Thoennes, 1998b). One early inquiry concluded that relationships typified by a moderate amount of jealousy are more likely to be *successful* than those relatively void of jealousy (Mathes & Severa, 1981). It is also common to classify the *consequences* of jealousy as either positive, such as increasing intimacy, or negative, such as fostering violence (Pines, 1998; Sheets, Fredendall, & Claypool, 1997). Whatever the case may be, experiencing jealousy is usually a negative feeling.

*Jealousy and relationship quality.* Research on the link between jealousy and relationship satisfaction is one area where *past* research findings have been fairly consistent. Not surprisingly, jealousy and lack of interpersonal trust appear to have a bearing on attachment disorders and dependency needs in partner-violent men. More than one study has reported that the association between jealousy and relationship satisfaction is significant and negative (see Tonizzo et al., 2000). Despite the regularity of past reports, *current investigations* have demonstrated that the association between jealousy and marital satisfaction can be positive, but only if the jealous individual loves his partner (Dugosh, 2000; Barelds & Barelds-Dijkstra, 2007).

*Jealousy and homicide.* The correlation between jealousy and intimate partner homicides (IPHs) is generally positive. An intimate partner's extreme jealousy poses a risk for possible fatal violence, even if there has been no previous violence. Of centrality to most jealousy specialists is the emergence of gender as a salient variable in homicides. As one illustration, analysts found that 41% of male-to-female murders were motivated by jealousy, compared with 7% of female-to-male IPHs (Cazenave & Zahn, 1992; see also Glass, Laughon, Rutto, Bevaqua, &

Campbell, 2008). Another evaluation attributed 39% of 2,556 IPHs by males in Chicago to jealousy (C. R. Block, 2003; Block & Christakos, 1995). (See www.sagepub.com/barnett3e about cautioning the assumption of jealousy as a motive for IPH.)

## Marital Dissatisfaction/Satisfaction

The question of *marital satisfaction* levels among male-to-female intimate partner violence perpetrators has been a perennial topic for MFIPV researchers, attracting considerable attention from the beginning of academic inquiry. Investigations have shown that MFIPV perpetrators have self-reported significantly lower marital satisfaction scores than men categorized as nonmaritally violent. Even before publication of research results, one of the most basic conceptions held by family violence experts is that marital dissatisfaction is an exceptionally *strong impetus* for male partner violence. Several experts presupposed that happily married men would simply not hit their wives. Only unhappily married men in a conflicted relationship would perpetrate assaultive behavior. These beliefs had such a powerful influence on the field of family violence in the 1980s that they shaped the type of *control groups* selected by researchers. (See www.sagepub.com/barnett3e for assessment of marital satisfaction.)

*Marital dissatisfaction and MFIPV.* Several lines of research have lent credence to the importance of marital dissatisfaction as an element of partner violence. First, researchers reported statistically significant correlations between marital dissatisfaction and MFIPV (e.g., Byrne & Arias, 1997; K. E. Leonard & Senchak, 1993). Second, researchers demonstrated that CTS1 aggression scores discriminated between separated/divorced couples and those who were still married. The methodology used in this second study consisted of tracing marital dissatisfaction over a 4-year period, starting with newlyweds and ending at the time of relationship dissolution (Rogge & Bradbury, 1999). Third, marital discord plays an important role in *predicting male battering recidivism* (P. R. Kropp, Hart, Webster, & Eaves, 1995). Finally, investigators conducting a path analysis identified a strong direct link between marital dissatisfaction and CTS2 aggression, thus finding that marital dissatisfaction is a strong predictor of MFIPV (K. D. O'Leary et al., 2007).

Surprisingly, research has *not* uniformly shown that couples involved in low-level IPV inevitably report marital dissatisfaction (S. L. Williams & Frieze, 2005). Indicative of these results are those of a study revealing that a subset of male perpetrators scored above the mean on marital satisfaction tests, while a number of nonperpetrators scored below the mean (e.g., Lawrence & Bradbury, 2001; Pan, Neidig, & O'Leary, 1994; Sagrestano, Heavey, & Christensen, 1999; L. E. Simpson, Atkins, Gattis, & Christensen, 2008).

Fortunately, a well-executed meta-analysis of the relationship between marital satisfaction/dissatisfaction and partner violence has helped clarify reasons for the inconsistency of the findings. The overall result was that IPV is negatively correlated with marital satisfaction and positively correlated with marital dissatisfaction, but a number of **moderator variables** (variables affecting the strength and direction of the relationship between predictor and criterion variables) influence the results. For example, the use of *standardized* versus nonstandardized assessments influenced the magnitude of the **effect sizes** (i.e., strength of the relationship) (Stith, Green, Smith, & Ward, 2008). (See www.sagepub.com/barnett3e for additional information.)

*Correlation of marital satisfaction with other traits.* Studies of both violent and nonviolent couples have examined the correlations of marital dissatisfaction with individual trait scores. Some of the findings are as follows: (a) Marital *dissatisfaction* is significantly related to *wives' low decision-making power* (Frieze & McHugh, 1992); (b) Marital *dissatisfaction* is correlated to some forms of *insecure attachment* (H. S. Kane et al., 2007); (c) The association between relationship satisfaction and jealousy is significant and negative (see Tonizzo et al., 2000); (d) Marital *satisfaction* can be positively correlated with jealousy, but only if the jealous individual loves his partner (Dugosh, 2000); (e) General marital adjustment measures are significantly and negatively associated with trait anger and hostile cognition measures (K. G. Baron et al., 2006); and (f) Continuing marital *dissatisfaction* may predict MFIPV *recidivism* (P. R. Kropp et al., 1995).

---

### SECTION SUMMARY

## Attitudes and Classifications of Batterers

The public, while becoming somewhat more intolerant of partner abuse, takes a lenient approach. Research indicates that many people are still willing to blame female victims rather than hold abusers accountable. MFIPV perpetrators themselves attribute negative intentions to their female partners. Some advocates believe that it is pivotal that batterers acknowledge the harm they are causing and accept responsibility for their own behavior. To that end, research has found that internalizing responsibility is a sign of progress toward stopping male battering.

One of the most significant contributions to the field of intimate partner violence is Johnson's theory differentiating couples involved in IPV. He used both partner violence (PV) levels and controlling behaviors to separate couples into *two basic types:* Situational Couple Violence (SCV—low level) and Intimate Terrorism (IT—frequent and severe). In subsequent work, he categorized IPV into four categories: SCV, MVC, VR, IT (MVC—Mutual Violent Control; VR—Violent Resistance). Some data have supported the existence of the two anchor categories, but confirmation of the four categories awaits further clarification. A team of investigators cleverly demonstrated how the concept of mutual couple violence would be inaccurate if it asserted that the IPV was gender equivalent.

Batterers differ significantly in regard to personality traits and situations that evoke responses. Battered women were some of the first people to describe batterers' traits. Turning to trait psychology correlational data from an array of single and broad-based inventories have revealed a number of individual differences between partner-violent and nonpartner-violent men. In general, male offenders have higher scores on a number of traits measures:

*(Continued)*

(Continued)

(a) *Denial and minimization*

(b) *Anger and hostility*—There are numerous connotations for anger and hostility. Some experts view anger as a trait, while others think of it as a temporary state. Anger has cognitive, behavioral, and physiological components. MFIPV perpetrators are definitely angrier and more hostile than nonperpetrators. It is possible to categorize batterers along an anger dimension and correlate levels of anger with other variables, such as childhood abuse and drug use, but studies have not uniformly shown that anger motivates male assaults. One study found that batterers suffer from intermittent explosive disorder.

(c) *Depression, shame, humiliation, guilt, and low self-esteem*—Batterers' feelings of shame, humiliation, and guilt, probably stemming from parent-to-child punishment and situations in adulthood (e.g., unemployment), contribute to their feelings of depression and low self-esteem.

(d) *Lack of awareness*—Some batterers do not know why they are abusive.

(e) *Lack of empathy*

(f) *Attachment issues*—Many batterers suffer from insecure attachment stemming from childhood. They have abandonment fears that can trigger violence. They are often emotionally dependent upon their partners, and they have difficulties regulating closeness.

(g) *Jealousy*—Jealousy has several meanings, and there are a number of measurement scales. Jealousy may be a sign of love or insecurity, and jealousy can be either sexual or emotional. There are gender differences in jealousy. Some batterers appear to be very jealous, and jealousy seems to reduce marital quality. Jealousy can also trigger violence and marital dissatisfaction.

(h) *Marital dissatisfaction*—Many batterers rate their marital satisfaction as low, but many do not.

Although experts in the field seem willing to acknowledge that jealousy is characteristic of male offenders, it is less clear if jealousy is a primary motivator in partner violence. The same is true of anger and hostility. If jealousy were the impetus for many incidents of IPV, it probably is not the only, or even the most powerful, instigator of partner violence. Jealousy can be a potent precursor to intimate partner homicide.

## BECOMING AND REMAINING A BATTERER: CAUSES OF MFIPV

A very popular approach extending from early in the study of abusive males to the present has been to look for differences between battering and nonbattering men that might explain their violence. This section addresses some of the more traditional rationales for partner violence along with a newer section on possible biological precursors. The discussion covers the topics of (a) socialization, (b) verbal skills/communication deficits, (c) alcohol or drug abuse, (d) stress, (e) emotional volatility, a history of trauma/PTSD, (f) biological/genetic influences, and (g) severe personality disorders and psychopathology (mental illness—brain disorders), such as antisocial personality disorder, and (h) differences between batterers grouped into typologies (see Henning & Holdford, 2006; Holtzworth-Munroe & Stuart, 1994). Appreciation of the research in the latter part of this section requires some understanding of several constructs that often comprise part of the content of classes in individual differences, personality, or abnormal psychology. Some of the topics covered include (a) **personality disorder,** such as antisocial, borderline, dysphoric, and narcissistic personality disorders, (b) **psychopathology,** such as bipolar disorder, and (c) **brain disorders.** In attempting to present their findings in the most empirical way possible, researchers have often used sophisticated statistical methodology to analyze their data.

## Socialization

This section summarizes some socialization practices that appear to contribute to battering. Violence is most likely a learned behavior with biological underpinnings, and socialization plays a pivotal role in transgenerational explanations of partner violence. On the other hand, socialization alone cannot account for the number of people who perpetrate IPV but do not come from abusive homes or for the large number of people from abusive households who do not engage in IPV (Bennett, Tolman, Rogalski, & Srinivasaraghavan, 1994). Research has frequently shown that men exposed to parental violence and men who themselves have been abused are substantially more likely to be violent toward their spouses than are their counterparts (e.g., G. Margolin, John, & Foo, 1998; Moffitt & Caspi, 1999). A number of researchers have carefully examined socialization variables, such as observing the behavior of a parent that might promote MFIPV. *Generalized modeling* may convey approval of violence, and *specific modeling* may teach that certain behaviors are acceptable and certain people are the proper targets of violence (e.g., Kalmuss, 1984). Even observation of community violence may increase violence in the home (see Kubrin & Weitzer, 2003).

*Childhood socialization.* Studies are beginning to evaluate the role of socialization as it applies to the learning of *cognitive or attitudinal variables that allow or encourage partner aggression,* such as hostility (e.g., Barnett, Fagan, & Booker, 1991). One team of investigators, for example, has proposed that *ineffective problem-solving strategies* learned in childhood carry over into adult relationships and precipitate IPV (Choice, Lamke, & Pittman, 1995). Another research team found evidence linking proneness to shame learned in childhood with adult marital abusive behaviors (D. G. Dutton, van Ginkel, & Starzomski, 1995). Fear of abandonment and emotional dependency stemming from childhood experiences may also **mediate** IPV (i.e., type of intervening variable) (C. M. Murphy et al., 1994). Abandonment fears are realistic because female victims seem to be more desirous of ending their relationship than male partners (Henning et al., 2003). Last, socialized expectations for men generate specific types of masculine gender role stress (T. M. Moore et al., 2008).

*Childhood abuse.* Harsh treatment in childhood may also lead to development of an **antisocial orientation** that in turn is associated with chronic partner violence (R. L. Simons, Wu, Johnson, & Conger, 1995; see also Ehrensaft et al., 2003). Commencing in 1975, a longitudinal study of men and women randomly sampled from communities searched for relationships between childhood maltreatment and IPV. Child maltreatment measures consisted of the following: (a) power-assertive punishment reported by the mother at child age 9, and (b) a retrospective report of parental IPV, and retrospective accounts of *child physical abuse, child sexual abuse,* and *neglect.* Both *exposure to parental battering* and *power-assertive punishment* were significantly and independently linked with perpetration of adult IPV (CTS1-assessed). *Neglect* was not a significant predictor. Furthermore, concurrent *personality disorders,* such as antisocial personality disorder and borderline-narcissistic disorder, were significantly associated with adult violence by both men and women. Hence, these childhood socialization factors increased the odds of adult IPV by increasing the risk of antisocial personality disorder (Ehrensaft et al., 2006).

*Exposure to interparental violence.* A relatively large volume of literature indicates that exposure to interparental violence during childhood is associated with later aggression (e.g., Trull, 2001; Widom & Maxfield, 2001). A meta-analysis of *intergenerational transmission* of MFIPV found a moderate correlation ($r = .35$) for males exposed to parental violence (Stith et al., 2000). Observing abuse, according to Hotaling and Sugarman (1986), may be a more powerful predictor of future IPV than experiencing abuse directly, and paternal violence may be a better predictor than maternal violence (see also Blumenthal, Neeman, & Murphy, 1998). As a general rule, certain kinds of childhood abuse and trauma (e.g., child sexual abuse) are capable of triggering a wide variety of problematic and long-lasting behaviors (e.g., PTSD, alcohol/drug problem).

*Childhood attachment.* From an *intergenerational transfer point of view,* researchers have shown that the insecure romantic attachment status of fathers is closely associated with the self-reported insecure attachment status of their children (Roelofs, Meesters, & Muris, 2008). One inquiry has revealed that adults who were insecure and fearful during infancy are likely to worry about abandonment when interacting with a partner who is cold and rejecting (Henning et al., 2003; also see Corvo, 1992).

*Childhood trauma.* Children may be exposed to traumatic events where they see or experience a threat to their own life or physical safety or to that of others. Traumas cause fear, terror, helplessness, or even **dissociation.** *As an example of dissociation, a child repeatedly raped, may survive by coming to believe that someone else, another child, is going through the experience.* Dissociative disorder may imply a number of symptoms, such as a sense of being detached or having amnesia. Many occurrences in the lives of children living in violent families qualify as traumas (e.g., physical abuse, sexual abuse, witnessing abuse). Experiencing childhood traumas is especially relevant to the study of family violence because researchers can connect *childhood trauma* with *adult dissociative experience.* Approaching the issue from a different direction, an investigation measured *general dissociative experiences* and *violence-specific dissociation.* The dimensions were significantly associated with each other and both were associated with the occurrence, frequency, and severity of partner violence behaviors (Simoneti, Scott, & Murphy, 2000; see also Cuartas, 2001; S. Watson, Chilton, Fairchild, & Whewell, 2006). (Go to www.sagepub.com/barnett3e for additional information. See the box on the etiology of MFIPV.)

Data from a random sample of men and women produced results supportive of the link between childhood trauma and adult IPV (Ehrensaft et al., 2006). The relationships between childhood exposure to parental IPV predicted two types of *personality disorders* (DSM-III-assessed; clusters A and B), which in turn, *partially* **mediated** *adult partner abuse.*

---

**Two Types of Personality Disorders**

*Cluster A*—Paranoid, schizoid, and schizotypal traits displayed as mistrust of others, suspiciousness, cognitive distortions, jealousy

*Cluster B*—Borderline, narcissistic, and antisocial group of features typified by emotional dysregulation, anger, stress reactivity, aggression

**Partial Mediation**

Exposure to Parental IPV → [Personality Disorder] → Adult IPV
[ Partial Mediation ]
[ Clusters A and B ]
[Transmits the Effects of Exposure to IPV]

---

*Male gender socialization—Attitude and beliefs.* To understand the role of attitudes in male-to-female intimate partner violence, social scientists have enlisted several types of attitude and belief scales. A number of these indices, however, seem unable to detect noticeable differences between male perpetrators and other males. Some investigations found that only scores on the *Adversarial Sexual Beliefs* (ASB) scale (Burt, 1980) were significantly correlated with CTS1 scores (B. M. Hastings, 2000). High scores on the ASB scale indicate assumptions that *sexual relationships* will be exploitative and manipulative.

*Masculinity-femininity.* One index of sex-role adherence measures the degree to which individuals endorse self-descriptions of masculine, feminine, undifferentiated (neither male nor female), and androgynous (both male and female) traits on the Bem Sex-Role Inventory (e.g., Bem, 1979). An early assessment on the Bem scale found that male offenders scored in the undifferentiated quadrant compared with normative data. Undifferentiated men lack both positive masculine skills (e.g., leadership) and positive feminine skills (nurturance) (LaViolette, Barnett, & Miller, 1984). A later meta-analysis found somewhat similar results. Batterers scored significantly lower on masculinity and femininity than nonbatterers (Sugarman & Frankel, 1993).

*Approval of aggression.* Another scale established that approval of aggression increases the **odds ratio** of assaultive behavior by 2.7 times. An analysis of proabuse attitudes also yielded positive results: Men who held proviolence attitudes exhibited more MFIPV than those who did not (Kantor, Jasinski, & Aldarondo, 1994). In a meta-analysis of seven studies, proabuse attitudes were significantly associated with abusive behavior ($r = .25$) (Hanson & Wallace-Capretta, 1998).

*Entitlement.* Men can be socialized to expect their wives to treat them with deference. Men's feelings of entitlement to power and their use of dominance in marital conflicts to control female partners hinge on sex-role socialization (Birns, Cascardi, & Meyer, 1994). According to Mihalic and Elliott (1997), patriarchal socialization confers upon males the roles of primary wage earner, head of the household, dominant marital partner, and the right to exert power and control, through the use of force if necessary.

## Verbal Skills/Communication

The possibility that *inadequate communication style* might be a *cause* of intimate partner violence was a popular speculation of early family violence researchers working within the context of conflict theory. Poor communication might trigger a quarrel that eventually ended in physical abuse.

*Assertion deficits.* Some practitioners/researchers thought that male perpetrators might suffer from *assertion deficits* (i.e., inadequacy in stating one's views forcefully or in making requests appropriately; see, e.g., D. G. Dutton & Strachan, 1987). Actually, these deficits are associated with greater verbal hostility (Maiuro, Cahn, & Vitaliano, 1988). Across studies, research conducted during the 1980s indicated that lack of assertiveness may be a risk marker for intimate partner violence (e.g., Hotaling & Sugarman, 1986), but findings vary depending on whether measures assess *general assertiveness* or *spouse-specific assertiveness.* MFIPV perpetrators tend to show the largest *deficits in spouse-specific assertiveness.*

*Misperception of communication.* Communication patterns predict couples' scores on marital satisfaction (Locke & Wallace, 1959). As already pointed out, marital dissatisfaction is a powerful correlate of MFIPV. Misperception of communication is another difficulty that some violent men experience (Margolin, John, & Gleberman, 1988). In one study, partner-violent men underestimated the quality and number of caring gestures received from their wives. They saw themselves as "doing more and getting less" in their relationships (Langhinrichsen-Rohling, Smutzler, & Vivian, 1994).

*Problem solving among MFIPV perpetrators.* Several studies have shown that, compared with nonpartner-violent men, partner-violent men are poor problem solvers (e.g., Anglin & Holtzworth-Munroe, 1997; Barnett & Hamberger, 1992; Hastings & Hamberger, 1988). Poor problem solving may play a role in men's negative reactions to marital stress. The inability to utilize effective *conflict resolution strategies* and *high marital distress* may serve as mediating factors between childhood exposure to interparental violence and wife battering (Choice et al., 1995). Partner-violent men exhibit particular difficulty generating adequate responses to situations involving jealousy and rejection by and challenges from their wives. Ridley and Feldman (2003) reasoned that their results from a communication study were consistent with a problem-solving skills deficit model of IPV (see J. C. Babcock, Waltz, Jacobson, & Gottmann, 1993). Without the necessary skills to resolve problems, a violent partner may turn to either verbal or physical aggression, or both.

# Alcohol/Drug Abuse and Battering

Although research has uniformly found associations between alcohol/substance abuse (AOD) and interpersonal violence, one cannot assume an inevitable causal link (e.g., Combs-Lane & Smith, 2002). Notwithstanding the very strong association between IPV and alcohol/drug abuse, the role of alcohol in family violence is complex. Male IPV perpetrators in one survey reported using drugs and alcohol as follows: (a) 19% consumed only alcohol, (b) 18% used only illicit drugs, and (c) 30% both drank and used drugs. Further, violent intimates may use alcohol and other drugs *before, during, or after IPV* (Barnett & Fagan, 1993; Willson et al., 2000).

*Alcohol and MFIPV.* Evidence from several lines of research shows that certain partner-violent men commit much *more severe and frequent violence* when intoxicated than when not intoxicated (Fals-Stewart, 2003; O'Farrell, Fals-Stewart, Murphy, & Murphy, 2003). In fact, there is a direct effect between alcohol abuse and the commission of male-partner abuse according to one duo of investigators (Stalans & Ritchie, 2008). A different comparison, nevertheless, found a significant correlation between excessive drinking and IPV *only* when analyzing cross-sectional data, not when using longitudinal data (Schumacher, Homish, Leonard, Quigley, & Kearns-Bodkin, 2008). Men in treatment for partner violence usually need to be in addiction treatment as well (S. Jackson, 2003). In fact, the probability of a dual diagnosis is high in MFIPV perpetrator groups. PTSD, alcoholism, and antisocial personality disorder may be present in male-to-female IPV offenders, thus indicating the need for *thorough screening at intake.* Certainly, health personnel should routinely screen all men for violence as well as more ordinary problems, such as depression and substance abuse (Riggs, Caulfield, & Street, 2000).

Nevertheless, it is not yet totally clear whether alcohol use is *causally* related to adult IPV (Zubretsky & Digirolamo, 1994). Men who batter when they are drinking may also batter when they are sober, and the vast majority of men who consume even large quantities of alcohol never batter female partners at all (Bennett, 1995; Fals-Stewart, 2003). Relatedly, in one sample, 30% of women experienced IPV perpetrated by male partners who had no histories of drug or alcohol use (Willson et al., 2000). A pair of researchers stated that, "Evidence from cross-cultural research, laboratory studies, blood tests of men arrested for wife beating, and survey research all indicates that although alcohol use may be associated with intimate violence, alcohol is *not* a primary *cause* of the violence" (Gelles & Cavanaugh, 2005, p. 177).

*Explaining the alcohol/drug abuse—Male-partner abuse connection.* In a careful critique, O'Farrell et al. (2003) enumerated several alternative explanations for the link between AOD and MFIPV. They suggest that a third variable, such as antisocial personality traits, might account for the relationship between IPV and alcohol consumption (see Agrawal, Lynskey, Madden, Bucholz, & Heath, 2006). A more recent study may have elucidated these uncertainties by isolating **moderator variables.** "Alcohol was longitudinally predictive of husband violence among *hostile* men with high levels of *avoidance coping*" (Schumacher et al., 2008, p. 894; see also Copenhaver, Lash, & Eisler, 2000). That is, hostility and avoidance coping **moderated** (influenced the strength) of MFIPV.

Using a path model (of risk factors), Schafer, Caetano, and Cunradi (2004) produced a more complex representation of the relationship between alcohol consumption and IPV based on the personality trait of *impulsivity*. Although some of the risk factors varied significantly by gender and ethnicity, an overall model was able to capture a fairly consistent single path. Childhood abuse was a risk factor for impulsivity for all the men and Hispanic women. Impulsivity was a risk factor for alcohol problems among all groups, and alcohol problems were a risk factor for MFIPV and FMIPV. Huss and Langhinrichsen-Rohling (2006) emphasized that alcohol consumption is not only a strong risk marker for MFIPV, but it can serve as a discriminating variable between subgroups of batterers. A different study of 453 representative community couples also used a path model and surprisingly did *not* uncover a direct path from alcohol misuse to commission of IPV (K. D. O'Leary et al., 2007). In a separate analysis, investigators found that *jealousy is a mediator* between problem drinking and male partner abuse. In this study, community men ($N = 453$) who had very high jealousy scores but did not have anger control problems were those more apt to aggress against a female partner. Foran and O'Leary (2008, p. 147) state that:

> If he is jealous, but does not have anger control problem, problem drinking may "push him" over the threshold and he may be more likely to engage in severe physical aggression.... when sober, his high anger control may enable him to inhibit angry and aggressive responses to his jealousy, but when intoxicated, his inhibitions may be reduced and lead to less ability to control angry and aggression responses.

Researchers have added some clarity to this patchwork of findings by including additional variables in their analyses. They found that several factors, including alcohol abuse, had a *direct* effect on the perpetration of IPV. These investigators had access to a very large pool of research participants ($N = 19,131$) from the nationally representative National Household Survey on Drug Abuse. On the negative side, the questionnaire data included only *one* question on IPV (an item about hitting or threatening to hit one's partner). Other scales assessed variables such as *socioeconomic status*. A multiplicity of statistical analyses involving racial and socioeconomic differences generated some of their most interesting findings. Marijuana use/abuse was a stronger predictor of IPV among minorities than Caucasians, and lower socioeconomic status was a stronger predictor of IPV than higher socioeconomic status. Among minorities, marijuana use/abuse increased psychological abuse and mutual yelling and insulting behavior, which in turn, **mediated** the drug's effects on IPV (Stalans & Ritchie, 2008).

### Alcohol/Drug Abuse Risk Marker Studies

- Child abuse is a risk factor for impulsivity; impulsivity is a risk factor for alcohol consumption; and alcohol consumption is a risk factor for IPV (Schafer et al., 2004).
- Alcohol consumption is a strong risk marker for MFIPV (Huss & Langhinrichsen-Rohling, 2006).
- Alcohol abuse has a direct effect on the perpetration of IPV (Stalans & Ritchie, 2008).

- Marijuana use is a stronger predictor of IPV among minorities than Caucasians. Marijuana use increases psychological abuse with mutual yelling and insulting behavior, which in turn, mediates the drug's effects on IPV (Stalans & Ritchie, 2008).
- Alcohol use is *not* predictive of either male-to-female or female-to-male IPV (K. D. O'Leary et al., 2007).

## Stress, Emotions, Mood States, Trauma, and Posttraumatic Stress Disorder (PTSD)

Just as early scholars surmised that jealousy or marital dissatisfaction provided an impetus for MFIPV, they similarly speculated that the male partner's stress and experiences with trauma might be a trigger for abuse. Accordingly, a large number of researchers undertook investigations of the role of these factors in male-to-female intimate partner violence.

*Stress.* As so frequently happens in social science research, researchers lack a uniform definition of stress, and the connotations of stress are manifold. The most common understanding is that stress refers to a *physiological and psychological response to a stressor* (e.g., pain). "Stress dysregulates the immune system and compromises health" (Kiecolt-Glaser, 2009). As described previously, both perpetrators and victims of IPV suffer from a high level of debilitating stress that affects cognitions, emotions, and physiology.

A review of studies shows that there are multiple pathways, both direct and indirect, between stress and male partner violence. Researchers found that *negative life events* are significantly associated with male IPV (McHenry, Julian, & Gavazzi, 1995). Another inquiry based its findings on sociodemographic information and **proxy measures** for male partner abuse (i.e., female partners' assessments of their male partners on the CTS). **Multiple regression** analyses of these responses revealed that younger age, unemployment status, and violence toward nonfamily members were all predictors of MFIPV. Because variables such as unemployment are stressful, the authors concluded that their findings supported a stress-level *model of male-to-female partner abuse* (Torres & Han, 2003). In a later **path model** analysis, investigators found that *perceived stress* was first linked with *anger expression,* and that anger expression was then linked to CTS2 aggression (O'Leary et al., 2007).

*Trauma and posttraumatic stress disorder.* Traumatized persons have painful memories, trouble concentrating, flashbacks, extreme startle reactions, and numbing of emotions (VandenBos, 2007). Research in child abuse and wife abuse has documented high levels of PTSD in a significant number of survivors, and some victims have symptoms for many years.

Using the Millon Clinical Multiaxial Inventory (Millon, 1995), D. G. Dutton (1995) detected a PTSD-like profile among a group of 132 partner-violent men. Unlike profiles of PTSD men, however, profiles of partner-violent men included *higher scores for antisocial personality.* Partner-violent males' trauma symptoms were significantly related to retrospective reports of parental treatment, especially rejection and physical abuse. Later, D. G. Dutton (1999) formulated a theory of intimate rage founded on a triad of traumatic childhood events. These include observation of father-to-mother violence, experiencing violence directed at the self, shaming, and insecure attachment (see also Beckham, Feldman, Kirby, Hertzberg, & Moore, 1997).

*Masculine gender-role stress.* Another line of inquiry concerns a unique type of stress labeled *masculine gender-role stress (MGRS)* (Eisler & Skidmore, 1987). High levels of MGRS are related to a number of disruptive behaviors. Male gender-role perceptions encompass socially mandated expectations and rules prescribing appropriate and inappropriate male behaviors. Masculine gender-role stress also refers to the name of a test for this type of stress. Factor analysis of the MGRS test has identified types of stress-eliciting situations that comprise five dimensions: (a) *physical inadequacy,* (b) *emotional expressiveness,* (c) *subordination to women,* (d) *intellectual inferiority,* and (e) *performance failure.* Researchers have found that high levels of MGRS are associated with problematic behaviors, such as physical health problems (including heart disease), psychological problems, problems in interpersonal relationships, and MFIPV (e.g., Copenhaver & Eisler, 1996; Lash, Copenhaver, & Eisler, 1998; Lash, Eisler, & Schulman, 1990; see also Copenhaver, Lash, & Eisler, 2000).

A compelling newer inquiry has provided some fascinating information about significant relationships between individual male gender-role stress subscales and CTS2 subscales. These results indicate that male gender-role stress is *not a unitary construct,* and researchers and clinicians should take *specific types of MGRS and IPV* into account in their work. As an example, an abuser prone to using sexual coercion against his female partner may suffer from feeling physically inadequate (T. M. Moore et al., 2008). Data derived from men court-mandated to treatment for male-to-female partner abusers indicated the following multivariate correlations significant at the p ≤ .05 level appear in Table 9.4.

| TABLE 9.4 | Significant Relationships Between MGRS Factors and MFIPV Factors |

| *MGRS Subscales* | *CTS2 (MFIPV) Subscales* | *Correlation* |
|---|---|---|
| Physical inadequacy | Sexual coercion | .15 |
| Intellectual inferiority | Injury to partner | .16 |
| Performance failure | Psychological aggression | .13 |

*Emotions and mood states.* Emotions, such as anger and fear, play significant roles in adult family violence. Anger can serve as a motive for both male and female IPV, and fear may be a hallmark of female victimization by male partners. Fear also plays a role in trauma reactions and PTSD. Certain emotions may play havoc with immune responses, providing evidence for the association between emotions and physical illnesses. Questions have arisen about the extent to which individual emotional reactions may reflect individual differences in the brain. Identification of brain behavior gives rise to the possibility of developing *psychotropic drugs* that would assist individuals in managing their emotions and moods.

Physiological psychologists, medical researchers, and others have made rapid advances during the last decade in understanding the *biological basis of behavior.* This research is providing more and more evidence that biological anomalies underlie many behavioral symptoms. In a review of studies linking individual and group differences, researchers described a number of intriguing findings. Some electroencephalographic (EEG) experiments, for instance, demonstrated a biological basis for **affective style** (emotional responding). Emotions, such as *fear* as opposed to attraction, activated different prefrontal lobe regions of the brain, and there were individual response differences in these brain regions (Kosslyn et al., 2002).

## Biology and Genetics

A number of social scientists believe that evolutionary biology has fashioned men to be aggressive (M. Daly & Wilson, 1998). More and more psychologists have searched for genetic contributions to behavior and mental disorders (Kagan, 2007). One question that has attracted increasing research scrutiny is whether male (or female) violence might have a biological basis, rather than being wholly attributable to the consequences of learning experiences. Could it be, for instance, that the intergenerational transfer of abuse springs from genetic transmission rather than from learning based on exposure to violent parents (Hines & Saudino, 2002)?

Newer discoveries about relationships between biology and aggression suggest that the traditional "nature/nurture" dichotomy no longer fits empirical data and must be replaced by a **biopsychosocial model** (Bassarath, 2001). Evidence suggests that biological determinants, such as hormones and *neurotransmitters* (brain chemicals), may drive general male violence. In one experiment, scientists collected data from men and women, with and without a history of aggression. Using a competitive shock paradigm, augmentation of serotonin (a calming neurotransmitter) weakened aggressive responding (M. E. Berman, McCloskey, Fanning, Schumacher, & Coccaro, 2009). Furthermore, criminal behavior and psychopathology may have their roots in genetic differences. *Victims* of aggression may suffer long-term structural changes in the brain (Covington, Tropea, Rajadhyaksha, Kosofsky, & Miczek, 2008).

*Biological hormone studies.* According to Alan Mazur, the major male hormone *testosterone* has earned a bad reputation (cited in Bower, 2003). In a review of testosterone studies, for example, J. A. Harris (1999) found greater aggression in males relative to females and also found that aggression is dimorphic; that is, aggression takes different forms in men and women. One group of researchers conducted a meta-analysis of 45 independent studies covering 9,760 research participants and found that testosterone-aggression correlations ranged from 0.28 to 0.71. The weighted correlation was $r = 0.14$, a significant but weak correlation (Book, Starzyk, & Quinsey, 2001). Other scientists contend that testosterone forms part of a configuration of components contributing to a general *latent predisposition* toward aggression but that social factors moderate its influence (Royce & Coccaro, 2001; Soler, Vinayak, & Quadagno, 2000; Virkkunen et al., 1994). One inquiry showed that testosterone was significantly associated with verbal and physical levels of violence as measured by CTS1. Because demographic variables (e.g., age) and *alcohol consumption* also helped explain the

**variance** in aggressive responses, the researchers concluded that a biosocial model best fit the data (Soler et al., 2000; see also Bernhardt, 1997). (See www.sagepub.com/barnett3e for a theoretical account of testosterone and dominance behavior.)

*Genetic studies.* Essentially, genes set the reaction range for traits and may set a patient's therapeutic range for change. "Traits contribute to the expression of symptoms of common psychiatric disorders, are moderately heritable, and relatively stable (yet also dynamic to some extent)" (Zinbarg, Uliaszek, & Adler, 2008, p. 1649). Genetic comparisons have shown, for example, that testosterone level is highly heritable (J. A. Harris, Vernon, & Boomsma, 1998).

One of the most accurate ways to isolate genetic from environmental contributions to criminality is with adoption studies. Children share 50% of their genetic inheritance with each biological parent and none with genetically unrelated persons, such as adoptive parents. Comparing children's behavior with both their biological fathers and their adoptive fathers represents an excellent test of the gene-crime relationship. A meta-analysis authenticated a low to moderate but significant association between heredity variables and indices of crime, despite the methodological weakness of many of the studies. An analysis of 13 adoption studies suggests that the individual genetic inheritance of criminal behavior is 11% to 17%. These studies demonstrate a *gene-crime relationship* (Walters, 1992).

Two other twin studies found significant heritability for *antisocial personality disorder symptoms* (Coccaro, Bergeman, Kavoussi, & Seroczynski, 1997) and the results of genetic studies of antisocial personality disorder may, by logical extension, apply to maritally assaultive men (Dunford, Huizinga, & Elliott, 1990). The overlap between MFIPV and general violence may have additional implications. In the last decade, more and more research has documented genetic contributions to traits characterizing male-partner assaulters. Typical of such studies are those pinpointing genetic variations relevant to *alcohol dependence* (Schumann et al., 2008; see also Hutchinson et al., 2008; Brans et al., 2008; Zandi et al., 2008).

*Sex differences in the brain.* New technologies have led to new discoveries in neuropsychology that have pinpointed a number of sex differences in the structures of the brain. Although research has not advanced sufficiently to indicate how these differences are translated into behavior, the knowledge may prove relevant to understanding male aggression (see Tyre & Scelfo, 2006). Females have smaller amygdalas (locus of strong emotions and anger) than males and some larger brain areas in the prefrontal cortex (restrains the amygdala's aggressive impulses). A third divergence is that women possess a larger hippocampus (emotional memory center) than men. It is probable, therefore, that men get angrier than women and have a harder time controlling their aggression. Men also may not remember such events as well as women might when answering questions about their aggressive behavior.

*Brain dysfunctions.* Another biological postulation is that MFIPV perpetrators may suffer from various *brain disorders*. A number of brain regions are involved in controlling aggression: prefrontal cortex, limbic system, septum, hippocampus, caudate nucleus, thalamus, and the amygdala (Raine, 1993). A few analyses have discriminated the effects of damage to these regions. Volavka (1995), for instance, discovered frontal lobe dysfunction in some criminal and violent individuals. Others have shown that psychopaths have interpersonal/affective deficits that may be related to an information-processing deficit in hemispheric arousal (Bernstein, Newman, Wallace, & Luh, 2000). In addition, a meta-analysis revealed that of 39 studies encompassing 4,589 research participants, antisocial groups performed .62 standard deviations worse on executive functioning tests (frontal lobe reactions) (A. B. Morgan & Lilienfeld, 2000; see also Warnken, Rosenbaum, Fletcher, Hoge, & Adelman, 1994).

*PET scans of batterers.* One investigation using *neuroimaging* (e.g., positron emission tomography—PET) enlisted a group of alcoholic batterers and two control groups, one of alcoholics (nonbattering) and one that consisted of nonalcoholic, nonbattering men. The PET scans revealed that the alcoholic batterers showed evidence of *decreased metabolism* in the right hypothalamus and reduced relationships between cortical/subcortical brain structures (G. T. George et al., 2004). Replication of brain scans, however, is obligatory because of the possibility of interpretations arising from methodological problems (see L. Sanders, 2009). Another breakthrough by a research team headed by psychiatrist Harold Koenigsberg (cited in Bower, 2009) has been the discovery of *unusual brain circuits* in some personality-disordered people. Individuals diagnosed with borderline personality disorder have brain circuits that foster *extreme emotional oversensitivity* and an inability to see that people have both positive and negative attributes. (See www.sagepub.com/barnett3e for addition examples of relevant physiological studies.)

## Personality Disorders

Personality disorders are "a group of disorders involving pervasive patterns of perceiving, relation to, and thinking about the environment and the self that interfere with long-term functioning of the individual and are not limited to isolated episodes" (VandenBos, 2007, p. 659). *Borderline personality disorder* refers to "a personality disorder characterized by a long-standing pattern of instability in mood, interpersonal relationships, and self-image that is severe enough to cause extreme distress or interfere with social and occupational functioning" (VandenBos, 2007, p. 130).

A variety of researchers have conceptualized borderline personality disorder differently, using various tests (e.g., the MMPI and MCMI) to assess these pathologies. From the very first, inventories of psychopathology showed that a subsample of male batterers are diagnosable with some form of disorder (e.g., Faulk, 1974). In a seminal study using the MCMI, investigators contrasted 43 nonviolent community volunteers with 78 alcoholic batterers and 47 nonalcoholic batterers. They were able to classify 88% of their batterer populations as suffering from some level of psychopathology, and they discerned several types of personality disorders: **passive dependent/compulsive**, **narcissistic/antisocial**, and **schizoidal/borderline** (Hamberger & Hastings, 1986; see also S. D. Hart, Dutton, & Newlove, 1993).

*Psychopathology (mental illness, "brain disorders") among batterers.* Psychopathology (mental illness) refers to patterns of behavior or thought processes that are distinctly abnormal or maladaptive. *Schizophrenia and bipolar disorders* are two examples of debilitating psychopathology. Because of a confluence of evidence from neuroimaging, genetics, and other biological sciences, these forms of mental illness are now designated as *brain disorders.* Scientists have made the name change because individuals diagnosed with psychopathology clearly suffer from brain and/or other physiological abnormalities. In addition, there is every reason to believe that mental illness exacerbates interpersonal conflicts and that relationship discord and mental disorders commonly co-occur (Denton & Brandon, 2007; see Silver, 2002). (See www.sage pub.com/barnett3e for additional information on criminal courts and the mentally ill.)

The extent to which batterers suffer from psychopathology has become another source of debate in the field. Professional practitioners and researchers have speculated from the beginning that a proportion of maritally violent men have some form of psychopathology. Others, especially feminists, have argued against this view on the grounds that attributions of mental illness serve as an *abuse excuse* for batterers ("Focus: Call for Help," 1994; see Dershowitz, 2000). They also express concern about attributing MFIPV to mental illness because it diminishes the role of patriarchy as the prime motivation for male aggression. Possibly, scientific practitioners and feminists are both right because a number of assessments of psychopathology have substantiated that about half the men classified as male IPV offenders test in the normal range (e.g., Chambers & Wilson, 2007). (See the website for more details on antisocial personality disorder.)

*Mentally ill and criminal MFIPV offenders.* Criminologist Eric Silver (2006) has pointed out that an individual can be either *mentally disordered, criminal,* or *both* (see also Hodgins, 2001). One cannot assume, therefore, that attenuating a person's mental illness alone will automatically curb his violence or criminal behavior (or marital violence). According to Silver's (2006) premise, reducing the psychopathology of male perpetrators will not inevitably eliminate their violent partner abuse. Much more research is needed in this area. Research efforts should focus on understanding the risk factors for both psychopathology and criminality. (See Teasdale, Silver, & Monahan, 2006, for a study about violence as a coping strategy.)

## Similarities and Differences Between Partner-Violent-Only Men and Other Violent Men

Advances in knowledge highlighted the shortsightedness of conceptualizing abusers as a homogeneous group. It has become clear, for example, that not every wife assaulter grew up in a violent home or has problems with unemployment. Consequently, researchers devised alternative methods for understanding wife assault. They began looking for subgroups of violent men. More specifically, questions have arisen about how partner-violent-only men compare with generally violent men. Generally violent men are violent toward many people, not only their female partners, but other family members, acquaintances, and strangers. These are the group of men commonly thought of as criminal. The question of most interest is whether it is possible and useful to classify violent men into subgroups that are separate, yet exhibit some continuities.

*Differences in targets (victims).* Several early investigations determined that maritally violent men were truly generally violent. In an evaluation based on interviews with female victims, almost half of all spouse abusers had been arrested previously for other violence (Fagan, Stewart, & Hansen, 1983; see also Dunford, Huizinga, & Elliott, 1990; Gondolf, 1999; Keilitz, Davis, & Eikeman, 1998). Using data from 2,291 males included in the National Family Violence Survey-2, Kandel-Englander (1992) identified 311 men (15%) who had been violent during the previous 12-month period. From the violent group, 208 (67%) had been violent only toward their wives, 71 (23%) had been violent only toward persons outside their families, and 32 (10%) had been violent toward both wives and nonfamily individuals. Thus the selection of the target (assaulted person) clearly differentiated these groups.

*Social and behavioral differences.* Other research sought to unravel social/behavioral dissimilarities between subsamples of violent men. One study found that men charged with domestic homicide experienced more behavioral problems in childhood (e.g., truancy) than did men charged with nondomestic homicide. Nonetheless, both groups were more likely than nonviolent men to have disturbed childhoods, such as a missing parent (Anasseril & Holcomb, 1985). Finally, men who are severely violent differed from less violent men on some dimensions, such as drug usage, unemployment, range of deviant acts, and psychopathology (D. S. Elliott, 1994; Huss & Langhinrichsen-Rohling, 2000; Loeber & Farrington, 1997). Some argue that the most dangerous wife assaulters are very likely to be generally violent men who have prior arrest records. Personal characteristics of these offenders, such as pernicious drug use and impulsive rages, render them practically unfazed by arrest (Buzawa & Buzawa, 2003; see also Brookman & Maguire, 2005). (See www.sagepub.com/barnett3e for a comparison of IPV and non-IPV offenders on probation.)

## Typologies of Male (MFIPV) Perpetrators

There are different ways of separating the causes of male partner violence into groups. Isolating commonalities among abusers initially provided a basis for intervention, but it concomitantly postponed recognition of their heterogeneity. As research advanced, it became clear that individuals involved in partner violence are not identical. Some experts began to propose that subgroups of perpetrators existed within the larger classification of violent IPV offenders.

Most important, typology research held the promise of providing keys to achieving more effective treatment for an individual or couples involved in partner aggression. Presumably, therapists could match treatments to the specific needs of subgroups of individuals who are similar in order to enhance treatment effectiveness (**responsivity principle**). Researchers have made relatively rapid advances in this area of inquiry. In fact, a consensus about which types exist empirically and about the terminology enlisted to designate them is on the horizon. This section includes descriptions of some typologies of male perpetrators.

*Holtzman-Munroe and Stuart typology study (1994).* Although not the first to call attention to the heterogeneity of male offenders, Holtzworth-Munroe and her colleagues have been the primary researchers to successfully develop empirically based subtypes of male aggressors. These researchers undertook an industrious series of research projects to search for types of male IPV perpetrators among samples of violent and nonviolent men. They first constructed a theoretical prototype of violent men using both rational/**deductive** and empirical/**inductive** concepts culled from the literature. This work yielded three major descriptive dimensions: (a) *severity of violence,* (b) *generality of violence,* and (c) *psychopathology.* On the basis of previous research findings, they hypothesized that MFIPV perpetrators could be classified into three subtypes: (a) FAMILY ONLY (FO—low level of violence, little pathology, and little violence outside the family), (b) BORDERLINE/DYSPHORIC (BD—unwell, unhappy/normality mixed with abnormality), and (c) GENERALLY VIOLENT/ANTISOCIAL (GVA—violent/little sense of responsibility, morality, concern for others). Next, they speculated how important variables, such as *attachment and skill deficits,* might be associated with the three purported groups.

Later, Holtzworth-Munroe, Meehan et al. (2000) tested this theoretical typology (FO, BD, GVA) using 102 violent and nonviolent *community volunteers.* In this highly scientific demonstration, the researchers used an extremely large number of measures, several compiled from both the husband's and wife's responses about the husband's violence. The three broad measures included items and scales from many inventories including the following: (a) CTS 2—level and severity of violence; (b) generality of violence (GVQ; experimenter-designed); and (c) MCMI-III (Choca & Van Denburg, 1997; Millon, 1983) measures of antisocial and borderline/dysphoric disorder (i.e., especially fear of abandonment). These data underwent **cluster analysis** to establish subtypes. The results confirmed the three subtypes, but unexpectedly detected a fourth subtype, low-level antisocial (LLA). Although a majority of researchers value representative samples, some have questioned whether typologies based on *community samples* are applicable to *clinical samples.* Hence, the continuing problem of definitions comes to the fore. (See www.sagepub.com/barnett3e for a listing of some of the tests and a modified table for a summary of the subtypes accompanied by their related characteristics.)

*Sexually violent–only men?* Over the years, academicians have been uncertain whether a sexually violent–only group of men existed. After Holtzworth-Munroe, Meehan et al.'s (2000) typology work, A. D. Marshall and Holtzworth-Munroe (2002) investigated whether any men in their samples could be classed as sexually violent only. In the first sample, they identified only 3 of 105 men as sexually abusive only, and these men came from the "nonviolent" comparison sample. In the second sample, they found two outcomes: (a) Men in the more severely partner-violent group engaged primarily in sexual coercion, and (b) Men in the generally violent/antisocial group engaged more frequently in threatened/forced sex rather than sexual coercion (see also Raghavan, Swan, Snow, & Mazure, 2005).

*Testing Holtzworth-Munroe and Stuart's study.* In a 2003 review of all typology research to that date (9 studies), researchers found evidence *converging* with Holtzworth-Munroe and Stuart's (1994) three-dimensional model of male perpetrators (Dixon & Browne, 2003). Despite the general corroboration of the model, some discrepancies came to light. As an example, one replication detected no significant differences between groups on family-of-origin violence (Lawson et al., 2003; see also Huss & Langhinrichsen-Rohling, 2006; Waltz, Babcock, Jacobson, & Gottman, 2000). (See www.sagepub.com/barnett3e for descriptions of several other typologies.)

*Evaluating typologies.* As research on typologies continues, experts have made additional criticisms and proposals. One research has proposed the need to focus more heavily on anger (Prentky, 2004). Another recommended including race, socioeconomic status, educational level, employment, or occupational status as potential differentiating variables (Gondolf, 1999). Some experts judged statistical approaches as inadequate (e.g., Saunders, 2004; Widiger & Mullins-Sweatt, 2004). On the basis of a **cluster analysis** of behavior-based measures, other scholars have recently grouped data from 671 male batterers into three types: (a) 25.6% low-level criminality, (b) 42.2% **dysphoric** (i.e., sad mood, restless volatile behavior); and (c) 32.2% dysphoric general violence (Stoops, Bennett, & Vincent, 2010). Finally, other scholars suggested expanding the idea of typologies to other areas of marital violence, such as to child abusers or to responses of IPV victims (e.g., Cavanaugh & Gelles, 2005). Already, Hamberger and Guse (2005) have categorized *spouses' responses* to batterers.

---

**SECTION SUMMARY**

### Becoming and Remaining a Batterer: Causes of MFIPV

In terms of socialization, it is clear that there are strong links between childhood exposure to violence in the home and later partner violence. Violent men (and possibly women) are apt to come from *dysfunctional homes* typified by *parental abuse, alcoholism,* and *psychopathology.* Newer research has been successful in illuminating how other childhood experiences, such as being *anxiously attached,* are associated with male partner violence. Abusive male-to-female perpetrators' fears of abandonment are excessive.

*(Continued)*

(Continued)

Male *gender socialization* has been another focal point of investigation as an anteced-ent of male partner violence. First, society generally requires men to display aggression. Some men seem to learn that women are opportune targets for their violence. Although attitude measurements have not revealed a large number of significant differences in attitudes between partner-violent and partner-nonviolent men, they have discerned a relation-ship between *exploitive/manipulative sexual beliefs* and male partner violence. *Approval of aggression* is also linked with male partner violence. Verbal skills/communication deficits are apparent in male offenders.

Research on relationship factors has frequently shown that lack of verbal skills, stress, interpersonal control issues, jealousy, and lack of trust are related to partner violence. Male partner abusers appear to be insufficiently assertive in communications and display considerable negative affect (i.e., emotional reactions) during conflictual conversations. They have inadequate problem-solving skills and consequently may become embroiled in considerable relational conflict. They frequently express feelings of "getting a raw deal," and often misperceive their partners' intentions.

The role of alcohol or drugs in male violence toward partners is clear in some respects but not others. Excessive drinking is associated with more frequent and severe male IPV. Two sets of researchers describe the alcohol/drug problem—male-to-female intimate partner abuse relationship as direct. That is, alcohol or drug misuse can be a cause of male partner violence, but a third study did not find a direct link. Reasons for the lack of clarity are that batterers perpetrate IPV whether they are drunk or not. Perhaps the association can be explained by the use of a mediator, such as antisocial personality disorder (alcohol/drug misuse → antisocial personality disorder → male partner violence). Another mediator seems to be impulsivity (childhood abuse → impulsivity → alcohol/drug misuse → male-to-female partner abuse). Alcohol/drug problems also discriminate between subtypes of batterers. Race is yet another differentiating variable in the alcohol/drug—male partner abuse link.

Practitioners have long hypothesized that stress was a precursor to male-to-female intimate partner violence, and research has validated this perception. Batterers expe-rience high levels of stress, particularly in terms of reactions to their female partners. Some argue that batterers are more vulnerable to stress because of childhood abuse. Events such as unemployment also cause stress that becomes focused on female part-ners. A path analysis specified an indirect association between stress and MFIPV. (stress → anger → male IPV). An additional and newer conception of stress is termed *mas-culine gender-role stress (*e.g., physical inadequacy, performance failure). Masculine gender-role stress is an explicit type of stress linked with male partner violence. Of substantial interest is the finding that specific subcomponents of male gender-role stress are correlated with specific CTS2 subscales

Several biological elements of maleness and individual defects may exacerbate part-ner violence. It is conceivable that male hormones make a nuanced contribution to aggression. The major male hormone, *testosterone,* is significantly but weakly correlated with aggression. Social factors **moderate** testosterone's effects. Serotonin, a neural trans-mitter with calming effects, appears to be at lower levels in partner-abusive men, possibly leading to lowering the ability to tolerate frustration. Head trauma and various brain dysfunctions, observed more frequently in abusive men than in nonabusive men in some samples, also seem to influence aggression. This kind of research has suggested the need for a *biosocial model of aggression.*

The biological research on emotions and mood states is shedding some light on individual differences in biological anomalies underlying some behavioral symptoms, such as anxiety. Traumatized persons have a number of emotional reactions such as fear to certain stimuli that can last a lifetime, as evidenced in PTSD symptoms (flashback, startle reactions, trouble concentrating, etc.). Partner-violent males also have relatively high levels of PTSD, probably stemming from parental mistreatment. Evolutionary theories propose that men's violence and jealous mate-guarding has a biological basis, rather than being a legacy of learned behaviors. Studies using specific tests of jealousy indicate that partner-abusive men suffer from high levels of jealousy.

Genetic studies demonstrate that criminal behavior, mental illness, and personality disorders have a genetic component. It is believable that male aggressors have inherited unfavorable *genetic predispositions* for these disorders. Various sources of information, family of origin violence, assessment of biological traits, personality tests, and inventories of psychopathology all implicate antisocial personality disorder, borderline personality organization, and borderline disorders as the constellation of traits most typical of men who aggress against their partners.

It now seems clear that male partner offenders are a heterogeneous group differing along many personality and psychopathology dimensions. Although incomplete, available information has shown that subsamples of violent men (violent toward family only, toward nonfamily only, or toward both family and nonfamily) vary in important ways but also share some important attributes (e.g., disturbed childhoods). These men may range on a continuum extending from partner-only violent men, who select primarily their female partners as targets, to men who are assaultive toward a broad range of family and nonfamily individuals. It has become possible to categorize violent men into subgroups that have distinctive qualities (i.e., typologies), although the distribution of types varies by sample.

# FEMALE-TO-MALE INTIMATE PARTNER ABUSE (FMIPV)

### CASE HISTORY   Zaida and Kumar—"I Just Bopped Him One"

Zaida was one of three women arrested in one jurisdiction over a year's time for female-to-male partner violence and diverted into a counseling program. All other members of the group were men. Zaida was 57 years old and had been married for 35 years. She worked in a factory and admitted having a problem with alcohol. She looked haggard and perhaps unwell.

The evening that she completed her 26 sessions in the program, she finally opened up about her reasons for hitting Kumar. He seldom talked to her, she complained, and she was "damned mad about it." When she came home from work and saw Kumar drinking a beer in front of the

TV, she often greeted him with a question, such as "What's for supper?" If she didn't like his answer, she just "bopped him one on the head." If she got "really pissed off," she grabbed his beer and threw it on the floor. Kumar never defended himself even once, but if she socked him, he would not speak to her the rest of the evening.

The group therapist tactfully pointed out that he "thought he saw a connection" between Zaida's assaults and Kumar's refusal to speak to her. Zaida was stunned into silence, but she listened attentively as men in the group commented. The men told her that Kumar probably would talk to her if he didn't have to worry about getting socked. Zaida was thoughtful but said nothing more until the final good-byes. As she proudly marched off, she told the group members that they would never see her again, and they didn't.

It is difficult to say how typical Zaida's FMIPV assaultive case is. Her behavior and that of some other women, nonetheless, has made it abundantly clear that men are *not* the sole perpetrators of intimate violence. There are some women who abuse men, and a rare few who even kill their male partners. Much more research is needed before investigators will know if female-to-male intimate partner abusers are a homogenous or heterogeneous group. The scarcity of empirical data available, coupled with the belief that much of women's interpersonal violence is self-defensive (violent resistance), has initially created a state of ambiguity about the nature of female abuse.

Researchers have attempted *to study female partner aggression using* the same variables and the same methodologies as they used in examining MFIPV. In the last decade, scholarship about abusive females has mushroomed, yet knowledge and understanding of women's violence remains insufficient, simplistic, and controversial. To offset these quandaries, one duo of academicians developed an interpretive framework for explaining female IPV offenders (Swan & Snow, 2006). Their premise is that to understand female violence, academicians must take into account a host of variables: (a) female victimization, (b) motivations for FMIPV, (c) coping style used to counter male partner abuse, (d) childhood traumas, (e) outcomes of male partner violence (e.g., PTSD, substance abuse), (f) the broader sociocultural and historical context, and (g) the **intersectionality** of gender, race, and class.

## Self-Defensive Female Violence (Violent Resistance, VR)

With the recognition that female violence is a reality, researchers initially emphasized its *self-defensive nature* (Cascardi, Langhinrichsen-Rohling, & Vivian, 1992; Hamberger & Potente, 1994; Saunders, 1995). A unanimity of empirical evidence has, in fact, validated the claim that much of FMIPV is self-defensive. Women are very often reacting to what is being done to them, rather than initiating confrontations (Melton & Belknap, 2003; Seamans, Rubin, & Stabb, 2007). In M. P. Johnson's (2000) four-group classification of intimate partner violence described previously, 80% of female perpetrators asserted that they were reacting to ongoing male abuse. Johnson classified these women as *violent resisters (VR)*. Another researcher/practitioner reported that nearly 60% of women who provided attributions for their female aggression against men cited self-defense (Hamberger, 1997). In yet another account of men court-ordered into treatment, their female partners attributed 66% of their own female partner aggression as aggression in self-defense and 22% to fear (Gondolf, 1998). As a side note, one study found that prior sexual abuse was the *only* predictor of using self-defense against a male partner (Kernsmith, 2005a).

It is difficult, however, to interpret the data gathered to assess self-defensive aggression, because the definition of self-defense may be too narrow. Partner-assaultive persons do not necessarily base their self-reports of self-defense on the customary specification of the sequence of the violent events, that is who hits first, or on the measurement of other background factors (e.g., Barnett et al., 1997; Browne, Salomon, & Bassuk, 1999; Hamberger & Arnold, 1991). Instead, victims of MFIPV often factor into their meaning of self-defense, a *pre-emptive* strike to ward off impending harm or to minimize potential harm (Kernsmith, 2005a).

---

**CASE HISTORY**   Mark and Cheryl—Running for Our Lives

Mark suddenly jumped on me from behind, knocking me to the living room floor. He started choking me and calling me a bitch. Then he forced sex on me right in front of our 12-year-old son, Danny. Danny grabbed the poker near the fireplace and hit his dad on the head, stunning him. I got up and hit Mark on the head as hard as I could with a dining room chair. Then I began to kick him as hard as I could anywhere that I could. I knew he would come after me again when he came to, so I grabbed Danny with one hand and my purse with the other and we ran for our lives.

---

The preceding case history exemplifies one type of female violence and highlights the problems of classifying this behavior. To what extent should society and family violence experts classify Cheryl's actions as self-defensive, retaliatory, or mutual IPV? Is her behavior typical of battered women? Is "a slap is a slap is a slap" true no matter who does the slapping (McHugh, Livingston, & Ford, 2005, p. 323)? If not, why not? Should women who use violence against their male partners be termed "batterers" (Saunders, 2002)?

## Motives for FMIPV

Over time, it has become clear that self-defense could not account for all of women's female-to-male intimate partner violence. Rather, there seemed to be a group of women who appeared to be as aggressive as their male counterparts. An insightful finding is that the higher women's status in a society and the greater the amount of individualism allowed, the higher the rate of female-to-male IPV. As women become more emancipated, they perpetrate more violence against men (Archer, 2006). Although it is unclear whether designating these women as female batterers is warranted, it is fair to say that some women are the *primary aggressors.* It is also fair to say that identification of these women is not an artifact of measurement. The extent to which female perpetrators are comparable to male perpetrators is very much the focus of current research.

Social scientists began examining motivations other than self-defense for female partner abuse by using comparative paradigms, such as (a) female abuse contrasted with male abuse, and (b) MFIPV *victims* with female nonvictims. There are a number of other motives, such as demanding attention, escaping abuse, and punishing the abuser (Dasgupta, 2002; Hamberger 1994, 1997; see also Barnett, Martinez, & Bluestein, 1995). In a different inquiry, female aggressors endorsed various reasons for their violence from a list of 29 possible rationales (Stuart et al., 2006). In a different inquiry, a factor analytic approach, investigators identified seven motive factors among four groups of women who varied in the severity of female-to-male violence from none to severe. The researchers did not use CTS but made use of L. L. Marshall's (1992a) Severity of Violence Against Women Scales (Weston, Marshall & Coker, 2007). See Table 9.5 for the reasons for the women's violence provided by the Stuart et al. (2006) study and the Weston, Marshall, & Coker, (2007) factor analysis.

**TABLE 9.5**   Motivation for Female-to-Male Intimate Partner Violence

| Stuart et al. (2006) Study [Six Motives] (N = 87) | Weston et al. (2007) Study [eight motives] (N = 580) |
|---|---|
| 38.9% – partner provoked the violence | Partner's negative behaviors |
| 38.0% – self-defense | To increase intimacy |
| 36.5% – stress | My own personal problems |
| 35.3% – retaliation for emotional abuse | Retaliation |
| 28.0% – to show feelings hard to explain in words | My childhood experiences |
| 26.1% – to feel more powerful | The situation/mood |
| | Partner's personal problems |
| | Self-defense |

*Anger among female offenders.* The literature contains very little experimental data concerning anger among female *perpetrators* other than as a motive for aggressive behavior. Most of the research on anger focuses on the anger response among female *victims.* Generally speaking, society considers anger to be unfeminine (Gilligan, 1990). Anger, nevertheless, can serve as a motive for female partner abuse (Kosslyn et al., 2002). In a path analysis, anger was significantly correlated with FMIPV, but in a separate model with numerous other variables, anger dropped out of the model (K. D. O'Leary et al., 2007).

*Violence of battered female victims.* A study using a different methodology also found that the violence of female *victims* included variables beyond self-defense or retaliation. In this appraisal, investigators recruited women *incarcerated* for *violent crimes* to serve as research participants. Using a *life-events calendar research methodology,* they examined data drawn from 106 incidents of violence that occurred 36 months prior to incarceration. Some of the women's actions were reactions to perceived *threats to their status* as *good mothers* or *faithful partners.* The *motives* for much female abuse were *jealousy, male violence by the male victim,* and *mutual violence.* FMIPV perpetrators frequently directed their violence at either the men they thought were unfaithful or at other women deemed threatening to their relationships (Kruttschnitt & Carbone-Lopez, 2006).

*Female-to-male partner control.* The evidence for *partner-control* behaviors as a motive for female partner violence has been mixed. In one inquiry, female aggression did not appear to be a true female power strategy but a *reaction* to male batterers. Furthermore, women's use of violence did not succeed in expanding the women's decision-making power (Frieze & McHugh, 1992; see also Hamberger, 2005). Another investigation, however, found that women's controlling behaviors were significantly correlated with both male violence and their own violence (Graham-Kevan & Archer, 2005; see also K. D. O'Leary et al., 2007; Swan, Gambone, Caldwell, Sullivan, & Snow, 2008).

## Correlates of Female-to-Male IPV

A number of associations between female-to-male intimate partner violence have emerged from data analyses.

*Childhood abuse and later perpetration of FMIPV.* Several studies have found a significant relationship between childhood maltreatment and female IPV perpetration (J. A. Siegel, 2000; T. P. Sullivan et al., 2005; Swan & Snow, 2006). J. Miller (2006) believes that her analyses, based on the National Violence Against Women Survey (Tjaden & Thoennes, 1999) data, allow the inference that childhood abuse helps explain not only women's *perpetration* of female aggression but also its *severity* (see also Weston et al., 2007). In two other accounts, correlational data revealed positive associations between child abuse and women's partner violence, but *not* women's victimization by male batterers (T. P. Sullivan et al., 2005; Swan et al., 2005). Both *exposure to parental IPV* and *power-assertive punishment* were significantly and independently linked with perpetration of adult female assaults. In addition, childhood socialization factors increased the risk of *antisocial personality disorder,* which, in turn, elevated the odds of adult female partner violence (Ehrensaft et al., 2006). A unique investigation revealed that women's unfortunate childhood environments tended to be *repeated* in adulthood, including poverty, substance abuse, early parenting, single marital status, and various types of mental illness. These findings, taken together with previous research, suggest that *stress* generated from negative life events contributes to FMIPV. (Dowd, Leisring, & Rosenbaum, 2005). Note that in Table 9.6, "fearing harm" evoked the largest percentage of FMIPV.

**TABLE 9.6**　Three Types of Behavioral Categories of Female-to-Male Intimate Partner Violence

| Generalized Violence—5% | Frustration Response—30% | Defensive Behavior—65% |
|---|---|---|
| Assaulted family member and others in many situations | Response to stress | When feared harm to self or children |
| Not similar to male batterers | | |
| Did not gain control | | |
| Did not induce fear | | |

As representative of defensive behavior, one woman jumped in her car *after* being assaulted by her partner. After numerous attempts to drive off while her partner tried to break in through a car window, the woman pinned her partner against the garage door with the car. The police arrested *her* for assault with a deadly weapon.

*Jealousy and FMIPV.* There is some scholarship suggesting that jealousy may be more troublesome for women than men in the *general* population: (a) Women may be equally or even more concerned about sexual infidelity than men; (b) Women are more likely than men to try purposely to evoke jealousy in their partner; (c) Women rated both their levels of reactive and anxious jealousy higher than men did and tended to rate themselves higher on possessive jealousy as well; (d) Women were more likely than men to compare themselves with other same-sex persons in terms of a rival's jealousy-evoking traits; and (e) Women rated physical attractiveness of a rival as more jealousy-evocative than men did (e.g., Dijkstra & Buunk, 2002; Puente & Cohen, 2003). Several others studies of female offenders established that these women are especially jealous and appear to be more jealous and untrusting than nonviolent women (Goldenson et al., 2007). The most conclusive finding to date revealed that a combined *dominance/jealousy score* is one of the *strongest predictors* of both male and female *aggression* (O'Leary et al., 2007).

*Powerlessness.* In the Caetano et al. (2008) research described above, females in both the *perpetrator-only* and *mutually violent groups* reported more powerlessness than partner-nonviolent women. This kind of research needs replication when a more robust measure becomes available.

*Suicide/depression.* Some evidence suggests that female perpetrators are at greater risk for suicide than are male perpetrators (Henning et al., 2003), and one study has, in fact, shown a link between FMIPV and depression (Vaeth, Ramisetty-Mikler, & Caetano, 2010). Several studies, however, have *not* found that depression is linked with female perpetration (Swan, Gambone, Fields et al., 2005; see also Lewis, Griffing et al., 2006). A possibility is that perpetrating violence against one's male partner offsets feelings of depression.

*Attachment styles.* As discussed above, females' anxious attachment, and the interaction between male avoidance and female anxious attachment patterns, predicted IPV for both men and women (Doumas et al., 2008).

# Battered Women Who Kill

When women kill, they most often kill male intimates. In many cases, these women are female victims. In situations where battered women have killed their abusers to stop the violence (i.e., self-defense), their own use of violence has necessarily become the paramount issue (e.g., Cazenave & Zahn, 1992; Mouradian, 2001).

*The battered woman syndrome.* During the 1980s, feminist clinicians began to claim that battered women often suffer from a trauma-induced condition they labeled **battered woman syndrome,** a subcategory of PTSD (L. E. Walker, 1983; 1991). The noncontingent, uncontrollable, cyclical nature of a perpetrator's violence creates a condition of *learned helplessness* in the female victim. Victims may become so overwhelmed by fear, feelings of helplessness, and stress symptoms, **coupled with a belief that there is** *no other way to escape,* **that they resort to killing their abuser. These women nearly always kill out of fear for their own life and/or for their children's safety (Melbin, Sullivan, & Cain, 2003; Walker, 1993; Wells & DeLeon-Granados, 2005). Essentially, the battered woman syndrome model expands the concept of legal self-defense to take into account the state of mind of a battered woman who kills. (See www.sagepub.com/barnett3e for a discussion of the mental state of battered women who kill, the case history of Francine Hughes, and for information on battered woman syndrome and the court.)

## SECTION SUMMARY

### Female-to-Male Intimate Partner Violence

The acceptance of females as partner aggressors has gained more traction, but little information about this subgroup of abusers is available. The lack of knowledge about female partner abuse has led to overly simplistic explanations. It is probable that women's violence toward male intimates has not as yet reached the level of a social problem. Two reasons are that women are far more injured than men, and much of women's IPV is actually self-defensive, a type of violent resistance. Research results have indicated a number of *motives for women's violence against men,* other than self-defense, such as feelings provoked by her partner, stress, retaliation, and problems associated with childhood experiences. Anger and control may also function as motives. A prison study demonstrated that motives for female partner violence included negative attributions about their skills as a mother, ascriptions of infidelity, and jealousy.

Some researchers have also examined traits of violent women, and some have attempted to classify female offenders into a typology. A few identified traits are jealousy, dominance/jealousy, feelings of powerlessness, and anxious attachment. Finally, some women actually kill their partners. Such events occur almost totally in situations in which the woman has been battered for a long period of time and has developed battered woman syndrome. Battered woman syndrome is a learned helplessness and/or PTSD-driven state of mind borne out of intense fear. When such a woman perceives there is no escape, she may resort to murder.

1. Discuss at least three different types of definitions of partner violence.

2. Describe sources of information for partner violence.

3. Discuss when it might be advisable to use either a broad or narrow definition of sexual assault.

4. List and explain why several types of behavior might be considered psychological abuse. Give an example from your own life or that of a friend's.

5. Discuss blame. Evaluate how it affects battered women and partner violent men.

6. Discuss Michael Johnson's four-category classification of "violent couples."

7. Discuss traits and typologies of batterers. Why is this information useful?

8. Discuss evidence for jealousy among partner-violent men and women.

9. Discuss childhood learning and how it impacts violent adult behavior toward partners.

10. Discuss the relationship between alcohol problems and IPV for both men and women.

11. Discuss what evidence there is for genetic causation of IPV.

12. List several personality disorders and explain how one of them is related to IPV.

13. Discuss what is known about female partner abuse offenders. Compare and contrast differences with male offenders.

For chapter-specific resources including audio and video links, SAGE research articles, additional case studies, and more, please visit www.sagepub.com/barnett3e.

# 10

# Abused and Abusive Partners in Understudied Populations

## Cross-Cultural, Immigrant/Ethnic/Racial, Rural, Same-Sex, and Military Groups

Over the years, several groups of people have received much less research and policy attention compared with the dominant Anglo-Saxon group in the United States. Racism, xenophobia, classism, language barriers, cultural beliefs, and other factors have combined to render intimate partner violence (IPV) invisible in certain segments of the American population. Included in this chapter is introductory information about partner abuse among the following groups: *cross-cultural, immigrant/ethnic/racial minority, rural, same-sex,* and *military personnel.* To obtain more knowledge of minority group IPV, the U.S. Congress has addressed the issue legislatively through the Violence Against Women Act (VAWA) of 1994 and its reauthorizations (Violence Against Women Office, 2000, 2005). These laws, initially focused on *traditional* American women, have expanded to assess partner violence in marginalized groups.

One intriguing contribution of research beyond the borders of the United States is the multiplicity of definitions of partner abuse. These definitions greatly affect individuals' judgments of whether certain actions constitute partner abuse (Caetano, Ramisetty-Mikler, & McGrath, 2004; Tang, Cheung, Chen, & Sun, 2002). If a woman believes a husband has a right to slap her for leaving the house without his permission, she will not define the slap as a form of male partner violence. In parallel fashion, definitions affect legislation and treatment. Differing definitions of male partner violence provide comparative information that broadens perspectives. As has been noted in U.S. research, many heterosexual European American individuals do not recognize they are being abused, and the same is true of persons living in other countries or of persons belonging to understudied populations (Distefano, 2009; Hammond & Calhoun, 2007). For a comprehensive discussion of definitions across cultures, see Malley-Morrison and Hines (2004).

The concept of **intersectionality** has special utility in the discussion of understudied populations. Intersectionality refers to the intersection (place of meeting) of important sociodemographic variables that influence behavior, such as gender, race, and class. One goal of intersectionality is to improve the understanding of certain marginalized groups such as African American women or Asian immigrants (Mahalingam, Balan, & Haritatos, 2008; Sokoloff & Dupont, 2005). As an example, one intersectional analysis explored IPV among *Japanese sexual minorities.* Race, male, gender, sexual orientation, and partner abuse status intersect to produce a subgroup of men that potentially has unique characteristics (Distefano, 2009). See the following case history that depicts an intersection between culture, age, gender, and sexual orientation.

**CASE HISTORY**   "Let's Rape Her 'Til She's Normal"

In Zimbabwe, a teenage girl was repeatedly raped by an older man—a violation mandated by her parents to "correct" her lesbianism: "They locked me up in a room and brought him in every-day to rape me so I would fall pregnant and be forced to marry him. They did this to me until I was pregnant." (Amnesty International, n.d.)

The first section of this chapter presents a brief overview of *cross-cultural research on intimate partner abuse.* For the most part, recognition of male-to-female IPV as a social problem in other countries has lagged behind recognition in the United States. The Japanese, for instance, did not officially acknowledge male battering until 1992 (Yoshihama, 2002). Research in these nations currently follows a similar path. After conducting national surveys to obtain information about violence against women (VAW), surveyors may go on to determine how much of the violence represents men's abuse of their female partners. At this time, not all published research disaggregates the details of *intimate partner violence* from the entirety of VAW. Along the same vein, researchers may combine intimate violence with intimate sexual assault or present data on intimate partner homicides.

## CROSS-CULTURAL INTIMATE PARTNER VIOLENCE

Violence against women stretches across the globe and has existed throughout history. Entire cultures permit or encourage violence against women. Most of the scholarship on male-to-female IPV is secondary to the overarching problem of the universal violence against women. Cross-cultural studies not only illuminate the terrible atrocities practiced against women, but they also show how male domination can affect every aspect of women's lives, robbing them of their personhood from cradle to grave.

In more recent times, the devaluation of women and the rampant violence perpetrated against them has emerged as an international *human rights* issue that demands redress (Levesque, 2001). Organizations such as Amnesty International and the World Health Organization (WHO) have undertaken surveys documenting the general violence against women and the more specific male-to-female intimate partner violence. While Amnesty International focuses upon the human rights aspect of the violence, WHO focuses upon the multiplicity of health problems caused by male violence against women, such as disability and even death (Diop-Sidibe, Campbell, & Becker, 2006; Neieren & Schel, 2008). Poor reproductive and mental health consequences are obvious. Other extremely serious health problems, such as the spread of HIV infection through forced sex, constitute another kind of scourge (e.g., Suffla, Van Niekerk, & Arendse, 2008).

In 48 population-based studies, 10% to 69% of women reported that they had been physically assaulted by an intimate partner (Heise, Ellsberg, & Gottemoeller, 1999). A multi-country assessment of interpersonal violence in 35 countries prior to 1999 reported that 10% to 52% of women had been physically abused by an intimate partner at some point in their lives. The range for marital rape was 10% to 30% (World Health Organization, 1997). Such overwhelming evidence of male-to-female violence has strongly factored into the conceptualization of intimate partner violence as an outgrowth of patriarchy.

Bias against women comes to light in an entire array of exaggerated and false beliefs, many of which reflect the misinterpretation of religious doctrines. Although all the major religions support male dominance, they commonly espouse *peace* toward men (and women) and *harmony* in living. When deluded clerics endorse an extreme view of male-female relationships, such as men have the right to "punish" women, their admonitions place women in great jeopardy (Erwin, 2006). As religious doctrines become integrated into mainstream thinking, they become part of the cultural mores that direct gender-based behavior.

Despite the distressing nature of the information emanating from cross-cultural studies, the research has illuminated and broadened the whole field of family violence. A particularly valuable contribution has been the promulgation of *explanatory frameworks* (e.g., patriarchal beliefs). Another is to use the new strategy of mapping (locating) brain areas where neural activation diverges between cultures. As one example, Westerners tend to look at an *object* in a box (activating one area of the brain), while East Asians tend to focus on *contextual* information (activating a different area of the brain) (Ambody & Bharucha, 2009). Although the attitudes underlying woman abuse are often similar across countries and the correlates of male partner violence overlapping, some types of abuse are more prevalent or even unique to a particular region of the world. One disheartening finding is that women tutored in the mores of their culture are just as likely as, or more so than men, to approve of bias against women.

One insightful admonition centers on social scientists trying to understand another culture to achieve *cultural competence*. They should *not* assume that individuals living in the same culture are uniformly indoctrinated into the mores of that culture. Many distinct subgroups continue living side by side, not to mention differences among individuals within a community. Cultures are not as stable over time as common definitions imply. As an illustration, the global economic structure is bringing many changes. To view information about a culture as a "packaged picture" obscures the ongoing changes. For an alternative view on assessing the attitudes and behaviors of people in other cultures, see the box on cultural relativism.

## BOX 10.1 Cultural Relativism

It may seem obvious that domestic abuse is a serious problem that must be stopped no matter where it occurs and no matter who perpetrates it, but this is only one perspective. From a different point of view, sociologists, anthropologists, political theorists, and philosophers all argue that an equally important issue concerns how cultures can best relate to each other. People should be extremely aware of how they affect foreign cultures. More directly, cultures must be on guard not to disrupt others' ways of life simply because these ways are distinct from their own. As the world continues to become more and more diverse, the need for respect and tolerance grows in equal part. A society cannot intrude on another simply because it has different attitudes and practices about marriage, child rearing, and education.

What an American feminist calls "abuse," an Asian male may call "teaching a woman how to be a wife." These academics argue that there is no unbiased way of deciding that one is right and another wrong.

Intuitions of this type are grouped together as the doctrine of cultural relativism. Formally, *cultural relativism is the position that one culture cannot justifiably judge the practices of another culture.* Evaluating other cultures is, indeed, not the right way for cultures to relate to each other. One cannot plausibly hold judgments about the habits, customs, and laws of a culture to which one does not belong. According to a relativist, such judgments are lacking in authority. A person's judgments are tied to a specific set of circumstances, and they can only make sense within those circumstances. In some fundamental and ultimate way, for example, a Scandinavian and Haitian do not and could never fully understand each other. They lack some crucial common ground. The Scandinavian has a different set of experiences that qualifies him to know about and to judge that set of experiences and that set of experiences only—likewise with the Haitian. Because of this fundamental truth, cultures, particularly Western ones, should decrease their tendency to judge practices other than their own. Otherwise, cultures run the risk of making serious and destructive mistakes, to which the history of imperialism, ethnocentrism, and racism can all attest.

Relativism is an old idea that dates back thousands of years, but it came into prominence in the twentieth century with considerable vigor and force. Relativism was reformulated and given a new sense of urgency with the work of cultural anthropologists such as Franz Boas and Melville Herskovits. As these anthropologists studied exotic cultures, their exposure led them to appreciate and better understand the diversity and variety among cultures. From their ethnographic research, they concluded that there could never be an authoritative *universal standard* for judging other cultures. Some people raise their family this way, and some do it that way—and on and on. It is futile at best and dangerous at worst to promote the idea of a universal standard.

The intersection between cultural relativism and family violence is obvious. The question is: Are domestic violence researchers and anti-abuse advocates misguided when studying and campaigning against the abuse that occurs in other countries? Should researchers refrain from such study? Should advocates worry only about their own culture? Are organizations like Amnesty International, the United Nations, and the World Health Organization overstepping some boundary? If they are, then any international attempt to litigate and regulate intimate partner violence would be a farce. If it is true that a Scandinavian cannot judge or understand a Haitian, then certainly a Scandinavian psychologist cannot fairly judge or understand the spousal interactions taking place in a Haitian marriage.

Far from being an abstract philosophical idea with no implications for real life, cultural relativism directly relates to the cross-cultural study of domestic violence. What exactly is the best way for someone to study the intimate relations of those in another culture? Are cultural relativists right?

SOURCE: An original piece written for this text by Devin Blake, M.A., John W. Draper Interdisciplinary Master's Program in Humanities and Social Thought, New York University

Each subsection that follows presents prevalence statistics of countries grouped by their global locations: Africa, Asia, Europe, Latin America, the Middle East, North America, and Russia.

## Africa

In Africa, the group of individuals permitted to assault women constitutes a broad group of both male and female relatives. The category of female behaviors cited as justification for abuse is also very broad. Forced early marriages typify Sierra Leone and other African countries. One practice more common in Africa than in some other parts of the world is **polygamy**. Polygamy occurs along with wives' inability to make unilateral decisions about contraception. **Men's sexual encounters with multiple partners expose their female partners to HIV.** Nonetheless, society expects women to remain silent about their victimization by male intimates and to accept the abuse (A. M. Fox et al., 2007).

One risk factor for male violence in *Ghana* and around the world is witnessing parental violence and experiencing physical violence during childhood (Gupta et al., 2008). As a result, intergenerational transmission of abuse likely explains much of the continuing abuse of female partners. See Table 10.1 for findings about male-to-female partner violence in a few African countries.

*Ghana.* Egalitarian decision making and equal economic contributions to the household are associated with reduced male battering in *Ghana* (Mann & Takyi, 2009). Within this framework, a duo of researchers attributed male partner violence to an *imbalance theory.* Imbalance theory proposes that when one partner has more resources (e.g., income) and power (male dominance or female dominance) than the other, partner violence will increase (S. Y. P. Choi & Ting, 2008).

| Country | Physical Abuse: H=Husband W=Wife; Percentages Are H→W Unless Otherwise Specified | Researchers/Compilers |
|---|---|---|
| Ghana | H→W homicides (IPHs) are 5 x more than W→H [2]IPHs[1] | Adinkrah, 2008 |
| Ethiopia—N = 673 partnered women; population sample | 10% last year<br>45% lifetime | [1]Heise, Ellsberg, & Gottemoeller, 1999 |
| Ethiopia—N = 3,016 ever partnered women (mainly Muslim; mainly rural) | 49% physical lifetime<br>29% physical last year<br>59% sexual lifetime<br>44% sexual last year | Garcia-Moreno, Jansen, Ellsberg, Heise, & Watts, 2006 |
| Kenya—N = 520 women in STD clinic | 26% lifetime; HIV women 50% to 74% lifetime violent, H→W | Fonck, Els, Kidula, Ndinya-Achola, & Temmerman, 2005 |
| Kenya—N = 4,876 currently married women | 36% physical lifetime<br>13% sexual lifetime | Djamba & Kimuna, 2008<br>Kenya Demographic and Health Survey |
| Namibia—N = 1,500 ever partnered women; representative sample | 31% physical lifetime<br>17% sexual lifetime | Garcia-Moreno et al., 2006 |
| Nigeria—N = 418 pregnant women | 47% lifetime hurt by anyone<br>78.7% H→W<br>28.7% when pregnant | Ezechi et al., 2004 |
| Nigeria—N = 334 pregnant women | 29% physical<br>10.2% sexual | Efetie & Salami, 2007 |
| South Africa—N = 834 men; health study | 27.5 % H→W | Gupta et al., 2008 |
| South Africa—N = 5,077 partnered women; national sample | 13% lifetime<br>6% last year | Heise et al., 1999 |
| South Africa—N = 3,797 female homicides | 50.3% H→W | Abrahams et al., 2009 |
| Uganda—N = 1,660 partnered women; two districts | 41% currently | Heise et al., 1999 |
| West Africa—N = 2,759 women; a representative sample | 78% victimization<br>H→W largest number of perpetrators | Moore, 2008 |

NOTES: [1]Compiled data. [2]IPH = Intimate Partner Homicide.

# Asia

Many of the same proscriptions for women's behavior in Asian countries are like those in African countries. Women lack even the most basic human rights concerning their own bodies and their own lives.

*Japan and Korea.* Japan is probably the most Westernized of the Asian countries. Its customs are no longer similar to some of the other Asian countries, such as Malaysia. Korea is becoming Westernized. See Table 10.2 for prevalence estimates for Japan and Korea.

**TABLE 10.2** Prevalence/Incidence of Husband-to-Wife IPV in Japan and Korea

| Country | Physical Abuse: H=Husband W=Wife; Percentages Are H→W Unless Otherwise Specified | Researchers/Compilers |
|---|---|---|
| Japan (Cabinet Office Survey on Domestic Violence) | 19.1% M→F sexual and physical threat; 11.2% M→F physical threat; 19.1% M→F sexual | United Nations Development Fund for Women, 2002 |
| Japan (Yokohama)—*N* = 1,371 ever partnered women; representative sample | 13% physical lifetime<br>6% sexual lifetime | Garcia-Moreno et al., 2006 |
| Korea—*N* = 707 partnered women | 38% any abuse<br>12% severe physical abuse | [1]Heise et al., 1999 |
| South Korea—*N* = 1,079 women; national random sample | 29.5% physical violence<br>3.7% sexual violence | J. Kim, Park, & Emery, 2009 |

ADDITIONAL SOURCE: See Boy & Kulczycki, 2008.

NOTE: [1]Compiled data.

*Korea—power structure and partner violence.* Other researchers gathered information about social norms, power structures, and conflict among Korean couples. **Logistic regression analyses** (e.g., prediction) uncovered a number of expected results: (a) The incidence of husband-to-wife and wife-to-husband violence is very high in *male-dominant marriages;* (b) The high wife-to-husband incidence reflects *wives' fighting back;* (c) Male-dominant and divided power marriages are highly associated with conflict, and *conflict is highly associated with husband-to-wife partner violence;* (d) As norm consensus (i.e., agreement on dominance) increases, partner violence decreases; (e) Male dominance first, followed by conflict, are the most highly correlated predictors of husband-to-wife IPV; and (f) Conflict followed by male dominance are the most highly associated predictors of wife-to-husband IPV (J. Y. Kim & Emery, 2003).

*Korea—patriarchal husbands.* Results of studies of couple violence in *Korea* are similar to those in other countries with patriarchal views. Korean wives are likely to stay with abusive husbands for several reasons: (a) Family members should stick together, (b) A wife's duty is to care for the family and sacrifice her own desires, (c) It is unnatural for women to have a position of authority in the family, (d) The first priority of marriage is obedience to husbands, and (e) Women should never talk back to husbands (M. Choi & Harwood, 2004).

*India.* India is a country with some relatively unique customs. Young women living in India customarily must obey all male family members and older women in the family. In addition to the husband, these family members may beat younger wives at will and employ other cruel practices. Presumably, it is women's behaviors that trigger violence against them—thus, women are to blame for men's violence. Since wives are responsible, society excuses and justifies male-to-female violence (e.g., A. R. Moore, 2008; Tang, Wong, & Cheung, 2002). See Table 10.3 for prevalence and incidence estimates of partner violence.

**TABLE 10.3**   Prevalence/Incidence of Husband-to-Wife Intimate Partner Violence in India

| Country | Physical Abuse: H=Husband W=Wife; Percentages Are H→W Unless Otherwise Specified | Researchers/Compilers |
| --- | --- | --- |
| India | Dowry murders = 7,618 | National Crime Records Bureau, 2008 |
| India—N = 90 MFIPV victims | 70% threatened with murder; 85% injured | Panchanadeswaran & Koverola, 2005 |
| India—N = 1,718 married women, 1,715 married men In eastern provinces; population-based sample | Women lifetime: 16% physical, 25% sexual; Men lifetime: 22% physical, 17% sexual | Babu & Kar, 2009 |
| India—N = 751 women | 17% last year | Pandey, Dutt, & Banerjee, 2009 |
| South India—N = 1,974 married women Poor, living in slums | 99% lifetime physical 75% lifetime sexual | S. Solomon et al., 2009 |
| Nepal—N = 63 married adult women; household interviews | 35% (primarily by husbands) | Paudel, 2007 |
| Sri Lanka—N = 417 ever partnered women; representative sample | 30% lifetime 22% last year | Subramaniam & Sivayogan, 2001 |

ADDITIONAL SOURCE: See Boy & Kulczycki, 2008.

NOTE: [1]Compiled data.

*India.* An inquiry with a sample of *Indian* women revealed that a lifetime of being blamed by parents, husbands, and in-laws contributed to female victims' beliefs that they were ultimately responsible for managing their home life and that they should be able to *adjust* to their husband's aggression. When asked, Indian women say they have lived in a state of prolonged captivity their entire lives (Purewal & Ganesh, 2000). Without options, even contraception is out of reach for many women, although some manage to use covert strategies to prevent pregnancies. For a wife to make a unilateral decision about contraception greatly increases her risk of male violence (Wilson-Williams, Stephenson, Juvekar, & Andes, 2008).

*Dowry murders,* although outlawed, are frequent and increase with economic downturns. As the dowry wealth of the bride is consumed by her husband and his family, their need for money mounts. If a man's current wife dies (accidentally in a kitchen fire), the husband is free to remarry and acquire another dowry (Rastogi & Therly, 2006; Rudd, 2001). One study identified two correlates of male IPV: (a) being in a "love" marriage, instead of an "arranged" marriage, and (b) having one's husband and in-laws ask for more *dowry resources.* Correlates associated with less male partner violence were participating in social groups and/or having vocational training. Thus, avoiding isolation is beneficial (Rocca, Rathod, Falle, Pande, & Krishnan, 2009).

*Nepal.* Attitudes toward women in Nepal seem medieval. In addition to dowry murders and acid throwing, customs require menstruating women and those giving birth to live in a cowshed because they are *unclean* at such times. Customs demand that the most nutritious and tastiest food be given to men in the family first, and women get the leftovers. During their stays in the cowshed, the family deprives women of good food because they are *untouchable* at these times. On the other hand, women's ascendancy into the labor market has begun to change societal responses. Newly empowered women are establishing nongovernmental organizations that are providing some of the services so badly needed by these cruelly abused female victims (Chowdhury, 2007).

*Southern Asia.* Most of the countries in the Southern Asian group are poverty stricken, except for those living in Hong Kong. See Table 10.4 for prevalence estimates for these nations.

**TABLE 10.4**   Prevalence/Incidence of Husband-to-Wife IPV in Southern Asian Nations

| Country | Physical Abuse: H=Husband W=Wife; Percentages Are H→W Unless Otherwise Specified | Researchers/Compilers |
|---|---|---|
| Dhaka, Bangladesh—N = 1,603; Matlab, Bangladesh—N = 1,527 partnered women; representative sample | Dhaka—40% physical 37% sexual lifetime Matlab—42% physical 50% sexual lifetime | Garcia-Moreno et al., 2006 |
| Bangladesh—N = 1,225 partnered women | 47% lifetime 19% current | [1]Heise et al., 1999 |

*(Continued)*

**TABLE 10.4**    (Continued)

| Country | Physical Abuse: H=Husband W=Wife; Percentages Are H→W Unless Otherwise Specified | Researchers/Compilers |
|---|---|---|
| Bangladesh—N = 2,780 married men; demographic and health surveys | 74% lifetime<br>37% last year | K. B. Johnson & Das, 2009 |
| Cambodia—N = 2,403 ever partnered women | 17.4% physical lifetime | Kishor & Johnson, 2006 |
| China—N = 2,673 couples; age groups: 20–29; 30–39; 40–49; 50–64 | 19%<br>20–29 significantly more hitting | T. Wang et al., 2009 |
| Hong Kong—N = 3,245 pregnant women | 9% last year | K. L. Chan et al., 2009 |
| Philippines—N = 1,660 partnered women in two provinces | 26% lifetime | Heise et al., 1999 |
| Vietnam—N = 465 married women | 36.8% lifetime<br>14.6% last year | Luke, Schuler, Mai, Thien, & Minh, 2007 |

ADDITIONAL SOURCE: See Boy & Kulczycki, 2008.

NOTE: [1]Compiled data.

*Bangladesh—acid throwing.* In *Bangladesh* and elsewhere, an all-too-common occurrence is the disfigurement of women's faces by men who *throw acid* at them. Although Bangladesh is a signatory to the United Nations Fourth World Conference on Women in Beijing, the government has continued to allow gendered violence against women. Laws against acid throwing are only ornamental. Many of the victims of these assaults are the perpetrators' wives, but some are girlfriends who have rejected the perpetrator as a marriage partner. The offenders are seldom arrested, much less prosecuted and convicted (Abdi, 2000). The government has failed to provide any satisfactory medical treatment or meaningful legal redress for this horrible crime.

*China—jealousy.* A large body of evidence has shown not only that jealousy-related violence is a global phenomenon but also it is the apparent precipitant of many male-to-female assaults and intimate partner homicides (e.g., Adinkrah, 2008; Rastogi & Therly, 2006). A fresh investigation examined the impact of sexual jealousy on partner abuse by both genders among a representative sample (N = 2,673) of Chinese adult couples. An unusual victim/perpetrator split emerged concerning the victim of hitting: Fewer people claimed to be victims than offenders.

- 11% of men said they hit a partner
- 5% of women said they were hit by partner
- 7% of women said they hit a partner
- 5% of men said they were hit by partner

The researchers suggested that this victim/perpetrator divide may indicate social disapproval of victimization (T. Wang et al., 2009). (See www.sagepub.com/barnett3e for a list of other significant results.)

*Hong Kong (Chinese Definition of IPV).* A novel inquiry determined the extent to which a population sample of 885 people in Hong Kong evaluated aggressive behaviors as abusive within the context of a specific victim category. The results had implications for how *Chinese in Hong Kong* define family violence. The inquiry also ascertained whether people would report the maltreatment to social services. (See www.sagepub.com/barnett3e for more details of this study.)

The results as a whole showed that the type of maltreatment and the category of victim elicited significantly different responses from the participants and impacted their intention to report the abuse. One individual result was that 28% of the participants had no intention of reporting an act of maltreatment, even though they judged it to be abusive. The researchers offered several interpretations of the findings. First, the Hong Kong population has no *common conception* of abusive family behaviors. People accept the traditional Chinese beliefs that families have a right to privacy and that others should not interfere in family matters. Consequently, judging an action as abusive is not translated into reporting the event to social services. Another explanation for not reporting the event may be that informing authorities is *difficult* in Hong Kong. Moreover, people may believe that social services would not be effective in helping the victim. By and large, the findings point out the need for changes in public policy, in particular the need for public awareness campaigns (Y. C. Chan, Chun, & Chung, 2008).

*Vietnam—attitudes toward gender.* In a study of gender similarities/differences in attitudes among 465 couples, both genders supported *inequitable gender norms* (e.g., "The husband should have the final say in all family matters."). Wives approved of these norms more than men did. In contrast to many other studies, men's IPV *increased with age*. More male partner violence occurred if a husband's or wife's *educational level was low* or if the husband's educational level was less than the wife's. Male IPV was highest among wives whose attitudes toward gender were the *most inequitable* and for women in marriages with the *greatest discrepancy of* attitudes. A few of the findings support a "backlash" effect against women with higher status (Luke et al., 2007).

*Australia, New Zealand, and Pacific Islanders.* Although many communities in Australia or New Zealand are similar to those in the United Kingdom or the United States, there are indigenous groups that are very different from the dominant English-speaking groups. See Table 10.5 for prevalence estimates for these groups.

**TABLE 10.5** Prevalence/Incidence of Husband-to-Wife IPV in Australia and New Zealand

| Country | Physical Abuse: H=Husband W=Wife; Percentages Are H→W Unless Otherwise Specified | Researchers/Compilers |
|---|---|---|
| Australia—N = 6,300 all women | 3% last year | [1]Heise et al., 1999 |
| New Zealand—N = 3,805 men and women; indigenous groups | 41% women<br>19.6% men | Morris & Reilly, 2003 |
| Auckland, New Zealand—N = 1,436 Waikato, New Zealand—N = 1,419 ever-partnered women; population based | Auckland—30% physical lifetime 14% sexual lifetime;<br>Waikato—38% physical lifetime 22% sexual lifetime | Garcia-Moreno et al., 2006 |
| Pacific Islanders—N = 1,095 currently partnered mothers who gave birth within last 12 months | H→W 11% severe physical last year (CTS)<br>W→H 19% severe physical last year (CTS) | Paterson, Feehan, Butler, Williams, & Cowley-Malcolm, 2007 |
| Samoa—N = 1,640 ever partnered women; national sample | 41% physical lifetime 20% sexual lifetime | Garcia-Moreno et al., 2006 |

ADDITIONAL SOURCE: See Boy & Kulczycki, 2008.

NOTE: [1]Compiled data.

*Pacific Islanders.* The New Zealand Pacific community is comprised of a variety of *Pacific Islanders,* indigenous population subgroups, such as Samoan, Tongan, and Cook Island Maori. A study of couple violence within this community determined that one risk factor for severe partner violence is being marginalized because of membership in an immigrant group. Some additional risk factors included sociodemographic variables such as cohabitation, no formal education, and low income (Paterson, Feehan, Butler, Williams, & Cowley-Malcom, 2007; see also S. Evans, 2005). One more study identified a number of developmental antecedents of partner abuse for both genders, such as exposure to abuse in childhood, family dysfunction and adversity, conduct problems, and alcohol dependence (Fergusson, Boden, & Horwood, 2008).

## Afghanistan, Pakistan, and Tajikistan

Afghanistan, Pakistan, and Tajikistan are similar in their attitudes toward women and the treatment of women because of their shared Muslim beliefs. See Table 10.6 for prevalence estimates for two of these nations.

*Afghanistan—the Taliban.* In *Afghanistan* under the *Taliban,* women may not leave their homes without their husband's permission and only if accompanied by a close male relative. They may not work outside the home or attend school. Women must wear head scarves and

| TABLE 10.6 | Prevalence of Husband-to-Wife IPV in Pakistan and Tajikistan | |
|---|---|---|
| Country | Physical Abuse: H=Husband W=Wife; Percentages Are H→W Unless Otherwise Specified | Researchers/Compilers |
| Pakistan—N = 100 obstetricians (95% female); stratified sample, screened patients | Physicians' estimates: more than 30% lifetime; 75% identified abuse victim last year | Fikree, Jafarey, Korejo, Khan, & Durocher, 2004 |
| Tajikistan—N = 400 women, 90% partnered | 36.1% physical lifetime<br>11.8% physical current<br>42.5% sexual lifetime | Haarr, 2007 |

ADDITIONAL SOURCE: See Boy & Kulczycki, 2008.

long veils (burkas), long robes, and keep every inch of skin covered no matter how hot the weather. Religious police roaming the cities do not hesitate to beat women they deem insufficiently covered (Norman & Finan, 2001). As of July 2009, it is legal for husbands to deny food (starve) any of their wives who do not meet their husband's sexual requirements. Although hard to believe, this law is an improvement over one that legalized rape of wives (Starkey, 2009). Perhaps it is no wonder that female suicide is high in countries where women have no rights (King, 2009).

## Middle East

Human rights abuses against women in Middle Eastern nations are rampant. In Muslim countries, for instance, fathers have total custody over children. If a woman divorces or leaves her husband, she must also leave her children (Chavez et al., 2005). In Saudi Arabia, society is struggling with the demands of globalization that call attention to women's lower status compared with men's. "Saudi business women [are] still shackled by some archaic rules. They are forbidden to drive a car, which mean that male chauffeurs have to be hired at extra cost. Moreover, they cannot leave the country without written permission from their husband or father" (Pharaon, 2004, p. 359).

Strong beliefs (perhaps fears) about women's sexuality encourage customs that place young girls in jeopardy for physical and sexual assault. Parents in these cultures *rush* to have their daughters marry as soon as possible, partially to maintain the daughter's virginity. It is not unusual for parents to pressure a girl as young as 12 into marrying a man in his forties or fifties. In *Afghanistan,* poverty-stricken parents may even sell very young girls (under 10) to men who want them as *brides.* Middle Eastern beliefs in honor killings provide insight into the culture's misogynistic attitudes toward sex and expectations for women's obedience (e.g., Amowitz, Kim, Reis, Asher, & Iacopino, 2004). See Box 10.2 for a discussion of honor killings.

## BOX 10.2 Honor Societies

Some scholars place the violence against women in honor cultures within the framework of male-to-female intimate partner violence, while others view the violence as a human rights issue. Even though twisted thinking about Islamic tenets justifies the killing of both partners for infidelity, the culture uniformly targets women more readily than men. These killings are "necessary" to preserve the family's honor. From this viewpoint, a man's honor depends upon a woman's public behavior, not the man's. Honor cultures not only allow brutal violence against wives, but they also proscribe extreme violence toward any women in the family whose behavior dishonors the family. Teenage daughters are most at risk for male violence.

To preserve their honor, men can kill women for virtually any offense, even a rumor. A partial list of dishonorable female behaviors includes sexual infidelity, dating/ marrying a man considered undesirable by her parents, seeking a divorce, wearing Western clothes and makeup, refusing to keep her hair covered, being raped, or refusing to enter into an arranged marriage.

Fathers, brothers, uncles, and cousins may kill, indeed should kill, daughters, sisters, nieces, and cousins who "shame" the family. (By comparison, fathers in Western cultures almost never kill their teenage daughters.) The United Nations Population Fund estimates that men kill 5,000 women annually for dishonoring their families. Question: Are honor killings a facet of male partner violence or not? The conflict between Muslims who defend and wish to continue honor practices and those working to end them is ongoing (Chesler, 2009; Kulwicki, 2002).

See Table 10.7 for a summary of MFIPV prevalence estimate for the Middle East.

**TABLE 10.7**  Prevalence Estimates of Male Partner Abuse in Middle Eastern Nations

| Country | Physical Abuse: H=Husband W=Wife; Percentages Are H→W Unless Specified | Researchers/Compilers |
| --- | --- | --- |
| Egypt—N = 5,612 women | 18.9% last year | Akmatov, Mikolajerczyk, Labeeb, Dharer, & Khan, 2008 |
| Egypt—N = 6,566 married women | 34% lifetime 16% last year | Diop-Sidibe et al., 2006 |
| Iran—N = 416 pregnant women | 35% | Salari & Nakhaee, 2008 |
| Iraq—N = 1,991 men and women; random sample, interviewed by physicians for *all* violence | 50/1,000 *documented;* 7.7/1,000 U.S. *documented* | Amowitz et al., 2004; (Rennison & Welchans, 2000, for U.S.) |

| Country | Physical Abuse: H=Husband W=Wife; Percentages Are H→W Unless Specified | Researchers/Compilers |
|---------|---------|---------|
| Israel—*N* = 2,410 partnered women | 37% lifetime any abuse<br>52% last year any abuse | [1]Heise et al., 1999 |
| Jordan—*N* = 1,011 reported IPV incidents | 97% H→W<br>3% W→H | Kulwicki, 2002 |
| Jordan—*N* = 390 pregnant women | 15% (83% H→W) | C. J. Clark, Hill, Jabbar, & Silverman, 2009 |
| Jordan—*N* = 356 ever married women | 19.6% lifetime physical | Al-Nsour, Khawaja, & Al-Kayyali, 2009 |
| Lebanon—*N* = 417 women | 22% lifetime; 9.1% last year; 6.9% while pregnant | Khawaja & Tewel-Salem, 2004 |
| Palestine—*N* = 1,410 women | 52% last year | Haj-Yahia, 1999 |
| Syria—*N* = 411 low-income women | 23.1% lifetime | Maziak & Asfar, 2003 |

ADDITIONAL SOURCE: See Boy & Kulczycki, 2008.

NOTE: [1]Compiled statistics.

*Egypt.* In the viewpoint of one observer, husbands' violence toward wives in Egypt is most often *ascribed to Islamic beliefs,* even though the real cause is *cultural tradition* (El-Safty, 2004). Reasons for wife beating are similar to those in other Islamic countries: a belief that beating is justified, economic issues, refusing sex, spending too much money, and any presumed inadequacies of the victim (e.g., poor parenting). As elsewhere, Muslim *women* also believe that wife beating is justified. Numerous individuals view wife beating as *well-intentioned discipline gone wrong.* As found elsewhere, women who are younger, less educated, and living in rural areas are at the greatest risk for abuse (see Jeyaseelan et al., 2004, for additional risk factors).

Reporting abuse to the police accomplishes little, and judges are reluctant to punish wife beaters severely. Instead, the judges prefer to use their discretion to lighten sentences as a form of mercy. Shelters in Egypt rarely allow IPV victims refuge; instead, they help widows or displaced women. In 2000, laws changed to allow women to divorce. If a woman seeks a divorce, though, she must accept the fact that she is not entitled to any money or property. In fact, she must give back the dowry price. Thus, she has two choices: (a) she can be free of beatings and be pauperized, or (b) she may stay married and be subjected to beating that may cause disability or even death. Thankfully, some individuals are beginning to *rethink gender in Islam,* but as yet there are no extensive changes in the customs or legal structures. (See Ammar, 2006, for a review.)

*Israel.* Findings from the First *Israeli* National Survey of Domestic Violence revealed some of the proviolence attitudes prevalent in the Middle East. Both men (23.4%) and women (17.8%) subscribe to the acceptability of wife beating for *infidelity.* A much smaller percentage of men (14.9%) and women (13.0%) approve of wife beating if she "does as she pleases." Somewhat more than 25% of both genders believe that a woman should not break up a marriage even if the husband uses quite a bit of force against his wife. About 16% think a wife can be happy even if she is beaten (Eisikovits, Winstock, & Fishman, 2004). It is interesting to note that in the *Kibbutzim* collective communities where gender equality is the norm, violence against women is almost unheard of (Shoham, 2005).

*Palestine.* A contemporary survey of 395 married Palestinian refugees in Jordan has uncovered strong approval of wife-beating by both men (60.1%) and women (61.8%). Although a few gender differences occurred, risk factors for male-to-female IPV for both men and women included age, labor force participation, and views about women's autonomy. Acceptance of male partner violence was strongly linked with their individual experience of either victimization or perpetration, statistically adjusted by other risk factors (Khawaja, Linos, & El-Roueiheb, 2008).

*Health professionals.* In Arab and Islamic countries, medical professionals collude in a conspiracy of silence about violence against women. Medical personnel deny reports of abuse, tell the woman she is delusional, and interpret her behavior as masochistic. They also systematically downplay the consequences of abuse (Douki, Nacef, Belhadj, Bousaker, & Ghachem, 2003).

## Europe

Some initial theorizing about wife abuse originated in England with the writings of R. E. Dobash and R. P. Dobash (1988), and it was Erin Pizzey (1974) who opened the first shelter for battered women. Theoretical frameworks from the United Kingdom (e.g., patriarchal explanations) have greatly impacted the field of family violence. Still, European research, advocacy efforts, and responses to intimate partner violence across the European continent have lagged behind advances made in the United States. Despite accumulated evidence, individuals in European countries seem to believe that women can and should *simply leave* their abusive partners. A few countries are relatively archaic in their practices. Arranged marriages of young girls, for instance, remains a problem in Romania (Oprea, 2005). See Table 10.8 for a summary of prevalence findings about IPV in Europe.

An interesting qualitative analysis from *Scotland* detailed a series of vacillating cognitive processes and behaviors emblematic of battered women's coping responses to their partners' IPV. Women's strategies of resistance and their attempts to keep themselves and their children safe occur interactively along with men's various efforts to control them.

**TABLE 10.8** Prevalence/Incidence of Husband-to-Wife IPV in European Nations

| Country | Physical Abuse: H=Husband W=Wife; Percentages Are H→W Unless Otherwise Specified | Researchers/Compilers |
|---|---|---|
| Albania—N = 1,039 married women; representative sample | 37% Last year | Burazeri, Roshi, Jewkes, Jordan, Bjegovic, & Laaser, 2005 |
| Denmark—N = 3,300 persons charged with violence | 20% H→W<br>2% W→H | Minister for Gender Equality, 2007 |
| England/Wales | 20% Homicides are [2]IPHs | Brookman & Maguire, 2005 |
| Finland—N = 4,955 current/former partnered/ex-partnered women | 64% current partner physical and sexual<br>26% former male partner | Lundgren, 2002 (Cited in Kury, Obergfell-Fuchs, & Woessner, 2004) |
| Germany—N = 5,711 German 59 or younger; past 5 years | West Germany: 18.7%<br>East Germany: 16.6% | Wetzels et al., 1995 (Cited in Kury et al., 2004) |
| Greece | 45% IPHs jealousy-related | Chimbos, 1998 |
| Ireland—N = 2,598 police-identified IPV cases; 128 cases identified victims or offenders | 96.2% MFIPV<br>3.8% FMIPV | Stevenson, Goodall, & Moore, 2008 |
| Italy—N = 1,872 partnered/ex-partnered women; Rome, Milan | 18% physical<br>20% forced sexual contact | Morgani (in Gulotta, 1984)—Cited in McCloskey, Treviso, Scionti, & dal Pozza, 2002) |
| Netherlands—N = 989 all women; national sample | 21% any abuse<br>11% severe | [1]Heise et al., 1999 |
| Norway—N = 2,143 women | 26.8% lifetime<br>5.5% last year | Neieren & Schel, 2008 |
| Norway N = 111 married women | 18% lifetime | Heise et al., 1999 |
| Poland—N = 2009 women; random selection | 15.1% physical lifetime<br>5.1% sexual lifetime | International Violence Against Women, 2007 |
| Spain—N = 400 women | 22.8% lifetime | Ruiz-Pérez, Mata-Pariente, & Plazaola-Castaño, 2006 |
| Spain—N = 2,015 women | 13% severe physical<br>16.2% severe sexual | Medina-Ariza & Barberet, 2003 |

*(Continued)*

**TABLE 10.8**  (Continued)

| Country | Physical Abuse: H=Husband W=Wife; Percentages Are H→W Unless Otherwise Specified | Researchers/Compilers |
|---|---|---|
| Sweden—*N* = 6,926 females | 8% to 20% physical and sexual by partners/ex-partners | Lundgren, 2002 (Cited in Kury et al., 2004) |
| Switzerland—*N* = 1,500 women; national sample | 21% lifetime<br>6% last year | Heise et al., 1999 |
| Turkey—*N* = 599 all women; one area | 58% lifetime | Heise et al., 1999 |
| Turkey—*N* = 116 married women | 41.4%<br>8.6% sexual assault | Mayda & Akkuş, 2005 |
| Turkey—*N* = 475 Married, pregnant women | 64.6% lifetime<br>33.3% pregnant | Sahin & Sahin, 2003 |
| United Kingdom—partnered men and women; British Crime Survey | 23% women lifetime<br>15% men lifetime<br>by current/former partner | Mirrlees-Black & Byron, 1999 (Cited in Kury et al., 2004) |
| United Kingdom—*N* = 430 all women; North London | 30% lifetime<br>12% last year | Heise et al., 1999 |

ADDITIONAL SOURCE: Boy & Kulczycki, 2008.

NOTE: [1]Compiled statistics. [2]IPH = Intimate Partner Homicide.

Because the women wanted to save their relationship, while ending the violence, they selected responses presumed to achieve that goal. See Box 10.3 for a discussion of active responses among Scottish battered women (Cavanagh, 2003).

### BOX 10.3 Understanding Survival (Agency) in Scottish Battered Women

First, women usually had to experience several episodes of male violence directed at them before they recognized their male partner's behavior as battering. They treated the first incident as an aberration by minimizing or outright denying the man's violence. Men nearly always apologized, and women most frequently accepted the apology; many even felt sorry for their partner. The men made *rules* (e.g., scrubbing the kitchen floor daily) and blamed their own assaultive behaviors on the women because of their *failure to comply*. Most men felt justified in establishing rules.

Many women made efforts to comply with such demands, but eventually they noted that compliance did not eliminate the violence, and they recognized that they could not control it. Most women did not disclose it to others because they felt ashamed and continued to hope their male partner would change. They had understood the message from their gender socialization—it was their responsibility to improve the relationship.

Second, many women hoped a dialogue would enable their partner to reconsider his male IPV for what it was and stop it. Although women broached the topic of violence, the men were usually reluctant or refused to discuss it. Many women tried to become more sensitive to their partner's moods or his alcohol intake. They often mulled over the best course of action to take at that time. Despite their fear, women tried to help their partner become more aware of his violence. They hoped his awareness would convince him to stop it, but it did not.

Third, some women adopted various "cajoling" strategies they thought might end the violence. For example, a woman might start agreeing with everything her partner said, or repeatedly tell him how much she loves him. Although such tactics may have produced some transient periods of nonviolence, the male partner violence persisted, and the women's fear increased.

Fourth, a number of women discontinued these ineffective tactics and challenged the men's use of aggression. As women began to consider the violence as life-threatening, they became more confrontational. They might verbally or physically confront their partner, leave the relationship (temporarily), and tell others about their partner's battering behavior. The women felt terrified, angry, and frustrated. Some began to retaliate by hitting their partner back. Retaliation seemed to induce some men to stop their violence at least for a time, but it antagonized other men even more.

Fifth, many women decided to *go public* about their partner's violence. As an illustration, a woman might leave her house, letting others see her black eyes. The women hoped that letting others see what was going on would shame their partner. At this juncture, the reactions of others were critical in terms of what happened next. If women were criticized and blamed by the community, rather than understood and helped, they often did not seek assistance again.

Sixth, at long last some women left their homes or called the police to have their partners forcefully removed; however, many women returned only to be battered once more.

## Russia

Scholarship on male-to-female intimate partner violence in Russia is almost nonexistent. Russia is behind many other countries in adopting legislation protecting women and in providing other assistance such as shelters (e.g., Zakirova, 2005). Battered women in Russia suffer from a lack of employment caused by gender bias, lack of political power, an unresponsive police force, and the alcoholism of their male partners. In one inquiry of 510 men and 680 women from the Moscow Public Health Survey, less than half of the research participants evaluated male-to-female battering as a serious problem. A small number of interviewees judged violence to be permissible/justifiable (A. Stickley, Kislitsyna, Timofeeva, & Vågerö, 2008). Table 10.9 displays incidence estimates of male partner abuse in Russia.

**TABLE 10.9**    Incidence of Husband-to-Wife Partner Violence and Homicide in Russia

| Country | Physical Abuse | Researchers/Compilers |
|---|---|---|
| Russia | 16,800 intentional IPV<br>10,300 [1]IPHs | Veltishchev, 2004 |
| Russia | 14,000 women killed by family members, 1997 | Violence Against Women: 10 Reports/Year 2003 |

NOTE: [1]IPH = Intimate Partner Homicide.

*Risk factors for IPV.* One *risk factor* analysis gathered data from 45 female IPV victims attending crisis centers and 33 pregnant nonvictims. In addition to alcoholism, another risk factor was the male partner's exposure to his *father's physical* abuse of his mother. An interesting *protective factor* was living in a communal-style apartment where families shared bathrooms and kitchens. The authors concluded that the presence of others, relative to the privacy of living in a separate apartment, inhibited male partner violence. Possibly, living in a separate area emphasized the notion that partner violence is a private family matter (A. Stickley, Timofeeva, & Sparén, 2008).

## Latin America

In addition to patriarchal practices already described, Latin countries often endorse the cultural value of *machismo* (exaggerated masculinity, male supremacy, sexual prowess, important responsibilities). Alcoholism rates are high among Latin partner-violent men, as in most other areas of the world. The family structure of Latin America is often authoritarian, with the father making all the decisions and controlling everyone in the family. Young impoverished Mexican brides often live in the husband's home and come under the authority of the husband's family. If the woman's husband has a job, he may give all of his income to his mother, thus increasing his wife's economic dependence and struggle for scarce resources. The culture expects wives to sacrifice their lives for the well-being of other family members. Latin Americans also blame women for their partners' violence just as they do in other countries (Agoff, Herrera, & Castro, 2007). See Table 10.10 for a summary of prevalence of male partner aggression in Latin America.

**TABLE 10.10** Prevalence of Husband-to-Wife IPV in Latin American Nations

| Country | Physical Abuse: H=Husband W=Wife; Percentages Are H→W Unless Otherwise Specified | Researchers/Compilers |
|---|---|---|
| Bolivia—N = 289 All women, 3 districts | 17% Last year | [1]Heise et al., 1999 |
| Brazil—São Paulo: N = 1,172 partnered; Pernambuco daMata: N = 1,473 partnered; representative samples | São Paulo: 27% physical lifetime, 10% sexual lifetime; Pernambuco daMata: 34% physical lifetime, 14% sexual lifetime | Garcia-Moreno et al., 2006 |
| Chile—N = 1,000 currently partnered women; Santiago | 60% physical violence 26% severe physical violence | Creel, Lovera, & Ruiz, 2001 |
| Colombia—N = 6,097 partnered women | 19% current relationship | [1]Heise et al., 1999 |
| Costa Rica—N = 1,312 women; San Jose | 10% | Creel et al., 2001 |
| Dominican Republic—N = 6,807 ever-partnered women | 22% Lifetime | Kishor & Johnson, 2006 |
| Ecuador—N = 200 low-income women; Quito sample | 60% | Creel et al., 2001 |
| Guatemala—N = 1,000 women | 49% | Creel et al., 2001 |
| Haiti—N = 2,347 ever-partnered women | 28.8% physical lifetime | Kishor & Johnson, 2006 |
| Jamaica—N = 187 (of 247) women at domestic crisis center | 90% physical 59% sexual assault | Arscott-Mills, 2001 |
| Mexico—N = 1,064 ever-married women; Monterey | 17% lifetime | Creel et al., 2001 |
| Mexico—N = 1,789 medical outpatients | 41% lifetime | Diaz-Olavarrieta, Blertson, Paz, de Leon, & Alarcon-Segovia, 2002 |
| National Institute of Statistics, Geography, and Informatics of Mexico, 2004 | 47% last year | Cited in Quelopana, Champion, & Salazar, 2008 |
| Mexico—N = 253 pregnant women; prenatal care clinic, Monterey | 35% abuse during pregnancy 64% of abuse by current/former male partner | Quelopana et al., 2008 |

*(Continued)*

**TABLE 10.10** (Continued)

| Country | Physical Abuse: H=Husband W=Wife; Percentages Are H→W Unless Otherwise Specified | Researchers/Compilers |
|---|---|---|
| Nicaragua—*N* = 8,507 ever-married women; national sample | 52% any abuse lifetime <br> 37% severe lifetime <br> 27% any abuse last year <br> 20% severe last year | Heise et al., 1999 |
| Nicaragua—*N* = 378 ever-partnered women | 69% lifetime <br> 33% any abuse last year | Creel et al., 2001 |
| Paraguay—*N* = 5,940 ever-married women; national | 10% lifetime | [1]Heise et al., 1999 |
| Lima, Peru—*N* = 1,414 ever-partnered women <br> Cusco, Peru: *N* = 1,837 ever-partnered women, representative samples | Lima: 49% physical lifetime <br> 23% sexual lifetime <br> Cusco: 61% physical lifetime <br> 47% sexual lifetime | Garcia-Moreno et al., 2006 |
| Puerto Rico—*N* = 7,121 ever-married women; national | 13% lifetime | Creel et al., 2001 |
| Uruguay—*N* = 545 currently partnered women | 10% last year | Creel et al., 2001 |

ADDITIONAL SOURCES: Boy & Kulczycki, 2008; Creel et al., 2001.

NOTE: [1]Compiled statistics.

---

**CASE HISTORY** **Awaiting the Birth of a First Baby Is a Joyous Occasion**

In papers filed for an asylum case, Ms. Alvarado from Guatemala described some of the abuse she endured during a 10-year marriage to Francisco Osorio. Osorio was a former Guatemalan soldier who married Ms. Alvarado when she was 16. When she became pregnant, Osorio began beating her to try and induce an abortion. In the process, "Mr. Osorio dislocated her jaw and kicked her repeatedly. He also 'pistol-whipped her, broke windows and mirrors with her head, punched and slapped her, threatened her with his machete, and dragged her down the street by her hair'" (Preston, 2009).

*Mexican pregnant women.* One study of 253 pregnant outpatients in *Mexico* specified several variables associated with abuse of pregnant women: *being unmarried, not living with their partner,* and *having a lower income* (Quelopana et al., 2008). In contradistinction, women's employment reduces their risk of violence (Villarreal, 2007). Attitudes toward rape defy logic. "In 12 Latin American countries, a rapist can be exonerated if he offers to marry the victim and she accepts. . . . The family of the victim frequently pressures her to marry the rapist, which they believe restores the family's honour" (Bunch, 1997, p. 43).

Many abused *Mexican* pregnant women had a negative attitude toward the pregnancy—the pregnancy was unintended and unwanted. When asked why they did not use contraception, the abused women said that the man said he would "take care of it" but did not (Quelopana et al., 2008).

*Mexican social ties—not supportive.* A different study of social support among battered women in Mexico has provided a fresh analysis of the effects of *social ties (i.e., family, in-laws) on male partner abuse.* In this qualitative evaluation of 26 women's narratives, researchers made a strong case for designating women's social ties as representing a *negative rather than a positive feature* of their lives. The reason is that social ties are most likely to *foster women's victimization.* When living with her in-laws, a wife becomes a focus of their negative evaluations of her character—she is *morally deficient* and *blameworthy.* When she complains to her natal family (e.g., her mother) about her husband's violence, she receives unsympathetic platitudes such as, "This is your cross to bear." These messages from her family are harmful because they help to justify her husband's violence against her (Agoff et al., 2007). Fortunately over the last decade, more women are starting to report improved autonomy (Heaton & Forste, 2008).

## North America

In addition to the United States, Canada and Greenland have recognized male-to-female intimate partner violence as a social problem. Both Canada and Greenland have experienced assimilation problems with indigenous populations. In Greenland, alcohol is associated with sexual assault in 63% of the cases reported to the police (Mejlvang & Boujida, 2007). Academicians are unsure about the causes of male partner violence. One academician attributes male IPV to rapid social change, while another attributes it to men's desire to be dominant (B. W. Sørensen, 2001).

Canada, of course, has many prominent researchers and practitioners investigating intimate partner violence. Some very generalizable research has centered on the causes and treatment of male violence toward female partners (D. Dutton, University of British Columbia) and risk assessment research (R. Kropp, Simon Fraser University). Overall, the research output of Canadians has become closely intermingled with that of Americans. See Table 10.11 for a summary of prevalence estimates for male-to-female intimate partner violence in North America.

| Country | Physical Abuse: H=Husband W=Wife; Percentages Are H→W Unless Otherwise Specified | Researchers/Compilers |
|---|---|---|
| Canada—$N$ = 12,300 all lifetime partnered women | 3% last year<br>29% lifetime | [1]Heise et al., 1999 |
| Canada—$N$ = 2,461 emergency room patients | 4.1% to 17.7% physical last year (varied by screening instrument) | H. L. MacMillan et al., 2006 |
| Canada (Statistics Canada, 1999a) | 29% | Cited in G. E. Robinson, 2003 |
| Canada—$N$ = 6,983 non-Aboriginal $N$ = 143 Aboriginal; currently partnered women; Statistics Canada | 3.5% non-Aboriginal last 5 years physical<br>12.6% Aboriginal last 5 years, physical | Brownridge, 2003 |
| Greenland—$N$ = 173 (2002) rapes, attempted rapes; reported to police | 15% Perpetrated by current partner ($n$ = 2) or ex-partner ($n$ = 10) | Mejlvang & Boujida, 2007 |
| Greenland Sexual Assaults (1993–1994) Health Interview Survey | 25% of all women<br>6% of all men | Cited in G. E. Robinson, 2003 |

NOTE: [1]Compiled statistics.

## SECTION SUMMARY

### Cross-Cultural Intimate Partner Violence

Violence against women occurs everywhere in the world. People living in Western industrialized countries find the treatment of women across the globe horrifying and incredible. Within the sphere of overwhelming violence against women generally, there exists a lesser but still vast amount of male violence against female partners. There are many commonalities among types of male-to-female partner violence across cultures, yet there remain some distinctive types that are more prevalent in some regions than others.

Male abusive behavior is so entrenched and attitudes permitting it so broadly held that recognition of the problem is still not universal. The majority of the countries are just now becoming aware of the problem and a number are beginning to respond to the violence as a serious social problem. Information about the extent of the violence is uneven from one locality to the next. First, the availability of adequate assessment tools varies. Second, conditions conducive to executing high-quality research vary.

Lack of economic resources is one of the strongest correlates of male intimate partner violence everywhere. It is clear that low-income couples around the world are significantly more likely to be abusive than higher income couples. Because of poverty and customs, young brides often move into their husband's family home and become vulnerable to ill-treatment from in-laws. These young women cannot return to a natal home because their family cannot provide economic support for them either. Women lack any type of financial independence that would enable them to escape. Male gender violence takes many forms and often revolves around women's and young girls' sexual behavior or men's jealousy (Fields-Meyer & Benet, 1998; Levesque, 2001). In India, these girls may "accidentally" burn themselves to death in a cooking accident, leaving the husband to seek a new bride with another dowry.

There are several other obvious correlates of male-to-female violence. First, immigrant status is associated with male assaultiveness. Immigrants must cope with a new language and new customs, and trying to earn a living while being under threat of deportation. Second, alcohol is highly associated with family violence. Generally, the higher the consumption of alcohol in a country, the higher the rates of intimate partner violence. Third, the chaos generated by wars or civil unrest inflates the level of violence against women. Fourth, proviolence attitudes are related to more male partner violence. Fifth, the lack of a legal structure that protects women permits male partner violence to occur unabated.

In addition to the correlates noted, gender inequality plays a large role in a society's acceptance of male partner violence. Where partner abuse is widespread, *expectations for women* dictate that they are to be subservient to men. Wives *must obey* their husbands and probably their in-laws. Women have no option to refuse sex. The husband may decide if his wife can (or must) *work* outside the home, if she can *leave the confines of her home,* whom she *may befriend, what clothes* she must wear, and how she *must behave.* Women are as likely or as more likely than men to believe wife beating is justified.

On the surface, Islamic dogma appears to be at the core of a large share of violence against women. Still, it is *not* Islam or any other religion *per se* that proscribes the cruel and inhumane treatment of women. Instead, it is religious precepts *gone wrong* that harm women. *Fundamentalist* religious beliefs contribute to violence perpetrated against women by supporting male dominance and by promulgating certain antiwoman biases. It is individuals within Islamic communities that have misinterpreted the Koran to tolerate, if not promote, intimate partner violence against women. "A fair reading of the Koran shows that wife abuse, genital mutilation and honour killings are a result of *culture* rather than religion" (Douki et al., 2003, p. 165). Tenets of other religion, such as the Catholic ban on divorce, also shape society's beliefs about leaving an abusive relationship.

South Asian women have incorporated a mental model of the *good wife* and the *good daughter* presumably based on the Muslim faith. South Asian women believe that a good wife is *totally subservient* to her husband's needs. She accepts the blame associated with any punishment she receives. She may also be motivated to tolerate abuse to shield her children from punitive retributions. "South Asian ideals of womanhood and wifehood help to create a mind-set whereby South Asian women are reluctant to advocate for themselves and are reluctant to leave" abusive men (Goel, 2005, p. 639).

The conclusion of one prominent academician is that social role theory explains all the cross-cultural data (Archer, 2006). The definition of **social role theory** is that "all psychological differences between men and women can be attributed to cultural expectations about gender, rather than to biological factors" (VandenBos, 2007, p. 868). Whether social role theory is *totally explanatory*, culturally endorsed gender inequality undoubtedly promotes male-to-female IPV.

# IMMIGRANT AND ETHNIC/RACIAL INTIMATE PARTNER VIOLENCE

The U.S. Census Bureau (2008) projects that by the year 2050, 54% of the U.S. population will have diverse ethnic backgrounds. This estimate calls attention to the need to prepare service providers with the knowledge they need to work with minority groups. The terms *race* and *ethnicity* have distinct meanings although people use the terms interchangeably. Initially, *biologists* classified humans into different racial groups based on observable genetic variation (phenotypic; e.g., skin color) just as they classify plants and animals. Genomic researchers continue to look for racial differences, and they find some that are related to physical vulnerabilities or illnesses. Medical researchers are interested in understanding the link between genes and disease.

> SOME SCIENTISTS CLAIM THAT RACE, AS A *PSYCHOLOGICAL VARIABLE* IN RESEARCH, CANNOT PREDICT ANYTHING. GENETICISTS HAVE *NOT* BEEN ABLE TO TIE GENETIC MARKERS TO ANY BEHAVIORAL TRAITS. ETHNICITY IS A BETTER PREDICTOR OF BEHAVIOR THAN RACE.

*Ethnicity* implies a psychological and *social identity* based on one's *heritage—one's cultural allegiance.* From this point of view, an Asian is likely to have recognizable external features of his *race,* but his choice of religious beliefs is not tied directly to his physical features. Over time, social scientists have been less inclined to classify people on the basis of race and more inclined to group them by their *cultural identification* (Helms, Jernigan, & Mascher, 2005).

Certain minority groups have attracted considerably more research attention than others, creating an uneven patchwork of findings. Research on African American partner violence, for example, has grown faster than that of Native American Indians, and research on Asian immigrant IPV has proliferated more than that of Arab American immigrants. In addition, the study samples recruited for immigrant and ethnic/racial partner violence research overlap. As a case in point, most Latino and Asian American ethnic samples contain large percentages of immigrants who are undergoing different stages of acculturation. Research on African American partner violence, on the other hand, uses samples that contain few, if any, immigrants. When study samples lack comparability on such a fundamental variable as country of origin, the results are apt to vary dramatically, and the interpretations of the findings can only be considered speculative.

## Immigrants

Immigrants in the United States face a host of special problems that compound female victimization by male intimate partners. Although each group brings with it remnants from its own culture's mores, immigrants still share commonalities. They share stressors such as feeling oppressed and marginalized by their minority status, acculturation demands, and isolation from their families. In some cases an abusive male partner will elevate his isolation tactics by including acts such as locking a woman in a house, removing telephones, and taking all her clothes (Abraham, 2000). Another stressor that immigrants encounter is having to send money home to poverty-stricken families.

## Ethnic/Racial Minorities

Having minority status in America is *painful* for most members of minority groups. Little *stings*, like name-calling, and more serious *oppressions*, like unequal work opportunities, occur frequently and they have a *cumulative negative effect*. Another type of hurt experienced by minorities is to feel shamed by the actions (e.g., high rate of out-of-wedlock births) of other members of their own minority group, to be "tarred with the same brush." Even though some experiences of discrimination come about through the *unconscious biases* of other racial groups, they are still capable of causing deep-down hurt—a wounding of one's soul. Yet another practice, grouping all minorities together as if they were like-minded, leads to additional *tactless misconceptions*. To make matters worse, minorities themselves hold prejudices against other minorities causing serious frictions. Last, there are many *within-group variations* related to various advantages (e.g., higher income) and disadvantages (lower level of education) that must be recognized as individual differences (Farberman, 2007).

There are both general similarities and dissimilarities among intimate partner violence victims and offenders across ethnicities and racial groups. To obtain *survey data* on minority groups, the U.S. Congress has had to address and re-address minority issues legislatively, through the Violence Against Women Act (VAWA) of 1994 and reauthorization of that act in 2000. These laws have included requirements to assess the levels of partner abuse in *marginalized groups*, such as Native Americans, and to improve the coverage of ethnic minority groups in general (see Raj & Silverman, 2002; Violence Against Women Office, 2000).

As observed throughout the text, when *data* from diverse racial groups *are aggregated*, rates of intimate partner violence are significantly higher among members of minority groups than among nonminorities. One research team suggests that aggregating data is misleading. It leads to attributions about racial effects when *other factors, such as socioeconomic status,* more validly account for the dissimilarities (Sokoloff & Dupont, 2005). Since races *may* tend to perpetrate *subtypes of abuse in different forms* (i.e., physical, sexual, verbal, homicide), these differences may further confound understanding.

One especially important factor in ethnic minority research is the *context of questionnaires*—whether inventories are *labeled as crime surveys* or as *personal safety surveys* (McFarlane, Groff, O'Brien, & Watson, 2005). If research participants do *not perceive their victimization as a crime,* and the questionnaire they receive is labeled a crime survey, their disclosure of partner violence decreases. Another factor that impacts obtained rates of partner violence is the culturally influenced variation in *willingness to disclose IPV abuse* (Hamby, 2009). Finally, dissimilarities that are identified are not definitive, and there is *no empirical evidence* suggesting that racial differences in partner violence are rooted in biology.

## Laws Affecting Immigrant Women

Immigrant battered women have unique problems with United State immigration laws. Initially, immigration laws followed the model of **coverture** (a married couple has a single legal entity). Because the antiquated meaning of coverture gives the husband control over the property and the body of the wife and their children, battered immigrant women were *legally dependent on their husband (possibly an abuser)*. Consequently, immigrant wives could not pursue visa petitions or other legal protections on their own. Rather, they were legally dependent on others (e.g., husband, brother) to sponsor and pursue visa petitions for them. These laws enabled abusive husband-sponsors to use a wife's dependency status as a weapon to threaten her with deportation. Of particular concern were so-called "mail-order brides" who were at particular risk for sexual abuse (Morash, Bui, Stevens, & Zhang, 2008).

One goal of the Violence Against Women Act (2005) was to rectify immigrant women's legal dependency on husbands. Legislative changes made it possible for undocumented abused women to *self-petition* (on their own, not through a sponsor) to obtain a green card and to stay in the United States. It became the responsibility of the United States Citizenship and Immigration Service (USCIS) to oversee this change. More specifically, USCIS must provide *linguistically appropriate services* that enable battered wives to access legal remedies. Of potential assistance also is a *U-visa* that lets *victims of a crime* (e.g., trafficking) who have been helpful in the crime's investigation to apply for a *nonimmigrant visa* and a work permit. Many immigrant women are not aware of these laws and so they remain entrapped in abusive relationships (Erez, Adelman, & Gregory, 2009; "New Rule," 2007). Among the general public there has been a growing anti-immigrant bias. (See www.sagepub.com/barnett3e for more details.)

*Cultural insensitivity and the law.* Courts are increasingly compelled to address crimes committed by immigrants whose homeland customs differ from those of the United States. A number of commentators have expressed concern about *cultural insensitivity* toward immigrant groups and the unfairness of penalties for behaviors that are legal in the immigrants' home countries but outlawed in the United States. Defense attorneys for immigrants may try to represent their clients by using *cultural defenses.* As one illustration, an immigrant father might try to force his 12-year-old daughter to marry a much older man. In the United States, the groom could be prosecuted for child sexual assault (B. Murray, 1999; Torry, 2000). The following case history exemplifies this cultural clash of laws.

## CASE HISTORY  Honor Killing in New York

On February 17, 2009, Muzzammil Hassan entered a police department near Buffalo, New York, and announced that his wife was dead—nothing more. Later the district attorney of Erie County, Frank Seditat III, charged the 44-year-old man with second-degree murder for *beheading* his 37-year-old wife, Aasiya Hassan. Attorney Seditat said that Muzzammil was a pretty "vicious and remorseless bastard." Psychology Professor Dr. Phyllis Chesler said, "The fierce and gruesome nature of this murder signals it's an honor killing."

What precipitated Muzzammil's actions? Aasiya had filed for divorce on February 6 and obtained a protective order after multiple episodes of domestic violence. According to experts, Muslim men often consider divorce a dishonor on their family.

Rabbi Brad Hirschfield, a producer and host for Bridges TV, said that it would be inappropriate to leap to the conclusion that beheadings of women are intrinsic to Islam. He asked whether one should consider drunkenness as intrinsic to Irish Catholics.

It is especially troubling to note that Muzzammil and Aasiya had founded Bridges TV in 2004 to counter anti-Islam stereotypes . . . (J. R. Miller, 2009)

## Prevalence of Intimate Partner Violence
## Among Racial/Ethnic Groups

The following *two lists* highlight prevalence estimates of racial intimate partner violence *before* NCVS and other data-gathering groups *changed their classification scheme* by combining Hispanic Whites with Whites and non-Hispanic Blacks with Blacks.

### General observations

- First, surveys do *not usually* uncover major differences in partner abuse between *various ethnic groups,* such as Latinos and Pacific Islanders.
- Second, minority groups are likely to show significant variations within their own group.
- Third, some racial disparities do appear if analysts *aggregate* data into a *single minority category of "other"* and then contrast the "other" group against the majority group.
- Fourth, NCVS data have revealed significantly higher IPV rates for Blacks relative to Whites and members of some other racial groups.

### Comparisons of male-to-female intimate partner violence by ethnic groups based on the federal government's previous classification systems

- *American Indian/Alaska Natives* reported the *most male partner violence* (30.7%) and Asian/Pacific Islanders reported the least (12.8%) (Tjaden & Thoennes, 2000a).
- *Black female* victims have a rate 35% higher than that for *White females* and 2.5 times higher than that for other races (Rennison & Welchans, 2000).
- *Native American Indians* reported a 58% lifetime rate of male-to-female IPV, a 30.1% past year rate, a 9.3% rate while pregnant, a 12.2% sexual assault lifetime rate, and a 42% rate for those on welfare in the past year (Malcoe, Duran, & Montgomery, 2004)
- The rate for *Hispanics* was 21.2% and for mixed races it was 27% (Tjaden & Thoennes, 2000a).
- Relative to *African American women,* about 4 times as many *Hispanic* women and 3 times as many *White* women reported *sexual abuse* (Grossman & Lundy, 2008).
- No large *Black/White differences* appeared in the National Violence Against Women Survey (Tjaden & Thoennes, 2000a).
- Partner victimization rates of *South Asian men/women* were 16.4% (Leung & Cheung, 2008).
- Sexual coercion among 292 *Latinas* including migrant workers was 20.9% (Hazen & Soriano, 2007).

## Distinctive Features of Immigrants
## and Minority Intimate Partner Violence

There are some features of IPV that vary somewhat between ethnic groups.

*African Americans.* Studies of partner violence with samples of African Americans are relatively extensive. Almost without exception, the surveys show higher rates for both African American men and women. It is challenging to pinpoint the exact reason for racial discrepancies, but one theory is the failure to account for socioeconomic status. What is sorely missing within this body of research is any substantial investigation of *contextual factors* that would help explain the disparities.

Some commentators are concerned about the dwindling marriage rate among African Americans. One investigator suggests that Black women are especially concerned about entering patriarchal marriages because of the potential for negative outcomes, such as loss of autonomy (S. A. Hill, 2006). Risk factor appraisals have uncovered numerous risk factors for partner violence, such as poverty, unemployment, and alcohol/drug misuse. Possibly the most salient risk factors are *economic distress* (including male joblessness) combined with *residency in socially disadvantaged neighborhoods* (Benson, Fox, DeMaris, & Van Wyk, 2003; see also Williams, Oliver, & Pope, 2008).

*Arab Americans.* One researcher comprehensively tested 67 Arab immigrant women about the amount of partner abuse they experienced, their attitudes toward gender role traditions, wife beating, their endorsement of patriarchal beliefs, and their use of service agencies. The research participants emigrated from Palestine, Syria, Lebanon, Egypt, and other countries. Prevalence rates for several variables are as follows: (a) severe physical abuse—73%, (b) severe sexual coercion—40%, (c) minor physical abuse—100%, and (d) severe injuries—40%. More than half the women disagreed with the statement that a woman should divorce her husband as a solution to partner abuse. Nevertheless, more than half the women were divorced or separated.

Attitudes toward women and wife beating were ambiguous. The majority of the women (88%) agreed that "it is very important for a woman to be a virgin before marriage." Nearly all the women disagreed with the idea that "a man has a right to have sex with his wife when he wants, even though she may not want to." Research participants (25%) considered wife beating to be justifiable under certain circumstances, such as "challenging a husband's manhood." A shocking 25% agreed that "killing a woman for sexual infidelity was justified" (e.g., the "honor" imperative). A sizeable majority (88%) did *not* endorse the view that "battered wives are responsible for their abuse because they intended it to happen." Inconsistently, 31% endorsed the statement that "a battered woman is solely responsible for being beaten because she obviously did something that irritated her husband" and 87% *disagreed* with the statement "in most cases, it is the woman's fault that she was beaten by her husband."

In addition to calling the police, the women sought help for partner abuse from several sources. They were most likely to go to an Arab family service organization or seek legal services. They were least likely to seek mental health services or mainstream social services. Women who endorsed ideas that wife beating is justifiable and that women are responsible for their own abuse were less likely than women who disagreed with these ideas to seek services. Despite living in the United States for an average of 10 years (range 1–29 years), the attitudes of these immigrants remain dissimilar to those of people living in the United States (Abu-Ras, 2007).

*Native American Indians.* Native American Indian women are the most victimized ethnic/racial group of women in the United States. It is important to note, however, that no research has examined the possibility of cultural differences in disclosure rates (Wahab, 2005). Some additional prevalence rates for lifetime intimate partner violence among American Indians are the following: (a) $N = 28,139$ women—27.8% (Silverman, Decker, Saggurti, Balaiah, & Raj, 2008); (b) $N = 341$ women—52% (Fairchild, Fairchild, & Stoner, 1998); (c) Lifetime $N = 88$—61.4% (Tjaden & Thoennes, 2000a).

One comparison, contrasting the viewpoints of 20 *American Indian* women with those of 20 *European American* women, identified some significant differences. Native American Indian women were more likely than European American women to endorse the next two statements: (a) "If a person hits you, you should hit them back," and (b) "It's okay to beat up a person for badmouthing me or my family." In contrast, they were less likely to endorse the statement "If someone tries to start a fight with you, you should walk away." The two groups also had significantly different ideas about the *meaning of partner violence.* First, Native American Indian women emphasized physical IPV, while European American women included both physical and verbal abuse. Second, Native American Indian women thought partner abuse was rare, while European American women thought it was hidden (Tehee & Esqueda, 2008).

One distinctive condition affecting Native American Indians is a type of *historical trauma,* caused by oppression that is passed down across generations. An entire family may be suffering from something akin to *learned helplessness.* A lack of knowledge about the *historical context* of abuse clouds the interpretation of research findings. In addition, Native Americans face a combination of legal inequality, poverty, racism, and continuing federal neglect. These conditions translate into haphazard law enforcement, if any, and lack of treatment services or shelter-like facilities. Many criminal offenders come onto reservation from other areas, few are convicted, and penalties are extremely lenient, such as a 6-month jail term for rape. Tribal laws usually rely on *restorative justice,* a victim-centered approach. VAWA funds are finally reaching the tribes, suggesting that more research will be conducted soon (Hamby, 2009; Jones, 2008).

*Asian Americans.* Immigrants from *Southern Asian countries* come to the United States with strong cultural beliefs that do not merge easily with those of the majority culture. Asian Americans may not define a partner's violent behavior as abusive. When asked to list their personal problems, battered Asian women might mention financial management or their fear that their children will lose their cultural roots. There is almost no chance that they would volunteer the information that their partner's violence is a problem, although they might provide a hint. They are not comfortable disclosing their problems to strangers, and they are prone to tolerating partner abuse in a way that makes their victimization invisible (Leung & Cheung, 2008; see Raj & Silverman, 2002, for a comprehensive review).

*Haitian immigrants.* Haitian immigrants are likely to have experienced and witnessed acts of violence on the street or even suffered torture. Wife beating is *normal* and occurs openly, outside of homes. Some people even clap their hands in approbation because some particular woman is "getting what she deserves." At least half of all Haitians in the United States are undocumented and thus vulnerable to deportation. In a qualitative study of 15 individuals from three groups (service providers, courts/police, and culture-specific clinics or churches), researchers gathered narrative statements that revealed problems for the immigrants. The primary goal of most Haitian battered women is basic survival (food, housing). In addition to the aforementioned difficulties with religiously linked behavior and acceptance of violence against women, the researchers obtained a sampling of problematic attitudes: (a) Haitians are confused about the role of police and services such as counseling; and (b) they are misinformed about women residing in shelters and hence they are reluctant to go to shelters (Latta & Goodman, 2005).

*Latinos.* Latino culture strongly affects the meaning and the measurement of male-to-female partner violence. Latinas face many barriers associated with disclosure of male-to-female IPV: *language, fear of deportation,* and *poverty* (e.g., Acevedo, 2000; Torres, 1998; Vogel & Marshall, 2001). Country-of-origin differences and degree of acculturation further contribute to these barriers (Aldarondo, Kantor, & Jasinski, 2002). For both men and women in a study of 387 Latino couples, *low acculturation led to stress and stress led directly to male partner violence.* For women, however, a second path led from *high acculturation directly to IPV.* Hence, either acculturation or acculturation stress are related to intimate partner violence (Caetano, Ramisetty-Mikler, Vaeth, & Harris, 2007).

## Disclosure Patterns

One study ($N = 164$) found that acculturated *Latina* patients at health clinics were significantly more likely to report victimization by their male partner than less acculturated Latinas (Garcia, Hurwitz, & Kraus, 2004). *African American* women have an especially difficult time reporting male partner abuse for several *reasons,* including the following (C. C. Bell & Mattis, 2000; Donovan & Williams, 2002; S. A. Hill, 2006; Moss, Pitula, Campbell, & Halstead, 1997):

- The stereotype of *strong, invulnerable Black woman*
- *Urging by clergy to fight collective racism—do not disclose to police*
- Exposure may appear as *disloyalty to members of the community*
- Already experienced *unhelpful/biased responses from the criminal justice system*
- May not receive the type of *help they need* even if they do disclose their MFIPV

## Trait Comparisons

What little research has been conducted has shown that trait differences among minority individuals involved in partner violence vary along some of the same dimensions as those of the majority White individuals.

*Gender trait comparison.* In one inquiry, researchers compared the personality traits of 2,254 male and 281 female IPV perpetrators in a primarily *African American* sample. The *men* were more likely than the women to have had *prior conduct disorders and substance abuse problems.*

The women were more likely than the men to have previously *attempted suicide,* to *have personality dysfunction and mood disorders,* and to have taken *psychotropic medications* prior to arrest. More women than men also reported *observing severe interparental violence* and having received *corporal punishment* during childhood. Regardless of the observed dissimilarities, male and female perpetrators obtained scores on the questionnaires that were more alike than different (Henning, Jones, & Holdford, 2003).

*Differences among Latina partner-violent offenders (FMIPV).* A newer investigation looked for differences between English- and Spanish-speaking women's partner violence. Reports of 125 women court-ordered into a program for batterers comprised the data for the study. Analyses indicated that the *Spanish speakers* were significantly *less likely* to be citizens of the United States and therefore less likely to be acculturated. As expected, the English-speaking Latinas perpetrated a greater frequency of female partner violence than the Spanish-speaking Latinas. The investigators suggested that the findings reflect the lesser acceptability of female aggression in the Hispanic culture. Of the women ordered into treatment, 94% said that their male partner committed physical assaults against them. The male partners also used significantly more control tactics than the female partners used. Almost 89% of the women had called the police for assistance, and more than 50% had separated from their partner because of the violence. Of these female "aggressors," 19% sought medical treatment compared with 3.3% of their male partners. Thus, Hispanic females were *primarily victims* rather than perpetrators (Tower & Fernandez, 2008).

**CASE HISTORY** "Don't Send Me Back"

Budhwantie Ferri, a 41-year-old nursing student, gave $15,000 to a police informant as a "down payment" to murder her 64-year-old husband, Antonio Ferri, a wealthy businessman. Before trying to hire a hit man, Budhwantie tried to kill her husband by injecting him with dirty needles from the medical center where she worked. The plan was to have the hit man help her inject her husband with HIV, and if that didn't work, to run him over with a car. According to a police lieutenant, Antonio wanted to annul his marriage to Budhwantie, an action that could have resulted in Budhwantie's deportation to Venezuela (de la Cruz, 2001).

## Immigrant and Ethnic Batterers

There is relatively little information over and above prevalence data that compares immigrant and ethnic batterers. A team of researchers undertook a *qualitative* investigation of 15 incarcerated *Latino* male partner abusers. One appraisal pinpointed several factors that seemed to precipitate Latino partner abuse: (a) anger, (b) gender role expectations, (c) acculturation stresses, and (d) lack of self-control. From these male immigrants' perspectives, the effect of incurring a criminal record because of their partner abuse was a serious problem. The men also felt that raising community awareness about battering would be helpful (Saez-Betacourt, Lam, & Nguyen, 2008).

A survey of *Korean* immigrant batterers revealed that 80% reported being exposed to parental violence (Shin, 1995). *African American men* tend to drop out of treatment programs at higher rates than European American (Gondolf & Williams, 2001). In contrast, being *Latino* was a *strong predictor of program completion,* according to a system-wide analysis of 30 batterer intervention programs (L. W. Bennett, Stroops, Call, & Flett, 2007).

## Motives for Intimate Partner Violence

Just as motives for partner violence vary among the majority White male and female partner abusers, so do they vary among minority members by gender and culture.

*Motives for female-to-male IPV.* One inquiry examined motivations for female-to-male intimate partner abusers among *White, African American, and Mexican American* poor women. A sample of these motivations appears below (Weston, Marshall, & Coker, 2007).

1. *African American* and *Mexican American* women, relative to White women, were significantly more likely to report *childhood experiences* as a motivating factor.
2. Both *Mexican American* and *African American* women rated motives *to increase intimacy* and for *retaliation* significantly higher than White women did.
3. Overall, no two groups had similar patterns.
4. *African American women* in a *female-primary-perpetrator group* committed significantly more female-to-male IPV than did women in either the male-primary-perpetrator or the mutually violent groups.

*Motives for African American female-to-male intimate partner violence (FMIPV).* A team of researchers conducted a path analysis in a complex, four-model design based on a range of variables. They provided information about the motivations for female-to-male partner violence among African American women. The analyses revealed several significant associations:

1. Female victimization was directly correlated with female aggression. That is, female *victimization* was a *cause* of female offending.
2. Female victimization was indirectly related to female offenders' post-traumatic stress disorder (PTSD). Female victimization was correlated with *PTSD,* then PTSD was correlated with both *anger-out* and *anger-control.* Anger-out (but not anger-control) was then correlated with female offending.
3. Female victimization was also correlated with depression, and depression was correlated with anger-in. Anger-in, however, was not linked with FMIPV.

These findings support the long-held supposition that a female victim's *abuse-instigated anger may* function as the motivation for her violence against her male partner (Swan, Gambone, Fields, Sullivan, & Snow, 2005).

*Male motivation for partner abuse.* Role strain associated with immigration and acculturation help explain *male partner violence,* but highly acculturated *Mexican men* perpetrated even more frequent partner violence. The researchers suggest that this relationships stems from the frustration of their "unrealized aspirations" (Kantor, Jasinski, & Aldarondo, 1994).

## Differences in Attitudes Toward the Criminal Justice System

Researchers have uncovered a small number of racial disparities in regard to attitudes about the actions of the criminal justice system.

*Calling the police.* African American women are *more likely* than *European American* women to seek help for male partner violence from police (see Goodman, Bennett & Dutton, 1999; Hutchison & Hirschel, 1998). NCVS data show that 67% of *Black* women, compared with 50% of *White* women, made reports to police (Rennison & Welchans, 2000). *Latinos were marginally more likely* (p = .071) to call the police than *non-Latinos* (Ingram, 2007). Asian battered women are especially unlikely to ask the police for assistance (Chavez et al., 2005). A small study of 67 Arab Muslim women found that of the 73% of severely battered women, 72% had called the police, and 40% had obtained protective orders (Abu-Ras, 2007). In regard to prosecuting partner violent men, one study found that *White* women are more likely to favor prosecution than *Latinas* and *African American* women (Bui, 2001).

*Police behavior.* One persistent allegation has been that the police treatment of minorities is biased. Despite such assumptions, a study of *police behavior* concluded that police treat partner violence cases involving minority group members about the same as cases involving non-minorities (e.g., Hutchison, Hirschel, & Pesackis, 1994). Likewise, a finding among *immigrant victims was* that 84% to 94% "felt police were responsive to their concerns" (e.g., R. C. Davis & Erez, 1998, p. 5). By comparison, evaluations of law enforcement's responses in a different study were far less positive. In a sample of 125 Latinas in a court-ordered treatment program for batterers, 51.4% asserted that the police treated them badly. The women's displeasure was probably the outcome of the policemen's focus when handling the call. The police concentrated so heavily on the violence, rather than the context, that they ignored the self-defensive nature of the women's actions. In this account, the women's experiences may have been so discouraging that only 35% said they would call the police in the future. The researchers concluded that, "It is not appropriate to criminalize women in violent relationships who respond to violence with violence" (Tower & Fernandez, 2008, p. 35).

## Consequences of Male-to-Female Intimate Partner Violence

A large number of serious physical and mental health effects stem from partner violence. Some of these are relatively temporary, but some are chronic and disabling.

*Health problems.* African American victims, compared with nonvictims, have significantly *more health problem,* more health problems per medical visit, and more emergency room visits (e.g., Schollenberger et al., 2003). Of 1,212 Latinas participating in an intimate partner violence study,

44% reported having poor to fair health compared with 21% of non-Latinos (Denham et al., 2007). A number of Asian victims of male partner violence suffered from burns and scalding. They also endured an increased number of miscarriages, broken bones, and other injuries (Raj & Silverman, 2003). To date, research has revealed that all the immigrant and minority battered women (Arab, Asian, Black, and Latina) are at greater risk for HIV infection than nonminority battered women (see Denham et al., 2007; Y. Lee & Hadeed, 2009). As an illustration, 22% of 28,139 physically and sexually abused married Indian women tested positive for HIV (Silverman et al., 2008).

*Mental health problems.* Not surprisingly, victimization also has negative *mental/emotional effects.* One assessment of *African American* women, for instance, revealed a significant effect of partner violence on *PTSD symptoms* (Lilly & Graham-Berman, 2009). Of 55 *Vietnamese* women, those who were abused experienced significantly more *fear* of their partners than did nonabused Vietnamese women (Morash et al. 2008).

Victimization contributes to *depression.* Half of a sample of *African American* victims interviewed in an emergency room had *attempted suicide.* The suicide attempters, contrasted with the nonattempters, scored significantly higher on a depression inventory (Houry, Kaslow, & Thompson, 2005). In a different comparison of 265 primarily *African American* women (74% from a prenatal clinic) researchers determined the effects of *cumulative abuse* on *depressive symptoms.* Using self-report data, the investigators divided the participants into four abuse/ nonabuse categories: (a) *no child sexual abuse (CSA) and no adult abuse;* (b) *CSA only;* (c) *adult abuse* only (intimate partner or family member); and (d) *both CSA and adult abuse.* The results supported the authors' hypotheses that child sexual abuse and adult abuse had a *cumulative effect* on depressive symptoms. The greater the amount of abuse suffered by women in the four groups, the greater the extent of their depressive symptoms. Both stress and feeling powerless were related to more frequent depressive symptoms, and family support was related to fewer depressive symptoms (McGuigan & Middlemiss, 2005). Studies of *Latinas* produced similar results (Hazen, Connelly, Soriano, & Landsverk, 2008).

*African Americans, Hispanics, and other races.* A study of 475 recently abused women included 328 *African American* women, 103 *Hispanic* women, and 44 *other race* women drawn from the Chicago Women's Health Risk Study. Psychologists specified a number of *predictors of the amount of help-seeking:* (a) *number of incidents a year,* (b) *experiencing a very severe assault,* (c) *being har*assed (e.g., stalked), and (d) *having a support network.* Having a *support network* was the most significant predictor of seeking help (Sabina & Tindale, 2008; see Greer, 2007).

*White, African Americans, and Latinas.* One survey focused on help-seeking actions of White, African American, and Latina *economically marginalized women* seeking medical care in Florida. Of 321 women responding to a mental health inquiry about *depression,* the most frequently cited rationale for not disclosing abuse was that the women thought *health care issues* and *partner violence issues* were *separate concerns* (Van Hook, 2000).

*Arab women.* For women in the *Arab* community, help-seeking was related to *attitudes toward women and beliefs about the justifiability of wife beating.* More specifically, participants who did *not* justify wife beating and who did *not* blame wives for male-partner victimization, were significantly more likely to seek help from shelters, hotlines, and safe homes (Abu-Ras, 2007).

*Latinos vs. non-Latinos.* One investigation conducted a random-digit-dial survey of 12,039 households in 20 selected sites matched on socioeconomic status: (a) 16.4% of the sample was *Latino and* (b) 82.9% was *non-Latino.* Within this *middle-aged sample,* about 48% was male and about 52% was female. Of *Latinos,* less than half (47.4%) had lived in the United States "all my life" compared with 90.5% of the *non-Latinos.* Analyses revealed interesting results about help-seeking for partner violence (Ingram, 2007; see also Brabeck & Guzmán, 2008).

- Latinos and non-Latinos were *not* significantly different in seeking help from informal sources.
- Latinos were significantly *more likely* than non-Latinos to *disclose their abuse* to a family member and to be asked about partner violence by a professional.
- Latinos were significantly *less likely* to have knowledge about community resources and to disclose their abuse to a health care worker or clergyman.
- Latinos, in particular, were *less* likely than non-Latinos to seek help from a shelter.

## Social Support

Several social scientists have identified the importance of social support to battered women (Fowler & Hill, 2004; M. P. Thompson et al., 2000). In a racial comparison between *African American* and *White* women, researchers ascertained the following: (a) *Satisfaction* with social support was equivalent across races, (b) both groups had a similar number of *available kin,* and (c) African American women had a *smaller number of available friends.* The researchers concluded, however, that previous assumptions that African American women can rely on a strong kinship network appear to be *unfounded* (Griffin, Armodeo, Clay, Fassler, & Ellis, 2006). A different assessment revealed that members of support networks were most likely to advise *African American and Hispanic women* to leave the abuser but advised *South Asian women* to stay (Yoshioka, Gilbert, El-Bassel, & Baig-Amin, 2003).

*Asian women.* For *battered Asian immigrant women,* social support is virtually nonexistent. Asian women are frequently isolated from their natal families and risk ostracism from their communities if they disclose their victimization status. It is extremely important to "save face" or maintain the family's honor. An Asian immigrant woman may not be able to seek refuge with a relative, neighbor, or friend because the entire community will know where she is and expose her whereabouts. The husband can easily find her and force her to return (Chavez et al., 2005). Asian sources of support are most likely to be medical doctors.

*Latinas.* In a study of 1,212 female blue collar workers, abused *Latinas* were significantly more likely to lack social support compared with nonabused Latinas. Of this group, 25% said they had no friend or family member nearby who could help them (Denham et al., 2007). The primary agents of social support for *Latinas* are their family and kinship/friendship networks. Although the presence of an extended family can be a protective factor, many immigrant Latinas may be separated from their families and thus unable to take advantage of this resource. (See Swan & Snow, 2006, for a review).

## Differences in Leave/Stay Decisions

Just as battered women in the majority group find it difficult to leave an abusive husband, so do minority women. Some concerns reach across nearly every group: (a) *emotional connection to the abuser,* (b) *economic dependency on the abuser,* (c) *reluctance to break up families,* and (d) *fear of more violence, control, and retaliation.*

*African American women. African American* women's attempts to leave were similar to those of *other racial groups'* attempts. They were *cyclical* in nature with several returns before leaving permanently (Bliss, Ogley-Oliver, Jackson, Harp, & Kaslow, 2008). Women who *left* experienced significantly more *harassment* (e.g., stalking), more efforts by the batterer to control them, and better physical health. Being a *homemaker,* rather than being employed, was a *significant hindrance* to leaving (Sabina & Tindale, 2008), and cuts in welfare services appeared to endanger the lives of *Black* women (Dugan, Nagin, & Rosenfeld, 1999). Despite such handicaps, one comparison found that *women of color* were significantly *more likely* to leave an abusive relationship than *Anglo* women (Panchanadeswaran & McCloskey, 2007).

*Vietnamese women.* An inquiry about the lives of 57 *Vietnamese* women living in an enclave revealed that those who escaped abusive husbands had been able to seek help from a variety of sources compared with those who did not escape. Those who did *not* escape were more likely than those who did to place a high value on *maintaining a family* and *living in a patriarchal family.* Those who did *not* escape were also more *fearful of their partner.* Some factors expected to influence leave/stay decisions, such as age, education level, and extent of male partner IPV, did *not* exert a substantial influence on their decision making (Morash et al., 2008).

*Mexican American.* In an evaluation of leave/stay decisions among a group of primarily *Mexican American rural women* receiving welfare for their children, 96% needed the welfare because of victimization by their abusive partners (Krishnan, Hilbert, McNeil, & Newman, 2004). As is true with male-to-female IPV in general, *surveys of women on welfare* show that minority women experience three times as much battering as nonminority women (see Connelly et al., 2006). Welfare programs, however, may reduce the level of MFIPV suffered by some victims.

---

### SECTION SUMMARY

### Immigrant/Ethnic/Racial Intimate Partner Violence

The information presented in this section clarifies how a woman's decisions about partner abuse are filtered through a cultural lens. The foregoing content describes how the beliefs and customs of immigrants are fundamental to the decisions women make about the acceptability of partner violence and the options available to them for responding to the violence. Understanding these decisions requires recognition of the basic *difference in worldview* held by immigrants and residents of the host nation. The meaning of a worldview, as used here, is whether one's *goals* are individualistic or collectivist:

---

*Individualism*—self-actualization—the individual is an authority unto himself—popular in Western societies

*Collectivism*—the betterment of the community—the community is the authority (especially widespread in Asian countries)

Connected to a culture's worldview is its *tolerance for diverse behaviors* and a *range of lifestyles.* A Western woman has the privilege of making choices about having a career and family, while an Asian woman must learn how to conform to a rigid gender role. A reality-based evaluation of *the options* available to her for handling partner violence is a second factor shaping her decisions. By necessity, she must take into account her *legal status,* the *services available* to her, her *ability to navigate these services* (e.g., language facility, transportation), and her *level of family and community support.*

An abused woman from a *Western* society might emphasize her need to leave her partner, to "move on," and how to make a new life that is more satisfying. An abused woman from another culture, by contrast, might use a collaborative process in considering what is best for her family and her community and how to "save face." In the final analysis, it is not surprising that an Asian immigrant will hesitate before leaving her abusive partner (based on Yoshioka & Choi, 2005).

*African Americans and Native American Indians* face somewhat similar obstacles in dealing with male IPV. They must overcome historical racism that has affected every aspect of their lives. Their prejudicial treatment has been humiliating and painful and has robbed them of equal opportunities to obtain an education and economic security. In addition, their legal and social status has jeopardized their very existence. The accessibility of services for battered women in these groups is limited and often culturally inappropriate.

*Latinas* face challenges from cultural influences and the forces of acculturation. Factors such as having to help support their poverty-stricken families in their native countries increase their poverty. Language proficiency poses another difficulty.

These briefly outlined group differences do not specify the many overlapping disadvantages. As stated at the beginning of the chapter, racism, classism, xenophobia, language barriers, cultural beliefs, and other factors have combined to render male partner violence hidden in many segments of the American population. Society as a whole, and family violence experts in particular, must continue their efforts to bring the complexities of male partner abuse into the light of scientific inquiry.

## RURAL MALE-TO-FEMALE INTIMATE PARTNER VIOLENCE

The term *rural* refers to a geographic location that is sparsely populated. As of 2000, the U.S. Census Bureau drew on population density to define rural areas as all territory outside of urbanized areas and urban clusters. Rural areas comprise open country and settlements with fewer than 2,500 residents (Congressional Research Service Reports), thus rural residents often live far apart.

Although it is common to think of Appalachia as America's rural area, there are rural areas in almost every state and some of them are multicultural. The most obvious extra burden battered women experience living in a rural community is lack of access to services. Essentially, rural abused women live in a cultural *enclave of patriarchy.* Close-knit families, kinships, and friendship networks typical of rural communities greatly diminish rural abuse victims' ability and willingness to seek help. In addition to the patriarchal social order, there is an entire spectrum of *barriers* blocking women's efforts to find help. Some of the most noteworthy include (a) *isolation,* (b) *lack of phones and transportation,* (c) *lack of confidentiality,* (d) *little, if any, social support,* (e) *lack of medical care and medical screening,* (f) *greater gun use,* (g) *inadequate or no criminal justice response,* and (h) *little or no legal representation.*

The American Prosecutors Research Institute (APRI, 2006) noted several conditions that impact rural communities: (a) *low employment linked with significantly higher crime rates than found in urban areas;* (b) *social problems such as teen pregnancies, single-parent households, low educational achievement, and high school drop-out rates;* and (c) *low economic growth.* These obstacles negatively impact the delivery of criminal justice system services. Overarching this already vast number of roadblocks, rural battered women, like battered women everywhere, have less income, are less educated, are less employed, and have more childhood abuse compared with their nonabused counterparts. This confluence of negative conditions makes rural battered women extremely vulnerable to male partner abuse (DeKeseredy & Schwartz, 2008; Krishnan, Hilbert, & Pase, 2001; Shannon, Logan, Cole, & Medley, 2006).

## Law Enforcement

Rural women are at a great disadvantage in calling police when they need assistance for several reasons. First, the police often must answer calls for service across vast distances, and the total number of law enforcement personnel is sparse. Second, police often participate in the "good ol' boys" network that oppresses women (Websdale, 1995). Police officers know the offenders, socialize with them, and may sympathize with them more than with the female victims. Third, the antiwoman, antivictim bias typical of the criminal justice system as a whole is more apparent in rural settings. Research clearly shows that rural women gauge law enforcement as less responsive than do urban women (Shannon et al., 2006; Shuman et al., 2008). The reports of a few women, nevertheless, show that there are some pockets of real support. One woman told of her favorable interaction with a judge.

> "'If I ever see you back in this court, or you ever lay a hand on her or that child,' he [the judge] said, 'I'll see you under the jail!'—and he meant it."
>
> (Van Hightower & Gorton, 2002, p. 855)

## Male-to-Female Intimate Partner Violence

The type of male partner violence characteristic of many rural communities could be designated *intimate terrorism* because of patriarchal control of women and the fear it generates. Refer to Table 10.12 for statistics on abuse of rural women.

**TABLE 10.12**    Male-to-Female Intimate Partner Violent Events Among Rural Women

| Dimension of Abuse From Male Partner | 378 Women With Protective Orders | 87 Emergency Room Patients | Women Attending Medical Clinics |
|---|---|---|---|
| Lifetime | 100% | 41% | |
| Lifetime physical | 97.6% | | |
| Lifetime sexual | 30.2% | | |
| Last year sexual | $m = 25.48$ | | |
| Last year physical | $m = 79.88$ | | |
| Current physical | | 29% | 26% of 81 women |
| Ex-partner physical | | 18% | 35% of 79 women |

SOURCES: Shannon et al., 2006; Krishnan et al., 2001; M. Johnson & Elliott, 1997.

*NCVS.* According to the National Crime Victimization Survey data for 2001 to 2005, the annual rate of intimate family violence for female victims was 5.5% and for male victims it was 0.8%. Homicides in rural areas top those occurring in urban and suburban areas (Catalano, 2007).

In addition to the lack of services for battered women, there are other rural-urban differences. A large-sample study highlighted several kinds of differences between female victims in different areas (urban vs. rural) and between different races (Black vs. White) (Grossman, Hinkley, Kawalski, & Margrave, 2005). Refer to Table 10.13 for a summary of shelter-seeking differences.

**TABLE 10.13**    A Comparison of Shelter-Seeking Among Rural/Urban and Black/White Women

| Dimension of Abuse From Male Partner | Seeking Shelter Service for the First Time in an Urban Area | | Seeking Shelter Service for the First Time in a Rural Area | |
|---|---|---|---|---|
| | Black—$n = 17,119$ 88.4% current/ ex-partner | White—$n = 17,510$ 90.1% current/ ex-partner | Black—$n = 1,420$ 97.1% current/ ex-partner | White—$n = 17,203$ 89% current/ ex-partner |
| Physical | 40.0% | 60.0% | 41.5% | 62.6% |
| Sexual | 48.4% | 30.0% | 45.6% | 26.5% |

SOURCE: Grossman et al., 2005.

## Sociodemographic Comparisons

A comparison of rural women ($n = 378$) and urban women ($n = 379$) revealed large *socioeconomic disparities* between groups. Rural women were significantly *more likely* than urban women to be White and married, and *less likely* to have a high school education, to be employed, and to have an income over $15,000 a year (Shannon et al., 2006).

One inquiry examined severely *abused rural women* ($n = 188$) (i.e., seeking emergency help from a shelter) with *nonabused rural women* ($n = 360$) recruited from local medical practices. Congruent with typical findings about abused women, abused women were significantly *less educated, less likely to be financially stable,* and had an *abusive family of origin.* Conversely, the risk of male partner abuse increased with age (Shuman et al., 2008). This significant age disparity is unusual given that abused women are nearly always *younger* than nonabused women.

A further analysis of the *characteristics of the partners* of the women uncovered other dissimilarities—the abusive partners had significantly more *drug problems.* Although the two groups did *not* differ statistically on gun ownership, the abusive men were significantly more likely to *carry a gun or knife.* Last, examination of the men's intimate relationships showed that the topics of a couple's arguments differed significantly. The abused group, compared with the nonabused group, experienced more *fighting over money* and the *female partner's family* (Shuman et al., 2008).

## Help-Seeking and Services Available

As previously mentioned, rural battered women have significantly more problems than urban battered women in disclosing their abuse and in seeking help to end the abuse. A major problem for those seeking formal sources of help (e.g., mental health counselors) is the *lack of funding* by the Violence Against Women Act and the Victims of Crime Act. Child abuse/neglect cases receive more funding than domestic violence cases, and urban services receive more than rural services. Victim advocates working in prosecutors' offices receive some funding. They spend the greatest amount of their time working with misdemeanor cases, a category that includes domestic violence. The second most time-consuming category is rape/sexual offenses. The geography of rural areas requires comparatively more of advocates' time. For instance, an advocate might need to drive a female victim to a shelter that is 100 miles away (American Prosecutors Research Institute, 2006).

*Help-seeking.* A comparison of urban and rural services disclosed many significant distinctions (Grossman et al., 2005).

- Of 19,239 clients in rural counties, service providers assisted 18.3%.
- Of 46,174 clients in one urban area, services providers assisted 43.9%.

See Table 10.14 for a summary of specific unmet needs of battered urban and rural women.

An assessment of *help-seeking strategies* among rural ($n = 378$) and urban ($n = 379$) women who had *obtained protective orders* found some group differences. *Urban women were more likely than rural women to make use of the following resources:* (a) *support from friends,* (b) *alcohol and drug treatment programs,* and (c) *victims' advocates* (Shannon et al., 2006).

**TABLE 10.14** Comparison of the Primary *Unmet* Service Needs of Urban and Rural Battered Women

| TOP THREE Unmet Needs | Seeking Shelter Service First Time in Urban Areas | | Seeking Shelter Service First Time in Rural Areas | |
|---|---|---|---|---|
| | Black *n* = 17,119 | White *n* = 17,530 | Black *n* = 1,420 | White *n* = 17,206 |
| Housing | 17.5% | 8.3% | 21.7% | 13.7% |
| Emotional support | 54.9% | 78.2% | 91.4% | 94.5% |
| Legal assistance | 46.9% | 55.0% | 62.5% | 71.3% |

SOURCE: Grossman et al., 2005.

*Coping strategies.* In regard to coping strategies, the *urban women* also sought more emotional support, used more positive self-talk, and participated in more exercise/meditation than the rural women. By contrast, rural women significantly more often relied on *denial* as a coping strategy and were more likely to *seek help from an attorney.* Women in either group who made *use of problem-focused coping,* relative to those who did not, sought out a significantly greater *number* of resources (Shannon et al., 2006).

---

**SECTION SUMMARY**

### Rural Battered Women

Although research on rural battered women is limited, it has expanded to form a steady stream year by year. The research findings about rural intimate partner violence are unusually consistent. Most investigators find that male partner physical violence is extremely high. There is a fairly high consensus that rural women are disadvantaged by several circumstances: (a) poverty; (b) unemployment; (c) isolation; (d) patriarchal attitudes; (e) lack of community awareness of male partner violence; (f) lack of community support, informal or formal; (g) a small number of underfunded geographically distant services, such as shelters; (h) unaware and untrained medical personnel; (i) heavy gun ownership; and (j) inadequately trained and funded law enforcement and criminal justice personnel. The sociodemographic profile of rural victims is quite similar to that of urban victims with one exception—age. The totality of these conditions makes escape very complicated.

---

## SAME-SEX INTIMATE PARTNER VIOLENCE (SSIPV)

In addition to heterosexual studies of IPV, researchers have increasingly broadened the scope and number of their investigations to include gay, lesbian, bisexual, and transgendered populations (see Lockhart, White, Causby, & Isaac, 1994). Research on same-sex intimate partner violence (SSIPV) is especially needed because of the many myths surrounding gays and lesbians, homophobia, homonegativity, and the vulnerabilities of these underserved groups (Fredriksen-Goldsen & Muraco 2010). Most research to date on homosexual IPV has used relatively more lesbian samples than gay samples.

For centuries, homophobia has been rampant in many cultures. *Global* authorities recognize these vulnerabilities and have declared discrimination against lesbian, gay, bisexual, and transgendered individuals to be a *human rights violation.* Attitudes of college students have become more tolerant of homosexuals. Although males, older persons, less educated persons, and conservatives are more homophobic than their counterparts, Black/White attitudes may not differ significantly (Jenkins, Lambert, & Baker, 2009). Being homosexual in America entails taxing experiences because of societal prejudice and the effects these biases have on them. Recently, there has been an upsurge in homophobic crimes, seemingly connected to worsened economic conditions (T. Anderson, 2009). See the listing below for explanation of such attitudes.

HOMOPHOBIA—An irrational fear, anger, hatred, contempt, or intolerance for lesbians and gays

HOMONEGATIVITY—A negative attitude (emotional, moral, or intellectual) toward homosexuality or homosexuals

HETEROSEXISM—Negative attitudes, biases, and discrimination favoring opposite-sex sexuality because they are "normal" and therefore "superior"

MINORITY STRESS—Attributions of *inferiority and defectiveness* toward various categories of people, even though people may have no control over their status, such as race (Brooks, 1981; see Balsam & Szymanski, 2005; Weinberg, 1972)

INTERNALIZED HOMOPHOBIA—A homosexual's incorporation of negative stereotypes into attitudes about himself/herself

*Same-Sex IPV definitions.* One definition of gay intimate partner violence is as follows:

> male-to-male intimate partner violence is "a means to control others through power, including physical and psychological threats (verbal and nonverbal) or injury (to the victim or others), isolation, economic deprivation, heterosexist control (threats to reveal homosexuality), sexual assaults, vandalism (destruction of property), or any combination of methods" (T. W. Burke, 1998, p. 164; National Coalition of Antiviolence Programs [NCAVP], 2001).

Based on anecdotal evidence, some social scientists have hypothesized the existence of a group of IPV tactics unique to same-sex partners: (a) threatening to *out* the partner (i.e., disclosing the partner's homosexuality to family, friends, and employers); (b) using heterosexist control or convincing the victims that they are *mutual batterers* when their same-sex IPV is self-defensive; and (c) threatening to *infect a gay partner with HIV* (see Giorgio, 2002; B. J. Hart, 1996; Letellier, 1996; N. E. Murphy, 1995). While most experts working in the field of female-to-male violence question whether female offenders should be categorized as *batterers,* some have surmised that women who hit other women (female-to-female IPV) probably *are* true batterers (Osthoff, 2002). In FFIPV, physical strength is more evenly matched than in female-to-male IPV. Thus, a female-to-female aggressor may be a batterer.

*Legal definitions.* Legal definitions of same-sex partner violence are crucial because they have a direct impact on victims' lives. Before the U.S. Supreme Court struck down the existing sodomy statutes in 13 states in 2003, the law's very existence prevented the legalizations of gay marriage. Because homosexuals are precluded from entering into legal marriages in nearly all jurisdictions, they are extremely vulnerable in matters of inheritance. Fortunately, they are able to surmount some problems through advance planning, wills, and other legal documents (Riggle, Rostosky, & Prather, 2006).

*Protective orders.* Homosexuals also encounter severe restrictions when it comes to obtaining protective orders following same-sex IPV-related crimes. Police in mandatory-arrest jurisdictions face an added dilemma in knowing whom to arrest—who the perpetrator is. Gay males subjected to a sexual assault are unable to obtain needed assistance from the courts *unless force is used.* Last, just as in heterosexual IPV, threats to lock a partner out of the house or threats to notify immigration authorities of a partner's illegal immigration status do not count as crimes.

*The genesis of homosexuality and the causes of violence.* Although a common belief has been that homosexuality is a lifestyle *choice,* budding neurobiological evidence suggests otherwise. Studies of birth order effects among latter-born sons (Bower, 2006), wiring of lesbians' brains (Associated Press, 2006a), and brain structure disparities (Levay & Hamer, 1994) all infer a *genetic/biological basis* for homosexuality (see DuPree, Mustanski, Bocklandt, Nievergelt, & Hamer, 2004).

Just as social learning theory can explain IPV among heterosexual partners, it may also explain intimate partner violence between homosexual partners. That is, gays and lesbians *learn to be violent* through *social learning (modeling).* Childhood exposure to parental violence and direct physical abuse are, in fact, influential in same-sex partner abuse. An investigation of family-of-origin violence and adult male-to-male IPV among a sample of HIV-positive men shed some light on the relationship between the two variables. The researchers used Revised Conflict Tactics Scales (CTS2) to assess male partner violence and the *Family-of-Origin Violence Scale* (L. L. Marshall & Rose, 1990) to assess witnessing abuse and being a direct victim of parental abuse during childhood. This inquiry with a sample of both offenders and victims (not partnered with each other) found a number of associations between subcomponents of the scales. See Table 10.15 for a composite of these significant associations.

Because there were no significant correlations between witnessing parental *male-to-female violence,* the researchers concluded that the results only partially supported the *intergenerational transmission of violence hypothesis* (Craft & Serovich, 2005). Others might argue that the intergenerational transmission of abuse hypothesis does *not* have to be sex-specific. (See www.sagepub.com/barnett3e for another formulation of the genesis of same-sex violence.)

**TABLE 10.15** Significant Associations Between Childhood Experiences and Adult Male-to-Male IPV

| | Same-Sex Adult Physical Assault | Same-Sex Adult Sexual Coercion | Injured as Adult |
|---|---|---|---|
| **Perpetrator of MMIPV** | | | |
| Saw father-to-mother IPV | | | |
| Saw mother-to-father IPV | | Significant+ | |
| Victim of direct parental abuse | Significant+ | Significant+ | |
| **Victim of MMIPV** | | | |
| Saw father-to-mother IPV | | Significant+ | |
| Saw mother-to-father IPV | | Significant+ | Significant+ |
| Victim of direct parental abuse | | | |

SOURCE: Adapted from Craft & Serovich, 2005 (*Journal of Interpersonal Violence*—Sage).

## Estimating the Prevalence/Incidence of Same-Sex IPV

Because measurement of same-sex IPV is unsatisfactory, research on homosexual violence cannot achieve its goals. What is more, finding research participants is especially difficult.

*Measurement.* First, there is an issue of measurement. One group of researchers concluded that the Conflict Tactics Scales (CTS) discriminate well along the severity of violence continuum within a sample of gay/bisexual men (Regan, Bartholomew, Oram, & Landolt, 2002). Other groups have expressed doubt about the suitability of the CTS for assessment of same-sex abuse. Even though CTS2 has made many substantial improvements over CTS, some scholars still feel obliged to modify the inventory (McHugh, Livingston, & Ford, 2005). In a survey of lesbians, for instance, researchers added IPV tactics, such as threatening to "out" a partner or "forcing a partner to be affectionate" in public (Balsam & Szymanski, 2005). One legal scholar contended that just as the CTS produces *gender-equivalent results* with reference to heterosexual IPV, so too does it produce gender-equivalent results when assessing same-sex partner violence. Thus, CTS abuse scores are often *higher for lesbians* than for gay men. As one scholar has commented, the CTS takes a nongendered approach to a gendered problem and in so doing creates a gender-biased viewpoint of same-sex IPV (Lilith, 2001). (See www.sagepub.com/barnett3e for information on research methodology.)

*Prevalence of same-sex IPV.* Along with measurement challenges, there are several reasons why researchers cannot determine accurate prevalence estimates of SSIPV. First, same-sex individuals habitually hide their sexual orientation because of stigma. Hence, for research participation they must self-identify their homosexuality, a potentially hazardous personal decision. As a consequence, there are no empirically sound sampling strategies available for obtaining a representative sample. Researchers usually must depend on handy samples with their many limitations. Even if these impediments did not exist, government agencies that would ordinarily obtain large samples have few mandates, if any, to assess the prevalence of SSIPV.

*Official reports.* Official reports of same-sex IPV are generally lacking because police and the FBI do not have categories suitable for classifying SSIPV. Instead, criminal justice system personnel place data from these offenders and victims into categories such as *friend or acquaintance.* Even the U.S. Census Bureau does not categorize homosexual couples as members of a household category during data collection. Instead, they must execute post-collection editing to estimate the number of same-sex households. For the 2000 census, statisticians estimated the number of homosexual households in the United States as ranging from 1.1 million to 1.6 million (O'Connell & Gooding, 2007).

*Estimates of same-sex IPV.* Same-sex partners classify partner abuse as their most serious *health problem* after AIDS, making it a very serious health problem indeed (Friedman, Marshal, Stall, Cheong, & Wright, 2008). As such, it is important to know the extent of same-sex intimate partner violence (Peterman & Dixon, 2003; see Island & Letellier, 1991). According to some accounts, same-sex IPV has varied from a low of 11% to 73% (Craft & Serovich, 2005). Most recently, investigators ascertained the prevalence rate of lesbian childhood abuse and IPV using a *unique matched control group* consisting of lesbians' heterosexual sisters. This study uncovered significant demographic dissimilarities. The lesbians were significantly older, better educated, more likely to live alone, and more likely to live in urban areas than their sisters. With regard to physical and sexual abuse during childhood and adulthood, the following *significant differences in incidence* between lesbians and their sisters occurred (Stoddard, Dibble, & Fineman, 2009):

| *Lesbians* suffered *more* abuse than *sisters* | *Both lesbians and sisters* suffered abuse |
| --- | --- |
| *Childhood* | *Childhood* |
| More incidents of physical abuse | More *physical* abuse by male relatives |
| More incidents of sexual abuse | *Adult* |
| *Adult* | More *sexual abuse* by male strangers |
| More sexual abuse incidents | |

An interesting interpretation of these results is that lesbians are *not* protected from male-to-female adult sexual assault because they have less exposure to men (Stoddard et al., 2009; see also Balsam, Rothblum, & Beauchaine, 2005). (For additional estimates of same-sex IPV, see the website for a tabular account of same-sex victimization rates, see Waldner-Haugrud, 1999.)

*Unwanted sexual experiences.* Assessment of 595 men attending a gay pride event provided data encompassing several aspects of sexual behavior. The researchers subdivided the men into four subgroups: (a) 385—no sexual abuse, (b) 81—adult sexual coercion, (c) 89—childhood sexual abuse only, and (d) 40—both childhood sexual abuse and adult coercion (revictimized). Forms of coercion primarily included *fear of abandonment, threat of force,* and *actual force.* Several significant differences between groups emerged from the data analyses: (a) men sexually abused as *either* a child *or* sexually coerced had more substance abuse problems, (b) *revictimized men* were most likely to have been treated for sexually transmitted diseases, and (c) men sexually coerced as *adults only* were the most *likely group to have had unprotected sex.* That is, this group was most at risk for HIV. This group also exhibited significantly more symptoms of dissociation, trauma-related anxiety, and borderline personality disorder.

The 89 men sexually abused as a child and the 40 men in the revictimized group did *not* participate in significantly more *risk behaviors* than the 81 men victimized only as adults. In this study, therefore, results did not support the revictimization hypothesis of participation in a greater number of risk behaviors than non-revictimized men (Kalichman et al., 2001).

*Reporting/disclosing same-sex IPV and crimes.* Both heterosexuals and homosexuals *underreport crimes* to the police, especially IPV crimes, and homosexuals report differently than heterosexuals. On balance, homosexuals contact the police significantly *less* often than heterosexual victims (C. R. Block, 2003). One noticeable distinction is that same-sex pairs may report IPV and hate (bias) incidents significantly differently (Kuehnle & Sullivan, 2003). See Table 10.16 for a summary of reported incidents.

**TABLE 10.16**   SSIPV and Bias Victimization Incidents Among Same-Sex Intimates

| | Number of Victimization Incidents Occurring | | Number Victimization Incidents Reported | |
|---|---|---|---|---|
| Incidents | Gays | Lesbians | Gays | Lesbians |
| IPV (*n* = 119) | 74 (62.2%) | 45 (37.8%) | 49% | 60% |
| Bias (hate) (*n* = 143) | 118 (82.5%) | 25 (17.5%) | 66% | 50% |

SOURCE: Kuehnle & Sullivan, 2003 (*Criminal Justice and Behavior*—Sage)

## Partner Violence

*Lesbians and public attitudes.* Lesbian FFIPV victims elicit very little sympathy from the public. Even individuals trained to help others in critical situations, such as mental health professionals, seem inclined to hold lesbian *victims responsible* for their own victimization. Most lay observers have an even more difficult time perceiving lesbian IPV victims as worthy victims. What is more, there appears to be a strong reluctance within the lesbian community to acknowledge FFIPV.

Some of the aversion stems from a strong belief in *partner equality* among lesbian intimates. Because feminists hold that IPV arises from *patriarchal practices,* they envisaged that lesbians would be free of such attitudes (Renzetti, 1992). A related problem is connected to the greater willingness of many critics to attach the label of *mutual combat* to homosexual abuse compared with heterosexual abuse (B. Hart, 1986).

*Attitudes of the public toward same-sex partner abuse.* One word academicians use to describe the rejecting attitude of society, police, juries, medical professionals, and others toward persons with a same-sex orientation is **homonegativity.** The public seems to accept many false beliefs (myths) about homosexuals and their sexual activities because of heterosexist socialization and victim blaming, according to some experts. Some of these include the following:

| | |
|---|---|
| Offender must be *butch;* victim must be *femme* | Gays deserve AIDS |
| Lesbian relationships are egalitarian | Homosexual have low morals |
| Same-sex abuse is actually mutual abuse | Homosexuals deserve abuse |
| Rape of a homosexual is not a serious crime | Gay IPV is less violent than heterosexual IPV |

SOURCES: C. Brown, 2008; Gold, Dickstein, Marx, & Lexington, 2009; Merrill, 1996; Potoczniak, Mourot, Crosbie-Burnett, & Potoczniak, 2003; Renzetti, 1992; Walsh, 1996.

*Sexual orientation and faith leaders.* One especially perplexing challenge for faith leaders is how to assist gay, lesbian, bisexual, or transgendered (GLBT) parishioners. Clergy's responses and those of non-GLBT congregants can be problematic for GLBT parishioners. Individuals facing conflicting paradigms of spirituality and homosexuality may feel forced to choose between their religious identity (e.g., Catholic) and their sexual identity (e.g., gay). How to reconcile these opposing identities can become insoluble for GLBT individuals, since disclosure can have calamitous repercussions. Pastoral counselors need to become educated about sexual orientation, examine their own biases toward sexual minorities, and be ready to refer clients they cannot treat because of their own reactions to homosexuality. Counselors can help clients determine the personal meaning of spirituality, clear up cognitive distortions, emphasize the value of every human being, and refer GLBT clients to accepting congregations (Heermann, Wiggins, & Rutter, 2007; see also Greene, 2009).

## Individual Differences (Traits) of Homosexuals

Some traits of SSIPV perpetrators are quite similar to those of heterosexual IPV perpetrators. Both groups tend to externalize blame and exhibit narcissistic personality characteristics (Merrill, 1998). FFIPV perpetrators, relative to nonperpetrators, report higher levels of childhood abuse and higher levels of alcohol problems. Their responses on the *Millon Clinical Multiaxial Inventory–III* (MCMI–III) reflect antisocial, borderline, paranoid traits, and delusional clinical symptoms (Fortunata & Kohn, 2003).

*Jealousy and sexual orientation.* Interestingly, a few investigators have studied romantic jealousy among homosexuals. The limited research available shows that an individual's sexual orientation *does* affect his or her experiences of jealousy. Jealousy, like many other concepts in the social sciences, has no agreed-upon definition. Usually, researchers define jealousy operationally via a jealousy scale. One popular definition separates jealousy into three types (Buunk, 1997).

---

REACTIVE JEALOUSY is the normal/rational jealousy that one feels when there is an *actual, direct threat* to one's romantic relationship. Example: feeling jealous upon seeing one's partner kissing a potential romantic rival.

ANXIOUS JEALOUSY refers to an *unhealthy rumination* about a mate's real, potential, or imagined involvement with another person. Example: brooding about why one's romantic partner did not answer a phone call.

POSSESSIVE JEALOUSY entails an individual's inclination to actually *prevent* his mate from having contact with a potential romantic rival. Example: demanding that a partner refrain from dancing with his rival at a disco club.

---

In one comparison, researchers examined whether groups differentiated on the basis of sexual orientation experienced different types of jealousy. The groups were as follows: (a) *heterosexual men,* (b) *heterosexual women,* (c) *gay men,* and (d) *lesbian*s. To measure jealousy, the investigators assessed three types of jealousy (reactive, anxious, possessive) developed by Buunk (1997). Similar to heterosexuals, results demonstrated that homosexual participants' most intense jealousy was *reactive jealousy* (i.e., *normal* jealousy based on a real threat to the relationship). Nonetheless, the participants differed significantly on the basis of sexual orientation (Barelds & Dijkstra, 2006):

- Heterosexual men reported lower levels of *anxious jealousy* than the other groups.
- Gay men reported lower levels of *reactive jealousy* than the other three groups.
- Lesbian women reported less *reactive jealousy* than heterosexual women.
- No significant differences between groups occurred in *possessive jealousy.*
- Anxious jealousy was negatively associated with relationship quality for *gays,* but not for lesbians.

*Power/dominance/control among gays.* An inquiry about power among gays involved in male-to-male IPV revealed significant differences among groups. Analyses of decision-making *power* highlighted a major dissimilarity on one abuse variable. *Psychological abuse* was significantly *higher* among MMIPV couples who *shared power* (each member was dominant in some area) than with couples whose *power was divided* (one member was dominant in most areas). Analyses of other dimensions showed three significant partner *similarities:* (a) level of abusiveness, (b) level of borderline personality traits (BPO), and (c) level of paternal rejection. Analyses of physical abuse uncovered significant distinctions between *bidirectionally* (mutually abusive) and *unidirectionally* (one member is abusive) violent couples. Specifically, the *couple level* of BPO, preoccupied attachment, and paternal rejection were all significantly higher in mutually abusive couples (Landolt & Dutton, 1997).

*Dynamics of abusive lesbian relationships.* One researcher gathered information from 80 lesbians who had experienced same-sex partner abuse in their first lesbian relationships and 45 feminist service providers. She concluded that as a paradigm, male-to-female partner abuse does *not* fit female-to-female partner pattern (Ristock, 2003; see also Kurdek, 2008). (See www.sagepub.com/barnett3e for details about identified differences.)

## Consequences of Same-Sex Intimate Partner Violence

Generally, same-sex victims and heterosexual victims respond in a like manner. Victims, for example, believe their partner will change (e.g., Walsh, 1996). Most investigators specify three common types of emotional reactions to same-sex IPV: *depression, anxiety, and PTSD.* These reactions are also extremely common among heterosexual IPV victims. Physical IPV is positively linked to depression levels in both lesbian and heterosexual women (Tuel & Russell, 1998).

*Responses of same-sex victims.* One survey found that both lesbian and heterosexual women primarily responded with *passive coping strategies* to their abuser's IPV: avoidance, talking to someone, and doing nothing (Bernhard, 2000). A new study of lesbian survivors of *sexual assault* uncovered three important variables (Gold et al., 2009):

- *Internalized homophobia* (i.e., negativity toward one's own homosexuality, self-blame)
- *Experiential avoidance* (i.e., avoidance of feelings through emotional suppression, substance abuse, etc. Experiential avoidance is *negatively reinforcing* because it prevents the individual from feeling or coming into contact with negative stimuli.)
- *PTSD symptoms* (i.e., reliving the trauma, flashbacks, nightmares, numbing)

Results of this study revealed that *experiential (actual) avoidance* completely **mediated** the relationships between *internalized homophobia* and PTSD symptoms. Simply put, avoiding thoughts and places that were related to the rape altered the relationship between feeling negative about being a lesbian and PTSD symptom severity—in the short term. In the long run, however, experiential avoidance postponed dealing with the trauma that must be processed.

*Leaving among lesbian women.* Investigators compared the factors that made it difficult for heterosexual and lesbian women to leave an abusive relationship (Lincoln & Guba, 1985). Although the two groups shared a number of reasons for not leaving in common (e.g., love, self-blame), other explanations advanced by the lesbian participants were somewhat novel. Some feelings of lesbian victims were as follows: (a) did not believe women could be violent, (b) shared a common community value entitled the bond of lesbianism (i.e., a strong feeling of connectedness to other lesbians, and (d) concerned that the ending of their relationship would contribute to the stereotype of troubled lesbians. Gay men infected with HIV stayed with their abuser for the following reasons: (a) poor health, (b) lack of financial independence, (c) fear of losing a caregiver, and (d) lack of available community resources (see Craft & Serovich, 2005).

## SECTION SUMMARY

### Same-Sex Intimate Partner Violence

Homosexuals face undeniable discrimination because of their sexual orientation. In addition to homophobic reactions directed at them and homonegativity, they suffer minority stress and internalized homophobia. They also must endure legal inequalities that prevent them from marrying, and they must make special plans to handle financial matters concerning end-of-life decisions. A full scientific explanation concerning the genesis of homosexuality is tentative. There are potential neurobiological, learning, and early sexual development factors involved, but there is little evidence to suggest homosexuality is a free lifestyle choice. The patriarchal explanation of same-sex IPV is seemingly inapplicable.

Quantification of same-sex partner violence is especially difficult to achieve, primarily because one's sexual orientation is not obvious and must be self-identified. Until this decade, even the U.S. Census Bureau has gathered no initial information on SSIPV and had to rely on post-collection editing estimates. As a result, researchers cannot recruit representative samples and must resort to techniques such as quota sampling. The most valid estimates place lifetime physical violence victimization at 44% for male-to-male IPV and 55% for female-to-female IPV. Gays suffer from wanted and especially unwanted sexual experiences that place them at great risk for HIV infections. Homosexuals are less willing to report crimes to the police than heterosexuals, and gays and lesbians are significantly different in their reporting proclivities.

As victims, homosexuals elicit very little sympathy from the public because of homonegativity and acceptance of myths about homosexuals. The faith community, in particular, is unwilling to accept homosexuality and homosexuals. Some personality trait studies have shown that gays and lesbians differ significantly from heterosexuals and from each other on *jealousy*. Also demonstrated were correlations between power/dominance/control traits and same-sex violence among gays. Some of the consequences of same-sex violence victimization—depression, anxiety, and PTSD—are similar to those found in heterosexual victims. Lesbians' attempts to cope with victimization relied on actual avoidance methods and avoidance coping styles.

# THE MILITARY AND INTIMATE PARTNER VIOLENCE

Whether IPV among military personnel qualifies as an understudied population has become debatable. On the one hand, women in the military began to contact women's advocates to find out how to handle the sexual harassment and rape they were experiencing. The recruits' complaints to their superiors went unheeded. When the advocates relayed the military women's problems to military commanders, nothing happened. The top brass took no remedial actions. Reporters began writing about a few dramatic cases of the military's extreme bias against women, not only in terms of sexual assault and male partner abuse, but also in terms of bias in promotions, medical treatment, and several other areas. After pressure from Pentagon officials and others, commanders in the field began to improve regulations, investigations, and prosecution of offenders.

On the other hand, the war in Iraq brought attention to a different problem, primarily experienced by combat soldiers: posttraumatic stress disorder (PTSD). Some PTSD symptoms include flashbacks, re-experiences of trauma, sleep disturbances, guilt, and other strong and disturbing emotions. Another type of injury also assumed a prominent role, traumatic brain injury (TBI). These problems, alongside inadequate medical and psychiatric care, attracted additional news exposures eventually followed by an influx of researchers and practitioners tasked with resolving remaining obstacles. Professionals began conducting more research on the prevalence of rape and intimate partner violence, mandating counseling for offenders and victims, developing prevention programs, and generally taking a more proactive approach.

As the government became energized to take action, Congress awarded $900 million to the Department of Defense for 2007 to 2008. Some of this money was targeted toward research on traumatic brain injury and some to expand mental health services. One innovation was the establishment of a Center for Deployment Psychology, a setting for training psychology interns. Currently, there is a growing body of knowledge about traumatic events, PTSD, IPV, sexual assault, gender differences, and interventions for these conditions (see Munsey, 2007a; M. Price, 2007).

An impression of early military research is that military philosophy may have guided the course of actions taken. The late entry of military research into the common domain, contrasted with research in other settings, may be one factor making some studies seem outmoded. In this group, shortcomings are the choices of topics and an overreliance on Conflict Tactics Scale measurements, without assessment of contextual differences. Another limitation is the use of unsophisticated research methodology. On the other hand, well-trained researchers are beginning to provide critical information about military personnel. Inclusion of anger, attachment, attitudes toward women, and jealousy tests, when possible, would shed additional light on veterans' difficulties. Prior arrest record is another important risk factor. An advantage of military research is that research samples are often very large, thus enhancing confidence in the statistical findings. Conversely, military samples are predominantly male and younger than civilian samples. Presumably, the influx of new funding will enhance scholarship leading to beneficial new findings.

When Omar attended a conference on male-to-female violence in Northern California, he was desperately seeking help for his unexpected bouts of violence. Omar was a Vietnam veteran, 38 years old, and married with two children. He was employed as a guard at a local mall. Although Omar loved his family dearly and would do anything for them, he was worried that he might accidentally kill his wife.

Omar had frequent flashbacks and nightmares about an event in which a Viet Cong soldier had jumped into his foxhole and tried to kill him. Sometimes, Omar woke up in the middle of the night believing he was still in his foxhole in 'Nam. With hair-trigger reactions, he would grab his wife by the throat and try to strangle her. So far, she was able to wake up and fend him off as he slowly "came to his senses." Omar apologized profusely on such occasions, but he was worried his wife would leave him. The two of them felt on-edge all the time; they never felt totally safe.

Moreover, Omar's condition had become an issue in the neighborhood. Whenever it rained, Omar thought he was back in 'Nam. If he was at work, he became so agitated that he could not trust himself. He did not know what he might do. He usually raced home, got his rifle out of his closet, loaded it, and began patrolling the outside of his house. A certain type of terror gripped him; his heart was pounding as he kept alert for Viet Cong. In time, the delusion left and he once again returned to "normal," grateful no one got hurt.

Omar had gone to the doctors at the VA after a 6-month wait for an appointment. They suggested he go on disability. They offered no medications and no therapy. They did not even suggest he put his rifle in storage. They seemed not to know how to diagnose his condition or how to provide treatment.

Luckily, an experienced counselor at the conference recognized Omar's symptoms as PTSD. Omar started seeing the counselor even though he had to foot the bill himself. At long last, he was finally getting help. There was light at the end of the tunnel.

*Prevalence of IPV.* One frequent question about batterers in the military is whether they perpetrate more partner violence than civilians do. To answer this question, nearly every military researcher has relied on the CTS. As of 2008, the U.S. Army had not collected incidence or prevalence data on IPV and compiled a central database. Data collected from some Army installations and compared with civilian rates, however, showed no significant differences based on self-report data (McCarroll, Castro et al., 2008). A duo of researchers examined a sample of 33,762 men and women in the military and discovered that, in comparison with 3,044 non-military men and women, the military personnel had significantly higher rates of severe partner abuse (Heyman & Neidig, 1999). Studies conducted in the last decade have frequently disclosed elevated rates of IPV for both men and women in the military (e.g., A. D. Marshall, Panuzio, & Taft, 2005).

Demographic data for military personnel involved in IPV reveal that as in other sectors of the population, age (youthfulness) is a risk factor for IPV. Because military personnel are generally younger than nonmilitary personnel, IPV data derived from military sources is expected to be higher than from civilian sources. Research on race is mixed. Although one study failed to find significant Black/White differences (Cronin, 1995), subsequent comparisons have found a striking divergence. One comparison indicated that Black males were significantly more partner-violent than White males (Rosen, Parmley, Knudson, & Fancher, 2002). A dataset of substantiated spouse abuse incidents found striking racial difference in IPV rates between White and Black married active-duty armed forces personnel: (a) Whites were counted as 61% of records in the database and 37% of IPV cases, and (b) Blacks were 28% of records in the database and 51% of IPV cases (S. L. Martin et al., 2007; McCarroll et al., 1999).

Gender differences in injury rates from military partner violence are higher and in the same direction as those among civilians. An analysis using a dataset of 10,864 family violence offenses of *substantiated spouse abuse* and *child abuse* cases reported highly significant gender disparity. The percentage of soldiers in the Army who are male is 84%; the percentage of male perpetrators of family violence offenses is 89% of the cases. The percentage of soldiers in the Army who are female is 16%; the percentage of females who perpetrated family offenses is 11% (S. L. Martin et al., 2007). This database, however, gathered data only about active-duty military and their civilian spouses. Within a comparison of 199 military spouses in treatment for IPV, 65% of the wives compared with 33% of the husbands reported injuries (Langhinrichsen-Rohling, Neidig, & Thorn, 1995). Paradoxically, a different evaluation of civilian spouses revealed that female-to-male IPV was severe and significantly greater against *unemployed* than employed male spouses. Measurement of female aggression relied on the CTS scores (Newby et al., 2003).

A second question is whether deployment with its many stressors affects IPV rates. An analysis of 26,835 individuals (95.1% men and 4.9% women) evaluated differences in CTS1 scores of military personnel who had been deployed and those who had not. Over a 1-year period, results demonstrated a small significant difference. Contrasted with nondeployed individuals, those who had been deployed were more severely violent. Statistical analyses, however, suggested other factors besides deployment affected IPV rates (McCarroll, Ursano et al., 2000; McCarroll, Newby, & Dooley-Bernard, 2008).

Other variables contribute to the rate of military IPV. One interesting inquiry used a sample of military men to compare the combined impact of individual-level and group-level variables on male abuse. Individual predictors of male IPV included race, depression, poor marital adjustment, alcohol problems, and childhood abuse. Group-level predictors included (a) lower levels of bonding between soldiers and their leaders, (b) a culture of hypermasculinity, and (c) lower levels of support for female spouses (Rosen, Kaminski, Parmley, Knudson, & Fancher, 2003). Of course, the association between substance abuse and partner violence is nearly always significant. An analysis of alcohol use by active-duty men disclosed that heavy drinking was a very strong and independent risk factor for MFIPV (Bell, Harford, McCarroll, & Senier, 2004). Researchers have also uncovered links between substance abuse and PTSD among female military veterans (e.g., Dobie, Maynard, Bush, Davis, & Bradley, 2004) and male veterans (e.g., Hankin et al., 1999).

*Family violence offenders.* Another investigation using the database of substantiated family violence cases categorized offenders into three groups: (a) SCO (12%)—both *spouse and child* offenders, (b) SOO (61%)—*spouse offenders only,* and (c) COO (27%)—*child offenders only.* Chi-square and ANOVA analyses provided one especially interesting revelation. The SCO group was significantly more likely than either of the other two groups to commit multiple offenses (i.e., more incidents) (S. L. Martin et al., 2007). (See www.sagepub.com/barnett3e for more details about this study.)

*Posttraumatic stress disorder.* Some victims have PTSD symptoms for many years. A third fundamental issue is the role of PTSD in military partner abuse. Several strands of research show a progression of PTSD rates among disparate populations. Civilian women have higher PTSD rates than civilian men. Women in the military have significantly higher rates than civilian women. Men in the military have significantly higher rates than civilian men, rates that may be comparable to those of military women. Although women usually suffer from higher rates of PTSD than men, men's trauma during combat most likely elevates their PTSD rates making them more comparable to those of military women (Magruder et al., 2005; M. Price, 2007).

Literature reviews have shown that the prevalence of traumatic events among male and female military veterans is high and extensive. Some of the traumas reported by female veterans are as follows: (a) 30% to 45%—military sexual trauma; (b)18% to 19%—male IPV; (c) 46% to 51%—physical assaults; (d) 27% to 49%—history of child sexual assaults; (e) 35%—history of child physical assaults; and (f) 81% to 93%—any trauma (Zinzow, Grubaugh, Monnier, Suffoletta-Maierle, & Frueh, 2007). These rates are significantly higher that those found in civilian populations (Kessler, Sonnega, Bromet, Hughes, & Nelson, 1995). Such high levels of trauma suggest that clinical personnel should screen clients for trauma history to make appropriate referrals. Clinicians should also consider using prolonged exposure (a type of cognitive behavioral therapy) to quell PTSD (Schnurr et al., 2007).

For women in the military, traumas other than combat are more prevalent, and as with nonmilitary women, childhood experiences exacerbate the impact of adult traumas. One inquiry examined child sexual abuse (CSA) among military women. Female veterans who reported a history of CSA, relative to veterans without such a history, had significantly worse physical and mental health, as well as a poorer quality of life. Likewise, the occurrence of a military sexual assault for CSA victims created a cumulative effect that further increased the negative consequences of their traumas (Suris, Lind, Kashner, & Borman, 2007).

*Relationship between PTSD and IPV.* Because of the elevated prevalence of PTSD among military men and women, its relationship to IPV has demanded considerable attention. One analysis of Vietnam combat veterans showed that *veterans with PTSD* were significantly more violent than veterans without PTSD. Severity of PTSD in this group was significantly correlated with partner abuse (Beckham, Feldman, Kirby, Hertzberg, & Moore, 1997).

In a later appraisal, researchers used data from a national sample of Vietnam combat veterans. The inventories captured information about a number of individual differences: (a) *combat exposure,* (b) *perceived level of threat posed by combat,* (c) *childhood exposure to violence,* (d) *current family functioning,* (e) *marital adjustment,* and (f) *psychiatric disorders.* The investigators randomly selected 109 case files and classified the data into three groups: (a) *partner-violent with PTSD;* (b) *partner-violent without PTSD;* and (c) *nonpartner-violent with PTSD.* Analyses revealed a large number of significant differences between groups. Results indicated that *risk factors for partner violence* were twofold: (a) *trauma-related experiences* combined with psychopathology, and (b) *relationship problems* associated with PTSD. Men with PTSD had been exposed to significantly more atrocities. Therefore, war-zone conditions pose risk factors for partner violence among men with PTSD (Taft et al., 2005).

The above results show that men in the military categorized with PTSD + PV (partner violence) had risk factors that are found among civilian populations. Furthermore, this group had significantly worse scores on the categorical and quantitative variables shown in the tables. The researchers suggest that because war-zone traumas may have special salience for IPV, clinicians should target men with PTSD and war-zone traumas for IPV prevention.

*Categorizing IPV offenders.* Just as nonmilitary researchers classified male perpetrators into typologies, a trio of military researchers undertook a similar assessment. They employed a convenience sample of male military veterans diagnosed with PTSD, depression, or a relationship problem and their spouses. Both members of the couple responded to the test inventories in a clinical setting where they were seeking treatment. Measurements included subsets of CTS1 and CTS2 questions about psychological, physical, and sexual IPV. Other indexes were a marital adjustment test and an intimacy measure. The researchers used ANOVAs of the CTS scores and other analyses to separate the research participants into three profiles: (a) partner-nonviolent (NV), (b) other-partner violent (OPV [male *or* female IPV], unidirectional), and (c) mutually violent (MV, both partners violent, bidirectional).

Although the three groups of men could not be differentiated on the basis of marital satisfaction or intimacy, they could be on the basis of the *men's mental health diagnoses.* Results indicated that mutually violent men had the highest PTSD scores. High levels of depression differentiated the nonviolent men from both the partner violent men and other-partner violent groups. The female partners differed significantly only in age, with the mutually violent women significantly younger than the other two groups of women. The PTSD and depression outcomes for male military personnel corresponded with previous research, both civilian and military, showing that PTSD is a risk factor for male aggression. Results disclosing that marital satisfaction levels did *not* vary significantly across groups are inconsistent with previous research. Most likely, the reason is that participants in this study had very low marital satisfaction scores in every group (Teten, Sherman, & Han, 2009).

## Military Intimate Partner Violence

Studies of IPV in the military have uncovered some aspects of IPV that seem both similar to and different from those found in nonmilitary studies. One similarity is the acknowledgement of specific risk markers for partner violence, such as age, minority status, alcohol or drug abuse, victim tries to separate from his or her abuser, PTSD, and stalking. In addition, IPV has common negative physical and psychological ramifications such as depression. There also may be common triggers for IPV, such as jealousy. Gender bias is evident among civilians and military personnel, but improvements were slower to begin in the military. Another correspondence is the mixed findings about gender symmetry that may depend on measurement disparities.

A substantial division occurs in the types and frequency of traumatic events experienced and in the prevalence of PTSD. Other distinctions turn up in the types of responses to IPV and in the capacity to institute prevention measures. These circumstances stem from the organization and judicial system of the military. With the influx of federal funding, medical and emotional treatment should improve for military personnel. It may not be overly optimistic to expect that the military setting will provide opportunities for investigation of alternative methods for reducing IPV.

**DISCUSSION QUESTIONS**

1. What is the meaning of intersectionality? Make up your own example.

2. Describe the organizations that study cross-cultural violence and their mandates.

3. Discuss the "general causes" of partner abuse in countries other than the United States. How are they the same and how are they different from causes in the United States?

4. Why do Middle Eastern men sometimes kill their sisters? Should America impose its own standards on these countries to make them stop the killings? Why and why not?

5. Discuss the severity of male-to-female violence within each group of countries.

6. Why are immigrant women at such great risk of partner violence?

7. Suggest one need for intervention for each of the three major ethnic groups in the United States.

8. Discuss the research methodology issues related to studying same-sex partner abuse.

9. Discuss the reasons why rural women are so disadvantaged in obtaining services for IPV.

10. What is the role of PTSD in military partner abuse? What advantages do the armed services have in quelling IPV?

For chapter-specific resources including audio and video links, SAGE research articles, additional case studies, and more, please visit www.sagepub.com/barnett3e.

# CHAPTER

## 11

# Adult Intimate Partner Violence

## *Practice, Policy, and Prevention*

This chapter presents three broad clusters of knowledge-based findings and evaluations that may translate into ideas for improving responses to violence against intimate partners: (a) *practice*—effective professional counseling, (b) *policy*—needed changes in guidelines or courses of action, and (c) *prevention*—innovative programs to help partners avoid victimization or perpetration of abuse. Frequently, practice, policy, and prevention overlap. An outreach program to help disabled women avoid rape, for instance, could provide guidelines for a law enforcement/shelter advocate alliance. Within this same framework, a specific type of police training might become a law enforcement policy. A broader example of how these entities might work with batterers is the following:

- *Practice:* What are the newer ideas for encouraging batterers to complete a counseling program?
- *Policy:* Would new guidelines requiring judges to grant permanent protective orders to partner abuse victims reduce post-separation assaults?
- *Prevention:* Would some innovative program conducted by marriage counselors motivate potentially abusive men to participate in counseling?

This chapter will cover evaluations and recommendations for therapists, treatments, legal approaches, government policies, public awareness campaigns, and for changing societal attitudes. It examines these topics from the point of view of changing problematic behaviors/beliefs of victims, perpetrators, service providers, and others connected with the burden of family violence.

## *ABUSED* PARTNERS: PRACTICE, POLICY, AND PREVENTION—PRIMARILY WOMEN

### National Domestic Violence Hotline: 1-800-799-SAFE

Counselors of battered women need to learn which actions are truly helpful and supportive. There are several different types of support, and each has its own benefits. Workers' preconceived ideas of which resources (e.g., police, shelters) may be helpful to battered women have not necessarily been accurate (see Bowker, 1983). Some supposedly supportive actions are actually unwelcome, and counseling personnel need to identify these.

### Agency Practices

In general, this section concentrates on the recognition of battered women's problems and presents recommendations for change. Research has currently brought to light principles for changing how social agencies should intervene to provide support for battered women. Some suggestions rest on research indicating that some actions taken by agencies are *not* considered helpful by battered women.

*Isolation of battered mothers.* From the beginning, advocates remarked on the social isolation of battered women, much of it manipulated by their abusers. To understand this phenomenon, a newer investigation used a sample of mothers, some of whom were battered. First they classified the mothers into three groups based on the severity of male partner violence: (a) *severely battered,* (b) *nonseverely battered* (e.g., few bruises), and (c) *nonbattered.* Second, they conducted a *social networks* analysis by quantifying four types of social contacts and using the results as a basis for classifying women's degree of *social isolation.* These measures consisted of the (a) number of supportive family members/number of friends, (b) number of contacts with family/friends, (c) number of *emotionally* supportive behaviors (e.g., "really listened to you"), and (d) number of *behaviorally* supportive behaviors (e.g., "babysat").

The results of the network analysis detected no significant differences between the three groups with regard to the *number of family members* who gave *emotional support,* but the battered groups received financial help from more family members. The most revealing outcome was that women in the *severely battered women* group had significantly *fewer friends, fewer contacts with friends, fewer long-term relationships, and fewer friends who really listened to them.* These results imply that very violent batterers successfully isolated their victims from their friends (Coohey, 2007), and therefore female victims usually need more social support.

### CASE HISTORY    Wendy Calls a Hotline

The third time the police arrested Wendy's husband for beating her, they handed Wendy a card with the name and phone number of a battered woman's hotline. The next day, while her cut lip was still hurting and she felt afraid and alone, she called the hotline and spoke with Judy. Judy provided Wendy with a lot of information and told her about the battered woman's outreach group she could attend on Wednesday mornings at 11:00. Although Wendy did not see how sitting around talking and listening to other battered women could possibly help her personally, she attended her first group meeting the following Wednesday. She was amazed to hear about the experiences of other women, how some were trying to get jobs, others were making plans to move in together to share expenses, and still others were seeking civil damages against their abusers in court. For the first time in 10 years, Wendy felt that maybe she really could do something to stop her husband's assaults, and she began to think more carefully about her safety needs.

As this case history illustrates, reaching out for help and interacting with other victims can be a vital link to a violence-free life. Although stopping male partner abuse is a crucial first step, helping the survivor heal must be an integral part of society's response (Arriaga & Capezza, 2005).

## Social Support

Scholars often refer to social support as *the availability of individuals who can provide various relational elements deemed helpful to people experiencing stress*. Experts have identified different types of social support, such as *instrumental, emotional,* and *informational.* For battered women, positive social support often helps to ameliorate the negative impact of battering on their physical and mental health, as well as on their ability to hold down a job (Goodkind, Gillum, Bybee, & Sullivan, 2003; Kocot & Goodman, 2003). Social support should help embolden a battered victim to redefine marriage as a relationship in which violence is not allowed (Bagarozzi & Giddings, 1983). Support should also help transform a battered woman into a self-saver rather than a relationship-saver or a husband-changer (Chang, 1989).

*What types of social support help?* The type of support provided is crucial. Advising a woman to stay with her abuser, giving mixed messages, or providing a low level of social support may backfire. Women survivors given such messages may experience heightened posttraumatic stress disorder (PTSD) or depression (Kokot & Goodman, 2005; see also Staggs, Long, Mason, Krishnan, & Riger, 2007). Research findings about the helpfulness of various social supports have varied somewhat in relationship to characteristics of the woman's victimization—its severity, type, and recency. Also affecting the evaluation of the social support provided was its kind and timing, and whether it was considered positive (see also Postmus, Severson, Berry, & Yoo, 2009).

In another appraisal, the findings indicated that friends and family members made far more positive responses than negative ones, but occasionally did hurtful things, such as (a) changed the subject, (b) spent less time with the victim, (c) insinuated that the survivor was stupid, or (d) refused to help in any way. The same assessment shed light on the helpful responses of friends and family: (a) offered a place to stay, (b) urged victims to call police or a lawyer, and (c) urged them to seek counseling (Goodkind et al., 2003; see also Morrison, Luchok, Richter, & Parra-Medina, 2006; Rose, Campbell, & Kub, 2000). (See the website for the Theran, Sullivan, Bogat, & Stewart, 2006, study of social support.)

*Helpful agency actions.* As a general matter, women want to have more control when working with staff, and they need staff to listen to their opinions before taking action. Some of the elements that enhance an agency's approach to its clients appear in Table 11.1.

| TABLE 11.1 | Helpful Behaviors of Social Service Agency Staff |
| --- | --- |

| ATTITUDES | ACTIONS |
| --- | --- |
| Displaying genuine concern | 24-hour availability of service |
| Respecting client's ideas | Providing an all-female group |
| Respecting client's choices | Having a female service provider |
| Acknowledging client's capabilities | Helping the client gain insurance coverage |
| Acknowledging client's intelligence | Advocating for the client's children |
| Sharing one's own relevant experiences | |
| Validating the client's experiences | **GROUP ACTIVITIES—PROGRESSION** |
| | a. Letting client share her experiences |
| **REFERRALS** | b. Hearing how other women solved problems |
| Legal services | c. Seeing the progress of other clients |
| Other community services | d. In time becoming role models themselves |

SOURCES: L. A. Goodman & Epstein, 2008; Zweig & Burt, 2007

*Improving shelter services.* There are a number of applications from research findings that could inform shelter workers about how to assist battered women. One useful action is to obtain a comprehensive abuse history, given that so many battered women have experienced multiple forms of abuse over a lifetime and may be suffering from the cumulative effects of all of them. Another important function is to screen female victims for alcohol/drug abuse. Although most shelters do screen, one survey uncovered a very uneven approach to alcohol/drug problems. Half of the programs had no policies covering alcohol/drug problems, and about one-fourth had agreements with local program providers for alcohol/drug services. Finally, about one-tenth had no staff or volunteers with training in alcohol/drug problems (S. L. Martin, Moracco, Chang, Council, & Dulli, 2008). Obviously, it would be useful for shelters to improve such services.

*Admittance policies.* A number of experts recommend that shelter staff change their policies concerning *women arrested for female-to-male intimate partner violence.* Even if wrongfully arrested, these women are ineligible for shelter residence because partner violence is a misdemeanor or felony. Currently, shelter staff are recognizing that battered women who strike back (female-to-male IPV) are usually *not* true female batterers. Addressing this issue calls attention to the need to *distinguish minor violence from battering.*

*Teaching parenting skills.* Shelter workers are often able to take advantage of battered mothers' desire to protect their children by offering a variety of services that might help the women find jobs, obtain health care, secure protective orders, and so forth. Another consequence of male violence is its deleterious effect on a mothers' ability to parent. Mothers in violent relationships commonly have their psychological energy absorbed by feelings of guilt, depression, low self-esteem, or fear for their own safety. Victimized mothers may be less consistent, sometimes more lenient, and sometimes more harsh in their discipline practices.

Shelter staff frequently offer parenting skills classes, even though some mothers resent the implications. Workers are sometimes successful in helping battered women change their thinking about the lives of their children. Workers may be able to help them understand the terrible damage that exposure to interparental violence is doing to their children (e.g., McCloskey, Figueredo, & Koss, 1995; Rossman & Ho, 2000). Enrollment in a shelter parenting class might make mothers eligible for custody once again if Child Protective Services has removed children from the home, possibly for exposure to male battering (Tower, 2007).

*Transitional supportive housing (TSH).* Transitional supportive housing (TSH) programs are so new and few in number that very little evaluation research has appeared in the literature. One duo of researchers found that TSH participants appreciated the services but tended to be *critical of their implementation* (L. V. Davis & Srinivasan, 1995). Findings from a qualitative undertaking indicated that participants thought TSH programs offer vital services and should be expanded. Their availability enabled women to avoid homelessness and to avoid returning to abusive partners. "They [the women] particularly appreciated having a safe home with supportive people around them, giving them the time and assistance necessary to rebuild their lives" (Melbin, Sullivan, & Cain, 2003, p. 457).

## Psychotherapists' Practices

C. S. Lewis, Griffing et al. (2006, p. 351) state that "the negative cycle of psychological control, damage to self-esteem, and subsequent ability to leave a relationship requires intense therapeutic intervention." Counseling is a crucial element in helping victims make decisions about how to avoid further violence. Victims may be aware of their need for counseling support but may not know whom to call or what sort of assistance they might receive. Exacerbating the situation is that some counseling techniques intended to help female victims have, in reality, been detrimental (Dutton-Douglas & Dionne, 1991; Hansen, Harway, & Cervantes, 1991; Stenius & Veysey, 2005).

## General Counseling Topics for Battered Women

*Clinical screening.* Mental health practitioners and addiction counselors working in clinics or in private practice should screen clients for male-to-female IPV, substance abuse, and trauma symptoms (L. A. Goodman & Epstein, 2008). In fact, many experts believe that screening by professionals should be universal and codified into law (e.g., P. G. Jaffe & Crooks, 2005). As discussed previously, victims may not recognize they are being abused or may be too afraid or ashamed to tell their counselors about the violence. Laffaye, Kennedy, and Stein (2003), for example, found that identification of male aggression can help to forestall development of PTSD and quality of life problems (e.g., finding adequate health care). (See www.sagepub.com/barnett3e for a list of appropriate screening instruments for male partner abuse compiled by an American Psychological Association task force [Harway et al., 2002].)

After screening clients to identify their specific needs, counselors usually work on safety planning first. In these sessions, experts help victims to think through various actions that will facilitate an emergency escape, such as having money hidden somewhere, having a bag packed, and locating a safe home where they and their children may reside temporarily (see Dutton-Douglas & Dionne, 1991). The large number of potential variables impacting a victim's response to trauma complicates treatment selections. Victims may have unusually diverse childhood abuse histories, live under wide-ranging social conditions, experience extremely disparate adult abuses, and react quite individually to these variations. A newer study has uncovered a strong link between a *harsh childhood* background and a *pro-inflammatory phenotype* (muscle/joint pain) in adolescence extending even into old age (G. E. Miller & Chen, 2010).

*Basic counseling goals.* Counseling for female victims should include helping them to define the meaning of male partner violence, to understand what causes it, and to be aware of the role it plays in their lives (Werner-Wilson, Zimmerman, & Whalen, 2000). It is important for counselors to accomplish the following tasks: (a) *emphasize that male-female intimate partner violence (MFIPV) is wrong,* (b) *impart information and options for managing male intimate partner violence (IPV),* (c) *ask each woman what she needs/wants,* (d) *communicate continuing support for her,* and (e) *help each woman develop a safety plan* (Chang et al., 2006).

*Alcohol/drug treatment.* A number of studies have disclosed that female IPV victims tend to abuse alcohol and drugs (AOD). Because AOD exposes victims to risk for continued partner violence, *sobriety treatment is urgent* (El-Bassel, Gilbert, Schilling, & Wada, 2000; Salomon, Bassuk, & Huntington, 2002; Swan & Snow, 2002). Conversely, two longitudinal investigations have *not confirmed* these studies (Panchanadeswaran & McCloskey, 2007; Zlotnick, Johnson, & Kohn, 2006). Whatever the case may be, counselors need to avoid substituting Alcoholics Anonymous or Al-Anon for shelter programs. The *sobriety first model* applied to chemically dependent women is almost certainly doomed to failure for intimate partner violence victims. It disregards the requisite *safety first* approach and the recognition that alcohol use is a method for coping with unremitting danger, fear, and pain (Zubretsky & Digirolamo, 1994).

*Remaking victims' belief system.* Wetzel and Ross (1983) contend that some of the most important therapeutic work with female victims is the *remaking of their belief system.* Victims may erroneously believe that male partner abuse is *normative* rather than abusive. Therapists can help victims stop believing that they caused or can stop the abuse and to make different **attributions** about the causes of male IPV (Massad & Hulsey, 2006).

*Dangers in leaving the abuser.* Apprising women of the added danger they face when leaving an abusive relationship falls heavily upon counselors. The high-priority task of recommending safety precautions to separated and divorced women applies not only to shelter workers, but also to psychotherapists. "The risk of intimate partner homicide is highest when a victim of domestic abuse tries to leave the relationship" (Dugan, Nagin, & Rosenfeld, 2003, p. 22). The period of separation or divorce also places battered woman in extreme danger of physical assaults, sexual assaults, threats, harm to children, stalking, harassment at work, and property damage (Byrne, Resnick et al., 1999; DeKeseredy, Schwartz, Fagen, & Hall, 2006). Court orders requiring *ongoing interaction* with a batterer (e.g., child visitation) place both the child and the mother at risk for assault or even a homicide-suicide. Cummings (1990) suggests that, along with other types of competency training, shelters should offer IPV victims self-defense training.

*Brain-based psychotherapy.* Therapists can improve their clinical efficacy by understanding and applying information about the brain's role in developing problem feelings, thoughts, and behaviors, and in modifying them. Of special significance are the facts that genes alone do not account for behavior and that the brain evidences plasticity through learning (e.g., through psychotherapy). As one illustration, a victim's reactions to abuse (e.g., PTSD) involve the brain's processing of traumatic memory and memory retrieval during flashbacks. The therapist needs to understand which methods, such as narrative therapy or extinction, can diminish and replace the client's painful memories (Cappas, Andres-Hyman, & Davidson, 2005).

Keeping abreast of new drug treatments for diminishing fear would be especially helpful (see Ressler et al., 2004, for drug-based therapies). Clinical personnel need to send clients for routine medical screening when indicated. One advance has been the demonstration that the drug sertraline (e.g., Zoloft) has shown significant benefits in reducing PTSD symptoms in a randomized double-blind treatment with a placebo control group (D. J. Stein, van der Kolk, Austin, Fallad, & Clary, 2006). On the other hand, over-prescribing powerful tranquilizers just to rush someone out of a doctor's office can pose another type of hazard.

*Individualized treatment.* Helpers need to put themselves in the victim's shoes (B. E. Carlson, 2006), because the "one size fits all" approach may be ineffective in reducing IPV (see Hovell, Seid, & Liles, 2006). Any intervention should be tailored to meet the *specific needs* of the individual woman and her family. Such complex variability demands thorough assessment and a multimodal approach including advocacy support, medical intervention, and cognitive-behavioral or psychodynamic counseling. Treatment should be *individualized* (Briere & Jordan, 2004).

*Victims' attachment and grief.* "Practitioners need to acknowledge not only the external constraints that prevent women from leaving abusive partners, but also the women's positive feelings toward their partners and the relationship" (Schiff, Gilbert, & El-Bassel, 2006, p. 135). Male partner offenders usually exhibit some forms of *positivity* (e.g., affection) that *mediates* (changes) the effects of their abuse on victims (L. L. Marshall, Weston, & Honeycutt, 2000). Strangely, therapists may also need help in dealing with the perpetrator's positivity because of their difficulty in understanding the client's life. When *counselors and advocates get frustrated* trying to facilitate the recovery of female victims, it may be because they fail to recognize the positive side of the victims relationship (e.g., how the abuser meets the victim's needs).

Attachment plays a large role in *leave/stay decision making.* In truth, both members of a violent couple may stay because they are so strongly *attached to* each other (Griffing et al., 2002). When a battering relationship ends, most women feel great deprivation and loss. It is not easy to give up one's future hopes and dreams for a happy marriage and a family. *Feelings of loneliness are so strong* that battered women may return only to be abused again. Male partners are not immune either. A frustrated emotionally dependent male partner may feel driven to violence if he feels his female partner is about to leave him.

Over the years, various conceptions of attachment and attachment orientations have emerged in the literature (e.g., Allison, Bartholomew, Mayseless, & Dutton, 2008; Dutton, Saunders, Starzomski, & Bartholomew, 1994).

## CASE HISTORY   I Can't Let Him Leave Me

When Pam Harris, age 45, learned her husband was having an affair with the receptionist in his dental office, she was devastated. He was her whole life. She had built her life around him. Her husband's parents and his children liked her and wanted her in the family. The pain was unbearable. In a desperate attempt to save her relationship, Pam cooked all his favorite meals, scheduled cosmetic surgery, hired a physical trainer, and had sex with him three times a night. Despite this Herculean effort, her husband said he wanted a divorce and he continued his affair. How could she go on without him? When Pam caught him at a hotel in another tryst with the receptionist, she waited until he left the hotel, and then she killed him by running over him with her car. After her arrest, she tried to commit suicide, but did not succeed. Without he husband, her life was over (P. Easton, 2003).

NOTE: Pam Harris is the real name of the person described in the case history.

The above case reflects Pam's extreme attachment to her philandering husband. Undoubtedly, many cases of murder/suicide stem from one partner's deep attachment to his or her partner. Often jealousy plays a role and intensifies one's heartbreak; and sometimes these feelings boil over into a murderous rage.

*Regulating closeness.* Violent individuals may have very *strong attachments* to their partner that are associated with *proximity/distance regulating strategies.* It is essential for counselors to help battered women gain awareness of their own and their partner's attachment needs and related pursuit-distancing strategies. As an example of such strategies, a partner might repeatedly telephone a partner in order to keep close—a *pursuit strategy.* Conversely, a partner might find ways to leave the house because he "needs more space"—a *distancing strategy.* Individuals whose attachment patterns are *primarily preoccupied* usually seek high levels of *closeness* and use pursuit strategies to achieve greater proximity. Individuals whose attachment patterns are primarily *dismissing or fearful* typically want to avoid too much closeness, and they tend to use *distancing strategies.* When one member of a couple desires more closeness than the other, a frustration response may occur and escalate into partner violence (Allison et al., 2008; see also K. C. Gordon & Christman, 2008).

*Coping styles.* The method a battered woman uses to cope with her victimization may mean the difference between life and death. A meta-analytic review of coping styles found that *escape-avoidance* coping styles are negatively associated with good health outcomes, while *problem-focused* coping styles are positively correlated (Penley, Tomaka, & Wiebe, 2002). Given the salience of coping proficiency, social scientists studied the *coping styles of battered women* and uncovered a number of relationships between coping and help-seeking (Dutton, Goodman, & Bennett, 1999; Taft, Resick, Panuzio, Vogt, & Mechanic, 2007a).

CORRELATES OF ENGAGEMENT (PROBLEM-FOCUSED) COPING TYLE

- Had higher levels of *personal and environmental resources* (e.g., babysitters, car) (.e.g., Cronkite & Moos, 1984).
- Had greater *economic resources* (Rusbult, Martz, & Agnew, 1998)
- *Had social support* (e.g., friends who listens) (Taft, Resick, Vogt, & Mechanic, 2007b)

CORRELATES OF DISENGAGEMENT (AVOIDANCE) COPING STYLE

- Had history of violence in childhood home (Mitchell & Hodson, 1983)
- Was victim of psychological aggression (Taft et al., 2007b)

*Personal empowerment strategies.* The authors of many articles on treatment for MFIPV victims advise counselors to provide some form of *personal empowerment strategy* as an essential component of a recovery plan (e.g., Busch & Valentine, 2000; Lempert, 1996; Peled, Eisikovits, Enosh, & Winstok, 2000). Empowerment involves two major elements: *gaining power* and *taking action.* A therapeutic empowerment strategy encourages a victim made powerless through a trauma to reduce fear by regaining a sense of mastery and control over frightening events. Women also fare better if they feel empowered, particularly women suffering from poverty (S. L. Williams & Mickelson, 2004; Wuest & Merritt-Gray, 1999).

*Forgiveness.* Although the idea of forgiving an abuser seems dangerous and an anathema to some experts, they need to realize that a victim's decision to *forgive the abuser* is a real possibility; it might happen. Because forgiveness is a value inculcated within many religious doctrines, some victims may feel more comfortable forgiving their abuser than simply leaving or seeking revenge. In addition to its possible spiritual value, failing to forgive an offender may contribute to *negative health consequences.* To forgive, however, should not be taken to imply acceptance of harmful behavior. Therapists need to explain the difference between forgiving, pardoning, forgetting, and condoning. Therapists also need to examine different *cultural definitions* of forgiveness (Reed & Enright, 2006; Stoia-Caraballo et al., 2008).

## Policy

Several broad elements of social customs contribute to the problems battered women experience in trying to survive battering and move forward. Several experts have suggested that the area of battered women would profit from treating *victims as experts* in guiding policy (Nabi & Horner, 2001). In a dissertation, J. A. West (2002) indicated that battered women had some excellent ideas about public awareness campaigns (e.g., posters in health clinics).

## Discrimination Against Women

Discrimination against women in the American political and legal systems allows practices that undermine women's attempts to achieve independence.

*Discrimination against women occurs in many other settings.* Illustrative of ongoing discrimination are the results of a 2007 study by Abel and Meltzer (2007). These investigators contrasted male (*n* = 41) and female (*n* = 46) undergraduates' *evaluations of male and female professors' identical written lectures.* Sadly, both men and women rated the male professor's lecture more positively than the female professor's lecture. Male students' sexist ratings of the lectures were significantly associated with the students' traditional and stereotyped attitudes toward women.

*Discrimination in housing.* Discrimination against women in housing complicates battered victims' efforts to secure economic stability. Some government-subsidized housing projects have established rules that allow the eviction of tenants involved in violence, even if the tenants are the victims. If a batterer harasses a woman by forcing his way into her apartment and then assaults her, housing authorities may evict her. Federal mandates to stop evicting female IPV victims need monitoring and expanding (reported in "Federal Sex Discrimination Lawsuit," 2001).

*Discrimination in the court system.* Another form of debilitating discriminatory practices occurs in the court system. When researchers examined judges' rulings involving female victims of partner violence, they found that judges ordered child support in only 13.2% of the cases (Ford, Rompf, Faragher, & Weisenfluh, 1995). Such practices severely penalize children, forcing some into poverty. It is unclear why judges may disregard laws passed by legislatures to protect women and children and suffer no adverse consequences to their careers. Without doubt, legislatures need to address such policies and make the necessary changes.

*Legal changes.* Battered victims are dependent on the criminal justice system for their very lives. Previous chapters have detailed some of the pitfalls of current practices in the criminal justice system, thus pointing out the kinds of policy changes needed. One dilemma that needs more attention is how policies can be changed to help women trying to escape from an abuser who has been stalking and threatening them. Given *separation violence* and the ineffectiveness of protective orders, achieving safety can be nearly impossible. Experts often advise endangered women to *relocate* as the only possible solution. These female victims have high safety needs that entail keeping their whereabouts *confidential.*

Confidentiality, however, has been difficult to attain. Without training about separation violence and other aspects of male-to-female intimate partner violence, courts have assumed that fathers had a legal right to know where their children were. In so doing, male offenders were able to know victims' new location through access to children's schools and medical records (Zorza, 1995). One policy change made by the Social Security Administration in 1998 was their modification of guidelines regarding the issuance of new Social Security numbers. With adequate evidence of abuse, Social Security agents will now consider issuing new Social Security numbers to female victims who need them. This provision allows women fleeing from male partner violence to open new bank accounts and obtain new driver's licenses. These amendments have substantially improved victims' abilities to start new lives safely (see "Getting New," 1999).

Even more help became available with the publication of an assortment of *guides* delineating the large number of obstacles that might be encountered during a relocation attempt and how to address them. In these guide booklets, Betsy Ramsey Enterprises (cited in Zorza, 2007) points out special actions that abusers might take to find a relocated victim. An abuser might issue a missing persons report or hire a detective to find the victim. Another challenge that victims may encounter is proving their educational attainments and possession of professional licenses. Making plans to relocate successfully may take from 3 to 10 months. The Washington State Department of Economic Security has also helped in the relocation process by expanding battered victims' *rights to leave their jobs* (which may be necessary to escape their abusers) and still be eligible to file for unemployment insurance (Shuman-Austin, 2000). What is more, women who are seriously injured as a result of partner violence may be eligible to take time off from work under the federal Family and Medical Leave Act (Runge & Hearn, 2000).

## Economic Support and Freedom From Battering

Female IPV victims often lack the financial resources and social support needed to surmount the host of institutional and social obstacles that impede their progress toward self-sufficiency (see Browne & Bassuk, 1997; P. N. Clarke, Pendry, & Kim, 1997). Some problems such as poverty, of course, not only impact abused women but women in general. The fact that poverty is so highly correlated with family violence implies that women's advocates and battered women's advocates in particular need to increase their antipoverty work (L. A. Goodman & Epstein, 2008).

*Discrimination in the workplace.* One related set of discriminations occurs in employment, income, and child care assistance. A woman still earns approximately 77 cents for every dollar a man earns, and in some occupations a man with only a high school diploma may earn more than a woman with a college degree (U.S. Bureau of Labor Statistics, 1999). A study conducted by the American Association of University Women revealed that as early as one year post graduation, women baccalaureates earn only 80% as much as men do, and this gender pay gap widens over time ("For Women," 2007). Women's low wages contribute to their economic dependence on abusive males and force women into poverty if they try to leave.

Gender discrimination continues despite research showing that women, relative to men, are as productive on the job, as committed to their jobs, and do not quit their jobs any more frequently than men do. Women perform well on the job even though they still shoulder the majority of household work and child care (Bianchi & Spain, 1996). Most recently, President

Barack Obama signed into law the *Lilly Ledbetter Fair Pay Act,* a law designed to eliminate a 180-day statute of limitations on bringing a gender-based unequal pay discrimination suit. In the Ledbetter case, gender discrimination was incremental as male workers received raises larger than hers over a 20-year period.

*Policies of corporations.* Even though the link between being abused by a partner and employment rates has received considerable attention, little research has described the *burdens placed upon employers* when the victim's problems spill over at work. One quandary centers on how the workplace is organized to respond to a worker's IPV victimization. Illustrative of these issues is the additional costs that may be involved in trying to keep the worker safe while at work. A few companies may have sufficient funds and be willing to assist battered victims, but many may not. (See Swanberg, Logan, & Macke, 2005, for a review.)

Working not only benefits a woman financially, but it also provides her with a crucial *survival strategy.* Working away from home probably lessens female victims' social and emotional dependence on their abusers (Wilson, Baglioni, & Downing, 1989). A few studies have shown that *coworkers* can function as a vital element of social support. If nothing else, coworkers may lessen battered women's isolation (Repetti, Matthews, & Waldron, 1989).

Employers may ignore signs that employees are victims of abuse and, even if they are aware of a problem, fail to offer supportive services. Employers may even intensify the woman's problems because of concern for other employees or customers. Currently, only a few corporations in the United States make any effort to support employees who are victims of male partner abuse (Isaac, 1998). Although laws are changing slowly, most states do *not* routinely protect women from losing their jobs because of victimization-related absenteeism (e.g., for court appearances or medical treatments) (Runge & Hearn, 2000). On the other hand, only 25% of female victims on welfare asserted that working actually decreased their level of victimization (Brush, 2003).

One female survivor told researchers that she was asked to come in early because her employer wanted to talk about "bringing my personal problems to work." The employer was referring to the woman's black eye, not about her discussing her abuse with others, which she was not doing. Although this woman considered herself to be a "good faithful worker," she worried about being asked to leave her job (Riger, Raja, & Camacho, 2002). Because of these practices, legislators need to enact laws requiring employers to assist employees who are being threatened, stalked, or harassed at work by taking preventive safety measures.

It is heartening to learn that despite some extremely negative reactions to disclosure of victimization at work, the majority of women who disclosed it in one study (46% to supervisors, 43% to coworkers) received both tangible and emotional support. Supervisors undertook measures such as transferring abused workers to other locations. With this support, battered women were able to focus on their work and retain their jobs much longer. Nonetheless, many women experienced job turnover because of the abuse (Swanberg & Logan, 2005).

*Shelter economic-skills services.* At a practical level, shelter workers sometimes help abuse victims improve their skills by role-playing job interviewing techniques and assertion skills (Holiman & Schilit, 1991). Also, if women can enhance their education by going to school and thus equalizing *gender power* to some extent, it may reduce their partner's aggression. Although the findings are mixed, a handful of studies has shown that the relationship between the partner's employment may affect abuse rates (e.g., Fox, Benson, DeMaris, & Van Wyk, 2002; Macmillan & Gartner, 1999; see also J. Miller, 2006). One policy change that would benefit all children is to improve the financial status of custodial parents. Government and criminal justice agencies should strengthen their efforts to make all noncustodial parents meet their child support obligations.

*Training unskilled males.* Poverty can affect men's ability to pay child support. Low-income men need programs that offer them support, incentives, and positive affirmation so they can better support their children. It seems apparent to many that one beneficial policy change would be to help unskilled males become more educated and employable. They would be more able to provide for their families, and they might be less likely to perpetrate abuse (R. M. Brown, 2002). Parenting classes for fathers are often helpful as well (see DeAngelis, 2004).

*Legislators.* Legislators should strengthen existing laws intended to protect women against sex discrimination or victim-related discrimination, and society should demand the enforcement of those laws. In particular, legislators need to increase their efforts to protect female victims and their children so that victims can safely work (e.g., Brush, 2000). It is imperative that state and local governments design policies aimed at bolstering battered women's income and at providing them with job support (D. K. Anderson & Saunders, 2003). Researchers, then, must continue to evaluate the outcomes of legislative changes.

## Victim Services

A review of assistance over the years 1986 to 2000 indicated vast improvements in victim services for battered women (Tiefenthaler, Farmer, & Sambria, 2005). Refer to Table 11.2 for numerical information on improvements from 1986 to 2000.

**TABLE 11.2**  Programs to Assist Victims of IPV by Type of Service

| Program | 1986 | 1994 | 2000 | % Change 1986–2000 |
|---|---|---|---|---|
| Shelters | 921 | 1,338 | 1,386 | +50 |
| Hotlines | 1,105 | 1,649 | 1,697 | +54 |
| Legal services | 336 | 1,190 | 1,441 | +329 |
| Counseling | 1,166 | 1,622 | 1,742 | +49 |
| Total programs | 1,229 | 1,850 | 1,887 | +54 |

SOURCE: Modified from Tiefenthaler et al., 2005.
NOTE: Two other programs (Child Services and Transportation) started up in 1994.

*Welfare programs.* The major goal of current Welfare to Work (WtW) programs is to help women find *any* job and exit welfare. It is important to note that WtW programs have successfully reduced welfare rolls. In 1996, the year that Congress passed the Temporary Assistance for Needy Families Act, 4.4.million families were on welfare. By 2001, the number had dropped to 2.1 million (U.S. Department of Health & Human Services, 2001). *Any* job, however, might be minimum wage, part-time, or temporary employment. Under the philosophy of WtW, women finding such jobs will have to leave the welfare rolls, even if they do not escape from poverty. Working for minimum wages, of course, does not provide adequate funds for women to be self-sufficient (Cooney, 2006), and problems with welfare regulations may actually increase the risk of battering for some recipients (Beechey & Payne, 2002). (See the website for information about the lack of psychosocial improvements tied to WtW programs.)

*Needed changes in welfare.* It is no surprise that putting into practice the massive changes in welfare, Temporary Assistance for Needy Families (TANF), Welfare to Work (WtW), and the Family Violence Option (FVO) have failed in some ways. For women suffering from male-to-female IPV, the failure of workers to screen for FVO is an acute problem. Some welfare workers' *limited knowledge base, their lack of social skills,* and their *negative attitudes toward welfare recipients* is disturbing. It is essential that welfare staff obtain appropriate training and that supervisors monitor workers' implementation of FVO (Lindhorst, Meyers, & Casey, 2008).

*Legislatures* need to mandate evaluations of welfare departments' policies and take action as needed. Other worthy proposals that might permit women to be less economically dependent include raising the minimum wage, making after-school programs available, and establishing an earned income tax credit. Another suggestion is providing reduced welfare benefits as an adjunct to the income of women with low-paying jobs (Scott, London, & Myers, 2002).

*Greater focus on MFIPV.* Because women whose children are among the child welfare population may suffer from partner abuse, child welfare workers need to focus more intensely on these *victims* and to make referrals for their treatment. Taking a more supportive, rather than a blaming attitude, toward abused mothers should contribute to improving the welfare of the children (Kohl & Macy, 2008).

*Misguided "wedfare" programs.* Other policies of the federal government can impact battered women negatively. In 2001, President George Bush proclaimed that the central goal of American welfare policy is *building and preserving stable families* (Bush, 2002). Entering the fray about how to end welfare and poverty, advocacy groups such as the politically conservative Heritage Foundation, have endorsed a *family values* orientation. Through this lens, proponents consider *marriage to be a safe haven for poor women and those needing protection from violence.*

Objecting to the politically conservative Heritage Foundation's assertions and agenda, the Family Violence Prevention Fund (2002) called attention to refined sets of government data conflicting with those presented by the Heritage Foundation. The support for the idea that marriage is protective is very slim. A newer analysis of abused women responding to the National Violence Against Women Survey (NVAWS) found that divorced women and women with children experienced a significantly heightened risk of male partner abuse than their counterparts (J. Miller, 2006). (See www.sagepub.com/barnett3e for details about the debate concerning MFIPV for married and unmarried women.)

To draw a causal inference between marriage and economic security represents flawed thinking. Moreover, the wedfare programs do not seem to recognize the growing diversity of family structures, such as same-sex unions or elective single parenting (DeKeseredy & Schwartz, 2006b). Teenage mothers, in particular, may not find salvation in marriage and may need welfare over their entire life trajectory. The following scenario is a condensed version of such a woman (from Fram, Miller-Cribbs, & Farber, 2006).

## CASE HISTORY   Terry and Her Disadvantaged Life

Terry grew up in a home with an alcoholic father who beat everyone in the family. He controlled everyone and everything. He did not allow his wife to work, even when he could not hold down a job, thus forcing the family to live in poverty or on welfare. Trying to escape from this environment, Terry married her boyfriend at age 16, forfeiting her chance to finish her high school education. After the birth of two children, Terry left her husband because of his substance abuse, unemployment, and violent assaults. She received no child support and did not have enough money even for food. She had a mental breakdown and was homeless from time to time.

She managed to obtain Medicaid for her children and Temporary Assistance for Needy Families, but welfare cut off her benefits after only two checks because of her so-called noncompliance. Eventually, she got her GED and with child care help from friends got a job in a nursing home. She became involved with another man who was supportive of her going to school to become a nurse. For awhile all was going fairly well. Her *family* had a car, enough to eat, and a place to live. Still, one of her sons was behaving badly at school.

Her boyfriend lost his low-paying job as a manual laborer and Terry lost her job as well because her boss said she was too outspoken at work. As she was applying for other jobs, she tested positive for tuberculosis and could no longer work as a nurse's aid. By now, she was several thousand dollars in debt, accumulated during her attempt to get an education. Social Services also claimed she owed them money for overpayments she *never received*. At the last interview, Terry said she was facing eviction, but she did not want to apply for Temporary Assistance for Needy Families.

The foregoing case history provides a picture of how difficult it can be for disadvantaged women to escape poverty *and* be free from intimate partner violence. Also, it provides insight into a generational transfer of poverty.

*Hiring and training welfare workers.* Judging from the research presented above concerning the behaviors of some welfare workers, the hiring standards of welfare departments need a review (Shim & Haight, 2006). One state's effort to measure training needs of its workers concluded that, "benefits workers are perceived as knowing less about domestic violence than other social service workers" (Payne & Triplett, 2009). Interventionists recommend basic skills training in several areas, such as being supportive and positive, knowing about other IPV resources, being flexible, knowing how to present referrals, and protecting the client's confidentiality. The most sensible recommendation made by this research team was to develop and use a short screening instrument to detect male partner abuse (Brush, 2003; Burt, Zweig, & Schlichter, 2000; Davies, 2000; Postmus, 2003).

Saunders, Holter, Pahl, Tolman, and Kenna (2005) found that training welfare workers achieved several important goals. Trained workers relative to untrained were more likely to discuss the women's fear and physical harm and more likely to help them develop safety plans. Clients also rated the trained workers as more helpful and more comfortable when talking about battering.

## Health Care Providers

The professional group that battered women disclose their abuse to most frequently appears to be health care providers (Van Hook, 2000). This choice may occur because victims suffer numerous debilitating and chronic health problems and are therefore in contact with health care personnel (Attala, Weaver, Duckett, & Draper, 2000; J. C. Campbell & Soeken, 1999). The medical community can play a pivotal role by assessing, intervening, and appropriately referring battered women (Naumann, Langford, Torres, Campbell, & Glass, 1999; Schornstein, 1997).

*Medical screening.* Going back as far as 1991, a number of physical and mental care organizations have advised adoption of *routine IPV screening* for women in medical offices, clinics, and other areas beyond the emergency room (e.g., Knapp, Dowd, Kennedy, Stallbaumer-Rouyer, & Henderson, 2006). Psychologists and others have specifically urged medical personnel to pay close attention to *suspicious injuries* manifested by pregnant or older women (McFarlane, Groff, O'Brien, & Watson, 2005; Sheridan & Nash, 2007). One especially overlooked health issue is identification of mild traumatic brain injuries (M. E. Banks, 2007). The Centers for Disease Control and Prevention have prepared a document on victimization assessments for use in health care settings (Basile, Hertz, & Back, 2007). Only 33% to 53% of health care providers, nonetheless, routinely screen women for abuse (Ramsey, Richardson, Carter, Davidson, & Feder, 2002).

*Mandated identification of battered women in the emergency room.* During the 1990s, the Joint Commission on Accreditation of Healthcare Organizations established a policy that hospital emergency room personnel "had to identify" battered women ("Focus," 1994). The thinking underlying the new mandate was that for some partner-assaulted victims, hospital *emergency room staff* might be their first contact with a potential community helper. Once a victim discloses her abuse, medical staff should find the time to hear her story and refer her to appropriate agencies. They should tell her that abuse is illegal, give her information about abuse, and arrange for follow-up with supportive services (Frasier, Slatt, Kowlowitz, & Glowa, 2001). Without this support, battered women may not be able to leave their abusers. In response to such policy changes, the American Medical Association began publishing booklets for doctors' use in addressing family violence (Children's Safety Network, 1992). (See the website for a study comparing women referred for assistance and women on routine visits.)

Nevertheless, medical screening can have both positive and negative effects for women. In one inquiry, *positive effects* for the victims included their *recognition that the violence* was a problem, decreased isolation, and feeling that the medical provider cared. *Negative outcomes* included the victims' feeling *judged* by the provider, *increased anxiety* about the unknown, finding the *screening process cumbersome and intrusive,* and *disappointment in the provider's reactions* to disclosure (Chang et al., 2003). One investigation compared three different screening tests. A total of 523 women, 181 physicians, and 169 medical staff participated. Results were positive: (a) All three groups were comfortable with all three screening tools; (b) disclosure was high; and (c) the internal reliability and validity of the tests were acceptable (Chen et al., 2007). Some other research, however, does not support screening in health care settings (MacMillian et al., 2009).

*Centers for Disease Control and Prevention (CDC).* As the federal government has become more involved in family violence, it has established more surveillance (monitoring) systems which provide extremely valuable information. The systems gather data about gender, relationships of perpetrator/offenders, types/locations of injuries, and other vital information. As noted previously, more and more emergency rooms are adding their treatment records to national databases, such as the *National Center for Injury Prevention and Control* (NCIPC) and the *Behavioral Risk Factor Surveillance System* (BRFSS). (See Intimate Partner Violence: Data Sources on the CDC website.)

*Medical training.* Medical professionals need training if they are to be effective in screening and referring IPV victims (J. R. Hill, 2005). They may need training to avoid non-nurturing responses, such as distancing, blaming the victim, and suggesting that the symptoms are not real. Recently, a team of scholars has shown that a routine inquiry intervention for doctors significantly increased doctors' probability of documenting the effects of IPV (Soglin, Bauchat, Soglin, & Martin, 2009). Medical psychologists have risen to the challenge by improving their knowledge base and then learning how best to train doctors (e.g., Hamberger & Phelan, 2004). Consequently, the health care community is increasingly joining society's efforts to stop partner abuse.

One especially supportive medical response is to recognize the *nonphysical* injury health repercussions of male partner violence. When patients present with problems closely linked to abuse such as PTSD and depression, doctors should investigate further. As Jaffe and Crooks (2005) have observed, there is a gap between knowing how to screen for IPV and knowing what to do to help the victim. Behavioral scientists can inform medical students about the dynamics of IPV and how they can contribute to the reduction of family violence (Wedding, 2008). (See Basile, Hertz, & Back, 2007, for practical guides for doctors.)

## Prevention Strategies

Given the serious consequences of male-to-female intimate partner violence for victims, their children, and society at large, it is essential that government and nongovernment organizations take steps to prevent it (Osofsky, 1999). Basic to prevention of violence against women is to bring about changes in attitudes. In particular, efforts must target the *sexist, patriarchal, and hostile attitudes toward women* that are so persistent. It is essential to change attitudes within families, communities, organizations, institutions, and societal norms. Other influential factors, such as the media and the law, impact all these groups (Flood & Pease, 2009).

*College classes.* Some universities now commonly require entering freshmen to attend violence prevention classes covering partner violence and rape. Sometimes, fraternities and sororities conduct antiviolence programs. Another prevention approach is for universities to offer more *personal relationship classes.* Research has shown that even a 20-minute oral presentation to university students about domestic violence can produce some favorable changes in attitudes (O'Neal & Dorn, 1998). The hope is that such programs will work forward to prevent violence even after students leave college.

*Public awareness programs.* Public awareness campaigns may enable some potential victims to avoid victimization. Trying to make the public responsive to the plight of female IPV victims, nevertheless, may run into two widely held cultural beliefs: (a) People "get what they deserve" (i.e., just world belief), and (b) victims "should have seen it coming" (i.e., hindsight bias) (Arriaga & Capezza, 2005). These beliefs suggest that it would be helpful if some public awareness campaigns took aim at victim-blaming. To make campaigns more beneficial to potential or real victims of battering, it would be wise to obtain feedback from victims. To this end, researchers conducted focus groups made up of victims whose task was to evaluate a public awareness campaign about male partner abuse. The data analysis indicated that the victims judged the information offered to be somewhat *inaccurate.* They suggested that the messages should have focused on *enhancing early identification, empowerment, and help-seeking.* A different group of victims, who *regretted their inactions* and lack of knowledge about male battering, thought that public awareness campaigns emphasizing *human rights* would have helped them recognize male IPV and take action sooner (Fry & Barker, 2001).

*PREVENT program.* The National Center for Injury Prevention and Control, along with domestic violence and rape education organizations, has launched an especially relevant prevention program named PREVENT. PREVENT staff identifies functioning *teams of practitioners* from within social service organizations (e.g., domestic violence, rape crisis). When the teams arrive at the training facility, the staff asks the practitioner participants, along with a coach, to develop an individualized program to take back and use in their own organization. To facilitate the process, PREVENT offers engaging, action-oriented, adult learning, and face-to-face training in the forms of workshops and institutes. They also provide fact sheets, tool kits, and other aids.

To understand how organizations might respond to PREVENT programs, researchers gathered interview data from practitioners within these organizations about two topics: (a) what do organizational personnel want to learn, and (b) what obstacles face personnel attempting to accomplish their training needs. Respondents were very interested in understanding primary prevention, how to work in the community, and about other associated activities. There were several barriers including lack of time and lack of money to attend training. On balance, PREVENT offers a bright future for preventing interpersonal violence (S. L. Martin et al., 2009).

## Research Needs

First, researchers have expanded the information available on how to enhance ethical and safety considerations in conducting research. They covered a wide breadth of topics, such as how to contact women without notifying abusers, the importance of staff training and supervision, and how to adequately compensate women for their participation. They compiled an exceptionally valuable 2-page table of safety protocols that should be mandatory reading for researchers planning to recruit battered women as participants (Sullivan & Cain, 2004). Second, there is need for a well-conceptualized set of research projects that call for both qualitative and quantitative studies (see the National Institute of Justice's Compendium of Research on Violence Against Women: 1993–2009, 2009).

---

**SECTION SUMMARY**

### Practice, Policy, and Prevention for Abused Partners

The first section of this chapter discusses how professionals can help battered women respond to male-to-female partner violence, what social organizations can do to help, and what might be done to prevent male abuse of their partners. Research has pinpointed the extreme *social isolation* that may occur in female victims' lives and their need for *social support*. There are many kinds of social support that family and friends can offer and other types that agencies, courts, and health care personnel can provide. At least three issues about social support are problematic. First, some support, such as advising a woman to stay with her abuser, may actually be detrimental. Second, the correlation between what agencies presuppose to be supportive and what battered women think is supportive is often incongruent. Third, the supports needed by women currently in a relationship are not the same as those of women who have exited a relationship. Researchers have ascertained the types of attitudes, actions, referral, and group activities women find helpful (e.g., showing concern, having 24-hour services available, knowing which attorneys might help, and group activities).

Shelters need to provide alcohol and drug services within or outside the shelter. Shelter policies need modification to allow women who are self-defensively violent to enter. Teaching parenting skills can be especially beneficial because mothers can learn to offset the violence-caused poorer parental functioning. For women whose children have been taken by Child Protective Services, parenting classes may help them regain custody. Women in Transitional Supportive Housing sometimes experience frustration if supervised in a unit with excessive regulations but experience a sense of progress in a unit with more flexible supervision.

*(Continued)*

---

(Continued)

Psychotherapists need to begin their work with battered women by conducting violence screening and problem identification. After following up with discussions about safety planning, they need to fashion an individualized plan for helping women cope with their particular situation. Some of the issues to cover include the following: (a) arrange for drug/alcohol treatment when needed; (b) address false beliefs such as battering is normal; (c) discuss that trying to leave can be dangerous; (d) recognize the devastation of marital rape and surrounding issues is an important topic; (e) obtain current information about brain-based psychotherapy; (f) be prepared that past victimization effects may surface as a discussion theme; (g) recognize that some victims are very attached to their abuser and very much want to save their relationships while managing to eliminate the violence. Because victims are probably strongly attached to their abuser, therapists can address how to regulate attachment needs and how best to cope with violence; (h) deal with victims' grief in losing the positive aspects of their relationship; (i) address the victim's fear; (j) help women with their coping and problem-solving skills, how to become empowered, and how to deal with workplace issues; and (k) address issues of forgiveness because the outcome can be either beneficial or perilous.

There are a number of proposed policy alterations that can be improved by allowing battered women to offer their opinions. Discrimination against women has been a staple of American life that is in dire need of change. Women often become the sole support of their children, yet they must work for much less money than men and receive little support with child care. Women face inexcusable discrimination in the court system where they may be maligned, disbelieved, and left alone to cope with risky situations. Discrimination in public housing constitutes yet another unfair burden placed on female victims. These types of discrimination alone may force women and children into unending poverty. Safety in relocating to a another location can still be uncertain, despite improvements, and advocates must still bear the brunt of providing such assistance.

Battered women face enormous challenges in becoming financially independent. Shelters and Transitional Supportive Housing have made some inroads in providing assistance but need to improve some aspects of their services. Corporations need to consider improving their work rules to accommodate battered women's special needs, and more government organizations need to determine how they might help women achieve safety. Providing work training for unskilled males would enhance their ability to support their children. On a positive note, society has increased its financial support for battered women's services every year.

*Welfare programs* geared to assist battered women have been quite disappointing. Not only has welfare staff received inadequate training on how to address partner abuse victims, but criteria for hiring of welfare workers need revision. The effectiveness of the entire Welfare to Work program is questionable. Women completing such programs are usually earning minimum wage or are still unemployed. One especially annoying intrusion has been the focus on marriage as a panacea for women's economic problems. Women cannot marry their way out of poverty.

> *Medical providers* have a heavy responsibility in reducing family violence because of their role as first responders, the first person to hear about the abuse. Having to identify battered women is time-consuming and not always rewarding. Providing referrals and making appropriate comments can be validating to a victim. Within the federal oversight of health care, new data systems are coming online that provide useful information about IPV.
>
> *The criminal justice system* has not been able to establish best practices that save women's lives. Not only do laws need to be changed, but also appropriate implementation is needed. Judges may pose an obstacle in attaining justice. Finally, much more prevention is needed at every level. In addition to posters and media announcements, college courses offer some hope of changing attitudes about acceptance of violence toward women.

## *ABUSIVE* ADULT PARTNERS: PRACTICE, POLICY, AND PREVENTION ISSUES

"Just get him to stop" is the urgent call of victims, society, and the criminal justice system, thus creating an exceptionally strong impetus for effective batterer interventions. Many abused women and partner-abusive men wish to save their relationship, a desire that nearly always requires counseling. In addition, society seems to favor counseling over jail time, so from both perspectives the treatment of choice is counseling. Cavanaugh and Gelles (2005, p. 164) state that "the illusion of the stereotypic batterer who is somehow miraculously going to desist without appropriate treatment has well past." Finding effective methods to help or coerce men to stop their IPV is no easy task. One encouraging probability, nevertheless, is that with scientific progress and more interdisciplinary collaboration, practitioners will be able to attain a deeper understanding of mental phenomena, and thus treatment will improve (Dingfelder, 2008). The section that follows unveils the many compelling problems encountered by practitioners attempting to stop IPV.

### Practice

Much of the work that must be done in batterers' treatment programs revolves around encouraging batterers to *recognize their* abuse—their various forms of intimidation. The end goal is to help batterers find ways to halt nonphysical as well as physical abuse, but change is difficult and demanding. One expert has provided a handy list of *subtypes of counseling* (R. B. Stuart, 2005):

- Insight therapy
- Empathy training
- Problem-solving skills
- Medication
- Training in relativistic thinking

- Relapse prevention
- Entry into social networks
- Overreaction and oversensitivity
- Job counseling

- Rejection of violence
- Reflection about gender roles
- Anger and conflict management

## Need for Screening

Without exception, experts are calling for practitioners to screen men for partner violence. Some mental health clinicians also advise the administration of tests, such as the Psychopathy Checklist for detecting psychopathology (S. D. Hart, Hare, & Forth, 1993) and tests to recognize the existence of cognitive deficits (e.g., difficulty in handling delayed reward, problems in processing contextual information) (Huss & Langhinrichsen-Rohling, 2000). Still other experts are suggesting screening to separate *family-only (FO)* or *partner-only (PO)* batterers from *generally violent (GV)* batterers. Although family-only and partner-only violent men may be suitable candidates for treatment, generally violent men may not be. For GV men, it may be best to call upon the justice system and/or medical interventionists. Under some situations, it seems possible that treatment for partner violence, substance abuse, and personality disorders—*within* rather than outside prison—might be less costly and safer (Rossen, Bartlett, & Herrick, 2008).

In a contemporary study, academicians devised screening tests that can be used by untrained group facilitators. These tests yield a simple, reliable, standardized system for classifying violent men (D. J. Boyle, O'Leary, Rosenbaum, & Hassett-Walker, 2008). Some of the most crucial information needed includes the following:

- Jealousy
- Dangerousness
- Attachment style
- Control/dominance
- Anger and hostility
- Socio-demographics

- Status with the court
- Alcohol/drug problems
- Type/severity/rate of IPV
- Tendency to blame others

## General Targets of Batterer Counseling

*Batterer intervention programs (BIPs).* BIPs are by far the most common and most preferred type of treatment for partner abuse. In one account, 86% of administrators of BIPs stated a preference for group programs (Austin & Dankwort, 1999; Carden, 1994). Group settings are preferable because they help partner-violent men work on male-to-male relationships. Such relationships are vital to men who experienced poor father-son relationships in childhood (Jennings & Murphy, 2000). In the late 1970s and early 1980s, batterer interventions programs were developing so rapidly that by the mid-1980s there were already more than 200 such programs in the United States (Stordeur & Stille, 1989).

Most batterer intervention programs work in conjunction with the criminal justice system. In fact, the justice system has institutionalized the BIP as a strategy for reducing partner violence (Gregory, 2004). Approximately *80%* of clients in batterer interventions attend the programs because the *courts* have ordered them to do so. Child abuse agency personnel and probation officers are representative of other referral sources (Healey, Smith, & O'Sullivan, 1998). A few clients may be volunteers, but these men may differ from men court-ordered into treatment (e.g., more likely employed) (Dutton & Starzomski, 1994).

## Type of Treatment—The Controversy

The choice of program content and format for batterer interventions has probably been the most contentious issue in the treatment field. The type of treatment offered has even become a legal issue. A major reason for the disagreement is the *philosophical split* between two major groups of batterer counselors. One faction consists of *trained, licensed mental health practitioners.* The other consists of *trained feminist advocates* and includes some members of professional organizations. Disparate *conclusions about the etiology* of male-to-female violence (i.e., sociopolitical, interpersonal, intrapersonal, or biological) dominate the debate because the conclusions determine the disparate modes of facilitating change. The dissent has polarized practitioners, advocates, and academicians in the field (Mankowski, Haaken, & Silvergleid, 2002; see also Silvergleid & Mankowski, 2006).

*The Duluth model: Psychoeducational approaches.* The Duluth model, initiated by feminist advocates, was the earliest mode of treatment. The goal of psychoeducational programs is for batterers to *unlearn socially/culturally* reinforced violent *behavior* directed toward women. Presumably, male partner violence is an extreme action falling on a *continuum of behaviors* through which *men control and oppress women.* Adherents of this perspective want to *resocialize men to abandon patriarchal power and control* tactics as well as *sexist attitudes* toward women. As an illustration, a man who beats his wife because dinner is late must first learn that he has no right to order her to make dinner or to make it on time (E. Pence & Paymar, 1993). Obviously, there is work to do on transforming basic conceptions of masculinity so that males are less violent, less controlling, more loving, more emotionally expressive, more nurturing, and more appreciative of women (see also Mankowski et al., 2002). The Duluth approach also capitalizes on criminal justice sanctions as an integral part of a successful feminist program.

Skeptics of the Duluth model question its scientific foundation and consider it more of a political statement than a psychological treatment. Indicative of this criticism is that feminist agendas do not focus on treating men's *psychiatric or medical problems.* Critics believe that the assumption that all partner abuse is motivated by issues of patriarchal power and control is overbroad at a minimum and risky at a maximum (Dutton, 2008). Indeed, R. B. Stuart (2005) believes that this faulty assumption, along with others, is a major factor in spawning *ineffective treatment* (see also Norlander & Eckhardt, 2005). R. B. Stuart (2005) also states that the Duluth model is one "that ignores individual differences, omits many potentially useful techniques and treatment formats, and in some cases falsely reassures victims that they are safe from further abuse" (p. 257). Currently, experienced practitioners/ researchers have become more actively involved in denouncing the model as unethical (Corvo, Dutton, & Chen, 2009).

Despite the lack of scientific evidence supporting the effectiveness of the Duluth model (Dutton, 1994), and evidence indicating it is not effective (e.g., Schrock & Padavic, 2007), many U.S. states have established regulations requiring the feminist approach. In fact, more batterer programs across the United States adhere to the Duluth model than any other (Jackson, 2003).

Feminist scholars have criticized psychological treatment approaches for male offenders on grounds that they serve as excuses for battering. As an example, a batterer who blames his assaults on his abusive parents is using his childhood experiences as a defense. Feminists further argue that batterers do *not* need counseling; they need *reeducation*. Psychoeducational therapists label some psychological treatment, such as training to overcome *skill deficits* or *anger management,* as misguided. In reality, male-to-female aggression stems from *patriarchy,* not from lack of communication skills or inability to control anger (e.g., Goldner, Penn, Sheinberg, & Walker, 1990). (For more on this important, ongoing controversy, see the website.)

*Cognitive-behavioral therapy.* The second most common treatment is cognitive-behavioral therapy. Therapists apply *learning principles* to help clients modify behavior recognized as problematic. Simply put, a therapist might help a client reduce his hostility toward women by restructuring his thinking. The following three-stage example shows how a typical batterer might think *before therapy:* First, he encounters external stimuli such as a wife's failure to have dinner ready on time. Second, he then internally interprets the event (e.g., in terms of past learning, current stress, or some other variable) as her "not caring about how he feels." He decides that he must "force her to treat him better." And third, in the final stage, he carries out an external response, such as throwing the food in her face.

In the preceding example, cognitive behavioral therapy would focus on teaching this male offender to *reinterpret the situation.* He might be able to recognize that his wife's lateness in preparing dinner occurred because she was ill and realize that there are *other behavioral options* (e.g., take the family out to a fast-food restaurant). Some other therapeutic techniques involve helping offenders accomplish goals, such as *managing adverse arousal and learning appropriate assertion and problem-solving skills* (see Faulkner, Stoltenberg, Cogen, Nolder, & Shooter, 1992). A therapist might use cognitive-behavioral therapy to focus on verbal and communication skills, because improving communication skills would improve the man's perceptions of his ability to control his aggression toward his female partner (see Hollin et al., 2008; O'Farrell, Murphy, Neavins, & Van Hutton, 2000). Another approach is to integrate feminist/cognitive-behavioral and psychodynamic group treatment for batterers (Lawson et al., 2001).

*Anger management.* Anger management is an important therapeutic focus of many batterer intervention programs because research has identified elevated levels of anger among male perpetrators (e.g., C. Gregory & Erez, 2002; Norlander & Eckhardt, 2005; Whatule, 2000). The goal of anger management is to identify feelings of anger, control inappropriate feelings, and learn how to express such feelings appropriately. Therapy aimed at anger management often uses cognitive methods and anger reduction techniques (e.g., relaxation training, time-out, anger logs). Because anger can sometimes be constructive rather than destructive, it is advisable to determine a point at which anger becomes dysfunctional (Davidson, MacGregor, Stuhr, Dixon, & MacLean, 2000; Tiedens, 2001). Although feminist advocates may question the need for anger management, many practitioners believe it is useful (Eckhardt, Samper, & Murphy, 2008; Orme, Dominelli, & Mullender, 2000).

In a dissertation, an investigator collected archival data from 1,150 male offenders in Massachusetts. A 5-year follow-up compared recidivism across eight different treatment groups: (1) *arrest only,* (2) *probation only,* (3) *incarceration,* or court-ordered completion of one of the following: (4) a *BIP,* (5) an *anger-management program,* (6) *substance abuse evaluation or treatment,* (7) *unspecified* "other counseling," or (8) placed in the *dropped out* category. Results of the data analyses ascertained that the *anger management* group fared best. Offenders in this group were both less likely to recidivate and had the fewest number of re-offenses relative to individuals in the other groups (Macvaugh, 2005).

*Eclectic approaches.* Many batterer intervention programs take an eclectic approach that includes anger management and consciousness-raising. Whatever treatment approaches are being used, one absolute obligation of all BIPs must be a consideration of battered women's safety (Hamberger & Barnett, 1995). In an effort to ensure victims' safety, some batterer programs have initiated sessions in which they provide female victims with safety planning information (Hamberger & Hastings, 1990). Practitioners also have the ethical and legal "duty to warn" potential victims (*Tarasoff v. Regents of the University of California,* 1976) while maintaining their primary duty to maintain confidentiality.

*Couples therapy (family therapy and systems therapy).* Systems theory has been an especially controversial approach to batterer treatment. In fact, 72% of the states have reporting standards labeling systems therapy as inappropriate, probably because of feminist advocacy efforts (Austin & Dankwort, 1999). This approach expands the focus of treatment to include *marital dynamics* and the *whole family system* as a context for marital violence. Underlying this modality is the goal of *family preservation.* A philosophical underpinning is that a batterer's violence is *not* attributable to him *alone,* but is somehow *attributable to his relationship* with his partner (Goodyear-Smith & Laidlaw, 1999). Two assets of couples' therapy are that it improves communication and allows male and female therapists to model nonviolent behavior (Geffner & Rosenbaum, 1990).

Some scholars believe such treatment is suitable under prescribed circumstances, such as when the violence is at a low level, the victim is not fearful, and the couple wants to stay together (O'Leary, 1996). One disturbing finding regarding therapists' use of couples' therapy is their *failure to comply with mandated assessment procedures.* One national survey of 620 counselors randomly selected from the register of the American Association for Marriage and Family Therapists asked respondents about their screening practices. Fewer than 4% reported that they followed published guidelines, such as screening members of a couple separately. Most did not take the victim's safety into consideration either. The researcher concluded that "therapists may be using conjoint therapy with couples for whom such therapy is contraindicated because of relationship violence" (Schacht, Dimidjian, George, & Berns, 2009).

A debate is ongoing whether couples' therapy is appropriate, or whether treatment should focus only on the behavior of the batterer.

## Alcohol and Drug Substance Abuse Treatment

Substance abuse is very prevalent among people in the United States. The National Institute of Alcohol Abuse and Alcoholism (National Institute on Drug Abuse, 2007) reported data from a survey of 43,093 American adults: (a) About 30% of American adults have engaged in harmful patterns of alcohol use; (b) about 18% have experienced alcohol-based absences from work and driving while drunk; and (c) about 12.5% say they have been or are alcohol dependent. What is more, others have pointed out that an overlap exists between substance abuse and *antisociality*. Both *genetic components* (see, e.g., Bower, 1994) and *learning components* (Vaillant & Milofsky, 1982) play a role in alcohol misuse.

Research consistently shows that spouse abusers in particular have alcohol- and drug-related problems. Because drunkenness can precipitate battering and may be used as an excuse for partner abuse, practitioners must address alcohol treatment. One *myth* that Zubretsky and Digirolamo (1994) have tried to debunk, however, is that *treatment* of alcohol or substance abuse problems *alone* will concomitantly eliminate problems with domestic violence. A batterer trying to stop drinking, in fact, may be more abusive because of the new, added stress of attempting sobriety.

*An integrated substance abuse/domestic violence treatment program.* Some experts have speculated that combining batterer treatment with alcohol/drug treatment might be especially effective in reducing battering. Another supposition was that using different types of community service sanctions might be effective. One investigation compared the efficacy of a *Twelve-Step Facilitation* group with an integrated *substance abuse/domestic violence* treatment. Men arrested for partner abuse who were seeking treatment for substance abuse were randomly assigned to either of the two groups for 12 weeks of treatment. The substance abuse/domestic violence group received *cognitive-behavioral therapy* following instructions in a manual focusing on both alcohol use and spouse abuse. Some of the many issues covered in structured handouts included the following: (a) identifying high-risk situations for substance abuse and partner abuse, (b) awareness of anger, and (c) coping with criticism.

The study used several assessments. Tests included *psychiatric diagnoses* from DSM-IV and the *addiction severity* index administered at three times: baseline, 12 weeks posttreatment, and at the 6-month follow-up. There were weekly assessments to *test for substance abuse* including such measures as onsite urine toxicology and self-reports. For physical and injury-producing male-to-female partner abuse, the participants completed the CTS2 at three times: baseline, 12 weeks posttreatment, and at the 6-month follow-up. Female partners added data about partner abuse at 12 weeks posttreatment and 6 months follow-up. Across both treatment types (Twelve-Step or substance abuse/domestic violence), 83% of the men completed 9 of the 12 sessions. Results indicated that the *substance abuse/domestic violence* participants used *alcohol on fewer days* during the treatment and demonstrated a statistical trend toward a *reduction in battering behavior*. These findings suggest that joint treatment for substance abuse and male violence can be combined effectively (Easton et al., 2007; see Labriola, Rempel, & Davis, 2005, for a review).

Appropriate *drugs* to assist in alcohol cessation are available and should be prescribed (Chaimowitz, Glancy, & Blackburn, 2000). One contemporary longitudinal controlled study of nearly a thousand alcoholics (not assessed for partner violence) revealed the efficacy of the drug *acamprosate.* In this controlled analysis, participants receiving the drug, relative to those receiving a placebo, significantly increased the number of days abstinent and time until first drink (Kranzler & Gage, 2008). (See www.sagepub.com/barnett3e for additional drug treatments for male partner violence.)

*Psychiatric-psychotropic medication treatments.* There is a sizable minority of male perpetrators who suffer from some form of psychopathology; yet, exactly how psychopathology is linked with violence is not well understood. Men in this subset of offenders are likely to be the most difficult to treat (e.g., Holtzworth-Munroe, Meehan et al., 2000). Perhaps individuals beset with traits such as antipersonality disorder cannot be helped sufficiently via any known kind of psychotherapy and should receive drug treatments. Psychotropic medications such as *antianxiety, antidepression, antiaggression, and antipsychotic drugs* should reduce associated behavioral correlates of these conditions (see Berman, McCloskey, Fanning, Schumacher, & Coccaro, 2009; Paschall & Fishbein, 2002). (See the website for more specific recommendations for treatment.)

## Are Batterer Programs Effective?

Treatment effectiveness studies have not permitted researchers to reach firm conclusions about the value of specific types of treatment but have allowed experts to hold opposing viewpoints about batterer intervention programs. The majority of experts are skeptical about the quality and *permanence of behavioral changes* made by abusers as the result of counseling (e.g., Feder & Wilson, 2005; Healey et al., 1998). Others hold out hope that counseling can at least achieve minimal or even modest positive results (Bennett, Stroops, Call, & Flett, 2007; A. A. Jones, D'Agostino, Gondolf, & Heckert, 2004). It is interesting to note the similarity of recidivism rates for male *criminals* exiting prison *not* categorized by offender status. For several states, the 2002 recidivism rates were 62.5% for 1983 and 67.5% for 1994 (Palermo, 2010a). (See the website for detail on typology-based treatments.)

*Reducing recidivism—The Plumas Program.* A promising newer approach for *reducing recidivism* is the *Plumas Program,* a goal-directed, *solution-based IPV program.* This therapy does *not* dwell on *deficits* or changes in sexist attitudes (M. Y. Lee, Sebold, & Uken, 2003); instead, it incorporates the following elements:

MALE/FEMALE COTHERAPISTS

EIGHT 1-HOUR SESSIONS OVER 3 MONTHS

PROGRESS TOWARD GOALS—PART OF GROUP INTERACTIONS

OFFENDERS ACCOUNTABLE FOR SOLUTIONS RATHER THAN PROBLEMS

In a subsequent evaluation of the Plumas Program, researchers assessed the progress of *both male and female intimate partner offenders* enrolled in the program. Data included the customary socioeconomic indicators and information about childhood abuse, brain injury, substance abuse, criminal records, and mental health status. The investigators tracked the relationship between several collections of variables and reoffending.

1. *Predictor variables:* aspects of goal setting: goal commitment, goal specificity, and goal agreement (between the participant and a therapist)
2. *Mediating* variable: *participants' confidence* that they would continue working on the goals after completing the intervention
3. *Dependent variables* for *recidivism:* reports from the district attorney's office, the probation office, the victim witness office, and victim's request for a protective order.

Results showed that the reoffense rate was 10.2% (an extremely low rate) and that the final statistical model accounted for 58% of the variance. "Goal specificity and goal agreement positively predicted confidence to work on goals, which negatively predicted recidivism indexes" (Lee, Uken, & Sebold, 2007, p. 30).

*Controlled comparison of batterer treatment effectiveness—The Brooklyn study.* In one controlled comparison, Taylor, Davis, and Maxwell (2001) employed a *randomized selection* procedure to examine outcomes for male offenders drawn from a population of 11,000 defendants in Brooklyn. A *treatment group* received a 40-hour *Duluth-type program,* while a *comparison group* received a 40-hour *community service intervention.* The researchers obtained several recidivism measures at 6 and 12 months: (a) *arrest reports,* (b) *crime complaints,* and (c) 48% to 51% of *victims' reports* (modified CTS1 index). Some insignificant problems occurred when judges overrode the researchers' random selection by assigning 14% of maritally violent men to a batterer intervention program when the researchers would have assigned them to community service.

Categories of outcome measures included *battering prevalence, frequency, severity,* and *time to first failure following counseling.* Results disclosed that men in treatment had *significantly less recidivism* based on two sources of official data (Criminal Justice Agency, New York City Police Department). Calculation provided an estimate of a 44% reduction in recidivism attributable to treatment. Analyses of victims' reports disclosed less recidivism on all four measures, but no single comparison reached statistical significance. While the findings supported the value of treatment, the total sample size was too small for generalizability.

*Narrow criteria.* Other commentators, such as D. C. Adams and Galibois (2004), have voiced concern over what they consider to be the narrow criteria for assessing the impact of batterer intervention programs (BIPs). They believe that a top priority of BIPs is to promote *batterer accountability,* rather than expecting abusers to modify either assault behavior or their attitudes toward women rapidly. Holding men more accountable prompted a number of female victims to report feeling empowered. Note that in a previously described study, accountability referred to *internalization of responsibility* rather than acknowledgement that their behavior was harmful (Costa, Canady, & Babcock, 2007). Others added that accountability efforts by intervention programs need to encompass a number of activities: (a) documenting batterer noncompliance, (b) informing the courts of noncompliance, (c) terminating batterers who do not comply with BIP requirements, (d) keeping victims informed of the program's goals and limitations, (e) stop blaming victims—and hold themselves more accountable, (f) collaborating with other community agencies, such as child welfare, and (g) trying to maximize victims' safety (Adams & Galibois, 2004).

*Meta-analytic reviews.* Two groups of researchers have conducted *meta-analyses* of the effectiveness of interventions aimed at diminishing male partner violence. In the first review of 22 carefully selected experimental and **quasi-experimental investigations,** researchers identified positive but very small improvement (Babcock, Green, & Robie, 2004).

In the second review, criminologists conducted a meta-analysis using 10 studies they deemed especially rigorous. They did not, for instance, include designs lacking pretreatment equivalence of groups. Their criteria also required that investigators collect follow-up data for at least 6 months. For outcome measures, they used both *official reports* and *victims' reports.* The meta-analyses found *mixed results* reflecting inconsistencies associated with differences in research designs and outcome measures. They concluded that their findings "raise doubts about the effectiveness of court-ordered batterer intervention programs" (Feder & Wilson, 2005, p. 239), and that practitioners need to develop diverse types of batterer treatment programs.

## Challenges in Treatment Evaluation

As a rule, methodological deficiencies plague batterer outcome studies. Two issues that have been especially acute in evaluation of program effectiveness are *lack of random assignment* and *attrition* (premature termination of treatment, dropout). Researchers cannot randomly assign men to the batterer group, nor can they control attrition. Premature termination of therapy occurs frequently in nearly any kind of psychological treatment, not just treatment for male IPV. The estimated noncompletion rate for psychotherapy outpatients is typically 47% (L. M. Miller, Southam-Gerow, & Allin, 2008; see also Topham & Wampler, 2008). Customarily, only 40% to 70% of batterers who begin treatment finish (e.g., Tutty, Bidgood, Rothery, & Bidgood, 2001; see also Olson & Stalans, 2001).

Illustrative of *treatment attrition* are findings in a study in which researchers tracked records of 200 inquiries about batterer programs (i.e., men calling about entering treatment): (a) From inquiry to first intake session, the attrition rate was 73%; (b) From inquiry to counseling attendance, attrition was 86%; and (c) From inquiry to completion of 12 sessions, the attrition rate was 93%. Altogether, only 1% of the original group completed the contracted 8-month treatment program (Gondolf & Foster, 1991). The high dropout rate not only undermines the generalizability of findings from program evaluations, but it also poses a serious safety issue for victims.

*Treatment completion/noncompletion.* For research purposes, investigators have frequently categorized batterers as *completers or noncompleters.* As one example, investigators matched up completers with noncompleters following a 16-week aggression abatement program (Hamberger & Hastings, 1990). These researchers reported that violence-free completers had fewer alcohol/drug *problems* both pre- and posttreatment, and following treatment they had lower scores *for narcissism* (self-centered/demanding). With few exceptions, studies have shown that the relationship between male abusers' treatment *dropout and violent recidivism* is high. (See the website for a partial list of completion/dropout studies.)

### Effectiveness of Counseling Programs

Because evaluation of batterer intervention programs is so compromised, it may not be surprising that the measured success of abuser counseling is less than impressive. Most batterer programs have shown little, if any, effectiveness especially if the mode of treatment lacks a scientific basis (R. B. Stuart, 2005; see also Cattaneo & Goodman, 2005).

*Consumer satisfaction.* Another perspective on the effectiveness of batterer programs is *consumer satisfaction.* In one appraisal, practitioners asked men in treatment and the majority of their female partners a number of open-ended questions about their satisfaction/ dissatisfaction with the male partners' program. Approximately half of this sample made no recommendations for change. Of the 14% of men suggesting change, their wish was to have *more supportive counseling.* Of the 13% of women advising change, the most common requests were for greater safety and for more information about the program. In addition, batterers *frequently wanted their partners to join them* because, they asserted, the women should share the blame. Averaging consumers' satisfaction levels indicated that consumers were generally satisfied (Gondolf & White, 2000).

*Batterer intervention program effectiveness—Gondolf.* Another method for determining BIP effectiveness has been to use more refined statistical techniques. Within the confines of a quasi-experimental study of *batterer reassaults,* investigators demonstrated how *propensity score analysis* provided a different view of program completion effects. **Propensity analysis** takes *dosage effects* (*degree* of program completed) into account for estimating the probability of reassault. This analysis led to a more scientifically sound estimate when the decision to complete or drop out was a classified as *batterer self-selection,* rather than of random assignment. "Program completion reduced the probability of reassault during the 15-month follow-up by 33% for the full sample and by nearly 50% for the court-ordered men" (A. S. Jones et al., 2004, p. 1002). These results are in stark contrast to the *no program effects* reported by others whose random assignment paradigm placed some men *without any treatment* into the treatment group (intention to treat) for statistical analyses (Feder & Ford, 2000).

Another group of researchers conducted a longitudinal evaluation of two distinctive male offender groups: (a) *convicted men on probation* and (b) *men diverted into treatment before conviction.* The outcome measures, taken at 6 months, 12 months, and 18 months, consisted of offender arrest records included in a computerized database. Of the 200 men, 17.5% reoffended, with most arrests occurring very early in the process. The progression in the number of men reoffending is as follows: (a) 4 before treatment started; (b) 17 within six months after treatment ended; (c) 8 within 6 to 12 months after treatment; and (d) 6 within the 12- to 18-month posttreatment period (Hendricks, Werner, Shipway, & Turinetti, 2006). See Table 11.3 for factors predicting reassault.

For a review of risk factors for male partner violence, see Gondolf, 2004; Schumacher, Feldbau-Kohn, Slep, & Heyman, 2001.

**TABLE 11.3**   Some Factors Predicting Reassault

| Reassault Factors | Outcomes | Researchers |
|---|---|---|
| Mental disorders | Did *not* predict reassault | Gondolf & White, 2001 |
| Stalking | Major predictor of reassault | M. E. Bell, Bennett-Cattaneo, Goodman, & Dutton, 2008 |
| Previous emotional abuse | Predicts reassault | Bell et al., 2008 |
| Recency of physical assault | Predicts reassault | Bell et al., 2008 |
| Batterer women's predictions | Excellent predictor of reassault | Heckert & Gondolf, 2004; many others |
| Some favorable changes | *No* reduction in reassault | Buttell & Pike, 2003 |
|  | Increased assault rate | Belaga, 2005 |
| Program completion is significant variable | Reduced reassault | Jones & Gondolf, 2004 |
| Minority status | Predicted reassault | Ménard, Anderson, & Godboldt, 2009 |
| Drug user | Predicted reassault | Ménard et al., 2009 |
| Court warrants–noncompliance | Predicted reassault | Kindness et al., 2009 |

*Other posttreatment changes.* Given that batterer intervention programs have not been able to modify recidivism rates successfully, questions have arisen about other possible benefits of counseling. To this end, D. C. Adams and Galibois (2004) proposed a broadening of the criteria of success. Whether or not batterers decrease their physical violence posttreatment, a number seem to make *some* favorable changes. See Table 11.4 for posttreatment changes among batterers.

**TABLE 11.4**  Some Posttreatment Changes Among Batterers

| Posttreatment Change | Researchers |
|---|---|
| Reduction in depression | Hamberger & Hastings, 1989 |
| Used own interruption techniques to avoid partner violence | Gondolf, 2000a |
| Used own problem-solving approach to avoid partner violence | Gondolf, 2000a |
| Stopped drinking, went to church, etc. | Gondolf, 2000a |
| Changes in cognitive processing styles | Porter, 2004 |
| More socially appropriate behavior | Porter, 2004 |
| Less aggressive responses | Porter, 2004 |
| Enhanced coping | Buttell & Pike, 2003 |
| Reduced male-to-female IPV | Buttell & Pike, 2003 |
| Reduced alcohol/drug use | Buttell & Pike, 2003 |
| Improved self-esteem | C. M. Murphy, Stosny, & Morrel (2005) |
| More personal relationship efficacy | Belaga, 2005 |
| Better goal achievement | Belaga, 2005 |
| Less partner control | Belaga, 2005 |

## Policy

The research available suggests several policy changes that might help reduce intimate partner violence. Just as advocates were very active in recommending changes in the legal system and the criminal justice system in the past, academicians have become more active in calling for the application of more scientific approaches to the problem of family violence.

*Need for evidence-based treatments.* Regrettably, the danger of reassaults during and after counseling remains extremely high because partner abuse is such an entrenched behavior. Lives may actually hang in the balance if counseling for male violence is unsuccessful. Practitioners and criminal justice personnel alike need to know why batterer intervention programs have been unsuccessful and find out how to improve them. All the disciplines including clinicians are currently undergoing a paradigm shift—practitioners in the various fields *must* use *empirically based interventions* and evaluate the outcomes empirically (Baker, McFall, & Shoham, 2008; Kazdin, 2008; Procter & Rosen, 2008; Stoltenberg & Pace, 2007). A duo of scholars, for instance, has made several recommendations for improving social work practice: (a) reduce attention to a theory-driven research agenda; (b) adopt ethical standards supporting the right to *effective* treatment; and (c) give up seeking discipline-specific knowledge and focus on interdisciplinary efforts instead (Mullen, Bledsoe, & Bellamy, 2008; see also Cnaan & Dichter, 2008).

*Alcoholism policies and drug courts.* Because alcoholism is a serious medical and social crisis, intervention and prevention have become a national priority. To understand, treat, and prevent alcoholism, the federal governments established the *National Institute on Drug Abuse* (NIDA) in 1974. One innovative approach to substance abuse disorders has been the establishment of *drug courts.* These special courts, established to combat alcohol/drug abuse and associated criminality, coerce participation in treatment programs via the use of various rewards. Treatment completion might earn dismissal of the original charges, a reduction in sentence, or a lesser penalty. Conversely, failure to complete treatment results in various sanctions (U.S. Department of Justice, 2004). These community-based addiction programs have been far more effective for participants who complete the program than for those who terminate prematurely and more effective than for those receiving simple probation (e.g., Galloway & Drapela, 2006; Kalich & Evans, 2006).

Regrettably, many drug court defendants do *not* complete their programs. Much more research is needed to identify the various characteristics of successful drug courts, programs, and defendants (e.g., Bouffard & Richardson, 2007; Giacomazzi & Bell, 2007; U.S. Department of Justice, 2006b). In a **quasi-experimental** research design, investigators did *not* offer rewards for participation and completion of treatment but *threatened jail time.* Participation rates in the *threatened group* did *not* differ significantly from those who were not threatened. The study "found no support for the widely held view that the threat of incarceration is needed to motivate offenders to participate in the drug court program" (Hepburn & Harvey, 2007, p. 271).

In 2007, the American Psychological Association (APA) organized a panel of experts to address Congress in an educational briefing entitled, "*Drug Abuse Treatment: The Blending of Research and Practice.*" Perhaps the most startling revelation was that a *17-year gap* existed between the publication of research findings and their influence on treatment delivery! Bridging this gap is crucial to treatment improvement. A synthesis of findings from clinical trials of alcohol treatment was that client improvement results from *combining pharmacological and behavioral therapies.* Collaboration among such specialists is especially useful in treating alcoholism, drug abuse, and their related problems (Carroll, 1997; see also Bettesworth, 2007).

## Preventing Treatment Attrition (Dropout)

Since completion of a batterer intervention program is almost uniformly associated with less recidivism, researchers turned their attention toward finding solutions to prevent batterer dropout.

*Predicting dropout.* Current studies are sharpening attention on predicting dropout from tests given at treatment intake, but selecting the most powerful tests may be often overlooked (e.g., Hendricks et al., 2006). One undertaking showed that it was possible not only to predict dropout but also to train batterer counselors to use a prediction protocol designed for their particular counseling program (Buttell & Carney, 2008). A second successful attempt to predict treatment outcomes (treatment dismissal/recidivism outcomes) involved the use of the MMPI-2 Restructured Clinical (RC) scales, along with historical variables, such as criminal history (Sellbom, Ben-Porath, Baum, Erez, & Gregory, 2008). A third investigation showed that two factors (low alcoholism risk and negative views about aggressive behavior) predicted persistence in treatment (Duplantis, Romans, & Bear, 2007).

One of the most interesting investigations of factors affecting treatment dropout involved the use of a **classification tree analysis (CTA).** Researchers sought to differentiate *noncompleters* from *completers* within a group of IPV perpetrators (males = 92.0%; females = 8%) ordered into a BIP. Of this group, 31.8% did *not* complete the program. Analyses disclosed that batterers within the failed group were significantly more likely than completers to be arrested for *a new crime* and significantly more likely to be arrested for a new *violent crime.*

Additional classification tree analyses uncovered 12 significant and generalizable predictors of unsatisfactory completion while eliminating other variables. The researchers identified three types of offenders with at least a 60% chance of treatment failure: (a) *unemployed, generally violent offenders;* (b) *high school dropouts ordered into AOD treatment;* and (c) *unemployed offenders ordered into substance abuse treatment.* The CTA classified 79.2% of the treatment failures correctly, while a regression analysis identified only 36.6%, thus demonstrating the superiority of CTA (Stalans & Seng, 2007). Judges, probation officers, and others could apply these findings to monitor more efficiently batterers prone to dropout. In addition, the American Probation and Parole Association has recently issued a booklet on responding to domestic violence (Crowe et al., 2009). (See www.sagepub.com/barnett3e for brief descriptions of a county-wide dropout prevention program and for a judicial monitoring program.)

## Community Intervention Programs

Community agencies focus on the overarching agenda of assisting independent groups to coordinate their efforts. Agencies involved in stopping violence against women are those offering batterer treatments, women's support groups, and groups for children exposed to interparental violence. Often the programs are under the direction of domestic violence councils and are embedded in a broader system including the justice system and other community services (see Douglas, Bathrick, & Perry, 2008). Over the years, family violence experts/advocates expressed confidence that collaborations by community agencies would be able to fashion especially effective interventions for partner violence (e.g., Fleury, Sullivan, Bybee, & Davidson, 1998).

*Police and treatment personnel.* One study examined the effects of a community collaboration between police and treatment personnel by examining the court records of men either charged, convicted, or both charged and convicted of IPV-related offenses. Analyses of data on demographics, criminal history, victim injuries, and recidivism measures indicated that the combined efforts of criminal justice and treatment personnel were effective. The *cumulative effect* of *successful prosecution, probation monitoring,* and *offender counseling did* reduce recidivism (Murphy, Musser, & Maton, 1998; see also Mears, 2003; Syers & Edleson, 1992).

Most reported collaborations have *not* produced promising results. One researcher investigated whether the Duluth Domestic Abuse Intervention Project (DDAIP) in collaboration with the criminal justice system was effective in changing male IPV behavior. The DDAIP offered a 22-week program of *anger management* and *recognition of and change of power and control behaviors.* The criminal justice component included mandatory arrest/prosecution and the use of sentencing guidelines. The recidivism rate was 40% after 5 years (Shepard, 1992). A 2001 multisite investigation found that community coordination efforts did *not* produce hoped for changes (Worden, 2001; also see Sartin, Hansen, & Huss, 2006, for reviews). (See the website for a box, Community Intervention Projects: "It Takes a Village.")

## Prevention

The prevention of battering has received very little attention. Most of the research has centered on interventions. Researchers need to identify new methods for reaching the public, and policymakers need to find funding to disseminate the information. A methodological review of prevention research offers some constructive suggestions (Murray & Graybeal, 2007).

*Public awareness campaigns.* Public awareness campaigns concerning partner abuse nearly always focus on the victims, rarely providing information about what perpetrators can do to stop their violence. Campaigns that might have spillover effects for IPV reduction are those aimed at *diminishing the stigma* attached to seeking treatment for depression. The federal government sponsors public awareness campaigns urging depressed men to seek treatment ("Real Men, Real Depression," 2003). Alcohol abuse awareness campaigns might also reduce partner violence.

*Public educational programs.* Since many members of the public hold ill-informed views about the nature and prevalence of intimate partner violence, educational campaigns are fitting. The community agencies most likely to provide such programs are the courts, social agencies, health care providers, and workplace counselors. Through all of these resources, it may be possible to use adult education as a catalyst for social change (C. E. Miller & Mullins, 2002).

*Male socialization.* Throughout this chapter, research has shown that some principles of male socialization are not only linked with partner violence, but they are also linked with diminished quality of life for men. Although patriarchy seems not to be a negative factor for men, masculine gender role stress certainly is. In line with masculine stress theories, "men feel intense demands to uphold gender role norms (e.g., appear strong) and aggressive behaviors may be reactions to the stress men experience in trying to abide by gender role expectation" (Moore et al., 2008, p. 83). Society needs to develop different expectations of men.

*Clinical screening of male IPV perpetrators.* Because male perpetrators suffer from wide-ranging difficulties and are not a homogeneous group, clinicians need to provide routine screening for customary problems as well as providing referrals for medical, psychiatric, and neurobiological examinations (e.g., Barber et.al, 2008; McCray & King, 2003).

Psychologists and psychiatrists as a group, however, have frequently failed to recognize male battering IPV in the clients they treat. As a case in point, Hansen, Harway, and Cervantes (1991) used two hypothetical cases to study family therapists' ability to recognize IPV and recommend appropriate protection strategies. In one of two "test" stories, Carol told her therapist privately that she had sought an order of protection against her partner, James, because he "grabbed her and threw her on the floor in a violent manner and then struck her" (p. 235). In the other vignette, Beth claimed that Tony "punched her in the back and stomach and caused her to miscarry" (p. 235). Tony asserted that Beth tried to hit him and punched herself in the back. Of the 362 therapists in the study sample, 22% identified the problem as violence and 17% as an abusive relationship. Others classified the problem as conflict (8%), anger (5%), a power struggle (4%), lack of control (1%), or other type of conflict (4%). The remaining 39% selected nonconflict options, such as lack of communication, trust, or secrecy. Only 45% of the therapists advised crisis intervention; 48% called for further assessment, 60% suggested work on a nonviolent marital problem, and 28% recommended couples' counseling. Only 10% addressed the need for protection.

It seems probable that some improvement has taken place since publication of the Hansen et al. (1991) study. In a later inquiry, researchers presented participants with vignettes containing *indicators of partner violence* (e.g., controlling behaviors), rather than vignettes that overtly included the word "violence." Statistical results indicated that 57.8% of the clinicians *recognized* that IPV might be an issue, and 45.9% actually *responded* to the violence in some manner (Dersch, Harris, & Rappleyea, 2006).

*Physician screening.* Some *health experts* believe that screening of male medical patients may be constructive. When physicians do screen for male violence against women, many men are willing to discuss their violence, thus opening a door for appropriate referrals (Hamberger, Phelan, & Zozel, 2001). Although men may appear disposed to accept referrals to treatment agencies, it is unclear whether they follow through. Research needs to examine follow-through.

*Criminal justice system responses.* A general rule for the justice system should be to *focus on the safety of battered women and their children.* Judges, for example, must monitor offenders post-adjudication to evaluate batterer compliance with judicial orders, and they must remove weapons from batterers as required by law. One constructive idea is to establish *specialized IPV prosecution units,* because they generally show higher conviction rates, 70% to 88% (Garner & Maxwell, 2008; J. Miller, 2006). Another idea is to revamp the justice system so that repeat batterers receive longer sentences (Teichroeb, 2009; see also Kindness et al., 2009).

*Reducing revictimization in Wales—community collaboration.* One program aimed at reducing repeat victimization in Cardiff, Wales, has proved to be surprisingly effective but time-consuming. Some of the key elements of the program include (a) leadership by the police, (b) participation by many agencies (e.g., police, probation, women's advocacy, health, social services, and homelessness), and (c) formation of the *Multi-Agency Risk Assessment Conference* (MARAC).

The MARAC meets once a month to share information and estimate the probability that the *victim* will be *safe* (*not* the perpetrator's probability of reoffending). Agencies update their files from information gained from other agencies.

The MARAC group develops a plan to ensure the woman's safety. Probation, for example, might look for a relapse in compliance and work with police to rearrest the man, and the agency for homelessness might place the woman in emergency housing. MARAC's collaboration for a study sample of 146 battered women's cases showed that of the women interviewed after 6 months, 70% reported no further domestic violence police calls and 63% had experienced no additional violence or threats. These results are remarkably better than any reported by programs in the United States (A. L. Robinson, 2006). (See also the COPS special report on police-community partnerships published by the U.S. Department of Justice [Reuland, Morabito, Preston, & Cheney, 2006] to address male-to-female IPV.)

*Increased court involvement.* Almost without exception, men ordered into treatment by the courts are more likely than other men to complete the necessary number of therapeutic sessions. Criminal justice authorities advise that a batterer should not be diverted into a counseling program and out of the justice system *before a plea is entered.* Court-mandated treatment of male offenders is essential to the justice system's objective of reducing recidivism (Dutton, 1988). If nothing else, arrest challenges a batterer's belief that his use of violence is justified (Ganley, 1981). It also places the responsibility for change on the batterer, a stance that is compatible with *deterrence themes* (Fagan, 1988). (See the boxed study on the website about *pretrial bail supervision* for a description of an interesting program to ensure battered women's safety.)

As long as the abuser is under the control of the court, the court can sentence him without having to reset a trial. According to a 1990 report from the Family Violence Project, without this leverage, a recalcitrant batterer may be able to leave treatment with no criminal record at all (cited in Pagelow, 1992). Clearly, the courts *must remain involved* whenever they mandate counseling for male perpetrators. Often, however, there is a lack of follow-through once a male IPV perpetrator has been mandated to treatment. Courts do not routinely apply sanctions to men who fail to attend as directed. Only specialized *domestic violence courts* appear to monitor batterers' compliance with court orders. An examination of victims' and offenders' reactions to one specialized domestic violence court was very positive. Both parties were satisfied (Gover, Brank, & MacDonald, 2007).

*Early identification.* Early diagnosis of antisocial personality disorder, excessive alcohol use, and other pathologies might allow practitioners an opportunity to institute effective preventative treatment via psychotherapy and medications. Prevention should focus on at-risk populations. Such populations include children referred to Child Protective Services, children of sheltered women, families contacted by the police for partner violence, and adolescents with conduct disorder or delinquency (D. J. Boyle et al., 2008). One team of social scientists prescribes targeting *young men,* because they comprise the largest segment of male IPV offenders. It would be wise to craft distinctive programs that address the special problems of this population (Bennett et al., 2007; see also Peacock & Rothman, 2001).

*Prevention through prison programs.* Men incarcerated in low-security federal prisons usually exhibit aggression, substance abuse, and mental health problems. Prison authorities have directed attention to the wisdom of combining batterer treatment with the AOD treatment commonly conducted in such institutions. Further scrutiny is warranted (R. J. White, Gondolf, Robertson, Goodwin, & Caraveo, 2002).

*Because We Have Daughters program.* A different intervention, *Because We Have Daughters,* helps men take advantage of opportunities to strengthen their understanding and connection with their daughters while improving their safety. A goal of this approach is to help men recognize that their daughters will be safer when all women are safer and that fathers can help create such a change.

*Profeminist men's contributions.* Many men are appalled by other men's treatment of women and children, and they wish to contribute to efforts to stop the violence. In the case of male partner violence, as D. C. Adams and McCormick (1982) note, "men have a particular role to play in educating other men about the nature of abuse and how men can change" (p. 171). One organization with this aim is the National Organization for Men Against Sexism (NOMAS). This group has created an umbrella Internet site, Ending Men's Violence Network (EMV.net), to provide resources, training, and support to local organizations that are combating battering. (See the NOMAS website at http://www.nomas.org.) There is a substantial need for researchers to examine methods for educating men about male partner violence.

*Men Stopping Violence program.* The fact that men who have received treatment are at risk of recidivism is only one problem encountered by communities trying to stop male violence. The risk of male IPV also exists for the 98% of batterers who are not receiving any treatment. To reach unidentified batterers in the community, one novel approach is to ask *BIP graduates to enlist other male "volunteers" to come to a batterer intervention program orientation meeting.* Here, the program director explains the Men's Education Program and invites/challenges the volunteers to work with the director to end abusive behavior. The volunteers may wish to join the BIP or serve as allies (mentors) to the men in the program. A BIP graduate then demonstrates his accountability for his partner abuse by describing the worst male assaultive incident that he ever enacted. Other graduates may testify at legislative hearings about bills affecting battered women or perhaps sign up in a speakers' bureau for service in community education.

Next, *community men serving as allies to batterer intervention program* participants attend a class midway through and at the end to witness the group work. Because the culture surrounds men with proviolence attitudes and beliefs that men have the inherent right to control women, an ally or sponsor (e.g., an "uncle") promises to challenge a participant's use of violence and to urge the participant to consider the effects of his violence on others. As the allies attend the meetings, they too reconsider whether some characteristic male behaviors may, in fact, be more controlling than they formerly thought. They may recognize the need to change some of their own beliefs and attitudes toward women. Another intervention includes holding occasional classes in public to inform community members about the purposes and processes of BIPs.

## Practice, Policy, and Prevention
## Issues for *Abusive* Partners

Finding effective methods for stopping male violence has taken central stage within the topic of adult family violence because couples often want to stay together, and society seems unwilling to punish batterers severely. One basic recommendation is for an increased number of professionals to screen people entering their offices, such as those conducting alcohol/drug programs. Therapists need to prepare to offer treatment beyond violence abatement. Some experts believe that a subgroup of extremely violent men suffering from psychopathy may be almost untreatable with current knowledge. Screening instruments need to include questions on an increased number of topics, such as psychopathology, addictions, jealousy, anger, and attachment.

A *controversy* over appropriate treatment for male partner abusers is ongoing. Feminists assume the sociopolitical system with its patriarchal structure is the cause of battering because it allows men to beat women. As a result, *feminists prefer Duluth* psychoeducational treatment, which emphasizes antisexist education coupled with criminal justice sanctions. For treatment of female offenders, the Duluth model seems especially inappropriate.

Although some work on entitlement beliefs and sexism may be useful, *research* favors *cognitive-behavioral therapy (CBT)* and medical treatments. Cognitive-behavioral advocates base their treatment on *evidence* of individual variability, as assessed by tests in personality (e.g., anger) and psychopathology (e.g., depression). Biological explanations embedded in genetics and brain functioning are also accepted as causal agents. CBT employs procedures premised on test findings to modify batterers' behavior. As a result, they focus on anger management; stress-reduction, attachment, and jealousy issues; controlling behaviors; and other specific problems.

Feminist are especially distressed by *couples' counseling* because it places some of the blame on the female victims. Couples counseling is consonant with the goal of family preservation. To make matters worse, therapists offering couples' counseling may not be following guidelines that ensure battered women's safety. A number of group treatment programs are eclectic, incorporating therapeutic approaches from several sources. Both feminist and CBT viewpoints include an appreciation for *alcohol/ drug* (AOD) treatment, although AOD treatment should *not* be substituted for batterer treatment. One study ascertained that a program addressing both AOD and battering can be effective.

A few new programs are showing promise, such as the *Plumas program.* This treatment focuses on solutions rather than deficits. Batterer intervention programs (BIPs), however, have not been very successful in reducing male partner violence. Posttreatment relapse into violence remains high among batterers.

*(Continued)*

(Continued)

Batterer treatment programs have shown *disappointing results* in terms of reducing violence, but they have shown some promise in ameliorating symptoms such as depression. Evaluation of treatment effectiveness is complex because of the nature and number of confounding variables. The ongoing problem of counseling dropouts, in particular, hampers the success of treatment and evaluation. Studies almost universally indicate that program completers have less recidivism than noncompleters. Offenders most likely to drop out of treatment tend to have difficulties with employment and drugs, and may have dropped out of high school. Despite hopes that community collaboration between police and treatment personnel would reduce recidivism, the cumulative effects of prosecution, probation monitoring, and offender counseling were more effective.

Policy recommendations have recently centered on the need for treatments to be evidence-based. Another policy recommendation is to treat alcohol and drug offenders in a special AOD court but to conduct research to determine what elements of the court reduce relapses. One problem is the lag between publication of research and implementation of the findings in treatment.

Experts have advanced many ideas for preventing male violence toward their partners: public awareness campaigns and educational programs, changes in male socialization, better clinical screening of offenders, and better training of treatment personnel. Police procedures need improvement, and ideas such as specialized prosecutor units are being evaluated. Pamphlets for police and probation officers are available on the Internet. Training of judges needs to be mandatory. Some experts suggest early identification of individuals with personality disorders followed by treatment would be beneficial. More and more practitioners are suggesting that treatment for incarcerated men would add safety for battered women. Last, several programs designed for male participants might help change attitudes toward male partner violence. Certainly, battering will continue as long as society delegates the responsibility for finding a solution to the victim.

## TREATMENT FOR FEMALE-TO-MALE INTIMATE PARTNER VIOLENCE PERPETRATORS

When policymakers conceive of IPV as gender neutral, they nearly always require the women arrested for female-to-male intimate partner violence (FMIPV) to enter treatment, the *same treatment* as male perpetrators. On the surface, this policy may seem justified because some treatment issues may be germane for both genders, such as anger management (Jacobson et al., 1994). If men's and women's IPV is *not* equivalent, however, which treatment techniques should counselors adopt? If many male batterer programs function to resocialize males to reject patriarchal beliefs, how do such goals apply to women (Dasgupta, 2002)?

*Gender distinctiveness.* As evidence has accumulated, the gender distinctiveness of partner violence has become increasingly clear. Male and female offenders have *dissimilar motivations,* experience *divergent consequences,* and perpetrate IPV in *diverse contexts* (Tower, 2007). By and large, female aggression does *not* fit the classic pattern of battering perpetrated by men.

Male partner violence is typified by fear-producing coercive control, coercive sex, injury, and severe physical assault. Although women arrested for abuse do not exhibit this male pattern of abuse, neither do they appear to be similar to the female victims encountered in shelters (C. A. Simmons, Lehmann, & Collier-Tenison, 2008).

Currently, experts agree that a gender-neutral approach to a gender-specific problem is inappropriate (Hamberger & Guse, 2002; Kernsmith, 2005b; S. L. Miller, Gregory, & Iovanni, 2005; Swan, Gambone, Caldwell, Sullivan, & Snow, 2008; Tower, 2007; Weston, Marshall, & Coker, 2007). The major concern voiced by professionals is that women's violence is nearly always perpetrated within the *context of male partner violence*. In several analyses, for example, over 90% of women arrested for female partner violence had been victimized by male IPV (Hamberger & Guse, 2002; also see Abel, 2001; G.L. Stuart, Moore et al., 2006).

As a result, female IPV intervention programs *must* address female *victimization* as well as female *perpetration*. Some scholars suggest that treatments for female offenders should acknowledge that these women form a unique group who are *violent resisters*. If mental health professionals fail to fashion new programs for women, judges will have no option but to assign women to whatever (male) programs are available. Some authorities are beginning to specify the types of counseling that might help women avoid further victimization and to avoid the legal consequences of arrests. These women may need "services designed to improve interpersonal coping skills, conflict management, and ability to regulate emotions/behavior" (C. A. Simmons et al., 2008, p. 391; see also S. L. Miller et al., 2005; Osthoff, 2002).

Despite these concerns, one research team reported that female offenders treated with interventions designed for male batterers did have value. In this pilot study, investigators employed a large number of scales to use in a pre- and posttreatment research design. Analyses indicated that after a 16-week program, the offenders were *less likely to use physical force on their partner*. Further, only one woman who completed the program was rearrested in the 12-month follow-up period (Buttell & Carney, 2004).

*Screening for FMIPV perpetrator treatment.* Just as practitioners should screen male IPV perpetrators for substance abuse, trauma exposure, and psychopathology, they should also screen female offenders (e.g., Bennett, 2008; Call & Nelsen, 2007; Kraemer, 2007). In parallel fashion, practitioners can integrate mental health treatments into IPV prevention programs for both genders.

*Female Offender Program (FOP).* One of the few specialized treatment programs for treating female offenders is the Female Offender Program (FOP), a program that draws on principles from *feminist philosophical traditions*. A central facet of the FOP is its emphasis on *contextualizing women's v*iolence and on the responses of the police and the criminal justice system to the women convicted of female-to-male aggression. The program focuses on women's options for action, accountability for their violence, and their previous choices. Although the scope of the study did not include outcome data, the researchers provided a number of interesting remedies for problems encountered in dealing with the criminal justice system (S. L. Miller et al., 2005; S. L. Miller & Meloy, 2006). (See the website for recommendations for treating violent resistors.)

*Other treatment suggestions.* Possibly, the earliest form of treatment for female offenders arose within the confines of alcohol/drug programs. Now, specialists advise therapists to focus treatment on *mediator variables* (e.g., hostility, avoidance coping) that intervene between excessive drinking and female aggression (Schumacher, Homish, Leonard, Quigley, & Kearns-Bodkin, 2008). A few other recommendations for female treatment have appeared as *isolated techniques,* not entire programs. Some suggestions are to prioritize accountability, to ask motivational questions (i.e., motivational interviewing) about self-defense and retaliation, as well as safety planning (Hamberger & Potente, 1994). Others recommend that women *learn nonviolent responses* to male assaultiveness because "there is no excuse for domestic violence" (Kernsmith, 2005a, p. 183). One team of researchers advised that psychotropic medications may be needed (Henning, Jones, & Holdford, 2003). Therapists might further benefit from knowing about two important *predictors* of female reassault: (a) the severity of assault, and (b) the ending of the abusive relationship (Ménard et al., 2009).

## CROSS-CULTURAL PRACTICE, POLICY, AND PREVENTION

Even a short perusal of cross-cultural intimate partner abuse makes it clear why some experts refer to violence against women as pandemic. Similarly, it is clear why such a broad spectrum of experts and especially feminists believe that it is the patriarchy that spawns male partner abuse. In reality, intimate partner violence is multidetermined. Thinking about how best to intervene in cross-cultural intimate partner violence has placed the issue within five broad contexts.

First, one widely accepted conception is that male-to-female IPV is a *human rights* issue. From this stance, the global community works toward condemning the violence against women on *moral grounds.* Various United Nations organizations write *treaties* that are presented to all nations with the hope that heads of state will sign the documents. Human rights workers, such as those in Amnesty International, urge the signatories to honor their commitment to abolish the injustice. Groups publicize information on any advancements or failures as a type of global feedback.

A second avenue is through *legal reforms.* When countries judge women as equal to men under the law, males are much less prone to be violent toward their partner (Broude & Greene, 1983; Heise, Pitanguy, & Germain, 1994; Levinson, 1989). Legal scholars have approached the problem of woman abuse by *writing legislation* that recognizes women's *human rights,* often by transporting statutes from the United States directly into another country. This path has not been as successful as hoped because of cultural clashes. The advance of societies globally, nevertheless, has laid the groundwork for the evolution of a fairly homogenous set of laws against male partner abuse. A number of countries, including the United States, Brazil, India, Japan, Bangladesh, and Ghana, have developed similar sets of human rights laws (Shahidullah & Derby, 2009). In 2008, senators in the United States introduced I-VAWA, an International Violence Against Women Act. I-VAWA extends protections to women beyond simply outlawing male-to-female intimate partner violence. This law bans honor killings, rape as a tool of war, and other gender-based atrocities.

A third method is to cast family violence as a *health problem.* The World Health Organization, for example, often centers its efforts on research and interventions geared toward improving women's health. Abused individuals have significantly more physical and mental illnesses than nonabused individuals. They visit doctors significantly more often, need hospitalization more often, and are disabled more often than nonabused individuals. The problem of HIV infections plays a large role in health approaches to stopping violence against women, because rape of intimate partners spreads this expensive and deadly disease.

A fourth approach is to couch family violence within the sphere of *economic concerns.* To make the case, experts document medical outlays, criminal justice expenditures, and welfare expenses that demonstrate the high cost of responding to the violence. Based on this information, some heads of state see the logic of trying to eradicate family violence on financial grounds. Other reformers hope to reduce woman abuse (child abuse and poverty) by helping countries *decrease poverty.* An especially strong correlate of woman abuse is poverty. There are bank lending programs, agricultural programs, educational programs, and other methods that anti-poverty experts use to accomplish their goals.

The fifth modality is to use *state interventions* by providing victims with more resources and options for safety, such as shelters and health clinics (Erwin, 2006; Stewart & Cherrin, 2008). Another possibility is for countries to offer asylum to victimized women.

## Practice

Some nations permit, if not encourage, so much violence against women that intimate partner violence becomes just one more form of cultural violence. As a consequence, formulating practice guidelines seems premature. It is policy changes that are so desperately needed. Experts have managed to make a few suggestions for coping with male partner abuse in specific countries.

*Africa.* Health care professionals need to be more supportive of battered women and screen their patients for violence (Adeyemi et al., 2008).

*Iran.* One group of practitioners, noting some of gender awareness and changes taking place in Iran, warn therapists not to make assumptions about the degree of egalitarianism between couples. Couples vary on a continuum—from those mired in male-dominant marriage to those somewhere in the middle, to those demonstrating a higher degree of egalitarianism (Moghadam, Knudson-Martin, & Mahoney, 2009).

*Israel.* Practitioners in Israel have conducted some research on treatment issues. One analysis examined 25 *partner-violent men's* experiences in a cognitive-behavioral therapy treatment that encompassed 25 sessions. Most of the participants, however, went through a *second cycle* of treatment voluntarily. The men almost uniformly found the experience positive, and they had magnanimous evaluations of the social-worker therapist. They credited the therapy with helping them gain self-control and stop their battering. Although the men changed their attitudes about the acceptability of violence, they continued to perceive personal relationships as power-based. They were unaware of some aspects of this approach to relationships, and the researchers suggested that some type of *self-awareness experience,* such as insight therapy, would be useful (Shamai & Buchbinder, 2009).

*Middle Eastern intimate partner violence.* One survey indicated that although poverty was highly associated with male-to-female violence against women, the strongest predictor of male partner violence is a positive attitude toward male dominance (Faramarzi, Esmailzadeh, & Mosavi, 2005). This association seems to hold in all of the Muslim countries. It is clear, therefore, that social support of male dominance must change if women are to be free of violence. Clerics can help by de-emphasizing any passages in religious texts and partnering with community efforts to stop MFIPV (see Solarsh & Frankel, 2005).

## Policy

Most obviously in need of change are patriarchal, gender-biased beliefs and attitudes that support violence against women. Although men's biased attitudes are usually more entrenched than women's, this is not uniformly the case. Sometimes, *women* hold antiwoman (patriarchal) beliefs as strongly as or more strongly than men. Although the Koran does not recommend stoning adulterous individuals or perpetrating honor killings, the practice is common. Saudi Arabia has begun to modernize by taking actions such as opening the first co-ed university (Dowd, 2010).

"Multi-strategy interventions that promote equity between women and men, provide economic opportunities for women, inform them of their rights, reach out to men and change societal beliefs and attitudes that permit exploitive behavior are urgently required" (Fawole, 2008, p. 167). Clerics need to rethink and reformulate their teachings. The following ideas emanate from a Western point of view, without taking cultural relativism into account, and therefore they need to be changed.

CROSS-CULTURAL CORRELATES OF MALE-TO-FEMALE IPV include the following:

| | |
|---|---|
| Attitudes | Low socioeconomic status |
| Poverty | Lack of family support |
| Religious beliefs | Failure to criminalize male IPV |
| Cultural beliefs | Lack of community support |
| Lack of education | Inadequate access to medical care |

SPECIFIC BELIEFS AND ATTITUDES CONDUCIVE TO WIFE ABUSE THAT NEED CHANGING

- Women have no rights, no human rights (e.g., women may not refuse sex).
- Controlling women is men's God-given right.
- Men's education is more important than women's.
- Women should not participate in government.
- Women must not leave their homes or must be accompanied by prescribed male relatives.
- Women must wear the clothing (e.g., burkas) that men require them to wear.
- Women have limited or no rights to divorce, and men automatically receive custody of the children.
- Women should be obedient and subservient to men. Men should make all important household decisions.
- To be considered a "good" wife, a woman must be totally self-sacrificing.
- A young bride must obey in-laws as well as her husband.
- Men have the right to chastise (i.e., beat, hurt, disable, sexually mutilate, or even kill) women as they see fit.
- Beating pregnant women is acceptable as well as forbidding them to go to clinics or to have help during a delivery.

- It is still suitable to chastise women for infractions such as burning the dinner.
- Young girls, 8 to 14 years of age, can be forced into marriage.
- A girl's virginity before marriage must be preserved at all costs.

## PRACTICE, POLICY, AND PREVENTION AMONG IMMIGRANT/ETHNIC/RACIAL GROUPS

The practice, policy, and prevention issues for immigrant, ethnic, and racial groups reveal a core of similarities and some differences. The field is relatively new, and it has only recently begun to generate research in these areas.

### Practice

The most common call for change in the area of minority counseling is for *cultural competence* of service providers. Not only should practitioners demonstrate cultural competence, but so too should policymakers and those devising prevention programs. To some extent there has been little disagreement with this edict, but operationalizing the concept of cultural competence into specific guidelines is still evolving (American Psychological Association, 2006). There are interconnected and overlapping factors inherent in culturally based psychotherapy (Burman, Smailes, & Chantler, 2004; La Roche & Christopher, 2008). The barriers to mental health care for ethnic diverse populations are multifactored (M. Rodriguez, Valentine, Son, & Muhammad, 2009).

*Immigrant batterers' intervention program.* A fresh study of *batterer program completion* in Massachusetts compared 480 nonimmigrants and immigrants (73% not U.S. citizens). The investigators also contrasted immigrants participating in non-English culturally specific groups with those in mainstream prevention programs. Chi-square and logistic regression analyses differentiated the completion rates for the groups.

First, significantly more immigrant batterers completed the programs than nonimmigrant batterers (54% vs. 38%). Second, immigrants enrolled in the *non-English groups completed more sessions* than immigrants in the mainstream groups (66% vs. 46%), but the differences did not reach significance. Some of the identified client demographic dimensions, such as older age and higher income, were significantly related to program completion, just as they are among nonethnic batterers. Although the reason for the superior attendance record of the immigrants was not empirically tested, the researchers conjectured that fear of repercussion from the criminal justice system was higher in the immigrant group than in the nonimmigrant group (Rothman, Gupta, Pavlos, Dang, & Coutinho, 2007).

A comparison of Asian Chinese immigrant batterers with nonviolent men disclosed that the groups differed significantly in regard to several factors: (a) *hostile attributional bias*, (b) *early abuse*, and (c) *social desirability* reporting (faking answers to look good) of their hostile attributional bias (i.e., believing behaviors of female partner were hostile). The batterer group consisted of 64 men court-ordered to treatment and 62 nonbattering participants. As has been found across the spectrum of studies on domestic violence, the batterer group was younger, less well educated, and had lower incomes than the nonbatterer group. The batterer group also had lived in the United States for a shorter period of time than the nonbatterer group.

The results provided helpful information for therapists. One result showed that the batterers' (but not the nonbatterers') childhood exposure to violence was linked with their hostile attributions about their wife's behavior. Researchers posited that the batterers wanted to hide their hostile attributions and anger toward their wife because of their assumptions that these feelings were not admirable (Jin, Eagle, & Keat, 2008).

*Latina.* A different study found that culturally competent treatment provided to Latina women *court-ordered into a male-oriented batterer intervention program* reduced depression symptomatology (Tower, Schiller, & Fernandez, 2008). An earlier study suggested that *group treatment* would provide mutual aid for Latinas, especially for Latina immigrant women.

*Interventions for Haitian women.* As mentioned in a previous chapter, 50% of Haitians are undocumented immigrants. Haitians do not understand the role of the police or the functioning of social services. A first remedy is to have medical, legal, and housing services manned by people who can speak the language. Haitian women are leery about shelters, and because shelters have no Haitian food, the women will go hungry rather than eat a fast-food hamburger. Some specific recommendations are as follows: (a) Have community workshops that explain the role of police, social services, and laws against intimate partner violence; (b) have workshops on changing community values regarding violence; (c) send trained workers to visit women in their homes to educate women; (d) offer community-based English-language programs; (e) help women wanting to leave abusive relationships not to feel ashamed; (f) discuss immigration status because it affects everything the woman is doing; and (e) have a program for religious leaders to encourage them to condemn violence against women (Latta & Goodman, 2005).

*Treatment for African American women.* Mainstream treatment for partner abuse may not be meeting the needs of African American women. In the past, findings about White women have been imposed upon Black women without any investigation of their applicability. Secondarily, some members of the African American community perceive the criminal justice system to be racially biased. As a result, women may not want to add to the high number of Black males in jails by disclosing their abuse, and/or they may be ostracized by their community if they do disclose (Hampton, LaTaillade, Dacey, & Marghi, 2008).

In a qualitative study of 14 African American IPV victims, research uncovered some of the major differences between mainstream services and culturally specific services. The culturally specific agency was able to provide a setting that was welcoming to African Americans and presented an atmosphere that indicated staff really cared about the victim's *healing*—not one of just doing a job. Staff were sensitive to the push/pull of loving a violent partner. Staff did not urge the woman to leave, and they did not "wash their hands of the victim" if she was not ready to leave. There were structures in place that increased staff's ability to assist in the following ways: (a) transportation to and from the group, (b) accompaniment to court, and a "big, burly man" to accompany a woman to her home to collect her belongings after she left. Staff were able to adopt a holistic approach that included assistance with finding a place to live and getting a job (Gillum, 2009). Other immigrant group service agencies should adopt these practices also.

Culturally appropriate support groups may be especially helpful for African American women. Battered women have an opportunity to listen, support, and reassure each other, and they sometimes can supply information about unique resources. Mutual aid may be just as important for battered African American as it is for Latinas (Gillum, 2009; Taylor, 2000).

*Native American Indians.* Very high rates of *alcoholism, unemployment, and HIV* infections plague Indian tribes. Consequently, alcohol/drug programs, jobs programs, and medical care and education for HIV programs are needed. Behaviors such as *respecting privacy* and *autonomy* are important. *Making informal connections* rather than holding formal groups sessions is basic to successful helping. Service providers need to know the laws and understand how the "jurisdictional maze" hampers law enforcement (Farberman, 2007; National Sexual Violence Resource Center, 2000).

## Policy

*Shelters.* Shelters should expand their outreach to meet the needs of marginalized groups such as immigrant, ethnic, or racial minority women. Shelters impose a number of exclusions on entry, such as prohibiting women with teenage boys from admission. They also may exclude women who have disabled children. To meet requirements of cultural competency, they try to keep basic food staples that are common to different cultures: (a) tortillas and beans for Latinas, (b) chicken teriyaki and rice for Asians, (c) maize and squash for Native American Indians, (d) grits and collard greens for African Americans, and (e) pita bread and falafel for Middle Eastern residents.

*Justice for African American women.* According to one group of experts, a better, more effective type of justice for African American batterers might be *restorative justice. Restorative justice* views male violence toward women (and other crimes) as a problem affecting both the partners *and* the community. Everyone must work together to repair the damage done and heal all the involved parties. One advantage of this approach is that it allows Black women to voice their opinions about how the abuser should be held accountable. There are others who condemn restorative justice on the grounds that it forces victims to interact with their abusers (Zorza, 2001). A related suggestion is that discretion be used when making an arrest. Perhaps minor acts of violence could be treated differentially by asking the victim what police response she would prefer (Hampton et al., 2008). Within the medical field, health providers should screen African American women for depression because it is highly associated with female IPV victimization (Houry, Kaslow, & Thompson, 2005).

*Native American Indians.* An influx of funding from the Violence Against Women Act has greatly assisted tribes to strengthen their response to intimate partner violence, particularly the "maze of law enforcement authority." One step forward has been the availability of protective orders in 93% of tribal court jurisdictions. Additional accomplishments included (a) coordination of law enforcement services through development of protocols (i.e., what to do when), (b) enhancement of law enforcement response as a result of officer training, (c) innovative approaches to tribal prosecution, (d) putting shelters on the reservation to make them more accessible and identifying safe houses where tribal women can stay for a short period, and (e) full faith and credit provisions (i.e., judgments made in one jurisdiction must be considered valid in other jurisdictions) (Luna-Firebaugh, 2006).

*Southern Asians.* A survey of organizations serving female victims of intimate partner violence uncovered what types of assistance were needed by South Asian women. Organizations, often informally structured and privately funded, offer a wide range of services: educational workshops, community outreach, and Internet information. More specifically, they present literacy classes, women's social groups, and training for police departments. Of explicit interest is their recognition of different religions and different *castes.* Those taking part in the organization believe in the necessity of making culturally matched service providers available.

> These agencies are influenced by the cultural values, traditions, and norms of the people they serve. Cultural behaviors that may be viewed with cynicism, disbeliefs, or disdain by mainstream agencies are embraced with understanding and acceptance. (Merchant, 2000)

*Latinas.* These findings suggest the need for more public education that informs members of society about the violence process and actions that they might take to help victims (S. L. Williams & Mickelson, 2004). Although one investigator suggested that family service providers might try to increase family support for abused victims (Ingram, 2007), a different study found that receiving higher levels of social support did *not* reduce male IPV. In addition, social support did *not* mediate the association between male violence and employment stability (Staggs et al., 2007). (See Kugel et al., 2009, for information about preventing male violence against Hispanic migrant workers).

## Prevention

The change most needed is clear: *Challenging cultural norms that encourage violence against women.* Promoting women's empowerment may be the second most important change, yet advocates trying to change attitudes should expect a backlash. Change will require "political commitment, sustained funding, and engagement with the public at large" (Garcia-Moreno, 2000, p. 333). There are several approaches to prevention (Ellsberg, 2006; Shefer et al., 2008):

Finding ways for women to become economically independent

Screening for partner violence wherever appropriate, followed by referrals

Training first responders such as medical personnel and law enforcement officers

Motivating ethnic clergy to preach against male-to-female partner violence

Encouraging women to disclose abuse wherever appropriate

Adapting public awareness campaigns to meet the needs of ethnic groups

Legislating changes and implementing existing laws (e.g., equal pay)

Going beyond simple translations of information from English into another language

Making a public awareness messages meaningful to the targeted community

Using "Edutainment" methods in getting messages to the public

## PRACTICE, POLICY, AND PREVENTION AMONG RURAL BATTERED WOMEN

Rural battered women face many challenges in achieving safety, and minorities, lesbians, and disabled women living in these communities face even more.

### Practice

One of the most important undertakings for service providers is to understand the culture of rural America: (a) the role of the church, (b) the patriarchal nature of rural society, (c) the lack of medical care, (d) the lack of transportation and shelters, and (e) the inadequacy of law enforcement. Service providers themselves may lack professional development opportunities (American Prosecutors Research Institute, 2006; Eastman, Bunch, Williams, & Carawan, 2007).

*Individual level.* If a rural woman wants to leave her abusive male partner, she may have to change her entire life and face almost total isolation from her family. Because of the lack of shelters and low employment opportunities, she may have to leave the entire area. Rural women need help in dealing with their extremely stressful emotional burdens. They need to understand that *emotion-focused coping* strategies may not help and how they might be able to learn and use better problem-focused coping alternatives.

### Policy

Highlighting the injustices suffered by rural women is the first step toward remedying them. At a community level, the most obvious issue is to provide access to shelters, telephones, and transportation. A few states have passed laws criminalizing the dismantling of telephones to prevent someone from calling for assistance. Medical personnel and law enforcement need training on how better to understand and assist women with problems related to battering. Shelter workers need to be especially mindful that any negative interactions with battered women may appear to be just one more barrier in their quest for safety. *Confidentiality* in a rural setting is far more difficult to ensure than in an urban setting (Shannon, Logan, Cole, & Medley, 2006).

*Medical screening.* A medical team of researchers concluded that given the wide geographic area that slowed a law enforcement response and the severity of the abuse, especially of older women, medical professionals urgently need to conduct *IPV screening*. To facilitate screening, the doctors might utilize the *risk factors* identified by the research team: *older than 25, financial problems, no education past high school, abused as a child, non-owner of a home,* and *low self-esteem.* Assisting abused women with referrals for counseling and other types of assistance as soon as possible might help prevent continued abuse (Shuman et al., 2008).

*Prosecution.* One encouraging endeavor has been a survey of rural prosecutors' offices, their staff size, their services, and the time they spent with victims conducted by the American Prosecutors Research Institute (2006). Despite laws mandating certain rights for victims and witnesses, prosecutors are too short-staffed to provide them. These rights are as follows: (a) legal counsel, (b) protection from intimidation and harm, (c) information concerning the criminal justice process, (d) preservation of property and employment, (e) reparations or restitution, (f) due process in criminal court proceedings, and (g) treatment characterized by dignity and compassion. The average percentage of time staff spent on fulfilling each of these rights varied from 22% to 30%.

*Funding inequities.* The major explanation for the deficiencies in prosecutors' offices is the shortfall in state funding and the disparity in funding priorities. As one illustration, 26 urban counties received $7.3 million from the Victims of Crime Act (VOCA) and $5 million from the Violence Against Women Act (VAWA). Conversely, 76 rural counties received less than $1 million from VOCA and less than 10% of VAWA funds (Sifferd, 1996).

*Collaborations.* There are compelling reasons for advocates and service providers to form collaborations in rural areas. Professionals may have considerable knowledge about services in their own profession (e.g., legal services) but much less about other services (e.g., social services). Collaborations can help close the gap in knowledge. The dearth of basic services makes it essential for various agencies to work together, to provide more coverage to large geographic areas. One challenge advocates may wish to consider is approaching faith communities as a resource for a meeting place. Advocates might also work to form cooperative relationships with local sources of transportation. They might make arrangements with taxi services and available law enforcement to provide transportation, and to provide gasoline cards for local gas stations. Because of the lack of shelters, advocates might be able to arrange temporary discount rates at local hotels.

*Collaboration: Law enforcement/shelter counselors.* One collaborative endeavor, the *Community Partnership Team,* tried to promote cooperation between agencies. To accomplish this goal, they identified group differences that presumably caused disagreements. See Table 11.5 for a summary of their findings (Sudderth, 2006).

The *Community Partnership Team* had some successes. One of the police departments established a link on their website to the advocates' office. Advocates realized it was better to try to change police protocols than try to change police ideology (i.e., patriarchy, military hierarchy). Advocates found that agreed-upon changes in police protocols needed to be *put into writing.* The researchers concluded that the most effective way to work with the police was to obtain a *commitment from the highest levels* of the department. It is "who you know" that makes the difference. Finding ways to *build trust* between groups with such disparate agendas presents yet another problem in collaborations (Sudderth, 2006).

**TABLE 11.5** Differences Between IPV Victims' Advocates and Law Enforcement

| Clashes | IPV Victims' Advocates | Law Enforcement |
|---|---|---|
| Clash of values | Advocates valued the *process* (talking/building a relationship to get acquainted); wanted to raise awareness, establish trust | Familiar with and valued a hierarchical command; getting acquainted took time from real issues; judged the advocates to be abrasive and disrespectful |
| Clash of protocols | Advocates strive for empowering battered women—support the victim's decision; take a flexible approach; most concerned with victim's safety | Actions dictated by law; updates every year; dislike extra paper work; empowerment model is frustrating |
| Victim empathy differences | Leaving is a complex process; let the victim decides when or if to leave. Police don't understand process of victimization; advocate went on a ride-along | Adult women can leave—they should do so; police want advocates to *make* women leave |
| Training disparities (police have little time for meetings) | Get extensive training in IPV. Focus on victim's safety. Want to raise policemen's awareness; explain victim's fear of leaving to police; explain the process of victimization | Receive very little training about IPV; willing to talk about needed changes in law; must establish truth and look for probable cause to arrest |
| Personnel turnover | New director; lacked authority to control follow-through; thought police had too much power; advocates needed police, not the reverse | New commander lacked interest in the alliance: Police stopped cooperating |

## Prevention

One recently described dilemma is the accessibility of pornography to teenage boys. As adults, pornography consumption, alcohol consumption, male peer support, and adherence to familial patriarchy are all associated with sexual assault of rural women (DeKeseredy & Joseph, 2006). These issues make a strong case for creating public awareness campaigns. In rural areas, the campaign might include not only information about partner abuse but also about pornography.

To address the severe staff shortage in prosecutors' offices, it is possible to establish a network of interns to provide more victim services. Some unique programs have developed to prevent male partner abuse in rural America. One is a CyberCrisis anonymous hotline available 24 hours a day. A person can anonymously ask a question about partner abuse over the Internet. A coordinator reviews the question, obtains an answer from a counselor, and sends the message back. Along the same lines, it is possible to provide programs using existing distance education technology (Bischoff, Hollist, Smith, & Flack, 2004). A different program trained hair stylists to detect signs of abuse and furnish referrals (American Prosecutors Research Institute, 2006). A middle-aged daughter of a formerly beaten mother founded a third program called Have Justice

Will Travel. Ford Motor Company provided the ex-trucker with a car, laptop, portable printer, and a cell phone so that she could drive through rural enclaves dispensing free legal advice to battered women (Schindehette & Duffy, 2002).

## PRACTICE, POLICY, AND PREVENTION FOR SAME-SEX INTIMATE PARTNER VIOLENCE

A number of experts question whether the Duluth model is culturally sensitive (Crichton-Hill, 2001; see also Schrock & Padavic, 2007).

### Practice

Therapists need to develop special expertise to offer services to members of some particular subpopulations. They need to be nonjudgmental, trusting, willing to provide unconditional regard, genuine, and nonblaming. They need to attend to the victim's safety and be familiar with gay-friendly resources and, finally, try to increase victim empowerment (Peterman & Dixon, 2003). Therapists should note the similarity of lesbian, gay, bisexual, and transgender (LGBT) traits with those of heterosexual perpetrators and victims. Lydia Sousa, a psychologist working with transgendered clients (cited in D. Schwartz, 2007), urges psychologists to avoid considering transgendered clients as either *moving* from male-to-female *or* female-to-male. There are many transgendered identities, she says.

When women seek help for female-to-female intimate partner violence (FFIPV), it concurrently exposes their sexual orientation, thereby risking isolation and rejection (Levy, 1997). Consequently, lesbians often do not have access to two of the most common sources of help and support: *family* and *peers* (see Boxer, Cook, & Herdt, 1991; D'Augelli, 1992; Rotheram-Borus, Rosario, & Koopman, 1991). Lesbians often find that other resources, such as access to experienced therapists, are sparse as well (Leeder, 1988; Los Angeles Department of Probation, 1998). The same is true of locating same-sex friendly service agencies (Todahl, Linville, Bustin, Wheeler, & Gau, 2009). Erroneous perceptions of same-sex abuse plague crisis center staffs as well (M. J. Brown & Groscup, 2008).

Standards in 59% of U.S. states prescribe *separate treatment* for FMIPV perpetrators, and standards in 38% of states advise that lesbians and gays should receive treatment in *separate groups*. Although standards in 57% of states call for culturally sensitive interventions, no guidelines specify what these techniques are (Austin & Dankwort, 1999). (Therapists can obtain help for working with GLBT clients from the National Coalition of Antiviolence Programs.)

### Policy

Lesbians may encounter difficulties obtaining help from the ordinary sources of help afforded MFIPV victims. Although shelters are becoming increasingly aware of the need to improve their services through outreach to marginalized groups, most have not yet done so. In the meantime, most shelters will not accept lesbian clients to enter. If a lesbian is in a shelter, she is less safe because her violent partners can sometimes find out her location and gain entry because of being the same sex (e.g., Moe, 2007). Altogether, FFIPV victims in one survey rated *shelters as the least helpful* source of support (Renzetti, 1992). Professional counselors and health care workers need specialized training to be of assistance to homosexuals, to have cultural competence. Communities need to become more aware of the needs of homosexuals and provide social services agencies that are same-sex friendly (Todahl et al., 2009).

## Prevention

Educating the lesbian community about serial abusers in first relationships might prevent the relationships from starting (Ristock, 2003). It seems as if preventing same-sex intimate partner violence (SSIPV) would entail a massive change in attitudes among heterosexual Americans in every walk of life. Some organization, perhaps a psychological organization, needs to take the lead in debunking myths accepted by the public (Potoczniak, Mourot, Crosbie-Burnett, & Potoczniak, 2003). Changing **homophobia** and **homonegativity** may be similar to changing racial discrimination (see Faulkner, 2001). If so, initial changes would need to begin with legal protections.

*Legal protections.* Legal protections would help prevent SSIPV more than most other changes and provide same-sex couples various protections and marital benefits. It is difficult for legislators to change laws, however, given the prevailing antihomosexual attitudes toward same-sex couples and their sexual relationships. Currently, there are two types of partially legalized same-sex relationships: (a) *informal*—contracts, will, powers of attorney, and so on, and (b) *institutional*—domestic partnerships, civil unions, and state marriage (Oswald & Kuvalanka, 2008).

*State marriage laws.* Because laws governing *marriage* are ordinarily under the purview of state governments, each state may fashion its laws regulating relationships between same-sex pairs. Overriding these customary state laws is the federal *Defense of Marriage Act* (Defense of Marriage Act, 1996), which allows state statutes to reject same-sex marriage laws enacted in another state. In some states, the legal definitions of individuals covered under domestic violence laws explicitly require that complainants be of the opposite sex. Often laws define partners as individuals who have a child together. Since most states disallow same-sex marriages, it follows that laws protecting heterosexual partners from SSIPV do not apply to same-sex unions.

*Neutrally worded statutes.* Although the Violence Against Women Act uses neutral language and therefore could apply to homosexuals, courts have not seen fit to *interpret* the law as applicable to homosexuals.

*Protective orders.* A particularly dangerous legal shortcoming is the inability of same-sex partners to obtain domestic violence protective orders (POs) because of laws that do not recognize same-sex pairs as domestic partners. In addition, some state laws require both partners to be present when a judge issues a ruling on a PO. Same-sex victims cannot obtain civil POs either, but they are eligible for types of POs preventing harassment and physical and sexual assault. Since these legal failures often force a financially dependent victim to remain with the abuser, they should be removed and appropriate laws expanded to embrace SSIPV (Aulivola, 2004).

*Police.* SSIPV victims have many problems with customary police responses to SSIPV, because police arriving at the scene of an incident may not be able to differentiate the victim from the perpetrator. To the police, the incident may appear to be mutual combat. A comparison based on NIBRS data containing 176,488 cases of persons arrested for IPV assaults and intimidations shed light on arrest decisions (Pattavina, Hirschel, Buzawa, Faggiani, & Bentley, 2007). Of those arrested, most were *heterosexuals* ($n = 175,411$); a minority were *homosexuals* ($n = 1,077$). One predominant variable in the analyses was the type of state statute that governed police in making these arrests: (a) *mandatory arrest,* (b) *preferred arrest,* or (c) *discretionary arrest.* Within the mandatory arrest group of eight states, six had statues with so-called *inclusive statutory language* (i.e., same-sex couples *are* specifically included). Some of the findings are as follows:

Differences in police arrest rates comparing heterosexual and homosexual couples were minor. When data within genders is combined and other variables are controlled, police treat same-sex couples about the same as heterosexual couples.

Data for *heterosexual victims only* revealed that *mandatory-arrest* requirements and *seriousness of the assault* variables were significant predictors of arrest for all victims combined and for each gender separately. For *same-sex couples,* several significant differences occurred along variables of *statutory context, gender,* and *seriousness* of assault as follows:

- Police made more arrests when arrest statutes were *mandatory, if* the couple were *female,* but *not* if the couple were *male.*
- Police made more arrests if the crime were *serious* if the couple were *male,* rather than female.
- For same-sex couples in *mandatory-arrest states,* two other significant differences emerged: (a) If the statute had inclu*sive language, police arrested mor*e victims in general and more male couples but not female couples, and (b) the seriousness of the *crime was a better predictor of arrest* for females than males.

These results may indicate police attitudes about the need to protect female victims more than male victims; if so, the attitudes of police may be consonant with those of the undergraduates detailed previously (Seelau, Seelau, & Poorman, 2003). Some researchers suggest that police training in every state needs overhauling to offer protection to same-sex victims (Aulivola, 2004). Just as police departments in large cities are increasingly establishing specially trained units to respond to heterosexual IPV, they need parallel units to respond to SSIPV. Above and beyond the police, other CJS personnel (e.g., judges) need training. On the other hand, a California survey found no significant homophobia among police officers; rather, officers seemed to comply with the mandates given to them (Younglove, Keer, & Vitello, 2002).

## PRACTICE, POLICY, AND PREVENTION IN THE MILITARY

### Practice

Past research has uncovered several specific treatment needs for military personnel, especially combat personnel. The need for treatment of PTSD is obvious given the high rates of exposure to traumatic events, especially among combat veterans. Another high-risk group in need of treatment encompasses the women with child sexual assault and/or military sexual assault histories, and the few exposed to combat traumas. The need for alcohol or drug treatment is ongoing. Some comparisons of treatment effectiveness utilize pre- and posttreatment designs. Many others contrast military findings with those of civilians. Some contrast the treatment group with a control group.

The *Family Advocacy Program* provides the primary response to IPV. Some services available to victims are financial counseling, relocation counseling, and deployment assistance. The Social Work Services section is primarily responsible for assistance to victims and offenders. An interesting aspect of the legal response to IPV is that commanders are ultimately responsible for soldiers in their unit. Commanders can punish offenders in several ways, ranging from revoking the soldier's off-base passes to demoting the soldier and even having him discharged from the military. (See Judith Beals for information about a military manual on responses to male partner violence at the Battered Women's Justice Project at http://www.bwjp.org).

A comparison of more than 34,000 military IPV offenders and 13,000 civilian offenders who had received treatment for IPV revealed significantly lower posttreatment recidivism rates among the military offenders (McCarroll, Thayer et al., 2000). Another researcher compared the effectiveness of four types of 12-month treatments offered to 861 married U.S. Navy male personnel with substantiated partner violence. Treatments were as follows: (a) *a men's group,* (b) *a conjoint group,* (c) *a rigorously monitored group,* and (d) *a control group* (no treatment). Outcome measures consisted of male self-reports, victims' reports (e.g., felt endangered), official police and court records, and date of first re-assault. Of the men treated, 83% did not re-injure their wives, but *no significant differences* between treatment groups or the control group appeared (Dunford, 2000).

## Policy

It is clear that service members suffering from PTSD are more likely to become violent with their spouses and that service women subjected to sexual assault are more likely to develop PTSD. The U.S. Department of Defense has funded new mental health specialists and those investigating traumatic brain injury. In addition to the progress the military has already made, a team of researchers has made further recommendations (Munsey, 2007b; Rentz et al., 2006; Zinzow, Grubaugh, Monnier, Suffoletta-Maierle, & Frueh, 2007).

- Researchers should examine partner abuse and child abuse simultaneously.
- Researchers need to create similar definitions, create central databases, and use consistent methodologies.
- Researchers should study differences in reporting methods and reach a consensus.
- Practitioners need to serve abuse victims both in the military and civilian families that are related to the military.
- Practitioners should undertake education about the deleterious effects of alcohol use by either offender or victim.
- Practitioners need to improve early identification through screening methods.

## Prevention

A team of researchers at one military installation crafted an innovative, low- or no-cost intervention/prevention program designed to assist victims of partner violence (McCarroll, Newby, & Dooley-Bernard, 2008). In the program, volunteer victim advocates receive training about how to respond to victims of physical or severe verbal IPV on scene. When military police respond to an IPV call and determine that it is safe to call the advocate, the advocate arrives and begins to assist the victim. Some of the services include safety planning and a determination of the victim's immediate danger. The advocate discusses possible actions the victim might take with the offender's commander or other authorities. The advocate discusses the victim's immediate needs and provides a resource packet of available services. During this undertaking, advocates collected data about variables such as the number of previous IPV incidents and whether a weapon was used.

One unforeseen finding was the impact of verbal abuse. Victims of *verbal abuse* had previously *sought help significantly more often* than had physical abuse victims. The four most frequently endorsed risk markers were (a) spouse had become more violent, (b) spouse preoccupied with or stalking victim, (c) increased frequency of assaults against victim, and (d) during past year victim tried to separate from abuser. The lack of significance between the two types of IPV attests to the importance of verbal IPV. Gender differences were evident in the number of incidents reported. Females made 1,236 (74%) incident reports, and males made 443 (26%). Male clients were more likely to be involved in physical IPV and females more likely in verbal IPV. Active-duty personnel were more likely than civilian family members to be involved in physical abuse. Triggers (i.e., presumed motives) for IPV in descending order of frequency were *marital discord, jealousy, infidelity, power/control issues, and substance abuse.* See the website for more details about the program (McCarroll, Newby et al., 2008).

## DISCUSSION QUESTIONS

1. Discuss the meaning and importance of practice, policy, and prevention issues.
2. Evaluate agency services versus individual counseling services. What problems do agencies appear to have?
3. Discuss cultural competence and why is it needed in practice, policy, and prevention.
4. Discuss the controversy over treatment of male abusers. What is your opinion?
5. What is avoidance coping, and why it is important?
6. Thoroughly discuss attachment and its role in battering relationships.
7. What violence-related issues should therapists plan to address with battered women *or* battering men and why?
8. Discuss the issues involved in *evaluating* treatment programs for male batterers. What do evaluations generally show? What is the major challenge in evaluation?
9. Why or why not should medical personnel in emergency rooms be required to screen women for male-to-female IPV? What are the challenges?
10. What steps should be taken to provide treatment for female-to-male violence offenders?

 For chapter-specific resources including audio and video links, SAGE research articles, additional case studies, and more, please visit www.sagepub.com/barnett3e.

# 12

# Abuse of Elderly and Disabled Persons

**CASE HISTORY**  Jenny and Jeff Jr.—Dwindling Assets, Dwindling Devotion

Several years after my husband's death, my mother-in-law, Jenny, who was 91, became unable to care for herself. She went to live with my brother-in-law, Jeff Jr., and his wife, Marianne. Although my own aging mother was dying, I took time to visit Jenny, who had always been a loving mother-in-law.

Over the next year, Jeff Jr. became Jenny's guardian, and she made out a new will giving one-third of her estate to each of us—myself, Jeff Jr., and Marianne. I didn't understand this sudden change from the previous division of half for each son, but I said nothing; after all, I was a widowed daughter-in-law. As Jenny continued to deteriorate, I asked Jeff Jr. if he was planning to put Jenny in a retirement home where she would receive around-the-clock care. He said he couldn't afford to place her in a home and that he and Marianne would care for her at home. I was amazed. Jeff Jr. had sold Jenny's home for a probable yield of $150,000 in cash. Jeff Jr. and Marianne owned a mini-estate as well as stocks and bonds; they were probably worth $2 million.

I was puzzled by what was going on with Jenny and Jeff Jr., but then I became seriously concerned when I heard a number of rumors from Jenny's other relatives and friends. They said that Jeff Jr. and Marianne had offered financial advice to several aging relatives. Each had changed his or her will to name Jeff Jr. and Marianne the beneficiaries, and each had died shortly thereafter of neglect and malnutrition.

Over the next few months, I became alarmed when Jenny "refused to come to the phone" to speak to me. Marianne told me that "Jenny couldn't walk far enough to get to the phone." After 2 weeks, I drove several hours to visit her. I was appalled when I arrived. There was Jenny, sitting alone in a hot room that smelled like urine. She would not speak to me. She was in the maid's quarters, with no television and no phone. She was dirty and unkempt. There were no diapers in the room, the small refrigerator held only a piece of moldy bologna, and Jenny had not taken her medications. Later, when I expressed my concern to Jeff Jr., he said that he was going to hire a couple to come in and take care of her. I left feeling some sense of relief that Jenny's ordeal would soon be over.

A week later, I received a call from the caretaker couple. Frightened by Jenny's condition when they arrived to care for her, they had called the paramedics, who took Jenny to the hospital, and then they called me. Doctors diagnosed Jenny's condition as malnutrition, dehydration, and "neglect." The caretakers said that Jeff Jr. and Marianne had gone on a vacation, leaving no money for food or diapers, no instructions, no telephone numbers or itinerary—not even any information about when they would return. Finally, I felt compelled to call the county adult protective services (APS) agency. Someone there promised to visit the premises and did so. I also called some other relatives, who started making unscheduled visits to see Jenny.

Jeff Jr. and Marianne continue to take unexpected vacations to visit other aging relatives who may "need financial management services in the near future." I fear that Jeff Jr. and Marianne hope to come home someday to find that Jenny has simply "passed away in her sleep." I am constantly uneasy about Jenny's situation. I frequently call APS to see if they can do something more, and I keep "popping in" to check up on Jenny when Jeff Jr. and Marianne are away from home.

Jenny, by all accounts, is doing better now. She is clean and has food in the refrigerator. The caretakers drop in every day briefly and bring in food and diapers on their own. Jenny is still alone most of the time, and she seems too frightened to say much. As Jenny's life is slowly ending, I feel that my life is "on hold." I wish I knew for sure that everything that can be done to protect Jenny is being done. It's in God's hands now.

## INTRODUCTION

Violence against elders has been a perpetual feature of American social history. As with other forms of family violence, however, there has been an ebb and flow in the visibility and invisibility of elder abuse. During the 1980s, violence against elders received heightened consideration, especially violence perpetrated by informal caretakers, such as relatives (Social Services Inspectorate, 1992). The year 2002 brought international attention to elder abuse through the work of the World Health Organization (cited in Cook-Daniels, 2003b). The U.S. Department of Social and Rehabilitation Services began funding APS programs in the late 1960s (Quinn, 1985). In 1978, the Subcommittee on Human Services of the House Select Committee held the first congressional investigation on elder abuse (see Olinger, 1991). Following the hearings, Congress in 1981 recommended the establishment of the National Center on Adult Abuse (Filinson, 1989). By 1985, every state had some form of APS program (Quinn, 1985), and by 1989, 42 states had enacted some form of mandatory elder abuse reporting law (U.S. General Accounting Office, 1991). Increasingly, government agencies and community professional groups have specified elder abuse as a *social problem* (Rinker, 2009).

Any type of problem afflicting the elderly, of course, is likely to multiply with the rapid increase of elderly in the population. As of July 2008, the U.S. Census Bureau estimates that there are over 36 million elders (65+ years of age) in the United States. There may be at least one elderly family member in 25% of American households (U.S. Census Bureau, 2000).

The Federal Interagency Forum on Aging-Related Statistics (2008) has presented a brief overview of well-being of elderly people in the United States:

- The population of elders is expected to grow from 35 million in 2002 to 71.5 million in 2030.
- Elderly people are far more prosperous now than in previous generations, yet they are poorer than other groups except persons under 18 years. Only 9% of elders now live below the poverty line. Women are poorer than men. Blacks are poorer than Whites.
- Life expectancy, while improving, ranks fourth in the world. Individuals who survive to age 65 can expect to live 18.7 more years (83.7).
- Literacy of elderly people has been improving yearly, but 34% are below basic literacy standards.
- Health care costs have risen steadily, with increases in drug costs rising the fastest.

The field of elder abuse has *not* yet produced a *scientific body of evidence* commensurate with that of other subareas in family violence, such as child abuse or spouse abuse. Swedish nursing researcher Christen Erlingsson (2007) deserves credit for clarifying the problem by reporting on a systematic review of database citations. Using the search term "elder abuse," she searched PUB MED (MEDLINE), CINAHL, and PsycINFO for all publications using the term through 2005. In something resembling a reverse pyramid, the number of citations dwindled as she applied more restrictions. She located 2,418 unique references, of which 1,986 were nonresearch articles (e.g., reviews, practice issues, books, editorial comments). She found 34 dissertations and 398 published research articles. (For greater understanding, readers may evaluate the methodology of a contemporary research study on the Internet.)

*Unique definitions, nonstandard measurements,* and *lack of control groups* have contributed to uncertainties about elder abuse, some of which are very basic: What is elder abuse? Who are the abused elders? Who are the elder abusers? Why do people abuse elders? (See www.sagepub .com/barnett3e for an overview of research flaws.) Disturbingly, it seems probable that the failure to conduct adequate research has had serious consequences. Misdirected social services, based on the now-rejected *caregiver stress model,* for example, could have been avoided with a moderate level of research. The question arises, why has information about elder abuse not been *evidence-based?*

This chapter begins with perhaps the greatest uncertainty of all, namely, the *lack of a clear definition* of elder abuse. This deficiency has compounded assessment, treatment, and legal resolutions. This chapter also includes a short overview of abuse in nursing homes and ends with coverage of abuse of disabled persons. The nexus between all three topics—abuse of elderly people in the community, abuse of elderly people in nursing homes, and abuse of disabled persons—helps to increase understanding of each topic separately.

## SCOPE OF THE PROBLEM

If an elderly father insists on wearing a food-stained jacket to church, are his offspring-caregivers supposed to enforce a cleanliness standard to avoid being neglectful? What can a caregiver do if an elder decides to drink too much alcohol or otherwise act foolishly? What if an adult son decides to let his increasingly dependent father fend for himself? Is the son abusive?

## Defining Elder Abuse

Arguably, the debate about what represents family violence is more pronounced in the area of elder abuse than in other subfields. State legislatures, social service agencies, and various professional groups (e.g., in the fields of medicine) all characterize elder abuse dissimilarly. To define elder abuse, one must, for example, specify the meanings of *elder* (i.e., age requirements), *dependency, self-neglect,* and *institutional abuse.* A lack of consensus continues to impede the writing of new legislation to protect elderly people from abuse.

*American Psychological Association definition.* "Elder abuse is the infliction of physical, emotional, or psychological harm on an older adult. Elder abuse can take the form of financial exploitation or intentional or unintentional neglect of an older adult by the caregiver" (Office on Aging, http://www.apa.org/pi/aging/eldabuse.html, 2007). Definitions by agencies dedicated to elder abuse provide a similar definition but expand on each type individually (e.g., National Center on Elder Abuse [NCEA], 2007).

*Public definitions of elder abuse.* Interest has broadened in how members of the public view elder abuse. In one study, people contacted through a random household survey endorsed a fairly *broad definition of elder abuse.* The unique methodology used in this survey was longitudinal and cross-sectional. The investigators queried 400 household participants about their *recognition of signs* of elder abuse. They collected data at three time periods over 10 years (1986–1996): (a) first sample, $n = 117$; (b) second sample, $n = 134$; and (c) third sample, $n = 159$. The researchers determined that 63% or more of the individuals endorsed all of physical abuse items (e.g., "hit") as *always* signifying elder abuse. A majority, with one exception ("not spending time with the elder"), also endorsed the neglect items as abusive but did so at a lower level. Endorsement of emotional abuse items (e.g., "criticizing the elder") as abuse grew over the years. The household participants were less uniform in their endorsement of what constitutes financial abuse. Overall, people *had a fairly accurate idea of what behaviors constitute elder abuse might include* (E. Morgan, Johnson, & Sigler, 2006).

*Definitional limitations.* The term *elder abuse,* within the field of *family violence,* requires that the parties involved be immediate family members or intimate partners, but it leaves out an essential subgroup of abusers—unrelated caregivers (see Straka & Montiminy, 2006). As a result, a duo of elder mistreatment experts has proposed a *broader term* to incorporate the conceptions of both abuse communities (Brandl & Raymond, 2004, p. 60).

> *Abuse in later life:* "Female and male victims age 50 and older who have been harmed by a known abuser. The perpetrator is someone with an ongoing, trusting relationship with the victim, such as a spouse/partner, an adult child, a grandchild, another family member, or a paid or unpaid caregiver. Physical abuse, sexual assault, stalking, isolation, harassment,

financial exploitation, and neglect are often used in combination against the victim. Most often the abuse occurs in the victim's home, whether it's a private dwelling in the community or a residential care facility, such as a nursing home."

## Examples of Specific Abuses

Many different types of organizations define elder abuse, and they may use slightly different definitions and overlapping definitions. Some are definitions promulgated by social services, legislatures, researchers, and others.

- *Emotional/psychological abuses.* Examples include verbal assaults, insults, threats, intimidation, humiliation, and harassment. Other examples are treating an elder person like an infant; isolating the person from his or her family, friends, or regular activities; giving the person the *silent treatment;* and enforced social isolation (National Center on Elder Abuse, 2007). It should be noted that emotional abuse is not illegal.

- *Physical abuses.* Some examples of physical abuses are striking a person with or without an object, hitting, beating, pushing, shoving, shaking, slapping, kicking, pinching, and burning. Other examples include inappropriate use of drugs, physical restraints, force-feeding, and physical punishment (National Center on Elder Abuse, 2007).

- *Financial abuse.* Financial abuse of elders consists of a number of behaviors: (a) abuse of a durable power of attorney, bank account, or guardianship; (b) failing to compensate transfers of real estate; (c) charging excessive amounts for goods and services delivered to an elder; (d) using undue influence to gain control of an elder's money or property; (e) confiscating pension or Social Security checks; (f) denying medical care to avoid paying the cost of care; and (g) refusing to repay loans (e.g., see Rabiner, O'Keeffe, & Brown, 2006; Shilling, 2008).

- *Sexual abuse.* Direct forms of sexual abuse of elders encompass intercourse, molestation, sexualized kissing, oral/genital contact, and digital penetration. Indirect forms of sexual abuse include unwanted sexual discussions, exhibitionism, and exposed masturbation (see Ramsey-Klawsnik et al., 2007). Recall that experts typify rape as a crime of violence rather than a crime of sexual passion.

- *Internet pornography.* A surprising newer type of sexual abuse has come to light in the form of pornographic websites that display older victims. These sites offer still photographs of elderly women posed in every conceivable sexual activity. Viewers can also play short video clips of elderly women engaged in sexual activities. These media materials are classified as pornography, but laws regarding the use of older women hinge on the adults' ability to consent. Police officers who are specially trained in child and elder sexual abuse investigate these cases (Calkins, 2003).

- *Neglect.* Examples of neglect include failure to provide an elderly person with food, water, clothing, shelter, personal hygiene, medicine, comfort, and personal safety (National Center on Elder Abuse, 2007).

- *Self-Neglect.* Examples of self-neglect include failure of an elder to provide food, water, clothing, shelter, personal hygiene, and medication for himself. Self-neglect can also be defined as behavior of an elderly person that threatens his life or safety. Self-neglect behaviors exclude those of a mentally competent adult who understands the consequences of his actions (National Center on Elder Abuse, 2007). (See the box on self-neglects on the website for additional ideas.)

- *Abandonment.* Examples of abandonment include putting an elder demented person on a bus to another state or dropping an elder off at the hospital with no identification (i.e., *granny dumping*). Hospitals concerned with expenses have dumped persons who are seriously mentally ill, elderly and homeless, veterans with PTSD, and the disabled onto the streets (Kahntroff & Watson, 2009; see also Toy, 2010).

- *Violation of human rights.* One example of a human rights violation occurs when a caregiver withholds an elder victim's mail. Two other examples include removing all the doors from the elder's room to deprive her of privacy or interfering with the elder's religious observances. A fourth example is to ignore the elder person's preferences in his selection of friends (e.g., McGarry & Simpson, 2009; see also G. Boyle, 2008).

- *Scams by strangers.* Although not a form of family violence, caregivers of the elderly may have to respond to a scam of an elder by a stranger. Some scams by strangers listed by a California court study include (a) valueless "sweepstakes" that elder must pay to collect; (b) fraudulent investment schemes; (c) requiring cash deposits for repairs; (d) predatory lending; and (e) lottery scams (Shilling, 2008).

## Attitudes Toward Abuse of Elderly Persons

Kosberg and Garcia (1995b) have formulated a list of six viewpoints that promote elder abuse: ageism, sexism, proviolence attitudes, reactions to abuse, negative attitudes toward people with disabilities, and family caregiving imperatives. Emblematic of negative attitudes toward elders is the concept of *postmaturity,* the idea that elders are living too long. Some suggest that elderly people have had their "day in the sun" and now should just "fade away." When caregivers hold such attitudes, they are likely to miss signs of elder abuse. The media show great bias in depicting elder characters in terms of both sexism and ageism (e.g., Fulmer et al., 1999; Lauzen & Dozier, 2005).

*Ageism.* Ageism is a serious consideration for seniors. One important outcome is that age biases cast elders in the role of *second-class citizens.* According to R. A. Mead (2007), there are three types of ageism: (a) *personal* (one's own beliefs), (b) *institutional* (e.g., mandatory retirement age), and (c) *unintentional* (unaware practices). Of interest to students reading this text is that knowledge gained more than 5 years ago is automatically out of date, a type of *ageism of knowledge* (Gottlieb, 2003). So wide-ranging is ageism that a team of medical researchers devised a program to change the attitudes of 237 medical students. This innovative program included meeting with a group of healthy elders and reflective writing sessions. Pre- and post-responses on a *Geriatric Attitude Scale* documented significant improvements in attitudes toward elderly people. The researchers did not, however, administer any long-term tests or determine whether real behavioral changes occurred. As discussed in a previous chapter, research concerning a translation of attitudes into behavioral change has rarely been demonstrated. Consequently, follow-up research is needed (Westmoreland et al., 2009).

An illustration of two blanket *generalizations* is younger people up to age 64 are working and *productive,* while *elder people are unproductive;* hence younger people are the givers/providers and older people are the takers/dependent. These stereotypes overlook the fact that some younger people are disabled and not working and that some elderly people are actively engaged in volunteer work or may still be working. Societies may also pressure elderly people to "age well." Seniors who are healthy and wealthy (presumably through their morality and self-discipline) meet the requirements for aging well (Holstein & Minkle, 2003). As has been emphasized throughout this text, however, early adversities such as poverty and abuse, beyond an individual's control, often set the stage for a lifetime of adversity. As a side note, the findings of one study have generated a modicum of curiosity. In one inquiry, employed elder persons experienced more abuse than nonemployed elders. Elders were the target of workplace abuse (usually emotional) (Acierno, Hernandez-Tejada, Muzzy, & Steve, 2009). With results from only one survey, researchers need to replicate these findings.

A few studies have disclosed the effects of *ageist attitudes in the courtroom.* Research has demonstrated that mock jurors (i.e., research participants acting as jurors in a fictional trial) *question the credibility of elders' testimony* in cases of elder sexual abuse (Hodell et al., 2009). Last, *doctors* surveyed in Australia revealed ageist attitudes. They were apt to view elder abuse as less severe than older people did. Elder caregivers and males, relative to their counterparts, also were less likely to acknowledge the severity of elder abuse (Helmes & Cuevas, 2007).

*Media stereotyping.* The media show great bias in depicting elderly people. Major male characters outnumber major female characters (73% vs. 27%), and the number of elder males and females continually drops off with age (Lauzen & Dozier, 2005). Entertainment media includes relatively few depictions of elders who lead rewarding lives. Instead, their only role in life is to serve as a *supportive character to children and grandchildren.* Alternatively, media may portray them as *cranky and laughable* (see M. London, 2003).

*Criminalization of elder abuse.* In the United States, adult children are *not* legally required to help elderly parents in need (Cahill & Smith, 2002). Because of a lack of moral and legal standards concerning responsibility for care of the elderly, it is difficult to know *whom society should hold accountable for elder care (or neglect).* Nonetheless, individuals who do commit crimes against the elderly are categorized as criminals. A group of 400 adults participating in a household survey over three time periods from 1986 to 1996 favored criminalization of elder abuse. Survey participants endorsed the idea of a *new felony statute* to cover elder abuse. Further, the idea of incarcerating elder abusers became more favorably received over the time period. Rationales for criminalization were that others will see, by enactment of a law, that *elder abuse is wrong, that it will help prevent elder abuse,* and *that such a law would be enforced* (Morgan et al., 2006).

A study with entirely different research samples examined the viewpoints of 119 police chiefs and 203 ombudsmen about their perceptions of crimes against the elderly. The researchers used reactions to six scenarios about fictional crimes against elderly persons as their data. Results indicated that both groups approved of criminalization of crimes against the elderly, but *police chiefs* tended to evaluate *street crimes as more serious* than crimes against elderly people. Nursing home *ombudsmen,* in contrast, judged *crimes against elderly persons* as *more serious* than either street crimes or white collar crimes (Payne & Berg, 2003).

## PREVALENCE OF ELDER/ADULT ABUSE

Fortunately, the incidence of physical abuse declines with age (Rennison & Rand, 2003). Several conditions exacerbate problems in obtaining accurate prevalence estimates of elder abuse. First, definitional ambiguity hinders assessment (Lowenstein, 2009). Second, the mutuality of abuse complicates definitions and hence counting. In cases of interpersonal violence involving elderly persons, it is not always clear who is the victim and who is the perpetrator (see Payne & Appel, 2007). *Elders may strike out at their caregivers,* for instance, in reaction to the loss of personal freedom (e.g., when the caregiver will not let the elder leave the house alone) or because they have dementia. Third, the cognitive decline of many elders may prevent them from reporting their abuse or prevent others from believing them (N. G. Choi & Mayer, 2000; Cook-Daniels, 2004).

*Disclosure reluctance.* Elder victims, like other victims, are often unaware they are being abused as legally defined, and elder abuse victims are notoriously unwilling to *disclose* their abuse. National Criminal Victimization Survey (NCVS) estimates failure-to-disclose rates as high as 50%. Disclosure rates are so low that obtained data must represent underreporting. Some *elements of reluctance to report* are as follows (Acierno et al., 2009; Bulman, 2010; Catalano, 2007; A. Klein, Tobin, Salomon, & Dubois, 2008):

| Stigma | "One is not being a burden" to one's children |
|---|---|
| Nonrecognition of abuse | Desire to protect the abuser |
| Fear of others' disbelief | Fear of losing care from a family member |
| Fear of loss of independence | "One doesn't air his dirty laundry in public" |
| Fear of being institutionalized | "What goes on at home stays at home" |
| Mental incapability | Guilt about adult children's abusiveness |

*Beliefs of elders.* A qualitative study of elder abuse uncovered *barriers to disclosure* that were similar to barriers to help-seeking. About one-third of the women participants were *victims of intimate male partners.* Focus group data from 134 women 45+ years of age uncovered the following five barriers: (a) *powerlessness,* (b) *self-blame,* (c) *secrecy,* (d) *protecting family,* and (e) *hopelessness.* Some elder women did not disclose their husband's abuse for fear of upsetting their adult children or fear of not being believed (Beaulaurier, Seff, Newman, & Dunlop, 2005).

*Methodology.* An English study claims that the lack of clear definitions of elder abuse has led to inadequate reporting by community workers. One important technique is to interview family members about possible abuse separately (see Zink, Fisher, Regan, & Pabst, 2005).

*Other issues.* Another issue for some is that *elder abuse reporters receive no feedback* about the results of an investigation (McGarry & Simpson, 2009). *Training of service providers* about elder abuse increases the number of cases reported. The *setting of the interview* and the *context of questions* (e.g., relationships of seniors, daily lives of seniors) *affects disclosure rates* (Laumann, Leitsch, & Waite, 2008). See Table 12.1 for a summary of persons who reported abuse of elderly women to a Rhode Island *police department* and/or adult protective services (APS).

**TABLE 12.1**  Reporters of Abuse of Elder Women in Rhode Island

| Who Reported | [1]Reported to Police in Rhode island N = 408 Elder Women | [2]Reported to APS in 2004 State Survey (Top 10) N = 567,747 |
|---|---|---|
| Victim | 60.5% | 6.3% |
| Family member | 18.6% | 17.0% |
| Friend/neighbor | 10.8% | 8.0% |
| Social Services staff | | 10.6% |
| Law enforcement | | 5.3% |
| Nursing home staff | | 5.5% |
| Nurses/nurses' aides | | 4.7% |
| Home health staff | | 2.9% |
| Other/unknown/ anonymous | 12.7% | 3.8% |

SOURCES: [1]A. Klein et al., 2008; [2]Teaster, Dugar, Mendiano, Abner, & Cecil. 2006.

*Sample differences.* The source of data samples varies widely in elder abuse prevalence studies. Some surveys are not comparable.

- Studies of elder abuse are based on *files from social agencies,* such as APS. These are second-hand reports. That is, researchers do not contact the abused elders directly.

- Studies of elder abuse are based on a *random sample of the population.* Researchers interview *elders directly, first-hand*—the preferred scientific methodology.

## Prevalence of Abuse in Rhode Island

In the Rhode Island study of abused elderly people, investigators obtained most of the data from the *police department's Domestic Violence Training and Monitoring Unit.* Although the primary focus of the study was on persons age 50 and over, data for women under 50 ($n = 6,200$) were available as well. As data integrity checks, the investigators examined court records and interviewed key informants in the area. The research sample consisted of 408 abused female victims age 50+ reported to police in 2002. Table 12.2 provides details about specific types of elder abuse (A. Klein et al., 2008).

**TABLE 12.2**  Specific Types of Abuse Reported to Police Departments in Rhode Island

| Type of Abuse | Specific Abuse | Percentage Past Year |
|---|---|---|
| Emotional | Infliction of anguish, pain, or distress via verbal/nonverbal acts | 5.0% |
| Physical | Physical force; could cause bodily harm | 2.0% |
| Sexual | Nonconsensual contact of any kind | 1.0% |
| | | Percentage Over Lifetime |
| Neglect (Potential) | Identified need; no one available to fulfill need | 5.1% |
| Neglect (Caregiver) | Assigned caregiver is not fulfilling the need | 0.5% |
| Financial (Family) | Illegal/improper use of elder's funds, property, or assets | 5.2% |
| Financial (Stranger) | Illegal/improper use of elder's funds, property, or assets | 6.5% |

SOURCES: A. Klein et al., 2008; $N = 408$; Age = 60+

## Prevalence of Elder Abuse in Two National Random Samples of Elders

Researchers conducted one of the few truly random samples of elderly people in the United States. The research sample consisted of 5,777 people 60+ years of age randomly selected by random digit dialing methodology. Table 12.3 summarizes elderly person's self-reports of types of abuse from two different national surveys (Acierno et al., 2009).

**TABLE 12.3**  Self-Reports of Abuse in Two National Elder Mistreatment Studies

| Type of Abuse | Brief Definition | [1]Abuse by Others N = 5,777; 60+ Years | [2]Abuse by Family Members N = 3,005; 57–85 Years |
|---|---|---|---|
| Emotional | Infliction of anguish, pain, or distress via verbal/nonverbal acts | 4.6% | 9% |
| Physical | Physical force could cause bodily harm | 1.6% | 0.27% |
| Sexual | Nonconsensual contact of any kind | 0.6% | Not asked |
| Neglect | Refusal/failure to fulfill any obligations/duties to elder | 5.1% | Not asked |
| Financial | Illegal/improper use of elder's funds, property, or assets | 5.2% | 3.5% |

SOURCES: [1]Acierno et al., 2009; [2]Laumann et al., 2008

## Prevalence of Elder Abuse Reported to State APSs: Abuse of Adults 60+ Years of Age

Researchers working for the National Committee on Elder Abuse (NCEA) conducted their second national survey of adult protective services in the 50 states. The research sample consisted of 253,426 cases of abuse of persons 60+ years of age reported to state adult protective services in 2004. Table 12.4 summarizes APS report findings that were received, investigated, and substantiated (Teaster et al., 2006).

**TABLE 12.4**  Summary of Reports Received, Investigated, and Substantiated of Elder Abuse of Persons 60 and Over in Contact With Adult Protective Services

| Type of Abuse | Brief Definition of Abuse Type | Percentage of Cases |
|---|---|---|
| Self-Neglect | Failure/inability of an elder to provide herself with food, water, clothing, shelter, personal hygiene, medication | 37.2% |
| Emotional | Infliction of anguish, pain, or distress via verbal/nonverbal acts | 14.8% |
| Physical | Physical force could cause bodily harm | 10.7% |
| Sexual | Nonconsensual sexual contact of any kind | 1.0% |
| Neglect | Refusal/failure to fulfill any obligations/duties to elder | 20.4% |
| Financial | Illegal/improper use of elder's funds, property, or assets | 14.7% |
| Other | | 1.2% |

SOURCES: Teaster et al., 2006; N = 253,426 Cases

(See the website for additional statistics on elder abuse.)

## Types of Injuries and Estimates

The latest official numerical summary from the *National Electronic Injury Surveillance System– All Injury Program* provides the most comprehensive and reliable data concerning injuries of elders seeking treatment at hospital emergency departments ("Public Health," 2003). This program furnishes national, annualized, weighted estimates of nonfatal, nonsexual, physical assaults categorized by intent. During 2001, roughly 33,026 elders received treatment in *emergency departments* (rate = 72/100,000). The majority of elders treated were men (55.4%). Primary injuries were as follows: (a) contusion/abrasion, 31.9%; (b) laceration, 21.1%; and (c) fracture, 12.7%. The primary sources of injury were assaults as follows: (a) by body part, 20.3%; (b) blunt object, 17.1%; (c) push, 14.4%; and (d) undetermined, 31.8%. *Perpetrators were most likely to be family members or acquaintances.*

## CONSEQUENCES OF ELDER ABUSE

### Health Consequences

One survey of 995 patients in a primary health care setting found significant differences between victims ($n = 31$) and nonvictims ($n = 964$) in regard to their health status. During the past year, *intimate partner abuse victims* suffered significantly more *chronic pain, depression, and high blood pressure* (Zink et al., 2005).

### Reactions of Professional Practitioners

Responding to elder mistreatment is a complex and confusing area of social work practice (Braun, Lenzer, Shumacher-Mukai, & Snyder, 1993). One aspect of the problem is the continuing ambiguity concerning who is responsible for dependent elders and what kind of care (or lack of care) constitutes mistreatment. Another is that there is no single response to elder abuse but *many different types of response* (Shilling, 2008).

*Social services agencies.* Screening elderly clients for abuse is a basic responsibility of several subgroups of professionals and others who work with the elderly. Some of these are *senior centers, adult day services,* and *community-based health services.* When abuse is suspected, most of these agencies refer the client to adult protective services (see Pagano, Mihaly, Dauenhauer, & Mason, 2007).

*Adult protective services.* APS agencies are most commonly assigned the responsibility of implementing legal policies concerning elders. When a suspected case of elder abuse is reported, APS has several duties (Rosenblatt, 1996):

- Determine whether the information available is sufficient to warrant an investigation
- Substantiate whether abuse/neglect actually occurred
- Assess the elder's decision-making capacity about his or her care
- Evaluate what services are needed to sustain the elder

*Investigations by APS.* The 2000 national survey of APS organizations cited previously indicated that all U.S. states have accorded APS statutory power to investigate reported abuse in domestic settings. In many circumstances, the needs of elder abuse victims exceed APS agencies' functions, and other community agents, such as *health care providers* or *law enforcement personnel,* have the responsibility to provide assistance. In fact, there are numerous other organizations charged with protecting elders, such as *ombudsman programs.* The complexity of responsibilities assigned to various agencies can be problematic, leading to some cases "falling through the cracks" (Shilling, 2008).

*In-home assessments.* An innovative approach to determining unmet needs of 211 abused female elders was the use of in-home assessments. An analysis of APS personnel's responses indicated considerable activity in the form of *referrals.* Workers prescribed one or more interventions for 46% of the elderly clients. In addition to services already being delivered, APS staff made the following referrals: (a) institutional placement (36%), guardianship (36%), urgent medications (25%), and acute hospitalization (20%) (Heath, Kobylarz, Brown, & Castano, 2005).

*Refusing service.* It is not uncommon for *elders to refuse the services offered* by APS workers (A. A. Klein et al., 2008). Refusing services may discourage practitioners who are trying to help. It is interesting to note that information from 8 states showed that only 16% of elders contacted by APS refused services (Teaster et al., 2006). In Vinton's (1991) study, elders who refused care often did so because the services offered (respite care and homemaker services) did *not meet their needs.* What these women needed were emergency shelters and restraining orders. Interestingly, not all elder victims meet statutory requirements for services. APS "discharges" elder victims from various support systems if APS personnel judge the elder to be capable of acting on her own behalf (Beaulaurier et al., 2005).

---

### SECTION SUMMARY

#### Definitions, Prevalence of Abuse, and Consequences of Abuse

Definitions of elder abuse are even more problematic than definitions in other areas of family violence. Definitions encompass a number of subtypes of abuse and types of abuse that are especially subjective and difficult to operationalize, such as violations of individuals' constitutional rights, or self-neglect. Especially troublesome is the failure to specify a uniform age for classifying individuals as elders. Definitions are so ambiguous that analysts cannot reach definitive conclusions about the prevalence of mistreatment and which kinds of perpetrator/victim relationships are most common. Despite ageism and unrealistic stereotypes of elderly people, the public is now more willing to criminalize it.

*(Continued)*

The usual reluctance of research participants to disclose their abuse and the additional problem of cognitive impairments hinders data collection. In previous assessments, researchers have most frequently relied on data provided in social workers' reports, police reports, and reports of caregivers or health care workers. In 2008–2009, scientists for the first time conducted two surveys based on self-report data from representative samples. Representative sample data provide estimates ranging from 0.27% to 9% depending on the type of abuse (e.g., sexual). Of particular interest is that the frequency of physical and sexual abuse tends to be less for elders than for other groups, but financial abuse is far greater.

The health consequences of abuse not only destroy an elder person's quality of life but also can be deadly. Social services agencies respond to elder abuse and adult protective services (APS) investigates alleged cases of elder abuse. APS has a number of services at its disposal such as food service delivery, finding different living arrangements, recommending placement in a nursing home, informing the police, and providing in-home caretakers.

## SEARCHING FOR PATTERNS: WHO IS ABUSED AND WHO ARE THE ABUSERS?

Elder abuse researchers have tried to classify types of elders who may be especially vulnerable to abuse and types of individuals who are most apt to abuse elders. They have examined issues of family relationship, gender, age, and race, as well as mental health and alcohol abuse. Kosberg and Nahmiash (1996) have developed a *conceptual framework for categorizing characteristics of victims and abusers* that includes living arrangements, gender, socioeconomic status, health, age, psychological factors, problem behaviors, dependence, isolation, financial problems, family violence, and lack of social support. Given definitional, sampling, and methodological limitations of available research, social scientists accept discriminated patterns as preliminary in nature.

### Characteristics of Abused Elders

Research on elder abuse has revealed few reliable differences, if any, between victims and non-victims. In their review of the literature, Brandl and Cook-Daniels (2002) were unable to uncover any standard victim profile.

*Age.* Because not all researchers and organizations define the status of elder in the same way, the victim characteristic of age is difficult to pin down. Some state APS agencies typically serve all adults, without regard to age, whereas others serve only elders, defined as persons 60 or 65 years of age or older. The fastest-growing group of elders in the United States today is made up of individuals *80 years old and older,* and these elders are targets of abuse and neglect significantly more often than others (NCEA, 1998). See Table 12.5 for a summary of female victims' ages in the Rhode Island inquiry.

**TABLE 12.5** Abused Female Victims in Rhode Island Over Age 50

| Age | Population | Percentage of 50+ Women | Reported to Social Agencies | Abuse per 1,000 of Female Population |
|------|-----------|-------------------------|-----------------------------|--------------------------------------|
| 50–59 | 65,265 | 37.7% | 187 | 2.90 |
| 60+ | 107,576 | 62.2% | 135 | 1.25 |
| Total | 172,841 | 100% | 408 | 2.36 |

SOURCE: A. Klein et al., 2008

*Gender.* The data available concerning gender are somewhat contradictory among studies examining intimate partner violence. Although many types of data, such as injury reports, suggest that males perpetrate more male-to-female intimate partner violence than female-to-male IPV, experts are less sure of similar gender differences among elders or the disabled. See Table 12.6 for a brief overview of crimes reported by the victim's gender.

**TABLE 12.6** Violent Crimes Reported by Victim's Gender

| Victim | Males | Females |
|--------|-------|---------|
| Parent | 32.0% | 68.0% |
| Spouse | 20.0% | 80.0% |

SOURCE: Federal Bureau of Investigations (NIBRS), 2000, $N = 207,571$

Additional gender statistics

66.9% female victims—BJS, $N = 734$ incidents (Catalano, 2007)

65.7% female victims—APS, $N = 15$ states reporting (Teaster et al., 2006)

52% male victims—Boston Study, $N = 2,020$ (Pillemer & Finkelhor, 1988)

*Race.* For information about the race of elderly abuse victims, see Tables 12.7 and 12.8.

**TABLE 12.7** Abused Elderly Women in Rhode Island by Race

|  | White | Black | White Hispanic* | Black Hispanic* | Asian | Native American |
|--|-------|-------|-----------------|-----------------|-------|-----------------|
| Number | 362 | 26 | 13 | 2 | 2 | 2 |
| Percentage | 88.9% | 6.4% | 3.2% | 0.5% | 0.5% | 0.5% |
| % State Population | 80.0% | 6.2% | 8.9% | 1.8% | 2.7% | 0.6% |

SOURCE: Klein et al., 2008, $N = 408$

| TABLE 12.8 | Abused Elderly People in APS State Survey by Race | | | | | |
|---|---|---|---|---|---|---|
| | *White* | *Black* | *Native American* | *Asian* | *Hawaiian/ Pacific Islander* | *Other* |
| Percentage | 77.1% | 21.2% | 0.6% | 0.5% | 0.2% | 0.2% |

SOURCE: Teaster et al., 2006, *N* = 13 states reporting.

*New racial classifications place Hispanics into Hispanic White or Hispanic Black categories.

## Characteristics of Elder Abusers

There are so many noncontinuities among research results that a high degree of uncertainty exists about the typical characteristics of elder/adult abusers. Customary risk factors for elder *homicide perpetrators* are gender (male) and race (African American) (Chu, 2001). One might think that women, however, would be the most likely abusers because they provide most informal family caregiving for elders (Arber & Ginn, 1999).

*Age.* With 7 states reporting, the 2004 APS survey determined that 75.1% of elder abusers were under the age of 60. Ages of elder abuse perpetrators were as follows (Teaster et al., 2006):

Under 18 → 4.3%    50–59 → 18.5%

18–29 → 10.6%    60–69 → 11.2%

30–39 → 16.1%    70–79 → 7.9%

40–49 → 25.6%    80+ → 5.8%

Many abusive caretakers in Pillemer and Finkelhor's (1988) community survey were over age 50 (75%), and some were over 70 (20%). Abusers who are elders themselves may suffer from dementia or other problems that render them less able to care for dependent elders and more likely to abuse those elders. Although some neglect by such elders may be conscious and premeditated, some may result from ignorance or incompetence. *Accounting for intentionality* of abuse in such cases is another important issue challenge (Glendenning, 1993).

*Gender.* Results are mixed concerning the gender of elder abusers. With 11 states reporting, the 2004 APS survey ascertained that 52.7% of abusers of elders 60+ years were female and 47.3% were male (Teaster et al., 2006). A number of studies have found sons to be more abusive than daughters toward elderly parents (e.g., Crichton, Bond, Harvey, & Ristok, 1998; Wolf & Pillemer, 1997). One study, however, found opposite results when neglect was included as a category of abuse (Anetzberger, 1998; Dunlop, Rothman, Condon, Hebert, & Martinez, 2000).

*Relationship to victim.* Most, but not all, surveys have found that *family members are the primary perpetrators of elder abuse* (e.g., Laumann et al., 2008). Intimates (spouses, partners, ex-intimates) also comprise a very large group (Acierno et al., 2009). Nonetheless, there has been considerable discussion about which group of family members or others are most likely to abuse elders/adults. With so much ambiguity about definitions and types of reporters, not to mention underreporting biases and large gaps in data caused by nonresponding organizations, there is much room for error. See Tables 12.9, 12.10, and 12.11 for summaries of perpetrators from various samples.

**TABLE 12.9**  Type of Abuse by Perpetrators' Relationship to Victim (Victim Self-Reports)

| Most Recent Abusive Event | Intimate Partner | Children/ Grand-Children | Other Relative | All Relatives | Acquain-tances | Stranger | Refused to Say |
|---|---|---|---|---|---|---|---|
| Emotional | 25% | 19% | 13% | (32%) | 25% | 9% | 9% |
| Physical | 57% | 10% | 9% | (19%) | 19% | 3% | 2% |
| Sexual maltreatment | 40% | — | 12% | (12%) | 40% | 3% | 5% |
| Neglect | 28% | 39% | 7% | (46%) | 23% | — | 3% |
| Financial | | 5.2% Current | | | | 6.5% Lifetime | |

SOURCE: Acierno et al., 2009; *N* = 5,777; Age = 60+ National Representative Sample.

**TABLE 12.10**  Abuser's Relationship to Elder Female Victim in Rhode Island (Police Records)

| Relationship to Victim | Number | Percentage | Relationship to Victim | Number | Percentage |
|---|---|---|---|---|---|
| INTIMATES | 207 | | FAMILY MEMBERS | 189 | |
| Married | 108 | 26.3% | One generation younger | 154 | |
| Ex-married | 10 | 2.4% | Son | 86 | 46.2% |
| Current intimate partner | 55 | 13.4% | Daughter | 50 | 26.9% |
| Ex-intimate partner | 26 | 6.3% | Stepson | 2 | 1.1% |
| Dating partner | 8 | 1.9% | Stepdaughter | 1 | 0.5% |
| | Total = 191 | | Son-in-law | 9 | 4.8% |
| COHABITANT (not related; nonintimate) | 16 | 3.9% | Daughter-in-law | 4 | 2.1% |
| | | | Nephew | 1 | 0.5% |
| | | | Niece | 1 | 0.5% |
| | | | Two generations younger | 20 | 10.8% |
| | | | Same generation–nonspouse | 10 | 4.8% |
| | | | One generation older | 2 | 1.5% |
| Intimates | 191 | **46.0%** | Family | 189 | **46.0%** |

SOURCE: A. Klein et al., 2008, (*N* = 411); Victim's Age = 50+; Police Reports.

**TABLE 12.11**    Abuser's Relationship to Elder Victim in APS State Survey

| Relationship to Victim | Percentage |
|---|---|
| Adult child | 32.8% |
| Other family member | 21.5% |
| Unknown | 16.3% |
| Spouse/intimate partner | 11.3% |

SOURCE: Teaster et al., 2006; 11 states reporting.

## EXPLAINING ABUSE OF ELDERLY PERSONS

It is not known with any certainty *why* relatives and intimates abuse elders. In the United States, only 21 states reporting to adult protective services maintained an *abuse registry* (database) of alleged perpetrators (Teaster et al., 2006). (See http://www.dhhs.mo.gov for an example of responses to elder abuse in Missouri.) Worldwide, experts have found several correlates of elder abuse, but the causal significance of these factors remains unclear (e.g., Ramsey-Klawsnik, 2006; H. Thompson & Priest, 2005):

| | |
|---|---|
| Isolation | Cultural heterogeneity |
| Married status | Acceptance of violence |
| Female gender | Impaired caretakers |
| Substance abuse | Lack of housing |
| Low socio-economic status | |

As in other subareas of family violence, there is no unicausal theory. The three theories most widely advanced in the United States to explain elder abuse are *social learning theory, social exchange theory* (encompassing situational stress and dependency), and *psychopathology* of the abuser (see Fulmer, 1991; Tomita, 1990).

## Social Learning Theory

Because learning theory has received wide acceptance as one explanation for child abuse and spouse abuse, it seems reasonable to suggest that it may offer a viable account of elder abuse by adult offspring. This view holds that children exposed to violence are likely to grow up to adopt proabuse norms that eventually contribute to their abusing their own parents or grandparents

(Fulmer & O'Malley, 1987). Others see the learning connection more as a retaliatory response for past abuse—You hurt me then; now I'll hurt you (Phillips, 1996). Research has *not* strongly supported a learning connection (e.g., Korbin, Anetzberger, & Austin, 1995).

## Social Exchange Theory

*Social exchange theory* assumes that "social interactions involve exchange of rewards and punishments between people and that people seek to maximize rewards and minimize punishments in these exchanges" (Ansello, 1996, p. 17). Proponents of this theory postulate that elders have little to offer in the way of rewards, so interacting with them is costly and rarely "pays off." Presumably, the high costs of assuming responsibility for elder care, in combination with the few tangible rewards, can result in abuse.

## Stress and Dependency Theories

*How burdensome is caregiving?* As an illustration of the extreme *stress some elder caregivers experience,* Mace (1981) coined the term *36-hour day.* Others invented phrases such as the "sandwich generation" to convey the burden of middle-aged adults who must care for their own children while concurrently caring for aging parents (S. Preston, 1984). A related type of strain occurs when adult siblings in a given family *designate a specific sibling* as the caretaker. Elder caregiving becomes the individual responsibility of one child, not the whole family (F. Russo, 2010).

Correlational analyses have revealed a link between some *burdensome caregiver tasks* and measures of *caregiver stress* (Hinrichsen, Hernandez, & Pollack, 1992). Similarly, a comparison of caregivers of spouses with dementia, relative to spouses with cancer, registered significantly more stress (Clipp & George, 1993; see also Bertrand, Fredman, & Saczynski, 2006).

*Dependency of abused elders.* The theory that caregiver stress causes elder abuse raises two questions: (a) Are abused *elders significantly more dependent* or impaired than nonabused elders? and (b) Are *caregivers of impaired elders more stressed* than caregivers of nonimpaired elders? Some research findings are the following: (a) *Elder dependency,* when it occurs, *is* a strong predisposing factor for abuse (Coyne, Reichman, & Berbig, 1993); (b) Alzheimer's-impaired elders were at greater risk for abuse than elders without the disease (Paveza et al., 1992); and (c) *Caregiver stress* was a risk factor for *emotional and financial mistreatment* of elders among a nationally representative sample of elderly people (Acierno et al., 2009). Although it is clear that elder care can be stressful, the majority of published studies do *not* support the *caregiver-stress model;* that is, it is *caregiver-induced stress* that engenders elder abuse (e.g., Brandl & Cook-Daniels, 2002; A. Klein et al., 2008).

*Problems with the caregiver-stress model.* Arguably, it is the *caregivers who are dependent.* The supposition that abuse stems from victim impairment and dependency may be yet one more disguised attempt to *blame victims* for the abusive behavior of others (Pillemer & Hudson, 1993). Research has indicated that abused elders are *not* significantly more impaired than nonabused elders (Wolf & Pillemer, 1989). Furthermore, elder abuse *victims* are significantly *less dependent* on abusers than are elder nonvictims (Pillemer, 2005.) Overall, stress arises from *caregivers' behavior* (e.g., getting arrested) rather than from strain engendered by caring for elders. An impressive amount of research has identified the *mental health and personality factors of caregivers* as risk factors for abuse of elders: The subset of variables that seems to be most descriptive of the elder abusers is as follows (Pillemer, 2005):

| | |
|---|---|
| • Social isolation | • Financial dependency |
| • Mental illnesses | • Cognitive impairments |
| • Employment problems | • Substance abuse problems |
| • Arrest records | |

The case history of Melvin and Charlie illustrates how the emotional and behavioral problems of adult offspring can lead to elder abuse.

## CASE HISTORY  Melvin and Charlie—The Voices Told Him to Do It

Melvin is a 79-year-old retired carpenter who currently lives with his son, Charlie. Charlie, a 53-year-old food server in a high school cafeteria, has worked for the school district off and on for 20 years. When Charlie was 38 years old, doctors diagnosed him as having paranoid schizophrenia. At 40, Charlie went broke, spending most of his money on home security devices and car alarms that he "needed" for self-protection. Eventually, Charlie's financial problems forced him to move back in with his father.

Melvin's approach to Charlie's problems was to "set Charlie straight" whenever he told unbelievable stories about his coworkers or neighbors. Melvin accused Charlie of "talking hogwash" and of "needing medicine because he was crazy." Charlie's response was to argue with Melvin to try to convince him that his stories about other people were true. The battle between the two loomed larger and larger until Charlie's problems became the focal point of Melvin's life. At the same time, Melvin was spending more and more of his limited income to feed Charlie. Without an income of his own, Charlie stole small amounts of cash from Melvin's wallet whenever he could.

To save himself the aggravation of dealing with Charlie, Melvin began staying in his own room as much as possible. Charlie reacted by standing in front of Melvin's bedroom door, yelling and screaming at him to come out. One time, Charlie got so mad that he ripped out the telephone so neighbors could not tell Melvin lies about him. Another time, he barricaded Melvin into his room for a day, and Melvin had to break a window to escape. Melvin sank into a deep depression. He loved Charlie, but he felt humiliated, afraid, and alone.

The next year, Melvin slipped on some ice and broke his leg. At first Charlie was the dutiful son who brought Melvin his meals, drove him to the doctor, and cleaned the apartment. Eventually, however, Charlie heard voices telling him that Melvin was plotting to have him locked up in a mental institution. One day, Charlie beat Melvin and pushed him out of his bed. Melvin lay on the floor for a day until a neighbor heard him groaning and called police.

The police kept Charlie in custody for a 3-day psychiatric evaluation and called social services. APS had Melvin admitted to a nursing home temporarily. In the psychiatric hospital, doctors started Charlie on strong antipsychotic drugs. Now, Charlie is kinder and "normal," as long as he takes his medicines. At the moment, things are better for both Melvin and Charlie, but no one knows for how long.

## Abuse by the Severely Mentally Ill (SMI)

The general question about a possible link between severe mental illness (SMI) and violence has permeated the literature on violence. In every area of family violence (i.e., child abuse, adolescent abuse, abuse of adult men and women), speculations have arisen about the mental health of the abusers. Of course, *most abusers are not mentally ill.* Looking at the broader field, Solomon, Cavanaugh, and Gelles (2005) have now taken the stance that an *unrecognized type of family violence* is abuse of family members by other family members who are SMI. Although several studies have determined that the *total amount of violence* perpetrated by those who are SMI is *actually very small,* media attention has led to a common *but FALSE belief that the frequency of such cases is very high.* According to Rep. Ted Strickland (D-Ohio; cited in Holloway, 2005), police arrest 284,000 people diagnosed with *bipolar disorder* or *schizophrenia* every day in America.

A proposed new statistical system has improved the accuracy of estimates about the number of incidents of violence connected with SMIs (Lidz, Banks, Simon, Schubert, & Mulvey, 2007). In this new survey of 3,438 individuals, researchers first identified 97 (*0.028%*) people with severe mental illness/major mental disorder. Within this group, 28.9% experienced 2 or more stressful life events, 25.0% suffered from impaired social support, and *8.3% were violent.* A significant *correlation between violence and SMI* emerged from the data analyses. Further, the risk of violence increased when the levels of stressful life events and impaired social relationships entered the statistical equations (Silver & Teasdale, 2005). The targets of perpetrators with SMIs were most frequently family members. (See www.sagepub.com/barnett3e for a classification of victims of perpetrators with SMIs.)

*Alcohol and drug use of mentally ill.* Risk factor analyses of the SMI data indicated that *alcohol or drug (AOD)* abuse by either patients or community members greatly increased the risk of assault, and those with SMIs had higher levels of AOD than those without SMIs. Estroff, Swanson, Lachicotte, Swartz, and Bolduc (1998) also examined the targets of perpetrators and the *risk factors* for assault by a mentally ill person:

- Being a mother co-resident of an individual with SMI who has a substance abuse disorder
- Being an immediate family member who has a relationship with the person with SMI
- Duration of time spent in co-residency with a person affected by an SMI
- Whether the individual with SMI is financially dependent on the family member

These results have raised a number of questions about suitable methods for *prevention of* SMI violence (see Appelbaum, 2006, for a short review; also see Simpson, Allnutt, & Chaplow, 2001).

*Criminality of elder abusers.* Several studies have confirmed earlier findings that elder abusers have high rates of criminality, and adult children who are abusive can be considered *predatory offspring*. Because of their children's criminality, drug/alcohol problems, personality disorders, or mental illness, elders sometimes report their victimization with the hope of getting *services for their children* (Klein et al., 2008).

## Revictimization Studies

Research cited throughout this text testifies to the phenomenon of revictimization. The survey of 408 abused elder women in Rhode Island found that 91 (20%) had been revictimized: (a) 84.6% by the *original abuser* identified in the study, (b) 17.1% by *a different abuser,* and (c) 3.3% by *same and a different abuser* (Klein et al., 2008). In the Acierno et al. (2009) survey of a nationally representative sample of abused elder women, analyses revealed that all prior traumatic experiences were associated with victimization of elders. After controlling for the effects of other variables, prior trauma still predicted emotional, sexual, and some forms of financial abuses. A secondary analysis of the *National Violence Against Women Survey* (NVAWS; Tjaden & Thonenes, 2000a) revealed that of women 45 years of age and older, approximately 64% had experienced some form of child abuse. Within this age group, 41% of the women had suffered intimate partner violence for an average of 14.5 years (Wilke & Vinton, 2005).

### SECTION SUMMARY

#### Characteristics of Victims/Abusers, and Explanations for the Abuse of Elderly People

The gender of victims is most often female, whether the victim is a parent or a spouse. On the surface it appears that most victims are White. Different ethnic classifications, such as combining Hispanic with Whites or Blacks, complicate comparisons. Despite this confound, it is safe to say that ethnic minorities do not report more elder abuse than Whites, and most likely elder abuse occurs less frequently among minorities than among Whites.

Among elder abusers, the most common age range is between 40 and 60. The gender of elder abusers is more equally divided between the sexes than among abusers of younger adults. One reason may be that in-home professional caretakers are often female. Among adult children who abuse their parents and intimates, however, the gender of the abuser is most often male. Depending on the sample, abusers are equally divided between adult children and intimates (intimate partner violence—IPV). The relationship and gender of the abuser, in contrast, depends heavily upon the type of elder abuse perpetrated. *Intimates* are more likely than nonintimates to abuse physically, while *adult children* are more likely than intimates to abuse financially.

Logicians have advanced several theories to account for elder abuse. So far, research has provided almost no support for either social learning theory or social exchange theory, as applied to elder abuse. Research may unveil unforeseen connections in the future. The most advocated theory is caregiver stress. This model assumes that the dependency of an elder, brought about by impairments, places inordinate demands upon caregivers. Presumably, dependent elders' needs create such overwhelming pressure upon caregivers that they lose control and abuse the elders. Certainly, the stress on middle-aged adult children caring for aging parents while still caring for their own children is taxing. Most social services personnel, regrettably, adopted the caregiver stress model without research evidence, and they continued relying upon it for many years after research discredited it.

A large body of evidence demonstrates that perpetrators of elder abuse, not the elder victims, are the persons most likely to be dependent, and they are also the persons most likely to cause stress in the household. Adult children who are elder abuse perpetrators have far-ranging problems, such as serious mental health problems, drug/alcohol problems, unemployment, and criminal histories. Recently, experts have proposed that a special category of elder abusers: the severely mentally ill (SMI) living in the community. What is more, their alcohol/drug usage exacerbates their mental illness, and they may seriously abuse vulnerable elders. As a result of all these findings, the psychological status of abusers may be a better predictor of elder abuse than characteristics of victims.

Finally, the tragedy of revictimization moves forward all the way from childhood, through adulthood, and into old age. Elders who were abused as children or traumatized in other ways continue to be more vulnerable to current abuses.

## PRACTICE, POLICY, AND PREVENTION ISSUES

Elder abuse hotline: 1-800-752–6200

Long-term care ombudsman: 1-800-372-2991; (TYY hearing impaired: 1-800-627-4702)

National Domestic Violence Hotline: 1-800-799-SAFE (7233)

Rape, Abuse and Incest National Network (RAINN) Hotline: 1-800-656-HOPE (4673)

Suspect elder abuse, neglect, and exploitation: 1-800-677-1116

## PRACTICE ISSUES FOR TREATING ELDER ABUSE

One issue in helping elderly victims of abuse is that they are reluctant to receive any services (Klein et al., 2008). Such reluctance hampers investigations and delivery of services. Nonetheless, practitioners working with elderly people should keep in mind that *elder abuse is always a possibility* (H. Thompson & Priest, 2005).

*Recognizing elder abuse.* Several research endeavors have examined caretakers' abilities to recognize elder abuse. An English study of 202 fourth-year medical students exposed to vignettes containing some abusive and nonabusive events disclosed five important results: (a) Many students were unable to detect abuse and neglect in the vignette; (b) In nearly every case, medical students were able to specify behaviors that were *not* abusive/neglectful (e.g., getting an ID bracelet for the elder); (c) Hands-on experience as a professional caregiver substantially improved their detection rates; (d) University instruction on elder abuse/neglect did not improve detection rates; and (e) Asian medical students were less likely to recognize abuse compared with Anglo students (Thompson-McCormack, Jones, & Livingston, 2009).

*Practitioner training.* The three most important group targets of elder abuse education are *professionals, community leaders,* and the *elderly* themselves. One inquiry reported that 33% of a group of various types of service providers said they would like more training and 40% had received no training (Pagano et al., 2007; see also Thompson-McCormack et al., 2009).

*Elder abuse investigator training.* Professionals who investigate cases of suspected elder abuse need to be well trained to avoid potential damage to victims and their families, offenders, care providers, and society. Professionals need to make logical links between data analyses and their substantiation decisions, and maintain consistency. Failing to validate cases of real abuse leaves victims vulnerable to ongoing or even escalating abuse. Conversely, falsely judging a situation to be elder abuse may cause extreme harm: lawsuits, forced registration of individuals on central registries, criminal prosecutions, loss of licenses, and other sanctions (Ramsey-Klawsnik, 2004).

*Guardianship dilemmas.* Geriatric social workers need knowledge about guardianship statutes. More specifically, social workers need a basic understanding of the decision-making process undertaken to determine the need for a guardianship appointment. How do authorities try to balance the benefits of autonomy for the elder against the questionable competency of an elder (Crampton, 2004)?

*REACH program.* In listening to older women's opinions, personnel at Project REACH in Maine learned to avoid using stigmatizing terms such as *domestic violence* and *battered woman* when placing advertisements about support groups. Using a trial-and-error procedure, they fashioned ads that used terminology suitable for attracting needy and isolated older women. They found that ads referring to the "concerns of older women," for example, were more palatable to their target audience than ads that mentioned the "abuse of older women" (see Brandl, Hebert, Rozwadowski, & Spangler, 2003; M. London, 2003; J. Mears, 2003). Finding ways to provide social support to elders does appear to have beneficial consequences. In one examination, social support was positively associated with proactive coping and was negatively associated with depression and functional disability (Greenglass, Fiksenbaum, & Eaton, 2006).

*Helping elders abused by offspring.* Ramsey-Klawsnik (2006) has made a number of recommendations for assisting elder victims of offspring abuse: (a) Help the victim-parent deal with feelings of guilt, fear, and embarrassment; (b) Avoid blaming either the victim or the offender and build rapport; (c) Individualize treatment; (d) Help raise the victim's self-esteem; (e) Know what services are available for the problematic offspring; (f) Help the victim-parent set ground rules if the offender-offspring stays in the house; and (g) Challenge the victim's thinking errors (e.g., offspring cannot control behavior). For treatment of *anxiety,* research identifies cognitive behavior therapy as probably the most effective (Stanley et al., 2009).

## Adult Protective Services (APS) Responses to Elder Abuse

Just as definitional ambiguity has hindered research progress it has also hampered efforts to respond to elder abuse. As practitioners obtain greater understanding of the precursors of elder abuse, they should be able to protect potential victims more readily. See Table 12.12 for lists of documented risk factors for elder abuse.

**TABLE 12.12**    Victim and Perpetrator Risk Factors

| Victim Characteristics | Perpetrator Characteristics |
|---|---|
| Dependence on the abuser | Dependence on the victim (e.g., financial) |
| Physical or mental frailty | Psychological disturbance |
| Social isolation | Psychiatric or substance abuse history |
| Psychiatric or substance abuse history | Past history of abusiveness |
| Shared living situation | Shared living situation |

SOURCES: Lachs & Pillemer, 2004; Stiegel, 1997; Stiegel, Heisler, Brandl, & Judy, 2000.

Many of the cases that APS agencies investigate are similar to the case of Jenny and Jeff Jr., described at the beginning of this chapter. Uncertainties abound: Would a judge find Jeff Jr. and Marianne guilty of neglect? Is Jenny's situation serious enough to warrant her removal from their house? Would Jenny be happier and safer living elsewhere? What is the former daughter-in-law's appropriate role in helping Jenny? Who should inherit the remainder of Jenny's estate when she dies? In the real world, there are few good answers, just more difficult questions.

*Treatment of elder abusers.* One useful treatment of elder abusers is to find ways for the abused elder to help the caregiver (Reid, Moss, & Hyman, 2005). An innovative program treated 9 individuals who had physically abused and 10 who had neglected their elderly relatives. The treatment included both an *educational component* and an *anger management* program. Using pre- and posttests, the researchers assessed the abusers via the Conflict

Tactics Scale (CTS1) and measures of caregiver stress, depression, anxiety, and cost of care. Results showed that both types of abusers experienced reductions in the test measures. Further, after anger management training, CTS1 scores and cost of care measures also fell. These significant improvements were still evident at the 6-month follow-up (Reay & Browne, 2002). One *ineffective approach* is to enroll elder abusers in batterer counseling groups; the counseling needs of elder abusers seem not to parallel those of younger batterers. One comparison of three approaches to reducing elder abuse, however, found that the *least effective* approach was to try to effect "changes in the circumstances of the perpetrator" (Klein et al., 2008).

*Gaps in service provision.* According to the New York State Office of Aging, a number of concerns about responding to elder abuse exist (Pagano et al., 2007). Klein et al. (2008) also listed gaps in service provision (see also Beaulaurier et al., 2005):

| | |
|---|---|
| • Elder-specific counseling groups | • Provider's lack of knowledge about resources |
| • Lack of community support | • Age-appropriate counseling groups |
| • Advocacy training and services | |

*Research findings on programs.* Some progress in empirical research in the area of elder care and prevention of seniors are as follows:

- Reduction in elders' loneliness by day care participation (Aday, Kehoe, & Farney, 2006)
- Reduction in depression through a life-review (i.e., focused reminiscence) (Mastel-Smith et al., 2006; Zauszniewski et al., 2004)
- Reduction in mortality associated with participation in day care services (Kuzuya et al., 2006)
- Higher rates of victim compliance (follow-through) with recommended agency referrals if abuser had substance abuse/mental illness problem (Powell & Berman, 2006)

### Criminal Justice System Responses

*Police responses.* The Rhode Island study of elder women revealed that, contrary to the experimental hypothesis, police were *not* reluctant to arrest elder abuse suspects. Arrest, prosecution, and incarceration, nonetheless, did *not* prevent reabuse, and revictimizers were particularly prone to violating orders of protection (A. Klein et al., 2008). *Improving police response* is the goal of a class offered by Florida's attorney general to law enforcement (Florida Crime Prevention Training Institute, 2009).

*Prosecutors.* According to one summary, prosecution of elder abuse and fraud is rarely successful. Few prosecutions continue beyond the investigatory phase, and most cases have been closed because evidence is lacking (see J. M. Otto, 2005). In the survey of victimized elderly women in Rhode Island, *prosecutors* were *more* likely to charge *elder* abusers than abusers of younger women with felonies instead of misdemeanors. As commented upon in previous chapters, there are significant drop-offs between arrest, decision to prosecute, guilty verdict, and incarceration. Upon examination of victim cooperation with the prosecutors, researchers determined that elder victims (60+ years old) were as cooperative with prosecutors as younger victims (50–59 years) (A. Klein et al., 2008).

## Legal Issues

State governments are extremely active in fashioning legislation to prevent or punish elder abuse. Some topics under discussion include (a) denying sex offenders residency and sex offender employment in nursing homes, (b) identifying "gray murders" (see p. 32 this text), (c) completely overhauling APS (in Texas), and (d) placing undercover patients in homes to identify abuse (Cook-Daniels, 2005). In addition to the forms of abuse mentioned previously, experts have added new types of abuse or new definitions as follows: (a) *abduction*—removing a vulnerable adult from the state or preventing his return to the state, (b) *abandonment*—a caregiver's desertion at a time when a reasonable person would continue providing care, and (c) *isolation*—false imprisonment or preventing the elder from communicating with the outside world (Shilling, 2008). Federal legislation would have the benefit of creating uniformity in the laws. As in other cases of family violence (e.g., child abuse), hard evidence of abuse may be challenging to produce for the court.

*The Elder Justice Act.* Currently pending in Congress are bills extending back to 2003 authorizing the Elder Justice Act. Officials have studied and amended the bills but not passed them. Initially the bill aimed to change the age of an elder to 60 years, down from 65, and enact or strengthen laws protecting elders (see "Congress Considers," 2003). Because the bill is stalled in Congress, an Elder Justice Coalition has formed to encourage Congress to pass the legislation; it has *not* succeeded. More recently a group termed *Elder Justice Now* has joined the movement to help get the bill passed (see http://www.elderjusticenow.org).

*Legal access.* Elders' access to legal services is a vital concern, because attorneys can provide abuse victims with services not available from other professionals. For example, attorneys can execute court and noncourt actions as well as legal and "nonlegal" actions that have the potential to help the elder person threaten court action. In addition, it can be especially challenging for elder victims to appear in court. More than 40% of senior citizens suffer from some form of disability. Some of these problems include poor hearing, mobility problems (cannot access the court building), no transportation to court, deafness or other communication problems, limited stamina, and some tendencies toward mental confusion. Elders frequently feel embarrassed, guilty, or worried about shaming the family by going to court (Shilling, 2008).

*Legal needs of elders.* By and large, abused elders most frequently need one of four types of legal interventions: (a) an *order of protection* to remove the abuser from the residence; (b) *guardianship* of the elder and/or his or her estate; (c) a *representative payeeship* to safeguard certain types of the elder's income, such as social security; and (d) *protection against involuntary commitment to a mental health care facility* (Segal & Iris, 1989; see also Heisler, 2004). Although abused elders may have many unmet legal needs, they tend to make sparse use of legal resources (see Korbin, Anetzberger, Thomasson, & Austin, 1991). There are a number of civil and criminal procedures that attorneys familiar with contract law and incapacitation can take to try to recover a senior's stolen assets (Seal, 2008). John E. B. Myers (2005) has provided information on understanding evidentiary proof for use in court. A website that originates in Ventura, California, provides a compendium of laws protecting the elderly (see M. Schwartz, 2000, at http://www.elderabuselaw.com).

*Reducing financial exploitation.* Across the nation, laws protecting elderly people from financial abuse generally require a complete overhaul. As highlighted previously in this chapter, *adult children* are likely to perpetrate the majority of these crimes. Legislation in 2009 in New York has made several advances to protect elderly and incapacitated people through changes in their *durable power of attorney laws* (Bailly, 2009). Laws are aimed at minimizing opportunities for exploitation by an incapacitated elder's agent.

> A power of attorney in common law or mandated in civil law systems is an authorization to act on someone else's behalf in a legal or business matter. The person authorizing the other to act is the principal, and the one authorized to act is the agent. ("Power of Attorney," 2010)

New York legislators specified the *standard of care* owed to a principal as follows: (a) to act in the best interests of the principal, (b) to keep the principal's property separate from the property of the agent, (c) to keep records of the agent's transactions on behalf of the principal, (d) to make records and a copy of the power of attorney available upon the request of key individuals, and (e) to avoid conflicts of interest (Bailly, 2009). Government officials have developed durable power of attorney documents that require new procedures. Now, the principal must personally "check" boxes giving the agent any *special* powers, two individuals must sign that they witnessed the principal's check-offs, and the whole document, of course, must be notarized. Third parties may refuse to honor certain powers of attorney under certain circumstances; if agents refuse to turn over records to APS, APS can compel the agent to do so.

*Medicare/Medicaid fraud.* Past laws totally failed to curb rampant *Medicare/Medicaid fraud* by health care workers, drug and medical supply companies, and nursing homes. Possibly as much as $60 billion of annual Medicare expenditures are fraudulent (See Potter, 2007). The siphoning off of these funds is an *indirect form of elder abuse,* because it reduces the amount of funding available for other needed elder services. In some cases, Medicare fraud has resulted in beneficiaries having to pay illegally high prices for drugs (e.g., for schizophrenia and bipolar disorder). Much fraud emanates from fraudulent billing practices. Improper *coding of claims* in one U.S. General Accounting Office (GAO) study, for example, found that more than 90% of the coding was incorrect, a practice undertaken to make higher claims for benefits. The fraud committed by drug companies has been exceptional. Thanks to whistleblowers and others, a number of drug companies have paid hefty *fines* and received other *punishments* for fraudulent practices.

> *Example of a fraud:* Schering-Plough misrepresented its best price for Claritin Redi-Tabs to the government agency overseeing Medicaid. Schering-Plough did not charge the same price to an HMO (Kaiser-Permanente) as it charged to Medicaid, as required by law. Schering-Plough found a fraudulent method for giving Kaiser-Permanente a deep discount. Although Schering-Plough kept the *stated price* for each tablet the same for the two groups, it provided the HMO with enough "free samples" to deeply discount the real price paid by the HMO (A. Schneider, 2007).

## Medical Responses

Doctors, nurses, and other medical personnel can play a vital role in assisting elder abuse victims. In fact, the responsibility of responding to elder mistreatment has fallen heavily upon health care professionals because elderly individuals are very likely to visit health care facilities. Studies have indicated that by 2005, the average number of visits to a physician was on average 13.9 times a year (Federal Interagency Forum on Aging-Related Statistics, 2008; Fulmer, Guadagno, Dyer, & Connolly, 2004).

*Medical screening.* Most hospital and medical center emergency departments have screening protocols for identifying and reporting elder abuse. Most often these instruments are based on theoretical frameworks, but they lack psychometric assessment (Yaffe, Wolfson, & Lithwick, 2009). Despite the strong acceptance of these scales by experts, scientific evaluations have not reported evidence *for or against* their use as of the mid-2000s (see U.S. Preventative Services Task Force, 2004). Nevertheless, there is forward movement in the construction of screening tools. "There is a new broad consensus that appropriate, conceptually consistent, and psychometrically sound EM [elder mistreatment] instruments are crucial if there is to be progress in the practice and research of this significant health concern" (Fulmer et al., 2004, p. 297). Moreover, medical experts in nearly every field (e.g., ophthalmology, neurology) should participate in *screening elders* suspected of being victims of elder abuse.

*Assessment tools.* One valuable advance has been the development of a one-page assessment and management tool for identifying *elder abuse* (Bomba, 2006). Israelis developed a reliable and valid screening instrument, the *Expanded Indicators of Abuse* (M. Cohen, Halevi-Levin, Gagin, & Friedman, 2006). Canadian researchers have conducted a scientific comprehensive multistage study that produced a 6-item medical screening tool for doctors, the Elder Abuse Suspicion Index (EASI; Yafee et al., 2009). See the website for a copy of the questions developed by Mount Sinai/Victim Services Agency, Elder Abuse Project (1988), *Elder Mistreatment Guidelines for Health Care Professionals: Detection, Assessment, and Intervention.*

*Documenting abuse.* In addition to using screening questions, nurses can check an elder's body for physical signs of abuse or inadequate care and conduct a psychological assessment. *Nurses and other medical personnel should photograph and document any evidence of elder abuse*

(Pearsall, 2005; see also the *Journal of Forensic Nursing* for guidelines nurses can follow in order to intervene most effectively).

*Possible physical signs of abuse.* In addition to screening questions (e.g., "Are you afraid of anyone"?), some experts suggest that certain conditions should be "red flags" to physicians that abuse may be or has been a problem for an elderly patient (Pearsall, 2005; Rinker, 2009; Zink et al., 2005):

| | | |
|---|---|---|
| Bruising | Chronic pain | Restraint trauma (e.g., rope burns) |
| Fractures | Depression | Time lapses: injury → medical treatment |
| Burns | Hygiene issues | Repeated unexplained injuries |
| Abrasions | Hypothermia | Use of many different emergency rooms |
| Lacerations | Weight loss | Sexual abuse trauma (e.g., STD, injury) |
| Bed sores | Dehydration | Cognitive/mental health problems |
| | Pain upon being touched | Injuries undisclosed by caregiver |

*Perceptions of abuse by care providers.* One topic in the field of elder abuse has garnered an elevated amount of research attention—Do emergency medical services (EMS) personnel accurately identify elder abuse? An inquiry of 399 prehospital/hospital workers demonstrated an apparent disconnect between what they believed about the frequency of elder abuse and what they actually encountered on the job. Although more than 95% believed that elder abuse was "*not a rare event,*" 51.3% said they had no reason to suspect that any of their clients had been abused. Workers had trouble (as others do also) with the ambiguity between abuse/neglect and self-abuse/self-neglect. The EMS workers might find an elder living in an unheated house with no electricity and little food, while the hospital workers might observe that the same elder had bed sores, was malnourished, and was wearing dirty clothing. It was not clear who was to blame for the elder's condition (Rinker, 2009; see also Nusbaum, Cheung, Cohen, Keca, & Mailey, 2006).

*Mandatory reporting compliance.* Most states have *resource hotlines that doctors (or elders) can call for assistance* in matters of abuse (Lachs & Pillemer, 1995). Evidence suggests that when states require mandated reporting by medical doctors, nursing home administrators, and others, significantly higher rates of investigations take place (Jogerst et al., 2003).

*Failure to report.* Research has suggested that medical personnel are often *reluctant to report suspected cases* of elder abuse (Blakely & Dolon, 1991). In one study, a significant number of interviewed doctors (36%) and nurses (60%) cited their *fear of becoming involved in lengthy court appearances* as a major reason for their failure to comply with mandated reporting laws. Some were simply *unaware of reporting laws* (O'Malley, Segel, & Perez, 1979). Other frequent reasons included beliefs that the *problem is not serious enough,* the *evidence is insufficient, services are inadequate,* and the *report would disrupt family relationships* (Clark-Daniels, Daniels, & Baumhover, 1989). Kosberg and Nahmiash (1996) believe that medical personnel's improved understanding of the dynamics of elder abuse would enhance their ability to detect it and presumably to report it.

*Reasons for reluctance to report.* In an effort to understand physicians' reluctance to report elder abuse, researchers conducted interviews with 20 family practice doctors/internists. Analysis of the data revealed three paradoxes (M. A. Rodriguez, Wallace, Woolf, & Mangione, 2006):

1. Working diligently to establish rapport with a patient can be undermined by disclosing suspected abuse.

2. Reporting elder abuse may lead to a response by APS or law enforcement that diminishes the victim's quality life.

3. Reporting abuse may lead to a loss of the physician's decision-making power about what needs to be done in the "best interest" of the elder patient.

Although physicians generally thought mandatory reporting was a good idea, their own considerations led them to disregard the mandate. *They wanted their reporting to result in something less forceful than a police investigation.*

*Physician education.* A 2005 report ascertained that among 392 primary care physicians in Ohio, 72% said they had received no exposure to elder abuse. They did not believe it was a significant problem, and a majority had neither encountered an abused patient nor asked any patient about being abused (Kennedy, 2005). Medical schools are slowly adding elements to their curriculums on managing elder abuse. One survey of 23 primary residency programs in Michigan uncovered significant differences between types of specialties and their management of elder abuse. Clustering of program types indicated that the intensity of training on elder abuse ranged from *high-intensity* programs in *family medicine,* downward through *preventative medicine,* and *emergency medicine,* to the lowest cluster of *internal medicine* residencies.

Results suggest that *emergency medicine* and *internal medicine* clusters should consider *adding clinical experience with abused elders to their training.* As mentioned throughout the text, medical schools as well as clinically oriented programs emphasize the need for doctors to be culturally competent when dealing with elders from diverse backgrounds (Wagenaar, Rosenbaum, Herman, & Page, 2009).

## Policy Issues for Combating Elder Abuse

Collaborative efforts between agencies often improve services for elder abuse victims. Professionals and service providers with expertise in divergent disciplines need to join forces to provide a coordinated response to elder abuse. Programs built on *interagency cross-training* have the potential to overcome mistrust and establish successful policy guidelines (Klein et al., 2008).

*Non-collaboration between adult protective services and domestic violence programs.* The primary current need for collaboration is for better coordination between adult protective services and domestic violence groups. The lack of understanding between the two networks has deprived abused elders of receiving the best services that society can provide. Otto and Quinn (2007) have drawn a number of distinctions and parallels that help clarify how the disconnect between the two networks evolved. How soon can this impasse be remedied? See Table 12.13 for a simplified account of some of the major distinctions.

**TABLE 12.13**    A Simplified Summary of Distinctions between APS and DV Programs

| Dimension | Adult Protective Services (APS) for Abused Elders 60+Years | Domestic Violence (DV) Programs for Abused Elders Under 60 Years of Age |
|---|---|---|
| Establishment | Authorized by federal/state agencies | Grassroots movement—feminism |
| Clientele | Abused (disabled) adults (men and women), not children | Abused women (few men) and their children |
| Abusers | Adult children, extended family, spouses/partners/ex-spouses/caregivers/friends | Intimates/ex-intimates; spouses/partners—implies sexual intimacy |
| Goal of organization | Protect the elder, not crisis-oriented | Shelter/safety for women and their children, crisis-oriented |
| Access | Business hours: 9 a.m. – 5 p.m., weekdays | 24 hours/day; 7 days/week |
| Definition of abuse | Physical, sexual, emotional, self-neglect, neglect, financial exploitation | Physical, sexual, emotional, theft, criminal, coercive control |
| Sexual assault | Inadequate response—need rape crisis centers to assume treatment | Respond, but may refer to multi-service rape crisis centers |
| Setting of abuse | Home or long-term facility | Home, work, other settings |
| Gender of victim | Available for both sexes | Focus almost entirely on women |
| Services | Multifaceted: refer, obtain services, e.g., medical, legal, in-home help | Help women obtain services, help her re-establish herself |
| Treatment | Do not provide group counseling | Provide group counseling; empower the survivor |
| Cultural accommodations | Challenge for APS—need interpreters; needs improvement | Some progress in providing culturally sensitive shelters |
| Mandatory reporting | Report to APS and notify law enforcement (some confidentiality requirements) | No mandatory reporting (confidentiality requirements) |
| Shelters | Not typically provided—must refer to long-term care | Have not typically provided, but working to improve |

SOURCES: Otto & Quinn, 2007; see also Vierthaler, 2008.

*A successful collaboration.* A very successful collaboration emerged from the first *Elder Abuse Forensic Center* (EAFC) at the University of California at Irvine. Key professionals from nine different organizations comprised the team: APS, long-term care ombudsman, the sheriff's department, district attorney's office, Vulnerable Adult Specialist Team [VAST], public guardian's office, Older Adult Services, the Victim Witness Assistance Program, and Human Options (domestic violence services).

Researchers provided these forensic team members with 3-question surveys for assessing each of 114 elder mistreatment cases needing processing in a year's time. Quantitative results disclosed that the members thought working together was both time-saving and more effective than working independently. Questions about the members' satisfaction with the collaboration were high. Although most members were enthusiastic about the accomplishments of the forensic team, there were some significant differences between groups. Members from the district attorney's office ranked the experience higher than some of the other members (Wiglesworth, Mosqueda, Burnight, Younglove, & Jeske, 2006).

*Shelters for elderly abused women.* As discussed in a previous chapter, there is a need for domestic violence programs and APS agencies to collaborate (e.g., Dunlop et al., 2000; S. B. Harris, 1996). Access to battered women's shelters, however, may not be as helpful to elderly women as better access to elder care facilities. There are several modifications that could make shelters more user-friendly to elders. As a case in point, a local school of architecture designed special furniture for a cottage housing abused elders. Representative of the architects' volunteer efforts were beds designed with bookshelf headboards containing lights (McFall, 2000). The expense of buying, permitting, and remodeling houses for use as shelters is often prohibitive.

*Converting an assisted-living center into a shelter is an excellent solution* (Reingold, 2006; see also Zink, Regan, Jacobson, & Pabst, 2003). One anecdotal account described the success of converting a nursing home into a shelter suitable for housing women of any age and their families. The supporting agency (Hopeline) was able to provide nine separate bedrooms with individual bathrooms and TV. There were shared rooms and kitchens and a playroom with a courtyard for children (Youngblood, 2006). Even when there are shelters available, victims usually have no idea about their accessibility. Those in social services need to inform elder abuse victims of their existence (A. Klein et al., 2008).

*Emergency disaster care.* The need for policy change in evacuating ill elders during disasters became evident during Hurricane Katrina (Mead, 2008). Elders experienced life-threatening situations in understaffed facilities that lacked medication. In retrospect, APS workers' disaster training was inadequate and to make matters worse, workers "just rolled with the punches," rather than make use of their training. Support services, such as databases containing clients' names, are not available to help workers keep track of elder clients. States in the gulf region have considered passing disaster management bills (Mixson, 2006). Florida placed the bill on a special order senate calendar but let the bill die on calendar without taking action (Florida Senate, 2007).

*Criminal justice system responses.* Newer research can inform practices throughout the criminal justice system.

*Training.* One type of training police need is about the timing of their reports of abuse to social service agencies (A. Klein et al., 2008). Dissemination of effective police procedures should help increase the arrest rate. A New York report on elder abuse prevalence found that one police department accounted for approximately 70% of 1,201 elder abuse cases. Other police departments may not know what this effective department is doing (Pagano et al., 2007). Police need training in how to deal with dementia.

*Funding police.* Police departments need funding to develop on-scene protocols for cases of possible elder abuse and abuse of disabled persons, to purchase special transportation vehicles (e.g., for transport of wheelchair-bound victims) and to hire specialists (e.g., sign-language interpreters). At least many police departments are already providing officers with some training in recognizing mentally ill perpetrators and where to take them (Briere, Woo, McRae, Foltz, & Sitzman, 1997). To assist police, the California State Legislature has passed directives requiring various agencies to establish *medical forensic forms* for use with abused elders (Dayton, 2002). Also available are several videotapes for police training (Law Enforcement Research Center, 1996). As in other areas of family violence, police departments are starting to create *specialized elder abuse police units* ("San Diego," n.d.; D. Jones, 2009).

*Improving the court's oversight of guardianship matters.* In the past and extending into the present, many courts have lacked sufficient powers to protect elders in guardianship matters (see Bailly, 2009; Myers, 2008). In 2007, the American Association of Retired Persons (AARP) and the American Bar Association (ABA) issued a report on the outcome of a 2-year assessment of court practices entitled *Guarding the Guardians: Promising Practices of Court Monitoring.* Although laws governing all 50 states permit courts to oversee guardianship appointments, court problems remain (Cook-Daniels, 2008a):

- 25% do not require guardians to file status reports.
- Over 33% do not require verification of information in the reports.
- Only 16% verify every report.
- 40% do not designate anyone to visit the incapacitated person.
- Many courts (for legal requirements governing judges' informal communications outside of the courtroom) decline to act on complaints about a guardian's behavior without a formal petition.
- Complicated procedures make it nearly impossible to locate specifics about guardianships.
- Lay people find it nearly impossible to follow procedural requirements for making complaints.

Some states, such as California, now have statutes permitting the court to assign an investigator to examine complaints or to take other appropriate actions. New York has a fiduciary inspector who can make random audits of guardianship reports. Also it is unclear whether courts report possible guardianship infractions to adult protective services.

The joint AARP and ABA report provides a menu of ideas available for selection by judges (http://assets.aarp.org/rgcenter/il/2007_21_guardians.pdf). A summary of actions undertaken by one court are as follows (Cook-Daniels, 2008a):

- Placing English and Spanish versions of court forms on the Internet
- Using court accountants to review the financial accounting of guardians' reports

- Inputting on the computer the due dates for guardians' reports to be filed
- Charging fees for filing of guardianship papers to offset the costs for the court's supervision

*Improving the court's response to elder mistreatment.* A philanthropic grant from the Archstone Foundation (2006) enabled a study of courts' handling of elder mistreatment cases (http://www.CourtInfo.ca.gov/programs/cfcc/resources/publications/articles/html). This study identified a number complicating factors for courts: (a) One factor is the *nature of a case.* An apparent landlord eviction of a tenant may, in reality, turn out to be a case of elder neglect requiring a conservatorship. Other court contexts, such as *criminal, civil,* and *probate,* may eventuate into an elder abuse case; (b) Another factor is the *slow pace of legal proceedings,* coupled with *elder victims' waning capacities,* hinders prosecution of elder abuse. Changes in court procedures could remedy some problems for elderly people; and (c) One advance would be to allow elders to submit testimony via videotape. This modification would resolve situations in which elders die or lose the capacity to testify before a trial starts. Panels examining the problems of elder victims in court periodically make recommendations for improving the courts (e.g., American Bar Association). (See the website for additional Internet resources.)

| | |
|---|---|
| Prioritize scheduling of elder abuse cases | Train and use victim/witness advocates |
| Provide training for conservators | Have referral service available |
| Have volunteer attorneys available to help as needed | Maintain continuity of elder's court contacts |
| Appoint appropriate experts for needed testimony | Draft individualized orders of protection |
| Coordinate activities of different courts | Accommodate impairments of elders |

SOURCE: American Bar Association, n.d.

| | |
|---|---|
| Advocate for needed legislation and for sufficient court budgets | Create a national court resource center on aging issues |
| Develop innovative solutions to elder abuse problems | Encourage courts/judges to participate in multi-agency initiatives |
| Train judges and other court personnel on aging and abuse | Issue standards for court performance and tracking of cases |
| | Provide information on model practices |

SOURCE: National Center for State Courts.

Courts can help prevent financial exploitation. As an illustration, courts can set up restricted accounts which require a court order for withdrawal of money, and they can restrict the sale of property (Seal, 2009). Some states, such as California, have *included financial institutions as mandated reporters.* Elders can also sign informed consent letters to banks to allow various organizations (e.g., APS) to review their banking activities (Seal, 2009).

*Legislation.* Legislators may need to pass laws governing *gifting of assets to members of professional organizations,* such as doctors and attorneys (Seal, 2009). Another legislative need is to modify bankruptcy laws to prevent elder abusers from confiscating an elder's assets and then declaring bankruptcy to escape responsibility for the abuse (Aaron, 2008). The California Assembly passed a law in 2008 that adds *undue influence* to the *definition of elder abuse.* In so doing, the adult civil protection code provides new remedies to vulnerable adults who have been defrauded. The law calls for fundamental changes in contract law. Some of the new remedies include recovery of damages, attorney fees, and court costs. The law makes it easier for victims to initiate lawsuits (Nerenberg, 2008).

One study emphasized that legislatures fashion laws regarding elder abuse without sufficient input from *police representatives* or other knowledgeable individuals from the *elder care community.* Legislators need to refashion their laws taking the opinions of these two groups into account (Payne & Berg, 2003). To promote understanding of *gerocriminology,* Payne (2005) had emphasized three major points: (a) the victimization experience of elderly people, (b) the victims' needs, and (c) rationales for this kind of criminal behavior.

*University courses on aging.* University courses on family violence have often failed to include the topic of elder abuse, but progress is starting to occur. Social work classes are finding student-friendly methods for strengthening the aging content of classes (Waites & Lee, 2006). In 2002, an American Psychological Association committee on aging addressed the U.S. Congress about the need for more geropsychologists (Levitt, 2002). To overcome knowledge gaps, states should require licensed professionals to take *continuing education courses* in health care, gerontology, elder abuse, and abuse of disabled persons (Otto, 2000). States are beginning to require continuing education. Commencing in 1995, social workers formed an organization (Action Network for Social Work Education) to advocate on behalf of social work educations and research.

## Community Involvement

Communities need to make a large number of changes in practices and policies to protect vulnerable elders. One modification communities can make is to *reduce the fragmentation of service delivery.* Usually there is no single community agency in charge of assisting abused elders. Some agencies provide certain services, such as Meals on Wheels, that are not available for use by other agencies, such as law enforcement. One problem is that personnel have a poor understanding of the role of other types of workers in different agencies.

*The Weinberg Center.* Fortunately, personnel working in the field of elder abuse seem more willing than personnel working in other areas of family violence (e.g., violence against female partners, rural workers) to join forces to provide protection and services. Professionals at the *Weinberg Center* for Prevention, Intervention and Research in Elder Abuse have mounted one of the most *comprehensive community responses detailed in the literature.* The multidisciplinary team works with a network of private and government agencies to address multiple needs, such as legal advocacy, housing, and education and support for informal caregivers (Reingold, 2006). One problem that can occur in multidisciplinary teams is different requirements for *maintenance of confidentiality.* Social workers, for instance, must meet standards that are different than those for law enforcement (Brandl et al., 2007).

Wayne County Michigan has a Senior Alliance dedicated to preserving and enhancing the independence of elder persons and those with disabilities named *Project Gatekeeper, Think S.A.F.E.* The program is a network of 50 programs and services, such as home delivery of meals, care management, and chore services. One seminal component of the network is to provide training to increase awareness of caregivers (Vail, 2008).

*Multidisciplinary teams.* Current approaches have identified *agency teamwork as the most viable form of response to the multifaceted problem of elder abuse* (e.g., Nerenberg, 2008). In other words, "it takes a village" to protect the vulnerable elderly. Such approaches improve victim identification as well as the quality of decision making concerning the most effective methods of intervening and which agencies are best suited to the task (Matlaw & Spence, 1994; Vinton, 2003).

A few communities have formed elderly *death review teams* to detect "gray murders" that may go undetected (Dayton, 2002). A web-based survey of 363 medical doctors determined that there was considerably amount of *death certificate inaccuracy* and *underreporting of injuries* in elderly people (Betz, Kelly, & Fisher, 2008). Discipline cross-training is the backbone of fatality review teams (Calkins, 2003).

Orange County, California, established an *Elder Abuse Forensic Center* to address elder abuse. A team of professionals, including a medical doctor, social worker, and police detective, meets at least once a week to assist each other in handling elder abuse reports. The team makes various decisions about cases, such as whether to prosecute alleged abusers or whether to provide caregiver support (J. Gross, 2006). In 2005, Lori Stiegel, a prominent elder law expert, worked with the American Bar Association to offer guidance on fatality review teams. She prepared a manual that presents "recipes" and "ingredients" that communities can adapt to their own needs (American Bar Association Commission on Law and Aging: http://wwwabanet.org/aging/fatalitymanual.pdf].

Several communities have inaugurated *Financial Abuse Specialist Teams (F.A.S.T.).* F.A.S.T. is a multidisciplinary team that includes a district attorney, a stock broker, a bank trust officer, a retired probate judge, and public guardian staff. Some of the team's duties include training APS representatives, public guardians, and ombudsmen in how to detect financial abuse of elders. Acting as a fiduciary SWAT team, F.A.S.T. sweeps into banks and other areas to safeguard seniors by suggesting that administrators put a hold on the seniors' assets (F.A.S.T., 2003).

Reports on most innovative programs aimed at reducing or preventing elder abuse have presented anecdotal accounts. Nerenberg (2003) tackled financial abuse by developing a *daily money management program* for elders. Weitzman and Weitzman (2003) designed a program to improve elders' communication skills, one element of which was the constructive handling of conflictual interactions. Project C.A.R.E. (Caregiver Alternatives to Running on Empty), which is available in 38 states, on the other hand, has provided assistance to caregivers of elders with dementia. The program may grant as much as $2,000 annually to minority and rural caregivers for such services as in-home and overnight respite care. C.A.R.E. has developed a network of community-based, comprehensive care support (C. M. Kelly & Williams, 2007).

*A research agenda.* A number of published appraisals, as well as previous editions of this text, have criticized the lack of empirical research on elder abuse (and the abuse of disabled persons). In 1991, an interdisciplinary group of researchers formulated a national agenda of research priorities on the subject of elder abuse. This group pinpointed the *need to make the following determinations* (Carp, 1999; Rabiner et al., 2006):

| Nature/extent of the problem | Societal costs/ consequences | Legal concerns |
|---|---|---|
| Etiology—Root causes Financial exploitation | Identification of abused elders | Prevention and treatment |

*Expanded research topics.* Further analyses revealed that the topics of research were quite limited. Prevalence estimates, typologies of abuse, and definitions represented the major content areas investigated. Another shortcoming was that the academic training of the first authors was also restricted, primarily to medicine, nursing, and social sciences. An analysis of the populations studied revealed an especially discouraging trend, because there were a disproportionate number of professionals, personnel, cases, and charts used, rather than elder participants. The bulk of the articles emanated from the United States with minimal research coming from developing countries.

Taking other weaknesses into account as well, Erlingsson (2007) typified the research as lacking in diversity. She states that "These patterns indicate that there is still, after 30 years, an unfulfilled need for basic knowledge-building material on elder abuse" (p. 72). She further laments the loss of dissertation writers as prospective researchers. Of this group, 59% do not appear as authors in additional research literature. Expansion of research should include any identifiable new types, such as pharmacological abuse (inappropriate control over sedation) (Acierno et al., 2009).

## Prevention

*Public awareness campaign.* One team of criminologists tested the prevention effects of a *public awareness campaign,* home visits, or *both* in a *public housing project.* The goal was to prevent revictimization of elders. This systematic controlled study of 403 abused elders and comparisons ascertained that *interventions had no impact on victims' knowledge about elder abuse or social services and did not improve elders' psychological well-being.* When victims received *both treatments,* however, they were *more likely to call police and report abuse incidents to researchers* (R. C. Davis, Medina, & Avitabile, 2001). The California State Legislature has devised a public awareness campaign to prevent elder abuse. One product to arise from the campaign is a booklet titled "A Citizen's Guide to Preventing and Reporting Elder Abuse" (cited in Cook-Daniels, 2003a). No outcome data about the effectiveness of the program are available.

*Improving official evaluations.* The National Center for Injury Prevention and Control (2002) has published recommendations for preventing elder abuse that focus primarily on improving evaluations of (a) efficacy of interventions, (b) strategies for changing recognized cultural norms supportive of abuse, (c) training programs for elder abuse and health professionals, (d) health consequences of abuse, (e) surveillance methods used for abuse, and (f) models for integrated community services. The center also notes that it is important to examine how individuals *come to be at risk* for both perpetration and victimization. In addition to social workers and physicians, laws have often required other personnel to serve as *mandated reporters*. Some of these individuals include law enforcement personnel, mental health professionals, dentists, and social workers. State social services departments are most frequently assigned the task of receiving reports of elder abuse (Wolf & Pillemer, 1989).

## Social Support/Social Connectedness

Because of the significant role social support plays in preventing elder abuse, the most important target of intervention should be the social environment of elders (Acierno et al., 2009). One innovative idea is that social support may not be as important to elder well-being and social connectedness. The connotation of *social support* includes four component types of support: (a) emotional, (b) instrumental (tangible aid), (c) informational, and (d) appraisal (evaluation). *Social connectedness* refers to pleasurable interaction (companionship), without requiring social support. Social connectedness is positively correlated with self-reported good health; social support may not be. Lack of social connectedness (loneliness) is associated with chronic health problems such as arthritis and lung disease (Ashida & Heaney, 2008; see also Shearer & Fleury, 2006). These findings point to a recommendation of modifying community centers, such as senior centers, to focus more intensely on *providing opportunities for elders to make friendships* (see Aday et al., 2006).

*Living arrangements—housing.* Some housing challenges faced by battered elderly women include (a) insufficient money, (b) no available roommates to share expenses, (c) limited job opportunities, (d) dependency on younger family, and (e) being considered a credit risk. Needing housing in a *rural community* presents even more acute challenges because shelters are nonexistent or too far away (Raymond, 2008; see also Teaster, Roberto, & Dugar, 2006).

*Innovative assisted-living facilities.* Thomas Day created a totally different type of facility—the *Eden Alternative.* In this holistic setting, elders take care of pets, visit school children, and accomplish other tasks that empower them. Costs of care greatly declined and health greatly improved. Day's newest conception for elder care is the Green House Project ("About Nursing Homes," n.d.)

*Aging in place.* A newer concept involving housing is referred to as *aging in place.* This idea encompasses the idea of finding ways to enable seniors to stay in their own homes. Services such as Meals on Wheels, for instance, may allow seniors to avoid going into long-term care (National Association for Home Care [http://www.NAHC.org/education/PDFs/HCAcert.pdf]; Sabia, 2008).

*Help from organizations.* Given the salience of living arrangements in *preventing elder mistreatment,* a wide variety of organizations has addressed the issue. As one illustration, there is an entire journal, the *Journal of Housing for the Elderly* (Haworth Press), that provides research on the topic. Examples of articles include one titled "'Smart Homes' for Patients at the End of Life," on the use of high-tech equipment for monitoring seniors to meet their needs more completely (Demiris & Hensel, 2009). Experts recommend that online-search capacity regarding housing for the elderly be improved. In addition to customary data such as the location of a facility, information should include data about bed size, services offered, and a *report card* of findings by objective organizations, patients, and the government (Castle & Sonon, 2006). The Administration on Aging (n.d.) provides some data comparing living arrangements (http://www.aoa.gov/aoaroot/elders_families/index.aspx).

*Elder fraud prevention.* For those attempting to prevent financial abuse, there is a list of *signs or clues of financial exploitation.* Some of these include the following (Rabiner et al., 2006):

| | |
|---|---|
| Unpaid bills | Caregiver's over-interest in money spent on the elder |
| Beneficiary changes | Care given to elder does not match elder's estate |
| Misuse of powers of attorney | Implausible explanations for use of elder's assets |
| Suspicious signatures on checks | Persons living with the elder refuse to pay rent |
| New "best friends" | Caregivers overcharge for their services |
| Many ATM withdrawals | Bank statements not delivered to house |
| Belongings or property missing | Significant changes in spending patterns |
| Unusual activity in bank account | |

One type of financial exploitation attracting increased attention is "death bed marriages." Typically, a much younger person would marry a wealthy senior, slowly isolate him/her, and manage to get access to bank accounts, become the beneficiary in a will, or at least try to exert spousal privilege for a share of the estate. Adult children or other relatives trying to get the marriage annulled face stiff legal challenges. Issues such as *competency* and *undue influence* come into question. Currently, it is very difficult to void these kinds of "unholy matrimony" (Krohn, 2010).

*Faith community fraud prevention programs.* A fraud prevention program developed in Denver, Colorado, has received high marks by the participants. The Office of Victims of Crime (OVC) reported on a successful *collaboration between the district attorney's office and 200 faith communities.* The goals of the program were to prevent, intervene, and provide services for elder fraud victims. Some of their activities included (a) clergy training seminars, (b) monthly fraud alerts, (c) "Power Against Fraud Seminars" provided for the whole congregation, or often provided at a lunch for seniors at the faith community's building (e.g., churches, temples), (d) establishment of a fraud assistance line to encourage disclosure, and (e) specialized program staff to function in needed capacities. District attorneys in other Colorado communities successfully replicated the program ("Partnership With Faith," 2006). An article by attorney Catherine Seal (2009) has covered a host of financial exploitation issues and outlined several preventive approaches (see also Curtis, 2004).

*Steps seniors can take themselves.* Seniors need to make a suitable choice for the agent of their power of attorney. They need to set up standards with respect to gifting of the senior's assets. What is more, the senior needs to require regular accountings of her assets and needs to designate someone to review the accounts. Having help with daily money management may be helpful. The senior may need someone to help pay his bills and help with budgeting. The *Social Security Administration stands ready to appoint a payee* for the incapacitated elder, but Social Security has put several safeguards in place, such as requiring an affidavit of incapacitation (Seal, 2009).

*Role of attorneys.* Attorneys could help safeguard dependent elders by *screening* their elderly clients for *financial exploitation.* There is a need for specially trained domestic violence and *elder law attorneys* to help elderly victims set up legal documents that more comprehensively prevent elder fraud. In particular, elder law attorneys need to focus on the stipulations included in a durable power of attorney. A third party, without a vested interest in the estate, needs to have access to the activities of the elder's agent to prevent fraudulent transfers of property and the like (Seal, 2009). (See the *Los Angeles Lawyer,* 2007, for an issue devoted to elder law.)

---

**SECTION SUMMARY**

### Practice, Policy, and Prevention Issues Related to Elder Abuse

Society has devoted a substantial amount of resources to combating elder abuse. In the area of elder abuse, social services such as adult protective services (APS) provide the bulk of assistance to the aged. This observation is less accurate for elder persons victimized by spouses. Shelters for victims of intimate partner violence (IPV) are ill-prepared to serve women 60+ years of age. To be precise, their focus has been limited to the needs of younger women with children. Domestic violence shelters, for instance, can rarely offer crisis accommodations to elderly women who require complicated medicine regimes, assistive devices, or architectural modifications (e.g., wheelchair ramps).

There are many gaps in service provision for abused elderly people. One example is the lack of age-specific counseling groups. A few studies evaluating programs for elders, such as following through with referrals for specialized help, consistently show benefits. Tracking of arrests of elder abusers showed no reduction in re-abuse rates.

*(Continued)*

(Continued)

Although evidence for prosecution was often lacking, prosecutors were likely to charge abusers of elders with more serious crimes than abusers of younger adults. Research on legal responses to elder abuse is growing. Examples include attempts to have sex offenders added to central registries and finding ways to reduce financial exploitation. A last example is modifying loopholes in the laws that allow Medicare/Medicaid fraud.

Health care providers have a special responsibility for screening elders and documenting identified abuse because elders so frequently consult doctors. There are debates about the value of mandatory reporting. Some outcome evaluations have found no significant benefit from screening, and most doctors are reluctant to report it. Rationales include impinging on a doctor's rapport with his patient and starting a chain-reaction that ultimately harms an elder. Medical researchers are working on effective screening protocols, and medical schools are incorporating more and more information about elder abuse into medical school curricula.

Policy revisions occur as issues come to light. The need for interagency collaboration has drawn considerable attention. Possibly the most noteworthy issue to arise in recent years has been the need for disaster preparedness. Responses during Hurricane Katrina focused national attention upon elders residing in nursing homes and hospitals. As usual, persons involved in delivering services to elders need to enroll in college courses on aging.

Improvements in the criminal justice system call for more training of police, prosecutors, and the judiciary. Judges, for example, need training in guardianship oversight and appropriate responses to elder abuse.

Community involvement in responding to elder abuse has been expanding. Some multidisciplinary teams, such as death review teams and financial abuse teams, all contribute to elders' safety. Last, methodologically sound research has been on the rise but lags behind research conducted in other fields of family violence.

Prevention of elder abuse extends beyond the customary public awareness campaigns. One proposal has been to improve official evaluations of programs such as training of health care workers. Recognition and amelioration of elders' needs for social connectedness should be a top priority. Day care programs may offer ideal settings for forming friendships. An elder's living arrangements have a profound impact on her well-being. Efforts to remove elder abusers (e.g., adult child) from an elder's home can bring about dramatic benefits. Some innovative thinkers have created very supportive villages for elders that improve social connectedness and feelings of empowerment by assigning tasks to elders such as taking on the responsibility for bird feeding. Finding ways to allow elderly people to "age in place" via services such as Meals on Wheels improves the independence and safety of many elders.

A number of preventive programs exist for preventing fraud against the elderly. Faith communities, for instance, may host luncheon seminars featuring expert speakers on legal matters such as selection of an individual to be the agent of a power of attorney. Engineers and architects have been working on "smart homes" for elders, homes that can monitor a senior's functioning while at home alone. Some attorneys have become experts in elder law to help seniors avoid fraud.

# SAME-SEX ELDER ABUSE: GAY, LESBIAN, BISEXUAL, AND TRANSGENDERED ELDERS

Very little is known about interpersonal violence against same-sex and gay, lesbian, bisexual, and transgendered (GLBT) elders. Abuse of individuals in this population often goes undetected and unassisted by medical and mental health personnel. Both *heterosexism* (denigration of nonheterosexual behavior) and *homophobia* (fear or hatred of a homosexual orientation) plague elders whose sexual orientation falls outside the typical range. Accordingly, scholarship on the topic must take into account individuals at the *intersection* of homophobia/heterosexism and abuse. It has not helped that the American Psychological Association categorized persons with GLBT orientations as mentally ill until 1973. Caretakers of GLBT elders may erroneously assume that the elderly people they encounter are not sexual. As a consequence, the caretakers ask embarrassing questions about their "opposite-sex" partner (Knauer, 2009).

*Prevalence of abuse.* There is little doubt that being an GLBT elder is a risk factor for abuse. In a survey of 56 GLBT seniors, the rates of reported abuse were as follows: (a) *Emotional psychological abuse—64.8%*, (b) *Health care discrimination—30.9%*, (c) *Sexual assault—12.7%*, and (d) *Self-Neglect—27.3%* (Cook-Daniels, 2008b). As described in a previous chapter, abusive partners among younger couples threaten to "out" their partner, a type of abuse unique to persons whose sexual orientation varies. In the case of elders, abusive *caregivers* compose another category of persons making the same threat (see Cahill & Smith, 2002).

*Gay, lesbian, bisexual, and transgendered elders.* Several issues for elders surfaced in a study of actual experiences of 56 GLBT elders (Cook-Daniels, 2008b). Two crucial problems occurred in the area of *housing* and *medical care.* First, some GLBT elders encountered such serious problems in gaining access to housing that they live in fear of abuse. Short of this concern, GLBT elders might have to live alone because other elders will not share housing with them. Moreover, some long-term care establishments deny them admission. Housing concerns are so acute that GLBT retirement villages have sprung up to serve this population. GLBT seniors have taken a "separation route" for housing needs. One such community is the Palms of Manasota in Florida (Knauer, 2009; D. Rosenberg, 2001).

Second, some GLBT seniors have come across problems with medical personnel. Occasionally, doctors will not provide treatment and nurses may mistreat this population even at locations such as the Veterans Administration (M. J. Brown & Groscup, 2008; Knauer, 2009). A case history provided by Loree Cook-Daniels (2007) tells the story of a transgendered man living in a nursing home.

---

**CASE HISTORY**   "They Laughed at My Genitals"

Mr. Adams approached a male social worker in his long-term care facility about abuse he suffered at the hands of two female nursing assistants. Over the recent past, the women noted unusual aspects of his genitalia. For one thing, Mr. Adam's urine did not get expelled in the customary fashion. First the women made fun of his small penis size. Next they tried different techniques to force him to have an erection, and when he didn't they ridiculed him. In the end, they used some objects to rape him anally.

The female nursing home workers abused him whenever they found him alone, and Mr. Adams was fearful of what they might do next to hurt him. Mr. Adams was in tears, but he did not want the social worker to tell his nephew, who was his guardian; nor did he want the women fired. What should the social worker do?

*Needs of homosexual elders.* Many policies tangential to elder abuse affect GLBT elders. Cahill and Smith (2002) found "legal" discrimination against GLBT elders in the following areas: (a) denial of senior center services; (b) noneligibility of longtime same-sex partners for spousal Social Security benefits, despite their having made payments into the system; (c) noneligibility of same-sex partners for pensions automatically set aside for spouses; (d) restriction of access to federally subsidized senior housing; and (e) barriers to receiving health care and long-term health care. Some states that allow civil unions have obviated some of these problems by giving a partner equivalent rights as a spouse (Riggle, Rostosky, & Prather, 2006).

Other unmet needs may include the *lack of a family to provide social support.* GLBT seniors often may either have no children or be estranged from their children, brothers, and sisters. GLBT seniors may choose to fulfill this shortfall with networks of other GLBT individuals (Knauer, 2009). A small qualitative investigation of rural lesbians ($N = 15$) outlined some of the additional burdens placed upon them. The need to create informal networks with other lesbians could easily mean that these lesbians would have to "leave their immediate communities and travel to access support networks" (Comerford, Henson-Stroud, Sionainn, & Wheeler, 2004, p. 431.). Lesbian elders with mobility or health problems faced more challenges in trying to leave the area.

## CROSS-CULTURAL ELDER ABUSE

The abuse of elders by caretakers appears to be a worldwide phenomenon. Some conceptions about elder abuse around the world are similar to those in the United States. By the mid-1980s, however, a few reports from other countries began to trickle in (see Bužgová & Ivanová, 2009; Kivela, 1995). Recognition of elder abuse worldwide has rested primarily on its "discovery" in the United States and Britain (see Kosberg & Garcia, 1995a; Kurrle & Naughtin, 2008). At first, experts in other countries tended to deny the existence of this form of abuse in their own countries (P. F. Dunn, 1995). In Ireland, for instance, the minister of health reportedly said that "no cases of abuse of the elderly were formally reported to me in 1989 or 1990" (quoted in Horkan, 1995, pp. 131–132).

*Conceptions of elder abuse* reveal some distinctions across the globe. According to a 2001 report published by the World Health Organization, younger adults may accuse elders of *witchcraft* or of causing too much rain and then banish them to isolated locations. In many areas of the world (e.g., Hong Kong, India) *abandonment* is particularly prevalent and oftentimes is associated with insufficient income (e.g., Shah, Veedon, & Vasi, 1995). Malley-Morrison (2004) provided a thorough review of international elder abuse. Some examples include the following: (a) showing *disrespect* to elders occurs frequently and is an especially painful type of abuse; (b) being abusive in public—failing to "save face" (Korea); (c) disregarding the opinions, advice, and feelings of elders (Somalia); (d) failing to enact one's appropriate gender role (Lebanon); (e) failing to be a good conversational partner (Japan); (f) placement in a nursing home (Nicaragua); and (g) and isolating/hiding them in cupboards and other place (China). The number of cross-cultural studies is growing. The following section provides a sample of cross-cultural and ethnic studies.

## Prevalence of Cross-Cultural Elder Abuse

Cross-cultural studies of *adult family violence* are relatively new. Most of them have limited their research to other forms of family violence. International studies of elder abuse usually rely on small qualitative studies. A few research endeavors have been able to obtain some indication of the prevalence of elder abuse in specific countries.

## Asian Countries

In Korea, a population-based study of 15,230 persons reported the rate of any one category of elder abuse at 6.3% (J. Oh, Kim, Martins, & Kim, 2006). Of older Chinese couples (aged 50–64), 5% reported hitting a partner (Wang, Parish, Laumann, & Luo, 2009). Because of China's one-child policy, fewer adult children are available to care for their parents, and more elders need to live in nursing homes (Zhan, Liu, Guan, & Bai, 2006). (See the website for statistics from other countries.)

## Israel

Researchers in some nations have been especially active in researching elder abuse. Researchers reported the following rates of abuse in rural Israel, where 18.4% of elderly people said they had been abused: (a) *Neglect—18.0%,* (b) *verbal abuse—8.0%,* (c) *economic abuse—6.6%,* (d) *physical or sexual abuse—2.0%,* and (e) *limitation of freedom—2.7%* (Eisikovits, Lowenstein, & Winterstein, 2005). A study of different techniques for assessing elder abuse demonstrated that *hospital workers* found *evidence of abuse much more frequently* than the elder residents disclosed it (Cohen, Halevi-Levin, Gagin, & Friedman, 2007). For an article containing case studies, see Band-Winterstein & Eisikovits, 2009. (See the website for information on Israeli nursing homes.)

## Spain

A team of investigators in Spain were able to obtain data about suspected elder abuse and its correlates. They interviewed 875 persons 75+ years of age and found that the prevalence of abuse ranged from 25.8% to 32.8% for any kind of abuse. In addition, they uncovered four kinds of behavior defined as abuse: (a) *neglect—*16.0%, (b) *psychosocial abuse—*15.2%, (c) *financial abuse—*4.7%, and (d) *physical abuse—*0.1%. The major risk factors for abuse included living with family members—excluding spouse, 85+ years of age, cognitive impairment, depression, social isolation, and frequent bladder incontinence (Garre-Olmo et al., 2009).

## United Kingdom

Between 2006 and 2007, researchers in England conducted a nationally representative survey of elder abuse in the community. Of the 2,111 elderly people 66+ years of age who responded to the survey items, about 2.6% reported abuse. This percentage is undoubtedly an underestimate because of reluctance to disclose and because a number of people in the specified age group suffered from dementia. More women than men were victimized. *Risk factors* for abuse were *loneliness, depression,* and *poor quality of life.* The most frequent form of abuse was neglect (1.1%), followed by financial exploitation (0.7%), psychological abuse (0.4%), physical abuse (0.4%), and sexual abuse/harassment (0.2%). Unexpectedly, almost 75% of elders queried had disclosed their abuse to someone, such as a family member, friend, health professional, or social worker. Given the percentage of self-disclosed abuse, the researchers wonder why so few official reports to social services occurred. One policy implication is that community nurses need more exposure to this type of research (Manthorpe et al., 2007).

## ETHNIC ELDER ABUSE

### African Americans

An inquiry of 35 African Americans disclosed that they found physical elder abuse especially intolerable, but they were less aware of the preponderance of financial exploitation of elderly persons and they expressed less concern about it (Tauriac & Scruggs, 2006). (See also Paranjape, Corbie-Smith, Thompson, & Kaslow, 2009).

### American Indians

A duo of investigators conducted an exploratory study of 56 tribal members: facility residents ($n = 13$) and nonresidents ($n = 43$). In contrast to a number of findings, the elders housed in assisted-living facilities were significantly happier, were less lonely, and felt they had significantly more social support than nonresident elders (C. M. Brown & Gibbons, 2008).

### Chinese Americans

A telephone survey of 77 Chinese Americans ascertained that 7.1% of women and 5.6% of men reported being victimized by minor physical violence using CTS1 (a nonsignificant difference). Men were more likely than women to believe that intimate partner violence (IPV) was justified. More men than women believed that IPV was a growing problem. Men were generally more acculturated than women, and less acculturated persons were less likely to think male-to-female violence was a form of IPV (Shibusawa & Yick, 2007).

### Korean Americans

Traditionally, Korean Americans participate in a type of co-ownership of elder parents' financial assets, an arrangement that many African Americans and Whites consider a form of financial exploitation. Korean Americans are also especially likely to blame elder victims for their own abuse (Moon & Benton, 2000).

## Cultural Competence

Some observers claim that most professionals who work with elder abuse victims in the United States *lack the competencies* needed to work with members of marginalized groups. For research purposes, a team of specialists, for example, have pondered the question of obtaining informed consent ethically using dementia patients. Their innovative approach is to require suitable consent proxies based on videotaped encounters that include a patient, a companion, and a physician (J. Sugarman et al., 2007).

## ABUSE OF DISABLED PERSONS

People of all ages can be disabled, but elderly people have a larger percentage than other age groupings. People with disabilities represent approximately 19% to 20% of the population (Rand & Harrell, 2009; D. D. Sorensen, 2004). Some major forms of disability include developmental disability (e.g., cerebral palsy), traumatic brain injury, major mental disorders, degenerative brain diseases (e.g., Parkinson's), and organic brain damage. Researchers have been slow to investigate crimes against the disabled, including those committed by family members. Emblematic of the problem is that researchers did not extract data about disabled persons from larger pools of data even when the data were available. The *invisibility* of handicapped people, possibly stemming from stigmatization, may be one reason for this *omission in research* (Mays, 2006). Despite the 1998 *Crime Victims with Disabilities Awareness Act* (Public Law 105–301) that required coverage of handicapped persons, it has taken years to obtain nationally representative data on abuse of disabled persons.

## Defining Disability

The U.S. Census Bureau's American Community Survey defines disability as *sensory, physical, mental, or emotional conditions, lasting six months or more, that make it difficult to perform activities of daily living, such as walking, climbing stairs, dressing, bathing, learning, or remembering.* Over the past decade, leaders in the field have recast initial conceptions of disability and moved away from the medical model of pathology, loss, and mental and physical deficit. The new social paradigm maintains that disability is the intersection between the traits of the individual (i.e., specific handicaps, mobility, socioeconomic status) and the characteristics of their environment (natural, structural, social, and cultural) (National Institute on Disability and Rehabilitation Research, 2003). In other words, society's concepts of disability play a role in the definition of disability, not just the individual's impairments. As an illustration, society's assumptions that disabled people cannot function in the workplace prevents employers from providing jobs that disabled people can do effectively (e.g., bag groceries).

*Types of disabilities.* Researchers have sharpened the meaning of abuse against disabled persons by including types of abuse that are seldom used against the nondisabled. Interwoven among very common forms of mistreatment (e.g., hitting) are *terrorizing behaviors, severe rejection, isolation, ignoring behaviors, and use of physical and medical restraints.* Other types of abuse may include withholding services that the disabled person cannot perform unaided, such as toileting, bathing, and feeding. It is not uncommon for abusive care providers to withhold food and water. Furthermore, an abuser might unplug an assistive device or place a walker just out of reach. Another form of abuse is exemplified by the utilization of targeted behaviors like moving furniture around in the house so that a blind person will stumble and fall.

## Attitudes Toward Disabled Persons

Society oppresses, socially devalues, and dehumanizes disabled women (and men), thus making them even more vulnerable to abuse than others (Hassounch-Phillips, & McNeff, 2005). Attitudes toward disabled women reflect negative stereotyping:

- Disabled mothers cannot perform satisfactorily as mothers.
- Disabled women are either asexual or promiscuous.
- Disabled women cannot discuss serious matters.

Researchers may unwittingly contribute to stereotyping by conducting studies on topics such as the *poor self-concept* and *over-compliance* of disabled women. It might be more beneficial to conceptualize disabled women as victims of *patriarchy* and to view their problems from a *feminist stance.* By placing disabled women in the position of deprivation, it allows others to have control over them (Mays, 2006).

## Estimates of Abuse of Disabled Persons

There is every reason to believe that nearly all prevalence estimates of abuse of disabled persons represent vast underreporting because of the nature of this population's handicaps (e.g., deafness, speech impairments). Nonetheless, it seems clear that disabled people are more likely to be abused than nondisabled people (e.g., S. L. Martin et al., 2006). Another feature hampering investigations of abuse of the disabled is the failure of a large proportion of disabled persons to recognize abuse. For many disabled women (and men), *abuse has been such a routine aspect of their living condition that it seems normal.*

There are not only family members around who might be abusive, but also an entire cadre of personal assistants and medical personnel who might perpetrate abuse. Because the services that caregivers provide are very personal and because caregivers have access to victims' bodies over long periods of time, the abuses they inflict can be markedly diverse. As with elders in nursing homes, it seems necessary to widen the category of abusers of disabled persons to anyone who provides care whether an intimate partner, a family member, or a paid caregiver (e.g., Barranti & Yuen, 2008; Nosek & Howland, 1998).

*National Criminal Victimization Survey (NCVS): handicapped prevalence rates.* In 2009, the first national representative survey of *noninstitutionalized* handicapped adults became available. This survey is unique because interviewers attempted to use *proxy interviews* when needed and safe to do so. (A proxy interview is one in which someone else answers for a communication-handicapped respondent, being careful to avoid perpetrators.) According to NCVS's special report on crimes against people with disabilities (Rand & Harrell, 2009), violent *victimization rates for nonfatal violence against disabled are as follows:*

- Male-to-*disabled female* IPV … … … … …16.1%
- Female-to-*disabled male* IPV … … … …….5.4%
- 56% of crimes against disabled persons were those against multiply disabled persons.
- Age-adjusted rates of nonfatal crimes against disabled persons were 1.5 times higher than the rate for persons without disabilities.
- 34% of crimes against persons with disabilities were nonfatal violent crimes (e.g., rape).

*Centers for Disease Control and Prevention (CDC) data.* One researcher used the Behavioral Risk Factor Surveillance System database ($N = 356,112$) to examine many dissimilarities associated with gender and disability. This study was unique because the data came from a large population-based database. In particular, she searched for dissimilarities regarding abuse and relationship to the abuser. She classified data by gender: Women ($n = 219,911$) and Men ($n = 136,201$) and identified disabled women ($n = 49,756$). Chi-square analyses compared participant variation on a number of additional dimensions such as employment status and demographics. Many significant differences emerged (D. L. Smith, 2008). A few *highlights of the abuse are* as follows:

- Disabled women suffer more abuse than nondisabled women *and* disabled men.
- Nondisabled women experience abuse almost exclusively from their male partners.
- Disabled women who experience multiple forms of abuse are older than nondisabled women.
- Disabled abused women are less educated, less employed, and less likely to be in a relationship than nondisabled women.
- Disabled women suffering multiple forms of abuse are less employed than disabled men.

*Estimates of abuse of disabled.*

- adults who are both mentally ill and have a substance abuse disorder are more likely to be victimized by physical abuse and IPV than those without a disability (Wolf-Branigin, 2007).
- Homeless and seriously mentally ill women experience a victimization rate of 97% (L. A. Goodman, Dutton, & Harris, 1995)
- Studies of male IPV against women with severe psychiatric disorders (e.g., schizophrenia) have rates varying from 21% to 75% (Briere et al., 1997).
- Disabled women suffer an average of 3.9 years of physical and sexual abuse before escaping compared with 2.5 years for nondisabled women (Young, Nosek, Howland, Chanpong, & Rintala, 1997).

Disparities in definitions for categorizing individuals as disabled or nondisabled, along with disparities in making statistical adjustments, may be responsible for some inconsistencies in outcomes. For one thing, the handicapped population as a whole is older than the non-handicapped population. Surveyors such as NCVS often statistically adjust results of groupings of individuals on the basis of age or other variables.

## Sexual Assault of Disabled Persons

As a rule, society has frequently overlooked handicapped individuals' constitutionally guaranteed sexual rights by curtailing their sexual activities. All the same, sexual assault/sexual coercion are very common in this population. Abusers frequently use deception to gain sexual access to disabled women (L. R. Taylor & Gaskin-Laniyan, 2007), leading to an abuse rate that is twice the rate of nondisabled women (e.g., Powers, Oschwald, Maley, Saxton, & Eckles, 2002). Inspection of rape crisis data provided a different type of evidence about disparities in sexual abuse. Therapists at these centers counseled adult survivors of child incest/sexual assault, adult victims of sexual assault, stalking victims, and others. Chi-square analyses disclosed that *47.6% of the disabled group of women* suffered adult sexual assault/abuse contrasted with 39.4% of the nondisabled group. Of women seeking counseling for childhood incest/sexual assault, 21.1% were disabled compared with 25.1% who were not disabled (Grossman & Lundy, 2008).

*Capacity to consent.* Complicating the issue of substantiating sexual assault of disabled victims is the issue of *capacity to consent.* Determining capacity to consent is complicated by many legal and ethical mandates. First, the *legal age for consent,* for example, varies widely across states (e.g., 14–18 years). Second, there are several criteria for inferring consent capacity: (a) safety, (b) voluntariness, (c) non-exploitiveness, (d) nonabusiveness, (e) ability to say "no," and (f) appropriateness of a time and location (Lyden, 2007; Stavis, 2005; see also Sundram, 2006a).

## Perpetrators of Abuse of Disabled Persons

The categories of offenders of disabled persons are relatively extensive because of additional caregivers (e.g., physical rehabilitation providers, bathing assistants) and a larger number of strangers (e.g., delivery persons—supplies for incontinence) eager to take advantage of disabled persons. See Table 12.14 for summaries of the relationship between perpetrators and disabled victims.

**TABLE 12.14**    Relationships of Abuser of Disabled Persons and Their Abusers

| Offender Relationship to Victim | | Disabled Victims | | |
|---|---|---|---|---|
| | | Relationship | Males | Females |
| Intimate male partner | 80% | Intimate partner | 5.4% | 16.1% |
| Family member | 31% | Relative | 3.0% | 12.5% |
| Acquaintance | 16% | Acquaintance | 39.1% | 31.6% |
| Caretaker/health professional | 12% | Stranger | 40.4% | 33.5% |
| Stranger | 8% | Don't know | 12.2% | 6.3% |

SOURCE: Milberger et al., 2003.          SOURCE: Rand & Harrell, 2009 (*N* = 1,068).

*Institutionalized disabled person and abuse.* A Swedish survey of caregivers of adult persons with intellectual disabilities yielded findings reminiscent to those obtained with institutionalized elders. Responses of 122 staff members yielded the following percentages: (a) 35% said they had been implicated in or witnessed a violent incidence toward a disabled adult, (b) 14% admitted to being the perpetrators in a violent incident, and (c) 61% said they had been the victim of a disabled adult's violence. Most of the abuse was physical and occurred in helping situations when the disabled person did not cooperate (M. Strand, Benzein, & Saveman, 2004).

## Criminal Justice System Responses

Laws attempting to end discrimination against handicapped persons have evolved over the last few decades. In 1990, Congress enacted the *Americans with Disabilities Act (ADA)*. Although rights under ADA were asserted (e.g., unwarranted firing) and were presented in court, the Supreme Court made decisions that weakened the intentions of the ADA. Illustrative of the debacle was the Court's definition of disability. If a person had extremely poor eyesight but glasses brought his vision back into normal range, he could not be considered disabled. Amendments to the ADA made in 2008 (ADAAA) and implemented in 2009 specifically rejected four of the Supreme Court's rulings. Arguably, the major improvement of ADAAA was to amend the legal definition of disability. Now, a person with extremely poor vision could be considered disabled whether glasses offsetting the problem were available or not (see Pardeck & Pardeck, 2007).

## Characteristics of Disabled Victims and Their Abusers

Disabled women suffer from a multitude of disabilities that included arthritis, cerebral palsy, visual and hearing impairments, multiple sclerosis, traumatic brain injuries, strokes, post-polio symptoms, spina bifida, spinal cord injuries, and amputations. One inquiry provided a summary of some demographic descriptions of disabled women. The average age of the research participants was 45.3 years, and 41% were laid-off or unemployed. Although most of the women (77%) lived independently, 60% had used at least one personal assistance service. In terms of relationship status, 42% were single, 28% were divorced or separated, 24% were married, and 5% were widowed. Over half of the abused women (53%) volunteered the information that their male partners were using alcohol or drugs at the time of the abuse (Milberger et al., 2003).

## Disclosure of Abuse and Help-Seeking Activities

A multipart investigation of safety-promoting behaviors among women with disabilities revealed encouraging findings. One reason for a favorable outcome may be that research participants were middle-aged ($m = 50.75$ years) and relatively well educated (70% had some college). Researchers factor analyzed questionnaire data obtained via a computer-assisted self-interview program and identified six categories of safety-promoting behaviors: (a) *seeking abuse-related safety information,* (b) *building abuse-related safety-promoting skills,* (c) *using relationship support,* (d) *planning for emergencies,* (e) *taking legal action,* and (f) *managing safety in personal assistance relationships* (Powers et al., 2009).

*Disclosure to police.* The NCVS (Rand & Harrell, 2009) survey found *no significant differences* between disabled and nondisabled persons in disclosing abuse to the police. The disabled persons relative to the nondisabled did, however, report that police did not respond to their calls. Moreover, the NCVS reported no significant differences in contacting victim services. A different study, though, found that disabled *sexually assaulted women* do *not* as readily turn to rape crisis centers after an assault as nondisabled women do. Of 44,000 research participants, with and without disabilities, social scientists found that only 2.5% of those served were disabled. Those who were disabled, however, received comparatively more hours of services, specific services, family and phone counseling, and medical and other advocacy services (Grossman & Lundy, 2008).

*Barriers facing deaf individuals.* An investigation of 51 *deaf people,* 15 *service providers,* and 10 *police officers* identified additional barriers encountered by *deaf sexual assault victims* seeking help. These barriers included the following unique circumstances: (a) facing stereotypes of both deaf people *and* sexual assault victims; (b) closeness of the deaf community, a situation that compromises privacy and anonymity, especially if the perpetrator is deaf; (c) service providers' failure to recognize that deaf people have established a deaf "culture" and do not necessarily view deafness as a medical problem; and (d) obtaining help via teletypewriter (TTY) devices when responders, such as those at 911, the police department, and social service agencies, do not know how to operate them. These impediments often create a *strong sense of isolation* among deaf sexual assault victims (Obinna, Krueger, Osterbaan, Sadusky, & DeVore, 2006). Language impairments may also place females and possibly males at elevated risk for sexual assault (Brownlie, Jabbar, Beitchman, Vida, & Atkinson, 2007).

## Practice, Policy, and Prevention

There are a number of interventions and policy initiatives that should improve the quality of life of persons with disabilities. Some of these are as follows:

- Psychologists and other professionals need to be aware of their own prejudices against disabled people (Behnke, 2009).
- Provide electronic memory aids that can be programmed for disabled persons (e.g., doctor's appointments) (Cohen-Mansfield et al., 2005).
- Develop learning DVDs with input from disabled persons (Boyden, Esscopri, Ogi, Brennan, & Kalsy-Lillico, 2009).
- Be aware that 32.3% of family-based disabled adults need financial support; 40% of these live in a household where the primary income earner is 60+ years of age (Fujiura, 2010).
- Provide transitional services for young disabled persons going to college (Kirkendall, Doueck, & Saladino, 2009).
- Foster independence through health-promoting activities in readiness for the Special Olympics (Mackey, Lynnes, Nichols, & Temple, 2009).

## ABUSE IN NURSING HOMES (LONG-TERM CARE FACILITIES)

Closely related to abuse of elders in their homes is abuse and neglect by caregivers in nursing homes. As the two areas of elder abuse and domestic violence have started to join together, some authorities have called for a redefinition of elder abuse as *abuse in later life* (Brandl & Raymond, 2004). Although abuse of residents in long-term care may not technically qualify as family violence, caregivers of the elderly and disabled often carry out very intimate tasks, such as providing bathing assistance. *The lack of adequate care and the abuse that take place in America's nursing homes is a national disgrace.*

*Complaints against nursing homes.* The U.S. Department of Health & Human Services (DHHS) receives numerous complaints of abuse, inadequate care, and fraud in the country's nursing homes. The top seven complaints of nursing home residents from 1996 to 2000 were as follows: (a) physical abuse, (b) resident-to-resident abuse, (c) verbal/mental abuse, (d) gross neglect, (e) other abuse or exploitation, (f) financial abuse, and (g) sexual abuse (U. S. Department of Health & Human Services, OIG Report, 2003). The 2004 APS Survey (Teaster et al., 2006) of abuse and neglect substantiated 6.2% of the cases in long-term care compared with 89.3% in domestic settings. Another 1.8% occurred in "other" settings. Thus, abuse of elders is less likely to occur in nursing homes than elsewhere. A report from the Office of Inspector General of the DHHS unveiled a number of disturbing findings: (a) 94% of for-profit nursing homes sustained citations for various violations and (b) about 17% of the facilities received citations for *actual harm* to patients. Abuses included infected bedsores, poor nutrition, medication mix-ups, and neglect (Levinson, 2008; Pear, 2008). Also, a contemporary study has highlighted the probability that if an elder suffers one type of abuse, she is likely to suffer at least one additional type—**polyvictimization** (Post et al., 2010).

*Sexual abuse in nursing homes.* In the past decade, research has advanced regarding *sexual abuse of nursing home residents.* One disturbing finding is that some residents are registered sex offenders. Another is that nursing home administrators are unclear about their obligations to warn other residents and staff about sex offenders (U.S. General Accounting Office, 2006). The most complete investigation and review of sexual abuse comes from the research of Ramsey-Klawsnik and her colleagues (2007). See Table 12.15 for a condensed version of her findings.

**TABLE 12.15**   Sexual Abuse in Long-Term Care Facilities

| | |
|---|---|
| Facilities fail to substantiate valid cases | Most victims are female—some male |
| Substantiation rate is 25% to 32% | Most offenders are long-term care employees |
| Facilities delay notification of law enforcement | Second largest category of offenders is residents |
| Police rarely arrest | Some employees have criminal records |
| Few prosecutions/convictions | Some residents are registered sex offenders |
| Most perpetrators are males | |

SOURCE: Modified summary of findings of Ramsey-Klawsnik, Teaster, Mendiondo, Marcum, and Abner, 2008.

*Operations of the DHHS.* The U.S. Department of Health & Human Services, following the dictates of Congress, has established regulations governing elder care in long-term facilities. The core mission of the Inspector General's Office of the DHHS is to promote honesty, economy, and efficiency in its *oversight role* of nursing home abuse. Data about abuse reach federal regulatory agencies through a long and circuitous route:

1. Congress establishes minimum standards of care.
2. The Centers for Medicare/Medicaid Services (CMS) translate these laws into regulations (about 150) and provide guidance and instructions for implementation.
3. Nursing home administrators must routinely report events/infractions to the state agencies.
4. States license/monitor their long-term health homes.
5. States must report infractions/events to CMS.
6. CMS inspects/monitors, withholds government funds, and informs law enforcement as necessary to combat abuse.

*Costs.* The bottom line for proving adequate care is cost. In 2005, the total amount spent on long-term care services in the United States was $206.6 billion. The costs are borne by the federal government, the states, private insurance, out-of-pocket funds, and by other sources. Regrettably, to avoid increased costs, state officials may falsify reports by claiming that nursing homes are in compliance with government regulations. (See the Medicare websites: "Nursing Home Compare," 2008, at http://www.medicare.gov/nhcompare/home.asp) and "Paying for Long-Term Care," 2009, at http://www.longtermcare.gov/LTC/main; see also Cook-Daniels, 2006, for a review of other interagency failures to cooperate.)

*Lack of interagency cooperation.* A report about possible fraud in New Mexico's Health Services Department stated that these state agencies stonewalled the federal Office of the Inspector General by refusing to turn over documents and by misdirecting the flow of information (Furlow, 2010). In testimony before Congress, the Inspector General provided an example of fraud. Medicare (in receipt of falsified documents) allowed reimbursement for renting equipment that was less expensive to buy, resulting in the waste of $3 billion over 5 years (Testimony, 2007). In 2008, David Hoffman wrote that *effective compliance,* however, does *not prevent institutional elder neglect* (cited in Mead, 2009).

*Nursing home personnel.* Relevant to cost considerations is the selection of personnel hired to care for elders. Often, long-term care facilities lack enough funding to hire more workers. Less than 10% have enough personnel to provide good care (U.S. Department of Health & Human Services, 2002; see also Castle, 2008). Several studies have pointed out that understaffing, along with low pay, contribute to burnout and a high turnover rate of employees (e.g., Purk & Lindsay, 2006). From a different viewpoint, the characteristics of the facility (e.g., staff cohesion, attractive location) are more closely tied to staff turnover than remuneration (Konetzka, Stearns, Konrad, Magaziner, & Zimmerman, 2005; see also Noelker, Ejaz, Menne, & Jones, 2006). One analysis discovered that quality of care decreased for patients whose cases required extensive history-taking, counseling, medication prescribing, and diabetes (Min et al., 2005). Estimates of additional costs to the Medicare/Medicaid budget for 2001 to improve the staff/resident ratio reached $7.6 billion (U.S. General Accounting Office, 2002b).

*Certified nursing assistants* (CNAs), who provide approximately 90% of patient care, are the employees *most likely to abuse patients*. They also are the employees *most likely to be abused* by nursing home residents (see Stanley, Martin, Michel, Welton, & Nemeth, 2007). The U.S. Bureau of Labor Statistics has shown that caregivers suffer a higher rate of injury from patient assaults and physical overextension (e.g., lifting) than do many other types of workers (Payne & Appel, 2007). One survey of CNAs ($N = 76$) established that CNAs experienced a median of 26 aggressive acts by nursing home residents but reported only about 5% (L. A. Snyder, Chen, & Vacha-Haase, 2007).

*Situational factors.* One investigation found that two situational factors were strongly related to CNAs' propensity to abuse: staff burnout and level of staff-patient conflict (Singer, 2002). Nursing home administrators do not routinely require nursing homes to use a number of hiring safeguards that experts have recommended, such as (a) checking prospective employees for criminal backgrounds, (b) screening unlicensed employees, (c) reporting candidates with questionable abuse backgrounds to appropriate nurses' registries, and (d) reporting suspected abuse to local law enforcement agencies.

*Registries.* A national survey of abusive nursing home workers showed that only 21 states maintain *central registries/databases* of abusive workers (Teaster et al., 2006). In addition, the registries are problematic because of liability, undetermined effectiveness, and cost issues (Duke, 1999). Not withstanding such concerns, nursing home administrators must screen employees thoroughly and report all abusive staff to local law enforcement and abuse registries. Missouri has provided other states with an example of an excellent response system to elder abuse ("Elder Abuse," 2006).

*Accountability.* No one is held accountable for unsatisfactory conditions in nursing homes. Although congressional committees decry nursing home abuse and neglect, their remedies are inadequate, frequently consisting of little more than calls for additional studies (Singer, 2002). *Suing a nursing home for failure to protect* its residents may be one remedy. On March 5, 2010, a 94-year-old woman with dementia won a $12 million settlement from a nursing home where she was raped by an undocumented immigrant employed as a dietary aide (City News Service, 2010).

*Preventing long-term care abuse.* If the underlying inability to prevent nursing home abuse is cost, the most obvious solution lies in the augmentation of government subsidies for certified nursing assistants (CNAs). CNAs usually pay to be trained for certification and then earn minimum wages. In 2005, the total amount spent on long-term care services in the United States was $206.6 billion. Another pivotal step is *better training for CNAs*. Effective training consists primarily of stress and anger management, conflict resolution skills, and abuse reporting information (Menio & Keller, 2000). Last, class action lawsuits on behalf of patients may be the best approach when regulatory protection in nursing homes has failed (e.g., Intagliata, 2002).

Experts have advanced several other proposals for eliminating nursing home abuse and improving quality of care: (a) *using gerontological clinical nurse specialists to support improvement* (Popejoy et al., 2000) and (b) *adopting national standards against which compliance could be judged empirically* (Huber, Borders, Badrak, Netting, & Nelson, 2001).

## DISCUSSION QUESTIONS

1. How does elder abuse compare with abuse of younger adults? What is elder self-neglect?
2. What sorts of individuals are most likely to abuse elders?
3. How is caregiver stress related to elder abuse?
4. Should society accept sexuality among elderly and disabled persons? Why or why not?
5. If you were an elder vulnerable to abuse, which country would be your least preferred choice? Why?
6. What factors impede effective criminal justice responses (police, prosecutors, and judiciary) to elder abuse and abuse of disabled persons?
7. What are the benefits of interagency collaboration between the various agencies, professional groups, and private organizations concerned with elder abuse?
8. Devise an elder abuse program and propose how you might test the program's effectiveness.
9. What are some of the forms of abusing disabled persons that appear to be unique?
10. What elder abuse problems and responses to abuse occur in nursing homes?
11. Should the "Average Joe or Jane" trained caretaker be required to provide services for a GLBT elder?

For chapter-specific resources including audio and video links, SAGE research articles, additional case studies, and more, please visit www.sagepub.com/barnett3e.

# Abbreviations

| | |
|---|---|
| AAPC | American Association for Protecting Children |
| AARP | American Association of Retired Persons |
| AAS | Abuse Assessment Screen |
| ABA | American Bar Association |
| ABI | Abusive Behavior Inventory |
| AFCARS | Adoption and Foster Care Analysis & Reporting System |
| ASA | adult sexual assault |
| AFDC | Aid to Families with Dependent Children |
| AOD | alcohol and other drugs |
| APA | American Psychological Association |
| APD/ASPD | antisocial personality disorder |
| APS | adult protective services |
| APSAC | American Professional Society on the Abuse of Children |
| AS | Accountability Scale |
| ASA | adult sexual assault |
| ASFA | Adoption and Safe Families Act |
| BIP | batterer intervention program |
| BIS | batterer intervention system |
| BJS | Bureau of Justice Statistics |
| BPD | borderline personality disorder |
| BPO | borderline personality organization |
| BRFSS | Behavioral Risk Factor Surveillance System |
| CAPTA | Child Abuse Prevention and Treatment Act–2006 (2010) |
| CBT | cognitive-behavioral therapy |
| CCV | common couple violence |
| CDC | Centers for Disease Control and Prevention |
| CES-D | Centers for Epidemiologic Studies Depression scale |
| CJS | criminal justice system |
| CP | corporal punishment |
| CPA | child physical abuse |
| CPS | Child Protective Services |

| | |
|---|---|
| CROWD | Center for Research on Women With Disabilities |
| CSA | child sexual abuse |
| CSI | Coping Strategies Inventory |
| CT | cognitive therapy |
| CTS1, CTS2 | Conflict Tactics Scales |
| CTSPC | Parent-Child Conflict Tactics Scale |
| DAS | Dyadic Adjustment Scale |
| DHHS | U.S. Department of Health & Human Services |
| DNA | deoxyribonucleic acid |
| DOJ | U.S. Department of Justice |
| DOMA | Defense of Marriage Act |
| DSM | Diagnostic and Statistical Manual of Mental Disorders |
| DV | dating violence |
| DVFRT | domestic violence fatality review team |
| EVA | Evaluation of Violence through Audiovisual |
| FAST | Financial Abuse Specialist Team |
| FBI | Federal Bureau of Investigation |
| FFIPV | female-to-female (lesbian) intimate partner violence |
| FMIPV | female-to-male intimate partner violence |
| FOP | female offender program (for FMIPV) |
| FTT | failure to thrive |
| FVO | family violence option |
| GAD | generalized anxiety disorder |
| GAO | U.S. Government Accountability Office |
| GLBTQ | gay, lesbian, bisexual, transgendered (transsexual), questioning |
| HFA | Healthy Families America |
| HIV | human immunodeficiency virus |
| IBS | intensive bail supervision |
| IED | intermittent explosive disorder |
| IPH | intimate partner homicide |
| ISPCAN | International Society for Prevention of Child Abuse and Neglect |
| IPV | intimate partner violence |
| IT | intimate terrorism |
| I-VAWA | International Violence Against Women Act |
| JCAHO | Joint Commission on Accreditation of Healthcare Organizations |
| LCA | latent class analysis |
| MANCOVA | multivariate analyses of covariance |
| MBP | Munchausen by proxy |

| | |
|---|---|
| MCMI | Millon Clinical Multiaxial Inventory |
| MCTS | Modified Conflict Tactics Scale |
| MFIPV | male-to-female intimate partner violence |
| MGRS | masculine gender-role stress |
| MI | motivational interviewing |
| MMIPV | male-to-male (gay) intimate partner violence |
| MMWR | Morbidity and Mortality Weekly Review |
| MMPI | Minnesota Multiphasic Personal Inventory |
| MSA | military sexual assault |
| MVC | mutual violent control |
| NAIARC | National Abandoned Infants Assistance Resource Center (2003) |
| NAMBLA | North American Man/Boy Love Association |
| NCANDS | National Child Abuse and Neglect Data System |
| NCCAN | National Center for Child Abuse and Neglect |
| NCEA | National Center on Elder Abuse |
| NCIPC | National Center for Injury Prevention and Control |
| NCJRS | National Criminal Justice Reference Service |
| NCMEC | National Center for Missing and Exploited Children |
| NCAVP | National Coalition of Antiviolence Programs |
| NCS | National Comorbidity Survey |
| NCS-R | National Comorbidity Survey Replication |
| NCVS | National Crime Victimization Survey |
| NDVH | National Domestic Violence Hotline |
| NEAIS | National Elder Abuse Incidence Study |
| NEISS | National Electronic Injury Surveillance System |
| NEISS–AIS | National Electronic Injury Surveillance System–All Injury System |
| NFVS-1, NFVS-2 | National Family Violence Surveys |
| NIBRS | National Incident-Based Reporting System |
| NIDA | National Institute on Drug Abuse |
| NIJ | National Institute of Justice |
| NIS | National Incidence Study |
| NOW | National Organization for Women |
| NSCAW | National Survey of Child and Adolescent Well-being |
| NSFH | National Survey of Families and Households |
| NVAWS | National Violence Against Women Survey |
| NVDRS | National Violent Death Reporting System |
| OVW | Office of Violence Against Women |
| PAI | Personality Assessment Inventory |

| | |
|---|---|
| PIM | Positive Impression Management |
| PMWI | Psychological Maltreatment of Women Inventory |
| PO | protective order (also called restraining order) |
| PRWORA | Personal Responsibility and Work Opportunity Reconciliation Act |
| PTSD | posttraumatic stress disorder |
| QOL | quality of life |
| RMA | rape myth acceptance |
| SA | sexual assault |
| SANE | Sexual Assault Nurses Examination |
| SART | Sexual Assault Response Team |
| SCV | situational couple violence |
| SDT | Self-Determination Theory |
| SES | socioeconomic status |
| SHR | Supplementary Homicide Reports |
| SMI | severely mentally ill (person) |
| SOC | sense of cohesion |
| SSA | Social Security Administration |
| SSI | Supplemental Security Income |
| SSIPV | same-sex intimate partner violence |
| ST | stalking |
| STD | sexually transmitted disease |
| SV | sexually violent-only |
| SVAMS | Severity of Violence Against Men Scale |
| SVAWS | Severity of Violence Against Women Scale |
| TANF | Temporary Assistance for Needy Families |
| TASS | traits as situational sensitivities |
| TSC-33 | Trauma Symptom Checklist |
| TSH | transitional supportive housing |
| TTM | Transtheoretical Model (of Change) |
| UCR | Uniform Crime Reports |
| VAWA | Violence Against Women Act |
| VOCA | Victims of Crime Act |
| WHO | The World Health Organization |
| VR | violent resistance |
| WtW | Welfare to Work program |
| YRBS | Youth Risk Behavior Survey |
| YRBSS | Youth Risk Behavior Surveillance System |

# Glossary

**acculturation**   Acculturation refers to the processes by which immigrants integrate the values and behavioral patterns of their original culture with those of a different culture.

**actuarial scales**   An actuarial instrument is one that provides weightings and published scores that have been shown through formal and independent research to predict (violent) outcomes.

**affective style**   Affective style refers to an individual's typical ways of responding emotionally.

**agency**   "The state of being active, usually in the service of a goal, or of exerting power or influence" (VandenBos, 2007, p. 29). Use of the term in IPV literature frequently occurs as an opposite construct to nonaction or helplessness.

**aggregate data**   "Information about aggregates or groups such as race, social classes, or nation" (Vogt, 1993, p. 4).

**Alzheimer's disease**   "A progressive neurological disease due to widespread degeneration of brain cells, with formation of senile plaques and neurofibrillary tangles" (VandenBos, 2007, p. 40).

**amygdala**   The amygdale is a brain structure within the limbic system that is active in memory and in processing emotions, especially negative emotions such as fear and anger.

**analysis of variance (ANOVA)**   "A test of statistical significance of the differences among the mean scores of two or more groups on one or more variables or factors" (Vogt, 1993, p. 7).

**anger (trait)**   A relatively stable (not temporary) tendency to perceive situations as frustrating, unfair, or threatening.

**antisocial behaviors**   Behaviors that suggest a disregard for the rights and feelings of others and include violating societal norms (e.g., aggression, unlawful behavior).

**antisocial orientation**   A term that designates exploitive and narcissistic behaviors that characterize some child molesters and partner-violent men.

**antisocial personality disorder**   "A type of personality disorder marked by impulsivity, inability to abide by the customs and laws of society, and lack of anxiety or guilt regarding behavior [synonyms: sociopathic personality, psychopathic personality]" (Atkinson, Atkinson, Smith, & Bem, 1990, p. A-2).

**anxious/insecure attachment**   A form of insecure attachment between a child and a caregiver associated with insufficient attachment. Anxiously attached children are overly dependent on caregivers (e.g., clingy, fussy).

**assortive mating**   "Mating behavior in which mates are chosen on the basis of a particular trait or group of traits (e.g., attractiveness, similarity of body size)" (VandenBos, 2007, p. 78).

**attachment (adult)**   An affectionate bond with a romantic partner that is a relatively long-lasting tie typified by wanting to be close to the partner, resulting in feelings of comfort and security; also incorporates seeing the partner as unique as an individual who is not exchangeable with any other (Feeney & Noller, 1996).

**attachment (infant/childhood)**   "The tendency of the young organism to seek closeness to particular individuals and to feel more secure in their presence" (Atkinson et al., 1990, p. A-2).

**attention-deficit/hyperactivity disorder**   A psychological disorder characterized by a consistent pattern of age-inappropriate behaviors, including inattention, impulsivity, and hyperactivity.

**attribution** "The process by which we attempt to explain the behavior of other people" (e.g., attributions of blame) (Atkinson et al., 1990, p. A-2).

**avoidance conditioning** another basic theory used to explain the connection between an animals' (or human's) behavior (e.g., fear *or* running away) and an aversive stimulus (e.g., shock or a spanking). Avoidance conditioning involves both classical conditioning (e.g., learning to fear) and operant conditioning (e.g., running away).

**base rate** "The unconditional, naturally occurring rate of a phenomenon in a population" (VandenBos, 2007, p. 103).

**battered woman syndrome (BWS)** A subcategory of posttraumatic stress disorder consisting of a cluster of cognitions, feelings, and behaviors brought about by the effects of trauma, learned helplessness, and the cycle of violence that culminates in the victim's belief that she cannot escape her abuser (L. E. Walker, 1991, 1993).

**battering** "A process whereby one member of an intimate relationship experiences vulnerability, loss of power and control, and entrapment as a consequence of the other member's exercise of power through the patterned use of physical, sexual, psychological, and/or moral force" (P. H. Smith, Thornton, DeVellis, Earp, & Coker, 2002, p. 1210).

**batterer intervention system (BIS)** A proactive domestic violence community that includes agencies and agents, such as the criminal justice system, battered women's networks, and political leaders. The BIS is broader than a batterer intervention program (BIP) and functions across a larger area, such as an entire county (L. W. Bennett, Stroops, Call, & Flett, 2007).

**Big Five Personality model** This model purports to cover the primary dimensions of individual differences in personality. The dimensions are extraversion, neuroticism, agreeableness, conscientiousness, and openness to experience (see VandenBos, 2007, p. 116).

**biopsychosocial model** An explanation of behavior inclusively in terms of biological, psychological, and social factors.

**bisexual(ity)** "sexual attraction to or sexual behavior with both men and women" (VandenBos, 1007, p. 123).

**bivariate association** "A relation (covariation) between two variables only" (Vogt, 1993, p. 24).

**brain disorder** "any condition marked by disruption of the normal functioning of the brain" (VandenBos, 2007, p. 133).

**borderline disorders** (BPD) "A group of psychological disturbances which exhibit various combinations of normality, neurosis, functional psychosis, and psychopathy" (Goldenson, 1970, p.172). The term borderline implies that there is no dominant pattern of deviance, but there are problems with impulsivity, instability of moods, and so forth. Antisocial disorder is characterized by long-standing problems, such as a disregard for the rights of others, irresponsibility, and resisting authority.

**cognitive-behavioral therapy** Strategies aimed at altering behaviors by altering maladaptive cognitions (thoughts).

**cognitive restructuring** "A technique used in cognitive therapy and cognitive-behavioral therapy to help the client identify his or her self-defeating beliefs or cognitive distortions, refute them, and then modify them so that they are adaptive and reasonable" (VandenBos, 2007, p. 191).

**claims-makers** Interest groups and individuals actively engaged in the process of raising awareness about a particular social condition.

**classical conditioning** "a basic theory used to explain connections between events. Pavlov's dog learned that food followed a tone. Saliva was the dependent variable. Humans also learn to connect two events. A child may learn that a mother's hug followed the mother's smile. Classical conditioning occurs automatically. The child does not take any action to get a hug."

**classification tree analysis (CTA)** CTA is a type of multivariate analysis that allows for the investigation of simultaneous influences of a series of independent variables on the one dependent variable (Jazbec, Todorovski, & Jereb, 2007). CTA is a test in which participants themselves are sorted into categories (e.g., of ability or psychological type) according to the responses given (see VandenBos, 2007, p. 177).

**cluster analysis** "Any of several procedures in multivariate analysis designed to determine whether individuals (or other units of analysis) are similar enough to fall into groups or clusters" (Vogt, 1993, p. 36).

**comorbidity**    "The simultaneous presence in the individual of two or more mental or physical illnesses, diseases, or disorders" (VandenBos, 2007, p. 202).

**compulsive disorders**    "Disorders of impulse control in which the individual feels forced to perform acts that are against his or her wishes or better judgment" (VandenBos, 2007, p. 208).

**conduct disorder**    One type of disruptive behavior disorder in which a child exhibits a consistent pattern of behavior characterized by antisocial behaviors, including aggression toward people or property, stealing, lying, truancy, and running away.

**confirmatory factor analysis**    A factor analysis conducted to test hypotheses (to confirm theories) about the factors one will find (Vogt, 1993, p. 43).

**coperpetrator**    A person who joins with a more dominant person to commit a crime.

**coping**    "The use of cognitive and behavioral strategies to manage the demands of a situation when these are appraised as taxing or exceeding one's resources or to reduce the negative emotions and conflict caused by stress" (VandenBos, 2007, p. 232).

**coping style**    "The characteristic manner in which an individual confronts and deals with stress, anxiety, provoking situations, or emergencies" (VandenBos, 2007, p. 232).

**corporal punishment**    Minor, "legitimate" violence accepted and sometimes encouraged in society because of its presumed positive effects on the behavior of children.

**coverture**    A legal doctrine under which a married woman's rights to own property are subsumed under her husband's property rights. His duty is to protect and care for her. This law was in force in the 19th century in most of the United States.

**cultural competency**    "Possession of the skills and knowledge that are appropriate for and specific to a given culture" (VandenBos, 2007, p. 249).

**deductive methods**    Research methods in which "conclusions [are] derived by reasoning rather than by data gathering" (Vogt, 1993, p. 64).

**dementia**    "A generalized, pervasive deterioration of cognitive functions, such as memory, language, and executive functions, due to any of various causes" (VandenBos, 2007, p. 266).

**deoxyribonucleic acid (DNA)**    "One of the two types of nucleic acid found in living organisms, which is the principal carrier of genetic information in chromosomes and, to a much lesser extent, in the mitochondria" (VandenBos, 2007, p. 294).

**disability**    "A product of the intersection of individual characteristics (e.g., conditions or impairments, functional status, or personal and socioeconomic qualities) and characteristics of the natural, built, cultural, and social environments" (National Institute on Disability and Rehabilitation Research, 2003, p. 2).

**disaggregate**    "To separate out for purposes of analysis the parts of an aggregate statistic" (Vogt, 1993, p. 70). An example would be sorting out a subgroup, such as college students, in an aggregate sample of young adults.

**discriminant functions analysis**    "A form of regression analysis designed for classification. It allows two or more continuous independent or predictor variables to be used to place individuals or cases into the categories of a categorical dependent variable" (Vogt, 1993, p. 71). Correlational analyses are designed to separate individuals into distinct categories based on their scores on various dependent variables. The analyses provide information on how to distinguish groups.

**disorganized attachment**    A form of attachment between a child and a caregiver that is characterized by insecurity and disorganization. Also referred to as Type D attachment.

**dispositional mood**    Ease with which one can be classically conditioned, especially negatively conditioned.

**disruptive behavior disorders**    A category in the Diagnostic Manual and Statistical Manual of Mental Disorders (American Psychiatric Association, 1994) that includes oppositional defiant disorder, *conduct disorder, and attention-deficit/hyperactivity disorder.*

**dissociation**    "The process whereby some ideas, feelings, or activities lose relationship to other aspects of consciousness and personality and operate automatically or independently" (Atkinson et al., 1990, p. A-8; see also Braun, 1988).

**dual arrest**    The arrest of both individuals involved in IPV regardless of who is the primary aggressor.

**dual diagnoses**    The diagnosis of the co-occurrence of two or more mental disorders. For example, the same individual might be diagnosed with antisocial personality and substance abuse disorder.

**dyadic effect**    "That part of the behavior of two interacting individuals that is due to their particular interaction, as distinct from the way in which each characteristically relates to others" (VandenBos, 2007, p. 305).

**dysphoria**    "Generalized feeling of anxiety, restlessness accompanied by depression" (Wolman, 1973, p. 109).

**dysthymia**    A form of depression characterized by a chronic rather than an acute pattern of symptoms.

**dyadic relationship**    "Any committed, intimate two-person relationship" (VandenBos, 2007, p. 305).

**effect size**    "Any of several measures of strength of a relation. The effect size is an estimate of the degree to which a phenomenon is present in a population and/or the extent to which the *null hypothesis* is false" (Vogt, 1993, p. 79).

**emotion-focused coping**    "A type of coping strategy that focuses on regulating negative emotional reactions to a stressor, as opposed to taking actions to change the stressor. Emotion-focused coping may include social withdrawal, disengagement, and acceptance of the situation" (VandenBos, 2007, p. 326).

**endangerment standard**    A standard used in defining child abuse and neglect that includes situations in which children are not yet harmed by maltreatment but have experienced maltreatment that puts them in danger of being harmed.

**exosystem**    "Those societal structures that function largely independently of the individual but which nevertheless affect the immediate context within which he or she develops. They include the government, the legal system, and the media" (VandenBos, 2007, p. 352).

**exposure reduction theory**    The assumption that a reduction in the amount of time a couple spend together leads to a reduction in their violence.

**exposure therapy**    "A form of behavior therapy that is effective in treating anxiety disorders. Exposure therapy involves systematic confrontation with a feared stimulus, either in vivo (live) or in the imagination. It works [partially] by habituation, in which repeated exposure reduces anxiety over time by a process of extinction" (VandenBos, 2007, p. 357).

**externalizing behaviors**    A dimension of childhood behaviors typically viewed as "acting-out" behaviors, including aggressive, delinquent, and impulsive behaviors.

**extinction**    In Pavlovian conditioning, a learning procedure to reduce responses (e.g., fear). One procedure involves presenting a "rat" with the conditioned stimulus ($CS^+$, e.g., tone) alone, without the customary unconditioned stimulus ($UCS^+$, e.g., shock). Over many $CS^+$ no $UCS^+$ trials, the rat slowly reduces responding to the $CS^+$ (e.g., tone).

**factor analysis**    "Any of several methods of analysis that enable researchers to reduce a large number of variables to a smaller number of variables, or 'factors,' or latent variables. Factor analysis is done by finding patterns among the variations in the values of several variables; a cluster of highly intercorrelated variables is a factor" (Vogt, 1993, p. 89).

**failure to thrive**    A disorder in infants characterized by failure to maintain age-appropriate weight.

**family violence**    "Includes family members' acts of omission or commission resulting in physical abuse, sexual abuse, emotional abuse, neglect, or other forms of maltreatment that hamper individuals' healthy development" (Levesque, 2001, p. 13).

**femicide**    "all killings of women, regardless of motive or perpetrator status" (J. C. Campbell & Runyan, 1998).

**feminist theories**    typically focus on accounting for gender and power relationships when understanding IPV, the historical salience of the family as an institution, the importance of understanding and validating women's experiences, and the use of family violence research findings to help women (see Bograd, 1988).

**filicide/siblicide**    Filicide/siblicide is the killing of one's brother or sister (Michalski, Russell, Shackelford, & Weekes-Shackelford, 2007).

**forensic psychology**  "The application of psychological principles and techniques to legal issues or situations involving the law or legal systems (both criminal and civil)" (VandenBos, 2007, p. 385).

**gay intimate partner violence**  "A means to control others through power, including physical and psychological threats (verbal and nonverbal) or injury (to the victim or others), isolation, economic deprivation, heterosexist control, sexual assaults, vandalism (destruction of property), or any combination of methods" (T. W. Burke, 1998, p. 164).

**generalized anxiety disorders (GAD)**  "Excessive anxiety and worry about a range of events and activities (e.g., world events, finances, health, appearance, activities of family members and friends, work, or school) accompanied by such symptom as restlessness, fatigue, impaired concentration, irritability, muscle tension, and disturbed sleep. The anxiety occurs on more days than not and is experienced as difficult to control" (VandenBos, 2007, p. 403).

**harm standard**  A standard used in defining child abuse and neglect that requires demonstrable harm to children as a result of maltreatment.

**heterosexism**  "An ideological system that denies, denigrates, and stigmatizes any nonheterosexual form of behavior, identity, relationship, or community" (Herek, 1990, p. 316).

**hierarchical regression**  "A type of regression model that assumes that, when a higher order interaction term is included, all the lower order terms (main effects) are also included" (Vogt, 1993, p. 104).

**homonegativity**  A negative attitude (emotional, moral, or intellectual) toward homosexuality or homosexuals.

**homophobia**  Heterosexuals' dread or fear of being in close quarters with homosexuals or aversion to nonheterosexuals or their lifestyles.

**hopelessness**  "The feeling that one will not experience positive emotions or an improvement in one's condition" (VandenBos, 2007, p. 447). Feeling hopeless occurs frequently in depressive episodes.

**hostility**  "An attitudinal disposition toward negative evaluation" (Eckhardt, Barbour, & Stuart, 1997, p. 335).

**incidence (of violence)**  The frequency of violent acts occurring within a subgroup of affected individuals.

**inductive methods**  "Research procedures and methods of reasoning that begin with (or put emphasis on) observation and then move from observation of particulars to the development of general hypotheses" (Vogt, 1993, p. 111).

**interaction effect**  "The joint effect of two or more independent variables on a dependent variable. Interaction effects occur when independent variables not only have separate effects but also have combined effects on a dependent variable" (Vogt, 1993, p. 112) (a statistical term). Hypothetical example: Exercise significantly improves muscle mass only in people under age 88.

**interactionism**  "A set of approaches, particularly in personality psychology, in which behavior is explained not in terms of personality attributes or situational influences but by references to interactions that typify the behavior of a certain type of person in a certain type of setting" (VandenBos, 2007, p. 490).

**intermittent explosive disorder (IED)**  Behavior "characterized by recurrent episodes of serious assaultive acts that are out of proportion to psychosocial stressors and that are not better accounted for either by another mental disorder or by the physiological effects of a substance with psychotropic properties" (Kessler, et al. 2006, p. 2)

**internalized homophobia**  "A set of negative attitudes, and affects toward homosexuality in other persons and toward homosexual features in oneself" (Shidlo, 1994, p. 178).

**internalizing behaviors**  A dimension of childhood behaviors typically viewed as "inhibited" behaviors, including depression, anxiety, and low self-esteem.

**intersectionality**  Intersectionality refers to the intersection (place or area of meeting) of important sociodemographic variables, such as gender, race, and class that influence behavior.

**intervention (in family violence)**  Societal responses to family violence after it occurs, including counseling, arrest, and medical attention.

**intimate partner violence (IPV)**  Violence between sexually intimate couples of almost any age, education level, marital status, living arrangement, or sexual orientation.

**latent class analysis (LCA)** "A method similar to factor analysis but used with categorical data … LCA is used to find latent categories or 'classes' of variables, such as questionnaire items that have categorical, not continuous, answers" (Vogt, 1993, p. 123).

**latent profile analysis (LPA)** A latent variable model that postulates some relationship between statistical properties of observable variables (indicators) and latent variables. A latent variable describes an unobservable construct that cannot be measured directly but must be inferred (http://www.Statistic.com).

**Lautenberg Amendment** An amendment (named after the bill's author, Senator Frank Lautenberg) that bans individuals who have been convicted of domestic assault from carrying weapons.

**learned helplessness** "A condition in which a subject does not attempt to escape from a painful or noxious situation after learning in a previous, similar situation that escape is not possible" (Gerow, 1989, p. 193).

**Likert scale** "A direct attitude measure that consists of statements reflecting strong positive or negative evaluations of an attitude object. Respondents indicate their reaction to each statement on a response scale ranging from "strongly agree" to "strongly disagree" (VandenBos, 2007, p. 537).

**logistic regression analysis** "A kind of regression analysis used when the dependent variable is dichotomous and scored 0.1. It is usually used for predicting whether something will happen or not, such as graduation, business failure, heart disease—anything that can be expressed as Event/Nonevent" (Vogt, 1993, p. 131).

**longitudinal study** "A study over time of a variable or a group of subjects" (Vogt, 1993, p. 131).

**macrosystem** "The level of environmental influence that is most distal to the developing individual and that affects all other systems. It includes values, traditions, and sociocultural characteristics of the larger society" (VandenBos, 2007, p. 548).

**mandatory arrest laws** Laws that require police to arrest violent intimates when probable cause exists; such laws currently exist in many U.S. states and local jurisdictions.

**mandatory reporting laws** Laws that require certain classes of professionals to report cases of suspected child or adult abuse; such laws currently exist in all U.S. states.

**matricide** Matricide is the killing of one's mother (Heide & Frei, 2010).

**maximum likelihood coefficients** "Statistical method for estimating the population parameters most likely to have resulted in the observed sample data" (Vogt, 1993, p. 137).

**mediator (variable)** "Another term for intervening variable, that is, a variable that 'transmits' the effects of another. Example: Parents' Status—Child's Education—Child's Status. Education is the mediating variable" (Vogt, 1993, p. 138). Another example would be "medication" use by a mentally ill person. The medication may alter the severity of the symptoms of the disorder.

**meta-analysis** "Quantitative procedure for summarizing or integrating the findings obtained from a literature review of a subject. Meta-analysis is, strictly speaking, more a kind of synthesis than analysis. The meta-analyst uses the results of individual research projects on the same topic (perhaps studies testing the same hypothesis) as data points for a statistical study of the topic" (Vogt, 1993, p. 138).

**microsystem (mesosystem)** "The groups and institutions outside the home (e.g., daycare, school, or a child's peer group) that influence the child's development and interact with aspects of the microsystem (relations in the home)" (VandenBos, 2007, p. 571).

**mirror cell** "A type of cell in the brains of primates that responds in the same way to a given action (e.g., reaching out to grasp an object) whether it is performed by the primate itself or whether the primates has merely observed another primate (which may be a human) perform the same action" (VandenBos, 2007, p. 583).

**moderator (variable)** "A variable that influences ('moderates') the relation between two other variables and thus produces an interaction effect" (Vogt, 1993, p. 142). Moderator variables refer to "variables that affect the strength and directions of the relationship between predictor and criterion variables" (Baron & Kenny, 1986, p. 1174).

**motivational interviewing**   a newer type of intake interview developed to help clients mandated into counseling become involved in changing their behavior. A counselor asks a client (e.g., an abusive parent or a batterer) what changes he wishes to make in his behavior. This approach differs from customary methods in which the counselor 'knows' how the client 'must' change (e.g., stop his battering). Motivational interviewing and treatment rest on a "stages of change" model that individualizes treatment.

**multiple regression (analysis)**   "Any of several related statistical methods for evaluating the effects of more than one independent variable on a dependent variable" (Vogt, 1993, p. 146).

**multivariate methods**   "Any of several methods for examining multiple variables at the same time.... Examples include path analysis, factor analysis, multiple regression analysis, MANOVA, LISREL, canonical correlations, and discriminant analysis" (Vogt, 1993, p. 147).

**Munchausen by proxy**   A constellation of behaviors whereby an adult uses a child as the vehicle for fabricated illness.

**narcissism**   "Inflated, grandiose, or unjustified favorable self-views" (Bushman & Baumeister, 1998, p. 220). "Excessive self-love or egocentrism" (VandenBos, 2007, p. 608).

**narrative therapy**   Treatment "that helps clients reinterpret and rewrite their life events into true but more life-enhancing narratives or stories" (VandenBos, 2007, p. 608).

**neurotransmitter**   "A chemical involved in the transmission of nerve impulses across the synapse from one neuron to another" (Atkinson et al., 1990, p. A-16).

**null hypothesis**   The concept that an experiment will find no (statistical) difference between the experimental and control groups (VandenBos, p. 634).

**obsessive-compulsive disorder (OCD)**   "An anxiety disorder characterized by recurrent obsessions, compulsions, or both that are time consuming (more than one hour per day), cause significant distress, or interfere with the person's functioning" (VandenBos, 2007, p. 638).

**odds**   "The ratio of success to failure in probability calculations. For example, the odds of drawing, at random, a heart (success) from an ordinary deck of cards are 13 to 39 or 1 to 3. By contrast, the probability (likelihood of success) of drawing a heart is .25 or 1 out of 4" (Vogt, 1993, p. 158).

**odds ratio**   "A ratio of one odds to another. The odds ratio is a measure of association, but unlike other measures of association, 1.0 means that there is no relationship between the variables. The size of any relationship between variables is measured in either direction from 1.0. An odds ratio less than 1.0 indicates an inverse or negative relation; and odds ratio greater than 1.0 indicates a direct or positive relation" (Vogt, 1993, p. 158).

**official statistics**   "statistics provided by official agencies, such as the FBI's Uniform Crime Reports, the Department of Justice, and the Department of Health and Human Services (see Chapter 1 for a list of some official surveys). Official statistics are contrasted with statistics provided by other organizations and other researchers. Examples include an individual researcher's statistical data derived from self-report surveys in a clinical setting."

**operationalization**   Refers to the definition of a construct (e.g., IQ), in terms of the variables and methods used to measure it (e.g., an IQ test, such as the Stanford-Binet Intelligence Scale).

**operant conditioning**   "another basic theory used to explain the connection between events. A monkey learns that getting a banana follows climbing a tree. A child learns that getting a cookie follows cleaning his room. Operant conditioning requires an active response to acquire a reward. The child must act (operate on the environment—clean his room) to get the cookie."

**oversampling**   "A procedure of stratified sampling in which the researcher selects a disproportionately large number of subjects from a particular group (stratum)" (Vogt, 1993, p. 162).

**parentification**   A distortion of boundaries among family members when a child becomes responsible for a parent's emotional or behavior needs (see Hooper, 2008).

**parricide**   Parricide usually refers to killing one's parents but can refer to killing a close relative (Heide & Frei, 2010).

**partial correlation**   "The correlation between two variables with the influence of a third variable removed from one (but only one) of the two variables" (VandenBos, 2007, p. 674).

**passive dependent (dependent personality disorder)**   "A personality disorder manifested in a long-term pattern of passively allowing others to take responsibility for major areas of life and of subordinating personal needs to the needs of others, due to lack of self-confidence and self-dependence" (VandenBos, 2007, p. 269).

**path model**   "A kind of multivariate analysis in which causal relations among several variables are represented by graphs (path diagrams) showing the "paths" along which causal influences travel. The causal relationships must be stipulated by the researcher" (Vogt, 1993, p. 167).

**patricide**   Patricide is the killing of one's father (Heide & Frei, 2010).

**pedophilia**   Abnormal "sexual acts or fantasies with prepubertal children are the persistently preferred or exclusive method of achieving sexual excitement" (VandenBos, 2007, p. 681).

**personality disorder**   "A group of disorders involving pervasive patterns of perceiving, relation to, and thinking about the environment and the self that interfere with long-term functioning of the individual and are not limited to isolated episodes (VandenBos, 2007, p. 689).

**personality trait**   "A relatively stable, consistent, and enduring internal characteristic that is inferred from a pattern of behaviors, attitudes, feelings, and habits in the individual" (VandenBos, 2007, p. 690).

**polygamy**   Being married to more than one woman (usually) or man at the same time.

**polyvictimization**   "Four or more different types of victimization in separate incidents within the previous year" (Finkelhor, Ormrod, Turner, & Hamby, 2005, p. 1297).

**posttraumatic stress disorder (PTSD)**   An anxiety disorder produced by an extremely stressful event(s) (e.g., assault, rape, military combat, death camp) and characterized by a number of adverse reactions: (a) re-experiencing the trauma in painful recollections or recurrent dreams; (b) diminished responsiveness (numbing), with disinterest in significant activities and with feelings of detachment and estrangement from others; and (c) symptoms such as exaggerated startle response, disturbed sleep, difficulty in concentrating or remembering, guilt about surviving when others did not, and avoidance of activities that call the traumatic event to mind (Goldenson, 1984).

**prevalence (of violence)**   The number of people in the population of interest who are affected by the occurrence of violent acts.

**primary prevention (of family violence)**   Efforts to prevent family violence from occurring in the first place. Some experts use the term prevention (as opposed to primary prevention) when referring to efforts to prevent recurrences of violence.

**probability sample**   "A sample in which each subject chosen has a known probability of being included. Usually a random sample" (Vogt, 1993, p. 180).

**problem-focused coping**   "A type of coping strategy that is directed toward decreasing or eliminating stressors, for example, by generating possible solutions to a problem. The coping actions may be directed at the self, the environment, or both" (VandenBos, 2007, p. 735).

**problem solving**   "The process by which individuals attempt to overcome difficulties, achieve plans that move them from a starting situation to a desired goal, or reach conclusions through the use of higher mental processes" (VandenBos, 2007, p. 735).

**process theories (of child abuse)**   Theories that emphasize specific precursors that lead to child abuse and neglect and/or processes that maintain the child abuse and neglect.

**propensity analysis**   "A statistical approach to the adjustment of group means to account for pre-existing group differences on a set of variables. Propensity analysis is an alternative to matching or analysis of covariance" (VandenBos, 2007, p. 741).

**protective factor**   A variable that precedes a negative outcome and decreases the chances that the outcome will occur.

**proxy interview**   Someone else answers for a communication-handicapped respondent.

**proxy measure**   A measure used in place of another when the preferred scores are unavailable. As an example, women might respond to the Conflict Tactics Scale (CTS) as if they were their male partner as a substitute for the men's actual responses, because the men's scores are unavailable.

**psychobiological bases**   "a broad theory that explains the causes of behavior as a reflection of biological, psychological, and social determinants. Example: Empathic behavior is assumed to result from favorable genetics, excellent parenting, and a positive evaluation by society."

**psychopathology**   Patterns of behavior or thought processes that are abnormal or maladapative. The term in this sense is sometimes considered to be synonymous with mental illness or mental disorder (VandenBos, 2007, p. 755).

**psychopathy**   "A former term for a personality trait marked by egocentricity, impulsivity, and lack of such emotions as guilt and remorse, which is particularly prevalent among repeat offenders" (VandenBos, 2007, p. 755).

**quasi-experimental research design**   "A type of research design for conducting studies in field or real-life situations where the researcher may be able to manipulate some independent variables but cannot randomly assign subjects to control and experimental group" (Vogt, 1993, p. 184).

**quota sampling**   A method somewhat similar to convenience sampling with the restriction of obtaining a certain distribution of individuals within specific demographic categories (e.g., 10 Asian women 30–44 years of age). If there are more participants than needed in the subcategory, a judgment is made (not random selection) as to which members within a category to retain for analysis.

**Q sort**   "A technique used in personality measurement in which cards representing personal traits are sorted, by the participant or a rater observing the participant, into piles (of predetermined size) ranging from 'most characteristic' to 'least characteristic' of the [trait or] participant" (VandenBos, 2007, p. 762).

**recidivism**   "Repetition of delinquent or criminal behavior, especially in the case of a habitual criminal" (repeat offender) (i.e., battering after arrest) (VandenBos, 2007, p. 776).

**reframing**   "The process of reconceptualizing an idea for the purposes of changing an attitude by seeing it from a different perspective" (VandenBos, 2007, p. 781).

**regression analysis**   "Any of several statistical techniques that are designed to allow the prediction of the score on one variable, the dependent variable, from the scores on one or more other variables, the independent variables" (VandenBos, 2007, p. 782).

**reliability**   The reliability of a test refers to the consistency of the answers furnished by research participants when responding to the questions a second time (test-retest reliability) or when responding to the same test presented in an alternative format.

**repression**   In Freudian analysis, repression is the basic defense mechanism. It "consists of excluding painful experiences and unacceptable impulses from consciousness. Repression operates on an unconscious level as a protection against anxiety produced by objectionable sexual wishes, feelings of hostility, and ego-threatening experiences of all kinds" (VandenBos, 2007, p. 790).

**responsivity principle**   "Focuses on client and program characteristics that influence the offender's ability to learn in a therapeutic situation. Treatment is a learning experience and individual factors that interfere with, or facilitate, learning are termed responsivity factors. These factors can also be understood as contextual variables, which may influence treatment outcome. These variables make a difference to the skills, strategies, or identities that individuals develop and to the support available when transitions are made. Factors such as age, ethnicity, gender, disability and socioeconomic status can be considered key responsivity factors" (Day, Howells, & Rickwood, 2004, pp. 2–3).

**revictimization**   An unfortunate type of "learning" that is evident when a response to an initial victimization is predictive of a second victimization (Fisher, Cullen, & Turner, 2000).

**risk factor**   A variable that precedes a negative outcome and increases the chances that the outcome will occur.

**risk marker**   An antecedent variable that is significantly correlated with a consequent variable. The antecedent variable predicts the consequent variable. Example: Female poverty is a risk factor for female IPV victimization.

**schema** "A collection of basic knowledge about a concept or entity that serves as a guide to perception, interpretation, imagination, or problem solving" (VandenBos, 2007, p. 814).

**schizoid (personality disorder)** "A personality disorder characterized by long-term emotional coldness, absence of tender feelings for others, indifference to praise or criticism and to the feelings of others ..." (VandenBos, 2007, p. 815).

**schizophrenia** "A psychotic disorder characterized by disturbances in thinking (cognition), emotional responsiveness, and behavior" (VandenBos, 2007, p. 815). There are several subtypes of schizophrenia (e.g., paranoid).

**secondary appraisal** "appraisal of one's ability to cope with the consequences of an interaction with the environment which follows a primary appraisal" (VandenBos, 2007, p. 821).

**sense of coherence** A tendency to view the world as comprehensible, manageable, and meaningful.

**sexual coercion** "Any situation in which one person uses verbal or physical means to obtain sexual activity against consent (including the administration of drugs or alcohol, with or without the other person's consent)" (Adams-Curtis & Forbes, 2004, p. 91).

**serotonin** "A neurotransmitter in both the peripheral and central nervous systems. It is an inhibitory transmitter whose actions have been implicated in various processes including sleep, the perception of pain, and mood disorders (depression and manic-depression)" (Atkinson et al., 1990, p. A-23).

**sexual violence** "A sex act completed against a victim's will or when a victim is unable to consent due to age, illness, disability, or the influence of alcohol or other drugs. It may involve actual or threatened physical force, use of guns or other weapons, coercion, intimidation, or pressure. Sexual violence also includes intentional touching of the genitals, anus, groin, or breast against a victim's will or when a victim is unable to consent, as well as voyeurism, exposure to exhibitionism, or undesired exposure to pornography. The perpetrator of sexual violence may be a stranger, friend, family member, or intimate partner" (Centers for Disease Control and Prevention, 2002, p. 3).

**shaken baby syndrome** A type of brain injury in a child that results from the child's being vigorously shaken.

**situationalism** "The view that an organism's interactions with the environment and situational factors, rather than personal characteristics and other internal factors, are the primary determinants of behavior" (VandenBos, 2007, p. 855).

**social comparison theory** "The propositions that people evaluate their abilities and attitudes in relation to those of others (i.e., through a process of comparison) when objective standards for the assessment of these abilities and attitudes are lacking (VandenBos, 2007, p. 863).

**social constructionism** A perspective that holds that societal reactions to a social condition are central to the process of that condition's redefinition as a social problem.

**social role theory** "All psychological differences between men and women can be attributed to cultural expectations about gender, rather than to biological factors" (VandenBos, 2007, p. 868)

**social support** "The provision of assistance or comfort to others, typically in order to help them cope with a variety of biological, psychological, and social stressors" (VandenBos, 2007, p. 869).

**somatization** "The organic expression of a psychological disturbance" (VandenBos, 2007, p. 874).

**somatoform disorders** "Somatoform disorders and functional somatic syndromes are defined as the presence of physical symptoms in the absence of sufficient tissue or organ damage to account for the degree of pain or dysfunction" (Arnd-Caddigan, 2006, p. 21).

**stalking** "A course of conduct directed at a specific person involving repeated visual or physical proximity; nonconsensual communication; verbal, written, or implied threats; of a combination thereof that would cause fear in a reasonable person, with 'repeated' meaning on two or more occasions" (Tjaden & Thoennes, 2000a, p. 5).

**stimulus generalization** "...in classical conditioning, the principle that once a conditioned response has been established to a given stimulus, similar stimuli will also evoke that response" (Atkinson, Atkinson, Smith, & Bem, 1990, p. A-10)

**structural equation**    "An equation representing the strength and nature of the hypothesized relations among (the 'structure' of) sets of variables in a theory" (Vogt, 1993, p. 224).

**structural equation models (SEM)**    "A statistical modeling technique that includes latent variables as causal elements. SEM is an advanced statistical method for testing causal models involving constructs that cannot be directly measured but are, rather, approximated through several measures presumed to assess part of the given construct" (VandenBos, 2007, p. 900; see also Vogt, 1993, p. 224).

**substantiated (allegation of maltreatment)**    "A type of investigation disposition that concludes that the allegation of maltreatment or risk of maltreatment was supported or founded by State law or State policy. This is the highest level of finding by a State Agency" (U.S. Department of Health & Human Services, 2003a, p. 92).

**survival analysis**    "A variety of event history analysis in which there are a limited number of states or conditions. Survival analysis focuses on how long subjects persist in a state ('survive')" (Vogt, 1993, p. 228). Example: How long before a machine fails, before an addict drinks alcohol again, or before someone dies.

**survivor theory**    A theory developed by Gondolf and Fisher (1988) in opposition to *learned helplessness* theory. Survivor theory supposes that the many actions battered women take indicate their attempts to survive spouse abuse. Battered women are not passive in response to spouse abuse.

**theory**    "An integrated set of ideas that explain a set of observations" (O'Neill, 1998, p. 459).

**therapeutic jurisprudence**    A justice approach that frames an offense to include the perpetrator, the victim, and the community. Family, peers, and advocates design an individualized perpetrator rehabilitation, victim restoration, and community social reintegration of all parties involved (Koss, 2000). Also known as restorative jurisprudence and communitarian jurisprudence.

**trait**    "An enduring personality characteristic that describes or determines an individual's behavior across a range of situations" (VandenBos, 2007, p. 950).

**transactional theories (of child abuse)**    Theories that emphasize the interactions among risk and protective factors associated with child abuse and neglect.

**transitional supportive housing (TSH)**    A post-shelter program for battered women that provides temporary housing and support services from 12 to 24 months.

**transtheoretical model (TTM)**    A stages of change model that suggests that changes in behavior (e.g., occurring in a batterer intervention program) go through four phases: precontemplation, contemplation, action, and maintenance.

**traumatic event**    A circumstance in which an individual experiences, witnesses, or is confronted with an event or events that involve actual or threatened death or serious injury, or a threat to the physical integrity of the individual or others. Responses to traumatic events entail intense fear, helplessness, and horror (American Psychiatric Association, 1994).

**typology**    "Any analysis of a particular category of phenomena (e.g., individuals, things) into classes based on common characteristics" (VandenBos, 2007, p. 964).

**validity**    Essentially, validity refers to whether a test is accurate, or the extent to which a test measures what it claims to measure. There are several connotations of validity including construct validity and concurrent validity. Often, a validity assessment reflects the degree to which a test predicts another criterion. Example: Does the SAT accurately predict success in college?

**variance (explained)**    The proportion of differences on one variable that is accounted for by differences in scores on another variable(s). Hypothetical example: Differences in anger levels account for 25% of the differences in the severity of assaults.

**vicarious traumatization (VT)**    "The impact on a therapist of repeated emotionally intimate contact with trauma survivor" (VandenBos, 2007, p. 982).

**victim precipitation**    "Behavior by the victim that initiates the subsequent behavior of the victimizer" (Muftić, Bouffard, & Bouffard, 2007, p. 327).

**violence**    "An act carried out with the intention of, or an act perceived as having the intention of, physically hurting another person" (Steinmetz, 1987, p. 729).

**vulnerable adult**    "A person who is either being mistreated or in danger of mistreatment and who, due to age and/or disability, is unable to protect him/herself" (Teaster, 2003, p. viii).

# References

Aaron, R. (2008). Bankruptcy to thwart responsibility for financial abuse of the elderly. *Marquette University Elder Law Advisor, 9,* 299.

Abbey, A. (1982). Sex differences in attribution for friendly behavior: Do males misperceive females' friendliness? *Journal of Personality and Social Psychology, 42,* 830–838.

Abbey, A., McAuslan, P., Zawacki, T., Clinton, A. M., & Buck, P. O. (2001). Attitudinal, experiential, and situational predictors of sexual assault perpetration. *Journal of Interpersonal Violence, 16,* 784–807.

Abdi, S. N. M. (2000, November 27). Women's worsening plight greeted with indifference. *South China Morning Post,* 14–15.

Abel, E. M. (2001). Comparing the social service utilization, exposure to violence, and trauma symptomatology of domestic violence female "victims" and female "batterers." *Journal of Family Violence, 16,* 401–420.

Abel, G. G., Becker, J. V., & Cunningham-Rathner, J. (1984). Complications, consent, and cognitions in sex between children and adults. *International Journal of Law and Psychiatry, 7,* 89–103.

Abel, M. H., & Meltzer, A. L. (2007). Student ratings of a male and female professors' lecture on sex discrimination in the workforce. *Sex Roles, 57,* 173–180.

About nursing homes. (n.d.). Retrieved from http://www.longtermcarelink.net/eldercare/nursing_home.htm

Abraham, M. (2000). Isolation as a form of marital violence: The South Asian immigrant experience. *Journal of Social Distress and the Homeless, 9,* 221–236.

Abrahams, N., Jewkes, R., Martin, L. J., Mathews, S., Vetten, L., & Lombard, C. (2009). Mortality of women from intimate partner violence in South Africa: A national epidemiological study. *Violence and Victims, 24,* 546–556.

Abram, S. (2010, June 24). Whooping cough epidemic declared. *Daily News,* A4.

Abu-Ras, W. (2007). Cultural beliefs and service utilization by battered Arab immigrant women. *Violence Against Women, 13,* 1002–1028.

Abusive relationships and Stockholm syndrome. (1991, September 23). *Behavior Today, 22*(39), 6–7.

Acevedo, M. (2000). Battered immigrant Mexican women's perspectives regarding abuse and help-seeking. *Journal of Multicultural Social Work, 8,* 243–282.

Achenbach, T. M., & Edelbrock, C. S. (1983). *Manual for the Child Behavior Checklist and Revised Child Behavior Profile.* Burlington: University of Vermont Press.

Acierno, R., Hernandez-Tejada, M., Muzzy, W., & Steve, K. (2009). *The national elder mistreatment study* (NCJ Publication No. 226456). Washington, DC: U.S. Department of Justice.

Ackard, D. M., & Neumark-Sztainer, D. (2002). Date violence and date rape among adolescents: Association with disordered eating behaviors and psychological health. *Child Abuse & Neglect, 26,* 455–473.

Adair, J. G., & Vohra, N. (2003). The explosion of knowledge, references, and citations. *American Psychologist, 58,* 15–23.

Adams, C. M. (2006). The consequences of witnessing family violence on children and implications for family counselors. *The Family Journal, 14,* 334–341.

Adams, D. C. (2007). *Why do they kill? Men who murder their intimate partners.* Nashville, TN: Vanderbilt University Press.

Adams, D. C., & Galibois, N. (2004, April/May). Batterer intervention program outcomes: Broadening the criteria. *Domestic Violence Reports, 9,* 49–50, 60.

Adams, D. C., & McCormick, A. J. (1982). Men unlearning violence: A group approach based on the collective model. In M. Roy (Ed.), *The abusive partner: An analysis of domestic battering* (pp. 170–197). New York: Van Nostrand Reinhold.

Adams, J. A., et al. (2007). Guidelines for medical care of children who may have been sexually abused. *Journal of Pediatric and Adolescent Gynecology, 20,* 163–172.

Adams, V., Miller, S., Craig, S., Sonam, N., Droyoung, P. V. L., & Varner, M. (2007). Informed consent in cross-cultural perspective: Clinical research in the Tibetan autonomous region, PRC. *Culture, Medicine and Psychiatry, 31,* 445–472.

Adams-Curtis, L. E., & Forbes, G. B. (2004). College women's experiences of sexual coercion: A review of cultural, perpetrator, victim, and situational variables. *Trauma, Violence, & Abuse, 5,* 91–122.

Aday, R. H., Kehoe, G. C., & Farney, L. A. (2006). Impact of senior center friendships on aging women who live alone. *Journal of Women & Aging, 18,* 57–73.

Adeyemi, A. B., Irinoye, O. O., Oladimeji, B. Y., Fatusi, A. O., Fatoye, F. O., Mosaku, S. K., & Ola, B. A. (2008). Preparedness for management and prevention of violence against women by Nigerian health professional. *Journal of Family Violence, 23,* 719–723.

Adinkrah, M. (2008). Spousal homicides in Ghana. *Journal of Criminal Justice, 36,* 209–216.

Adler, J. R. (1999). Strengthening victims' rights in domestic violence cases: An argument for 30-day mandatory restraining orders in Massachusetts. *Boston Public Interest Law Journal, 8,* 303–332.

Adler, N., & Schutz, J. (1995). Sibling incest offenders. *Child Abuse & Neglect, 19,* 811–819.

Administration on Aging. *Senior websites you can trust.* Washington, DC: U.S. Department of Health & Human Services. Retrieved from http://www.aoa.gov/AoARoot/Elders_Families/index.aspx

Advisory Council on Violence Against Women. (1996). *A community checklist: Important steps to end violence against women.* Retrieved from http://www.usdoj.gov/vawa/cheklist.htm

Afifi, T. O., Brownridge, D. A., Cox, B. J., & Sareen, J. (2006). Physical punishment, childhood abuse and psychiatric disorders. *Child Abuse & Neglect, 30,* 1093–1103.

Afifi, T. O., MacMillan, H., Cox, B. J., Asmundson, G. J. G., Stein, M. B., & Sareen, J. (2009). Mental health correlates of intimate partner violence in marital relationships in a nationally representative sample of males and females. *Journal of Interpersonal Violence, 24,* 1398–1417.

Agoff, C., Herrera, C., & Castro, R. (2007). The weakness of family ties and their perpetuating effects on gender violence. *Violence Against Women, 13,* 1206–1220.

Agrawal, A., Lynskey, M., Madden, P., Bucholz, K., & Heath, A. (2006). A latent class analysis of illicit drug abuse/dependence: Results from the National Epidemiological Survey on Alcohol and Related Conditions. *Addiction, 102,* 94–104.

Ahrens, C. E., Cabral, G., & Abeling, S. (2009). Healing or hurtful: Sexual assault survivors' interpretation of social reactions from support providers. *Psychology of Women Quarterly, 33,* 81–94.

Akers, R. L. (2000). Criminological theories: Introduction, evaluation, and application (3rd ed.). Los Angeles: Roxbury.

Akmatov, M. K., Mikolajerczyk, R. T., Labeeb, S., Dharer, E., & Khan, M. M. (2008). Factors associated with wife beating in Egypt: Analysis of two surveys (1995 and 2005). *BMC Women's Health, 8,* 15–23.

Alaggia, R. (2010). An ecological analysis of child sexual abuse disclosure: Considerations for child and adolescent mental health. *Journal of the Canadian Academy of Child and Adolescent Psychiatry, 19,* 32–39.

Alaggia, R., & Millington, G. (2008). Male child sexual abuse: A phenomenology of betrayal. *Clinical Social Work Journal, 36,* 1573–1674.

Aldarondo, E. (1996). Cessation and persistence of wife assault: A longitudinal analysis. *American Journal of Orthopsychiatry, 66,* 141–151.

Aldarondo, E., Kantor, G. K., & Jasinski, J. L. (2002). A risk marker analysis of wife assault in Latino families. *Violence Against Women, 8,* 429–454.

Al Eissa, M., & Almuneef, M. (2010). Child abuse and neglect in Saudi Arabia: Journey of recognition to implementation of national prevention strategies. *Child Abuse & Neglect, 34,* 28–33.

Alessandri, S. M. (1991). Play and social behavior in maltreated preschoolers. *Development and Psychopathology, 3,* 191–205.

Alexander, K. W., Quas, J. A., Goodman, G. S., Ghetti, S., Edelstein, R. S., & Redlich, A. D. (2005). Traumatic impact predicts long-term memory for documented child sexual abuse. *Psychological Science, 16,* 33–40.

Alexander, R., Baca, L., Fox, J. A., Frantz, M., Huffman, L., et al. (2003). *New hope for preventing child abuse and neglect: Proven solutions to save lives and prevent future crime.* Washington, DC: Fight Crime: Invest in Kids, http://www.fightcrime.org/

Allen, B. (2008). An analysis of the impact of diverse forms of childhood psychological maltreatment on emotional adjustment in early adulthood. *Child Maltreatment, 13,* 307–312.

Allen, C. T., Swan, S. C., & Raghavan, C. (2009). Gender symmetry, sexism, and intimate partner violence. *Journal of Interpersonal Violence, 24,* 1816–1834.

Allen, N. E., Lehrner, A., Mattison, E., Miles, T., & Russell, A. (2007). Promoting system change in the health care response to domestic violence. *Journal of Community Psychology, 35,* 103–120.

Allison, C. J., Bartholomew, K., Mayseless, O., & Dutton, D. G. (2008). Love as a battlefield: Attachment and relationship dynamics in couples identified for male partner violence. *Journal of Family Issues, 29,* 125–150.

Al-Nsour, M., Khawaja, M., & Al-Kayyali, G. (2009). Domestic violence against women in Jordan: Evidence from health clinics. *Journal of Family Violence, 24,* 569–575.

Alyahri, A., & Goodman, R. (2008). Harsh corporal punishment of Yemini children: Occurrence, type and association. *Child Abuse & Neglect, 32,* 766–773.

Amar, A. F. (2007). Behaviors that college women label as stalking or harassment. *Journal of the American Psychiatric Nurses Association, 13,* 210–220.

Ambody, N., & Bharucha, J. (2009). Culture and the brain. *Current Direction in Psychological Science, 18,* 342–345.

American Bar Association. (n.d.). *ABA Commission on Law and Aging.* Retrieved from http://www.abanet.org/aging/publications/docs/brochure2.pdf

American Bar Association. (2009). *National domestic violence pro bono directory,* sponsored by *Verizon Wireless' Hopeline Program.* Retrieved from http://www.abanews.org

American Professional Society on the Abuse of Children. (1995). *Guidelines for the psychosocial evaluation of suspected psychological maltreatment in children and adolescents.* Chicago: Author.

American Professional Society on the Abuse of Children. (2008). *Guidelines for the psychosocial evaluation of suspected psychological maltreatment in children and adolescents.* Chicago: Author.

American Prosecutors Research Institute. (2006). *Rural victim assistance* (NCJ No. 211106). Washington, DC: Author.

American Psychiatric Association. (1994). *Diagnostic and statistical manual of mental disorders* (4th ed.). Washington, DC: Author.

American Psychiatric Association. (2000). *Diagnostic and statistical manual of mental disorders* (DSM-IV-TR). Washington, DC: Author.

American Psychological Association. (2002). Ethical principles and code of conduct. *American Psychologist, 57,* 1060–1073.

American Psychological Association. (2003). Guidelines on multicultural education, training, research, practice, and organizational change for psychologists. *American Psychologist, 58,* 377–402.

American Psychological Association. (2006). Evidence-based practice in psychology: APA Presidential Task Force on Evidence-Based Practice. *American Psychologist, 61,* 271–285.

Ammar, N. H. (2006). Beyond the shadows: Domestic spousal violence in a "democratizing" Egypt. *Trauma, Violence, & Abuse, 7,* 244–259.

Amnesty International. *Violence against women.* Retrieved from http://www.amnestyusa.org/violence-against-women

Amoakohene, M. I. (2004). Violence against women in Ghana: A look at women's perception and review of policy and social responses. *Social Science & Medicine, 59,* 2373–2385.

Amowitz, L. L., Kim, G., Reis, C., Asher, J. L., & Iacopino, V. (2004). Human rights abuses and concerns about women's health and human rights in Southern Iraq. *Journal of the American Medical Association, 291,* 1471–1479.

Anasseril, D., & Holcomb, W. (1985). A comparison between men charged with domestic and nondomestic homicide. *Bulletin of the American Academy of Psychiatry and Law, 13,* 233–241.

Andersen, P. A., Eloy, S. V., Guerrero, L. K., & Spitzberg, B. H. (1995). Romantic jealousy and relational satisfaction: A look at the impact of jealousy experience and expression. *Communication Reports, 8,* 77–85.

Anderson, C. A., Berkowitz, L., Donnerstein, E., Huesman, L. R., Johnson, J. D., et al. (2003). The influence of media violence on youth [Monograph]. *Psychological Science in the Public Interest, 4,* 81–110.

Anderson, C. A., Shibuya, A., Ihori, N., Swing, E. L., Bushman, B. J., Sakamoto, A., et al. (2010). Violent video game effects on aggression, empathy, and prosocial behavior in Eastern and Western countries: A meta-analytic review. *Psychological Bulletin, 136,* 151–173.

Anderson, D. K., & Saunders, D. G. (2003). Leaving an abusive partner: An empirical review of predictors, the process of leaving, and psychological well-being. *Trauma, Violence, & Abuse, 4,* 163–191.

Anderson, D. K., Saunders, D. G., Yoshihama, M., Bybee, D. I., & Sullivan, C. M. (2003). Long-term trends in depression among women separated from abusive partners. *Violence Against Women, 9,* 807–838.

Anderson, K. L. (2007). Who gets out? *Gender and Society, 21,* 173–201.

Anderson, L. A., & Whiston, S. C. (2005). Sexual assault education programs: A meta-analytic examination of their effectiveness. *Psychology of Women Quarterly, 29,* 374–388.

Anderson, M. A., Gillig, P. M., Sitaker, M., McCloskey, K., Malloy, K., & Grigsby, N. (2003). "Why doesn't she just leave?":

A descriptive study of victim reported impediments to her safety. *Journal of Family Violence, 18,* 151–155.

Anderson, T. (2009, November 11). Religious, homophobic hate surges. *Daily News,* p. A11.

Anetzberger, G. J. (1998). Psychological abuse and neglect: A cross-cultural concern to older Americans. In Archstone Foundation (Ed.), *Understanding and combating elder abuse in minority communities* (pp. 141–151). Long Beach, CA: Archstone Foundation.

Ang, R. P., Chia, B. H., & Fung, D. S. S. (2006). Gender differences in life stressors associated with child and adolescent suicides in Singapore from 1995 to 2003. *International Journal of Social Psychiatry, 52,* 561–570.

Anglin, K., & Holtzworth-Munroe, A. (1997). Comparing the responses of violent and nonviolent couples to problematic marital and nonmarital situations: Are the skills deficits of violent couples global? *Journal of Family Psychology, 11,* 301–313.

Annerbäch, E., Svedin, C., & Gustafsson, P. (2010). Characteristics features of severe child physical abuse—multi-informant approach. *Journal of Family Violence, 25,* 165–172.

Ansello, E. F. (1996). Understanding the problem. In L. A. Baumhover & S. C. Beall (Eds.), *Abuse, neglect, and exploitation of older persons: Strategies for assessment and intervention* (pp. 9–29). Baltimore: Health Professions Press.

Anson, O., & Sagy, S. (1995). Marital violence: Comparing women in violent and nonviolent unions. *Human Relations, 48,* 285–305.

Antonovsky, A. (1993). The structure and properties of the Sense of Coherence Scale. *Social Science and Medicine, 36,* 725–733.

Appel, A. E., & Holden, G. W. (1998). The co-occurrence of spouse and physical child abuse: A review and appraisal. *Journal of Family Psychology, 12,* 578–599.

Appelbaum, P. S. (2006). Violence and mental disorders: Data and public policy. *The American Journal of Psychiatry, 163,* 1319–1321.

Appleyard, K., Egeland, B., van Dulmen, M. H., & Sroufe, L. A. (2005). When more is not better: The role of cumulative risk in child behavior outcomes. *Journal of Child Psychology and Psychiatry, 46,* 235–245.

Apsler, R., Cummins, M. R., & Carl, S. (2003). Perceptions of the police by female victims of domestic partner violence. *Violence Against Women, 9,* 1318–1335.

Arata, C. M. (1998). To tell or not to tell: Current functioning of child sexual abuse survivors who disclosed their victimization. *Child Maltreatment, 3,* 63–71.

Arber, S., & Ginn, J. (1999). Gender differences in informal caring. In G. Allan (Ed.), *The sociology of the family: A reader* (pp. 321–339). Oxford, England: Blackwell.

Arboleda-Florez, J., & Wade, T. J. (2001). Childhood and adult victimization as risk factors for major depression. *International Journal of Law and Psychiatry, 24,* 357–370.

Archer, J. (1999). An assessment of the reliability of the Conflict Tactics Scales: A meta-analytic review. *Journal of Interpersonal Violence, 14,* 1263–1289.

Archer, J. (2000). Sex differences in aggression between heterosexual partners: A meta-analytic review. *Psychological Bulletin, 126,* 651–680.

Archer, J. (2006). Cross-cultural differences in physical aggression between partners: A social-role analysis. *Personality and Social Psychology Review, 10,* 133–153.

Archstone Foundation. (2006). The Archstone Foundation grants. Elder abuse and neglect initiative. Retrieved from http://www.archstone.org

Arias, I., & Corso, P. (2005). Average cost per person victimized by and intimate partner of the opposite gender: A comparison of men and women. *Violence and Victims, 20,* 379–391.

Arias, I., & Pape, K. T. (1999). Psychological abuse: Implications for adjustment and commitment to leave violent partners. *Violence and Victims, 14,* 55–67.

Armstrong, T. G., Wernke, J. Y., Medina, K. L., & Schafer, J. (2002). Do partners agree about the occurrence of intimate partner violence? *Trauma, Violence, & Abuse, 3,* 181–193.

Army gender-integrated basic training (GIBT). (2003, May). *Summary of relevant findings and recommendations: 1993–2002.* Retrieved from http://www.cmrlink.org/cmrnotes/gibtsp01.pdf

Arnd-Caddigan, M. (2006). Somatoform disorders and a history of abuse: Comorbidity, dynamics, and practice implications. *Journal of Social Work, 6,* 21–31.

Arnold, D., Gelaye, B., Goshu, M., Berhane, Y., & Williams, M. A. (2008). Prevalence and risk factors of gender-based violence among female college students in Awassa, Ethiopia. *Violence and Victims, 23,* 787–800.

Arosarena, O. A., Fritsch, T. A., Hsueh, Y., Aynehchi, A., & Haug, R. (2009). Maxillofacial injuries and violence against women. *Facial Plastic Surgery, 11,* 48–52.

Arriaga, X. B., & Capezza, N. M. (2005). Targets of partner violence: The importance of understanding coping trajectories. *Journal of Interpersonal Violence, 20,* 89–99.

Arriaga, X. B., & Foshee, V. A. (2004). Adolescent dating violence: Do adolescents follow in their friends,' or their parents' footsteps? *Journal of Interpersonal Violence, 19,* 162–184.

Arscott-Millis, S. (2001). Intimate partner violence in Jamaica. *Violence Against Women, 7,* 1284–1302.

Arseneault, L., Walsh, E., Trzesniewski, K., Newcombe, R., Caspi, A., & Moffitt, T. E. (2010). Bully victimization uniquely contributes to adjustment problems in young children: A nationally representative cohort study. *Pediatrics, 118,* 130–138.

Ashcraft, C. (2000). Naming knowledge: A language for reconstructing domestic violence and gender inequity. *Women and Language, 23,* 3–10.

Ashida, S., & Heaney, C. A. (2008). Differential associations of social support and social connectedness with structural features of social networks and the health status of older adults. *Journal of Aging and Health, 20,* 872–893.

Associated Press. (2006a, May 9). Lesbians' brains wired like those of straight men. *Daily News,* 13.

Associated Press. (2006b, July 27). Woman not guilty in retrial in the deaths of her 5 children. *New York Times.* Retrieved from www.nytimes.com/2006/07/27/us/27yates.html

Atkinson, R. L., Atkinson, R. C., Smith, E. E., & Bem, D. J. (1990). *Introduction to psychology* (10th ed.). New York: Harcourt Brace Jovanovich.

Attala, J. M., Weaver, T. L., Duckett, D., & Draper, V. (2000). The implications of domestic violence for home care providers. *International Journal of Trauma Nursing, 6*(2), 48–53.

Auerhahn, K. (2007). Adjudication outcomes in intimate and nonintimate homicides. *Homicide Studies, 11,* 213–230.

Aulivola, M. (2004). Outing domestic violence: Affording appropriate protection to gay and lesbian victims. *Family Court Review, 42,* 162–177.

Austin, J. B., & Dankwort, J. (1999). Standards for batterer programs: A review and analysis. *Journal of Interpersonal Violence, 14,* 152–168.

Avakame, E. F., & Fyfe, J. J. (2001). Differential police treatment of male-on-female spousal violence. *Violence Against Women, 7,* 22–45.

Azar, B. (1997, March). APA task force urges a harder look at data. *APA Monitor on Psychology, 28,* 26.

Azar, S. T., Povilaitis, T. Y., Lauretti, A. F., & Pouquette, C. L. (1998). The current status of etiological theories in intrafamilial child maltreatment. In J. R. Lutzker (Ed.), *Handbook of child abuse research and treatment* (pp. 3–30). New York: Plenum.

Babcock, J. C., Green, C. E., & Robie, C. (2004). Does batterers' treatment work? A meta-analytic review of domestic violence treatment. *Clinical Psychology Review, 23,* 1023–1053.

Babcock. J. C., Green, C. E., Webb, S. A., & Graham, K. H. (2004). A second failure to replicate the Gottman et al. (1995) typology of men who abuse intimate partners . . . and possible reasons why. *Journal of Family Psychology, 18,* 396–400.

Babcock, J. C., Jacobson, N. S., Gottman, J. M., & Yerington, T. P. (2000). Attachment, emotional regulation, and the function of marital violence: Differences between secure, preoccupied, and dismissing violent and nonviolent husbands. *Journal of Family Violence, 15,* 391–409.

Babcock, J. C., Roseman, A., Green, C. E., & Ross, J. M. (2008). Intimate partner abuse and PTSD symptomatology: Examining mediators and moderators of the abuse-trauma link. *Journal of Family Psychology, 22,* 809–818.

Babcock, J. C., Waltz, J., Jacobson, N. S., & Gottman, J. M. (1993). Power and violence: The relation between communication patterns, power discrepancies, and domestic violence. *Journal of Consulting and Clinical Psychology, 61,* 40–50.

Babinski, L. M., Hartsough, C. S., & Lambert, N. M. (2001). A comparison of self-report of criminal involvement and official arrest records. *Aggressive Behavior, 27,* 44–54.

Babu, B. V., & Kar, S. K. (2009). Domestic violence against women in eastern India: A population-based study on prevalence and related issues. *BMC Public Health, 9,* 129–143.

Bachman, R., & Saltzman, L. E. (1995). *Violence against women: Estimates from the redesigned survey* (NCJ Publication No. 154348). Rockville, MD: U.S. Department of Justice.

Bader, S. M., Scalora, M. J., Cassady, T. K., & Black, S. (2008). Female sexual abuse and criminal justice intervention: A comparison of child protective service and criminal justice samples. *Child Abuse & Neglect, 32,* 111–119.

Bader, S. M., Welsh, R., & Scalora, M. J. (2010). Recidivism among female child molesters. *Violence and Victims, 25,* 349–361.

Bagarozzi, D., & Giddings, C. (1983). Conjugal violence: A critical review of current research and clinical practices. *American Journal of Family Therapy, 11,* 3–15.

Bailey, S. J. (2007). Unraveling the meaning of family: Voices of divorced nonresidential parents. *Marriage & Family Review, 42,* 81–102.

Bailly, R. M. (2009, March/April). Where there's a will there's a way. *Victimization of the Elderly and Disabled, 11,* 81–82, 86, 92, 94–95.

Baines, V. (2008). Online child sexual abuse: The law enforcement response. Brazil: ECPAT International. Retrieved from www.ecpat.net.../PDF/.../ICT.../thematic_paper_ICTLAW_ENG.pdf

Bair-Merritt., M. H., Feudtner, C., Localio, A. R., Feinstein, J. A., Rubin, D., & Holmes, W. C. (2008). Health care use of children whose female caregivers have intimate partner violence histories. *Archives of Pediatrics & Adolescent Medicine, 162,* 134–139.

Baker, C. K., Niolon, P. H., & Oliphant, H. (2009). Descriptive analysis of transitional housing programs for survivors of partner violence in the United States. *Violence Against Women, 15,* 460–481.

Baker, T. B., McFall, R. M., & Shoham, V. (2009). Current status and future prospects of clinical psychology toward a scientifically principled approach to mental and behavioral health care [Monograph]. *Psychological Science in the Public Interest, 9*(2), 67–103.

Baker-Ericzén, M. J., Hurlburt, M. S., Brookman-Frazee, L., Jenkins, M. M., & Hough, R. L. (2010). Comparing child, parent, and family characteristics in usual care and empirically supported treatment research samples for children with disruptive behavior disorder. *Journal of Emotional and Behavioral Disorders, 18,* 82–99.

Bakwin, H. (1949). Emotional deprivation in infants. *Journal of Pediatrics, 35,* 512–521.

Bala, N., Lee, K., Lindsay, R. C. L., & Talwar, V. (2010). Competency of children to testify. Psychological research informing Canadian law reform. *International Journal of Children's Rights, 18,* 53–77.

Baldry, A. C., & Farrington, D. P. (2007). Effectiveness of programs to prevent school bullying. *Victims and Offenders, 2,* 183–204.

Ball, B., Kerig, P. K., & Rosenbluth, B. (2009). "Like a family but better because you can actually trust each other": The Expect Respect dating violence prevention program for at-risk youth. *Health Promotion Practice, 10 (Suppl. 1),* 45S–58S.

Ball, H. A., Arseneault, L., Taylor, A., Maughan, B., Caspi, A., & Moffitt, E. T. (2008). Genetic and environmental influences on victims, bullies and bully-victims in childhood. *Journal of Child Psychology and Psychiatry, 49,* 104–112.

Balsam, K. F., Rothblum, E. D., & Beauchaine, T. P. (2005). Victimization over the life span: A comparison of lesbian, gay, bisexual, and heterosexual siblings. *Journal of Consulting and Clinical Psychology, 73,* 477–487.

Balsam, K. F., & Szymanski, D. M. (2005). Relationship quality and domestic violence in women's same-sex relationships: The role of minority stress. *Psychology of Women Quarterly, 29,* 258–269.

Bandstra, E., Morrow, C., Mansoor, E., & Accornero, V. H. (2010). Prenatal drug exposure: Infant and toddler outcomes. *Journal of Addictive Disease, 2,* 245–258.

Bandura, A. (1977). *Social learning theory.* Morristown, NJ: General Learning.

Bandura, A., Ross, D., & Ross, S. A. (1961). Transmission of aggression through imitation of aggressive models. *Journal of Abnormal and Social Psychology, 67,* 575–582.

Band-Winterstein, T., & Eisikovits, Z. (2009). "Aging out" of violence: The multiple faces of intimate violence over the life span. *Qualitative Health Research, 19,* 161–180.

Bane, V., Grant, M., Alexander, B., Kelly, K., Brown, S. A., Wegher, B., et al. (1990, December 17). Silent no more. *People,* 94–97, 99–100, 102, 104.

Banks, A. (2001). *PTSD: Relationships and brain chemistry* (Project Report No. 8). Wellesley, MA: Wellesley Centers for Women.

Banks, D., Dutch, N., & Wang, K. (2008). Collaborative efforts to improve system response to families who are experiencing child maltreatment and domestic violence. *Journal of Interpersonal Violence, 23,* 876–902.

Banks, L., Crandall, C., Sklar, D., & Bauer, M. (2008). A comparison of intimate partner homicide to intimate partner homicide-suicide. *Violence Against Women, 14,* 1065–1078.

Banks, M. E. (2007). Overlooked but critical. *Trauma, Violence, & Abuse, 8,* 290–298.

Banyard, V. L., Cross, C., & Modecki, K. L. (2006). Interpersonal violence in adolescence: Ecological correlates of self-reported perpetration. *Journal of Interpersonal Violence, 21,* 1314–1332.

Banyard, V. L., Ward, S., Cohn, E. S., Plante, E. G., Moorhead, C., & Walsh, W. (2007). Unwanted sexual contact on campus: A comparison of women's and men's experiences. *Violence and Victims, 22,* 52–70.

Barak, A. (2005). Sexual harassment on the Internet. *Social Science Computer Review, 23,* 77–92.

Barata, P. C., & Senn, C. Y. (2003). When two worlds collide: An examination of the assumptions of social science research and law within the domain of domestic violence. *Trauma, Violence, & Abuse, 4,* 3–21.

Barber, C. W., Azrael, D., Hemenway, D., Olson, L. M., Nie, C., Schaechter, J., et al. (2008). Suicide and suicide attempts following homicide: Victim-suspect relationship, weapon type, and presence of antidepressants. *Homicide Studies, 12,* 285–297.

Barelds, D. P. H., & Barelds-Dijkstra, P. (2007). Relations between different types of jealousy and self and partner perceptions of relationship quality. *Clinical Psychology & Psychotherapy, 14,* 176–188.

Barelds, D. P. H., & Dijkstra, P. (2006). Reactive, anxious and possessive forms of jealousy and their relation to relationship quality among heterosexuals and homosexuals. *Journal of Homosexuality, 51,* 183–198.

Barkin, S. L., Finch, S. A., Ip, E. H., Schneidlin, B., & Craig, J. S., et al. (2008). Is office-based counseling about media use, timeouts and firearm storage effective? Results from a cluster-randomized controlled trial. *Pediatrics, 122,* e15–e25.

Barnett, O. W. (2000). Why battered women do not leave, Part 1: External inhibiting factors within society. *Trauma, Violence, & Abuse, 1,* 343–372.

Barnett, O. W. (2001). Why battered women do not leave, Part 2: External inhibiting factors, social support, and internal inhibiting factors. *Trauma, Violence, & Abuse, 2,* 3–35.

Barnett, O. W., & Fagan, R. W. (1993). Alcohol use in male spouse abusers and their female partners. *Journal of Family Violence, 8,* 1–25.

Barnett, O. W., Fagan, R. W., & Booker, J. M. (1991). Hostility and stress as mediators of aggression in violent men. *Journal of Family Violence, 6,* 219–241.

Barnett, O. W., & Hamberger, L. K. (1992). The assessment of maritally violent men on the California Psychological Inventory. *Violence and Victims, 7,* 15–28.

Barnett, O. W., Lee, C. Y., & Thelen, R. E. (1997). Differences in forms, outcomes, and attributions of self-defense and control in interpartner aggression. *Violence Against Women, 3,* 462–481.

Barnett, O. W., Martinez, T. E., & Bluestein, B. W. (1995). Jealousy and anxious romantic attachment in maritally violent and nonviolent males. *Journal of Interpersonal Violence, 10,* 473–486.

Barnett, O. W., Martinez, T. E., & Keyson, M. (1996). The relationship between violence, social support, and self-blame in battered women. *Journal of Interpersonal Violence, 11,* 221–233.

Baron, K. G., Smith, T. W., Butner, J., Nealey-Moore, J., Hawkins, M. W., & Uchino, B. N. (2006). Hostility, anger, and marital adjustment: Concurrent and prospective associations with psychosocial vulnerability. *Journal of Behavioral Medicine, 30,* 1–10.

Baron, R. M., & Kenny, D. A. (1986). The moderator-mediator variable distinction in social psychological research: Conceptual, strategic, and statistical considerations. *Journal of Personality and Social Psychology, 51,* 1173–1182.

Barranti, C. C. R., & Yuen, F. K. O. (2008). Intimate partner violence and women with disabilities: Toward bringing visibility to an unrecognized population. *Journal of Social Work in Disability & Rehabilitation, 7,* 115–130.

Barrera, M., Jr., Palmer, S., Brown, R., & Kalaher, S. (1994). Characteristics of court-involved men and non-court-involved men who abuse their wives. *Journal of Family Violence, 9,* 333–345.

Barry, R. A., Lawrence, E., & Langer, A. (2008). Conceptualization and assessment of disengagement in romantic relationships. *Personal Relationships, 15,* 297–315.

Bartfield, J. (2000). Child support and the post-divorce economic well-being of mothers, fathers, and children. *Demography, 37,* 203–213.

Barth, R. P. (2009). Preventing child abuse and neglect with parent training: Evidence and opportunities. *The Future of Children, 19,* 95–118.

Bartholomew, K. (1997). Adult attachment processes: Individual and couple perspectives. *British Journal of Medical Psychology, 70,* 249–263.

Bartholomew, K., & Horowitz, L. M. (1991). Attachment styles among young adults: A test of a four-category model. *Journal of Personality & Social Psychology, 61,* 226–244.

Bartholomew, K., Regan, K. V., White, M. A., & Oram, D. (2008). Patterns of abuse in male same-sex relationships. *Violence and Victims, 5,* 617–636.

Bartkowski, J. P., & Wilcox, W. B. (2000). Conservative Protestant child discipline: The case of parental yelling. *Social Forces, 79,* 265–291.

Bartkowski, J. P., & Xu, X. (2000). Distant patriarchs or expressive dads? The discourse and practice of fathering in conservative Protestant families. *Sociological Quarterly, 41,* 465–485.

Barton, K., & Baglio, C. (1993). The nature of stress in child-abusing families: A factor analytic study. *Psychological Reports, 73,* 1047–1055.

Basile, K., Swahn, M., Chen, J., & Saltzman, L. (2006). Stalking in the United States: Recent national prevalence estimates. *American Journal of Preventive Medicine, 31,* 172–175.

Basile, K. C., Hertz, M. F., & Back, S. E. (2007). *Intimate partner violence and sexual violence victimization assessment instruments for use in healthcare settings: Version 1.* Atlanta, GA: Centers for Disease Control and Prevention, National Center for Injury Prevention and Control.

Basow, S. A., Cahill, K. F., Phelan, J. E., Longshore, K., & McGillicuddy-DeLise, A. (2007). Perceptions of relational and physical aggression among college students: Effects of perpetrator, target, and perceiver. *Psychology of Women Quarterly, 31,* 85–95.

Bass, E., & Davis, L. (1988). *The courage to heal.* New York: Harper & Row.

Bassarath, L. (2001). Neuroimaging studies of antisocial behavior. *Canadian Journal of Psychiatry, 46,* 728–732.

Bassuk, E. L., Weinreb, L. F., Buckner, J. C., Browne, A., Salomon, A., & Bassuk, S. S. (1996). The characteristics and needs of sheltered homeless and low-income housed mothers. *Journal of the American Medical Association, 276,* 640–646.

Baum, K., Catalano, S., Rand, M., & Rose, K. (2009). *Stalking victimization in the United States* (NCJ Publication No. 224527). U.S. Department of Justice, NCVS.

Baumann, E. A. (1989). Research rhetoric and the social construction of elder abuse. In J. Best (Ed.), *Images of issues: Typifying contemporary social problems* (pp. 55–74). New York: Aldine de Gruyter.

Baumeister, R. F., Dale, K., & Sommer, K. L. (1996). Relation of threatened egotism to violence and aggression: The dark side of high self-esteem. *Psychological Review, 103,* 5–33.

Bauserman, S. A. K., & Arias, I. (1992). Relationships among marital investment, marital satisfaction, and marital commitment in domestically victimized and nonvictimized wives. *Violence and Victims, 7,* 287–296.

Beach, S. R. H., Kim, S., Cercone-Keeney, J., Gupta, M., Arias, I., & Brody, G. H. (2004). Physical aggression and depressive symptoms: Gender asymmetry in effects. *Journal of Social and Personal Relationships, 21,* 341–360.

Beaulaurier, R. L., Seff, L. R., Newman, F. L., & Dunlop, B. (2005). Internal barriers to help seeking for middle-aged and older women who experience intimate partner violence. *Journal of Elder Abuse & Nelgect, 17,* 53–74.

Beck, A. T. (1978). *BDI (Beck Depression Inventory).* San Antonio, TX: Psychological Corporation.

Becker, H. W. (1963). *Outsiders.* New York: Free Press.

Becker-Blease, K. A. (2006). Research participants telling the truth about their lives: The ethics of asking and not asking about abuse. *American Psychologist, 61,* 218–226.

Becker-Blease, K. A., Friend, D., & Freyd, J. (2006, November 4–7). *Child sex abuse among male university students.* Poster presented at the 22nd annual meeting of the International Society for Traumatic Stress Studies, Hollywood, CA, http://hdl.handle.net/1794/4318

Beckham, J. C., Feldman, M. E., Kirby, A. C., Hertzberg, M. A., & Moore, S. D. (1997). Interpersonal violence and its correlates in Vietnam veterans with chronic posttraumatic stress disorder. *Journal of Clinical Psychology, 53,* 859–869.

Bedi, G., & Goddard, C. (2007). Intimate partner violence: What are the impacts on children? *Australian Psychologist, 42,* 66–77.

Beech, A. R., Ward, T., & Fisher, D. (2006). The identification of sexual and violence motivations in men who assault women: Implications for treatment. *Journal of Interpersonal Violence, 21,* 1635–1653.

Beechey, S., & Payne, J. (2002). *Surviving violence and poverty: A focus on the link between domestic and sexual violence, women's poverty, and welfare.* New York: NOW Legal Defense and Education Fund.

Behnke, S. (2009, June). Disability as an ethical issue. *Monitor on Psychology, 40,* 62–63.

Belaga, I. (2005). *Domestic violence: Typology of batterers and effectiveness of treatment* (Doctoral dissertation). Available from ProQuest Dissertations and Theses database. (UMI No. 3151695)

Belar, C. (2008, July). Internationalizing psychology education. *Monitor on Psychology, 39,* 86.

Belknap, J. (2000). *Factors related to domestic violence court dispositions in a large urban area: The role of victim/witness reluctance and other variables* (NCJ Publication No. 184232). Washington, DC: National Institute of Justice.

Belknap, J., Graham, D. L. R., Allen, P. G., Hartman, J., Lippen, V., & Sutherland, J. (1999, October/November). Predicting court outcomes in intimate partner violence cases: Preliminary findings. *Domestic Violence Report, 5,* 1–2, 9–10.

Bell, C. C., & Mattis, J. (2000). The importance of cultural competence in ministering to African American victims of domestic violence. *Violence Against Women, 6,* 515–532.

Bell, M. E., Bennett-Cattaneo, L., Goodman, L. A., & Dutton, M. A. (2008). Assessing the risk of future psychological abuse: Predicting the accuracy of battered women's predictions. *Journal of Family Violence, 23,* 69–80.

Bell, M. E., Goodman, L. A., & Dutton, M. A. (2007). The dynamics of staying and leaving: Implications for battered womens' emotional well-being and experiences of violence at the end of a year. *Journal of Family Violence, 22,* 413–428.

Bell, N. S., Harford, T., McCarroll, J. E., & Senier, L. (2004). Drinking and spouse abuse among U.S. Army soldiers. *Alcoholism: Clinical and Experimental Research, 28,* 1890–1897.

Bellamy, J. L. (2009). A national study of male involvement among families in contact with the child welfare system. *Child Maltreatment, 14,* 255–262.

Belli, R. F., Shay, W. L., & Stafford, F. P. (2001). Event history calendars and question list surveys: A direct comparison of interviewing methods. *Public Opinion Quarterly, 65,* 45–74.

Belsky, J. (2005). The development and evolutionary psychology of intergenerational transmission of attachment. In C. S. Carter, L. Ahmert, K. E. Grossman, S. B. Hardy, M. E. Lamb, S. W. Porges, & N. Sachser (Eds.), *Attachment and bonding: A new synthesis* (pp. 169–198). Cambridge, MA: The MIT Press.

Bem, S. L. (1979). *Bem Sex-Role Inventory: Professional manual.* Palo Alto, CA: Consulting Psychologists Press.

Ben-David, S., & Schneider, O. (2005). Rape perceptions, gender role attitudes, and victim-perpetrator acquaintance. *Sex-Roles, 53,* 385–399.

Bender, H. L., Allen, J. P., McElhaney, K. B., Antonishak, J., Moore, C. M., et al. (2007). Use of harsh physical discipline and developmental outcomes in adolescence. *Development and Psychopathology, 19,* 227–242.

Benedict, M., White, R., Wulff, L., & Hall, B. (1990). Reported maltreatment in children with multiple disabilities. *Child Abuse & Neglect, 14,* 207–217.

Bennett, D. S., Bendersky, M., & Lewis, M. (2008). Children's cognitive ability from 4 to 9 years old as a function of prenatal cocaine exposure, environmental risk, and maternal verbal intelligence. *Developmental Psychology, 44,* 919–928.

Bennett, D. S., Sullivan, M., Thompson, S. M., & Lewis, M. (2010). Early child neglect: Does it predict obesity or underweight in later childhood? *Child Maltreatment.* doi: 10.1177/1077559510363730

Bennett, L. W. (1995). Substance abuse and the domestic assault of women. *Social Work, 40,* 760–771.

Bennett, L. W. (2008). Substance abuse by men in partner abuse intervention programs: Current issues and promising trends. *Violence and Victims, 23,* 236–248.

Bennett, L. W., & Fineran, S. (1998). Sexual and severe physical violence among high school students: Power beliefs, gender, and relationship. *American Journal of Orthopsychiatry, 68,* 645–652.

Bennett, L. W., Stroops, C., Call, C., & Flett, H. (2007). Program completion and re-arrest in a batterer intervention system. *Research and Social Work Practice, 17,* 42–54.

Bennett, L. W., Tolman, R. M., Rogalski, C. J., & Srinivasaraghavan, J. (1994). Domestic abuse by male alcohol and drug addicts. *Violence and Victims, 9,* 359–368.

Bennett, S., Hart, S. N., & Svevo-Cianci, K. (2010). The need for a general comment for Article 19 of the UN Convention on the Rights of the Child: Toward enlightenment and progress for child protection. *Child Abuse & Neglect, 33,* 783–790.

Ben-Porat, A., & Itzhaky, H. (2009). Implications of treating family violence for the therapist: Secondary traumatization, vicarious traumatization, and growth. *Journal of Family Violence, 24,* 507–515.

Benson, M., Fox, G., DeMaris, A., & Van Wyk, J. (2003). Neighborhood disadvantage, individual economic distress and violence against women in intimate relationships. *Journal of Quantitative Criminology, 19,* 207–235.

Bent-Goodley, T. B. (2001). Eradicating domestic violence in the African American community: A literature review and action agenda. *Trauma, Violence, & Abuse, 2,* 316–330.

Bergen, R. K. (1996). *Wife rape: Understanding the response of survivors and service providers.* Thousand Oaks, CA: Sage.

Bergen, R. K., & Bukovec, P. (2006). Men and intimate partner rape. *Journal of Interpersonal Violence, 21,* 1375–1384.

Berger, L. M., Slack, K. S., Waldfogel, J., & Bruch, S. K. (2010). Caseworker-perceived substance abuse and child protective services outcomes. *Child Maltreatment, 15,* 199–210.

Berger, R., & Rosenberg, E. (2008). The experience of abused women with their children's law guardians. *Violence Against Women, 14,* 71–92.

Berk, R. A., Fenstermaker, S., & Newton, P. J. (1988). An empirical analysis of police responses to incidents of wife battery. In G. T. Hotaling, D. Finkelhor, J. T. Kirkpatrick, & M. A. Straus (Eds.), *Coping with family violence* (pp. 158–168). Newbury Park, CA: Sage.

Berkoff, M. C., Zolotor, A. J., Makoroff, K. L., Thackeray, J. D., Shapiro, R. A., & Runyan, D. K. (2008). Has this prepubertal girl been sexually abused? *Journal of the American Medical Association, 300,* 2779–2792.

Berkowitz, A. D. (2000, May/June). Critical elements of campus sexual assault prevention and risk reduction programs. *Sexual Assault Report, 3,* 67–68, 80.

Berliner, L. (1991). Clinical work with sexually abused children. In C. R. Hollin & K. Howells (Eds.), *Clinical approaches to sex offenders and their victims* (pp. 209–228). New York: John Wiley.

Berliner, L. (1994). The problem with neglect. *Journal of Interpersonal Violence, 9,* 556–560.

Berliner, L. (1998). Battered women and abused children: The question of responsibility. *Journal of Interpersonal Violence, 13,* 287–288.

Berliner, L. (2000). What is sexual abuse? In Dubowitz & D. DePanfilis (Eds.), *Handbook for child protection* (pp.18–22). Thousand Oaks, CA: Sage.

Berliner, L., & Conte, J. R. (1990). The process of victimization: The victim's perspective. *Child Abuse & Neglect, 14,* 29–40.

Berliner, L., & Saunders, B. (2010). Child sexual abuse: definitions, prevalence, and consequences. In J. E. B. Myers (Ed.), *The APSAC handbook on child maltreatment* (3rd ed., pp. 215–231). Thousand Oaks, CA: Sage

Berman, M. E., McCloskey, M. S., Fanning, J. R., Schumacher, J. A., & Coccaro, E. F. (2009). Serotonin augmentation reduces response to attack in aggressive individuals. *Psychological Science, 20,* 714–720.

Bernhard, L. A. (2000). Physical and sexual violence experienced by lesbian and heterosexual women. *Violence Against Women, 6,* 68–79.

Bernhardt, P. C. (1997). Influences of serotonin and testosterone in aggression and dominance: Convergence with social psychology. *Current Directions in Psychological Science, 6,* 44–48.

Berns, N. (2001). Degendering the problem and gendering the blame: Political discourse on women and violence. *Gender & Society, 15,* 262–281.

Bernstein, A., Newman, J. P., Wallace, J. F., & Luh, K. E. (2000). Left-hemisphere activation and deficient response modulation in psychopaths. *Psychological Science, 11,* 414–418.

Bernstein, D. M., & Loftus, E. F. (2009). How to tell if a particular memory is true or false. *Perspectives on Psychological Science, 4,* 370–374.

Berson, I. R., Berson, M. J., & Ferron, J. M. (2002). Emerging risks of violence in the digital age: Lessons for educators from an online study of adolescent girls in the United States. *Journal of School Violence, 1,* 51–71.

Berson, N., & Herman-Giddens, M. (1994). Recognizing invasive genital care practices: A form of child sexual abuse. *APSAC Advisor, 7*(1), 13–14.

Bertrand, R. M., Fredman, L., & Saczynski, J. (2006). Are all caregivers created equal? Stress in caregivers to adults with and without dementia. *Journal of Aging and Health, 16,* 534–551.

Best, J. (2001). *Damned lies and statistics: Untangling numbers from the media, politicians, and activists.* Berkley: University of California Press.

Bethell, C., Reuland, C. P., Halfon, N., & Schor, E. L. (2004). Measuring the quality of preventive and developmental services for young children: National estimates and patterns of clinicians' performance. *Pediatrics, 113*(Suppl.), 1973–1983.

Bethke, T., & De Joy, D. (1993). An experimental study of factors influencing the acceptability of dating violence. *Journal of Interpersonal Violence, 8,* 36–51.

Bettesworth, A. (2007, March). Friends of NIDA hold congressional briefing on drug abuse treatment. APA Online: *Psychological Science Agenda.* Retrieved from http://www.apa.org/science/psa/mar07fon.html

Betz, C. L. (2007). Editorial. Teen dating violence: An unrecognized health care need. *Journal of Pediatric Nursing, 22,* 427–429.

Betz, M. E., Kelly, S. P., & Fisher, J. (2008). Death certificate inaccuracy and underreporting of injury in elderly people. *Journal of the American Geriatriac Society, 56,* 2267–2272.

Bevc, I., & Silverman, I. (1993). Early proximity and intimacy between siblings and incestuous behavior: A test of the Westermarck theory. *Ethology and Sociobiology, 14,* 171–181.

Beyer, K., Mack, S. M., & Shelton, J. L. (2008). Investigative analysis of neonaticide: An exploratory study. *Criminal Justice and Behavior, 35,* 522–535.

Bianchi, S. M., & Spain, D. (1996). Women, work, and family in America. *Population Bulletin, 51,* 2–47.

Billingham, R. E. (1987). Courtship violence: The patterns of conflict resolution strategies across seven levels of emotional commitment. *Family Relations, 36,* 283–289.

Binggeli, N. J., Hart, S. N., & Brassard, M. R. (2001). *Psychological maltreatment of children.* Thousand Oaks, CA: Sage.

Birns, B., Cascardi, M., & Meyer, S. L. (1994). Sex-role socialization: Developmental influences on wife abuse. *American Journal of Orthopsychiatry, 64,* 50–59.

Birns, B., & Meyer, S. L. (1993). Mothers' role in incest: Dysfunctional women or dysfunctional theories? *Journal of Child Sexual Abuse, 2*(3), 127–135.

Bischoff, R. J., Hollist, C. S., Smith, C. W., & Flack, P. (2004). Addressing mental health needs of the rural underserved: Findings from a multiple case study of a behavioral telehealth project. *Contemporary Family Therapy, 26,* 179–198.

Bishop, D. M. (2010). Juvenile law reform: Ensuring the right to counsel [Editorial]. *Criminology, 9,* 321–325.

Bishop, D. M., Frazier, C. E., Lanza-Kaduce, L., & Winner, L. (1996). The transfer of juveniles to criminal court: Does it make a difference? *Crime and Delinquency, 42,* 171–191.

Bitensky, S. H. (2006). *Corporal punishment of children: A human rights violation.* Ardsley, NY: Transnational Publishers.

Blaauw, E., Winkel, F. W., Arensman, E., Sheridan, L. P., & Freeve, A. (2002). The toll of stalking: The relationship between features of stalking and psychopathology of victims. *Journal of Interpersonal Violence, 17,* 50–63.

Black, B. M., Tolman, R. M., Callahan, M., Saunders, D. G., & Weisz, A. N. (2008). When will adolescents tell someone about dating violence victimization? *Violence Against Women, 14,* 741–756.

Black, B. M., & Weisz, A. N. (2004). Dating violence: A qualitative analysis of Mexican-American youths' views. *Journal of Ethnic & Cultural Diversity in Social Work, 13,* 69–90.

Black, D. A., Heyman, R. E., & Slep, A. M. S. (2001). Risk factors for child physical abuse. *Aggression and Violent Behavior, 6,* 121–188.

Black, D. S., Sussman, S., & Unger, J. B. (2010). A further look at the intergenerational transmission of violence: Witnessing interparental violence in emerging adulthood. *Journal of Interpersonal Violence, 25,* 1022–1042.

Black, K. A., & Gold, D. J. (2008). Gender differences and socio-economic status biases in judgments about blame in date rape scenarios. *Violence and Victims, 23,* 115–128.

Black, M. C., & Black, R. S. (2007). A public health perspective on "the ethics of asking and not asking about abuse." *American Psychologist, 62,* 328–329.

Blakely, B. E., & Dolon, R. (1991). Area agencies on aging and the prevention of elder abuse: The results of a national study. *Journal of Elder Abuse & Neglect, 3*(2), 21–40.

Blanchard, B. D. (2001). Extremes of narcissism and self-esteem and the differential experience and expression of anger and use of conflict tactics in male batterers. *Dissertation Abstracts International, 62*(05), 2476B. (UMI No. 301619)

Bleecker, E. T., & Murnen, S. K. (2005). Fraternity membership, the display of degrading sexual images of women, and rape myth acceptance. *Sex Roles, 53,* 487–493.

Bliss, M. J., Ogley-Oliver, E., Jackson, E., Harp, S., & Kaslow, N. J. (2008). African American women's readiness to change abusive relationships. *Journal of Family Violence, 23,* 161–171.

Block, C. R. (2003). How can practitioners help an abused woman lower her risk of death? *National Institute of Justice Journal, Issue 250,* 4–7.

Block, C. R., & Christakos, A. (1995). Intimate partner homicide in Chicago over 29 years. *Crime & Delinquency, 41,* 496–526.

Block, C. R., Engel, B., Naureckas, S. M., & Riordan, K. A. (1999). The Chicago Women's Health Risk Study: Lessons in collaboration. *Violence Against Women, 5,* 1158–1177.

Block, R. W., & Krebs, N. F. (2005). Failure to thrive as a manifestation of child neglect. *Pediatrics, 116,* 1234–1237.

Blum, L. C. (1997). The impact of the rewards and costs of family functioning on the decisions made by battered women. *Dissertation Abstracts International, 57*(11), 4928A. (UMI No. 9711021)

Blumenthal, D. R., Neeman, J., & Murphy, C. M. (1998). Lifetime exposure to interparental physical and verbal aggression and symptom expression in college students. *Violence and Victims, 13,* 175–196.

Boba, R., & Lilley, D. (2009). Violence Against Women Act (VAWA) funding: A nationwide assessment of effects on rape and assault. *Violence Against Women, 15,* 168–185.

Boeringer, S. B. (1999). Associations of rape-supportive attitudes with fraternal and athletic participation. *Violence Against Women, 5,* 81–90.

Bogat, G. A., Levendosky, A. A., Theran, S., von Eye, A., & Davidson, W. S. (2003). Predicting the psychosocial effects of intimate partner violence (IPV): How much does a woman's history matter? *Journal of Interpersonal Violence, 18,* 1271–1291.

Bograd, M. (1988). Feminist perspectives on wife abuse: An introduction. In K. A. Yllö & M. Bograd (Eds.), *Feminist perspectives on wife abuse* (pp. 11–26). Newbury Park, CA: Sage.

Bolen, R. M. (2003). Nonoffending mothers of sexually abused children. *Violence Against Women, 9,* 1336–1366.

Bomba, P. A. (2006). Use of a single page elder abuse assessment and management tool: A practical clinician's approach to identifying elder mistreatment. *Journal of Gerontological Social Work, 46,* 103–122.

Bondurant, B. (2001). University women's acknowledgment of rape. *Violence Against Women, 7,* 294–314.

Boney-McCoy, S., & Finkelhor, D. (1995). The psychosocial sequelae of violent victimization in a national youth sample. *Journal of Consulting and Clinical Psychology, 63,* 726–736.

Boney-McCoy, S., & Sugarman, D. E. (1999, July). *Self-esteem and partner violence: A meta-analytic review.* Paper presented at the Sixth International Family Violence Research Conference, Durham, NH.

Bonomi, A. E., Allen, D. G., & Holt, V. L. (2005). Conversational silence, coercion, equality: The role of language in influencing who gets identified as abused. *Social Science & Medicine, 62,* 2258–2266.

Bonomi, A. E., Anderson, M. L., Reid, R. J., Rivara, F. P., Carrell, D., & Thompson, R. S. (2009). Medical and psychological diagnoses in women with a history of intimate partner violence. *Archives of Internal Medicine, 169,* 1692–1697.

Book, A. S., Starzyk, K. B., & Quinsey, V. L. (2001). The relationship between testosterone and aggression: A meta-analysis. *Aggression and Violent Behavior, 6,* 579–599.

Bookwala, J. (2002). The role of own and perceived partner attachment in relationship aggression. *Journal of Interpersonal Violence, 17,* 84–100.

Borochowitz, D. Y., & Eisikovits, Z. (2002). To love violently: Strategies for reconciling love and violence. *Violence Against Women, 8,* 476–494.

Borowski, A., & Ajzenstadt, M. (2007). Achieving justice for children. *International Journal of Offender Therapy and Comparative Criminology, 51,* 191–211.

Borrego, J., Timmer, S. G., Urzquiz, A. J., & Follette, W. C. (2004). Physically abusive mothers' responses following episodes of child noncompliance and compliance. *Journal of Consulting & Clinical Psychology, 72,* 897–903.

Bos, H. M. W., Sandfort, T. G. M., de Bruyn, E. D., & Hakvoort, E. M. (2008). Same-sex attraction, social relationships, psychosocial functioning, and school performance in early adolescence. *Developmental Psychology, 44,* 59–68.

Bossarte R. M., Simon, T. R., & Barker, L. (2006). Characteristics of homicide followed by suicide in multiple states, 2003–2004. *Injury Prevention 2006;12*(Suppl. 2), ii33–ii38.

Botash, A. S. (2008). Pediatrics, child sexual abuse. *Emedicine.* Retrieved July 11, 2010, from http://emedicine.medscape.com/article/800770-print, pp. 1–12.

Bothwell, R., & Scott, J. (1997). The influence of cognitive variables on recovery in depressed inpatients. *Journal of Affective Disorders, 43,* 207–212.

Bouffard, J. A., & Richardson, K. A. (2007). The effectiveness of drug court programming for specific kinds of offenders. *Criminal Justice Policy Review, 18,* 274–293.

Bourg, S., & Stock, H. V. (1994). A review of domestic violence arrest statistics in a police department using a pro-arrest police: Are pro-arrest policies enough? *Journal of Family Violence, 9,* 177–192.

Bowen, R., & Schneider, J. (2007). *Forensic databases: Paint, shoe prints, and beyond* (NIJ Journal No. 258; NCJ Publication No. 219606). Washington, DC: National Institute of Justice.

Bower, B. (1993, September 18). Sudden recall: Adult memories of child abuse spark heated debate. *Science News, 144,* 177–192.

Bower, B. (1994). Alcoholism exposes its "insensitive" side. *Science News, 145,* 118.

Bower, B. (2003, January 18). Testosterone's family ties: Hormone-linked problems reflect parent-child bond. *Science News, 163,* 36.

Bower, B. (2006, July). Gay males' sibling link. *Science News, 170,* 3.

Bower B. (2009, February 14). Neural circuits foster oversensitivity. *Science News, 175,* 13.

Bowker, L. H. (1983). *Beating wife beating.* Lexington, MA: Lexington.

Bowlby, J. (1980). *Attachment and loss: Vol. 3. Loss.* London: Hogarth.

Bowlus, A. J., & Seitz, S. (2006). Domestic violence, employment, and divorce. *International Economic Review, 47,* 1113–1149.

Boxer, A. M., Cook, J. A., & Herdt, G. (1991). Double jeopardy: Identity transitions and parent-child relations among gay and lesbian youth. In K. A. Pillemer & K. McCartney (Eds.), *Parent-child relations throughout life* (pp. 59–92). Hillsdale, NJ: Lawrence Erlbaum.

Boxer, P., & Terranova, A. M. (2008). Effects of multiple maltreatment experiences among psychiatrically hospitalized youth. *Child Abuse & Neglect, 32,* 637–647.

Boy, A., & Kulczycki, A. (2008). What we know about intimate partner violence in the Middle East and North Africa. *Violence Against Women, 14,* 53–70.

Boyden, P., Esscopri, N., Ogi, L., Brennan, A., & Kalsy-Lillico, S. (2009). Service users leading the way. *Journal of Intellectual Disabilities, 13,* 183–194.

Boyle, C. L., Sanders, M. R., Lutzker, J. R., Prinz, R. J., Shapiro, C., & Whitaker, D. J. (2010). An analysis of training, generalization, and maintenance effects of primary care Triple P for parents of preschool-aged children with disruptive behavior. *Child Psychiatry and Human Development, 41,* 114–131.

Boyle, D. J., O'Leary, K. D., Rosenbaum, A., & Hassett-Walker, C. (2008). Differentiating between generally and partner-only violent subgroups: Lifetime antisocial behavior, family of origin violence, and impulsivity. *Journal of Family Violence, 23,* 47–55.

Boyle, G. (2008). Autonomy in long-term care: A need, a right or a luxury? *Disability & Society, 23,* 299–210.

Brabeck, K. M., & Guzmán, M. R. (2008). Frequency and perceived effectiveness of strategies to survive abuse employed by battered Mexican-origin women. *Violence Against Women, 14,* 1274–1294.

Brace, A. M., Hall, M., & Hunt, B. P. (2008). Social, economic, and health costs of unintended teen pregnancy: The Circle of Care Intervention program in Troup County, Georgia.

*Journal of the Georgia Public Health Association 1(1),* 33–46.

Bradford, J. (1990). The antiandrogen and hormonal treatment of sex offenders. In W. L. Marshall, D. R. Laws, & H. E. Barbaree (Eds.), *Handbook of sexual assault: Issues, theories, and treatment of the offender* (pp. 297–327). New York: Plenum.

Bradley, A. R., & Wood, J. M. (1996). How do children tell? The disclosure process in child sex abuse. *Child Abuse & Neglect, 20,* 881–891.

Brandl, B., & Cook-Daniels, L. (2002). *Domestic abuse in later life.* Washington, DC: National Resource Center on Domestic Violence.

Brandl, B., Hebert, M., Rozwadowski, J., & Spangler, D. (2003). Feeling safe, feeling strong: Support groups for older abused women. *Violence Against Women, 9,* 1490–1503.

Brandl, B., Dyer, C. B., Heisler, C. J., Otto, J. M., Stiegel, L. A., & Thomas, R.W. (2007). *Elder abuse detection and intervention: A collaborative approach.* New York: Springer.

Brandl, B., & Raymond, J. (2004, November/December). Abuse in later life: Name it! Claim it! *Victimization of the Elderly and Disabled, 7,* 49, 60–62.

Brans, R. G., van Haren, N. E., van Baal, G. C., Schnack, H. G., Kahn, R. S., & Pol, H. E. (2008). Heritability of changes in brain volume over time in twin pairs discordant for schizophrenia. *Archives of General Psychiatry, 65,* 1259–1268.

Brassard, M. R., & Donovan, K. L. (2006). Defining psychological maltreatment. In M. M. Feerick, J. F. Knutson, P. K. Trickett, & S. M. Flanzer (Eds.), *Child abuse and neglect: Definitions, classifications, and a framework for research* (pp. 151–197). Baltimore: Paul H. Brookes.

Braun, B. G. (1988). The BASK model of dissociation. *Dissociation, 1,* 45–50.

Braun, K., Lenzer, A., Shumacher-Mukai, C., & Snyder, P. (1993). A decision tree for managing elder abuse and neglect. *Journal of Elder Abuse & Neglect, 5*(3), 89–103.

Braun-Courville, D. K., & Rojas, M. (2009). Exposure to sexually explicit web sites and adolescent sexual attitudes and behaviors. *Journal of Adolescent Health, 45,* 156–162.

Break the Cycle. (n.d.). Retrieved from http://www.breakthecycle.org/who-we-are

Breaslau, N., Peterson, E. L., & Schultz, L. R. (2008). A second look at prior trauma and the posttraumatic stress disorder effects of subsequent trauma. *Archives of General Psychiatry, 65,* 431–437.

Brecklin, L. R., & Ullman, S. E. (2005). Self-defense or assertiveness training and women's responses to sexual attacks. *Journal of Interpersonal Violence, 20,* 738–762.

Breen, A. B., & Karpinski, A. (2008). What's in a name: Two approaches to evaluating the label feminist. *Sex Roles, 58,* 299–310.

Breiding, M., Black, M. & Ryan, G. (2008). Prevalence and risk factors of intimate partner violence in eighteen U.S. states/territories. *American Journal of Preventive Medicine, 34,* 112–118.

Breitenbecher, K. H. (2008). The convergent validities of two measures of dating behaviors related to sexual victimization. *Journal of Interpersonal Violence, 3,* 1095–1107.

Brewin, C. R. (2001). A cognitive neuroscience account of posttraumatic stress disorder. *Behavior Research and Therapy, 39,* 373–393.

Brickman, J. (1984). Feminist, nonsexist, and traditional models of therapy: Implications for working with incest. *Women & Therapy, 3,* 49–67.

Briere, J., & Conte, J. R. (1993). Self-reported amnesia for abuse in adults molested as children. *Journal of Traumatic Stress, 6,* 21–31.

Briere, J., & Elliott, D. M. (1994). Immediate and long-term impacts of child sexual abuse. *Future of Children, 4*(2), 54–69.

Briere, J., & Jordan, C. E. (2004). Violence against women: Outcome complexity and implications for assessment and treatment. *Journal of Interpersonal Violence, 19,* 1252–1276.

Briere, J., Woo, R., McRae, B., Foltz, J., & Sitzman, R. (1997). Lifetime victimization history, demographics, and clinical status in female psychiatric emergency room patients. *Journal of Nervous and Mental Disease, 185,* 95–101.

Brinkerhoff, M. B., & Lupri, E. (1988). Interpersonal violence. *Canadian Journal of Sociology, 13,* 407–434.

Brook, D., Zhang, C., Rosenberg, G., & Brook, J. (2006). Maternal cigarette smoking during pregnancy and child aggressive behavior. *American Journal of Addiction, 15,* 450–456.

Brookman, F., & Maguire, M. (2005). Reducing homicide: A review of possibilities. *Crime, Law & Social Change, 42,* 325–403.

Brooks, V. R. (1981). *Minority stress and lesbian women.* Lexington, MA: Lexington Books.

Broude, G. J., & Greene, S. J. (1983). Cross-cultural codes on husband-wife relationship. *Ethnology, 22,* 263–280.

Brower, M., & Sackett, R. (1985, November 4). Split. *People,* 108, 111.

Brown, A. L., Testa, M., & Messman-Moore, T. L. (2009). Psychological consequences of sexual victimization resulting from force, incapacitation, or verbal coercion. *Violence Against Women, 15,* 898–919.

Brown, C. (2008). Gender-role implications on same-sex intimate partner violence. *Journal of Family Violence, 23,* 457–462.

Brown, C. M., & Gibbons, J. L. (2008). Taking care of our elders. *Journal of Applied Gerontology, 27,* 523–531.

Brown, C., Reedy, D., Fountain, J., Johnson, A., & Dichiser, T. (2000). Battered women's career decision-making self-efficacy: Further insights and contributing factors. *Journal of Career Assessment, 8,* 251–265.

Brown, E. J. (2003). Child physical abuse: Risk for psychopathology and efficacy of interventions. *Current Psychiatry Reports, 5,* 87–94.

Brown, J., Cohen, P., Johnson, J. G., & Salzinger, S. (1998). A longitudinal analysis of risk factors for child maltreatment: Findings of a 17-year prospective study of officially recorded and self-reported child abuse and neglect. *Child Abuse & Neglect, 22,* 1065–1078.

Brown, J. M., Hamilton, C., & O'Neill, D. (2007). Characteristics associated with rape attrition and the role played by skepticism or legal rationality by investigators and prosecutors. *Psychology, Crime, and Law, 13,* 355–370.

Brown, L. K., Puster, K. L., Vazquez, E. A., Hunter, H. L., & Lescano, C. M. (2007). Screening practices for adolescent dating violence. *Journal of Interpersonal Violence, 22,* 456–464.

Brown, M. J., & Groscup, J. (2008). Perceptions of same-sex domestic violence among crisis center staff. *Journal of Family Violence, 24,* 87–93.

Brown, R. M., III. (2002). The development of family violence as a field of study and contributors to family and community violence among low-income fathers. *Aggression and Violent Behavior, 7,* 499–511.

Brown, T. J., Sumner, K. E., & Nocera, R. (2002). Understanding sexual aggression against women: An examination of the role of men's athletic participation and related variables. *Journal of Interpersonal Violence, 17,* 937–952.

Browne, A., & Bassuk, S. S. (1997). Intimate violence in the lives of homeless and poor housed women: Prevalence and patterns in an ethnically diverse sample. *American Journal of Orthopsychiatry, 67,* 261–278.

Browne, A., Salomon, A., & Bassuk, S. S. (1999). The impact of recent partner violence on poor women's capacity to maintain work. *Violence Against Women, 5,* 393–426.

Browne, C., & Winkelman, C. (2007). The effect of childhood trauma on later psychological adjustment. *Journal of Interpersonal Violence, 22,.* 684–697.

Brownlie, E. B., Jabbar, A., Beitchman, J., Vida, R., & Atkinson, L. (2007). Language impairment and sexual assault of girls and women: Findings from a community sample. *Journal of Abnormal Child Psychology, 35,* 618–626.

Brownridge, D. A. (2003). Male partner violence against aboriginal women in Canada. *Journal of Interpersonal Violence, 18,* 65–83.

Brownridge, D. A., & Halli, S. S. (1999). Measuring family violence: The conceptualization and utilization of prevalence and incidence rates. *Journal of Family Violence, 14,* 333–350.

Brush, L. D. (2000). Battering, traumatic stress, and welfare-to-work transition. *Violence Against Women, 6,* 1039–1065.

Brush, L. D. (2003). Effects of work on hitting and hurting. *Violence Against Women, 9,* 1213–1230.

Bui, H. N. (2001). Domestic violence victims' behavior in favor of prosecution: Effects of gender relations. *Women and Criminal Justice, 12,* 51–75.

Bulman, P. (2010, April). Elder abuse emerges from the shadows of public consciousness. *NIJ Journal, 265,* 4–7.

Bunch, C. (1997). The intolerable status quo: Violence against women and girls. *The progress of nations 1997.* New Jersey: Center for Women's Global Leadership at Rutgers University.

Burazeri, G., Roshi, E., Jewkes, R., Jordan, S., Bjegovic, V., & Laaser, U. (2005). Factors associated with spousal physical violence in Albania: Cross sectional study. *British Medical Journal, 331,* 197–201.

Burgess, A. W., Hartman, C. R., & Clements, P. T., Jr. (1995). Biology of memory and childhood trauma. *Jounal of Psychosocial Nursing and Mental Health Services, 33,* 16–26.

Burgess, E. S., & Wurtele, S. K. (1998). Enhancing parent-child communication about sexual abuse: A pilot study. *Child Abuse & Neglect, 22,* 1167–1175.

Burgess, G. H. (2007). Assessment of rape-supportive attitudes and beliefs in college men. *Journal of Interpersonal Violence, 22,* 973–993.

Burke, T. W. (1998). Male-to-male gay domestic violence: The dark closet. In N. A. Jackson & G. C. Oates (Eds.), *Violence in intimate relationships: Examining sociological and psychological issues* (pp. 161–179). Woburn, MA: Butterworth-Heinemann.

Burman, E., & Smailes, S. L., & Chantler, K. (2004). 'Culture' as a barrier to service provision and delivery: Domestic violence services for minoritized women. *Critical Social Policy, 24,* 332–367.

Burt, M. R. (1980). Cultural myths and support for rape. *Journal of Personality and Social Psychology, 38,* 217–230.

Burt, M. R. (1991). Rape myths and acquaintance rape. In A. Parrott & L. Bechhofer (Eds.), *Acquaintance rape: The hidden crime* (pp. 26–40). New York: John Wiley.

Burt, M. R., Newmark, L. C., Olson, K. K., Aron, L. Y., & Harrell, A. V. (1997). *1997 report: Evaluation of the STOP formula grants under the Violence Against Women Act of 1994.* Washington, DC: Urban Institute.

Burt, M., Zweig, J., & Schlichter, K. (2000). *Strategies for addressing the needs of domestic violence victims within the TANF program: The experience of seven counties.* Final Report to the U.S. Department of Health & Human Services. June 30, 2000.

Burton, D. L. (2003). Male adolescents: Sexual victimization and subsequent sexual abuse. *Child and Adolescent Social Work Journal, 20,* 277–296.

Busch, N. B., & Valentine, D. (2000). Empowerment practice: A focus on battered women. *Affilia, 15*(1), 82–95.

Busch, N. B., & Wolfer, T. A. (2002). Battered women speak out: Welfare reform and their decision to disclose. *Violence Against Women, 8,* 566–584.

Bush, G. W. (2002, February 26). President announces welfare reform agenda. Retrieved June, 25, 2004, from http://www.whitehouse.gov/news/release/2002/02/20020226–11.html

Bushman, B. J., & Anderson, C. A. (2001). Media violence and the American public: Scientific facts versus media misinformation. *American Psychologist, 56,* 477–489.

Bushman, B. J., & Anderson, C. A. (2009). Comfortably numb: Desensitizing effects of violent media on helping others. *Psychological Science, 20,* 273–277.

Bushman, B. J., & Baumeister, R. F. (1998). Threatened egotism, narcissism, self-esteem, and direct and displaced aggression: Does self-love or self-hate lead to violence? *Journal of Personality and Social Psychology, 75,* 219–229.

Buss, A. H., & Durkee, A. (1957). An inventory for assessing different kinds of hostility. *Journal of Consulting Psychology, 2,* 343–349.

Buss, D. M., Larsen, R., Westen, D., & Semmelroth, J. (1992). Sex differences in jealousy: Evolution, physiology, and psychology. *Psychological Science, 3,* 251–255.

Buss, D. M., & Shackelford, T. K. (1997). From vigilance to violence: Mate retention tactics in married couples. *Journal of Personality and Social Psychology, 72,* 346–361.

Busseri, M. A., Willoughby, T., Chalmers, H., & Bogaert, A. R. (2006). Same-sex attraction and successful adolescent development. *Journal of Youth and Adolescence, 35,* 663–575.

Butler, K. (1994, June 26). Clashing memories, mixed messages. *Los Angeles Times,* p. 12.

Buttell, F. P., & Carney, M. M. (2004). A multidimensional evaluation of a treatment program for female batterers: A pilot study. *Research on Social Work Practice, 14,* 249–258.

Buttell, F. P., & Carney, M. M. (2008). A large sample investigation of batterer intervention program attrition: Evaluating the impact of state program standards. *Research on Social Work Practice, 18,* 177–188.

Buttell, F. P., & Pike, C. K. M. (2003). Investigating the differential effectiveness of a batterer treatment program on outcomes for African American and Caucasian batterers. *Research on Social Work Practice, 13,* 675–692.

Button, D. M., & Gealt, R. (2010). High risk behaviors among victims of sibling violence. *Journal of Family Violence, 25,* 131–140.

Buunk, B. P. (1997). Personality, birth order and attachment styles as related to various types of jealousy. *Personality and Individual Differences, 23,* 997–1006.

Buzawa, E. S., & Buzawa, C. G. (2003). *Domestic violence: The criminal justice response* (3rd ed.). Thousand Oaks, CA: Sage.

Buzawa, E. S., & Hotaling, G. T. (2006). The impact of relationship status, gender, and minor status in the police response to domestic assaults. *Victims and Offenders, 1,* 323–360.

Bužgová, R., & Ivanová, K. (2009). Elder abuse and mistreatment in residential settings. *Nursing Ethics, 16,* 110–126.

Byrd, K. K. (2007). Bringing science to society. *Observer, 20*(8), 31.

Byrne, B. M. (2001). *Structural equation modeling with AMOS: Basic concepts, applications, and programming.* New York: Taylor & Francis.

Byrne, C. A., & Arias, I. (1997). Marital satisfaction and marital violence: Moderating effects of attributional processes. *Journal of Family Psychology, 11,* 188–195.

Byrne, C. A., Resnick, H. S., Kilpatrick, D. G., Best, C. L., & Saunders, B. E. (1999). The socioeconomic impact of interpersonal violence on women. *Journal of Consulting and Clinical Psychology, 67,* 362–366.

Cacioppo, J. T. (2007, September). Better interdisciplinary research through psychological science. *Psychological Science, 20*(10), 3, 48–49.

Caetano, R., Field, C., Ramisetty-Mikler, S., & Lipsky, S. (2009). Agreement on reporting of physical, psychological, and sexual violence among White, Black, and Hispanic couples in the United States. *Journal of Interpersonal Violence, 24,* 1318–1337.

Caetano, R., Ramisetty-Mikler, S., & McGrath, C. (2004). Acculturation, drinking and intimate partner violence among Hispanic couples in the U.S.: A longitudinal analysis. *Hispanic Journal of Behavioral Science, 26*, 60–78.

Caetano, R., Ramisetty-Mikler, S., Vaeth, P. A., & Harris, T. R. (2007). Acculturation, stress, drinking and intimate partner violence among Hispanic couples in the U.S. *Journal of Interpersonal Violence, 22*, 1431–1447.

Caetano, R., Vaeth, P. A. C., & Ramisetty-Mikler, S. (2008). Intimate partner violence victim and perpetrator characteristics among couples in the United States. *Journal of Family Violence, 23*, 507–518.

Caffaro, J. V., & Conn-Caffaro, A. (1998). *Sibling abuse trauma: Assessment and intervention strategies for children, families, and adults.* New York: Haworth Maltreatment and Trauma Press.

Caffaro, J. V., & Conn-Caffaro, A. (2005). Treating sibling abuse families. *Aggression and Violent Behavior, 10*(5) 604–623.

Cahill, C., Llewelyn, S. P., & Pearson, C. (1991). Treatment of sexual abuse which occurred in childhood: A review. *British Journal of Clinical Psychology, 30*, 1–12.

Cahill, S., & Smith, K. (2002). Policy issues affecting lesbian, gay, bisexual, and transgender people in retirement. *Generations, 26*(2), 49–54.

California Penal Code Section 261.5. (2010). Statutory Rape Act, California Penal Code Secion 261.5.

California Secretary of State. (1998). *How does Safe at Home work?* Retrieved November 26, 2003, from http://www.ss.ca.gov/safeathome/Safe_at_Home_how.htm

Calkins, P. (2003, July/August). Cross-discipline gains in Indiana. *Victimization of the Elderly and Disabled, 6*, 17–18, 30.

Call, C. R., & Nelsen, J. C. (2007). Partner abuse and women's substance problems. *Affilia, 22*, 334–346.

Call, K. T., Finch, M. A., Huck, S. M., & Kane, R. A. (1999). Caregiver burden from a social exchange perspective: Caring for older people after hospital discharge. *Journal of Marriage and the Family, 61*, 688–699.

Callahan, M. R., Tolman, R. M., & Saunders, D. G. (2004). Dating violence among adolescents. *Archives of Pediatrics & Adolescent Medicine, 158*, 1132–1139.

Calif. Husband, wife arrested for elder abuse. (2009, May 14). *Daily Press,* Retrieved from http://www.lorain.oh.networkofcare.org/dv/news/detail.cfm?articleID=23384

Calvete, E., Corral, S., & Estévez A. (2007). Factor structure and validity of the revised Conflict Tactics Scales for Spanish women. *Violence Against Women, 13*, 1072–1087.

Campbell, J. C. (1989a). A test of two explanatory models of women's responses to battering. *Nursing Research, 38*(1), 18–24.

Campbell, J. C. (1989b). Women's responses to sexual abuse in intimate relationships. *Health Care for Women International, 8*, 335–347.

Campbell, J. C. (2002). Health consequences of intimate partner violence. *Lancet, 359*, 1331–1336.

Campbell, J. C. (2005). Assessing dangerousness in domestic violence cases: History, challenges, and opportunities. *Criminology & Public Policy, 4*, 653–672.

Campbell, J. C., & Alford, P. (1989). The dark consequences of marital rape. *American Journal of Nursing, 87*, 946–949.

Campbell, J. C. & Runyan, C. (1998). Femicide [Editorial]. *Homicide Studies, 4*, 347–352.

Campbell, J. C., & Soeken, K. L. (1999). Women's responses to battering over time. *Journal of Interpersonal Violence, 14*, 21–40.

Campbell, J. C., Webster, D., Koziol-McLain, J., Block, C. R., Campbell, D. W., Curry, M. A., et al. (2003). Risk factors for femicide in abusive relationships: Results from a multi-site case control study. *American Journal of Public Health, 93*, 1089–1097.

Campbell, R. (2008). The psychological impact of rape victims' experiences with the legal, medical, and mental health systems. *American Psychologist, 63*, 702–717.

Campbell, R. (2009). Rape survivors' experiences with the legal and medical system. *Violence Against Women, 12*, 30–45.

Campbell, R., Patterson, D., Bybee, D., & Dworkin, E. R. (2009). Predicting sexual assault prosecution outcomes. *Criminal Justice and Behavior, 36*, 712–727.

Campbell, R., Wasco, S. M., Ahrens, C. E., Sefl, T., & Barnes, H. E. (2001). Preventing the "second rape": Rape survivors' experiences with community service providers. *Journal of Interpersonal Violence, 16*, 1239–1259.

Canales-Portalatín, D. (2000). Intimate-partner assailants: Comparison of cases referred to a probation department. *Journal of Interpersonal Violence, 15*, 843–854.

Canavan, M. M., Meyer, W. J., & Higgs, D. C. (1992). The female experience of sibling incest. *Journal of Marital and Family Therapy, 18*, 129–142.

Candell, S., Frazier, P., Arikan, N., & Tofteland, A. (1993, August). *Legal outcomes in rape cases: Case attrition and postrape recovery.* Paper presented at the annual meeting of the American Psychological Association, Toronto.

Cantor, J. M., Kabani, N., et al. (2008). Cerebral white matter deficiencies in pedophilic men. *Journal of Psychiatric Research, 42,* 167–183.

Cantos, A. L., Neidig, P. H., & O'Leary, K. D. (1994). Injuries of women and men in a treatment program for domestic violence. *Journal of Family Violence, 9,* 113–124.

Capaldi, D. M., & Clark, S. (1998). Prospective family predictors of aggression toward female partners for at-risk young men. *Developmental Psychology, 34,* 1175–1188.

Capezza, N. M., & Arriaga, X. B. (2008). Why do people blame victims of abuse? The role of stereotypes of women on perceptions of blame. *Sex Roles, 59,* 839–850.

Cappas, N. M., Andres-Hyman, R., & Davidson, L. (2005). What psychotherapists can begin to learn from neuroscience: Seven principles of a brain-based psychotherapy. *Psychology, Theory, Research, Practice, Training, 42,* 374–383.

Cardemil, E. V. (2008). Commentary: Culturally sensitive treatments: Need for an organizing framework. *Culture & Psychology, 14,* 357–367.

Carden, A. D. (1994). Wife abuse and the wife abuser: Review and recommendations. *Counseling Psychologist, 22,* 539–582.

Carll, E. K. (2006, March 29). *What's in a game? State regulation of violent video games and the first amendment.* Testimony before the Senate Committee on the Judiciary Subcommittee on the Constitution, Civil Rights and Property Rights.

Carlson, B. E. (1996). Dating violence: Student beliefs about the consequences. *Journal of Interpersonal Violence, 11,* 3–18.

Carlson, B. E. (2006). Commentary on "You think you know me." *Trauma, Violence, & Abuse, 7* 64–65.

Carlson, B. E., & Dalenberg, C. J. (2000). A conceptual framework for the impact of traumatic experiences. *Trauma, Violence, & Abuse, 1,* 4–28.

Carlson, B. E., Maciol, K., & Schneider, J. (2006). Sibling incest: Reports from forty-one survivors. *Journal of Child Sexual Abuse, 15,* 19–34.

Carlson, B. E., McNutt, L. A., & Choi, D. Y. (2003). Childhood and adult abuse among women in primary health care: Effects on mental health. *Journal of Interpersonal Violence, 18,* 924–941.

Carlson, M. J., Harris, S. D., & Holden, G. W. (1999). Protective orders and domestic violence: Risk factors for re-abuse. *Journal of Family Violence, 14,* 205–226.

Carlstedt, A., Nilsson, T., Hofvander, B., Brimse, A., Innala, S., & Ackarsäter, H. (2009). Does victim age differentiate between perpetrators of sexual child abuse? A study of mental health, psychosocial circumstance, and crimes. *Sexual Abuse: A Journal of Research and Treatment, 21,* 442–459.

Carp, F. M. (1999). *Elder abuse in the family: An interdisciplinary model for research.* New York: Springer.

Carr, J. L., & VanDeusen, K. M. (2002). The relationship between family of origin violence and dating violence in college men. *Journal of Interpersonal Violence, 17,* 630–646.

Carrigan, T. D., Walker, E., & Barnes, S. (2000). Domestic violence: The shaken adult syndrome. *Journal of Accident and Emergency Medicine, 17,* 138–139.

Carroll, K. M. (1997). New methods of treatment efficacy research: Bridging clinical research and clinical practice. *Alcohol, Health & Research World, 21,* 352–359.

Carson, C. L., & Cupach, W. R. (2000). Fueling the flames of the green-eyed monster: The role of ruminative thought in reaction to romantic jealousy. *Western Journal of Communication, 64,* 308–329.

Casanueva, C., Martin, S. L., Runyan, D. K., Barth, R. P., & Bradley, R. H. (2008). Quality of maternal parenting among intimate-partner violence victims involved with the child welfare system. *Journal of Family Violence, 23,* 413–427.

Cascardi, M., Avery-Leaf, S., O'Leary, K. D., & Slep, A. M. S. (1999). Factor structure and convergent validity of the Conflict Tactics Scale in high school students. *Psychological Assessment, 11,* 546–555.

Cascardi, M., Langhinrichsen-Rohling, J., & Vivian, D. (1992). Marital aggression: Impact, injury, and health correlates for husbands and wives. *Archives of Internal Medicine, 152,* 1178–1184.

Casey. E. A., & Lindhorst, T. P. (2009). Toward a multilevel, ecological approach to the primary prevention of sexual assault. *Trauma, Violence, & Abuse, 10,* 91–114.

Cashell-Smith, M. L., Connor, J. L., & Kypri, K. (2007). Harmful effects of alcohol on sexual behaviour in a New England university community. *Drug and Alcohol Review, 26,* 645–651.

Cashin, J. R., Presley, C. A., & Meilman, P. W. (1996). Alcohol use in the Greek system: Follow the leader? *Journal of Studies of Alcohol, 57,* 63–70.

Caspi, A., McClay, J., Moffitt, T. E., Mill, J., Martin, J., Craig, I. W., et al. (2002). Role of genotype in the cycle of violence in maltreated children. *Science, 297,* 851–854.

Caspi, J. (2008). Building a sibling aggression treatment model: Design and development research in action. *Research in Social Work Practice, 18,* 575–585.

Castle, N. G. (2008). Nursing home caregiver staffing levels and quality of care. *Journal of Applied Gerontolgy, 27,* 375–405.

Castle, N. G., & Sonon, K. E. (2006). Internet resources and searching for a residential care setting: What information is available for consumers? *Journal of Applied Gerontology, 25,* 214–233.

Catalano, S. (2007). *Intimate partner violence in the United States* (NCJ Publication No. 210675). Washington, DC: U.S. Department of Justice Statistics, http://www.ojp.usdoj.gov

Cattaneo, L., & Goodman, L. A. (2005). Risk factors for reabuse in intimate partner violence: A cross-disciplinary review. *Trauma, Violence, & Abuse, 6,* 141–175.

Cauce, A. M., Tyler, K. A., & Whitbeck, L. B. (2004). Maltreatment and victimization in homeless adolescents: Out of the frying pan and into the fire. *The Prevention Researcher, 11*(1), 12–14.

Caustic ingestion as a manifestation of fabricated and induced illness (Munchausen syndrome by proxy). (2010). Letter to the editor. *Child Abuse & Neglect, 34,* 471.

Cavanagh, K. (2003). Understanding women's responses to domestic violence. *Qualitative Social Work 2,* 229–249.

Cavanaugh, M. M., & Gelles, R. J. (2005). The utility of male violence offender typologies: New directions for research, policy, and practice. *Journal of Interpersonal Violence, 20,* 155–166.

Cazenave, N. A., & Zahn, M. A. (1992). Women, murder, and male domination: Police reports of domestic violence in Chicago and Philadelphia. In E. C. Viano (Ed.), *Intimate violence: Interdisciplinary perspectives* (pp. 83–97). Washington, DC: Hemisphere.

Ceci, S. J., & Bjork, R. A. (2003). Science, politics, and violence in the media [Editorial]. *Psychological Science in the Public Interest, 4*(3), i–iii.

Ceci, S. J., & Bruck, M. (1993). Suggestibility of the child witness: A historical review and synthesis. *Psychological Bulletin, 113,* 403–439.

Centers for Disease Control and Prevention. (n.d.). *Child maltreatment prevention scientific information: Risk and protective factors.* Atlanta, Georgia: U.S. Centers for Disease Control.

Centers for Disease Control and Prevention. (2000, October 27). Building data systems for monitoring and responding to violence against women: Recommendations from a workshop. *Morbidity and Mortality Weekly Report, 49,* 1–19.

Centers for Disease Control and Prevention. (2002). *Injury fact book: 2001–2002.* Atlanta, GA: Author.

Centers for Disease Control and Prevention. (2006). *Youth Risk Behaviors Surveillance—United States. 2005.* Surveillance Summaries, 2006. *Morbidity and Mortality Weekly Report, 2006; 55:SS-5.*

Centers for Disease Control and Prevention. (2007). *Suicide trends among youths and young adults aged 10—24 years—United States, 1990–2004. Morbidity and Mortality Weekly Report, 2007; 56*(35); 905–908.

Centers for Disease Control and Prevention. (2008). *Nonfatal maltreatment of infants—United States, October 2005 – Septermber 2006. Morbidity and Mortality Weekly Report, 2008; 57*(13); 336–339.

Centers for Disease Control and Prevention (CDC). (2009a). *Parent training programs: Insight for practitioners.* Atlanta, Geororgia: Centers for Disease Control.

Centers for Disease Control and Prevention. (2009b). *Preventing teen pregnancy—An update in 2009.* Atlanta, GA: Author.

Cercone-Keeney, J. J., Beach, S. R. H., & Arias, I. (2005). Gender asymmetry in dating intimate partner violence: Does similar behavior imply similar constructs? *Violence and Victims, 20,* 207–218.

Cerezo, M. A., Pons-Salvador, G., & Trenado, R. M. (2008). Mother-infant interaction and children's socio-emotional development with high- and low-risk mothers. *Infant Behavior and Development, 31,* 578–589.

Chaffin, M. (1994). Research in action: Assessment and treatment of child sexual abusers. *Journal of Interpersonal Violence, 9,* 224–237.

Chaffin, M., Silovsky, J. F., et al. (2004). Parent-child interaction therapy with physically abusive parents: Efficacy for reducing future abuse reports. *Journal of Consulting & Clinical Psychology, 72,* 500–510.

Chaffin, M., Silovsky, J. F., & Vaughn, C. (2005). Temporal concordance of anxiety disorders and child sexual abuse: Implication for direct versus artifactual effects of sexual abuse. *Journal of Clinical Child & Adolescent Psychology, 34,* 210–222.

Chaimowitz, G. A., Glancy, G. D., & Blackburn, J. (2000). The duty to warn and protect: Impact on practice. *Canadian Journal of Psychiatry, 45,* 899–904.

Chalk, R., & King, P. A. (Eds.). (1998). *Violence in families: Assessing prevention and treatment programs.* Washington, DC: National Academy Press.

Chamberlin, J. (2008, March). Prenatal exposure triggers a taste for alcohol. *Monitor on Psychology, 39,* 12.

Chamberland, C., Fortin, A., Turgeon, J., & Laporte, L. ( 2007). Men's recognition of violence against women and spousal abuse: Comparison of three groups of men. *Violence and Victims, 22,* 419–436.

Chambers, A. L., & Wilson, M. N. (2007). Assessing male batterers with the personality assessment inventory. *Journal of Personality Assessment, 88,* 57–65.

Champagne, F. A., & Curley, J. P. (2009). Epigentic mechanisms mediating the long-term effects of maternal care on development. *Neuroscience and Biobehavioral Reviews, 33,* 593–600.

Chan, K. L., Tiwari, A., Fong, D. Y. T., Leung, W. C., Brownridge, D. A., & Ho, P. C. (2009). Correlates of in-law conflict and intimate partner violence against Chinese pregnant women in Hong Kong. *Journal of Interpersonal Violence, 24,* 97–110.

Chan, Y. C., Chun, P. R., & Chung, K. W. (2008). Public perception and reporting of different kinds of family abuse in Hong Kong. *Journal of Family Violence, 23,* 253–263.

Chang, D. B. K. (1989). An abused spouse's self-saving process: A theory of identity transformation. *Sociological Perspectives, 32,* 535–550.

Chang, J. C., Dado, D., Ashton, S., Hawker, L., Cluss, P. A., Buranosky, R., & Scholle, S. H. (2006). Understanding behavior change for women experiencing intimate partner violence: Mapping the ups and downs using the stages of change. *Patient Education and Counseling, 62,* 330–339.

Chang, J. C., Decker, M., Moracco, K. E., Martin, S. L., Petersen, R., & Frasier, P. Y. (2003). What happens when health care providers ask about intimate partner violence? A description of consequences from the perspective of female survivors. *Journal of the American Women's Medical Association, 58,* 76–81.

Chang, J. J., Theodore, A. D., Martin, S. L., & Runyan, D. K. (2008). Psychological abuse between parents: Associations with child maltreatment from a population-based sample. *Child Abuse & Neglect, 32,* 819–829.

Chapleau, K. M., Oswald, D L., & Russell, B. L. (2008). Male rape myths: The role of gender, violence, and sexism. *Journal of Interpersonal Violence, 23,* 600–615.

Chapple, C. L. (2003). Examining intergenerational violence: Violent role modeling or weak parental controls? *Violence and Victims, 18,* 142–162.

Chard, K. (2005). An evaluation of cognitive processing therapy for the treatment of posttraumatic stress disorder related to childhood sexual abuse. *Journal of Consulting and Clinical Psychology, 73,* 965–971.

Chard, K., Weaver, T., & Resick, P. (1997). Adapting cognitive processing therapy for child sexual abuse survivors. *Cognitive and Behavioral Practice, 4,* 31–52.

Chartier, M. J., Walker, J. R., & Naimark, B. (2010). Separate and cumulative effects of adverse childhood experiences in predicting adult health and health care utilization. *Child Abuse & Neglect, 34,* 454–464.

Chartrand, M. M., Frank, D. A., White, L. F., & Shope, T. R. (2008). Effects of parents' wartime deployment on the behavior of young children in military families. *Archives of Pediatrics & Adolescent Medicine, 11,* 1009–1014.

Chavez, V., Wie, S., Hurtado, E., Bui, M., Oweini, I., Walton, M., et al. (2005, September). *Cultural perspectives on domestic violence.* Symposium presented at the Tenth International Conference on Family Violence, San Diego, CA.

Chen, H-Y., Hou, T-W., & Chuang, C-H. (2009). Applying data mining to explore the risk factors of parenting stress. *Expert Systems With Applications: An International Journal, 37,* 598–601.

Chen, P-H, Rovi, S., Washington, J., Jacobs, A., Vega, M., Pan, K-Y, & Johnson, M. S. (2007). Randomized comparison of 3 methods to screen for domestic violence in family practice. *Annals of Family Medicine, 5,* 430–435.

Chesir-Teran, D., & Hughes, D. (2009). Heterosexism in high school and victimization among lesbian, gay, bisexual, and questioning students. *Journal of Youth and Adolescence, 38,* 963–975.

Chesler, P. (2009). Are honor killings simply domestic violence? *Middle East Quarterly, Spring,* 61–69.

Cheung, M. (2008). Promoting effective interviewing of sexually abused children: A pilot study. *Research on Social Work Practice, 18,* 137–143.

Child Abuse Prevention and Treatment Act (CAPTA), the Keeping Children and Families Safe Act of 2003. Public Law No. 108–36.

Child Abuse Prevention and Treatment Act (CAPTA), the Keeping Children and Families Safe Act of 2006 (42 U. S. C. 5101 et seq.)—section 106(b)(2)(A)(ii).

Child Welfare Information Gateway. (2006) *About CAPTA: A legislative history.* Washington, DC: Author.

Child Welfare Information Gateway. (2008). National Child Abuse and Neglect Data System (NCANDS; 2008). *Child abuse and neglect fatalities: Statistics and interventions.* Washington, DC: Author.

Child Welfare Information Gateway. (2009, July). *Definitions of child abuse and neglect.* Washington, DC: Author.

Children's Safety Network. (1992). *Domestic violence: A directory of protocols for health care providers.* Newton, MA: Education Development Center.

Chimbos, P. D. (1998). Spousal homicides in contemporary Greece. *International Journal of Comparative Sociology, 39,* 213–223.

Choca, J., & Van Denburg, E. (1997). *Interpretative guide to the Millon Clinical Multiaxial Inventory* (2nd ed.). Washington, DC: American Psychological Association.

Choi, H., Klein, C., Shin, M-S., & Lee, H-J. (2009). Posttraumatic stress disorder (PTSD) and disorders of extreme stress (DESNOS) symptoms following prostitution and childhood abuse. *Violence Against Women, 15,* 913–951.

Choi, M., & Harwood, J. (2004). A hypothesized model of Korean women's responses to abuse. *Journal of Transcultural Nursing, 15,* 207–216.

Choi, N. G., & Mayer, J. (2000). Elder abuse, neglect, and exploitation. *Journal of Gerontological Social Work, 32,* 5–25.

Choi, S. Y. P., & Ting, K-F. (2008). Wife beating in South Africa: An imbalance theory of resources and power. *Journal of Interpersonal Violence, 23,* 834–852.

Choice, P., Lamke, L. K., & Pittman, J. F. (1995). Conflict resolution strategies and marital distress as mediating factors in the link between witnessing interparental violence and wife battering. *Violence and Victims, 10,* 107–119.

Chowdhury, E. H. (2007). Negotiating state and NGO politics in Bangladesh. *Violence Against Women, 13,* 857–873.

Chrisler, J. C., & Ferguson, S. (2006). Violence against women as a public health issue. *Annals of the New York Academy of Sciences, 1087,* 235–249.

Chronister, K. M., Wettersten, K. B., & Brown, C. (2004). Vocational research for the liberations of battered women. *The Counseling Psychologist, 32,* 900–922.

Chu, L. D. (2001). Homicide and factors that determine fatality from assault in the elderly population. *Dissertation Abstracts International, 62*(11), 5063B. (UMI No. 3032861)

Chung, D. (2007). Making meaning of relationships. *Violence Against Women, 12,* 1274–1295.

Churchill, S. D. (1993). The lived meanings of date rape: Seeing through the eyes of the victim. *Family Violence and Sexual Assault Bulletin, 9*(1), 20–23.

Ciabattari, T. (2006). Single mothers and family values: The effects of welfare, race, and marriage on family attitudes. *Marriage & Family Review, 39,* 53–73.

Cicchetti, D., & Lynch, M. (1993). Toward an ecological/transactional model of community violence and child maltreatment: Consequences for child development. *Psychiatry: Interpersonal & Biological Processes, 56,* 96–119.

Cicchetti, D., & Rogosch, F. A. (in press). Neuroendocrine regulation and emotional adaptation in the context of child maltreatment. In T. Dennis, P. Hastings, & K. Buss (Eds.), *Physiological measures of emotion from a developmental perspective: State of the science.* SRCD Monographs in Child Development. New York: Wiley.

City News Service. (2010, March 5). Sex attack at nursing home nets $12 million. *Daily News,* p. A1.

City News Service. (2010, March 24). Molina: Social workers failing to visit children at risk. *Daily News,* p. A1.

City News Service. (2010a March 24). Molina: Social workers failing to visit children at risk. *Daily News,* p. A1.

Claerhout, S., Elder, J., & Jensen, C. (1982). Problem-solving skills of rural battered women. *American Journal of Community Psychology, 10,* 605–612.

Clark, C. J., Hill, A., Jabbar, K., & Silverman, J. G. (2009). Violence during pregnancy in Jordan. *Violence Against Women, 15,* 720–735.

Clark, K. A., Biddle, A. K., & Martin, S. L. (2002). A cost-benefit analysis of the Violence Against Women Act of 1994. *Violence Against Women, 8,* 417–428.

Clark-Daniels, C. L., Daniels, R. S., & Baumhover, L. A. (1989). Physicians' and nurses' responses to abuse of the elderly: A comparative study of two surveys in Alabama. *Journal of Elder Abuse & Neglect, 1*(4), 57–72.

Clarke, P. N., Pendry, N. C., & Kim, Y. S. (1997). Patterns of violence in homeless women. *Western Journal of Nursing Research, 19,* 490–500.

Clarke, S. N. (2006). Strictly liable: Governmental use of the parent-child relationship as a basis for holding victims liable for their child's witness to domestic violence. *Family Court Review, 44,* 149–173.

Claussen, A. H., & Crittenden, P. M. (1991). Physical and psychological maltreatment: Relations among types of maltreatment. *Child Abuse & Neglect, 15,* 5–18.

Clay, R. A. (2010, April). It's father's day. *Monitor on Psychology, 41,* 52–55.

Clay-Warner, J., & Burt, C. H. (2005). Rape reporting after reforms: Have times really changed? *Journal of Interpersonal Violence, 11,* 150–176.

Clegg, C., & Fremouw, W. (2009). Phallometric assessment of rapists: A critical review of the research. *Aggression & Violent Behavior, 14,* 115–125.

Clements, C. M., Oxtoby, C., & Ogle, R. L. (2008). Methodological issues in assessing psychological adjustment in child witnesses of intimate partner violence. *Trauma, Violence, & Abuse, 9,* 114–127.

Clements, C. M., Sabourin, C. M., & Spilby, L. (2004). Dysporia and hopelessness following battering: The role of perceived control, coping, and self-esteem. *Journal of Family Violence, 19,* 25–36.

Clements, C. M., & Sawhney, D. K. (2000). Coping with domestic violence: Control attributions, dysphoria, and hopelessness. *Journal of Traumatic Stress, 13,* 221–240.

Clements-Schreiber, M. E., & Rempel, J. K. (1995). Women's sexual pressure tactics and adherence to related attitudes: A step toward prediction. *The Journal of Sex Research, 35,* 1998.

Clemmons, J. C., Walsh, K., DiLillo, D., & Messman-Moore, T. L. (2007). Unique and combined contributions of multiple child abuse types and abuse severity to adult trauma symptomatology. *Child Maltreatment, 12,* 172–181.

Clipp, E. C., & George, L. K. (1993). Dementia and cancer: A comparison of spouse caregivers. *Gerontologist, 33,* 534–541.

Close, S. M. (2005). Dating violence prevention in middle school and high school. *Journal of Child and Adolescent Psychiatric Nursing, 18,* 2–9.

Cnaan, R. A., & Dichter, M. E. (2008). Thoughts on the use of knowledge in social work practice. *Research on Social Work Practice, 18,* 278–284.

Coccaro, E. F., Bergeman, C. S., Kavoussi, R. J., & Seroczynski, A. D. (1997). Heritability of aggression and irritability: A twin study of the Buss-Durkee Aggression Scales in adult male subjects. *Biological Psychiatry, 41,* 273–284.

Coffey, P., Leitenberg, H., Henning, K. R., Bennett, R. T., & Jankowski, M. K. (1996). Dating violence: The association between methods of coping and women's psychological adjustment. *Violence and Victims, 11,* 227–238.

Cohen, M., Halevi-Levin, S. H., Gagin, R., & Friedman, G. (2006). Development of a screening tool for identifying elderly people at risk of abuse by their caregivers. *Journal of Aging and Health, 18,* 60–685.

Cohen, M., Halevi-Levin, S. H., Gagin, R., & Friedman, G. (2007). Elder abuse: Disparities between older people's disclosure of abuse, evident signs of abuse, and high risk of abuse. *Journal of the American Geriatrics Society, 55,* 1224–1230.

Cohen, P., Brown, J., & Smailes, E. M. (2001). Child abuse and neglect and the development of mental disorders in the general population. *Development and Psychopathology, 13,* 981–999.

Cohen, S., & Felson, M. (1979). Social change and crime rate trends: A routine activities approach. *American Sociological Review, 44,* 588–608.

Cohen-Mansfield, J., Creedon, M. A., Malone, T. B., Kirkpatrick, M. J., III, Dutra, L. A., & Herman, R. P. (2005). Electronic memory aids for community-dwelling elderly persons:

Attitudes, preferences, and potential utilization. *Journal of Applied Gerontology, 24,* 3–20.

Coker, A. L., Davis, K. E., Arias, I., Desai, S., Sanderson, M., Brandt, H. M., et al. (2002). Physical and mental health effects of intimate partner violence for men and women. *American Journal of Preventive Medicine, 23,* 260–268.

Coker, A. L., Sanderson, M., Fadden, M. K., & Pirisi, L. (2000). Intimate partner violence and cervical neoplasia. *Journal of Women's Health and Gender-Based Medicine, 9,* 1015–1023.

Coker, A. L., Smith, P. H., McKeown, R. E., & Melissa, K. J. (2000). Frequency and correlates of intimate partner violence by type: Physical, sexual, and psychological battering. *American Journal of Public Health, 90,* 553–559.

Cole, D. A., et al. (2007). Early predictors of helpless thought and behaviors in children: Developmental precursors to depressive cognitions. *Clinical Psychology and Psychiatry, 12,* 295–312.

Collin-Vézina, D., Hébert, M., Manseau, H., Blais, M., & Fernet, M. (2006). Self-concept and dating violence in 220 adolescent girls in the Child Protective System. *Child & Youth Care Forum, 35,* 319–326.

Collins, N. L., Guichard, A. C., & Ford, M. B. (2006). Responding to need in intimate relationships: Normative processes and individual difference. In M. Mikulincer & G. S. Goodman (Eds.), *Dynamics of romantic love* (pp. 149–189). New York: Guilford.

Collishaw, S., et al. (2007). Resilience to adult psychopathology following childhood maltreatment: Evidence from a community sample. *Child Abuse & Neglect, 31,* 211–229.

Combs-Lane, A. M., & Smith, D. W. (2002). Risk of sexual victimization in college women: The role of behavioral intentions and risk-taking behavior. *Journal of Interpersonal Violence, 17,* 165–183.

Comerford, S. A., Henson-Stroud, M. M., Sionainn, C., & Wheeler, E. (2004). Crone songs: Voices of lesbian elders on aging in a rural environment. *Affilia, 19,* 418–436.

Committee on Child Abuse and Neglect and Committee on Children With Disabilities. (2001). Assessment of maltreatment of children with disabilities. *Pediatrics, 108,* 508–512.

Congress considers ways to stop crimes against the elderly. (2003, October 1). *Criminal Justice Newsletter,* pp. 4–5.

Congress votes to reauthorize Violence Against Women Act. (2000). *Criminal Justice Newsletter, 31*(2), 1–2.

Connell, C. M., et al. (2009). Maltreatment following reunification: Predictors of subsequent Child Protective Services contact after children return home. *Child Abuse & Neglect, 33,* 218–228.

Connelly, C. D., Hazen, A. L., Cohen, J. H., Kelleher, K. J., Barth, R. P., & Landsverk, J. A. (2006). Persistence of intimate partner violence among families referred to child welfare. *Journal of Interpersonal Violence, 21,* 774–797.

Conner, K. R., Cerulli, C., & Caine, E. D. (2002). Threatened and attempted suicide by partner-violent male respondents petitioned to family violence court. *Violence and Victims, 17,* 115–125.

Conner, K. R., Duberstein, P. R., & Conwell, Y. (2000). Domestic violence, separation, and suicide in young men with early onset alcoholism: Reanalyses of Murphy's data. *Suicide and Life-Threatening Behavior, 30,* 354–359.

Connolly, J., & Friedlander, L. (2009). Peer group influences on adolescent dating aggression. *The Prevention Researcher, 16,* 8–11.

Conrad, P., & Schneider, J. W. (1992). *Deviance and medicalization: From badness to sickness.* Philadelphia: Temple University Press.

Conron, K. J., Beardslee, W., Koenen, K. C., Buka, S. L., & Gortmaker, S. L. (2009). A longitudinal study of maternal depression and child maltreatment in a national sample of families investigated by Child Protective Services. *Archives of Pediatrics & Adolesent Medicine, 163,* 922–930.

Conroy, E., Degenhardt, L., Mattick, R. P., & Nelson, E. C. (2009). Child maltreatment as a risk factor for opioid dependence: Comparison of family characteristics and type and severity of child maltreatment with sa matched control group. *Child Abuse & Neglect, 33,* 343–352.

Conte, J. R. (1993). Sexual abuse of children. In R. L. Hampton, T. P. Gullotta, G. R. Adams, E. H. Potter III, & R. P. Weissberg (Eds.), *Family violence: Prevention and treatment* (pp. 56–85). Newbury Park, CA: Sage.

Conyers, J. Jr. (2007). The 2005 reauthorization of the Violence Against Women Act: Why Congress acted to expand protections to immigrant women. *Violence Against Women, 13,* 457-468.

Coohey, C. (2007). The relationship between mothers' social networks and severe domestic violence: A test of the social isolation hypothesis. *Violence and Victims, 22,* 503–512.

Coohey, C., & Braun, N. (1997). Toward an integrated framework for understanding child physical abuse. *Child Abuse & Neglect, 21,* 1081–1094.

Cook, P. W. (1997). *Abused men: The hidden side of domestic violence.* Westport, CT: Praeger.

Cook-Daniels, L. (2003a, July/August). Public information material. *Victimization of the Elderly and Disabled, 6,* 27–28, 32.

Cook-Daniels, L. (2003b, January/February). 2003 is the year elder abuse hits the international stage. *Victimization of the Elderly and Disabled, 5,* 65–66, 76.

Cook-Daniels, L. (2004, January/February). Wisconsin's dementia and aggressive/abusive behavior summit. *Victimization of the Elderly and Disabled, 6,* 69, 75.

Cook-Daniels, L. (2005, July/August). State legislation related to elder and disabled adult abuse victimization. *Victimization of the Elderly and Disabled, 10,* 1–2, 10.

Cook-Daniels, L. (2007, May/June). Transgender survivors of elder or disabled adult abuse, Part I. *Victimization of the Elderly and Disabled, 10,* 1–2, 10.

Cook-Daniels, L. (2008a, May/June). Guarding the guardians: Promising practices for court monitoring. *Victimization of the Elderly and Disabled, 11,* 1, 14–16.

Cook-Daniels, L. (2008b, September/October). What can a minority teach the majority about abuse of transgendered elders? *Victimization of the Elderly and Disabled, 11,* 33–34, 36, 46–47.

Coolidge, F. L., & Anderson, L. W. (2002). Personality profiles of women in multiple abusive relationships. *Journal of Family Violence, 2,* 117–131.

Cooney, K. (2006). Mothers first, not work first: Listening to welfare clients in job training. *Qualitative Social Work, 5,* 217–235.

Cooper, C. E., McLanahan, S. S., Meadows, S. O., & Brooks-Gunn, J. (2007). *Family structure transitions and maternal parenting stress.* Working Paper No. 2007–16-FF. Princeton, NJ: Center for Research on Child Wellbeing.

Cooper, H., Friedman, S., Tempalski, B., & Friedman, R. (2007). Residential segregation and injection drug use prevalence among Black adults in U.S. metropolitan areas. *American Journal of Public Health, 97,* 344–352.

Copenhaver, M. M., & Eisler, R. M. (1996). Masculine gender role stress: A perspective on men's health. In P. M. Kato (Ed.), *Health psychology of special populations: Issues in age, gender, and ethnicity.* New York: Plenum.

Copenhaver, M. M., Lash, S. J., & Eisler, R. M. (2000). Masculine gender-role stress, anger, and male intimate abusiveness: Implications for men's relationships. *Sex Roles, 42,* 405–414.

Corcoran, J. (2000). Family interventions with child physical abuse and neglect: A critical review. *Children and Youth Services Review, 22,* 563–591.

Corder, B. F., Haizlip, T., & DeBoer, P. A. (1990). A pilot study for a structured, time-limited therapy group for sexually abused pre-adolescent children. *Child Abuse & Neglect, 14,* 243–251.

Corporate Alliance to End Partner Violence. (2002). Retrieved September 4, 2010, from http://www.caepv.org/peaceat work.org/Peace@Work_DV-Workplace-Assaults_09.pdf

Cortoni, F., & Marshall, W. L. (2001). Sex as a coping strategy and its relationship to juvenile sexual history and intimacy in sexual offenders. *Sexual Abuse, 13*(1), 27–43.

Corvo, K. N. (1992). Attachment and violence in the families-of-origin of domestically violent men. *Dissertation Abstracts International, 54,* 1950A. (UMI No. 9322595)

Corvo, K. N., Dutton, D., & Chen, W-Y. (2009). Do Duluth model interventions with perpetrators of domestic violence violate mental health professionals' ethics? *Ethics & Behavior, 19,* 323–340.

Costa, D. M., Canady, B., & Babcock, J. C. (2007). Preliminary report on the Accountability Scale: A change and outcome measure for intimate partner violence research. *Violence and Victims, 22,* 515–531.

Cottrell, B., & Monk, P. (2004). Adolescent-to-parent abuse: A qualitative overview of common themes. *Journal of Family Issues, 25,* 1072–1095.

Coulter, M. L., Kuehnle, K., Byers, R., & Alfonso, M. (1999). Police-reporting behavior and victim-police interactions as described by women in a domestic violence shelter. *Journal of Interpersonal Violence, 14,* 1290–1298.

Cousins, A. J., & Gangestad, S. W. (2007). Perceived threats of female infidelity, male proprietariness, and violence in college dating couples. *Violence and Victims, 22,* 651–668.

Covell, C. N., & Scalora, M. J. (2002). Empathic deficits in sexual offenders: An integration of affective, social, and cognitive constructs. *Aggression and Violent Behavior, 7,* 251–270.

Covington, H. E., Tropea, T., Rajadhyaksha, A., Kosofsky, B. E., & Miczek, K. A. (2008). Intense cocaine taking and episodic social defeat distress in rates: Role of NMDA receptors in the ventral tegmental area. *Psychophamacology, 197,* 203–216.

Cox, L., & Speziale, B. (2009). Survivors of stalking. *Affilia, 24,* 5–18.

Coyle, J. P., Nochajski, T., Maguin, E., Safyer, A., DeWit, D., & Macdonald, S. (2009). An exploratory study of the nature of family resilience in families affected by parental alcohol abuse. *Journal of Family Issues, 30,* 1606–1623.

Coyne, A. C., Reichman, W. E., & Berbig, L. J. (1993). The relationship between dementia and elder abuse. *American Journal of Psychiatry, 150,* 643–663.

Craft, S. M., & Serovich, J. M. (2005). Family-of-origin factors and partner violence in the intimate relationships of gay men who are HIV positive. *Journal of Interpersonal Violence, 20,* 777–791.

Crampton, A. (2004). The importance of adult guardianship for social work practice. *Journal of Gerontological Social Work, 43,* 117.

Crawford, E., Wright, M. O., & Birchmeir, Z. (2008). Drug-facilitated sexual assault: College women's risk perception and behavioral choices. *Journal of American College Health, 57,* 261–272.

Crawford, N. (2002, November). Upcoming diversity conference is new and improved. *APA Monitor on Psychology, 33,* 19.

Creel, L., Lovera, S., & Ruiz, M. (2001). *Domestic violence: An ongoing threat to women in Latin America and the Caribbean.* Washington, DC: Population References Bureau.

Creighton, A., & Kivel, P. (1993). *Helping teens stop violence: A practical guide to counselors.* Alameda, CA: Hunter House.

Crichton, S. J., Bond, J. B., Jr., Harvey, C. D. H., & Ristok, J. (1998). Elder abuse: Feminist and ageist perspectives. *Journal of Elder Abuse & Neglect, 10*(3/4), 115–130.

Crichton-Hill, Y. (2001). Challenging ethnocentric explanations of domestic violence. *Trauma, Violence, & Abuse, 2,* 203–214.

Crittenden, P. M. (1992). Children's strategies for coping with adverse home environments: An interpretation using attachment theory. *Child Abuse & Neglect, 16,* 329–343.

Crittenden, P. M. (1996). Research on maltreating families: Implications for intervention. In J. Briere, L. Berliner, J. A. Bulkley, C. Jenny, & T. A. Reid (Eds.), *The APSAC handbook on child maltreatment* (pp. 158–174). Thousand Oaks, CA: Sage.

Crittenden, P. M. (1998). Dangerous behavior and dangerous contexts: A 35-year perspective on research on the developmental effects of child physical abuse. In P. K. Trickett & C. J. Schellenbach (Eds.), *Violence against children in the family and the community* (pp. 11–38). Washington, DC: American Psychological Association.

Crittenden, P. M., Kozlowska, K., & Landini, A. (2010). Assessing attachment in school-age children. *Clinical Child Psychology and Psychiatry, 15,* 185–208.

Crofford, L. J. (2007). Violence, stress, and somatic syndrome. *Trauma, Violence, & Abuse, 8,* 299–313.

Cronin, C. (1995). Adolescent reports of parental spousal violence in military and civilian families. *Journal of Interpersonal Violence, 10,* 117–122.

Cronkite, R. C., & Moos, R. H. (1984). The role of predisposing and moderating factors in the stress-illness relationship. *Journal of Health and Social Behavior, 25,* 372–393.

Crooks, C. V., Scott, K. L., Wolfe, D. A., Chiodo, D., & Killip, S. (2007). Understanding the link between childhood maltreatment and violent delinquency: What do school have to add? *Child Maltreatment, 12,* 269–280.

Cross, T. P., Jones, L. M., et al. (2008, August). *Evaluating children's advocacy centers' response to child sexual abuse.* Washington, D.C: U.S. Department of Justice (OJJDP), http://www.ojp.usdoj.gov/ojjdp

Cross, T. P., Finkelhor, D., & Ormrod, R. K. (2005). Police involvement in child protection services investigations. *Child Maltreamtent, 10,* 224–244.

Cross, T. P., Walsh, W. A., Simone, M., & Jones, L. M. (2003). Prosecution of child abuse: A meta-analysis of rates of criminal justice decisions. *Trauma, Violence, & Abuse, 4,* 323–340.

Crouch, J. L., et al. (2010). Automatic encoding of ambiguous child behavior in high and low risk for child physical abuse parents. *Journal of Family Violence, 25,* 73–80.

Crowe, A. H., Sydney, L., DeMichele, M., Keilitz, S., Neal, C., Frohman, S., et al. (2009, May). *Community corrections response to domestic violence: Guidelines for practice.* Washington, DC: Office of Violence Against Women (Department of Justice).

Cuartas, A. S. (2001). Dissociation in male batterers. *Dissertation Abstracts International, 62,* 3698A. (UMI No. 3033918)

Cuevas, C. A., Finkelhor, D., Ormrod, R. & Turner, H. (2009). Psychiatric diagnosis for victimization in a national sample of children. *Journal of Interpersonal Violence, 24,* 636–652.

Culp, R. E., Little, V., Letts, D., & Lawrence, H. (1991). Maltreated children's self-concept: Effects of a comprehensive treatment program. *American Journal of Orthopsychiatry, 61*(1), 114–121.

Cummings, N. (1990). Issues of the 1990s. *Response, 13*(1), 4.

Cunningham, S. (2003). The joint contribution of experiencing and witnessing violence during childhood on child abuse in the parent role. *Violence and Victims, 18,* 619–639.

Cunradi, C. B., Caetano, R., & Schafer, J. (2002). Socioeconomic predictors of intimate partner violence among White, Black, and Hispanic couples in the United States. *Journal of Family Violence, 17,* 377–389.

Cunradi, C. B., Bersamin, M., & Ames, G. (2009). Agreement on intimate partner violence among a sample of blue-collar couples. *Journal of Interpersonal Violence, 24,* 551–568.

Currie, D. H. (1998). Violent men or violent women? Whose definition counts? In R. K. Bergen (Ed.), *Issues in intimate violence* (pp. 97–111). Thousand Oaks, CA: Sage.

Currie, J., & Widom, C. S. (2010). Long-term consequences of child abuse and neglect on adult economic well-being. *Child Maltreatment, 15,* 11–120.

Currier, D. M., & Carlson, J. H. (2009). Creating attitudinal change through teaching. *Journal of Interpersonal Violence, 24,* 1735–1754.

Curtis, L. (2004, March/April). Older fraud prevention, intervention, and victim services through faith communities. *Victimization of the Elderly and Disabled, 6,* 81–82, 95.

Cuthbert, C., Sloat, K., Driggers, M. G., Mesh, C. J., Bancroft, L., & Silverman, J. (2002). *Battered mothers speak out: A human rights report on domestic violence and child custody in the Massachusetts Family Courts.* Wellesley, MA: Wellesley Centers for Women.

CyberBully Alert. (2008, October 8). *Cyber bullying state laws and policies.* http://cyberbullyalert.com/blog/2008/10/cyber-bullying-state-laws-and-policies/

Cyr, M., Wright, J., McDuff, P., & Perron, A. (2002). Intrafamilial sexual abuse: Brother-sister incest does not differ from father-daughter and stepfather-stepdaughter incest. *Child Abuse & Neglect, 26,* 957–973.

Dadds, M. R., & Salmon, K. (2003). Punishment insensitivity and parenting: Temperament and learning as interacting risks for antisocial behavior. *Clinical Child and Family Psychology Review, 6,* 69–86.

Dagenais, C., Briére, F. N., Gratton, G., & Dupont, D. (2009). Brief and intensive family support program to prevent emergency placements: Lessons learned from a process evaluation. *Children and Youth Services Review, 31,* 594–600.

Daka, K. (2009). Why nurses underreport suspected child abuse cases. *The Journal of Undergraduate Nursing Writing, 3,* 11–17.

Dalal, R., & Fulcher, J. (2006, December/January). Teen dating violence prevention education: Does it work? *Domestic Violence Report, 11,* 26–27.

Dalsbeimer, J. (1998). Battered men: A silent epidemic. *Topics in Emergency Medicine, 20*(4), 52–59.

Daly, M., & Wilson, M. (1998). The evolutionary social psychology of family violence. In C. Crawford & D. L. Krebs (Eds.), *Handbook of evolutionary psychology: Ideas, issues, and applications* (pp. 431–455). Mahwah, NJ: Lawrence Erlbaum.

Danese, A., et al. (2009). Adverse childhood experiences and adult risk factors for age-related disease. *Archives of Pediatrics & Adolescent Medicine, 163,* 1135–1143.

Daniels, V. (2001). Navajo male batterers' and battered Navajo females' therapeutic preferences. *Dissertation Abstracts International, 62*(03), 1570B. (UMI No. 3007081)

Danis, F. S., Lewis, C. M., Trapp, J., Reid, K., & Fisher, E. R. (1998, July). *Lessons from the first year: An evaluation of the National Domestic Violence Hotline.* Paper presented at Program Evaluation and Family Violence Research: An International Conference, Durham, NH.

Dannerbeck, A. M. (2005). Differences in parenting attributes, experiences, and behaviors of delinquent youth with and without a parental history of incarceration. *Youth Violence and Juvenile Justice, 3,* 199–213.

Daro, D. (1988). *Confronting child abuse: Research for effective program design.* New York: Free Press.

Daro, D., & Donnelly, A. C. (2002). Charting the waves of prevention: Two steps forward, one step back. *Child Abuse & Neglect, 26,* 731–742.

Daro, D., & Gelles, R. J. (1992). Public attitudes and behaviors with respect to child abuse prevention. *Journal of Interpersonal Violence, 7,* 517–531.

Daro, D., & McCurdy, K. (1994). Preventing child abuse and neglect: Programmatic interventions. *Child Welfare, 73,* 405–430.

Dasgupta, S. D. (2002). A framework for understanding women's use of non-lethal violence in intimate heterosexual relationships. *Violence Against Women, 8,* 1364–1389.

D'Augelli, A. R. (1992). Lesbian and gay male undergraduates' experiences of harassment and fear on campus. *Journal of Interpersonal Violence, 7,* 383–395.

D'Augelli, A. R., Grossman, A. H., & Starks, M. T. (2006). Childhood gender atypicality, victimization, and PTSD among lesbian, gay, and bisexual youth. *Journal of Interpersonal Violence, 21,* 1462–1482.

Daversa, M. T., & Knight, R. A. (2007). A structural examination of the predictors of sexual coercion against children and adolescent sexual offenders. *Criminal Justice and Behavior, 34,* 1313–1333.

Davey, G. C. L. (1992). Classical conditioning and the acquisition of human fears and phobias: A review and synthesis of the literature. *Advances in Behaviour Research and Therapy, 14,* 29–66.

Davidson, H. A. (1994). *The impact of domestic violence on children: A report to the president of the American Bar Association* (2nd rev. ed., Report No. 549–0248). Chicago: American Bar Association.

Davidson, H. A. (1995). Child abuse and domestic violence: Legal connections and controversies. *Family Law Quarterly, 29,* 357–373.

Davidson, K., MacGregor, M. W., Stuhr, J., Dixon, K., & MacLean, D. (2000). Constructive anger verbal behavior predicts blood pressure in a population-based sample. *Health Psychology, 19,* 55–64.

Davies, J. (2000) *Recommendations for training TANF and child support enforcement staff about domestic violence.* Harrisburg, PA: National Resource Center on Domestic Violence. Retrieved October 11, 2000, from http://www.vawnet.org

Davies, S. L., Glaser, D., & Kossoff, R. (2000). Children's sexual play and behavior in pre-school settings: Staff's perceptions, reports, and responses. *Child Abuse & Neglect, 24,* 1329–1343.

Davis, K. C., Stoner, S. A., Norris, J., George, W. H., & Masters, N. T. (2009). Women's awareness of and discomfort with sexual assault cues. *Violence Against Women, 15,* 1106–1125.

Davis, K. E., Frieze, I. H., & Maiuro, R. D. (2002). *Stalking: Perspectives on victims and perpetrators.* New York: Springer.

Davis, K. E., Ace, A., & Anda, M. (2000). Stalking perpetrators and psychological maltreatment of partners: Anger-jealousy, attachment insecurity, and break-up context. *Violence and Victims, 15,* 407–425.

Davis, L. V., & Srinivasan, M. (1995). Listening to the voices of battered women: What helps them escape the violence. *Affilia, 10,* 49–69.

Davis, M. K., & Gidycz, C. A. (2000). Child sexual abuse prevention programs: A meta-analysis. *Journal of Clinical Child Psychology, 29,* 257–265.

Davis, R. C., & Erez, E. (1998, May). *Immigrant populations as victims: Toward a multicultural criminal justice system* (NCJ Publication No. 167571). Washington, DC: U.S. Department of Justice.

Davis, R. C., Medina, J., & Avitabile, N. (2001). *Reducing repeat incidents of elder abuse: Results of a randomized experiment, final report* (NCJ Publication No. 189086). Washington, DC: U.S. Department of Justice.

Davis, R. E. (2002). "The strongest women": Exploration of the inner resources of abused women. *Qualitative Research, 12,* 1248–1263.

Davis, R. L. (1998). *Domestic violence: Facts and fallacies.* Westport, CT: Praeger.

Day, A., Howells, K., & Rickwood, D. (2004). Trends and issues in crime and criminal justice. *No. 284: Current trends in rehabilitation of juvenile offenders.* Australia: Australian Institute of Criminology.

Dayton, K. (2002, November/December). Legislative roundup: New state laws protecting vulnerable adults. *Victimization of the Elderly and Disabled, 5,* 53–54, 61.

DeAngelis, T. (1993, November). APA panel is examining memories of child abuse. *APA Monitor on Psychology, 24,* 44.

DeAngelis, T. (2001, October). Making 'welfare-to-work' work. *Monitor on Psychology, p.* 71.

DeAngelis, T. (2004, September). Marriage promotion: A simplistic 'fix'? *Monitor on Psychology, 35,* 42.

De Bellis, M. D., & Kuchibhatla, M. (2006). Cerebral volumes in pediatric maltreatment-related posttraumatic stress disorder. *Biological Psychiatry, 60,* 697–703.

De Bellis, M. D., & Thomas, L. (2003). Biologic findings of posttraumatic stress disorder and child maltreatment. *Current Psychiatry Reports, 5,* 108–117.

Deblinger, E., Thakkar-Kolar, R. R., Berry, E. J., & Schroeder, C. M. (2010). Caregivers' efforts to educate their children about child sexual abuse. *Child Maltreatment, 15,* 91–100.

Deering, C., Templer, D. I., Keller, J., & Canfield, M. (2001). Neuropsychological assessment of battered women: A pilot study. *Perceptual and Motor Skills, 92,* 682–686.

Defense of Marriage Act (DOMA). (1996). Public Law No. 104-199, Stat. 2419.

DeGue, S., & DiLillo, D. (2004). Understanding perpetrators of nonphysical sexual coercion: Characteristics of those who cross the line. *Violence and Victims, 19,* 673–688.

De Jong, A. R. (1989). Sexual interactions among siblings and cousins: Experimentation or exploitation? *Child Abuse & Neglect, 13,* 271–279.

DeKeseredy, W. S., & Joseph, C. (2006). Separation and/or divorce sexual assault in rural Ohio. *Violence Against Women, 12,* 301–311.

DeKeseredy, W. S., & Kelly, K. D. (1993). The incidence and prevalence of woman abuse in Canadian university and college dating relationships. *Canadian Journal of Sociology, 18,* 137–159.

DeKeseredy, W. S., & Schwartz, M. D. (1998). *Measuring the extent of woman abuse in intimate heterosexual relationships: A critique of the Conflict Tactics Scales.* Retrieved December 10, 2003, from http://www.vaw.umn.edu/documents/vawnet/ctscritique/ctscritique.pdf

DeKeseredy, W. S., & Schwartz, M. D. (2006a). Separation/divorce sexual assault: The contribution of male peer support. *Feminist Criminology, 1,* 228–250.

DeKeseredy, W. S., & Schwartz, M. D. (2006b). An economic exclusion/male peer support model looks at "wedfare" and woman abuse. *Critical Criminology, 14,* 23–41.

DeKeseredy, W. S., & Schwartz, M. D. (2008). *Escaping abusive relationships in rural America.* New Jersey: Rutgers University Press.

DeKeseredy, W. S., Schwartz, M. D., Fagen, D., & Hall, M. (2006). Separation/divorce sexual assault: The contribution of male support. *Feminist Criminology, 1,* 228–250.

de la Cruz, D. (2001, August 21). Angry wife needles her hubby, with ugly results. *Los Angeles Daily News, p.* 8.

DeLago, C., Deblinger, W., Schroeder, C., & Finkel, M. A. (2008). Girls who disclose sexual abuse: Urogenital symptoms and signs after genital contact. *Pediatrics, 122,* e281–286.

Deliramich, A. N., & Gray, M. J. (2008). Changes in women's sexual behavior following sexual assault. *Behavior Modification, 32,* 611–621.

DeLongis, A., & Holtzman, S. (2005). Coping in context: The role of stress, social support, and personality in coping. *Journal of Personality, 73,* 1633–1656.

De Luca, M. (2010). Incest et scarifications: Inceste fraternal et register partiel. *L'évolution Psychiatrique, 75,* 165–181.

DeMaris, A. (2000). Till discord do us part: The role of physical and verbal conflicts in union disruption. *Journal of Marriage and the Family, 62,* 683–692.

DeMatteo, D., & Marczyk, G. (2005). Risk factors, protective factors, and the prevention of antisocial behavior among juveniles (pp. 9–44). In K. Heilbrun, N. E. Sevin Goldstein, & R. E. Redding (Eds.), *Juvenile delinquency: Prevention, assessment, and intervention.* New York: Oxford University Press.

deMause, L. (1974). The evolution of childhood. In L. deMause (Ed.), *The history of childhood* (pp. 1–74). New York: Psychotherapy Press.

Demiris, G., & Hensel, B. (2009). "Smart homes" for patients at the end of life. *Journal of Housing for the Elderly, 23,* 106–115.

Dempsey, J. P., Fireman, G. D., & Wang, E. (2006). Transitioning out of peer victimization in school children: Gender and behavioral characteristics. *Journal of Psychopathology and Behavioral Assessment, 28,* 271–280.

Denham, A. C., Frasier, P. Y., Hooten, E. G., Belton, L., Newton, W., Gonzalez, P., et al. (2007). Intimate partner violence among Latina in eastern North Carolina. *Violence Against Women, 13,* 123–140.

Dennison, S. M. (2007). Interpersonal relationships and stalking: Identifying when to intervene. *Law and Human Behavior, 31,* 353–367.

Dennison, S. M., & Thomson, D. M. (2005). Criticisms or plaudits for stalking laws? What psychological research tells us about proscribing stalking. *Psychology, Public Policy, and the Law, 11,* 384–406.

Denton, W. H., & Brandon, A. R. (2007). Couple therapy in the presence of mental disorders. *Journal of Couple and Relationship Therapy, 6 1/2,* 17–29.

DePanfilis, D. (1996). Social isolation of neglectful families: A review of social support assessment and intervention models. *Child Maltreatment, 1,* 37–52.

de Paúl, J., Asla, M., Pérez-Albéniz, A., & Torres-Gómez de Cádiz, B. (2006). Impact of stress and mitigating information on evaluations, attributions, disciplinary choices and expectations of compliance in mothers at high and low risk for child physical abuse. *Journal of Interpersonal Violence, 21,* 1018–1045.

de Paúl, J., Pérez-Albéniz, A., Guibert, M., Asla, M., & Ormaechea, A. (2008). Dispositional empathy in neglectful mothers and mothers at high risk for child physical abuse. *Journal of Interpersonal Violence, 23,* 670–684.

De Ridder, D. (1997). What is wrong with coping assessment? A review of conceptual and methodological issues. *Psychological Health, 12,* 417–431.

Dersch, C. A., Harris, S. M., & Rappleyea, D. L. (2006). Recognizing and responding to partner violence: An analog study. *The American Journal of Family Therapy, 34,* 317–331.

Dershowitz, A. M. (2000). Moral judgment: Does the abuse excuse threaten our legal system? *Buffalo Criminal Law Review, 3,* 775–784.

Deyo, G., Skybo, T., & Carroll, A. (2008). Secondary analysis of the "Love Me . . . Never Shake Me" SBS education program. *Child Abuse & Neglect, 32,* 1017–1025.

Dias, M. S., Smith, K. S., deGuehery, K., Mazur, P., Li, V., & Shaffer, M. L. (2005). Preventing abusive head trauma among infants and young children: A hospital-based, parent education program. *Pediatrics, 115,* e470–e477.

Diaz-Olavarrieta, C., Blertson, C., Paz, F., de Leon, S.P., & Alarcon-Segovia, D. (2002). Prevalence of battering among 1,789 outpatients at an internal medicine institution in Mexico. *Society Scientific Medicine, 55,* 1589–1602.

Di Bartolo, L. (2001). The geography of reported domestic violence in Brisbane: A social justice perspective. *Australian Geographer, 32,* 321–341.

Dienemann, J., Boyle, E., Resnick, W., Wiederhorn, N., & Campbell, J. C. (2000). Intimate partner abuse among women diagnosed with depression. *Issues in Mental Health Nursing, 21,* 499–513.

Dietz, N. A., & Martin, P. Y. (2007). Women who are stalked: Questioning the fear standard. *Violence Against Women, 13,* 750–776.

Dijkstra, P., & Buunk, B. P. (2002). Sex differences in the jealousy-evoking effect of rival characteristics. *European Journal of Social Psychology, 32,* 829–852.

DiLalla, L. F., & Gottesman, I. (1991). Biological and genetic contributors to violence: Widom's untold tale. *Psychological Bulletin, 109,* 125–129.

Dingfelder, S. F. (2006a, July/August). Banishing bullying. *Monitor on Psychology, 37,* 76–78.

Dingfelder, S. F. (2006b, October). Violence in the home takes many forms. *Monitor on Psychology, 37,* 18.

Dingfelder, S. F. (2008, July). Do psychologists have 'neuron envy'? *Monitor on Psychology 39,* 26–27.

DiNitto, D. M., Busch-Armendariz, N. B., Bender, K., Woo, H., Tackett-Gibson, M., & Dyer, J. (2008). Testing telephone and web surveys for studying men's sexual assault perpetration behaviors. *Journal of Interpersonal Violence, 23,* 1483–1493.

Diop-Sidibe, N., Campbell, J. C., & Becker, S. (2006). Domestic violence against women in Egypt—wife beating and health outcomes. *Social Science & Medicine, 65,* 1260–1277.

Distefano, A. S. (2009). Intimate partner violence among sexual minorities in Japan: Exploring perceptions and experiences. *Journal of Homosexuality, 56,* 121–146.

Dissanaike, S. (2010). Burns as child abuse: Risk factors and legal issues in West Texas and Eastern New Mexico. *Journal of Burn Care Research, 31,* 176–183.

Diviney, C. L., Parekh, A., & Olson, L. M. (2009). Outcomes of civil protection orders: Results from one state. *Journal of Interpersonal Violence, 24,* 1209–1221.

Dixon, C. (2005). Best practices in the response to child abuse. *Mississippi College Law Review, 25,* 73–100.

Dixon, L., & Browne, K. (2003). The heterogeneity of spouse abuse: A review. *Aggression and Violent Behavior, 8,* 107–130.

Djamba, Y. K., & Kimuna, S. R. (2008). Intimate partner violence among married women in Africa. *Journal of Asian and African Studies, 43,* 457–469.

Dobash, R. E., & Dobash, R. P. (1978). Wives: The "appropriate" victims of marital violence. *Victimology, 2,* 426–442.

Dobash, R. E., & Dobash, R. P. (1979). *Violence against wives: A case against patriarchy.* New York: Free Press.

Dobash, R. E., & Dobash, R. P. (1988). Research as social action: The struggle for battered women. In K. A. Yllö & M. Bograd (Eds.), *Feminist perspectives on wife abuse* (pp. 51–74). Newbury Park, CA: Sage.

Dobie, D. J., Kaviahan, D. R., Maynard, C., Bush, D.R., Davis, T. M., & Bradley, K. A. (2004). Posttraumatic stress disorder in female veterans. *Archives of Internal Medicine, 164,* 394–400.

Dolan, M. M., Casanueva, C., Smith, K. R., & Bradley, R. H. (2008). Parenting and the home environment provided by grandmothers of children in the child welfare system. *Children and Youth Services Review, 31,* 784–796.

Dolan, M., & Völlm, B. (2009). Antisocial personality disorder and psychopathy in women: A literature review on the reliability and validity of assessment instruments. *International Journal of Law and Psychiatry, 32,* 2–9.

D'Olvidio, R., & Doyle, J. (2003). A study on cyberstalking: Understanding investigative hurdles. *FBI Law Enforcement Bulletin, 72*(3), 10–17.

Domestic violence conviction bars gun possession by officers. (1997, January 2). *Criminal Justice Newsletter,* pp. 2–3.

Donohue, B., & Van Hasselt, V. B. (1999). Development and description of an empirically based ecobehavioral treatment program for child maltreatment. *Behavioral Interventions, 14,* 55–82.

Donovan, R., & Williams, M. (2002). Living at the intersection: The effects of racism and sexism on Black rape survivors. *Women & Therapy, 25,* 95–105.

Doroszewicz, K., & Forbes, G. B. (2008). Experiences with dating aggression and sexual coercion among Polish college students. *Journal of Interpersonal Violence, 23,* 58–73.

Dougall, A. L., Hyman, K. B., Hayward, M. C., McFeeley, S., & Baum, A. (2001). Optimism and traumatic stress: The importance of social support and coping. *Journal of Applied Social Psychology, 31,* 223–245.

Douglas, E. M., & Straus, M. A. (2006). Assault and injury of dating partners by university students in 19 countries and its relation to corporal punishment experienced as a child. *European Journal of Criminology, 3,* 293–318.

Douglas, H., & Walsh, T. (2010). Mothers, domestic violence, and child protection. *Violence Against Women, 16,* 489–508.

Douglas, J. E., Burgess, A. W., Burgess, A. G., & Ressler, R. K. (1997). *Crime classification manual.* San Francisco: Jossey-Bass.

Douglas, M. A. (1987). The battered woman syndrome. In D. J. Sonkin (Ed.), *Domestic violence on trial: Psychological and legal dimensions of family violence* (pp. 39–54). New York: Springer.

Douglas, U., Bathrick, D., & Perry, P. A. (2008). Decontructing male violence against women. *Violence Against Women, 14,* 247–261.

Douki, S., Nacef, A., Belhadj, A., Bousaker, A., & Ghachem, R. (2003). Violence against women in Arab and Islamic countries. *Archives of Women's Mental Health, 6,* 165–171.

Doumas, D. M., Pearson, C. L., Elgin, J. E., & McKinley, L. L. (2008). Adult attachment as a risk factor for intimate partner violence: The "mispairing" of partners' attachment styled. *Journal of Interpersonal Violence, 23,* 616–634.

Dowd, M. (2010, March 4). Saudi Arabia creeps closer to a more modern society. *Daily News,* A13.

Dowd, L. S., Leisring, P. A., & Rosenbaum, A. (2005). Partner aggressive women: Characteristics and treatment attrition. *Violence and Victims, 20,* 219–233.

Downs, W. R., Rindels, B., & Atkinson, C. (2007). Women's use of physical and nonphysical self-defense strategies during incidents of partner violence. *Violence Against Women, 13,* 28–45.

Doyle, A. B., Markiewicz, D., Brendgen, M., Lieberman, M., & Voss, K. (2000). Child attachment security and self-concept: Associations with mother and father attachment style and marital quality. *Merrill-Palmer Quarterly, 46,* 514–540.

Dubner, A. E., & Motta, R. W. (1999). Sexually and physically abused foster care children and posttraumatic stress disorder. *Journal of Consulting and Clinical Psychology, 67,* 367–373.

Dubowitz, H. (1994). Neglecting the neglect of neglect. *Journal of Interpersonal Violence, 9,* 556–560.

Dubowitz, H. (2010). Neglect of children's health care. In J. E. B. Myers (Ed.), *The APSAC handbook on child maltreatment* (3rd ed., pp. 145–166). Thousand Oaks, CA: Sage.

Dubowitz, H., Black, M., Harrington, D., & Verschoore, A. (1993). A follow-up study of behavior problems associated with child sexual abuse. *Child Abuse & Neglect, 17,* 743–754.

Dubowitz, H., Black, M. M., Kerr, M. S., Starr, R. H., Jr., & Harrington, D. (2000). Fathers and child neglect. *Archives of Pediatrics & Adolescent Medicine, 154,* 135–141.

Dubowitz, H., Black, M., Starr, R., & Zuravin, S. J. (1993). A conceptual definition of child neglect. *Criminal Justice and Behavior, 20,* 8–26.

Dubowitz, H., Pitts, S. C., Litrownik, A. J., Cox, C. E., Runyan, D., & Black, M. M. (2005). Defining child neglect based on child protective service data. *Child Abuse & Neglect, 29,* 493–511.

Ducharme, L. J., Knudsen, H. K., & Roman, P. M. (2008). Emotional exhaustion and turnover intention in human service occupations: The protective role of coworker support. *Sociological Spectrum, 28,* 81–104.

Dugan, L., Nagin, D. S., & Rosenfeld, R. (1999). Explaining the decline in intimate partner homicide: The effects of changing domesticity, women's status, and domestic violence resources. *Homicide Studies, 3,* 187–214.

Dugan, L., Nagin, D. S., & Rosenfeld, R. (2003). Do domestic violence services save lives? *National Institute of Justice Journal, Issue 250,* 20–25.

Dugmore, L., & Channell, J. (2010). Developing a training programme for detecting and tackling childhood sexual abuse. *Nursing Times, 106,* 14–15.

Dugosh, J. W. (2000). On predicting relationship satisfaction from jealousy: The moderating effects of love. *Current Research in Social Psychology, 5,* 254–263.

Duke, J. (1999, January/February). Summary of findings of a national survey of adult abuse central registries. *Victimization of the Elderly and Disabled, 1,* 73–74, 77.

Dumont, K., Mitchell-Herzfeld, S., Greene, R., Lee, E., Lowenfels, A., et al. (2008). Healthy Families New York randomized trial: Effects on early child abuse and neglect. *Child Abuse and Neglect, 32,* 295–315.

Dunford, F. W. (2000). The San Diego Navy Experiment: An assessment of interventions for men who assault their wives. *Journal of Consulting and Clinical Psychology, 68,* 468–476.

Dunford, F. W., Huizinga, D., & Elliott, D. S. (1990). The role of arrest in domestic assault: The Omaha police experiment. *Criminology, 28,* 183–206.

Dunifon, R., & Kowaleski-Jones, L. (2007). The influence of grandparents in single-mother families. *Journal of Marriage and Family, 69,* 465–481.

Dunlap, E., Golub, A., Johnson, B. D., & Wesley, D. (2002). Intergenerational transmission of conduct norms for drugs, sexual exploitation and violence: A case study. *British Journal of Criminology, 41,* 1–20.

Dunlop, B. D., Rothman, M. B., Condon, K. M., Hebert, K. S., & Martinez, I. L. (2000). Elder abuse: Risk factors and use of case data to improve policy and practice. *Journal of Elder Abuse & Neglect, 12*(3/4), 95–122.

Dunn, P. F. (1995). "Elder abuse" as an innovation to Australia: A critical overview. In J. I. Kosberg & J. L. Garcia (Eds.), *Elder abuse: International and cross-cultural perspectives* (pp. 13–30). Binghamton, NY: Haworth.

Dunne, M. P., et al. (2009). ISPCAN child abuse screening tools retrospective version (ICAST-R): Delphi study and field testing in seven countries. *Child Abuse & Neglect, 33,* 815–825.

Duplantis, A. D., Romans, J. S. C., & Bear, T. M. (2007). Persistence in domestic violence treatment and self-esteem, locus of control, risk of alcoholism, level of abuse, and beliefs about abuse. *Journal of Aggression, Maltreatment & Trauma, 13,* 1–18.

DuPree, M. G., Mustanski, B. S., Bocklandt, S., Nievergelt, C., & Hamer, D. H. (2004). A candidate gene study of CYP19 (aromatase) and male sexual orientation. *Behavior Genetics, 34,* 243–250.

Durose, M., Harlow, C. W., Langan, P. A., Motivans, M., Rantala, R. R., & Smith, E. L. (2005). *Family violence statistics: Including statistics on strangers and acquaintances* (NCJ Publication No. 207846). Washington, DC: Bureau of Justice Statistics.

Durose, M. R., Landon, P. A., & Schmitt, E. L. (2003). Recidivism of sex offenders released from prison in 1994 (NCJ Publication No. 198281). Washington, DC: Bureau of Justice Statistics.

Dussich, J. P. J., & Maekoya, C. (2007). Physical child harm and bullying-related behaviors: A comparative study in Japan, South Africa, and the United States. *International Journal of Offender Therapy & Comparative Criminology, 51,* 495-509.

Dutton, D. G. (1988). *The domestic assault of women.* Boston: Allyn & Bacon.

Dutton, D. G. (1994). Patriarchy and wife assault: An ecological fallacy. *Violence and Victims, 9,* 167–182.

Dutton, D. G. (1995). Trauma symptoms and PTSD-like profiles in perpetrators of intimate abuse. *Journal of Traumatic Stress, 8,* 299–316.

Dutton, D. G. (1998). *The abusive personality: Violence and control in intimate relationships.* New York: Guilford.

Dutton, D. G. (1999). Traumatic origins of intimate rage. *Aggression and Violent Behavior, 4,* 431–447.

Dutton, D. G. (2008). My back pages: Reflections on thirty years of domestic violence research. *Trauma, Violence, & Abuse, 9,* 131–143.

Dutton, D. G., & Painter, S. L. (1981). Traumatic bonding: The development of emotional attachments in battered women and other relationships of intermittent abuse. *Victimology, 6*(1–4), 139–155.

Dutton, D. G., & Painter, S. L. (1993a). The battered woman syndrome: Effects of severity and intermittency of abuse. *American Journal of Orthopsychiatry, 63,* 614–622.

Dutton, D. G., & Painter, S. L. (1993b). Emotional attachments in abusive relationships: A test of traumatic bonding theory. *Violence and Victims, 8,* 105–120.

Dutton, D. G., Saunders, K., Starzomski, A. J., & Bartholomew, K. (1994). Intimacy-anger and insecure attachment as precursors of abuse in intimate relationships. *Journal of Applied Social Psychology, 24,* 1367–1386.

Dutton, D. G., & Starzomski, A. J. (1994). Psychological differences between court-referred and self-referred wife assaulters. *Criminal Justice and Behavior, 21,* 203–222.

Dutton, D. G., & Strachan, C. E. (1987). Motivational needs for power and spouse-specific assertiveness in assaultive and nonassaultive men. *Violence and Victims, 2,* 145–156.

Dutton, D. G., van Ginkel, C., & Landolt, M. A. (1996). Jealousy, intimate abusiveness, and intrusiveness. *Journal of Family Violence, 11,* 411–423.

Dutton, M. A., & Goodman, L. A. (2005). Coercion in intimate partner violence: Toward a new conceptualization. *Sex Roles, 52,* 743–756.

Dutton, M. A., Goodman, L. A., & Bennett, L. (1999). Court-involved battered women's responses to violence: The role of psychological, physical, and sexual abuse. *Violence and Victims, 14,* 89–104.

Dutton, M. A., Holtzworth-Munroe, A., Jouriles, E. N., McDonald, R., Krishnan, S. P., McFarlane, J., et al. (2003). *Recruitment and retention in intimate partner violence research* (NCJ Publication No. 201943). Washington, DC: U.S. Department of Justice.

Dutton-Douglas, M. A., & Dionne, D. (1991). Counseling and shelter services for battered women. In M. Steinman (Ed.), *Woman battering: Policy responses* (pp. 113–130). Cincinnati, OH: Anderson.

Dye, M. L., & Davis, K. E. (2003). Stalking and psychological abuse: Common factors and relationship-specific characteristics. *Violence and Victims, 18,* 163–180.

Dyslin, C. W., & Thomsen, C. J. (2005). Religiosity and risk of perpetrating child physical abuse: An empirical investigation. *Journal of Psychology and Theology, 33,* 291–298.

Eastman, B. J., Bunch, S. G., Williams, A. H., & Carawan, L. W. (2007). Exploring the perceptions of domestic violence service providers in rural localities. *Violence Against Women, 13,* 700–716.

Easton, C. J., Mandel, D. L., Hunkele, K. A., Nich, C., Rounsaville, B. J., & Carroll, K. M. (2007). A cognitive-behavioral therapy for alcohol-dependent domestic violence offenders: An integrated substance abuse—domestic violence treatment approach (SADV). *The American Journal on Addictions, 16,* 24–31

Easton, J. A., Shackelford, T. K., & Schipper, L. D. (2008). Delusional disorder-jealous type: How inclusive are the DSM-IV diagnostic criteria? *Journal of Clinical Psychology, 64,* 264-275.

Easton, P. (2003, February 14). Wife convicted of murder for running over husband. *The Daily News,* p. 10.

Eby, K. K. (2004). Exploring the stressors of low-income women with abusive partners: Understanding their needs and developing effective community responses. *Journal of Family Violence, 19,* 211–232.

Eckenrode, J., Izzo, C., & Smith, E. (2007). Physical abuse and adolescent outcomes. In R. Haskins, F. Wulczyn, & M. B. Webb (Eds.), *Child protection: Using research to improve policy and practice* (pp. 226–242).

Eckhardt, C. I., Barbour, K. A., & Stuart, G. L. (1997). Anger and hostility in maritally violent men: Conceptual distinctions, measurement issues and literature review. *Clinical Psychology Review, 17,* 333–358.

Eckhardt, C. I., Jamison, T. R., & Watts, K. (2002). Anger experience and expression among male dating violence perpetrators during anger arousal. *Journal of Interpersonal Violence, 17,* 1102–1114.

Eckhardt, C. I., Norlander, B. J., & Deffenbacher, J. L. (2004). The assessment of anger and hostility: A critical review. *Aggression and Violent Behavior, 9,* 17–43.

Eckhardt, C. I., Samper, R. E., & Murphy, C. M. (2008). Anger disturbances among perpetrators of intimate partner violence. *Journal of Interpersonal Violence, 23,* 1600–1617.

Edens, J, F., Skopp, N. A., & Cahill, M. A. (2008). Psychopathic features moderate the relationship between harsh and inconsistent parental discipline and adolescent antisocial behavior. *Journal of Clinical & Adolescent Psychology, 37 (2),* 472–476.

Edin, K., & Lein, L. (1997*). Making ends meet: How single mothers survive welfare and low-wage work.* New York: Russell Sage.

Edinburgh, L. D., & Saewyc, E. M. (2009). A novel, intensive home-visiting intervention for runaway sexually exploited girls. *Journal of Specialists in Pediatric Nursing, 14,* 41–48.

Edleson, J. L. (1998). Responsible mothers and invisible men: Child protection in the case of adult domestic violence. *Journal of Interpersonal Violence, 13,* 294–298.

Educational Testing Service (ETS). (2009). Scholastic Aptitude Test (SAT). Princeton, NJ: Author.

Edwards, A., & Lutzker, J. R. (2008). Iterations of the SafeCare model. *Behavior Modification, 32,* 736–756.

Edwards, V. J., Dube, S. R., Felitti, V. J., & Anda, R. (2007). It's OK to ask about past abuse. *American Psychologist, 62,* 327–328.

Efetie, E. R., & Salami, H. A. (2007). Domestic violence on pregnant women in Abuja, Nigeria. *Journal of Obstetrics and Gynaecology, 27,* 379–382.

Egeland, B. (1993). A history of abuse is a major risk factor for abusing the next generation. In R. J. Gelles & D. R. Loseke (Eds.), *Current controversies on family violence* (pp. 197–208). Newbury Park, CA: Sage.

Egeland, B. (1997). Mediators of the effects of child maltreatment on developmental adaptation in adolescence. In D. Cicchetti & S. L. Toth (Eds.), *Rochester Symposium on Developmental Psychopathology: Vol. 8. The effects of trauma on the developmental process* (pp. 403–434). Rochester, NY: University of Rochester Press.

Egeland, B., Sroufe, L. A., & Erickson, M. F. (1983). The developmental consequences of different patterns of maltreatment. *Child Abuse & Neglect, 7,* 459–469.

Ehlers, A., Michael, T., Chen, Y., Payne, E., & Shan, S. (2006). Enhanced perceptual priming for neutral stimuli in a traumatic context: A pathway to intrusive memories. *Memory, 14,* 316–328.

Ehrensaft, M. K., Cohen, P., & Johnson, J. G. (2006). Development of personality disorder symptoms and the risk for partner violence. *Journal of Abnormal Psychology, 115,* 474–483.

Ehrensaft, M. K., Cohen, P., Brown, J., Smailes, E. M., Chen, H., & Johnson, J. G. (2003). Intergenerational transmission of partner violence: A 20-year prospective study. *Journal of Consulting and Clinical Psychology, 71,* 741–753.

Ehrensaft, M. K., Langhinrichsen-Rohling, J., Heyman, R. E., O'Leary, K. D., & Lawrence, E. (1999). Feeling controlled in marriage: A phenomenon specific to physically aggressive couples. *Journal of Family Psychology, 13,* 20–32.

Eisikovits, Z., Lowenstein, A., & Winterstein, T. (2005). Report of the first national survey on elder abuse and neglect in Israel. Haifa: The Center for Research and Study of Aging. The University of Haifa, Israel (Hebrew). Presented to ESHEL and the Insurance Institute.

Eiskovits, Z., Winstock, Z., & Fishman, G. (2004). The First National Survey on Domestic Violence. *Violence Against Women, 7,* 729–748.

Eisler, R. M., & Skidmore, J. R. (1987). Masculine gender-role stress: Scale development and component factors in the appraisal of stressful situations. *Behavior Modification, 11,* 123–136.

Eitle, D. (2005). The influence of mandatory arrest policies, police organizational characteristics, and situational variables on the probability of arrest in domestic violence cases. *Crime & Delinquency, 51,* 573–597.

El-Bassel, N., Gilbert, L., Schilling, R., & Wada, T. (2000). Drug abuse and partner violence among women in methadone treatment. *Journal of Family Violence, 15,* 209–228.

Elbow, M. (1977). Theoretical considerations of violent marriages. *Social Casework, 58,* 515–526.

Elder abuse, neglect, and financial exploitation—2006. (www.dhss.mo.gov).

Elder Justice Coalition. (2009). *The Elder Justice Act Introduced.* Retrieved May 11, 2009, from webmaster@elderjustice coalition.com

Eliot, M., & Cornell, D. G. (2009). Bullying in middle school as a function of insecure attachment and aggressive attitudes. *School Psychology International, 30,* 201–214.

Elliott, D. S. (1994). Serious violent offenders: Onset, developmental course, and termination. *Criminology, 32,* 1–21.

Elliott, I. A., Eldridge, H. J., Ashfield, S., & Beech, A. R. (2010). Exploring risk: Potential static, dynamic, protective and treatment factors in the clinical histories of female sex offenders. *Journal of Family Violence, 25,* 595–602.

Ellis, K. K., et al. (2008). Rural mothers experiencing the stress of intimate partner violence or not: Their newborn health concerns. *Journal of Midwifery and Women's Health, 53,* 556–562.

Ellis, L., Widmayer, A., & Palmer, C. T. (2009). Perpetrators of sexual assault continuing to have sex with their victims following the initial assault. *International Journal of Offender Therapy and Comparative Criminology, 53,* 454–463.

Ellison, C. G., Bartkowski, J. P., & Segal, M. L. (1996). Do conservative Protestant parents spank more often? Further evidence from the national survey of families and households. *Social Science Quarterly, 77,* 663–673.

Ellison, C. G., & Bradshaw, M. (2009). Religious beliefs, sociopolitical ideology, and attitudes toward corporal punishment. *Journal of Family Issues, 30,* 320–340.

Elliston, E. J. W. (2001). Why don't they just leave? The effects of psychological abuse on sheltered women. *Dissertation Abstracts International, 62*(07), 2570A. (UMI No. 3019516)

Ellsberg, M. (2006). Violence against women and the Millennium Development Goals: Facilitating women's access to support. *International Journal of Gynecology and Obstetrics, 94,* 325–332.

El-Safty, M. (2004). Women in Egypt: Islamic rights versus cultural practice. *Sex Roles, 51,* 273–281.

Else-Quest, N. M., Hyde, J. S., Goldsmith, H. H., & Van Hulle, C. A. (2006). Gender differences in temperament: A meta-analysis. *Psychological Bulletin, 132,* 33-72.

Emery, R. E., & Laumann-Billings, L. (1998). An overview of the nature, causes, and consequences of abusive family relationships: Toward differentiating maltreatment and violence. *American Psychologist, 53,* 121–135.

Emmers-Sommer, T. M., Pauley, P., Hanzal, A. & Triplett, L. (2006). Love, suspense, sex, and violence: Men's and women's film predilections, exposure to sexually violent media, and their relationship to rape myth acceptance. *Sex roles, 55,* 311–320.

Emotional judgments seek respect. (1999, July 24). *Science News, 156,* 59.

Empey, L. T., Stafford, M. C., & Hay, H. H. (1999). *American delinquency: Its meaning and construction.* Belmont, CA: Wadsworth.

Enander, V., & Holmberg, C. (2008). Why does she leave? The leaving process(es) of battered women. *Health Care for Women International, 29,* 200–226.

English, D. J., et al. (2008). At-risk and maltreated children exposed to intimate partner aggression/violence. *Child Maltreatment, 14,* 157–171.

English, D. J., Graham, J. C., Litrownik, A. J., Everson, M., & Bangdiwala, S. I. (2005). Defining maltreatment chronicity: Are there differences in child outcomes? *Child Abuse & Neglect, 29,* 575–595.

English, D. J., Upadhyaya, M. P., Litrownik, A. J., Marshall, J. M., Runyan, D. K., Graham, J. C., et al. (2005). Maltreatment's wake: The relationship of maltreatment dimensions to child outcomes. *Child Abuse and Neglect, 29,* 597–619.

English, D. J., Widom, C. S., & Brandford, C. (2004). Another look at the effects of child abuse. *NIJ Journal, 251,* 23–24.

Epstein, D. (1999). In search of effective intervention in domestic violence cases: Rethinking the roles of prosecutors, judges, and the court system. *Yale Journal of Law & Feminism, 11,* 3–50.

Erez, E., Adelman, M., & Gregory, C. (2009). Intersection of immigration and domestic violence: Voices of battered immigrant women. *Feminist Criminology, 4,* 32–56.

Erez, E., & Belknap, J. (1998). In their own words: Battered women's assessment of the criminal processing system's response. *Violence and Victims, 13,* 251–268.

Erez, E., & Tontodonato, P. (1990). The effect of victim participation in sentencing outcomes. *Criminology, 28,* 451–474.

Erickson, M. F., & Egeland, B. (2010). Child neglect. In J. E. B. Myers (Ed.), *The APSAC handbook on child maltreatment* (3rd ed., pp. 103–124). Thousand Oaks, CA: Sage.

Erickson, N. S. (2000). The role of the law guardian in a custody case involving domestic violence. *Fordham Urban Law Journal, XXVII,* 817–848.

Erickson, N. S. (2006). Problems with custody evaluations. (2006, June/July). *Domestic Violence Report, 11,* 67.

Eriksen, S., & Jensen, V. (2009). A push or a punch: Distinguishing the severity of sibling violence. *Journal of Interpersonal Violence, 24,* 183–208.

Erlingsson, C. L. (2007). Searching for elder abuse: A systematic review of database citations. *Journal of Elder Abuse & Neglect, 19,* 59–78.

Erwin, P. E. (2006). Exporting U.S. domestic violence reforms: An analysis of human rights frameworks and U.S. "best practices." *Feminist Criminology, 1,* 188–206.

Espelage, D. L. (2004). An ecological perspective to school-based bullying prevention. *The Prevention Researcher, 11*(3), 3–6.

Espelage, D. L., Bosworth, K., & Simon, T. R. (2001). Short-term stability and prospective correlates of bullying in middle school students: An examination of potential demographic, psychosocial, and environmental influences. *Violence and Victims, 16,* 411–426.

Espelage, D. L., & Swearer, S. M. (2003). Research on school bullying and victimization: What have we learned and where do we go from here? *School Psychology Review, 12,* 365–383.

Estacion, A., & Cherlin, A. (2010). Gender distrust and intimate unions among low-income Hispanic and African American women. *Journal of Family Issues, 31,* 475-498.

Estes, R. J., & Weiner, N. A. (2010). The commercial sexual exploitation of children in the U. S., Canada and Mexico. Retrieved from meridian.pmhclients.com/.../Univ.%20PA20Complete_CSEC_020220.pdf

Estimates of child sexual abuse. (2004). Retrieved July 16, 2010, from www.bishop-accountability.org/reports/2004.../1_2_JJ_EstimatesOf.pdf

Estroff, S., Swanson, J., Lachicotte, W., Swartz, M., & Bolduc, M. (1998). Risk reconsidered: Targets of violence in the social networks of people with serious psychiatric disorders. *Social Psychiatry and Psychiatric Epidemiology, 33*(Suppl. 1), 95–101.

Euser, E., M., Ijendoorn, M. H., Prinzie, P., & Bakerman-Kranenburg, M. J. (2010). Prevalence of child maltreatment in the Netherlands. *Child Maltreatment, 15,* 5–17.

Evans, G. W., Gonnella, C., Marcynszyn, L. A., Gentile, N., & Salpekar, N. (2005). The role of chaos in poverty and children's socioemotional adjustment. *Psychological Science, 16,* 560–565.

Evans, S. (2005). Beyond gender: Class, poverty and domestic violence. *Australian Social Work, 58,* 36–43.

Everson, M. D., et al. (2008). Concordance between adolescent reports of childhood abuse an Child Protective Service determinations in an at-risk sample of young adolescents. *Child Maltreatment, 13,* 14–26.

Ewing, C. P., & Aubrey, M. (1987). Battered women and public opinion: Some realities about myths. *Journal of Family Violence, 2,* 257–264.

Eyssel, F., Bohner, G., & Siebler, F. (2006). Perceived rape myth acceptance of others predicts rape proclivity: Social norm or judgmental anchoring. *Swiss Journal of Psychology, 65,* 93–99.

Ezechi, O. C., Kalu, B. K., Ezechi, L. O., Nwokoro, C. A., Ndududa, V. L., & Okeke, G. C. E. (2004). Prevalence and pattern of domestic violence against pregnant women. *Journal of Obstetrics and Gynaecology, 24,* 652–656.

Fagan, A. A. (2005). The relationship between adolescent physical abuse and criminal offending: Support for an enduring and generalized cycle of violence. *Journal of Family Violence, 20,* 279–290.

Fagan, J. A. (1988). Contributions of family violence research to criminal justice policy on wife assault: Paradigms of science and social control. *Violence and Victims, 3,* 159–186.

Fagan, J. A. (1993). Interactions among drugs, alcohol, and violence. *Health Affairs, 12,* 65–79.

Fagan, J. A., Stewart, D., & Hansen, K. (1983). Violent men or violent husbands? Background factors and situational correlates. In D. Finkelhor, R. J. Gelles, G. T. Hotaling, & M. A. Straus (Eds.), *The dark side of families: Current family violence research* (pp. 49–67). Beverly Hills, CA: Sage.

Fairchild, D. G., Fairchild, M. W., & Stoner, S. (1998). Prevalence of adult domestic violence among women seeking routine care in a Native American health care facility. *American Journal of Public Health, 88,* 1515–1518.

Faller, K. C. (1988). *Child sexual abuse: An interdisciplinary manual for diagnosis, case management, and treatment.* New York: Columbia University Press.

Faller, K. C. (1993a). *Child sexual abuse: Intervention and treatment issues: Definitions, scope, and effects of child sexual abuse.* Washington, DC: Child Welfare Information Gateway.

Faller, K. C. (1993b). Research on false allegations of sexual abuse in divorce. *APSAC Advisor, 6*(1), 7–10.

Fals-Stewart, W. (2003). The occurrence of partner physical aggression on days of alcohol consumption: A longitudinal diary study. *Journal of Consulting and Clinical Psychology, 71,* 41–52.

Family Violence Project of the National Council of Juvenile and Family Court Judges. (1995). Family violence in child custody statutes: An analysis of state codes and legal practice. *Family Law Quarterly, 29,* 197–227.

Family Violence Prevention Fund. (2002, April 19). *Coercing marriage among welfare recipients.* http://www.endabuse.org

Famularo, R., Fenton, T., Kinscherff, R. T., Ayoub, C. C., & Barnum, R. (1994). Maternal and child posttraumatic stress disorder in cases of child maltreatment. *Child Abuse & Neglect, 18,* 27–36.

Fanniff, A. M., & Becker, J. V. (2006). Specialized assessment and treatment of adolescent sex offenders. *Aggression and Violent Behavior, 11,* 265–282.

Fantuzzo, J. W., Bulotsky-Shearer, R., Fusco, R. A., & McWayne, C. (2005). An investigation of preschool classroom behavioral adjustment problems and social-emotional school readiness competencies. *Early Childhood Research Quarterly, 20,* 256–275.

Fantuzzo, J. W., & Fusco, R. (2007). Children's direct sensory exposure to types of substantiated domestic violence crimes. *Journal of Family Violence and Victims, 22,* 543–552.

Faramarzi, M., Esmailzadeh, S., & Mosavi, S. (2005). A comparison of abused and non-abused women's definition of domestic violence and attitudes to acceptance of male dominance. *European Journal of Obstetrics & Gynecology and Reproductive Biology, 122,* 225–231.

Farberman, R. A. (2007, March). Empowerment through inclusions. *APA Monitor on Psychology, 38,* 36–38.

Farrell, M. L. (1996). Healing: A qualitative study of women recovering from abusive relationships with men. *Perspectives in Psychiatric Care, 32,* 23–32.

Farris, C., & Holtzworth-Munroe, A. (2007). Representative sampling of maritally violent and nonviolent couples: A feasibility study. *Journal of Interpersonal Violence, 22,* 1613–1622.

F.A.S.T. (2003, April). *Financial abuse specialist team* video (NCJ Publication No. 198153). Washington, DC: Office of Victims of Crime.

Fast, N. J., Gruenfeld, D. H., Sivanathan, N., & Galinsky, A. D. (2009). Illusory control: A generative force behind power's far-reaching effects. *Psychological Science, 20,* 502–508.

Faul, M., Xu, L., Wald, M. M., & Coronado, V. G. (2010, March). Traumatic brain injury in the United States: Emergency department visits, hospitalizations and deaths 2002–2006, Atlanta, GA: Centers for Disease Control and Prevention, National Center for Injury Prevention and Control.

Faulk, M. (1974). Men who assault their wives. *Medicine, Science, and the Law, 14,* 180–183.

Faulkner, A. H., & Cranston, K. (1998). Correlates of same-sex sexual behavior in a random sample of Massachusetts high school students. *American Journal of Public Health, 88,* 262–266.

Faulkner, M.E. (2001). Empowering victim advocates: Organizeing against anti-gay/lesbian violence in Canada. *Critical Criminology,10,*123–135.

Faulkner, K., Stoltenberg, C. D., Cogen, R., Nolder, M., & Shooter, E. (1992). Cognitive-behavioral group treatment for male spouse abusers. *Journal of Family Violence, 7,* 37–55.

Fawole, O. I. (2008). Economic violence to women and girls. *Trauma, Violence, & Abuse, 9,* 167–177).

Fay, K. E., & Medway, F. J. (2006). An acquaintance rape education program for students transitioning to high school. *Sex Education: Sexuality, Society and Learning, 6,* 223–236.

Feder, L. (1998). Police handling of domestic and nondomestic assault calls: Is there a case for discrimination? *Crime & Delinquency, 44,* 335–349.

Feder, L., & Ford, D. A. (2000). A test of the efficacy of court-mandated counseling for domestic violence offenders: The Broward Experiment. Washington, DC: National Institute of Justice Final Report (Grant NIJ-96-WT-NX-0008).

Feder, L., & Wilson, D. B. (2005). A meta-analytic review of court-mandated batterer intervention programs: Can courts affect abusers' behavior? *Journal of Experimental Criminology, 1,* 239–262.

Federal Bureau of Investigation. (2000). National Incident-Based Reporting System (NIBRS).

Federal Interagency Forum on Aging-Related Statistics. Older Americans 2008: Key indicators of well-being. Federal Interagency Forum on Aging-Related Statistics, Washington, DC: Government Printing Office, March 2008.

Federal sex discrimination lawsuit settled, company agrees to end housing discrimination against battered women. (2001). *Family Violence and Sexual Assault Bulletin, 17*(7), 42.

Feeney, J. A., & Noller, P. (1996). *Adult attachment.* Thousand Oaks, CA: Sage.

Fehringer, J. A., & Hindin, M. J. (2009). Like parent, like child: Intergenerational transmission of partner violence in Cebu, the Phillipines. *Journal of Adolescent Health, 44,* 363–371.

Feigelman, S., et al. (2009). Screening for harsh punishment in a pediatric primay care clinic. *Child Abuse & Neglect, 33,* 269–277.

Feiring, C., & Cleland, C. (2007). Childhood sexual abuse and abuse-specific attributions of blame over 6 years following discovery. *Child Abuse & Neglect, 31,* 1169–1186.

Feiring, C., Deblinger, E., Hoch-Espada, A., & Haworth, T. (2002). Romantic relationship aggression and attitudes in high school students: The role of gender, grade, and attachment and emotional styles. *Journal of Youth and Adolescence, 31,* 173–385.

Feld, B. C., & Schaefer, S. (2010). The right to counsel in juvenile court: Law reform to deliver legal services and reduce justice by geography. *Criminology & Public Policy, 9,* 327–356.

Feldman, P. H., Nadash, P., & Gursen, M. (2001). Improving communication between researchers and policy makers in long-term care: Or, researchers are from Mars; policy makers are from Venus. *Gerontologist, 41,* 312–321.

Feldman, R. S., Salzinger, S., Rosario, M., Alvarado, L., Caraballo, L., & Hammer, M. (1995). Parent, teacher, and peer ratings of physically abused and nonmaltreated children's behavior. *Journal of Abnormal Child Psychology, 23,* 317–334.

Felix, E. D., & McMahon, S. D. (2006). Gender and multiple forms of peer victimization: How do they influence adolescent psychosocial adjustment. *Violence and Victims, 21,* 707–743.

Felson, R. B. (1992). "Kick 'em when they're down": Explanation of the relationship between stress and interpersonal aggression and violence. *Sociological Quarterly, 33,* 1–16.

Felson, R. B. (2000). The normative protection of women from violence. *Sociological Forum, 15,* 91–116.

Felson, R. B., Messner, S. F., Hoskin, A. W., & Deane, G. (2002). Reasons for reporting and not reporting domestic violence to the police. *Criminology, 40,* 617–647.

Felson, R. B., & Tedeschi, J. T. (Eds.). (1993). *Aggression and violence: Social interactionist perspectives.* Washington, DC: American Psychological Association.

Felthous, A. R., Hempel, A. G., Heredia, A., Freeman, E., Goodness, K., Holzer, C., et al. (2001). Combined homicide-suicide in Galveston County. *Journal of Forensic Sciences, 46,* 586–592.

Ferguson, C. U. (1998). Dating violence as a social phenomenon. In N. A. Jackson & G. C. Oates (Eds.), *Violence in intimate relationships: Examining sociological and psychological issues* (pp. 83–118). Woburn, MA: Butterworth-Heinemann.

Fergusson, D. M., Boden, J. M., & Horwood, L. J. (2008). Developmental antecedents of interpartner violence in a New Zealand birth cohort. *Journal of Family Violence, 23,* 737–753.

Fergusson, D. M., & Horwood, L. J. (1998). Exposure to interparental violence in childhood and psychosocial adjustment in young adulthood. *Child Abuse & Neglect, 22,* 339–357.

Fernández, M. (2006). Cultural beliefs and domestic violence. *Annals of the New York Academy of Science, 1087,* 250–260.

Fewer new laws passed in Sacramento. (2006, January 5). *Thousand Oaks Acorn*, p. 2.

Field, J., Crothers, L., & Kolbert, J. B. (2007). Adolescent female gender identity and attraction to male bullies and victims. *Journal of Emotional Abuse, 7,* 1–15.

Field, T. (2010). Postpartum depression effects on early interactions, parenting, and safety practices: A review. *Infant Behavior and Development, 33,* 1–6

Field, T., Diego, M., Hernandez-Reif, M., Deeds, O., & Figuerido, B. (2009). Pregnancy massage reduces prematurity, low birthweight and postpartum depression. *Infant Behavior & Development, 32,* 454–460.

Fields-Meyer, T., & Benet, L. (1998, November 16). Speaking out. *People, 232,* 234.

Fikree, F. F., Jafarey, S. N., Korejo, R., Khan, A., & Durocher, J. M. (2004). Pakistani obstetricians' recognition of and attitude towards domestic violence screening. *International Journal of Gynecology and Obstetrics, 87,* 59–65.

Filinson, R. (1989). Introduction. In R. Filinson & S. R. Ingman (Eds.), *Elder abuse: Practice and policy* (pp. 17–34). New York: Human Sciences Press.

Filson, J., Ulloa, E., Runfola, C., & Hokado, A. (2010). Does powerlessness explain the relationship between intimate partner violence and depression? *Journal of Interpersonal Violence, 25,* 400–415.

Fincham, F. D. (2000). Family violence: A challenge for behavior therapists. *Behavior Therapy, 31,* 685–693.

Fincham, F. D., Cui, M., Braithwaite, S., & Pasley, K. (2008). Attitudes toward intimate partner violence in dating relationships. *Psychological Assessment, 30,* 260–269.

Finkel, M. A. (2009). Physical examination. In M. A. Finkel & A. P. Giardino (Eds.), *Medical evaluation of child sexual abuse* (3rd ed., pp. 53–104). Chicago, IL: American Academy of Pediatrics.

Finkelhor, D. (1980). Sex among siblings: A survey of prevalence, variety, and effects. *Archives of Sexual Behavior, 9,* 171–193.

Finkelhor, D. (2006). *Updated trends in child maltreatment, 2006.* Retrieved July 16, 2010, from http://www.cyber.law .harvard.edu/.../cyber.law.harvard.../Trends%20in %20Child%20Maltreatment.pdf

Finkelhor, D. (1996). Introduction. In J. Briere, L. Berliner, J. A. Bulkley, C. Jenny, & T. A. Reid (Eds.), *The APSAC handbook on child maltreatment* (pp. ix–xiii). Thousand Oaks, CA: Sage.

Finkelhor, D., Asdigian, N., & Dziuba-Leatherman, J. (1995). The effectiveness of victimization prevention instruction: An evaluation of children's responses to actual threats and assaults. *Child Abuse & Neglect, 19,* 141–153.

Finkelhor, D., & Dziuba-Leatherman, J. (1994). Victimization of children. *American Psychologist, 49,* 173–183.

Finkelhor, D., & Jones, L. M. (2004). *Sexual abuse decline in the 1990s: Evidence for possible causes* (NCJ Publication No. 199298, pp. 1–12). Washington, DC: U.S. Department of Justice.

Finkelhor, D., & Jones, L. (2006). Why have child maltreatment and child victimization declined? *Journal of Social Forces, 62,* 685–716.

Finkelhor, D., Moore, D., Hamby, S. L., & Straus, M. A. (1997). Sexually abused children in a national survey of parents: Methodological issues. *Child Abuse & Neglect, 21,* 1–9.

Finkelhor, D., & Ormrod, R. (2001). *Child abuse reported to the police* (NCJ Publication No. 187238). Washington, DC: U.S. Bureau of Justice Statistics.

Finkelhor, D., Ormrod, R. K., & Turner, H. A. (2007a). Polyvictimization: A neglected component in child victimization trauma. *Child Abuse & Neglect, 31,* 7–26.

Finkelhor, D., Ormrod, R. K, & Turner, H. A. (2007c). Re-victimization patterns in a national longitudinal sample of children and youth. *Child Abuse & Neglect, 31,* 479–502.

Finkelhor, D., Ormrod, R. K., Turner, H. A., & Hamby, S. L. (2005). Measuring poly-victimization using the Juvenile Victimization Questionnaire. *Child Abuse & Neglect, 29,* 1297–1312.

Finkelhor, D., Turner, H. A., Ormrod, R. K., & Hamby, S. L. (2009). Violence, crime, and exposure in a national sample of children and youth. *Pediatrics, 124,* 1411–1423.

Finkelhor, D., Turner, H., Ormrod, R. K., Hamby, S. L., & Kracke, K. (2009, October). *Children's exposure to violence: A comprehensive national survey.* Washington, DC: U.S. Department of Justice, (OJJDP/CDC), http://www.ojp .usdoj.gov

Finkelhor, D., & Yllö, K. A. (1982). Forced sex in marriage: A preliminary research report. *Crime & Delinquency, 82,* 459–478.

Finkelhor, D., & Yllö, K. A. (1987). *License to rape: Sexual abuse of wives.* New York: Free Press.

Finn, J. (1985). The stresses and coping behavior of battered women. *Social Casework: The Journal of Contemporary Social Work, 66,* 341–349.

Finn, J., & Atkinson, T. (2009). Promoting the safe and strategic use of technology for victims of intimate partner violence: Evaluation of the Technology Safety Project. *Violence Against Women, 15,* 1402–1414.

Finn, J., & Banach, M. (2000). Victimization online: The downside of seeking services for women on the Internet. *Cyberpsychology and Behavior, 3,* 776–785.

Finn, M. A., & Bettis, P. (2006). Punitive action or gentle persuasion: Exploring police officers' justifications for using dual arrest in domestic violence cases. *Violence Against Women, 12,* 268–287.

Finn, M. A., Blackwell, B. S., Stalans, L. J., Studdard, S., & Dugan, L. (2004). Dual arrest decisions in domestic violence cases: The influence of departmental polices. *Crime & Delinquency, 50,* 565–589.

Finn, M. A., & Stalans, L. J. (2002). Police handling of the mentally ill in domestic violence situations. *Criminal Justice and Behavior, 29,* 278–307.

Finzi-Dottan, R., & Karu, T. (2006). From emotional abuse in childhood to psychopathology in adulthood: A path mediated by immature defense mechanisms and self-esteem. *Journal of Nervous and Mental Disease, 194,* 616–621.

Fischer, K., & Rose, M. (1995). When "enough is enough": Battered women's decision making around court orders of protection. *Crime & Delinquency, 4,* 414–429.

Fischer, S., Stojek, M., & Hartzell, E. (2010). Effects of multiple forms of childhood abuse and adult sexual assault on current eating disorder symptoms. *Eating Behaviors, 11,* 190–192.

Fisher, B. S., Cullen, F. T., & Turner, M. G. (2000). *The sexual victimization of college women* (NCJ Publication No. 182369). Washington, DC: U.S. Department of Justice.

Fisher, B. S., Cullen, F. T., & Turner, M. G. (2002). Being pursued: Stalking victimization in a national study of college women. *Criminology & Public Policy, 1,* 257–308.

Fisher, B. S., Daigle, L. E., Cullen, F. T., & Santana, S. A. (2007). Assessing the efficacy of the protective action—Completion nexus for sexual victimization. *Violence and Victims, 22,* 18–42.

Fitzpatrick, L. (2009, September 14). Brief history: Stockholm syndrome. *Time,* p. 19.

Flanagan, T. J., & Maguire, K. (Eds.). (1991). *Bureau of Justice sourcebook of criminal justice statistics—1991* (NCJ Publication No. 137369). Washington, DC: U.S. Department of Justice.

Fleury, R. E., Sullivan, C. M., & Bybee, D. I. (2000). When ending the relationship does not end the violence: Women's experiences of violence by former partners. *Violence Against Women, 6,* 1363–1383.

Fleury, R. E., Sullivan, C. M., Bybee, D. I., & Davidson, W. S. (1998). What happened depends on whom you ask: A comparison of police records and victim reports regarding arrests for woman battering. *Journal of Criminal Justice, 26,* 53–59.

Flood, M., & Pease, B. (2009). Factors influencing attitudes to violence against women. *Trauma, Violence, & Abuse, 10,* 125–142.

Florida Crime Prevention Training Institute, http://www.fcpti.com/

Florida Senate. (2007). Emergency management/major disaster, S 0010. Retrieved from *Senate daily calendars* at http://www.flsenate.gov

Flowe, H. D., Ebbensen, E. B., & Putcha-Bhagavatula, A. (2007). Rape shield laws and sexual behavior evidence: Effects of consent level and women's sexual history on rape allegations. *Law and Human Behavior, 31,* 159–175.

Flynn, A., & Graham, K. (2010). "Why did it happen?" A review and conceptual framework for research on perpetrators' and victims' explanation for intimate partner violence. *Aggression and Violent Behavior, 15,* 239–251.

Flynn, C. P. (1996). Normative support for corporal punishment: Attitudes, correlates, and implications. *Aggression and Violent Behavior, 1,* 47–55.

Focus: Call for help. (1994, June 23). *MacNeil/Lehrer NewsHour* [Transcript]. Overland Park, KS: Strictly Business.

Follette, V. M., Polusny, M. A., Bechtle, A. E., & Naugle, A. E. (1996). Cumulative trauma: The impact of child sexual abuse, adult sexual assault, and spouse abuse. *Journal of Traumatic Stress, 9,* 25–35.

Follingstad, D. R., Bradley, R. G., Helff, C. M., & Laughlin, J. E. (2002). A model for predicting dating violence: Anxious attachment, angry temperament, and need for relationship control. *Violence and Victims, 17,* 35–47.

Follingstad, D. R., & DeHart, D. D. (2000). Defining psychological abuse of husbands toward wives. *Journal of Interpersonal Violence, 15,* 891–920.

Follingstad, D. R., Runge, M. M., Ace, A., Buzan, R., & Helff, C. (2001). Justifiability, sympathy level and internal/external locus of the reasons battered women remain in abusive relationships. *Violence and Victims, 16,* 621–643.

Fonck, K., Els, L., Kidula, N., Ndinya-Achola, J., & Temmerman, M. (2005). Increased risk of HIV in women experiencing physical partner violence in Nairobi, Kenya. *AIDS and Behavior, 9,* 335–339.

Fontana, V. J., & Moohnan, V. (1994). Establish more crisis intervention centers. In D. Bender & B. Leone (Eds.), *Child abuse: Opposing viewpoints* (pp. 227–234). San Diego, CA: Greenhaven.

Fontes, L. A. (2002). Child discipline and physical abuse in immigrant Latino families: Reducing violence and misunderstandings [Electronic version]. *Journal of Counseling & Development, 80,* 31–41.

Foo, L., & Margolin, G. (1995). A multivariate investigation of dating aggression. *Journal of Family Violence, 10,* 351–377.

For women, equal pay? No way. (2007, May 7). *Time, 169,* 20.

Foran, H. M., & O'Leary, K. D. (2008). Problem drinking, jealousy, and anger control: Variables predicting physical aggression against a partner. *Journal of Family Violence, 23,* 141–148.

Forbes, G. B., & Adams-Curtis, L. (2001). Experiences with sexual coercion in college males and females. *Journal of Interpersonal Violence, 16,* 865–889.

Forbes, G. B., Adams-Curtis, L. E., & White, K. B. (2004). First- and second-generation measures of sexism, rape myths and related beliefs and hostility toward women. *Violence Against Women, 10,* 236–261.

Forbes, G. B., Jobe, R. L., White, K. B., Bloesch, E., & Adams-Curtis, L. E. (2005). Experiences with sexual coercion in college males and females. *Sex Roles, 52,* 165–173.

Forcier, M., Patel, R., & Kahn, J. A. (2003). Pediatric residents' attitudes and practices regarding adolescent dating violence. *Ambulatory Pediatrics, 3,* 317–323.

Ford, D. A. (1999, July). *Coercing victim participation in domestic violence prosecutions.* Paper presented at the Sixth International Family Violence Research Conference, Durham, NH.

Ford, D. A., & Regoli, M. J. (1992). The preventive impact of policies for prosecuting wife batterers. In E. S. Buzawa & C. G. Buzawa (Eds.), *Domestic violence: The changing criminal justice response* (pp. 181–207). Westport, CT: Greenwood.

Ford, J. D., Racusin, R., Daviss, W. B., Ellis, C. G., Thomas, J., Rogers, K., et al. (1999). Trauma exposure among children with attention deficit hyperactivity disorder and oppositional defiant disorder. *Journal of Consulting and Clinical Psychology, 67,* 786–789.

Ford, J. P., Rompf, E. L., Faragher, T. M., & Weisenfluh, S. M. (1995). Case outcomes in domestic violence court: Influence of judges. *Psychological Reports, 77,* 587–594.

Forliti, A. (2009, May 16). Judge rules family can't refuse chemo for son. *Daily News,* pp. A1, 16.

Fortunata, B., & Kohn, C. S. (2003). Demographic, psychosocial, and personality characteristics of lesbian batterers. *Violence and Victims, 18,* 557–568.

Foshee, V. A. (1996). Gender differences in adolescent dating abuse prevalence, types and injuries. *Health Education Research, 11,* 275–286.

Foshee, V. A., Bauman, K. E., Arriaga, X. R., Helms, R. W., Koch, G. G., & Linder, G. F. (1998). An evaluation of Safe Dates, an adolescent prevention program. *American Journal of Public Health, 88,* 45–50.

Foshee, V. A., Bauman, K. E., Greene, W. F., Koch, G. G., Linder, G. F., & MacDougall, J. E. (2000). The Safe Dates program: 1-year follow-up results. *American Journal of Public Health, 90,* 1619–1622.

Foshee, V. A., Bauman, K. E., Linder, F., Rice, J., & Wilcher, R. (2007). Typologies of adolescent dating violence. *Journal of Interpersonal Violence, 22,* 498–519.

Foshee, V. A., Linder, G. F., MacDougall, J. E., & Bangdiwala, S. (2001). Gender differences in the longitudinal predictors of adolescent dating violence. *Preventive Medicine, 32,* 128–141.

Foster, J. (2008). Incorporating personality into the investment model: Probing commitment processes across individual difference. *Journal of Social and Personal Relationships, 25,* 211–223.

Foubert, J. D., & Marriott, K. A. (1997). Effects of a sexual assault peer education program on men's belief in rape myths. *Sex Roles, 36,* 257–266.

Fowler, D. N., & Hill, H. M. (2004). Social support and spirituality as culturally relevant factors in coping among African American women survivors of partner abuse. *Violence Against Women, 10,* 1267–1282.

Fox, A. M., Jackson, S. S., Hanson, N. B., Gasa, N., Crewe, M., & Sikkema, K. J. (2007). In their own voices: A qualitative study of women's risk for intimate partner violence and HIV in South Africa. *Violence Against Women, 13,* 583–602.

Fox, C. L., & Boulton, M. J. (2006). Longitudinal associations between submissive/nonassertive social behavior and different types of peer victimization. *Violence and Victims, 21,* 383–400.

Fox, G. L., Benson, M. L., DeMaris, A. A., & Van Wyk, J. (2002). Economic distress and intimate violence: Testing family stress and resources theories. *Journal of Marriage and Family, 64,* 793–807.

FoxNews. (2008, January 8). Missouri lawmakers consider harassment law after teen's Internet suicide. Retrieved from http://www.foxnews.com/story/0,2933,321183,00.html

Fraley, R. C., & Waller, N. G. (1998). Adult attachment patterns: A test of the typological model. In J. A. Simpson & W. S. Rholes (Eds.), *Attachment Theory and Close Relationships* (pp. 77–114) New York: Guilford.

Fram, M. S., Miller-Cribbs, J., & Farber, N. (2006). Chicks aren't chickens: Women, poverty, and marriage in an orthodoxy of conservatism. *Affilia, 21,* 256–271.

Francis, K. J., & Wolfe, D. A. (2008). Cognitive and emotional differences between abusive and non-abusive fathers. *Child Abuse & Neglect, 32,* 1127–1137.

Franiuk, R., Seefelt, J. L., Cepress, S. L., & Vandello, J. A. (2008). Prevalence and effects of rape myths in print journalism: The Kobe Bryant case. *Violence Against Women, 14,* 287–309.

Fraser, J. A., Mathews, B., Walsh, K., Chen, L., & Dunne, M. (2010). Factors influencing child abuse and neglect recognition and reporting by nurses: A multivariate analysis. *International Journal of Nursing Studies, 47,* 146–153.

Frasier, P. Y., Slatt, L., Kowlowitz, V., & Glowa, P. T. (2001). Using the stages of change model to counsel victims of intimate partner violence. *Patient Education and Counseling, 43,* 211–217.

Frazier, P. A., Byer, A. L., Fischer, A. R., Wright, D. M., & DeBord, K. A. (1996). Adult attachment style and partner choice: Correlational and experimental findings. *Personal Relationships, 3,* 117–136.

Fredriksen-Goldsen, K. I., & Muraco, A. (2010). Aging and sexual orientation: A 25-year review. *Research on Aging, 32,* 372–413.

Freed, L. H., Gupta, R., Hynes, C., & Miller, E. (2003). Detecting adolescent dating violence in the clinical setting. *Journal of Adolescent Health, 32,* 151–152.

Freedman, D., Thornton, A., Camburn, D., Alwin, D., & Young-DeMarco, L. (1988). The life history calendar: A technique for collecting retrospective data. In C. C. Clogg (Ed.), *Sociological methodology* (pp. 37–68). San Francisco: Jossey-Bass.

Freedner, N., Freed, L. H., Yang, Y. W., & Austin, S. B. (2002). Dating violence among gay, lesbian, and bisexual adolescents: Results from a community survey. *Journal of Adolescent Health, 31,* 469–474.

Freeman, D. H., Jr., & Temple, J. R. (2010). Social factors associated with history of sexual assault among ethnically diverse adolescents. *Journal of Family Violence, 25,* 349–356.

Friday. P., Lord, V., Exum, M., & Hartman, J. (2006, May). *Evaluating the impact of a specialized domestic violence police unit* (NCJ Publication No. 215916). Washington, DC: U.S. Department of Justice, National Institute of Justice.

Friedman, M. S., Marshal, M. P., Stall, R., Cheong, J., & Wright, E. R. (2008). Gay-related development, early abuse and adult health outcomes among gay males. *AIDS and Behavior, 12,* 891–902.

Friedrich, W. N. (1993). Sexual victimization and sexual behavior in children: A review of recent literature. *Child Abuse & Neglect, 17,* 59–66.

Friedrich, W. N., Dittner, C. A., Action, R., Berliner, L., Butler, J., Damon, L., et al. (2001). Child Sexual Behavior Inventory: Normative, psychiatric and sexual abuse comparisons. *Child Maltreatment, 6,* 37–49.

Frieze, I. H. (2003). Violence in close relationships: Development of a research area: Comment on Archer (2000). *Psychological Bulletin, 126,* 681–684.

Frieze, I. H. (2008a). Publishing qualitative research in *Sex Roles. Sex Roles, 58,* 1–2.

Frieze, I. H. (2008b). Social policy, feminism, and research on violence in close relationships. *Journal of Social Issues, 64,* 665–684.

Frieze, I. H., & McHugh, M. C. (1992). Power and influence strategies in violent and nonviolent marriages. *Psychology of Women Quarterly, 16,* 449–466.

Fry, P. S., & Barker, L. A. (2001). Female survivors of violence and abuse: Their regrets of action and inaction in coping. *Journal of Interpersonal Violence, 16,* 320–342.

Fujiura, G. T. (2010). Aging families and the demographics of family financial support of adults with disabilities. *Journal of Disability Policy Studies, 20,* 241–250.

Fulmer, T. T. (1991). Elder mistreatment: Progress in community detection and intervention. *Family and Community Health, 14*(2), 26–34.

Fulmer, T. T., Guadagno, L., Dyer, C. B., & Connolly, M. T. (2004). Progress in elder abuse screening and assessment instruments. *Journal of the American Geriatrics Society, 52,* 297–304.

Fulmer, T. T., & O'Malley, T. A. (1987). *Inadequate care of the elderly.* New York: Springer.

Fulmer, T. T., Ramirez, M., Fairchild, S., Holmes, D., Koren, M. J., & Teresi, J. (1999). Prevalence of elder mistreatment as reported by social workers in a probability sample of adult day health care clients. *Journal of Elder Abuse & Neglect, 11*(3), 25–36.

Furlow, B. (2010, January 28). State hindered Medicaid fraud investigations, Attorney General office report claims. *The New Mexico Independent,* http://newmexicoindependent.com/45491/state-hindered-medicaid-fraud-investigations-attorney-general

Fyfe, J. J., Klinger, D. A., & Flavin, J. M. (1997). Differential police treatment of male-on-female spousal violence. *Criminology, 35,* 455–473.

Gaarder, E., & Belknap, J. (2002). Tenuous borders: Girls transferred to adult court. *Criminology, 40,* 481–517.

Gage, E. A. (2008). Gender attitudes and sexual behaviors. *Violence Against Women, 14,* 1014–1032.

Gaidos, S. (2010, June 5). A pregnant question. *Science News,* 22–25.

Gallopin, C., & Leigh, L. (2009). Teen perceptions of dating violence, help-seeking, and the role of schools. *The Prevention Researcher, 16,* 17–20.

Galloway, A. L., & Drapela, L. A. (2006). Are effective drug courts an urban phenomenon? *International Journal of Offender Therapy and Comparative Criminology, 50,* 280–293.

Ganaway, G. K. (1989). Historical versus narrative truth: Clarifying the role of exogenous trauma in the etiology of MPD and its variants. *Dissociation, 2,* 205–220.

Ganley, A. L. (1981). *Court-mandated counseling for men who batter: A three-day workshop for mental health professional* [Participants' manual]. Washington, DC: Center for Women's Policy Studies.

Gannon, T. A., & Rose, M. R. (2008). Female child sexual offenders: Towards integrating theory and practice. *Aggression and Violent Behavior, 13,* 442–461.

Gao, Y., Glenn, A. L., Schug, R. A., Yang, Y., & Raine, A. (2009). The neurobiology of psychopathy: A neurodevelopmental perspective. *The Canadian Psychiatric Association Journal, 54,* 813–823.

Garbarino, J. (2005). Corporal punishment in perspective. In M. Donnelly & M. A. Straus (Eds.), *Corporal punishment in theoretical perspective* (pp. 8–18). New Haven, CT: Yale University Press.

Garcia, L., Hurwitz, E. L., & Kraus, J. F. (2004). Acculturation and reported intimate partner violence among Latinas in Los Angeles. *Journal of Interpersonal Violence, 20,* 569–590.

Garcia, L., Soria, C., & Hurwitz, E. L. (2007). Homicides and intimate partner violence: A literature review. *Trauma, Violence, & Abuse, 8,* 370–383.

Garcia-Moreno, C. (2000). Violence against women international perspectives. *American Journal of Preventative Medicine, 19,* 330–333.

Garcia-Moreno, C., Jansen, H., Ellsberg, M., Heise, L., & Watts, C. H. (2006). Prevalence of intimate partner violence: Findings from the WHO multi-country study on women's health and domestic violence. *The Lancet, 368,* 1260–1269.

Garner, J. H., & Clemmer, E. (1986). *Danger to police in domestic disturbances: A new look.* Washington, DC: U.S. Department of Justice.

Garner, J. H., & Maxwell, C. D. (2008). Coordinated community responses to intimate partner violence in the 20th and 21st centuries. *Criminology, 7,* 525–526.

Garner, J. H., & Maxwell, C. D. (2009). Prosecution and conviction rates for intimate partner violence. *Criminal Justices Review, 34,* 44–49.

Garre-Olmo, J., Planas-Pujol, X., López-Pousa, S., Juvinyà, D., Vilà, A., & Vilalta-Franch, J. (2009). Prevalence and risk factors of suspected elder abuse subtypes in people aged 75 or older. *Journal of the American Geriatric Society, 57,* 815–822.

Gartner, R. (1993). Methodological issues in cross-cultural large-survey research on violence. *Violence and Victims, 8,* 199–215.

Gaudin, J. M. (1993). Effective intervention with neglectful families. *Criminal Justice and Behavior, 20,* 66–89.

Geffner, R., & Rosenbaum, A. (1990). Characteristics and treatment of batterers. *Behavioral Sciences and the Law, 8,* 131–140.

Gelles, R. J. (1983). An exchange/social control theory. In D. Finkelhor, R. J. Gelles, G. T. Hotaling, & M. A. Straus (Eds.), *The dark side of families: Current family violence research* (pp. 151–165). Beverly Hills, CA: Sage.

Gelles, R. J. (2004). Family violence against men is a serious problem. In K. F. Balkin (Ed.), *Violence against women.* Farmington Hills, MI: Greenhaven Press.

Gelles, R. J. (2007). The politics of research: The use, abuse, and misuse of social science data: The cases of intimate partner violence. *Family Court Review, 45,* 42–51.

Gelles, R. J., & Cavanaugh, M. M. (2005). Association is not causation. In D. R. Loseke, R. J. Gelles, & M. M. Cavanaugh (Eds.), *Current controversies on family violence* (2nd ed., pp. 175–189). Thousand Oaks, CA: Sage.

Gelles, R. J., & Cornell, C. P. (1990). *Intimate violence in families* (2nd ed.). Newbury Park, CA: Sage.

Gelles, R. J., & Loseke, D. R. (1993). Conclusions: Social problems, social policy, and controversies on family violence. In R. J. Gelles & D. R. Loseke (Eds.), *Current controversies on family violence* (pp. 357–366). Newbury Park, CA: Sage.

Gelles, R. J., & Straus, M. A. (1987). Is violence toward children increasing? A comparison of 1975 and 1985 national survey rates. *Journal of Interpersonal Violence, 2,* 212–222.

Gelles, R. J., & Straus, M. A. (1988). *Intimate violence.* New York: Simon & Schuster.

Gentile, D. A., Lynch, P. J., Linder, J. R., & Walsh, D. A. (2004). The effects of violent video game habits on adolescent hostility, aggressive behaviors, and school performance. *Journal of Adolescence, 27,* 5–22.

George, G. T., et al. (2004). A select group of perpetrators of domestic violence: Evidence of decreased metabolism in the right hypothalamus and reduced relationships between cortical/subcortical brain structures in positron emission tomography. *Psychiatry Research: Neuroimaging, 130,* 11–25.

George, M. J. (2003). Invisible touch. *Aggression and Violent Behavior, 8,* 23–60.

George, W. H., Stoner, S. A., Davis, K. C., Lindgren, K. P., Norris, J., & Lopez, P. A. (2006). Postdrinking sexual perceptions and behaviors toward another person: Alcohol expectancy set and gender differences. *The Journal of Sex Research, 43,* 282–292.

Geraerts, E., et al. (2009). Cognitive mechanisms underlying recovered-memory experiences of childhood sexual abuse. *Psychological Science, 20,* 92–98.

Gerber, G. L., & Cherneski, L. (2006). Sexual aggression toward women: Reducing the prevalence. *Annals of the New York Academy of Science, 1087,* 35–46.

Gerow, J. R. (1989). *Psychology: An introduction* (2nd ed.). Glenville, IL: Scott, Foresman.

Gershater-Molko, R., Lutzker, J. R., & Wesch, D. (2003). Project SafeCare: Improving health, safety, and parenting skills in families reported for, and at-risk for child maltreatment. *Journal of Family Violence, 18,* 377–386.

Gershoff, E. T. (2002). Corporal punishment by parents and associated child behaviors and experiences: A meta-analytic and theoretical review. *Psychological Bulletin, 128,* 539–579.

Gershoff, E. T. (2008). *Report on physical punishment in the United States: What research tells us about its effects on children.* Columbus, OH: Center for Effective Discipline.

Gery, I., Miljkovitch, R., Berthoz, S., & Soussignan, R. (2009). Empathy and recognition of facial expressions of emotion in sex offenders, non-sex offenders and normal controls. *Psychiatry Research, 165,* 252–262.

Gessner, B. D. (2008). The effect of Alaska's home visitation program for high-risk families on trends in abuse and neglect. *Child Abuse & Neglect, 32,* 317–333.

Getting new Social Security numbers for battered women. (1999, April/May). *Domestic Violence Report, 4,* 52.

Giacomazzi, A. L., & Bell, V. (2007). Drug court program monitoring. *Criminal Justice Policy Review, 18,* 294–312.

Gibb, B. E., Chelminski, L., & Zimmerman, M. (2007). Childhood emotional, physical, and sexual abuse, and diagnoses of depressive and anxiety disorders in adult psychiatric patients. *Depression and Anxiety, 24,* 256–263.

Gibbs, D. A., Martin, S. L., Kupper, L. L., & Johnson, R. E. (2007). Child maltreatment in enlisted soldiers' families during combat-related deployment. *Journal of the American Medical Association, 298,* 528–535.

Gibson, J. W., & Gutierrez, L. (1991). A service program for safe-home children. *Families in Society, 72,* 554–562.

Gibson-Davis, C. M., & Glassman-Pines, A. (2010). Early childhood family structure and mother-child interactions: Variation by race and ethnicity. *Developmental Psychology, 46,* 151–164.

Gidycz, C. A., Van Wynsberghe, A., & Edwards, K. M. (2008). Prediction of women's utilization of resitance strategies in a sexual assault situation. *Journal of Interpersonal Violence, 23,* 571–588.

Gil, A., et al. (2009). The association of child abuse and neglect with adult disability in schizophrenia and the prominent role of physical neglect. *Child Abuse & Neglect, 33,* 618-624.

Gil, D. G. (1970). *Violence against children: Physical child abuse in the United States.* Cambridge, MA: Harvard University Press.

Gil, E. (1996). *Treating abused adolescents.* New York: Guilford Press.

Gilbert, R., et al. (2008). Burden and consequences of child maltreatment in high-income countries. *The Lancet, 373,* 68–81.

Giles-Sims, J. (1983). *Wife battering: A systems theory approach.* New York: Guilford.

Gilligan, C. (1990). Joining the resistance: Psychology, politics, girls and women. *Michigan Quarterly Review, 29,* 241–251.

Gillum, T. L. (2009). Improving services to African American Survivors of IPV. *Violence Against Women, 15,* 57–80.

Giltay, E. J., & Gooren, L. J. G. (2009). Potential side effects of Androgen Deprivation Treatment in sex offenders. *Journal of the American Academy of Psychiatry and the Law, 37,* 53–58.

Gini, G., & Pozzoli, T. (2006). The role of masculinity in children's bullying. *Sex Roles, 54,* 585–588.

Giorgio, G. (2002). Speaking silence: Definitional dialogues in abusive lesbian relationships. *Violence Against Women, 8,* 1233–1259.

Girard, A. L., & Senn, C. Y. (2008). The role of the new "date rape drugs" in attributions about date rape. *Journal of Interpersonal Violence, 23,* 3–20.

Givertz, M., & Segrin, C. (2005). Explaining personal and constraint commitment in close relationships: The role of satisfaction, conflict responses, and relational bond. *Journal of Social and Personal Relationships, 22,* 757–775.

Glaser, D. (2002). Emotional abuse and neglect (psychological maltreatment): A conceptual framework. *Child Abuse & Neglect, 26,* 697–714.

Glass, N., Laughon, N., Rutto, C., Bevaqua, J., & Campbell, J. C. (2008). Young adult intimate partner femicide. *Homicide Studies, 12,* 177–187.

Glendenning, F. (1993). What is elder abuse and neglect? In P. Decalmer & F. Glendenning (Eds.), *The mistreatment of elderly people* (pp. 1–34). London: Sage.

Glowa, P. T., Frasier, P. Y., & Newton, W. P. (2002). Increasing physician comfort level in screening and counseling patients for intimate partner violence: Hands-on practice. *Patient Education and Counseling, 46,* 213–220.

Godbout, N., Sabourin, S., & Lussier, Y. (2009). Child sexual abuse and adult romantic adjustment. *Journal of Interpersonal Violence, 24,* 693–705.

Godenzi, A., & De Puy, J. (2001). Overcoming boundaries: A cross-cultural inventory of primary prevention programs against wife abuse and child abuse. *Journal of Primary Prevention, 21,* 455–475.

Goel. R. (2005). Sita's trousseau: Restorative justice, domestic violence, and South Asian culture. *Violence Against Women, 11,* 639–665.

Gold, S. D., Dickstein, B. D., Marx, B. P., & Lexington, J. M. (2009). Psychological outcomes among lesbian sexual assault survivors: An examination of the roles of internalized homophobia and experiential avoidance. *Psychology of Women Quarterly, 33,* 54–66.

Gold, S. N., Hyman, S. M., & Andrés-Hyman. (2004). Family of origin environment in two clinical samples of survivors of intra-familial, extra-familial, and both types of sexual abuse. *Child Abuse & Neglect, 28,* 1199–1212.

Goldberg, L. R., et al. (2010). Methamphetamine exposure, iron deficiency, and implications for cognitive-communicative function: Case study. *Communication Disorders Quarterly, 31,* 183–192.

Goldberg-Ambrose, C. E. (1992). Unfinished business in rape law reform. *Journal of Social Issues, 48*(1), 173–185.

Goldenson, J., Geffner, R., Foster, S. L., & Clipson, C. R. (2007). Female domestic violence offenders: Their attachment security, trauma symptoms, and personality organization. *Violence and Victims, 22,* 532–545.

Goldenson, R. M. (Ed.). (1970). *The encyclopedia of human behavior: Psychology, psychiatry, and mental health* (Vol. 1). Garden City, NY: Doubleday.

Goldenson, R. M. (Ed.). (1984). *Longman dictionary of psychology and psychiatry.* New York: Longman.

Golding, J. M. (1999). Intimate partner violence as a risk factor for mental disorders: A meta-analysis. *Journal of Family Violence, 14,* 99–132.

Goldman, J. D. G., & Padayachi, U. K. (2000). Some methodological problems in estimating incidence and prevalence in child sexual abuse research. *Journal of Sex Research, 4,* 305–314.

Goldner, V., Penn, P., Sheinberg, M., & Walker, G. (1990). Love and violence: Gender paradoxes in volatile attachments. *Family Process, 29,* 343–364.

Goldstein, D. S., & Kopin, I. J. (2007). Evolution of concepts of stress. *Stress, 10,* 109–120.

Goldstein, D., & Rosenbaum, A. (1985). An evaluation of self-esteem of maritally violent men. *Family Relations, 34,* 425–428.

Goldstein, S. E., Chesir-Teran, D., & McFaul, A. (2008). Profiles and correlates of relationship aggression in young adults' romantic relationships. *Journal of Youth and Adolescence, 37,* 251–265.

Gomes-Schwartz, B., Horowitz, J. M., & Cardarelli, A. P. (1990). *Child sexual abuse: The initial effects.* Newbury Park, CA: Sage.

Gondolf, E. W. (1988). The effect of batterer counseling on shelter outcome. *Journal of Interpersonal Violence, 3,* 275–289.

Gondolf, E. W. (1998). The victims of court-ordered batterers. *Violence Against Women, 4,* 659–676.

Gondolf, E. W. (1999). Characteristics of court-mandated batterers in four cities. *Violence Against Women, 5,* 1277–1293.

Gondolf, E. W. (2000a). How batterer program participants avoid reassault. *Violence Against Women, 6,* 1204–1222.

Gondolf, E. W. (2000b). Mandatory court review and batterer program compliance. *Journal of Interpersonal Violence, 15,* 428–437.

Gondolf, E. W. (2004). Evaluating batterer counseling programs: A difficult task showing some effects and implications. *Aggression and Violent Behavior, 9,* 605–631.

Gondolf, E. W., & Fisher, E. R. (1988). *Battered women as survivors: An alternative to treating learned helplessness.* Lexington, MA: Lexington Books.

Gondolf, E. W., & Foster, R. A. (1991). Pre-program attrition in batterer programs. *Journal of Family Violence, 6,* 337–349.

Gondolf, E. W., & White, R. J. (2000). "Consumer" recommendations for batterers programs. *Violence Against Women, 6,* 198–217.

Gondolf, E. W., & White, R. J. (2001). Batterer program participants who repeatedly reassault. *Journal of Interpersonal Violence, 16,* 361–380.

Gondolf, E. W., & Williams, O. (2001). Culturally focused batterer counseling for African American men. *Trauma, Violence, & Abuse, 4,* 283–295.

Gone, J. P. (2008). So I can be like a whiteman: The cultural psychology of space and place in American Indian mental health. *Culture & Psychology, 14,* 369–399.

Gonzalez, M., Durrant, J. E., Chabot, M., Trocmé, N., & Brown, J. (2008). What predicts injury from physical punishment? A test of the typologies of violence hypothesis. *Child Abuse & Neglect, 32,* 752–765.

Goodfriend, W., & Agnew, C. R. (2008). Sunken costs and desired plans: Examining different types of investments in close relationships. *Personality and Social Psychology Bulletin, 34,* 1639–1652.

Goodkind, J. R., Gillum, T. L., Bybee, D. I., & Sullivan, C. M. (2003). The impact of family and friends' reactions on the well-being of women with abusive partners. *Violence Against Women, 9,* 347–373.

Goodman, C. C., & Silverstein, M. (2006). Grandmothers raising grandchildren. *Journal of Family Issues, 27,* 1605–1626.

Goodman, G. S., & Quas, J. A. (2008). Repeated interviews and children's memory. *Current Directions in Psychological Science, 17,* 386–390.

Goodman, G. S., Taub, E. P., Jones, D. P. H., England, T., Port, L. K., Rudy, L., et al. (1992). Testifying in criminal court. *Monographs of the Society for Research in Child Development, 57*(5, Serial No. 229).

Goodman, L. A., Bennett, L., & Dutton, M. A. (1999). Obstacles to victims' cooperation with the criminal prosecution of their abusers: The role of social support. *Violence and Victims, 14,* 427–444.

Goodman, L. A., Dutton, M. A., & Harris, M. (1995). Episodically homeless women with serious mental illness: Prevalence of physical and sexual assault. *American Journal of Orthopsychiatry, 65,* 468–478.

Goodman, L. A., Dutton, M. A., Weinfurt, K., & Cook, S. (2003). The Intimate Partner Violence Strategies Index. *Violence Against Women, 9,* 163–186.

Goodman, L. A., & Epstein, D. (2008). *Listening to battered women: A survivor-centered approach to advocacy, mental health and justice.* Washington, DC: American Psychological Association.

Goodman, L. A., Koss, M. P., & Russo, N. F. (1993). Violence against women: Physical and mental health effects. Part I: Research findings. *Applied and Preventive Psychology, 2,* 79–89.

Goodyear-Smith, F. A., & Laidlaw, T. M. (1999). Aggressive acts and assaults in intimate relationships: Towards an understanding of the literature. *Behavioral Sciences and the Law, 17,* 285–304.

Gordon, K. C., Burton, S., & Porter, L. (2004). Predicting the intentions of women in domestic violence shelters to return to partners: Does forgiveness play a role? *Journal of Family Psychology, 18,* 331–338.

Gordon, K. C., & Christman, J. A. (2008). Integrating social information processing and attachment style research with cognitive-behavioral couples therapy. *Journal of Contemporary Psychotherapy, 38,* 129–138.

Gordon, L. (2001). Who deserves help? Who must provide help? *Annals of the American Academy of Political and Social Science, 577,* 12–25.

Gordon, M. (2000). Definitional issues in violence against women: Surveillance and research from a violence research perspective. *Violence Against Women, 6,* 747–783.

Gore-Felton, C., Gill, M., Koopman, C., & Spiegel, D. (1999). A review of acute stress reactions among victims of violence: Implications for early intervention. *Aggression and Violent Behavior, 4,* 203–306.

Gormley, B., & Lopez, F. G. (2010). Psychological abuse perpetration in college dating relationships. *Journal of Interpersonal Violence, 25,* 204–218.

Gortner, E., Berns, S. B., Jacobson, N. S., & Gottman, J. M. (1997). When women leave violent relationships: Dispelling clinical myths. *Psychotherapy, 34,* 342–352.

Gottlieb, L. N. (2003). Editorial: Ageism of knowledge: Outdated research. *Canadian Journal of Nursing Research, 33,* 3.

Gough, H. G. (1975). *Manual for the California Psychological Inventory.* Palo Alto, CA: Consulting Psychologists Press.

Gover, A. R., Brank, E. M., & MacDonald, J. M. (2007). A specialized domestic violence court in South Carolina. *Violence Against Women, 13,* 603–626.

Gover, A. R., Kaukinen, C., & Fox, K. A. (2008). The relationship between violence in the family of origin and dating violence among college students. *Journal of Interpersonal Violence, 23,* 1667–1693.

Graham, D. L. R., Rawlings, E., & Rimini, E. (1988). Survivors of terror: Battered women, hostages, and the Stockholm syndrome. In K. A. Yllö & M. Bograd (Eds.), *Feminist perspectives on wife abuse* (pp. 217–233). Newbury Park, CA: Sage.

Graham-Bermann, S. A. (2002). Child abuse in the context of domestic violence. In J. E. B. Myers, L. Berliner, J. Briere, C. T. Hendrix, C. Jenny, & T. A. Reid (Eds.), *The APSAC handbook on child maltreatment* (2nd ed., pp. 119–129). Thousand Oaks, CA: Sage.

Graham-Bermann, S. A., Cutler, S. E., Litzenberger, B. W., & Schwartz, W. E. (1994). Perceived conflict and violence in childhood sibling relationships and later emotional adjustments. *Journal of Family Psychology, 8,* 85–97.

Graham-Bermann, S. A., Gruber, G., Howell, K. H., & Girz, L. (2009). Factors discriminating among profiles of resilience and psychopathology in children exposed to intimate partner violence. *Child Abuse & Neglect, 33,* 648–660.

Graham-Bermann, S. A., & Howell, K. H. (2010). Child maltreatment in the context of intimate partner violence. In J. E. B. Myers (Ed.), *APSAC handbook on child maltreatment* (3rd ed., pp. 167–179). Thousand Oaks, CA: Sage.

Graham-Bermann, S. A., & Hughes, H. M. (2003). Intervention for children exposed to interparental violence (IPV): Assessment of needs and research priorities. *Clinical Child and Family Psychology Review, 6,* 189–204.

Graham-Bermann, S. A., Lynch, S., Banyard, V., & Halabu, H. (2007). Community-based intervention for children exposed to intimate partner violence: An efficacy trial. *Journal of Consulting and Clinical Psychology, 75,* 199–209.

Graham-Kevan, N., & Archer, J. (2003). Intimate terrorism and common couple violence: A test of Johnson's predictions in four British samples. *Journal of Interpersonal Violence, 18,* 1247–1270.

Graham-Kevan, N., & Archer, J. (2005). Investigating three explanations of women's relationship aggression. *Psychology of Women Quarterly, 29,* 270–277.

Grasmick, H. G., Blackwell, B. S., Bursik, R. J., & Mitchell, S. (1993). Changes in perceived threats of shame, embarrassment, and legal sanctions for interpersonal violence, 1982–1992. *Violence and Victims, 8,* 313–325.

Graves, K. N., Sechrist, S. M., White, J. W., & Paradise, M. J. (2005). Intimate partner violence perpetrated by college women with the context of a history of being victimized. *Psychology of Women Quarterly, 29,* 278–289.

Graziano, A. M., & Namaste, K. A. (1990). Parental use of physical force in child discipline: A survey of 679 college students. *Journal of Interpersonal Violence, 5,* 449–463.

Green, M. C., & Sabini, J. (2006). Gender, socioeconomic status, age, and jealousy: Emotional responses to infidelity in a national sample. *Emotion, 6,* 330–334.

Green, R. (2006). Parental alienation syndrome and the transsexual parent. *International Journal of Transgenderism, 9,* 9–13.

Greene, B. (2009). The use and abuse of religious beliefs in dividing and conquering between socially marginalized groups: The same-sex marriage debate. *American Psychologist, 64,* 698–709.

Greenfeld, L. A., Rand, M. R., Craven, D., Klaus, P. A., Perkins, C. A., Ringel, C., et al. (1998). *Violence by intimates* (NCJ Publication No. 167237). Washington, DC: U.S. Department of Justice.

Greenfeld, L. A. (1998). Alcohol and crime. (NCJ Publication No. 168632). Washington, DC: U.S. Department of Justice.

Greenfield, E. A. (2010). Child abuse as a life-course social determinant of adult health. *Maturitas, 66,* 51–58.

Greenfield, E. A., & Marks, N. F. (2010). Identifying experiences of physical and psychological violence in childhood that jeopardize mental health in adulthood. *Child Abuse & Neglect, 34,* 161–171.

Greenglass, E., Fiksenbaum, L., & Eaton, J. (2006). The relationship between coping, social support, functional disability and depression in the elderly. *Anxiety, Stress & Coping, 19,* 15–31.

Greer, M. (2004, June). Families' finanicial woes can foster child depression and disobedience. *Monitor on Psychology, 35,* 14.

Greer, T. M. (2007). Measuring coping strategies among African Americans: An exploration of the latent structure of the COPE inventory. *Journal of Black Psychology, 33,* 260–277.

Gregory, C., & Erez, E. (2002). The effects of batterer intervention programs. *Violence Against Women, 8,* 206–232.

Gregory, C. R. (2004, November). Assessing amenability to treatment in community corrections: Creating a valid and reliable instrument for male batterers. *Dissertation Abstracts International* (DAI-A 65/05) p. 1992.

Gregory, J. (2010). (M)Others in altered states: Prenatal drug-use, risk, choice, and responsible governance. *Social & Legal Studies, 19,* 49–66.

Griffin, M. L., Armodeo, M., Clay, C., Fassler, I., & Ellis, M. A. (2006). Racial differences in social support: Kin versus friends. *American Journal of Orthopsychiatry, 76,* 374–380.

Griffin, T., Miller, M. K., Hoppe, J., Rebideaux, A., & Hammack, R. (2007). A preliminary examination of Amber alert's effects. *Criminal Justice Policy Review, 18,* 378–394.

Griffing, S., Ragin, D. F., Sage, R. E., Madry, L., Bingham, L. E., & Primm, B. J. (2002). Domestic violence survivors' self-identified reasons for returning to abusive relationships. *Journal of Interpersonal Violence, 17,* 306–319.

Grigsby, N., & Hartman, B. R. (1997). The barriers model: An integrated strategy for intervention with battered women. *Psychotherapy, 34,* 484–497.

Grogan-Kaylor, A. (2005). Corporal punishment and the growth trajectory of children's antisocial behavior. *Child Maltreatment, 10,* 263–292.

Gross, J. (2006, September 27). Forensic skills seek to uncover hidden patterns of elder abuse. *The New York Times*, p. A23.

Grossman, S. F., Hinkley, S., Kawalski, A., & Margrave, C. (2005). Rural versus urban victims of violence: The interplay of race and region. *Journal of Family Violence, 20,* 71–81.

Grossman, S. F., & Lundy, M. (2008). Double jeopardy: A comparison of persons with and without disabilities who were victims of sexual abuse and/or sexual assault. *Journal of Social Work in Disability & Rehabilitation, 7,* 19–46.

Groth, A. N., & Burgess, A. W. (1980). Male rape: Offenders and victims. *The American Journal of Psychiatry, 137,* 806–810.

Groves, B. M. (2002). *Children who see too much.* Boston: Beacon.

Groves, B. M., & Gewirtz, A. (2006). Interventions and promising approaches for children exposed to domestic violence. In M. M. Feerick & G. B. Silverman (Eds.), *Children exposed to violence* (pp. 107–135). Baltimore: Paul H. Brooke.

Gruber, J. E., & Fineran, S. (2007). The impact of bullying and sexual harassment on middle and high school girls. *Violence Against Women, 13,* 627–643.

Guetzkow, J. (2010). Beyond deservingness: Congressional discourse on poverty, 1964–1996. *The Annals of the American Academy of Political and Social Science, 629,* 173–197.

Gupta, J., Silverman, J. G., Hemenway, D., Acevedo-Garcia, D., Stein, D. J., & Williams, D. R. (2008). Physical violence against intimate partners and related exposures to violence among South African men. *Canadian Medical Association Journal, 179,* 535–541.

Gwinn, C. (2006). Domestic violence and firearms: Reflections of a prosecutor. *Evaluation Review, 30,* 237–244.

Haarr, R. N. (2007). Wife abuse in Tajikistan. *Feminist Criminology, 2,* 245–270.

Hackett, G., McKillop, P., & Wang, D. (1988, December 12). A tale of abuse. *Newsweek, 117,* 56–61.

Haj-Yahia, M. M. (1999). Wife abuse and its psychological consequences as revealed by the First Palestinian National Survey on Violence Against Women. *Journal of Family Psychology, 13,* 642–662.

Halambie, A. M., & Klapper, S. A. (2005). The impact of maltreatment on child development. In *Child welfare law and practice: Representing children, parents, and state agencies in abuse, neglect, and dependency cases* (pp. 53–77). Denver, CO: Bradford Publishing Co.

Hall, C. C. I. (1997). Cultural malpractice: The growing obsolescence of psychology with the changing U.S. population. *American Psychologist, 52,* 642–651.

Hall, K. (2008). Childhood sexual abuse and adult sexual problems: A new view of assessments and treatment. *Feminism & Psychology, 18,* 546–556.

Halligan, S. L., Michael, T., Clark, D. M., & Ehlers, A. (2003). Posttraumatic stress disorder following assault: The role of cognitive processing, trauma memory, and appraisals. *Journal of Consulting and Clinical Psychology, 71,* 419–431.

Halpern, C. T., Young, M. L., Waller, M. W., Martin, S. L., & Kupper, L. L. (2004). Prevalence of partner violence among same-sex romantic and sexual relationships in a national sample of adolescents. *Journal of Adolescent Health, 35,* 131.

Halter, S. (2010). Factors that influence police conceptualizations of girls involved in prostitution in six U.S. cities: Child sexual exploitation victims or delinquents? *Child Maltreatment, 15,* 152–160.

Hamarman, S., & Bernet, W. (2000). Evaluating and reporting emotional abuse in children: Parent-based, action-based focus aids in clinical decision-making. *Journal of the American Academy of Child and Adolescent Psychiatry, 39,* 928–930.

Hamarman, S., Pope, K. H., & Czaja, S. J. (2002). Emotional abuse in children: Variations in legal definitions and rates across the United States. *Child Maltreatment, 7,* 303–311.

Hamberger, L. K. (1994). Domestic partner abuse: Expanding paradigms for understanding and intervention. *Violence and Victims, 9,* 91–94.

Hamberger, L. K. (1997). Cognitive behavioral treatment of men who batter their partners. *Cognitive & Behavioral Practice, 4,* 147–169.

Hamberger, L. K. (2005). Men's and women's use of intimate partner violence in clinical samples: Toward a gender-sensitive analysis. *Violence and Victims, 20,* 131–151.

Hamberger, L. K., & Ambuel, B. (1998). Dating violence. *Pediatric Clinics of North America, 45,* 381–390.

Hamberger, L. K., & Arnold, J. (1991). The impact of mandatory arrest on domestic violence perpetrator counseling services. *Family Violence Bulletin, 6*(1), 11–12.

Hamberger, L. K., & Barnett, O. W. (1995). Assessment and treatment of men who batter. In L. Vandecreek, S. Knapp, & T. L. Jackson (Eds.), *Innovations in clinical practice: A source book* (Vol. 14, pp. 31–54). Sarasota, FL: Professional Resource Press.

Hamberger, L. K., & Guse, C. E. (2002). Men's and women's use of intimate partner violence in clinical samples. *Violence Against Women, 8,* 1301–1331.

Hamberger, L. K., & Guse, C. E. (2005). Typology of reactions to intimate partner violence among men and women arrested for partner violence. *Violence and Victims, 20,* 303–317.

Hamberger, L. K., & Hastings, J. E. (1986). Personality correlates of men who abuse their partners: A cross-validation study. *Journal of Family Violence, 1,* 323–341.

Hamberger, L. K., & Hastings, J. E. (1989). Counseling male spouse abusers: Characteristics of treatment completers and dropouts. *Violence and Victims, 4,* 275–286.

Hamberger, L. K., & Hastings, J. E. (1990). Recidivism following spouse abuse abatement counseling: Treatment implications. *Violence and Victims, 5,* 157–170.

Hamberger, L. K., & Hastings, J. E. (1991). Personality correlates of men who batter and nonviolent men: Some continuities and discontinuities. *Journal of Family Violence, 6,* 131–147.

Hamberger, L. K., & Phelan, M. B. (2004). *Domestic violence screening and intervention in medical and mental health-care settings.* New York: Springer.

Hamberger, L. K., Phelan, M. B., & Zozel, A. (2001, August). *Male victims of domestic violence in an emergency department.* Paper presented at the meeting of the American Psychological Association, San Francisco.

Hamberger, L. K., & Potente, T. (1994). Counseling heterosexual women arrested for domestic violence: Implications for theory and practice. *Violence and Victims, 9,* 125–137.

Hamby, S. L. (1996). The Dominance Scale: Preliminary psychometric properties. *Violence and Victims, 11,* 199–212.

Hamby, S. L. (1998). Partner violence: Prevention and intervention. In J. L. Jasinski & L. M. Williams (Eds.), *Partner violence: A comprehensive review of 20 years of research* (pp. 210–256). Thousand Oaks, CA: Sage.

Hamby, S. L. (2005). Measuring gender differences in partner violence: Implications from research on other forms of violent and socially undesirable behavior. *Sex Roles, 52,* 725–742.

Hamby, S. L. (2009). Walking with American Indian victims of sexual assault: A review of legal obstacles and legal resources affecting victims in Indian country. *Family & Intimate Partner Violence Quarterly, 1,* 293–305.

Hamby, S. L., Poindexter, V. C., & Gray-Little, B. (1996). Four measures of partner violence: Construct similarity and classification differences. *Journal of Marriage and the Family, 58,* 127–139.

Hamby, S. L., & Gray-Little, B. (2009). Can battered women cope? A critical analysis of research on women's responses to violence. *Family and Intimate Partner Violence Quarterly, 1,* 229–251.

Hammond, C. B., & Calhoun, K. S. (2007). Labeling of abuse experiences and rates of victimization. *Psychology of Women Quarterly, 31,* 371–380.

Hammond, M., Miller, M. K., & Griffin, T. (2010). Safe haven laws as crime control theater. *Child Abuse and Neglect, 34,* 545–552.

Hampton, R. L., LaTaillade, J. J., Dacey, A., & Marghi, J. R. (2008). Evaluating domestic violence interventions for Black women. *Journal of Aggression, Maltreatment & Trauma, 16,* 330–353.

Hampton, R. L., & Newberger, E. H. (1988). Child abuse incidence and reporting by hospitals: Significance of severity, class, and race. In G. T. Hotaling, D. Finkelhor, J. T. Kirkpatrick, & M. A. Straus (Eds.), *Coping with family violence: Research and policy perspectives* (pp. 212–221). Newbury Park, CA: Sage.

Handelsman, M. M., Gottlieb, M. C., & Knapp, S. (2005). Training ethical psychologists. *Professional Psychology: Research and Practice, 36,* 59–65.

Hankin, C. S., Skinner, K. M., Sullivan, L. M., Miller, D. R., Frayne, S., & Tripp, T. J. (1999). Prevalence of depressive and alcohol abuse symptoms among women VA outpatients who report experiencing sexual assault while in the military. *Journal of Traumatic Stress, 12,* 601–612.

Hannon, R., Hall, D. S., Nash, H., Formanti, J., & Hopson, T. (2000). Judgments regarding sexual aggression as a function of sex of aggressor and victim. *Sex Roles, 5–6,* 311–322.

Hansen, M., Harway, M., & Cervantes, N. (1991). Therapists' perceptions of severity in cases of family violence. *Violence and Victims, 6,* 225–235.

Hanson, R. K., Gizzarelli, R., & Scott, H. (1994). The attitudes of incest offenders. *Criminal Justice and Behavior, 21,* 187–202.

Hanson, R. K., Morton, K. E., & Harris, A. J. R. (2003). Sexual offender recidivism risk. What we know and what we need to know. *The Annals of the New York Academy of Science, 989,* 154–166.

Hanson, R. K., & Wallace-Capretta, S. (1998, July). *Attitudinal support for wife assault: New findings and cumulative evidence.* Paper presented at Program Evaluation and Family Violence Research: An International Conference, Durham, NH.

Harding, H. G., & Helweg-Larsen, M. (2008). Perceived risk for future intimate partner violence among women in a domestic violence shelter. *Journal of Family Violence, 24,* 75–85.

Hardy, M., Beers, B., Burgess, C., & Taylor, A. (2010). Personal experience and perceived acceptability of sibling aggression. *Journal of Family Violence, 25,* 65–71.

Hargrove, T., & Bowman, L. (2007). Saving babies: Exposing sudden infant death in America. Scripps Howard News Service. Retrieved November 21, 2009, from http://dx.doi.org/10.1136/ip.2006.012542

Harper, D. W., & Voigt, L. (2007). Homicide followed by suicide: An integrated theoretical perspective. *Homicide Studies, 11,* 295–318.

Harris, A. J. R., & Hanson, R. K. (2004). *Sex offender recidivism. A simple question* (No. 2004-03). Ottawa Public Safety and Emergency Preparedness.

Harris, C. R. (2003). A review of sex differences in sexual jealousy, including self-report data, psychophysiological responses, interpersonal violence, and morbid jealousy. *Personality and Social Psychology Review, 7,* 102–128.

Harris, H. N., & Valentiner, D. P. (2002). World assumptions, sexual assault, depression, and fearful attitudes toward relationships. *Journal of Interpersonal Violence, 17,* 286–305.

Harris, J. A. (1999). Review and methodological considerations in research on testosterone and aggression. *Aggression and Violent Behavior, 4,* 273–291.

Harris, J. A., Vernon, P. A., & Boomsma, D. I. (1998). The heritability of testosterone: A study of Dutch adolescent twins and their parents. *Behavior Genetics, 28,* 165–171.

Harris, L. H., & Paltrow, L. (2003). The status of pregnant women and fetuses in U.S. criminal law. *Journal of the American Medical Association, 289,* 1697–1699.

Harris, S. B. (1996). For better or for worse: Spouse abuse grown old. *Journal of Elder Abuse & Neglect, 8*(1), 1–33.

Hart, B. (1986). Lesbian battering: An examination. In K. Lobel (Ed.), *Naming the violence: Speaking out about lesbian battering* (pp. 173–189). Seattle, WA: Seal.

Hart, B. J. (1996). Battered women and the criminal justice system. In E. S. Buzawa & C. G. Buzawa (Eds.), *Do arrests and restraining orders work?* (pp. 98–114). Thousand Oaks, CA: Sage.

Hart, S. D., Dutton, D. G., & Newlove, T. (1993). The prevalence of personality disorder among wife assaulters. *Journal of Personality Disorder, 7,* 329–341.

Hart, S. D., Hare, R. D., & Forth, A. E. (1993). Psychopathy as a risk marker for violence: Development and validation of a screening version of the Revised Psychopathy Checklist. In J. Monahan & H. Steadman (Eds.), *Violence and mental disorder: Developments in risk assessment* (pp. 81–98). Chicago: University of Chicago Press.

Hart, S. N., & Brassard, M. R. (1991). Psychological maltreatment: Progress achieved. *Development and Psychopathology, 3,* 61–70.

Hart, S. N., & Brassard, M. R. (1993). Psychological maltreatment. *Violence Update, 3*(7), 4, 6–7, 11.

Hart, S. N., Brassard, M. R., Binggeli, N. J., & Davidson, H. A. (2002). Psychological maltreatment. In J. E. B. Myers, L. Berliner, J. Briere, C. T. Hendrix, C. Jenny, & T. A. Reid (Eds.), *The APSAC handbook on child maltreatment* (2nd ed., pp. 79–103). Thousand Oaks, CA: Sage.

Hart, S. N., Brassard, M. R., & Davidson, H. A. (2010). Psychological maltreatment. In J. E. B. Myers (Ed.), *The APSAC handbook on child maltreatment* (3rd ed., pp. 125–146). Thousand Oaks, CA: Sage.

Hartfield, D. S. (2010). Reversible sideropenic dysphagia in a toddler with iron deficiency. *Clinical Pediatrics, 49,* 180–182.

Hartley, C., & Frohmann, L. (2003, August). *Cook County Target Abuser Call (TAC): An evaluation of a specialized domestic violence court* (NCJ Publication No. 202944). U.S. Department of Justice, National Institute of Justice.

Harvey, S. T., & Taylor, J. E. (2010). A meta-analysis of the effects of psychotherapy with sexually abused children and adolescents. *Clinical Psychology Review, 30*(5), 517–535.

Harway, M., Geffner, R., Ivey, D., Koss, M. P., Murphy, B. C., Mio, J. S., et al. (2002). *Intimate partner abuse and relationship violence.* Washington, DC: American Psychological Association.

Hasday, J. E. (2000). Contest and consent: A legal history of marital rape [Electronic version]. *California Law Review, 88,* 1373–1505.

Haskett, M. E., Allaire, Kreig, S., & Hart, K. C. (2008). Protective and vulnerability factors for physically abused children: Effects of ethnicity and parenting context. *Child Abuse & Neglect, 32,* 567–576.

Hassounch-Phillips, D., & McNeff, E. (2005). "I thought I was less worthy": Low sexual and body esteem and increased vulnerability to intimate partner abuse in women with physical disabilities. *Sexuality and Disability, 23,* 227–240.

Hastings, B. M. (2000). Social information processing and the verbal and physical abuse of women. *Journal of Interpersonal Violence, 15,* 651–664.

Hastings, J. E., & Hamberger, L. K. (1988). Personality characteristics of spouse abusers: A controlled comparison. *Violence and Victims, 3,* 31–48.

Hathaway, J. E., Mucci, L. A., Silverman, J. G., Brooks, D. R., Mathews, R., & Pavlos, C. A. (2000). Health status and health care use of Massachusetts women reporting partner abuse. *American Journal of Preventive Medicine, 19,* 302–307.

Haugaard, J. J. (2000). The challenge of defining child sexual abuse. *American Psychologist, 55,* 1036–1039.

Haugaard, J. J., & Reppucci, N. D. (1988). *The sexual abuse of children.* San Francisco: Jossey-Bass.

Hay, T., & Jones, L. (1994). Societal interventions to prevent child abuse and neglect. *Child Welfare, 73,* 379–403.

Hayashino, D. S., Wurtele, S. K., & Klebe, K. J. (1995). Child molesters: An examination of cognitive factors. *Journal of Interpersonal Violence, 10,* 106–116.

Hays, D. G., & Emelianchik, K. (2009). A content analysis of intimate partner violence assessments. *Measurement and Evaluation in Counseling and Development, 42,* 139–153.

Hazan, C., & Shaver, P. (1987). Conceptualizing romantic love as an attachment process. *Journal of Personality and Social Psychology, 52,* 511–524.

Hazen, A. L., Connelly, C. D., Soriano, F. I., & Landsverak, J. A. (2008). Intimate partner violence and psychological functioning in Latina women. *Health Care for Women International, 29,* 282–299.

Hazen, A. L., & Soriano, F. I. (2007). Experiences with intimate partner violence among Latina women. *Violence Against Women, 13,* 562–582.

Healey, K. M. (1995). *Victim and witness intimidation: New developments and emerging responses* (NCJ Publication No. 156555). Washington, DC: U.S. Department of Justice.

Healey, K. M., Smith, C., & O'Sullivan, C. (1998, February). *Batterer intervention: Program approaches and criminal justice strategies* (NCJ Publication No. 168638). Washington, DC: U.S. Department of Justice.

Hearn, J. (2006). Collateral damage: Men's 'domestic' violence seen through men's relations with men. *Probation Journal, 53,* 38–56.

Heath, I. (2001). Domestic violence as a women's health issue. *Women's Health Issues, 11,* 376–381.

Heath, J. M., Kobylarz, F. A., Brown, M., & Castano, S. (2005). Interventions from home-based geriatric assessments of adult protective service clients suffering elder mistreatment. *Journal of the American Geriatric Society, 53,* 1538–1542.

Heaton, T. B., & Forste, R. (2008). Domestic violence, couple interaction and children's health in Latin America. *Journal of Family Violence, 23,* 183–193.

Hébert, M., Lavoie, F., & Parent, N. (2002). An assessment of outcomes following parents' participation in a child abuse prevention program. *Violence and Victims, 17,* 355–372.

Hébert, M., Lavoie, F., Vitaro, F., McDuff, P., & Tremblay, R. E. (2008). Association of child sexual abuse and dating victimization with mental health disorder in a sample of adolescent girls. *Journal of Traumatic Stress, 21,* 181–189.

Hechler, D. (1988). *The battle and the backlash: The child sexual abuse war.* Lexington, MA: Lexington.

Heckert, D. A., & Gondolf, E. W. (2004). Battered women's perceptions of risk versus risk factors and instrument in predicting repeat reassault? *Journal of Interpersonal Violence, 19,* 778–800.

Heermann, M., Wiggins, M. I., & Rutter, P. A. (2007). Creating a space for spiritual practice: Pastoral possibilities with sexual minorities. *Pastoral Psychology, 55,* 711–721.

Heese, M., & Tutenges, S. (2008). Gender differences in self-reported drinking-induces disinhibition of sexual behaviors. *American Journal of Addiction, 17,* 293–297.

Hegarty, K., Bush, R., & Sheehan, M. (2005). The composite abuse scale: Further development and assessment of reliability and validity of a multidimensional partner abuse measure in clinical settings. *Violence and Victims, 20,* 529–547.

Heggen, C. H. (1996). Religious beliefs and abuse. In C. C. Kroeger & J. R. Beck (Eds.), *Women, abuse, and the Bible: How scripture can be used to hurt or heal* (pp. 15–27). Grand Rapids, MI: Baker Books.

Heide, K. M. (1992). *Why kids kill parents: Child abuse and adolescent homicide.* Columbus: Ohio State University Press.

Heide, K. M., & Frei, A. (2010). Matricide: A critique of the literature. *Trauma, Violence, & Abuse, 11,* 3–17.

Heinze, J. E., & Horn, S. S. (2009). Intergroup contact and beliefs about homosexuality in adolescence. *Journal of Youth and Adolescence, 38,* 937–951.

Heise, L. L., Ellsberg, M., & Gottemoeller, M. (1999). Ending violence against women. *Population Reports, Series L, No. 11.* Baltimore: Johns Hopkins University School of Public Health.

Heise, L. L., Pitanguy, J., & Germain, A. (1994). *Violence against women: The hidden health burden.* Washington, DC: The World Bank.

Heisler, C. J. (2004, January/February). Domestic abuse court orders: An overview. *Victimization of the Elderly and Disabled, 6,* 65–66, 76–78.

Helfrich, C. A., Fujiura, G. T., & Rutkowski-Kmitta, V. (2008). Mental health disorders and functioning of women in domestic violence shelters. *Journal of Interpersonal Violence, 23,* 437–453.

Helmes, E., & Cuevas, M. (2007). Perceptions of elder abuse among Australian older adults and general practitioners. *Australasian Journal on Ageing, 26,* 120–124.

Helms, J. E., Jernigan, M., & Mascher, J. (2005). The meaning of race in psychology and how to change it: A methodological perspective. *American Psychologist, 60,* 27–36.

Hemmens, C., Strom, K., & Schlegel, E. (1998). Gender bias in the courts: A review of the literature. *Sociological Imagination, 35,* 22–42.

Henderson, A. J. Z., Bartholomew, K., & Dutton, D. G. (1997). He loves me; he loves me not: Attachment and separation resolution of abused women. *Journal of Family Violence, 12,* 169–191.

Henderson, A. J. Z., Bartholomew, K., Trinke, S. J., & Kwong, M. J. (2005). When loving means hurting: An explanation of attachment and intimate abuse in a community sample. *Journal of Family Violence, 20,* 219–230.

Hendricks, B., Werner, T., Shipway, L., & Turinetti, G. J. (2006). Recidivism among spousal abusers: Predictions and program evaluation. *Journal of Interpersonal Violence, 21,* 703–716.

Hendy, H. M., Eggen, D., Gustitus, C., McLeod, K. C., & Ng, P. (2003). Decision to leave scale: Perceived reasons to stay in or leave violent relationships. *Psychology of Women Quarterly, 27,* 162–173.

Henggeler, S. W., Schoenwald, S. K., Borduin, C. M., Rowland, M. D., & Cunningham, P. B. (1998). *Multisystem treatment of antisocial behavior in children and adolescents.* New York: Guilford.

Hennessy, E. (2009). Economic stress impacts child abuse rates. *Inside Hanscom Air Force Base.*

Hennighausen, K., & Lyons-Ruth, K. (2010). Disorganization of attachment strategies in infancy and childhood. Cambridge, MA: *Encyclopedia on Early Childhood Development.*

Henning, K. R., & Holdford, R. (2006). Minimization, denial, and victim blaming by batterers. *Criminal Justice and Behavior, 33,* 110–130.

Henning, K. R., Jones, A., & Holdford, R. (2003). Treatment needs of women arrested for domestic violence: A comparison with male offenders. *Journal of Interpersonal Violence, 18,* 839–856.

Henning, K. R., & Klesges, L. M. (2003). Prevalence and characteristics of psychological abuse reported by court-involved battered women. *Journal of Interpersonal Violence, 18,* 857–871.

Henning, K. R., Leitenberg, H., Coffey, P., Turner, T., & Bennett, R. T. (1996). Long-term psychological and social impact of witnessing physical conflict between parents. *Journal of Interpersonal Violence, 11,* 35–51.

Henningsen, D. D. (2004). Flirting with meaning: An examination of miscommunication in flirting interactions. *Sex Roles, 50,* 481–489.

Hensing, G., & Alexanderson, K. (2000). The relation of adult experience of domestic harassment, violence, and sexual abuse to health and sickness absence. *International Journal of Behavioral Medicine, 7,* 1–18.

Hepburn, J. R., & Harvey, A. N. (2007). The effect of the threat of legal sanction on program retention and completion: Is that why they stay? *Crime & Delinquency, 53,* 255–280.

Herbert, T. B., Silver, R. C., & Ellard, J. H. (1991). Coping with an abusive relationship: How and why do women stay? *Journal of Marriage and the Family, 53,* 311–325.

Herek, G. M. (1990). The context of anti-gay violence: Notes on cultural and psychological heterosexism. *Journal of Interpersonal Violence, 5,* 316–333.

Herman-Smith, R. L. (2009). CAPTA referrals for infants and toddlers. *Topics in Early Childhood Special Education, 29,* 181–191.

Hernandez, A. (2009). An integrated approach to treating non-offending parents affected by sexual abuse. *Social Work in Mental Health, 7,* 533–555.

Herrenkohl, E. C., Herrenkohl, R. C., Rupert, L. J., Egolf, B. P., & Lutz, J. G. (1995). Risk factors for behavioral dysfunction: The relative impact of maltreatment, SES, physical health problems, cognitive ability, and quality of parent-child interaction. *Child Abuse & Neglect, 19,* 191–203.

Herrenkohl, R. C., Egolf, B. P., & Herrenkohl, E. C. (1997). Preschool antecedents of adolescent assaultive behavior: A longitudinal study. *American Journal of Orthopsychiatry, 67,* 422–432.

Herrenkohl, T. I., Huang, B., Tajima, E., & Whitney, S. D. (2003). Examining the link between child abuse and youth violence: An analysis of mediating mechanisms. *Journal of Interpersonal Violence, 18,* 1189–1208.

Herrenkohl, T. I., Mason, W. A., Kosterman, R., Lengua, L., Hawkins, J. D., & Abbott, R. D. (2004). Pathways from physical childhood abuse to partner violence in young adulthood. *Violence and Victims, 19,* 123–136.

Hersch, K., & Gray-Little, B. (1998). Psychopathic traits and attitudes associated with self-reported sexual aggression in college men. *Journal of Interpersonal Violence, 13,* 456–471.

Hesse, E., & Main, M. (2000). Disorganized infant, child, and adult attachment: Collapse in behavioral and attentional strategies. *Journal of the American Psychoanalytic Association, 48,* 1097–1127.

Hettrich, E. L., & O'Leary, K. D. (2007). Females' reasons for their physical aggression in dating relationships. *Journal of Interpersonal Violence, 23,* 1131–1143.

Hetzel-Riggin, M. D. (2009). A test of structural invariance of post-traumatic stress symptoms in female survivors of sexual and/or physical abuse or assault. *Traumatology, 15,* 46–59.

Hewitt, B., Podesta, J. S., & Longley, J. (2002, June 3). No time to wait. *People, 57,* 21.

Hewitt, S. K. (1998). *Small voices: Assessing allegations of sexual abuse in preschool children.* Thousand Oaks, CA: Sage.

Heyman, R. E., & Neidig, P. H. (1999). A comparison of spousal aggression prevalence rates in U.S. Army and civilian representative samples. *Journal of Consulting and Clinical Psychology, 67,* 239–242.

Heyman, R. E., & Slep, A. M. S. (2006). Creating and field-testing diagnostic criteria for partner and child maltreatment. *Journal of Family Psychology, 20,* 397–408.

Hickman, L. J., Jaycox, L. H., & Aronoff, J. (2004). Dating violence among adolescents. *Trauma, Violence, & Abuse, 5,* 123–142.

Hildyard, K. L., & Wolfe, D. A. (2002). Child neglect: Developmental issues and outcomes. *Child Abuse & Neglect, 26,* 679–695.

Hill, J. B., & Amuwo, S. A. (1998). Understanding elder abuse and neglect. In N. A. Jackson & G. C. Oates (Eds.), *Violence in intimate relationships: Examining sociological and psychological issues* (pp. 195–223). Woburn, MA: Butterworth-Heinemann.

Hill, J. R. (2005). Teaching about family violence: A proposed model curriculum. *Teaching and Learning in Medicine, 17,* 169–178.

Hill, M. S., & Fischer, A. R. (2001). Does entitlement mediate the link between masculinity and rape-related variables? *Journal of Counseling Psychology, 48,* 39–50.

Hill, S. A. (2006). Marriage among African American women: A gender perspective. *Journal of Comparative Family Studies, 37,* 421–440.

Hilton, N. Z. (1992). Battered women's concerns about their children witnessing wife assault. *Journal of Interpersonal Violence, 7,* 77–86.

Hilton, N. Z., Harris, G. T., & Rice, M. E. (1998). On the validity of self-reported rates of interpersonal violence. *Journal of Interpersonal Violence, 16,* 865–889.

Hinduja, A., & Patchin, J. W. (2008). Cyberbullying: An exploratory analysis of factors related to offending and victimization. *Deviant Behavior, 29*(2), 129–156.

Hines, D. A. (2007). Postraumatic stress symptoms among men who sustain partner violence: An international multisite study of university students. *Psychology of Men & Mascuinity 8,* 225–239.

Hines, D. A., & Saudino, K. J. (2002). Intergenerational transmission of partner violence. *Trauma, Violence, & Abuse, 3,* 210–225.

Hines, D. A., & Saudino, K. J. (2003). Gender differences in psychological, and sexual aggression among college students using the revised Conflict Tactics Scale. *Violence and Victims, 18,* 197–217.

Hines, T. (2003). *Pseudoscience and the paranormal* (2nd ed.). Amherst, NY: Prometheus.

Hinrichsen, G. A., Hernandez, N. A., & Pollack, S. (1992). Difficulties and rewards in family care of depressed older adults. *Gerontologist, 32,* 486–492.

Hirschel, J. D., & Buzawa, E. S. (2002). Understanding the context of dual arrest with directions for future research. *Violence Against Women, 8,* 1449–1473.

Hirschel, J. D., Buzawa, E., Pattavina, A., & Faggiani, D. (2007 April). *Explaining the prevalence, context, and consequences of dual arrest in intimate partner cases* (NCJ Publication No. 218355). Washington, DC: U.S. Department of Justice, National Institute of Justice.

Ho, S-M., et al. (2009). Effectiveness of a discharge education program in reducing the severity of postpartum: A randomized controlled evaluation study. *Patient Education and Counseling, 77,* 68–71.

Hodell, E. C., Golding, J. M., Yozwiak, J. A., Brandshaw, G. S., Kinstle, T. L., & Marsil, D. F. (2009). The perception of elder sexual abuse in the courtroom. *Violence Against Women, 16,* 678–698.

Hodgins, S. (2001). The major mental disorders and crime: Stop debating and start treating and preventing. *International Journal of Law and Psychiatry, 24,* 427–446.

Hoefnagels, C., & Baartman, H. (1997). On the threshold of disclosure: The effects of a mass media field experiment. *Child Abuse & Neglect, 21,* 557–573.

Hofeller, K. (1982). *Social, psychological and situational factors in wife abuse.* Palo Alto, CA: R & E Research Associates.

Hoffman, K. L., Kiecolt, K. J., & Edwards, J. N. (2005). Physical violence between siblings: A theorectical and empirical analysis. *Journal of Family Issues, 26,* 1103–1130.

Hoffman, N. D., Swann, S., & Freeman, K. (2003). Communication between health care providers and gay, lesbian, bisexual, transgender, and questioning youth. *Journal of Adolescent Health, 32,* 131.

Hofford, M., & Harrell, A. D. (1993). *Family violence: Interventions for the justice system.* Washington, DC: Bureau of Justice Assistance.

Holahan, C. J., Moos, R. H., Holahan, C. K., Brennan, P. L., & Schutte, K. K. (2005). Stress generation, avoidance coping, and depressive symptoms: A 10-year model. *Journal of Consulting and Clinical Psychology, 73,* 658–666.

Holahan, C. J., Moos, R. H., Moerkbak, M. L., Cronkite, R. C., Holahan, C. K., & Kenney, B. A. (2007). Spousal similarity in coping and depressive symptoms over 10 years. *Journal of Family Psychology, 21,* 551–559.

Holcomb, D. R., Savage, M. P., Seehafer, R., & Waalkes, D. M. (2002). A mixed-gender date rape prevention intervention targeting freshmen college athletes. *College Student Journal, 36,* 165–180.

Holden, G. W. (1998). Introduction: The development of research into another consequence of family violence. In G. W. Holden, R. A. Geffner, & E. N. Jouriles (Eds.), *Children exposed to marital violence: Theory, research, and applied issues* (pp. 1–18). Washington, DC: American Psychological Association.

Holden, G. W. (2003). Children exposed to domestic violence and child abuse: Terminology and taxonomy. *Clinical Child and Family Psychology Review, 6,* 151–160.

Holden, G. W., & Ritchie, K. L. (1991). Linking extreme marital discord, child rearing, and child behavior problems: Evidence from battered women. *Child Development, 62,* 311–327.

Holiman, M. J., & Schilit, R. (1991). Aftercare for battered women: How to encourage the maintenance of change. *Psychotherapy, 28,* 345–353.

Hollin, C. R., McGuire, J., Hounsome, J. C., Hatcher, R. M., Bilby, C. A. L., & Palmer, E. J. (2008). Cognitive skills behavior programs for offenders in the community: A reconviction analysis. *Criminal Justice and Behavior, 35,* 269–283.

Hollins, L. D., & Hankin, B. L. (2005, September 19). Link between childhood psychological maltreatment and adult mental health functioning. Paper presented at the Tenth International Conference on Family Violence, San Diego, CA.

Holloway, J. D. (2005, November). Striking a balance between correction and care. *APA Monitor on Psychology, 36,* 48–49.

Holloway, M. (1994, August). Trends in women's health: A global view. *Scientific American,* 76–83.

Holmes, W. M. (1993). Police arrests for domestic violence. *American Journal of Police, 12,* 101–125.

Holstein, M. B., & Minkler, M. (2003). Self, society and the "new gerontology." *The Gerontologist, 43,* 787–796.

Holt, V. L., Kernic, M. A., Wolf, M., & Rivara, F. P. (2003). Do protection orders affect the likelihood of future partner violence and injury? *American Journal of Preventive Medicine, 24,* 16–21.

Holtzworth-Munroe, A. (2005). Female perpetration of physical aggression against an intimate partner: A controversial new topic of study. *Violence and Victims, 20,* 251–259.

Holtzworth-Munroe, A., Bates, L., Smutzler, N., & Sandin, E. (1997). A brief review of the research on husband violence: Part I. Maritally violent versus nonviolent men. *Aggression and Violent Behavior, 2,* 65–99.

Holtzworth-Munroe, A., & Hutchinson, G. (1993). Attributing negative intent to wife behavior: The attributions of maritally violent versus nonviolent men. *Journal of Abnormal Psychology, 102,* 206–211.

Holtzworth-Munroe, A., Meehan, J. C., Stuart, G. L., Herron, K., & Rehman, U. (2000). Testing the Holtzworth-Munroe and Stuart (1994) batterer typology. *Journal of Consulting and Clinical Psychology, 68,* 1000–1019.

Holtzworth-Munroe, A., Meehan, J. C., Stuart, G. L., Herron, K., & Rehman, U. (2003). Do subtypes of maritally violent men continue to differ over time? *Journal of Consulting and Clinical Psychology, 71,* 728–740.

Holtzworth-Munroe, A., Rehman, U., & Herron, K. (2000). General and spouse-specific anger and hostility in subtypes of maritally violent men and nonviolent men. *Behavior Therapy, 31,* 603–630.

Holtzworth-Munroe, A., & Stuart, G. L. (1994). Typologies of male batterers: Three subtypes and the differences among them. *Psychological Bulletin, 116,* 476–497.

Holtzworth-Munroe, A., Stuart, G. L., & Hutchinson, G. (1997). Violent versus nonviolent husbands: Differences in attachment patterns, dependency, and jealousy. *Journal of Family Psychology, 11,* 314–331.

Hooper, L. M. (2008). Defining and understanding parentification: Implications for all counselors. *The Alabama Counseling Association Journal, 34,* 34–43.

Hooper, L. M., Marotta, S. A., & Lanthier, R. P. (2008). Predictors of growth and distress following childhood parentification: A retrospective exploratory study. *Journal of Family Studies, 17,* 693–705.

Horkan, E. M. (1995). Elder abuse in the Republic of Ireland. In J. I. Kosberg & J. L. Garcia (Eds.), *Elder abuse: International and cross-cultural perspectives* (pp. 119–137). Binghamton, NY: Haworth.

Horn, S. S. (2007). Adolescents' acceptance of same-sex peers based on sexual orientation and gender expression. *Journal of Youth and Adolescence, 36,* 363–371.

Horn, S. S., Kosciw, J. G., & Russell, S. T. (2009). Editorial: Special issue introduction: New research on lesbian, gay, bisexual, and transgendered youth: Studying lives in context. *Journal of Youth and Adoslcence, 38,* 863–866.

Hornor, G., & Ryan-Wenger, N. A. (1999). Aberrant genital care practices: An unrecognized form of child abuse. *Journal of Pediatric Health Care, 13,* 12–17.

Horton, A. L., & Johnson, B. L. (1993). Profile and strategies of women who have ended abuse. *Families in Society, 74,* 481–492.

Hotaling, G. T., Straus, M. A., & Lincoln, A. J. (1990). Intrafamily violence and crime and violence outside the family. In M. A. Straus & R. J. Gelles (Eds.), *Physical violence in American families: Risk factors and adaptations to violence in 8,145 families* (pp. 431–470). New Brunswick, NJ: Transaction.

Hotaling, G. T., & Sugarman, D. B. (1986). An analysis of risk markers in husband to wife violence: The current state of knowledge. *Violence and Victims, 1,* 101–124.

Hotaling, G. T., & Sugarman, D. B. (1990). A risk marker analysis of assaulted wives. *Journal of Family Violence, 5,* 1–13.

Houry, D., Kaslow, N. J., & Thompson, M. P. (2005). Depressive symptoms in women experiencing intimate partner violence. *Journal of Interpersonal Violence, 20,* 1467–1477.

Hovell, M. F., Seid, A. G., & Liles, S. (2006). Evaluation of a police and social services domestic violence program: Empirical evidence needed to inform public health policy. *Violence Against Women, 12,* 137–159.

Howard, D. E., Wang, M. Q., & Yan, F. (2007a). Psychosocial factors associated with reports of physical dating violence among U.S. adolescent females. *Adolescence, 42,* 311–324.

Howard, D. E., Wang, M. Q., & Yan, F. (2007b). Prevalence and psychosocial correlates of forced sexual intercourse among U.S. high school adolescents. *Adolescence, 42,* 629–643.

Howe, D. (1995). Pornography and the paedophile: Is it criminogenic? *British Journal of Medical Psychology, 68*(1), 15–27.

Howells, K. H., Graham-Bermann, S. A., Czyz, E., & Lilly, M. (2010). Assessing resilience in preschool children exposed to intimate partner violence. *Violence and Victims, 25,* 150–164.

Hoyle, C., & Sanders, A. (2000). Police response to domestic violence: From victim choice to victim empowerment? *British Journal of Criminology, 40,* 14–36.

Huber, R., Borders, K. W., Badrak, K., Netting, F. E., & Nelson, H. W. (2001). National standards for the long-term care ombudsman program and a tool to assess compliance: The Huber Badrak Borders Scales. *Gerontologist, 41,* 264–271.

Hughes, H. M., & Luke, D. A. (1998). Heterogeneity in adjustment among children of battered women. In G. W. Holden, R. A. Geffner, & E. N. Jouriles (Eds.), *Children exposed to marital violence: Theory, research, and applied issues* (pp. 185–221). Washington, DC: American Psychological Association.

Hughes, P. P., Marshall, D., & Sherrill, C. (2003). Multidimensional analysis of fear and confidence of university women relating to crimes and dangerous situations. *Journal of Interpersonal Violence, 18,* 33–49.

Hulbert, S. N. (2008). Children exposed to violence in the child protection system: Practice-based assessment of the system processs can lead to practical strategies for improvement. *Journal of Emotional Abuse, 6,* 217–234.

Humenik, A. L. F., & Fingerhut, R. (2007). A pilot study assessing the relationship between child harming thoughts and postpartum depression. *Journal of Clinical Psychology in Medical Settings, 14,* 360–366.

Humphreys, J. C., Lee, K. A., Neylan, T. C., & Marmar, C. R. (1999). Trauma history of sheltered battered women. *Issues in Mental Health Nursing, 20,* 319–332.

Humphreys, K. L., Sauder, C. L., Martin, E. K., & Marx, B. P. (2010). Tonic immobility in childhood sexual abuse survivors and its relationship to posttraumatic stress symptomatology. *Journal of Interpersonal Violence, 25,* 358–373.

Humphrey, S. E., & Kahn, A. S. (2000). Fraternities, athletic teams, and rape: Importance of identification with a risky group. *Journal of Interpersonal Violence, 15,* 1313–1322.

Humphreys, T. & Herold, E. (2007). Sexual consent in heterosexual relationships: Development of a new measure. *Sex Roles, 57,* 305–315.

Hunnicutt, G. (2009). Varieties of patriarchy and violence against women. *Violence Against Women, 15,* 553–573.

Hunt, P., & Baird, M. (1990). Children of sex rings. *Child Welfare, 69,* 195–207.

Hunter, S. V. (2010). Evolving narratives about childhood sexual abuse: Challenging the dominance of the victim and survivor paradigm. *Australian and New Zealand Journal of Family Therapy, 31,* 176190.

Hurlburt, M., Barth, R. P., Leslie, L. K., Landsverk, J. A., & McCree, J. S. (2007). Building on strengths: Current status and opportunities for improvement of parent training for families in child welfare services. In R. Haskins, F. Wulczyn, & M. B. Webb (Eds.), *Child protection: Using research improves policy and practice* (pp. 81–106). Washington, DC: Brookings.

Hurlburt, M. S., Zhang, J., Barth, R. P., Leslie, L. K., & Burns, B. J. (2010). Posttraumatic stress symptoms in children and adolescents referred for child welfare investigation. *Child Maltreatment, 15*, 48–63.

Huss, M. T., & Langhinrichsen-Rohling, J. (2000). Identification of the psychopathic batterer: The clinical, legal, and policy implications. *Aggression and Violent Behavior, 5*, 403–422.

Huss, M. T., & Langhinrichsen-Rohling, J. (2006). Assessing the generalization of psychopathy in a clinical sample of domestic violence perpetrators. *Law and Human Behavior, 30*, 571–586.

Hussey, J. M., Chang, J. J., & Kotch, J. B. (2008). Child maltreatment in the United States: Prevalence, risk factors, and adolescent health factors. *Pediatrics, 118*, 933–942.

Hussey, J. M., Marshall, J. M., et al. (2005). Defining maltreatment according to substantiation: Distinction without a difference. *Child Abuse & Neglect, 29*, 342–357.

Hussong, A. M., Wirth, R. J., Edwards, M. C., Curran, P. J., Chassin, L. A., & Zucker, R. A. (2007). Externalizing symptoms among children of alcoholic parents: Entry points for an antisocial pathway to alcoholism. *Journal of Abnormal Psychiatry, 116*, 529–542.

Hutchison, I. W. (1999). *Influence of alcohol and drugs on women's utilization of the police for domestic violence* (NCJ Publication No. 179277). Washington, DC: U.S. Bureau of Justice Statistics.

Hutchison, K. E. et al. (2008). The incentive salience of alcohol. *Archives of General Psychiatry, 65*, 841–850.

Hutchison, I. W., & Hirschel, J. D. (1998). Abused women: Help-seeking strategies and police utilization. *Violence Against Women, 4*, 436–456.

Hutchison, I. W., Hirschel, J. D., & Pesackis, C. E. (1994). Family violence and police utilization. *Violence and Victims, 9*, 299–313.

Huth-Bocks, A. C., & Hughes, H. M. (2008). Parenting stress, parenting behavior, and children's adjustment in families experiencing intimate partner violence. *Journal of Family Violence, 23*, 243–251.

Hydén, M. (1999). The world of the fearful: Battered women's narratives of leaving abusive husbands. *Feminism and Psychology, 9*, 449–469.

Hydén, M. (2005). 'I must have been an idiot to let it go on': Agency and positioning in battered women's narratives of leaving. *Feminism & Psychology, 15*, 169–188.

Hyman, A., Schillinger, D., & Lo, B. (1995). Laws mandating reporting of domestic violence: Do they promote patient well-being? *Journal of the American Medical Association, 273*, 1781–1787.

I am just a poor boy though my story's seldom told. (2009, April 4–10). *The Economist*, 82–83.

Ignoring warning proves tragic in Texas. (2007, May 07). Houston *Chronicle (KRT)*. Houston, TX. Retrieved from http://www.lorain.oh.networkofcare.org/dv/news/detail.cfm?articleID=14572

Ingram, E. M. (2007). A comparison of help-seeking between Latino and non-Latino victims of intimate partner violence. *Violence Against Women, 13*, 159–171.

Intagliata, K. L. (2002). Improving the quality of care in nursing homes: Class action impact litigation. *University of Colorado Law Review, 73*, 1013–1045.

Inter-Agency Council on Child Abuse and Neglect (ICAN). (2009). *Child death review team report for 2009*. El Monte, CA: Author.

Inter-Agency Council on Child Abuse and Neglect (ICAN). (2010). *Safely surrendered and abandoned infants in Los Angeles County – 2002–2009*. El Monte, CA: Author.

International Society for Prevention of Child Abuse and Neglect (ISPCAN). (2008). World perspectives on child abuse (8th ed.). Retrieved May 10, 2010, from http://www.ispcan.org/wp/index.htm

International Violence Against Women. (2007). Officyna Wolters Kluwer, Warszawa.

Ireland, T. O., Smith, C. A., & Thornberry, T. (2002). Developmental issues in the impact of child maltreatment on later delinquency and drug use. *Criminology, 40*, 359–400.

Isaac, N. E. (1998). Corporate sector response to domestic violence. In National Institute of Justice & American Bar Association, *Legal interventions in family violence: Research findings and policy implications* (NCJ Publication No. 171666, pp. 76–77). Washington, DC: U.S. Department of Justice.

Isaac, N. E., & Enos, V. P. (2001, September). *Documenting domestic violence: How health care providers can help victims* (NCJ Publication No. 188564). Washington, DC: U.S. Department of Justice.

Island, D., & Letellier, P. (1991). Men who beat the men who love them: Battered gay men and domestic violence. New York: Haworth Press.

Ismail, F., Berman, H., & Ward-Griffin, C. (2007). Dating violence and the health of young women: A feminist narrative study. *Health Care for Women International, 28*, 453–477.

Jackson, K. F., & Hodge, D. R. (2010). Native American youth and culturally sensitive interventions: A systematic review. *Research on Social Work Practice, 20,* 260–270.

Jackson, S. (2003). Analyzing the studies. In S. Jackson, L. Feder, D. R. Forde, R. C. Davis, C. D. Maxwell, & B. G. Taylor, *Batterer intervention programs: Where do we go from here?* (NCJ Publication No. 195079, pp. 23–29). Washington, DC: National Institute of Justice.

Jackson, S. M. (1998). Issues in the dating violence research: A review of the literature. *Aggression and Violent Behavior, 4,* 233–247.

Jacobson, N. S. (1994). Rewards and dangers in researching domestic violence. *Family Process, 33,* 81–85.

Jacobson, N. S., & Gottman, J. M. (1993, August). *New picture of violent couples emerges from UW study.* Paper presented at the annual meeting of the American Psychological Association, Toronto.

Jacobson, N. S., Gottman, J. M., Gortner, E., Berns, S., & Shortt, J. W. (1996). Psychological factors in the longitudinal course of battering. *Violence and Victims, 11,* 625–629.

Jacobson, N. S., Gottman, J. M., Waltz, J., Rushe, R., Babcock, J. C., & Holtzworth-Munroe, A. (1994). Affect, verbal content and psychophysiology in the arguments of couples with a violent husband. *Journal of Consulting and Clinical Psychology, 62,* 982–988.

Jaffe, E. (2007, May). Mirror neurons. *Observer, 20,* 20–23, 25.

Jaffe, P. G., & Crooks, C. V. (2005). *Understanding women's experiences parenting in the context of domestic violence: Implications for community and court-related service providers.* Retrieved from http://www.vaw.umn.edu/documents/commissioned/parentingindv/parentingindv.html

Jaffe, P. G., Wolfe, D. A., & Wilson, S. K. (1990). *Children of battered women.* Newbury Park, CA: Sage.

Jaffee, S. R., & Caspi, A., et al. (2005). Nature X nurture: Genetic vulnerabilities interact with physical maltreatment to promote conduct problems. *Development and Psychopathology, 17,* 67–84.

Jakupcak, M. (2003). Masculine gender role stress and men's fear of emotions as predictors of self-reported aggression and violence. *Violence and Victims, 18,* 533–541.

James, K. (1996). Truth or fiction: Men as victims of domestic violence? *Australian & New Zealand Journal of Family Therapy, 17,* 121–125.

Jankowski, M. K., Leitenberg, H., Henning, K. R., & Coffey, P. (1999). Intergenerational transmission of dating aggression as a function of witnessing only same sex parents vs. opposite sex parents vs. both parents as perpetrators of domestic violence. *Journal of Family Violence, 14,* 267–279.

Jayakumar, P., Barry, M., Ramachandran, M. (2010). Orthopaedic aspects of non-accidental injury. *Journal of Bone & Joint Surgery, British Volume, 92,* 189–195.

Jaycox, L. H., Mcaffrey, D., Eiseman, B., Aronoff, J., Shelley, G. A., et al. (2006). Impact of a school-based dating violence prevention program among Latino teens: Randomized controlled effectiveness trial. *Journal of Adolescent Health, 39,* 694–704.

Jazbec, J., Todorovski, L., & Jereb, B. (2007). Classification tree analysis of second neoplasms in survivors of childhood cancer. *BMC Cancer, 7,* 27–36.

Jenkins, M., Lambert, E. G., & Baker, D. N. (2009). The attitudes of Black and White college students toward gays and lesbians. *Journal of Black Studies, 39,* 589–613.

Jennings, J. L., & Murphy, C. M. (2000). Male-male dimensions of male-female battering: A new look at domestic violence. *Psychology of Men & Masculinity, 1*(1), 21–29.

Jensen, G. F., & Karpos, M. (1993). Managing rape: Exploratory research on the behavior of rape statistics. *Criminology, 31,* 363–385.

Jesperson, A. F., Lalumière, M. L., & Seto, M. C. (2009). Sexual abuse history among adult sex offenders and non-sex offenders: A meta-analysis. *Child Abuse & Neglect, 33,* 179–192.

Jesse, D. E., Dolbier, C. L., & Blanchard, A. (2008). Barriers to seeking help and treatment suggestions for prenatal depressive symptoms: Focus groups with rural low-income women. *Issues in Mental Health Nursing, 29,* 3–19.

Jeyaseelan, L., Sadowski, L. S. Kumar, S., Hassan, F., Ramiro, L., & Vizcarra, B. (2004). World studies of abuse in the family environment—Risk factors for physical intimate partner violence. *International Journal of Injury Control and Safety Promotion, 11,* 117–124.

Jin, X. A., Eagle, M., & Keat, J. E. (2008). Hostile attributional bias, early abuse, and social desirability in reporting hostile attributions among Chinese Immigrant batterers and nonviolent men. *Violence and Victims, 23,* 773–786.

Jogerst, G. J., Daly, J. M., Brinig, M. F., Dawson, J. D., Schmuch, G. A., & Ingram, J. G. (2003). Domestic elder abuse and the law. *American Journal of Public Health, 93,* 2131–2136.

Johnson, C., & Gorchynski, J. (2004). Intimate partner violence among men presenting to a university emergency department. *Western Journal of Emergency Medicine, 5,* 40–44.

Johnson, C. F. (2004). Child sexual abuse. *The Lancet, 364,* 462–470.

Johnson, H., & Bunge, V. P. (2001). Prevalence and consequences of spousal assault in Canada. *Canadian Journal of Criminology, 43,* 27–45.

Johnson, I. M., Crowley, J., & Sigler, R. T. (1992). Agency response to domestic violence: Services provided by battered women. In E. C. Viano (Ed.), *Intimate violence: Interdisciplinary perspectives* (pp. 191–202). Bristol, PA: Taylor & Francis.

Johnson, J. M., & Bondurant, D. M. (1992). Revisiting the 1982 church response survey. *Studies in Symbolic Interaction, 13,* 287–293.

Johnson, K. B., & Das, M. B. (2009). Spousal violence in Bangladesh as reported by men. *Journal of Interpersonal Violence, 24,* 977–995.

Johnson, M. C., & Kercher, G. A. (2009). Identifying predictors of negative psychological reactions to stalking victimization. *Journal of Interpersonal Violence, 24,* 866–882.

Johnson, M. P. (1995). Patriarchal terrorism and common couple violence: Two forms of violence against women. *Journal of Marriage and the Family, 57,* 283–294.

Johnson, M. P. (2000). Conflict and control: Images of symmetry and asymmetry in domestic violence. In A. Booth, A. C. Crouter, & M. Clements (Eds.), *Couples in conflict.* Mahwah, NJ: Lawrence Erlbaum.

Johnson, M. P. (2006). Conflict and control: Gender symmetry and asymmetry in domestic violence. *Violence Against Women, 12,* 1003–1018.

Johnson, M., & Elliott, B. A. (1997). Domestic violence among family practice patients in midsized and rural communities. *The Journal of Family Practice, 44,* 391–400.

Johnson, M. P., & Ferraro, K. J. (2000). Research on domestic violence in the 1990s: Making distinctions. *Journal of Marriage and the Family, 62,* 948–963.

Johnson, P. J., McCreary, D. R., & Mills, J. S. (2007). Effects of exposure to objectified male and female media images on men's psychological well-being. *Psychology of Men & Masculinity, 8,* 95–102.

Johnson, R. M., Kotch, J. B., Catellier, D. J., Winsor, J. R., Dufort, V., Hunter, W., et al. (2002). Adverse behavioral and emotional outcomes from child abuse and witnessed violence. *Child Maltreatment, 7,* 179–186.

Johnson, S., & Lebow, J. (2000). The "coming of age" of couples therapy. *Journal of Marital and Family Therapy, 26,* 23–38.

Johnson, S. P., & Sullivan, C. M. (2008). How child protection workers support or further victimize battered mothers. *Affilia, 23,* 242–258.

Johnson-Reid, M., Chung, S., Way, I., & Jolley, J. (2010). Understanding service use and victim patterns associated with re-reports of alleged maltreatment perpetrators. *Children and Youth Services Review, 32,* 790–797.

Jones, A. S. (2000). The cost of batterer programs: How much and who pays? *Journal of Interpersonal Violence, 15,* 566–586.

Jones, A. S., D'Agostino, R. B., Jr., Gondolf, E. W., & Heckert, A. (2004). Assessing the effect of batterer program completion on reassault using propensity scores. *Journal of Interpersonal Violence, 19,* 1002–1020.

Jones, A. S., & Gondolf, E. W. (2004). Assessing the effects of batterer program completion on reassault: An instrumental variables analysis. *Journal of Quantitative Criminology, 18,* 71–98.

Jones, D. (2009). Spotlight on elder abuse. Retrieved from http://www.elder-abuse-spotlight.blogspot.com/2009/03/police-training-in-elder-abuse.html

Jones, D. P. H. (1994). Editorial: The syndrome of Munchausen by proxy. *Child Abuse & Neglect, 18,* 769–771.

Jones, H. E. (2006). Drug addiction during pregnancy. *Psychological Science, 15,* 126–130.

Jones, L. (2008). The distinctive characteristics and needs of domestic violence victims in a Native American community. *Journal of Family Violence, 23,* 113–118.

Jones, L. M., et al. (2010). Nonoffending caregiver and youth experiences with child sexual abuse investigations. *Journal of Interpersonal Violence, 25,* 291–314.

Jones, N. T., Ji, P., Beck, M., & Beck, N. (2002). The reliability and validity of the Revised Conflict Tactics Scale (CTS2) in a female incarcerated population. *Journal of Family Issues, 23,* 441–457.

Jordan, C. E., Logan, T., Walker, R., & Nigoff, A. (2003). Stalking: An examination of the criminal justice response. *Journal of Interpersonal Violence, 18,* 148–165.

Jouriles, E. N., McDonald, R., Slep, A. M. S., Heyman, R. E., & Garrido, E. (2008). Child abuse in the context of domestic violence: Prevalence, explanations, and practice implications. *Violence and Victims, 23,* 221–235.

Jouriles, E. N., McDonald, R., Stephens, N., Norwood, W. D., Spiller, L. C., & Ware, H. S. (1998). Breaking the cycle of violence: Helping families departing from battered women's shelters. In G. W. Holden, R. A. Geffner, & E. N. Jouriles (Eds.), *Children exposed to marital violence: Theory, research, and applied issues* (pp. 337–369). Washington, DC: American Psychological Association.

Jouriles, E. N., Platt, C., & McDonald, R. (2009). Violence in adolescent dating relationships. *The Prevention Researcher, 16,* 3–7.

Journal of Clinical Psychology in Medical Settings. (2008, *15,* 1).

Ju, S., & Lee, Y. (2010). Experiences of family maltreatment of Korean children in Korean National Protective Services. *Child Abuse & Neglect, 34,* 18–27.

Judge OKs retrial in alleged abuse case. (2003, February 1). *Los Angeles Times,* p. B3.

Julian, T. W., & McHenry, P. C. (1993). Mediators of male violence toward female intimates. *Journal of Family Violence, 8,* 39–56.

Kaffman, A. (2009). The silent epidemic of neurodevelopmental injuries [Commentary]. *Biological Psychiatry, 66,* 624–626.

Kagan, J. (2007). A trio of concerns. *Perspectives on psychological science, 2,* 361–376.

Kahn, J. M., & Schwalbe, C. (2010). The timing and risk factors associated with child welfare recidivism at two decision-making points. *Children & Youth Services Review, 32,* 1035–1044.

Kahntroff, J., & Watson, R. (2009). Refusal of emergency care and patient dumping. *American Medical Association Journal of Ethics, 1,* 49–53.

Kalich, D. M., & Evans, R. D. (2006). Drug court: An effective alternative to incarceration. *Deviant Behavior, 27,* 569–590.

Kalichman, S. C., Benotsch, E., Rompa, D., Gore-Felton, C., Austin, J., Luke, W., et al. (2001). Unwanted sexual experiences and sexual risks in gay and bisexual men: Associations among revictimization, substance use, and psychiatric symptoms. *The Journal of Sex Research, 38,* 1–9.

Kalmuss, D. S. (1984). The intergenerational transmission of marital aggression. *Journal of Marriage and the Family, 46,* 11–19.

Kandel-Englander, E. (1992). Wife battering and violence outside the family. *Journal of Interpersonal Violence, 7,* 462–470.

Kane, H. S., Jaremka, L. M., Guichard, A. C., Ford, M. B., Collins, N. L., & Feeney, B. C. (2007). Feeling supported and feeling satisfied: How one partner's attachment style predicts the other partner's relationships experiences. *Journal of Social and Personal Relationships, 24,* 535–555.

Kane, R. (1999). Patterns of arrest in domestic violence encounters: Identifying a police decision-making model. *Journal of Criminal Justice, 27,* 65–80.

Kane, T. A., Staiger, P. K., & Ricciardelli, L. A. (2000). Male domestic violence: Attitudes, aggression, and interpersonal dependency. *Journal of Interpersonal Violence, 15,* 16–29.

Kanin, E. J. (1957). Male aggression in dating-courting relations. *American Journal of Sociology, 63,* 197–204.

Kantor, G., & Straus, M. A. (1990). The "drunken bum" theory of wife beating. In M. A. Straus & R. J. Gelles (Eds.) *Physical Violence in American Families* (pp. 203–224). New Brunswick, NJ: Transaction.

Kantor, G. K., Jasinski, J. L., & Aldarondo, E. (1994). Sociocultural status and incidence of marital violence in Hispanic families. *Violence and Victims, 9,* 207–222.

Kantor, G. K., & Little, L. (2003). Defining the boundaries of child neglect: When does domestic violence equate with parental failure to protect? *Journal of Interpersonal Violence, 18,* 338–355.

Kaplan, S. J., Pelcovitz, D., Salzinger, S., Mandel, F. S., & Weiner, M. (1997). Adolescent physical abuse and suicide attempts. *Journal of the American Academy of Child and Adolescent Psychiatry, 36,* 799–808.

Karch, D. L., Dahlberg, L. L., Patel, N., Davis, T. W., Logan, J. E., et al. (2009, March 20). *Surveillance for violent deaths—national violent death reporting system, 16 states, 2006, Morbidity and Mortality Weekly Report (MWR) Surveillance Summary, 58,* 1–44.

Kasl, C. D. (1990). Female perpetrators of sexual abuse: A feminist view. In M. Hunter (Ed.), *The sexually abused male: Prevalence, impact, and treatment* (pp. 259–274). Lexington, MA: Lexington Books.

Katz, J., Carine, A., & Hilton, A. (2002). Perceived verbal conflict behaviors associated with physical aggression and sexual coercion in dating relationships: A gender-sensitive analysis. *Violence and Victims, 17,* 93–109.

Katz, L. F., & Windecker-Nelson, B. (2006). Domestic violence, emotion coaching, and child adjustment. *Journal of Family Psychology, 20,* 56–67.

Kaufman, J., & Cicchetti, D. (1989). The effects of maltreatment on school-aged children's socioemotional development: Assessments in a day-camp setting. *Developmental Psychology, 25,* 516–524.

Kaukinen, C., & DeMaris, A. (2009). Sexual assault and current mental health: The role of help-seeking and police responses. *Violence Against Women, 15,* 1331–1357.

Kaura, S. A., & Lohman, B. J. (2009). Does acceptability of violence impact the relationship between satisfaction, victimization, and commitment levels in emerging adult dating relationships? *Journal of Family Violence, 24,* 349–359.

Kazdin, A. (2008). Evidence-based treatment and practice. *American Psychologist, 63,* 146–159.

Keel, B. (2007, August 20). "I'm not ashamed." *People,* 89–90.

Keilitz, S. L. (1994). Civil protection orders: A viable justice system tool for deterring domestic violence. *Violence and Victims, 9,* 79–84.

Keilitz, S. L., Davis, C., & Eikeman, H. S. (1998). *Civil protection orders: Victims' views on effectiveness.* Washington, DC: U.S. Department of Justice.

Keller, C. S., Gonzales, A., & Fleuriet, K. J. (2005). Retention of minority participants in clinical research studies. *Western Journal of Nursing Research, 27,* 292–306.

Kelley, S. J. (2002). Child maltreatment in the context of substance abuse. In J. E. B. Myers, L. Berliner, J. Briere, C. T. Hendrix, C. Jenny, & T. A. Reid (Eds.), *The APSAC handbook on child maltreatment* (2nd ed., pp. 105–117). Thousand Oaks, CA: Sage.

Kellogg, N. D., Burge, S., & Taylor, E. R. (2000). Wanted and unwanted sexual experiences and family dysfunction during adolescence. *Journal of Family Violence, 15,* 55–68.

Kelly, C. M., & Williams, I. C. (2007). Providing dementia-specific services to family caregivers: North Carolina's project C.A.R.E. program. *Journal of Applied Gerontology, 26,* 399–412.

Kelly, J. B., & Johnson, M. P. (2008). Differentiation among types of intimate partner violence: Research update and implications for interventions. *Family Court Review, 46,* 476–499.

Kemp, A., Green, B. L., Hovanitz, C., & Rawlings, E. I. (1995). Incidence and correlates of posttraumatic stress disorder in battered women: Shelter and community samples. *Journal of Interpersonal Violence, 10,* 43–55.

Kempe, C. H., & Helfer, R. E. (Eds.). (1972). *Helping the battered child and his family.* Philadelphia: J. B. Lippincott.

Kempe, C. H., Silverman, F. N., Steele, B. F., Droegemueller, W., & Silver, H. K. (1962). The battered child syndrome. *Journal of the American Medical Association, 17,* 17–24.

Kempe, R. S., Cutler, C., & Dean, J. (1980). The infant with failure-to-thrive. In C. H. Kempe & R. E. Helfer (Eds.), *The battered child* (3rd ed., pp. 163–182). Chicago: University of Chicago Press.

Kendall-Tackett, K. A., & Eckenrode, J. (1996). The effects of neglect on academic achievement and disciplinary problems: A developmental perspective. *Child Abuse & Neglect, 20,* 161–169.

Kendall-Tackett, K. A., Williams, L. M., & Finkelhor, D. (1993). Impact of sexual abuse on children: A review and synthesis of recent empirical studies. *Psychological Bulletin, 113,* 164–180.

Kendall-Tackett, K.A. (2009). Taking our family violence work to the next level. *Family & Intimate Partner Violence Quarterly, 1,* 195–196

Kennair, N., & Mellor, D. (2007). Parent abuse: A review. *Child Psychiatry and Human Development, 38,* 203–219.

Kennedy, R. D. (2005). Elder abuse and neglect: The experience, knowledge, and attitudes of primary care physicians. *Family Medicine, 37,* 481–485.

Kent, A., & Waller, G. (2000). Childhood emotional abuse and eating psychopathology. *Clinical Psychology Review, 20,* 887–903.

Kernic, M. A., Holt, V. L., Stoner, J. A., Wolf, M. E., & Rivara, F. P. (2003). Resolution of depression among victims of intimate partner violence: Is cessation of violence enough? *Violence and Victims, 18,* 115–129.

Kernsmith, P. (2005a). Exerting power or striking back: A gendered comparison of motivations for domestic violence perpetration. *Violence and Victims, 20,* 173–185.

Kernsmith, P. (2005b). Treating perpetrators of domestic violence: Gender differences in the applicability of the theory of planned behavior. *Sex Roles, 52,* 757–770.

Kernsmith., P., & Craum, S. W. (2008). Predictors of weapon use in domestic violence incidents reported to law enforcement. *Journal of Family Violence, 23,* 589–596.

Kerzner, B. (2009). Clinical investigation of feeding difficulties in young children: A practical approach. *Clinical Pediatrics, 48,* 960–965.

Kesmodal, U. S., et al. (2010). Lifestyle during pregnancy: Neurodevelopmental effects at 5 years of age. The design and implementation of a prospective follow-up study. *Scandinavian Journal of Public Health, 38,* 208–219.

Kesner, J. E., Julian, T., & McKenry, P. C. (1997). Application of attachment theory to male violence toward female intimates. *Journal of Family Violence, 12,* 211–228.

Kesner, J. E., & McKenry, P. C. (1998). The role of childhood attachment factors in predicting male violence toward female intimates. *Journal of Family Violence, 13,* 417–432.

Kessler, A. (2002). State laws on human research subjects. *APS Observer, 15*(8), 9–10.

Kessler, R. C., Borges, G., & Walters, E. E. (1999). Prevalence of and risk factors for lifetime suicide attempts in the National Comorbidity Survey. *Archives of General Psychiatry, 56,* 617–625.

Kessler, R. C., Coccaro, E. F., Fava, M., Jaeger, S., Jin, R., & Walters, E. (2006). The prevalence and correlates of DSM-IV intermittent explosive disorder in the National Comorbidity Survey replication. *Archives of General Psychiatry, 63,* 669–678.

Kessler, R. C., McGonagle, K. A., Zhao, S., Nelson, C. B., Hughes, M., Eshelman, S., et al. (1994). Lifetime and 12-month prevalence of *DSM-III-R* psychiatric disorders in the United States: Results from the National Comorbidity Survey. *Archives of General Psychiatry, 51,* 8–19.

Kessler, R. C., Molnar, B. E., Feurer, I. D., & Appelbaum, M. (2001). Patterns and mental health predictors of domestic violence in the United States: Results from the National Comorbidity Survey. *International Journal of Law and Psychology, 24,* 487–508.

Kessler, R. C., Sonnega, A., Bromet, E., Hughes, M., & Nelson, C. B. (1995). Posttraumatic stress disorder in the National Comorbidity Survey. *Archives of General Psychiatry, 52,* 1048–1060.

Kethineni, S., & Beichner, D. (2009). A comparison of civil and criminal orders of protection as remedies for domestic violence victims in a Midwestern county. *Journal of Family Violence, 24,* 311–321.

Khan, R., & Cooke, D. J. (2008). Risk factors for severe inter-sibling violence: A preliminary study of youth forensic sample. *Journal of Interpersonal Violence, 23,* 1513–1530.

Khawaja, M., & Tewel-Salem, M. (2004). Agreement between husband and wife reports of domestic violence: Evidence from poor refugee communities in Lebanon. *International Journal of Epidemiology, 33,* 526–533.

Khawaja, M., Linos, N., & El-Roueiheb, Z. (2008). Attitudes of men and women towards wife beating: Findings from Palestinian refugee camps in Jordan. *Journal of Family Violence, 23,* 211–218.

Kids Count. (2008). Kids Count fact sheet. Georgia Family Connections Partnership. Retrieved June 30, 2008, from http://www.gafcp.org/kidscount/kidscountfm.html

Kiecolt-Glaser, J. K. (2009). Psychoneuroimmunology: Psychology's gateway to the biomedical future. *Perspectives on Psychological Science, 4,* 367–369.

Kiely, M., El-Mohandes, A. A., El-Khorazaty, M. N., & Gantz, M. G. (2010). An integrated intervention to reduce intimate partner violence in pregnancy: A randomized controlled trial. *Obstetrics & Gynecology, 115,* 273–283.

Kiever, P. (2005). Multigenerational stress and nuclear family functioning. *Contemporary Family Therapy, 27,* 233–250.

Kilpatrick, D. G., & McCauley, J. (2009, September). *Understanding national rape statistics.* Harrisburg, PA: Vane. Retrieved August 31, 2010, from http://www.vawnet.org

Kim, J. (2008). Type-specific intergenerational transmission of neglectful and physically abusive parenting behaviors among young parents. *Children and Youth Services Review, 31,* 761–767.

Kim, J. Y., & Emery, C. (2003). Marital power, conflict, norm consensus, and marital violence in a nationally representative sample of Korean couples. *Journal of Interpersonal Violence, 18,* 197–219.

Kim, J. Y., McHale, S. M., Crouter, A. C., & Osgood, D. W. (2007). Longitudinal linkages between sibling relationships and adjustment from middle childhood through adolescence. *Developmental Psychology, 43,* 960–973.

Kim, J., Park, S., & Emery, C. R. (2009). The incidence and impact of family violence on mental health among South Korean women: Results of a national survey. *Journal of Family Violence, 24,* 193–202.

Kim, N. S., & Ahn, W. (2002). Clinical psychologists' theory-based representations of mental disorders predict their diagnostic reasoning and memory. *Journal of Experimental Psychology: General, 131,* 451–476.

Kimball, C., & Golding, J. (2004). Adolescent maltreatment: An overview of the research. *The Prevention Researcher, 11*(1), 3–6

Kim-Godwin, Y. S., Clements, C., McCuiston, A. M., & Fox, J. A. (2010). Dating violence among high school students in Southeastern North Carolina. *Journal of School Nursing, 25,* 141–151.

Kimmel, M. S. (2002). "Gender symmetry" in domestic violence: A substantive and methodological research review. *Violence Against Women, 8,* 1332–1363.

Kimmerling, R. E., Alvarez, J., Pavao, J., Kaminiski, A., & Baumrind, N. (2007). Epidemiology and consequences of women's revictimization. *Women's Health Issues, 17,* 101–106.

Kimmerling, R. E., Alvarez, J., Pavao, J., Mack, K. P., Smith, M. W., & Baumrind, N. (2009). Unemployment among women: Examining the relationship of physical and psychological intimate partner violence and posttraumatic stress disorder. *Journal of Interpersonal Violence, 24,* 450–463.

Kinard, E. M. (2001). Recruiting participants for child abuse research: What does it take? *Journal of Family Violence, 16,* 219–236.

Kindler, H. (2008). Developing evidence-based child protection practice: A view from Germany. *Research on Social Work Practice, 18,* 319–324.

Kindness, A., Kim, H., Alder, S., Edwards, A., Parekh, A., & Olson, L. M. (2009). Court compliance as a predictor of postadjudication recidivism for domestic violence offenders. *Journal of Interpersonal Violence, 24,* 1222–1238.

King, A. (2009). Islam, women and violence. *Feminist Theology, 17,* 292–328.

Kinkade, P., Burns, R., & Fuentes, A. I. (2005). Criminalizing attraction: Perceptions of stalking and the stalker. *Crime & Delinquency, 51,* 3–25.

Kirkendall, A., Doueck, H. J., & Saladino, A. (2009). *Research on Social Work Practice, 19,* 434–445.

Kirsch, L. G., Fanniff, A. M., & Becker, J. V. (2010). Treatment of adolescent and adult sex offenders. In J. E. B. Myers (Ed.), *The APSAC handbook on child maltreatment* (3rd ed., pp. 289–306). Thousand Oaks, CA: Sage.

Kiselica, M. S., & Morrill-Richards, M. (2007). Sibling maltreatment: The forgotten abuse. *Journal of Counseling and Development, 85,* 148–161.

Kishor, S., & Johnson, K. (2006). Reproductive health and domestic violence: Are the poorest women uniquely disadvantaged? *Demography, 43,* 293–307.

Kitchener, K. S. (2000). *Foundations of ethical practice, research, and teaching in psychology.* Mahwah, NJ: Lawrence Erlbaum.

Kivela, S. L. (1995). Elder abuse in Finland. In J. I. Kosberg & J. L. Garcia (Eds.), *Elder abuse: International and cross-cultural perspectives* (pp. 31–44). Binghamton, NY: Haworth.

Klein, A. (2004, April/May). To the editor: Missing the point of batterer intervention programs. *Domestic Violence Report, 9,* 49–64.

Klein, A. (2009, June). *Practical implications of current domestic violence research: For law enforcement, prosecutors, and judges* (NCJ Publication No. 225722). Washington, DC: U.S. Department of Justice, National Institute of Justice.

Klein, A., Tobin, T., Salomon, A., & Dubois, J. (2008). *A statewide profile of abuse of older women and the criminal justice response* (NCJ Publication No. 222459). Washington, DC: U.S. Department of Justice.

Klein, A., Wilson, A., Crowe, A., & DeMichele, M. (2005). *Evaluation of the Rhode Island probation specialized domestic violence supervision unit* (NCJ Publication No. 222912). Washington, DC: National Institute of Justice.

Klein, E., Campbell, J. C., Soler, E., & Ghez, M. (1997). *Ending domestic violence: Changing public perceptions/halting the epidemic.* Thousand Oaks, CA: Sage.

Klein, J. (2006). An invisible problem: Everyday violence against girls in schools. *Theoretical Criminology, 10,* 147–177.

Kleinbaum, J. (2005, July 27). Report: Many restraining orders go unserved. *Los Angeles Daily News,* pp. 1, 16.

Klevens, J., & Leeb, R. (2010). Child maltreatment fatalities in children under 5: Findings from the National Violent Death Reporting System. *Child Abuse & Neglect, 34,* 262–266.

Klonsky, E. D., & Moyer, A. (2008). Childhood sexual abuse and non-suicidal self-injury: Meta-analysis. *The British Journal of Psychiatry, 192,* 166–170.

Knapp, J. F., Dowd, M. D., Kennedy, C. S., Stallbaumer-Rouyer, J., & Henderson, D. P. (2006). Evaluation of a curriculum for intimate partner violence screening in a pediatric emergency department. *Pediatrics, 117,* 110–116.

Knauer, N. J. (2009, Winter). LGBT elder law: Toward equity in aging. *Harvard Journal of Law and Gender, 32.*

Knight, C. (2004). Working with survivors of childhood trauma: Implications for clinical supervision. *The Clinical Supervisor, 23,* 81–105.

Knickerbocker, L., Heyman, R. E., Slep, A. M. S., Jouriles, E. N., & McDonald, R. (2007). Co-occurrence of child and partner maltreatment. *European Psychologist, 12,* 36–44.

Knox, M. (2010). On hitting children: A review of corporal punishment in the United States. *Journal of Pediatric Health Care, 24,* 103–107.

Kocot, T., & Goodman, L. (2003). The roles of coping and social support in battered women's mental health. *Violence Against Women, 9,* 323–346.

Koenig, B. L., Kirkpatrick, L. A., & Ketelaar, T. (2007). Misperception of sexual and romantic interest in opposite-sex friendships: Four hypotheses. *Personal Relationships, 14,* 411–429.

Koepsell, J. K., Kernic, M. A., & Holt, V. L. (2006). Factors that influence battered women to leave their abusive relationships. *Violence and Victims, 21,* 131–147.

Kohl, P. L., & Macy, R. J. (2008). Profiles of victimized women among the child welfare population: Implications for targeted child welfare policy and practices. *Journal of Family Violence, 23,* 57–68.

Kolko, D. J., & Feiring, C. (2002). "Explaining why": A closer look at attributions in child abuse victims. *Child Maltreatment, 7,* 5–8.

Kolko, D. J., & Kolko, R. P. (2009). Psychological impact and treatment of child physical abuse. In C. Jenny (Ed.), *Child abuse and neglect: Diagnosis, treatment, and evidence.* Philadelphia: Saunders/Elsevier.

Kolko, D. J., Moser, J., & Hughes, J. (1989). Classroom training in sexual victimization awareness and prevention skills: An extension of the Red Flag/Green Flag People program. *Journal of Family Violence, 4,* 25–45.

Kominkiewicz, F. B. (2004). The relationship of child protection service caseworker discipline-specific education and definition of sibling abuse: An institutional hiring impact study. *Journal of Human Behavior in the Social Environment, 9,* 69–82.

Konetzka, R. T., Stearns, S. C., Konrad, T. R., Magaziner, J., & Zimmerman, S. (2005). Personal care aide turnover in residential care settings: An assessment of ownership, economic, and environmental factors. *Journal of Applied Gerontology, 24,* 87–107.

Korbin, J. E., Anetzberger, G. J., & Austin, C. (1995). The intergenerational cycle of violence in child and elder abuse. *Journal of Elder Abuse & Neglect, 7*(1), 1–15.

Korbin, J. E., Anetzberger, G. J., Thomasson, R., & Austin, C. (1991). Abused elders who seek legal recourse against their adult offspring: Findings from an exploratory study. *Journal of Elder Abuse & Neglect, 3*(3), 1–18.

Korkman, J., Santtila, P., Drzewiecki, T., & Sandnabba, N. K. (2007). Failing to keep it simple: Language use in child sexual abuse interviews with 3-8-year-old children. *Psychology, Crime & Law, 14,* 41–60.

Korn, A. (2009). Jews' and Arabs' perception of inter-group and intra-group date rape. *Journal of Family Violence, 24,* 255–262.

Kosberg, J. I., & Garcia, J. L. (1995a). Common and unique themes on elder abuse from a world-wide perspective. In J. I. Kosberg & J. L. Garcia (Eds.), *Elder abuse: International and cross-cultural perspectives* (pp. 183–197). Binghamton, NY: Haworth.

Kosberg, J. I., & Garcia, J. L. (1995b). Introduction to the book. In J. I. Kosberg & J. L. Garcia (Eds.), *Elder abuse: International and cross-cultural perspectives* (pp. 1–12). Binghamton, NY: Haworth.

Kosberg, J. I., & Nahmiash, D. (1996). Characteristics of victims and perpetrators and milieus of abuse and neglect. In L. A. Baumhover & S. C. Beall (Eds.), *Abuse, neglect, and exploitation of older persons: Strategies for assessment and intervention* (pp. 31–49). Baltimore: Health Professions Press.

Koss, M. P. (1990). The women's mental health research agenda. *American Psychologist, 45,* 374–380.

Koss, M. P. (1992). The underdetection of rape: Methodological choices influence incidence estimates. *Journal of Social Issues, 48*(1), 61–76.

Koss, M. P. (1993). Detecting the scope of rape. *Journal of Interpersonal Violence, 8,* 198–222.

Koss, M. P. (2000). Blame, shame, and community justice: Responses to violence against women. *American Psychologist, 55,* 1332–1343.

Koss, M. P., Abbey, A., Campbell, R., Cook, S., Norris, J., Testa, M., Ullman, S., West, C., & White, J. (2007). Revising the SES: A collaborative process to improve assessment of sexual aggression and victimization. *Psychology of Women Quarterly, 31,* 357–370.

Koss, M. P., Gidycz, C. A., & Wisniewski, N. (1987). The scope of rape: Incidence and prevalence of sexual aggression and victimization in a national sample of higher education students. *Journal of Consulting and Clinical Psychology, 55,* 162–170.

Koss, M. P., Goodman, L. A., Browne, A., Fitzgerald, L. F., Puryear-Keita, G., & Russo, N. F. (1994). *Male violence against women at home, at work, and in the community.* Washington, DC: American Psychological Association.

Kosslyn, S. M., Cacioppo, J. T., Davidson, R. J., Hugdahl, K., Lovallo, W. R., Spiegel, D., et al. (2002). Bridging psychology and biology: The analysis of individuals in groups. *American Psychologist, 57,* 341–351.

Kotch, J. B., et al. (2008). Importance of early neglect for childhood aggression. *Pediatrics, 121,* 725–732.

Kovan, N. M., Chung, A. L., & Sroufe, L. A. (2009). The intergenerational continuity of observed early parenting: A prospective, longitudinal study. *Developmental Psychology, 45,* 1205–1213.

Koverola, C., Murtaugh, C. A., Connors, K. M., Reeves, G., & Papas, M. A. (2007). Children exposed to intra-family violence: Predictors of attrition and retention in treatment. *Journal of Aggression, Maltreatment & Trauma, 14,* 19–42.

Kracke, K., & Cohen, E. P. (2008). The Safe Start initiative: Building and disseminating knowledge to support children exposed to violence. *Journal of Emotional Abuse, 8,* 155–174.

Kracke, K., & Hahn, H. (2008). The nature and extent of childhood exposure to violence: What we know, why we don't know more, and why it matters. *Journal of Emotional Abuse, 8,* 29–49.

Kraemer, K. L. (2007). The cost-effectiveness and cost-benefit of screening and brief intervention for unhealthy alcohol use in medical settings. *Substance Abuse, 28,* 67–77.

Kranzler, H. R., & Gage, A. (2008). Acamprosate efficacy in alcohol-dependent patients: Summary of results from three pivotal trials. *American Journal on Addictions, 17,* 70–76.

Krienert, J. L., & Fleisher, M. S. (2005). "It ain't happening here": Working to understand prison rape. *The Criminologist, November/December, 30,* 2–6.

Krishnan, S. P., Hilbert, J. C., McNeil, K., & Newman, I. (2004). From respite to transition: Women's use of domestic violence shelters in rural New Mexico. *Journal of Family Violence, 19,* 165–173.

Krishnan, S. P., Hilbert, J. C., & Pase, M. (2001). An examination of intimate partner violence in rural communities: Results from a hospital emergency department study from Southwest United States. *Family and Community Health, 24*(1), 1–14.

Krohn, S. (2010, May/June). Nonprofits fight financial abuse. *Victimization of the Elderly and Disabled, 13,* 1–2, 13–14.

Kropp, P. R., Hart, S. D., Webster, C. W., & Eaves, D. (1995). *Manual for the Spousal Assault Risk Assessment Guide* (2nd ed.). Vancouver, BC, Canada: Institute of Family Violence.

Krueger, R. F., Moffitt, T. E., Caspi, A., Bleske, A., & Silva, P. A. (1998). Assortive mating for antisocial behavior: Developmental and methodological implications. *Behavior Genetics, 23,* 173–186.

Krugman, S. D., Witting, M. D., Furuno, J. P., Hirshon, J. M., Limcangco, R., Perisse, A. R., et al. (2004). Perceptions of help resources for victims of intimate partner violence. *Journal of Interpersonal Violence, 19,* 766–777.

Kruttschnitt, C., & Carbone-Lopez, K. (2006). Moving beyond the stereotypes: Women's subjective accounts of their violent crime. *Criminology, 44,* 321–351.

Kruttschnitt, C., & Dornfeld, M. (1992). Will they tell? Assessing preadolescents' reports of family violence. *Journal of Research in Crime and Delinquency, 29,* 136–147.

Kubrin, C., & Weitzer, R. (2003). New direction in social disorganization theory. *Journal of Research in Crime and Delinquency, 40,* 374–402.

Kuehnle, K., & Sullivan, A. (2003). Gay and lesbian victimization: Reporting factors in domestic violence and bias incidents. *Criminal Justice and Behavior, 30,* 85–96.

Kugel, C., Retzlaff, C., Hopfer, S., Lawson, D. M., Daley, E., Drewes, C., & Freedman, S. (2009). *Familias con Voz:* Community survey results from an intimate partner violence (IPV) prevention projects with migrant workers. *Journal of Family Violence, 24,* 649–660.

Kuleshnyk, I. (1984). The Stockholm syndrome: Toward an understanding. *Social Action and the Law, 10*(2), 37–42.

Kulwicki, A. D. (2002). The practice of honor crimes: A glimpse of domestic violence in the Arab world. *Issues in Mental Health Nursing, 23,* 77–87.

Kurdek, L. A. (2008). A general model of relationship commitment: Evidence from same-sex partners. *Personal Relationships, 15,* 391–405.

Kurlychek, M. C., & Johnson, B. D. (2004). The juvenile penalty and young adult sentencing outcomes in criminal court. *Criminology, 42,* 485–515.

Kurrle, S. E., & Naughtin, G. (2008). An overview of elder abuse and neglect in Australia. *Journal of Elder Abuse & Neglect, 20,* 108–125.

Kurtz, P. D., Gaudin, J. M., Wodarski, J. S., & Howing, P. T. (1993). Maltreatment and the school-aged child: School performance consequences. *Child Abuse & Neglect, 17,* 581–589.

Kury, H., & Ferdinand, T. (1997). The victim's experience and fear of crime. *International Review of Victimology, 5,* 93–140.

Kury, H., Obergfell-Fuchs, J., & Woessner, G. (2004). The extent of family violence in Europe. *Violence Against Women, 10,* 749–769.

Kurz, D. (1989). Social science perspective on wife abuse. *Gender & Society, 3,* 489–505.

Kuzuya, M., Masuda, Y., Hirakawa, Y., Iwata, M., Enoki, H., Hasegawa, J., et al. (2006). Day care service use is associated with lower mortality in community-dwelling frail older people. *Journal of the American Geriatric Society, 54,* 1364–1371.

Laakso, J. H., & Drevdahl, D. J. (2006). Women, abuse, and the welfare bureaucracy. *Affilia, 21,* 84–96.

La Bash, H. A. J., Vogt, D. S., King, L. A., & King, D. W. (2009). Deployment stressors of the Iraq war. *Journal of Interpersonal Violence, 24,* 231–258.

LaBell, L. S. (1979). Wife abuse: A sociological study of battered women and their mates. *Victimology: An International Journal, 4,* 257–267.

Labriola, M., Rempel, M., & Davis, R. C. (2005). *Testing the effectiveness of batterer programs and judicial monitoring.* New York: New York Unified Court System, Center for Court Innovation.

Lacayo, R., Barovick, H., Cloud, J., & Duffy, M. (1998, October 26). The new gay struggle. *Time, 152,* 32–36.

Lachs, M. S., & Pillemer, K. A. (1995). Abuse and neglect of elderly persons. *New England Journal of Medicine, 332,* 437–443.

Lachs, M. S., & Pillemer, K. A. (2004). Elder abuse. *Lancet, 364,* 1263–1272.

Lackie, L., & de Man, A. F. (1997). Correlates of sexual aggression among male university students. *Sex Roles, 37,* 451–457.

Laffaye, C., Kennedy, C., & Stein, M. (2003). Post-traumatic stress disorder and health-related quality of life in female victims of intimate partner violence. *Violence and Victims, 18,* 227–238.

Lamb, M. E. (2010). How do fathers affect children's development? Let me count the ways. In M. E. Lamb (Ed.), *The role of father in child development* (5th ed., pp. 1–26). New York: John Wiley.

Lambert, L. C., & Firestone, J. M. (2000). Economic context and multiple abuse techniques. *Violence Against Women, 6,* 49–67.

Landenburger, K. M. (1998). The dynamics of leaving and recovering from an abusive relationship. *Journal of Obstetric, Gynecologic, and Neonatal Nursing, 27,* 684–691.

Landolt, M. A., & Dutton, D. (1997). Power and personality: An analysis of gay male intimate abuse. *Sex Roles, 37,* 333–359.

Landy, C. K., Sword, W., & Valaitis, R. (2009). The experiences of socioeconomically disadvantaged postpartum women in the first 4 weeks at home. *Qualitative Health Research, 19,* 194–206.

Lane, G., & Russell, T. (1989). Second-order systemic work with violent couples. In P. L. Caesar & L. K. Hamberger (Eds.), *Treating men who batter* (pp. 134–162). New York: Springer.

Lang, A. J., Gartstein, M. A., Rodgers, C. S., & Lebeck, M. M. (2010). The impact of maternal childhood abuse on parenting and infant temperament. *Journal of Child & Adolescent Psychiatric Nursing, 23,* 100–110.

Langford, L., Isaac, N. E., & Kabat, S. (1998). Homicides related to intimate partner violence in Massachusetts. *Homicide Studies, 2,* 353–377.

Langhinrichsen-Rohling, J. (2006). An examination of sheltered battered women's perpetration of stalking and other unwanted pursuit behaviors. *Violence and Victims, 21,* 579–595.

Langhinrichsen-Rohling, J. (2010). Controversies involving gender and intimate partner violence in the United States. *Sex Roles, 62,* 179–193.

Langhinrichsen-Rohling, J., Neidig, P., & Thorn, G. (1995). Violent marriages: Gender differences in levels of current violence and past abuse. *Journal of Family Violence, 10,* 159–176.

Langhinrichsen-Rohling, J., Palarea, R. E., Cohen, J., & Rohling, M. L. (2000). Breaking up is hard to do: Unwanted pursuit behaviors following the dissolution of a romantic relationship. *Violence and Victims, 15,* 73–89.

Langhinrichsen-Rohling, J., Smutzler, N., & Vivian, D. (1994). Positivity in marriage: The role of discord and physical aggression against wives. *Journal of Marriage and the Family, 56,* 69–79.

Lanier, C. A., & Green, B. A. (2006). Principal component analysis of the college data rape Attitude Scale (CDRAS): An instrument for the evaluation of date rape programs. *Journal of Aggression, Maltreatment & Trauma, 13,* 79–93.

Lanning, K. V. (2002). Criminal investigation of sexual victimization of children. In J. E. B. Myers, L. Berliner, J. Briere, C. T. Hendrix, C. Jenny, & T. A. Reid (Eds.), *The APSAC handbook on child maltreatment* (2nd ed., pp. 329–347). Thousand Oaks, CA: Sage.

Lansford, J. E., Dodge, K. A., Petit, G. S., & Bates, J. E. (2010). Does physical abuse in early childhood predict substance use in adolescence and early adulthood? *Child Maltreatment, 15,* 190–194.

Lansford, J. E., Malone, P. S., et al. (2006). Developmental trajectories of externalizing and internalizing behavior: Factors underlying resilience in physically abused children. *Development and Psychopathology, 18,* 35–55.

Largen, M. A. (1987). A decade of change in the rape reform movement. *Response, 10*(2), 4–9.

La Roche, M., & Christoper, M. S. (2008). Culture and empirically supported treatments: On the road to a collision? *Culture and Psychology, 14,* 333–356.

Lash, S. J., Copenhaver, M. M., & Eisler, R. M. (1998). Masculine gender-role stress and substance abuse among substance-dependent males. *Journal of Gender, Culture, and Health, 3,* 183–191.

Lash, S. J., Eisler, R. M., & Schulman, R. S. (1990). Cardiovascular reactivity to stress in men: Effects of masculine gender-role stress appraisal and masculine performance challenge. *Behavior Modification, 14,* 3–20.

Latta, R. E., & Goodman, L. A. (2005). Considering the interplay of cultural context and service provision in intimate partner violence. *Violence Against Women, 11,* 1441–1464.

Laumann, E. O., Leitsch, S. A., & Waite, L. J. (2008). Elder mistreatment in the United States: Prevalence estimate from a nationally representative study. *Journals of Gerontology: Series B, Psychological Sciences and Social Sciences, 63*(4), S248–S254.

Launius, M. H., & Jensen, B. L. (1987). Interpersonal problem-solving skills in battered, counseling, and control women. *Journal of Family Violence, 2,* 151–162.

Lauritsen, J. L., & White, N. A. (2001). Putting violence in its place: The influence of race, ethnicity, gender, and place on the risk for violence. *Criminology & Public Policy, 1,* 37–59.

Lauzen, M. M., & Dozier, D. M. (2005). Maintaining the double standard: Portrayals of age and gender in popular films. *Sex Roles, 52,* 437–446.

Laviola, M. (1992). Effects of older brother–young sister incest: A study of the dynamics of 17 cases. *Child Abuse & Neglect, 16*, 409–421.

LaViolette, A. D., & Barnett, O. W. (2000). *It could happen to anyone: Why battered women stay* (2nd ed.). Thousand Oaks, CA: Sage.

LaViolette, A. D., Barnett, O. W., & Miller, C. L. (1984, August). *A classification of wife abusers on the Bem Sex-Role Inventory.* Paper presented at the Second Family Violence Research Conference, Durham, NH.

Lavis, V., Horrocks, C., Kelly, N., & Barker, V. (2005). Domestic violence and health care: Opening Pandora's box—challenges and dilemmas. *Feminism & Psychology, 15*, 441–460.

Lavoie, F., Vezina, L., Piche, C., & Boivin, M. (1995). Evaluation of a prevention program for violence in teen dating relationships. *Journal of Interpersonal Violence, 10*, 516–524.

Lawson, L. (2008). Female sex offenders' relationship experiences. *Violence and Victims, 23*, 331–341.

Law Enforcement Research Center. (1996). *Police and people with disabilities.* Minneapolis, MN: Author.

Lawrence, E., & Bradbury, T. N. (2001). Physical aggression and marital dysfunction: A longitudinal analysis. *Journal of Family Psychology, 15*, 135–154.

Lawrence, E., Yoon, J., Langer, A., & Ro, E. (2009). Is psychological aggression as detrimental as physical aggression? The independent effects of psychological aggression. *Violence and Victims, 24*, 20–35.

Lawson, D. M. (2008). Attachment, interpersonal problems, and family of origin functioning: Differences between partner violent and nonpartner violent men. *Psychology of Men & Masculinity, 9*, 90–105.

Lawson, D. M., Dawson, T. E., Kieffer, K. M., Perez, L. M., Burke, J., & Kier, F. J. (2001). An integrated feminist/ cognitive-behavioral and psychodynamic group treatment for men who abuse partners. *Psychology of Men & Masculinity, 2*(1), 86–99.

Lawson, D. M., Weber, D., Beckner, H. M., Robinson, L., Marsh, N., & Cool, A. (2003). Men who use violence: Intimate violence versus non-intimate violence profiles. *Violence and Victims, 18*, 259–277.

Lawson, L. (2008). Female sex offenders' relationship experiences. *Violence and Victims, 23*, 331–343.

Leander, L. (2010). Police interviews with child sexual abuse victims: Patterns of reporting, avoidance, and denial. *Child Abuse & Neglect, 34*, 192–205.

Leclerc, B., Proulx, J., & Beauregard, E. (2009). Examining the modus operandi of sexual offenders against children and its practical implications. *Aggression and Violent Behavior, 14*, 8–12.

Lee, B-J. (2007). Moderating effects of religious/spiritual coping in the relation between perceived stress and psychological well-being. *Pastoral Psychology, 55*, 751–759.

Lee, J., Busch, N. B., Kim, J., & Lim, H. (2007). Attitudes toward date rape among university students in South Korea. *Sex Roles, 57*, 641–649.

Lee, J. K. P., Jackson, H. J., Pattison, P., & Ward, T. (2002). Developmental risk factors for sexual offending. *Child Abuse & Neglect, 26*, 73–92.

Lee, M. Y., Sebold, J., & Uken, A. (2003). *Solution-focused treatment with domestic violence offenders: Accountability for change.* New York: Oxford University Press.

Lee, M. Y., Uken, A., & Sebold, J. (2007). Role of self-determined goals in predicting recidivism in domestic violence offenders. *Research on Social Work Practice, 17*, 30–41.

Lee, Y-Y., Kam, C. C-S., & Bond, M. H. (2007). Predicting emotional reactions after being harmed by another. *Asian Journal of Social Psychology, 10*, 85–92.

Lee, Y., & Hadeed, L. (2009). Intimate partner violence among Asian immigrant communities. *Trauma, Violence, & Abuse, 10*, 143–170.

Lee-Baggley, D., Preece, M., & DeLongis, A. (2005). Coping with interpersonal stress: Role of big five traits. *Journal of Personality, 73*, 1141–1180

Leeder, E. (1988). Enmeshed in pain: Counseling the lesbian battering couple. *Women & Therapy, 7*(1), 81–99.

Leff, S. (2005). Gaining a better understanding of peer group contributions to dating aggression—Implications for prevention and programming: Comment on Kinsfogel and Grych (2004). *Journal of Family Psychology, 18*, 516–518.

Legal: Terms, definitions & dictionary. (2010). Retrieved from http://www.USLegal.com, 2010

Legislation advances in Congress keeping grant system unchanged. (2007, July 16). *Criminal Justice Newsletter*, pp. 2–3.

Leifer, M., Shapiro, J. P., & Kassem, L. (1993). The impact of maternal history and behavior upon foster placement and adjustment in sexually abused girls. *Child Abuse & Neglect, 17*, 755–766.

Leisenning, A. (2008). Controversies surrounding mandatory arrest policies and the police response to intimate partner violence. *Sociology Compass, 2*, 451–466.

Lempert, L. B. (1996). Women's strategies for survival: Developing agency in abusive relationships. *Journal of Family Violence, 11,* 269–289.

Leonard, E. D. (2001). Convicted survivors: Comparing and describing California's battered women inmates. *The Prison Journal, 81,* 73–86.

Leonard, I. M. (2003). The historiography of American violence. *Homicide Studies, 7,* 99–153.

Leonard, J. (2001, September 13). Sheriff's sergeant accused of child abuse. *Los Angeles Times,* p. B1.

Leonard, K. E., & Senchak, M. (1993). Alcohol and premarital aggression among newlywed couples. *Journal of Studies on Alcohol, 11,* 96–108.

Lerner, C. F., & Kennedy, L. T. (2000). Stay-leave decision making in battered women: Trauma, coping and self-efficacy. *Cognitive Therapy and Research, 24,* 215–232.

Lesch, K. P., & Merschdorf, U. (2000). Impulsivity, aggression, and serotonin: A molecular psychobiological perspective. *Behavioral Sciences and the Law, 18,* 581–604.

Lesher, M. (2009, February/March). Justice for child victims of incest. *Domestic Violence Report, 33,* 42–48.

Leslie, L. K., et al. (2005). The physical, developmental, and mental health needs of young children in child welfare by initial placement type. *Journal of Developmental and Behavioral Pediatrics, 26,* 1–4.

Lester, B. M., LaGasse, L. L., Shrankaran, S., Bada, H. S., Bauer, C. R., Lin, R., et al. (2010). Prenatal cocaine exposure related to cortisol stress reactivity in 11-year-old children. *The Journal of Pediatrics, 157,* 288–295.

Letarte, M-J., Normandeau, S., & Allard, J. (2010). Effectiveness of a parent training program "Incredible Years" in a child protection service. *Child Abuse & Neglect, 34,* 253–261.

Letellier, P. (1996). Twin epidemics: Domestic violence and HIV infection among gay and bisexual men. In C. M. Renzetti & C. H. Miley (Eds.), *Violence in gay and lesbian domestic partnerships* (pp. 69–82). Binghamton, NY: Haworth.

Letiecq, B. L., Bailey, S. J., & Porterfield, F. (2008). We have no rights, we get no help. *Journal of Family Issues, 29,* 995–1012.

Letourneau, E. J., & Levenson, J. S. (2010). Preventing sexual abuse: Community protection policies and practice. In J. E. B. Myers (Ed.), *The APSAC handbook on child maltreatment* (3rd ed., pp. 307–321). Thousand Oaks, CA: Sage.

Leung, C., Tsang, S., Heung, K., & Yiu, I. (2009). Effectiveness of Parent-Child Interaction Therapy (PCIT) among Chinese families. *Research on Social Work Practice, 19,* 304–313.

Leung, P., & Cheung, M. (2008). A prevalence study on partner abuse in six Asian American ethnic groups in the USA. *International Social Work, 51,* 635–649.

Leung, P., Curtis, R. L., Jr., & Mapp, S. C. (2010). Incidences of sexual contacts of children: Impacts of family characteristics and family structure. *Children and Youth Services Review, 32,* 650–656.

LeVay, S., & Hamer, D. H. (1994, May). Evidence for a biological influence in male homosexuality. *Scientific American, 270,* 20–25.

Levendosky, A. A., Huth-Bocks, A. C., Semel, M. A., & Shapiro, D. L. (2002). Trauma symptoms in preschool-age children exposed to domestic violence. *Journal of Interpersonal Violence, 17,* 150–164.

Levendosky, A. A., Lynch, S. M., & Graham-Bermann, S. A. (2000). Mothers' perceptions of the impact of woman abuse on their parenting. *Violence Against Women, 6,* 247–271.

Leventhal, J. M., Murphy, J. L., & Asnes, A. G. (2010). Evaluations of child sexual abuse: Recognition of overt and latent family concerns. *Child Abuse & Neglect, 34,* 289–295.

Levesque, R. J. R. (2001). *Culture and family violence.* Washington, DC: American Psychological Association.

Levin, R. (1999). Participatory evaluators. *Violence Against Women, 5,* 1213–1227.

Levinson, D. (1989). *Family violence in cross-cultural perspective.* Newbury Park, CA: Sage.

Levinson, D. R. (2008, September). Trends in nursing home deficiencies and complaints (Publication Number, OEI-02–08–00140). Washington, DC: U.S. Department of Health & Human Services.

Levitt, H. M., & Ware, K. N. (2006). Religious leaders' perspectives on marriage, divorce, and intimate partner violence. *Psychology of Women Quarterly, 30,* 212–222.

Levitt, N. (2002, June). APA tells the Senate why we need more geropsychologists. *APA Monitor on Psychology, 33,* 17.

Lev-Wiesel, R., Daphna-Tekoah, S., & Hallak, M. (2009). Childhood sexual abuse as a predictor of birth-related posttraumatic stress and postpartum stress. *Child Abuse & Neglect, 33,* 877–887.

Levy, B. (1991). *Dating violence: Young women in danger.* Seattle: Seal.

Levy, B. (1997). Common stereotypes contribute to invisibility of battered lesbians. *Update* (Newsletter of the Statewide California Coalition for Battered Women), *3*(1), 1, 6.

Levy, D. L. (2009). Lending a hand one child at a time: The Children's Rights Council's child access and transfer centers. *The American Journal of Family Therapy, 37,* 396–413.

Lewis, C. S., Griffing, S., Chu, M., Sage, R. E., Madry, L., & Primm, B. J. (2006). Coping and violence exposure as predictors of psychological functioning in domestic violence survivors. *Violence Against Women, 12,* 340–354.

Lewis, C. S., Jospitre, T., Griffing, S., Chu, M., Sage, R. E., Madry, L., et al. (2006). Childhood maltreatment, familial violence, and retraumatization: Assessing inner-city battered women. *Journal of Emotional Abuse, 6,* 47–67.

Lewis, T. (2010, March 21). Rethinking sex offender laws for youths and 'sexting.' *The New York Times* (Reprinted in the *Daily News,* p. A12).

Lidz, C. W., Banks, S., Simon, L., Schubert, C., & Mulvey, E. P. (2007). Violence and mental illness: A new analytic approach. *Law and Human Behavior, 31,* 23–31.

Lien, L., Jacquet, S. E., Lewis, C. M., Cole, P. R., & Williams, B. B. (2001). With the best of intentions: Family violence option and abused women's needs. *Violence Against Women, 7,* 193–210.

Light, D., & Monk-Turner, E. (2009). Circumstances surrounding male sexual assault and rape. *Journal of Interpersonal Violence, 24,* 1849–1858.

Lilith, R. (2001). Reconsidering the abuse that dare not speak its name: A criticism of recent legal scholarship regarding same-gendered domestic violence. *Michigan Journal of Gender & Law, 7,* 181–219.

Lilly, M. M., & Graham-Berman, S. A. (2009). Ethnicity and risk for symptoms of posttraumatic stress following intimate partner violence. *Journal of Interpersonal Violence, 24,* 3–19.

Lincoln, Y., & Guba, E. (1985). *Naturalistic inquiry.* Beverly Hills, CA: Sage.

Lindgren, A. S., Parkhill, M. R., George, W. H., & Hendershot, C. S. (2008). Gender differences in perceptions of sexual intent: A qualitative review and integration. *Psychology of Women Quarterly, 32,* 423–439.

Lindgren, A. S., & Renck, B. (2008). 'It is still so deep-seated, the fear': Psychological stress reactions as a consequence of intimate partner violence. *Journal of Psychiatric and Mental Health Nursing, 15,* 219–228.

Lindhorst, T., & Meyers, M., & Casey, E. (2008). Screening for domestic violence in public welfare offices: An analysis of case manager and client interactions. *Violence Against Women, 14,* 5–28.

Lindhorst, T., & Tajima, E. (2008). Reconceptualizing and operationalizing context in survey research on intimate partner violence. *Journal of Interpersonal Violence, 23,* 362–388.

Litrownick, A. J., et al. (2005). Measuring the severity of child maltreatment. *Child Abuse & Neglect, 29,* 553–573.

Littel, K., Malefyt, M. B., Walker, A., Buel, S. M., & Tucker, D. D. (1998). *Assessing justice system response to violence against women: A tool for law enforcement, prosecution and the courts to use in developing effective responses.* Retrieved from http://www.vaw.umn.edu/documents/promise/pplaw/pplaw.html

Littleton, H., Axsom, D., & Grills-Taqueschel, A. (2009). Sexual assault victims' acknowledgment status and revictimization risk. *Psychology of Women Quarterly, 33,* 34–42.

Liu, R. T. (2010). Early life stressors and genetic influences on the development of bipolar disorder: The roles of childhood abuse and brain-derived neurotrophic factor. *Child Abuse & Neglect, 34,* 516–572.

Livingston, J. A., Hequembourg, A., Testa, M., & VanZile-Tamsen, C. (2007). Unique aspects of adolescent sexual victimization experiences. *Psychology of Women Quarterly, 31,* 331–343.

Livingstrong.com (2009). Retrieved from http://www.livingstrong.com/article/12483-age-consensual-sex/

Lloyd, S. A. (1988, November). *Conflict and violence in marriage.* Paper presented at the annual meeting of the National Council on Family Relations, Philadelphia.

Lloyd, S. A. (1991). The dark side of courtship: Violence and sexual exploitation. *Family Relations, 40,* 14–20.

Lobach, K. S. (2008). Child and adolescent health. *Journal of Urban Health, 85,* 807–811.

Locke, H. J., & Wallace, K. M. (1959). Short Marital Adjustment and Prediction Tests: Their reliability and validity. *Journal of Marriage and Family Living, 21,* 251–255.

Lockhart, L. L., White, B. W., Causby, V., & Isaac, A. (1994). Letting out the secret: Violence in lesbian relationships. *Journal of Interpersonal Violence, 9,* 469–492.

Loeber, R., & Farrington, D. P. (1997). Strategies and yields of longitudinal studies on antisocial behavior. In D. M. Stoff, J. Breiling, & J. D. Maser (Eds.), *Handbook of antisocial behavior* (pp. 125–139). New York: John Wiley.

Loftus, E. (1993). The reality of repressed memories. *American Psychologist, 48,* 518–537.

Loftus, E. F. (2005). Planting misinformation in the human mind: A 30-year investigation of the malleability of memory. *Learning & Memory, 12,* 361–366.

Loftus, E., & Ketcham, K. (1991). *Witness for the defense: The accused, the eyewitness, and the expert who puts memory on trial.* New York: St. Martin's.

Logan, T., & Cole, J. (2007). The impact of partner stalking on mental health and protective order outcomes over time. *Violence and Victims, 22,* 546–562.

Logan, T., Shannon, L., & Cole, J. (2007). Stalking victimization in the context of intimate partner violence. *Violence and Victims, 22,* 669–683.

Logan, T., Shannon, L., Cole, J., & Swanberg, J. (2007). Partner stalking and implications for women's employment. *Journal of Interpersonal Violence, 22,* 268–291.

Logan, T., & Walker, R. (2009a). Civil protection order outcomes. *Journal of Interpersonal Violence, 24,* 675–692.

Logan, T., & Walker, R. (2009b). Partner stalking: Psychological dominance or "business as usual"? *Trauma, Violence, & Abuse, 10,* 247–270.

Logsdon, M. C., Wisner, K., Billings, D. M., & Shanahan, B. (2006). Raising the awareness of primary care providers about postpartum depression. *Issues in Mental Health Nursing, 27,* 59–73.

Loh, C., Orchowski, L. M., Gidycz, C. A., & Elizaga, R. A. (2007). Socialization and sexual aggression in college men: The role of observational influence in detecting risk cues. *Psychology of Men & Masculinity, 8,* 129–144.

Lohr, B. A., Adams, H. E., & Davis, M. J. (1997). Sexual arousal to erotic and aggressive stimuli in sexually coercive and noncoercive men. *Journal of Abnormal Psychology, 106,* 230–242.

London, K., Bruck, M., Wright, D. B., & Ceci, S. J. (2008). Review of the contemporary literature on how children report sexual abuse to others: Findings, methodological issues, and implications for forensic interviews. *Memory, 16,* 29–47.

London, M. (2003, May/June). Crafting support services for older women. *Victimization of the Elderly and Disabled, 6,* 5–6.

Long, N. (2008). Editorial: Closing the gap between research and practice—The importance of practitioner training. *Clinical Child Psychology and Psychiatry, 13,* 187–190.

Lonsway, K. A., & Conis, P. (2003, October). Officer domestic violence. *Law and Order, 51,* 132–134.

Lopez, P. A., George, W. H., & Davis, K. C. (2007). Do hostile sexual beliefs affect men's perceptions of sexual-interest messages? *Violence and Victims, 22,* 226–242.

Lorenz, L., Davis, B., Ramakrishnan, K., & Chun, S. (2008). Do state domestic violence laws protect teens? *Family & Intimate Partner Violence Quarterly, 1,* 71–79.

Loring, M. T. (1994). *Emotional abuse.* Lexington, MA: Lexington.

Loring, M. T., Smith, R. W., & Bolden, T. (1997). Distal coercion: Case studies. *Psychology: A Journal of Human Behavior, 34,* 10–14.

Los Angeles Department of Probation. (1998). *Los Angeles Department of Probation approved batterers' programs.* Los Angeles: Author.

Los Angeles Lawyer. (2007, October). Retrieved from http://www.lacba.org/lalawyer

LLoseke, D. R. (2003). *Thinking about social problems: An introduction to constructionist perspectives* (2nd ed.). New York: Aldine de Gruyter.

Loseke, D. R., & Kurz, D. (2005). Men's violence toward women is the serious social problem. In D. R. Loseke, R. J. Gelles, & M. M. Cavanaugh (Eds.), *Current controversies on family violence* (2nd ed., pp. 79–95). Thousand Oaks, CA: Sage.

Lount, M., & Hargie, O. (1997). The priest as counselor: An investigation of critical incidents in the pastoral work of Catholic priests. *Counseling Psychology Quarterly, 10,* 246–258.

Lowenberg, K., & Fulcher, J. (2008). Thoughts on designing domestic violence laws and services to protect teens. *Family & Intimate Partner Violence Quarterly, 1,* 115–125.

Lowenstein, A. (2009). Elder abuse and neglect—"old phenomenon": New directions for research, legislation, and service developments. *Journal of Elder Abuse & Neglect, 21,* 278–287.

Lucente, S. W., Fals-Stewart, W., Richards, H. J., & Goscha, J. (2001). Factor structure and reliability of the Revised Conflict Tactics Scales for incarcerated female substance abusers. *Journal of Family Violence, 16,* 437–450.

Luke, N., Schuler, S. R., Mai, B. T. T., Thien, P. V., & Minh, T. H. (2007). Exploring couple attributes and attitudes and marital violence in Vietnam. *Violence Against Women, 13,* 5–27.

Luna-Firebaugh, A. M. (2006). Violence against American Indian women and the Services-Training-Officers-Prosecutors violence against Indian women (STOP VAIW) program. *Violence Against Women, 12,* 125–136.

Lundhal, B., & Harris, N. (2006). Delivering parent training to families at risk to abuse: Lessons from three meta-analyses. *APSAC Advisor, 18*(3), 7–11.

Lyden, M. (2007). Assessment of sexual consent capacity. *Sexuality and Disability, 25,* 3–20.

Lynam, D. R., Loeber, R., & Stouthamer-Loeber, M. (2008). The stability of psychopathy from adolescence into adulthood: The search for moderators. *Criminal Justice and Behavior, 35,* 228–243.

Lynch, S. M., & Graham-Bermann, S. A. (2000). Woman abuse and self-affirmation. *Violence Against Women, 6,* 178–197.

Lyon, E. (2010). The spiritual implications of interpersonal abuse: Speaking of the soul. *Pastoral Psychology, 59,* 233–247.

Lysova, A., & Douglas, E. (2008). Intimate partner violence among male and female Russian university students. *Journal of Interpersonal Violence, 23,* 1579–1599.

Mace, N. L. (1981). *The 36-hour day: A family guide to caring for persons with Alzheimer's disease, related dementing illness, and memory loss in later life.* Baltimore: Johns Hopkins University Press.

Macfie, J., Cicchetti, D., & Toth, S. L. (2001). The development of dissociation in maltreated preschool-aged children. *Development and Psychopathology, 13,* 233–254.

Mackey, A. L., Fromuth, M. E., & Kelly, D. B. (2009). The association of sibling relationship and abuse with later psychological adjustment. *Journal of Interpersonal Violence, 25,* 955–968.

Mackey, A. L., Lynnes, M. D., Nichols, D., & Temple, V. A. (2009). Fostering independence in health-promoting exercise. *Journal of Intellectual Disabilities, 13,* 143–159.

MacMillan, H. L, Wathen, C. N,. Barlow, J., Fergusson, D. M., Leventhal, J. M, & Taussig, H. N. (2009). Interventions to prevent child maltreatment and associated impairments. *Lancet, 373,* 250–266.

MacMillan, H. L, Wathen, C. N., Jamieson, E., Boyle, M., McNutt, L., Worster, A., Lent, B., & Webb, M. (2006). Approaches to screening for intimate partner violence in health care settings. *Journal of the American Medical Association, 296,* 530–536.

Macmillan, R., & Gartner, R. (1999). When she brings home the bacon: Labor-force participation and the risk of spousal violence against women. *Journal of Marriage & the Family, 61,* 947–958.

Macmillan, R., & Kruttschnitt, C. (2004). *The patterns of violence against women: Risk factors and consequences, final report* (NCJ Publication No. 208346). Washington, DC: National Institute of Justice.

Macvaugh, G. S., III. (2005). *Outcomes of court intervention and diversionary program for domestically violent offenders* (AAT 3143323). Proquest Digital Dissertations, DAI-B 65/08, p. 4294, Feb 2005.

Macy, T. J., Nurius, P. S., & Norris, J. (2007). Latent profiles among sexual assault survivors: Understanding survivors and their assault experiences. *Journal of Interpersonal Violence, 22,* 520–542.

Madsen, M. D., & Abell, N. (2010). Trauma resilience scale: Validation of protective factors associated with adaptation following violence. *Research on Social Work Practice, 20,* 223–233.

Magdol, L., Moffitt, T. E., Caspi, A., Newman, D. L., Fagan, J. A., & Silva, P. A. (1997). Gender differences in partner violence in a birth cohort of 21-year-olds: Bridging the gap between clinical and epidemiological approaches. *Journal of Consulting and Clinical Psychology, 65,* 68–78.

Magdol, L., Moffitt, T. E., Caspi, A., & Silva, P. A. (1998). Sex effects in risk predictors for antisocial behavior: Are males exposed to more risk factors for antisocial behavior: In T. E. Moffitt, A. Caspi, M. Rutter, & P. A. Silva (Eds.), *Sex differences in antisocial behaviour: Conduct disorder, delinquency, and violence in the Dunedin longitudinal study* (pp. 109–122). Cambridge, UK: Cambridge University Press.

Magruder, K. M., Frueh, B. C., Knapp, R. G., Davis, L., Hamner, M. V., Martin, R. H., et al. (2005). Prevalence of posttraumatic stress disorder in Veterans Affairs primary care clinics. *General Hospital Psychiatry, 27,* 169–179.

Mahalingam, R., Balan, S., & Haritatos, J. (2008). Engendering immigrant psychology: An intersectional perspective. *Sex Roles, 59,* 326–336.

Mahlstedt, D. L, & Keeny, L. (1993). Female survivors of dating violence and their social networks. *Feminism and Psychology, 3,* 319–333.

Mahlstedt, D. L., & Welsh, L. A. (2005). Perceived causes of physical assault in heterosexual dating relationships. *Violence Against Women, 11,* 447–472.

Maier, S. F., Amat, J., Baratta, M. V., Bland, S. T., Christianson, J. C., Thompson, B., Rozeske, R. R., & Watkins, L. R. (2009). The role of the medial prefrontal cortex in mediating resistance and vulnerability to the impact of adverse events. In C. M. Pariente, R. M. Nesse, D. Nutt, & L. Wolpert (Eds.), *Understanding depression: A translational approach* (pp. 157–171). Oxford University Press.

Maikovich-Fong, A. K., & Jaffee, S. R. (2010). Sex differences in childhood sexual abuse characteristics and victims' emotional and behavioral problems: Findings from a national sample of youth. *Child Abuse & Neglect, 34,* 429-437.

Maiuro, R. D., Cahn, T. S., & Vitaliano, P. P. (1988). Anger, hostility, and depression in domestically violent versus generally assaultive men and nonviolent control subjects. *Journal of Consulting and Clinical Psychology, 56,* 17–23.

Majdan, A. (1998, March). *Prevalence and personality correlates of women's aggressive behaviors against male partners.* Poster presented at the biennial meeting of the American Psychology-Law Society, Redondo Beach, CA.

Makepeace, J. M. (1981). Courtship violence among college students. *Family Relations, 30,* 97–102.

Maker, A. H., & deRoon-Cassini, T. A. (2007). Prevalence, perpetrators, and characteristics of witnessing parental violence and adult dating violence in Latina, East Asian, South Asian, and Middle Eastern women. *Violence and Victims, 22,* 632–647.

Maker, A. H., Kemmelmeier, M., & Peterson, C. (1998). Long-term psychological consequences in women of witnessing parental physical conflict and experiencing abuse in childhood. *Journal of Interpersonal Violence, 13,* 574–589.

Maker, H., Shah, P. V., & Agha, Z. (2005). Child physical abuse. *Journal of Interpersonal Violence, 20,* 1406–1428.

Malamuth, N. M. (1989). Predictors of naturalistic sexual aggression. In M. A. Pirog-Good & J. E. Stets (Eds.), *Violence in dating relationships: Emerging social issues* (pp. 219–240). New York: Praeger.

Malcoe, L. H., Duran, B. M., & Montgomery, J. M. (2004). Socioeconomic disparities in intimate partner violence against Native American women: A cross-sectional study. *BioMed Central Medicine, 2,* 20–33.

Maletzky, B. M., & Field, G. (2003). The biological treatment of dangerous sexual offenders, A review and preliminary report of the Oregon pilot Depo-Provera program. *Aggression and Violent Behavior, 8,* 391–412.

Malkin, C., & Stake, J. E. (2004). Changes in attitudes and self-confidence in the women's gender studies classroom: The role of teacher alliance and student cohesion. *Sex Roles, 50,* 455–468.

Mallett, C. A., Dare, P. S., & Seck, M. M. (2009). Predicting juvenile delinquency: The nexus of childhood maltreatment, depression and bipolar disorder. *Criminal Behaviour and Mental Heatlh, 19,* 235–246.

Malley-Morrison, K. (2004). *Family violence in a cultural perspective: Defining, understanding, and combating abuse.* Hillsdale, NJ: Lawrence Erlbaum.

Malley-Morrison, K., & Hines, D. A. (2004). *Family violence in a cultural perspective: Defining, understanding, and combating abuse.* Thousand Oaks, CA: Sage.

Malsch, M. (2007). Stalking: Do criminalization and punishment help? *Punishment & Society, 9,* 201–209.

Mammen, O., Kolko, D., & Pilkonis, P. (2003). Parental cognition and satisfaction: Relationship to aggressive parental behavior. *Child Maltreatment, 8,* 288-301.

Manders, J. E., & Stoneman, Z. (2008). Children with disabilities in the child protective services system: An analog study of investigation and case management. *Child Abuse & Neglect, 33,* 229–237.

Mandeville-Norden, R., & Beech, A. R. (2009). Development of a psychometric typology of child molesters. *Journal of Interpersonal Violence, 24,* 307–325.

Man held after wife found chained [Associated Press article]. (2003, April 5). *Los Angeles Daily News,* p. 15.

Mandel, D. (2010). Child welfare and domestic violence: Tackling the themes and thorny questions that stand in the way of collaboration and improvement of child welfare practice. *Violence Against Women, 16,* 530–536.

Mankowski, E. S., Haaken, J., & Silvergleid, C. S. (2002). Collateral damage: An analysis of the achievements and unintended consequences of batterer intervention programs and discourse. *Journal of Family Violence, 17,* 167–184.

Mann, J. R., & Takyi, B. K. (2009). Autonomy, dependence or culture: Examining the impact of resources and socio-cultural processes on attitudes towards intimate partner violence in Ghana, Africa. *Journal of Family Violence, 24,* 323–335.

Mann, R., Webster, S., Wakeling, H., & William, M. (2007). The measurement and influence of child sexual abuse supportive beliefs. *Psychology, Crime & Law, 13,* 443–458.

Manthorpe, J., et al. (2007, October). The UK national study of abuse and neglect among older people. *Nursing Older People, 19*(8), 24–26.

Marcus, R. F., & Swett, B. (2002). Violence and intimacy in close relationships. *Journal of Interpersonal Violence, 17,* 570–586.

Marcus, R. F., & Swett, B. (2003). Multiple-precursor scenarios: Predicting and reducing campus violence. *Journal of Interpersonal Violence, 18,* 553–571.

Margolin, G., Burman, B., & John, R. S. (1989). Home observations of married couples reenacting naturalistic conflicts. *Behavioral Assessment, 11,* 101–118.

Margolin, G., Chien, D., Duman, S. E., Fauchier, A., Gordis, E. B., et al. (2005). Ethical issues in couple and family research. *Journal of Family Psychology, 19,* 157–167.

Margolin, G., Fernandez, V. (1987). The "spontaneous" cessation of marital violence: Three case examples. *Journal of Marital and Family Therapy, 13,* 241–250.

Margolin, G., John, R. S., & Foo, L. (1998). Interactive and unique risk factors for husbands' emotional and physical abuse of their wives. *Journal of Family Violence, 13,* 315–341.

Margolin, G., John, R. S., & Gleberman, L. (1988). Affective responses to conflictual discussions in violent and non-violent couples. *Journal of Consulting and Clinical Psychology, 56,* 24–33.

Margolin, L., Moran, P. B., & Miller, M. (1989). Social approval for violations of sexual consent in marriage and dating. *Violence and Victims, 4,* 45–55.

Marino, R., Weinman, M. L., & Soudelier, K. (2001). Social work intervention and failure to thrive in infants and children. *Health and Social Work, 26,* 90–98.

Markiewicz, D., Lawford, H., Doyle, A., & Haggart, N. (2006). Developmental differences in adolescents' and young adults' use of mothers, fathers, best friends, and romantic partners to fulfill attachment needs. *Journal of Youth and Adolescence, 35,* 121–134.

Marques, J., Nelson, C., West, M. A., & Day, D. M. (1994). The relationship between treatment goals and recidivism among child molesters. *Behavior Research and Therapy, 32,* 577–588.

Marshall, A. D., & Holtzworth-Munroe, A. (2002). Varying forms of husband sexual aggression: Predictors and subgroup differences. *Journal of Family Psychology, 16,* 286–296.

Marshall, A. D., Panuzio, J., & Taft, C. T. (2005). Intimate partner violence among military veterans and active duty servicemen. *Clinical Psychology Review, 25,* 862–876.

Marshall, C. E., Benton, D., & Brazier, J. M. (2000). Elder abuse: Using clinical tools to identify clues of mistreatment. *Geriatrics, 55*(2), 42, 44, 47–50, 53.

Marshall, L. L., (1992a). Development of the Severity of Violence Against Women Scales. *Journal of Family Violence, 7,* 103–121.

Marshall, L. L., (1992b). The Severity of Violence Against Men Scales. *Journal of Family Violence, 7,* 189–203.

Marshall, L. L., & Rose, P. (1990). Premarital violence: The impact of family of origin violence, stress, and reciprocity. *Violence and Victims, 5,* 51–64.

Marshall, L. L., Weston, R., & Honeycutt, T. C. (2000). Does men's positivity moderate or mediate the effects of their abuse on women's relationship quality? *Journal of Social and Personal Relationships, 17,* 660–675.

Marshall, M. A., & Brown, J. D. (2006). Trait aggressiveness and situational provocations: A test of the traits as situational sensitivities (TASS) model. *Personality and Social Psychology Bulletin, 32,* 1100–1113.

Marshall, P. (1997). *The prevalence of convictions for sexual offending.* Home Office Research and Statistics Directorate, Research Findings No. 55. London: Home Office.

Marshall, W. L., Jones, R., Ward, T., Johnston, P., & Barbaree, H. E. (1991). Treatment outcome with sex offenders. *Clinical Psychology Review, 11,* 465–485.

Marshall, W. L., & Moulden, H. (2001). Hostility toward women and victim empathy in rapists. *Sexual Abuse: A Journal of Research and Treatment, 13,* 249–255.

Marshall, W. L., & Marshall, L. E. (2000). The origins of sexual offending. *Trauma, Violence, & Abuse, 1,* 250–263.

Marshall, W. L., & Pithers, W. (1994). A reconsideration of treatment outcome with sex offenders. *Criminal Justice and Behavior, 21,* 10–27.

Martin E. P. Seligman. (2007). Martin E. P. Seligman 2006 award for distinguished scientific contributions. *American Psychologist, 61,* 772–788.

Martin, J. A., Hamilton, B. F., et al. (2007). Births: Final data for 2005. *National Vital Statistics Report 2007*; 56(6).

Martin, M. E. (1997). Double your trouble: Dual arrest in family violence. *Journal of Family Violence, 12,* 139–157.

Martin, P. Y., & Hummer, R. A. (1995). Fraternities and rape on campus. In P. Searles & R. J. Berger (Eds.), *Rape and society: Readings on the problem of sexual assault* (pp. 139–151). Boulder, CO: Westview.

Martin, S. L., Coyne-Beasley, T., Hochn, M., Matthew, M., Runyan, C. W., Orton, S., & Royster, L. A. (2009). Primary prevention of violence against women: Training needs of violence practitioners. *Violence Against Women, 15,* 44–56.

Martin, S. L., Moracco, K. E., Chang, J. C., Council, C. L., & Dulli, L. S. (2008). Substance abuse issues among women in domestic violence programs. *Violence Against Women, 14,* 985–997.

Martin, S. L., Ray, N., Sotres-Alvarez, D., Kupper, L., Morocco, K., Dickens, P., et al. (2006). Physical and sexual assault of women with disabilities. *Violence Against Women, 12,* 823–837.

Martin, S. L., Young, S. K., Billings, D. L., & Bross, C. C. (2007). Health care-based interventions for women who have experienced sexual *violence. Trauma, Violence, & Abuse, 8,* 3–18.

Martin, S. L., Gibbs, D. A., Johnson, R. E., Rentz, E. D., Clinton-Sherrod, M., & Hardison, J. (2007). Spouse abuse and child abuse by army soldiers. *Journal of Family Violence, 22,* 587–595.

Marx, B. P., Calhoun, K. S., Wilson, A. E., & Meyerson, L. A. (2001). Sexual revictimization prevention: An outcome evaluation. *Journal of Consulting and Clinical Psychology, 69,* 25–32.

Marx, B. P., Heidt, J. M., & Gold, S. D. (2005). Perceived uncontrollability and unpredictability, self-regulation, and sexual revictimization. *Review of General Psychology, 9,* 67–90.

Mash, E. J., & Wolfe, D. A. (2008). *Abnormal child psychology* (4th ed.). Belllingham, WA: Wadsworth Publishing.

Masho, S. W., & Alvanzo, A. (2009). Help-seeking behavior of men sexual assault survivors. *American Journal of Men's Health.* Published online doi:10.1177/1557988309336365.

Massad, P. M., & Hulsey, T. L. (2006). Causal attributions in post-traumatic stress disorder: Implications for clinical research and practice. *Psychotherapy: Theory, Research, Practice, Training, 43,* 201–215.

Mastel-Smith, B., Binder, B., Malecha, A., Hersch, G., Symes, L., & McFarlane, J. (2006). Testing therapeutic life review offered by home care workers to decrease depression among home-dwelling older women. *Issues in Mental Health Nursing, 27,* 10–37, 1049.

Mastrofski, S. D., Parks, R. B., Reiss, A. J., & Worden, R. E. (1998). *Policing neighborhoods: A report from Indianapolis.* Washington, DC: U.S. Department of Justice.

Mathes, E. W., & Severa, N. (1981). Jealousy, romantic love, and liking: Theoretical considerations and preliminary scale development. *Psychological Reports, 49,* 23–31.

Mathews, B., & Bross, D. C. (2008). Mandated reporting is still a policy with reason: Empirical evidence and philosophical grounds. *Child Abuse & Neglect, 32,* 511–516.

Matlaw, J. R., & Spence, D. M. (1994). The hospital elder assessment team: A protocol for suspected cases of elder abuse and neglect. *Journal of Elder Abuse & Neglect, 6*(2), 23–37.

Matthew Hale (jurist). In *Wikipedia, the free encyclopedia.* Retrieved January 6, 2010, from http://en.wikipedia.org/wiki/Matthew_Hale_(jurist)

Maurer, T. W., & Robinson, D. W. (2008). Effects of attire, alcohol, and gender on perception of date rape. *Sex Roles, 58,* 423–434.

Mauricio, A. M., & Gormley, B. (2001). Male perpetration of physical violence against female partners: The interaction of dominant needs and attachment insecurity. *Journal of Interpersonal Violence, 16,* 1066–1081.

Mauricio, A. M., Tein, J. Y., & Lopez, F. G. (2007). Borderline and antisocial personality scores as mediators between attachment and intimate partner violence. *Violence and Victims, 22,* 139–157.

Max, W., Rice, D. P., Finkelstein, E., Bardwell, R. A., & Leadbetter, S. (2004). The economic toll of intimate partner violence against women in the United States. *Violence and Victims, 19,* 259–272.

Maxwell, C. D., Garner, J. H., & Fagan, J. A. (June, 2001). *The effects of arrest on intimate partner violence: New evidence from the Spouse Assault Replication Program* (NCJ Publication No. 188199). Washington, DC: U.S. Department of Justice.

Mayda, A. S., & Akkuş, D. (2005). Domestic violence against 116 Turkish housewives: A field study. *Women & Health, 40,* 95–108.

Mays, J. M. (2006). Feminist disability theory: Domestic violence against women with a disability. *Disability & Society, 21,* 147–158.

Mayseless, O. (1991). Adult attachment patterns and courtship violence. *Family Relations, 40,* 21–28.

Maziak, W., & Asfar, T. (2003). Physical abuse in low-income women in Aleppo, Syria. *Health Care for Women International, 24,* 313–326.

Mazzeo, S. E., & Espelage, D. L. (2002). Association between childhood physical and emotional abuse and disordered eating behaviors in female undergraduates: An investigation of the mediating role of alexithymia and depression. *Journal of Counseling Psychology, 49,* 86–100.

McCarroll, J. E., Castro, S., Nelson, E. M., Fan, Z., Evans, P. K., & Rivera, A. (2008). Characteristic of domestic violence incidents reported at the scene by volunteer victim advocates. *Military Medicine, 173,* 865–870.

McCarroll, J. E., Newby, J. H., & Dooley-Bernard, M. (2008). Responding to domestic violence in the U.S. Army—The family advocacy program. *Family & Intimate Partner Violence Quarterly, 1,* 5–23.

McCarroll, J. E., Newby, J. H., Thayer, L. E., Norwood, A. E., Fullerton, C. S., & Ursano, R. J. (1999). Reports of spouse abuse in the U.S. Army Central Registry (1989–1997). *Military Medicine, 164,* 77–84.

McCarroll, J. E., Thayer, L. E., Liu, X., Newby, J. H., Norwood, A. E., Fullerton, C. S., et al. (2000). Spouse abuse recidivism in the U.S. Army by gender and military status. *Journal of Consulting and Clinical Psychology, 68,* 521–525.

McCarroll, J. E., Ursano, R. J., Liu, X., Thayer, L. E., Newby, J. H., Norwood, A. E., et al. (2000). Deployment and the probability of spousal aggression by U.S. Army soldiers. *Military Medicine, 165,* 41–44.

McCarthy, G., & Taylor, A. (1999). Avoidant/ambivalent attachment style as a mediator between abusive childhood experiences and adult relationship difficulties. *Journal of Child Psychology & Psychiatry & Allied Disciplines, 40,* 465–477.

McCloskey, L. A., Figueredo, A. J., & Koss, M. P. (1995). The effects of systemic family violence on children's mental health. *Child Development, 66,* 1239–1261.

McCloskey, L. A., & Lichter, E. L. (2003). The contribution of marital violence to adolescent aggression across different relationships. *Journal of Interpersonal Violence, 18,* 390–412.

McCloskey, L. A., Treviso, M., Scionti, T., & dal Pozza, G. (2002). A comparative study of battered women and their children in Italy and the United States. *Journal of Family Violence, 17,* 53–74.

McClung, J. J., Murray, R., & Braden, N. J. (1988). Intentional ipecac poisoning in children. *American Journal of Diseases in Children, 142,* 637–639.

McColgan, M. D. et al. (2010). Results of a multifaceted intimate partner violence training program for pediatric residents. *Child Abuse & Neglect, 34,* 275–283

McCourt, J., Peel, J. C. F., & O'Carroll, P. (1998). The effects of child sexual abuse on the protecting parent(s): Identifying a counseling response for secondary victims. *Counseling Psychology Quarterly, 11,* 283–299.

McCray, J. A., & King, A. R. (2003). Personality disorder attributes as supplemental goals for change in interpersonal psychotherapy. *Journal of Contemporary Psychotherapy, 33,* 79–92.

McFall, C. (2000, March/April). Rainbow services: A new beginning for older battered women. *Victimization of the Elderly and Disabled, 2,* 86.

McFarlane, J. M., Campbell, J. C., & Watson, K. (2002). Intimate partner stalking and femicide: Urgent implications for women's safety. *Behavioral Sciences and the Law, 20,* 51–68.

McFarlane, J. M., Groff, J. Y., O'Brien, J. A., & Watson, K. (2005). Prevalence of partner violence against 7,443 African American, White, and Hispanic women receiving care at urban public primary care clinics. *Public Health Nursing, 22,* 98–107.

McGarry, J., & Simpson, C. (2009). Raising awareness of elder abuse in the community practice setting. *British Journal of Community Nursing, 14,* 305–308.

McGowan, P. O., Sasaki, A., D'Alessio, Dymov, S., Labonte, B., et al. (2009). *Nature Neuroscience, 12,* 342–348.

McGrath, R. J., Cumming, G. F., & Burchard, B. L. (2003). *Current practices and trends in sexual abuser management: Safer Society 2002 nationwide survey.* Brandon, VT: Safer Society Press.

McGregor, K., Jolich, S., Glover, M., & Gautam, J. (2010). Health professionals' responses to disclosure of child sexual abuse history: Female child sexual abuse survivors' experiences. *Journal of Child Sexual Abuse, 19,* 239–254.

McGuigan, W. M., & Middlemiss, W. (2005). Sexual abuse in childhood and interpersonal violence in adulthood: A cumulative impact on depressive symptoms in women. *Journal of Interpersonal Violence, 10,* 1271–1287.

McHenry, P. C., Julian, T. W., & Gavazzi, S. M. (1995). Toward a biopsychosocial model of domestic violence. *Journal of Marriage and the Family, 57,* 307–320.

McHugh, M. C., Livingston, N. A., & Ford, A. (2005). A postmodern approach to women's use of violence: Developing multiple and complex conceptualizations. *Psychology of Women Quarterly, 29,* 323–336.

McKay, M. M. (1994). The link between domestic violence and child abuse: Assessment and treatment considerations. *Child Welfare, 73,* 29–39.

McKell, A. J., & Sporakowski, M. J. (1993). How shelter counselors' views about responsibility for wife abuse relate to services they provide. *Journal of Family Violence, 8,* 101–112.

McKelvey, L. M., et al. (2008). Validity of the short form of the parenting stress index. *Journal of Child and Family Studies, 18,* 102–11.

McKenzie, R. B. (Ed.). (1998). *Rethinking orphanages for the 21st century.* Thousand Oaks, CA: Sage.

McKinney, C. M., Caetano, R., Ramisetty-Mikler, & Nelson, S. (2009). Childhood family violence and perpetration and victimization of intimate partner violence: Findings from a national population-based study of couples. *Annals of Epidmiology, 19,* 25–32.

McLean, L. M., & Gallop, R. (2003). Implications of childhood sexual abuse for adult borderline personality disorder and complex posttraumatic stress disorder. *American Journal of Psychiatry, 160,* 369–371.

McMahon, M., & Pence, E. (2003). Making social change: Reflections on individuals and institutional advocacy with women arrested for domestic violence. *Violence Against Women, 9,* 47–74.

McNally, R. J., & Geraerts, E. (2009). A new solution to the recovered memory debate. *Perpsectives on Psychological Science, 4,* 126–134.

McNutt, L. A., Carlson, B. E., Rose, I. M., & Robinson, D. A. (2002). Partner violence intervention in the busy primary care environment. *American Journal of Preventive Medicine, 22,* 84–91.

McPherson, A. V., Lewis, K. M., Lynn, A. E., Haskett, M. E., & Behrend, T. S. (2009). Predictors of parenting stress for abusive and nonabusive mothers. *Journal of Child and Family Studies, 18,* 61–69.

McWhirter, P. T. (1999). Domestic violence in Chile. *American Psychologist, 54,* 47–40.

Mead, R. A. (2007, May/June). Ageism in America. *Victimization of the Elderly and Disabled, 10,* 8–9.

Mead, R. A. (2008, May/June). Emergency preparedness and the St. Rita's nursing homes catastrophe. *Victimization of the Elderly and Disabled, 11,* 25.

Mead, R. A. (2009, July/August). Worth reading, worth watching. *Victimization of the Elderly and Disabled, 12,* 25.

Mears, J. (2003). Survival is not enough: Violence against older women in Australia. *Violence Against Women, 9,* 1478–1489.

Mechakra-Tahiri, S., Zunzunegui, M. V., & Seguin, L. (2007). Self-rated health and postnatal depressive symptoms among immigrant mothers in Québec. *Women & Health, 45(4),* 1–17.

Medina-Ariza, J., & Barberet, R. (2003). Intimate partner violence in Spain. *Violence Against Women, 9,* 302–322.

Medley, A., & Sachs-Ericsson, N. (2009). Predictors of parental physical abuse: The contribution of internalizing and externalizing disorders and childhood experiences of abuse. *Journal of Affective Disorders, 113,* 244–254.

Mega, L. T., Mega, J. L., Mega, B. T., & Harris, B.M. (2000). Brainwashing and battering fatigue. Psychological abuse in domestic violence. *North Carolina Medical Journal, 61,* 260–265.

Meichenbaum, D. (2004). What "expert" therapists do: A constructive narrative perspective. *International Journal of Existential Psychology & Psychotherapy, 1,* 50–56.

Mejlvang, P., & Boujida, V. (2007). Sexual assaults in Greenland: Characteristics of police-reported rapes and attempted rapes. *International Journal of Circumpolar Health, 66,* 257–263.

Melbin, A., Sullivan, C. M., & Cain, D. (2003). Transitional supportive housing programs: Battered women's perspectives and recommendations. *Affilia, 18,* 445–460.

Melton, G. B. (2002). Chronic neglect of family violence: More than a decade of reports to guide US policy. *Child Abuse and Neglect, 26,* 569–586.

Melton, G. B. (2005). Mandated reporting: A policy with reason. *Child Abuse & Neglect, 29,* 9–18.

Melton, H. C. (2007). Predicting the occurrence of stalking in relationships characterized by domestic violence. *Journal of Interpersonal Violence, 22,* 3–25.

Melton, H. C., & Belknap, J. (2003). He hits, she hits: Assessing gender differences and similarities in officially reported intimate partner violence. *Criminal Justice and Behavior, 30,* 328–348.

Melville, R. (2005). Human research ethics committees and ethical review: The changing research culture for social workers. *Australian Social Work, 58,* 370–383.

Ménard, K. S., Anderson, A. L., & Godboldt, S. M. (2009). Gender differences in intimate partner recidivism: A 5-year follow-up. *Criminal Justice and Behavior, 36,* 61–76.

Menio, D., & Keller, B. H. (2000). CARIE: A multifaceted approach to abuse prevention in nursing homes. *Generations, 24*(2), 28–32.

Merchant, M. (2000). A comparative study of agencies assisting domestic violence victims: Does the South Asian community have special needs? *Journal of Social Distress and Homelessness, 9,* 249–259.

Merrill, G. S. (1996). Ruling the exception: Same-sex battering and domestic violence theory. In C. Renzetti & C. H. Miley (Eds.), *Violence in gay and lesbian domestic partnerships* (pp. 9–21). Binghamton, NY: Harrington Park Press.

Merrill, G. S. (1998). Understanding domestic violence among gay and bisexual men. *Journal of Homosexuality, 39,* 1–30.

Merschman, J. C. (2001). The dark side of the web: Cyberstalking and the need for contemporary legislation. *Harvard Women's Law Journal, 24,* 255–292.

Mersky, J. P., Berger, L. M., Reynolds, A. J., & Gromoske, A. N. (2009). Risk factors for child and adolescent maltreatment. *Child Maltreatment, 14,* 73–88.

Mertin, P. G., & Mohr, P. B. (2001). A follow-up study of post-traumatic stress disorder, anxiety, and depression in Australian victims of domestic violence. *Violence and Victims, 16,* 645–653.

Messing, J. T. (2007a, December/January). Research & practice in cahoots: A guide to research for practitioners (Part I). *Domestic Violence Report, 12,* 17–32.

Messing, J. T. (2007b, February/March). Research & practice in cahoots: A guide to research for practitioners (Part II). *Domestic Violence Report, 12,* 35–43.

Messing, J. T., & Heeren, J. W. (2004). Another side of multiple murder: Women killers in the domestic context. *Homicide Studies, 8,* 123–158.

Messman-Moore, T. L., & Brown, A. L. (2006). Risk perception, rape, and sexual revictimization: A prospective study of college women. *Psychology of Women Quarterly, 30,* 159–172.

Messman-Moore, T. L., & Coates, A. A. (2007). The impact of childhood psychological abuse on adult interpersonal conflict: The role of early maladaptive schemas and patterns of interpersonal behavior. *Journal of Emotional Abuse, 7,* 75–92.

Messman-Moore, T. L., Coates, A. A., Gaffey, K. J., & Johnson, C. F. (2008). Sexuality, substance use, and susceptibility to victimization predictors of revictimization. *Journal of Interpersonal Violence, 23,* 1731–1746.

Mezzich, A. C., Bretz, W. A., Day, B-S., Corby, P.M., Kirisci, L., et al. (2007). Child neglect and oral health in offspring of substance-abusing fathers. *American Journal of Addictions, 16,* 397–402.

Michalski, R. L., Russell, D. P., Shackelford, T. K., & Weekes-Shackelford, V. A. (2007). Siblicide and genetic relatedness in Chicago, 1870–1930. *Homicide Studies, 11,* 231–237.

Migliaccio, T. A. (2002). Abused husbands. *Journal of Family Issues, 23,* 26–52.

Mihalic, S. W., & Elliott, D. (1997). A social learning theory model of marital violence. *Journal of Family Violence, 12,* 21–47.

Milberger, S., Israel, N., LeRoy, B., Martin, A., Potter, L., & Patchak-Schuster, P. (2003). Violence against women with physical disabilities. *Violence and Victims, 18,* 581–590.

Miles, A. (2002). Holding Christian men accountable for abusing women. *Journal of Religion & Abuse, 4*(3), 15–27.

Millburn, M. A., Mathes, R., & Conrad, S. D. (2000). The effects of viewing R-rated movie scenes that objectify women on perceptions of date rape. *Sex Roles, 43,* 645–664.

Miller, B., & Marshall, J. (1987). Coercive sex on the university campus. *Journal of College Student Development, 28,* 38–47.

Miller, C. E., & Mullins, B. K. (2002). Lifelong learning to reduce domestic violence. *International Journal of Lifelong Education, 21,* 474–484.

Miller, G. E., & Chen, E. (2010). Harsh family climate in early life presages the emergence of a proinflammatory phenotype in adolescence. *Psychological Science, 21,* 846–856.

Miller, J. (2006). A specification of the types of intimate partner violence experienced by women in the general population. *Violence Against Women 12,* 1105–1131.

Miller, J. R. (2009, February 17). Beheading in New York appears to be honor killing, experts say. Retrieved from htpp://www.foxnews.com/story/0,2933,494785,00.html

Miller, L. M., Southam-Gerow, M. A., & Allin, R. B., Jr. (2008). Who stays in treatment? Child and family predictors of youth client retention in a public mental health agency. *Child & Youth Care Forum, 37,* 153–170.

Miller, S. L. (2001). The paradox of women arrested for domestic violence. *Violence Against Women, 7,* 1339–1376.

Miller, S. L., Gregory, C., & Iovanni, L. (2005). One size fits all? A gender-neutral approach to a gender-specific problem: Contrasting batterer treatment programs for male and female offenders. *Criminal Justice Policy Review, 16,* 336–359.

Miller, S. L., & Meloy, M. L. (2006). Women's use of force: Voices of women arrested for domestic violence. *Violence Against Women, 12,* 89–115.

Miller, S. L., & Simpson, S. S. (1991). Courtship violence and social control: Does gender matter? *Law & Society Review, 2,* 335–365.

Miller, T. R., Cohen, M.A., & Wiersema, B. (1996). *Victim costs and consequences: A new look* (NCJ Publication No. 155282). Washington, DC: National Institute of Justice.

Miller-Perrin, C. L., & Perrin, R. D. (1999). *Child maltreatment: An introduction.* Thousand Oaks, CA: Sage.

Millon, T. (1983). *Millon Clinical Multiaxial Inventory manual.* Minneapolis: Interpretive Scoring Systems.

Millon, T. (1995). *Millon Clinical Multiaxial Inventory–II manual (Brief form).* Minneapolis, MN: National Computer Systems.

Milner, J. S. (2003). Social information processing in high-risk and physically abusive parents. *Child Abuse & Neglect, 27,* 7–20.

Milner, J. S., & Chilamkurti, C. (1991). Physical child abuse perpetrator characteristics: A review of the literature. *Journal of Interpersonal Violence, 6,* 336–344.

Milner, J. S., Thomsen, C. J., et al. (2010). Do trauma symptoms mediate the relationship between childhood physical abuse and adult child abuse risk? *Child Abuse & Neglect, 34,* 332–344.

Min, L.C., et al. (2005). Predictors of overall quality of care provided to vulnerable older people. *Journal of the American Geriatric Society, 53,* 1705–1711.

Min, P. G. (2001). Changes in Korean immigrants' gender role and social status, and their marital conflicts. *Sociological Forum, 16,* 301–320.

Mineka, S., & Zinbarg, R. (2006). A contemporary learning theory perspective on the etiology of anxiety disorders: It's not what you thought it was. *American Psychologist, 61,* 10–26.

Minister for Gender Equality, National Institute of Public Health, Denmark (Helweg-Larsen & Frederiksen). (2007). *Men's violence against women: Extent, characteristic and the measures against violence—2007.* Denmark: Department of Gender Equality.

Minow, J. C., & Einolf, C. J. (2009). Sorority participation and sexual assault risk. *Violence Against Women, 15,* 835–851.

Mischel, W. (2009). Connecting clinical practice to scientific progress (Editorial). *Psychological Sciences in the Public Interest, 9,* i–ii.

Misri, S., Reebye, P., Millis, L., & Shah, S. (2006). The impact of treatment intervention on parenting stress in postpartum depressed mothers: A prospective study. *American Journal of Orthopsychiatry, 76,* 115–119.

Mitchell, R. E., & Hodson, C. A. (1983). Coping with domestic violence: Social support and psychological health among battered women. *American Journal of Community Psychology, 11,* 629–654.

Mixson, P. M. (2006, July/August). Florida: Lessons from the storms. *Victimization of the Elderly and Disabled, 9,* 17–18, 31.

Mize, K. D., & Shackelford, T. K. (2008). Intimate partner homicide methods in heterosexual, gay, and lesbian relationships. *Violence and Victims, 23,* 98–114.

Moe, A. M. (2007). Silenced voices and structured survival: Battered women's help seeking. *Violence Against Women, 13,* 676–699.

Moe, A. M., & Bell, M. P. (2004). Abject economics: The effects of battering and violence on women's work and employability. *Violence Against Women, 10,* 29–55.

Moe, B. K., King, A. R., & Bailly, M. D. (2004). Retrospective accounts of recurrent parental physical abuse as a predictor of adult laboratory-induced aggression. *Aggressive Behavior, 30,* 217–228.

Moffitt, T. E. (1997). *Partner violence among young adults.* Washington, DC: U.S. Department of Justice.

Moffitt, T. E., & Caspi, A. (1999). *Findings about partner violence from the Dunedin Multidisciplinary Health and Development Study* (NCJ Publication No. 170018). Washington, DC: U.S. Department of Justice.

Moghadam, S., Knudson-Martin, C., & Mahoney, A. R. (2009). Gendered power in cultural contexts: Part III. Couple relationships in Iran. *Family Process, 48,* 41–54.

Mohandie, K., Meloy, J. R., McGowan, M. G., & Williams, J. (2006). The RECON typology of stalking: Reliability and validity based upon a large sample of North American stalkers. *Journal of Forensic Science, 51,* 147–166.

Mohler-Kuo., M., Dowdall, G. W., Koss, M. P., & Wechsler, H. (2004). Correlates of rape while intoxicated in a nation sample of college women. *Journal of Studies on Alcohol, 65*(1), 37–45.

Mohr, W. K. (1998, August/September). Bringing together the town and the gown: NIJ initiative for practitioner synthesis. *Domestic Violence Report, 3,* 89.

Molidor, C. E., & Tolman, R. M. (1998). Gender and contextual factors in adolescent dating violence. *Violence Against Women, 4,* 180–194.

Molnar, B. E., Buka, S. L., & Kessler, R. C. (2001). Child sexual abuse and subsequent psychopathology: Results from the National Comorbidity Survey. *American Journal of Public Health, 91,* 753–760.

Mom's Opportunity to Access Health, Education, Research, and Support for Postpartum Depression (MOTHERS) Act, H.R. 20, 111th Cong. (2009), Introduced as S.324.

Monahan, K., & O'Leary, K. D. (1999). Head injury and battered women: An initial inquiry. *Health and Social Work, 24,* 269–278.

Moon, A., & Benton, D. (2000). Tolerance of elder abuse and attitudes toward third-party intervention among African American, Korean American, and White elderly. *Journal of Multicultural Social Work, 8,* 283–303.

Moor, A., & Silvern, L. (2006). Identifying pathways linking child abuse to psychological outcome: The mediating role of perceived parental failure of empathy. *Journal of Emotional Abuse, 6,* 91–144.

Moore, A. R. (2008). Types of violence against women and factors influencing intimate partner violence in Togo (West Africa). *Journal of Family Violence, 23,* 777–783.

Moore, C. G. (2005). *Poverty, parental stress, and violent disagreements in the home among rural families.* Office of Rural Health Policy, South Carolina. Retrieved July 18, 2010, from http://www.ruralhealthresearch.org/projects/100000775/

Moore, T. M., Stuart, G. L., McNulty, J. K., Addis, M. E., Cordova, J. V., & Temple, J. R. (2008). Domains of masculine gender role stress and intimate partner violence in a clinical sample of violent men. *Psychology of Men & Masculinity, 9,* 82–89.

Morash, M., Bui, H. N., Stevens, T., & Zhang, Y. (2008). Getting out of harm's way: One-year outcomes for abused women in a Vietnamese immigrant enclave. *Violence Against Women, 14,* 1413–1429.

Morbidity and Mortality Weekly Report. (2008, February 8). Adverse health conditions and health risk behaviors associated with intimate partner violence—United States, 2005 (pp. 113–117) Atlanta, GA: Centers for Disease Control and Prevention.

Mordini, N. M. (2004). Mandatory state interventions for domestic abuse cases: An examination of the effects on victim safety and autonomy. *Drake Law Review, 52,* 295–306.

Morency, N. L., & Krauss, R. M. (1982). The nonverbal encoding and decoding of affect in first and fifth graders. In R. S. Feldman (Ed.), *Development of nonverbal behavioral skill.* New York: Springer.

Morgan, A. B., & Lilienfeld, S. O. (2000). A meta-analytic review of the relation between antisocial behavior and neuropsychological measures of executive function. *Clinical Psychology Review, 20,* 113–136.

Morgan, E., Johnson, I., & Sigler, R. (2006). Public definitions and endorsement of criminalization of elder abuse. *Journal of Criminal Justice, 34,* 275–283.

Moriarty, L. J., & Freiberger, K. (2008). Cyberstalking: Utilizing newspaper accounts to establish victimization patterns. *Victims & Offenders, 3,* 131–141.

Morris, A., & Reilly, J. (2003). *New Zealand national survey of crime victims, 2001.* New Zealand: New Zealand Ministry of Justice.

Morrison, K. E., Luchok, K. J., Richter, D. L., & Parra-Medina, D. (2006). Factors influencing help-seeking from informal networks among African American victims of intimate partner violence. *Journal of Interpersonal Violence, 21,* 1493–1511.

Morrow, M., Hankivsky, O., & Varcoe, C. (2004). Women and violence: The effects of dismantling the welfare state. *Critical Social Policy Limited, 24,* 358–384.

Morse, B. J. (1995). Beyond the Conflict Tactics Scale: Assessing gender differences. *Violence and Victims, 10,* 251–272.

Morton, E., Runyan, C. W., Moracco, K. E., & Butts, J. (1998). Partner homicide-suicide involving female homicide victims: A population-based study in North Carolina, 1988–1992. *Violence and Victims, 13,* 91–106.

Morton, N., & Browne, K. D. (1998). Theory and observation of attachment and its relation to child maltreatment: A review. *Child Abuse & Neglect, 22,* 1093–1104.

Mosher, D. L., & Sirkin, M. (1984). Measuring a macho personality constellation. *Journal of Research in Personality, 18,* 150–163.

Moskowitz, S. (1997). Private enforcement of criminal mandatory reporting laws. *Journal of Elder Abuse & Neglect, 9*(3), 1–22.

Moss, V. A., Pitula, C. R., Campbell, J. C., & Halstead, L. (1997). The experience of terminating an abusive relationship from an Anglo and African American perspective: A qualitative descriptive study. *Issues in Mental Health Nursing, 18,* 433–454.

Mount Sinai/Victim Services Agency, Elder Abuse Project. (1988). *Elder mistreatment guidelines for health care professionals: Detection, assessment, and intervention.* New York: Author.

Mouradian, V. E. (2001). Applying schema theory to intimate aggression: Individual and gender differences in representation of contexts and goals. *Journal of Applied Social Psychology, 31,* 376–408.

Mowat-Leger, V. (2002). Risk factors for violence: A comparison of domestic batterers and other violent and nonviolent men. *Dissertation Abstracts International, 63*(04), 2046B. (UMI No. NQ67053)

Moylan, C. A., Herrenkohl, T. I., Sousa, C., Tajima, E. A., Herrenkohl, R. C., & Russo, M. J. (2010). The effects of child abuse and exposure to domestic violence on adolescent internalizing and externalizing behavior problems. *Journal of Family Violence, 25,* 53–63.

Muftic, L. R., Bouffard, L. A., & Bouffard, J. A. (2007). An exploratory analysis of victim precipitation among men and women arrested for intimate partner violence. *Feminist Criminology, 2,* 327–346.

Muldary, P. S. (1983). Attribution of causality of spouse assault. *Dissertation Abstracts International, 44,* 1249B. (UMI No. 8316576)

Mulford, C., & Giordano, P. C. (2008). *Teen dating violence: A closer look at adolescent romantic relationships* (NCJ Publication No. 224089). Washington, DC: National Institute of Justice.

Mulford, C. F., & Redding, R. E. (2008). Training the parents of juvenile offenders: State of the art and recommendations for service delivery. *Journal of Child and Family Studies, 17,* 629–648.

Mullen, E. J., Bledsoe, S. F., & Bellamy, J. L. (2008). Implementing evidence-based social work practice. *Research on Social Work Practice, 18,* 325–338.

Mullins, S. M., Bard, D. E., & Ondersma, S. J. (2005). Comprehensive services for mothers of drug-exposed infants: Relations between program participation and subsequent Child Protective Services reports. *Child Maltreatment, 10,* 72–81.

Municipal liability for domestic violence homicides. (1998, August/September). *Domestic Violence Report, 3,* 90.

Munsey, C. (2007a, September). Transforming military mental health. *APA Monitor on Psychology, 38,* 38–41.

Munsey, C. (2007b, September). Fixing the institutional review board system. *APA Monitor on Psychology, 38,* 50.

Murnen, S. K., & Kohlman, M. K. (2007). Athletic participation, fraternity membership, and sexual aggression among college men: A meta-analtyic review. *Sex Roles, 57,* 145–157.

Murphy, C. M., & Dienemann, J. A. (1999). Informing the research agenda on domestic abuser intervention through practitioner-research dialogues. *Journal of Interpersonal Violence, 14,* 1314–1326.

Murphy, C. M., Meyer, S. L., & O'Leary, K. D. (1993). Family of origin violence and MCMI-II psychopathology among partner assaultive men. *Violence and Victims, 8,* 227–238.

Murphy, C. M., Meyer, S. L., & O'Leary, K. D. (1994). Dependency characteristics of partner assaultive men. *Journal of Abnormal Psychology, 103,* 729–735.

Murphy, C. M., Musser, P. H., & Maton, K. L. (1998). Coordinated community intervention for domestic abuser: Intervention system involvement and criminal recidivism. *Journal of Family Violence, 13,* 263–284.

Murphy, C. M., Stosny, S., & Morrel, T. M. (2005). Change in self-esteem and physical aggression during treatment for partner violent men. *Journal of Family Violence, 20,* 210–210.

Murphy, K. A., & Smith, D. L. (2010). Adolescent girls' responses to warning signs of abuse in romantic relationships. *Journal of Interpersonal Violence, 25,* 626–647.

Murphy, N. E. (1995). Queer justice: Equal protection for victims of same-sex violence. *Valparaiso University Law Review, 30,* 335–340.

Murray, B. (1999, October). Cultural insensitivity leads to unfair penalties. *APA Monitor on Psychology.* Retrieved October 4, 2002, from http://apa.org/monitor/oct99/mv2.html

Murray, C. E., & Graybeal, J. (2007). Methodological review of intimate partner violence prevention research. *Journal of Interpersonal Violence, 22,* 1250–1269.

Murray, S. L., Bellavia, G. M., Rose, P., & Griffin, D. W. (2003). Once hurt, twice hurtful: How perceived regard regulates daily marital interactions. *Journal of Personality and Social Psychology, 84,* 126–147.

Murray, S. L., Rose, P., Bellavia, G. M., Holmes, J. G., & Kusche, A. G. (2002). When rejection stings: How self-esteem constrains relationship-enhancement processes. *Journal of Personality and Social Psychology, 83,* 556–573.

Murty, K. S., & Roebuck, J. B. (1992). An analysis of crisis calls by battered women in the city of Atlanta. In E. C. Viano (Ed.), *Intimate violence: Interdisciplinary perspectives* (pp. 61–81). Bristol, PA: Taylor & Francis.

Myers, D. L. (2005). *Boys among men: Trying and sentencing juveniles as adults.* Westport, CT: Praeger.

Myers, J. E. B. (1992). *Evidence in child abuse and neglect cases.* New York: John Wiley.

Myers, J. E. B. (2005). *Myers on evidence in child, domestic and elder abuse cases.* New York: Aspen.

Myers, R. (2008, Septermber/October). Court's discretion to appoint guardians. *Victimization of the Elderly and Disabled, 11,* 35–36.

Myers, J. E. B. (2010). Criminal prosecution of child maltreatment. In J. E. B. Myers (Ed.), *The APSAC handbook on child maltreatment* (3rd ed., pp. 87–99). Thousand Oaks, CA: Sage.

"Myths and Facts": Current research on managing sex offenders. (2008, April). Retrieved August 2, 2010, from http://www.criminaljustice.state.ny.us/nsor/som_mythsandfacts.htm

Nabi, R. L., & Horner, J. R. (2001). Victims with voices: How abused women conceptualize the problem of spousal abuse and implications for intervention and prevention. *Journal of Family Violence, 16,* 237–253.

Nakajima, Y. (2005). The need for gender-sensitive medical interpreters for victims with limited English proficiency in sexual assault examinations. *Journal of Immigrant & Refugee Services, 3,* 57–72.

Nansel, T. R., Overpectk, M., Pilla, R. S., Ruan, W. J., Simons-Morton, B., & Scheidt, P. (2001). Bullying behaviors among U.S. youth: Prevalence and association with psychosocial adjustment. *Journal of the American Medical Association, 285,* 2094–2100.

Nason-Clark, N. (1997). *The battered wife: How Christians confront family violence.* Louisville, KY: Westminster John Knox Press.

National Abandoned Infants Assistance Resource Center (NAIARC; 2010). http://aia.berkeley.edu/information_resources/substance_exposed_newborns.php

National Association for Home Care. (n.d.). *Home care aide national certification program.* Retrieved from http://www.NAHC.org/education/PDFs/HCAcert.pdf

National Center for Injury Prevention and Control. (2000). *Dating violence.* Retrieved from http://www.cdc.gov/ncipc/factsheets/datviol.htm

National Center for Injury Prevention and Control. (2002). *CDC injury research agenda.* Atlanta, GA: Centers for Disease Control and Prevention.

National Center for Missing and Exploited Children. (n.d.). Pornographic images of children. In *Child sexual exploitation.* Retrieved January 25, 2004, from http://www.ncmec.org/missingkids/servlet

National Center for Prosecution of Child Abuse. (2001, August). *OJJDP fact sheet.* Alexandria, VA: Author.

National Center for Victims of Crime. (1992). *Sexual violence.* Retrieved from http://www.ncvc.org

National Center for Victims of Crime. (2002, January). Enforcement of protective orders (NCJ Publication No. 189190). *VC Legal Series Bulletin, 4,* 1–7.

National Center on Elder Abuse. (2007). *NCEA definition.* Retrieved from NCEA.aoa.gov/NCEAroot/Main_Site/FAQ/Basics/Definition.aspx

National Center on Substance Abuse and Child Welfare [NCSACW]. (2009). Retrieved from www.ncsacw.samhsa.gov/

National Child Abuse and Neglect Data System [NCANDS]. (2008). Retrieved from http://www.ceufast.com/

courses/viewcourse.asp?id=220#Child_characteristics_ (NCANDS, 2008).

National Coalition of Antiviolence Programs. (2001). *Lesbian, gay, bisexual and transgender domestic violence in 2000.* New York: Author.

National Council of Juvenile and Family Court Judges. (1994). *Model code on domestic and family violence.* Reno, NV: Author.

National Crime Records Bureau. (2008). *Crime in India, 2006.* Author.

National Criminal Justice Reference Service. (2007). *Family violence.* (An update on the cycle of violence, NIJ, 2001). Author.

National Institute of Justice. (2009). Compendium of research on violence against women: 1993-2009 (NCJ Publication No. 223572). Washington, DC: Author.

National Institute of Neurological Disorders and Stroke. (2010, May). *Shaken baby syndrome.* Retrieved June 6, 2010, from www.ninds.nih.gov/disorders/shakenbaby/shakenbaby .htm

National Institute on Disability and Rehabilitation Research. (2003). *Long-range plan 1999–2003.* Washington, DC: U.S. Department of Education.

National Institute on Drug Abuse. (2007, May 7). NIH survey shows most people with drug use disorders never get treatment. http://www.drugabuse.gov

National Low Income Housing Coalition. (1998). *Women and housing.* Retrieved from http:www.nlihc.org/template/page.cfm?id=21

National Opinion Research Center. (1998). *General Social Survey: 1972–2000 cumulative codebook.* Retrieved May 17, 2002, from http://www.icpsr.umich.edu/GSS

National Research Council. (1993). *Understanding child abuse and neglect.* Washington, DC: National Academy Press.

National Sexual Violence Resource Center. (2000). *Sexual assault in Indian country.* www.VAW.UMN.edu

National Survey of Child and Adolescent Well-Being (NSCAW). (n.d.). *No. 11. Adolescents involved with child welfare: A transition to adulthood.* Wave 5 data: 2006–2007. Washington, DC: Author.

National Survey on Drug Use and Health. (2009, May). Substance use among women during pregnancy and following childbirth. Washington, DC: Author.

National Symposium on Alcohol Abuse and Crime: Recommendations to the Office of Justice Programs. (1998, April). (NCJ Publication No. 172209). Washington, DC: Office of Justice Programs.

Naumann, P., Langford, D., Torres, S., Campbell, J., & Glass, N. (1999). Woman battering in primary care practice. *Family Practice, 16,* 343–352.

Nebbitt, V. E., House, L. E., Thompson, S. J., & Pollio, D. E. (2007). Successful transitions of runaway/homeless youth from shelter care. *Journal of Child and Family Studies, 16,* 545–555.

Neergaard, J. A., Lee, J. W., Anderson, B., & Wong Gengler, S. (2007). Women experiencing intimate partner violence: Effects of confiding in religious leaders. *Pastoral Psychology, 55,* 773–787.

Neidig, P., Friedman, D., & Collins, B. (1986). Attitudinal family violence characteristics of men who have engaged in spouse abuse. *Journal of Family Violence, 1,* 223–233.

Neieren, A. I., & Schel, B. (2008). Partner violence and health: Results from the first national study on violence against women in Norway. *Scandinavian Journal of Public Health, 36,* 161–168.

Neigh, G. N., Gillespie, C. F., & Nemeroff, C. B. (2009). The neurobiological toll of child abuse and neglect. *Trauma, Violence, & Abuse, 10,* 389–410.

Nerenberg, L. (2003). *Daily money management programs: A protection against elder abuse.* Washington, DC: National Center on Elder Abuse.

Nerenberg, L. (2008). *Elder abuse prevention: Emerging trends and promising strategies.* New York: Springer.

Neuger, C. C. (2002). Premarital preparation: Generating resistance to marital violence. *Journal of Religion & Abuse, 4*(3), 43–59.

New rule drafted to encourage cooperation by aliens with police. (2007, August 15). *Criminal Justice Newsletter,* p. 1.

Newby, J. H., Ursano, R. J., McCarroll, J. E., Martin, L. E., Norwood, A. E., & Fullerton, C. S. (2003). Spousal aggression by U.S. Army female soldiers toward employed and unemployed civilian husbands. *Military Medicine, 170,* 643–647.

Newcomb, M. D., & Locke, T. F. (2001). Intergenerational cycle of maltreatment: A popular concept obscured by methodological limitations. *Child Abuse & Neglect, 25,* 1219–1240.

Newman, C. J., Holenweg-Gross, C., Vuillerot, C., Jeannet, P.Y., & Roulet-Perez, E. (2010). Recent skin injuries in children with disabilities. *Archives of Disease in Childhood, 95,* 387–390.

News @ a Glance. (2007, January/February). *Assistant attorney general promotes national teen dating violence awareness and prevention week.* Author.

New U.S. crime reports: Flawed methodology sharply underestimates rape rates against women and persons with disabilities. (2009, October 26). *Legal Momentum Briefing Room.*

Newton, R. R., Connelly, C.D., & Landsverk, J. A. (2001). An examination of measurement characteristics and factorial validity of scores on the Revised Conflict Tactics Scale. *Educational and Psychological Measurement, 61,* 317–335.

New York Alliance Against Sexual Assault. (n.d.). Retrieved from http://www.syfreenyc.org

Ney, P. G., Fung, T., & Wickett, A. R. (1994). The worst combinations of child abuse and neglect. *Child Abuse & Neglect, 18,* 705–714.

Ng Tseung, C., & Schott, G. (2004). The quality of sibling relationships during late adolescent: Are there links with other significant relations? *Psychological Studies, 49,* 20–30.

Nichols, L., & Feltey, K. M. (2003). "The woman is not always the bad guy": Dominant discourse and resistance in the lives of battered women. *Violence Against Women, 9,* 784–806.

Niebuhr, G. (1998, June 10). Baptists laud submission by women. *Los Angeles Daily News,* pp. 8, 10.

Nielsen, J. M., Endo, R. K., & Ellington, B. L. (1992). Social isolation and wife abuse: A research report. In E. C. Viano (Ed.), *Intimate violence: Interdisciplinary perspectives* (pp. 40–59). Bristol, PA: Taylor & Francis.

Nock, M. K., & Kazdin, A. E. (2002). Parent-directed physical aggression by clinic-referred youth. *Journal of Clinical and Child Psychology, 31,* 193–205.

Noelker, L. S., Ejaz, F. K., Menne, H. L., & Jones, J. A. (2006). The impact of stress and support on nursing assistant satisfaction. *Journal of Applied Gerontology, 25,* 307–323.

Nomura, Y., & Chemtob, C. M. (2007). Conjoined effects of low birth weight and childhood abuse on adaptation and well-being in adolescence and adulthood. *Archives of Pediatric & Adolescent Medicine, 161,* 186–192.

Noonan, R. K., & Charles, D. (2009). Developing teen dating violence prevention strategies: Formative research with middle school youth. *Violence Against Women, 15,* 1087–1105.

Nooner, K. B., et al. (2010). Youth self-report of physical and sexual abuse: A latent class analysis. *Child Abuse & Neglect, 34,* 146–154.

Norlander, B. & Eckhardt, C. (2005). Anger, hostility, and male perpetrators of intimate partner violence: A meta-analytic review. *Clinical Psychology Review, 25,* 119–152.

Norman, P., & Finan, E. (2001, November 12). Veil of tears. *People, 56,* 107–110.

Norris, J., George, W. H., Stoner, S. A., Masters, N. T., Zawacki, T., & Davis, K. C. (2006). Women's responses to sexual aggression: The effects of childhood trauma, alcohol, and prior relationship. *Experimental and Clinical Psychopharmacology, 14,* 402–411.

North American Man/Boy Love Association. (2002). *Statement of purpose.* Retrieved May 14, 2002, from http://qrd.tcp.com/qrd/orgs/NAMBLA/statement.of.purpose

Nosek, M. A., & Howland, C. A. (1998). *Abuse of women with disabilities.* Minneapolis: Minnesota Center Against Violence and Abuse.

Nugent-Borakove, M. E., Fanflik, P., Troutman, D., Johnson, N., Burgess, A., & O'Connor, A. L (2006). Testing the efficacy of SANE/SART programs: Do they make a difference in sexual assault arrest & prosecution outcomes? (NCJ Publication No. 214252). Washington, DC: U.S. Department of Justice.

Nunes, K. L., Firestone, P., Wexler, A. F., Jensen, T. L., & Bradford, J. M. (2007). Incarceration and recidivism among sexual offenders. *Law and Human Behavior, 31,* 305–318.

Nurius, P. S., Furrey, J., & Berliner, L. (1992). Coping capacity among women with abusive partners. *Violence and Victims, 7,* 229–243.

Nusbaum, N. J., Cheung, V. M., Cohen, J., Keca, M., & Mailey, B. (2006). Role of first responders in detecting and evaluating elders at risk. *Archives of Gerontology and Geriatrics, 43,* 361–367.

Nuttall, R., & Jackson, H. (1994). Personal history of childhood abuse among clinicians. *Child Abuse & Neglect, 18,* 455–472.

NYC official: Ban Japanese 'rape' video game (2009, February 20). *Fox News.* Retrieved from http://www.foxnews.com/story/0,2993,499284,00.html

Obinna, J., Krueger, S., Osterbaan, C., Sadusky, J. M., & DeVore, W. (2006). *Understanding the needs of the victims of sexual assault in the deaf community* (NCJ Publication No. 212867). Washington, DC: U.S. Department of Justice.

O'Brien, M., John, R. S., Margolin, G., & Erel, O. (1994). Reliability and diagnostic efficacy of parents' reports regarding children's exposure to marital aggression. *Violence and Victims, 9,* 45–62.

O'Connell, M., & Gooding, G. (2007, July). *Editing unmarried couples in Census Bureau data.* Washington, DC: U.S. Bureau of the Census.

October is domestic violence awareness month. (2007, October 4). *Thousand Oaks Acorn,* p. 5.

O'Donnell, C. J., Smith, A., & Madison, J. R. (2002). Using demographic risk factors to explain variations in the incidence of violence against women. *Journal of Interpersonal Violence, 17,* 1239–1262.

O'Donohue, W., Benuto, L., & Fanetti, M. (2010). Children's allegations of sexual abuse: A model for forensic assessment. *Psychological Injury and Law, 3,* 148–154.

O'Farrell, T. J., Fals-Stewart, W., Murphy, M., & Murphy, C. M. (2003). Partner violence before and after individually based alcoholism treatment for male alcoholic patients. *Journal of Consulting and Clinical Psychology, 71,* 92–102.

O'Farrell, T. J., Murphy, C. M., Neavins, T. M., & Van Hutton, V. (2000). Verbal aggression among male alcoholic patients and their wives in the year before and two years after alcoholism treatment. *Journal of Family Violence, 15,* 295–310.

Office for Victims of Crime. (1999). *Breaking the cycle of violence: Recommendations to improve the criminal justice response to child victims and witnesses.* Washington, DC: U.S. Department of Justice.

Office for Victims of Crime. (2002). *Strengthening antistalking statutes* (NCJ Publication No. 189192). Washington, DC: U.S. Department of Justice.

Office of the Surgeon General. (2001). Youth Violence: A report of the Surgeon General. Washington, DC: Office of Public Health and Science, http://www.surgeongeneral.gov/library/youthviolence.

Office of Violence Against Women. (2009, August). Violence against women online resources. The facts about sexual violence. http://www.vaw.umn.edu

Office on Aging. (2007). www.apa.org/pi/aging/eldabuse .html, 2007)

Ofuro, bathing ritual in Japan. (1995, June 30). Retrieved from http://www.travbuddy.com/travel-blogs/9389/Ofuro-Bathing-ritual-Japan-1#

Oh, J., Kim, H. S., Martins, D., & Kim, H. (2006). A study of elder abuse in Korea. *International Journal of Nursing Studies, 43,* 203–214.

O'Hagan, K. (1995). Emotional and psychological abuse: Problems of definition. *Child Abuse & Neglect, 19,* 449–461.

Ohlin, L., & Tonry, M. (1989). Family violence in perspective. In L. Ohlin & M. Tonry (Eds.), *Violence in marriage* (pp. 1–18). Chicago: University of Chicago Press.

OJJDP News @ a Glance. (2006, November/December). *International conference focuses on Children's Advocacy Centers.* Rockville, MD: U.S. Department of Justice at http://www.ipscan.org

O'Keefe, M. (1994). Adjustment of children from maritally violent homes. *Families in Society, 75,* 403–415.

O'Keefe, M. (1997). Incarcerated battered women: A comparison of battered women who killed their abusers and those incarcerated for other offenses. *Journal of Family Violence, 12,* 1–18.

O'Keefe, M. (1998). Factors mediating the link between witnessing interparental violence and dating violence. *Journal of Family Violence, 13,* 39–57.

O'Keefe, M., & Treister, L. (1998). Victims of dating violence among high school students. *Violence Against Women, 4,* 195–223.

Okie, S. (2005). Traumatic brain injury in the war zone. *New England Journal of Medicine, 352,* 2043–2047.

Okun, L. E. (1986). *Woman abuse: Facts replacing myths.* Albany: State University of New York Press.

Olafson, E., Corwin, D. L., & Summit, R. C. (1993). Modern history of child sexual abuse awareness: Cycles of discovery and suppression. *Child Abuse & Neglect, 17,* 7–24.

Olaya, B., Ezpeleta, L., de la Osa, N., Granero, R., & Doménech, J. M. (2010). Mental health needs of children exposed to intimate partner violence seeking help from mental health services. *Children and Youth Services Review, 32,* 1004–1011.

Olds, D. L. (2006). The nurse-family partnership: An evidence-based preventive intervention. *Infant Mental Health Journal, 27*(1), 5–25.

O'Leary, K. D. (1993). Through a psychological lens: Personality traits, personality disorders, and levels of violence. In R. J. Gelles & D. R. Loseke (Eds.), *Current controversies on family violence* (pp. 7–30). Newbury Park, CA: Sage.

O'Leary, K. D. (1996). Physical aggression in intimate relationships can be treated within a marital context under certain circumstances. *Journal of Interpersonal Violence, 11,* 450–452.

O'Leary, K. D. (1999). Psychological abuse: A variable deserving critical attention in domestic violence. *Violence and Victims, 14,* 3–23.

O'Leary, K. D., Slep, A. M. S., & O'Leary, S. G. (2007). Multivariate models of men's and women's partner aggression. *Journal of Consulting and Clinical Psychology, 75,* 752–764.

O'Leary, K. D., & Williams, M. C. (2006). Agreement about acts of aggression in marriage. *Journal of Family Psychology, 20,* 656–662.

O'Leary, K. D., Woodin, E. M., & Fritz, P. T. (2006). Can we prevent the hitting? Implications for the prevention of partner violence. *Journal of Aggression, Maltreatment and Trauma, 13,* 125–181.

Olinger, J. P. (1991). Elder abuse: The outlook for federal legislation. *Journal of Elder Abuse & Neglect, 3*(1), 43–52.

Oliver, J., & Washington, K. T. (2009). Treating perpetrators of child physical abuse. *Trauma, Violence, & Abuse, 10,* 115–124.

Olshen, E., McVeigh, K. H., Wunsch-Hitzig, R. A., & Rickert, V. I. (2007). Dating violence, sexual assault, and suicide attempts among urban teenagers. *Archives of Pediatric and Adolescent Medicine, 161,* 539–545.

Olson, D. E., & Stalans, L. J. (2001). Violent offenders on probation: Profile, sentence, and outcome differences among domestic violence and other violent probationers. *Violence Against Women, 7,* 1164–1185.

Olson, L. N., & Lloyd, S. A. (2005). "It depends on what you mean by starting": An exploration of how women define initiation of aggression and their motives for behaving aggressively. *Sex Roles, 53,* 603–617.

O'Malley, H. C., Segel, H. D., & Perez, R. (1979). *Elder abuse in Massachusetts: Survey of professionals and paraprofessionals.* Boston: Legal Research and Services to the Elderly.

Omer, S. B., Salmon, D. A., Orenstein, W. A., deHart, M. P., & Halsey, N. (2009). Vaccine refusal, mandatory immunization, and the risks of vaccine-preventable diseases. *New England Journal of Medicine, 360,* 1981–1988.

Ondersma, S. J., Simpson, S. M., Brestan, E. V., & Ward, M. (2000). Prenatal drug exposure and social policy: The search for an appropriate response. *Child Maltreatment, 5,* 93–108.

O'Neal, M. F., & Dorn, P. W. (1998). Effects of time and an educational presentation on student attitudes toward wife-beating. *Violence and Victims, 13,* 149–157.

O'Neill, D. (1998). A post-structuralist review of the theoretical literature surrounding wife abuse. *Violence Against Women, 4,* 457–490.

Oprea, A. (2005). The arranged marriage of Ana Maria Cioba, intra-community oppression and Romani feminist ideals. *European Journal of Women's Studies, 12,* 133–148.

Orchowsky, S., & Weiss, J. (2000). Domestic violence and sexual assault data collection systems in the United States. *Violence Against Women, 6,* 904–911.

O'Reilly, R., Wilkes, L., Luck, L., & Jackson, D. (2010). The efficacy of family support and family preservation services on reducing child abuse and neglect: What the literature reveals. *Journal of Child Health Care, 14,* 82–94.

Orlov, R. (2008, October, 30). Rape kit analysis advances. *Daily News,* p. A4.

Orme, J. (2003). 'It's feminist because I say so.' *Qualitative Social Work, 2,* 131–153.

Orme, J., Dominelli, L., & Mullender, A. (2000). Working with violent men from a feminist social work perspective. *International Social Work, 43,* 89–105.

Ortiz, J. (2006, October 21). Court won't consider Neb, 'rape' testimony issue. *Associated Press,* USA Today.com.

Osborne, C. & Berger, L. M. (2009). Parental substance abuse and child well-being. *Journal of Family Issues, 30,* 341–370.

Osgood, N. J., & Manetta, A. A. (2002). Developing a service response to elder abuse. *Generations, 24,* 86–93.

Osmond, M., Durham, D., Leggett, A., & Keating, J. (1998). *Treating the aftermath of sexual abuse: A handbook for working with children in care.* Washington, DC: Child Welfare League of America.

Osofsky, J. D. (1999). The impact of violence on children. *Future of Children, 9*(3), 33–49.

Osofsky, J. D., et al. (2007). The development and evaluation of the intervention model for the Florida Infant Mental Health Pilot Program. *Infant Mental Health Journal, 28,* 299–280.

Ost, J. (2003). Seeking the middle ground in the "memory wars." *British Journal of Psychology, 94,* 125–139.

Osthoff, S. (2002). But, Gertrude, I beg to differ, a hit is not a hit is not a hit. *Violence Against Women, 8,* 1521–1544.

Osthoff, S., & Maguigan, H. (2005). Explaining without pathologizing. In D. R. Loseke, R. J. Gelles, & M. M. Cavanaugh (Eds.), *Current controversies on family violence* (2nd ed., pp. 225–240). Thousand Oaks, CA: Sage.

Oswald, R. F., & Kuvalanka, K. A. (2008). Same-sex couples: Legal complaints. *Journal of Family Issues, 29,* 1051–1066.

Otto, J. M. (2000, May/June). Fitting elder abuse into the family violence continuum. *Victimization of the Elderly and Disabled, 3,* 5–6.

Otto, J. M. (2005, May/June). Twenty years of a community review team. *Victimization of the Elderly and Disabled, 8,* 3, 14–16.

Otto, J. M., & Quinn, K. (2007, May). *Barriers to and promising practices for collaboration between adult protective services and domestic violence programs.* Washington, DC: The National Center on Elder Abuse.

Otto, R. K., & Melton, G. B. (1990). Trends in legislation and case law on child abuse and neglect. In R. T. Ammerman & M. Hersen (Eds.), *Children at risk: An evaluation of factors contributing to child abuse and neglect* (pp. 55–83). New York: Plenum.

Outlaw, M. (2009). No one type of intimate partner abuse: Exploring physical and non-physical abuse among intimate partners. *Journal of Family Violence, 24,* 263–272.

Owen, A. E., Mitchell, M. D., Paranjape, A., & Hargrove, G. L. (2008). Perceived social support as a mediator of the link between intimate partner conflict and child adjustment. *Journal of Family Violence, 23,* 221–230.

Oz, S. (2010). Treatment of individuals and families affected by child sexual abuse: Defining professional expertise. *Journal of Child Sexual Abuse, 19,* 1–19.

Packard, E. (2007, March). $20,000 grant awarded to fight sexual violence. *Monitor on Psychology, 38,* 68–69.

Pagano, N., Mihaly, C., Dauenhauer, A., & Mason, A. (2007, September/October). County-based needs assessment. *Victimization of the Elderly and Disabled, 10,* 33, 44–46.

Page, A. D. (2008). Gateway to reform? Policy implications of police officers' attitudes toward rape. *American Journal of Criminal Justice, 33,* 44–58.

Page, R. M., & O'Hegarty, M. (2006). Type of student residence as a factor in college students' alcohol consumption and social normative perceptions regarding alcohol use. *Journal of Child and Adolescent Substance Abuse, 15*(3), 15–31.

Pagelow, M. D. (1981). *Woman-battering: Victims and their experiences.* Beverly Hills, CA: Sage.

Pagelow, M. D. (1984). *Family violence.* New York: Praeger.

Pagelow, M. D. (1992). Adult victims of domestic violence. *Journal of Interpersonal Violence, 7,* 87–120.

Palermo, G. B. (2010a). Editorial: Reintegration and recidivism. *International Journal of Offender Therapy and Comparative Criminology, 53,* 3–4.

Palermo, G. B. (2010b). Editorial: Parricide. *International Journal of Offender Therapy and Comparative Criminology, 54,* 3–5.

Palusci, V. J., & Haney, M. L. (2010, Winter). Strategies to prevent child maltreatment and integration into practice. *APSAC Advisor, 22*(1), 8–17.

Pan, H. S., Neidig, P. H., & O'Leary, K. D. (1994). Predicting mild and severe husband-to-wife physical aggression. *Journal of Consulting and Clinical Psychology, 62,* 975–981.

Panchanadeswaran, S., & Koverola, C. (2005). The voices of battered women in India. *Violence Against Women, 11,* 736–758.

Panchanadeswaran, S., & McCloskey, L. A. (2007). Predicting the timing of women's departure from abusive relationships. *Journal of Interpersonal Violence, 22,* 50–65.

Pandey, G. K., Dutt, D., & Banerjee, B. (2009). Partner and relationship factors in domestic violence. *Journal of Interpersonal Violence, 24,* 1175–1191.

Panicker, S. (2008, January). Experts examine vulnerability and risk in behavioral research. *APA Online, 22.*

Paranjape, A., Corbie-Smith, G., Thompson, N., & Kaslow, N. J. (2009). When older African American women are affected by violence in the home. *Violence Against Women, 15,* 975–990.

Pardeck, J. T., & Pardeck, J. A. (2007), An overview of and comments on the American with Disabilities Act (ADA). *Journal of Social Work in Disability & Rehabilitation, 6,* 67–91.

Paris, J. (2001). Why behavioral genetics is important for psychiatry [Editorial]. *Canadian Journal of Psychiatry, 46,* 223–224.

Pariset, J. M., Feldman, K. W., & Paris, C. (2010). The pace of signs and symptoms of blunt abdominal trauma in children. *Clinical Pediatrics, 49,* 24–28.

Parish, S. L., Magaña, S., & Cassiman, S. A. (2008). It's just that much harder. *Affilia, 23,* 51–65.

Parker, J. G., & Herrera, C. (1996). Interpersonal processes in friendship: A comparison of abused and nonabused children's experiences. *Developmental Psychology, 32,* 1025–1038.

Parrott, D. J., & Zeichner, A. (2003a). Effects of hypermasculinity on physical aggression against women. *Psychology of Men & Masculinity, 4*(1), 70–78.

Parrott, D. J., & Zeichner, A. (2003b). Effects of trait anger and negative attitudes towards women on physical assault in dating relationships. *Journal of Family Violence, 18,* 301–307.

*Partnership with faith communities to provide elder fraud prevention, intervention, and victim services.* (2006). Washington, DC: Office of Victims of Crime.

Pascall, G., Lee, S. J., Morley, R., & Parker, S. (2001). Changing housing policy: Women escaping domestic violence. *Journal of Social Welfare and Family Law, 23,* 293–309.

Paschall, M. J., & Fishbein, D. H. (2002). Executive cognitive functioning and aggression: A public health perspective. *Aggression and Violent Behavior, 7,* 215–235.

Patchin, J. W., & Hinduja, S. (2006). Bullies move beyond the schoolyard: A preliminary look at cyberbullying. *Youth Violence and Juvenile Justice, 4,* 148–169.

Paterson, J., Feehan, M., Butler, S., Williams, M., & Cowley-Malcolm, E. (2007). Intimate partner violence within a cohort of mothers living in New Zealand. *Journal of Interpersonal Violence, 22,* 698–721.

Paterson, R., Luntz, H., Perlesz, A., & Cotton, S. (2002) Adolescent violence toward parents: Maintaining family connections when the going gets tough. *Australian and New Zealand Journal of Family Therapy, 23,* 90–100.

Pattavina, A., Hirschel, D., Buzawa, E., Faggiani, D., & Bentley, H. (2007). A comparison of the police response to heterosexual versus same-sex intimate partner violence. *Violence Against Women, 13,* 374–394.

Patterson, G. R. (1982). *Coercive family process.* Eugene, OR: Castalia.

Paudel, G. S. (2007). Domestic violence against women in Nepal. *Gender, Technology and Development, 11,* 199–223.

Paul, L., & Galloway, J. (1994). Sexual jealousy: Gender differences in response to partner and rival. *Aggressive Behavior, 3,* 203–211.

Paulozzi, L. J., Saltzman, L. E., Thompson, M. P., & Holmgreen, P. (2001, October 12). Surveillance for homicide among intimate partners—United States, 1981–1998. *Morbidity and Mortality Weekly Report, 50,* 1–15.

Paveza, G. J., Cohen, D., Eisdorfer, C., Freels, S., Semla, T., Ashford, J. W., et al. (1992). Severe family violence and Alzheimer's disease: Prevalence and risk factors. *Gerontologist, 32,* 493–497.

Paying for long-term care. (2009, December). Retrieved from http://www.longtermcare.gov/LTC/main

Payne, B. K. (2005). *Crime and elder abuse: An integrated perspective.* Springfield, IL: Charles C. Thomas.

Payne, B. K. (2007). Victim advocates' perceptions of the role of health care workers in sexual assault cases. *Criminal Justice Policy Review, 18,* 81–94.

Payne, B. K., & Appel, J. K. (2007). Workplace violence and worker injury in elderly care settings: Reflective of a setting vulnerable to elder abuse? *Journal of Aggression, Maltreatment & Trauma, 14*(4), 43–56.

Payne, B. K., & Berg, B. L. (2003). Perceptions about the criminalization of elder abuse among police chiefs and omsbudsmen. *Crime & Delinquency, 49,* 439–459.

Payne, B. K., Carmody, D. C., Plitchta, S., & Vandecar-Burdin, T. (2007). Domestic violence training policies: Influence on participation in training and awareness of abuse. *Affilia, 22,* 292–301.

Payne, B. K., & Triplett, R. (2009). Assessing the domestic violence training needs of benefit workers. *Journal of Family Violence, 24,* 243–253.

Peace, K. A., Porter, S., & ten Brinke, L. (2008). Are memories for sexually traumatic events "special"? A within-subjects investigation of trauma and memory in a clinical sample. *Memory, 16,* 10–21.

Peacock, D., & Rothman, E. (2001*). Working with young men who batter: Current strategies and new directions.* VAWnet

Applied Research Forum: National Online Resources Center on Domestic Violence.

Pear, R. (2008, September 28). Violations reported at 94% of nursing homes. *New York Times.* Retrieved from http://www.nytimes.com/2008/09/30/us/30nursing.html

Pearl, J. (2000). *Causality: Models, reasoning, and inference.* New York: Cambridge University Press.

Pearsall, C. (2005), Forensic biomarkers of elder abuse: What clinicians needs to know. *Journal of Forensic Nursing, 1,* 182–186.

Pelcovitz, D., Kaplan, S., Goldenberg, B., & Mandel, F. (1994). Posttraumatic stress disorder in physically abused adolescents. *Journal of the American Academy of Child and Adolescent Psychiatry, 33,* 305–312.

Peled, E., Eisikovits, Z., Enosh, G., & Winstok, Z. (2000). Choice and empowerment for battered women who stay. *Social Work, 45,* 9–25.

Pelligrini, A. D., & Long, J. (2002). A longitudinal study of bullying, dominance, and victimization during the transition from primary to secondary school. *British Journal of Developmental Psychology, 20,* 259–280.

Pence, D. M. (2010). Child abuse and neglect investigations. In J. E. B. Myers (Ed.), *The APSAC handbook on child maltreatment* (3rd ed., pp. 325–336). Thousand Oaks, CA: Sage.

Pence, E., & Paymar, M. (1993). *Education groups for men who batter: The Duluth model.* New York: Springer.

Penke, L., & Asendorpf, J. B. (2007). Evidence for conditional sex differences in emotional but not in sexual jealousy at the automatic level of cognitive processing. *European Journal of Personality, 22,* 3–30.

Penley, J. A., Tomaka, J., & Wiebe, J. S. (2002). The association of coping to physical and psychological health outcomes: A meta-analytic review. *Journal of Behavioral Medicine, 25,* 551–603.

Pereda, N., Guilera, G., Forns, M., & Gómez-Benito, J. (2009). The prevalence of child sexual abuse in community and student samples. *Clinical Psychology Review, 29,* 328–338.

Perilla, J. L., Bakeman, R., & Norris, F. H. (1994). Culture and domestic violence: The ecology of abused Latinas. *Violence and Victims, 9,* 325–339.

Perrin, R. D., & Miller-Perrin, C. L. (2004, April 15–18). *Statistical claims-making in family violence advocacy.* Paper presented at the annual meeting of the Pacific Sociological Association, San Francisco.

Perry, A. (2007, August/September). Florida appellate court finds no child abuse where father told six-year-old son to kill his mother. *Domestic Violence Report, 12,* 84.

Peter, T. (2008). Speaking about the unspeakable: Exploring the impact of mother-daughter sexual abuse. *Violence Against Women, 14,* 1033–1053.

Peter, T. (2009). Exploring taboos: Comparing male- and female-perpetrated child sexual abuse. *Journal of Interpersonal Violence, 24,* 1111–1128.

Peterman, L. M., & Dixon, C. G. (2003). Intimate partner abuse between same-sex partners: Implication for counseling. *Journal of Counseling and Development, 81,* 40–59.

Peters, J. (2008). Measuring myths about domestic violence: Development and initial validation of the domestic violence myth acceptance scale. *Journal of Aggression, Maltreatment & Trauma, 16,* 1–21.

Peters, J. M. (1989). Criminal prosecution of child abuse: Recent trends. *Pediatric Annals, 18,* 505–509.

Peterson, C., Maier, S. F., & Seligman, M. E. P. (1993). *Learned helplessness: A theory for the age of personal control.* New York: Oxford University Press.

Pfeifer, S. (2002, November 21). Tough love or abuse? *Los Angeles Times,* p. A1.

Pfeifer, S., & Anton, M. (2002, December 17). Parents' action not conspiracy, jury says. *Los Angeles Times,* p. B1.

Pfeiffer, S. M., & Wong, P. T. P. (1989). Multidimensional jealousy. *Journal of Social and Personal Relationships, 6,* 181–196.

Pflieger, J. C., & Vazsonyi, A. T. (2005). Parenting process and dating violence: The mediating role of self-esteem in low- and high-SES adolescents. *Journal of Adolescence, 29,* 495–512.

Pfohl, S. J. (1977). The "discovery" of child abuse. *Social Problems, 24,* 310–323.

Pharaon, N. A. (2004). Saudi women and the Muslim state in the twenty-first century. *Sex Roles, 51,* 349–366.

Phelan, M. B., Hamberger, L. K., Guse, C. E., Edwards, S., Walczak, S., & Zosel, A. (2005). Domestic violence among male and female patients seeking emergency medical services. *Violence and Victims, 20,* 187–206.

Phillips, D. A. (2007). Punking and bullying. *Journal of Interpersonal Violence, 22,* 158–178.

Phillips, L. R. (1996). *Final report of the causal and cultural factors affecting the quality of family caregiving project.* Unpublished manuscript, University of Arizona, Tucson.

Phillipsen, N. C. (2003). Abandoned-baby laws. *The Journal of Perinatal Education, 12,* 41–43.

Phillips-Green, M. J. (2002). Sibling incest. *The Family Journal: Counseling and Therapy for Couples and Families, 10,* 195–202.

Physical violence and injuries in intimate relationships—New York, Behavioral Risk Factor Surveillance System, 1994. (1996). *Morbidity and Mortality Weekly Report, 45,* 765–767.

Pianta, R. C., & Egeland, B. (1994). Relation between depressive symptoms and stressful life events in a sample of disadvantaged mothers. *Journal of Consulting and Clinical Psychology, 62,* 1229–1234.

Pico-Alfonso, M. A. (2005). Psychological intimate partner violence: The major predictor of posttraumatic stress disorder in abused women. *Neuroscience, 29,* 181–193.

Piers, M. W. (1978). *Infanticide: Past and present.* New York: Norton.

Pillemer, K. A. (2005). Elder abuse is caused by the deviance and dependence of abusive caregivers. In D. R. Loseke, R. J. Gelles, & M. M. Cavanaugh (Eds.), *Current controversies on family violence* (2nd ed., pp. 207–220). Thousand Oaks, CA: Sage.

Pillemer, K. A., & Finkelhor, D. (1988). The prevalence of elder abuse: A random sample survey. *Gerontologist, 28,* 51–57.

Pillemer, K. A., & Hudson, B. (1993). A model abuse prevention program for nursing assistants. *Gerontologist, 33,* 128–131.

Pines, A. M. (1998). *Romantic jealousy: Causes, symptoms, cures.* New York: Routledge.

Pinto-Foltz, M. D., & Logsdon, M. C. (2008). Stigma towards mental illness: A concept analysis using postpartum depression as an examplar. *Issues in Mental Health Nursing, 29,* 21–36.

Pittman, F. (1987). *Turning points: Treating families in transition and crisis.* New York: Norton.

Pitzner, J. K., & Drummond, P. D. (1997). The reliability and validity of empirically scaled measures of psychological/verbal control and physical/sexual abuse: Relationship between mood and a history of abuse independent of other negative events. *Journal of Psychonomic Research, 43,* 125–142.

Pizzey, E. (1974). *Scream quietly or the neighbours will hear.* Harmondsworth, UK: Penguin.

Pleck, E. (1987). *Domestic tyranny: The making of American social policy against family violence from colonial times to present.* New York: Oxford University Press.

Pledger, C. (2003). Discourse on disability and rehabilitation issues: Opportunities for psychology. *American Psychologist, 58,* 279–284.

Pogarsky, G., Thornberry, T. P., & Lizotte, A. J. (2006). Developmental outcomes for children of young mothers. *Journal of Marriage and Family, 68,* 332–344.

Police agencies lack experience investigating cyberstalking. (2001). *Criminal Justice Newsletter, 31*(19), 6–7.

Police: N.M. suspect shot unborn son. (2009, June 05). Santa Fe Mexican, NM. Retrieved from http://www.lorain.oh.networkofcare.org/dv/news/detail.cfm?articleID=23699

Pollak, S. D., Vardi, S., Bechner, A. M. P., & Curtain, J. J. (2005). Physically abused children's regulation of attention in response to hostility. *Child Development, 76,* 968–977.

Pollet, S. L., & Lombreglia, M. (2008). A nationwide survey of mandatory parent education. *Family Court Review, 46,* 375–396.

Polusny, M. A., & Follette, V. M. (2008). Long-term correlates of child sexual abuse: Theory and review of the empirical literature. *Applied and Preventive Psychology, 4,* 143–166.

Pontius, A. A. (2002). Impact of fear-inducing violence on neuropsychological visuo-spatial test in warring hunter-gatherers: Analogies to violent Western environments. *Aggression and Violent Behavior, 7,* 69–84.

Poole, A., Beran, T., & Thurston, W. E. (2008). Direct and indirect services for children in domestic violence shelters. *Journal of Family Violence, 23,* 679–686.

Popejoy, L. L., Rantz, M. J., Conn, V., Wipke-Tevis, D., Grando, V. T., & Porter, R. (2000). Improving quality of care in nursing facilities. *Journal of Gerontological Nursing, 26*(4), 6–13.

Porter, A. (2004, November). Cognitive processing patterns associated with completion of treatment for domestic violence. *Dissertation Abstracts International* (DAI-B 65/05), p. 2646.

Portwood, S. G. (1999). Coming to terms with a consensual definition of child maltreatment. *Child Maltreatment, 4,* 56–68.

Post, D. (2008). Mothers file international court complaint against the U.S. *Family and Intimate Partner Violence Quarterly, 1,* 61–66.

Post, L., Page, C., Conner, T., Prokhorov, A., Fang, & Biroscak, B. J., (2010). Elder abuse in long-term care: Types, patterns, and risk factors. *Research on Aging, 32,* 323–348.

Postmus, J. L. (2003). Valuable assistance or missed opportunities? *Violence Against Women, 9,* 1278–1288.

Postmus, J. L., & Merritt, D. H. (2010). When child abuse overlaps with domestic violence: The factors that influence child protection workers' beliefs. *Children and Youth Services Review, 32,* 309–317.

Postmus, J. L., Severson, M., Berry, M., & Yoo, J. A. (2009). Women's experiences of violence and seeking help. *Violence Against Women, 15,* 852–868.

Poteat, V. P., & Espelage, D. L. (2008). Predicting psychosocial consequences of homophobic victimization in middle school students. *Journal of Early Adolescence, 27,* 175–191.

Poteat, V. P., Espelage, D. L., & Koenig, B. W. (2009). Willingness to remain friends and attend school with lesbians and gay peers: Relational expressions of prejudice among heterosexual youth. *Journal of Youth and Adolescence, 38,* 952–962.

Potoczniak, M. J., Mourot, J. E., Crosbie-Burnett, M., & Potoczniak, D. J. (2003). Legal and psychological perspectives on same-sex domestic violence: A multisystemic approach. *Journal of Family Psychology, 17,* 252–259.

Potter, M. (2007, December 11). Blatant Medicare fraud costs taxpayers billions. Retrieved from http://msbc.com

Powell, M. E., & Berman, J. (2006). Effects of dependency on compliance rates among elder abuse victims at the New York City Department for the Aging, Elderly Crime Victim's Unit. *Journal of Gerontological Social Work, 46,* 229–247.

Power of attorney. In *Wikipedia, the free encyclopedia.* Retrieved May 4, 2010, from http://en.wikipedia.org/wiki/Power_of_attorney

Power, C., Koch, T., Kralik, D., & Jackson, D. (2006). Lovesick: Women, romantic love and intimate partner violence. *Contemporary Nurse, 21,* 174–185.

Powers, J. L., & Eckenrode, J. (1988). The maltreatment of adolescents. *Child Abuse & Neglect, 12,* 189–199.

Powers, L. E., Oschwald, M., Maley, S., Saxton, M., & Eckles, K. (2002). Barriers and strategies in addressing abuse: A survey of disabled women's experiences. *Journal of Rehabilitation, 68,* 4–13.

Powers, L. E., Renker, P., Robinson-Whelen, S., Oschwald, M., Hughes, R., Swank, P., & Curry, M. A. (2009). Interpersonal violence and women with disabilities. *Violence Against Women, 15,* 1040–1069.

Pratt, T. C., Gaffney, M. J., Lovrich, N. P., & Johnson, C. L. (2006). This isn't CSI: Estimating the backlog of forensic DNA cases and the barriers associated with case processing. *Criminal Justice Policy Review, 17,* 32–47.

Prentky, R. A. (2004). Can sex offender classification inform typologies of male batterers? A response to Holtzworth-Munroe and Meehan. *Journal of Interpersonal Violence, 19,* 1405–1411.

President signs legislation to increase child protection. (2006, August 17). *Criminal Justice Newsletter,* p. 3.

Preston, J. (2009, October 29). U.S. may be open to asylum for spouse abuse. *The New York Times,* p. A14.

Prevalence of individual adverse childhood experiences (ACE). (2006). Centers for Disease Control and Prevention. Retrieved from http://www.cdc.gov/print.do?url=http://www.cdc.gov/nccdphp/ace/prevalence.htm

Price, D. L., & Gwin, J. F. (2007). *Pediatric nursing: An introductory text.* Philadelphia, PA: Elsevier Health Sciences.

Price, M. (2007, October). Overseas, but under care. *APA Monitor on Psychology, 38,* 44.

Prison rape panel releases 'zero tolerance' standards. (2008, May 15). *Criminal Justice Newsletter,* pp. 1–3.

Procci, W. R. (1990). *Medical aspects of human sexuality.* New York: Cahners.

Procter, E. K., & Rosen, A. (2008). From knowledge production to implementation: Research challenges and imperatives. *Research on Social Work Practice, 18,* 285–291.

Próspero, M. (2008). The effect of coercion on aggression and mental health among reciprocally violent couples. *Journal of Family Violence, 23,* 185–202.

Pruett, K. D. (2007). Perspectives on family law and social science research: Social science research and social policy: Bridging the gap. *Family Court Review, 45,* 52–56.

Pryce, J. M., & Samuels, G. M. (2010). Renewal and risk: The dual experience of young motherhood and aging out of the child welfare system. *Journal of Adolescent Research, 25,* 205–230.

Pryor, D. W. (1996). *Unspeakable acts: Why men molest children.* New York: New York University Press.

Ptacek, J. (1999). *Battered women in the courtroom: The power of judicial responses.* Boston: Northeastern University Press.

Public health and aging: Nonfatal physical assault-related injuries among persons aged > 60 years treated in hospital emergency departments—United States, 2001. (2003). *Morbidity and Mortality Weekly Report, 52,* 812–816.

Puente, S., & Cohen, D. (2003). Jealousy and the meaning (or nonmeaning) of violence. *Personality and Social Psychology Bulletin, 29,* 449–460.

Purdie, V., & Downey, G. (2000). Rejection sensitivity and adolescent girls' vulnerabilities to relationship-centered difficulties. *Child Maltreatment, 5,* 338–349.

Purewal, J., & Ganesh, I. (2000). Gender violence, trauma, and its impact on women's mental health. *Journal of Indian Social Work, 61,* 542–557.

Purk, J. K., & Lindsay, S. (2006). Job satisfaction and intention to quit among frontline assisted living employees. *Journal of Aging and Health, 20,* 117–131.

Puzzanchera, C. (2009). *Juvenile arrests 2008* (NCJ No. 228–479). Office of Juvenile Justice and Delinquency Prevention (OJJDP). Rockville, MD: U.S. Department of Justice.

Pyles, L. (2007). The complexities of the religious response to domestic violence. *Affilia, 22,* 281–291.

Pyles, L., & Postmus, J. L. (2004). Addressing the problem of domestic violence: How far have we come? *Affilia, 19,* 376–368.

Quelopana, A. M., Champion, J. D., & Salazar, B. C. (2008). Health behavior in Mexican pregnant women with a history of violence. *Western Journal of Nursing Research, 30,* 1005–1018.

Quinn, M. J. (1985). Elder abuse and neglect. *Generations, 10*(2), 22–25.

Quinsey, V. L., Lalumière, M. L., Rice, M. E., & Harris, G. T. (1995). Predicting sexual offenses. In J. C. Campbell (Ed.), *Assessing dangerousness: Violence by sexual offenders, batterers, and child abusers* (pp. 114–137). Thousand Oaks, CA: Sage.

Rabiner, D. J., O'Keeffe, J. O., & Brown, D. (2006). Financial exploitation of older persons: Challenges and opportunities to identify, prevent, and address it in the United States. *Journal of Aging & Social Policy, 18,* 47–68.

Rabinowitz, S. S., Katturupalli, M., & Rogers, G. (2010). Failure to thrive. Retrieved from http://emedicine.medscape.com/article/985007-print, updated May 4, 2010.

Radford, L., & Gill, A. (2006). Losing the plot? Researching community safety partnership work against domestic violence. *The Howard Journal, 45,* 369–387.

Radosevich, A. C. (2000). Thwarting the stalker: Are anti-stalking measures keeping pace with today's stalker? *University of Illinois Law Review, 2000,* 1371–1395.

Rafnsson, F. D., Jonsson, F. H., & Windle, M. (2006). Coping strategies, stressful life events, problem behaviors, and depressed affect. *Anxiety, Stress, and Coping, 19,* 241–257.

Raghavan, C., Rajah, V., Gentile, K., Collado, L., & Kavanagh, A. M. (2009). Community violence, social support networks, ethnic group differences, and male perpetration of intimate partner violence. *Journal of Interpersonal Violence, 24,* 1615–1622.

Raghavan, C., Swan, S. C., Snow, D. L., & Mazure, C. M. (2005). The mediational role of relationship efficacy and resource utilization in the link between physical and psychological abuse and relationship termination. *Violence Against Women, 11,* 65–88.

Raine, A. (1993). *The psychopathology of crime: Criminal behavior as a clinical disorder.* San Diego, CA: Academic Press.

Raj, A., & Silverman, J. (2002). Violence against immigrant women: The roles of culture, context, and legal immigrant status on intimate partner violence. *Violence Against Women, 8,* 367–398.

Raj, A., & Silverman, J. (2003). Immigrant South Asian women at greater risk for injury from intimate partner violence. *American Journal of Public Health, 93,* 435–437.

Rajah, V., Frye, V., & Haviland, M. (2006). "Aren't I a victim?" Notes on identity challenges relating to police action in a mandatory arrest jurisdiction. *Violence Against Women, 12,* 897–916.

Ramsey, J., Richardson, J., Carter, Y, H., Davidson, L. L., & Feder, G. (2002). Should health professionals screen women for domestic violence? Systematic review. *BMJ: British Medical Journal, 325,* 314–318.

Ramsey-Klawsnik, H. (2004, July/August). Clinical practice: Alleged victimization. *Victimization of the Elderly and Disabled, 7,* 17, 31–32.

Ramsey-Klawsnik, H. (2006, November/December). Victimization of elders by offspring. *Victimization of the Elderly and Disabled, 9,* 51–52, 64.

Ramsey-Klawsnik, H., Teaster, P. B., Mendiondo, M. S., Abner, E. L., Cecil, K. A., & Tooms, M. R. (2007). Sexual abuse of vulnerable adults in care facilities: Clinical findings and a research initiative. *Journal of the American Psychiatric Nurses Association, 12,* 332–339.

Ramsey-Klawsnik, H., Teaster, P. B., Mendiondo, M. S., Marcum, J. L., & Abner, E. L. (2008). Sexual predators who target elders: Findings from the First National Study of Sexual Abuse in Care Facilities. *Journal of Elder Abuse & Neglect, 20,* 353–376.

Rand, M. R. (1997). *Violence-related injuries treated in hospital emergency departments* (NCJ Publication No. 156921). Rockville, MD: U.S. Department of Justice.

Rand, M. R. (2009, September). *National Crime Victimization Survey, Criminal Victimization, 2008* (NCJ Publication No. 227777). U.S. Department of Justice, Bureau of Justice Statistics.

Rand, M. R., & Harrell, E. (2009). *Crime against people with disabilities, 2007* (NCJ Publication No. 227814). U.S. Department of Justice, NCVS.

Rand, M. R., & Saltzman, L. E. (2003). The nature and extent of recurring intimate partner violence against women in the United States. *Journal of Comparative Family Studies, 34,* 137–149.

Randolf, M. K., & Conkle, L. K. (1993). Behavioral and emotional characteristics of children who witness parental violence. *Family Violence and Sexual Assault Bulletin, 9*(2), 23–27.

Raphael, J. (1996). *Prisoners of abuse: Domestic violence and welfare receipt.* Chicago: Taylor Institute.

Raphael, J., & Tolman, R. M. (1997). *Trapped by poverty/trapped by abuse: New evidence documents the relationship between domestic violence and welfare* (A research compilation from the Project for Research on Welfare, Work, and Domestic Violence, a collaborative project). Ann Arbor: Taylor Institute and University of Michigan.

Rapoza, K. A., & Baker, A. T. (2008). Attachment styles, alcohol, and childhood experiences of abuse: An analysis of physical violence in dating couples. *Violence and Victims, 23,* 52–65.

Rastogi, M., & Therly, P. (2006). Dowry and its link to violence against women in India. *Trauma, Violence, & Abuse, 7,* 66–77.

Ratner, C. (2008). Cultural psychology and qualitative methodology: Scientific and political considerations. *Culture & Psychology, 14,* 259–288.

Rausch, S. L., van der Kolk, B. A., Fisler, R. F., & Alpert, N. M. (1996). A symptom provocation study of posttraumatic stress disorder using positron emission tomography and script-driven imagery. *Archives of General Psychiatry, 53,* 380–387.

Rawlings, E. I., Allen, G., Graham, D. L. R., & Peters, J. (1994). Chinks in the prison wall: Applying Graham's Stockholm syndrome theory in the treatment of battered women. In L. Vandecreek, S. Knapp, & T. L. Jackson (Eds.), *Innovations in clinical practice: A source book* (Vol. 13, pp. 401–417). Sarasota, FL: Professional Resource Press.

Raymond, J. A. (2008). Housing and the older battered woman. *Family & Intimate Partner Violence Quarterly, 1,* 135–140.

Real men, real depression. (2003). National Institute of Mental Health. Retrieved from http://www.nimh.nih.gov

Reay, A. C., & Browne, K. D. (2002). The effectiveness of psychological interventions with individuals who physically abuse or neglect their elderly dependents. *Journal of Interpersonal Violence, 17,* 416–431.

Rebovich, D. J. (1996). Prosecution response to domestic violence: Results of a survey of large jurisdictions. In E. S. Buzawa & C. G. Buzawa (Eds.), *Do arrests and restraining orders work?* (pp. 176–191). Thousand Oaks, CA: Sage.

Records show uneven domestic violence effort. (1994, September 25). *Boston Globe,* pp. 1, 28–29.

Reece, R. M. (2010). Medical evaluation of physical abuse. In J. E. B. Myers (Ed.), *The APSAC handbook on child maltreatment* (3rd ed., pp. 183–193). Thousand Oaks, CA: Sage.

Reece, R. M., & Nicholson, C. E. (Eds.). (2003). *Inflicted childhood neurotrauma.* Elk Grove Village, IL: American Academy of Pediatrics.

Redding, R. E. (2001). Sociopolitical diversity in psychology. *American Psychologist, 56,* 205–215.

Reed, D. (1999). Where's the penalty flag? A call for the NCAA to promulgate an eligibility rule revoking a male student-athlete's ability to participate in intercollegiate athletics for committing violent acts against women. *Women's Rights Law Reporter, 21,* 41–56.

Reed, G. L., & Enright, R. D. (2006). The effects of forgiveness therapy on depression, anxiety, and posttraumatic stress for women after spousal emotional abuse. *Journal of Clinical and Consulting Psychology, 74,* 920–929.

Reeves, C., & O'Leary-Kelly, A. M. (2007). The effects and costs of intimate partner violence for work organization. *Journal of Interpersonal Violence, 22,* 327–344.

Regan, K. V., Bartholomew, K., Kwong, M. J., Trinke, S. J., & Henderson, A, J. Z. (2006). The relative severity of acts of physical violence in heterosexual relationships: An item response theory analysis. *Personal Relationships, 13,* 37–52.

Regan, K. V., Bartholomew, K., Oram, D., & Landolt, M. A. (2002). Measuring physical violence in male same-sex relationships: An item response theory analysis of the Conflict Tactics Scales. *Journal of Interpersonal Violence, 17,* 235–252.

Regoeczi, W. C. (2001). Exploring racial variations in the spousal sex ratio of killing. *Violence and Victims, 16,* 591–606.

Reid, C. E., Moss, S., & Hyman, G. (2005). Caregiver reciprocity: The effect of reciprocity, carer self-esteem and motivation on the experience of caregiver burden. *Australian Journal of Psychology, 57,* 186–196.

Reid-Cunningham, A. R. (2009). Parent-child relationship and mother's sexual assault history. *Violence Against Women, 15,* 920–932.

Reingold, D. A. (2006). An elder abuse shelter program: Build it and they will come, a long term care based program to address elder abuse in the community. *Journal of Gerontological Social Work, 46,* 123–135.

Reitzel, L. R., & Carbonell, J. L. (2006). The effectiveness of sexual offender treatment for juveniles as measured by recidivism: A meta-analysis. *Sexual Abuse: A Journal of Research and Treatment, 18,* 401–421.

Reitzel-Jaffe, D., & Wolfe, D. A. (2001). Predictors of relationship abuse among young men. *Journal of Interpersonal Violence, 16,* 99–115.

Remillard, A. M., & Lamb, S. (2005). Adolescent girls' coping with relationship aggression. *Sex Roles, 53,* 221–229.

Renk, K., Liljequist, L., Steinberg, A., Bosco, G., & Phares, V. (2002). Prevention of child sexual abuse: Are we doing enough? *Trauma, Violence, & Abuse, 3,* 68–84.

Renner, L. M. (2009). Intimate partner violence victimization and parenting stress: Assessing the mediating role of depressive symptoms. *Violence Against Women, 15,* 1380–1401.

Rennison, C. M. (2007). Reporting to the police by Hispanic victims of violence. *Violence and Victims, 22,* 754–772.

Rennison, C. M., & Rand, M. R. (2003). *Nonlethal intimate partner violence against women: A comparison of three age cohorts* (NCJ Publication No. 203207). U.S. Department of Justice, NCVS.

Rennison, C. M., & Welchans, S. (2000). *Intimate partner violence* (NCJ Publication No. 178247). Washington, DC: U.S. Department of Justice.

Rentz, E. D., Martin, S. K., Gibbs, D. A., Clinton-Sherrod, M., Hardison, J., & Marshall, S. W. (2006). Family violence in the military: A review of the literature. *Trauma, Violence, & Abuse,* 93–108.

Rentz, E. D., Marshall, S. W., Loomis, D., Casteel, C., Martin, S. L., & Gibbs, D. A. (2007). Effect of deployment on the occurrence of child maltreatment in military and non-military families. *American Journal of Epidemiology, 165,* 1199–1206.

Renzetti, C. M. (1992). *Violent betrayal: Partner abuse in lesbian relationships.* Newbury Park, CA: Sage.

Repetti, R. L., Matthews, K. A., & Waldron, I. (1989). Employment and women's health: Effects of paid employment on women's mental and physical health. *American Psychologist, 44,* 1394–1401.

Repetti, R. L., Taylor, S. E., & Seeman, T. E. (2002). Risky families: Family social environments and the mental and physical health of offspring. *Psychological Bulletin, 128,* 330–366.

Reppucci, N. D., Land, D., & Haugaard, J. J. (1998). Child sexual abuse prevention programs that target young children. In P. K. Trickett & C. J. Schellenbach (Eds.), *Violence against children in the family and the community* (pp. 317–337). Washington, DC: American Psychological Association.

Resnick, J. L. (2006). Strategies for implementation of the multicultural guidelines in university and college counseling centers. *Professional Psychology, Research and Practice, 37,* 14–20.

Ressler, K. J., Rothbaum, B. O., Tannenbaum, L., Anderson, P., Graap, K., Zimand, E., et al. (2004). Cognitive enhancers as adjuncts to psychotherapy: Use of D-cycloserine in phobic individuals to facilitate extinction of fear. *Archives of General Psychiatry, 61,* 1136–1144.

Restrictions on gun crime data headed for debate in congress. (2007, June 1). *Criminal Justice Newsletter,* 4–5.

Reuland, M., Morabito, A. S., Preston, C., & Cheney, J. (2006, March). *Police-community partnerships to address domestic violence.* Washington, DC: U.S. Department of Justice, Office of Community Oriented Policing Services. Retrieved from http://www.cops.usdoj.gov

Reyes, K. (1999, Spring). Domestic violence prevention for clergy proves slow-going. *Focus, 4,* 1–3.

Reynolds, A. J., Mathieson, L. C., & Topitzes, J. W. (2009). Do early childhood interventions prevent maltreatment? A review of research. *Child Maltreatment, 14,* 182–206.

Rhatigan, D. L., Moore, T. M., & Stuart, G. L. (2005). An investment model analysis of relationship stability among women court-mandated to violence interventions. *Psychology of Women Quarterly, 29,* 313–322.

Rhodes, N. R., & McKenzie, E. B. (1998). Why do battered women stay? Three decades of research. *Aggression and Violent Behavior, 3,* 391–406.

Rich, A. (1976). *Of woman born.* New York: Norton.

Richie, B. E. (2004). *Research on violence against women and family violence: The challenges and the promise* (NCJ Publication No. 199731). National Criminal Justice Reference Service. Retrieved from http://ncjrs.gov/App/publications/Abstract.aspx?id=199731

Rickert, V. I., Sanghvi, R., & Wiemann, C. M. (2002). Is lack of sexual assertiveness among adolescent and young adult women a cause for concern? *Perspectives on Sexual and Reproductive Health, 34,* 178–183.

Ridley, C. A., & Feldman, C. M. (2003). Female domestic violence toward male partners: Explaining conflict responses and outcomes. *Journal of Family Violence, 18,* 157–170.

Rigakos, G. S. (1995). Constructing the symbolic complainant: Police subculture and the nonenforcement of protection orders for battered women. *Violence and Victims, 10,* 227–247.

Riger, S., & Krieglstein, M. (2000). The impact of welfare reform on men's violence against women. *American Journal of Community Psychology, 28,* 631–647.

Riger, S., Raja, S., & Camacho, J. (2002). The radiating impact of intimate partner violence. *Journal of Interpersonal Violence, 17,* 184–205.

Riger, S., & Staggs, S. L. (2004). Welfare reform, domestic violence, and employment: What do we know and what do we need to know? *Violence Against Women, 10,* 961–990.

Riggle, E. B., Rostosky, S. S., & Prather, R. A. (2006). Advance planning by same-sex couples. *Journal of Family Issues, 27,* 58–776.

Riggs, D. S., & Caulfield, M. B. (1997). Expected consequences of male violence against their female dating partners. *Journal of Interpersonal Violence, 12,* 229–240.

Riggs, D. S., Caulfield, M. B., & Street, A. E. (2000). Risk for domestic violence: Factors associated with perpetration and victimization. *Journal of Clinical Psychology, 56,* 1289–1316.

Riggs, D. S., O'Leary, K. D., & Breslin, F. C. (1990). Multiple correlates of physical aggression in dating couples. *Journal of Interpersonal Violence, 5,* 61–73.

Riley, N. E. (1996). China's "missing girls": Prospects and policy [Electronic version]. *Population Today, 24*(2), 4.

Rinker, A. G. (2009). Recognition and perception of elder abuse by prehospital and hospital-based care providers. *Archives of Gerontology and Geriatrics, 48,* 110–115.

Ristock, J. L. (2003). Exploring dynamics of abusive lesbian relationships: Preliminary analysis of a multisite, qualitative study. *American Journal of Community Psychology, 31,* 329–341.

Robbins, K. (1999). No-drop prosecution of domestic violence: Just good policy, or equal protection mandate? *Stanford Law Review, 52,* 205–233.

Roberts, K. A. (2005). Women's experiences of violence during stalking by former romantic partners: Factors predictive of stalking violence. *Violence Against Women, 11,* 89–114.

Robinson, A. L. (2006). Reducing repeat victimization among high-risk victims of domestic violence. *Violence Against Women, 12,* 761–788.

Robinson, A. L., & Chandek, M. S. (2000). The domestic violence arrest decision: Examining demographic, attitudinal, and situational variables. *Crime & Delinquency, 46,* 18–37.

Robinson, D. T., Gibson-Beverly, G., & Schwartz, J. P. (2004). Sorority and fraternity membership and religious behaviors: Relation to gender attitudes. *Sex Roles, 50,* 871–877.

Robinson, G. E. (2003). Violence against women in North America. *Archives of Women's Mental Health, 6,* 185–191.

Rocca, C. H., Rathod, S., Falle, T., Pande, R. P., & Krishnan, S. (2009). Challenging assumptions about women's empowerment: Social and economic resources and domestic violence among young married women in urban South India. *International Journal of Epidemiology, 38,* 577–585.

Rodriguez, C. M. (2010). Personal contextual characteristics and cognition: Predicting child abuse potential and disciplinary style. *Journal of Interpersoanl Violence, 25,* 315–335.

Rodriguez, C. M., & Henderson, R. C. (2010). Who spares the rod? Religious orientation, social conformity, and child abuse potential. *Child Abuse & Neglect, 34,* 84–94.

Rodriguez, E. (2001). How do women cope with family violence? Moving ahead in our understanding of international issues. *Journal of Epidemiology and Community Health, 55,* 531.

Rodriguez, M. A., Wallace, S. P., Woolf, N. H., & Mangione, C. M. (2006). Mandatory reporting of elder abuse: Between a rock and a hard place. *Annals of Family Medicine, 4,* 403–409.

Rodriguez, S. F., & Henderson, V. A. (1995). Intimate homicide: Victim-offender relationship in female-perpetrated homicide. *Deviant Behavior, 16,* 45–57.

Rodriguez, M., Valentine, J. M., Son, J. B., & Muhammad, M. (2009). Intimate partner violence and barriers to mental health care for ethnically diverse populations of women. *Trauma, Violence & Abuse, 10,* 358–374.

Roelofs, J., Meesters, C., & Muris, P. (2008). Correlates of self-reported attachment (in)security in children: The role of parental romantic attachment status and rearing behaviors. *Journal of Child and Family Studies, 17,* 555–566.

Roe-Sepowitz, D., & Krysik, J. (2008). Examining the sexual offenses of female juveniles: The relevance of childhood maltreatment. *American Journal of Orthopsychiatry, 78,* 405-412.

Rogan, M. T. (1997). Fear conditioning induces associative long-term potentiation in the amygdala. *Nature, 390,* 604–607.

Rogers, P., Krammer, L., Podesta, J. S., & Sellinger, M. (1998, August 31). Angry and hurt, but no quitter. *People,* 61–62, 64.

Rogge, R. D., & Bradbury, T. N. (1999). Till violence does us part: The differing roles of communication and aggression in predicting adverse marital outcome. *Journal of Clinical and Consulting Psychology, 67,* 340–351.

Roisman, G. I. (2009). Adult attachment: Toward a rapprochement of methodological cultures. *Current Directions in Psychological Science, 18,* 122–126.

Rollstin, A. O., & Kern, J. M. (1998). Correlates of battered women's psychological distress: Severity of abuse and duration of the postabuse period. *Psychological Reports, 82,* 387–394.

Roloff, M. E., Soule, K. P., & Carey, C. M. (2001). Reasons for remaining in a relationship and responses to relational transgressions. *Journal of Social and Personal Relationships, 18,* 362–385.

Romano, E., & De Luca, R. V. (2001). Male sexual abuse: A review of effects, abuse characteristics, and links with later psychological functioning. *Aggression and Violent Behavior, 6,* 55–78.

Römkens, R. (2006). Protecting prosecution: Exploring the powers of law in an intervention program for domestic violence. *Violence Against Women, 12,* 166–186.

Rondfeldt, H. M., Kimmerling, R., & Arias, I. (1998). Satisfaction with relationship power and perception of dating violence. *Journal of Marriage and the Family, 60,* 70–78.

Rose, C. A., Espelage, D. L., & Monda-Amaya, L. E. (2009). Bullying and victimization rates among students in general and special education: A comparative analysis. *Educational Psychology, 29,* 761–776.

Rose, K. (2007, October). Sexual assault: Virtual training takes responders from exam room to courtroom. *National Institute of Justice Journal* (Publication No. 258).

Rose, L. E., Campbell, J., & Kub, J. (2000). The role of social support and family relationships in women's responses to battering. *Health Care for Women International, 21,* 27–30.

Rosemond, J. Proper socialization requires powerful love and equally powerful discipline. (2005). In D. R. Loeseke, R. J. Gelles, & M. M. Cavanaugh (Eds.), *Current controversies on family violence* (2nd ed., pp. 131–136). Thousand Oaks, CA: Sage.

Rosen, K. H., & Stith, S. M. (1995). Women terminating abusive dating relationships: A qualitative study. *Journal of Social and Personal Relationships, 12,* 155–160.

Rosen, L. N., Kaminski, R. J., Parmley, A. M., Knudson, K. H., & Fancher, P. (2003). The effects of peer group climate on intimate partner violence among married male U.S. Army soldiers. *Violence Against Women, 9,* 1045–1071.

Rosen, L. N., Parmley, A. M., Knudson, K. H., & Fancher, P. (2002). Intimate partner violence among married males U.S. army soldiers: Ethnicity as a factor in self-reported perpetration and victimization. *Violence and Victims, 17,* 607–622.

Rosenbaum, A. (1988). Methodological issues in marital violence research. *Journal of Family Violence, 3,* 91–104.

Rosenbaum, A., & O'Leary, K. D. (1981). Marital violence: Characteristics of abusive couples. *Journal of Consulting and Clinical Psychology, 49,* 63–76.

Rosenberg, D. (2001, January 15). A place of their own. *Newsweek,* 54–55.

Rosenberg, D. A. (1987). Web of deceit: A literature review of Munchausen syndrome by proxy. *Child Abuse & Neglect, 11,* 547–563.

Rosenblatt, D. E. (1996). Documentation. In L. A. Baumhover & S. C. Beall (Eds.), *Abuse, neglect, and exploitation of older persons: Strategies for assessment and intervention* (pp. 145–161). Baltimore: Health Professions Press.

Rosencrans, B. (1997). *The last secret: Daughters sexually molested by mothers.* Brandon, VT: Safe Society Press.

Rosenfeld, A. A., Bailey, R., Siegel, B., & Bailey, G. (1986). Determining incestuous contact between parent and child: Frequency of children touching parents' genitals in a non-clinical population. *Journal of the American Academy of Child Psychiatry, 25,* 481–484.

Rosenfeld, A. A., Siegel, B., & Bailey, R. (1987). Familial bathing patterns: Implications for cases of alleged molestation and for pediatric practice. *Pediatrics, 79,* 224–229.

Rosenfeld, B. D. (2000). Assessment and treatment of obsessional harassment. *Aggression and Violent Behavior, 5,* 529–549.

Rossegger, A., Endrass, J., Urbaniok, F., & Maercker, A. (2010). Abstract: From victim to offender: Characteristics of sexually abused violent sex offenders. Nervenarzt, June. [Epub ahead of print].

Rossen, E. K., Bartlett, R., & Herrick, C. A. (2008). Interdisciplinary collaboration: The need to revisit. *Issues in Mental Health Nursing, 29,* 387–396.

Rossman, B. B. R. (2001). Longer term effects of children's exposure to domestic violence. In S. A. Graham-Bermann & J. L. Edleson (Eds.), *Domestic violence in the lives of children* (pp. 35–65). Washington, DC: American Psychological Association.

Rossman, B. B. R., & Ho, J. (2000). Posttraumatic response and children exposed to parental violence. *Journal of Aggression, Maltreatment, & Trauma, 3,* 85–106.

Rothbaum, F., Weisz, J., Pott, M., Miyake, K., & Morelli, G. (2000). Attachment and culture: Security in the United States and Japan. *American Psychologist, 55,* 1093–1104.

Rotheram-Borus, M. J., Rosario, N., & Koopman, C. (1991). Minority youths at high risk: Gay males and runaways. In M. E. Colton & S. Gore (Eds.), *Adolescent stress: Causes and consequences* (pp. 181–200). New York: Aldine de Gruyter.

Rothman, E. F., Gupta, J., Pavlos, C., Dang, Q., & Coutinho, P. (2007). Batterer Intervention Program enrollment and completion among immigrant men in Massachusetts. *Violence Against Women, 13,* 527–543.

Roudsari, B. S., Leahy, M. M., Walters, S. T. (2009). Correlates of dating violence among male and female heavy-drinking college students. *Journal of Interpersonal Violence, 24,* 1892–1905.

Rowntree, M. (2007). Responses to sibling sexual abuse: Are they harmful or helpful? *Australian Social Work, 60,* 347–361.

Royce, L., & Coccaro, E. (2001). The neuropsychopharmacology of criminality and aggression. *Canadian Journal of Psychiatry, 46,* 35–43.

Royzman, E. B., Leeman, R. F., & Sabini, J. (2008). "You make me sick": Moral dyspepsia as a reaction to third-party sibling incest. *Motivation and Emotion, 32,* 100–108.

Rubin, A. (2007). Improving the teaching of evidence-based practice: Introduction to the special issue [Special issue]. *Research on Social Work Practice, 17,* 541–552.

Rudd, J. (2001). Dowry-murder: An example of violence against women. *Women's Studies International Forum, 24,* 613–622.

Rudin, M. M., Zalewski, C., & Bodmer-Turner, J. (1995). Characteristics of child sexual abuse victims according to perpetrator gender. *Child Abuse & Neglect, 19,* 963–973.

Ruggiero, K. J., McLeer, S. V., & Dixon, J. F. (2000). Sexual abuse characteristics associated with survivor psychopathology. *Child Abuse & Neglect, 24,* 951–964.

Ruiz-Peréz, I., Mata-Pariente, N., & Plazaola-Castaño. J. (2006). Women's response to intimate partner violence. *Journal of Interpersonal Violence, 21,* 1156–1168.

Runge, R. R., & Hearn, M. E. (2000, December/January). Employment rights advocacy for domestic violence victims. *Domestic Violence Report, 5,* 17–18, 26–29.

Runyan, D. K., Curtis, P. A., Hunter, W. M., Black, M. M., Kotch, J. B., Bangdiwala, S., et al. (1998). LONGSCAN: A consortium for longitudinal studies of maltreatment and the life course of children. *Aggression and Violent Behavior, 3,* 275–285.

Runyan, D. K., Hunter, W. M., & Everson, M. D. (1992). *Maternal support for child victims of sexual abuse: Determinants and implications* (Grant No. 90-CA-1368). Washington, DC: National Center on Child Abuse and Neglect.

Runyon, M. K., Deblinger, E., & Schroeder, C. (2009). Pilot evaluation of outcomes of combined parent-child cognitive-behavioral therapy for families at risk for child physical abuse. *Cognitive and Behavioral Practice, 16,* 101–118.

Runyon, M. K., & Urquiza, A. J. (2010). Child physical abuse: Interventions for parents who engage in physically abusive parenting practices and their children. In J. E. B. Myers (Ed.), *The APSAC handbook on child maltreatment* (3rd ed., pp. 195–211). Thousand Oaks, CA: Sage.

Rusbult, C. E. (1980) Commitment and satisfaction in romantic associations: A test of the investment model. *Journal of Experimental Social Psychology, 45*, 101–117.

Rusbult, C. E., Martz, J. M., & Agnew, C. R. (1998). The investment model scale: Measuring commitment level, quality of alternatives, and investment size. *Personal Relationships, 5*(35), 7–391.

Russell, D., Springer, K. W., & Greenfield, E. A. (2010). Witnessing domestic abuse in childhood as an independent risk factor for depressive sysmptoms in young adulthood. *Child Abuse & Neglect, 34*, 448–453.

Russell, D. E. H. (1982). *Rape in marriage.* New York: Macmillan.

Russell, D. E. H. (1983). The incidence and prevalence of intra-familial and extrafamilial sexual abuse of female children. *Child Abuse & Neglect, 7,* 133–146.

Russell, D. E. H. (1990). *Rape in marriage* (Rev. ed.). Bloomington: Indiana University Press.

Russo, F. (2010). *They're your parents too! How siblings can survivie their parents' aging without driving each other crazy.* New York: Bantam/Dell.

Ryan, J. P., & Testa, M. F. (2005). Child maltreatment and juvenile delinquency: Investigating the role of placement instability. *Children and Youth Services Review, 27,* 227–349.

Sabia, J. J. (2008). There's no place like home. *Research on Aging, 30,* 3–35.

Sabina, C., & Straus, M. A. (2008). Polyvictimization by dating partners and mental health among U.S. college students. *Violence and Victims, 23,* 667–682,

Sabina, C., & Tindale, R. S. (2008). Abuse characteristics and coping resources as predictors of problem-focused coping strategies among battered women. *Violence Against Women, 14,* 437–456.

Sable, M. R., Libbus, M. K., Huneke, D., & Anger, K. (1999). Domestic violence among AFDC recipients: Implications for welfare-to-work programs. *Affilia, 14,* 199–216.

Sacramento Police Department. (n.d.). *How to obtain and use sex offender information.* Retrieved December 4, 2003, from Sacramento Police Department website: http://sacpd.org

Sadler, A. G., Booth, B. M., Mengeling, M. A., & Doebbeling, B. N. (2004). Life span and repeated violence against women during military service: Effects on health status and outpatient utilization. *Journal of Women's Health, 13,* 799–811.

Saewye, E. M. (2003). Influential life contexts and environments for out-of-home pregnant adolescents. *Journal of Holistic Nursing, 21,* 343–367.

Saey, T. H. (2009, September 12). Human cells play Simon Says: Research uncovers evidence for mirror neurons in people. *Science News, 11.*

Saez-Betacourt, A., Lam, B. T., & Nguyen, T. (2008). The meaning of being incarcerated on a domestic violence charge and its impact on self and family among Latino immigrant batterers. *Journal of Ethnic and Cultural Diversity in Social Work, 17,* 130–156.

Sagarin, B. J. (2005). Reconsidering evolved sex differences in jealousy: Comment on Harris (2003). *Personality and Social Psychology Review, 9,* 62–75.

Sagrestano, L. M., Heavey, C. L., & Christensen, A. (1999). Perceived power and physical violence in marital conflict. *Journal of Social Issues, 55*(1), 65–79.

Sahin, H., & Sahin, H. (2003). An unaddressed issue: Domestic violence and unplanned pregnancies among pregnant women in Turkey. *European Journal of Obstetrics and Gynecology and Reproductive Biology, 103,* 26–29.

Sahr, R. (2006). *Consumer Price Index (CPI).* Retrieved form http://www.oregonstate.edu/cla/polisci/sahr/sahr

Sakalli-Uğurlu, N., Yalçin, Z. S., & Glick, P. (2007). Ambivalent sexism, Belief in a Just World, and empathy as predictors of Turkish students' attitudes toward rape victims. *Sex Roles, 57,* 889–895.

Salari, Z., & Nakhaee, N. (2008). Identifying types of domestic violence and its associated risk factors in a pregnant population in Kerman Hospitals, Iran Republic. *Asian-Pacific Journal of Public Health, 20,* 49–55.

Salazar, L. F., & Cook, S. L. (2006). Preliminary findings from an outcome evaluation of an intimate partner violence prevention program for adjudicated, African American, adolescent males. *Youth Violence and Juvenile Justice, 4,* 368–385.

Salisbury, E. J., Henning, K., & Holdford, R. (2009). Fathering by partner-abusive men: Attitudes on children's exposure to violence and risk factors for child abuse. *Child Maltreatment, 14,* 232–242.

Salomon, A., Bassuk, S. S., & Huntington, N. (2002). The relationship between intimate partner violence and the use of addictive substances in poor and homeless single mothers. *Violence Against Women, 8,* 785–815.

Saltzman, L. E., Fanslow, J. L., McMahon, P. M., & Shelley, G. A. (1999). *Intimate partner violence surveillance: Uniform definitions and recommended data elements* (Version 1.0). Retrieved from Centers for Disease Control and Prevention website: http://www.cdc.gov/ncipe

Salzinger, S., Rosario, M., & Feldman, R. S. (2007). Physical child abuse and adolescent violent delinquency: The mediating and moderating roles of personal relationships. *Child Maltreatment, 12,* 208–219.

Sanders, L. (2009, December 10). Trawling the brain: New findings raise questions about reliability of MRI as gauge of neural activitiy. *Science News,* 16–20.

Sanders, M. J., & Bursch, B. (2002). Forensic assessment of illness falsification, Munchausen by proxy, and factitious disorder, NOS. *Child Maltreatment, 7,* 112–124.

San Diego Elder Abuse/Dependent Unit.(n.d.). Retrieved from http://www.sandiego.gov/police/about/elderdependent.shtml

Sandnabba, N. K., Santtila, P., Wannas, M., & Krook, K. (2003). Age and gender-specific sexual behaviors in children. *Child Abuse & Neglect, 27,* 579–605.

Sanford, L. D., Tang, X., Ross, R. J., & Morrison, A. R. (2003). Influence of shock training and explicit fear-conditioned cues on sleep architecture in mice: Strain comparison. *Behavior Genetics, 33,* 43–58.

Sappington, A. A., Pharr, R., Tunstall, A., & Rickert, E. (1997). Relationships among child abuse, date abuse, and psychological problems. *Journal of Clinical Psychology, 53,* 318–329.

Saradjian, J. (1996). *Women who sexually abuse children: From research to clinical practice.* Chichester, England: John Wiley.

Sartin, R. M., Hansen, D. J., & Huss, M. T. (2006). Domestic violence treatment response and recidivism: A review and implications for the study of family violence. *Aggression and Violent Behavior, 11,* 425–440.

Saunders, B. E., Berliner, L., & Hanson, R. F. (Eds.) (2004). *Child physical and sexual abuse: Guideline for treatment* (final report: January 15, 2004). Charleston, SC: National Crime Victims Research and Treatment Center.

Saunders, D. G. (1995). The tendency to arrest victims of domestic violence: A preliminary analysis of officer characteristics. *Journal of Interpersonal Violence, 10,* 147–158.

Saunders, D. G. (2002). Are physical assaults by wives and girlfriends a major social problem? *Violence Against Women, 8,* 1424–1448.

Saunders, D. G. (2004). The place of a typology of men who are maritally violent within a nested ecological model. *Journal of Interpersonal Violence, 19,* 1390–1395.

Saunders, D. G., Holter, M. C., Pahl, L. C., Tolman, R. M., & Kenna, C. E. (2005). TANF workers' reponses to battered women and the impact of brief worker training: What survivors report. *Violence Against Women, 11,* 227–254.

Sawyer, C. (2006). The child is not a person: Family law and other legal cultures. *Journal of Social Welfare & Family Law, 28,* 1–14.

Saywitz, K. J., Goodman, G. S., & Lyon, T. D. (2002). Interviewing children in and out of court. In J. E. B. Myers, L. Berliner, J. Briere, C. T. Hendrix, C. Jenny, & T. A. Reid (Eds.), *The APSAC handbook on child maltreatment* (2nd ed., pp. 349–377). Thousand Oaks, CA: Sage.

Saywitz, K. J., Mannarino, A. P., Berliner, L., & Cohen, J. A. (2000). Treatment for sexually abused children and adolescents. *American Psychologist, 55,* 1040–1049.

Saywitz, K. J., & Snyder, L. (1993). Improving children's testimony with preparation. In G. S. Goodman & B. L. Bottoms (Eds.), *Child victims, child witnesses: Understanding and improving testimony* (pp. 117–146). New York: Guilford.

Sbarra, D. A., & Ferrer, E. (2006). The structure and process of emotional experience following nonmarital relationship dissolution: Dynamic factor analyses of love, anger, and sadness. *Emotion, 6,* 224–238.

S.C. husband jailed for assaulting wife. (2009, May 21). *Sun News,* Myrtle Beach. http://www.lorain.oh.networkofcare.org/dv/news/detail.cfm?articleID=23490

Scarce, M. (1997). Same-sex rape of male college students. *Journal of American College Health, 45,* 171–173.

Schacht, R. L., Dimidjian, S., George, W. H., & Berns, S. B.(2009) Domestic violence assessment procedures among couple therapists. *Journal of Marital and Family Therapy, 35,* 47–59.

Schafer, J., Caetano, R., & Clark, C. (1998). Rates of intimate partner violence in the United States. *American Journal of Public Health, 88,* 1702–1704.

Schafer, J., Caetano, R., & Cunradi, C. B. (2004). A path model of risk factors for intimate partner violence among couples in the United States. *Journal of Interpersonal Violence, 19,* 127–142.

Schechter, S. (1988). Building bridges between activists, professionals, and researchers. In K. A. Yllö & M. Bograd (Eds.), *Feminist perspectives on wife abuse* (pp. 299–312). Newbury Park, CA: Sage.

Schell, B. H., Martin, M. V., Hung, P. C. K., & Rueda, L. (2007). Cyber child pornography: A review paper of the social and legal issues and remedies and a proposed technological solution. *Aggression and Victim Behavior, 12,* 45–63.

Schiff, M., Gilbert, L., & El-Bassel, N. (2006 ). Perceived positive aspects of intimate relationships among abused women in methadone maintenance treatment programs (MMTP). *Journal of Interpersonal Violence, 21,* 121–138.

Schindehette, S. (1998, September 7). High infidelity. *People,* 52–59.

Schindehette, S., & Duffy, T. (2002, December 9). Help on wheels. *People, 58,* 185–187.

Schmitt, B. D. (1987). The child with nonaccidental trauma. In R. E. Helfer & R. S. Kempe (Eds.), *The battered child* (4th ed., pp. 178–196). Chicago: University of Chicago Press.

Schneider, A. (2007, February 14). *The role of the False Claims Act in combating Medicare and Medicaid fraud by drug manufacturers: An update.* Taxpayers Against Fraud, http://www.taf.org.

Schneider, R., Baumrind, N., & Kimerling, R. (2007). Exposure to child abuse and risk for mental health problems in women. *Violence & Victims, 22,* 620–631.

Schnurr, P. P., Friedman, M. J., Engel, C. C., Foa, E. B., Shea, M. T., Chow, B. K., et al. (2007). Cognitive behavioral therapy for posttraumatic stress disorder in women: A randomized controlled trial. *The Journal of the American Medical Association, 297,* 820–830.

Schollenberger, J., Campbell, J. C., Sharps, P. W., O'Campo, P., Gielen, A. C., Dienemann, J., et al. (2003). African American HMO enrollees: Their experiences with partner abuse and its effect on their health. *Violence Against Women, 9,* 599–618.

Schornstein, S. L. (1997). *Domestic violence and health care: What every professional needs to know.* Thousand Oaks, CA: Sage.

Schrock, D. P., & Padavic, I. (2007). Negotiating hegemonic masculinity in a batterer intervention program. *Gender & Society, 21,* 625–649.

Schuler, M. E., & Nair, P. (1999). Brief report: Frequency of maternal cocaine use during pregnancy and infant neurobehavioral outcome. *Journal of Pediatric Psychology, 24,* 511–514.

Schuller, R. A., & Klippenstine, M. A. (2004). The impact of complainant sexual history evidence on jurors' decisions. *Psychology, Public Policy, and Law, 10,* 321–342.

Schumacher, J. A. (2002). Battering and common couple violence: A construct validation. *Dissertation Abstracts International, 63*(03), 1573B. (UMI No. 3044966)

Schumacher, J. A., Feldbau-Kohn, S., Slep, A. M. S., & Heyman, R. E. (2001). Risk factors for male-to-female partner physical abuse. *Aggression and Violent Behavior, 6,* 281–352.

Schumacher, J. A., Homish, G. G., Leonard, K. E., Quigley, B. M., & Kearns-Bodkin, J. N. (2008). Longitudinal moderators of the relationship between excessive drinking and intimate partner violence in the early years of marriage. *Journal of Family Psychology, 22,* 894–904.

Schumacher, J. A., Slep, A. M. S., & Heyman, R. E. (2001). Risk factors for male-to-female partner psychological abuse. *Aggression and Violent Behavior, 6,* 255–268.

Schumann, G. et al. (2008). Systemic analysis of glutamtatergic neurotransmission genes in alcohol dependence and adolescent risky drinking behavior. *Archives of General Psychiatry, 65,* 826–838.

Schwartz, D. (2007, October). The special challenges of counseling transgendered clients. *Monitor on Psychology, 38,* 19.

Schwartz, J. P., Magee, M. M., Griffin, L. D., Dupuis, L. D. (2004). Effects of a group preventive intervention on risk and protective factors related to dating vaiolence. *MGroup Dynamics: Theroy, Research, and Practice, 8,* 331–231.

Schwartz, M. (2000). *Elder abuse law: Elder abuse, nursing homes, and fiduciaries.* Retrieved September 5, 2003, from http://www.elderabuselaw.com

Schwartz, M., O'Leary, S. G., & Kendziora, K. T. (1997). Dating aggression among high school students. *Violence and Victims, 12,* 295–305.

Schwartz, M. D. (2000). Methodological issues in the use of survey data for measuring and characterizing violence against women. *Violence Against Women, 6,* 815–838.

Schwartz, M. D., & Pitts, V. (1995). Exploring a feminist routine activities approach to explaining sexual assault. *Justice Quarterly, 12,* 9–31.

Schwartz, R. H., Milteer, R., & LeBeau, M. A. (2000). Drug-facilitated sexual assault ("date rape"). *Southern Medical Journal, 93,* 558–561.

Scott, C. L., & Holmberg, T. (2003). Castration of sex offenders: Prisoners' rights versus public safety. *Journal of the American Academy of Psychiatry and the Law, 31,* 502–509.

Scott, E. K., London, A. S., & Myers, N. A. (2002). Dangerous Dependencies. The intersection of welfare reform and domestic violence. *Gender & Society, 16,* 878–897.

Scott, K., & Straus, M. (2007). Denial, minimization, partner blaming, and intimate aggression in dating partners. *Journal of Interpersonal Violence, 22,* 851–871.

Seal, C. A. (2008). *Colorado elder law.* (Vol. 24, Colorado Practice Series) St. Paul, MN: West Publishing Co.

Seal, C. A. (2009, July/August). Financial exploitation of seniors, Part II. *Victimization of the Elderly and Disabled, 12,* 19, 27–30.

Seamans, C. L., Rubin, L. J., & Stabb, S. D. (2007). Women domestic violence offenders: Lessons of violence and survival. *Journal of Trauma & Dissociation, 8,* 47–68.

Sedlak, A. J. (1990). *Technical amendment to the study findings: National incidence and prevalence of child abuse and neglect: 1988.* Rockville, MD: Westat.

Sedlak, A. J., & Broadhurst, D. D. (1996). *Third National Incidence Study on child abuse and neglect.* Washington, DC: U.S. Department of Health and Human Services.

Sedlak, A. J., Mettenberg, J., Basena, M., Petta, I., McPherson, K., Greene, A., et al. (2010). *Fourth National Incidence Study of Child Abuse and Neglect (NIS-4): Report to Congress, Executive Summary.* Washington, D.C: U.S. Department of Health & Human Services, Administration for Children and Families.

Sedlar, G., & Hansen, D. J. (2001). Anger, child behavior, and family distress: Further evaluation of the Parental Anger Inventory. *Journal of Family Violence, 16,* 361–373.

Seedat. S., Stein, M. B., & Forde, D. (2005). Association between physical partner violence, posttraumatic stress, childhood trauma, and suicide attempts in a community sample of women. *Violence and Victims, 20,* 87–98.

Seelau, E. P., Seelau, S. M., & Poorman, P. B. (2003). Gender and role-based perceptions of domestic abuse: Does sexual orientation matter? *Behavioral Sciences and the Law, 21,* 199–214.

Segal, S. R., & Iris, M. A. (1989). Strategies for service provision: The use of legal interventions in a systems approach to casework. In R. Filinson & S. R. Ingman (Eds.), *Elder abuse: Practice and policy* (pp. 104–116). New York: Human Services Press.

Sege, R. D., & Flaherty, E. G. (2008). Forty years later: In consistencies in reporting child abuse. *Archives of Disease in Childhood, 93,* 822–824.

Seiffge-Krenke, I. (2006). Coping with relationship stressor: The impact of different working models of attachment and links to adaptation. *Journal of Youth and Adolescence, 35,* 25–39.

Sellbom, M., Ben-Porath, Y. S., Baum, L. J., Erez, E., & Gregory, C. (2008). Predictive validity of the MMPI-2 Restructured Clinical (RC) scales in a batterers' intervention program. *Journal of Personality Assessment, 90,* 129–135.

*Seneca Falls Convention, Seneca Falls, New York, July 19–20, 1848, including the Declaration of Sentiments and Resolutions.* (1848). Retrieved November 10, 2003, from E. C. DuBois website: http://www.sscnet.ucla.edu/history/dubois/classes/995/98F/doc5.html

Seng, A. C., & Prinz, R. J. (2008). Parents who abuse: What are they thinking? *Clinical Child and Family Review, 11,* 163–175.

Senn, C. Y., Desmarais, S., Verberg, N., & Wood, E. (2000). Predicting coercive sexual behavior across the lifespan in a random sample of Canadian men. *Journal of Social and Personal Relationships, 17,* 95–113.

Serbin, L., & Karp, J. (2003). Intergenerational studies of parenting and the transfer of risk from parent to child. *Current Directions in Psychological Science, 12,* 138–142.

Seto, M. C., & Lalumière, M. L. (2010). What is so special about male adolescent sexual offending? A review and test of explanation through meta-analysis. *Psychological Bulletin, 136,* 526–575.

Shaffer, A., Huston, L., & Egeland, B. (2008). Identification of child maltreatment using prospective and self-report methodologies: A comparison of maltreatment incidence and relation to later psychopathology. *Child Abuse & Neglect, 32,* 682–692.

Shah, G., Veedon, R., & Vasi, S. (1995). Elder abuse in India. In J. I. Kosberg & J. L. Garcia (Eds.), *Elder abuse: International and cross-cultural perspectives* (pp. 101–118). Binghamton, NY: Haworth.

Shahidullah, S. M., & Derby, C. N. (2009). Criminalisation, modernisation, and globalisation: The US and international perspective on domestic violence. *Global Crime, 10,* 196–223.

Shainess, N. (1979). Vulnerability to violence: Masochism as process. *American Journal of Psychotherapy, 33,* 174–189.

Shalansky, C., Ericksen, J., & Henderson, A. (1999). Abused women and child custody: The ongoing exposure to abusive ex-partners. *Journal of Advanced Nursing, 29,* 416–426.

Shamai, M., & Buchbinder, E. (2009). Control of the self: Partner-violent men's experiences of therapy. *Journal of Interpersonal Violence, 25*(7), 1338–1362.

Shannon, L., Logan, T., Cole, J., & Medley, K. (2006). Help-seeking and coping strategies for intimate partner violence in rural and urban women. *Violence and Victims, 21,* 167–181.

Sharps, P., Campbell, J. C., Campbell, D., Gary, F., & Webster, D. (2003). Risky mix: Drinking, drug use, and homicide. *National Institute of Justice Journal, Issue 250,* 8–12.

Sharpsteen, D. J. (1991). The organization of jealousy knowledge: Romantic jealousy as a blended emotion. In P. Salovey (Ed.), *The psychology of jealousy and envy* (pp. 31–52). New York: Guilford.

Shaw, J. A., Lewis, J. E., Loeb, A., Rosado, J., & Rodriguez, R. (2000). Child on child sexual abuse: Psychological perspectives. *Child Abuse & Neglect, 24,* 1591–1600.

Shearer, N., & Fleury, J. (2006). Social support promoting health in older women. *Journal of Women & Aging, 18(3),* 3–17.

Sheets, V. L., Fredendall, L. L., & Claypool, H. M. (1997). Jealousy evocation, partner reassurance, and relationship stability: An exploration of the potential benefits of jealousy. *Evolution and Human Behavior, 18,* 387–402.

Shefer, T. et al. (2008). Gender, power and resistance to change among two communities in the Western Cape, South Africa. *Feminism & Psychology, 18,* 157–182.

Shen, A. C-T. (2009). Self-esteem of young adults experiencing interparental violence and child physical maltreatment. *Journal of Interpersonal Violence, 24,* 770–794.

Shepard, M. F. (1992). Predicting batterer recidivism five years after community intervention. *Journal of Family Violence, 7,* 167–178.

Shepard, M. F., & Pence, E. L. (1988). The effect of battering on the employment status of women. *Affilia, 3*(2), 55–61.

Shepard, M. F., & Pence, E. L. (Eds.). (1999). *Coordinating community responses to domestic violence: Lessons from Duluth and beyond.* Thousand Oaks, CA: Sage.

Sheridan, D. J., & Nash, K. R. (2007). Acute injury patterns of intimate partner violence victims. *Trauma, Violence, & Abuse, 8,* 281–289.

Sheridan, L. P., Blaauw, E., & Davies, G. M. (2003). Stalking: Knowns and unknowns. *Trauma, Violence, & Abuse, 4,* 148–162.

Sheridan, L. P., Gillett, R., Blaauw, E., Davies, G. M., & Patel, D. (2003). "There's no smoke without fire": Are male ex-partners perceived as more "entitled" to stalk than stranger or acquaintance stalkers? *British Journal of Psychology, 94,* 87–98.

Shibusawa, T., & Yick, A. (2007). Experiences and perceptions of intimate partner violence among older Chinese migrants. *Journal of Elder Abuse & Neglect, 19,* 1–17.

Shidlo, A. (1994). Internalized homophobia: Conceptual and empirical issues in measurement. In B. Greene & G. M. Herek (Eds.), *Lesbian and gay psychology: Theory, research, and clinical applications* (pp. 176–205). Thousand Oaks, CA: Sage.

Shields, A., Ryan, R. M., & Cicchetti, D. (2001). Narrative representations of caregivers and emotion dysregulation as predictors of maltreated children's rejection by peers. *Developmental Psychology, 37,* 321–337.

hilling, D. (2008, November/December). Improving the court system's response to elder abuse. *Victimization of the Elderly and Disabled, 11,* 49, 51–52, 59, 62–63.

Shim, W.S., & Haight, W.L. (2006). Supporting battered women and their children: Perspectives of battered mothers and child welfare professionals. *Children and Youth Services Review, 28,* 620–637.

Shin, H. L. (1995). Violence and intimacy: Risk markers and predictors of wife abuse among Korean immigrants. Unpublished doctoral dissertation, University of Southern California, Los Angeles.

Shir, J. S. (1999). Battered women's perceptions and expectations of their current and ideal marital relationship. *Journal of Family Violence, 14,* 71–82.

Shoham, E. (2005). Gender, traditionalism, and attitudes toward domestic violence within a closed community. *International Journal of Offender Therapy and Comparative Criminology, 49,* 427–449.

Shor, R. (2000). Child maltreatment: Differences in perceptions between parents in low income and middle income neighbourhoods. *British Journal of Social Work, 30,* 165–178.

Short, L. M., McMahon, P. M., Chervin, D. D., Shelley, G. A., Lezin, N., Sloop, K. S., et al. (2000). Survivors' identification of protective factors and early warning signs for intimate partner violence. *Violence Against Women, 6,* 272–285.

Shuman, R. D., Jr., McCauley, J., Waltermaurer, E., Roche, W. P., Hollis, H., Gibbons, A. K., Dever, A. et al. (2008). Understanding intimate partner violence against women in the rural South. *Violence and Victims, 23,* 390–405.

Shuman-Austin, L. A. (2000). Is leaving work to obtain safety "good cause" to leave employment? Providing unemployment insurance to victims of domestic violence in Washington State. *Seattle University Law Review, 23,* 797–847.

Sidebotham, P., & Heron, J. (2003). Child maltreatment in the "children of the nineties": The role of the child. *Child Abuse & Neglect, 27,* 337–352.

Siegel, J. A. (2000). Aggressive behavior among women sexually abused as children. *Violence and Victims, 15,* 235–255.

Sierra, L. (1997). Representing battered women charged with crimes for failing to protect their children from abusive partners. *Double-Time* (Newsletter of the National Clearinghouse for the Defense of Battered Women), *5*(1/2), 1, 4–7.

Sifferd, K. (1996). Victim services stretched far in rural areas. *Illinois Criminal Justice Information Authority. The Compiler 17*(4), 11–14.

Sigler, R. T. (1989). *Domestic violence in context: An assessment of community attitudes.* Lexington, MA: Lexington.

Signs of physical abuse. (n.d.). Retrieved on June 20, 2010, from http://www.child-abuse-effects.com/signs-of-physical-abuse.html

Silbert, M., & Pines, A. M. (1983). Early sexual exploitation as an influence in prostitution. *Social Work, 28,* 285–289.

Silver, E. (2002). Mental disorder and violent victimization: The mediating role of involvement in conflicted social relationships. *Criminology, 40,* 191–212.

Silver, E. (2006). Understanding the relationship between mental disorder and violence: The need for a criminological perspective. *Law and Human Behavior, 30,* 685–706.

Silver, E., & Teasdale, B. (2005) Mental disorder and violence: An examination of stressful life events and impaired social support. *Social Problems, 52,* 62–78.

Silvergleid, C. S., & Mankowski, E. S. (2006). How batterer intervention programs work. *Journal of Interpersonal Violence, 21,* 139–159.

Silverman, A. B., Reinherz, H. Z., & Giaconia, R. M. (1996). The long-term sequelae of child and adolescent abuse: A longitudinal community study. *Child Abuse & Neglect, 8,* 709–723.

Silverman, J. G., Decker, M. R., Saggurti, N., Balaiah, D., & Raj, A. (2008). Intimate partner violence and HIV infection among married Indian women. *Journal of the American Medical Association, 300,* 703–710.

Silverman, J. G., Raj, A., Mucci, L. A., & Hathaway, J. E. (2001). Dating violence against adolescent girls and associated substance use, unhealthy weight control, sexual risk behavior, pregnancy, and suicidality. *Journal of the American Medical Association, 286,* 572–579.

Silvern, L., Karyl, J., Waelde, L., Hodges, W. F., Starek, J., Heidt, E., et al. (1995). Retrospective reports of parental partner abuse: Relationships to depression, trauma symptoms and self-esteem among college students. *Journal of Family Violence, 10,* 177–202.

Simao, P. (2009 March 14). Brazil says leave U. S. custody case to courts. *Reuters.*

Simmons, A. N., Paulus, M. P., Thorp, S. R., Norman, S. B., & Stein, M. B. (2008). Functional activation and neural networks in women with posttraumatic stress disorder related to intimate partner violence. *Biological Psychiatry, 15,* 681–690.

Simmons, C. A., Lehmann, P., & Collier-Tenison, S. (2008). Men's use of controlling behaviors: A comparison of reports by women in a domestic violence shelter and women in a domestic violence offender program. *Journal of Family Violence, 23,* 387–394.

Simon, T. R., Anderson, M., Thompson, M. P., Crosby, A. E., Shelley, G., & Sacks, J. J. (2001). Attitudinal acceptance of intimate partner violence among U.S. adults. *Violence and Victims, 16,* 115–126.

Simon, T. R., Miller, S., Gorman-Smith, D., Orpinas, P., & Sullivan, T. (2010). Physical dating violence norms among sixth-grade students from four U. S. sites. *The Journal of Early Adolescence, 30,* 395–409.

Simonelli, C. J., Mullis, T., Elliott, A. N., & Pierce, T. W. (2002). Abuse by siblings and subsequent experiences of violence within the dating relationship. *Journal of Interpersonal Violence, 17,* 103–121.

Simoneti, S., Scott, E. C., & Murphy, C. M. (2000). Dissociative experiences in partner-assaultive men. *Journal of Interpersonal Violence, 15,* 1262–1283.

Simons, D. A., Wurtele, S. K., & Durham, R. L. (2008). Developmental experiences of child sexual abusers and rapists. *Child Abuse & Neglect, 32,* 549–560.

Simons, D. A., Wurtele, S. K., & Durham, R. L. (2008). Developmental experiences of child sexual abusers and rapists. *Child Abuse & Neglect, 32,* 540–560.

Simons, L. G., Burt, C. H., & Simons, R. L. (2008). A test of explanations for the effect of harsh parenting on the perpetration of dating violence and sexual coercion among college males. *Violence and Victims, 23,* 66–82.

Simons, R. L., Lin, K., & Gordon, L. C. (1998). Socialization in the family of origin and male dating violence. *Journal of Marriage and the Family, 60,* 467–478.

Simons, R. L., Wu, C.-I., Johnson, C., & Conger, R. D. (1995). A test of various perspectives on the intergenerational transmission of domestic violence. *Criminology, 33,* 141–170.

Simpson, A. I. F., Allnutt, S., & Chaplow, D. (2001). Inquiries into homicides and serious violence perpetrated by psychiatric patients in New Zealand: Need for consistency of method and result analysis. *Australian and New Zealand Journal of Psychiatry, 35,* 36369.

Simpson, L. E., Atkins, D. C., Gattis, K. S., & Christensen, A. (2008). Low-level relationship aggression and couple therapy outcomes. *Journal of Family Psychology, 22,* 102–111.

Simpson, S. S., Bouffard, L. A., Garner, J., & Hickman, L. J. (2006). The influence of legal reform on the probability of arrest in domestic violence cases. *Justice Quarterly, 23,* 297–316.

Singer, D. (2002). *Quality of care project.* Denver, CO: Denver Regional Council on Government Aging Services.

Sirles, E. A., & Franke, P. J. (1989). Factors influencing mothers' reactions to intrafamily sexual abuse. *Child Abuse & Neglect, 13,* 131–139.

Sitren, A. H., & Applegate, B. K. (2007). Testing the deterrence effects of personal and vicarious experience with punishment and punishment avoidance. *Deviant Behavior, 28,* 29–55.

Skilling, T. A., Quinsey, V. L., & Craig, W. M. (2001). Evidence of a taxon underlying serious antisocial behavior in boys. *Criminal Justice and Behavior, 4,* 450–470.

Slashinski, M. J., Coker, A. L., & Davis, K. E. (2003). Physical aggression, forced sex, and stalking victimization by a dating partner: An analysis of the National Violence Against Women Survey. *Violence and Victims, 18,* 595–617.

Slattery, S. M., & Goodman, L. A. (2009). Secondary traumatic stress among domestic violence advocates: Workplace risk and protective factors. *Violence Against Women, 15,* 1358–1379.

Sledjeski, E. M., Speisman, B., & Dierker, L. C. (2008). Does the number of lifetime traumas explain the relationship between PTSD and chronic medical conditions? Answers from the National Comorbidity Survey-Replication (NCS-R). *Central European Journal of Medicine, 31,* 341–349.

Slep, A. M. S., Heyman, R. E., Williams, M. C., Van Dyke, C. E., & O'Leary, S. G. (2006). Using random telephone sampling to recruit generalizable samples for family violence studies. *Journal of Family Psychology, 20,* 680–689.

Slep, A. M. S., & O'Leary, S. G. (2007). Multivariate models of mothers' and fathers' aggression toward their children. *Journal of Consulting and Clinical Psychology, 75,* 739–751.

Slesnick, N., Prestopnik, J. L., Meyers, R. J., & Glassman, M. (2004). Treatment outcome for street-living, homeless youth. *Addictive Behaviors, 32,* 1237–1251.

Smallbone, S. W., & Dadds, M. R. (2001). Further evidence for a relationship between attachment insecurity and coercive sexual behavior in nonoffenders. *Journal of Interpersonal Violence, 16,* 22–35.

Smiljanich, K., & Briere, J. (1996). Self-reported sexual interest in children: Sex differences and psychological correlates in a college sample. *Violence and Victims, 11,* 39–50.

Smith, A., & Chiricos, T. (2003). Structural antecedents of aggravated assault: Exploratory assessment of female and male victimization. *Violence and Victims, 18,* 55–70.

Smith, C. A. (2009). Substance abuse, chronic sorrow, and mothering loss: Relapse triggers among female victims of child abuse. *Journal of Pediatric Nursing, 24,* 401–412.

Smith, C. A., Thornberry, T. P., & Ireland, T. O. (2004). Adolescent maltreatment and its impact: Timing matters. *The Prevention Researcher, 11(1),* 7–11.

Smith, D. L. (2008). Disability, gender, and intimate partner violence: Relationships from the Behavioral Risk Factor Surveillance System. *Sexuality and Disability, 26,* 15–28.

Smith, J. P., & Williams, J. G. (1992). From abusive household to dating violence. *Journal of Family Violence, 7,* 153–165.

Smith, M. (1999, March 2). Judge dismisses charges in "false memories" case. *Houston Chronicle,* p. A1.

Smith, P., & Welchans, S. (2000). Peer education: Does focusing on male responsibility change sexual assault attitudes? *Violence Against Women, 6,* 1255–1268.

Smith, P. H., Smith, J. B., & Earp, J. L. (1999). Beyond the measurement trap: A reconstructed conceptualization and measurement of women battering. *Psychology of Women Quarterly, 23,* 179–195.

Smith, P. H., Thornton, G. E., DeVellis, R., Earp, J. L., & Coker, A. L. (2002). A population-based study of the prevalence and distinctiveness of battering, physical assault, and sexual assault in intimate relationships. *Violence Against Women, 10,* 1208–1232.

Smith, R. (2009, October 19). Lesbian honor student's fight to wear tuxedo in yearbook photo may end in court. CBS/AP.

Smith, R., Pine, C., & Hawley, M. (1988). Social cognitions about adult male victims of female sexual assault. *Journal of Sex Research, 24,* 101–112.

Smith, S. G. (2008). Disclosing sexual assault to parents: The influence of parental messages about sex. *Violence Against Women, 14,* 1326–1348.

Smith, S. G., & Cook, S. L. (2008). Disclosing sexual assault to parents: The influence of parental messages about sex. *Violence Against Women, 14,* 1326–1348.

Smolak, L., & Murnen, S. K. (2002). A meta-analytic examination of the relationship between child sexual abuse and eating disorders. *International Journal of Eating Disorders, 31,* 136–150.

Smolowe, J., Herbert, D., Egan, N. W., Rakowsky, J., & Mascia, K. (2010, April 26). Inside her torment. *People, 66,* 68, 70,

Snow, D. A. (2001). Extending and broadening Blumer's conceptualization of symbolic interactionism. *Symbolic Interactionism, 24,* 367–377.

Snyder, H. N., & McCurley, C. (2008). *Domestic assaults by juvenile offenders.* Washington, DC: Office of Juvenile Jusice Delinquency Prevention.

Snyder, L. A., Chen, P. Y., & Vacha-Haase, T. (2007). The underreporting gap in aggressive incidents from geriatric patients against certified nursing assistants. *Violence and Victims, 22,* 367–379.

Sobsey, D. (1994). *Violence in the lives of people with disabilities.* Baltimore: Paul H. Brookes.

Social Services Inspectorate. (1992). *Confronting elder abuse: An SSI London Region Survey.* London: Her Majesty's Stationery Office.

Soglin, L. F., Bauchat, J., Soglin, D. F., & Martin, G. J. (2009). Detection of intimate partner violence in a general medicine practice. *Journal of Interpersonal Violence, 24,* 338–348.

Sokoloff, N. J., & Dupont, I. (2005). Domestic violence at the intersections of race, class, and gender: Challengers and contributions to understanding violence against marginalized women in diverse communities. *Violence Against Women, 11,* 38–64.

Solarsh, B., & Frankel, J. (2005). Domestic violence in the South African Jewish community: A model of service delivery. *Journal of Religion & Abuse, 6,* 113–128.

Solberg, M. E., & Olweus, D. (2003). Prevalence estimation of school bullying with the Olweus Bully/Victim Questionnaire. *Aggressive Behavior, 29,* 239–268.

Soler, H., Vinayak, P., & Quadagno, D. (2000). Biosocial aspects of domestic violence. *Psychoneuroendocrinology, 25,* 721–739.

Solomon, P. L., Cavanaugh, M. M., & Gelles, R. J. (2005). Family violence among adults with severe mental illness: A neglected area of research. *Trauma, Violence, & Abuse, 6,* 40–54.

Solomon, S., Subbaraman, R., Solomon, S. S., Srikrishnan, A. K., Johnson, S. C., Vasudevan, C. K., et al. (2009). Domestic violence and forced sex among the urban poor in South India. *Violence Against Women, 15,* 753–773.

Somer, E., & Braunstein, A. (1999). Are children exposed to interparental violence being psychologically maltreated? *Aggression and Violent Behavior, 4,* 449–456.

Sommers, M. S. (2007). Defining pattern of genital injury from sexual assault. *Trauma, Violence, & Abuse, 8,* 270–280.

Sørensen, B. W. (2001). Men in transition: The representation of men's violence against women in Greenland. *Violence Against Women, 7,* 826–847.

Sorensen, D. D. (2004, July/August). Invisible victims 2003. *Victimization of the Elderly and Disabled, 7,* 17–18, 28–30.

Sorenson, S. B., Stein, J. A., Siegel, J. M., Golding, J. M., & Burnam, M. A. (1987). Prevalence of adult sexual assault: The Los Angeles Epidemiologic Catchment Area Study. *American Journal of Epidemiology, 126,* 1154–1164.

Sorenson, S. B., & Taylor, C. A. (2005). Females' aggression toward intimate male partners: An examination of social norms in a community-based sample. *Psychology of Women Quarterly, 29,* 78–96).

Sorenson, S. B., & Wiebe, D. J. (2004). Weapons in the lives of battered women. *American Journal of Public Health, 94,* 1412–1417.

Sousa, C. A. (1999). Teen dating violence: The hidden epidemic. *Family and Conciliation Courts Review, 37,* 356–374.

Southworth, C., Finn, J., Dawson, S., Fraser, C., & Tucker, S. (2007). Intimate partner violence, technology, and stalking. *Violence Against Women, 13,* 842–856.

Spaccarelli, S., Sandler, I. N., & Roosa, M. (1994). History of spouse violence against mother: Correlated risks and unique effects in child mental health. *Journal of Family Violence, 9,* 79–98.

Spears, J. W., & Spohn, C. G. (1997). The effect of evidence factors and victim characteristics on prosecutors' charging decisions in sexual assault cases. *Justice Quarterly, 14,* 501–524.

Spector, M., & Kitsuse, J. I. (1977). *Constructing social problems.* Menlo Park, CA: Benjamin Cummings.

Spielberger, C. D. (1988). *Manual for the State-Trait Anger Expression Inventory.* Odessa, FL: Psychological Assessment Resources.

Spitzberg, B. H. (2002). The tactical topography of stalking victimization and management. *Trauma, Violence, & Abuse, 30,* 261–288.

Spitzberg, B. H., & Hoobler, G. (2002). Cyberstalking and the technologies of interpersonal terrorism. *New Media & Society, 4,* 71–92.

Spitzberg, B. H., & Veksler, A. E. (2007). The personality of pursuit: Personality attributions of unwanted pursuers and stalkers. *Violence and Victims, 22,* 275–289.

Sprecher, S. (2001). Equity and social exchange in dating couples: Associations with satisfaction, commitment, and stability. *Journal of Marriage and Family, 63,* 599–613.

Springer, K. W., Sheridan, J., Kuo, D., & Carnes, M. (2007). Long-term physical and mental health consequences of childhood physical abuse: Results from a large population-based sample of men and women. *Child Abuse & Neglect, 31,* 517–530.

Sroufe, L. A., Egeland, B., Carlson, E. A., & Collins, W. A. (2005). *The development of the person: The Minnesota study of risk and adaptation from birth to adulthood.* New York: Guilford Publications.

Sroufe, L. A., Coffino, B., & Carlson, E. A. (2010). Conceptualizing the role of early experience: Lessons from the Minnesota longitudinal study. *Developmental Review, 30,* 36–51.

Stacey, W. A., & Shupe, A. (1983). *The family secret.* Boston: Beacon.

Staggs, S. L., Long, S. M., Mason, G. E., Krishnan, S., & Riger, S. (2007). Intimate partner violence, social support, and employment in the post-welfare reform era. *Journal of Interpersonal Violence, 22,* 345–367.

Stahly, G. (2007). Domestic violence child custody: A critique of recent JCC articles. *Journal of Child Custody, 4,* 1–29.

Stahmer, A. C., Sutton, D. T., Fox, L., & Leslie, L. K. (2008). State Part C agency practices and the Child Abuse Prevention and Treatment Act (CAPTA). *Topics in Early Childhood Special Education, 28,* 99–108.

Stalans, L.J., & Ritchie, J. (2008). Relationship of substance use/abuse with psychological and physical intimate partner violence: Variations across living situations. *Journal of Family Violence, 23,* 9–24.

Stalans, L. J., & Seng, M. (2007). Identifying subgroups at high risk of dropping out of domestic batterer treatment: The buffering effects of a high school education. *International Journal of Offender Therapy and Comparative Criminology, 51,* 151–169.

Stalking Resource Center, National Center for Victims of Crime. (n.d.) Retrieved from http://www.ncvc.org/src/main.aspx?dbID=DB_Online_National111

Stambor, Z. (2006, July/August). Bullying stems from fear, apathy. *Monitor on Psycholgy, 37,* 71–73.

Stankiewicz, J.M., & Rosselli, F. (2008). Women as sex objects and victims in print advertisements. *Sex Roles, 58,* 579–589.

Stanley, K. M., Martin, M. M., Michel, Y., Welton, J. M., & Nemeth, L. S. (2007). Examining lateral violence in the nursing workforce. *Issues in Mental Health Nursing, 28,* 1247–1265.

Stanley, M. A., Wilson, N. L., Novy, D. M., Rhoades, H. M., Wagener, P. D., Greisinger, A. J., et al. (2009). Cognitive behavior therapy for generalized anxiety disorder among older adults in primary care. *Journal of the American Medical Association, 302,* 1460–1467.

Stanley, S. M., Amato, P. R., Johnson, C. A., & Markman, H. J. (2006). Premarital education, marital quality, and marital stability: Findings from a large, random household survey. *Journal of Family Psychology, 20,* 117–126.

Stark, E. (2007). *Coercive control: How men entrap women in personal life.* New York: Oxford University Press.

Starkey, J. (2009). Afghan leader accused of bid to 'legalise rape.' http://www.independent.co.uk/news

Starr, K., Hobart, M., & Fawcett, J. (2004, December). *Every life lost is a call for change: Findings and recommendations from the Washington State Domestic Violence Fatality Review.* Seattle, WA: Washington State Coalition Against Domestic Violence.

Staske, S. A. (1999). Creating relational ties in talk: The collaborative construction of relational jealousy. *Symbolic Interaction, 22,* 213–246.

State of California, Department of Social Services, Office of Child Abuse Prevention. (2003). *The California child abuse & neglect reporting law.* Sacramento, CA: Author.

Stavis, P. F. (2005). Harmonizing the right to sexual expression and the right to protection from harm for persons with mental disability. *Sexuality and Disability, 9,* 131–141.

Steel, J., Sanna, L., Hammond, B., Whipple, J., & Cross, H. (2004). Psychological sequelae of childhood sexual abuse: Abuse-related characteristics, coping strategies, and attributional style. *Child Abuse & Neglect, 28,* 785–801.

Steele, B. F., & Alexander, H. (1981). Long-term effects of sexual abuse in childhood. In P. B. Mrazek & C. H. Kempe (Eds.), *Sexually abused children and their families* (pp. 223–233). New York: Pergamon.

Steffensmeir, D., & Hayne, D. L. (2000). The structural sources of urban female violence in the United States. *Homicide Studies, 4,* 107–134.

Stein, A.L, Tran, G. Q., & Fisher, B. S. (2009). Intimate partner violence experience and expectations among college women in dating relationships: Implications for behavioral interventions, *Violence and Victims, 24,* 153–162.

Stein, D. J., van der Kolk, B., Austin, C., Fallad, R., & Clary, C. (2006). Efficacy of Sertraline in posttraumatic stress disorder secondary to interpersonal trauma or childhood abuse. Annals of *Clinical Psychiatry, 18,* 243–249.

Stein, R. F., & Nofziger, S. D. (2008). Adolescent sexual victimization. *Youth Violence and Juvenile Justice, 6,* 158–177.

Stein, T. J. (1993). Legal perspectives on family violence against children. In R. L. Hampton, T. P. Gullotta, G. R. Adams, E. H. Potter III, & R. P. Weissberg (Eds.), *Family violence: Prevention and treatment* (pp. 179–197). Newbury Park, CA: Sage.

Steinman, M. (1991). The public policy process and woman battering: Problems and potentials. In M. Steinman (Ed.), *Woman battering: Policy responses* (pp. 1–18). Cincinnati, OH: Anderson.

Steinmetz, S. K. (1977). The battered husband syndrome. *Victimology, 2,* 499–509.

Steinmetz, S. K. (1987). Family violence: Past, present, and future. In M. B. Sussman & S. K. Steinmetz (Eds.),

*Handbook of marriage and the family* (pp. 725–765). New York: Plenum.

Stenius, V. M., & Veysey, B. M. (2005). "It's the little things": Women, trauma, and strategies for healing. *Journal of Interpersonal Violence, 20,* 1153–1174.

Stenner, P., & Rogers, R. S. (1998). Jealousy as a manifold of divergent understandings: A Q methodological investigation. *European Journal of Social Psychology, 28,* 71–94.

Stephens, B. J., & Sinden, P. G. (2000). Victims' voices: Domestic assault victims' perceptions of police demeanor. *Journal of Interpersonal Violence, 15,* 534–547.

Stermac, L., Del Bove, G., & Addison, M. (2001). Violence, injury, and presentation patterns in spousal sexual assaults. *Violence Against Women, 7,* 1218–1233.

Stermac, L., Del Bove, G. & Brazeau, P., & Bainbridge, D. (2006). Patterns in sexual assault violence as a function of victim perpetrator degree of relatedness. *Journal of Aggression, Maltreatment & Trauma, 13,* 41–58.

Sternberg, K. J., Lamb, M. E., Greenbaum, C., Cicchetti, D., Dawud, S., Cortes, R. M., et al. (1993). Effects of domestic violence on children's behavior problems and depression. *Developmental Psychology, 29,* 44–52.

Sternberg, K. J., Lamb, M. E., Guterman, E., & Abbott, C. B. (2006). Effects of early and later family violence on children's behavior problems and depression: A longitudinal, multi-informant perspective. *Child Abuse & Neglect, 30,* 283–306.

Stets, J. E., & Straus, M. A. (1990). Differences in reporting marital violence and its medical and psychological consequences. In M. A. Straus & R. J. Gelles (Eds.), *Physical violence in American families: Risk factors and adaptations to violence in 8,145 families* (pp. 151–166). New Brunswick, NJ: Transaction.

Stevenson, T. R., Goodall, E. A., & Moore, C. B. (2008). A retrospective audit of the extent and nature of domestic violence cases identified over a three year period in the two district command units of the police service of Northern Ireland. *Forensic Legal Medicine, 15,* 430–436.

Stewart, A. (2000). Who are the respondents of domestic violence protection orders? *Australian and New Zealand Journal of Criminology, 33,* 77–90.

Stewart, K., & Cherrin, A. (2008, April/May). Landmark International Violence Against Women Act introduced. *Domestic Violence Report, 13,* 51, 59–60.

Stickley, A., Kislitsyna, O, Timofeeva, I., & Vågerö, D. (2008). Attitudes toward intimate partner violence against women in Moscow, Russia. *Journal of Family Violence, 23,* 447–456.

Stickley, A., Timofeeva, I., & Sparén, P. (2008). Risk factors for intimate partner violence against women in St. Petersburg, Russia. *Violence Against Women, 14,* 483–495.

Stiegel, L. A. (2007, January/February). Washington report. *Victimization of the Elderly and Disabled, 9,* 65–66, 73–77.

Stiegel, L. A., & Klem, E. M. (2007, September/October). Washington Report. *Victimization of the Elderly and Disabled, 9,* 37–38, 48.

Stiegel, L. A., Heisler, C. J., Brandl, B., & Judy, A. (2000, November/December). Developing services for older victims of domestic or sexual assault: The approach of Wisconsin coalitions. *Victimization of the Elderly and Disabled, 3,* 49–50, 58–60.

Stipanicic, A., Nolin, P., Fortin, G., & Gobeil, M-F. (2008). Comparative study of the cognitive sequelae of school-aged victims of shaken baby syndrome. *Child Abuse & Neglect, 32,* 415–428.

Stirling, J. Jr. (2007). Beyond Munchausen syndrome by proxy. Identification and treatment of child abuse in a medical setting. *Pediatrics, 119,* 1026–1030.

Stith, S. M., Green, N. M., Smith, D. B., Ward, & D. B. (2008). Marital satisfaction and marital discord as risk markers for intimate partner violence: A meta-analytic review. *Journal of Family Violence, 23,* 149–160.

Stith, S. M., et al. (2009). Risk factors in child maltreatment: A meta-analyatic review of the literature. *Aggression and Violent Behavior,* 14, 13–29

Stith, S. M., Rosen, K. H., Middleton, K. A., Busch, A. L., Lundberg, K., & Carlton, R. P. (2000). The intergenerational transmission of spouse abuse: A meta-analysis. *Journal of Marriage and the Family, 62,* 640–654.

Stoddard, J. P., Dibble, S. L., & Fineman, N. (2009). Sexual and physical abuse: A comparison between lesbians and their heterosexual sisters. *Journal of Homosexuality, 56,* 407–420.

Stoia-Caraballo, R., Rye, M. S., Pan, W., Kirschman, K. J. B., Lutz-Zois, C., & Lyons, A. M. (2008). Negative affect and anger rumination as mediators between forgiveness and sleep quality. *Journal of Behavior Medicine, 31,* 478–488.

Stoltenberg, C. D., & Pace, T. M. (2007). The scientific-practitioner model: Now more than ever [Special issue]. *Journal of Contemporary Psychotherapy, 37*(4), 195–203.

Stoner, S. A., Norris, J., George, W. H., Davis, K. C., Masters, N. T., & Hessler, D. M. (2007). Effects of alcohol intoxication and victimization history on women's sexual assault resistance intentions: The role of secondary appraisals. *Psychology of Women Quarterly, 31,* 344–356.

Stoops, C., Bennett, L., & Vincent, N. (2010). Development and predictive ability of a behavior-based typology of men who batter. *Journal of Family Violence, 25,* 325–335.

Stop Prisoner Rape. (2002, October 30). *Stop Prisoner Rape accuses FBI of ignoring male rape in new crime report* [Press release]. Retrieved November 16, 2003, from Stop Prisoner Rape website: http://www.spr.org

Stordeur, R. A., & Stille, R. (1989). *Ending men's violence against their partners: One road to peace.* Newbury Park, CA: Sage.

Stosny, S. (1995). *Treating attachment abuse: A compassion approach.* New York: Springer.

Stouthamer-Loeber, M., van Kammen, W., & Loeber, R. (1992). Researchers' forum: The nuts and bolts of implementing large-scale longitudinal studies. *Violence and Victims, 7,* 63–78.

Straight, E. S., Harper, F. W. K., & Arias, I. (2003). The impact of partner psychological abuse on health behaviors and health status in college women. *Journal of Interpersonal Violence, 18,* 1035–1054.

Straka, S. M., & Montiminy, L. (2006). Responding to the needs of older women experiencing domestic violence. *Violence Against Women, 12,* 251–267.

Strand, M., Benzein, E., & Saveman, B. (2004). Violence and aggression: Violence in the care of adult persons with intellectual disabilities. *JCN: Journal of Clinical Nursing, 13,* 506–514.

Strand, V. C. (2000). *Treating secondary victims: Intervention with the nonoffending mother in the incest family.* Thousand Oaks, CA: Sage.

Strauchler, O., McCloskey, K., Malloy, K., Sitaker, M., Grisby, N., & Gillig, P. (2004). Humiliation, manipulation, and control: Evidence of centrality in domestic violence against an adult partner. *Journal of Family Violence, 19,* 339–354.

Straus, M. A. (1976). Sexual inequality, cultural norms, and wife beating. *Victimology, 1,* 54–76.

Straus, M. A. (1979). Measuring intrafamily conflict and aggression: The Conflict Tactics Scale (CT). *Journal of Marriage and the Family, 41,* 75–88.

Straus, M. A. (1980). Societal stress and marital violence in a national sample of American families. *Annals of the New York Academy of Sciences, 34,* 229–250.

Straus, M. A. (1983). Ordinary violence, child abuse, and wife beating: What do they have in common? In D. Finkelhor, R. J. Gelles, G. T. Hotaling, & M. A. Straus (Eds.), *The dark side of families: Current family violence research* (pp. 213–234). Beverly Hills, CA: Sage.

Straus, M. A. (1990). The Conflict Tactics Scales and its critics: An evaluation of new data on validity and reliability (pp. 49–73). In M. A. Straus and R. J. Gelles (Eds.). *Physical violence in American families: Risk factors and adaptations to violence in 1,845 families.* New Brunswick, NJ: Transaction Books.

Straus, M. A. (1991a, September). *Children as witness to marital violence: A risk factor for life long problems among a nationally representative sample of American men and women.* Paper presented at the Ross Roundtable on Children and Violence, Washington, DC.

Straus, M. A. (1991b). Discipline and deviance: Physical punishment of children and violence and other crime in adulthood. *Social Problems, 38,* 133–154.

Straus, M. A. (1991c). New theory and old canards about family violence research. *Social Problems, 38,* 180–197.

Straus, M. A. (1992). Children as witnesses to marital violence: A risk factor for life-long problems among a nationally representative sample of American men and women. In *Children and violence: A report of the Twenty-Third Ross Roundtable on Initial Approaches to Common Paediatric Problems.* Columbus, OH: Ross Laboratories.

Straus, M. A. (1993). Physical assaults by wives: A major social problem. In R. J. Gelles & D. R. Loseke (Eds.), *Current controversies on family violence* (pp. 67–87). Newbury Park, CA: Sage.

Straus, M. A. (1994). *Beating the devil out of them: Corporal punishment in American families.* Lexington, MA: Lexington.

Straus, M. A. (2001). *Beating the devil out of them: Corporal punishment in American families and its effects on children* (2nd ed.). New Brunswick, NJ: Transaction.

Straus, M. A. (2004a). Prevalence of violence against dating partners by male and female university students worldwide. *Violence Against Women, 10,* 790–811.

Straus, M. A. (2004b). Women's violence toward men is a serious social problem. In D. R. Loseke, R. J. Gelles, & M. M. Cavanaugh (Eds.), *Current controversies on family violence* (2nd ed., pp. 55–77). Newbury Park, CA: Sage.

Straus, M. A. (2005). Children should never, ever, be spanked no matter what the circumstances. In D. R. Loeseke, R. J. Gelles, & M. M. Cavanaugh (Eds.), *Current controversies on family violence* (2nd ed., pp. 137–157). Thousand Oaks, CA: Sage.

Straus, M. A. (2006). Cross-cultural reliability and validity of the Multidimension Neglectful Behavior Scale Adult Recall Short Form. *Child Abuse and Neglect, 30,* 1257–1279.

Straus, M. A., & Gelles, R. J. (1986). Societal change and change in family violence from 1975 to 1985 as revealed by two national surveys. *Journal of Marriage and the Family, 48,* 465–479.

Straus, M. A. & Gelles, R. J. (Eds.). (1990). *Physical violence in American families: Risk factors and adaptations to violence in 8,145 families.* New Brunswick, NJ: Transaction.

Straus, M. A., Gelles, R. J., & Steinmetz, S. K. (1980). *Behind closed doors: Violence in the American family.* Garden City, NY: Doubleday.

Straus, M. A., Hamby, S. L., Boney-McCoy, S., & Sugarman, D. B. (1996). *The Revised Conflict Tactics Scales (CTS2): Development and preliminary psychometric data.* Durham, NH: Family Violence Research Laboratory.

Straus, M. A., Hamby, S. L., Finkelhor, D., Moore, D. W., & Runyan, D. (1998). Identification of child maltreatment with the Parent-Child Conflict Tactics Scales: Development and psychometric data for a national sample of American parents. *Child Abuse & Neglect, 22,* 249–270.

Straus, M. A., & Kaufman Kantor, G. (2005). Definition and measurement of neglectful behavior: Some principles and guidelines. *Child Abuse & Neglect, 29,* 19–29.

Straus, M. A., & Savage, S. A. (2006). Neglectful behavior by parents in the life history of university students in 17 countries and its relation to violence against dating partners. *Child Maltreatment, 10,* 124–135.

Straus, M. A., & Smith, C. (1990). Family patterns of primary prevention of family violence. In M. A. Straus & R. J. Gelles (Eds.), *Physical violence in American families: Risk factors and adaptations to violence in 8,145 families* (pp. 507–526). New Brunswick, NJ: Transaction.

Straus, M. A., Sugarman, D. B., & Giles-Sims, J. (1997). Spanking by parents and subsequent antisocial behavior of children. *Archives of Pediatric and Adolescent Medicine, 151,* 761–767.

Street, A. E. (1998). Psychological abuse and posttraumatic stress disorder in battered women: Examining the role of shame. *Dissertation Abstracts International, 59*(05), 2438B. (UMI No. 9908648)

Streissguth, A. (1997). *Fetal alcohol syndrome: A guide for families and communities.* Baltimore: Paul H. Brookes.

Strickland, J. (2010, April 1). Is cyber bullying illegal? Discovery News. Retrieved from http://news.discovery.com/tech/is-cyber-bullying-illegal.html, http://news.discovery.com/tech/is-cyber-bullying-illegal.html

Strickland, S. (2008). Female sex offenders: Exploring issues of personality, trauma, and cognitive distortions. *Journal of Interpersonal Violence, 23,* 474–489.

Stripe, T. S., & Stermac, L. E. (2003). An exploration of childhood victimization and family-of-origin characteristics of sexual offenders against children. *International Journal of Offender Therapy and Comparative Criminology, 46,* 542–555.

Strom, T. O., & Kosciulek, J. (2007). Stress, appraisal and coping following mild traumatic brain injury. *Brain Injury, 21,* 1137–1145.

Stroshine, M. S., & Robinson, A. L. (2003). The decision to end abusive relationships: The role of offender characteristics. *Criminal Justice and Behavior, 30,* 97–117.

Struther, R., Lauderdale, J., Tom-Orme, L., & Strickland, G. J. (2005). Respecting tribal traditions in research and publications: Voices of five Native American scholars. *Journal of Transcultural Nursing, 16,* 193–201.

Stuart, G. L., Moore, T. M., Gordon, K. C., Hellmuth, J. C., Ramsey, S. E., & Kahler, C. W. (2006). Reasons for intimate partner violence perpetration among arrested women. *Violence Against Women, 12,* 609–621.

Stuart, R. B. (2005). Treatment for partner abuse: Time for a paradigm shift. *Professional Psychology: Research and Practice, 36,* 254–263.

Studer, M. (1984). Wife-beating as a social problem: The process of definition. *International Journal of Women's Studies, 7,* 412–422.

Stuewig, J., & McCloskey, L. A. (2005). The relation of child maltreatment to shame and guilt among adolescents: Psychological routes to depression and delinquency. *Child Maltreatment, 10,* 324–336.

Subramanian, P., & Sivayogan, S. (2001). The prevalence and pattern of wife beating in the Trincomalee district in eastern Sri Lanka. *Southeast Asian Journal of Tropical Medicine and Public Health, 32,* 186–195.

Successes seen in making arrests for Internet-related sex crimes. (2003, November 17). *Criminal Justice Newsletter,* pp. 1–2.

Sudderth, L. K. (2006). An uneasy alliance: Law enforcement and domestic violence victim advocates in a rural area. *Feminist Criminology, 1,* 329–353.

Sue, S. (1998). In search of cultural competence in psychotherapy and counseling. *American Psychologist, 53,* 440–448.

Suffla, S., Van Niekerk, A., & Arendse, N. (2008). Female homicidal strangulation in urban South Africa. *BMC Public Health, 8,* 363–374.

Sugarman, D. B., & Frankel, S. L. (1993, August). *A meta-analytic study of wife assault and patriarchal beliefs.* Paper presented at annual meeting of the American Psychological Association, Toronto.

Sugarman, D. B., & Hotaling, G. T. (1989). Dating violence: Prevalence, context, and risk markers. In M. A. Pirog-Good & J. E. Stets (Eds.), *Violence in dating relationships: Emerging social issues* (pp. 3–32). New York: Praeger.

Sugarman, J., Roter, D., Cain, C., Wallace, R., Schmechel, D., & Welsh-Bohmen, K. A. (2007). Proxies and consent discussion for dementia research. *Journal of the American Geriatrics Society, 55,* 556–561.

Suk, J. (2006). Criminal law comes home. *Yale Law Journal, 116,* 2–70.

Sullivan, C. M. (1991). Battered women as active helpseekers. *Violence Update, 1*(1), 8, 10.

Sullivan, C. M., & Cain, D. (2004). Ethical and safety considerations when obtaining information from or about battered women for research purposes. *Journal of Interpersonal Violence, 19,* 603–618.

Sullivan, T. P., Meese, K. J., Swan, S. C., Mazur, C. M., & Snow, D. L. (2005). Precursors and correlates of women's violence: Child abuse traumatization, victimization of women, avoidance coping, and psychological symptoms. *Psychology of Women Quarterly, 29,* 290–301.

Sundram, C. J. (2000, January/February). Sex and mental disability: A responsible approach. *Victimization of the Elderly and Disabled, 2,* 67–68.

Sundram, C. J. (2006a, January/February). New treaty on disability and legal capacity, Part II. *Victimization of the Elderly and Disabled, 9,* 65–78, 80.

Sundram, C. J. (2006b, May/June). Children with disabilities in Eastern Europe. *Victimization of the Elderly and Disabled, 9,* 3, 13.

Suris, A., Lind, L., Kashner, T. M., & Borman, P. D. (2007). Mental health, quality of life, and health functioning in women veterans. *Journal of Interpersonal Violence, 22,* 179–197.

Suyemoto, K. L., Liem, J. H., Kuhn, J. C., Mongillo, E. A., & Tauriac, J. J. (2007). Therapists' cultural competence training. *Women & Therapy, 30,* 209–227.

Swahn, M. H., Simon, T. R., Arias, I., & Bossarte, R. M. (2008). Measuring sex differences in violence victimization and perpetration within date and same-sex peer relationships. *Journal of Interpersonal Violence, 23,* 1120–1138.

Swan, S. C., Gambone, L. J., Caldwell, J. E., Sullivan, T. P., & Snow, D. L. (2008). A review of research on women's use of violence with male intimate partners. *Violence and Victims, 23,* 301–314.

Swan, S. C., Gambone, L. J., Fields, A. M., Sullivan, T. P., & Snow, D. L. (2005). Women who use violence in intimate relationships: The role of anger, victimization, and symptoms of posttraumatic stress and depression. *Violence and Victims, 20,* 267–285.

Swan, S. C., & Snow, D. L. (2002). A typology of women's use of violence in intimate relationships. *Violence Against Women, 8,* 286–319.

Swan, S. C., & Snow, D. L. (2006). The development of a theory of women's use of violence in intimate relationships. *Violence Against Women, 12,* 1026–1045.

Swanberg, J. E., & Logan, T. (2005). Domestic violence and employment: A qualitative study. *Journal of Occupational Health Study, 10,* 3–17.

Swanberg, J. E., Logan, T. K., & Macke, C. (2005). Intimate partner violence, employment, and the workplace. *Trauma, Violence, & Abuse, 6,* 286–312.

Swearer, S. M., Espelage, D. L., Vaillancourt, T., & Hymel, S. (2010). What can be done about school bullying? Linking research to educational practice. *Educational Researcher, 19,* 38–47.

Sweeny, K., Carroll, P. J., & Shepperd, J. A. (2006). Is optimism always best? Future outlooks and preparedness. *Current Directions in Psychological Science, 15,* 302–306.

Swenson, C. C., & Kolko, D. J. (2000). Long-term management of the developmental consequences of child physical abuse. In R. M. Reece (Ed.), *Treatment of child abuse: Common ground for mental health, medical, and legal practitioners* (pp. 135–154). Baltimore: Johns Hopkins University Press.

Syers, M., & Edleson, J. L. (1992). The combined effects of coordinated criminal justice intervention in woman abuse. *Journal of Interpersonal Violence, 7,* 490–502.

Taft, C. T., Pless, A. P., Stalans, L. J., Koenen, K. C., King, L. A., & King, D. W. (2005). Risk factors for partner violence among a national sample of combat veterans. *Journal of Counseling and Clinical Psychology, 73,* 151–159.

Taft, C. T., Resick, P. A., Panuzio, J., Vogt, D. S., & Mechanic, M. B. (2007a). Coping among victims of relationship abuse: A longitudinal examination. *Violence and Victims, 22,* 408–418.

Taft, C. T., Resick, P. A., Panuzio, J., Vogt, D. S., & Mechanic, M. B. (2007b). Examining the correlates of engagement and disengagement coping among help-seeking battered women. *Violence and Victims, 22,* 3–17.

Taft, C. T., Street, A. E., Marshall, A. D., Dowdall, D. J., & Riggs, D. S. (2007). Posttraumatic stress disorder, anger, and partner abuse among Vietnam combat veterans. *Journal of Family Psychology, 21,* 270–277.

Tajima, E., & Harachi, T. W. (2010). Parenting beliefs and physical discipline among Southeast Asian immigrants: Parenting in the context of cultural adaptation to the United States. *Journal of Cross-Cultural Psychology, 41,* 212–235.

Talley, P., Heitkemper, M., Chiez-Demet, A., & Sandman, C. A. (2006). Male violence, stress, and neuroendocrine parameters in pregnancy: A pilot study. *Biological Research in Nursing, 7,* 222–233.

Tamraz, D. N. (1996). Nonoffending mothers of sexually abused children: Comparison of opinions and research. *Journal of Child Sexual Abuse, 5*(4), 75–99.

Tang, C. S. (1997). Psychological impact of wife abuse: Experiences of Chinese women and their children. *Journal of Interpersonal Violence, 12,* 466–478.

Tang, C. S., Cheung, F. M., Chen, R., & Sun, X. (2002). Definition of violence against women. *Journal of Interpersonal Violence, 17,* 671–688.

Tang, C. S., Wong, D., & Cheung, F. M. (2002). Social construction of women as legitimate victims of violence in Chinese societies. *Violence Against Women, 8,* 968–996.

Tang, S. S. S., Freyd, J. J., & Wang, M. (2007). What do we know about gender in the disclosure of child sexual abuse? *Journal of Psychological Trauma, 6,* 1–26.

Tarasoff v. Regents of the University of California, 529 P.2d 553 (Cal. 1974), vac., reheard in bank and aff'd, 131 Cal Rptr. 14, 551 P.2d 334 (1976).

Tauriac, J. J., & Scruggs, N. (2006). Elder abuse among African Americans. *Educational Gerontology, 32,* 37–48.

Taylor, J. Y. (2000). Sisters of the yam: African American women's healing and self-recovery from intimate male partner violence. *Issues in Mental Health Nursing, 21,* 515–531.

Taylor, B. G., Davis, R. C., & Maxwell, C. D. (2001). The effects of a group batterer treatment program: A randomized experiment in Brooklyn. *Justice Quarterly, 18,* 171–201.

Taylor, L. R. & Gaskin-Laniyan, N. (2007, June). *Study reveals unique issues faced by deaf victims of sexual assault* (NIJ Journal No. 257; NCJ Publication No. 219606). Washington, DC: National Institute of Justice.

Teasdale, B., Silver, E., & Monahan, J. (2006). Gender, threat/control-override delusions and violence. *Law and Human Behavior, 30,* 649–658.

Teaster, P. B. (2003). *A response to the abuse of vulnerable adults: The 2000 survey of State Adult Protective Services.* Washington, DC: National Center on Elder Abuse.

Teaster, P. B., Dugar, T. A., Mendiano, M. S., Abner, E. L., & Cecil, K. A. (2006). *The 2004 survey of state adult protective services: Abuse of adults 60 years of age and older.* National Committee for the Prevention of Elder Abuse, http://www.elderabusecenter.org

Teaster, P. B., Roberto, K. A., & Dugar, T. A. (2006). Intimate partner violence of rural aging women. *Family Relations, 55,* 636–648.

Tebo, M. G. (2005). We need to talk. *ABA Journal, 91,* 60.

Tehee, M., & Esqueda, C. W. (2008). American Indian and European American women's perceptions of domestic violence. *Journal of Family Violence, 23,* 25–35.

Teichroeb, R. ( 2009, January 7). McKenna targets repeat batterers. *Seattle Post-Intelligence,* p. A8.

Temple, J. R., Weston, R., Rodriguez B. F., & Marshall, L. L. (2007). Differing effects of partner and nonpartner sexual assault on women's mental health. *Violence Against Women, 13,* 285–297.

Terry, K. J. (2004). Understanding the sexual abuse crisis in the Catholic church: Challenges with prevention policies. *Victims & Offender, 3,* 31–44.

Terry, K. J., & Tallon, J. (2004). Child sexual abuse: A review of the literature. Retrieved July 17, 2010, from http://www.jj.cuny.edu/criminaljustice/pdfs/terry-cv.pdf

Terry, K. J., & Tallon, J. (2008). Understanding the sexual abuse crisis in the Catholic Church: Challenges with prevention policies. *Victims & Offenders, 3,* 31–44.

Testimony, House Committee on Ways and Means Subcommittees on Health and Oversight. (2007, March 8). Retrieved from http://www.waysandmeans.house.gov

Teten, A. L., Sherman, M. D., & Han, X. (2009). Violence between therapy-seeking veterans and their partners. *Journal of Interpersonal Violence, 24,* 111–127.

Thackeray, J. D., Scribano, P. V., & Rhoda, D. (2010). Domestic violence assessment in the child advocacy center. *Child Abuse & Neglect, 34,* 172–182.

Thakker, J., Ward, T., & Tidmarsh, P. (2006). A reevaluation of relapse prevention with adolescents who sexually offend: A Good-Lives Model. In H. E. Barbaree & W. L. Marshall (Eds.), *The juvenile sex offender,* 2nd ed. (pp. 313–335). New York: Guilford.

Thanasiu, P. L. (2004). Childhood sexuality: Discerning healthy from abnormal sexual behavior. *Journal of Mental Health Counseling, 26,* 309–319.

Theran, S. A., Sullivan, C. M., Bogat, G. A., & Stewart, C. S. (2006). Abusive partners and ex-partners: Understanding the effects of relationship to the abuser on women's well-being. *Violence Against Women, 12,* 950–969.

Thiel de Bocanegra, H., Rostovtseva, D. P., Khera, S., & Godhwani, N. (2010). Birth control sabotage and forced sex: Experiences reported by women in domestic violence shelters. *Violence Against Women, 16,* 601–612.

Thompson, C. (1989). Breaking through walls of isolation: A model for churches in helping victims of violence. *Pastoral Psychology, 38,* 35–38.

Thompson, H., & Priest, B. (2005, Fall). Elder abuse and neglects: Considerations for mental health practitioners. *Adultspan, 4,* 116–119.

Thompson, K. D. (1995). *Officially reported characteristics of spouse abuse victims seeking assistance in Utah, 1992* [CD-ROM]. Abstract obtained from ProQuest File: Dissertation Abstracts Item 1358266.

Thompson, K. M. (2009). Sibling incest: A model for group practice with adult female victims of brother-sister incest. *Journal of Family Violence, 24,* 531–537.

Thompson, M. P., Kaslow, N. J., Kingree, J. B., Rashid, A., Puett, R., Jacobs, D., et al. (2000). Partner violence, social support, and distress among inner-city African American women. *American Journal of Community Psychology, 28,* 127–143.

Thompson, R. (2007). Mother's violence victimization and child behavior problems: Examining the link. *American Journal of Orthopsychiatry, 77,* 306–315.

Thompson, R. A., Laible, D. J., & Robbennolt, J. K. (1997). Child care and preventing child maltreatment. In C. J. Dunst & M. Wolery (Eds.), *Advances in early education and day care* (pp. 173–202). Greenwich, CT: JAI.

Thompson, R. A., & Wilcox, B. L. (1995). Child maltreatment research: Federal support and policy issues. *American Psychologist, 50,* 789–793.

Thompson-McCormick, J., Jones, L., & Livingston, G. (2009). Medical students' recognition of elder abuse. *International Journal of Geriatric Psychiatry, 24,* 770–777.

Thorensen, S., & Øverlien, C. (2009). Trauma victim: Yes or no?: Why it may be difficult to answer questions regarding violence, sexual abuse, and other traumatic events. *Violence Against Women, 15,* 699–719.

Thornberry, T. P., Henry, K. L., Ireland, T. O., & Smith, C. A. (2010). The causal impact of childhood-limited maltreatment and adolescent maltreatment on early adult adjustment. *Journal of Adolescent Heatlh, 46,* 359–365.

Thornberry, T. P., Ireland, T. O., & Smith, C. A. (2001). The importance of timing: The varying impact of childhood and adolescent maltreatment on multiple problem outcomes. *Development and Psychopathology, 13,* 957–979.

Tiedens, L. Z. (2001). Anger and advancement versus sadness and subjugation: The effect of negative emotion expressions on social status conferral. *Journal of Personality and Social Psychology, 80,* 86–94.

Tiefenthaler, J., Farmer, A., & Sambria, A. (2005). Services and intimate partner violence in the United States: A county-level analysis. *Journal of Marriage and Family, 67,* 565–578.

Tilden, V. P. (1989). Response of the health care delivery system to battered women. *Issues in Mental Health Nursing, 10,* 309–320.

Timmer, S. G., Zebell, N. M., Culver, M. A., & Urquiza, A. J. (2010). Efficacy of adjunct in-home coaching to improve outcomes in Parent-Child Interaction Therapy. *Research on Social Work Practice, 20,* 36–45.

Timnick, L. (1985, August 25). 22% in survey were child abuse victims. *Los Angeles Times,* p. 1.

Tjaden, P., & Thoennes, N. (1992). Predictors of legal intervention in child maltreatment cases. *Child Abuse & Neglect, 16,* 807–821.

Tjaden, P., & Thoennes, N. (1998a). *Prevalence, incidence, and consequences of violence against women: Findings from the National Violence Against Women Survey* (NCJ Publication No. 172837). Washington, DC: U.S. Department of Justice.

Tjaden, P., & Thoennes, N. (1998b). *Stalking in America: Findings from the National Violence Against Women Survey* (NCJ Publication No. 169592). Washington, DC: U.S. Department of Justice.

Tjaden, P., & Thoennes, N. (1999). Violence and threats of violence against women and men in the United States, 1994–1996. Denver, CO: Center for Policy Research.

Tjaden, P., & Thoennes, N. (2000a). *Extent, nature, and consequences of intimate partner violence* (NCJ Publication No. 181867). Washington, DC: U.S. Department of Justice.

Tjaden, P., & Thoennes, N. (2000b). *Full report of the prevalence, incidence, and consequences of violence against women: Findings from the National Violence Against Women Survey* (NCJ Publication No. 183781). Washington, DC: U.S. Department of Justice.

Todahl, J. L., Linville, D., Bustin, A., Wheeler, J., & Gau, J. (2009). Sexual assault support services and community systems: Understanding critical issues and needs in the LGBTQ community. *Violence Against Women, 15,* 952–976.

Toews, M. L., McHenry, P. C., & Catless, B. S. (2003). Male-initiated partner abuse during marital separation prior to divorce. *Violence and Victims, 18,* 387–402.

Tokunaga, R. S. (2010). Following you home from school: A critical review and synthesis of research on cyberbullying victimization. *Computers in Human Behavior, 26,* 277–287.

Tolan, P. H., & Guerra, N. (1998). Societal causes of violence against children. In P. K. Trickett & C. J. Schellenbach (Eds.), *Violence against children in the family and the community* (pp. 195–209). Washington DC: American Psychological Association.

Tolin, D. F., & Foa, E. B. (2008). Sex differences in trauma and posttraumatic stress disorder: A quantitative review of 25 years of research. *Theory, Research, Practice, and Policy, 1(Supp.1),*37–85.

Tollefson, D. R. (2002, March). Factors associated with batterer treatment success and failure. *Dissertation Abstracts International, 62,* 3191A. (UMI No. 3026165)

Tolman, R. M. (1989). The development of a measure of psychological maltreatment of women by their male partners. *Violence and Victims, 4,* 159–178.

Tolman, R. M., & Raphael, J. (2000). A review of research on welfare and domestic violence. *Journal of Social Issues, 56,* 655–681.

Tomita, S. K. (1990). The denial of elder mistreatment by victims and abusers: The application of neutralization theory. *Violence and Victims, 5,* 171–184.

Tomkins, A. J., Mohamed, S., Steinman, M., Macolini, R. M., Kenning, M. K., & Afrank, J. (1994). The plight of children who witness woman battering: Psychological knowledge and policy implications. *Law and Psychology Review, 18,* 137–187.

Tomoda, A., Suzuki, H., Rabi, K., Sheu, Y-S., Polcari, A., & Teicher, M. H. (2009). Reduced prefrontal cortical gray matter in young adults exposed to harsh corporal punishment. *NeuroImage, 47,* T66–T71.

Tomz, J. E., & McGillis, D. (1997). *Serving crime victims and witnesses* (2nd ed.) (NCJ Publication No. 163174). Washington, DC: U.S. Department of Justice.

Tonin, E. (2004). The attachment styles of stalkers. *The Journal of Forensic Psychiatry and Psychology, 15,* 584–590.

Tonizzo, S., Howells, K., Day, A., Reidpath, D., & Froyland, I. (2000). Attributions of negative partner behavior by men who physically abuse their partners. *Journal of Family Violence, 15,* 155–167.

Topham, G. L., & Wampler, K. S. (2008). Predicting dropout in a filial therapy program for parents and young children. *The American Journal of Family Therapy, 36,* 60–78.

Topping, K. J., & Barron, K. J. (2009). School-based child sexual abuse prevention programs: A review of effectiveness. *Review of Educational Research, 79,* 431-463.

Torres, J. (2008). Rape shield laws and game theory: The psychological effects on complainants who file false rape allegations. *Law & Psychology Review, 135,* 135.

Torres, S. L. (1991). A comparison of wife abuse between two cultures: Perceptions, attitudes, nature and extent. *Issues in Mental Health Nursing, 12,* 113–131.

Torres, S. L. (1998). Intervening with battered Hispanic pregnant women. In J. C. Campbell (Ed.), *Empowering survivors of abuse: Health care for battered women and their children* (pp. 259–270). Thousand Oaks, CA: Sage.

Torres, S. L. & Han, H-R. (2003). Women's perceptions of their male batterers' characteristics and level of violence. *Issues in Mental Health Nursing, 24,* 667–679.

Torry, W. I. (2000). Culture and individual responsibility: Touchstones of the cultural defense. *Human Organization, 59,* 58–71.

Totura, C. M. et al. (2009). Bullying and victimization among boys and girls in middle school. *Journal of Early Adolescence, 29,* 571–609.

Tovino, S. A. (2010). Scientific understanding of postpartum illness: Improving health law and policy? *Harvard Journal of Law & Gender, 33,* 99–173.

Tower, L. E. (2007). Group work with a new population: Women in domestic relationships responding to violence with violence. *Women & Therapy, 30,* 35–60.

Tower, L. E., & Fernandez, M. E. (2008). English- and Spanish-speaking women's use of violence. *Journal of Interpersonal Violence, 23,* 21–38.

Tower, L. E., Schiller, D., & Fernandez, M. E. (2008). Women court-ordered for domestic violence: Improvements in depression. *Journal of Aggression, Maltreatment & Trauma,* 40–54.

Towns, A., & Adams, P. (2000). "If I really loved him enough, he would be okay." *Violence Against Women, 6,* 558–585.

Toy, A. (2010, December/February). Leading the fight for disability rights. *Open Forum, 86,* 6.

Tresniowski, A., Atlas, D., Lang, A., & Cardwell, C. (2009, March 23). The children of the cult. *People,* 60–67.

Trull, T. J. (2001). Structural relations between borderline personality disorder features and putative etiological correlates. *Journal of Abnormal Psychology, 110,* 471–481.

Truman-Schram, D. M., Cann, A., Calhoun, L., & Vanwallendael, L. (2000). Leaving an abusive dating relationship: An investment model comparison of women who stay versus women who leave. *Journal of Social and Clinical Psychology, 19,* 161–183.

Tuel, B. D., & Russell, R. K. (1998). Self-esteem and depression in battered women: A comparison of lesbian and heterosexual survivors. *Violence Against Women, 4,* 344–362.

Turchik, J. A., Probst, D. R., Irvin, D. R., Chau, M., & Gidycz, C. A. (2009). Prediction of sexual assault experiences in college women based on rape scripts: A prospective analysis. *Journal of Counseling and Clinical Psychology, 77,* 351–366.

Turner, H. A., Finkelhor, D., & Ormrod, R. (2010). Child mental health problems as risk factors for victimization. *Child Maltreatment, 15,* 132–143.

Turner, R. J., & Noh, S. (1983). Class and psychological vulnerability among women: The significance of social support and personal control. *Journal of Health and Social Behavior, 33,* 10–24.

Turner, S. F., & Shapiro, C. H. (1986). Battered women: Mourning the death of a relationship. *Social Work, 31,* 372–376.

Turney, D. (2000). The feminizing of neglect. *Child and Family Social Work, 5,* 47–56.

Turrell, S. C. (2000). A descriptive analysis of same-sex relationship violence for a diverse sample. *Journal of Family Violence, 15,* 281–294.

Tutty, L. M., Bidgood, B. A., Rothery, M. A., & Bidgood, P. (2001). An evaluation of men's batterer treatment groups. *Research on Social Work Practice, 11,* 645–670.

Twemlow, S. W., & Fornagy, P. (2005). The prevalence of teachers who bully students in schools with differing levels of behavioral problems. *American Journal of Psychiatry, 162,* 2387–2389.

Tyler, K. A., & Johnson, K. A. (2006). A longitudinal study of the effects of early abuse on later victiminization among high-risk adolescents. *Violence and Victims, 21,* 287–306.

Tyre, P., & Scelfo, J. (2006, July 31). Why girls will be girls. *Newsweek, 147,* 46–47.

Tyrell, D. E. (2002). Understanding the coping strategies of men who batter through a stress and coping framework. *Dissertation Abstracts International, 63*(02), 1053B. (UMI No. 3043418)

Tyrka, A. R., Wyche, M. C., Kelly, M. M., Price, L. H., & Carpenter, L. L. (2009). Childhood maltreatment and adult personality disorder symptoms: Influence of maltreatment type. *Psychiatry Research, 165,* 281–287.

Ullman, S. E. (2007). A 10-year update of "review and critique of empirical studies of rape avoidance." *Criminal Justice and Behavior, 34,* 411–429.

Ullman, S. E., & Townsend, S. M. (2007). Barriers to working with sexual assault survivors. *Violence Against Women, 13,* 412–443.

Ulrich, Y. C., Cain, K. C., Sugg, N. K., Rivara, F. P., Rubanovice, D. M., & Thompson, R. S. (2003). Medical care utilization patterns in women with diagnosed domestic violence. *American Journal of Preventive Medicine, 24,* 9–15.

Ulrich, Y. C., McKenna, L. S., et al. (2006). Postpartum mothers' disclosure of abuse, role, and conflict. *Health Care for Women International, 27,* 343–345.

Umberson, D., Anderson, K., Glick, J., & Shapiro, A. (1998). Domestic violence, personal control, and gender. *Journal of Marriage and the Family, 60,* 442–452.

UNICEF. (n.d.). Conventions on the Rights of the Child. Retrieved May 8, 2010, from http://www.unicef.org/cre/?q=printme

UNICEF. (2006). Behind closed doors—The impact of domestic violence on children. New York: Author.

United Nations Development Fund for Women. (2002). Retrieved from http://www.unifem.org/

Urban, B. Y., & Bennett, L. W. (1999). When the community punches a time clock. *Violence Against Women, 5,* 1178–1193.

Urbaniok, F., Noll, T., Grunewald, S., Steinbach, J., & Endrass, J. (2006). Prediction of violent and sexual offences: A replication study of the VRAG in Switzerland. *Journal of Forensic Psychiatry and Psychology, 17,* 23–31.

Urquiza, A. J., & McNeil, C. B. (1996). Parent-child interaction therapy: An intensive dyadic intervention for physically abusive families. *Child Maltreatment, 1,* 134–144.

Urquiza, A. J., & Timmer, S. G. (2002). Patterns of interaction within violent families: Use of social interaction research methodology. *Journal of Interpersonal Violence, 17,* 824–835.

U.S. Bureau of Justice Statistics. (1992). *Criminal victimization in the United States, 1991* (NCJ Publication No. 139563). Washington, DC: U.S. Department of Justice.

U.S. Bureau of Labor Statistics. (1999). *Usual weekly earnings of wage and salary workers: Fourth quarter 1998* (USDL Publication No. 99–15). Washington, DC: U.S. Department of Labor.

U.S. Census Bureau. (2000). *U.S. population estimates, by age, sex, race, and Hispanic origin* (Current Population Reports No. P25–1095). Retrieved December 8, 2003, from http://www.census.gov/population/estimates/nation/intfile2–1.txt

U.S. Bureau of Justice Statistics (BJS). (2006). *Criminal victimization 2005* (NCJ Publication No. 214644). Washington, DC: Author.

U.S. Bureau of Justice Statistics (BJS). (2007). *Homicide trends in the U. S.* http://www.ojp.usdoj.gov.bjs/homicide/intimates.html

U.S. Census Bureau. (2008, August 14). An older and more diverse nation by mid-century. Retrieved from http://www.census.gov/popest/archives/files/MRSF-01-US1.html>

U.S. Department of Health & Human Services, Administration on Children, Youth and Families. (1981). *Study findings: National study of the incidence and severity of child abuse and neglect* (DHHS Publication No. OHDS 81–30325). Washington, DC: Government Printing Office.

U.S. Department of Health & Human Services, Administration on Children, Youth and Families. (1988). *Study findings: Study of national incidence and prevalence of child abuse and neglect* (DHHS Publication No. ADM 20–01099). Washington, DC: Government Printing Office.

U.S. Department of Health & Human Services, Administration on Children, Youth and Families. (1993). *A report on the maltreatment of children with disabilities* (DHHS Contract No. 105–89–1630). Washington, DC: Government Printing Office.

U.S. Department of Health & Human Services, Administration on Children, Youth and Families. (1999). Chapter 6. Additional research based on NCANDS data. Washington, DC: Government Printing Office. Retrieved from http://www.acf.hhs.gov/programs/cb/pubs/cm99/cpt6.htm

U.S. Department of Health & Human Services, Administration on Children, Youth and Families. (2001). *Child maltreatment 1999.* Washington, DC: Government Printing Office.

U.S. Department of Health & Human Services, Administration on Children, Youth and Families. (2002). *Appropriateness of minimum nurse staffing ratios in nursing homes.* Retrieved May 27, 2002, from http://www.house.gov/reform/min

U.S. Department of Health and Human Services, Administration on Children, Youth and Families. (2002b). *National Child Abuse and Neglect Data System (NCANDS) summary of key findings from calendar year 2000.* Retrieved May 16, 2002, from http://www.calib.com/nccanch/prevmnth/scope/ncands.cfm

U.S. Department of Health & Human Services, Administration on Children, Youth and Families. (2003a). *Child maltreatment 2001.* Washington, DC: Government Printing Office.

U.S. Department of Health & Human Services, Administration on Children, Youth and Families. (2003b, May 19). *Foster care and adoption statistics current reports.* Retrieved from http://www.acf.dhhs.gov/programs/cb/publications/index.htm

U.S. Department of Health & Human Services. (2003, July). OIG Report: *State ombudsman data: Nursing home complaints* (OEI-09–02–00160). Washington, DC: U.S. DHHS, Office of the Inspector General.

U.S. Department of Health & Human Services. (2005, January). *Male perpetrators of child maltreatment: Findings from NCANDS.* Washington, DC: DHHS, Office of the Assistant Secretary for Planning and Evaluation.

U.S. Department of Health & Human Services. (2008). Child maltreatment. Washington, DC: DHHS, Office of the Inspector General.

U.S. Department of Health & Human Services. (2009a). The AFCARS report. Washington, DC: Author.

U.S. Department of Health & Human Services, Administration on Children, Youth and Families. (2009). *Child Maltreatment 2008.* Retrieved from http://www.childwelfare.gov

U.S. Department of Health & Human Services, Administration on Children, Youth and Families. (2009b). *Child maltreatment 2008.* Retrieved from http://www.childwelfare.gov

U.S. Department of Health & Human Services, Administration for Children & Families, Office of Planning, Research & Evaluation. (n.d.). *Findings from secondary analyses of runaway and homeless youth datasets.* http://www.acf.hhs.gov/programs/opre/fys/sex_abuse/reports/sex abuse_hmless/sex_Chp5.html

U.S. Department of Justice. (2000). *Measuring violence against women: Recommendations from an interagency workshop* (NCJ Publication No. 184447). Washington, DC: Author.

U.S. Department of Justice. (2004). *Defining drug courts: The key components* (NCJ Publication No. 205621). Washington, DC: Author.

U.S. Department of Justice. (2006a). *Supplemental Victimization Survey (SVS) from the National Crime Victimization Survey.* Washington, DC: Author.

U.S. Department of Justice. (2006b). *Drug courts: The second generation* (NCJ Publication No. 211081). Washington, DC: Author.

U.S. Department of Justice. (2008). *Criminal victimization in the United States, 2006 statistical table* (NCJ Publication No. 223436). Washington, DC: Author.

U.S. Department of Justice, Federal Bureau of Investigation. (2002). *Crime in the United States 2001: Uniform crime reports.* Washington DC: Government Printing Office.

U.S. Department of Justice. (2009, April). Office of Justice Programs. *Juvenile Arrests 2007*, Juvenile Justice Bulletin. Office of Juvenile Justice and Delinquency Prevention (OJJDP). Washington, DC: Author.

U.S. Department of Justice, Federal Bureau of Investigation. (2010). *Crime in the United States 2008.* Expanded homicide data, Table 10—Murder circumstances. Washington, DC: Author.

U.S. General Accounting Office. (1991). *Elder abuse: Effectiveness of report laws and other factors* (Publication No. HRD-91-74). Washington, DC: Government Printing Office.

U.S. General Accounting Office. (2002a). *Gun control: Opportunities to close loopholes in the National Instant Criminal Background Check System* (Publication No. GAO-02-720). Washington, DC: Government Printing Office.

U.S. General Accounting Office. (2002b). *Nursing homes: More can be done to protect residents from abuse.* Retrieved May 27, 2002, from http://aging.senate.gov/hr78.htm

U.S. Government Accounting Office. (1998, November). *Domestic violence: Prevalence and implications for employment among welfare recipients* (HEHS-12). Author.

U.S. Government Accounting Office. (2006, March). *Long-term care facilities: Information on residents who are registered sex offenders or are paroled for other crimes* (GAO-06-326). Author.

U.S. Preventative Services Task Force. (2004). Screening for family and intimate partner violence: Recommendation Statement. *American Family Physician, 70,* 747–751.

U.S. Public Health Service. Office of the Surgeon General. (2001, January). Youth violence: A report of the Surgeon General. Washington, DC: United States Public Health Service. Office of the Reports of the Surgeon General.

Vaeth, P. A. C., Ramisetty-Mikler, S., & Caetano. (2010). Depression among couples in the United States in the context of intimate partner violence. *Journal of Interpersonal Violence, 25,* 771–790.

Vail, L. (2008, July/August). Project Gatekeeper, Think S.A.F.E. *Victimization of the Elderly and Disabled, 11,* 22–24.

Vaillant, G. E., & Milofsky, E. S. (1982). The etiology of alcoholism: A prospective viewpoint. *American Psychologist, 37,* 494–503.

Valentiner, D. P., Foa, E. B., Riggs, D. S., & Gershuny, B. S. (1996). Coping strategies and posttraumatic stress disorder in female victims of sexual and nonsexual assault. *Journal of Abnormal Psychology, 105,* 455–458.

Valera, E. M., & Berenbaum, H. (2003). Brain injury in battered women. *Journal of Consulting and Clinical Psychology, 71,* 797–804.

van Bakel, H. J. A., & Riksen-Walraven, J. M. (2002). Parenting and development of one-year-olds: Links with parental, contextual, and child characteristics. *Child Development, 73,* 256–273.

Vandello, J. A., & Cohen, D. (2003). Male honor and female fidelity: Cultural scripts that perpetuate domestic violence. *Journal of Personality and Social Psychology, 84,* 997–1010.

Vandello, J. A., Cohen, D., Grandon, R., & Franiuk, R. (2009). Stand by your man: Indirect prescriptions for honorable violence and feminine loyalty in Canada, Chile, and the United States. *Journal of Cross-Cultural Psychology, 40,* 81–104.

van den Boom, D. C. (1994). The influence of temperament and mothering on attachment and exploration: An experimental manipulation of sensitive responsiveness among lower-class mothers with irritable infants. *Child Development, 65,* 1457–1477.

van den Boom, D. C. (1995). Do first-year intervention effects endure? Follow-up during toddlerhood of a sample of Dutch irritable infants. *Child Development, 66,* 1798–1816.

VandenBos, G. R. (2007). *APA Dictionary of Psychology.* Washington, DC: American Psychological Association.

van den Bree, M. B. M., Svikis, D. S., & Pickens, R. W. (1998). Genetic influences in antisocial personality and drug use disorders. *Drug and Alcohol Dependence, 49,* 177–187.

van der Vegt, E. J. M., van der Ende, J., Kirschbaum, C., Verhulst, F. C., & Tiemeier, H. (2009). Early neglect and abuse predict diurnal cortisol patterns in adults: A study of international adoptees. *Psychoneuroendocriminology, 34,* 660–669.

Van Daalen, R. (2010). Children and childhood in Dutch society and Dutch sociology. *Current Sociology, 58,* 351–368.

Vandiver, D. M., & Kercher, G. (2004). Offender and victim characteristics of registered female sexual offenders in Texas: A proposed typology of female sexual offenders. *Sexual Abuse: A Journal of Research and Treatment, 16,* 121–137.

Van Hightower, N. R., & Gorton, J. (2002). A case study of community-based responses to rural woman battering. *Violence Against Women, 7,* 845–872.

Van Hook, M. P. (2000). Help seeking for violence: Views of survivors. *Affilia, 15,* 390–408.

Van Ijzendoorn, M. H. (1992). Intergenerational transmission of parenting: A review of studies in nonclinical populations. *Developmental Review, 12,* 76–99.

Van Wie, V. E., & Gross, A. M. (2001). The role of women's explanations for refusal on men's ability to discriminate unwanted sexual behavior in a date rape scenario. *Journal of Family Violence, 16,* 331–344.

Vashchenko, M., Lambidoni, E., & Brody, L. R. (2007). Late adolescents' coping styles in interpersonal and intrapersonal conflicts using the narrative disclosure task. *Clinical Social Work Journal, 35,* 245–255.

Vass, J. S., & Gold, S. R. (1995). Effects of feedback on emotion in hypermasculine males. *Violence and Victims, 10,* 217–226.

Veenema, A. H. (2009). Early life stress, the development of aggression and neuroendocrine and neurobiological correlates: What can we learn from animal models? *Frontiers in Neuroendocrinology, 30,* 497–518.

Veltishchev, D. Y. (2004). Violence and health in Russia: Statistical Review. Moscow: Moscow Research Institute of Psychiatry and the World Health Organization.

Veneziano, C., Veneziano, L., & LeGrand, S. (2000). The relationship between adolescent sex offender behaviors and victim characteristics with prior victimization. *Journal of Interpersonal Violence, 15,* 363–374.

Vennemann, B., et al. (2004). Suffocation and poisoning—The hard-hitting side of Munchausen syndrome by proxy. *International Journal of Legal Medicine, 119,* 98–102.

Ventura, L. A., & Davis, G. (2006). Domestic violence: Court case conviction and recidivism. *Violence Against Women, 11,* 255–277.

Verhoek-Oftedahl, W., Pearlman, D. N., & Babcock, J. C. (2000). Improving surveillance of intimate partner violence by use of multiple data sources. *American Journal of Preventive Medicine, 19,* 308–315.

Vesga-López, O. et al. (2008). Psychiatric disorders in pregnant and postpartum women in the United States. *Archives of General Psychiatry, 65,* 805–815.

Vézina, J., & Hébert, M. (2007). Risk factors for victimization in romantic relationships of young women. *Trauma, Violence, & Abuse, 8,* 33–66.

Victims office to grant funds for field-generated projects. (2008, April, 18). *Criminal Justice Newsletter,* 7–8.

Vierthaler, K. (2008). Best practices for working with rape crisis centers to address elder sexual abuse. *Journal of Elder Abuse & Neglect, 20,* 306–322.

Vigdor, A. R., & Mercy, J. A. (2006). Do laws restricting access to firearms by domestic violence offenders prevent intimate partner homicide? *Evaluation Review, 30,* 313–346.

Villarreal, A. (2007). Women's employment status, coercive control, and intimate partner violence in Mexico. *Journal of Marriage and Family, 69,* 418–434.

Vinton, L. (1991). Factors associated with refusing services among maltreated elderly. *Journal of Elder Abuse & Neglect, 3*(2), 89–103.

Vinton, L. (2003). A model collaborative project toward making domestic violence centers elder ready. *Violence Against Women, 9,* 1504–1513.

Violence Against Women: 10 Reports/Year 2003. (2005). Committee on Economic, Social and Cultural Rights: Russian Federation.

Violence Against Women Office. (2000, 2005). *The Violence Against Women Act of 2000, 2005 (VAWA 2000, 2005).* Retrieved from http://www.ojp.usdoj.gov/vawo/laws/vawa_summary2.htm

Virginia Coalition for the Homeless. (1995). *1995 shelter provider survey.* Richmond: Author.

Virkkunen, M., Rawlings, R., Tokola, R., Poland, R. E., Giuidotti, A., Nemeroff, C., et al. (1994). CSF biochemistries, glucose metabolism, and diurnal activity rhythms in alcoholic, violent offenders, fire setters, and healthy volunteers. *Archives of General Psychiatry, 51,* 20–27.

Vissing, Y. M., Straus, M. A., Gelles, R. J., & Harrop, J. W. (1991). Verbal aggression by parents and psychosocial problems of children. *Child Abuse & Neglect, 15,* 223–238.

Vittrup, B., & Holden, G. W. (2010). Children's assessments of corporal punishment and other practices: The role of age, race, SES, and exposure to spanking. *Journal of Applied Developmental Psychology, 31,* 211–220.

Vogel, L. C. M., & Marshall, L. L. (2001). PTSD symptoms and partner abuse: Low income women at risk. *Journal of Traumatic Stress, 14,* 569–584.

Vogt, W. P. (1993). *Dictionary of statistics and methodology: A nontechnical guide for the social sciences.* Newbury Park, CA: Sage.

Volavka, J. (1995). *Neurobiology of violence.* Washington, DC: American Psychiatric Association.

Von Eye, A., & Anne Bogat, G. (2006). Mental health in women experiencing intimate partner violence as the efficiency goal of social welfare functions. *International Journal of Social Welfare, 15* (Suppl. 1), S31–S40.

Vossekuil, B., Fein, R. A., Reddy, M., Borum, R., & Modzeleski, W. (2002). *The final report and findings of the Safe School*

Initiative: Implications for the prevention of school attacks in the United States. Washington, DC: United States Secret Service & U.S. Department of Education.

Waaland, P., & Keeley, S. (1985). Police decision making in wife abuse: The impact of legal and extralegal factors. *Law and Human Behavior, 9,* 355–366.

Wagar, J. M., & Rodway, M. R. (1995). An evaluation of a group treatment approach for children who have witnessed wife abuse. *Journal of Family Violence, 10,* 295–306.

Wagenaar, D. B., Rosenbaum, R., Herman, S., & Page, C. (2009). Elder abuse education in primary care residency programs: A cluster group analysis. *Family Medicine, 41,* 481–486.

Wahab, S. (2005). Motivational interviewing and social work practice. *Journal of Social Work, 5,* 45–60.

Waites, C. E., & Lee, E. O. (2006). Strengthening aging content in the baccalaureate social work curricula: What students have to say. *Journal of Gerontological Social Work, 48,* 47–62.

Walden, L. M., & Beran, T. N. (2010). Attachment quality and bullying behavior in school-aged youth. *Canadian Journal of School Psychology, 25,* 5–18.

Waldner-Haugrud, L. K. (1999). Sexual coercion in lesbian and gay relationships: A review and critique. *Aggression and Violent Behavior, 4,* 139–149.

Waldner-Haugrud, L. K., Gratch, L. V., & Magruder, B. (1997). Victimization and perpetration rates of violence in gay and lesbian relationships: Gender issues explored. *Violence and Victims, 12,* 173–184.

Waldrop, A. E., & Resick, P. A. (2004). Coping among adult female victims of domestic violence. *Journal of Family Violence, 19,* 291–302.

Walker., C. A., & Davies, J. (2009). A critical review of the psychometric evidence base of the Child Abuse Potential Inventory. *Journal of Family Violence, 25,* 215–227.

Walker, C. E., Bonner, B. L., & Kaufman, K. L. (1988). *The physically and sexually abused child.* New York: Pergamon.

Walker, E., Downey, G., & Bergman, A. (1989). The effects of parental psychopathology and maltreatment on child behavior: A test of the diathesis-stress model. *Child Development, 60,* 15–24.

Walker, L. E. (1979). *The battered woman.* New York: Harper & Row.

Walker, L. E. (1983). The battered woman syndrome study. In D. Finkelhor, R. J. Gelles, G. T. Hotaling, & M. A. Straus (Eds.), *The dark side of families: Current family violence research* (pp. 31–48). Beverly Hills, CA: Sage.

Walker, L. E. (1984). *The battered woman syndrome.* New York: Springer.

Walker, L. E. (1991). Post-traumatic stress disorder in women: Diagnosis and treatment of battered woman syndrome. *Psychotherapy, 28,* 21–29.

Walker, L. E. (1993). The battered woman syndrome is a psychological consequence of abuse. In R. J. Gelles & D. R. Loseke (Eds.), *Current controversies on family violence* (pp. 133–153). Newbury Park, CA: Sage.

Wallace, R., & Nosko, A. (1993). Working with shame in the group treatment of male batterers. *International Group Psychotherapy, 43,* 45–61.

Walsh, C. A., Jamieson, E., MacMillan, H., & Boyle, M. (2007). Child abuse and chronic pain in a community survey of women. *Journal of Interpersonal Violence, 22,* 1536–1554.

Walsh, F. (1996). Partner abuse. In D. Davies & C. Neal (Eds.), *Pink therapy: A guide for counselors and therapists working with lesbian, gay, and bisexual clients* (pp. 187–198). Philadelphia: Open University Press.

Walsh, J. A., & Krienert, J. L. (2009). A decade of child-initiated family violence. *Journal of Interpersonal Violence, 24,* 1450–1477.

Walsh, W. A., Dawson, J., & Mattingly, M. J. (2010). How are we measuring resilience following childhood maltreatment? Is the research adequate and consistent? *Trauma, Violence, & Abuse, 11,* 27–41.

Waltermaurer, E. S., Ortega, C. A., & McNutt, L. A. (2003). Issues in estimating the prevalence of intimate partner violence. *Journal of Interpersonal Violence, 18,* 959–974.

Walters, G. D. (1992). A meta-analysis of the gene-crime relationship. *Criminology, 30,* 595–613.

Waltz, J., Babcock,. J. C., Jacobson, N. S., & Gottman, J. M. (2000). Testing a typology of batterers. *Journal of Consulting and Clinical Psychology, 68,* 658–669.

Wang, C. T., & Holton, J. (2007). *Total estimated cost of child abuse and neglect in the United States.* Chicago: Prevent Child Abuse America.

Wang, T., Parish, W. L., Laumann, E. O., & Luo, Y. (2009). Partner violence and sexual jealousy in China. *Violence Against Women, 15,* 774–798.

Ward, M. J., Lee, S. S., & Lipper, E. G. (2000). Failure-to-thrive is associated with disorganized infant-mother attachment and unresolved maternal attachment. *Infant Mental Health Journal, 21,* 428–442.

Warnken, W. J., Rosenbaum, A., Fletcher, K. E., Hoge, S. K., & Adelman, S. A. (1994). Head-injured males: A population at risk for relationship aggression. *Violence and Victims, 9,* 153–166.

Washington State Coalition Against Domestic Violence. (2000). *Honoring their lives, learning from their deaths.* Seattle: Author.

Washington State Department of Health. (2009). Retrieved from http://www.doh.wa.gov

Wasik, B., & Roberts, R. N. (1994). Survey of home visiting programs for abused and neglected children and their families. *Child Abuse & Neglect, 18,* 271–283.

Watson, J. M., Cascardi, M., Avery-Leaf, S., & O'Leary, K. D. (2001). High school students' responses to dating aggression. *Violence and Victims, 16,* 339–348.

Watson, S., Chilton, R., Fairchild, H., & Whewell, P. (2006). Association between childhood trauma and dissociation among patients with borderline personality disorder. *Australian and New Zealand Journal of Psychiatry, 40,* 478–481.

Watts-English, T., Fortson, B. L., Gibler, N., Hooper, S. R., & De Bellis, M. D. (2006). The psychobiology of maltreatment in childhood. *Journal of Social Issues, 62,* 717–736.

Waxman, L., & Trupin, R. (1997). *A status report on hunger and homelessness in America's cities: 1997.* Washington, DC: U.S. Conference of Mayors.

Weak laws encourage sex abuse of federal inmates, auditors find. (2005, May 2). *Criminal Justice Newsletter,* 1–3.

Weaver, A. J. (1993). Psychological trauma: What clergy need to know. *Pastoral Psychology, 41,* 385–408.

Weaver, S. E., & Coleman, M. (2010). Caught in the middle: Mothers in stepfamilies. *Journal of Social and Personal Relationships, 27,* 305–326.

Weaver, T. L., & Clum, G. A. (1995). Psychological distress associated with interpersonal violence: A meta-analysis. *Clinical Psychology Review, 15,* 115–140.

Websdale, N. (1995). Rural woman abuse: The voices of Kentucky women. *Violence Against Women, 1,* 309–338.

Webster-Stratton, C. (2009). *The Incredible Years: Parents, teachers, and children training series.* Seattle, WA: Incredible Years, http://www.incredibleyears.com

Wechsler, H., Lee, J. E., Kuo, M., & Lee, H. (2000). College binge drinking in the 1990s: A continuing problem. Results of the Harvard School of Public Health 1999 college alcohol study. *Journal of American College Health, 48,* 199–210.

Wedding, D. (2008). Innovative methods for making behavioral science relevant to medical education. *Journal of Clinical Psychology in Medical Settings, 15,* 89–91.

Weinberg, G. (1972). *Society and the healthy homosexual.* New York: St. Martin's.

Weinberger, L. E., Sreenivasan, S., Garrick, T., & Osran, H. (2005). The impact of surgical castration on sexual recidivism risk among sexually violent predatory offenders. *Journal of the American Academy of Psychiatry and the Law, 33,* 16–36.

Weinhardt, L. S., Bickham, N. L., & Carey, M. P. (1999). Sexual coercion among women living with severe and persistent mental illness: Review of the literature and recommendations for mental health providers. *Aggression and Violent Behavior, 4,* 307–317.

Weis, J. G. (1989). Family violence research methodology and design. In L. Ohlin & M. Tonry (Eds.), *Family violence* (pp. 117–162). Chicago: University of Chicago Press.

Weisz, A. N., & Black, B. M. (2001). Evaluating a sexual assault and dating violence prevention program for urban youth. *Social Work Research, 25,* 89–100.

Weisz, A. N., & Black, B. M. (2009). *Programs to reduce teen dating violence and sexual assault.* New York: Columbia University Press.

Weisz, A., Tolman, R. M., Callahan, M. R., Saunders, D. G., & Black, B. M. (2007). Informal helpers' response when adolescents tell them about dating violence or romantic relationship problems. *Journal of Adolescence, 30,* 853–868.

Weitzman, P. F., & Weitzman, E. A. (2003). Promoting communication with older adults: Protocols for resolving interpersonal conflicts and for enhancing interactions with doctors. *Clinical Psychology Review, 23,* 523–535.

Wekerle, C., & Wolfe, D. A. (1996). Child maltreatment. In E. J. Mash & R. A. Barkley (Eds.), *Child psychopathology* (pp. 492–537). New York: Guilford.

Wekerle, C., & Wolfe, D. A. (1998). Windows for preventing child and partner abuse: Early childhood and adolescence. In P. K. Trickett & C. J. Schellenbach (Eds.), *Violence against children in the family and the community* (pp. 339–369). Washington, DC: American Psychological Association.

Wekerle, C., & Wolfe, D. A. (1999). Dating violence in mid-adolescence: Theory, significance, and emerging prevention initiatives. *Clinical Psychology Review, 19,* 435–456.

Wekerle, C., & Wolfe, D. A. (2003). Child maltreatment. In E. J. Mash & R. A. Barkley (Eds.), *Child psychopoathology* (2nd ed., pp. 632–684). New York: Guilford.

Welcome to the Commission on Youth at Risk. (2009). American Bar Association. Retrieved from http://abanet.org/abanet/

common/print/newprintview.cfm?ref=http%3A//www
.abanet.org/youthatrisk

Wells, W., & DeLeon-Granados, W. (2005). The decline of intimate partner homicide. *National Institute of Justice Journal,
252,* 33–34.

Werner-Wilson, R. J., Zimmerman, T. S., & Whalen, D. (2000).
Resilient response to battering. *Contemporary Family
Therapy, 22,* 161–188.

West, A., & Wandrei, M. L. (2002). Intimate partner violence: A
model for predicting interventions by informal helpers.
*Journal of Interpersonal Violence, 17,* 972–986.

West, J. A. (2002). Public service advertising in the 21st century:
Exploration of unintended effects of domestic violence cam-
paigns. *Dissertation Abstracts International, 63*(04), 1174A.
(UMI No. 3049494)

Westcott, H. L., & Kynan, S. (2006). Interviewer practice in
investigative interview for suspected child sexual abuse.
*Crime and Law, 12,* 367–382.

Westfall, S. S., Triggs, C., & Grossman, W. (2008, April 14).
*People,* 107–108.

Westmoreland, G. R., Counsell, S. R., Sennour, Y., Schubert, C. C.,
Frank, K. I., Wu, J., et al. (2009). Improving medical student
attitudes toward older patient through a "council of elders"
and reflective writing experience. *Journal of the American
Geriatric Society, 57,* 315–320.

Weston, R., Marshall, L. L., & Coker, A. L. (2007). Women's
motives for violent and nonviolent behaviors in conflicts.
*Journal of Interpersonal Violence, 22,* 1043–1065.

Weston, R., Temple, J. R., & Marshall, L. L. (2005). Gender symmetry and asymmetry in violent relationships: Patterns of
mutuality among racially diverse women. *Sex Roles, 53,*
553–571.

Westrup, D., Fremouw, W. J., Thompson, R. N., & Lewis, S. F.
(1999). The psychological impact of stalking on female
undergraduates. *Journal of Forensic Sciences, 44,* 554–557.

Wethington, H. R., et al. (2008). The effectiveness of interventions to reduce psychological harm from traumatic events
among children and adolescents: A systematic review.
*American Journal of Preventive Medicine, 35,* 287–313.

Wetzel, L., & Ross, M. A. (1983). Psychological and social rami-
fication of battering: Observations leading to a counseling
methodology for victims of domestic violence. *Personnel
and Guidance Journal, 61,* 423–428.

Whaley, A. L., & Davis, K. E. (2007). Cultural competence and
evidence-based practice in mental health service.
*American Psychologist, 62,* 563–574.

Wharton, R. H., Rosenberg, S., Sheridan, R. L., & Ryan, D. P. (2000).
Long-term medical consequences of physical abuse. In R. M.
Reece (Ed.), *Treatment of child abuse: Common ground for
mental health, medical, and legal practitioners* (pp. 537–548).
Baltimore: Johns Hopkins University Press.

Whatley, M. A., & Riggio, R. E. (1991, August). *Attributions of
blame for female and male victims.* Paper presented at the
annual meeting of the American Psychological Association,
San Francisco.

Whatule, L. J. (2000). Communication as an aid to resocializa-
tion: A case of men's anger groups. *Small Group Research,
31,* 424–446.

Whipple, E. E., & Finton, S. E. (1995). Psychological mistreatment by siblings: An unrecognized form of abuse. *Child
and Adolescent Social Work Journal, 20,* 21–36.

Whipple, E. E., & Webster-Stratton, C. (1991). The role of parental stress in physically abusive families. *Child Abuse &
Neglect, 15,* 279–291.

Whisman, M. A., Snyder, D. K., & Beach, S. R. H. (2009).
Screening for marital and relationship discord. *Journal of
Family Psychology, 23,* 247–254.

Whitaker, D. J., Haileyesus T., Swahn, M., & Saltzman, L. S.
(2007). Differences in frequency of violence and reported
injury between relationships with reciprocal and nonre-
ciprocal intimate partner violence. *American Journal of
Public Health, 97,* 941–947.

Whitaker, D. J., Le, B., et al. (2008). Risk factors for the perpetration of child sexual abuse: A review and meta-analysis.
*Child Abuse & Neglect, 32,* 529–548.

Whitaker, D. J., Morrison, S., Lindquist, C., Hawkins, S. R., O'Neil,
J. A., Nesius, A. M., et al. (2006). A critical review of interventions for the primary prevention of perpetration of
partner violence. *Aggression and Violent Behavior, 11,*
151–166.

Whitaker, R. C., Orzol, S. M., & Kahn, R. S. (2006). Maternal
mental health, substance abuse, and domestic violence in
the year after delivery and subsequent behavior problems
in children at age 3 years. *Archives of General Psychiatry,
63,* 551–560.

White, G. L. (1980). Inducing jealousy: A power perspective.
*Journal of Personality and Social Psychology, 6,* 222–227.

White, G. L., & Mullen, P. (1980). *Jealousy: Theory, research, and
clinical strategies.* New York: Guilford.

White, H. A. (2003). Refusing to blame the victim for the aftermath of domestic violence: Nicholson v. Williams is a step
in the right direction. *Family Court Review, 41,* 527–532.

White, J. W., Smith, P. H., Koss, M. P., & Figueredo, A. J. (2000). Intimate partner aggression: What have we learned? Comment on Archer 2000. *Psychological Bulletin, 126,* 690–696.

White, R. J., Gondolf, E. W., Robertson, D. U., Goodwin, B. J., & Caraveo, L. E. (2002). Extent and characteristics of woman batterers among federal inmates. *International Journal of Offender Therapy and Comparative Criminology, 46,* 412–426.

Widiger, T. A., & Mullins-Sweatt, S. N. (2004). Typology of men who are maritally violent: A discussion of Holtzworth-Munroe and Meehan. *Journal of Interpersonal Violence, 19,* 1396–1400.

Widom, C. S. (1989a). Child abuse, neglect, and violent criminal behavior. *Criminology, 27,* 251–271.

Widom, C. S. (1989b). Does violence beget violence? A critical examination of the literature. *Psychological Bulletin, 106,* 3–28.

Widom, C. S. (1995, March). Victims of childhood sexual abuse: Later criminal consequences. *National Institute of Justice Journal,* 1–8.

Widom, C. S., Czaja, S. J., & Dutton, M. A. (2008). Childhood victimization and lifetime revictimization. *Child Abuse & Neglect, 32,* 785–796.

Widom, C. S., & Maxfield, M. G. (2001). *An update on the "Cycle of Violence"* (NCJ Publication No. 184894). Washington, DC: U.S. Department of Justice.

Widom, C. S., & Morris, S. (1997). Accuracy of adult recollections of childhood victimization: Part 2. Childhood sexual abuse. *Psychological Assessment, 9,* 34–46.

Wiehe, V. R. (1990). *Sibling abuse: Hidden physical, emotional, and sexual trauma.* Lexington, MA: Lexington.

Wiehe, V. R. (1997). *Sibling abuse: Hidden physical, emotional, and sexual trauma* (2nd ed.). Thousand Oaks, CA: Sage.

Wiglesworth, A., Mosqueda, L., Burnight, K., Younglove, T., & Jeske, D. (2006). Findings from an elder abuse forensic center. *The Gerontologist, 46,* 277–283.

Wigman, S. A., Graham-Kevan, N., & Archer, J. (2008). Investigating subgroups of harassers: The roles of attachment, dependency, jealousy and aggression. *Journal of Family Violence, 23,* 557–568.

Wiist, W. H., & McFarlane, J. (1998). Utilization of police by abused pregnant Hispanic women. *Violence Against Women, 4,* 677–693.

Wilber, K. H., & McNeilly, D. P. (2001). Elder abuse and victimization. In J. E. Birren & K. W. Schai (Eds.), *Handbook of the psychology of aging* (5th ed., pp. 569–591). San Diego, CA: Academic Press.

Wilke, D. J., & Vinton, L. (2005). The nature and impact of domestic violence across age cohorts. *Affilia, 20,* 326–328.

Wilkens, S. L. (2002). The social problem-solving skills of preschoolers who witness domestic violence as measured by the MacArthur Story-Stem Battery. *Dissertation Abstracts International, 63*(01), 555B. (UMI No. 3040112)

Willard, N. (2005–2007). Educator's guide to cyberbullying and cyberthreats. Retrieved from http://cyber-safe-kids.com

Williams, K. R. (1992). Social sources of marital violence and deterrence: Testing an integrated theory of assaults between partners. *Journal of Marriage and the Family, 54,* 620–629.

Williams, L. M. (1994). Recall of childhood trauma: A prospective study of women's memories. *Journal of Consulting and Clinical Psychology, 62,* 1167–1176.

Williams, O. J. M., Oliver, W., & Pope, M. (2008). Domestic violence in the African American community. *Journal of Aggression, Maltreatment & Trauma, 16,* 229–237.

Williams, S. L., & Frieze, I. H. (2005). Patterns of violent relationships, psychological distress, and marital satisfaction in a national sample of men and women. *Sex Roles, 52,* 771–784.

Williams, S. L., & Frieze, I. H. (2008). Courtship behaviors, relationship violence, and breakup persistence in college men and women. *Psychology of Women Quarterly, 29,* 248–257.

Williams, S. L., & Mickelson, K. D. (2004). The nexus of domestic violence and poverty: Resilience in women's anxiety. *Violence Against Women, 10,* 283–293.

Williamson, C., & Folaron, G. (2003). Understanding the experiences of street level prostitutes. *Qualitative Social Work, 2,* 271–287.

Williamson, J. M., Borduin, C. M., & Howe, B. A. (1991). The ecology of adolescent maltreatment: A multilevel examination of adolescent physical abuse, sexual abuse, and neglect. *Journal of Consulting and Clinical Psychology, 59,* 449–457.

Willson, P., McFarlane, J., Malecha, A., Watson, K., Lemmey, D., Schultz, P., et al. (2000). Severity of violence against women by intimate partners and associated use of alcohol and/or illicit drugs by perpetrators. *Journal of Interpersonal Violence, 15,* 996–1008.

Wilsnack, S. C., Wonderlich, S. A., Kristjanson, A. F., Vogeltanz-Holm, N. D., & Wilsnack, R. W. (2002). Self-reports of forgetting and remembering childhood sexual abuse in a nationally representative sample of U.S. women. *Child Abuse & Neglect, 26,* 139–147.

Wilson, D. G., & Wilson, A. V. (1991). *Spousal abuse cases: Perceptions and attitudes of service providers* (Report prepared for Attorney General's Task Force on Domestic Violence Crime). Louisville: Kentucky Criminal Justice Statistical Analysis Center.

Wilson, H. W., & Widom, C. S. (2009). From child abuse and neglect to illicit drug use in middle adulthood: A prospective examination of the potential mediating role of four risk factors. *Journal of Youth and Adolescence, 38,* 340–354.

Wilson, M. N., Baglioni, A. J., Jr., & Downing, D. (1989). Analyzing factors influencing readmission to a battered women's shelter. *Journal of Family Violence, 4,* 275–284.

Wilson-Williams, L., Stephenson, R., Juvekar, S., & Andes, K. (2008). Domestic violence and contraceptive use in a rural Indian village. *Violence Against Women, 14,* 1181–1198.

Wind, T. W., & Silvern, L. (1992). Type and extent of child abuse as predictors of adult functioning. *Journal of Family Violence, 7,* 261–281.

Windle, M., & Mrug, S. (2009). Cross-gender violence perpetration and victimization among early adolescents and associations with attitudes toward dating conflict. *Journal of Youth Adolescence, 38,* 429–439.

Windle, M., & Windle, R. C. (1996). Coping strategies, drinking motives, and stressful life events among adolescents. Associations with behavioral and emotional problems, and academic functioning. *Journal of Abnormal Psychology, 105,* 551–560.

Winerman, L. (2006, November). Coping through cognition. *Monitor on Psychology, 37,* 16–17.

Wingood, G. M., DiClemente, R. J., & Raj, A. (2000). Identifying the prevalence and correlates of STDs among women residing in domestic violence shelters. *Women & Health, 30*(4), 15–26.

Witvliet, M., Olthof, T., Hoeksma, J. B., Goossens, F. A., Smits, M. S. I., & Koot, H. M. (2009). Peer group affiliation of children: The role of perceived popularity, likeability, and behavioral similarity. *Social Development, 19,* 285–303.

Wiwanitkit, V. (2005). Male rape, some notes on the laboratory investigation. *Sexuality and Disability, 23,* 41–46.

Wodarski, J. S., Kurtz, P. D., Gaudin, J. M., & Howing, P. T. (1990). Maltreatment and the school-age child: Major academic, socioemotional, and adaptive outcomes. *Social Work, 35,* 506–513.

Woffordt, S., Mihalic, D. E., & Menard, S. (1994). Continuation in marital violence. *Journal of Family Violence, 9,* 195–225.

Wolak, J., Mitchell, K. J., & Finkelhor, D. (2007). Does online harassment constitute bullying? An exploration of online harassment by known peers and online-only contacts. *Journal of Adolescent Health, 41,* S51–S58.

Wolf, M. E., Ly, U., Hobart, M. A., & Kernic, M. A. (2003). Barriers to seeking police help for intimate partner violence. *Journal of Family Violence, 18,* 121–129.

Wolf, R. S. (2000). The nature and scope of elder abuse. *Generations, 24*(2), 6–12.

Wolf, R. S., & Pillemer, K. A. (1988). Intervention, outcome, and elder abuse. In G. T. Hotaling, D. Finkelhor, J. T. Kirkpatrick, & M. A. Straus (Eds.), *Coping with family violence* (pp. 257–274). Newbury Park, CA: Sage.

Wolf, R. S., & Pillemer, K. A. (1989). *Helping elderly victims: The reality of elder abuse.* New York: Columbia University Press.

Wolf, R. S., & Pillemer, K. A. (1997). The older battered woman: Wives and mothers compared. *Journal of Mental Health and Aging, 3,* 325–336.

Wolf-Branigin, W. (2007). Disability and abuse in relation to substance abuse: A descriptive analysis. *Journal of Social Work in Disability & Rehabilitation, 6,* 65–74.

Wolfe, D. A. (1991). *Preventing physical and emotional abuse of children.* New York: Guilford.

Wolfe, D. A., Crooks, C. C., Chiodo, D., & Jaffe, P. G. (2003). Child maltreatment, bullying, gender-based harassment, and adolescent dating violence: Making the connections. *Psychology of Women Quarterly, 33,* 21–24.

Wolfe, D. A., & Jaffe, P. G. (1999). Emerging strategies in the prevention of domestic violence. *Future of Children, 9*(3), 133–141.

Wolfe, D. A., et al. (2009). A school-based program to prevent adolescent dating violence; a cluster randomized trial. *Archives of Pediatric and Adolescent Medicine, 163,* 692–699.

Wolfner, G. D., & Gelles, R. J. (1993). A profile of violence toward children: A national study. *Child Abuse & Neglect, 17,* 197–212.

Wolitzky-Taylor. K. B., Ruggiero, K. J., Danielson, C. K., Resnick, H. S., Hanson, R. F., Smith, D. W., et al. (2008). Prevalence and correlates of dating violence in a national sample of adolescents. *Journal of American Academy of Child and Adolescent Psychiatry, 47,* 755–762.

Wolman, B. B. (1973). *Dictionary of behavioral science.* New York: Van Nostrand Reinhold.

Wolock, T., & Horowitz, B. (1984). Child maltreatment as a social problem: The neglect of neglect. *American Journal of Orthopsychiatry, 54,* 530–542.

WomensLaw. Retrieved in August 2009 at http://www.murdoch .edu.au/elaw/issues/v9n2/netw92.html

Woods, S. J. (2000). Prevalence and patterns of posttraumatic stress disorder in abused and postabused women. *Issues in Mental Health Nursing, 21,* 309–324.

Woody, J. D., D'Souza, H. J., & Dartman, R. (2006). Do master's in social work programs teach empirically supported interventions? A survey of dean and directors. *Research on Social Work Practice, 16,* 469–479.

Worden, A. P. (2001). *Models of community coordination in partner violence cases: A multi-site comparative analysis, final report* (NCJ Publication No. 187351). Washington, DC: U.S. Department of Justice.

Worden, H. A. (2002). The effects of race and class on women's experience of domestic violence. *Dissertation Abstracts International, 62*(12), 4346A. (UMI No. 3034787)

Wordes, M., & Nunez, M. (2002). *Our vulnerable teenagers: Their victimization, its consequences, and directions for prevention and intervention.* Oakland, CA: National Council on Crime and Delinquency.

Working With Athletes to Prevent Dating Violence. (2007, December 7). *Prevention Researcher, 6.*

World Health Organization. (1997). *Gender, women and health.*

Worling, J. R. (1995). Adolescent sibling-incest offenders: Differences in family and individual functioning when compared to adolescent nonsibling sex offenders. *Child Abuse & Neglect, 19,* 633–643.

Wright, J., Fredrich, W., Cinq-Mars, C., & McDuff, P. (2004). Self-destructive and delinquent behaviors of adolescent female victims of child sexual abuse: Rates and covariates. *Violence & Victims, 19,* 627–643.

Wright, R., Powell, M. B., & Ridge, D. (2006). What criteria do police officers use to measure the success of an interview with a child. *Psychology, Crime & Law, 13,* 395-404.

Wuest, J., & Merritt-Gray, M. (1999). Not going back: Sustaining the separation in the process of leaving abusive relationships. *Violence Against Women, 5,* 110–133.

Wuest, J., & Merritt-Gray, M. (2008). A theoretical understanding of abusive intimate partner relationships that become non-violent: Shifting the pattern of abusive control. *Journal of Family Violence, 23,* 281–293.

Wurtele, S. K. (2002). School-based child sexual abuse prevention. In P. A. Schewe (Ed.), *Preventing violence in relationships: Interventions across the lifespan* (pp. 9–26). Washington, DC: American Psychological Association.

Wurtele, S. K., Kast, L. C., & Melzer, A. M. (1994). Sexual abuse prevention education for young children: A comparison of teachers and parents as instructors. *Child Abuse & Neglect, 16,* 865–876.

Wurtele, S. K., & Miller-Perrin, C. L. (1992). *Preventing child sexual abuse: Sharing the responsibility.* Lincoln: University of Nebraska Press.

Xiying Wang, & Petula, S. Y. H. (2007). *My Sassy Girl:* A qualitative study of women's aggression in dating relationships in Beijing. *Journal of Interpersonal Violence, 22,* 623–638.

Yaffe, M., Wolfson, C., & Lithwick, M. (2009). Professions show different enquiry strategies for elder abuse detection: Implications for training and interprofessional care. *Journal of Interprofessional Care, 23,* 646–654.

Yamawaki, N., & Tschanz, B. T. (2005). Rape perception differences between Japanese and American college students: On the mediating influence of gender role traditionality. *Sex Roles, 52,* 379–392.

Yampolskaya, S., & Banks, S. M. (2006). An assessment of the extent of child maltreatment using administrative databases. *Assessment, 13,* 342–355.

Yardley, J. (2002, March 16). Mother who drowned 5 children in tub avoids a death sentence. New York: *New York Times.* Retrieved from www.nytimes.com/2002/03/16/us/mother-who-drowned-5-children-in-tub-avoids-death-sentence.html

Yates, T. M. (2007). The developmental consequences of child emotional abuse: A neurodevelopmental perspective. *Journal of Emotional Abuse, 7,* 9–34.

Ybarra, M. L., Diener-West, M., & Leaf, P. J. (2007). Examining the overlap in Internet harassment and school bullying: Implications for school intervention. *Journal of Adolescent Health, 41,* S42–S50.

Ybarra, M. L., & Mitchell, J. K. (2004). Online aggressor/target, aggressors and target: A comparison of associated youth characteristics. *Journal of Child Psychology and Psychiatry, 45,* 1308–1316.

Yelsma, P. (1996). Affective orientation of perpetrators, victims, and functional spouses. *Journal of Interpersonal Violence, 11,* 141–161.

Yim, I. S., et al. (2009). Risk of postpartum depressive symptoms with elevated corticotrophin-releasing hormone in human pregnancy. *Archives of General Psychiatry, 66,* 162–169.

Yllö, K. A. (1993). Through a feminist lens: Gender, power, and violence. In R. J. Gelles & D. R. Loseke (Eds.), *Current controversies on family violence* (pp. 47–62). Newbury Park, CA: Sage.

Yllö, K. A. (2005). Through a feminist lens: Gender, diversity, and violence. In D. R. Loseke, R. J. Gelles, & M. M. Cavanaugh (Eds.), *Current controversies on family violence* (2nd ed., pp. 19–34). Thousand Oaks, CA: Sage.

Yoshihama, M. (2002). The definitional process of domestic violence in Japan. *Violence Against Women, 8,* 339–366.

Yoshihama, M., & Gillespie, B. W. (2002). Age adjustment and recall bias in the analysis of domestic violence data: Methodological improvements through the application of survival analysis method. *Journal of Family Violence, 17,* 199–221.

Yoshihama, M., Hammock, A. C., & Horrocks, J. (2006). Intimate partner violence, welfare receipt, and health status of low-income African American women: A lifecourse analysis. *American Journal of Community Psychology, 37,* 95–109.

Yoshioka, M. R., & Choi, D. Y. (2005). Culture and interpersonal violence research: A paradigm shift to create a full continuum of domestic violence services. *Journal of Interpersonal Violence, 20,* 513–519.

Yoshioka, M. R., DiNoia, J., & Ullah, K. (2001). Attitudes toward marital violence: An examination of four Asian communities. *Violence Against Women, 7,* 900–926.

Yoshioka, M. R., Gilbert, L., El-Bassel, N., Baig-Amin, M. (2003). Social support and disclosure of abuse: Comparing South Asian, African American, and Hispanic battered women. *Journal of Family Violence, 18,* 171–180.

Young, A. (2009, January 1). Nurturing our interdisciplinary science. *APA Online, 23.* Retrieved from http://www.apa.org/science/psa/jan09-nurturing.html

Young, B. J., & Furman, W. (2008). Interpersonal factors in the risk for sexual victimization and its recurrence during adolescence. *Journal of Youth and Adolescence, 37,* 297–309.

Young, M. E., Nosek, M. A., Howland, C. A., Chanpong, G., & Rintala, D. H. (1997). Prevalence of abuse of women with physical disabilities. *Archives of Physical Medicine and Rehabilitation, 78*(12, Suppl. 5), S34–S38.

Youngblade, L. M., & Belsky, J. (1990). Social and emotional consequences of child maltreatment. In R. T. Ammerman & M. Hersen (Eds.), *Children at risk: An evaluation of factors contributing to child abuse and neglect* (pp. 109–140). New York: Plenum.

Youngblood, P. (2006, Spring). Hopeline moves to new facility. *Hope Lines. Albemarle Hopelines's Quarterly Newsletter,* 3.

Younglove, J. A., Keer, M. G., & Vitello, C. J. (2002). Law enforcement officers' perceptions of same sex domestic violence. *Journal of Interpersonal Violence, 17,* 760–772.

Yozwiak, J. A. (2010). Postpoartum depression and adolescent mothers: A review of assessment and treatment approaches. *Journal of Pediatric and Adolescent Gynecology, 23,* 172–178.

Zahn, M. A., et al. (2008). *Girls study group: Violence by teenage girls: Trends and contexts.* Washington, DC: U.S. Department of Justice, Office of Juvenile and Delinquency Prevention.

Zakirova, V. (2005). War against the family: Domestic violence and human rights in Russia—A view from the Bashkortostan Republic. *Current Sociology, 53,* 75–91.

Zandi, P. P., et al. (2008). Association study of signaling pathway genes in bipolar disorder. *Archives of General Psychiatry, 65,* 785–793.

Zauszniewski, J. A., Eggenschwiler, K., Preechawon, S., Chung, C. W., Airey, T. F., Wilke, P. A., et al. (2004). Focused reflection reminiscence group for elders: Implementation and evaluation. *Journal of Applied Gerontology, 23,* 429–442.

Zayas, V., & Shoda, Y. (2007). Predicting preferences for dating partners from past experiences of psychological abuse: Identifying the psychological ingredients of situations. *Personality and Social Psychology Bulletin, 33,* 123–138.

Zeanah, C. H., et al. (2004). Reactive attachment disorder in maltreated toddlers (2004). *Child Abuse & Neglect, 28,* 877–888.

Zeanah, C. H., Egger, H. L., Smyke, A. T., Nelson, C. A., Fox, N. A., Marshall, P. J., et al. (2009). Institutional rearing and psychiatric disorders in Romanian preschool children. *American Journal of Psychiatry, 166,* 777–785.

Zebian, A., Alamuddin, R., Maalouf, M., & Chatila, Y. (2007). Developing an appropriate psychology through culturally sensitive research practices in the Arabic-speaking world. *Journal of Cross-Cultural Psychology, 38,* 91–122.

Zeelenberg, R., Wagenmakers, E. M., & Rotteveel, M. (2006). The impact of emotion on perception: Bias or enhanced processing? *Psychological Science, 17,* 287–291.

Zellman, G. L., & Fair, C. C. (2002). Preventing and reporting abuse. In J. E. B. Myers, L. Berliner, J. Briere, C. T. Hendrix, C. Jenny, & T. A. Reid (Eds.), *The APSAC handbook on child maltreatment* (2nd ed., pp. 449–475). Thousand Oaks, CA: Sage.

Zgoba, K. M. (2004). Spin doctors and moral crusaders: The moral panic behind child safety legislations. *Criminal Justice Studies, 17,* 385–404.

Zhan, H. J., Liu, G., Guan, X., & Bai, H-G. (2006). Recent developments in institutional elder care in China: Changing concepts and attitudes. *Journal of Aging & Social Policy, 18,* 85–108.

Zielinski, D. S. (2009). Child maltreatment and adult socioeconomic well-being. *Child Abuse & Neglect, 33,* 666–678.

Zinbarg, R. E., Uliaszek, A. A., & Adler, J. M. (2008). The role of personality in psychotherapy for anxiety and depression. *Journal of Personality, 76,* 1649–1688.

Zingraff, M. T., Leiter, J., Myers, K. A., & Johnsen, M. C. (1993). Child maltreatment and youthful problem behavior. *Criminology, 31,* 173–202.

Zink, T., Fisher, B. S., Regan, S., & Pabst, S. (2005). The prevalence and incidence of intimate partner violence in older women in primary care practice. *Journal of General Internal Medicine, 20,* 884–888.

Zink, T., Klesges, L., Stevens, S., & Decker, P. (2009). The development of a sexual abuse severity score: Characteristics of childhood sexual abuse associated with trauma symptomatology, somatization, and alcohol abuse. *Journal of Interpersonal Violence, 24,* 537–546.

Zink, T., Regan, S., Jacobson, C. J., Jr., & Pabst, S. (2003). Cohort, period, and aging effects: A qualitative study of older women's reasons for remaining in abusive relationships. *Violence Against Women, 9,* 1429–1441.

Zinzow, H. M., Grubaugh, A. L., Frueh, B. C., & Magruder, K. M. (82007). Sexual assault, mental health, and service use among male and female veterans seen in Veterans Affairs primary care clinics: A multi-site study. *Psychiatry Research, 159,* 226–236.

Zinzow, H. M., Grubaugh, A. L., Monnier, J., Suffoletta-Maierle, S., & Frueh, B. C. (2007). Trauma among female veterans: A critical review. *Trauma, Violence, & Abuse, 8,* 384–400.

Zinzow, H. M., & Jackson, J. L. (2009). Attributions for different types of traumatic events and post-traumatic stress among women. *Journal of Aggression, Maltreatment & Trauma, 18,* 499–515.

Zinzow, H. M, Seth, P., Jackson, J., Niehaus, A., & Fitzgerald, M. (2010). Abstract: Abuse and parental characteristics, attributions of blame, and psychological adjustment in adult survivors of child sexual abuse. *Journal of Child Sexual Abuse, 19,* 79–96.

Zlotnick, C., Johnson, D. M., & Kohn, R. (2006). Intimate partner violence and long-term psychosocial functioning in a national sample of American women. *Journal of Interpersonal Violence, 21,* 262–275.

Zolotor, A. J., Theodore, A. D., Coyne-Beasley, T., & Runyan, D. K. (2007). Intimate partner violence and child maltreatment: Overlapping risk. *Brief Treatment and Crisis Intervention, 7,* 305–321.

Zolotor, A. J., Theodore, A. D., Chang, J. J., Berkoff, M. C., & Runyan, D. K. (2008). Speak softly—and forget the stick: Corporal punishment and child physical abuse. *American Journal of Preventive Medicine, 35,* 364–369.

Zorza, J. (1995). Recognizing and protecting the privacy and confidentiality needs of battered women. *Family Law Quarterly, 29,* 273–311.

Zorza, J. (2001, October/November). Some controversies concerning classifying and treating stalkers. *Domestic Violence Report, 7,* 3–5.

Zorza, J. (2003, April/May). Battered mothers speak out: Part II. The recommendations. *Domestic Violence Report, 4,* 49, 57–60.

Zorza, J. (2007, February/March). A guide to relocation and legal identity change. *Domestic Violence Report, 12,* 36.

Zubretsky, T. M., & Digirolamo, K. M. (1994). Adult domestic violence: The alcohol connection. *Violence Update, 4*(7), 1–2, 4, 8.

Zurbriggen, E. L. (2009). Understanding and preventing adolescent dating violence: The importance of developmental, sociocultural, and gendered perspectives. *Psychology of Women Quarterly, 33,* 30–33.

Zweig, J. M., & Burt, M. R. (2007). Predicting women's perceptions of domestic violence and sexual assault agency helpfulness. *Violence Against Women, 13,* 1149–1178.

Zwi, K. J., Woolfenden, S. R., Wheeler, D. M., O'Brien, T. A., Tait, P., & Williams, K. W. (2008). School-based education programmes for the prevention of child sexual abuse [Review]. *Evidence-Based Child Health, 3,* 6–34.

# Author Index

Aaron, R., 618
Abbey, A., 330, 335
Abbott, C. B., 163, 252
Abbott, R. D., 172, 255, 310
Abdi, S. N. M., 478
Abel, G. G., 567, 2320
Abeling, S., 354
Abell, N., 118
Abner, E. L., 587, 591, 593, 595, 597, 598, 600, 635, 637
Abraham, M., 494
Abrahams, N., 474
Abrams, S., 92
Abu-Ras, W., 498, 503, 505
Accornero, V. H., 87
Ace, A., 316, 363, 424
Acevedo, M., 500
Acevedo-Garcia, D., 72, 474
Acharsäter, H., 198
Achenbach, T. M., 66
Acierno, R., 589, 590, 592, 593, 599, 601, 604, 620, 621
Ackard, D. M., 271
Adair, J. G., 8
Adams, C. M., 115
Adams, D. C., 390, 554, 555, 557, 564
Adams, H. E., 333
Adams, J. A., 202
Adams, P., 366, 376, 408
Adams, V., 77
Adams-Curtis, L. E., 288, 317, 322, 328
Aday, R. H., 608, 621
Addis, M. E., 69, 445, 452, 561
Addison, M., 329
Adelman, M., 496
Adelman, S. A., 455
Adeyemi, A. B., 569
Adinkrah, M., 474, 478
Adler, J. M., 454
Adler, J. R., 387
Adler, N., 266
Afifi, T. O., 153, 177, 372
Afrank, J., 114
Agha, Z., 181
Agnew, C. R., 408, 535
Agoff, C., 488, 491

Agrawal, A., 449
Ahn, W., 46
Ahrens, C. E., 336, 354
Airey, T. E., 608
Ajzenstadt, M., 30
Akers, R. L., 273
Akkuş D., 486
Akmatov, M. K., 482
Al Eissa, M., 191
Al-Kayyali, G., 483
Al-Nsour, M., 483
Alaggia, R., 201, 227
Alamuddin, R., 77
Alarcon-Segovia, D., 489
Aldarondo, E., 419, 420, 447, 500, 503
Alder, S., 557, 562
Alexander, B., 331
Alexander, H., 268
Alexander, K. W., 203
Alexander, R., 128, 135
Alexanderson, K., 372
Alfonso, M., 31, 394
Alford, P., 422
Allard, J., 187
Allen, B., 111, 124
Allen, C. T., 311, 317
Allen, D. G., 63, 64
Allen, G., 375
Allen, J. P., 6
Allen, N. E., 15
Allen, P. G., 395, 396
Allin, R. B., Jr., 555
Allison, C. J., 376, 410, 437, 534
Allnutt, S., 604
Almuneef, M., 191
Alpert, N. M., 370
Alvamzo, A., 336
Alvarado, L., 160
Alvarez, J., 303, 332, 382
Alwin, D., 66
Alyahri, A., 190
Amar, A. F., 342
Amat, J., 377
Amato, P. R., 318

Bechtle, A. E., 371
Beck, A. T., 435
Beck, M., 69
Becker, J. V., 230, 241, 245, 274
Becker, S., 471, 482
Becker-Blease, K. A., 59, 231
Beckham, J. C., 451, 524
Beckner, H. M., 459
Bedi, G., 115
Beech, A. R., 216, 217, 238, 239, 333
Beechey, S., 540
Beers, B., 267, 272
Behnke, S., 634
Behrend, T. S., 171, 179
Beichner, D., 388
Beitchman, J., 634
Belaga, I., 557, 558
Belar, C., 45
Belhadj, A., 484, 493
Belknap, J., 44, 391, 395, 396, 397, 462
Bell, C. C., 500
Bell, M. E., 402, 557
Bell, M. P., 382
Bell, N. S., 523
Bell, V., 559
Bellamy, J. L., 86, 121, 559
Bellavia, G. M., 435
Belli, R. F., 66
Belsky, J., 98, 177, 178
Belton, L., 504, 505
Bem, S. L., 447
Ben-David, S., 355
Ben-Porat, A., 78
Ben-Porath, Y. S., 560
Bender, H. L., 6
Bender, K., 325
Bendersky, M., 87
Benedict, M., 166
Benet, L., 493
Bennett, D. S., 87
Bennett, D. S., 99
Bennett, L., 396, 459, 503, 535
Bennett, L. W., 29, 296, 309, 363, 365, 445, 449, 502, 553, 563, 567
Bennett, R. T., 116, 172, 317, 318
Bennett, S., 246
Bennett-Cattaneo, L., 557
Benotsch, E., 516
Benson, M., 498
Benson, M. L., 539
Bent-Goodley, T. B., 394
Bentley, H., 580
Benton, D., 404, 628
Benuto, L., 203

Benzein, E., 633
Beran, T. N., 161
Beran, T., 129
Berbig, I. J., 601
Berenbaum, H., 370
Berg, B. L., 590, 618
Bergeman, C. S., 454
Bergen, R. K., 422
Berger, L. M., 120, 171, 256, 257
Berger, R., 122
Bergman, A., 173
Berhane, Y., 356
Berk, R. A., 390
Berkhoff, M. C., 113, 181, 192, 202
Berkowitz, A. D., 338
Berkowitz, L., 289
Berliner, L., 84, 113, 163, 199, 206, 220, 226, 236, 237, 272, 365, 369, 374
Berman, H., 310
Berman, J., 608
Berman, M. E., 453, 553
Bernard, L. A., 374, 519
Bernhardt, P. C., 454
Berns, N., 364
Berns, S. B., 400, 401, 402, 420, 551, 566
Bernstein, A., 455
Bernstein, D. M., 202
Berry, E. J., 246
Berry, M., 529
Bersamin, M., 70
Berson, I. R., 281
Berson, M. J., 281
Berson, N., 197
Berthoz, S., 229
Bertrand, R. M., 601
Best, C. L., 403, 533
Best, J., 10
Bethell, C., 184
Bethke, T., 315
Bettesworth, A., 559
Bettis, P., 70, 309, 393
Betz, C. L., 282
Betz, M. E., 619
Bevaque, J., 441
Bevc, I., 270
Bewnab, J. P., 455
Beyer, K., 149
Bharucha, J., 471
Bianchi, S. M., 537
Biddle, A. K., 32
Bidgood, B. A., 555
Bidgood, P., 555
Bilby, C. A. L., 550

Bradley, R. G., 313, 318
Bradley, R. H., 121, 171, 187, 192, 523
Bradshaw, M., 180
Braithwaite, S., 317
Brandford, C., 153
Brandl, B., 586, 596, 601, 606, 607, 619, 635
Brandon, A. R., 456
Brandshaw, G. S., 589
Brandt, H. M., 310
Brank, E. M., 563
Brans, R. G., 454
Brassard, M. R., 12, 106, 107, 108, 109, 111, 133, 135, 185
Braun, B. G., 435, 446
Braun, K., 594
Braun, N., 172
Braun-Courville, D. K., 290
Brazeau, P., 338
Brazier, J. M., 404
Breaslau, N., 52
Brecklin, L. R., 338
Breen, A. B., 41, 245
Breiding, M., 310
Breitenbecher, K. H., 338
Brendgen, M., 120, 178
Brennan, A., 634
Brennan, P. L., 374
Breslin, F. C., 315
Brestan, E. V., 87, 89
Bretz, W. A., 91
Brewin, C. R., 370
Brickman, J., 268
Briére, F. N., 188
Briere, J., 32, 205, 219, 230, 533, 616, 631
Brimse, A., 198
Brinig, M. F., 612
Brinkerhoff, M. B., 5, 49
Broadhurst, D. D., 87, 94
Brody, G. H., 370, 379
Brody, L. R., 286
Bromet, E., 524
Brook, D., 87
Brook, J., 87
Brookman, E., 485
Brookman, F., 457
Brookman-Frazee, L., 125
Brooks, D. R., 370, 372
Brooks, V. R., 512
Brooks-Gunn, J., 119
Bross, C. C., 332, 523, 524
Bross, D. C., 244
Broude, G. J., 568
Brower, M., 427
Brown, A. L., 52, 323
Brown, C., 75, 406, 517

Brown, C. M., 628
Brown, D., 587, 620, 622
Brown, E. J., 156
Brown, J., 50, 51, 97, 166, 169, 180, 226, 314, 445
Brown, J. D., 430
Brown, J. M., 327
Brown, L. K., 298
Brown, M., 595
Brown, M. J., 578, 625
Brown, R., 427
Brown, R. M., 539
Brown, S. A., 331
Brown, T. J., 334
Browne, A., 65, 407, 463, 537
Browne, C., 226
Browne, K., 53, 459
Browne, K. D., 436, 608
Brownlie, E. B., 634
Brownridge, D. A., 72, 153, 177, 492
Bruanstein, A., 113
Bruch, S. K., 171
Bruck, M., 201, 202
Brush, L. D., 538, 539, 542
Bruyn, E. D., 294
Buchbinder, E., 569
Bucholz, K., 449
Buck, P. O., 330
Buckner, J. C., 407
Buel, S. M., 327
Bui, H. N., 496, 503, 504, 506
Bui, M., 481, 503, 505
Buka, S. L., 97, 225
Bukovec, P., 422
Bulman, P., 590
Bulotsky-Shearer, R., 187
Bunch, S. G., 575
Bunge, V. P., 403
Buranosky, R., 400, 532
Burazeri, G., 485
Burchard, B. L., 274
Burge, S., 287
Burgess, A., 332
Burgess, A. G., 220
Burgess, A. W., 220, 271, 329
Burgess, C., 267, 272
Burgess, E. S., 246
Burgess, G. H., 328
Burke, J., 416, 550
Burke, T. W., 512
Burman, E., 571
Burman, B., 63
Burnam, M. A., 62
Burnight, K., 615
Burns, B. J., 162

Burns, R., 342
Bursch, B., 176
Bursik, R. J., 7
Burt, C. H., 16, 310, 322, 324
Burt, M., 542
Burt, M. R., 35, 328, 397, 447, 530
Burton, D. L., 234
Burton, S., 403
Busch, A. L., 51, 446
Busch, N. B., 32, 43, 356, 535
Busch-Armendariz, N. B., 325
Bush, G. W., 540
Bush, R., 71
Bushman, B. J., 7, 288, 289
Buss, A. H., 434
Buss, D. M., 441
Busseri, M. A., 293
Bustin, A., 578
Butler, K., 204
Butler, S., 480
Butner, J., 443
Buttell, F. P., 557, 558, 560, 567
Button, D. M., 162, 268, 271, 272, 273, 278, 280
Butts, J., 365
Buunk, B. P., 466, 518
Buzan, R., 363
Buzawa, E., 580
Buzawa, C. G., 31, 61, 391, 457
Buzawa, E. S., 24, 31, 61, 386, 391, 392, 393, 457
Bužgová, R., 626
Bybee, D. I., 327, 379, 410, 529, 560
Byer, A. L., 313
Byers, R., 31, 394
Byrd, K. K., 75
Byrne, B. M., 59
Byrne, C. A., 403, 442, 533

Cabral, G., 354
Cacioppo, J. T., 75, 453, 464
Caetano, R., 70, 72, 155, 178, 417, 424, 450, 466, 469, 500
Caffaro, J. V., 265, 266, 268, 273, 275, 276
Cahill, C., 237
Cahill, K. F., 316, 317
Cahill, M. A., 157
Cahill, S., 589, 625.626
Cain, C., 629
Cain, D., 59, 406, 407, 467, 531, 545
Cain, K. C., 25
Caine, E. D., 421
Caldwell, J. E., 70, 465, 567
Calhoun, K. S., 271, 322, 469
Calhoun, L., 318
Calkins, P., 587, 619
Call, C. R., 296, 502, 553, 563, 567

Call, K. T., 56
Callahan, M. R., 286, 287, 298
Calvete, E., 20, 69, 72, 77
Camacho, J., 369, 387, 404, 538
Camburn, D., 66
Campbell, D. W., 389, 403
Campbell, J. C., 7, 51, 331, 339, 372, 379, 389, 401, 403, 407, 408, 422, 442, 471, 482, 500, 503, 529, 542
Campbell, R., 327, 332, 336
Canady, B., 555
Canales-Portalatín, D., 395
Canavan, M. M., 268
Candell, S., 337
Canfield, M., 370
Cann, A., 318
Cantor, J. M., 229, 231
Cantos, A. L., 373, 427, 438
Capaldi, D. M., 314
Capezza, N. M., 364, 425, 529, 544
Cappas, N. M., 533
Caraballo, L., 160
Caraveo, L. E., 564
Carawan, L. W., 575
Carbone-Lopez, K., 465
Carbonell, J. L., 241, 274
Cardarelli, A. P., 219, 225, 228, 234
Cardemil, E. V., 79
Carden, A. D., 548
Cardwell, C., 21
Carey, C. M., 407
Carine, A., 316
Carl, S., 394
Carll, E. K., 289
Carlson, B. E., 44, 227, 259, 269, 270, 295, 313, 371, 379, 533
Carlson, E. A., 97, 98, 152, 171, 177
Carlson, J. H., 338
Carlson, M. J., 387
Carlstedt, A., 198
Carlton, R. P., 51, 446
Carmody, D. C., 79
Carnes, M., 155, 159
Carney, M. M., 560, 567
Carp, F. M., 620
Carpenter, L. L., 99
Carr, J. L., 50, 317
Carrigan, T. D., 370
Carroff, A., 159
Carroll, K. M., 553, 559
Carroll, P. J., 409
Carson, C. L., 441
Carter, Y. H., 542
Casanueva, C., 121, 171, 187, 192
Cascardi, M., 68, 69, 286, 448, 462
Casey, E. A., 337, 339, 406, 540

Chung, D., 316
Chung, K. W., 479
Chung, S., 171
Churchill, S. D., 337
Ciabattari, T., 365
Cicchetti, D., 96, 124, 159, 160, 171, 182
Cinq-Mars, C., 229
Claerhout, S., 372
Clark, C., 417
Clark, C. J., 483
Clark, D. M., 370, 372
Clark, K. A., 32
Clark, S., 314
Clark-Daniels, C. L., 613
Clarke P. N., 537
Clarke, S. N., 18
Clary, C., 533
Claussen, A. H., 119
Clay, C., 505
Clay, R. A., 188
Clay-Warner, J., 16, 322, 324
Claypool, H. M., 441
Clegg, C., 231
Cleland, C., 213, 223
Clements, C., 283
Clements, C. M., 114, 373, 374, 378, 379
Clements, P. T., Jr., 271
Clements-Schreiber, M. E., 329
Clemmer, E., 390
Clemmons, J. C., 371
Clinton, A. M., 330
Clinton-Sherrod, M., 120, 209, 581
Clipp, E. C., 601
Clipson, C. R., 438, 466
Close, S. M., 298
Cloud, J., 21
Clum, G. A., 370
Cluss, P. A., 400, 532
Cnaan, R. A., 559
Coates, A. A., 112, 172, 359
Coccaro, E. F., 32, 434, 453, 454
Coffey, P., 116, 172, 314, 317, 318
Coffino, B., 97, 98, 152, 171, 177
Cogen, R., 550
Cohen, D., 7, 313, 319, 356, 357, 407, 438, 440, 441, 466, 601
Cohen, E. P., 130
Cohen, J., 346, 612
Cohen, J. A., 236
Cohen, J. H., 420, 506
Cohen, M., 611, 627
Cohen, M. A., 25
Cohen, P., 50, 51, 97, 166, 169, 226, 314, 430, 445, 446, 447, 465
Cohen, S., 56
Cohen-Mansfield, J., 634

Cohn, E. S., 322
Coker, A. L., 56, 66, 155, 310, 326, 341, 372, 423, 464, 465, 502, 567
Cole, D. A., 163
Cole, J., 17, 345, 349, 350, 351, 374, 508, 509, 510, 511, 575
Cole, P. R., 383, 384
Coleman, M., 120
Collado, L., 358
Collier-Tension, S., 567
Collin-Vézina, D., 286
Collins, B., 435
Collins, N. L., 312, 376
Collishaw, S., 157
Combs-Lane, A. M., 449
Comerford, S. A., 626
Condon, K. M., 598, 615
Conger, R. D., 445
Conis, P., 389
Conkle, L. K., 66
Conn, V., 638
Conn-Caffaro, A., 265, 266, 268, 273, 275, 276
Connell, C. M., 188
Connelly, C. D., 420, 504, 506
Connelly, D. C., 69
Conner, K. R., 421
Conner, T., 635
Connolly, J., 279, 288, 296
Connolly, M. T., 611
Connor, J. L., 333, 336
Connors, K. M., 260, 261
Conrad, P., 32
Conron, K. J., 97
Conroy, E., 160
Conte, J. R., 205, 220, 231
Conwell, Y., 421
Conyers, J., Jr., 308
Coohey, C., 172, 178, 279
Cook, S. L., 201, 578
Cook, P. W., 413
Cook, S., 21, 374, 377, 406
Cook, S. L., 298
Cook-Daniels, L., 17, 584, 590, 596, 601, 609, 616, 621, 625, 636
Cooke, D. J., 268
Cool, A., 459
Coolidge, F. L., 380
Cooney, K., 540
Cooper, C. E., 119
Cooper, H., 55
Copenhaver, M. M., 49, 449, 452
Corbie-Smith, G., 628
Corby, P. M., 91
Corcoran, J., 126
Corder, B. F., 237
Cordova, J. V., 69, 445, 452, 561

Cornell, D. G., 161
Cornell, C. P., 33, 251, 265
Coronado, V. G., 158
Corral, S., 20, 69, 72, 77
Corso, P., 25
Cortes, R. M., 124
Cortoni, F., 230, 231
Corvo, K. N., 549
Corwin, D. L., 196
Costa, D. M., 555
Cotton, S., 262
Cottrell, B., 263
Coulter, M. L., 31, 394
Council, C. L., 530
Counsell, S. R., 589
Cousins, A. J., 314
Coutinho, P., 571
Covell, C. N., 235
Covington, H. E., 453
Cowley-Malcolm, E., 480
Cox, B. J., 153, 177, 372
Cox, C. E., 85, 86
Cox, L., 341, 344, 345, 346, 347, 349, 350
Coyle, J. P., 119
Coyne, A. C., 601
Coyne-Beasley, T., 545
Craft, S. M., 50, 513, 514, 515, 520
Craig, I. W., 155
Craig, J. S., 192
Craig, S., 77, 202
Craig, W. M., 254
Crampton, A., 606
Crandall, C., 421
Cranston, K., 293
Craun, S. W., 389
Craven, D., 35, 55, 373, 378, 394, 425
Crawford, E., 329, 338
Crawford, N., 67
Creedon, M. A., 634
Creel, L., 489, 490
Creighton, A., 296
Crewe, M., 473
Crichton, S. J., 598
Crichton-Hill, Y., 578
Crittenden, P. M., 97, 98, 119, 177, 234
Crofford, L. J., 310
Cronin, C., 62, 420, 523
Cronkite, R. C., 374, 535
Crooks, C. C., 111, 155, 161, 279, 531
Crooks, C. V., 121, 154, 180
Crosbie-Burnett, M., 517, 579
Crosby, A. E., 47
Cross, C., 284
Cross, H., 237

Cross, T. P., 132, 243, 244
Crothers, L., 279
Crouch, J. L., 171
Crouter, A. C., 270, 271, 273
Crowe, A., 388, 389
Crowe, A. H., 560
Crowley, J., 402
Crutis, R. L., Jr., 209
Cuartas, A. S., 446
Cuevas, C. A., 177, 181
Cuevas, M., 589
Cui, M., 317
Cullen, F. T., 52, 324, 326, 344, 345, 349, 350, 359
Cully, J. A., 607
Culp, R. E., 187
Culver, M. A., 185
Cumming, G. F., 274
Cummings, N., 533
Cummins, M. R., 394
Cunningham, P. B., 274
Cunningham, S., 50
Cunningham-Rathner, J., 230
Cunradi, C. B., 70, 72, 450
Cupach, W. R., 441
Curley, J. P., 86
Curran, P. J., 56
Currie, D. H., 35, 423
Currie, J., 89, 126
Currier, D. M., 338
Curry, M. A., 389, 633
Curtain, J. J., 163
Curtis, L., 623
Curtis, P. A., 66, 211
Curtis, R. L., Jr., 209, 211, 213, 229, 234, 245
Cuthbert, C., 122
Cutler, C., 99
Cutler, S. E., 271
Cyr, M., 269, 272
Czaja, S. J., 97, 107, 162
Czyz, E., 118

Dacey, A., 572, 573
Dadds, M. R., 144, 355
Dado, D., 400, 532
Dagenais, C., 188
D'Agostino, R. B., Jr., 553, 556
Dahlberg, L. L., 4
Daigle, L. E., 326
Daka, K., 86, 146
dal Pozza, G., 485
Dalal, R., 299
Dale, K., 435
Dalenberg, C. J., 371
D'Alessio, D., 24

Dunifon, R., 192
Dunlap, E., 50
Dunlop, B. D., 591, 595, 598, 608, 615
Dunn, P. E., 626
Dunne, M. P., 146, 189
Duplantis, A. D., 560
Dupont, D., 188
Dupont, I., 20, 470, 495
DuPree, M. G., 513
Dupuis, L. D., 318
Duran, B. M., 497
Durham, D., 237, 240
Durham, R. L., 232, 273
Durkee, A., 434
Durocher, J. M., 481
Durose, M. R., 241, 307, 357, 417, 420
Durrant, J. E., 180
Dussich, J. P. J., 161, 162
Dutch, N., 134
Dutra, L. A., 634
Dutt, D., 476
Dutton, D., 491, 519, 549
Dutton, D. G., 8, 20, 48, 255, 376, 409, 410, 412, 435, 436, 437, 438, 440, 445, 448, 451, 455, 534, 549, 550, 563
Dutton, M. A., 18, 21, 66, 97, 162, 365, 374, 377, 396, 402, 406, 423, 503, 535, 557, 631
Dutton-Douglas, M. A., 531, 532
Dworkin, E. R., 327
Dye, M. L., 316, 346, 349
Dyer, C. B., 611, 619
Dyer, J., 325
Dymov, S., 24
Dyslin, C. W., 180
Dziuba-Leatherman, J., 245, 265

Eagle, M., 572
Earp, J. L., 66, 70, 423
Eastman, B. J., 575
Easton, C. J., 553
Easton, J. A., 291
Eaton, J., 606
Eaves, D., 442, 443
Ebbensen, E. B., 324
Eby, K. K., 370
Eckenrode, J., 86, 98, 251
Eckhardt, C. I., 551
Eckhardt, C. L., 315, 318, 432, 433, 434, 435, 549, 550
Eckles, K., 632
Edelbrock, C. S., 66
Edens, J. F., 157
Edin, K., 364
Edinburgh, L. D., 222
Edleson, J. L., 134, 364, 365, 561
Edwards, A., 557, 562

Edwards, J. N., 274
Edwards, K. M., 316, 359
Edwards, M. C., 56
Edwards, S., 44, 369
Edwards, V. J., 59
Efetie, E. R., 474
Egan, N. W., 280
Egeland, B., 34, 90, 91, 97, 98, 126, 132, 153, 157, 164, 177, 182, 208, 370
Eggen, D., 401, 408, 410
Eggenschwiler, K., 608
Egger, H. L., 93
Egolf, B. P., 156, 254
Ehlers, A., 318, 370, 372
Ehrensaft, M. K., 50, 51, 314, 378, 430, 445, 446, 447, 465
Eikeman, H. S., 457
Einolf, C. J., 335
Eisdorfer, C., 601
Eiseman, B., 282
Eisikovits, Z., 374, 484, 535, 627
Eisler, R. M., 49, 449, 452
Eitle, D., 392
Ejaz, F. K., 636
El-Bassel, N., 505, 532, 533
El-Khorazaty, M. N., 88
El-Mohandes, A. A., 88
El-Roueiheb, Z., 484
El-Safty, M., 483
Elbow, M., 430
Elder, J., 372
Eldridge, H. J., 216, 217
Elgin, J. E., 438, 466
Eliot, M., 161
Elizaga, R. A., 322, 338
Ellard, J. H., 402
Elliott, A. N., 287
Elliott, B. A., 509
Elliott, D., 50, 448
Elliott, D. M., 219
Elliott, D. S., 454, 457
Elliott, I. A., 216, 217
Ellis, C. G., 177
Ellis, K. K., 180
Ellis, L., 332
Ellis, M. A., 505
Ellison, C. G., 47, 180
Elliston, E. J. W., 71
Ellsberg, M., 471, 474, 475, 477, 478, 480, 483, 485, 486, 489, 490, 492, 574
Eloy, S. V., 438
Els, L., 474
Else-Quest, N. M., 178
Emelianchik, K., 309
Emery, C. R., 475

Emery, R. E., 35, 189, 200, 265, 266
Emmers-Sommer, T. M., 329
Empey, L. T., 10, 11
Enander, V., 407
Endrass, J., 73
Endress, J., 232
Engel, B., 76
Engel, C. C., 524
England, T., 190
English, D. J., 86, 129, 153, 157
Enoki, H., 608
Enos, V. P., 396
Enosh, G., 535
Enright, R. D., 535
Epstein, D., 365, 386, 397, 404, 530, 531, 537
Erel, O., 114
Erez, E., 391, 395, 496, 503, 550, 560
Ericksen, J., 369
Erickson, M. F., 90, 91, 97, 98, 126, 132, 177
Erickson, N. S., 121, 122
Eriksen, S., 266
Erlingsson, C. L., 585, 620
Erwin, P. E., 471, 569
Eshelman, S., 177
Esmailzadeh, S., 570
Espelage, D. L., 160, 161, 162, 294, 401
Esqueda, M. W., 499
Esscopri, N., 634
Estacion, A., 171
Estes, R. J., 221, 222
Estévez, A., 20, 69, 72, 77
Estroff, S., 603
Euser, E. M., 92
Evans, G. W., 213, 372
Evans, P. K., 522
Evans, R. D., 559
Evans, S., 480
Everson, M. D., 86, 157, 201, 228
Ewing, C. P., 363
Exum, M., 394
Eyssel, F., 337
Ezechi, L. O., 474
Ezechi, O. C., 474
Ezpeleta, L., 129

Fadden, M. K., 372
Fagan, A. A., 287
Fagan, J. A., 48, 56, 60, 67, 355, 457, 563
Fagan, R. W., 434, 445, 449
Fagen, D., 402, 533
Faggiani, D., 386, 391, 392, 580
Fair, C. C., 29, 30
Fairchild, D. G., 499
Fairchild, H., 446

Fairchild, M. W., 499
Fairchild, S., 588
Fallad, R., 533
Falle, T., 477
Faller, K. C., 198, 199, 211, 230, 234, 242, 271
Fals-Stewart, W., 69, 449
Famularo, R., 52
Fan, Z., 522
Fancher, P., 523
Fanetti, M., 203
Fanflik, p., 332
Fanniff, A. M., 241, 245, 274
Fanning, J. R., 453, 553
Fanslow, J. L., 23
Fantuzzo, J. W., 117, 187
Faqgan, R. W., 35
Faragher, T. M., 536
Faramarzi, M., 570
Farber, N., 541
Farberman, R. A., 573
Farmer, A., 539
Farney, L. A., 608, 621
Farrell, M. L., 21
Farrington, D. P., 280, 457
Farris, C., 77
Fassler, I., 505
Fast, N. J., 378
Fatoye, F. O., 569
Fatusi, A. O., 569
Faul, M., 158
Faulk, M., 455
Faulkner, K., 579
Faulkner, A. H., 293
Faulkner, K., 550
Fava, M., 434
Fawcett, J., 413
Fawole, O. I., 570
Fay, K. E., 245
Feder, G., 542
Feder, L., 60, 390, 553, 555, 556
Feehan, M., 480
Feeney, J. A., 312, 376, 436
Fehringer, J. A., 178
Feigelman, S., 192
Fein, R. A., 280
Feinstein, J. A., 115, 129
Feiring, C., 44, 156, 213, 223
Feld, B. C., 296
Feldbau-Kohn, S., 557
Feldman, C. M., 448
Feldman, K. W., 191
Feldman, M. E., 451, 524
Feldman, P. H., 73
Feldman, R. S., 153, 154, 160

Foster, R. A., 555
Foster, S. L., 438, 466
Foubert, J. D., 338
Fountain, J., 406
Fowler, D. N., 505
Fox, A. M., 473
Fox, C. L., 161
Fox, G., 498
Fox, G. L., 539
Fox, J. A., 128, 135, 283
Fox, K. A., 314, 315
Fox, L., 133
Fox, N. A., 93
Foz, E. B., 524
Fraley, R. C., 312, 376
Fram, M. S., 541
Francis, K. J., 171
Franiuk, R., 290, 328, 407
Frank, D. A., 179
Frank, K. I., 589
Frankel, J., 570
Frankel, S. L., 447
Frantz, M., 128, 135
Franuik, R., 356, 357, 440
Fraser, C., 343, 349, 351
Fraser, J. A., 189
Frasier, P. Y., 180, 404, 504, 505, 542, 543
Frayne, S., 523
Frazier, C. E., 297
Frazier, P. A., 313, 337
Fredendall, L. L., 441
Fredman, L., 601
Fredrich, W., 229
Fredriksen-Goldsen, K. I., 512
Freed, L. H., 298, 353
Freedman, D., 66
Freedner, N., 353
Freels, S., 601
Freeman, D. H., Jr., 214
Freeman, K., 295
Freeve, A., 350
Frei, A., 264, 265
Freiberger, K., 17
Fremouw, W. J., 231, 344
Freyd, J. J., 59, 201, 231
Friday, P., 394
Friedlander, L., 279, 288, 296
Friedman, G., 611
Friedman, D., 435
Friedman, G., 627
Friedman, M. J., 524
Friedman, R., 55
Friedman, S., 55
Friedrich, W. N., 223

Friend, D., 59, 231
Frieze, I. H., 67, 70, 73, 341, 379, 412, 419, 423, 424, 442, 443, 465
Fritsch, T. A., 373
Fritz, P. T., 314
Frohman, S., 560
Frohmann, L., 396
Fromuth, M. E., 266
Froyland, I., 428, 441
Frueh, B. C., 209, 213, 524, 581
Fry, P. S., 366, 544
Frye, V., 392
Fuentes, A. I., 342
Fujiura, G. T., 369, 634
Fulcher, J., 297, 299
Fullerton, C. S., 22, 523, 581
Fulmer, T. T., 588, 600, 601, 611
Fung, D. S. S., 286
Fung, T., 106
Furlow, B., 636
Furnam, W., 292
Furrey, J., 369, 374
Furuno, J. P., 404
Fusco, R. A., 117, 187
Fyfe, J. J., 390, 391, 392

Gaarder, E., 44
Gaffey, K. J., 359
Gaffney, M. J., 327
Gage, A., 553
Gage, E. A., 337
Gagin, R., 611, 627
Gaidos, S., 88, 173, 174
Galibois, N., 554, 555, 557
Galinsky, A. D., 378
Gallop, R., 225
Gallopin, C., 299
Galloway, A. L., 559
Galloway, J., 314
Gambone, L. J., 70, 379, 465, 466, 502, 567
Ganaway, G. K., 205
Ganesh, I., 401, 476
Gangestad, S. W., 314
Ganley, A. L., 563
Gannon, T. A., 216
Gantz, M. G., 88
Gao, Y., 230
Garbarino, J., 180
Garcia, J. L., 626
Garcia, L., 420, 480, 500
Garcia-Moreno, C., 474, 475, 477, 480, 489, 490, 574
Garner, J. H., 60, 390, 395, 562
Garre-Olmo, J., 627
Garrick, T., 239

Gonnella, C., 213, 372
Gonzales, A., 20, 77
Gonzalez, M., 180
Gonzalez, P., 504, 505
Goodall, E. A., 485
Goodfriend, W., 408
Gooding, G., 515
Goodkind, J. R., 529
Goodman, L. A., 529
Goodman, C. C., 192
Goodman, G. S., 190, 203, 244
Goodman, L., 529
Goodman, L. A., 21, 65, 78, 332, 365, 374, 377, 396, 402, 404, 406, 423, 500, 503, 530, 531, 535, 537, 556, 557, 572, 631
Goodman, R., 190
Goodwin, B. J., 564
Goodyear-Smith, F. A., 551
Gooren, L. J. G., 240
Goossens, F. A., 160
Gorchynski, J., 413
Gordon, K. C., 376, 403, 437, 464, 534, 567
Gordon, L. C., 314, 364
Gordon, M., 72
Gore-Felton, C., 371, 410, 516
Gorman-Smith, D., 285
Gormley, B., 312, 315
Gortmaker, S. L., 97
Gortner, E., 400, 401, 402, 420, 566
Gorton, J., 508
Goscha, J., 69
Goshu, M., 356
Gottemoeller, M., 471, 474, 475, 477, 478, 480, 483, 485, 486, 489, 490, 492
Gottesman, L., 53
Gottlieb, L. N., 588
Gottlieb, M. C., 74
Gottman, J. M., 63, 379, 400, 401, 402, 420, 432, 436, 448, 459, 566
Gough, H. G., 430
Gover, A. R., 314, 315, 563
Graap, K., 533
Graham, D. L. R., 375, 395, 396, 409
Graham, J. C., 86, 157
Graham, K., 178
Graham, K. H., 438
Graham-Bermann, S. A., 35, 112, 113, 115, 118, 129, 271, 410, 423, 504
Graham-Kevan, N., 70, 313, 346, 349, 350, 429, 465
Grando, V. T., 638
Grandon, R., 356, 357, 407, 440
Granero, R., 129
Grant, M., 331
Grasmic, H. G., 7
Gratch, L. V., 48

Gratton, G., 188
Graves, K. N., 307
Gray, M. J., 332, 336
Gray-Little, B., 71, 330, 377, 402
Graybeal, J., 59, 283, 561
Graziano, A. M., 142
Green, B. A., 338
Green, B. L., 374
Green, C. E., 52, 438, 555
Green, M. C., 314, 440
Green, N. M., 443
Green, R., 120
Greenbaum, C., 124
Greene, A., 83, 85, 90, 91, 93, 94, 101, 102, 103, 108, 112, 117, 119, 146, 153, 156, 165, 167, 169, 170, 178, 179, 193, 206, 209, 211, 212, 213, 214, 253
Greene, B., 517
Greene, R., 126, 128
Greene, S. J., 568
Greene, W. F., 299
Greenfeld, L. A., 35, 55, 373, 378, 394, 425
Greenfield, E. A., 115, 129, 154, 182
Greenglass, E., 606
Greer, T. M., 213, 374, 504
Gregory, C. R., 496, 549, 550, 560, 567
Gregory, J., 89
Greisinger, A. J., 607
Griffin, L. D., 318
Griffin, M. L., 505
Griffin, T., 133, 242
Griffing, S., 71, 292, 313, 354, 410, 423, 466, 531, 534
Grigsby, N., 6, 363, 393, 399, 403, 409, 410, 419, 424
Grills-Taqueschel, A., 359
Grisby, N., 71, 419
Groff, J. Y., 20, 495, 542
Grogan-Kaylor, A., 144
Gromley, B., 424
Gromoske, A. N., 256, 257
Groscup, J., 578, 625
Gross, A. M., 333
Gross, J., 619
Grossman, A. H., 294
Grossman, S. F., 497, 509, 510, 511, 632, 634
Groth, A. N., 329
Groves, B. M., 127, 129
Grubaugh, A. L., 209, 213, 524, 581
Gruber, G., 118
Gruber, J. E., 161
Gruenfeld, D. H., 378
Grunewald, S., 73
Guadagno, L., 611
Guan, X., 627
Guba, E., 519
Guerra, N., 6

Harrop, J. W., 278
Hart, B. J., 512, 517
Hart, K. C., 157
Hart, S. D., 442, 443, 455, 548
Hart, S. N., 12, 106, 107, 108, 109, 133, 135, 185, 246
Hartfield, D. S., 88
Hartley, C., 396
Hartman, B. R., 393, 399
Hartman, C. R., 271
Hartman, J., 394, 395, 396
Hartsough, C. S., 420
Hartzell, E., 156, 227
Harvey, A. N., 559
Harvey, C. D. H., 598
Harvey, S. T., 238, 240, 241
Harway, M., 67, 74, 404, 425, 531, 532, 562
Harwood, J., 476
Hasday, J. E., 15
Haskett, M. E., 157, 171, 179
Hassan, F., 483
Hassett-Walker, C., 548, 563
Hassounch-Phillips, D., 630
Hastings, B. M., 328, 409, 435, 447, 448, 455, 551, 556, 558
Hatcher, R. M., 550
Hathaway, J. E., 332, 370, 372
Haug, R., 373
Haugaard, J. J., 27, 196, 198, 200, 236, 245, 246, 258
Haviland, M., 392
Hawker, L., 400, 532
Hawkins, J. D., 172, 255, 310
Hawkins, M. W., 443
Hawkins, S. R., 298
Hawley, M., 329
Haworth, T., 44
Hay, H. H., 10, 11
Hay, T., 187
Hayashino, D. S., 232
Hayne, D. L., 43
Hays, D. G., 309
Hayward, M. C., 374
Hazan, C., 376
Hazen, A. L., 420, 497, 504, 506
Healey, K. M., 31, 49, 549, 553
Heaney, C. A., 621
Hearn, J., 59
Hearn, M. E., 537, 538
Heath, A., 449
Heath, I., 419
Heath, J. M., 595
Heaton, T. B., 491
Heavey, C. L., 442
Hebert, M., 606
Hébert, K. S., 598, 615

Hebert, M., 28, 285, 286, 303
Hechler, D., 12, 203
Heckert, A., 553, 556
Heckert, D. A., 366, 557
Heeren, J. W., 48
Heermann, M., 517
Heese, M., 334
Hegarty, K., 71
Heggen, C. H., 48
Heide, K. M., 264, 265
Heidt, E., 116
Heidt, J. M., 52
Heinze, J. E., 295
Heise, L. L., 471, 474, 475, 477, 478, 480, 483, 485, 486, 489, 490, 492, 568
Heisler, C. J., 607, 610, 619
Heitkemper, M., 88
Helfer, R. E., 173
Helff, C. M., 313, 318, 363
Helfrich, C. A., 369
Hellmuth, J. C., 464, 567
Helmes, E., 589
Helms, J. E., 494
Helms, R. W., 299
Helweg-Larson, M., 402
Hemenway, D., 72, 421, 473, 474, 562
Hemmens, C., 396
Hendershoot, C. S., 335
Henderson, A., 369
Henderson, A. J. Z., 410, 420, 436, 438
Henderson, D. P., 542
Henderson, R. C., 56, 180
Hendricks, B., 557, 560
Hendy, H. M., 401, 408, 410
Henggeler, S. W., 274
Hennessy, E., 165
Henning, K. R., 116, 121, 172, 314, 317, 318, 401, 431, 438, 445, 446, 466, 501
Henninghausen, K., 98, 177
Henry, K. L., 254
Hensel, B., 622
Hensing, G., 372
Henson-Stroud, M. M., 626
Hepburn, J. R., 559
Hequembourg, A., 258, 259
Herbert, D., 280
Herbert, T. B., 402
Herdt, G., 578
Herman, R. P., 634
Herman, S., 613
Herman-Giddens, M., 197
Herman-Smith, R. L., 100
Hernandez, A., 240
Hernandez-Reif, M., 175

Jacobs, A., 543
Jacobson, C. J., Jr., 615
Jacobson, N. S., 41, 63, 379, 400, 401, 420, 432, 436, 448, 459, 566
Jacquet, S. E., 383, 384
Jaeger, S., 434
Jafarey, S. N., 481
Jaffe, E., 51, 436
Jaffe, P. G., 27, 29, 111, 121, 129, 155, 161, 180, 279, 531
Jaffee, S. R., 153, 155, 225, 226
Jakupcak, M., 337
James, K., 413
Jamieson, E., 154, 492
Jamison, T. R., 315, 318
Jankowski, M. K., 314, 318
Jansen, H., 474, 475, 477, 480, 489, 490
Jasinski, J. L., 447, 500, 503
Jayakumar, P., 158
Jaycox, L. H., 282, 298
Jeannet, P. Y., 191
Jenkins, M., 512
Jenkins, M. M., 125
Jennings, J. L., 435, 548
Jensen, B. L., 372
Jensen, C., 372
Jensen, G. F., 61
Jensen, T. L., 49
Jensen, V., 266
Jernigan, M., 494
Jeske, D., 615
Jesperson, A. F., 232
Jesse, D. E., 174
Jewkes, R., 474, 485
Jeyaseelan, L., 483
Ji, P., 69
Jin, R., 434
Jin, X. A., 572
Jobe, R. L., 317
Jogerst, G. J., 612
John, R. S., 63, 114, 445, 448
Johnsen, M. C., 254, 278
Johnson, A., 406
Johnson, B. D., 50, 297
Johnson, B. L., 402, 404, 410
Johnson, C., 413, 445
Johnson, C. A., 318
Johnson, C. F., 208, 237, 359
Johnson, C. L., 327
Johnson, D. M., 370, 400, 402, 532
Johnson, H., 403
Johnson, I., 586, 589
Johnson, I. M., 402
Johnson, J. D., 289
Johnson, J. G., 50, 51, 166, 169, 314, 430, 445, 446, 447, 465
Johnson, J. M., 405

Johnson, K., 478, 489
Johnson, K. A., 223, 227
Johnson, K. B., 478
Johnson, M., 509
Johnson, M. C., 345
Johnson, M. P., 428, 429, 462
Johnson, M. S., 543
Johnson, N., 332
Johnson, P. J., 6
Johnson, R. E., 179
Johnson, R. M., 111
Johnson, S., 54
Johnson-Reid, M., 171
Johnston, P., 240
Johsson, F. H., 360
Jolich, S., 201, 226
Jolley, J., 171
Jones, A., 438, 445, 446, 466, 501
Jones, A. A., 553
Jones, A. S., 3, 556, 557
Jones, D., 616
Jones, D. P. H., 176, 190
Jones, H. E., 88
Jones, J. A., 636
Jones, L., 151, 187, 209, 499, 606
Jones, L. M., 243, 244
Jones, N. T., 69
Jones, R., 240
Jordan, C. E., 32, 347, 533
Jordan, S., 485
Joseph, C., 577
Jospitre, T., 292
Jouriles, E. N., 18, 24, 66, 112, 127, 172, 285
Ju, S., 191
Judy, A., 607
Julian, T. W., 435
Julian, T. W., 374, 451
Juvekar, S., 477
Juvinyà, D., 627

Kabani, N., 229, 231
Kabat, S., 61
Kadrak, K., 638
Kaffman, A., 86, 96
Kagan, J., 171, 453
Kahler, C. W., 567
Kahler, D. W., 464
Kahn, A. S., 334
Kahn, J. A., 298
Kahn, J. M., 156
Kahn, R. S., 173, 454
Kahntroff, J., 588
Kalaher, S., 427
Kalich, D. M., 559

Kalichman, S. C., 516
Kalmuss, D. S., 445
Kalsy-Lillico, S., 634
Kalu, B. K., 474
Kam, C. C. -S., 355
Kaminski, A., 303, 332
Kaminski, R. J., 523
Kandel-Englander, E., 457
Kane, R. A., 56
Kane, T. A., 436
Kanin, E. J., 307
Kantor, G. K., 35, 113, 447, 500, 503
Kaplan, S. J., 254
Kar, S. K., 476
Karch, D. L., 4
Karp, J., 330
Karpinski, A., 41
Karpos, M., 61
Karu, T., 111
Karyl, J., 116
Kashner, T. M., 524
Kasl, C. D., 216
Kaslow, N. J., 504, 505, 506, 573, 628
Kassem, L., 271
Kast, L. C., 246
Katturupalli, M., 99, 100
Katz, J., 316
Katz, L. E., 129
Kaufman, K. L., 10
Kaufman, J., 160
Kaufman Kantor, G., 85
Kaukinen, C., 314, 315
Kaura, S. A., 317
Kavanagh, A. M., 358
Kaviahan, D. R., 523
Kavoussi, R. J., 454
Kawalski, A., 509, 510, 511
Kazdin, A. E., 263, 558
Kearns-Bodkin, J. N., 449, 568
Keat, J. E., 572
Keating, J., 237, 240
Keca, M., 612
Keel, B., 262
Keeley, S., 390
Keeny, L., 344
Keer, M. G., 580
Kehoe, G. C., 608, 621
Keilitz, S. L., 388, 457, 560
Kelleher, K. J., 420, 506
Keller, B. H., 637
Keller, C. S., 20, 77
Keller, J., 370
Kelley, S. J., 88
Kellogg, N. D., 287

Kelly, C. M., 620
Kelly, D. B., 266
Kelly, J. B., 428, 429
Kelly, K., 331
Kelly, K. D., 310
Kelly, M. M., 99
Kelly, N., 366
Kelly, S. P., 619
Kemic, M. A., 394
Kemmelmeier, M., 116
Kemp, A., 374
Kempe, C. H., 11, 173
Kempe, R. S., 99
Kendall-Tackett, K. A., 8, 98, 223, 227
Kendziora, K. T., 284
Kenna, C. E., 405, 542
Kennair, N., 262, 263
Kennedy, C. S., 531
Kennedy, C. S., 542
Kennedy, L. T., 371, 374
Kennedy, R. D., 613
Kenney, B. A., 374
Kenning, M. K., 114
Kent, A., 125
Kercher, G. A., 216, 217, 345
Kerig, P. K., 301
Kern, J. M., 372
Kernic, M. A., 380, 389, 399, 400, 406
Kernsmith, P., 25, 368, 389, 392, 393, 425, 428, 463, 567
Kerr, M. S., 103
Kerzner, B., 100
Kesmodal, U. S., 88
Kesner, J. E., 374, 436
Kessler, R. C., 53, 62, 74, 177, 225, 421, 434, 435, 524
Ketcham, K., 202
Ketelaar, T., 335
Kethineni, S., 388
Keyson, M., 366
Khan, A., 481
Khan, M. M., 482
Khan, R., 268
Khawaja, M., 483, 484
Khera, S., 422
Kidula, N., 474
Kiecolt, K. J., 274
Kiecolt-Glaser, J. K., 370, 451
Kieffer, K. M., 416, 550
Kiely, M., 88
Kier, F. J., 416, 550
Kiever, P., 49
Killip, S., 154
Kilpatrick, D. G., 324, 403, 533
Kim, G., 481, 482
Kim, H., 557, 562, 627

Kozlowska, K., 97
Kracke, K., 115, 130, 150, 208, 212, 226
Kraemer, K. L., 567
Kralik, D., 315
Krammer, L., 407
Kranzler, H. R., 553
Kraus, J. F., 500
Krauss, R. M., 203
Krebs, N. F., 99
Kreig, S., 157
Krieglstein, M., 383
Krienert, J. L., 262, 263, 265, 333
Krishman, S., 384, 477, 574
Krishnan, S. P., 66, 178, 506, 508, 509, 529
Kristjanson, A. F., 203
Krohn, S., 622
Krook, K., 200
Kropp, P. R., 442, 443
Kropp, R., 491
Krueger, R. F., 53
Krueger, S., 634
Krugman, S. D., 404
Kruttschnitt, C., 62, 413, 465
Krysik, J., 216, 217
Kub, J., 401, 529
Kubrin, C., 445
Kuchibhatla, M., 159
Kuehnle, K., 31, 394, 516
Kugel, C., 574
Kuhn, J. C., 79
Kulczycki, A., 486, 490
Kuleshnyk, I., 375
Kulwicki, A. D., 7, 483
Kumar, S., 483
Kunik, M. E., 607
Kuo, D., 155, 159
Kuo, M., 319
Kupper, L., 630
Kupper, L. L., 179, 284
Kurdek, L. A., 519
Kurlychek, M. C., 297
Kurrle, S. E., 626
Kurtz, P. D., 96, 98, 156
Kury, H., 369, 485, 486
Kurz, D., 17, 68
Kusche, A. G., 435
Kuvalanka, K. A., 579
Kuzuya, M., 608
Kwong, M. J., 420, 436
Kynan, S., 242
Kypri, K., 333, 336

La Bash, H. A. J., 120
La Roche, M., 80, 571

La Taillade, J. J., 572, 573
Laakso, J. H., 406
Laaser, U., 485
Labeeb, S., 482
LaBell, L. S., 35
Labonte, B., 24
Labriola, M., 553
Lacayo, R., 21
Lachicotte, W., 603
Lachs, M. S., 607
Lackie, L., 334, 335
Laffaye, C., 531
LaGasse, L. L., 88
Laible, D. J., 187
Laidlaw, T. M., 551
Lalumière, M. L., 223, 230, 232, 233
Lam, B. T., 501
Lamb, M. E., 121, 124, 163, 252
Lamb, S., 286
Lambert, E. G., 512
Lambert, L. C., 49
Lambert, N. M., 420
Lambidoni, E., 286
Lamke, L. K., 116, 445, 448
Land, D., 27, 245, 246
Landenburger, K. M., 401
Landini, A., 97
Landolt, M. A., 435, 438, 440, 514, 519
Landon, P. A., 241
Landsverk, J. A., 69, 104, 420, 504, 506
Landy, C. K., 119
Lane, G., 54
Lang, A., 21
Lang, A. J., 178
Langan, P. A., 307, 357, 417, 420
Langer, A., 313, 401
Langford, D., 542
Langford, L., 61
Langhinrichsen-Rohling, J., 16, 68, 346, 366, 376, 378, 379, 402, 429, 448, 450, 457, 459, 462, 523, 548
Lanier, C. A., 338
Lanning, K. V., 203
Lansford, J. E., 154, 155, 156, 254
Lanthier, R. P., 108
Lanza-Kaduce, L., 297
Laporte, L., 64, 435
Larsen, R., 441
Lash, S. J., 49, 449, 452
Latta, R. E., 500, 572
Lauderdale, J., 79
Laughlin, J. E., 313, 318
Laughon, N., 441
Laumann, E. O., 438, 478, 479, 591, 593, 599, 627
Laumann-Billings, L., 35, 189, 200, 265, 266

Lien, L., 383, 384
Light, D., 331
Liles, S., 533
Lilienfeld, S. O., 455
Lilith, R., 514
Liljequist, L., 246
Lilley, D., 326
Lilly, M. M., 118, 504
Lim, H., 356
Limcangco, R., 404
Lin, K., 314
Lin, R., 88
Lincoln, A. J., 3
Lincoln, Y., 519
Lind, L., 524
Linder, F., 285
Linder, G. F., 288, 299
Linder, J. R., 289
Lindgren, A. S., 73, 335, 366, 369, 374, 378, 379, 380
Lindgren, K. P., 335
Lindhorst, T. P., 337, 339, 406, 540
Lindquist, C., 298
Lindsay, R. C. L., 242
Lindsay, S., 636
Linos, N., 484
Linville, D., 578
Lippen, V., 395, 396
Lipper, E. G., 55
Lipsky, S., 70
Lithwick, M., 611
Litrownik, A. J., 85, 86, 157, 227
Littel, K., 327
Little, L., 113
Little, V., 187
Littleton, H., 359
Litzenberger, B. W., 271
Liu, G., 627
Liu, R. T., 162
Liu, X., 22, 581
Livingston, G., 606
Livingston, J. A., 258, 259
Livingston, N. A., 64, 463, 514
Lizotte, A. J., 27
Llewelyn, S. P., 237
Lloyd, S. A., 36, 288, 366
Lo, B., 30
Lobach, K. S., 283
Localio, A. R., 115, 129
Locke, H. J., 448
Locke, T. F., 50
Lockhart, L. L., 511
Loeb, A., 270
Loeber, R., 72, 254, 457
Loftus, E. F., 202, 205

Logan, J. E., 4
Logan, T., 17, 343, 345, 347, 349, 350, 351, 374, 389, 508, 509, 510, 511, 538, 575
Logan, T. K., 382
Logsdon, M. C., 173, 174
Loh, C., 322, 338
Lohman, B. J., 317
Lohr, B. A., 333
Lombard, C., 474
Lombreglia, M., 33
London, A. S., 384, 405, 540
London, K., 201
London, M., 589, 606
Long, J., 160
Long, N., 78
Long, S. M., 178, 384, 529, 574
Longley, J., 327
Longshore, K., 316, 317
Lonsway, K. A., 389
Loomis, D., 179
Lopez, E. G., 438
Lopez, F. G., 312, 318
Lopez, P. A., 335
López-Pousa, S., 627
Lord, V., 394
Lorenz, L., 290, 291
Loring, M. R., 12
Loring, M. T., 375
Loseke, D. R., 9, 41, 67
Lount, M., 404
Lovallo, W. R., 453, 464
Lovera, S., 489, 490
Lovrich, N. P., 327
Lowenberg, K., 297
Lowenfels, A., 126, 128
Lowenstein, A., 590
Lucente, S. W., 69
Luchok, K. J., 529
Luck, L., 126, 127
Luh, K. E., 455
Luke, D. A., 115
Luke, N., 478, 479
Luke, W., 516
Luna-Firebaugh, A. M., 574
Lundberg, K., 51, 446
Lundhal, B., 127
Lundy, M., 497, 632, 634
Luntz, H., 262
Luo, Y., 438, 478, 479, 627
Lupri, E., 5, 49
Lussier, Y., 226
Lutz, J. G., 156
Lutz-Zois, C., 535
Lutzker, J. R., 128, 172, 185

Ly, U., 394
Lyden, M., 632
Lynam, D. R., 254
Lynch, M., 182
Lynch, P. J., 289
Lynch, S., 115, 129
Lynch, S. M., 35, 410, 423
Lynn, A. E., 171, 179
Lynnes, M. D., 634
Lynnes, M. D., 271
Lynskey, M., 449
Lyon, E., 367
Lyon, T. D., 202, 203
Lyons, A. M., 535
Lyons-Ruth, K., 98, 177
Lysova, A., 354

Maalouf, M., 77
MacDonald, J. M., 563
Macdonald, S., 119
MacDougall, J. E., 288, 299
Mace, N. L., 601
Macfie, J., 159
MacGregor, M. W., 551
Maciol, K., 269, 270
Mack, K. P., 382
Mack, S. M., 149
Macke, C., 382, 538
Mackey, A. L., 266, 271
MacLean, D., 551
MacMillan, H., 154, 372
MacMillan, H. L., 127, 234, 492, 543
Macmillan, R., 413, 539
Macolini, R. M., 114
Macvaugh, G. S., III, 551
Macy, R. J., 55, 383, 540
Macy, T. J., 333, 336, 338
Madden, P., 449
Madison, J. R., 417
Madry, L., 71, 292, 313, 354, 410, 466, 531, 534
Madsen, M. D., 118
Maekoya, C., 161, 162
Maercker, A., 232
Magaña, S., 121
Magaziner, J., 636
Magdol, L., 48, 67, 255, 298, 355
Magee, M. M., 318
Magruder, B., 48
Magruder, K. M., 209, 524
Maguigan, H., 78
Maguin, E., 119
Maguire, K., 324
Maguire, M., 457, 485
Mahalingam, R., 470, 471

Mahlstedt, D. L., 311, 344
Mahoney, A. R., 569
Mai, B. T. T., 478, 479
Maier, S. F., 377, 378
Maikovich-Fong, A. K., 225, 226
Mailey, B., 612
Main, M., 162
Maiuro, R. D., 341
Majdan, A., 309
Maker, A. H., 116, 356, 358
Maker, H., 181
Makoroff, K. L., 202
Malamuth, N. M., 333
Malcoe, L. H., 497
Malecha, A., 449, 608
Malefyt, M. B., 327
Maletzky, B. M., 32, 239
Maley, S., 632
Malkin, C., 338
Mallett, C. A., 154, 278
Malley-Morrison, K., 19, 626
Malloy, K., 6, 71, 363, 399, 403, 409, 410, 419, 424
Malone, P. S., 154, 156
Malone, T. B., 634
Malsch, M., 350
Mammen, O., 171
Mandel, D., 134
Mandel, D. L., 553
Mandel, F. S., 254
Manders, J. E., 167
Mandeville-Norden, R., 238, 239
Manetta, A. A., 56
Mangione, C. M., 613
Mankowski, E. S., 549
Mann, J. R., 473
Mann, R., 201, 232
Mannarino, A. P., 236
Manseau, H., 286
Mansoor, E., 87
Manthorpe, J., 628
Mapp, S. C., 209, 211, 213, 229, 234, 245
Marciol, K., 259
Marcum, J. L., 587, 635
Marcus, R. F., 54, 315, 319
Marcynszyn, L. A., 213, 372
Marczyk, G., 257
Margolin, G., 36, 63, 74, 114, 315, 445, 448
Margolin, L., 323
Margrave, C., 509, 510, 511
Marino, R., 100
Markiewicz, D., 120, 178, 288, 376
Markman, H. J., 318
Marks, N. F., 111
Marmar, C. R., 21

Marotta, S. A., 108
Marques, J., 240
Marriott, K. A., 338
Marsh, N., 459
Marshall, A. D., 52, 458, 522
Marshall, C. E., 404
Marshall, D., 338
Marshall, J., 323
Marshall, J. M., 201
Marshall, L. E., 235
Marshall, L. L., 155, 422, 429, 464, 465, 500, 502, 513, 533, 567
Marshall, M. A., 430
Marshall, P., 215
Marshall, P. J., 93
Marshall, S. W., 120, 179, 209
Marshall, W. L., 230, 231, 235, 240, 241, 328
Marsil, D. F., 589
Martin, A., 56, 632, 633
Martin, E. K., 225
Martin, G. J., 543
Martin, J., 155
Martin, J. A., 192
Martin, L. E., 523
Martin, L. J., 474
Martin, M. E., 391
Martin, M. M., 637
Martin, M. V., 221
Martin, P. Y., 334, 343, 348
Martin, R. H., 524
Martin, S. K., 120, 209, 581
Martin, S. L., 32, 114, 121, 171, 179, 187, 284, 332, 523, 524, 530, 543, 545, 630
Martinez, I. L., 598, 615
Martinez, T. E., 366, 440, 464
Martins, D., 627
Martz, J. M., 535
Marx, B. P., 52, 225, 271, 517, 519
Mascher, J., 494
Mascia, K., 280
Mash, E. J., 156
Masho, S. W., 336
Mason, A., 594, 606, 608, 616
Mason, G. E., 178, 384, 529, 574
Mason, W. A., 172, 255, 310
Massad, P. M., 532
Mastel-Smith, B., 608
Masters, N. T., 334, 336, 359
Mastrofski, S. D., 390
Masuda, Y., 608
Mata-Pariente, N., 485
Mathes, E. W., 440, 441
Mathews, B., 189, 244
Mathews, R., 370, 372
Mathews, S., 474

Mathieson, L. C., 126, 128
Matlaw, J. R., 619
Maton, K. L., 397, 561
Matthew, M., 545
Matthews, K. A., 538
Mattick, R. P., 160
Mattingly, M. J., 117, 118
Mattis, J., 500
Mattison, E., 15
Maughan, B., 162
Maurer, T. W., 329
Mauricio, A. M., 425, 438
Max, W., 25, 341
Maxfield, M. G., 446
Maxwell, C. D., 60, 395, 562
Mayda, A. S., 486
Mayer, J., 590
Mays, J. M., 629, 630
Mayseless, O., 288, 376, 410, 437, 534
Maziak, W., 483
Mazur, C. M., 371, 380, 465
Mazur, P., 159
Mazure, C. M., 379, 400, 401, 402, 459
Mazzeo, S. E., 401
Mcaffrey, D., 282
McAuslan, P., 330
McCarroll, J. E., 22, 522, 523, 581, 582
McCarthy, G., 318, 436
McCauley, J., 324, 508, 510, 576
McClay, J., 155
McCloskey, K., 6, 71, 363, 399, 403, 409, 410, 419, 424
McCloskey, L. A., 114, 116, 287, 400, 401, 402, 406, 485, 506, 531, 532
McCloskey, M. S., 453, 553
McClung, J. J., 176
McColgan, M. D., 129
McCormick, A. J., 564
McCourt, J., 271
McCray, J. A., 562
McCreary, D. R., 6
McCree, J. S., 104
McCuiston, A. M., 283
McCurdy, K., 245
McCurley, C., 263, 272, 284
McDonald, R., 18, 24, 66, 112, 127, 172, 285
McDuff, P., 229, 269, 272, 303
McElhaney, K. B., 6
McFall, C., 615
McFall, R. M., 558
McFarlane, J. M., 20, 66, 341, 394, 449, 495, 542
McFaul, A., 315
McFeeley, S., 374
McGarry, J., 588, 591
McGillicuddy-DeLise, A., 316, 317

Middleton, K. A., 51, 446

Migliaccio, T. A., 413

Mihalic, D. E., 419

Mihalic, S. W., 50, 448

Mihaly, C., 594, 606, 608, 616

Mikjkovitch, R., 229

Mikolajerczyk, R. T., 482

Milberger, S., 56, 632, 633

Miles, A., 405

Miles, T., 15

Mill, J., 155

Miller, B., 323

Miller, C. E., 561

Miller, D. R., 523

Miller, E., 298

Miller, G. E., 111, 532

Miller, J., 465, 541, 562

Miller, J. R., 496

Miller, L. M., 555

Miller, M., 323

Miller, M. K., 133, 242

Miller, S., 77, 202, 285

Miller, S. L., 18, 315, 392, 567

Miller, T. R., 25

Miller-Cribbs, J., 541

Miller-Perrin, C. L., 32, 200, 208, 221, 222, 234, 235, 246

Millington, G., 201

Millis, L., 175

Millon, T., 451

Mills, J. S., 6

Milner, J. S., 53, 157, 171, 178

Milofsky, E. S., 552

Milteer, R., 323

Min, L. C., 637

Min, P. G., 43

Mineka, S., 369, 377

Minh, T. H., 478, 479

Minkle, M., 589

Minow, J. C., 335

Mio, J. S., 67, 74, 404, 425, 532

Mischel, W., 78

Misri, S., 175

Mitchell, J. K., 280

Mitchell, K. J., 280

Mitchell, M. D., 121

Mitchell, R. E., 535

Mitchell, S., 7

Mitchell-Herzfeld, S., 126, 128

Mixson, P. M., 615

Miyake, K., 54

Mize, K. D., 20

Modecki, K. L., 284

Modzeleski, W., 280

Moe, A. M., 382, 397, 405, 425, 578

Moe, B. K., 153

Moerkbak, M. L., 374

Moffitt, T. E., 48, 50, 53, 67, 155, 161, 162, 255, 298, 309, 355, 445

Moghadam, S., 569

Mohamed, S., 114

Mohandie, K., 347

Mohler-Kuo, M., 35

Mohr, P. B., 371

Mohr, W. K., 76

Molidor, C. E., 291, 315

Molnar, B. E., 53, 62, 225, 435

Monahan, J., 456

Monahan, K., 370

Monda-Amaya, L. E., 161

Mongillo, E. A., 79

Monk, P., 263

Monnier, J., 213, 524, 581

Mont-Turner, E., 331

Montgomery, J. M., 497

Moohnan, V., 125, 126

Moon, A., 628

Moor, A., 157

Moore, A. R., 474, 476

Moore, C. B., 485

Moore, C. G., 213

Moore, C. M., 6

Moore, D. W., 70, 95, 110, 150

Moore, S. D., 451, 524

Moore, T. M., 69, 408, 445, 452, 464, 561, 567

Moorhead, C., 322

Moos, R. H., 374, 535

Morabito, A. S., 563

Moracco, K. E., 365, 530, 543

Moran, P. B., 323

Morash, M., 496, 504, 506

Mordini, N. M., 390

Morelli, G., 54

Morency, N. L., 203

Morgan, A. B., 455

Morgan, E., 586, 589

Moriarty, L. J., 17

Morley, R., 407

Morocco, K., 630

Morrel, T. M., 558

Morrill-Richards, M., 267

Morris, A., 480

Morris, S., 205

Morrison, A. R., 372

Morrison, K. E., 529

Morrison, S., 298

Morrow, C., 87

Morrow, M., 404

Morse, B. J., 62

Morton, E., 365

Paulozzi, L. J., 389
Paulus, M. P., 44
Pavao, J., 303, 332, 382
Paveza, G. J., 601
Pavlos, C. A., 370, 372, 571
Paymar, M., 549
Payne, B. K., 79, 332, 541, 590, 618, 637
Payne, E., 318
Payne, J., 540
Paz, F., 489
Peace, K. A., 203
Peacock, D., 296, 563
Pear, R., 635
Pearl, J., 59
Pearlman, D. N., 61, 71
Pearsall, C., 612
Pearson, C. L., 237, 438, 466
Pease, B., 544
Peel, J. C. F., 271
Pelcovitz, D., 254
Peled, E., 535
Pelligrini, A. D., 160
Pence, D. M., 132
Pence, E. L., 7, 33, 382, 549
Pendry, N. C., 537
Penke, L., 440
Penley, J. A., 373, 535
Penn, P., 550
Pereda, N., 212
Perez, L. M., 416, 550
Perez, R., 612
Pérez-Albéniz, A., 181
Perilla, J. L., 57
Perisse, A. R., 404
Perkins, C. A., 35, 55, 373, 378, 394, 425
Perlesz, A., 262
Perrin, R. D., 32, 200
Perron, A., 269, 272
Perry, P. A., 560
Pesackis, C. E., 503
Peter, T., 216, 227
Peterman, L. M., 515, 578
Peters, J. M., 33, 176, 375
Petersen, R., 543
Peterson, C., 116, 378
Peterson, E. L., 52
Petit, G. S., 155, 254
Petta, I., 83, 85, 90, 91, 93, 94, 101, 102, 103, 108, 112, 117, 119, 146, 153, 156, 165, 167, 169, 170, 178, 179, 193, 206, 209, 211, 212, 213, 214, 253
Petula, S. Y. H., 355
Pfeifer, S., 251
Pfeiffer, S. M., 440
Pflieger, J. C., 287

Pfohl, S. J., 10, 11
Pharaon, N. A., 481
Phares, V., 246
Pharr, R., 287
Phelan, J. E., 316, 317
Phelan, M. B., 44, 369, 543, 562
Philipsen, N. C., 133
Phillips, D. A., 280
Phillips, L. R., 601
Pianta, R. C., 370
Picke, C., 335
Pickens, R. W., 45
Pico-Alfonso, M. A., 71, 380
Pierce, T. W., 287
Piers, M. W., 10
Pike, C. K. M., 557, 558
Pilkonis, P., 171
Pilla, R. S., 160, 279
Pillemer, K. A., 17, 56, 597, 598, 601, 602, 607, 621
Pine, C., 329
Pines, A. M., 221, 441
Pinto-Foltz, M. D., 174
Pirisi, L., 372
Pitanguy, J., 568
Pithers, W., 241
Pittman, F., 268
Pittman, J. F., 116, 445, 448
Pitts, S. C., 85, 86
Pitts, V., 56
Pitula, C. R., 407, 408, 500
Pitzner, J. K., 423
Pizzey, E., 484
Planas-Pujol, X., 627
Plante, E. G., 322
Platt, C., 285
Plazaolo-Castaño, J., 485
Pleck, E., 11, 14, 15
Pledger, C., 121
Pless, A. P., 525
Plichta, S., 79
Podesta, J. S., 327, 407
Pogarsky, G., 27
Poindexter, V. C., 71
Pol, H. E., 454
Poland, R. E., 453
Polcari, A., 143
Pollak, S. D., 162
Pollet, S. L., 33
Pollio, D. F., 256
Polusny, M. A., 226, 371
Pons-Salvador, G., 171, 177
Pontius, A. A., 369, 370
Poole, A., 129
Poorman, P. B., 354, 580

Pope, K. H., 107
Pope, M., 498
Popejoy, L. L., 638
Port, L. K., 190
Porter, A., 558
Porter, L., 403
Porter, R., 638
Porter, S., 203
Porterfield, F., 192
Portwood, S. G., 64
Post, L., 635
Postmus, J. L., 8, 134, 365, 529, 542
Poteat, V. P., 161, 162, 294
Potente, T., 68, 462, 568
Potoczniak, D. J., 517, 579
Potoczniak, M. J., 517, 579
Pott, M., 54
Potter, L., 56, 632, 633
Potter, M., 610
Pouquette, C. L., 103
Povilaitis, T. Y., 103
Powell, M. B., 244
Powell, M. E., 608
Power, C., 315
Powers, J. L., 251
Powers, L. E., 632, 633
Pozzoli, T., 161
Prather, R. A., 513, 626
Pratt, T. C., 327
Preece, M., 374
Preechawon, S., 608
Prentky, R. A., 459
Presley, C. A., 334
Preston, C., 563
Preston, J., 490
Preston, S., 601
Prestopnik, J. L., 256
Price, D. L., 192
Price, L. H., 99
Price, M., 521, 524
Priest, B., 600, 605
Primm, B. J., 71, 313, 466, 531, 534
Prinz, R. J., 128, 171, 172
Prinzie, P., 92
Probst, D. R., 338
Procci, W. R., 409
Procter, E. K., 558
Prokhorov, A., 635
Proulx, J., 220
Pruett, K. D., 75, 80
Pryce, J. M., 119
Pryor, D. W., 220
Ptacek, J., 378, 387, 389, 397
Puente, S., 313, 319, 356, 438, 441, 466

Puett, R., 505
Purdie, V., 287
Purewal, J., 401, 476
Purk, J. K., 636
Puryear-Keita, G., 65
Puster, K. L., 298
Putcha-Bhagavatula, A., 324
Puzzanchera, C., 278
Pyles, L., 8, 367

Quadagno, D., 453, 454
Quas, J. A., 244
Quelopana, A. M., 88, 489, 491
Quigley, B. M., 449, 568
Quinn, K., 614
Quinn, M. J., 584
Quinsey, V. L., 53, 230, 254, 453

Rabi, K., 143
Rabiner, D. J., 587, 620, 622
Rabinowitz, S. S., 99, 100
Racusin, R., 177
Radford, L., 75
Radosevich, A. C., 346
Rafnsson, F. D., 360
Raghavan, C., 311, 317, 358, 379, 400, 401, 402, 459
Ragin, D. F., 313, 410, 534
Raine, A., 230, 455
Raj, A., 332, 372, 495, 499, 504
Raja, S., 369, 387, 404, 538
Rajadhyaksha, A., 453
Rajah, V., 358, 392
Rakowsky, J., 280
Ramachandran, M., 158
Ramakrishnan, K., 290, 291
Ramirez, M., 588
Ramiro, L., 483
Ramisetty-Mikler, S., 70, 155, 178, 424, 466, 469, 500
Ramsey, J., 542
Ramsey, S. E., 464, 567
Ramsey-Klawsnik, H., 587, 600, 606, 607, 635
Rand, M., 342, 344, 345, 347, 348
Rand, M. R., 4, 35, 55, 284, 309, 325, 373, 378, 394, 419, 425, 590, 629, 631, 632, 634
Randolf, M. K., 66
Rantala, R. R., 307, 357, 417, 420
Rantz, M. J., 638
Raphael, J., 43, 364, 382, 383
Rapoza, K. A., 154, 288
Rappleyea, D. L., 562
Rashid, A., 505
Rastogi, M., 477, 478
Rathod, S., 477
Ratner, C., 71

Ruiz-Pérez, I., 485
Runfola, C., 318
Runge, M. M., 363
Runge, R. R., 537, 538
Runyan, C. W., 365, 545
Runyan, D. K., 66, 70, 85, 86, 95, 110, 113, 114, 121, 150, 171, 181, 187, 192, 202, 228
Runyon, M. K., 163, 184, 186, 234
Rupert, L. J., 156
Rusbult, C. E., 408, 535
Rushe, R., 379, 432
Russell, A., 15
Russell, B. L., 392
Russell, D., 115, 129
Russell, D. E. H., 48, 219, 422
Russell, D. P., 268
Russell, R. K., 519
Russell, S. T., 293
Russell, T., 54
Russo, F., 601
Russo, M. J., 287
Russo, N. F., 65, 332
Rutlowski-Kmitta, V., 369
Rutter, P. A., 517
Ryan, D. P., 154
Ryan, G., 310
Ryan, J. P., 278
Ryan, R. M., 96
Ryan-Wenger, N. A., 216
Rye, M. S., 535

Sabia, J. J., 621
Sabina, C., 283, 310, 504, 506
Sabini, J., 268, 314, 440
Sable, M. R., 384
Sabourin, C. M., 378, 379
Sabourin, S., 226
Sachs-Ericsson, N., 178
Sackett, R., 427
Sacks, J. J., 47
Saczynski, J., 601
Sadler, A. G., 179
Sadowski, L. S., 483
Sadusky, J. M., 634
Saewye, E. M., 222, 259
Saey, T. H., 51, 436
Saez-Betacourt, A., 501
Safyer, A., 119
Sagarin, B. J., 440
Sage, R. E., 71, 292, 313, 354, 410, 466, 531, 534
Saggurti, N., 499, 504
Sagrestano, L. M., 442
Sagy, S., 374
Sahin, H., 486

Sahin, H., 486
Sahr, R., 341
Sakalli-U urlu, N., 356
Sakamoto, A., 289
Saladino, A., 634
Salami, H. A., 474
Salari, Z., 482
Salazar, B. C., 88, 489, 491
Salazar, L. F., 298
Salisbury, E. J., 121
Salmon, D. A., 92
Salmon, K., 144
Salomon, A., 463, 532, 590, 591, 592, 595, 597, 599, 601, 604, 605, 608, 609, 613, 615, 616
Salpekar, N., 213, 372
Saltzman, L. E., 343
Saltzman, L. E., 3, 23, 44, 65, 308, 328, 389, 403, 418, 419, 425
Saltzman, L. S., 308, 429
Salzinger, S., 153, 154, 160, 166, 169, 254
Sambria, A., 539
Samper, R. E., 433, 551
Samuels, G. M., 119
Sanders, A., 394
Sanders, L., 455
Sanders, M. J., 176
Sanders, M. R., 128, 172
Sanderson, M., 310, 372
Sandfort, T. G. M., 294
Sandin, E., 434, 438
Sandino, K. J., 284
Sandman, C. A., 88
Sandnabba, N. K., 200, 242
Sanford, L. D., 372
Sanghvi, R., 318
Sanna, L., 237
Santana, S. A., 326
Santtila, P., 200, 242
Sappington, A. A., 287
Saradjian, J., 216, 217
Sareen, J., 153, 177, 372
Sartin, R. M., 561
Sasaki, A., 24
Sauder, C. L., 225
Saudino, K. J., 453
Saunders, B. E., 163, 199, 206, 220, 226, 403, 533
Saunders, D. G., 17, 68, 286, 287, 298, 379, 404, 405, 412, 459, 462, 463, 539, 542
Savage, M. P., 29
Saveman, B., 633
Sawhney, D. K., 373, 374
Sawyer, C., 9
Saxton, M., 632
Saywitz, K. J., 202, 203, 236
Sbarra, D. A., 312, 356

Scalora, M. J., 201, 216, 235
Scarce, M., 354
Scelfo, J., 62, 335, 454
Schacht, R. I., 551
Schaechter, J., 421, 562
Schaefer, S., 296
Schafer, J., 70, 72, 417, 450
Scheidt, P., 160, 279
Schel, B., 471, 485
Schell, B. H., 221
Schiff, M., 533
Schilit, R., 538
Schiller, D., 572
Schillinger, D., 30
Schindehette, S., 407, 577
Schipper, L. D., 291
Schlegel, E., 396
Schlichter, K., 542
Schmechel, D., 629
Schmitt, B. D., 157
Schmitt, E. L., 241
Schmuch, G. A., 612
Schnack, H. G., 454
Schneider, A., 611
Schneider, J., 259, 269, 270, 327
Schneider, J. W., 32
Schneider, O., 355
Schneider, R., 225, 227
Schneidlin, B., 192
Schnurr, P. P., 524
Schoenwald, S. K., 274
Scholle, S. H., 400
Schollenberger, J., 422, 503
Schor, E. L., 184
Schornstein, S. L., 542
Schott, G., 274
Schrock, D. P., 550, 578
Schroeder, C., 163, 186, 226, 234
Schroeder, C. M., 246
Schubert, C., 603
Schubert, C. C., 589
Schug, R. A., 230
Schuler, M. E., 88
Schuler, S. R., 478, 479
Schuller, R. A., 324
Schulman, R. S., 452
Schultz, L. R., 52
Schultz, P., 449
Schumacher, J. A., 64, 71, 433, 449, 453, 553, 557, 568
Schumann, G., 454
Schutte, K. K., 374
Schutz, J., 266
Schwalbe, C., 156
Schwartyz, W. E., 271

Schwartz, D., 578
Schwartz, J. P., 318, 335
Schwartz, M., 610
Schwartz, M. D., 24, 56, 70, 73, 284, 288, 402, 508, 533, 541
Schwartz, R. H., 323
Scionti, T., 485
Scott, C. L., 239
Scott, E. C., 446
Scott, E. K., 384, 405, 540
Scott, H., 53
Scott, J., 435
Scott, K., 317
Scott, K. L., 154
Scribano, P. V., 244
Scruggs, N., 628
Seal, C. A., 610, 618, 623
Seamans, C. L., 462
Sebold, J., 553, 554
Sechrist, S. M., 307
Seck, M. M., 154, 278
Sedlak, A. J., 83, 85, 87, 90, 91, 93, 94, 101, 102, 103, 108, 112, 117, 119, 146, 153, 156, 165, 167, 169, 170, 178, 179, 193, 206, 209, 211, 212, 213, 214, 253
Sedlar, G., 53
Seedat, S., 379
Seefelt, J. L., 290, 328
Seehafer, R., 29
Seelau, E. P., 354, 580
Seelau, S. M., 354, 580
Seeman, T. E., 115
Seff, L. R., 591, 595, 608
Sefl, T., 336
Segal, M. L., 47
Segal, S. R., 610
Sege, R. D., 86, 146
Segel, H. D., 612
Segrin, C., 408
Seid, A. G., 533
Seiffge-Krenke, I., 312
Seitz, S., 402
Seligman, M. E. P., 376, 378
Sellbom, M., 560
Sellinger, M., 407
Semel, M. A., 62
Semla, T., 601
Semmelroth, J., 441
Senchak, M., 442
Seng, A. C., 171
Seng, M., 560
Senier, L., 523
Senn, C. Y., 45, 55, 288, 319, 323, 329
Sennour, Y., 589
Sequin, L., 173
Serbin, L., 330

Simpson, L. E., 401, 442
Simpson, S. M., 87, 89
Simpson, S. S., 315, 395
Sinden, P. G., 394
Singer, D., 637
Sionainn, C., 626
Sirkin, M., 316
Sitaker, M., 6, 71, 363, 399, 403, 409, 410, 419, 424
Sitren, A. H., 49
Sitzman, R., 616, 631
Sivanathan, N., 378
Sivayogan, S., 476
Skidmore, J. R., 452
Skilling, T. A., 254
Skinner, K. M., 523
Sklar, D., 421
Skopp, N. A., 157
Skybo, T., 159
Slack, K. S., 171
Slashinski, M. J., 326, 341
Slatt, L., 542
Slattery, S. M., 78
Sledjeski, E. M., 371
Slep, A. M. S., 18, 24, 35, 54, 59, 68, 69, 71, 77, 172, 179, 183, 369, 433, 440, 442, 450, 451, 464, 465, 466, 557
Slesnick, N., 256
Sloat, K., 122
Sloop, K. S., 401, 408, 410, 576
Smailes, E. M., 50, 51, 97, 226, 314, 445, 571
Smallbone, S. W., 355
Smiljanich, K., 230
Smith, A., 20, 417
Smith, C., 31, 49, 379, 549, 553
Smith, C. A., 160, 226, 251, 252, 254, 255, 257, 260, 261
Smith, D. B., 443
Smith, D. L., 296, 631
Smith, D. W., 295, 449
Smith, E., 86
Smith, E. L., 307, 357, 417, 420
Smith, J. B., 70
Smith, J. P., 314
Smith, K., 589, 625, 626
Smith, K. R., 192, 523
Smith, K. S., 159
Smith, M., 204
Smith, M. W., 382
Smith, P., 318
Smith, P. H., 56, 66, 70, 423
Smith, R., 294, 329
Smith, R. W., 375
Smith, T. W., 443
Smits, M. S. I., 160
Smolak, L., 226
Smolowe, J., 280

Smutzler, N., 434, 438, 448
Smyke, A. T., 93
Snow, D. A., 56
Snow, D. L., 18, 70, 371, 379, 380, 400, 401, 402, 420, 459, 462, 465, 466, 502, 505, 532, 567
Snyder, D. K., 78
Snyder, H. N., 263, 272, 284
Snyder, L., 202
Snyder, L. A., 637
Snyder, P., 594
Sobourin, C. M., 374
Sobsey, D., 21
Soeken, K. L., 542
Soglin, D. F., 543
Soglin, L. F., 543
Sokoloff, N. J., 20, 470, 495
Solarsh, B., 570
Solberg, M. E., 161
Soler, E., 7, 453, 454
Solomon, P. L., 603
Solomon, S., 476
Solomon, S. S., 476
Somer, E., 113
Sommer, K. L., 435
Sommers, M. S., 331, 332
Son, J. B., 571
Sonam, N., 77, 202
Sonnega, A., 524
Sonon, K. E., 622
Sorensen, B. W., 491
Sorensen, D. D., 629
Sørenson, S. B., 62, 390, 427
Soria, C., 420, 480
Soriano, F. I., 497, 504
Sotres-Alvarez, D., 630
Soudelier, K., 100
Soule, K. P., 407
Sousa, C. A., 287, 318
Soussignan, R., 229
Southam-Gerow, M. A., 555
Southworth, C., 343, 349, 351
Spain, D., 537
Spangler, D., 606
Sparén, P., 488
Spears, J. W., 327
Spector, M., 9
Speilberger, C. D., 316
Speisman, B., 371
Spence, D. M., 619
Speziale, B., 341, 344, 345, 346, 347, 349, 350
Spiegel, D., 371, 410, 453
Spilby, L., 374, 378, 379
Spiller, L. C., 112, 127
Spitzberg, B. H., 292, 331, 341, 342, 346, 347, 350, 438

Spohn, C. G., 327
Sporakowski, M. J., 364
Sprecher, S., 56
Springer, K. W., 115, 129, 155, 159
Sreenivasan, S., 239
Srikrishnan, A. K., 476
Srimivasaraghavan, J., 363
Srinivasan, M., 404
Srinivasaraghavan, J., 445
Sroufe, L. A., 97, 98, 120, 152, 153, 171, 177, 182
Stabb, S. D., 462
Stacey, W. A., 404
Stafford, E. P., 66
Stafford, M. C., 10, 11
Staggs, S. L., 178, 384, 529, 574
Stahly, G., 121
Stahmer, A. C., 133
Staiger, P. K., 436
Stake, J. E., 338
Stalans, L. J., 44, 393, 417, 449, 450, 525, 555, 560
Stallbaumer-Rouyer, J., 542
Stambor, Z., 280
Stankiewicz, J. M., 6
Stanley, K. M., 637
Stanley, M. A., 607
Stanley, S. M., 318
Starek, J., 116
Stark, E., 423
Starkey, J., 481
Starks, M. T., 294
Starr, K., 413
Starr, R., 85
Starr, R. H., Jr., 103
Starzomski, A. J., 445, 549
Starzyk, K. B., 53, 453
Staske, S. A., 441
Stavis, P. F., 632
Stearns, S. C., 636
Steel, J., 237
Steele, B. F., 11, 268
Steffensmeir, D., 43
Stein, D. J., 531
Stein, A. L., 318
Stein, D. J., 474, 533
Stein, J. A., 62
Stein, M. B., 44, 372, 379
Stein, R. F., 277
Stein, S. J., 72
Stein, T. J., 189
Steinbach, J., 73
Steinberg, A., 246
Steinman, M., 61, 114
Steinmetz, S. K., 17, 18, 23, 412
Stenius, V. M., 404, 531

Stenner, P., 313, 440
Stephens, B. J., 394
Stephens, N., 112, 127
Stephenson, R., 477
Stermac, L. E., 229, 329, 338
Sternberg, K. J., 124, 163, 252
Stets, J. E., 366
Steve, K., 589, 590, 592, 593, 599, 601, 604, 620, 621
Stevens, S., 219, 236
Stevens, T., 496, 504, 506
Stevenson, T. R., 485
Stewart, A., 389
Stewart, C. S., 529
Stewart, D., 457
Stewart, K., 569
Stickley, A., 488
Stiegel, L. A., 17, 607, 619
Stille, R., 548
Stipanicic, A., 159
Stith, S. M., 51, 118, 181, 318, 443, 446
Stock, H. V., 20, 390
Stoddard, J. P., 515
Stoia-Caraballo, R., 535
Stojek, M., 156, 227
Stoltenberg, C. D., 78, 550, 558
Stoneman, Z., 167
Stoner, J. A., 380
Stoner, S., 499
Stoner, S. A., 334, 335, 336, 359
Stoops, C., 459
Stordeur, R. A., 548
Stosny, S., 435, 558
Stouthamer-Loeber, M., 72, 254
Strachan, C. E., 448
Straight, E. S., 331
Strand, M., 633
Strand, V. C., 234, 271
Strauchler, O., 71, 419
Straus, M. A., 3, 14, 17, 18, 22, 33, 34, 35, 36, 41, 48, 67, 68, 70, 73, 85, 95, 110, 116, 142, 144, 149, 150, 151, 173, 208, 278, 283, 310, 317, 354, 356, 366, 379, 412, 417, 420, 424, 442
Street, A. E., 52, 423, 449
Streissguth, A., 87
Strickland, G. J., 79
Strickland, S., 216, 217
Stripe, T. S., 229
Strom, K., 396
Strom, T. O., 372
Stroops, C., 296, 502, 553, 563
Stroshine, M. S., 402
Struther, R., 79
Stuart, G. L., 53, 69, 408, 420, 434, 436, 438, 440, 445, 452, 458, 459, 464, 553, 561, 567
Stuart, R. B., 402, 549, 556

Vindiver, D. M., 216
Vinton, L., 595, 604, 619
Virkkunen, M., 453
Vissing, Y. M., 278
Vitaro, F., 303
Vitello, C. J., 580
Vittrup, B., 145
Vivian, D., 68, 448, 462
Vizcarra, B., 483
Vogel, L. C. M., 500
Vogeltanz-Holm, N. D., 203
Vogt, D. S., 120, 535
Vogt, W. P., 73
Vohra, N., 8
Voigt, L., 365, 421
Volavka, J., 455
von Eye A., 368, 380
Voss, K., 120, 178
Vossekuil, B., 280
Vuillerot, C., 191
Vågerö, D., 488
Völlm, B., 216

Waaland, P., 390
Waalkes, D. M., 29
Wada, T., 532
Wade, T. J., 379
Waelde, L., 116
Wagar, J. M., 129
Wagenaar, D. B., 613
Wagener, P. D., 607
Wagenmakers, E. M., 369
Waite, L. J., 591, 593, 599
Waites, C. E., 618
Wakeling, H., 201, 232
Walczak, S., 44, 369
Wald, M. M., 158
Walden, L. M.., 161
Waldfogel, J., 171
Waldner-Haugrud, L. K., 48, 515
Waldron, I., 538
Waldrop, A. E., 374
Walker, C. E., 10
Walker, A., 327
Walker, C. A., 179
Walker, E., 173, 370
Walker, G., 550
Walker, J. R., 156, 182, 227
Walker, L. E., 378, 402, 419, 467
Walker, M. W., 284
Walker, R., 343, 345, 347, 350, 389
Wallace, J. F., 455
Wallace, K. M., 448
Wallace, R., 435, 629

Wallace, S. P., 613
Wallace-Capretta, S., 447
Waller, G., 125
Waller, N. G., 312, 376
Walsh, C. A., 154
Walsh, D. A., 289
Walsh, E., 161, 162
Walsh, F., 519
Walsh, J. A., 262, 263, 265
Walsh, K., 189, 371
Walsh, T., 134
Walsh, W. A., 117, 118, 244, 322
Waltermaurer, E. S., 62, 508, 510, 576
Walters, E. E., 421, 434
Walters, G. D., 454
Walters, S. T., 359
Walton, M., 481, 503, 505
Waltz, J., 379, 432, 448, 459
Wampler, K. S., 130, 555
Wandrei, M. L., 316
Wang, C. T., 25, 135
Wang, D., 362
Wang, E., 161
Wang, K., 134
Wang, M., 201
Wang, M. Q., 295
Wang, T., 478, 479, 627
Wannas, M., 200
Ward, D. B., 443
Ward, M. J., 55, 87, 89
Ward, S., 322
Ward, T., 73, 240, 274, 333, 438
Ward-Griffin, C., 310
Ware, H. S., 112, 127
Ware, K. N., 367
Warnken, W. J., 455
Wasco, S. M., 336
Washington, J., 543
Washington, K. T., 183, 184, 191
Wasik, B., 187
Wathen, C. N., 127, 234, 492, 543
Watson, J. M., 286
Watson, K., 20, 339, 449, 495, 542
Watson, R., 588
Watson, S., 446
Watts, C. H., 474, 475, 477, 480, 489, 490
Watts, K., 315, 318
Watts-English, T., 137, 142, 158
Waxman, L., 407
Way, I., 171
Weaver, A. J., 367
Weaver, S. E., 120
Weaver, T. L., 275, 370, 401, 542
Webb, M., 492

Yick, A., 628
Yim, I. S., 174
Yiu, I., 185
Yllö, K. A., 48, 70, 422
Yoo, J. A., 529
Yoon, J., 401, 423
Yoshihama, M., 19, 66, 364, 379, 470
Yoshioka, M. R., 47, 505, 507
Young, A., 46
Young, B. J., 292
Young, M. E., 631
Young, M. L., 284
Young, S. K., 332, 523, 524
Young-DeMarco, L., 66
Youngblade, L. M., 177
Youngblood, P., 615
Younglove, T., 580, 615
Yozwiak, J. A., 175, 589
Yuen, F. K. O., 630

Zahn, M. A., 279, 438, 441, 467
Zakirova, V., 487
Zalewski, C., 216
Zandi, P. P., 454
Zauszniewski, J. A., 608
Zawacki, T., 330, 359
Zayas, V., 311, 312
Zeanah, C. H., 93, 162
Zebell, N. M., 185
Zebian, A., 77

Zeelenberg, R., 369
Zeichner, A., 316, 317
Zellman, G. L., 29, 30
Zgoba, K. M., 240
Zhan, H. J., 627
Zhang, C., 87
Zhang, J., 162
Zhang, Y., 496, 504, 506
Zhao, S., 177
Zielinski, D. S., 119, 120, 178
Zimand, E., 533
Zimmerman, M., 111
Zimmerman, S., 636
Zimmerman, T. S., 369, 532
Zinbarg, R., 369, 377
Zinbarg, R. E., 454
Zingraff, M. T., 254, 278
Zink, T., 219, 236, 591, 594, 612, 615
Zinzow, H. M., 209, 213, 214, 225, 524, 581
Zlotnick, C., 370, 400, 402, 532
Zolotor, A. J., 113, 181, 192, 202
Zorza, J., 89, 348, 536, 547
Zozel, A., 44, 562
Zubretsky, T. M., 35, 449, 532, 552
Zucker, R. A., 56
Zunzunigui, M. V., 173
Zuravin, S. J., 85
Zurbriggen, E. L., 296
Zweig, J. M., 530, 542
Zwi, K. J., 245

# Subject Index

825

child sexual abuse and, 225, 226 (table)
interparental violence, child exposure to, 115 (table)
Afghanistan:
female maltreatment/abuse in, 19, 480–481
*See also* Central Asian intimate partner violence
African Americans:
child physical abuse and, 165, 166
elder abuse and, 628
family violence research and, 72
intersectionality and, 470
intimate partner violence and, 497, 498, 501–502, 503, 504, 505, 506, 507, 572–573
restorative justice and, 573
African intimate partner violence, 473, 474 (table)
forced early marriages and, 473
Ghana and, 473
imbalance theory and, 473
intergenerational transmission of abuse and, 473
polygamy and, 473
practice guidelines for, 569
risk factors for violence, 473
*See also* Cross-cultural intimate partner violence
Ageism, 588–589
Agency practices. *See* Practice issues
Aggregated data, 495
Aggressive behavior:
child physical abuse and, 153 (table), 154–155, 159–162
genetic factors in, 155, 454
*See also* Antisocial behavior; Bullying
Alcohol abuse:
abusive heterosexual partners and, 449–450, 453–454, 455
adolescents and, 56
alcoholism policies, 559
binge drinking and, 35, 286
cross-cultural intimate partner violence and, 488, 491, 493
dating violence and, 319, 359
family violence and, 35, 55–56
genetic factors in, 454
mentally ill people and, 603–604
sexual assault and, 333–334, 334 (table), 359
treatments for, 359–360, 532, 552–553
*See also* Alcohol and drug use (AOD); Alcoholism
Alcohol and drug use (AOD), 55–56, 58, 449–450, 532, 564, 603–604
Alcoholics Anonymous (AA), 532
Alcoholism, 45, 56, 124, 249, 287, 359–360, 449, 488
Alternative for Families-Cognitive Behavioral Therapy (AF-CBT), 185–186, 186 (table)
Alzheimer's disease, 601
Ambiguous attachment, 97
American Academy of Pediatrics, 167
American Association of Retired Persons (AARP), 616
American Bar Association (ABA), 297, 303, 387, 616
American with Disabilities Act (ADA) of 1990, 633

American Indians. *See* Native Americans/Alaska Natives
American Medical Association, 542
American Prosecutors Research Institute (APRI), 508, 576, 577
American Psychiatric Association, 99, 371
American Psychological Association (APA), 19, 23, 45, 66, 72, 74, 77, 206, 289, 559, 586, 625
Amnesia, 205
Amnesty International (AI), 470, 471
Amygdala, 454, 455
Analysis of variance (ANOVA), 524, 525
Anger, 8, 59, 225, 237, 315–316, 368, 431–432
control problems, 171
intimate partner violence, motive for, 432, 464
male offender disturbances, abusive behaviors and, 433, 433 (table)
meta-analytic review of, 432–433
multidimensional concept of, 432
Anger management programs, 550–551, 561, 607–608
Anonymity, 62, 74, 281
Antisocial behaviors:
adolescent abuse victims and, 253 (table)
adult child sexual abusers and, 230
child physical abuse and, 153 (table), 154–155, 159–162
child psychological maltreatment and, 108 (table)
deterrence theory and, 49
genetic factors in, 155
intergenerational transfer of violence and, 314–315
social support programs and, 127
spanking and, 144
stalking behaviors, 346–347
*See also* Antisocial personality disorder; Bullying
Antisocial orientation, 445
Antisocial personality disorder, 45, 53, 347, 446, 449, 451, 454, 563
Antisocial stalkers, 346
Anxiety:
batterers and, 315
child neglect/psychological maltreatment and, 97, 98, 99, 107, 110, 111, 112, 115, 116, 117
child physical abuse and, 153, 155, 161, 170
child sexual abuse and, 222, 223, 225, 226, 227, 233, 234, 237, 241, 245, 247
sibling abuse and, 270
victimization and, 303, 368
Anxious attachment, 97, 120, 466
Arab population:
Arab Americans, partner abuse and, 498, 504–505
justifiable wife beating and, 498
rape and, 355
*See also* Cross-cultural sexual assault; Middle Eastern intimate partner violence; Saudi Arabia; Yemen
Archstone Foundation, 617
Arranged marriages, 357, 477, 482, 484

intimate partner violence and, 477–478 (table), 478

*See also* Cross-cultural intimate partner violence; Southern Asian intimate partner violence

Base rate, 255

Battered child syndrome, 11, 29

Battered men, 17–18, 25

Battered woman syndrome (BWS), 467

Battered women:

adult alcohol/drug use and, 56

advocacy movement for, 14–15, 18, 41

battering, definition of, 64

battery, costs of, 25, 25 (table)

children of, services for, 129

Conflict Tactics Scale survey and, 17–18

criminal justice response and, 31

early marriage laws and, 13–14

fear reactions of, 44

health consequences for, 15

immigrant battered women, legal limbo for, 495–496

legal protections for, 14–15

mandatory reporting laws and, 30

media attention on, 14

mutual combat argument and, 25

perfect victim role and, 7

posttraumatic stress disorder and, 52

psychological abuse, impact of, 35

radiating impact of abusive relationships, 404

responses to battering and, 378

rural populations and, 21

self-defense argument and, 25

self-defensive attempts and, 378

shelters for, xx, 14, 32

social acceptance of violence and, 7, 14, 31

social services for, 14

social support for, inadequacy of, 404

stalking incidence and, 16, 16 (table)

treatment for, 32

*See also* Abused heterosexual partners; Abusive heterosexual partners; Battered men; Battered woman syndrome (BWS); Batterer intervention programs (BIPs); Leave/stay decisions

Battered Women's Justice Project, 581

Batterer intervention programs (BIPs), 548, 554–555, 564

Battering, 64

Because We Have Daughters program, 564

Behavior-based treatment programs, 185

Alternative for Families-Cognitive Behavioral Therapy, 185–186, 186 (table)

child protective services parenting training programs, 187

Combined Parent-Child Cognitive Behavioral Treatment, 186

family preservation programs, 187–188

Fathers Supporting Success program, 188

Incredible Years Teacher Training Series, 187

out-of-home placements, 188

Parent-Child Interaction Therapy, 185

parental support interventions, 187

therapeutic day care, 186–187

*See also* Cognitive behavioral therapy (CBT)

Behavioral problems:

adolescent abuse victims and, 253, 253–254 (Table)

bullying, 160–162

child physical abuse and, 153 (table), 159–162

child psychological treatment and, 111 (table)

child sexual abuse and, 225, 226 (table)

interparental violence, child exposure to, 115 (table)

*See also* Aggressive behavior; Antisocial behavior

Behavioral Risk Factor Surveillance System (BRFSS), 543

Belgium:

dating violence and, 355 (Table)

*See also* Cross-cultural sexual assault

Bem Sex-Role Inventory, 447

Biobehavioral research, 45

Biopsychosocial model:

hormone studies and, 453–454

psychobiological bases for violence and, 53–54, 453

*See also* Brain function; Genetics

Bipolar disorder, 162

Birth control options, 13, 260, 422, 473, 477, 491

Bisexual attraction (BSA), 293

Bisexuals:

adolescent development and, 293–294

anti-harassment programs and, 294–295, 299

bisexual adolescents, prejudice/victimization of, 294–295

revictimization experiences and, 52

same-sex adolescent assaults and, 293–295

same-sex elder abuse and, 625–626

*See also* Gays; Lesbians; Same-sex intimate partner violence (SSIPV)

Blame:

batterers, attributions for, 427–428

self-blame, 366

sexual assault, 329

*See also* Victim blaming

Blitz rape, 35

Body mass index (BMI), 372

Borderline personality disorder (BPD), 99, 111, 153, 162, 254, 435, 455

Brain function:

abused heterosexual partners and, 370, 372

aggressive/antisocial behaviors, neurotransmitter regulation and, 155

amygdala and, 454, 455

biological stress reaction and, 159

brain dysfunctions, violent behavior and, 454–455

brain-based psychotherapy and, 533

child abuse and, 24

child physical abuse and, 152 (table), 157–159

Child Abuse Prevention and Treatment Act (CAPTA), 11, 89, 133, 142, 198

Child Advocacy Centers (CACs), 242, 243–244, 243 (table), 248

Child Behavior Checklist (CBCL), 66

Child care, 14, 183, 186–187, 384

Child death. *See* Death review teams; Fatalities; Homicide

Child labor laws, 10

Child maltreatment, 4, 10

    child protection laws and, 10, 11

    corporal punishment and, 22

    dysfunctional families, rehabilitation of, 5

    foster care system and, 30

    historical context of, 10–12

    infanticide and, 10, 19

    institutionalization of children and, 92–93

    intergenerational transmission of maltreatment and, 119–120

    mandatory reporting of, 30, 86

    marital violence-child maltreatment link, 18

    one-child policy and, 19

    polyvictimization and, 92

    psychological maltreatment, 12

    rates of, 150–151

    risk factors for, 103–104

    *See also* Child abuse; Child neglect; Child physical abuse (CPA); Child psychological maltreatment; Child sexual abuse (CSA)

Child molestation, 43

Child neglect, 12, 23, 83

    attachment difficulties and, 96 (table), 97–98

    basic needs criteria and, 85, 87, 93

    case history of, 83

    child death data, 4

    chronicity of, 86

    cognitive/academic deficits and, 96 (table), 98

    costs of, 25, 26 (table)

    cross-cultural child neglect/abuse, 92–93

    cultural issues in, 86–87

    definitions of, 85–87, 93, 123

    disabled children, neglect of, 102–103

    early neglect, effects of, 96

    effects of, 96–101, 96–97 (table)

    effects research, methodological issues of, 123–125

    emotional neglect vs. psychological maltreatment and, 90

    emotional/behavioral problems and, 97 (table), 98–99

    failure to thrive and, 97 (table), 99–100 (box)

    family structure/functioning and, 119

    frequency/duration of, 86

    harm vs. endangerment standards and, 86, 95

    historical perspective on, 84

    inattention on, 84

    infant attachment, disturbed patterns of, 54–55

    intentionality, parent failure and, 85

    intergenerational transmission of maltreatment and, 119–120

    interventions/treatments for, 126–128

    laws concerning child neglect, 24, 86

    long-term consequences of, 97 (table)

    mandatory reporting of, 86

    medical neglect, 90, 90 (table), 91–92

    neglected children, characteristics of, 101–103, 102 (table), 104

    neglectful parents, characteristics of, 103–104

    observable harm and, 12

    offenders, treatment for, 32

    parent-child interaction patterns and, 104

    parenting problems and, 120–122

    paternal neglect, 89, 103

    physical consequences of, 97 (table), 99–100

    physical neglect, 90

    polyvictimization and, 124

    postnatal maternal stress and, 88

    prenatal neglect, 87–89

    prevalence/incidence of, 93–95, 94–95 (tables), 102–103, 102 (table)

    psychological maltreatment and, 12

    scenarios of, 84

    social problem of, 12

    socioeconomic status and, 119, 120, 123

    specific behaviors of, 89–90

    treatment strategies for, 86

    typology of, 89–92, 90–91 (table)

    unique effects of, 96

    *See also* Child abuse; Child maltreatment; Child physical abuse (CPA); Child sexual abuse (CSA)

Child physical abuse (CPA), 10, 106, 140, 145

    abused children, characteristics of, 164–167, 181 (table)

    adult abusers, characteristics of, 167–172, 167–171 (tables), 181 (table)

    adult biological factors in, 171, 171 (table)

    adult emotional/behavioral characteristics in, 170 (table), 171

    adult family/interpersonal factors in, 170 (table), 171–172

    age factor in, 164, 167

    aggressive/antisocial behaviors and, 153 (table), 154–155, 159–162

    anticipatory guidance and, 192

    battered child syndrome and, 11

    behavior-based treatment programs and, 185–188, 186 (table)

    bullying and, 160–162

    case history of, 139–140

    child death review teams and, 148

    child protection laws and, 10, 11

    child-saving movement and, 11

    claims-making activities and, 11

    cognitive/academic deficits and, 98, 152 (table), 159

Asian/Latinas, dating violence and, 358
ethnic/racial differences in sexual assault, 357–359, 357 (table)
honor societies and, 356, 357
jealousy, cultural effects on, 356, 357
male victims' stress reactions, 356
multi-nation dating violence, 356
*See also* Cross-cultural intimate partner violence
Cultural competence:
culturally sensitive care, barriers to, 79
culturally sensitive therapy and, 79–80
diversity awareness and, 67, 77
ethical research methods and, 74
ethnic elder abuse and, 629
evidence-based practice and, 79–80
family violence assessment and, 71–72
guidelines for, 79
legal system, cultural insensitivity and, 496
practice issue of, 78–79, 578–579
social science practice and, 471
Cultural factors:
child neglect and, 86–87
child sexual abuse and, 12
cross-cultural family abuse, 19
cultural context, transformation of, 79–80
cultural relativism, abusive practices and, 8
definitions of violence and, 10
ethnic/racial minorities, violence among, 20
ethnicity and, 494
evidence-based therapies and, 80
family violence and, 7, 10, 18–20, 47
immigrant family violence, 19–20
patriarchal ideology, 20, 21, 47–48, 57
saving face, 505, 507, 626
subculture of violence and, 57
*See also* Cultural competence; Ethnic minority groups; Immigrant and ethnic/racial intimate partner violence; International human rights protections; Racial minority groups
Cultural relativism, 471, 472–473 (box), 570
Custody issues, 121–122
Cyberbullying, 280–281 (box), 302, 352
CyberCrisis anonymous hotline, 577
Cyberstalking, 17, 342–343, 346, 351
Cycle of violence pattern, 419

Data:
aggregated data, 495
campus crime reports, 319
comparison group data, 66
correlational data, 124
direct observation data, 62–63
disaggregated data, 308, 343, 470
electronic databases, 3, 60
family violence data, 2–3, 4–5
fatal intrafamilial abuse data, 4–5
forensic databases, 327
informant data, 62
interviews, 71
intimate violence data, 19
Life History Calendar collection method, 66
nonfatal intrafamilial abuse data, 3–4
official statistical data, 61
operationalized definitions of abuse and, 24
qualitative data, 71, 73
quantitative data, 71
questionnaires, 71
retrospective data, 62, 66, 124
self-report surveys, 61–62
sources of, 60–63
survey data, 3, 61–62
victimization/perpetration surveys, 61–62
*See also* Measurement instruments; Statistical analysis
Date rape, 16, 35, 323, 328, 329
Date-rape drugs, 323, 329
Dating violence (DV), 15–16, 28–29, 50
age factor in, 307
alcohol abuse and, 319, 359
anger and, 315–316
attachment issues and, 312–313, 312 (table), 321
attitudes about, 316–317, 321
benevolent sexism and, 317
case history of, 305–306
consequences of, 310, 320
controlling behaviors and, 305–306, 314, 316
cross-cultural dating violence, 354–355, 355 (table)
dating vs. marital violence and, 307
definition of, 308
early research on, 307
ethnic/racial differences and, 357–359, 357 (table)
explanations for, 310–312
gender factor in, 309, 309–310 (tables)
gender-role socialization and, 315, 321
hostile sexism and, 317
hypermasculinity, power and, 316
infidelity, reactions to, 314
intergenerational transfer of violence and, 314–315
internship/mentoring programs and, 319
interpartner aggression, high relationship commitment and, 313
jealousy, role of, 313–314
personality characteristics and, 315–316
precursor variables and, 314, 321
preference for abusive relationships and, 311–312
prevalence estimates, factors in, 307–308, 309–310 (tables), 310
prevention of, 28–29, 318–319, 321
reciprocal/mutual dating violence, 308–309, 320

marital dysfunction/dyadic relationship stress, 54

social exchange theory and, 56

Dysphoria, 224, 379, 459

Dysthymia, 97, 155

child neglect/maltreatment investigations and, 132–133, 189–190

child sexual abuse victims, interviewing of, 244

disabled persons abuse, reporting of, 634

DNA evidence, mishandling of, 327

domestic abuse by officers and, 389

Domestic Abuse Intervention Project and, 33

dual arrest policy, 392, 394

elder abuse, responses to, 17, 590, 608, 616

family violence, reporting of, 2

family violence, trivialization of, 390–393

gender-neutral law enforcement approaches, 393

intimate partner violence, arrest for, 7, 31, 390–393

mandatory arrest policies, 391–392

police-treatment personnel collaboration, 560–561, 576, 577 (table)

primary aggressor provisions and, 392

protective orders and, 345, 353, 387–388

Rape Myth Acceptance score and, 327

rape, responses to, 326–327, 340

rural populations and, 508

same-sex intimate partner violence, response to, 579–580

sex crime units and, 327

sex offender registries, 31, 242

sibling abuse reports and, 276–277

stalking, responses to, 345, 351

tag-along charges and, 133

victim-offender dichotomy, law enforcement philosophy and, 393

*See also* Court system; Legal issues; Mandatory arrest policies; Rape laws

Law Enforcement Management and Administrative Statistics (LEMAS), 391, 392

Law guardians, 122

Learned helplessness, 363, 376–377, 467, 499

Learned hopefulness, 408–409

Learning theories, 50, 58

avoidance conditioning, 52

classical conditioning, 51, 273

intergenerational transmission of maltreatment and, 119–120

offender learning, 52

operant conditioning, 52

physical punishment/discipline and, 143

revictimization model and, 52

social learning theory, 50–51, 178, 273

trauma theory, 51–52, 58

*See also* Family violence theories; Microtheory framework

Leave/stay decisions, 398–399, 411–412

approach-avoidance conflicts and, 401–402, 410

attachment needs and, 410, 533–534, 534 (table)

backlash effect and, 402–403

battered women, leave/return data and, 402

child custody issues and, 410

child safety concerns and, 410

dangers of leaving abusive partners, 402–403, 532–533

decision process, 399–402

emotional factors in, 407–410

entrapment and, 401

fear response and, 410

forgiveness and, 403

gender differences in, 413

help-seeking activities and, 400

immigrant and ethnic/racial intimate partner violence and, 505, 506

investment model and, 408

leave decision, variables in, 399–400

lesbian partners and, 519–520

marital dissatisfaction and, 410

physical assaults and, 400–401, 403

psychological/emotional abuse and, 401

radiating impact of abusive relationships, 404

relationship commitment and, 407–408

relationship hope and, 408–409

shelter services and, 406–407

stay decision, childhood abuse experience and, 400

transitional supportive housing and, 407

traumatic bonding and, 409

women's beliefs about relationship and, 400

*See also* Abused heterosexual partners; Battered women; Intimate partner violence (IPV)

Legal issues:

abuse, mandatory reporting laws and, 29–30, 151–152, 189

abused heterosexual partners and, 386–393

adolescent dating violence and, 290–291, 292–293, 296–297 (box), 297–298

battered women and, 13–14, 15

child maltreatment, mandated record keeping and, 109

child physical abuse and, 188–189

child pornography, 221

child protection laws, 10, 11, 12, 133

child sexual abuse and, 242–244, 243 (table)

cross-cultural intimate partner violence and, 568

cultural insensitivity and, 496

customary laws, victimization and, 19

elder abuse and, 17, 609–611

English common law, 14

family relationships, legal protection of, 5, 133

family violence, legal definition of, 24–25

father-violent families, mothers' legal difficulties and, 121–122

gender-based disparities and, 24–25

harm/endangerment risk, child neglect definition and, 86

human research subjects and, 74

immigrant battered women and, 495–496

injury outcome focus and, 24

interparental violence, child exposure to, 113

intimate partner violence, arrest rate and, 7, 390–393

Matriarchal ideology, 48

Matricide, 264–265

Meals on Wheels, 621

Measurement instruments, 67
    Child Behavior Checklist, 66
    composite abuse scales, 71
    Conflict Tactics Scale, 17–18, 67–68, 69
    Conflict Tactics Scale/Revised, 68–69, 69–70 (boxes), 72
    cultural competence and, 71–72
    multiple measurements, need for, 71
    Parent-Child Conflict Tactics Scale, 70–71
    penile plethysmography, 231
    prevalence vs. incidence rates, 72
    psychological abuse, growing recognition of, 71
    rates of violence, estimation of, 72
    Violence Risk Appraisal Guide, 73
    *See also* Data; Family violence research methodology; Statistical analysis

Media:
    adolescent dating violence and, 288–290, 302–303
    child sexual abuse and, 235
    domestic violence problem and, 14
    family violence prevention campaigns, 29
    family violence, reporting on, 1–2, 8
    objectification/sexualization effects and, 6
    sensationalism in, 2
    sexual assault findings, 16
    sexually explicit media, 290
    sexually violent media, rape myth acceptance and, 328–329
    social acceptance of violence and, 7
    social learning, media violence and, 6
    television violence, 289
    Triple-P program and, 128
    video game violence, 6, 289, 302–303
    youth violence and, 6

Mediator variables, 156, 254, 315, 359, 403, 445, 447, 450, 519, 568

Medical consequences. *See* Health consequences; Physical illnesses

Medical neglect, 90, 90 (table), 91–92, 108 (table), 251

Medical research, 44

Medical resources:
    abuse/neglect mandatory reporting, 11, 29–30, 86
    adolescent dating violence and, 298
    birth control options, 13
    child protection support, 191
    child sexual abuse, disclosure of, 202
    child sexual abuse treatments, 239–240
    domestic violence, mandatory reporting of, 366
    elder abuse, responses to, 611–613
    federal government research agencies, 60
    interpersonal violence, screening for, 319
    male sexual assault medical needs and, 333

    mandated identification of battered women, emergency room personnel and, 542–543
    medical professionals, training enhancements, 543
    medical screening of abuse victims, 542
    Nurse-Family Partnership program, 128
    nurse-practitioner model and, 128
    patient dumping practice and, 588
    psychiatric medications, 32
    sexual assault nurse examiner protocol, 332
    sexual assault response teams, 332
    vaccination programs, 92
    *See also* Medications

Medicalization trend, 32

Medicare/Medicaid, 610–611, 636

Medications:
    alcohol cessation treatment, 553
    child sexual abuse treatments, 239–240
    date-rape drugs, 323
    drug-based therapies and, 533
    postpartum depression, antidepressants for, 175
    prenatal neglect and, 88
    psychiatric medications, 32, 553
    psychobiological bases for violence and, 53–54
    psychotropic drugs, 452, 501, 553
    *See also* Medical resources

Memory issues:
    accuracy of memory, 202–203
    capacity of memory, 202
    child sexual abuse and, 202–206
    repressed/recovered memory, 203–206
    victim fabrications, 203

Men's Education Program, 564

Mental health child maltreatment, 108 (table)

Mental illness model, 32

Mental illness/disorders, 8
    abused heterosexual partners and, 379–381
    abusive heterosexual partners and, 455, 456
    adolescent dating violence and, 287
    alcohol/drug use and, 602–604
    child psychological maltreatment and, 111
    dating violence and, 310
    elder abuse and, 602–603
    family-violent individuals and, 31–32, 53
    genetic inheritance and, 53
    postpartum depression/psychosis, 173–176
    stalking behaviors and, 345–347, 347–348 (table)
    victims of intimate partner violence and, 32
    *See also* Personality disorders; Psychiatric disorders; Psychopathology

Mentoring programs, 319

Meta-analysis, 73, 118, 131, 237–238, 336, 432–433, 442, 555

Methodology. *See* Effects research; Family violence research methodology

National Center on Elder Abuse (NCEA), 586, 587, 588
National Center for Injury Prevention and Control (NCIPC), 3, 20–21, 543
National Center for Missing and Exploited Children, 221
National Center for Prosecution of Child Abuse, 133
National Center for Victims of Crime, 35, 388
National Child Abuse and Neglect Data System (NCANDS), 3, 147, 151, 164, 179, 201, 207, 208
National Coalition Against Domestic Violence, 14–15
National Coalition of Antiviolence Programs (NCAVP), 512
National Committee on Elder Abuse (NCEA), 593
National Committee for the Prevention of Elder Abuse (NCPEA), 17
National Comorbidity Survey (NCS), 3, 119, 177, 225, 371
National Council on Child Abuse and Family Violence, 15
National Council of Juvenile and Family Court Judges, 397
National Crime Victimization Survey (NCVS), 3, 4, 65, 68, 81, 151, 308, 309, 325, 328, 357, 378, 412, 417, 418, 422, 425, 509, 590, 630–631
National Crime Violence Survey, 339
National Criminal Justice Reference Service, 50
National Data Archive on Child Abuse and Neglect (NDACAN), 60
National Domestic Violence Hotline (NDVH), 32, 386, 407, 410
National Domestic Violence Pro Bono Directory, 387
National Electronic Injury Surveillance System (NEISS), 3, 61
National Electronic Injury Surveillance System-All Injury Program, 594
National Epidemiological Survey on Alcohol and Related Conditions, 173
National Family Violence Re-survey, 17, 379
National Family Violence Surveys (NFVS), 3, 65, 81
National Health and Social Life Survey, 209, 211
National Household Survey on Drug Abuse, 450
National Incidence Studies/Fourth (NIS-4), 93, 101, 102, 103, 117, 146, 147, 151, 164, 165, 166, 167, 169, 206, 207, 211, 212, 213, 214, 215
National Incidence Study/Second (NIS-2), 86, 92, 147
National Incidence Study/Third (NIS-3), 90, 147, 151
National Incident-Based Reporting System (NIBRS), 3, 61, 207, 208, 263, 272, 391, 392, 425, 580
National Institute of Child Health and Development, 60
National Institute on Disability and Rehabilitation Research, 629
National Institute on Drug Abuse, 552
National Institute of Justice (NIJ), 3, 332
National Institute of Mental Health (NIMH), 16, 60
National Institutes of Health (NIH), 60
National Longitudinal Study of Adolescent Health, 284
National Low Income Housing Commission, 407
National Opinion Research Center (NORC), 6
National Organization for Men Against Sexism (NOMAS), 564
National Organization for Victim Assistance, 15
National Organization for Women (NOW), 14

National Prison Rape Elimination Commission, 63
National Research Council (NRC), 66
National Survey of Child and Adolescent Well-Being (NSCAW), 255, 262
National Survey of Children Exposed to Violence (NatSCEV), 164, 212, 280
National Survey of Families and Households (NSFH), 3, 401, 413
National Teen Dating Abuse Helpline, 281
National Teen Dating Awareness Week, 298
National Violence Against Women Survey (NVAWS), 3, 4, 25, 65, 150, 151, 209, 309, 310, 331, 348, 422, 425, 540, 604
National Violent Death Reporting System (NVDRS), 3, 4, 147, 421
National Youth Victimization Prevention Study, 245
National Youth Violence Prevention Resource Center, 283
Nationally Representative Survey of Children Exposed to Violence, 208–209
Native Americans/Alaska Natives, 20, 72
    elder abuse and, 628
    historic trauma and, 499
    intimate partner violence and, 497, 498–499, 507, 573–574
    learned helplessness and, 499
    physical fighting and, 499
    reservation life and, 499
    tribal law, restorative justice and, 499
Neglect. *See* Child neglect; Elder abuse; Prenatal neglect
Neighborhood disadvantage, 55
Neonaticidal mothers, 148–149
Nepal:
    acid throwing and, 477
    dowry murders and, 477
    intimate partner violence, 476 (table), 477
    untouchable women, privations of, 477
    *See also* Asian intimate partner violence; Cross-cultural intimate partner violence
Netherlands:
    child abuse/neglect study, 92
    intimate partner violence and, 485 (table)
    negative parent-child interactions, 131
    *See also* Cross-cultural child abuse/neglect
Neuroscience research, 44–45, 137
    *See also* Brain function
Neurotransmitters, 453
New York Alliance Against Sexual Assault, 323
New Zealand:
    intimate partner violence and, 479, 480 (table)
    *See also* Cross-cultural intimate partner violence; Oceania/ intimate partner violence
News reporting. *See* Media
Nineteenth Amendment, 13
No-drop prosecution policy, 31
Nonfatal abuse, 3–4
Nonverbal abuse, 71

reporting biases in, 62
response errors and, 62
retrospective nature of, 62
Semitheories, 55
Seneca Falls Convention, 13
Sense of coherence (SOC), 374, 424
September 11, 2001 terrorist attacks, 18–19
Serotonin, 453
Severely mentally ill (SMI), 603–604
Severity of Violence Against Men Scale (SVAMS), 429
Severity of Violence Against Women Scale (SVAWS), 3, 429, 464
Sex offender registry, 31, 242
Sex With Children (SWCH) scale, 232
Sexting, 292–293
Sexual activity:
　　adolescent abuse victims, sexual risk taking and, 253 (table)
　　adolescent dating violence and, 286
　　child physical abuse, sexual risk taking and, 153 (table)
　　gender factor in, 309, 309–310 (tables)
　　same-sex attractions, 293
　　sexual adjustment, child sexual abuse and, 226 (table)
　　sexual assault, sexual risk behavior and, 332
Sexual Assault Nurse Examination (SANE) protocol, 332, 340
Sexual assault response teams, 332
Sexual assault (SA), 16, 55, 56, 321–322
　　adversarial sexual beliefs and, 328
　　alcohol, harmful effects of, 333–334, 334 (table), 359
　　athletes and, 334–335, 336–337, 339
　　attitudes about, 328–330, 338, 340
　　blame for, 329
　　brain structures, gender differences in, 335–336
　　car license plate replacement and, 324
　　case history of, 330–331
　　college-based prevention initiatives, 338
　　consent criterion and, 323
　　consequences of, 330–332
　　cross-cultural sexual assault, 354–357, 355 (table)
　　definitions of, 322–324, 339, 421
　　disabled persons abuse and, 632
　　DNA evidence, mishandling of, 327
　　elder population, 587
　　empathy, lack of, 328
　　ethnic/racial differences and, 357–359, 357 (table)
　　explanations for, 333–336, 340–341
　　fear reactions and, 332
　　fraternity men and, 334–335, 339
　　gender-role socialization and, 335
　　hypermasculinity and, 316, 336, 337, 341
　　injuries/negative health outcomes and, 331
　　legal definitions of, 322–323, 337
　　male misperceptions of sexual/romantic interest and, 335, 336
　　media, sexual violent content and, 328–329
　　medical responses to, 332–333

mental health consequences of, 332
nondisclosure of, 324, 339
oral sex, 324, 422
perpetrator-focused prevention programs, 338
perpetrators, traits of, 330
policy changes and, 336–337
prevalence estimates of, 307–308, 324–326, 325 (table), 328
prevention of, 337–339
prosecutorial discretion and, 327
psychological outcomes and, 331–332
rape myth acceptance and, 327, 328–329, 333
rape myths/female victims and, 328–329
rape myths/male victims and, 329
same-sex sexual assault, 353–354
school-based prevention programs and, 319
situational components in, 330
subjective definitions of, 322
substance abuse and, 359
treatment of, 336
underreporting of, 324–325
victim-focused prevention programs, 337
women's resistance, believability of, 333
See also Abused heterosexual partners; Dating violence (DV); Rape; Sexual coercion; Sexual violence
Sexual coercion, 321
　　adolescent abuse victims and, 254 (table)
　　definition of, 22, 322, 339
　　disabled persons abuse and, 632
　　Hispanic female population and, 497
　　See also Child sexual abuse (CSA); Rape; Sexual violence
Sexual dysfunction, 332
Sexual Experiences Survey (SES), 328
Sexual violence:
　　blitz rape, 35
　　dating couples, sexual assault among, 16
　　revictimization risk and, 52
　　routine activities theory and, 56
　　See also Child sexual abuse (CSA); Rape; Sexual assault (SA); Sexual coercion
Sexually transmitted diseases (STDs), 253 (table), 331, 333, 372
Sexually violent-only men, 458–459
Shaken adult syndrome, 370
Shaken baby syndrome (SBS), 158–159
Shame, 287, 431, 434, 435, 444, 451
Shelter services, xx, 14, 32, 75, 129, 368–369, 388, 393, 402, 406–407, 484, 487, 500, 505, 509, 530, 531, 538, 539, 569, 572, 615
Siblicide, 264, 268
Sibling abuse, 265
　　age factor and, 272
　　attitudes toward, 267
　　conflict theory and, 273
　　dating violence and, 287

women's higher status, backlash effect and, 479
   *See also* Cross-cultural intimate partner violence; Southern
      Asian intimate partner violence
Violence, 2
   definition of, 23, 64
   media violence, social learning and, 6
   social acceptance of, 7
   social tolerance of, 6–7
   transgenerational abuse patterns and, 3
   witnesses of, 3
   *See also* Family violence; Intimate partner violence (IPV);
      Sexual violence
Violence Against Women Act (VAWA), 32, 290, 308, 387, 389,
   469, 495, 499, 510, 576, 579
Violence Against Women Office, 469
Violence Risk Appraisal Guide, 73
Violent Resistance (VR), 428, 443, 462–463
Visitation issues, 121, 533
Voting rights, 13
Vulnerable Adult Specialist Team (VAST), 615
Vulnerable adults:
   battered wives and, 13–15
   child sexual abuse offenders and, 53
   revictimization risk and, 52
   stalking behaviors and, 350
   *See also* Disabled persons abuse; Elder abuse

Wales:
   revictimization reduction, community collaboration in,
      562–563
   *See also* Cross-cultural intimate partner violence; European
      intimate partner violence
War-time violence, 8, 52, 521
Weapons possession, 388, 389–390
Wedfare, 540-541
Weinberg Center for Prevention, Intervention and Research in
   Elder Abuse, 618–619

Welfare:
   family violence and, 27
   family violence option and, 384–385, 405–406
   intimate partner violence and, 25, 383–385
   leave/stay decisions, welfare failures and, 405–406
   minority women, battering incidence and, 506
   misguided welfare programs, 540–541
   needed changes in, 540
   social entrapment and, 378
   Temporary Assistance for Needy Families Act,
      384–385, 540
   victim blaming and, 364–365
   welfare workers, hiring/training of, 541–542
   welfare-to-work programs, 384, 540
   young adults and, 262
Welfare-to-work (WtW) programs, 540
Withdrawal, 97, 115 (Table)
Woman's Right Convention, 13
Women's movements, xx
   abortion rights and, 14
   birth control and, 13
   child care, public funding for, 14
   feminist movement, 13, 14, 15, 22
   marital exemption law and, 15
   marital rape, recognition of, 15
   marriage, women's legal status and, 13–14, 15
   Suffrage movement, 13
   women workers and, 13, 14
Work. *See* Employment
World Conference on Women (Beijing), 478
World Health Organization (WHO), 470, 471, 568, 626

Yemen:
   child discipline practices, 190
   *See also* Cross-cultural child abuse/neglect
Youth Risk Behavior Surveillance United States 2005, 291
Youth Risk Behavior Survey (YRBS), 3, 283

impoverished children, brain deficits and, 24
intergenerational transmission of maltreatment and, 120
violence, incidence of, 33–34, 55
   *See also* Poverty
Socioemotional deficits:
   child physical abuse and, 153 (table), 155, 162–163
   child sexual abuse and, 230
   *See also* Affective-behavioral problems; Interpersonal
      maladjustment
Sociological research, 43
Sociopolitical conservatism, 180
Somatization, 162, 219, 219 (table)
Somatoform disorders, 381
Southern Asian intimate partner violence,
   477, 477–478 (table)
   Bangladesh and, 477–478 (table), 478
   China and, 478–479, 478 (table)
   good wife/good daughter model and, 493
   Hong Kong and, 478 (table), 479
   jealousy-related violence and, 478–479
   policy for, 574
   Vietnam and, 478 (table), 479
   *See also* Asian intimate partner violence; Central Asian
      intimate partner violence; Cross-cultural intimate
      partner violence; Oceania/intimate partner violence
Spain:
   elder abuse, 627
   *See also* Cross-cultural elder abuse
Spanking, 6, 22, 47, 57, 142, 181
   children's assessment of, 145
   harm of, 142–143
   spillover effects of, 144, 145
   *See also* Physical punishment/discipline
Spillover effect, 6, 144, 145, 270–271
Spouse abuse. *See* Domestic violence; Intimate partner
   violence (IPV); Marriage
Spouse Assault Replication Program, 391
Spurning, 107 (table)
Stalking Resource Center, 343
Stalking (ST), 16, 341, 379
   antisocial stalkers, 346
   antistalking legislation and, 351
   car license plate replacement and, 324
   college campuses and, 350
   consequences of, 345
   controlling behaviors and, 349
   courtship persistence and, 341–342, 349, 352–353
   criminal justice system responses to, 345, 350, 351
   cross-cultural stalking and, 354–356
   cyberstalking, 17, 342–343, 346, 351, 352
   definitions of, 16, 16 (table), 341–343, 350, 351–352
   disclosure/reporting of, 344, 352
   environmental protective reactions to, 345
   ethnic/racial differences and, 357–359, 357 (table)

explanations of, 348–349, 352–353
fear standard and, 343
femicide and, 341
gender factor in, 309, 309–310 (tables)
legal definition of, 343
love-obsessional stalkers, 346
measurement ambiguity and, 344
paraphilic stalkers, 346
perpetrators, traits of, 345–347, 347–348 (table), 352
policy responses to, 350–351
prevalence estimates of, 307–308, 343–345
prevention of, 351, 353
protective orders and, 345, 353
psychological effects of, 345
*Rapelay* video game and, 6
safety planning and, 349–350, 351, 352
same-sex stalking, 353–354
stalking with technology, 343, 352
subjective definitions of, 342
treatments of, 349–350, 353
typology of stalkers, 347, 347–348 (table), 352
victims' responses to, 348, 352
   *See also* Dating violence (DV); Sexual assault (SA)
State-Trait Anger Expression Inventory, 316
Statistical analysis, 59
   advocacy, researcher role in, 73
   analysis of variance, 524, 525
   causality, identification of, 59
   chi-square analysis, 524, 632
   cluster analysis, 414, 458, 459
   correlational data and, 124
   discriminate functions analysis, 429
   factor analysis, 232, 338
   family violence, data on, 2–3, 4–5
   fatal intrafamilial abuse, 4–5
   meta-analysis and, 73, 118, 131, 237–238, 336, 432–433,
      442, 555
   multiple regression analysis, 451
   nonfatal intrafamilial abuse, 3–4
   path analysis, 311, 335, 442, 450, 451, 460, 464, 502
   regression analysis, 560
   researcher training and, 72–73, 82
   risk markers, assessments of, 73
   structural equation modeling and, 59
   underestimation and, 2
   weighted frequency scores, 429
   *See also* Data; Family violence research methodology
Statutory rape, 199, 252, 292, 302
Stockholm syndrome, 374, 375, 381
Street Youth at Risk for AIDS (SYRA), 256
Stress:
   abused heterosexual partners and, 370–371
   abusive heterosexual partners and, 451
   biological stress reaction, 159

# SAGE Research Methods Online

## The essential tool for researchers

impoverished children, brain deficits and, 24
    intergenerational transmission of maltreatment and, 120
    violence, incidence of, 33–34, 55
    *See also* Poverty
Socioemotional deficits:
    child physical abuse and, 153 (table), 155, 162–163
    child sexual abuse and, 230
    *See also* Affective-behavioral problems; Interpersonal
        maladjustment
Sociological research, 43
Sociopolitical conservatism, 180
Somatization, 162, 219, 219 (table)
Somatoform disorders, 381
Southern Asian intimate partner violence,
        477, 477–478 (table)
    Bangladesh and, 477–478 (table), 478
    China and, 478–479, 478 (table)
    good wife/good daughter model and, 493
    Hong Kong and, 478 (table), 479
    jealousy-related violence and, 478–479
    policy for, 574
    Vietnam and, 478 (table), 479
    *See also* Asian intimate partner violence; Central Asian
        intimate partner violence; Cross-cultural intimate
        partner violence; Oceania/intimate partner violence
Spain:
    elder abuse, 627
    *See also* Cross-cultural elder abuse
Spanking, 6, 22, 47, 57, 142, 181
    children's assessment of, 145
    harm of, 142–143
    spillover effects of, 144, 145
    *See also* Physical punishment/discipline
Spillover effect, 6, 144, 145, 270–271
Spouse abuse. *See* Domestic violence; Intimate partner
        violence (IPV); Marriage
Spouse Assault Replication Program, 391
Spurning, 107 (table)
Stalking Resource Center, 343
Stalking (ST), 16, 341, 379
    antisocial stalkers, 346
    antistalking legislation and, 351
    car license plate replacement and, 324
    college campuses and, 350
    consequences of, 345
    controlling behaviors and, 349
    courtship persistence and, 341–342, 349, 352–353
    criminal justice system responses to, 345, 350, 351
    cross-cultural stalking and, 354–356
    cyberstalking, 17, 342–343, 346, 351, 352
    definitions of, 16, 16 (table), 341–343, 350, 351–352
    disclosure/reporting of, 344, 352
    environmental protective reactions to, 345
    ethnic/racial differences and, 357–359, 357 (table)

explanations of, 348–349, 352–353
    fear standard and, 343
    femicide and, 341
    gender factor in, 309, 309–310 (tables)
    legal definition of, 343
    love-obsessional stalkers, 346
    measurement ambiguity and, 344
    paraphilic stalkers, 346
    perpetrators, traits of, 345–347, 347–348 (table), 352
    policy responses to, 350–351
    prevalence estimates of, 307–308, 343–345
    prevention of, 351, 353
    protective orders and, 345, 353
    psychological effects of, 345
    *Rapelay* video game and, 6
    safety planning and, 349–350, 351, 352
    same-sex stalking, 353–354
    stalking with technology, 343, 352
    subjective definitions of, 342
    treatments of, 349–350, 353
    typology of stalkers, 347, 347–348 (table), 352
    victims' responses to, 348, 352
    *See also* Dating violence (DV); Sexual assault (SA)
State-Trait Anger Expression Inventory, 316
Statistical analysis, 59
    advocacy, researcher role in, 73
    analysis of variance, 524, 525
    causality, identification of, 59
    chi-square analysis, 524, 632
    cluster analysis, 414, 458, 459
    correlational data and, 124
    discriminate functions analysis, 429
    factor analysis, 232, 338
    family violence, data on, 2–3, 4–5
    fatal intrafamilial abuse, 4–5
    meta-analysis and, 73, 118, 131, 237–238, 336, 432–433,
        442, 555
    multiple regression analysis, 451
    nonfatal intrafamilial abuse, 3–4
    path analysis, 311, 335, 442, 450, 451, 460, 464, 502
    regression analysis, 560
    researcher training and, 72–73, 82
    risk markers, assessments of, 73
    structural equation modeling and, 59
    underestimation and, 2
    weighted frequency scores, 429
    *See also* Data; Family violence research methodology
Statutory rape, 199, 252, 292, 302
Stockholm syndrome, 374, 375, 381
Street Youth at Risk for AIDS (SYRA), 256
Stress:
    abused heterosexual partners and, 370–371
    abusive heterosexual partners and, 451
    biological stress reaction, 159

child physical abuse and, 153 (table), 179–180
child psychological maltreatment and, 112
child testimony and, 30
childhood poverty, brain volume and, 24
dyadic relationship stress, 54
family stress, 156
increased sensitivity, brain changes and, 24
intimate partner violence and, 180
masculine gender-role stress, 452, 452 (table), 561
maternal stress, prenatal/postnatal effects of, 88
minority stress, 512
specific patterns of activation, specific stressors and, 371
stress-free working environments, 29
See also Posttraumatic stress disorder (PTSD)
Strong families, 5–6
Structural equation modeling (SEM), 59
Student Right-to-Know and Campus Security Act of 1990, 319
Substance abuse:
    abusive heterosexual partners and, 449–450, 500
    adolescent abuse victims and, 254, 254 (table)
    child neglect and, 87
    child physical abuse and, 153 (table), 155
    cocaine use, 87, 88
    conduct disorder and, 315
    dating violence and, 359
    drug courts, 559
    family-violent individuals and, 31, 35, 55–56
    heroin, 88
    marijuana use/abuse, 450
    maternal drug use, criminalization vs. treatment of, 89
    newborns, drug testing for, 88–89
    paternal substance abuse, child risk and, 120
    prenatal neglect and, 87–88, 89
    sexual assault and, 332, 359
    treatment for, 532, 552–553
    victimization and, 303
    See also Alcohol abuse
Sudden infant death syndrome (SIDS), 148
Sudden unexpected infant death (SUID), 148
Suffragist movement, 13
Suicide:
    abused heterosexual partners and, 379, 501
    adolescent abuse victims and, 253–254 (table)
    adolescent dating violence and, 286
    child physical abuse and, 153 (table)
    combined homicide-suicides, 5
    female-to-male violence offenders and, 466
    homicide-suicide events, 421, 533
    interparental violence, child exposure to, 115 (table)
    intimate partner violence victimization and, 504
    partner-violent males and, 421
    sexual assault and, 332
    teen suicide rates, 151

Supervisory neglect, 91 (table)
Supplementary Homicide Reports, 151, 412, 421
Support initiatives:
    child neglect intervention, 86
    Fathers Supporting Success program, 188
    parental support interventions, 187
Survivor theory, 378
Survivors Network for those Abused by Priests (SNAP), 204
Symbolic interactionism, 56
Systems theory, 54, 551

Tag-along charges, 133
Tajikistan:
    intimate partner violence, 481 (table)
    See also Central Asian intimate partner violence; Cross-cultural intimate partner violence
Taliban practices, 480–481
Task Force on Statistical Inference, 72
Teach Early campaign, 29
Teen Dating Violence Prevention Act of 2009, 290
Teen pregnancy, 119, 123, 151, 259–260, 541
Television violence, 289, 302–303
Temperamental features, 157, 177, 178
Temporary Assistance for Needy Families (TANF), 384–385, 540
Terrorist attacks, 18–19
Terrorizing behaviors, 107 (table), 111, 123, 428, 629
Theory, 47
    See also Family violence theories; Macrotheory framework; Microtheory framework; Transtheoretical model (TTM)
Therapy. See Psychotherapy; Therapy/treatment drop-outs
Therapy/treatment drop-outs, 130–131, 555, 559–560
Think S.A.F.E. program, 619
Third National Incident Study (NIS-3), 90
Threats, 8
Tobacco use:
    prenatal maternal smoking, 87, 88
    See also Substance abuse
Touching:
    normal/acceptable touching, 200
    See also Child sexual abuse
Trait differences, 52
    homosexual trait differences, 517–519
    psychological traits, family violence and, 53–54
    See also Individual factors; Individual/intrapersonal differences theories; Personality traits
Traits, 430, 454
Traits as Situational Sensitivities (TASS) model, 430
Transactional theories of child abuse, 182–183
Transgender population:
    adolescent development and, 293–294
    anti-harassment programs, 294–295, 299
    same-sex elder abuse, 625–626